OLD ENGLISH SYNTAX

VOLUME I

CONCORD, THE PARTS OF SPEECH, AND THE SENTENCE

The aim of this work is to chart the whole realm of the syntax of Old English. It adopts the formal descriptive approach and the traditional Latin-based grammar because, in the author's opinion, these remain the most serviceable for the study of Old English syntax. As far as is at present possible, Old English usage is described and differences between Old and Modern English noted, with special reference to those phenomena which are the seeds of characteristic Modern English idioms.

Volume I sets out the general principles of concord in Old English and examines the parts of speech, the elements of the simple sentence and the types of simple and multiple sentences, and the complex sentence (including sections on punctuation, subordination and hypotaxis, correlation and anticipation, and the order and arrangement of clauses). Volume II deals with subordinate clauses, independent elements, and element order. It also offers a discussion of particular problems related to poetry, although poetry as well as prose is used illustratively throughout the book.

Old English syntax has been much less intensively studied than the syntax of the classical languages. There are many difficulties in the way of making definitive statements. They include the absence of native informants and of a knowledge of intonation patterns, limitations in the size and range of the corpus, the difficulty in assigning definite dates and locations to texts, problems of punctuation, and the possibility of later scribal changes. Hence this book does not lay down 'rules' but rather offers suggestions, demonstrates, where appropriate, the possibility of different interpretations, summarizes the present state of knowledge about the phenomena discussed, and indicates possible lines of future research.

This is the first work of its kind to be published; it will provide an essential foundation for more accurate and detailed exploration of Old English and of the English language by new generations of scholars equipped with the full collections of *A Microfiche Concordance to Old English*.

OLD ENGLISH SYNTAX

BY

BRUCE MITCHELL

VOLUME I

CONCORD, THE PARTS OF SPEECH, AND
THE SENTENCE

CLARENDON PRESS · OXFORD

1985

Oxford University Press, Walton Street, Oxford OX2 6DP

London New York Toronto
Delhi Bombay Calcutta Madras Karachi
Kuala Lumpur Singapore Hong Kong Tokyo
Nairobi Dar es Salaam Cape Town
Melbourne Auckland
and associated companies in
Beirut Berlin Ibadan Mexico City Nicosia

Oxford is a trade mark of Oxford University Press

Published in the United States
by Oxford University Press, New York

British Library Cataloguing in Publication Data

Mitchell, Bruce
Old English syntax.
1. Anglo-Saxon language—Syntax
I. Title
429'.5 PE131
ISBN 0-19-811935-6

Typeset by Joshua Associates, Oxford
Printed in Great Britain
at the Thetford Press

In Memoriam

ALISTAIR CAMPBELL

*who would have written
a better book*

ANGUS CAMERON

'dead ere his prime'

*Generous scholars and
good men*

FOREWORD

THIS book is, as far as I know, the first to try to chart the whole realm of the syntax of Old English—'the name applied . . . to the vernacular language of Great Britain as it is recorded in manuscripts and inscriptions dating from before about 1100' (*OEG*, §1). Like all early maps—including those of Captain James Cook, who missed both Bass Strait and Sydney Harbour—it is inevitably incomplete. Its aims and its limitations are defined in more detail in the Introduction. For the reasons given there, my syntactical approach is Latin-based. While I do not expect the work to be hailed as a triumphant vindication of traditional methods, I hope that it will not be condemned as a useless monument to outmoded theories.

My aim throughout has been clarity and ease of reading. Hence my use of heavy punctuation to replace the insetting and tabulation which considerations of space did not permit; the comparative absence of distracting footnotes containing references or material which should have been absorbed into the argument; and my reluctance to use technical terms—a prolific source of terminological controversy— except when it was inevitable. My concern has been to describe and to appreciate the tomato rather than to label it 'fruit' or 'vegetable'.

I have tried to avoid the common error of using the verb 'to feel' as a synonym for the verb 'to think' and to use the former only in those contexts where I am putting myself forward as the nearest equivalent I shall ever find of a native informant—a position in which every reader of Old English literature inevitably finds himself. Here we must all be aware of the dangers of unconsciously assuming that we actually are native informants and of dogmatically defending theories which depend on that assumption.

I am of course responsible for all errors and omissions, including any unintentional failure to mention helpers in the lists which follow. To them I apologize. Special obligations have been recognized in the appropriate sections. But it is a pleasurable duty to acknowledge here debts to the *eucalyptus gunnii* in my garden at Oxford; to three Australian schoolmasters—H. J. Tuck, C. A. Pledge, and H. J. Sutton; to Arthur Sandell; to Dorothy Coldicutt, Alec Hope, Vera Jennings, Keith Macartney, and Ian Maxwell, who taught me at the University of Melbourne; to all those scholars from whose printed work on Old English syntax I have profited, especially to Bacquet, Visser, and Wülfing, for their collections of examples; to Paul Foote, David

Budgen, Nikolai Dejevsky, Mary Dejevsky, Mary MacRobert, and Ralph Cleminson, for assistance with Russian and other Slavonic material; to Jeannine Alton, John Bell, Claire Catalini, John Cowdrey, Richard and Mary Fargher, George Gellie, Justin Gosling, Sandra Raphael, Ken Segar, Jennifer Speake, John Waś, Christopher Wells, and Jelly Williams, for specialist advice; to Eileen Crampton, Marge Edwards, Martin Garrett, Esther Gelling, Alice Gibbons, Ivan Herbison, Andrew Lynch, Melinda Measor, James Simpson, Margaret Swan, and Henry Wickens, for help in the preparation and checking of the typescript; to Sacha Wernberg-Møller, Librarian at St. Edmund Hall; to Margaret Weedon and Eileen Davies of the English Faculty Library, Oxford; to the staffs of the Bodleian Library and of the Taylor Institution Library, Oxford, too numerous to name but uniformly helpful; to the bibliographers of *Anglo-Saxon England, Neuphilologische Mitteilungen*, and *The Year's Work in Old English Studies*; to many scholars of Old English, including Christopher Ball, Janet Bately, Joyce Bazire, Carl Berkhout, Alan Bliss, Val Bonnell, Peter Clemoes, Jimmy Cross, Bob Farrell, Malcolm Godden, Pamela Gradon, Richard Hamer, Richard Hogg, Dennis Horgan, Dorothy Horgan, Nicolas Jacobs, Leena Kahlas, Bob Kaske, Matti Kilpiö, Lars Malmberg, Ray Page, Malcolm Parkes, John Pope, Matti Rissanen, Jim Rosier, Donald Scragg, Celia Sisam, Michael Samuels, Ruth Waterhouse, Edward Wilson, and David Yerkes; to three Oxford professors—Norman Davis, Eric Dobson, and Peter Ganz—for valued advice; to Eric Stanley for generous encouragement, especially since he took up the Rawlinson–Bosworth Chair of Anglo-Saxon at Oxford in 1976; to Reggie Alton and Graham Midgley, of St. Edmund Hall, for their never-failing understanding of the fact that I have been 'fiddling about with *þonne*'; to Tauno Mustanoja for fraternal support and sympathy; to Angus Cameron and the staff of *The Dictionary of Old English* for regular interchanges of material and of ideas; to generations of pupils for their stimulus and interest; to the English Faculty Board and to the University of Oxford for research grants and for granting me sabbatical leave for 1980-1; to the Principal and Fellows of St. Edmund Hall for granting me leave in the same year and for their support since 1954; to the British Academy for a grant which enabled me to make the best use of that year; to the Oxford Secretary of the Oxford and Cambridge Schools Examination Board, Robin Davis, and his staff, for the use of and help with their technical facilities; to various members of the staff of the Oxford University Press, who modestly insist on preserving their traditional anonymity, for their consistent thoughtfulness and valued advice; to the staff of Joshua Associates, especially Vera Keep, for their skill, care, and consideration, while turning typescript into print; to Sarah Ogilvie-Thomson for valuable and unselfish aid in the final stages of preparation; to Tom Dobson, sometime Reader in English in the University of Melbourne, who taught me Old English when I began to learn it in 1947 and who since then has encouraged and helped me continually; to Fred Robinson, who has constantly uplifted me in person and by 'Fred-letter days' since we first met in 1966; to Alistair Campbell, who gave me his own scheme for an *Old English Syntax* and was always ready with stimulating comment and wise counsel, and to Kathleen Campbell who, after his death, allowed me to use and to quote from his lecture notes; to my parents Donovan Frederick and Irene Kilbey Mitchell for their example and their sacrifices; and above all to my wife Mollie, who, while turning practically all the book from difficult manuscript to immaculate typescript and reading all the proofs, tried to keep within bounds the sense of humour, but succeeded in providing the Ivory Tower, without which I could never have finished it.

BRUCE MITCHELL

St. Edmund Hall, Oxford
Easter, 1984

Grateful acknowledgement is made to the
British Academy for a generous grant towards
the cost of printing this book

SUMMARY OF CONTENTS

VOLUME I

VOLUME II

CONTENTS OF VOLUME I

CHAPTER III: THE SIMPLE SENTENCE: ELEMENTS   529

CHAPTER IV: THE SIMPLE SENTENCE: TYPES

CHAPTER V: PARATAXIS AND THE 'MULTIPLE SENTENCE'

ABBREVIATIONS AND SYMBOLS

LANGUAGES AND DIALECTS

Ecc.Lat.	Ecclesiastical Latin	NHG	New High German
Gmc.	Germanic	nW-S	non-West-Saxon
Goth.	Gothic	OE	Old English
IE	Indo-European	OFr.	Old French
Lat.	Latin	OFris.	Old Frisian
ME	Middle English	OHG	Old High German
Merc.	Mercian	ON	Old Norse
MnE	Modern English	OS	Old Saxon
MnFr.	Modern French	WGmc.	West Germanic
Nb.	Northumbrian	W-S	West-Saxon

Before the name of a language or dialect: e = Early; l = Late; pr/Pr = Primitive

GRAMMATICAL TERMS

a., acc.	accusative	m., masc.	masculine
adj.	adjective	n., neut.	neuter
adv.	adverb	n., nom.	nominative
art.	article	p., pl.	plural
aux.	auxiliary	part.	partitive
compar.	comparative	pass.	passive
conj.	conjunction	pers.	person
correl.	correlative	poss.	possessive
d., dat.	dative	prep.	preposition
def.	definite	pres.	present
dem.	demonstrative	pret.	preterite
f., fem.	feminine	pret.-pres.	preterite-present
g., gen.	genitive	pron.	pronoun
i., inst.	instrumental	ptc.	participle
imp.	imperative	refl.	reflexive
impers.	impersonal	rel.	relative
ind.	indicative	s., sg.	singular
indef.	indefinite	st.	strong
inf.	infinitive	subj.	subjunctive
infl.	inflected	super.	superlative
interj.	interjection	tr.	transitive
interr.	interrogative	vb.	verb
intr.	intransitive	wk.	weak

's' may be added where appropriate to form a plural

SYMBOLS INVOLVING LETTERS

C	Complement	P	*See* §1901
O	Object	Sc	*See* §1911
S	Subject	Sp	*See* §1901
V	Verb	(Sp)	*See* §1901
v	Auxiliary verb	Ss	*See* §1901
Vv	Infinitive or participle + auxiliary verb	(Ss)	*See* §1901
vV	Auxiliary verb + infinitive or participle		

OTHER SYMBOLS

>	gives, has given
<	derived from
*	a reconstructed form
☆	an emendation or a reconstructed group of words
|, ||	(in verse) the medial and end caesura respectively
. . .	(in quotations) word or words omitted
/	(in citation of forms) alternatives. Thus *mid þæm/þam/þan/þon/þi/þy þe* means that in this formula *mid* and *þe* can be separated by any one of the six given forms.
( )	(in citation of forms) optional elements. Thus *(sona) hraðe/hraþe (. . .) þæs (. . .) þe* means that this particular combination occurs either with or without initial *sona*, with the given alternative spellings, and with the elements together or separated by other speech elements: *hraðe þæs þe; hraðe . . . þæs þe; hraðe þæs . . . þe; hraðe . . . þæs . . . þe.*
╳	(preceding a section number). See chapter XI (§§3977-4000) for an addition to this section.

OLD ENGLISH TEXTS: SHORT TITLES AND SYSTEM OF REFERENCE

The abbreviations for, and the method of reference to, OE texts are those proposed in 'Short titles of Old English texts', by Bruce Mitchell, Christopher Ball, and Angus Cameron (*ASE* 4 (1975), 207-21, and *ASE* 8 (1979), 331-3). These depend on 'A List of Old English Texts' by Angus Cameron (*Plan*, pp. 25-306). The whole basis of the system is that reference to Cameron's 'List'—which will form part of the first fascicle of the *DOE*—is inevitable for everything except the poetry and a few well-known prose texts. It is obviously impossible to reproduce all this material here. I can give only the short titles to the two groups excepted above, crave the reader's indulgence for the inevitable inconvenience, and at the same time warn him that, unless otherwise stated, I use the texts specified in Cameron's 'List' (1973), which sometimes differs from *The List of Texts* published in 1980 to accompany *A Microfiche Concordance to Old English*. But I can explain a few special points which may help him to recognize the short titles for some other prose texts.

Where necessary, a reference is made to a particular manuscript by the addition in brackets of the appropriate sigil, e.g. *Bede(T)*, or to a particular edition by the addition of (an obvious abbreviation for) the name of the editor.

Standard abbreviations are used for the books of the Bible and the reference is to chapter, or psalm, and verse.

For the Heptateuch and the Psalms respectively, reference to the manuscripts will be by means of the abbreviations set out by S. J. Crawford, *The Old English Version of the Heptateuch* (EETS 160), p. 1, and by C. and K. Sisam, *The Salisbury Psalter* (EETS 242), pp. ix–x. So *Ps(A)* = the Vespasian Psalter, *Ps(F)* = the Stowe Psalter, and *Ps(P)* = the prose psalms of the Paris Psalter.

For the gospels the following system will obtain:

Li	Lindisfarne Gospels
Ru1	Rushworth Gospels (Mercian)
Ru2	Rushworth Gospels (Northumbrian)
WS	West-Saxon Gospels
WSA	Cambridge, University Library, MS Ii. 2. 11
WSB	Oxford, Bodleian Library, MS Bodley 441
WSC	British Museum, MS Cotton Otho C. i
WSCp	Cambridge, Corpus Christi College, MS 140
WSH	Oxford, Bodleian Library, MS Hatton 38
WSR	British Museum, MS Royal 1. A. xiv

Thus *Matt(Li)* means the Lindisfarne version of St. Matthew and *Mark(WSH)* the West-Saxon version of St. Mark in Hatton 38.

The charters present a special problem because there is no one complete edition. For short charters the Sawyer numbers will suffice, but something more may be needed for longer ones. Where this is so, an editorial designation is added after the charter number according to the following system:

B	*Cartularium Saxonicum*, ed. W. de Gray Birch
BMFacs	*Facsimiles of Ancient Charters in the British Museum*, ed. E. A. Bond
H	*Select English Historical Documents of the Ninth and Tenth Centuries*, ed. F. E. Harmer
Ha	*Anglo-Saxon Writs*, ed. F. E. Harmer
K	*Codex Diplomaticus Ævi Saxonici*, ed. J. M. Kemble
N	*The Crawford Collection of Early Charters and Documents*, edd. A. S. Napier and W. H. Stevenson
OSFacs	*Facsimiles of Anglo-Saxon Manuscripts*, ed. W. B. Sanders
R	*Anglo-Saxon Charters*, ed. A. J. Robertson
W	*Anglo-Saxon Wills*, ed. D. Whitelock

and so on, as necessary. References such as *Ch* 1188 *H* 2. 11 (page 2, line 11, of Harmer's *Select Documents*) and *Ch* 1428 *Ha* 113. 40 (line 40 of charter 113 in Harmer's *Writs*) are thus possible. Unless otherwise stated, I use the most recent of the editions cited by Sawyer.

Legal references follow the system used by F. Liebermann in *Die Gesetze der Angelsachsen* (Halle, 1903–16). In volume iii of *Leechdoms* (*Lch* iii), I have followed the pagination of the Singer reprint (London, 1961), where *De Tonitru* begins at p. 224, and not that of the Rolls Series 35 (London, 1864–6) and the Kraus reprint (Wiesbaden, 1965), where *De Tonitru* begins at p. 280. Both versions have the same numbering until p. 159; after that, there is a discrepancy of 56 pages.

Roman numerals refer to volume numbers except in the abbreviations for the titles of those poems whose title includes a roman numeral. Arabic numerals are used for sequences of separate texts, such as the charters, homilies, riddles, and psalms.

For continuous prose texts references are by page and line. When a prose text consists of a number of separated items numbered continuously from beginning to end, the reference is given by piece and line number; an example is Pope's *Homilies of Ælfric* (EETS 259 and 260). When this is not possible—as in Napier's *Wulfstan*, where the line numbers begin afresh on each page, and in Morris's *Blickling Homilies*, where no line numbers are given—page and line numbers are used. (This explains why, in *Ch* 1188 *H* 2. 11 and *Ch* 1428 *Ha* 113. 40 above, 2 is a page number and 113 a charter number.) When numbering the lines in such texts, I have counted the headings which occur within the page. So my numbers may not always agree with those given by other scholars. I am particularly conscious of variations in the *Blickling Homilies*.

When a passage is referred to but not quoted, the reference is to the line number in which the passage containing the discussed phenomenon begins, unless the example has been quoted elsewhere to illustrate something different. In that event, the reference is to the line at which the quotation begins, and the section number in which it is to be found is given in brackets. When a particular word or phrase is singled out for comment, the reference is to the line in which it occurs, again provided that the passage has not been quoted elsewhere, in which case the procedure just outlined obtains.

The OE and Latin examples are printed without length marks and in general without editorial italics, brackets, and the like. I have occasionally permitted myself a silent emendation, e.g. in §2490, where I read *Bede(B)* 144. 21 *Is* instead of *S* (space).

Verse texts

With the exception of *Beowulf*, for which I use the text (but not the diacritics) of Klaeber 3, the poems are cited according to the lineation of The Anglo-Saxon Poetic Records or, in the case of the few poems not found there, according to the lineation of the editions specified in the list. With the charms, *Metres*, and riddles, the item number precedes the line number. In the Paris Psalter, of course, the reference is by psalm and verse. References consisting of a roman numeral followed by an arabic one are to volume and page number in The Anglo-Saxon Poetic Records:

Aldhelm	Aldhelm (vi. 97)
Alms	Alms-Giving (iii. 223)
And	Andreas (ii. 3)
Az	Azarias (iii. 88)
BDS	Bede's Death Song (vi. 107)
Beo	Beowulf (iv. 3)
Brun	Battle of Brunanburh (vi. 16)
BrussCr	Brussels Cross (vi. 115)
Cæd	Cædmon's Hymn (vi. 105)
Capt	Capture of the Five Boroughs (vi. 20)
CEdg	Coronation of Edgar (vi. 21)
ChristA	Christ (iii. 3), lines 1–439
ChristB	Christ (iii. 15), lines 440–866
ChristC	Christ (iii. 27), lines 867–1664

Cnut	Cnut's Song (*Liber Eliensis*, ed. E. O. Blake (R. Hist. Soc., Camden Soc. 3rd ser. 92) (London, 1962), 153)
CPEp	The Metrical Epilogue to the Pastoral Care (vi. 111)
CPPref	The Metrical Preface to the Pastoral Care (vi. 110)
Creed	Creed (vi. 78)
DAlf	Death of Alfred (vi. 24)
Dan	Daniel (i. 111)
DEdg	Death of Edgar (vi. 22)
DEdw	Death of Edward (vi. 25)
Deor	Deor (iii. 178)
Dream	Dream of the Rood (ii. 61)
Dur	Durham (vi. 27)
El	Elene (ii. 66)
Exhort	Exhortation to Christian Living (vi. 67)
Ex	Exodus (i. 91)
Fates	Fates of the Apostles (ii. 51)
Finn	Battle of Finnsburh (vi. 3)
Fort	Fortunes of Men (iii. 154)
FrCask	The Franks Casket (vi. 116)
GDPref	Metrical Preface to Gregory's Dialogues (vi. 112)
GenA	Genesis (i. 1), lines 1–234 and 852–2936
GenB	Genesis (i. 9), lines 235–851
Gifts	Gifts of Men (iii. 137)
Glor i	Gloria i (vi. 74)
Glor ii	Gloria ii (vi. 94)
Godric	Godric's Prayer (*EStudien*, 11 (1888), 423)
Grave	The Grave (*Erlanger Beiträge zur englischen Philologie*, 2 (1890), 11)
GuthA	Guthlac (iii. 49), lines 1–818
GuthB	Guthlac (iii. 72), lines 819–1379
Hell	Descent into Hell (iii. 219)
HomFr i	Homiletic Fragment i (ii. 59)
HomFr ii	Homiletic Fragment ii (iii. 224)
Husb	Husband's Message (iii. 225)
Instr.	Instructions for Christians (*Ang.* 82 (1964), 4)
JDay i	Judgement Day i (iii. 212)
JDay ii	Judgement Day ii (vi. 58)
Jud	Judith (iv. 99)
Jul	Juliana (iii. 113)
Kenelm	Distich on Kenelm (N. R. Ker, *Catalogue of Manuscripts Containing Anglo-Saxon* (Oxford, 1957), 124)
KtHy	Kentish Hymn (vi. 87)
KtPs	Psalm 50 (vi. 88)
LEProv	Latin-English Proverbs (vi. 109)
Loth	Distich on the Sons of Lothebrok (N. R. Ker, *Catalogue of Manuscripts Containing Anglo-Saxon* (Oxford, 1957), 124)
LPr i	Lord's Prayer i (iii. 223)
LPr ii	Lord's Prayer ii (vi. 70)
LPr iii	Lord's Prayer iii (vi. 77)
LRid	Leiden Riddle (vi. 109)
Mald	Battle of Maldon (vi. 7)

Max i	Maxims i (iii. 156)
Max ii	Maxims ii (vi. 55)
MCharm	Metrical Charms (vi. 116)
Men	Menologium (vi. 49)
MEp	Metrical Epilogue to MS 41 (vi. 113)
Met	Metres of Boethius (v. 153)
MRune	Rune Poem (vi. 28)
MSol	Solomon and Saturn (vi. 31)
OrW	Order of the World (iii. 163)
Pan	Panther (iii. 169)
Part	Partridge (iii. 174)
Pha	Pharaoh (iii. 223)
Phoen	Phoenix (iii. 94)
PPs	Metrical Psalms of the Paris Psalter (v. 3)
Pr	A Prayer (vi. 94)
Prec	Precepts (iii. 140)
ProvW	A Proverb from Winfrid's Time (vi. 57)
PsFr	Fragments of Psalms (vi. 80)
Res	Resignation (iii. 215)
Rid	Riddles (iii. 180, 224, 225, and 229)
Rim	Riming Poem (iii. 166)
Ruin	Ruin (iii. 227)
RuthCr	Ruthwell Cross (vi. 115)
Sat	Christ and Satan (i. 135)
Sea	Seafarer (iii. 143)
Seasons	Seasons for Fasting (vi. 98)
Soul i	Soul and Body i (ii. 54)
Soul ii	Soul and Body ii (iii. 174)
Summons	A Summons to Prayer (vi. 69)
Thureth	Thureth (vi. 97)
Vain	Vainglory (iii. 147)
WaldA	Waldere i (vi. 4)
WaldB	Waldere ii (vi. 5)
Wan	Wanderer (iii. 134)
Whale	Whale (iii. 171)
Wid	Widsith (iii. 149)
Wife	Wife's Lament (iii. 210)
Wulf	Wulf and Eadwacer (iii. 179)

Major prose texts

ÆCHom i, ii	*The Sermones Catholici* or *Homilies of Ælfric*, volumes i and ii, ed. B. Thorpe (London, 1844 and 1846)[1]
ÆGram	*Ælfrics Grammatik und Glossar*, ed. J. Zupitza (Berlin, 1880)
ÆHom	*The Homilies of Ælfric*, ed. J. C. Pope (EETS, 1967 and 1968)
ÆLS	*Ælfric's Lives of Saints*, ed. W. W. Skeat (EETS, 1881-1900)[2]

[1] I have used Thorpe's edition because the EETS edition is not yet complete (March, 1981).

[2] Here I now use Skeat's homily number and not the Cameron number; see *ASE* 8 (1979), 331. But there may still remain an occasional uncorrected reference with the Cameron number.

Alex	*Letter of Alexander the Great to Aristotle* in *Three Old English Prose Texts*, ed. S. Rypins (EETS, 1924)
ApT	*The Old English Apollonius of Tyre*, ed. P. Goolden (Oxford, 1958)
Bede	*The Old English Version of Bede's Ecclesiastical History of the English People*, ed. T. Miller (EETS, 1890-8)
BenR	*Die angelsächsischen Prosabearbeitungen der Benedictinerregel*, ed. A. Schröer (BASPr. ii, 1888)
BlHom	*The Blickling Homilies*, ed. R. Morris (EETS, 1874-80)
Bo	*King Alfred's Old English Version of Boethius*, De Consolatione Philosophiae, ed. W. J. Sedgefield (Oxford, 1899)
ByrM	*Byrhtferth's Manual*, ed. S. J. Crawford (EETS, 1929)
Ch	Charter. *See* p. xxxi
Chron	*The Anglo-Saxon Chronicle*[3]
CP	*King Alfred's West-Saxon Version of Gregory's Pastoral Care*, ed. H. Sweet (EETS, 1871)
GD	*Bischofs Wærferth von Worcester Übersetzung der Dialoge Gregors des Grossen*, ed. H. Hecht (BASPr. v, 1900)
Law	Law. *See* p. xxxi
Lch i, ii, iii	*Leechdoms, Wortcunning and Starcraft of Early England*, volumes i, ii, and iii, ed. O. Cockayne (London, 1864-6). *See* p. xxxi
Marv	*Wonders of the East* in *Three Old English Prose Texts*, ed. S. Rypins (EETS, 1924)
Or	*King Alfred's Orosius*, ed. H. Sweet (EETS, 1883)[4]
Solil	*König Alfreds des Grossen Bearbeitung der Soliloquien des Augustinus*, ed. W. Endter (BASPr. xi, 1922)
WHom	*The Homilies of Wulfstan*, ed. D. Bethurum (Oxford, 1957)

BOOKS AND PERIODICALS

The system of reference to books, periodicals, and the like, is explained in the introductory paragraphs to the Select Bibliography.

LATIN TEXTS

When the editor of an OE text provides a Latin original, I quote his Latin. The following separate editions of Latin texts have been used:

for *Bede*, *Bede's Ecclesiastical History of the English People*, edd. Bertram Colgrave and R. A. B. Mynors (Oxford, 1969);

for *Bo*, *Boethius, The Consolation of Philosophy with the English Translation of 'I.T.' (1609)*, rev. H. F. Stewart (Loeb Classical Library, 1953);

for *Cp*, *S. Gregorii Magni Regulæ Pastoralis Liber*, ed. H. R. Bramley (Oxford and London, 1874);

for *GD*, *Gregorii Magni Dialogi Libri IV*, ed. Umberto Moricca (Rome, 1924).

---

[3] Reference to Earle and Plummer by Chronicle letter, page and line, and annal, e.g. *ChronA* 94. 1 (905).

[4] My copy of *The Old English* Orosius, ed. J. Bately (EETS, 1980), reached me in December 1980. It was then more than I could face to change all the *Or* references.

SELECT BIBLIOGRAPHY

THIS Bibliography does not, and is not intended to, contain all the books, monographs, theses, articles, and notes, which have dealt with topics of interest to OE syntacticians. It merely lists in alphabetical order those works for which it was desirable to have an abbreviated reference. Some of these have been allotted a cue-title; these are explained in the appropriate place(s) below. For the rest, I use the author's name for this purpose when only one of his or her works is listed, e.g. Ahrens and Raw; the author's name and the date of publication when more than one is listed, e.g. Robinson 1973 or 1979 or 1980, or when there are two authors of the same name, e.g. Bock 1887 and Bock 1931; and, when the same author produced more than one work in the same year, the letter *a*, *b*, or *c*, after the date, following the order in which the items appear, e.g. Mitchell 1968*c* refers to *Neophil.* 52 (1968), 292–9. If page numbers are not added, the word *passim* is to be understood. I give references to the edition(s) I have used. But for reasons of space, I have not given details of all the editions of all Old English prose and verse texts. I have had to assume that, when I quote *Mald* 5 and say 'see Gordon's note' (§2706), the reader will be familiar with the work to which I refer, or will be able to trace it with the help of Greenfield and Robinson. The system of transliteration adopted for the Russian and other Slavonic items is the international philological one in the modification employed by *The Slavonic and East European Review*.

Some works which are concerned with one special topic receive mention as they become relevant. Others have been silently passed over as saying nothing new. So, although oversights and omissions are inevitable, the fact that a work is not mentioned within these covers does not certify that I am unaware of it or have not read it. My planned *A Critical Bibliography of Writings on Old English Syntax* (tentatively subtitled *Clearing the Decks*) will aim at completeness.

I am conscious of the fact that those who have to work in library systems less well equipped than that of Oxford may sometimes be exasperated by references to works not available to them or may wish that I had given in more detail my reasons for holding a particular view, whether I have stated it elsewhere, e.g. my dismissal of Krapp on *Ex* 326 (§2), or not, e.g. my disagreement with Goolden on *ApT* 18. 16 (§18). I can appreciate their feelings, but must plead lack of space. However, when I contemplate the money that is spent on the ephemeral trivia which adorn some library shelves in Oxford and elsewhere, I dare to suggest that some of it be diverted to the purchase of xerox, microfilm, or microfiche, copies of works on OE syntax.

Considerations of space also explain my failure to give in the body of the work full references to all the relevant discussions on any particular point in the standard grammars and monographs. A wider range of reference for most of the topics treated in Chapter VII will be found in Mitchell 1959. There is another gap. I began by attempting to read all the reviews of the works which appear in my Bibliography and of those which do not. I was compelled to abandon this plan because I found it more time-consuming and often less profitable than I had hoped. However, I have no doubt that there is still gold for the finding and hope to recover some of it in my *Critical Bibliography*.

I have had to set as my bibliographical deadline 30 June 1981. I cannot guarantee to have taken cognizance of the findings of any works which came to my notice after that date. But I have been able to include references to some important books and articles.

Adams, A., *The Syntax of the Temporal Clause in Old English Prose* (Yale Studies in English, 32) (1907).
AF = Anglistische Forschungen.
Ahlgren, A., *On the Use of the Definite Article with 'Nouns of Possession' in English* (Uppsala, 1946).
Ahrens, J., *Darstellung der Syntax im angelsächsischen Gedicht 'Phoenix'* (Rostock diss., 1904).
AJP = American Journal of Philology.
Åkerlund, A., *On the History of the Definite Tenses in English* (Lund and Cambridge, 1911).
Amati, A., 'Analisi contrastiva delle congiunzioni anglosassoni e latine nella versione dei Vangeli', *Annali della Facoltà di lingue e letterature straniere* (Univ. di Bari), 6 (1975) [1978], 141-203.
Amos, A. C. *Linguistic Means of Determining the Dates of Old English Literary Texts* (Cambridge, Mass., 1980)
Andrew, *Postscript* = Andrew, S. O., *Postscript on 'Beowulf'* (Cambridge, (1948).
Andrew, *SS* = id., *Syntax and Style in Old English* (Cambridge, 1940).
Ang. = Anglia.
Ang. B. = Anglia Beiblatt.
Anklam, E., *Das englische Relativ im 11. und 12. Jahrhundert* (Berlin diss., 1908).
Ann. Bib. = Annual Bibliography of English Language and Literature (Modern Humanities Research Association).
Archiv = Archiv für das Studium der neueren Sprachen und Literaturen.
Arch. L. = Archivum Linguisticum.
Ardenne, S. R. T. O. d', *An Edition of þe Liflade ant te Passiun of Seinte Iuliene* (Liège and Paris, 1936).
Ardern, P. S., *First Readings in Old English* (Wellington, 1948).
Aronstein, Ph., 'Die periphrastische Form im Englischen', *Ang.* 42 (1918), 1-84.
ASE = Anglo-Saxon England.
ASLIB *Index*, 1-   = *Index to Theses accepted for Higher Degrees in the Universities of Great Britain and Ireland* (ASLIB, 1950-   ).
ASPR i-vi = The Anglo-Saxon Poetic Records, volumes i-vi.
ASPR *Concordance* = Bessinger, J. B. Jr. (ed.) and Smith, P. H. Jr. (programmer), *A Concordance to the Anglo-Saxon Poetic Records* (Ithaca and London, 1978). [See Stanley, *RES* 30 (1979), 328-31, and Mitchell, *NQ* 224 (1979), 347-9.]
Bacquet, P., *La Structure de la phrase verbale à l'époque Alfrédienne* (Paris, 1962). [See Mitchell, *MÆ* 34 (1965), 244-5.]
Bale, C. E., *The Syntax of the Genitive Case in the Lindisfarne Gospels* (Iowa Studies in Language and Literature, 1) (1907).
Barela, R. E., 'A Descriptive Syntax of King Alfred's "Soliloquies" ' (University of Southern California Ph.D. diss., 1971).
BASP i-iii = Bibliothek der angelsächsischen Poesie, i-iii.
BASPr. i-xiii = Bibliothek der angelsächsischen Prosa i-xiii.
Bauch, H., *Die Kongruenz in der angelsächsischen Poesie* (Kiel diss., 1912).

Bauer, G., 'Über Vorkommen und Gebrauch von ae. *sin*', *Ang.* 81 (1963), 323–34.

Behaghel, *DS* i–iv = Behaghel, O., *Deutsche Syntax. Eine geschichtliche Darstellung*, i–iv (Heidelberg, 1923–1932).

Behre, F., *The Subjunctive in Old English Poetry* (Gothenburg, 1934).

Belden, H. M., 'The Prepositions "in", "on", "to", "for", "fore", and "æt" in Anglo-Saxon Prose. A Study of Case-Values in Old English' (Johns Hopkins University diss., 1897).

Benham, A. R., 'The Clause of Result in Old English Prose', *Ang.* 31 (1908), 197–255.

Bethurum, D., *The Homilies of Wulfstan* (Oxford, 1957).

Blain, H. M., *Syntax of the Verb in the Anglo-Saxon Chronicle from 787 A.D. to 1001 A.D.* (University of Virginia Monographs, School of Teutonic Languages, no. 2) (New York, 1901).

Bliemel, W., *Die Umschreibung des Personalpronomens im Englischen* (Breslau, 1933).

Bliss, A. J., *The Metre of 'Beowulf'* (Oxford, 1958; rev. edn. 1967).

—— *An Introduction to Old English Metre* (Oxford, 1962).

BM = *The Battle of Maldon and Other Old English Poems*, translated by K. Crossley-Holland and introduced by Bruce Mitchell (London, 1965).

Bock, H., 'Studien zum präpositionalen Infinitiv und Akkusativ mit dem *to*-Infinitiv', *Ang.* 55 (1931), 114–249.

Bock, K., *Die Syntax der Pronomina und Numeralia in König Alfreds Orosius* (Göttingen diss., 1887).

Bødtker, A. Trampe, *Critical Contributions to Early English Syntax* (First Series Christiania, 1908; Second Series Christiania, 1910).

Böhme, W., *Die Temporalsätze in der Übergangszeit vom Angelsächsischen zum Altenglischen (circa 1150–1250)* (Leipzig diss., 1903).

Bourcier, G., *Les Propositions relatives en vieil-anglais* (Paris, 1977). [See Mitchell, *MÆ* 48 (1979), 121–2.]

Braasch, Th., *Vollständiges Wörterbuch zur sog. Cædmonschen Genesis* (AF 76) (1933).

Braunmüller, K., 'Remarks on the Formation of Conjunctions in Germanic Languages', *NJL* 1 (1978), 99–120.

Breitkreuz, O., *Ein Beitrag zur Geschichte der Possessivpronomen in der englischen Sprache* (Erlangen diss., 1882).

Britannica 1929 = *Britannica. Max Förster zum sechzigsten Geburtstage* (Leipzig, 1929).

Brodeur, A. G., *The Art of Beowulf* (Berkeley and Los Angeles, 1959).

Brook, G. L., *An Introduction to Old English* (Manchester, 1955).

Brown, W. H., Jr., 'A Descriptive Syntax of King Alfred's "Pastoral Care" ' (Ph.D. diss., University of Michigan, 1963).

—— *A Syntax of King Alfred's 'Pastoral Care'* (The Hague and Paris, 1970).

Brunner, i, ii = Brunner, K., *Die englische Sprache* (2nd edn., Halle, 1960–2), i, ii.

BT = *An Anglo-Saxon Dictionary based on the manuscript collections of the late Joseph Bosworth . . . edited and enlarged by T. Northcote Toller* (Oxford, 1882–98).

BTC = *An Anglo-Saxon Dictionary based on the manuscript collections of Joseph Bosworth. Supplement by T. Northcote Toller: Enlarged Addenda and Corrigenda by A. Campbell* (Oxford, 1972).

BTS = Toller, T. N., *An Anglo-Saxon dictionary based on the manuscript collections of the late Joseph Bosworth. Supplement* (Oxford, 1908-21).

BT(S) = BT and BTS.

BT(S, C) = BT, BTS, and BTC.

Burkhart, R. S., 'The Syntax of Place in Old English Prose' (Ph.D. diss., University of Pittsburgh, 1935).

Burnham, J. M., *Concessive Constructions in Old English Prose* (Yale Studies in English, 39) (1911).

Calder, Daniel G. (ed.), *Old English Poetry: Essays on Style* (Berkeley, 1979).

Callaway, M., Jr., 'The Absolute Participle in Anglo-Saxon' (Johns Hopkins University diss., 1889).

—— 'The Appositive Participle in Anglo-Saxon', *PMLA* 16 (1901), 141-360.

—— *The Infinitive in Anglo-Saxon* (Washington, 1913).

—— *Studies in the Syntax of the Lindisfarne Gospels* (Baltimore, 1918).

—— *The Temporal Subjunctive in Old English* (Texas, 1931).

—— *The Consecutive Subjunctive in Old English* (*MLA* Monographs, 4) (1933).

Campbell, A., 'The Old English Epic Style', *English and Medieval Studies. Essays Presented to J. R. R. Tolkien*, edd. Davis, N. and Wrenn, C. L. (London, 1962), 13-26.

—— 'Verse Influences in Old English Prose', *Philological Essays in Old and Middle English Language and Literature in Honour of Herbert Dean Meritt*, ed. Rosier, J. L. (The Hague, 1970), 93-8.

—— Lecture Notes. [I am grateful to Mrs Campbell for allowing me to use these notes. They will ultimately be placed with the rest of Professor Campbell's papers in the Robarts Library, University of Toronto.]

Carkeet, D., 'Old English Correlatives: an exercise in internal syntactic reconstruction', *Glossa*, 10 (1976), 44-63.

—— 'Aspects of Old English Style', *Language and Style*, 10 (1977), 173-89.

Carlton, C. R., 'Syntax of the Old English Charters' (Ph.D. diss., University of Michigan, 1958).

—— *Descriptive Syntax of the Old English Charters* (The Hague and Paris, 1970). [See Mitchell, *MÆ* 40 (1971), 181-4.]

Carnicelli, T. A. (ed.), *King Alfred's Version of St. Augustine's Soliloquies* (Harvard, 1969).

Caro, G., 'Zur Lehre vom altenglischen Perfectum', *Ang.* 18 (1896), 389-449.

—— 'Das englische Perfectum und Praeteritum in ihrem Verhältnis zu einander historisch untersucht', *Ang.* 21 (1899), 56-88.

CB = Stanley, E. G. (ed.), *Continuations and Beginnings* (London, 1966).

CBEL = *Cambridge Bibliography of English Literature.*

Christophersen, P., *The Articles. A study of their theory and use in English* (Copenhagen and London, 1939).

CHum. = *Computers and the Humanities.*

Clark, C. (ed.), *The Peterborough Chronicle, 1070-1154* (Oxford, 1958; 2nd edn., 1970). [See Mitchell, *The Oxford Magazine*, 23 October 1958, p. 48.]

Closs, O. E. E., 'A Grammar of Alfred's "Orosius" ' (Ph.D. diss., University of California, Berkeley, 1964).

Cobb, G. W., 'The Subjunctive Mood in Old English Poetry', *Philologica: The Malone Anniversary Studies* (Baltimore, 1949), 43-55.

Conradi, B., *Darstellung der Syntax in Cynewulf's Gedicht 'Juliana'* (Leipzig diss., 1886).

Cook, A. S., *A First Book in Old English Grammar. Reader, Notes and Vocabulary* (3rd edn., Boston, 1921).

Curme, G. O., 'Development of the Progressiv Form in Germanic', *PMLA* 28 (1913), 159–87.

—— *A Grammar of the English Language*, iii. *Syntax* (Boston, 1931).

CV = Cleasby, R., and Vigfusson, G., *An Icelandic-English Dictionary*, 2nd edn., with a supplement by Sir William Craigie (Oxford, 1957).

DA/DAI = *Dissertation Abstracts* (formerly *Microfilm Abstracts*) (University Microfilms, Ann Arbor, Michigan). [From volume 30 (1969–70) *Dissertation Abstracts International.*]

Dančev, A., 'The Syntactic Functions of the Preposition *mid* in Old English Poetry and Prose. Part I'—'Sintaktičeskite funkcii na predloga *mid* v staroanglijskata poezija i proza. Čast I', *Godišnik na Sofijskija Universitet* (Fakultet po zapadni filologii), 61. 2 (1967), 51–130.

—— 'The Parallel Use of the Synthetic Dative Instrumental and Periphrastic Prepositional Constructions in Old English'—'Usporednata upotreba na sintetičnija instrumentalen datelen padež i predložni săčetanija v staroanglijski ezik', *Godišnik na Sofijskija Universitet* (Fakultet po zapadni filologii), 63. 2 (1969), 39–99.

Daniels, A. J., *Kasussyntax zu den [echten und unechten] Predigten Wulfstans* (Leiden diss., 1904).

Delbrück, B., 'Der germanische Optativ im Satzgefüge', *Beiträge zur Geschichte der deutschen Sprache und Literatur*, 29 (1904), 201–304.

Dethloff, R., *Darstellung der Syntax im angelsächsischen Gedicht 'Daniel'* (Rostock diss., 1907).

Dickins Studies = Clemoes, P. (ed.), *The Anglo-Saxons. Studies in some aspects of their history and culture presented to Bruce Dickins* (London, 1959).

Dissertations. See *DA/DAI*; 'The eighteen German dissertations'; 'The prose text dissertations'.

Dobbie, E. V. K. (ed.), *Beowulf and Judith* (ASPR iv, 1953).

Dodd, L. H., *A Glossary of Wulfstan's Homilies* (Yale Studies in English, 35) (1908).

DOE = *Dictionary of Old English* (in preparation at the University of Toronto).

Dowsing, A., 'Some Syntactic Structures Relating to the Use of Relative and Demonstrative "Ðæt" and "Se", in Late Old English Prose', *NM* 80 (1979), 289–303.

Dunning and Bliss = Dunning, T. P. and Bliss, A. J. (edd.), *The Wanderer* (London, 1969).

Dusenschön, F., *Die Präpositionen 'æfter', 'æt' und 'be' in der altenglischen Poesie* (Kiel diss., 1907).

Éa = Études anglaises.

Earle and Plummer = *Two of the Saxon Chronicles parallel*, i, ii. *A revised text edited by C. Plummer on the basis of an edition by J. Earle* (Oxford, 1892).

EETS = Early English Text Society.

EGS = English and Germanic Studies.

Eighteen German dissertations. See 'The eighteen German dissertations'.

Einenkel, E., 'On the History of the x-Genitive in the English Language', *An English Miscellany presented to Dr. Furnivall in Honour of his seventy-fifth Birthday* (Oxford, 1901), 68–79.

Ekwall, E., *Studies on the Genitive of Groups in English* (Lund, 1943).

Ellegård, A., *The Auxiliary 'Do'. The establishment and regulation of its use in English* (Stockholm, 1953).

ELN = *English Language Notes.*

EPS = *English Philological Studies.*

Erickson, J., '*An* and *Na þæt an* in late Old English Prose: Some Theoretical Questions of Derivation', *Arch. L.* 4 (1973), 75–88.

—— 'Subordinator Topicalization in Old English', *Arch. L.* 8 (1978 for 1977), 99–111.

Ericson, E. E., 'The Use of Old English *Swa* in Negative Clauses', *Studies in Honor of Hermann Collitz* (Baltimore, 1930), 159–75.

—— 'Old English *Swa* in worn-down Correlative Clauses', *EStudien*, 65 (1930–1), 343–50.

—— 'The Use of Old English *Swa* as a Pseudo-Pronoun', *JEGP* 30 (1931), 6–20.

—— *The Use of 'Swa' in Old English* (Göttingen and Baltimore, 1932).

E&S = *Essays and Studies.*

EStudien = *Englische Studien.*

EStudies = *English Studies.*

Exter, O., '*Beon' und 'wesan' in Alfreds Übersetzung des Boethius, der Metra und der Soliloquien. Eine syntaktische Untersuchung* (Kiel diss., 1911).

Fakundiny, L., 'The Art of Old English Verse Composition', *RES* 21 (1970), 129–42 and 257–66.

Farr, J. M., 'Intensives and Reflexives in Anglo-Saxon and Early Middle-English' (Johns Hopkins University diss., 1905).

Faulkner, W. H., *The Subjunctive Mood in the Old English Version of Bede's Ecclesiastical History* (University of Virginia Monographs, no. 6, 1902).

Fischer, A., *Der syntaktische Gebrauch der Partikeln 'of' und 'from' in Ælfric's Heiligenleben und in den Blickling-Homilien* (Leipzig diss., 1908).

Flamme, J., *Syntax der Blickling Homilies* (Bonn diss., 1885).

Fleischhauer, W., *Über den Gebrauch des Conjunctivs in Alfreds altenglischer Übersetzung von Gregors Cura Pastoralis* (Erlangen, 1885).

Fraatz, P., *Darstellung der syntaktischen Erscheinungen in den angelsächsischen Waldere-Bruchstücken* (Rostock diss., 1908).

Frank, T., 'On Constructions of Indirect Discourse in Early Germanic Dialects', *JEGP* 7 (1908), 64–80.

Frary, L. G., *Studies in the Syntax of the Old English Passive with special reference to the use of 'wesan' and 'weorþan'* (Baltimore, 1929).

Fricke, R., *Das altenglische Zahlwort, eine grammatische Untersuchung* (Erlangen, 1886).

Fritsche, P., *Darstellung der Syntax in dem altenglischen Menologium. Ein Beitrag zu einer altenglischer Syntax* (Berlin diss., 1907).

Fröhlich, J., *Der indefinite Agens im Altenglischen: unter besonderer Berücksichtigung des Wortes 'man'* (Berne, 1951).

Funke, O., 'On the Use of the Attributive Adjective in OE Prose and early ME', *EStudies*, 30 (1949), 151–6.

Furkert, M., *Der syntaktische Gebrauch des Verbums in dem angelsächsischen Gedichte vom heiligen Guthlac* (Leipzig diss., 1889).

Gardner, F. F., *An Analysis of Syntactic Patterns of Old English* (The Hague and Paris, 1971). [See Mitchell, *RES* 23 (1972), 461–3.]

Gehse, H., *Die Kontaminationen in der englischen Syntax* (Breslau, 1938).

Geoghegan, S. G., 'Relative Clauses in Old, Middle, and New English', *Working Papers in Linguistics* (Ohio State University), 18 (1975), 30–71.

Giles, i, ii = Giles, J. A. (ed.), *The Whole Works of King Alfred the Great*, i, ii (London, 1858).

GK = Grein, C. W. M., and Köhler, J. J., *Sprachschatz der angelsächsischen Dichter* (Heidelberg, 1912–14).

GL = Gildersleeve, B. L., and Lodge, G., *Latin Grammar* (3rd edn., London, 1930).

Gleason, H. A., Jr., *An Introduction to Descriptive Linguistics* (rev. edn., New York, Chicago, San Francisco, Toronto, and London, 1967).

Glogauer, E., *Die Bedeutungsübergänge der Konjunktionen in der angelsächsischen Dichtersprache* (Leipzig, 1922).

Glunz, H. H., *Die Verwendung des Konjunktivs im Altenglischen* (Leipzig, 1929).

Goodwin, C. W., *The Anglo-Saxon Version of the Life of St. Guthlac* (London, 1848).

Gorrell, J. Hendren, 'Indirect Discourse in Anglo-Saxon', *PMLA* 10 (1895), 342–485.

Gottweis, R., *Die Syntax der Präpositionen 'æt', 'be', 'ymb' in den Ælfric-Homilien und andern Homilien-Sammlungen* (Halle, 1905). [This is an off-print of *Ang.* 28 (1905), 305–93. Those who have access only to the latter can get the appropriate page number by adding 304 to that given in this book.]

Green, A., *The Dative of Agency* (Columbia, 1913).

——— 'The Analytic Agent in Germanic', *JEGP* 13 (1914), 514–52.

Greenfield, S. B., *The Interpretation of Old English Poems* (London, 1972).

——— and Robinson, F. C., *A Bibliography of Publications on Old English Literature to the end of 1972* (Toronto and Manchester, 1980).

Grimm, P., *Beiträge zum Pluralgebrauch in der altenglischen Poesie* (Halle diss., 1912).

Grossmann, H., *Das angelsächsische Relativ* (Berlin diss., 1906).

Guide = Mitchell, Bruce, *A Guide to Old English* (Oxford, 1964; 2nd edn. 1968, reprinted 1971, 1975, 1978, 1981), *or* Mitchell, Bruce and Robinson, Fred C., *A Guide to Old English Revised with Texts and Glossary* (Oxford, 1982, re-printed 1983).

Haarstrick, A., *Untersuchung über die Praepositionen bei Alfred dem Grossen* (Kiel diss., 1890).

Haddock, N. L., 'The Syntax of "The Lindisfarne Gospels" ' (M.A. diss., University of Birmingham, 1951–2).

Hahn, E. A., *Naming-Constructions in some Indo-European Languages* (Cleveland, Ohio, 1969).

Halfter, O., *Die Satzverknüpfung in der älteren Genesis* (Kiel diss., 1915).

Hamer, R. F. S., *A Choice of Anglo-Saxon Verse*, selected with an introduction by Richard Hamer (London, 1970).

Harlow, C. G., 'Punctuation in Some Manuscripts of Ælfric', *RES* 10 (1959), 1–19.

Harrison, J. A., 'The Anglo-Saxon Perfect Participle with *habban*', *MLN* 2 (1887), 134–5 (cols. 268–70).

Harrison, T. P., 'The Separable Prefixes in Anglo-Saxon' (Johns Hopkins University diss., 1892).

Harsh, W. C., 'A Historical Study of the English Subjunctive' (Ph.D. diss., University of California, Berkeley, 1963).

Healey, A. di P. and Venezky, R. L., *A Microfiche Concordance to Old English* (Toronto, 1980).

Heltveit, T., 'The Old English Appositional Construction Exemplified by *sume his geferan*', *EStudies*, 50 (1969), 225–35.

—— 'Aspects of the Syntax of Quantifiers in Old English', *NTS* 31 (1977), 47–94.

Hendrickson, J. R., *Old English Prepositional Compounds in Relationship to their Latin Originals* (Baltimore, 1948).

Henk, O., *Die Frage in der altenglischen Dichtung. Eine syntaktische Studie* (Kiel diss., 1903).

Henshaw, A. N., *The Syntax of the Indicative and Subjunctive Moods in the Anglo-Saxon Gospels* (Leipzig diss., 1894).

Hermodsson, L., *Reflexive und Intransitive Verba im älteren Westgermanischen* (Uppsala, 1952).

Hittle, E., *Zur Geschichte der altenglischen Präpositionen 'mid' und 'wið' mit Berücksichtigung ihrer beiderseitigen Beziehungen* (AF 2) (1901).

Höser, J., *Die syntaktischen Erscheinungen in 'Be Domes Dæge'* (Leipzig, 1889).

Hofer, O., 'Der syntaktische Gebrauch des Dativs und Instrumentals in den Cædmon beigelegten Dichtungen', *Ang.* 7 (1884), 355–404.

Hoffmann, G., *Die Entwicklung des umschriebenen Perfektums im Altenglischen und Frühmittelenglischen* (Breslau diss., 1934).

Holtbuer, Fr., 'Der syntaktische Gebrauch des Genitives in Andreas, Guðlac, Phönix, dem Heiligen Kreuz und Höllenfahrt', *Ang.* 8 (1885), 1–40.

Holthausen, F., *Altenglisches etymologisches Wörterbuch* (Heidelberg, 1934).

Horn, W., 'Untersuchungen zur historischen englischen Syntax', *Archiv*, 154 (1928), 213–23.

Hotz, G., *On the Use of the Subjunctive Mood in Anglo-Saxon and its Further History in Old English* (Zürich diss., 1882).

Hüllweck, A., *Ueber den Gebrauch des Artikels in den Werken Alfreds des Grossen* (Berlin diss., 1887).

IAF = Issledovanija po anglijskoj filologii.

IF = Indogermanische Forschungen.

Ingersoll, S. M., *Intensive and Restrictive Modification in Old English* (Heidelberg, 1978). [This is a revised version of Most 1969.]

Jacobsen, J., *Der syntaktische Gebrauch der Präpositionen 'for', 'geond', 'of' und 'ymb' in der altenglischen Poesie* (Kiel diss., 1908).

Jacobsen, R., *Darstellung der syntaktischen Erscheinungen im angelsächsischen Gedichte vom 'Wanderer'* (Rostock diss., 1901).

JEGP = Journal of English and Germanic Philology.

Jespersen, *Ess.* = Jespersen, O., *Essentials of English Grammar* (London, 1933).

Jespersen Gram. Misc. = *A Grammatical Miscellany offered to Otto Jespersen on his seventieth birthday*, edd. Bøgholm, N., Bousendorff, A., and Bodelsen, C. A. (Copenhagen and London, 1930).

Jespersen, *GS* = Jespersen, O., *Growth and Structure of the English Language.* [Edition and date specified in text.]

Jespersen, *MnEG* = id., *A Modern English Grammar on Historical Principles*, I–VII (London, Heidelberg and Copenhagen, 1909–49).

Jespersen, *Neg.* = id., *Negation in English and Other Languages* (Copenhagen, 1917).

Jespersen, *Phil. Gr.* = id., *The Philosophy of Grammar* (London, 1948).

Joint Committee Report = *On the Terminology of Grammar, being the Report of the Joint Committee on Grammatical Terminology* (revised 1911; tenth impression, London, 1947).

Joly, A., *Negation and the Comparative Particle in English* (Quebec, 1967).

Joly, A., 'La négation dite *explétive* en vieil anglais et dans d'autres langues indo-européennes', *Éa* 25 (1972), 30–44.

Jost, K., *'Beon' und 'wesan'. Eine syntaktische Untersuchung* (AF 26) (1909).

—— *Wulfstanstudien* (Bern, 1950).

JP = Jahrbuch für Philologie.

Kageyama, T., 'Relational Grammar and the History of Subject Raising', *Glossa*, 9 (1975), 165–81.

Karlberg, G., *The English Interrogative Pronouns* (Stockholm, 1954).

Kärre, K., *Nomina agentis in Old English, Part I* (Uppsala diss., 1915).

Kellner, L., *Historical Outlines of English Syntax* (London, 1892).

Kempf, E., *Darstellung der Syntax in der sogenannten Cædmon'schen Exodus* (Leipzig diss., 1888).

Kennedy, A. G., *A Bibliography of Writings on the English Language from the Beginning of Printing to the end of 1922* (Cambridge and New Haven, 1927).

Ker, N. R., *Catalogue of Manuscripts containing Anglo-Saxon* (Oxford, 1957).

Kershaw, N. (ed.), *Anglo-Saxon and Norse Poems* (Cambridge, 1922).

Kivimaa, K., *þe and þat as Clause Connectives in Early Middle English, with Especial Consideration of the Emergence of the Pleonastic þat* (Helsinki, 1966).

Klaeber, 1, 2, 3 = Klaeber, Fr., *Beowulf and The Fight at Finnsburg* (1st, 2nd, 3rd edition with second Supplement, Boston, etc., 1922–50).

Klaeber, Fr., 'Eine Bemerkung zum altenglischen Passivum', *EStudien*, 57 (1923), 187–95.

—— 'Eine germanisch-englische Formel: ein stilistisch-syntaktischer Streifzug', *Britannica. Max Förster Festschrift* (Leipzig, 1929), 1–22.

Klingebiel, J., *Die Passivumschreibungen im Altenglischen* (Berlin diss., 1937).

Klinghardt, H., *'þe* und die relative Satzverbindung im Angelsächsischen', *Beiträge zur deutschen Philologie* (Halle, 1880), 193–202.

Knispel, E., *Der altenglische Instrumental bei Verben und Adjektiven und sein Ersatz im Verlaufe der englischen Sprachgeschichte* (Ohlau, 1932).

Knörk, M., *Die Negation in der altenglischen Dichtung* (Kiel diss., 1907).

Knüpfer, H., 'Die Anfänge der periphrastischen Komparation im Englischen', *EStudien*, 55 (1921), 321–89.

Kock, E. A., *The English Relative Pronouns. A Critical Essay* (Lund, 1897).

Kock Studies = Studia Germanica tillägnade Ernst Albin Kock den 6. Dec. 1934 (Lund, 1934).

Kohonen, V., 'On the Problem of Sample Length in the Study of Major Word Order Patterns in Old English and Early Middle English Narrative Prose', *Reports on Text Linguistics*, ed. Enkvist, N. E. (Åbo, 1974), 94–117.

—— 'A Note on Factors affecting the Position of Accusative Objects and Complements in Ælfric's *Catholic Homilies*, I', *Reports on Text Linguistics: Approaches to Word Order*, edd. Enkvist, N.E. and Kohonen, V. (Åbo, 1976), 175–96.

—— *On the Development of English Word Order in Religious Prose around 1000 and 1200 A.D.* (Åbo, 1978).

Kopas, W., *Die Grundzüge der Satzverknüpfung in Cynewulfs Schriften* (Breslau diss., 1910).

Krapp, G. P., 'The Parenthetic Exclamation in Old English Poetry', *MLN* 20 (1905), 33–7.

Kress, J., *Ueber den Gebrauch des Instrumentalis in der Angelsaechsischen Poesie* (Marburg diss., 1864).

Krohmer, W., *Altenglisch 'in' und 'on'* (Berlin diss., 1904).

Krohn, R., *Der Gebrauch des schwachen Adjektivs in den wichtigsten Prosa-schriften der Zeit Alfreds des Grossen* (Breslau diss., 1914).

Kuhn, H., 'Zur Wortstellung und -betonung im Altgermanischen', *Beiträge zur Geschichte der deutschen Sprache und Literatur*, 57 (1933), 1–109.

Kuntz, M., 'Considérations élémentaires sur les verbes: "estre" et "avoir" de l'ancien français, et "beon" et "habban" du vieil anglais' (Thèse de 3ᵉ cycle (Paris), 4 (1979)).

Kurtz, G., *Die Passivumschreibungen im Englischen* (Breslau diss., 1931).

Lang. = *Language*.

Lange, F., *Darstellung der syntaktischen Erscheinungen im angelsächsischen Gedichte von 'Byrhtnoþ's Tod'. Ein Beitrag zur angelsächsischen Syntax* (Rostock diss., 1906).

Lebow, D. B., 'An Historical Study of Syntax: The Evolution of English from Inflectional to Prepositional Constructions' (Ph.D. diss., New York University, 1954).

Lee, D. W., *Functional Change in Early English* (Menasha, 1948).

Lehmann, A., *Der syntaktische Gebrauch des Genetivs in Ælfreds Orosius* (Leipzig diss., 1891).

Lehmann, W. P., *The Development of Germanic Verse Form* (Austin, 1956).

Leslie, R. F., *Three Old English Elegies* (Manchester, 1961: rev. 1966).

Lewis and Short = Lewis, C. T. and Short, C., *A Latin Dictionary* (Oxford, 1879).

Liedtke, E., *Die numerale Auffassung der Kollektiva im Verlaufe der englischen Sprachgeschichte* (Königsberg diss., 1910).

Liggins, E. M., 'The Expression of Causal Relationship in Old English Prose' (Ph.D. diss., University of London, 1955).

—— 'The Clause of "Denied Reason" in Old English', *JEGP* 59 (1960), 457–62.

—— 'The Authorship of the Old English *Orosius*', *Ang.* 88 (1970), 289–322.

LM = *Language Monographs*.

LSE = *Leeds Studies in English*.

Lüttgens, C., *Über Bedeutung und Gebrauch der Hilfsverba im frühen Altenglischen 'sculan' und 'willan'* (Kiel diss., 1888).

Lumby, J. Rawson, *Be Domes Dæge* (EETS, OS 65) (1876).

Lussky, G. F., 'The Verb Forms Circumscribed with the Perfect Participle in the *Beowulf*', *JEGP* 21 (1922), 32–69.

Macháček, J., *Complementation of the English Verb by the Accusative-with-Infinitive and the Content Clause* (Prague, 1965).

—— 'Historical Aspect of the Accusative with Infinitive and the Content Clause in English', *Brno Studies in English*, 8 (1969), 123–32.

Madert, A., *Die Sprache der altenglischen Rätsel des Exeterbuches und die Cynewulffrage* (Marburg diss., 1900).

McIntosh, A., 'The Relative Pronouns *þe* and *þat* in Early Middle English', *EGS* 1 (1947–8), 73–87.

MÆ = *Medium Ævum*.

Mätzner, i, ii, iii = Mätzner, E., *Englische Grammatik*, i, ii, iii (Berlin, 1880–5).

Magoun Festschrift = *Medieval and Linguistic Studies in Honour of Francis Peabody Magoun Jr.*, edd. Bessinger, J. B., Jr. and Creed, R. P. (London, 1965).

Mahn, E., *Darstellung der Syntax in dem sogenannten angelsächsischen Physiologus* (Rostock diss., 1903).

Maisenhelder, C., *Die altenglische Partikel 'and' mit Berücksichtigung anderer germanischer Sprachen* (Königsfeld diss., 1935).

Mann, G., *Konjunktionen und Modus im Konsekutiven und finalen Nebensatz des Altenglischen* (Sprache und Kultur der germanischen und romanischen Völker, A. Anglistische Reihe, 33) (Breslau, 1939).

March, F. A., *A Comparative Grammar of the Anglo-Saxon Language* (New York, 1873).

Mather, F. J., Jr., 'The Conditional Sentence in Anglo-Saxon' (Johns Hopkins University diss., 1893).

Matsunami, T., 'On the Old English Participles', *SEL* (Tokyo), 34 (1958), 161–80.

—— 'Functional Development of the Present Participle in English', *Collected Papers in Commemoration of the 40th Anniversary of the Faculty of Literature, Kyushu University* (1966), 314–48.

—— 'Functional Development of the Present Participle in English', *The Proceedings of the Faculty of Literature, Kyushu University, Studies in Literature*, 63 (1966), 1–81.

Maxwell Studies = Iceland and the Mediaeval World. Studies in Honour of Ian Maxwell, edd. Turville-Petre, G. and Martin, J. S. (Melbourne, 1974).

MED = Middle English Dictionary, edd. Kurath, H. and Kuhn, S. M. (Michigan and Oxford, 1952–   ).

Meritt Essays = Philological Essays: Studies in Old and Middle English Language and Literature in Honour of Herbert Dean Meritt, ed. Rosier, J. L. (The Hague, 1970).

Meritt, H. D., *The Construction ἀπὸ κοινοῦ in the Germanic Languages* (Stanford, 1938).

Meyer, E., *Darstellung der syntaktischen Erscheinungen in dem angelsächsischen Gedicht 'Christ und Satan'* (Rostock diss., 1907).

Microfiche Concordance = Healey, A. di P. and Venezky, R. L., A Microfiche Concordance to Old English (Toronto, 1980).

Migne = *Patrologiae cursus completus sive bibliotheca universalis . . . omnium sanctorum patrum, doctorum, scriptorumque ecclesiasticorum . . . Series Latina.*

Miller, i, ii. See Bede in list of *Short Titles of Old English Texts*, p. xxxv.

Millward, C. M., *Imperative Constructions in Old English* (The Hague and Paris, 1971). [See Mitchell, *ES* 55 (1974), 387–9.]

Mitchell, Bruce, 'Subordinate Clauses in Old English Poetry' (unpublished D.Phil. thesis, University of Oxford, 1959). [See §1931.]

—— ' "Until the Dragon Comes . . ." Some thoughts on *Beowulf*', *Neophil.* 47 (1963), 126–38.

—— 'Old English Syntactical Notes', *NQ* 208 (1963), 326–8.

—— 'Adjective Clauses in Old English Poetry', *Ang.* 81 (1963), 298–322.

—— See *Guide* above.

—— 'Pronouns in Old English Poetry: Some Syntactical Notes', *RES* 15 (1964), 129–41.

—— 'Syntax and Word-Order in *The Peterborough Chronicle* 1122–1154', *NM* 65 (1964), 113–44.

—— 'Some Problems of Mood and Tense in Old English', *Neophil.* 49 (1965), 44–57.

—— 'Bede's *Habere* = Old English *Magan*?', *NM* 66 (1965), 107–11.

—— 'The Status of *Hwonne* in Old English', *Neophil.* 49 (1965), 157–60.

—— 'P. Bacquet, *La Structure de la phrase verbale à l'époque Alfrédienne*', *NM* 67 (1966), 86–97.

—— 'An Old English Syntactical Reverie: *The Wanderer*, lines 22 and 34-36', *NM* 68 (1967), 139-49.

—— '*Swa* in Cædmon's *Hymn*, Line 3', *NQ* 212 (1967), 203-4.

—— 'Old English Prose and the Computer', *Modern Language Association of America, Old English Newsletter*, 1. 2 (December 1967), 4-5.

—— 'More Musings on Old English Syntax', *NM* 69 (1968), 53-63.

—— 'Some Syntactical Problems in *The Wanderer*', *NM* 69 (1968), 172-98.

—— 'Two Syntactical Notes on *Beowulf*', *Neophil.* 52 (1968), 292-9.

—— 'Five Notes on Old English Syntax', *NM* 70 (1969), 70-84.

—— 'Postscript on Bede's *Mihi cantare habes*', *NM* 70 (1969), 369-80.

—— 'Report from a Meeting in London', *Computers and Old English Concordances*, edd. Cameron, A., Frank, R., and Leyerle, J. (Toronto, 1970), 83-7.

—— 'The Subject-Noun Object-Verb Pattern in *The Peterborough Chronicle*. A Reply', *NM* 71 (1970), 611-14.

—— 'The Narrator of *The Wife's Lament*. Some Syntactical Problems Reconsidered', *NM* 73 (1972), 222-34.

—— 'The "fuglas scyne" of *The Phoenix*, line 591', *Old English Studies in Honour of John C. Pope*, edd. Burlin, R. B. and Irving, E. B. Jr. (Toronto, 1974), 255-61.

—— 'Bede's Account of the Poet Cædmon: Two Notes', *Iceland and the Mediaeval World. Studies in Honour of Ian Maxwell*, edd. Turville-Petre, G. and Martin, J. S. (Melbourne, 1974), 126-31.

—— 'Linguistic Facts and the Interpretation of Old English Poetry', *ASE* 4 (1975), 11-28.

—— [with C. Ball and A. Cameron], 'Short Titles of Old English Texts', *ASE* 4 (1975), 207-21.

—— 'The Expression of Extent and Degree in Old English', *NM* 77 (1976), 25-31.

—— 'Some Problems involving Old English Periphrases with *beon/wesan* and the Present Participle', *NM* 77 (1976), 478-91.

—— 'No "house is building" in Old English', *EStudies*, 57 (1976), 385-9.

—— 'Old English *ac* as an Interrogative Particle', *NM* 78 (1977), 98-100.

—— 'Prepositions, Adverbs, Prepositional Adverbs, Postpositions, Separable Prefixes, or Inseparable Prefixes, in Old English?', *NM* 79 (1978), 240-57.

—— 'Old English "Oð þæt" Adverb?', *NQ* 223 (1978), 390-4.

—— 'Old English *Self*: Four Syntactical Notes', *NM* 80 (1979), 39-45.

—— 'F. Th. Visser, *An Historical Syntax of the English Language*: Some Caveats Concerning Old English', *EStudies*, 60 (1979), 537-42.

—— [with C. Ball and A. Cameron], 'Short Titles of Old English Texts: Addenda and Corrigenda', *ASE* 8 (1979), 331-3.

—— 'The Dangers of Disguise: Old English Texts in Modern Punctuation', *RES* 31 (1980), 385-413.

—— [with A. Kingsmill], 'Prepositions, Adverbs, Prepositional Adverbs, Postpositions, Separable Prefixes, or Inseparable Prefixes, in Old English? A Supplementary Bibliography', *NM* 81 (1980), 313-17.

—— 'Old English *man* "one": two notes', at press (*a*). [This has appeared in *Current Issues in Linguistic Theory*, 15 (Series IV, Amsterdam Studies in the Theory and History of Linguistic Science, 1982), 277-84.]

—— '*Beowulf*, Lines 3074-3075: The Damnation of Beowulf?', at press (*b*). [This has appeared in *Poetica* (Tokyo), 13 (1982 for 1980), 15-26.]

Mitchell, Bruce, 'The Origin of Old English Conjunctions: Some Problems', at press (c). [Accepted May 1981 for publication in *Historical Syntax*, ed. Fisiak, J. (The Hague and Paris).]

—— 'A Note on Negative Sentences in *Beowulf*', in progress (a). [This has appeared in *Poetica* (Tokyo), 15-16 (1983), 9-12.]

—— '*Cædmon's Hymn*, Line 1: What is the subject of *scylun* or its variants?', in progress (b).

—— 'The Syntax of *The Seafarer*, Lines 50-52', in progress (c).

Miyabe, K., 'Some Notes on Negative Sentences in *Beowulf*', *Poetica* (Tokyo), 2 (1974), 25-35.

MLJ = *Modern Language Journal.*

MLN = *Modern Language Notes.*

MLQ = *Modern Language Quarterly.*

MLR = *Modern Language Review.*

Möllmer, H., *Konjunktionen und Modus im Temporalsatz des Altenglischen* (Sprache und Kultur der germanischen und romanischen Völker, Reihe A, 24) (Breslau, 1937).

Mohrbutter, A., *Darstellung der Syntax in den vier echten Predigten des angelsächsischen Erzbischofs Wulfstan* (Münster diss., 1885).

Moore, R. W., *Comparative Greek and Latin Syntax* (London, 1934).

Mossé, F., *Histoire de la forme périphrastique être + participe présent en germanique, Première Partie: Introduction. Ancien germanique- Vieil-anglais* (Paris, 1938).

—— *Manuel de l'anglais du moyen âge des origines au XIVe siècle, I. Vieil-anglais* (Paris, 1945).

Most, S. M., 'Intensive and Restrictive Modification in a Select Corpus of Old English Poetry and Prose' (Ph.D. diss., Northwestern University, 1969). [A revised version appeared as AF 124 (1978). See Ingersoll, S. M.]

Mourek, V. E., 'Zur Syntax des Konjunktivs im *Beowulf*', *Präger deutsche Studien*, 8 (1908), 121-37.

MP = *Modern Philology.*

MS = *Medieval Studies.*

Müllner, A., *Die Stellung des attributiven Adjektivs im Englischen* (New York, 1909).

Mustanoja, T. F., *A Middle English Syntax, Part I* (Helsinki, 1960).

Muxin, A. M., *Functional Analysis of Syntactic Elements on the material of Old English—Funkcional'nyj analiz sintaksičeskix èlementov na materiale drevne-anglijskogo jazyka* (Moscow and Leningrad, 1964).

Nader, E., 'Dativ und Instrumental im *Beowulf*' in *22. Jahresbericht der Wiener Communal-Ober-Realschule* (1882-3).

—— 'Tempus und Modus im *Beowulf*', *Ang.* 10 (1887-8), 542-63, and ibid. 11 (1888-9), 444-99.

—— 'Zur Syntax des *Beowulf*', in *Programme der Staats-Ober-Realschule in Brünn am Schlusse des Schuljahres*, 1879 (nominativ und akkusativ), 1880 (akkusativ), 1882 (genitiv).

Nadler, H., *Studien zum attributiven Genetiv des Angelsächsischen* (Berlin diss., 1916).

Nagashima, D., 'A Historical Study of the Introductory *There*, Part I. The Old English Period', *Studies in Foreign Languages and Literature* (Osaka), 8 (1972), 135-68.

Neckel, G., *Über die altgermanischen Relativsätze* (Palaestra, 5) (1900).

Neophil. = *Neophilologus.*

Nesfield, J. C., *Manual of English Grammar and Composition* (rev. edn., London, 1924).

Nickel, G., *Die expanded Form im Altenglischen. Vorkommen, Funktion und Herkunft der Umschreibung 'beon/wesan' + Partizip Präsens* (Neumünster, 1966).

—— 'An Example of a Syntactic Blend in Old English', *IF* 72 (1967), 261-74.

Nicolai, O., *Die Bildung des Adverbs im Altenglischen* (Kiel diss., 1907).

NJL = *Nordic Journal of Linguistics*, 1-   (1978-   ). [See *NTS*.]

NM = *Neuphilologische Mitteilungen.*

Noack, P., *Eine Geschichte der relativen Pronomina in der englischen Sprache* (Göttingen, 1882).

NQ = *Notes and Queries.*

NS = *Die neueren Sprachen.*

NTS = *Norsk Tidsskrift for Sprogvidenskap*, 1-31 (1928-77). [After 1978, see *NJL*.]

Nummenmaa, L., *The Uses of 'So', 'Also' and 'As' in Early Middle English* (Mémoires de la Société néophilologique de Helsinki, 39) (1973).

Nunn, H. P. V., *An Introduction to Ecclesiastical Latin* (3rd edn., Eton, 1951).

Nusser, O., *Geschichte der Disjunktivkonstruktionen im Englischen* (AF 37) (1913).

OED = *Oxford English Dictionary.*

OEG = Campbell, A., *Old English Grammar* (reprinted Oxford, 1969).

OEN = *Old English Newsletter* (published for the Old English Division of the Modern Language Association of America).

Ogawa, H., 'Modal Verbs in Noun Clauses after Volitional Expressions in the Old English *Orosius*', *Studies in English Literature* (Tokyo), English Number (1979), 115-37.

Ogura, M., '*Verba Dicendi* in Old English Poetry', *Bunken Ronshu* (Senshu University), 3 (1978), 1-26.

—— '*Cweðan* and *Secgan* in Old English Prose', *Bunken Ronshu* (Senshu University), 4 (1979), 1-30.

Ohlander, U., 'Omission of the Object in English', *SN* 16 (1943-4), 105-27.

Okasha, E., *Hand-List of Anglo-Saxon Non-Runic Inscriptions* (Cambridge, 1971).

Oldenburg, K., *Untersuchungen über die Syntax in dem altenglischen Gedicht 'Judith'* (Rostock diss., 1907).

O'Neil, W., 'Clause Adjunction in Old English', *General Linguistics*, 17 (1977), 199-211.

Onions, C. T., *An Advanced English Syntax* (2nd edn., London, 1905).

Ono, S., 'The Old English Verbs of Knowing', *Studies in English Literature* (Tokyo), English Number (1975), 33-60.

Palm, B., *The Place of the Adjective Attributive in English Prose* (Lund diss., 1911).

Palmer, F. R., *A Linguistic Study of the English Verb* (London, 1965).

PB = *Société de linguistique de Paris, Bulletin.*

PBA = *Proceedings of the British Academy.*

PBB = *Beiträge zur Geschichte der deutschen Sprache und Literatur.*

Peltola, N., 'On the "identifying" *swa (swa)* phrase in Old English', *NM* 60 (1959), 156-73.

—— 'On appositional constructions in Old English prose', *NM* 61 (1960), 159-203.

Penning, G. E., *A History of the Reflective Pronouns in the English Language* (Leipzig diss., 1875).

Penttilä, E., *The Old English Verbs of Vision. A Semantic Study* (Mémoires de la Société néophilologique de Helsinki, 18) (1956).

Pessels, C., 'The Present and Past Periphrastic Tenses in Anglo-Saxon' (Johns Hopkins University diss., 1896).

PG = Pei, M. and Gaynor, F., *A Dictionary of Linguistics* (New York, 1954).

Ph. = Philologus.

Philipsen, H., *Über Wesen und Gebrauch des bestimmten Artikels in der Prosa König Alfreds auf Grund des* Orosius *(Hs. L) und der* Cura Pastoralis (Greifswald diss., 1887).

Philologica = Philologica. The Malone Anniversary Studies, edd. Kirby, T. A. and Woolf, H. B. (Johns Hopkins, 1949).

Phoenix, W., *Die Substantivierung des Adjektivs, Partizips und Zahlwortes im Angelsächsischen* (Berlin diss., 1918).

Pillsbury, P. W., *Descriptive Analysis of Discourse in Late West Saxon Texts* (The Hague and Paris, 1967).

Pingel, L., *Untersuchungen über die syntaktischen Erscheinungen in dem angelsächsischen Gedicht von den 'Wundern der Schöpfung'* (Rostock diss., 1905).

Pinsker, H., *Altenglisches Studienbuch* (Düsseldorf, 1976).

PL = Papers in Linguistics (Illinois).

Plan = A Plan for the Dictionary of Old English, edd. Frank, R. and Cameron, A. (Toronto, 1973).

Plezia, M. (ed.), *Lexicon Mediae et Infimae Latinitatis Polonorum. Słownik Łaciny Średniowiecznej w Polsce* (Academia Scientiarum Polona, 1953–   ).

PLL = Papers in Language and Literature.

PMLA = Publications of the Modern Language Association of America.

Pogatscher, A., 'Unausgedrücktes Subjekt im Altenglischen', *Ang.* 23 (1901), 261–301.

Pope, *Ælfric*, i, ii = Pope, J. C. (ed.), *Homilies of Ælfric*, i (EETS, OS 259) (1967); ii (ibid. 260) (1968).

Pope Studies = Old English Studies in Honour of John C. Pope edd. Burlin, R. B. and Irving, E. P., Jr. (Toronto, 1974).

Postscript. See Andrew.

PQ = Philological Quarterly.

Prollius, M., *Über den syntaktischen Gebrauch des Conjunctivs in den Cynewulfschen Dichtungen 'Elene', 'Juliana' und 'Crist'* (Marburg diss., 1888).

Prose text dissertations. See 'The prose text dissertations'.

PSt. = Studies in English by members of the English Seminar of the Charles University, Prague.

Püttmann, A., 'Die Syntax der sogenannten progressiven Form im Alt- und Frühmittelenglischen', *Ang.* 31 (1908), 405–52.

Quirk, R., *The Concessive Relation in Old English Poetry* (Yale Studies in English, 124) (1954). [See Mitchell, *MÆ* 25 (1956), 36–40.]

Quirk, R., Greenbaum, S., Leech, G., and Svartnik, J. (edd.), *A Grammar of Contemporary English* (London, 1972).

QW = Quirk, R. and Wrenn, C. L., *An Old English Grammar* (2nd edn., London, 1958).

Raith, J., *Untersuchungen zum englischen Aspekt* (Munich, 1951).

Rauert, M., *Die Negation in den Werken Alfreds* (Kiel diss., 1910).

Raw, B. C., *The Art and Background of Old English Poetry* (London, 1978).

RES = *Review of English Studies.*

Reszkiewicz, A., 'Split Constructions in Old English', *Studies in Language and Literature in Honour of Margaret Schlauch* (Warsaw, 1966), 313–26.

—— *Ordering of Elements in Late Old English Prose in Terms of their Size and Structural Complexity* (Komitet Neofilologiczny Polskiej Akademii Nauk) (1966).

Reussner, H. A., *Untersuchungen über die Syntax in dem angelsächsischen Gedichte vom heiligen Andreas (Ein Beitrag zur angelsächsischen Grammatik, I. Das Verbum)*. (Leipzig diss., 1889.)

Reuter, O., *On Continuative Relative Clauses in English. A Feature of English Syntax and Style ascribed to Latin Influence* (Helsingfors, 1936).

Riggert, G., *Der syntaktische Gebrauch des Infinitivs in der altenglischen Poesie* (Kiel diss., 1909).

Rissanen, M., *The Uses of 'One' in Old and Middle English* (Helsinki, 1967). [This work is sometimes referred to as Rissanen instead of Rɨssanen 1967a.]

—— 'Old English *þæt an* "only" ', *NM* 68 (1967), 409–28.

Robertson, W. A., *Tempus und Modus in der altenglischen Chronik, Hss. A und E (C.C.C.C. 173, Laud 636)* (Marburg diss., 1906).

Robinson, F. C., 'Syntactical Glosses in Latin Manuscripts of Anglo-Saxon Provenance', *Speculum*, 48 (1973), 443–75.

—— 'Two Aspects of Variation in Old English Poetry', *Old English Poetry. Essays on Style*, ed. Calder, D. G. (Berkeley, 1979), 127–45.

—— 'Old English Literature in Its Most Immediate Context', *Old English Literature in Context: Ten Essays*, ed. Niles, J. D. (Bury St. Edmunds, 1980), 11–29.

Rössger, R., 'Über den syntaktischen Gebrauch des Genitivs in Cynewulf's *Elene, Crist* und *Juliana*', *Ang.* 8 (1885), 338–70.

Ropers, K., *Zur Syntax und Stilistik des Pronominalgebrauchs bei Ælfric* (Kiel diss., 1918).

Rose, A., *Darstellung der Syntax in Cynewulfs Crist* (Leipzig diss., 1890).

Royster, J. F., 'The Causative Use of *Hatan*', *JEGP* 17 (1918), 82–93.

—— 'Old English Causative Verbs', *SP* 19 (1922), 328–56.

Rübens, G., *Parataxe und Hypotaxe in dem ältesten Teil der Sachsenchronik* (Göttingen diss., 1915).

Rynell, A., *Parataxis and Hypotaxis as a Criterion of Syntax and Style, especially in Old English Poetry* (Lund, 1952).

SAP = *Studia Anglicana Posnaniensia.*

Sawyer, P. H., *Anglo-Saxon Charters. An Annotated List and Bibliography* (London, 1968).

SB = *Altenglische Grammatik nach der Angelsächsischen Grammatik von Eduard Sievers*, rev. K. Brunner (2nd, rev. edn., Halle, 1951).

Schaar, C., *Critical Studies in the Cynewulf Group* (Lund Studies in English, 17) (1949).

Schabram, H., '*Andreas* 303A und 360B–362A. Bemerkungen zur Zählebigkeit philologischer Fehlurteile', *Geschichtlichkeit und Neuanfang im sprachlichen Kunstwerk*, edd. Erlebach, P., Müller, W. G., and Reuter, K. (Tübingen, 1981), 39–47.

Schaubert, E. von, *Vorkommen, gebietsmässige Verbreitung und Herkunft altenglischer absoluter Partizipialkonstruktionen in Nominativ und Akkusativ* (Paderborn, 1954).

Scheler, M., *Altenglische Lehnsyntax. Die syntaktischen Latinismen im Altenglischen* (Berlin, 1961).

Schlauch Studies = *Studies in Language and Literature in Honour of Margaret Schlauch*, edd. Brahmer, M., Helsztyński, S., and Krzyzanowski, J. (Warsaw, 1966).

Schrader, B., *Studien zur Ælfricschen Syntax* (Jena, 1887).

Schuchardt, R., *Die Negation im Beowulf* (Berlin diss., 1910).

Schücking, L. L., *Die Grundzüge der Satzverknüpfung im Beowulf* (Halle, 1904).

Schürmann, J., *Darstellung der Syntax in Cynewulfs* Elene (Münster diss., 1884).

Sehrt, E. H., *Vollständiges Wörterbuch zum Heliand und zur altsächsischen Genesis* (Göttingen and Baltimore, 1925).

SEL (Tokyo) = *Studies in English Literature* (Tokyo).

Shannon, A., *A Descriptive Syntax of the Parker Manuscript of the Anglo-Saxon Chronicle from 734 to 891* (The Hague, 1964).

Shearin, H. G., *The Expression of Purpose in Old English Prose* (Yale Studies in English, 18) (1903).

—— 'The Expression of Purpose in Old English Poetry', *Ang.* 32 (1909), 235-52.

Shipley, G., 'The Genitive Case in Anglo-Saxon Poetry' (Johns Hopkins University diss., 1903).

Shippey, T. A., *Old English Verse* (London, 1972).

Sisam, K., *Studies in the History of Old English Literature* (Oxford, 1953).

Small, G. W., *The Comparison of Inequality* (Baltimore, 1924).

—— 'The Syntax of *The* with the Comparative', *MLN* 41 (1926), 300-13.

—— *The Germanic Case of Comparison with a special study of English* (Language Monographs of the Linguistic Society of America, 4) (1929).

—— 'The Syntax of *The* and OE *þon ma þe*', *PMLA* 45 (1930), 368-91.

Smith, C. A., 'The Order of Words in Anglo-Saxon Prose', *PMLA* 8 (1893), 210-44.

SN = *Studia Neophilologica*.

Sorg, W., *Zur Syntax und Stilistik des Pronominalgebrauches in der älteren angelsächsischen Dichtung* (Breslau diss., 1912).

SP = *Studies in Philology*.

Spec. = *Speculum*.

SPET = Society for Pure English Tracts.

Sprockel, C., *The Language of the Parker Chronicle*, i. *Phonology and Accidence;* ii. *Word-Formation and Syntax* (The Hague, 1965 and 1973). [See Mitchell, *RES* 25 (1974), 452-4.]

SS. See Andrew.

Standop, E., *Syntax und Semantik der modalen Hilfsverben im Altenglischen 'magan', 'motan', 'sculan', 'willan'* (Bochum-Langendreer, 1957). [See Mitchell, *NQ* 7 (1960), 273-4.]

Steadman, J. M., Jr., 'The Origin of the Historical Present in English', *North Carolina Studies in Philology*, 14 (1917), 1-46.

Steche, G., *Der syntaktische Gebrauch der Conjunctionen in dem angelsächsischen Gedichte von der Genesis* (Leipzig diss., 1895).

Stewart, A. H., 'The Old English "Passive" Infinitive', *Journal of English Linguistics*, 7 (1973), 57-68.

—— 'The Development of the Verb-Phrase Complement with Verbs of Physical Perception in English: Historical Linguistics as a Source of Deep Structures', *Journal of English Linguistics*, 10 (1976), 34-53.

Stieger, F., *Untersuchungen über die Syntax in dem angelsächsischen Gedicht vom 'Jüngsten Gericht'* (Rostock diss., 1902).

Stoelke, H., *Die Inkongruenz zwischen Subjekt und Prädikat im Englischen und in den verwandten Sprachen* (AF 49) (1916).

Süsskand, P., *Geschichte des unbestimmten Artikels im Alt- und Frühmittelenglischen* (Halle, 1935).

Suter, K., *Das Pronomen beim Imperativ im Alt- und Mittelenglischen* (Aarau, 1955).

Sweet, *NEG* i, ii = Sweet, H., *A New English Grammar, Part I. Introduction, Phonology, Accidence; Part II. Syntax* (Oxford, 1892 and 1898).

Sweet, *Pr.* 9 = *Sweet's Anglo-Saxon Primer*, 9th edn., rev. N. Davis (Oxford, 1953).

Sweet, *R.* 1-14 = Sweet, H., *An Anglo-Saxon Reader in Prose and Verse* (Oxford). 1-14 = 1st-14th editions.

Sweet, *R.* 15 = *Sweet's Anglo-Saxon Reader in Prose and Verse*, revised throughout by D. Whitelock (Oxford, 1967). [See Mitchell, *RES* 19 (1968), 415-16.]

TAPS = *American Philological Society Transactions and Proceedings.*

Taubert, E. M., *Der syntactische Gebrauch der Präpositionen in dem angelsächsischen Gedicht vom heiligen Andreas* (Leipzig diss., 1894).

Tellier, A., *Les Verbes perfecto-présents et les auxiliaires de mode en anglais ancien* (Paris, 1962).

Terasawa, Y., Review of F. Th. Visser, *An Historical Syntax of the English Language, Studies in English Literature* (Tokyo), English Number (1971), 125-36.

'The eighteen German dissertations'. These are the dissertations on individual OE poems by Ahrens, Conradi, Dethloff, Fraatz, Fritsche, Höser, Jacobsen, R., Kempf, Lange, Madert, Mahn, Meyer, Oldenburg, Pingel, Reussner, Rose, Schürmann, Stieger.

'The prose text dissertations'. These are the dissertations on individual prose texts by Barela, Brown (1963, 1970), Carlton (1958, 1970), Closs, Flamme, Haddock, Mohrbutter, Schrader, Shannon, Tilley, Wülfing (1888), Zuck.

Thomas, R., *Syntactical Processes Involved in the Development of the Adnominal Periphrastic Genitive in the English Language* (Michigan diss., 1931).

Thorpe, *Dip. Ang.* = Thorpe, B., *Diplomatarium Anglicum Ævi Saxonici* (London, 1865).

Tilley, M. P., *Zur Syntax Wærferths* (Leipzig diss., 1903).

Timmer, B. J., *Studies in Bishop Wærferth's Translation of the Dialogues of Gregory the Great* (Wageningen, 1934).

—— 'The Place of the Attributive Noun-Genitive in Anglo-Saxon with special reference to Gregory's "Dialogues" ', *EStudies*, 21 (1939), 49-72.

TLS = *Times Literary Supplement.*

TPS = *Philological Society Transactions.*

Traugott, E. Closs, *A History of English Syntax. A Transformational Approach to the History of English Sentence Structure* (New York, 1972).

Trnka, B., *Syntaktická charakteristika řeči anglosaských památek básnických* (Prague Studies in English, 2 (1925). [English subtitle: *A Syntactical Analysis of the Language of Anglo-Saxon Poetry.*]

TSLL = *Texas Studies in Literature and Language.*

Twaddell, W. P., *The English Verb Auxiliaries* (2nd edn. rev., Providence, 1963).

UZLGU = *Učenye zapiski Leningradskogo gosudarstvennogo universiteta, Serija filologičeskix nauk.*

UZLIJ = *Učenye zapiski I Leningradskogo gosudarstvennogo pedagogičeskogo instituta Inostrannyx jazykov.*

van Dam, J., *The Causal Clause and Causal Prepositions in early Old English Prose* (Groningen and Djakarta, 1957).

van der Gaaf, W., 'The Passive of a Verb accompanied by a Preposition', *EStudies*, 12 (1930), 1-24.

Varnhagen, H., *An Inquiry into the Origin and Different Meanings of the English particle 'but'* (Göttingen, 1876).

Visser, i, ii, iii = Visser, F. Th., *An Historical Syntax of the English Language*, iii vols. (Leiden, 1963-73).

Vleeskruyer, R. (ed.), *The Life of St Chad* (Amsterdam, 1953).

Voges, F., 'Der reflexive Dativ im Englischen', *Ang.* 6 (1883), 317-74.

Vogt, A., *Beiträge zur Konjunktivgebrauch im Altenglischen* (Borna and Leipzig, 1930).

Wack, G., 'Artikel und Demonstrativpronomen in *Andreas* und *Elene*', *Ang.* 15 (1893), 209-20.

Wagner, R., *Die Syntax des Superlativs im Gotischen, Altniederdeutschen, Althochdeutschen, Frühmittelhochdeutschen, im Beowulf und in der älteren Edda* (Palaestra, 91) (1910).

Wahlén, N., *The Old English Impersonalia, Part I. Impersonal Expressions containing Verbs of Material Import in the Active Voice* (Göteborg diss., 1925). [No Part II seems to have appeared.]

Waterhouse, R., 'The Two-to-One Construction in Ælfric's *Lives of Saints*', *Working Papers of the Speech and Language Research Centre, Macquarie University*, 1, no. 4 (July 1976), 173-200.

—— 'Some Syntactic and Stylistic Aspects of Ælfric's "Lives of Saints" ' (Macquarie University diss., 1978).

Wattie, J. M., 'Tense', *ES* 16 (1930), 121-43.

Wende, F., *Über die nachgestellten Präpositionen im Angelsächsischen* (Palaestra, 70) (1915).

West, F., 'The Cumulative Sentence in Old and Middle English' (University of Nevada diss., 1969).

Whitelock, D. (ed.), *Sermo Lupi ad Anglos* (3rd edn., London, 1963).

Wilde, H. O., 'Aufforderung, Wunsch und Möglichkeit', *Ang.* 63 (1939), 209-391, and ibid. 64 (1940), 10-105.

Williams, R. A., *The Finn Episode in Beowulf* (Cambridge, 1924).

Wood, F. T., 'Some Aspects of Conditional Clauses in English', *Moderna Språk*, 54 (1960), 355-64.

Wrenn–CH = *Beowulf and the Finnesburg Fragment. A Translation into Modern English Prose by J. R. Clark Hall, completely revised with Notes and an Introduction* by C. L. Wrenn (London, 1950).

Wülfing, i, ii = Wülfing, J. E., *Die Syntax in den Werken Alfreds des Grossen*, 2 vols. (Bonn, 1894 and 1901).

Wülfing, (J.) E., *Darstellung der Syntax in König Alfred's Übersetzung von Gregor's des Grossen 'Cura Pastoralis'* (Bonn diss., 1888).

Wullen, F., *Der syntaktische Gebrauch der Präpositionen 'fram', 'under', 'ofer', 'þurh' in der angelsächsischen Poesie. I. Teil, 'fram', 'under'* (Kiel diss., 1908); *II. Teil, 'ofer', 'þurh'* (*Ang.* 34 (1911), 423-97).

Wyss, S., *Le Système du genre en vieil anglais jusqu'à la conquête* (Thèse pour le doctorat d'État, l'Université de Paris, III, Sorbonne Nouvelle, n.d.). [This has now been published under the same title by Atelier de publication des thèses de Lille, 1982.]

Yamakawa, K., 'The Imperative accompanied by the Second Personal Pronoun', *Hitotsubashi Journal of Arts and Sciences*, 7 (1966), 6-25.

——— 'The Development of *When* as Subordinate Conjunction or Relative Adverb', *Hitotsubashi Journal of Arts and Sciences*, 10 (1969), 8–42.

——— 'OE *þær* and *hwær*: A Study of *Where* developing in the subordinating function (I)', *Hitotsubashi Journal of Arts and Sciences*, 12 (1971), 1–19.

——— 'The Adverbial Accusative of Duration and Its Prepositional Equivalent, Part I. Old and Middle English', *Hitotsubashi Journal of Arts and Sciences*, 21 (1980), 1–39.

Yerkes, D., 'Studies in the Manuscripts of the Old English Translation of the "Dialogues" of Gregory the Great' (Oxford diss., 1976). [The findings of this thesis have been distilled in two works: those on the vocabulary in *The Two Versions of Wærferth's Translation of Gregory's Dialogues: An Old English Thesaurus* (Toronto, 1979) and those on syntax in *Syntax and Style in Old English: A Comparison of the Two Versions of Wærferth's Translation of Gregory's Dialogues* (Binghamton N.Y., 1982)——a book which demands the close attention of those interested in the development of the English language.]

Yoshino, Y., 'A Restriction on Passivization in Old English', *Studies in English Linguistics* (Tokyo), 5 (1977), 281–90.

YWES = *The Year's Work in English Studies*.

Zadorožny, B., 'Zur Frage der Bedeutung und des Gebrauchs der Partizipien im Altgermanischen', *PBB* (Halle), 94 (1973), 52–76, and ibid. 95 (1974), 339–87.

Zeitlin, J., *The Accusative with Infinitive and Some Kindred Constructions in English* (New York, 1908).

ZfdA = *Zeitschrift für deutsches Altert(h)um.*

ZfdP = *Zeitschrift für deutsche Philologie.*

Zuck, L., 'The Syntax of the Parker Manuscript of the Anglo-Saxon Chronicle from the year 892 through 1001' (University of Michigan diss., 1966).

Postscript

Campbell, *OEG* = *OEG*.

Doyle, D., 'Coordination, Subordination, and Sentence Structure in Old English Poetry: An Inquiry into Aspects of the Interplay between Syntax and Style' (University of Pennsylvania Ph.D. diss., 1981).

McLaughlin, J., *Old English Syntax. A Handbook* (Tübingen, 1983). [See Mitchell, *RES* 35 (1984), 217–18.]

Mitchell, Bruce, '*Old English Syntax*: a Review of the Reviews' (to be published posthumously).

INTRODUCTION

THE study of OE syntax needs no defence. In *RES* 3 (1952), 166, Alistair Campbell wrote:

Nothing is more to be deplored in Old English studies than the prevailing neglect of style and syntax by the ordinary 'specialist' (student or teacher). Scholars with a sound knowledge of the syntactic structure of Old English have published work every decade or so since about 1880, but the working Old English scholar seldom familiarizes himself with their results sufficiently to benefit his own work, and hence, efficient as he usually is in phonology and metrics, he is ever ready to emend absurdly, mispunctuate, and mistranslate.

He could have added a tendency to utter banalities and to forget the dictum—beloved of my sometime headmaster—that 'nonsense is always wrong'; consider the ASPR notes on *WaldB* 27 ff. (last sentence) and on *Seasons* 83b–86 (first sentence) and see Mitchell 1964*a*, pp. 130-1. There has no doubt been some improvement in the thirty years since Campbell wrote. But we still find unnecessary emendations being made, e.g. *sið* to *siðe* in *Wife* 2 (see Mitchell 1972); unnecessary difficulties being created, e.g. the interpretation of *butan* in *GenB* 243 (see Mitchell 1969*a*, pp. 70-2, and Vickrey, *NM* 71 (1970), 191-2); and wrong interpretations being proffered, e.g. Bright's idea (followed by Krapp in ASPR) that *æfter* can be a conjunction in *Ex* 109 (see Irving's note and my §2654) and (I believe) the reading *me aht* in *Bede* 344. 1 (see Mitchell 1969*b*). But the study of OE syntax has more than therapeutic value. It can throw light on inflexional problems (see Mitchell 1969*a*, pp. 72-5); help to resolve semantic difficulties (see Mitchell 1969*b*, pp. 374-6, and Mitchell 1974*b*, pp. 126-8); aid our literary appreciation, e.g. in *Max i* 97 (§2318) and in *Ex* 280, where Tolkien's *nu* for MS *hu* (§3100) disposes of Legouis and Cazamian's charge that Moses becomes 'an artless gossip whom the miracle seems to amaze as much as it does his people'; and can lead to investigations of unsuspected complexity and value (consider where Robinson's simple self-question concerning *eac* in *MetEp* 1—' "Also" in addition to what?' (Robinson 1980, p. 15)—led him).

The syntactician of OE cannot, however, hope to answer all relevant questions. He lacks native informants and a knowledge of the intonation patterns of the language. His corpus is limited in size and in range. It is limited to written texts, the punctuation of which presents difficulties; see §§1879-82. Few if any of these texts can be localized and dated definitely or guaranteed free from later scribal changes; see Mitchell, *MÆ* 48 (1979), 121. There is little, if any, colloquial material. A study of the passages in direct speech (§§1635 and 1935) and of texts like *ApT* suggests itself here but is, I would think, unlikely to produce an effective distillation of the colloquial or spoken language. Another possibly valuable approach is suggested by Royster 1922, pp. 342-3:

The behavior of the superior-class language of the Old English record must be regarded in relation to the practices and conditions of Middle English writing. The bearing of Old English language habits observable in the record upon Middle English language forms and manner of expression has received an undue share of consideration in comparison with the attention which has been given to the possible bearing of the facts of usage to be found in the Middle English record upon the form and structure of the unrecorded language of the Old English period. In a more nearly colloquial Middle English document may be represented habits and practices of the widely used Old English language that do not appear in one of our formal Old English literary compositions. So far as its language is concerned, a document of the year one thousand may have been old at the time of its writing; its traditional language may have been many years behind the speech current when it was written. This consideration has been too easily overlooked by students of our language, intent upon establishing an orderly development of that institution, and too desirous of 'deriving' the Middle English written language directly from the models of the Old English language whose record we have inherited. In its intention to establish a smoothly flowing descent, the historical method has been too nearly unwilling to recognize genetic gaps.

Two stray points about prepositions serve to remind us that we are dealing with a written language which may be cut off from the spoken language in many ways. First, there is at least the possibility that the dative after *þurh*, which Ælfric used and subsequently rejected (§1207), was a feature of his spoken language. Second, there is Lebow's observation (p. 574) that because the percentage of prepositional phrases is higher and that of case phrases is lower (according to his figures) in *Chron* than in contemporary texts, 'we are forced to assume that the Chronicle was kept by men who wrote as they spoke and who spoke in a manner much more modern than the other writers of the time indicate'. A systematic examination of these and other variations might throw some light on spoken Old English.

The fact that the corpus is so limited means that the existence of syntactical *hapax legomena* is a very real possibility. Old English scholars have not yet defined their attitude to these. There is a conflict between syntax and metre in *Ex* 248 (§2780) and between literary considerations and linguistic arguments or, as I prefer to call them, facts in *Wan* 41 (§2608 and Mitchell 1975a, pp. 11-12 and 25-8). Here I venture to point out that of the four arguments set out below—all of which have been used consciously or unconsciously

by writers on OE syntax; see Mitchell 1968*c*, p. 297, Mitchell 1972,
p. 224 fn. 4 and pp. 231-2, and Mitchell, at press (*b*)—only the last
is respectable: 'There are examples, therefore this must be one';
'There are not many examples, therefore this can't be one'; 'There
are no examples, therefore this can't be one'; and 'There are no
examples, but this may be one'. Kaske (ΠΑΡΑΔΟΣΙΣ. *Studies in
Memory of Edwin A. Quain* (New York, 1976), 59) has posed the
question neatly: 'What degree of syntactic adventurousness can be
justified in cases where all other approaches are demonstrably unsatisfactory, and where the resulting construction, if it can be accepted,
seems neatly to solve all the other outstanding problems?' But the
problem remains: it is that of deciding and agreeing 'where all other
approaches are demonstrably unsatisfactory'. It will remain even
when we have a record of all the constructions which occur in the
extant corpus.

'There is', remarks Mather (p. 7), 'a certain humble satisfaction
even in an unintelligent knowledge of the facts.' As full a knowledge of the facts as is possible must be acquired before 'rules' can
be erected and theories formulated. It was my ignorance of many
facts which compelled me to abandon my hopes of producing an *Old
English Syntax* along the lines of Goodwin's *Greek Grammar* or
Gildersleeve and Lodge's *Latin Grammar*. Works such as these depend
on continuous study—admittedly of varying degrees of intensity—
over a period of more than two thousand years; see R. H. Robins,
Ancient and Mediæval Grammatical Theory in Europe (London,
1951), 6 and *passim*. The study of Old English is much less well
documented. Even now, I cannot agree with the implications of Heltveit's remark (*EStudies* 50 (1969), 229-30) that in Einenkel's time
'Old English syntax had not yet been very thoroughly investigated'.
That this stage has not been reached even yet has been regularly
brought home to me as I considered unusual or rare constructions,
for I have never been in a position to say that there are no such constructions in the prose and have not always been able to say that
there are none in the poetry. Not being a native informant, I have
not been able to say that such a construction did not or could not
exist or that such an interpretation was impossible. I can appreciate
the reason for the sampling procedures described by Kohonen (1974)
when one is studying something like element order. But by using
them one runs the risk of missing the vital rarity; see Mitchell 1975*a*,
pp. 24-7. In these circumstances, it seemed to me premature to follow Quirk (p. 1) and other modern scholars in preferring the functional to the formal approach; one does not retire the horse before
the engine has been installed in the horseless carriage.

Quirk (p. 1) sums up an important article by Small—'On the Study of Old English Syntax' (*PMLA* 51 (1936), 1–7)—thus: 'We must concentrate, says Small, on relationship and function, in a combination of the descriptive, historical, and comparative approaches. There is now, he adds, no room for the pure descriptivism of 1910.' The last eight words, which Bacquet (p. 22) seems to have picked up and of which, like Quirk, he seems to approve, were not actually used by Small and in my opinion are likely to mislead those who do not read his article. They appear to be based on this passage (p. 6):

> It is conceivable that an investigator may wish to confine his research to the purely descriptive method, deliberately avoiding any historical or comparative comment. Old English syntax a generation ago went through a vogue for this kind of study. The results of this poorly digested tabulation placed in our hands a mass of statistics seldom looked at by present-day investigators. . . . To bury one's head in an Old English text, expecting to interpret a construction through its context alone, can no longer be considered a scientific procedure.

But just before this (pp. 5–6), Small wrote:

> Whether the study is to be descriptive, historical, or comparative, the statistics upon which it is based should embrace all the available examples in Old English literature. This requirement, may at first seem too exacting, but the condition set forth above—namely, that scattered and somewhat artificial groups of writings compose the body of Old English literature—makes it dangerous to generalize upon selected examples.

So Small was not rejecting descriptivism. On the contrary, he was urging that it was an essential foundation.

I am not sure whose work Small had in mind when he spoke of 'a mass of statistics seldom looked at by present-day investigators'. It is unlikely that he was referring to 'the eighteen German dissertations' or to those of Flamme, Mohrbutter, and the like, which contain lists of examples rather than masses of statistics and some of which were written more than 'a generation ago'. He was certainly not tilting at Burnham (1911), who did not bother to give a list of *þeah (þe)* clauses; see §§3401 and 3427. It is most likely that his targets were the unwieldy and certainly 'seldom looked at' by me endpapers such as those provided by (among others) Shearin (1903), Adams (1907), and Callaway (1913). Yet Small's criticism is too damning for these investigators. All of them give collections of examples which I have found invaluable. And, though they have their faults, none of them can, in my opinion, be convicted of 'pure descriptivism'.

However, the important thing is Small's demand that the OE syntactician's statistics 'should embrace all the available examples in Old English literature'. For the reasons given later in this Introduction,

I have not been able to achieve such completeness, but have presented what statistics I could where they seemed relevant and helpful. *A Microfiche Concordance to Old English* puts this completeness within the reach of future workers, who might do well to meditate on the 'need for a more thoughtful use of statistics' urged by Edwards when writing on the language of Hesiod in *Publications of the Philological Society*, 22 (1971), 208.

As a result of all this, I found myself compelled to continue the formal descriptive approach which—in agreement with Sweet's dictum (*NEG* i. 204) that 'it is evident that all study of grammar must begin with being purely descriptive'—I used in my Oxford D.Phil. thesis 'Subordinate Clauses in Old English Poetry' (Mitchell 1959, pp. ix–xiv). My aims here then are to set out descriptively what I take to be the basic principles of the syntax of OE prose and poetry; to indicate the problems which need resolution or call for clarification; and (subject to the reservations made in my introductory comments to the Select Bibliography) to give some idea of the value of the various books, monographs, articles, and notes, on OE syntax. The justification for reviewing such works—some are still important, some are collections of examples which may be superseded by the microfiche concordance, and some have no value except possibly an admonitory or sentimental one—is that the time is past when OE syntacticians should ostrich-like pretend that no one has ever heard of OE syntax or, while citing authorities but apparently working from first principles, should utter with the air of a Jack Horner such observations as 'On listing all clauses introduced by *þa*, I found that word order is pertinent to the solution' (see Mitchell, *MÆ* 40 (1971), 182, and *RES* 25 (1974), 453).

I have adopted the old-fashioned formal Latin-based grammar of the Joint Committee because I am persuaded that, with all its faults, it remains the most serviceable for the study of OE syntax. OE is an Indo-European language and shares many of the structures of Latin. The conventional categories work for OE and do not have to be scrapped merely because they do not work for some non-Indo-European languages. Much of extant OE literature is translated from or based on Latin originals. We have therefore to study Latin loan syntax. And in his *Grammar*, Ælfric, a native speaker of OE, related his language to the structures of Latin. So my reluctance to abandon this traditional grammar is due, not to a stubborn refusal to acknowledge the existence of systems such as those proposed by Jespersen and by Sandfeld (§1884), by Long (*American Speech*, 32 (1957), 12–30), by West (§1898), and by Pilch (§1633), but to a genuine inability to agree that what I had to say could have been said more clearly or more simply through any other system. Here a study of H. Pilch, *Altenglische Grammatik* (Munich, 1970) and the same author's *Altenglischer Lehrgang* (Munich, 1970) and of Lars-G. Hallander's review of both (*SN* 50 (1978), 135–41) is revealing. While praising the former as marking 'a new approach to the field of Old English: a refreshing case of heterodoxy, especially as regards syntax' (p. 135), Hallander goes on to observe that 'there are, happily, few references to the syntactic section of the grammar' in the latter (p. 141).

It may be objected that I have failed to take full advantage of computers. It is true that computers can make lists, produce tables, find combinations, reveal unsuspected patterns, and perform other operations, faster than the human brain—and sometimes beyond its scope. But, as I suggest in §3957, I believe that (at present at any rate) the brain of a scholar is an instrument both more speedy and more sensitive for OE syntactical analysis than any computer. A recent 'progress report on the use of computer methods to analyse some aspects of the syntax of Old English prose texts' (in *The Computer in Literary and Linguistic Studies*, edd. A. Jones and R. F. Churchhouse (Cardiff, 1976), pp. 285-92) rather gives the game away (p. 289):

> As there were so many different parameters, (some 15), it was very difficult to see the correlation between the various parameters. It was therefore necessary to impose certain limitations on the treatment of complex relationships.
>
> First, they had to be limited to certain combinations, which were thought central, and second, it was desirable to be able to look at the results in an understandable form.
>
> Therefore a program was written to produce the results in tabular form, which made it much easier to evaluate these.

What is the point of evaluating material—in tabular or any other form—which has been limited by the arbitrary imposition of constraints enforced by a computer and shaped by what can only be the preconceived notions of the investigator? The tool is too crude. It is as if one were to remove an appendix with hacksaw and pliers.

'Other reviewers [of A. Campbell, *Old English Grammar* (Oxford, 1959)]', remarked Bazell (*MÆ* 29 (1960), 28), 'will make a more general objection: this is an Oxford book and hence does not profit from the development of linguistic theory over the last three decades.' I have to state categorically my opinion that, on the evidence so far available to me, the techniques of the various forms of linguistics fashionable today have little to offer students of OE syntax. They depend on a knowledge of intonation patterns and a supply of native informants, neither of which is available. Some of them are apparently already out of date; for examples, see *OEN* 11. 1 (1977), 31–4. Some of the practitioners seem to know little Old English—a desire to be charitable restrains me here, but examples will be found within the covers of this book. Few of them are really interested in Old English for itself; witness such typical remarks as those of Pillsbury (p. 24) —'the purpose here is to test an analytical procedure against a specific language corpus'—and of Joly (1967, p. 44)—'However, the main interest of this study, if any, is the technique of analysis I have adopted.' See further Mitchell, *MÆ* 48 (1979), 121–2. A reviewer of Mitchell 1975*a* said in *OEN* 10. 1 (1976), 37, that 'the newer practice of linguistics seems to infuriate some OE scholars'. What infuriates me is its misuse. While acknowledging the debt I owe to some of its products, I have to say that in my opinion anything in them that was new to an OE syntactician could have been said more clearly in ordinary language. Many of its products, however, have led me to some dim understanding of what A. E. Housman might have been feeling when he penned his more bitter remarks.

The absence of a complete descriptive syntax of OE prose and poetry makes it inevitable that this book does not lay down 'rules' but asks questions, offers suggestions, and demonstrates the possibility of different interpretations. It also makes it inevitable that readers will detect a certain capriciousness in the range of examples quoted in different sections. Space has not always permitted that regular presentation of examples from 'Alfredian' texts, the *Blickling Homilies*, the works of Ælfric and Wulfstan, and the early and late poetry, which is desirable. In such situations, I have tried to select a variety of relevant examples or to illustrate the phenomenon from Ælfric and *Beowulf*, as best suited to my purpose. But if some other text yielded a particularly interesting set of comparative examples I have used them.[1] For constructions which occur rarely I have had to be content with an incomplete collection. I have, I fear, been beset by a constant dilemma in the prose and (to a slightly lesser extent because of my D.Phil. thesis) in the poetry. When first collecting examples, I had to be selective. But I was not then always aware what was to prove significant or rare. Now that I have acquired some understanding, I am not in a position to reread the corpus in an endeavour to find what I want or what I suspect to be there. It may seem strange that a man in this situation has not made full use of *A Microfiche Concordance to Old English*. There are two reasons. First, the *Concordance* was not available until the whole book was in final draft and even then the high frequency function words were not

---

[1] Examples from *GenesisB* have been included where relevant, but (as has been pointed out where necessary) are not always typical; see Capek, *Neophil.* 55 (1971), 89–96.

concorded. So its use would have meant delay and starting again to produce a book which would have been larger than the Press could have accepted. Second, I believe that the arrival of the *Concordance* means that the time is ripe for this book to be published as a base from which a new generation of scholars, armed with new material, can produce definitive monographs on the various constructions and on the peculiarities of different periods and genres and of individual texts and authors. For the benefit of such scholars, I confess some of my omissions in my Conclusion.

The preparation of these monographs will open the way for an authoritative *Old English Syntax* which will supersede this book—I shall have failed in my primary purpose if it is not superseded—and which in its turn will provide a basis for a comparative syntax of the cognate Germanic dialects and for a historical treatment of English syntax from the beginnings to the twentieth—or perhaps by then to the twenty-first—century. Even for such designs, I could not expect the sun to stand still upon Gibeon or the moon in the valley of Ajalon.

I

CONCORD

A. INTRODUCTORY REMARKS

§1. This chapter sets out the basic principles of concord in Old English, with references to the more detailed discussions which follow in later chapters. On the 'parts of speech', see §§48-53.

B. ELEMENTS CONCERNED IN CONGRUENCE

1. SOME AMBIGUITIES

§2. It is a recognized truth that Old English was becoming more analytic than its ancestors had been. It often had to rely on element order and prepositions to make distinctions which in a more fully inflected language would have been made by unambiguous case-endings (§§8-13). That the Old English verb was (comparatively speaking) a blunt instrument, a system of minimal morphological distinction—even though (as we see in §§1093-9) it held in embryo practically all the patterns found in the more flexible verb system of today—is clear from §§600-601a. Ambiguities often arise as a result of these and other factors—the long time span of the period and the consequent early and late forms, the dialectal variations, and the changes introduced by later scribes. Whether the full extent of these ambiguities has been widely enough recognized sometimes seems doubtful. Examples and forms which give rise to this feeling include

Ex 326   þracu wæs on ore,
   heard handplega,   hægsteald modige
    . . .   wigend unforhte . . . ,

where it is better to take *hægsteald* as nominative plural—cf. *wigend* in the next line—than to believe with Krapp that 'the noun is singular and *modige* is plural' (Mitchell 1969a, p. 73); *Max i* 78 *Deop deada wæg dyrne bið lengest holen*, where *deada* or (if we prefer to emend) *deaða* can be taken as a surviving genitive singular of the *u*-declension to which *deað* originally belonged (ibid., p. 73 fn. 4); the verb form *syn*, which in Wulfstan and elsewhere can be indicative as well as subjunctive (ibid., pp. 74-5), whereas Ælfric appears to use *syndon*, not only as an indicative, but also a subjunctive (see Pope, *Ælfric*, i. 101-2); and

Dan 399   We þec bletsiað
          . . .   . . .
          hæleða helpend,   and þec, halig gast,
          wurðað in wuldre,   witig drihten!

where *wurðað* is usually emended to *wurðiað*, but (as Farrell suggests in his edition of *Daniel and Azarias*, pp. 17 and 71) might stand as a late analogical plural form. As *Sea* 49 *wongas wlitigað* and *Rul somnaþ* beside *somniaþ* (*OEG*, §757) testify, it is not alone. See further §§18 and 20. More generally, there are the problems of un-accented vowels (§§14-16), of changes of class and gender in nouns (§§62-5), and (in syntax) our uncertainty about the exact signifi-cance of the various OE element orders (§§10-11). Some of these difficulties have been obscured by standardization, emendation, or misinterpretation; see G. L. Brook, 'The Relation between the Tex-tual and the Linguistic Study of Old English', *Dickins Studies*, pp. 280-91. There is, I believe, room for more work on morphology along the lines of Pope, *Ælfric*, i. 182-5.

2. GENDER

§3. Old English distinguished three categories of grammatical gender ('gender') as opposed to natural gender ('sex')—masculine, feminine, and neuter—in nouns, adjectives, some pronouns, and sometimes in numerals and participles. On the conflict between 'gender' and 'sex', see §§69-71. On other problems, see §§54-61 and 66-8.

3. PERSON

§4. First, second, and third, persons were distinguished in personal pronouns and in the *singular* of verbs. See §17.

4. NUMBER

§5. Singular and plural were distinguished in nouns, adjectives, par-ticiples, pronouns, and verbs. See §§9 and 18-20. The dual appeared in the first and second personal pronouns only. The plural was used in agreement with the dual where no dual form existed and some-times where one did. See §§257-9.

5. CASE

§6. It is an oft-stated commonplace that Old English had four cases —nominative, accusative, genitive, and dative—and significant remnants of a fifth—the instrumental—in the masculine and neuter singular of the demonstratives *se* and *þes*, of the interrogative *hwa*, and of the strong declension of the adjective. The dative serves where there is no instrumental and sometimes where there is. But see §§8-15.

6. MOOD, TENSE, AND VOICE

§7. Four moods can be distinguished—indicative, subjunctive, imperative, and infinitive—and two participles. But it is important to recognize that there are many ambiguous forms; see §§16-22 and 601a. There are two tenses—past and present—and one voice— the active—apart from the forms *hatte* 'is/was called', plural *hatton*. On 'attraction of mood', see the references given in the General Index; on the 'sequence of tenses', §§859-64; and on the development of forms involving *habban, wesan,* and *weorþan,* with participles, §§681-858.

C. INTRODUCTORY REMARKS ON CASE

1. GENERAL

§8. The simple statement made in §6 that Old English had four cases and significant remnants of a fifth requires qualification. It is well known that there are vestiges of other cases, such as the locative in *-i* and the endingless locative (*OEG,* §571). The instrumental subsumed forms of different origin.[1] Other aspects of case syncretism have not been neglected.[2] But the extent to which the case forms already overlapped is less often mentioned. It is difficult (indeed,

---

[1] According to Anderson (*JEGP* 57 (1958), 21-6), the forms of 'the fifth case in Old English' are in origin variously accusative, perhaps dative, instrumental, locative, and ablative. See also Sievers, *PBB* 8 (1882), 324-33, and Hofer, *Ang.* 7 (1884), 357-8. J. Kress's gallant attempt to distinguish the dative and instrumental on syntactical grounds where no formal difference existed was foredoomed to failure; see the first paragraph of his *Ueber den Gebrauch des Instrumentalis in der Angelsaechsischen Poesie* (Marburg, 1864).

[2] Discussions on syncretism in OE include: on accusative/dative syncretism Blakeley, *EGS* 1 (1947-8), 6-31, and Ross, *JEGP* 32 (1933), 481-2; on genitive/dative syncretism Shipley, pp. 12-13; and on dative/instrumental syncretism Green 1913. Green (1913, pp. 113-19, and 1914, pp. 516-17) attempts to draw a distinction between a real dative of agency which had its origin in the dative of interest and a dative/instrumental of agency which derived from a Gmc. sociative-comitative, or instrumental of association. For further discussion and references, see Stewart, *PL* 8 (1975), 165-76.

impossible) for us to know how real a problem it was for an Anglo-Saxon speaker, writer, hearer, or reader, that *wine* was nominative, accusative, and dative, in form, or that *giefe* could be accusative, genitive, or dative. But in my view the typical *Introduction to Old English* leaves the beginner with the impression that Old English depended on inflexions to a larger degree than in practice it did and does not sufficiently emphasize the fact that element order and prepositions were already important grammatical devices. I take up these points now. A. Campbell's *Old English Grammar* is the basis for my summary of the Old English inflexional system before the late reductions in the variety of vowels in unaccented syllables. On these reductions see §§14-15 and 18-22.

2. NOMINATIVE, ACCUSATIVE, AND ELEMENT ORDER

§9. There is no distinction between nominative and accusative anywhere in OE in the plural (except in the first and second person pronouns, where there are also different forms in the dual). This inability to distinguish inflexionally between doers and those done-to is not, however, peculiar to OE. The same situation obtains, for example, in OHG. There is also no distinction between nominative and accusative in the singular of neuter nouns, adjectives, or pronouns. This leaves only the masculine and feminine singular. Here all strong masculine nouns and some strong feminine nouns have the same forms. But the nominative and accusative are distinguished in the singular of the first and second person possessives, the demonstratives, and all other pronouns; in the strong and weak declensions of the adjectives; in the strong feminine *o*-nouns; and in the masculine and feminine weak nouns.

§10. In sentences where we have the order OVS, the distinction between subject and object often rests on these distinctions, sometimes without the help of number, e.g. *ÆCHom* i. 86. 3 *Hine gelæhte unasecgendlic adl* and *ÆCHom* i. 232. 33 *þisne anweald forgeaf Crist þam apostolum*, and sometimes with it, e.g. *ÆCHom* i. 142. 35 *Hine ne gesawon na ealle men lichomlice*, *ÆCHom* i. 144. 5 *Ealle ðas word spræc se Symeon . . .* , and probably *ÆCHom* ii. 126. 32 *Ðas lareowas asende se eadiga papa Gregorius* (but *asende* may be ambiguous in form; see §19). Sentences with OVS in which the sense and context are the only guides are not common, but do exist, e.g. *ÆCHom* i. 290. 34 *Hit ne mihte eal mancynn gedon*, *ÆCHom* i. 306. 18 *þa ærran wundra worhton ægðer ge gode men ge yfele*, *ChronE* 19. 11 (565) *Ða stowe habbað nu git his erfewærdes*, where *ða stowe* is accusative singular rather than nominative plural, and (from the poet's account of the sacrifice of Isaac) *GenA* 2887 *Wudu bær sunu, ‖ fæder fyr and sweord.*[3] Such sentences run directly contrary to the instinct of the modern reader, who tends to take it for granted that, when two nouns and/or pronouns not distinguished by inflexions are separated by a transitive verb, the first is the subject and the second the object. In sentences like *ÆCHom* i. 136. 35 *He bær þæt cild, and þæt cild bær hine* and *ÆCHom* i. 64. 21 *Ge gehældon untruman* the pronouns *he, hine*, and *ge*, distinguish subject from object and so testify that the element order is SVO. But there are numerous examples where there are no inflexional differences, and where only external evidence—such as the Latin original, the context, or historical sources—tells us which is the subject and certifies the element order as SVO: examples are *Gen* 4. 18 *Soðlice Enoch gestrynde Irad and Irad gestrynde Mauiahel and . . .* , *ChronA* 52.2 (784) *Her Cyneheard ofslog Cynewulf cyning, ChronE* 141.12 (1011) *Hi heafdon þa ofergan East Engla ·i· and East Seaxe ·ii· . . .* , and *ÆCHom* i. 24. 31 *God Fæder geworhte mancynn*. These suggest that the order SVO was already to some degree established as a grammatical device in OE. For further examples of SVO and OVS, see Carlton 1970, pp. 189-91.

§11. No doubt intonation would have helped native speakers to recognize the order OVS both in prose and in poetry, where greater variety is possible. It would have helped too to make it clear whether the order is SOV or OSV. Examples of the former include *ÆCHom* i. 50. 17 *Ða reðan Iudei wedende þone halgan stændon, ÆCHom* i. 50. 30 *Stephanus soðlice gebigedum cneowum Drihten bæd þæt he Saulum alysde*, and *ÆCHom* i. 88. 2 *He ða his cempan to ðam slege genamode*. Examples of the latter include *ÆCHom* i. 14. 29 *ealle gesceafta God gesceop and geworhte, ÆCHom* ii. 582. 33 *þæt andgit we understandað swa, ÆCHom* i. 44. 18 *Ðas seofon hi gecuron*, and *ÆCHom* i. 544. 33 *Deoflu hi oferswyðdon and afligdon*. In all these examples, inflexions and/or context distinguish the subject from the object. But how do we determine which order we have when both inflexions and context fail, as they do in *Finn* 18 *Ða gyt Garulf Guðere styrde* and

Mald 304 Oswold and Eadwold ealle hwile,
      begen þa gebroþru, beornas trymedon,
      hyra winemagas wordon bædon
      þæt hi þær æt ðearfe þolian sceoldon . . . ?

[3] This particular example provides a striking illustration of a difficulty which dogs the student of OE syntax and indeed literature. See Mitchell 1975a, pp. 13–14.

However, ambiguities such as these are rare in OE, and the modern reader who unconsciously resolves them by assuming that the first word or group of words is the subject and the second the object unless the context clearly directs otherwise may perhaps be not so wrong. On element order in prose and poetry, see further chapter IX.[4]

3. OTHER CASES

§12. If we consider first the W-S paradigms presented by *OEG*, disregarding the early, late, and dialectal, forms, and the variations due to later scribes, we find coincidence of forms in cases other than the nominative and accusative. In the weak nouns (apart from the nominative singular, all genders, and accusative singular neuter), all cases except the gen. pl. -*ena* and dat. pl. -*um* had -*an*. There were difficulties too in the strong nouns. In *ia*-nouns, forms such as *ende* (masc.) and *wite* (neut.) could be nominative, accusative, or dative, singular. In masc. *i*-nouns like *wine*, this ambiguity extended to the nom./acc. plural. In the fem. *o*-nouns *giefu* and *lar* and the fem. *i*-noun *dæd*, only the nom. sg. and the dat. pl. -*um* were distinctive. Five of the eight case forms of the masc. and fem. *u*-nouns *sunu* and *duru* ended in -*a*. Similar lack of distinction in the minor noun declensions need not be itemized. These ambiguities, it is true, were often resolved by an accompanying demonstrative and/or adjective —though in these too some forms did duty for more than one case or number, e.g. *þæm* and *þissum* (dative singular masculine and neuter, and dative plural), *þære* and *þisse* (genitive and dative feminine singular), *tilum* (dative singular masculine and neuter, and dative plural), and the almost ubiquitous *tilan*. In the first and second person pronouns, the accusative and dative often coincided in the singular, dual, and plural, while in the third person *him* could be dative singular or dative plural and *hire* genitive singular or dative singular.

§13. It is clear therefore that even before the confusion and ultimate levelling of vowels in unstressed syllables (*OEG*, §§368–80 and *passim*, and §15 below), the W-S case system was such that important distinctions often depended on something other than case. Thus the meaning of the verbs points to the different functions of *me* and

---

[4] The whirligig of time produces strange results. If we 'translate' three of the sentences quoted above into MnE, retaining the OE element order, we will find that *ÆCHom* i. 86. 3 (§10) is unambiguous in both OE and MnE by virtue of the pronoun *hine* 'him'; that *ÆCHom* ii. 126. 32 (§10), unambiguous in OE by virtue of the three nominative singular inflexions, reverses its meaning in MnE; and that *ÆCHom* i. 44. 18 (§11), ambiguous out of context in OE, demands the unambiguous 'they' for the ambiguous *hi*.

ðe in *ÆCHom* ii. 182. 8 *'Agif me minne sunu, agif me minne sunu'*
. . . *'Hwæt la, ætbræd ic ðe þinne sunu?'*—if indeed they are different and not examples of the 'dative of interest'; see § 1345. But, as a
study of

ÆHex 505	forðamðe ure Hælend Crist	ðæs heofonlican Godes sunu,
	on ðære syxtan ylde	ðyssere worulde
	wearð to menn geboren	of ðam mædene Marian,
	and he mid his agenum deaðe	ðone deofol oferwann
	and he us swa alysde	of his laðum ðeowdome;
	and he of deaðe aras	on ðam ðriddan dæge
	and awende ðæt swurd	of ðam wæge mid ealle
	ðæt we inn moton gaan	to ðam upplican Paradise . . .

will show, the preposition was already indispensable in some situations. But not in all: cf. *GD(C)* 137. 4 *þa þe beoð Godes geþeahtunge*
with *GD(H)* 137. 3 *þa þing þe beoð on Godes geþeahtunge* and
ÆCHom ii. 64. 3 *þa spræc God to his witegan Samuhele ðisum wordum* . . . with *ÆCHom* ii. 112. 22 *Drihten andwyrde his apostolum
mid þisum wordum*. . . . On such variations, see further § § 1226 and
1347.

4. VARIANT CASE ENDINGS

§ 14. A full catalogue of early, late, and dialectal, forms would be
out of place here. But the seeds of further confusion existed in the
following forms noted by Campbell: neuter plural in *-a* for *-u, -o*,
and genitive plural in *-o* for *-a* (*OEG*, § 569); endingless locatives
(§ 572); lW-S dat. pl. *-an, -on* (§ 572); the confusion of endings in
the singular of *o*-nouns (§ 587) and of *u*-nouns (§ 613); and the
lNb. loss of *-n* in the weak nouns (§ 617)—to take only one example
of the chaotic (or progressive) tendencies of late Northumbrian.
Some useful examples of these tendencies will be found in T. Dahl,
Form and Function (Copenhagen, 1936), 13 ff. On the break-up of
the OE inflexional system, see further Mustanoja, pp. 67 ff., and the
references given there, and Yerkes, *NM* 83 (1982), 260–5.

§ 15. There still appears to be a difference of opinion about the significance of certain spellings of vowels in inflexional endings. Kemp
Malone (*LM* 7 (Baltimore, 1930), 117) concludes that 'the transition
period from Old to Middle English is not the twelfth century . . . nor
even the eleventh . . . but rather the tenth'. Wrenn (*TPS* 1943, p. 30)
holds a similar view: 'But it is a fact, I believe, that by the tenth century the unstressed vowels *a, e, o* and *u* had all been levelled in final

syllables in Old English to a *schwa* [ə], and that the final *m* in the unstressed position had come to be sounded as *n*.' Yet Campbell, while recognizing *m/n* confusion in lW-S dative plurals (*OEG,* §572 and fn. 4) and loss of final -*n* in certain dialects and forms (§§472-3), remarks: 'In the eleventh century unaccented *e* (< *æ, e, i*) and the unaccented back vowel in which *a, o, u* had largely coalesced, became confused. . . . It is doubtful if significance should be attached to earlier spellings of this type, e.g. *Beow.* 63 -*scilfingas* (gen. sg.), 519 -*ræmes* (acc. pl.)' (§379). In private conversation just before his death in 1974, Campbell explained to me the main reason behind this doubt. The fact that the 'errors' are so few in comparison with the enormous number of 'correct' forms suggests, he claimed, that till *c.*1000 the distinction was audible and not something artificially kept alive in manuscripts by scribes belonging to a people who had no native tradition of grammar. In reply, one might argue first, that in general the mistakes are not random ones, but are those predictable according to the vowel reductions which actually occurred; and second, that the frequency of the aberrant forms may appear to be less than it actually is because of automatic editorial emendation of such forms as present indicative plurals in -*eþ* (see §20). A study of the forms in the non-runic inscriptions in Okasha's *Hand-List* may throw more light on this problem, which has been pursued by Derolez in 'Periodisering en continuïteit of: "When did Middle English begin?" (K. Malone)', *Album Edgard Blancquaert* (Tongeren, 1958), 77-84. He gives some fascinating glimpses into the dying Anglo-Saxon scribal tradition by considering alterations in spelling and inflexions made as 'corrections' by copyists and readers in documents of the 'transitional' period. In particular he notes the absence of any one criterion by which we can distinguish OE from ME; the relevance of a problem often neglected by linguists, viz. the varying distance between the language as it is and the language as it is supposed to be and the related question of who or what decides linguistic usage; and the linguistic unreality of attempting to draw a sharp borderline, for languages continue even when undergoing major changes. We need, he says, a complete study of all the relevant phenomena before we attempt to answer the question 'When did Middle English begin?' or (to put it another way) 'How long did Old English last?' But the burden of the article, it seems to me, is that, although each of the various criteria can be studied with profit, the questions posed above are too vague to be answered with a date or dates. With this I agree.

D. INTRODUCTORY REMARKS ON VERB FORMS

§16. Similar problems arise in connection with verbs. This simplified account is based on Campbell's *Old English Grammar*, chapter XVI, where full details of dialectal and other variations will be found. But it is important to bear in mind a simple but vital truth expressed by Peeters ('A Formal Description of the Use of Some Verbal Endings in Old English', *Linguistique contemporaine: Hommage à Eric Buyssens*, edd. J. Dierickx and Y. Lebrun (Brussels, 1970), 159): 'in Classical Old English the relatively numerous verbal endings that were used could in most cases functionally be dispensed with. This is indeed what happened in the course of time.'

1. PERSON

§17. In common with Old Saxon and Old Frisian, Old English did not distinguish person in the plural of any verb. Person can be distinguished in the present indicative singular of both strong and weak verbs, but not in either the present or the preterite subjunctive. In the preterite indicative singular of strong and weak verbs, the first and third person singular forms are the same, e.g. *nam* and *nerede*. On confusion of the second and third person present indicative in strong and weak verbs in *Ru1* and Nb., see *OEG*, §§735(*b*) and 752.

2. NUMBER

§18. The singular and plural are normally distinguishable. But note the Nb. confusion of forms in -*eð*, -*að*, -*es*, -*as*, in third singular and in plural present indicative (*OEG*, §735(*b*) and (*c*)); the sporadic confusion of -*eð*/-*að* and -*að*/-*iað* in the present indicative plural in W-S (see §§2 and 20); Nb. loss of final -*n* in present and preterite subjunctive plural (*OEG*, §§472, 735(*f*) and (*g*), and 752); and the eW-S preterite subjunctive plural forms in -*e* (*OEG*, §§473, 735(*g*), and 752). That these forms did not completely disappear in lW-S is, however, implied in *OEG*, §735(*g*). That forms in -*e* may be present subjunctive plural in eW-S and lW-S is suggested by examples like *Bede(T)* 270. 2 *Forþon us gedafenað, þæt we his heofonlicre monunge . . . ondswarige*, *ThCap1* 478. 58 *7 hit gedafenað þ gehwylce cristene men þa þurhteon magon on Sæternesdæg cume to cyrcean 7 him leoht mid bringe 7 þær æfensang gehyran*, *ApT* 18. 16 *and genihtsumige unc bam mine litlan æhta* (where Goolden's explanation that we have a 'sing. verb with a pl. subject following' does not deserve acceptance), *Ex* 270 . . . *þæt ge gewurðien wuldres aldor*, ǁ *and eow liffrean lissa bidde*, and *Jul* 648 . . . *þæt ge eower hus* ǁ *gefæstnige. . . .*

§19. Campbell makes no mention of preterite indicative plural forms in *-e* in these sections or in §735(*e*), though he does hint at the possibility in §472, where he speaks of *-n* not being lost 'as a rule in the past indic. pl. (except in *Li* in the pres. of pret.-pres. verbs)'. Klaeber, in his note on *lemede* in *Beo* 905 (3, p. 165), remarks: 'Only sporadically do we find the ending *-on* of the pret. ind. plur. of wk. verbs weakened to *-e*.' But this (Campbell suggested to me verbally) may be scribal. Klaeber's two other examples (3, pp. lxxxiv and xciii) can be otherwise explained—*Beo* 1408 *ofereode* as preterite indicative singular and *Beo* 2164 *weardode* as preterite subjunctive plural in dependent speech (cf. *Beo* 2719 *healde*, which can be taken as preterite subjunctive singular or plural). I have no hesitation in rejecting Klaeber's suggestion (3, p. lxxxiv) that these 'can be accounted for by lack of congruence', despite the fact that Visser (i. 71-2) seems to accept it; cf. his 'plural subject with singular verb' with Klaeber's 'the coupling of a singular verb with a plural subject' (3, p. xciii). Marckwardt (*Philologica*, pp. 79-88) draws attention to eighteen examples found by Kemp Malone (*LM* 7 (1930), 110-17) of preterite indicative plural in *-en* and *-e* in the great codices of OE poetry and claims to have found twenty-eight in *-e* in the fifteen late OE texts he examined. As far as I can see, the only forms in *-e* in Kemp Malone's list are the three weak verbs from *Beowulf* already cited. Marckwardt must presumably have found some preterite indicative plurals of strong verbs in *-e*, for he suggests that this reduction began in the strong verbs, where in the first and third person the absence of *-e* in the singular and (except in classes VI and VII) the ablaut variations made the singular/plural distinction which rested only on the *-e/-on* opposition in weak verbs. But he gives no specific references. So it is impossible to decide whether any of his examples can be otherwise explained. Some may be 'mere scribal omission of the consonant' (*OEG*, §735(*e*) fn. 1)—though I do not know of any criterion for deciding when this rather desperate explanation is valid —some may follow the pattern 'verb + *we/ge*' (*OEG*, §730), some may be taken as subjunctives (see *OEG*, §473, and *Beo* 2164 *weardode* above) or as preterite singulars (e.g. *Beo* 1408 *ofereode* above and *sceolde* in *ÆCHom* i. 18. 25 *ac sceolde Adam and his ofspring tyman on asettum tyman*). Pending a fully documented study, however, it would seem dangerous to rely on *-e* in the preterite as an unambiguous sign of the singular or of the subjunctive plural; sometimes it might well stand as an indicative plural.

§20. The problem of distinguishing number in verbs can be illustrated from H. Stoelke's *Die Inkongruenz zwischen Subjekt und*

Prädikat im Englischen . . . (AF 49 (1916)). Apart from a few obvious errors of his own[5] and the exceptions discussed in §563, his OE examples display plural subjects accompanied by verbs in *-eþ* (rather than *-aþ*), *-aþ* (rather than *-iaþ*), and (in the preterite) *-e*. To remove the apparent lack of concord, editors often emend the *-eþ* forms to *-aþ*, e.g. *ChristA* 322, or vice versa, e.g. *ChristC* 1595, and those with *-aþ* to *-iaþ*, e.g. *Dan* 403 (§2). Such emendation is likely to eliminate important evidence about the pronunciation of unstressed vowels in OE. Of the preterites in *-e* which Stoelke notes, some at least are to be explained as subjunctive plural, e.g. the verbs in *Bede* 438. 9 *ðy læs him ætwite ᵹ on edwit sette his geðoftan*. But some must be indicative and those variations in manuscript readings to which Stoelke does draw our attention suggest that in some places at least they are preterite indicative plural rather than singular. Thus, in *Bede* 384. 22, in what seems clearly a result clause, Miller reports *T* as having *meahton*, *B* and *O mihton*, *C meahte*, and *Ca mihte*. Similar examples are not uncommon; see Stoelke, pp. 75-8, for several more. These, of course, may be examples of the 'mere scribal omission of the consonant' referred to in §19.

3. MOOD

§21. The indicative and subjunctive can be distinguished in the present plural of strong and weak verbs by the opposition *-(i)aþ/-e(n)*. In the present singular, there is no distinction in the first person, e.g. *binde* and *lufie*, but a clear one in the third by the opposition *-(e)þ, -t/-e*. The second person present indicative ends in *-est*, the subjunctive in *-e*. Campbell makes no mention of the extension of *-est* to the present subjunctive and Mustanoja (p. 452) says that the difference between these two forms was retained as long as they remained in use.

§22. In the preterite singular of strong verbs, the second person preterite indicative singular coincides with the subjunctive form for all three persons, e.g. *nime*; the first and third do not, e.g. *nam/nime*. There is no distinction between the preterite singular indicative and subjunctive of weak verbs; the lW-S extension of *-st* to the second person subjunctive (*OEG*, §752) makes it dangerous to rely on this ending in syntactical discussions in view of the possibility of scribal confusion. Because of their ambiguity, the endings *-an, -en, -on, -un*, do not distinguish the two moods in the preterite plural of strong or

---

[5] He sometimes fails to take into account manuscript variations (e.g. p. 76, in *Bo* 35. 23 and *CP* 234. 20) or to note that a verb may be impersonal (e.g. p. 77, in *Or* 178. 7 and 192. 15).

weak verbs (*OEG*, §§735(*f*) and (*g*) and 752). The same may be true of preterite plural forms in -*e*; see §19.

4. THE 'SECOND PARTICIPLE'

§23. The periphrastic perfect/pluperfect and the periphrastic passive discussed in §§702–43 and 744–858 involve combinations of *habban*, *wesan*, and *weorþan*, with what most Old English grammars (including my own *Guide*) call 'the past participle'. The use of this term for all verbs is better avoided, since it has been argued that in transitive verbs the participle 'expresses pure passivity, not necessarily passivity in past time', whereas in 'intransitive verbs the part. is past' (*OEG*, §727 and fn. 2). Campbell observes this distinction with admirable consistency, but it is not to be wondered at that he occasionally nods as, for example, in *OEG*, §744, where he writes: 'the pass. part. fluctuates between *æ* and *a*, e.g. *færen, faren, slægen, slagen* . . .'. But is the distinction a real one? This is discussed at length in §§768–81, where I conclude that there is room for doubt about its universal validity in OE. For this reason, I do not follow Campbell in distinguishing the *passive* participles of transitive verbs from the *past* participles of intransitive verbs, but use the unfamiliar yet neutral term 'second participle' for all verbs.

§24. However, it seems sound enough to accept that the second participles of transitive verbs are passive, those of intransitive verbs active. The existence of 'passive participles with active meaning' is denied by Khomiakov (*JEGP* 63 (1964), 675–8). He convincingly disposes of the examples he considers by dividing them into three groups:

(1) 'pure adjectives or participial adjectives', i.e. words with the prefix *un-* and *forwered, nyten, gelyfed*, and *besceawod*;[6]

(2) participles which 'were derived from the intransitive verbs and therefore naturally received active meaning', e.g. *forsyngod*;

(3) participles which 'were derived from verbs of double character: transitive–intransitive'. These, he says (p. 677), would 'acquire lexical meaning similar to that of the verb being treated as intransitive. Therefore it is quite natural that these participles would receive active meaning: e.g., "He dranc of tham wine, tha wearth he druncen".' But one important qualification must be made. In the periphrasis with *habban*, the participle is often declined in agreement with an

---

[6] On an example which tests his assertion that all the forms with the prefix *un–* must be adjectives rather than participles, see §713 fn. But he deals with all the points made by Callaway (1901, p. 290).

object and can be regarded as a passive participle used as an adjective. But when the periphrasis reaches the stage of being a verbal combination, we have not an adjectival use of a passive participle, but an *active* verbal use of the same participle. Whether this stage was reached in OE is arguable. On the whole question see §§724-8.

E. THE BASIC CONCORDS OF OE

1. GENERAL

§25. These are:

(1) agreement between subject and predicate (§§26-39);

(2) agreement of attributive or appositive elements with the substantive (§§40-4);

(3) agreement of pronoun with its antecedent (§§45-7).

Exceptions occur mainly through a preference for the natural rather than the artificial, e.g. *Judg* 4. 21 *seo wifman* and *ÆCHom* ii. 10. 5 *þonne hwilc mæden mid luste weres bricð, þonne bið hire mægðhad æfre siððan adylegod, hæbbe heo cild næbbe heo*; through a preference for the nearer rather than the more remote, e.g. *ÆCHom* ii. 40. 27 *ða wæs þæt wæter and ealle wyllspringas gehalgode* and *ÆGram* 259. 18 *ne lingua nec manus oculiue peccent, ne tunge ne handa oððe eagan syngion*; or because two alternatives are equally acceptable, e.g. *BlHom* 71. 7 *Eal þæt folc þæt þær beforan ferde, streowodan heora hrægl him togeanes.*

2. AGREEMENT BETWEEN SUBJECT AND PREDICATE

a. *Agreement of subject and verb*

§26. In the singular the verb agrees with its subject in number and person, e.g. *ÆCHom* i. 8. 9 *Nu bidde ic, ÆCHom* i. 198. 9 *þu acenst sunu*, and *ÆCHom* i. 198. 29 *Se Halga Gast cymð*. Person is not distinguished in the plural of verbs (§17), e.g. *ÆCHom* i. 8. 8 *We sind Godes gefylstan* and *ÆCHom* i. 10. 14 *Her sindon nigon engla werod*. Hence examples like *Si tu et Tullia, lux nostra, valetis, ego et suavissimus Cicero valemus* do not arise in OE. The changes of person seen in *CP* 3. 1 *Ælfred kyning hateð gretan Wærferð biscep his wordum luflice 7 freondlice; 7 ðe cyðan hate ðæt me com swiðe oft on gemynd* can be paralleled from charters and similar documents; see Carlton 1970, p. 32.

§27. The occasional exceptions can usually be explained as the result of changes in the author's viewpoint, e.g. *ChronA* 126. 1 (993) *Her on ðissum geare com Unlaf mid þrim 7 hund nigentigon scipum to Stane 7 forhergedon þ on ytan* . . ., where Unlaf and his men do the plundering, and *BlHom* 199. 12 *þa gesamnode he mycel weorod his manna 7 hwearf æfter wegum . . . 7 sohton þæt forwlencte hryþær*, where the members of the band all search; cf. §367. But sometimes confusion on the part of the author or an error on the part of a scribe may be responsible; see, for example, §1521.

§28. Dual pronouns are followed by plural verbs, e.g. *Bede* 392. 33 *þa bær unc mon lið forð, 7 wit butu druncon*. But plural pronouns may be used of two persons even where a dual exists, e.g. *ÆCHom* i. 62. 32 *forðan ðe ge eowre speda þearfum dældon* . . . ; *gað nu* . . . *and heawað incre byrðene gyrda*. See further §258.

§29. When two or more singular subjects are joined by *and*, the verb is often plural, e.g. *ÆCHom* i. 2. 16 *his gebyrd and goodnys sind gehwær cuþe*, *ÆCHom* i. 296. 13 *On ðyssere geferrædene wæron Petrus and Iohannes, Iacob and Andreas* . . . , and *ÆCHom* i. 470. 20 *æt ðam Ælmihtigan Scyppende, ðam ðe gehyrsumiað lif and deað, untrumnys and gesundfulnys*. The same is true in the poetry, e.g.

Wid 45   Hroþwulf ond Hroðgar   heoldon lengest
            sibbe ætsomne   suhtorfædran.

On number after two singular subjects joined by *mid, ne,* and *oððe*, see §§1502, 1526, and 1525.

§30. But two or more singular subjects joined by *and* may have a singular verb

(1) when they are thought of as a unit, e.g. *ÆCHom* i. 118. 23 *Se frumsceapena man and eall his ofspring wearð adræfed of neorxena-wanges myrhðe*, *ÆCHom* i. 364. 22 *flæsc and blod þe ne onwreah ðisne geleafan* (but cf. *ÆCHom* i. 272. 11 *þær beoð geþwære sawul and lichama, þe nu on ðisum life him betweonan winnað*), and

And 1684   þær fæder ond sunu   ond frofre gast
            in þrinnesse   þrymme wealdeð . . .

(but cf.

ChristA 124   God wæs mid us
            gesewen butan synnum;   somod eardedon
            mihtig meotudes bearn   ond se monnes sunu
            geþwære on þeode,

which raises the possibility that *wealdeð* in *And* 1685 is for *wealdað*; see §§2, 18, and 20). *ÆCHom* ii. 60. 28 *her is fyr and wudu*, *ÆCHom* ii. 192. 2 *Betwux ðisum asprang Moyses and his broðer Aaron*, and

Beo 1210   Gehwearf þa in Francna fæþm   feorh cyninges,
            breostgewædu,   ond se beah somod,

may belong here or to (2) below;

(2) when the verb precedes the first subject and is not repeated with any following subject(s), e.g. *ÆCHom* ii. 202. 20 *On ðam munte Synay . . . wearð micel ðunor gehyred, and stemn, and liget gesewen* and *ÆCHom* i. 550. 7 *On þas wisan wæs Abraham ðearfa, and Iacob, and Dauid*;

(3) when the two subjects are idiomatically separated (§1464), e.g. *ÆCHom* i. 464. 30 *þu Ælmihtiga God, on ðam ðe Abraham gelyfde, and Isaac, and Iacob*, *ÆCHom* i. 92. 30 *God bebead Abrahame, þæt he sceolde and his ofspring his wed healdan*, and *GenB* 350 *oð hine his hyge forspeon ‖ and his ofermetto*;

(4) when the second subject is more important or subsumes the first, e.g. *ÆCHom* i. 238. 29 *Ælc bisceop and ælc lareow is to hyrde gesett Godes folce*. The examples from *Beowulf* given by Woolf in *MLQ* 4 (1943), 51-3, belong to one of these four groups with the exception of *Beo* 2461, where *eall* is the subject (§31). More prose examples like those in §§29 and 30 will be found in Sprockel, ii. 214-16 (note especially his comments about scribal corrections), Flamme, pp. 76-7, and Mohrbutter, p. 54. Visser (i, §§77-110) gives examples from both prose and poetry. On the poetry alone, see Bauch, pp. 57-64, and the dissertations by Conradi, Höser, Kempf, Lange, Meyer, Oldenburg, Pingel, and Schürmann.

§31. (1) When one of a group of subjects preceding the verb is plural, the verb is also plural, e.g. *ÆCHom* i. 302. 14 *Gærs and treowa lybbað butan felnysse* and *GuthB* 1176 *siþþan lic ond leomu ond þes lifes gæst ‖ asundrien. . . .* The alleged examples to the contrary cited by Bauch from the poetry (p. 59) involve present subjunctive plurals in -*e*.

(2) When the second of two idiomatically separated subjects is plural, the verb is singular in agreement with the first, e.g. *ÆCHom* i. 358. 29 . . . *ða gastlican drohtnunga þe Crist siððan gesette, and his apostoli* and *GenA* 2045 *Him þa Abraham gewat and þa eorlas þry*.

(3) When the verb precedes a group of subjects of which the first is singular, the verb may remain singular even if one of the other subjects is plural, e.g. *ÆCHom* ii. 40. 27 (§25), *ÆCHom* i. 10. 34

þa wearð he and ealle his geferan forcuþran and wyrsan þonne ænig oðer gesceaft,

GenA 1514　　　　　　　　Eow is eðelstol
　　and holmes hlæst　　and heofonfuglas
　　and wildu deor　　on geweald geseald . . . ,

and (with the plural subject in apposition) *Beo* 2461 *þuhte him eall to rum,* || *wongas ond wicstede.* The verb similarly remains singular before the combination of a singular and a plural complement joined by *and,* e.g. *Deut* 32. 20 *soðlice hit is ungeleafful cynryn* 7 *ungetrywe bearn.*

§32. Exceptions

(1) On examples in which a plural subject is (or appears to be) construed with a singular verb, see §§1520 and 1522-4.

(2) On agreement with collective nouns and numerals, see §§78-86 and 561-5.

(3) On agreement with indefinite pronouns, see (*inter al.*) §§395, 428-31, 433, and 452.

(4) On the person and number of the verb in adjective clauses, see §§2338-62.

(5) On the number of the verb after *þara þe,* see §§2343-50.

(6) The verbs *wesan, weorþan* may take the number of the subject, e.g. *ÆCHom* i. 514. 30 *Middangeard is her gecweden þa ðe þisne ateorigendlican middangeard lufiað,* or of the complement, e.g. *Bo* 54. 8 *Ða getriewan friend . . . sie ðæt deorwyrðeste ðing ealra þissa weoruldgesælða.* Both occur in *ÆCHom* i. 530. 22 *þa inran þeostru sind þære heortan blindnys. þa yttran þeostru is seo swearte niht þære ecan geniðerunge.*

b. Agreement of subject and adjective/participle

§33. The adjective/participle with *wesan* and *weorþan* (and also with verbs like *cuman, hweorfan, licgan, lifian, sittan,* and *standan*) agrees with its subject in number, case, and gender. But since it is declined strong (except in the comparative; see §101), it is of course impossible to say whether it is inflected or not when the subject is masculine or neuter singular, e.g. *ÆCHom* i. 238. 17 *Crist is good* and *ÆCHom* i. 34. 23 *Næs þæt cild forði gecweden hire frumcennede cild. . . .* A distinctive form can occur in the nominative singular feminine of short-stemmed adjectives (*OEG,* §639), e.g. *CP* 3. 13 *Swæ clæne hio wæs oðfeallenu . . . , GD(O)* 31. 2 *heo . . . wæs swiþe geswencedu, Rid* 20. 20 *ne weorþeð sio mægburg gemicledu,* and

Wulf 10 *ond ic reotugu sæt.* But the form without *-u* is more common, e.g. *CP* 7. 15 . . . *hu sio lar Lædengeðiodes ær ðissum afeallen wæs, GD(C)* 31. 2 *heo . . . wæs swiþe geswenced, GD(H)* 31. 3 *heo swiðe wæs gedreht,* and *Beo* 2913 *Wæs sio wroht scepen* ‖ *heard wið Hugas.* The adjective/participle is always uninflected in the nominative singular in the *Catholic Homilies,* e.g. *ÆCHom* ii. 306. 3 *His modor wæs cristen, Elena gehaten, swiðe gelyfed mann, and ðearle eawfæst, ÆCHom* i. 84. 2 *Eadig is heora yld, ÆCHom* i. 308. 19 . . . *hu seo clænnys wæs ðeonde,* and *ÆCHom* i. 244. 15 . . . *þæt ðeos gehealdsumnys wurde aræred.*[7] Agreements of the type seen in *ÆCHom* i. 10. 34 *þa wearð he and ealle his geferan forcuþran and wyrsan þonne ænig oðer gesceaft* need no comment beyond that made about the number of the verb in §31(3).

§34. In the plural the adjective/participle can be uninflected or inflected with the generalized *-e* for all genders (see §37). Feminine plurals in *-a* like *Or* 106. 18 *þonne wæron ealle þa dura betyneda* and neuter plurals in *-u* like *GD(O)* 76. 3 *fela þinga, Petrus, beoð god gesegnu* are rare; in the latter, both MSS *C* and *H* have *gode gesewene* and all three manuscripts go on (with minor variations) *ac hi ne beoð na gode.* The form in *-e* is the norm in all manuscripts of Gregory's *Dialogues,* but uninflected forms do occur, e.g. *GD(H)* 51. 13 . . . *ealle þa fatu wæron hwæthwega ongoten mid bledsunge þæs ylcan eles;* MS *O* has *geoten,* but MS *C gegotene.* Uninflected forms occur in other texts, e.g. *BlHom* 209. 14 *7 manigfeald onlic wundor ðysum . . . ðær wæron 7 gyt beoð æteowed 7 gecyðed,* and *BlHom* 209. 22 *Englas beoð . . . fram Gode hider on world sended,* but in general seem to be the exception rather than the rule; see *BlHom* 105. 20 for a sequence of six participles inflected in *-e.* But note *-u* in *BlHom* 175. 32 *7 his weorc syndon deofollicu.* The adjective/participle in the *Catholic Homilies* always has *-e,* e.g.

---

[7] We have much information about the presence or absence of fem. sg. *-u* in this situation. Thus there are no feminine singular forms in *-u* in the *Chronicle* entries 734–1001 or in *ÆHom*; see Pope, *Ælfric,* i. 184. 5. Flamme (p. 81) records only one—*BlHom* 5.5 *Heo wæs ful cweden næs æmetugu.* Brown's selected corpus contains *CP* 3. 13 above. But he did not record this or any similar examples (1963, p. 93, and 1970, pp. 54–8). The unbelievable *þa he geendodu wæs* cited by Carlton (1970, p. 125) from Birch 1063 (*Ch* 1447) is an error of copying; Birch has *geendod.*

More work would no doubt produce more statistics and give us more information about the variations in different manuscripts, texts, and authors. We would then be able to confirm or deny, for example, the impression that all manuscripts of Gregory's *Dialogues* prefer the uninflected form, that *H* has no *-u* forms, *C* a very occasional one (e.g. 28. 25), and *O* a few more.

Vleeskruyer (pp. 137–8) is inclined to see in these and similar forms 'the peculiar usage of an early school of translation' artificially imitating the more distinctive inflexions of Latin.

ÆCHom i. 62. 6 *þas gymstanas synd tocwysede, ÆCHom* i. 238. 25
gode wæron ða apostoli, and *ÆCHom* i. 10. 29 *and hi ealle wurdon
awende of þam fægeran hiwe, þe hi on gesceapene wæron,* where the
antecedent of *hi* is *gastas* (line 15). Wulfstan's *Homilies* also have *-e*
in the plural, without exception as far as I have noted; see Mohrbutter, pp. 65-7. The only uninflected plural quoted by Shannon
and Zuck in *Chron* 734-1001 is *ChronA* 87. 25 (894) *7 þa oþre
wæron hungre acwolen* (Zuck, p. 25). Shannon (p. 28) reads *ChronA*
48. 22 (755) *þæt hie gesund from eodon.* But the *d* of *gesund* has
a tag read by Earle and Plummer as '*e*' and by Whitelock in Sweet, *R.*
15 as '*e*', and *ChronE* 49. 21 (755) and all other manuscripts apart
from *A* have *gesunde.* M. B. Parkes has told me that in his opinion
the form in *A* was intended to be, and should be read as, *gesunde.*
Brown notes two examples in his limited corpus—*CP* 439. 35 and
449. 6 (1963, p. 93). Flamme (pp. 80-3) gives three neuter examples
—*BlHom* 29. 10, 117. 32, and 187. 3—but misses the two quoted
above. See also Pope, *Ælfric,* i. 184. 5.

§35. The participle may be inflected in the genitive plural after *fela*
and *ma,* e.g. *ChronA* 132. 23 (1001) *7 ðær wearð fela ofslegenra*
and *ChronA* 132. 9 (1001) *7 þær wearð þara Denescra micle ma
ofslegenra.* But, as Zuck (p. 26) points out, the uninflected form is
found in *ChronA* 94. 16 (905) *7 þara Deniscena þær wearð ma
ofslægen,* probably in agreement with *ma.* So it is possible that in
El 990 *Næs þa fricgendra ‖ under goldhoman gad in burgum ‖ feorran geferede, geferede* is in apposition with *fricgendra.* But it could
be its object (cf. *Max i* 1 and *OrW* 3) and this interpretation is sufficiently attractive in the context to make the ASPR comment 'undoubtedly the word goes as an appositive' seem too dogmatic.

§36. Generally speaking, the situation in the poetry is the same as
that in the prose. Forms in *-e* are more common in the plural than
uninflected ones and neuter plurals in *-u* are exceptional; the only
example recorded in 'the eighteen German dissertations' is *Wan* 87
idlu and Bauch (pp. 66-74) adds only *Met* 21. 29 *lænu . . . ‖ . . .
fleondu.* Bauch (pp. 65-73) cites examples from the poetry of both
inflected and uninflected adjective/participles with a plural subject
and *beon* or *wesan*; they include

GenB 460   And him bi twegin   beamas stodon
                     þa wæron utan   ofætes gehlædene,
                     gewered mid wæstme . . .

and *El* 1308 *Hie asodene beoð, ‖ asundrod fram synnum,* in which
both forms appear. The examples he gives mostly involve second

participles, but even here his citations are not complete and it is difficult to determine what principles dictated his choice. Thus he quotes
all the examples from *Judith*—three in -*e* (lines 31, 32, and 305) and
two uninflected (lines 18 and 196)—but gives only two in -*e* for
Beowulf—which has four in -*e* (two in line 361, lines 1821 and 2063)
and one uninflected (line 1620). He therefore does not provide the
evidence by which we can test this remark (apparently made about
second participles only): 'Es ist auffällig, daß in den jüngeren Denk-
mälern der unflectierte Plural sich viel seltener findet als in den
älteren' ['It is striking that the uninflected plural occurs much less
frequently in the later than in the earlier monuments'] (pp. 73-4). In
view of the difficulties of dating OE poems, this is too vague to be
meaningful, especially when the examples he cites—they include
Daniel (6 in -*e*, 1 uninflected); *Andreas* (6 and 5); *Christ* (6 and 2);
Guthlac (6 and 0)—do not prove anything and do not even illustrate
his point. If we plan to replace Lichtenheld's test (§114) with that
of Bauch, we shall need full figures covering all adjectives and participles after verbs like *licgan, sittan, standan, cuman*, and *gangan*, as
well as *wesan* and *weorþan*. Such a compilation is now possible with
the publication of the *ASPR* and *Microfiche Concordances*, though
my feeling is that it will give little help in dating the poems and is
unlikely to reveal much of significance. Points which would have to
be considered by anyone willing to undertake such a task would include the relative percentages of adjectives, strong second participles,
and weak second participles, which are uninflected and which show
endings such as -*e* and -*u*, and also the gender of the subject to which
each refers. Metre too may have something to do with it; cf. *El* 382
Heo to salore eft ‖ ymb lytel fæc laðode wæron with *El* 556b . . .
þa hie laðod wæron. Meanwhile there is nothing in Bauch's material
or in 'the eighteen German dissertations' to contradict the general
statement with which this paragraph began.[8]

---

[8] A count of the examples Bauch does quote (pp. 68-74) yields the following table:

Second participles after		with -*e*		without -*e*	
		Weak	Strong	Weak	Strong
wesan and *weorþan*	in *Paris Psalter*	53	20	2	2
	in other poems	45	56	20	13
sittan, cuman, etc.	in *Paris Psalter*	1	1	—	—
	in other poems	6	9	2	2

Two points emerge:
(1) the marked preference for the form with -*e*;
(2) a possible tendency in poems other than the *Paris Psalter* for the second participle of
the strong verb to have -*e* more regularly than that of the weak verb. One might speculate
that this may perhaps have something to do with the fact that the latter when inflected with

§37. Agreement of gender in the plural of the adjective/participle is frequently obscured by the fact that the masculine ending *-e* in the nominative and accusative plural of adjective/participles is often used for feminine and neuter, especially in later texts (*OEG*, §641), e.g. *ÆCHom* ii. 432. 14 *ure dæda beon gode geðuhte* (feminine plural), *ÆCHom* i. 140. 6 *þas læssan lac . . . wæron for Criste geoffrode* (neuter plural), and *ÆCHom* i. 2. 16 *his gebyrd and goodnys sind gehwær cuþe* (two feminine singular subjects).

§38. It is therefore difficult to determine 'rules' for the priority of genders and/or sexes. Is *ofwundrode* common gender or masculine agreeing with Joseph, in *ÆCHom* i. 144. 14 *þa Maria, þæt halige mæden, and þæs cildes fostorfæder, Ioseph, wæron ofwundrode . . . ? GenB* 811b *and wit her baru standað* (Adam speaks of Eve and himself) is sometimes made the basis for a 'rule' that 'a mixture of genders requires neuter concord in the modifiers' (QW, §124). How much reliance should be placed on this is uncertain; the OS has *uuit hier thus bara standat*, where *bara* could be masculine or feminine. Is *baru* the result of a purposive change or careless handwriting in either an OE or an OS manuscript? Or was *bara* an error for neut. *baru* in the surviving OS manuscript? Similarly it has been said that 'when both men and women are referred to by the same adjective, it is sometimes put in the neuter' (Sweet, *Pr.* 9, §83). The example cited is *Judg* 16. 25 *ealle þa heafodmen 7 eac swilce wimmen . . . 7 þa þa hig bliðust wæron. . . .* But this does not establish the rule. Indeed it need not exemplify it, for *bliðust* may be uninflected. So too may *onsund* in *Jul* 714 *þenden gæst ond lic geador siþedan* ‖ *onsund on earde*, described by Conradi (p. 11) as neuter after two masculine nouns. If we accepted this 'rule', we should (I suppose) have to think of *ofwundrode* in *ÆCHom* i. 144. 14 above as neuter despite its form. But the use of *-e* as a common ending and the fact that adjective/participles in such contexts could be uninflected make it dangerous to think of the 'rule' as more than a possibility in the absence of clinching examples. One's confidence in its existence is not fostered by the use of the masc. *he* and *oþrum* (it would be perverse to claim this as neuter after *he*) to refer to both Malchus and his wife in *LS* 35. 269 *and uncer laþette ægþer oþer þeah þe he hit oþrum ne sæde.*

−e was identical in form with the preterite singular (and sometimes with the preterite plural; see §19). (The Miltonic distinction between, for example, past tense 'advanc'd' and second participle 'advanc't' comes to mind here; see also *GenB* 460 and *El* 1308, both quoted above.) But full examination is likely to prove that there was really no such tendency. Certainly, if there was, Ælfric and the poet of the *Paris Psalter* were unmoved by it.

c. Agreement of subject and complement

§39. A noun or pronoun in the complement[9] agrees with its subject in case and, in *ÆCHom* i. 138. 19 *Gif hit þonne unclæne nyten wære* and *ÆCHom* i. 64. 24 *ge sind earmingas gewordene*, in number and gender. But the latter two agreements are obviously not always possible, e.g. (for number) *ÆCHom* i. 530. 22 (§32(6)), and (for gender) *ÆCHom* i. 10. 7 *Ðeos þrynnys is an God*. On idiomatic uses of *þæt*, *hwæt*, and *hit*, without regard to gender or number, see §47(3).

3. AGREEMENT BETWEEN A NOUN OR PRONOUN AND ATTRIBUTIVE OR APPOSITIVE ELEMENTS

a. Attributive elements

§40. Demonstratives, adjectives, or participles, agree with a noun, pronoun, or noun equivalent, in gender, number, and case, e.g. *ÆCHom* i. 82. 3 *on ðam timan*, *ÆCHom* i. 44. 5 *ealra worulda woruld*, *ÆCHom* i. 80. 23 *be ðam acennedan cilde*, *ÆCHom* i. 6. 31 *se Ælmihtiga*, *ÆCHom* i. 84. 23 *ealle we cumað*, *ÆCHom* i. 106. 24 . . . *niwne steorran beorhtne*, and *ÆCHom* i. 434. 7 *hwider tihst ðu me gebundenne mid scearpum racenteagum?*

§41. An adjective and/or demonstrative qualifying two nouns need not be repeated, e.g. *ÆCHom* i. 100. 33 *Ælc bletsung is of Gode, and wyrigung of deofle* and *ÆCHom* ii. 58. 18 *ða ealdan æ oððe witegan*. If different forms are required, the adjective and/or demonstrative agrees with the nearest noun, e.g. *CP* 39.14 *ða he fægnode ðæs miclan weorces 7 fægernesse ðærre ceastre*, *ÆCHom* i. 114. 5 *He lufað ælc god and rihtwisnysse*, and *ÆCHom* i. 282. 9 *oðer is se leoma oððe beorhtnys æfre of ðære sunnan*. When the adjective is repeated, its form varies if necessary, e.g. *CP* 87. 1 *mæstne demm 7 mæste scande*. The situation in the poetry is generally the same, but the demands of metre and alliteration produce variations such as

Phoen 192 þonne feor ond neah
    þa swetestan   somnað ond gædrað
    wyrta wynsume   ond wudubleda . . . ,

Phoen 430 in þam he getimbreð   tanum ond wyrtum
    þam æþelestum   eardwic niwe,

and (with one possessive doing duty with two nouns) *El* 534 *nu ge*

---

[9] I retain the traditional distinction between object 'She hit *her daughter*' and complement 'She is *her daughter*'.

fyrhðsefan || *ond modgeþanc minne cunnon.* On the use of the strong and weak forms of the adjective, see §§136–41.

× §42. **Exceptions**

(1) For examples in which an adjective qualifying a noun does not have the inflected form we should expect, see §§114–22.

(2) The participle in a phrase does not always seem to agree with its noun, e.g. *ÆCHom* i. 46. 28 *Se halga Stephanus . . . geseah . . . þone Hælend standende æt his Fæder swiðran* and *Beo* 372 *Ic hine cuðe cnihtwesende.* On possible ambiguities arising from this lack of morphological distinction, see §§1438–9.

(3) After *habban*, the participle may agree with its object or may remain uninflected; see §§706 and 709.

(4) On the conflict of sex and gender which produces examples like *Judg* 4. 21 *seo wifman*, see §69.

(5) On other problems of gender, see §§69–71.

(6) On the sg. *heafde* in *ÆCHom* i. 236. 22 *Ne sceal eow beon for- loren an hær of eowrum heafde* and similar examples, see §§87–91.

(7) On fem. sg. and pl. all genders *ana* 'alone', see §§537–41 and cf. Vercelli Book, f. 87ᵛ. 15 *seo hel sylfa.*

(8) In the poetry, 'a parallel may be uninflected if the case is clearly indicated in the expressions which it parallels' (Campbell 1962, p. 22), e.g. *Beo* 2703 *wællseaxe gebræd* || *biter ond beadu- scearp*; cf. §§44(3) and 1438.

b. Appositive elements

§43. The element in apposition agrees with the principal word or words in case and, in *ÆCHom* ii. 284. 6 *Gregorius, se halga papa* and *ÆCHom* i. 78. 26 *mid Marian his meder* (cf. *ÆCHom* ii. 8. 19 *þære eadigan Marian*), in number and gender. But again the two latter agree- ments are not always possible, e.g. (for number) *ÆCHom* ii. 430. 25 *ða feower godspelleras, Matheus, Marcus, Lucas, Iohannes* and *ÆCHom* ii. 172. 18 *hi awocon, se ealdor and his profost,* and (for gender) *ÆCHom* i. 32. 9 *of þam mædene Marian* and *ÆCHom* i. 78. 14 *Beth- leem, Iudeisc land* (cf. *ÆCHom* i. 78. 3 *on þære Iudeiscan Bethleem*). On concord in appositional elements, see further §§1437–44, Peltola 1960, pp. 197–200, and for the poetry, Bauch, Abschnitt I.

§44. **Exceptions**

(1) The nominative of address; see §§1242–7.

(2) Examples involving proper names and/or the participles *gehaten, geciged,* etc.; see §§1473–81.

(3) Elements in 'extraposition', e.g. *ÆCHom* ii. 238. 2 *Iohannes se Godspellere awrat, þæt Drihten cwæde to Nichodeme, an ðæra Iudeiscra ealdra* ... ; for further examples see Peltola 1960, pp. 198-9. Here we may have to do with asyndetic parataxis or the suppression of a relative (or some similar element) rather than with apposition; cf. *ÆCHom* ii. 226. 26 . . . *ða Iudeiscan . . . geeuenlæcende heora fæder, þæt is, deofol.* . . .

(4) Examples involving *fela* or a numeral, e.g. *ÆLS* 35. 51 *He funde eac sona fif mædena him to, wlitige and rance*; see Peltola 1960, pp. 199-200, and cf. §35.

(5) Examples like *ÆCHom* i. 146. 4 . . . *ealle ða wundra þe he worhte, ealle hit wæron tacna* . . . ; see §1489.

(6) On the form of the adjective/participle, see §§130-1. On the 'appositive participle', see further §§1434-6.

(7) On partitive apposition see §§409-16 and 1455.

4. AGREEMENT BETWEEN ANTECEDENT AND PRONOUN

§45. Demonstrative, personal, and relative, pronouns agree with their antecedent in number and gender, e.g. the sequences *se apostol . . . him* and *anre wydewan . . . hire . . . heo* in *ÆCHom* i. 60. 11 *Mid þam ðe se apostol Iohannes stop into ðære byrig Ephesum, þa bær man him togeanes anre wydewan lic to byrigenne; hire nama wæs Drusiana. Heo wæs swiðe gelyfed and ælmesgeorn* . . . ; *Babilonia . . . Seo* . . . in *ÆCHom* ii. 66. 22 *Babilonia . . . is gereht 'gescyndnys'. Seo getacnað helle; þæt cild . . . hit* in *ÆCHom* i. 24. 33 *Seo halige moder . . . afedde þæt cild . . . and hit weox* . . . ; and (of particular interest for its extended triumph of gender over sex) *ænne wimman . . . þurwif hatte se wimman . . . þone mann . . . hine* in *Ch* 1447 *Se fruma wæs þ mon forstæl ænne wimman æt Ieceslea Ælfsige Byrhsiges suna. þurwif hatte se wimman. þa befeng Ælfsige þone mann* [the woman] *æt Wulfstane Wulfgares fæder. þa tymde Wulfstan hine* [her] *to Æþelstane æt Sunnanbyrg.* It is clear from these examples that agreement in case between pronoun and antecedent is a matter of chance, not principle, despite QW, §121(*c*).

§46. When in the poetry a group of nouns in apposition is followed by an adjective clause, the gender of the relative points sometimes to the first noun as the grammatical antecedent, e.g.

GenA 228   þonne seo æftre   Ethiopia
            land and liodgeard   beligeð uton,
            ginne rice,   þære is Geon noma,

and sometimes to the nearest, e.g.

Beo 2749   ... þæt ic ðy seft mæge
                  æfter maððumwelan   min alætan
                  lif ond leodscipe,   þone ic longe heold.

The former type justifies Robinson's retention of MS *þone* (in preference to the syntactically violent emendation *þonne*) in

Beo 67   Him on mod bearn,
                  þæt healreced   hatan wolde,
                  medoærn micel   men gewyrcean
                  þone yldo bearn   æfre gefrunon ...

as an accusative singular masculine relative pronoun referring to
reced, which can be masculine (as in *Beo* 412 *reced selesta*) as well as
neuter; see *Tennessee Studies in Literature*, 11 (1966), 151-5, and,
for my comments on the mood of *gefrunon*, Mitchell 1968*c*, p. 296.

§47. Exceptions

(1) On those with personal pronouns resulting from conflict between sex and gender, e.g. the sequences *ænne wifman . . . heo* in
ÆCHom i. 14. 21 *and [God] geworhte of ðam ribbe ænne wifman,
and axode Adam hu heo hatan sceolde*; *ænne arc . . . hit* in *ÆCHom*
i. 20. 31 *Wyrc þe nu ænne arc . . . gehref hit eall*; and *þeos race . . .
hit* in *ÆLS* 4. 139 *þeos race is swiðe langsum fullice to gereccenne ac
we hit sæcgað eow on þa scortostan wisan*, see §69. MnE would of
course have 'it' where Ælfric has *hit* in *ÆCHom* ii. 382. 21 *þa geleaffullan cwædon þæt hit nære Petrus, ac wære his engel*. But note the
variation of *hit* in *ÆCHom* ii. 246. 14 *Hi ða cwædon þæt hi Crist
sohton. Ða sæde he him 'Ic hit soðlice eom'* but *se* in *ÆCHom* ii.
246. 20 *'Ic eow sæde ær þæt ic se eom'*.

(2) On similar exceptions with the ambiguous demonstrative/rela-
tive *se* and with other relatives, see §§2356-8.

(3) On the formulae *þæt is/þæt sindon/þæt wæron* and *þis is/þis
sindon*, see §§324-5 and 342, and on agreement after interrogative
hwa and *hwæt*, §352. The general 'rule' is that the verb is singular
unless followed by a plural complement. This also obtains with *hit*;
cf. *ÆCHom* ii. 382. 21 *þa geleaffullan cwædon þæt hit nære Petrus
. . .* with *Gen* 32. 17-18 *þa ðing . . . þe ge mid farað . . . hit synd
Iacobes, 7 he hi sent hys hlaforde Esauwe . . .* and *ÆCHom* ii. 274.
11 *Hit wæron ða ylcan ðe we nu offriað*. The variation between
hit in *ÆCHom* i. 172. 8 *Eorðe and eall hire gefyllednys, and eal
ymbhwyrft and þa ðe on ðam wuniað, ealle hit syndon Godes æhta*
and *hi* in *ÆCHom* i. 172. 15 *Ealle gesceafta, sunne, and mona, and*

ealle tunglan, land, and sæ, and nytenu, ealle hi ðeowiað hyra Scyppende may point to a difference of meaning—'the whole lot' but 'all of them'. Further examples of these variations will be found in Wülfing, i, §238; Visser, i, §§51-64; and (for the poetry) Bauch, pp. 27-9, and also the dissertations by Conradi, Fritsche, Höser, Kempf, Meyer, Pingel, and Schürmann.

(4) On conflict of number between pronouns and collective nouns, see §§81-2.

II

THE PARTS OF SPEECH AND
THEIR FUNCTIONS

A. INTRODUCTORY REMARKS

§48. 'In dealing with linguistic subjects', writes Jespersen (*Ess.*, p. 66), 'it is necessary to have names for the various classes into which words fall naturally, and which are generally, but not very felicitously, called "parts of speech". It is practically impossible to give exact and exhaustive definitions of these classes; nevertheless the classification itself rarely offers occasion for doubt. . . .' This will, I hope, excuse the lack of any attempt to define the terms used below; we may remember that girl number twenty Sissy Jupe, whose father belonged to the horse-riding and who no doubt knew a horse when she saw one, was unable to define one for Mr Gradgrind. Following therefore the conventional terminology, I distinguish in Old English the following parts of speech: nouns, adjectives, numerals, pronouns (including articles), verbs (including infinitives and participles), adverbs, prepositions, conjunctions, and interjections.

§49. There are few, if any, forms in OE which tell us unambiguously that we have to do with one part of speech rather than with another. There is no opposition between any particular vowels or consonants. The ending *-an* belongs equally to the oblique cases of weak nouns and of adjectives declined weak and to verbs, especially infinitives. It can occur in adverbs and elsewhere. The ending *-ne* often signals an accusative singular masculine form of a personal pronoun, demonstrative, or strong form of an adjective, but can present itself in nouns like *fæmne*, adjectives like *grene*, pronominal forms like *mine*, and verb forms like *hrine*. The ending *-aþ*, predominantly found in verbs (but with varying significance), appears in nouns like *fiscaþ* and *hergaþ*. Even the validity of the opposition *-ende* participle and *-end* agent noun is at best extremely dubious; see §974.

§50. 'Functional change' or 'conversion'—'the process whereby a word comes to be used in a new grammatical function with no salient change of form, i.e. without the addition or subtraction of a derivative syllable or other similar element' (Lee, p. 2)—is unknown in OE. But inevitably there is some overlap in form. Words like *dolwillen, leoht, soþ*, and *riht*, can be nouns or adjectives. (Mutt has some comments on this in *NM* 69 (1968), 582). The imperative singular of some verbs, e.g. *drinc*, coincides in form with the nominative singular of the noun. *Fæste* can be an adverb or an oblique form of the adjective *fæst*; on this overlap see §1108. In these particular examples the position of the word in relation to other words in the phrase or sentence shows its function. Thus we have nouns in *Jul* 202 *þurh þin dolwillen, And* 124 *Leoht æfter com*, and *BlHom* 129. 32 *gif we nu soþ 7 riht on urum life don willaþ* (see §51), but adjectives in *Jul* 451 *þeah ic þec gedyrstig ond þus dolwillen ‖ siþe gesohte, And* 1251 *Him wæs leoht sefa, Coll* 5 *riht spræc*, and *BlHom* 33. 33 *he wæs soþ man*. We have no difficulty in distinguishing between *drinc* in *Matt(WSCp)* 10. 42 *anne drinc cealdes wæteres* and in *Gen(C)* 24. 18 *Drinc þu, leofa man*; between *fæste* in *Bede* 268. 21 *þonne eode he to cirican . . . 7 on sealmsonge fæste moode awunade* and in *Bede* 138. 8 *þa sceat he mid þy spere, þæt hit sticode fæste on þæm herige*; and (to take one example from §49) between the words ending in *-ne* in *Rid* 53. 1 *Ic seah on bearwe beam hlifian, ‖ tanum torhtne, Rid* 74. 1 *Ic wæs fæmne geong, Rid* 15. 6 *in grene græs, Rid* 8. 4 *mine wisan*, and *Rid* 66. 5 *Grundum ic hrine*.

§51. Sometimes the problem is purely terminological. Thus adjectives and participles can qualify nouns, e.g. *ÆCHom* i. 282. 21 *se Ælmihtiga God* and *ÆCHom* i. 34. 23 *hire frumcennede cild*, and can be used where we would expect nouns, e.g. *ÆCHom* i. 6. 31 *se Ælmihtiga* and *ÆCHom* i. 32. 31 *his gecorenan*. In the latter, they can be called 'adjective/participles used as nouns' or 'nouns'. Some, no doubt, will detect the same ambiguity in *soþ* and *riht* in *BlHom* 129. 32 (§50). On a similar problem with *geþafa*, see BTS, s.v.[1]

§52. But there are occasions when identity of form creates problems which the syntactician of today, working without native informants and intonation patterns, cannot always solve. Thus *se* may be used dependently, e.g. *ÆCHom* i. 4. 16 *se gesewenlica deofol*, or

---

[1] Walker (*PQ* 27 (1948), 264–72) offers some detailed comments on OE adjectival suffixes. He concludes that the situation in OE was different from that in MnE, where 'the tendency . . . is to discard the suffix as a signal of grammatical usage and to rely entirely on position, forcing the distinction on to syntax. The suffixes that are left are very likely to be chiefly used for semantic alteration' (p. 265). There is room for further work here.

On *-lic* see further K. Uhler, *Die Bedeutungsgleichheit der altenglischen Adjektiva und Adverbia mit und ohne -lic (-lice)* (AF 62) (1926).

independently, as either a demonstrative or a relative, e.g. *ÆCHom*
i. 134. 1 *Geleafa is ealra mægena fyrmest; buton þam ne mæg nan
man Gode lician, ÆCHom* i. 514. 18 *Se æswicað oðrum þe hine on
Godes dæle beswicð*, and *ÆCHom* i. 20. 26 *an man . . . se wæs Noe
gehaten*. (I follow Mustanoja in using the terms 'dependent' and 'independent'; see further §239.) It is often impossible to decide which
independent use we have; see §§322, 327, and 2109. Similar difficulties arise from the fact that words like *nu, siþþan, þær, þa*, and
þonne, can be either adverbs or conjunctions; for references, see the
Index of Words and Phrases.

§53. The parts of speech are treated in the standard grammars and
primers. The nearest approach to a general work is J. E. Wülfing,
Die Syntax in den Werken Alfreds des Grossen, i (Bonn, 1894) and
ii (Bonn, 1901). This was unfinished and there exists only 'der erste
"Hauptteil" des Werkes, die Syntax der einzelen Wortklassen' ['the
first "major part" of the work, the syntax of the individual classes of
words'].[2] But there are numerous articles and monographs on the
various topics. Reference is made to these as they become relevant.
Collections of examples from the prose will be found in 'the prose
text dissertations' and from the poetry in 'the eighteen German dissertations'; see the Bibliography under these titles.

B. NOUNS

1. CLASSIFICATION

§54. OE nouns are usually divided according to their inflexions into
strong, weak, and minor, declensions; see *OEG*, §568 and chapter
XI *passim*. On compounds see *Guide*, §137, and on loan-words,
OEG, chapter X. Traditionally nouns are classified according to
meaning as concrete—the name of a person or thing—or abstract—
the name of a quality or characteristic, e.g. *(se) wisdom* 'wisdom',
(seo) beorhtnes 'brightness, splendour', and *(þæt) mod* 'soul, spirit,
courage'. Concrete nouns are further divided into proper nouns—
the name of a particular person, place, or thing, e.g. *Ælfric, Hierusalem*, and *Temese*—or common nouns—the name of a member of

---

[2] Wülfing, ii, p. iva. Wülfing planned to treat 'die Syntax des Satzes' in a further volume.
But his wide selection of examples and broad interpretation of 'die Syntax der einzelen
Wortklassen' means that his work has a wider range than my chapter II.

Significant differences in the syntax of the parts of speech in Wærferth's translation of
Gregory's *Dialogues* and in the revision in MS *H* (made at Worcester during or just before
the first half of the eleventh century) are discussed by Yerkes in his thesis (pp. 124–227).

a class, e.g. *se munuc* 'the monk', *seo burg* 'the city', and *þæt scip* 'the ship'. These distinctions are of some slight value in the discussions which follow.

2. GENDER

a. Introductory remarks

§55. OE distinguishes three genders—masculine, feminine, and neuter. The system of gender is essentially that inherited from Pr. Gmc. and IE—'grammatical' rather than 'natural' or 'gender' as opposed to 'sex'. In the sections which follow, the words 'sexual', 'asexual', 'male', and 'female', refer to sex; 'masculine', 'feminine', and 'neuter', to gender. For a fuller treatment than is possible here of problems concerning gender, the reader is referred to the thesis by Wyss, to two articles by Wyss which are based thereon (*Linguistique et Philologie (applications aux textes médiévaux). Actes du Colloque des 29 et 30 avril 1977*, Centre d'Études Médiévales, Université de Picardie, 119-33; and *Confluents*, 4 (1978), 177-98), and to Mōri, 'Grammatical Gender in Old English', *Thought Currents in English Literature* (Aoyama Gakuin University), 52 (1979), 35-50, and 53 (1980), 1-9.

b. Distinctions of gender in nouns

§56. Nouns used of males are normally masculine, e.g. *Ælfric, se mann Adam, se fæder*; those used of females are normally feminine, e.g. *Eua, seo eadige Maria, seo modor, seo mægþ* 'maiden'.

Exceptions

(1) Neuter are *wif* 'woman', *mægden* 'maiden', and (more understandably) *bearn* and *cild* 'child'.

(2) The compound *wifmann* 'woman' is masculine, after the second element.

The same form may have two different meanings distinguished by gender, e.g. *leod* (masc.) 'man' but *leod* (fem.) 'people' and *secg* (masc.) 'man' but *secg* (fem.) 'sword' and *secg* (masc. or neut.) 'sedge'; see further BT, s.v. *secg*.

§57. Some nouns referring to male and female have only one gender, e.g. *fisc* 'fish', *freond* 'friend', *fugol* 'bird',[3] *hræfn* 'raven', *mearh*

---

[3] Note the compounds *karlfugel* and *cwenefugel* in *HomU* 17. 148. 4, and cf. *cucealf*, which (according to BTS, s.v.) means both 'a cow-calf, young cow' and 'a cow's calf'.

'horse', all masculine; *hyrnett* 'hornet', *geoguþ* 'the youth, young persons', *ylfett* 'swan', all feminine; *bearn, cild, cealf, lamb*, all neuter. *Leo* can be masculine, 'lion', e.g. *Bo* 102. 6 *nanne leon* or feminine, 'lioness', e.g. *Bo* 57. 9 *seo leo*.

§58. But there are also both words of different stems, e.g. *cniht* (masc.) 'boy, young man' but *mæden* (neut.) 'girl, maiden' and *oxa* (masc.) 'ox' but *cu* (fem.) 'cow', and feminine derivatives from masculine nouns, e.g. *hana* 'cock' (masc.), *henn* (fem.); *hunta* 'hunter' (masc.), *hunticge, huntigestre* (fem.); *þeow* 'slave' (masc.), *þeowenn* (fem.); *wulf* 'wolf' (masc.), *wylf, wylfenn* (fem.); see further Platt, *Ang.* 6 (1883), 178.

§59. Most neuter nouns are asexual, e.g. *scip* 'ship', *word* 'word', *cynn* 'race', *wite* 'punishment', *searu* 'device', *eage* 'eye'. For exceptions see §56(1).

§60. But asexual nouns are not necessarily neuter. Abstract nouns may be masculine, e.g. *wisdom* 'wisdom', or feminine, e.g. *mildheortnes* 'mercy', as well as neuter, e.g. *mod* 'courage'. Concrete nouns too may be masculine, e.g. *se mona* 'the moon', or feminine, e.g. *seo sunne* 'the sun' (but see §65), as well as neuter, e.g. *þæt scip* 'the ship'.

§61. So the gender of most nouns must be learnt. The following endings of the nominative singular are significant:

Weak Masculine:	-a
Strong Masculine:	-að/oð, -dom, agent nouns in -end (but see Kärre, pp. 131–2 and 192–4), -els, -ere, -had, names of persons in -ing and -ling, -scipe
Strong Feminine:	-nes(s), abstract nouns in -ing/ung, -ræden, -ðo/ðu
Strong Neuter:	-et(t), -lac

The ending -*e* is particularly ambiguous: see §66.

c. Change of class and gender in nouns

§62. Examples of change of class alone include the masculine and feminine *u*-nouns (*OEG,* §613), the short-syllabled feminine weak nouns with *o*-declension by-forms (*OEG,* §620(4); see also Platt, *Ang.* 6 (1883), 175–6), and possibly such variations as *fleah* 'flea' (masc. or neut.?)/*flea* (masc.) (*OEG,* §574(2)). The form *freos* in

Dan 66 may be a strong accusative plural of the usually weak *frea* (masc.) 'lord'; so Blackburn's note. But a good many changes of class in nouns appear to be associated with what is often called a 'change of gender'. Thus, Platt cited some forty nouns which (he claimed) had different genders in eOE and lOE (*Ang.* 6 (1883), 171-4). The phenomenon is not confined to OE, as Ælfric knew; see *ÆGram* 19. 16 ff. In 1889, von Fleischhacker (*TPS* 1888-90, pp. 235-54) listed a considerable number of OE 'nouns of more than one gender' divided into thirteen groups according to their suffixes or declensions, concluding with the observation that the words noted 'do not exhaust the list'. The glossary of Dunning and Bliss's 1969 edition of *The Wanderer* gives at least seven nouns which are said to have more than one gender. Similar lists could be prepared from other OE poems. In discussing the form *welle* in *CPEp* 24, Cross observes that 'Bosworth-Toller Dict. distinguishes the words, *will, well, wyll* -es (m); *wille* -es (m); *wille* -*an* (f); and *willa* -*an* (m)' but adds the proviso 'If these distinctions are valid . . .' (*NM* 70 (1969), 382 fn. 5). However, *Beo* 1614 *þa hilt*, taken by Klaeber (3, Glossary, s.v.) as accusative singular feminine, could be accusative plural neuter; cf. *Beo* 1574 *be hiltum*.

§63. What do we mean when we speak of a noun as 'having more than one gender' or as showing 'change of gender'? Would we be wiser—for the time being at least—to avoid terminological controversy by following Campbell, who speaks, for example, of OE *ewe* as declining 'both like *giefu* (acc. *eowe*, &c.) and as a weak noun, *eowe*, -*an*; there is also a masc. g.s. *eowes*' (*OEG*, §593(2))? For Jones (fn. 4 below) has pointed out that in *Li* and *DurRitGl* no noun shows 'change of gender' throughout its whole declension. This criterion has its difficulties. Thus *cealf* has a lW-S nom. acc. *cealfas*. But, when the word had gone over to the *a*-nouns, the nom. acc. pl. is the only form where there could be a difference between strong masculine and neuter (*OEG*, §635). However, that Jones has a point becomes clear when we consider another of his observations—that many of the apparent 'changes of gender' in his texts depend on unhistorical congruence of demonstrative and/or adjective and that, while some of them are explicable in terms of 'neutralization'— the replacement of the gender-categories (masculine, feminine, and neuter) by those of sex (male, female, and asexual) which, according to Ross, 'is first apparent in a tendency to use neuter forms with etymologically masculine or feminine asexuals' (*JEGP* 35 (1936), 324)—many show the use of the phonetically more distinctive forms of the demonstrative and/or adjective (e.g. the strong masculine endings -*ne* and -*(e)s*) as case indicators irrespective of gender.[4]

§64. Are we then justified in speaking of *wæstm* as neuter because of *GenB* 255 *his wæstm . . . þæt him com from weroda drihtne* (where *þæt* might be used without regard to gender or might be the result of resolution of *þ* which might stand for *þe*; but see §1930) or of the gloss *ofet, wæstm fruges, frumenta* (where *wæstm* might be singular; see BT, s.v. *wæstm* I. (1))? Does *ÆCHom* ii. 578. 11 *þæt east portic* certify *portic* (masc.) as neuter after the sequence *þæt tempel . . . swilc hus . . . þæt tempel*? See Platt, *Ang.* 6 (1883), 172. A similar example is *ÆLS,* 4. 336 *oðþæt þæt ad*. BT is cautious when it says that *wæter* 'seems to be feminine' in *BlHom* 247. 25 *ealle þa þe on þisse wætere syndon* (where *þisse* might be a reduction of *þissum* or an analogical form (*blacum : blace :: þissum : þisse*)) and *Ps(P)* 17. 11 *þa hangode swiðe þystru wæter on þam wolcnum and on þære lyfte* for *tenebrosa aqua in nubibus aeris* (could *þystru* be feminine under the influence of *aqua* or could it be plural?).[5] But we also have *ealle wæteras and ealle wyllas*—masculine by contextual analogy? See BTS, s.v. *wæter*.

§65. The same explanation will not do for all examples. Some may well be errors arising from ignorance of what was already a dying system—after all situations in which gender is the only guide to number, e.g. *Dan* 279 *Ða Azarias . . . þa word acwæð*, are not numerous. Some at least could be the result of analogical confusion explicable in and confined to the particular context. Some seem to show variation (or confusion) of gender and class in Gmc, others in OE. Clear examples of the last include the neut. *wange* 'cheek' which 'can be weak, but has also strong forms partly masc., partly fem.: g.s. *wonges*, d.s. -*wange*, n.p. *wangas*, -*wonge*, -*wonga*, g.p. -*wonga*; so (*þun*)*wenge*, a strong form, has weak inflexion, d.s. -*wengan*' (*OEG,* §618). We have *sunna* (masc.) alongside *sunne* (fem.) and *mone* (fem.) alongside *mona* (masc.). See BT, s.vv. In view of these variations

---

[4] See the two works here given, *passim*: C. Jones, 'Grammatical Gender in late Old English and Early Middle English' (unpublished B.Litt. thesis, University of Glasgow, 1964) and id., 'The Functional Motivation of Linguistic Change. A study of the development of the grammatical category of gender in the late Old English period' (*EStudies* 48 (1967), 97–111). (This distillation of part of his thesis does not in my view benefit from the use of modern linguistic terminology.)

. [5] See BT, s.v. *wæter*. For *hangode* as a possible preterite indicative plural see §19. The translator got *aquae = wæter* (pl.) right in *PPs* 76. 13. In *PPs* 77. 18 he rendered *aquam* as *wæter* (neut. pl.) and in the same sentence *aquas* as *wætera þryðe*. We would have to believe that in *Ps(P)* 17. 11 he drowsily took *aqua* as neuter or altered the singular to plural as he did—quite understandably—in *PPs* 77. 18 (first occurrence).

is it too long a shot to suggest that Dunning and Bliss may be wrong when they remark in their note on *Wan* 7 that '*hryre* cannot be genitive'? If we can take '*hrusan* for *hruse* in line 23 and *hruse* for *hrusan* in line 102 as examples of the levelling of endings in late Old English' (their note to line 23a), can we dismiss the possibility that *hryre* is for *hryran*, a late weak genitive singular form of the usually strong *hryre*? Such confusion of a strong masculine with a weak feminine or neuter noun may seem far-fetched, but is perhaps not impossible if we consider the various forms of *wange, -wenge, sunne*, and *mona*.[6] My aim, however, is not to establish the correctness or otherwise of this hypothesis, but to suggest that at the moment we may lack some evidence which might enable us to settle such problems. On this question, see now Wyss, pp. 34–53.

d. Congruential distinctions in adjectives, participles, and pronouns

§66. OE distinguished gender less by the form of the noun itself than by special forms of the adjective, participle, and pronoun. For, as the list of endings given in §61 suggests, the distinctions in the nouns themselves were often obscured—strong nouns of all genders can have nominative singular ending in a consonant, e.g., *stan* (masc.) 'stone', *lar* (fem.) 'learning', *word* (neut.) 'word'; OE *-e* can be nominative singular of a strong masculine (*wine* 'lord'), weak feminine (*sunne* 'sun'), strong neuter (*spere* 'spear'), or weak neuter (*eage* 'eye'), noun, and can occur somewhere in the oblique case of most strong nouns; *-u* appears in the nominative singular of strong nouns of all genders (*bearu* (masc.) 'grove', *searu* (neut.) 'device', *giefu* (fem.) 'gift') and in the nominative and accusative plural of strong neuter nouns such as *scipu* 'ships'. What distinctions remained disappeared in eME; indeed, in lNb. *Li* and *DurRitGl*, gender can generally be distinguished only by the congruential forms of the accompanying adjective or pronoun.[7] But even here 'grammatical gender largely survived intact' (Jones, *EStudies*, 48 (1967), 99 and 107), despite the examples of unhistorical use of the gender-distinguishing forms discussed in §68.

[6] The fact that there are no strong feminine nouns with nominative singular in *-e* might militate against explaining *hryre* as a genitive singular by analogy with *giefu* or the like. But could the scribe have pronounced *-u* as [ɔ]? Cf. the remarks by Wrenn quoted in §15. Of course, if we took too literally Klaeber's remark that 'lack of concord as shown in the interchange of cases . . . should cause no surprise or suspicion' (Klaeber, 3, p. xciii), the problem would disappear. So too would much else. I discuss this further in *ASE* 4 (1975), 14–15.

[7] See *OEG*, §569, and Ross, *JEGP* 35 (1936), 321 ff. On the use of the nominative and accusative singular form for the dative singular of nouns in *Li*, see Blakeley, *EGS* 1 (1947–8), 6–31.

§67. The agreement which obtained in OE between the noun, and pronouns, adjectives, or participles, referring to it, was an essential part of the gender system of the IE language family in historical times. This system was pretty well preserved in OE, though there were difficulties. Thus in *Matt(WSCp)* 7. 24 *ælc þæra þe ðas mine word gehyrð 7 þa wyrcð* there is no clue that *word* is accusative plural neuter and not accusative singular feminine; even the distinction *min/mine* has been lost (*OEG*, §§707 and 641). This is symptomatic of the general change from OE to ME which resulted in the eventual loss of the distinctions between the nouns themselves and of the accompanying congruential forms. In this process, grammatical gender, being formal and non-essential, did not find other means of expression as did the meaningful distinctions of number and case.

§68. Many of the OE exceptions to the rule that attributes of a noun agree with it in gender (see §40) can be explained as triumphs of 'sex' over 'gender'. (On nouns with more than one gender, see §§62-5.) A particular manifestation of this is the use in *Li* and *DurRitGl* of neuter forms of the demonstrative with historically masculine or feminine nouns denoting asexuals, e.g. *þ lofsong*. Ross called this 'neutralization' (my §63). But there are departures from historical gender in these two texts which this process cannot account for. The usual explanation for these is that there was a change of gender in the nouns involved; cf. Heltveit's suggestion that the elimination of these inflexional distinctions led to the association in eME of different word patterns with particular genders and so to eME changes in the gender of nouns (*NTS* 18 (1958), 357-69). But Jones, rejecting both this explanation and the suggestion that the influence of Latin gender was important except in a few isolated instances, provides new and (it seems to me) convincing explanations for the departures from historical gender unaccounted for by 'neutralization'; see his thesis (my §63 fn. 1), pp. 36-7 and 73-8. He detects two further influences—first, a tendency to use *þ* and its variants (e.g. *ðæt, ðet*) without regard to gender either to indicate object as opposed to subject or as an emphatic alternative to the article; second, a tendency to use the more phonetically distinctive endings *-ne, -(e)s, -(u)m*, again without regard to gender, to indicate respectively accusative, genitive, and dative, cases.[8] Examples of unhistorical congruence involving these forms, he argues, are not evidence of

---

[8] In *Li -r(e)* is sometimes used in the same way for genitive and dative (Jones, thesis, pp. 299-301), while *ða* may replace *ðone* as a sign of the accusative (Jones, thesis, pp. 23 and 77); see *EStudies*, 48 (1967), 103-7. Forms of *ðes* are discussed by Jones in the two works already cited and in *NQ* 214 (1969), 122-5; the last is in reply to Ross in *NQ* 212 (1967), 284-8. Jones returns to the question in *IF* 75 (1970), 198-219.

gender change in the nouns involved; see §§63 and 66. Similar investigations into all the examples of unhistorical congruence elsewhere in OE are needed. Roberts has supplied some striking confirmation of this in *EStudies*, 51 (1970), 30-7, by giving five (possibly six) examples of *-re* and one of *-ra* with dative singular forms of masculine and neuter nouns, one of *-re* with the dative plural of a neuter noun, and one of *þa* with the accusative singular of a masculine noun, in the prose *Life of St. Guthlac*. All of these were emended by both Goodwin and Gonser, along with other examples of 'unhistorical gender congruence'.

e. Triumphs of sex over gender

§ 69. These fall into three groups:

(1) the attributive demonstrative, e.g. *Judg* 4. 21 *seo wifman*, Latin *Iahel uxor*, and *Bede* 332. 25 *seo ærest wiifa* 'the first among women', Latin *quae prima feminarum fertur in prouincia . . .* contrasted with the grammatical *Or* 46. 27 *from ðæm wifmonnum* and *ÆCHom* i. 16. 34 *þæt wif*. This triumph is especially common in glosses like *Li* and *Ru2*, where, as in the two examples above, Latin influence is certainly involved, if not responsible.

(2) the ambiguous demonstrative/relative, e.g. *ÆCHom* i. 24. 22 *to anum mædene . . . seo wæs Maria gehaten*; see §52. On the gender of the relative pronoun when it refers to more than one noun of different genders, see §46.

(3) the anaphoric pronoun, the most common type. Examples fall into two groups:

(*a*) those in which *he* follows a neuter noun referring to a male, e.g. *ÆCHom* i. 24. 27 *Ðæt cild . . . he*; or in which *heo* follows a masculine or neuter noun referring to a female, e.g. *ÆCHom* i. 14. 21 *ænne wifman . . . heo* and *ÆCHom* i. 16. 32 *to ðam wife . . . hire to*. (For examples of this type from the poetry, see Bauch, pp. 29-32.) Ropers (pp. 28-9), quoting *Exod* 2. 3, *Exod* 14. 16, and *Gen* 2. 22 *7 geworhte ðæt rib . . . to anum wifmen 7 gelædde hi to Adame*, Latin *Et ædificauit Dominus Deus costam . . . in mulierem et adduxit eam ad Adam*, suggests that the change of gender is the result of Latin influence. This may be true for these three examples. But if his corpus had contained sentences from the *Homilies* like those quoted above, he would (I imagine) have had to admit a triumph of sex over gender in OE itself. In *ÆCHom* i. 440. 18 *Nis nanum deadlicum men cuð hu, oððe on hwylcere tide hyre halga lichama þanon gebroden wære, oððe hwider he ahafen sy, oððe hwæðer heo of deaðe arise, he* of course refers to the body and *heo* to the Virgin herself; the sequence 'it . . . she' is quite possible today, as Thorpe's translation attests.

(b) those in which masculine or feminine nouns referring to asexuals or non-personals are followed by *hit* instead of *he* or *heo*, e.g. *ÆCHom* i. 20. 31 *ænne arc . . . hit* and *ÆLS* 4. 139 *þeos race . . . hit*; cf. *ÆCHom* i. 98. 35 *þes monað . . . he* and *ÆCHom* i. 108. 16–21 *Sæ . . . hyre yða . . . Sunne . . . hire leoman . . . Seo eorðe . . . heo . . . Hell . . . heo . . .* , where we find the expected grammatical concord.

§ 70. Examples of the *ænne arc . . . hit* type are much less common than those of the *seo eorðe . . . heo* type. It was chiefly Moore's failure to note this that enabled him to make the startling but false claim that the OE personal pronoun referred to sex ('natural gender', as he called it) '(say) 98 per cent of the time' (*PMLA* 36 (1921), 90). Moore's conclusions give a false picture for two reasons. First, as Heltveit shows (*NTS* 18 (1958), 357–69), he did not study enough texts and, by an unfortunate coincidence, selected those in which the writers were more concerned with persons (where, except for *wif, wifmann*, and the like, sex and gender coincide) than with asexuals (where sex and gender conflict if the words are masculine or feminine rather than neuter). This point, well made by Heltveit's analysis of *Byrtferth's Manual* and *De Temporibus Anni*, can be illustrated by an analysis of Ælfric's Homily *Inuentio Scæ Crucis* (*ÆCHom* ii. 302. 26–306. 28), which will also serve to make clear the second reason why Moore's statistics give a false picture, viz. that they are insufficiently analysed. The Homily contains in all fifty-one occurrences of the pron. *he* in its various genders, numbers, and cases, distributed as follows:

masculine nouns referring to male persons—	
he and oblique cases	35
feminine nouns referring to female persons—	
heo and oblique cases	6
þæt folc . . . hi . . . him	2
seo rod . . . heo and oblique cases	8

So we could say that in some 15.7 per cent of these (the last eight examples) gender triumphs over sex. The startling contrast with Moore's figure of 0.047 per cent in *ÆCHom* i. 2. 1–160. 18 (*PMLA* 36 (1921), 98) is due to the presence of the asexual feminine noun *rod* in the Homily I have analysed. So we could say that in this Homily sex prevails in some 84.3 per cent of examples. But on the other hand we could also say that gender prevails in some 96.1 per cent of examples, that is, everywhere except in the two instances with *þæt folc*. Both statements are equally misleading and valueless. What we should say is that in forty-one out of fifty-one examples the requirements of sex and gender coincide and there is therefore no possibility of a conflict (except by error) and that in the remaining ten, gender triumphs after a feminine asexual noun eight times and change of number after a collective noun (rather than sex) triumphs twice. So sex unaided nowhere in this Homily prevails over gender. Heltveit's use of figures invites similar criticism. The really significant points are that in *Byrtferth's Manual, he* refers back to both masculine personal antecedents and masculine asexuals, *heo* refers to feminine asexuals only (this no doubt reflects the subject-matter), and *hit* never refers to masculine or feminine asexuals, rather than that the percentage of conflicts is 63.1; this means little or nothing. But basically Heltveit's conclusions are sound.

§71. The agreement of the anaphoric pronoun and its noun can be summed up as follows:

(*a*) Masculine/feminine nouns referring to males/females take *he/heo*. Here sex and gender coincide.

(*b*) Neuter nouns referring to males/females tend to take *he/heo* rather than *hit* and masculine nouns referring to females tend to take *heo* rather than *he*. Here sex triumphs over gender.

(*c*) Masculine/feminine nouns referring to asexuals tend to take *he/heo*. Here gender triumphs over sex. But occasional examples of *hit* anticipate the MnE situation.

(*d*) OE *hit* (like *þæt*) may refer back to an idea expressed in a previous clause or sentence; see §1490. Here too MnE is anticipated.

Thus, as Heltveit puts it, 'the use of *hit* in reference to persons was in conflict with the speaker's recognition of personality and sex to a greater degree than was the use of *he* and *heo* in reference to asexuals' (*NTS* 18 (1958), 366). The essential difference then between OE and MnE is that *hit* covered only part of the domain of the non-personal while its MnE equivalent 'it' covers the whole. This change is, Heltveit believes, part of the general process of the loss of gender, for the use of *he/heo* for asexuals could remain firm only as long as the *se/seo* distinction existed. When this went, *hit* (already used to some extent in accordance with sex and not used for male or female except sometimes in those rare examples where gender required it) came into general use for asexuals.

3. NUMBER

a. The three numbers of OE

§72. In the noun, two numbers are distinguished—singular and plural, though there are nouns in which the nominative/accusative singular and plural coincide, e.g. *word* (neut.), or may coincide, e.g. *tungol* (neut.) and *wine* (masc.). See further E. Ekwall, *On the Origin and History of the Unchanged Plural in English* (Lund and Leipzig, 1912). On some possibly dual forms in *duru* and in words referring to parts of the body, see *OEG*, §612, and my §§88-9. For the dual in first and second person pronouns, see §243. On collective nouns, see §79; on concord, §§5 and 80-6.

b. Singular and plural

§73. The singular usually denotes one, the plural more than two, e.g. *ÆCHom* i. 30. 5 *þa ferde Ioseph . . . mid Marian . . . þaða hi on þære byrig Bethleem wicodon*, *ÆCHom* ii. 268. 33 *þæt halige fantwæter, þe is gehaten lifes wylspring, is gelic on hiwe oðrum wæterum*, and *ÆCHom* i. 604. 20 . . . *þæt he Godes beboda ne forgæge, na on oferætum and druncennyssum* (where the reference is to repeated acts of gluttony and drunkenness). We can perhaps similarly explain *BlHom* 219.9 *manige cleopodan mid mycelre stefne. þa gestod he 7 ahsode hwæt seo cleopung wære* and *ÆCHom* ii. 32. 5 *seo cyrce wearð gefylled mid clypungum ðæs blissigendan folces*. But there are more difficult examples.

c. Some special uses of singular and plural

§74. We find singular forms where the MnE equivalent is plural, e.g. *gealga* 'gallows', and plural forms where modern speakers detect no plurality, e.g. *Beo* 87 *in þystrum* (but cf. *Rid* 47. 4 *in þystro*). Similar fluctuations are common.[9] Some are no longer current, e.g. *ÆCHom* i. 424. 17 . . . *æteowiað his gesihðum eal þæt witatol* and *ÆCHom* ii. 162. 32 . . . *on heora gesihðum* (but *ÆCHom* i. 64. 22 *ge forgeafon blindum gesihðe* and *And* 620 *on wera gesiehðe*). (For examples of -*wylm* compounds in singular and plural, see Grimm, pp. 105-7.) Others can be paralleled from MnE, e.g. *Beo* 52 *under*

---

[9] For examples from the prose, see Flamme, pp. 12-13; Mohrbutter, p. 1; and Wülfing, i. 275-7. For the poetry, see Grimm, pp. 38-43; Klaeber, 3, p. xcii; and, among 'the eighteen German dissertations', those of Ahrens, Conradi, Dethloff, Fritsche, Jacobsen, Kempf, Lange, Mahn, Meyer, Oldenburg, Pingel, Rose, Schürmann, and Stieger.

heofenum (but *Beo* 1571 *of hefene*) (see Wülfing, i, p. 276), *Matt (WSCp)* 25. 10 *seo duru wæs belocyn* (but *Finn* 20 *to ðære healle durum*) (see *OEG,* §612 and Grimm, pp. 20-2), and *LS* 23. 680 *hu heo mihte iordanes wæteru oferfaran*—the 'plural to denote quantity' (Bøgholm, *Jespersen Gram. Misc.,* p. 221)—(but *Exod* 7. 17 *þises flodes wæter . . . hit byð geworden to blode*).

§75. Grimm collects many examples of plurals in OE but often fails to cite parallel instances with the singular. Thus he notes the plural in such formulae as *Beo* 721 *dreamum bedæled* (but *Beo* 1275 *dreame bedæled*) and *GenB* 440 *wordum and dædum* (but *WHom* 20(C). 129 *wordes oððe dæde*). For further examples, see Grimm, pp. 156-63. He explains *Beo* 2088 *fellum* as due to the influence of *cræftum* in the same line (pp. 161-2). But I suppose *dracan* might be a late genitive plural form, in which event the dat. pl. *fellum* would be possible, but not obligatory; see §87. His other examples are less troublesome. The plural forms *bearnum* and *broðrum* in *Beo* 1074 where we ought to have the singular may be due to mental confusion, perhaps created by the plural *leofum* line 1073; see Gehse, p. 91. But Klaeber, 3, notes to lines 1074 and 565, sees them as 'generic plural', like *Beo* 565-7 *mecum . . . sweordum*. Grimm also gives other groups of words in which the plural is common in OE. These include names of weapons, e.g. *Beo* 565-7 *mecum . . . sweordum* (but *Beo* 561 *deoran sweorde*) and *Beo* 1574 *be hiltum* (but *Beo* 1668 *þæt hilt*) (Grimm, pp. 33-7; see also E. V. K. Dobbie, *Beowulf and Judith* (ASPR iv), note to *Beo* 565); names of places, e.g. *Beo* 53 *on burgum* and *Beo* 1138 *of geardum* (but *GenA* 2594 *of byrig* and *Men* 109 *on geard*) (Grimm, pp. 43-77); periods of time, e.g. *Ex* 97 *dagum and nihtum* (but *ÆCHom* i. 68. 7 *dæges oþþe nihtes*), *Beo* 175 *hwilum* and *Beo* 1423 *stundum* (Grimm, pp. 77-91); words like *rodor, wolcen, brim, flod,* and *lyft* (Grimm, pp. 91-101); and *gestreon, hord, æht, lean,* and *laf* (Grimm, pp. 103-5).

§76. The dative plural is frequently used adverbially, either without preposition, e.g. (in addition to those quoted above) *Beo* 1638 *weorcum* and *Beo* 296 *arum,* or with one, e.g. *Beo* 643 *on sælum* and *El* 714 *mid arum*; see Grimm, pp. 30-2, 102-3, and 117-56. But the singular is also found, though less commonly, e.g. *Beo* 893 *elne, Beo* 1418 *weorce,* and *Beo* 2378 *mid are*; note also the accusative singular in *Beo* 618 *on lust.*

§77. Ambiguous pronominal forms such as *hie, þa, þas* (accusative singular feminine/nominative and accusative plural) and *him* (dative singular masculine and neuter/dative plural) sometimes seem to produce a change in number, e.g. *CP* 9. 5 *forðy ic wolde ðæt[te] hie ealneg æt ðære stowe wæren, buton se biscep hie mid him habban wille, oððe hio hwær to læne sie, oððe hwa oðre biwrite* and *ÆCHom* i. 256. 26 *ac beon hi rice on godum weorcum, and syllan Godes ðearfum mid cystigum mode, and God him forgylt mid hundfealdum swa hwæt swa he deð þam earman for his lufon.*[10] But the true explanation would appear to lie deeper than a mere mechanical switch, since similar changes occur where there is no ambiguous form, e.g. *CP* 351. 18 *Eac sint to manianne ða gesibsuman ðæt hie to ungemetlice ðære sibbe ne wilnigen, ðylæs hie for ðære wilnunga ðisse eorðlican sibbe forlæten untælde oðerra monna yfele unðeawas, 7 hiene ðonne selfne swa aðiede from ðære sibbe his Scippendes mid ðære geðafunga ðæs unryhtes* and *CP* 453. 6 *Ymbe ðæt, hu mon monige scyndan scyle to ðæm ðætte his godan dæda ne weorðen to yflum dædum.* In *ÆLet* 1. 51 *And hi sceolon gebiddan geornlice for þone cyning and for heora bisceop, and for þa þe him god doð and for eall cristen folc.* [52] *He sceal habban eac þa wæpna to þam gastlicum weorce, him* may refer either to *hi* or to *cyning . . . bisceop.* If the former, we would have the sequence *hi . . . him . . . he* as in *ÆCHom* i. 256. 26 above. Bøgholm, quoting these and similar examples from OE and MnE, remarks, 'The teacher who is trying to bring home his lesson to the individual is prone to contract his field of operations and put a singular for a former plural.'[11]

d. Collective nouns and nouns referring to species

§78. The singular may denote a class or species as a whole while the plural refers to the individual members thereof, e.g. *PPs* 103. 15 *hlaf trymeð heortan mannes* and *Coll* 289 . . . *fisc 7 cyse . . . ic ete* (Latin *pisces et caseum . . . manduco*), but *Mark(WSCp)* 6. 38 *fif hlafas, ÆCHom* i. 276. 4 *Mannum he gesealde uprihtne gang,* and *Coll* 100 *Hwilce fixas gefehst þu?* (Latin *Quales pisces capis?*).

---

[10] The change from sg. *nis* to pl. *wæron* in *Beo* 2458-9 is probably due to a combination of factors—*gomen* (nominative singular/nominative plural?) *swylce* (conjunction 'such as'/ nominative plural pronoun?) and the presence of two parallel subjects *sweg* and *gomen.* Consider also such sequences as *his . . . hie . . . him . . . hine* in *GenB* 339-42.

[11] Bøgholm, *Jespersen Gram. Misc.* 216-18. See also *ÆHex* 68. 459-72. It is perhaps possible for those who accept MS *guþmod grummon* in *Beo* 306 as a separate sentence to claim that the sg. *heold* might be another example of such a switch, possibly helped by *fah* and *fyrheard* (nominative plural neuter/nominative singular neuter). For another example, see *CP* 235. 16-21. The sequence *hie bið aswunden* in the Cotton MSS (234. 20), where Hatton MS has *he,* is probably the result of some sort of scribal confusion rather than evidence for the sequence plural subject + singular verb, as Stoelke (p. 76) takes it.

§79. Slightly different are collective nouns, which in the singular designate a group of individuals and in the plural more than one such group, e.g. *ChronE* 75. 25 (878) *Her hine bestæl se here . . . 7 mycel þæs folces ofer sæ adræfdon* and *ÆCHom* i. 60. 24 *on ealles þæs folces gesihðe*, but *ChronA* 70. 27 (871) *þa hergas begen* and *Luke (WSCp)* 2. 31 *beforan ansyne eallra folca*. On *leod* and *folc*, see further Grimm, pp. 101–2. On 'the sing. of concrete nouns . . . used in a collective sense' in conjunction with words like *genehost* and *oft*, as in *Beo* 794 *þær genehost brægd* ‖ *eorl Beowulfes ealde lafe*, see Klaeber, 3, note to *Beo* 794.

§80. When the collective noun and the verb are in the same clause, the verb is normally singular. The element order may be SV or VS and the collective noun may or may not be accompanied by a genitive plural, e.g. *BlHom* 143. 4 *ne wep, þæt þin folc ne sy gedrefed*, *Ex* 106 *Folc wæs on salum*, *ÆLS* 31. 1012 *þa com him færinga to micel folc manna*, and *ChristC* 1607 *scyldigra scolu ascyred weorþeð*. The verb in a subsequent clause may also be singular, e.g. *Or* 210. 11 *. . . þæt him nan folc ne getruwade þe him underþeow wæs*, *ChronA* 70. 3 (869) *Her for se here eft to Eoforwicceastre, 7 þær sæt i gear*, and, with a preceding genitive plural, *ChronA* 76.3 (878) *. . . Ælfred cyning . . . was winnende wiþ þone here, 7 Sumursætna se dæl se þær niehst wæs*. For further examples from the poetry see Bauch, pp. 35–42. On the number of the verb in adjective clauses when the direct antecedent is a genitive plural, see §§2343–50.

§81. But (as in MnE) the idea of the *several* individuals in the group often triumphs over the idea of the *one* group. This is most common when two clauses are involved. Thus we find a collective noun with a singular verb in one clause followed by a plural pronoun with a plural verb in another. The singular verb may follow the collective, e.g. *Or* 134. 20 *. . . eall þæt folc wearð mid him anum agæled þæt hie þæs wealles nane gieman ne dydon*, *Or* 118. 4 *þa his here geseah þæt he mid þy horse afeoll, hie þa ealle flugon*, *ChronA* 87. 30 (894) *7 se dæl þe þær aweg com wurdon on fleame generede*, and

Ex 223   . . .   fyrd wæs on ofste.
Siððan hie getealdon   wið þam teonhete
on þam forðherge   feðan twelfe,

or precede it, e.g. *ChronA* 70. 5 (870) *Her rad se here ofer Mierce innan East Engle 7 wintersetl namon æt þeodforda*, *Or* 21. 13 *7 þær is mid Estum an mægð þæt hi magon cyle gewyrcan*, and

El 1286   þonne on þreo dæleð
in fyres feng   folc anra gehwylc,
þara þe gewurdon   on widan feore
ofer sidne grund.

Ropers gives more prose examples of this and the next type (pp. 26–7). For further examples from the poetry, see Bauch, pp. 42–6. A similar change from a singular to a plural verb may occur after a genitive plural, e.g. *Jud* 261 *Mægen nealæhte, ‖ folc Ebrea, fuhton þearle.*

§82. We also find a collective noun without a singular verb followed by another clause containing a plural pronoun and a plural verb, e.g. *ÆCHom* i. 212. 19 *þæt folc ðe heora reaf wurpon under þæs assan fet, þæt sind þa martyras* (on the pl. verb *sind* see §§324–5), and (with a change of case) *Or* 44. 11 . . . *þæt swa oferwlenced cyning sceolde winnan on swa earm folc swa hie wæron* and

El 1204   þa seo cwen ongan
læran leofra heap   þæt hie lufan dryhtnes,
ond sybbe swa same   sylfra betweonum,
freondræddenne   fæste gelæston.

§83. The shift from a singular verb in one clause to a plural verb in the next may occur without an intervening plural element, both when the collective precedes the singular verb, e.g. *BlHom* 71. 7 *Eal þæt folc þæt þær beforan ferde, streowodan heora hrægl him togeanes,* *ÆCHom* ii. 88. 10 . . . *micel menigu samod com to ðam Hælende, and fram gehwilcum burgum to him genealæhton, John(WSCp)* 12. 29 *Seo menio þe þær stod, ⁊ þ gehyrde, sædon þ hyt þunrode* (but Latin *Turba ergo quae stabat et audierat, dicebat tonitruum esse factum*), and *Beo* 3030 *Weorod eall aras; ‖ eodon unbliðe . . . ,*[12] and when the collective follows the singular verb, e.g. *ÆCHom* i. 316. 17 *þa arn micel menigu to . . . and brohton heora untruman, ChronA* 70. 5 (870) (§81), and

Dan 52   Gesamnode þa   suðan and norðan
wælhreow werod,   and west foran,
herige hæðencyninga   to þære hean byrig.

✕§84. But the verb of a clause may be plural when the subject is a collective noun in the singular. In some examples, the collective is accompanied by the genitive plural of a noun or pronoun, e.g. (with the order SV) *BlHom* 87. 17 *þa sona seo unarimede menigo haligra saula mid Drihtnes hæse wæron of þæm cwicsusle ahafena,*

---

[12] Cf. *Beo* 1424 and *El* 870. For more examples, see Woolf, *MLQ* 4 (1943), 54–5.

ÆHom 11. 153 *Micel heap* [MS *C* inserts *manne*] *andbidað þær ura
holdra freonda ures tocymes to him, hohfull git embe us, orsorh be
him sylfum* (note the uninflected adjectives), *ChristC* 927 *heofonengla
þreat* ‖ *ymbutan farað,* and *Dan* 10 *þenden þæt folc mid him hiera
fæder wære* ‖ *healdan woldon,* and (with the order VS) *ChronA* 89. 4
(896) *þa þæs on sumera foron micel dæl þara burgwara* and *Beo* 1626
Eodon him þa togeanes, Gode þancodon, ‖ *ðryðlic þegna heap.*[13] But
the verb may be plural even when no such plural element is present;
thus we find (with the order SV) *ChronA* 86. 2 (894) . . . *mid þære
scire þe mid him fierdedon, ÆCHom* i. 348. 26 *eal þæt heofonlice
mægen samod beoð onælede mid his lufe, ÆCHom* ii. 112. 32 *he
geseah þæt se mæsta dæl ðære ðeode his lare forsawon, Beo* 1422
folc to sægon (but *folc* may be plural), and (with the order VS)
BlHom 91. 6 *forþon hyhton nu 7 blissian eall geleaffull folc, BlHom*
191. 9 *þa coman þær tosamne unarimedlico mengeo,* and *Ex* 144
Ealles þæs forgeton siððan grame wurdon ‖ *Egypta cyn* (where, however, the collective may be in apposition with an unexpressed plural
subject; see §1508).[14]

§85. Liedtke's general conclusion (pp. 48-9) that the sequence
singular collective subject + singular verb in the same clause is the
'rule' before 1000 seems sound. But he failed to record some of the
examples quoted above from poems which he read of singular collective subject + plural verb, and read only *Orosius,* the Chronicle, and
parts of the Bible, from the prose. Of the four examples of this sort
he noted in the Gospels, three have a plural verb in both Latin and
OE; see §84 fnn. 13 and 14. The fourth is *Mark* 4. 1, where the
Corpus MS reads *7 eall seo menegu ymbe þa* [*sæ*] *wæron on lande,*
but the other manuscripts have *wæs* for Latin *erat.* His observation
that a singular verb is relatively infrequent in subordinate clauses also
seems well-based; the sequence 'collective + singular verb' followed
by '(some plural element) + plural verb' in a succeeding subordinate
—and indeed coordinate clause—is the usual one. But examples
have been quoted above in which the verb of the second clause is
singular; some of these are subordinate.

§86. Occasionally there is a change back to the singular. Thus in
ÆCHom i. 190. 14 *þæt folc, ða þe þæt wundor geseah, cwædon*

---

[13] For further examples from the poetry, see Bauch, p. 41. The plural verb in *Matt*
(*WSCp*) 21. 8 (cited by Liedtke, pp. 47-8) represents a Latin plural verb.

[14] The remark in the previous footnote is true of *Matt(WSCp)* 9.8 and of *Matt(WSCp)*
12. 15. For further examples from the poetry, see Bauch, pp. 41-2. *Beo* 1626 is one of two
examples cited by Woolf in *MLQ* 4 (1943), 53, of a singular subject with a plural verb. In
the other, *Beo* 1032, Klaeber reads *meahte.*

... we find the sequence 'collective noun... plural pronoun... singular verb . . . plural verb'. *ChronE* 77. 22 (879) *þy geare gegaderodon an hloð wicinga 7 gesæt æt Fullanhamme* (where *ChronA* has *gegadrode*) may be merely the result of scribal error or may genuinely present a usage possible when MS *E* was copied. For more examples from the Chronicle, see Liedtke, pp. 48-9, and Sprockel, ii. 221-5. The only example from the poetry cited by Bauch (p. 42) is

And 1609   þeh þe fell curen
                    synnigra cynn.   Swylt þrowode,
                    witu be gewyrhtum.

Here *þrowode* may be plural; see §19.

e. *The idiom* on heora bedde *'in their beds'*

§87. This construction, seen in *ÆLS* 32. 74 *þæs ic gewilnige and gewisce mid mode þæt ic ana ne belife æfter minum leofum þegnum þe on heora bedde wurdon mid bearnum and wifum færlice ofslægene fram þysum flotmannum*, has been well explained by Davis in his note on the word *bedde* in this passage: 'OE sometimes uses a singular noun in this way when the number of individual possessors is plural, but each has only one of the things in question' (Sweet, *Pr.* 9, p. 102). The importance of the word 'sometimes' will be apparent from the fact that in this very passage three of the four manuscripts read *beddum*. So the statement by Dunning and Bliss needs qualification: 'Different languages adopt different ways of expressing the concept that each of a number of persons possesses one specimen of a class of things: Modern English puts the "thing" in the plural; Old English, like the majority of languages, puts the "thing" in the singular' (*The Wanderer* (London, 1969), 23). The word *wifum* above does not prove that Edmund's thanes were polygamists.

✕ §88. The singular is used particularly with words denoting (parts of) the body or the human mind or spirit. But here too the plural is often found.[15] There are first those things of which each individual has one only, such as *heafod* 'head', e.g. *PsCa6* 6. 24 *heafud maehtigra bið onstyred*, Latin *capita potentium movebuntur*[16] (but *PsCa6* 6. 23

---

[15] For a general discussion, see Grimm, pp. 14-20 and 22-30. Grimm misses most of these phenomena by restricting himself (p. 23) to those parts of the body which, appearing as a unity, are expressed by a dual or plural. Those he mentions in addition to *heafod* and *breost* are *nosu* and *sculdor*. All four are discussed here. Wülfing (i. 276) gives further examples for *heafod* and *breost*.

[16] This explanation is, I think, preferable to Stoelke's suggestion (p. 68) that we have a plural subject but a singular verb.

in heafudu unrehtra, Latin *in capita iniquorum*) and *ÆCHom* i. 236.
22 *Ne sceal eow beon forloren an hær of eowrum heafde* (but *BlHom*
151. 5 *7 heora heafdu slogan on þa wagas*);[17] *heorte* 'heart', e.g.
ÆCHom i. 68. 8 *biddað forði mid inweardre heortan* and *ChronD*
156. 24 (1023) . . . *eallon þam* . . . *þe his halgan lichoman þær mid
estfulre heortan* . . . *seceað* (but *Rid* 26. 19 *hy beoð* . . . ‖ *heortum
þy hwætran* and *ÆCHom* ii. 370. 23 *awurpað forði hire lufe fram
eowerum heortum*);[18] *lichoma* 'body', e.g. *ÆCHom* i. 10. 15 *hi
nabbað nænne lichaman* and *ÆCHom* ii. 608. 6 *þonne betæcð Crist
ða manfullan, mid lichaman and mid sawle into hellewite* (*lichaman*
is presumably singular here and in *ÆLet* 6. 289 *on sawle and on
lichaman* but may be singular or plural in *GenB* 845 *þa hie heora
lichoman leafum beþeahton* and in *ÆLet* 6. 290 *and we sceolon eft
agifan ure sawla urum scyppende þam ðe hi ær gesceop and asende to
þam lichaman*, where *sawla* too is ambiguous;[19] I have found no certain examples with the plural); *mod* 'mind', e.g. *BlHom* 149. 28 *þa
wæron hie swiþe erre on heora mode* (but *BlHom* 81. 7 . . . 7 *Drihtnes weg gegearwian to heora modum*); *muð* 'mouth', e.g. *ÆCHom*
ii. 192. 21 . . . *mid hundes lusum, ða flugon into heora muðe* (but
PPs 143. 9 *þara muðas sprecað manidel word*), and *nosu* 'nose' (possibly in origin a dual formation; see *OEG*, §612), e.g. *CP* 65. 20
mid ðære nose we tosceadað ða stencas (but *CP* 433. 21 *mid ðæm
nosum we tosceadað . . . stencas*).

§89. Second are those things of which each individual has two, such
as *fot* 'foot', e.g. *CP* 359. 3 . . . *he* . . . *trit mid ðæm fet* (but *CP*
31. 2 . . . *ge gedrefdon hiora wæter mid iowrum fotum*) and *hand*
'hand', e.g. *BlHom* 73. 1 *Nu on twam nihtum biþ mannes sunu
geseald on synfulra hand,*[20] *Dream* 59 *þam secgum to handa*, and
Beo 814 *be honda* (but *ÆCHom* i. 60. 3 *Domicianus on ðam ylcan
geare wearð acweald æt his witena handum, Beo* 1461 *manna ængum
þara þe hit mid mundum bewand* (editors talk about two-handed
swords. This seems unnecessary in view of the examples here cited:
more than one warrior had held the sword), and *Sat* 267 *be hondum*).
These variations can be paralleled in MnE. The plural seems to be

---

[17] On the locatival dat. sg. *heafdum*, see *OEG*, §574(4), and Grimm, pp. 25–30.

[18] The ambiguity of the *-an* ending makes it difficult to find more convincing examples
of the singular. Thus, despite Schrader, p. 14, *heortan* in *ÆCHom* i. 46. 26 *ða Iudeiscan þa
wurdon þearle on heora heortan astyrode* may be plural; cf. *Deut* 28. 65, *BlHom* 143. 8,
PPs 72. 1, and *GuthA* 796 ff. Is *Mark(WSCp)* 16. 14 *hyra heortan heardnysse* the equivalent
of 'their hardness of heart' or 'the hardness of their heart(s)'?

[19] So also *ÆCHom* ii. 608. 4 *sawle* but *Ps(P)* 32. 16 *sawla*.

[20] Here *hand* comes close to having the sense of MnE 'control, power, sway'; cf.
ÆCHom i. 436. 30, *Or* 134. 18, *BlHom* 203. 23, and *Beo* 2208. The dat. sg. *handa* represents *manu* in *Ps(P)* 21. 18 (of one) and *PPs* 106. 2 (of more than one).

used with singular reference in *MEp* 4 *þone writre . . . ‖ þe ðas boc awrat bam handum twam* (but perhaps he was ambidextrous—or used a two-handed pen?). *Sculdor* (masc.) 'shoulder' has an 'apparently neut. pl. *sculdru* [which] is to be regarded as dual in origin' (*OEG*, §574(3) fn. 1).

§90. As in MnE, *breost* 'breast' is used of females in both singular and plural, e.g. *Beo* 2175 *hyre syððan wæs ‖ . . . breost geweorðod* and *Luke(WSCp)* 11. 27 *Eadig is se innoð þe þe bær, 7 þa breost þe ðu suce*, and of males in the singular, e.g. *Luke(WSCp)* 18. 13 *he beot his breost* and *Or* 134. 22 *Ðær wearð Alexander þurhscoten mid anre flan underneoðan oþer breost*, Latin *sub mamma*. But the plural is sometimes found referring to males, usually in the dative, e.g. *John(WSCp)* 13. 25 *he hlinode ofer ðæs hælendes breostum* and *Beo* 550 *me . . . ‖ . . . on breostum*, but occasionally in other cases, e.g. *Rid* 15. 15 *hine berað breost* and *GenA* 1606 *he . . . ‖ . . . breosta hord.*[21]

§91. Third are those things of which each individual has more than two, such as *finger* 'finger', e.g. *CP* 357. 19 *Aworpen man . . . spricð mid ðæm fingre* (but *CP* 359. 3 . . . *ðæt he . . . sprece mid ðæm fingrum*) and—not quite the same in kind—*hær* 'hair', e.g. *ÆCHom* ii. 38. 8 *Eall his reaf wæs geworht of oluendes hære* (but *ÆCHom* i. 330. 2 . . . *he wæs mid olfendes hærum gescryd*). These variations too can be paralleled in MnE. *Beard* 'beard' is found in both numbers, e.g. *ÆCHom* i. 466. 24 *mid sidum bearde* but *ÆCHom* i. 456. 18 *side beardas*.

f. Plurals of proper nouns

§92. As in ME and MnE, plurals of proper nouns may imply 'individuals of this name', e.g. *ÆCHom* ii. 382. 34 *þry Herodes we rædað on bocum. An . . . oðer . . . þridda . . .* , or 'people like this individual', e.g. *ÆCHom* i. 334. 29 *Manega Lazaras ge habbað nu licgende æt eowrum gatum. . . .* Wülfing (i. 277) gives further examples.

g. Nouns used in the plural only

§93. Certain words—the so-called *pluralia tantum*—occur only in the plural. These include names of peoples, e.g. *Engle* 'English'

---

[21] The word *breost* presents problems of gender. If it can be feminine, as *Lch* ii. 140. 27 *on þa winstran breost* suggests, then it could be accusative plural or feminine accusative singular in *GD(C)* 19. 12 *on ða breost þæs dæadan lichaman* and *CP* 137. 8 *sio mildheortnes ðæs lareowes . . . gelecð ða breost ðæs gehierendes*. Grimm, pp. 14–20, cites only examples of *breost* in the plural.

(*OEG,* §610(7)), *firas* 'men', *higan hiwan* 'family', *ilde* 'men', and compounds in *-dagas* and *-stafas* (*OEG,* §574(6), and Grimm, pp. 164-8). To these may be added certain 'agent-nouns' or perhaps rather 'substantival participles' which occur only in the plural, e.g. *GenA* 1089 *burhsittende, MSol* 290 *lyftfleogendra, laguswemmendra,* and *ThCap1* 7. 3 *He sceal gretan his ymbstandenda.* See Kärre, pp. 127-30 and 133-91. Grimm, pp. 105-17 and 163-8, gives further examples of *pluralia tantum,* though he perhaps uses the term a little loosely at times.

4. CASE

§94. Case syntax has many ramifications and much that applies to nouns applies *mutatis mutandis* to adjectives and participles and to pronouns. The main functions of the various cases are set out in §§1240-427. But see also the Subject Index, s.v. *case.*

5. REPETITION AND NON-REPETITION OF NOUNS

§95. In both OE and MnE, a noun is often repeated in a different number, e.g. *ÆCHom* ii. 478. 6 . . . *ofer hire heafod, and ofer ealra ðæra mædena heafdu,* or case, e.g. *ÆCHom* ii. 20. 7 *þæt fyr . . . on ðam fyre.* When it is in the same number and case, there are situations in which both OE and MnE can repeat the noun, e.g. *ChronA* 38. 13 (685) *Her Ceadwalla ongan æfter rice winnan; se Ceadwalla was Coenbryhting* (but cf. *ChronA* 34. 23 (674) *Her feng Æscwine to rice on Wesseaxum, se wes Cenfusing*). But there are also situations in which OE repeats a noun where MnE would not, e.g. *Or* 20. 35 *on fif milum oððe on syx milum, BlHom* 103. 15 *þone deopan grund þæs hatan leges 7 þæs heardan leges,* and *ÆCHom* i. 20. 8 *and he leofode nigon hund geara and þrittig geara.*

§96. But, when the sense is clear, a noun is frequently not repeated in OE or MnE. This may happen when the constructions are different, e.g. *ÆCHom* i. 30. 7 . . . *to Iudeiscre byrig, seo wæs Dauides* and *ÆCHom* ii. 156. 31 *forðan ðe he awende þone unlust to sarnysse, and þurh þa yttran ontendnysse acwencte þa inran.* But of course it is most frequent when the two constructions are parallel. The noun in question may be the subject (e.g. *ÆCHom* ii. 58. 3 *Seo þridde yld wæs fram Abrahame oð Dauid. Seo feorðe fram Dauide oðþæt Nabochodonosor hergode on Iudeiscre leode*), the object (e.g. *ÆCHom* ii. 354. 21 *Maran cyle ic geseah and wyrsan . . . Stiðran and wyrsan ic geseah*), the complement (e.g. *ÆCHom* ii. 182. 12 *nis*

ðis na ure dæd, ac is ðæra halgena apostola), a genitive (e.g. ÆCHom
ii. 442. 30 On Marthan wæs getacnung ðises andwerdan lifes, on
Marian ðæs toweardan), or part of a prepositional phrase (e.g.
ÆCHom i. 498. 26 . . . on ðyssere worulde, ne on ðære towerdan).
Interesting for its repetition of the demonstrative + adjective group
without its noun is ÆCHom i. 20. 14 ac se ylca God þe gesceop
Adam . . . he gescypð ælces mannes lichaman . . . ; and se ylca seðe
ableow on Adames lichaman . . . , se ylca forgyfð cildum sawle and
lif. . . . Further examples include ÆCHom ii. 192. 29 and 430. 11
(subject); ÆCHom i. 340. 28 and ÆCHom ii. 354. 22 (object);
ÆCHom ii. 400. 14 (complement); ÆCHom i. 190. 9 (genitive);
ÆCHom i. 56. 4 and 162. 13, ÆCHom ii. 494. 26 and 594. 4 (in
a prepositional phrase). Thorpe's translation of the last is wrong; the
reference is the old church (Solomon's) and the new (Christ's). It
may be worth observing that the non-repetition of the noun produces a technical ambiguity in examples like ÆCHom i. 616. 28 and
þær bið seo twæming rihtwisra manna and arleasra and ÆCHom ii.
68. 16 þus sind gemengde þa godan ceastergewaran and ða yfelan;
cf. ÆCHom i. 232. 29 . . . hi bodedon freolice Godes naman reðum
cynegum and wælreowum, where the two adjectives refer to the
same, not to different, kings.

C. ADJECTIVES

1. INFLEXION AND CLASSIFICATION

§97. We may slightly adapt the conventional terminology by distinguishing 'adjectives proper'—those which have a comparative and
a superlative[22]—from demonstratives (se, þes; §§311–45), possessives (e.g. min; §§289–310), interrogatives (e.g. hwelc; §§346–60),
and indefinites (e.g. sum; §§361–519)—all of which can function
as adjectives and as pronouns but cannot be compared. The sections
which follow deal mainly with 'adjectives proper', but some discussion of the other types is inevitable.[23]

§98. The details of OE adjectival inflexions are set out in OEG.
'Adjectives proper', participles, and some indefinites (my §241), e.g.
fea and manig, can be declined according to a strong and a weak

---

[22] See H. A. Gleason, An Introduction to Descriptive Linguistics (rev. edn., London,
1969), 95–6.
[23] Scheinert, in PBB 30 (1905), 345–430, classifies the adjectives in Beowulf according
to the type of person, object, quality, etc., which they designate or to which they refer.
On 'intensifying adjectives', see §1146.

declension; for exceptions see *OEG,* §638.[24] The distinction was syntactical, at least in extant OE; see §§136-41. These inflexions were subject to the confusion between front and back vowels and between *n* and *m* already discussed in §15; see Schrader, pp. 21-5, for examples of this confusion in the *Catholic Homilies* and *Lives of the Saints.* On the comparison of adjectives, see §§181-91.

§99. Adjectives may be used attributively (§§102-27), predicatively (§§128-9), or in apposition (§§130-1). That these three uses cannot always be distinguished is clear from such examples as *ÆCHom* ii. 256. 18 *þes sceaða gesælig siðode to heofenum.* This point is further discussed in §§160, 1429, and 1434. On the use of adjectives where we should expect nouns, see §§132-5, and where we should expect adverbs, §1108. On the possibility of an attributive use of nouns, consider such compounds as *guð-rinc* and *storm-sæ,* and see Mutt, *NM* 69 (1968), 582-3.

§100. Onions (§84) speaks of the genitive as 'primarily an *Adjectival Case*'. Thus we find adjectives used where the genitives of the various types of nouns described in §54 would serve, e.g. *ÆCHom* i. 80. 11 *to Iudeiscum rice* but *ÆCHom* i. 80. 4 *of Egypta lande* (proper noun), *ÆCHom* i. 60. 29 *on sumum gyldenum wecge* but *ÆCHom* i. 450. 21 *goldes and seolfres . . . ungerime hypan* (common noun), and *ÆCHom* i. 70. 23 *þa deofolgyldan þe þa gyt ungeleaffulle wæron* but *ÆCHom* ii. 392. 16 *þu lytles geleafan* (abstract noun). Waterhouse, 'Affective language, especially alliterating qualifiers, in Ælfric's Life of St. Alban', *ASE* 7 (1978), 131-48, discusses Ælfric's use of alliterating qualifiers, including nouns in the genitive and adjectives, 'to point a moral'. See also W. Becker, *Studien zu Ælfrics Homiliae Catholicae* (Marburg diss., 1969).

§101. Participles can function as 'adjectives proper'; for a full list of participial functions, see §§1556-60. Seelig cites occasional examples of comparative and superlative, e.g. *Bo* 69. 4 *nan mon ne bið . . . no þy mærra ne no þy geheredra* and *Bede* 270. 17 *se halgesta wer 7 se forhæfdesta* (AF 70 (1930), *passim.* See also §1556, Closs, pp. 130 ff., and Visser, ii, §1045). As noted above, both present and second participles can be declined strong or weak as syntactically appropriate. Present participles, however, show a considerable mixture of

---

[24] Here Campbell rightly corrects the statement in SB, §291 Anm. 1, that *monig* is always declined strong. But no weak forms of *eall* or *genog* have yet come to my notice. Should *agen* 'own' be added to the list of those declined strong? See BT(S) and GK, s.v. *agen,* and note *ÆCHom* i. 112. 5 *his agen cyre* (nom.) and 112. 8 *heora agenne cyre.* But see §501.

substantival and adjectival endings; see *OEG*, §§632-4; Callaway, *PMLA* 16 (1901), 141-360, especially pp. 150-1 and 353-4; Kärre, pp. 77-130; and Mitchell 1969*a*, p. 73. So we find acc. sg. masc. *-ende* as well as *-endne* and dat. sg. masc. and neut. *-ende* as well as *-endum*. Kärre (p. 82) attempts to distinguish 'substantival words [which] . . . have sometimes adopted adjectival flexion . . . instead of, or as well as, their own' from 'ptcc [which] are sometimes used substantivally with retained adjectival flexion'. But he has to admit that, if there is a difference, 'the flexion is . . . no absolutely decisive criterion', for the substantival form is found in contexts which are traditionally regarded as adjectival, e.g. *ÆCHom* i. 496. 17 . . . *swa swa digelne leahter on menniscre heortan lutigende* alongside *ÆCHom* ii. 418. 9 *underfoh me nu behreowsiendne*, and vice versa, e.g. *ÆCHom* i. 48. 29 *Setl gedafenað deman, and steall fylstendum oððe feohtendum* alongside the nominative forms *fylstend, gefylstend* recorded by BTS, and *CP* 279. 1 *to fultome ðæm wiðfeohtende*. This confusion creates no difficulty when the participle is used attributively (cf. *ÆCHom* ii. 326. 1 *on yfelwyllende sawle* with *ÆCHom* ii. 100. 26 *mid weallendre lufe*; see Schrader, p. 68, for further pairs of examples from Ælfric), but may do so when the participle is appositive. The fact that Hrothgar is speaking resolves the ambiguity in *Beo* 372 *Ic hine cuðe cnihtwesende*, while in *ÆCHom* i. 46. 30, 46. 32, 48. 7, and 48. 31 *and se eadiga cyðere Stephanus hine geseah standende, standende* must be accusative. (Similar examples can occur with adjectives and second participles, e.g. *ÆCHom* i. 20. 31 *Wyrc þe nu ænne arc, þreo hund fæðma lang, and fiftig fæðma wid, and þritig fæðma heah* and

GenB 454   oððæt he Adam   on eorðrice,
              godes handgesceaft,   gearone funde,
              wislice geworht.[25])

But even after study of the context doubt remains about the case of *blissigende* in *ÆCHom* i. 56. 34 *nu todæg hi* [= *englas*] *underfengon Stephanum blissigende on heora geferrædene* and of *sweltende* in *ÆCHom* i. 480. 21 *ic wylle deaðe sweltan for mancynnes alysednysse, and ðe sweltende æfterfyligan* (where both Christ *ic* and John the Baptist *ðe* were to suffer death).

---

[25] In view of this sort of example, the participles under discussion could be described as uninflected rather than accusative. The distinction is exquisite.

2. ATTRIBUTIVE USE

a. *Adjective before noun*

(1) *The basic rule*

§102. The attributive adjective before a noun is declined weak if it is preceded by a demonstrative (*se, þes*) or by a possessive (e.g. *min, his*),[26] but strong when without one of these elements, e.g. *ÆCHom* i. 58. 32 *se Ælmihtiga Hælend*, *ÆCHom* ii. 84. 25 *be ðyssere and-werdan tide*, *ÆCHom* ii. 6. 21 *his ancennedan Æðeling*, and (with an intervening personal pronoun) *Or* 22. 31 *seo us nearre Ispania* and *Or* 26. 3 *sio us fyrre Ægyptus*, but *ÆCHom* i. 90. 21 *Ælmihtig Drihten.*[27] The same is true when the adjective follows the noun; for examples see §§126-7. This is the basic 'rule'; on its possible origin and significance see §§136-41. (For further examples see Flamme, pp. 86-8.) But there are qualifications and difficulties of classification.

(2) *The possessive and demonstrative with (adjective +) noun*

§103. It is important to keep separate the various patterns which may occur. They are lettered for convenience of reference.

§104. (*a*) The pattern possessive + demonstrative + weak form of adjective + noun occurs in *Bede*, e.g. 342. 17 *his þa æfestan tungan*, in *Orosius*, e.g. 270. 26 *his sio gode modor*, and in *Cura Pastoralis*, e.g. 389. 20 *ðin sio winestre hond*. (For further examples see Krohn, pp. 17-18, 30, 41, 55-6, and 75; Philipsen, pp. 35-6; Hüllweck, p. 45; and Wülfing, i, §248(*a*).) It is common in the *Dialogues*. Here, however, the reviser is often content to omit the demonstrative in MS *H*, e.g. *GD(C)* 4. 9 *min þæt ungesælige mod*, but *GD(H)* 4. 9 *min ungesælige mod*; *GD(C)* 43. 25 *his þæt æwfæste lif* but *GD(H)* 43. 25 *his eawfæste lif*; and *GD(C)* 5. 23 *mines þæs ærran lifes* but *GD(H)* 5. 21 *mines ærran lifes*. In *GD(C)* 64. 27 *to þæs þam manig-fealdum 7 ungefohlicum stefnum*, *þæs* appears instead of *his* in an unusual combination of two demonstratives. Again, the reviser keeps the possessive, dispensing with *þam*: *GD(H)* 64. 27 *to þæs ungefohli-cum hreame*. Sometimes MSS *O* and *C* differ, e.g. at *GD* 13. 28, where MS *C* reads *þa mycclan mægnu* but MS *O* has *his* before *þa*. But the construction is not entirely absent in MS *H*. Thus, in eliminating

---

[26] For the reasons given in §239, I do not use the terms 'possessive adjective' or 'posses-sive pronoun', though they do of course occur in quotations from other writers.

[27] The examples cited here and in the rest of this section are those with one attributive adjective only. The 'rules' given for the form of such adjectives also apply when more than one qualifies the same noun. On the syntactical patterns then involved see §§166-74.

(as he often does) the split construction of *GD(C)* 3. 26 *ða com to me min sunu Petrus 7 min se leofesta diacon*, the reviser writes in MS *H* at 3. 25 *þa com to me min se leofesta sunu Petrus diacon.* Krohn does not seem to have thought this tendency of MS *H* to eliminate the demonstrative worthy of comment. It may be noted that examples with the superlative form of the adjective (like the last and *Or* 194. 3 *heora þa welegestan burg*) are more common than those with the positive form in the 'Alfredian' examples given in the three dissertations already mentioned.

§105. This pattern is not restricted to 'Alfredian' texts. It occurs in *Blickling Homilies*, e.g. 5. 1 *mid hire þære yfelan sceonesse 7 facne* and 13. 10 *ure se trumesta staþol* (see further Flamme, §43(1) and (5)), in Ælfric, e.g. *ÆCHom* i. 192. 6 *ure se Ælmihtiga scyppend, ÆCHom* i. 168. 3 *urne ðone ecan deað*, and *ÆCHom* i. 364. 5 *ðurh his ðæs mæran Forryneles and Fulluhteres ðingunge*, and in poetry, e.g. *Sat* 241 *his se deora sunu, Dan* 608 *Ðu eart seo micle and min seo mære burh, Dream* 95 *hæleð min se leofa*, and *Jul* 166 *min se swetesta sunnan scima.*

§106. The pattern possessive + demonstrative + noun, i.e. with no attributive adjective, is rare. The only example noted by Krohn, Hüllweck, and Philipsen, is *Bo* 69. 23 *mid his þam anwealde*. There are some with adjectives used as nouns, e.g. *Bede* 212. 30 *ussa þara neahstena, Bede* 370. 7 *þinne ðone nehstan*, and *BlHom* 117. 12 *his þam halgum*. The vocative expression in *BlHom* 229. 27 can be explained as an example of post-position—*Matheus, min se leofa*—(see §126) or as a combination of two separate elements—*Matheus min, se leofa.*[28]

§107. (*b*) The pattern demonstrative + possessive + weak form of adjective + noun also occurs, e.g. *GD(H)* 150. 32 *seo his gemæne spræc* (but *GD(C)* 150. 32 *his seo gemæne spræc*), *Bede* 282. 23 *in þis user ciriclice stær, Bo* 8. 16 *þ min murnende mod, BlHom* 201. 24 *se heora halga bisceop*, and possibly *ChronE* 135. 10 (1003) *ac he teah forð þa his ealdan wrenceas*, where *þa* may be the adverb. But here the reverse of pattern (*a*) is true—the form without an attributive adjective is much more common and is found in a variety of texts, e.g. *Or* 56. 31 *se heora cyning, CP* 147. 10 *sio hira lufu*,[29]

---

[28] See Wülfing, i, §248(*b*). *CP* 389. 20 and 21 *ðin sio swiðre* are special cases; *hand* occurs seven times in the preceding ten lines and again in line 21.

[29] For further examples from the 'Alfredian' texts see Philipsen, p. 35, and Hüllweck, pp. 44–5. Note also *Bo* 84. 27 *þone urne* and the similar example from the *Laws* quoted by Hüllweck, p. 45.

Matt(WSCp) 7. 24 *ðas mine word*, Latin *verba mea hæc*, *Matt(WSCp)* 20. 21 *þas mine twegen suna*, Latin *hi duo filii mei*, *Ch* 204 *ðas mine gesaldnisse*, *Ch* 126 *ðas mine geoue*, and *BlHom* 175. 20 *se heora lareow.*[30] Here too the reviser of *GD* usually dispenses with the demonstrative, e.g. *GD(C)* 35. 21 *hwæt se his wisdom wære* but *GD(H)* 35. 22 *hwæt his wisdom wære* and *GD(C)* 141. 20 *Exilatus þes ure gefera* but *GD(H)* 141. 20 *Exhilaratus ure gefera*. But he retains it at *GD(H)* 57. 15 *on þære his wædle*. Heltveit (1977, p. 69) quotes two examples from Ælfric which I had dismissed—*ÆCHom* i. 50. 25 *Swiðor he besorgade þa heora synna þonne his agene wunda*, where *þa* again may be the adverb, and *ÆLS* 36. 367 *Hwæt is se eower god þe awent þurh þe swa ure wif us fram?*, where Skeat's translation reads 'What is He, your God, who . . . ?' (such an interpretation could be extended to other examples)—but, like me, has noted none in Wulfstan. However, we find the pattern in the poetry, e.g. *Wife* 50 *se min wine* and *Met* 20. 29 *þæt ðin good*. *Res* 9 *ond þa manigfealdan mine geþohtas* of course reflects the demands of metre.

§108. This pattern is perhaps less frequent in OE than the last, but is common in eMnE, e.g. 'this our old friend' and 'these my gifts'. Whether it has had a continuous existence since OE and whether it was in origin a *calque* on Latin remains to be established.[31]

§109. (c) In *Ps(A)* we find a pattern which suggests that the glossator had trouble with Latin *suus* and *eius* or tried to render them very accurately (see the quotation from Vleeskruyer below). In this the demonstrative precedes the noun and the possessive follows. Examples are *Ps(A)* 2. 6 *mont ðone halgan his*, Latin *montem sanctum eius* and (without an attributive adjective or, perhaps better, without a noun) *Ps(A)* 4. 4 *ðone halgan his*, Latin *sanctum suum*.

Vleeskruyer (p. 48) writes of

the use of a possessive pronoun together with a demonstrative, a device no doubt originally adopted to render as literally as possible the clear inflexional distinctions

---

[30] The only three examples cited by Brown 1963, p. 55, are of this type—*CP* 301. 10, 301. 12, 451. 32. For further examples from *Blickling Homilies* see Flamme, §43(5). All the examples he cites of pattern (*a*) are with adjective, whereas all those of pattern (*b*) are without; cf. *BlHom* 201. 30 *heora þa leasan godas* with *BlHom* 201. 32 *þæm hera bisceope*. According to Flamme, the former is more common in the first three-fifths, the latter in the second two-fifths, of *Blickling Homilies*. However, his citations are not complete. Heltveit (1977, pp. 67–71) offers more examples from *BlHom*—and also from other texts in his selected corpus, which did not include *Bede* or *GD*—and draws our attention to the high preponderance of examples of my types (*a*) and (*b*), both with and without adjectives, in *BlHom*.

[31] I do not understand why the idiom seen in *BlHom* 163. 3 *seo heora iugoþ* was so attractive to writers in search of a source for the MnE construction 'a friend of mine'. It is to be compared rather with examples like *BlHom* 7. 31 *se Cristes brydbur* (discussed in §1318) and 'this my friend'. See Einenkel, *Ang.* 28 (1905), 504 ff., and my §§409–16 and 1201, fn. 2.

of the Latin possessive. This remarkable glossing artifice, which cannot be presumed to have had any but a paper existence, is still a feature of Wærferð's literary Mercian, and was also adopted in Alfred's Orosius, where it may be viewed as a further sign of Mercian influence. The stable character of this Mercian literary dialect is well illustrated by the occurrence of the device in a wide range of Mercian texts, including the VPs. gloss.

Later (p. 140), he cites further examples with the observation that 'this archaic usage' is found in other texts, including the *Blickling Homilies* and the prose texts of the *Beowulf* manuscript.

§110. Two points should be noted here. First, Vleeskruyer makes no distinction between the three patterns which I have noted above. He asterisks 'the possessive with demonstrative (§64)' as one of the 'particularly significant cases of agreement [in *St. Chad*] with the dialect of the Vespasian Psalter gloss'.[32] But the examples he quotes from *Ps(A)* belong to pattern (*c*), while the rest (except for *LS* 3 (*St. Chad*) 178 *his monunge þere heofonlican*, where demonstrative + adjective follow the noun) belong to patterns (*a*) and (*b*). Second, when Vleeskruyer (p. 139 (§62)) speaks of 'a possessive pronoun' he does not mean to exclude a 'possessive adjective'. The latter seems to be less common, but this is because the possessives of the third person are indeclinable and because we cannot classify forms like *min, uncer*, and *ure*, as either declined or not declined. But he does not mean to include the genitive of nouns—nowhere does he cite such an example. This is important. For when Grünberg comes to discuss this problem she at first follows Vleeskruyer and talks of 'the possessive with demonstrative', but comments that the group '*þæt godes word . . .* could be called closely parallel'.[33] It is indeed like some examples of pattern (*b*). But Grünberg fails to remember that 'closely parallel' does not mean 'identical'. For, a little later on, she expands Vleeskruyer's phrase to read 'groups consisting of a possessive (or genitive) + demonstrative which precede a noun' (p. 317, §58). This adds a variety of examples with the genitive of a noun to patterns (*a*), (*b*), and (*c*), which Vleeskruyer had already embraced under the one term. And so, when (rightly noting the above-mentioned peculiarity (my §104) of MS *H* of *Gregory's Dialogues* which others had missed) she writes 'From instances of this construction in the MSS. of GD. it is apparent that it is an archaic feature, the late MS. H avoiding it' (p. 391 n. 56), she includes as examples not only *GD* 4. 9,

[32] His p. 65 (item 21) and p. 63 respectively. '§64' in the first quotation should read '§62'; cf. his p. 48 fn. 5.

[33] M. Grünberg, *The West-Saxon Gospels* (Amsterdam, 1967), 261-2 (§33 f.). Flamme (p. 22) similarly compares *BlHom* 45. 24 *on Godes þone soþan þeowdom* to examples of pattern (*a*).

5. 23 (both in §104), and the like, and *GD(C)* 28. 19 *to Godes þam upplican wyllan* (MS *H* has *to þam upplicum gewilnungum*)—which does seem to be closely parallel—but also *GD(C)* 40. 33 *in þam diglan Godes dome* (MS *H* has *on Godes diglan dome*). This last pattern, which I shall call (*d*), is one of a number of variants of a basic pattern discussed in §1318;[34] it occurs in *GD(H)*, e.g. 28. 16 *se Godes þeow* and 44. 11 *se forecwedena Godes þeow*, and is common in Ælfric; Grünberg herself cites *ÆCHom* i. 18. 22 *þæt eaðelice Godes bebod* (§58).[35]

§111. So Grünberg's remark 'this construction . . . is an archaic feature' covers at least four patterns and seems to be based on the assumption that every change made in MS *H* of *Gregory's Dialogues* is the result of a desire to avoid archaism. But it will be apparent from the examples cited above that pattern (*a*) is not always eliminated in MS *H* and is found in Ælfric, that pattern (*b*) appears in MS *H* and in *Blickling Homilies*, and that pattern (*d*) occurs in MS *H* and in Ælfric. It is hard to see in what sense they can be 'archaic'.

§112. This leaves pattern (*c*). Now, as we have already seen, Vleeskruyer confused patterns (*a*), (*b*), and (*c*), when he spoke of the combination of a possessive and a demonstrative as a 'remarkable glossing artifice, which cannot be presumed to have had any but a paper existence' and as 'this archaic usage' (pp. 48 and 140). We can, I think, dismiss the latter as an unfortunate variation on the former; to describe as 'archaic' something which never existed in the spoken language is confusing. It seems reasonable to apply the former to pattern (*c*); it is unlikely that *his* in *ðone halgan his* was felt as a pronoun, 'the holy [thing] of him'. If Gradon's question 'Is it not in fact a normal Old English construction?'[36] is applied to this particular pattern, the answer is 'Probably not'. But if it is asked of any of patterns (*a*), (*b*), or (*d*), the answer is 'It would seem so', for it is hard to see how they can be denied real existence, since all occur in prose of different periods and in the poetry. Nevertheless, it is interesting to note that, in his fifty charters (see my §143), Carlton cites just one example—*his þære haligran unlu[st]* (*JEGP* 62 (1963), 781.

---

[34] *WHom* 8c. 107 *Godes agen þæt forme bebod*, quoted by Grünberg in §58 (p. 317), is a different pattern again. One suspects that the two elements were felt separately and that the implication was that of *Matt(WSCp)* 22. 38 *þ mæste 7 þ fyrmyste bebod*. Examples like *Dream* 95 *hæleð min se leofa* may also have been felt as two elements. Cf. §106.

[35] The distinction between this pattern and those involving the possessive will be apparent from the respective positions of the genitive of a noun and of the possessive in the table given in §143.

[36] *RES* 20 (1969), 202. The fact that Gradon repeats Grünberg's formula accounts for her use of the singular 'it' in the question quoted.

But this is suspect; see §144)—and that I have noted no examples in the *Anglo-Saxon Chronicle*. However, this does not justify the failure of Spamer (*Glossa*, 13 (1979), 241-50) to take cognizance of these constructions or of those like *BlHom* 7. 31 *se Cristes brydbur* discussed in §§1316-24. This failure must vitiate his conclusions about the development of the definite article in English.

(3) *Noun genitive (group) + weak form of adjective + noun*

§113. When a genitive of a noun or a genitive group precedes the combination 'adjective + noun', it too is followed by the weak form of the adjective, e.g. *GD(H)* 40. 30 *on Godes diglan dome*, *CP* 131. 14 *mid ðæs folces eorðlican ðeowote*, *ÆCHom* i. 24. 7 *of Noes eltstan suna*, *ÆCHom* i. 128. 16 *to þæs cyninges untruman bearne*, and *ÆCHom* ii. 162. 33 *þa geseah se halga wer þæs arleasan preostes niðfullan ehtnysse*. (Schrader gives more examples from the *Catholic Homilies* at p. 29. See also Krohn, pp. 18 and 31.) If the genitive follows the adjective, it does not affect its form, e.g. *ÆCHom* ii. 290. 33 *of yðigendre sæ þyssere worulde*. Further on the position of genitives and genitive groups, see §§1304-30.

(4) *Weak form of adjective + noun*

§114. The adjective is often declined weak in both prose and poetry when used in the vocative without a demonstrative or possessive; see §§1245-7. In the poetry it is commonly so found in the other cases. Examples (all from *Beowulf*) are 1792 *gamela Scylding*, 2330 *ofer ealde riht*, 1859 *widan rices*, 561 *deoran sweorde*, 963 *heardan clammum*,[37] and (with the adjective after the noun) 1801 *hrefn blaca* and 1343 *hreþerbealo hearde*. Campbell (*OEG*, §638) rightly observes that 'the later the verse the less it diverges from the syntax of prose in this matter'. This phenomenon was discussed by Lichtenheld and used by Barnouw as a criterion for a comparative dating of OE poems—hence 'Lichtenheld's test'. There is no point in rehearsing here the details of these studies and of the criticisms they provoked;[38] we can, I think, be content to agree with Funke that 'no one would attempt to-day to group OE poems in a strict chronological order according to the proportion of weak adj. forms with and without the

---

[37] These last two are dubious. Cf. *Beo* 1335 *heardum clammum* and see §15; Klaeber, 3, p. xcii; Funke, pp. 151-2; and the references there quoted. The possibility of *-an/-um* confusion arises frequently in the next few pages. Note also *ÆCHom* i. 284. 1 *se Halgan Gast*.

[38] Lichtenheld, 'Das schwache Adjektiv im AGS', *ZfdA* 16 (1873), 325-93; A. J. Barnouw, *Textkritische Untersuchungen nach dem Gebrauch des bestimmten Artikels und des schwachen Adjektivs in der altenglischen Poesie* (Leiden, 1902); R. W. Chambers, *Beowulf. An Introduction to the Study of the Poem* (3rd edn., with a Supplement by C. L. Wrenn, Cambridge, 1959), 105-7; Funke, pp. 151-2; and the references cited by the last two writers.

article' (p. 151) and with Amos (p. 124) that 'the "Lichtenheld tests" of the definite article and the weak adjective are not reliable for either prose or verse'.

§115. There are spasmodic examples of this combination in the prose of all periods. Those in which we have -*an* where we should expect -*um* in the dative singular masculine or neuter or in the dative plural can probably be dismissed, e.g. *GD(C)* 42. 32 *mid grimman sare* (but MS *H* 42. 35 *mid teartum sare*); *Bede(Ca)* 42. 10 *clænan muðe 7 clænre heortan* (MS *B* has *clæne muðe*); *ÆCHom* i. 12. 19 *to mæran engle* (but *ÆCHom* i. 12. 23 *mære engel*); and *WHom* 20(*BH*). 16 *mid swiðe micelan earnungan*, but *WHom* 20(*BH*). 15 *mid miclum earnungan.*[39]

§116. Taking as his authorities Krohn, Schrader, and Mohrbutter, Funke (pp. 152-3) claims that there were examples in which an adjective in -*an* was used alone with a feminine noun. On reference to the text the examples Funke cites all seem to disappear. The phrase from Bede *on godgundan lare* appears only in the later MS *B* where *T* has 268. 9 *in godcundre lare*. Krohn (p. 59) gives both these readings. Funke does not. *WHom* 7. 45 *to soðan helpe* is another example of -*an* for -*um*; cf. *WHom* 11. 179 *helpes bedæled*. Since the phrase *godcundan mihte* is preceded by *his* in the three examples cited by Mohrbutter (*WHom* 6. 138, 7. 65, 7. 67),[40] the weak form is regular (my §102). There are no examples of this in Ælfric, as far as I know at the moment. But cf. *Beo* 1104 *frecnan* (MS *frecnen*) *spræce*.

§117. Examples involving cases other than the dative have been cited. Some can be explained away, e.g. *GD(C)* 146. 29 *he seleð halgan witedomes gast*, where MS *O* has *his* before *halgan* to give the expected syntax. But some remain, e.g. *Bede(T)* 438. 31 *þeostran onseone* (so, with spelling variations, all MSS except *C þeosterran onseones*—which does not solve the problem) and *CP* 391. 9 *unnyttan men* (nom.), and leave in the mind the possibility that *GD(C)* 5. 16 *mycclan sæs* may not be an error, despite MS *O micles sæs*. Whether these are to be regarded, like their equivalents in the poetry, as examples of 'a presumable archaism' (Klaeber, 3, p. xcii), as the result of scribal error, or of phonetic and/or analogical confusion, is

---

[39] A comparison of the various manuscripts here is instructive. For further examples from various texts see Krohn, pp. 20-1, 44-5, 59-60, and 73; Funke, pp. 152-3; and Mohrbutter, pp. 72-6.

[40] Mohrbutter, pp. 73-4. He also includes *WHom* 20(*EI*). 20 *mid miclan earnungan* and *WHom* 20(*BH*). 104 *for godan dædan*; cf. *yfelan dædan* in the next line. But these are to be taken as dative plurals.

not certain. But pending complete examination of the OE corpus, we should perhaps bear in mind here too what I take to be the warning given by Funke (p. 152): 'we must be cautious to see in these dative types genuine archaic traits'.

(5) *Demonstrative + strong form of adjective + noun*

§118. The real existence of this pattern in OE is a matter of considerable doubt. Apart from *ÆCHom* ii. 478. 23 *þæt cristen folc* (described by Schrader, p. 29, as 'corrumpiert'), all the alleged examples in the *Catholic Homilies* involve the possibility of -*um*/-*an* confusion in dative singular masculine or dative singular neuter, e.g. *ÆCHom* ii. 84. 21 *fram ðisum andwerdum dæge* (but *ÆCHom* ii. 86. 12 *fram ðisum andwerdan dæge*). There are none with feminine nouns.

§119. The situation is the same in 'Alfredian' prose. No examples with feminine nouns have been produced, but we frequently find that, while one manuscript has -*um*, another has -*an*, e.g. *ChronE* 75. 19 (877) *æfter þam gehorsedum here* where *ChronA* 74. 17 has *æfter þam gehorsudan here* and *Bede(O)* 262. 23 *to þam heofonlicum timbre*, where MS *T* has *to þæm heofonlican timbre*. Krohn, who cites further examples (pp. 27-8, 36-7, 49, and 64), is (in the words of Christophersen, p. 91) 'unwilling to recognize the forms in question as strong, but ingeniously explains them as weak adjectives with an ending -*um* due to the analogy of the strong paradigm (p. 37)'. Since it suits his theory to claim that these were archaic survivals of an earlier pattern, Christophersen is reluctant to admit Krohn's explanation. But he can find no unambiguous examples of the pattern demonstrative + strong form of adjective + noun in OE prose[41] and, like Curme (*JEGP* 9 (1910), 449-51), the only example from the poetry he can call to his support is *Beo* 2860 *æt ðam geongū*. With disarming ingenuity, he almost succeeds in turning this scarcity of examples into an argument in his favour: 'Seeing that Beowulf is archaic enough to have preserved, in a large number of instances, the old articleless combination of weak adjective and noun, it is rather to be wondered at that the usage *article + strong adjective* is not more common in the poem' (p. 92). There are, of course, examples in the poetry like *Dream* 109 *on þyssum lænum life*, but any possibility that this is significant would seem to be wiped out by *Dream* 138 *on þysson lænan life*; *geongum* in *Beo* 2860 is almost certainly for *geongan*.

[41] He admits (p. 91) that all his examples seem 'to be confined to the dative masc. and neut.' but calls to his aid the pattern discussed in the next section. *Or* 274. 10 *þara cristenra monna* will not serve; see §141.

§120. I do not claim that I have proved that this pattern never existed in OE.[42] But the slightness of the evidence supplied by Christophersen seems to support both Funke's dismissal of the *Beowulf* example and his comment that he seems 'to be justified in the assumption that in OE prose traces of an older usage of strong adj. forms after the def. article cannot be proved' (p. 155). *GD* 217. 26 . . . *þæt he sylfa naht ne cuðe ne nyste buton þone hælendan Crist 7 þysne hangiendne 7 þrowiendne for ealles mancynnes hæle* is to be taken as a special case; *hangiendne* and *þrowiendne* are emphatic —note the change of demonstrative—and can be said to hover uneasily between functioning as nouns or adjectives.

(6) *Possessive + strong form of adjective + noun*

§121. In *Catholic Homilies*—with the exception quoted below— this pattern too appears only in contexts where *-an/-um* confusion in dative singular masculine and dative singular neuter is possible, e.g. *ÆCHom* ii. 200. 18 *on urum gastlicum fulluhte*; cf. the dative plural in *-an* in *ÆCHom* ii. 300. 9 *be his ærran dædum*. Similar examples occur in 'Alfredian' prose, e.g. *GD(H)* 75. 15 *mid his lyttlum suna*, where MS *C* has *mid his lytlan suna*, and *Or* 202. 6 *æfter hiera hæðeniscum gewunan*. But we find also unambiguous instances, e.g. *CP* 393. 8 *his getreowne ðegn*, *GD* 212. 17 *mid hire scamleasre bælde*, *Bede(T)* 238. 22 *his unrihtes sleges*, where the later MS *B* has *his unrihtan sleges*, *BlHom* 131. 24 *his ful leof fæder*, and *ÆCHom* ii. 32. 14 *his broðerlicere and moderlicere yrmðe*.[43] Heltveit (1977, pp. 82-5) adds several more examples, including *CP* 252. 25 *ure worldcunde fæderas* and *LS* 8. 122 *þurh þin sigefæst gefeoht*, but goes on to draw conclusions which do not seem to me proved by the evidence he presents. See further §§123 and 409-16, Krohn, pp. 17, 30, 41, 55, and 71-2, and Funke, p. 155.

§122. 'In the poetry', remarks Christophersen (p. 91), 'the strong form seems to have been more common than the weak in this position (Lichtenheld, p. 379).' An analysis of Lichtenheld's examples does not really support this. Of the eleven he cites, only one— *GenB* 654 *his holdne hyge*—is strictly parallel to those from the prose cited above. In *GenA* 1936 *drugon heora selfra ‖ ecne unræd* the possessive element is in a different half-line and is perhaps therefore in a less close relationship. In the remaining nine also, the possessive is always in a different half-line from the adjective + noun (on

---

[42] On the question of its existence in Germanic, see Curme, *JEGP* 9 (1910), 439-82.

[43] *Beo* 373, quoted by Andrew (*Postscript*, p. 79) as *his eald fæder*, is not a case in point. Klaeber has *his ealdfæder*.

the principle involved, see §§152-7) and sometimes at any rate can be taken apart from it, e.g. *GenA* 166 *Gesette yðum heora* || *onrihtne ryne* (where *yðum heora* could be taken together; note *lago* in line 163), *GenA* 1827 *þæt þu min sie* || *beorht gebedda* (where we could translate 'that you are mine, a noble consort'), and

GenA 1533   æðelum fyllað
       eowre fromcynne   foldan sceatas,
       teamum and tudre

(where the possibility of apposition again presents itself: 'with nobles, with your offspring, with children and progeny').[44] Since Lichtenheld himself (p. 379) noted six examples of the regular prose pattern possessive adjective + weak form of adjective + noun in *Gen*, e.g. *GenA* 2609 *heora ealdan fæder* and *GenB* 245 *his halige word* (he found none in *Beowulf*), his evidence does not justify Christophersen's conclusion quoted above. Nevertheless, the existence of some examples of the pattern possessive + strong form of adjective + noun in both prose and poetry must be admitted. According to Curme (*JEGP* 9 (1910), 449 and *passim*) and Christophersen (pp. 91-2), they are survivals. I must concede that this theory is possible. But I am reluctant to endorse it because the alternative of analogical confusion presents itself; see Heltveit (1977, pp. 82-5). Most of the rare examples involve dative singular masculine and neuter *-um*, where the possibility of confusion with the weak ending *-an* exists; cf. §§118-19. Of Heltveit's 435 examples, 404 (92.9 per cent) have the expected weak form, twenty-four (5.5 per cent) have *-um*, and only seven (1.6 per cent) have an unambiguously strong form.

(7) An/sum *(sg.)* + *adjective* + *noun*

§123. In this pattern the adjective is usually declined strong, e.g. *ÆCHom* ii. 452. 31 *an stunt wif*, *ÆCHom* ii. 252. 11 *ænne bealdne ðeof*, *ÆCHom* ii. 514. 26 *sum earm wif*, and *ÆCHom* i. 58. 25 *sum wælhreow casere*. But the weak form is found, e.g. *ÆCHom* ii. 160. 22 *on anes blacan cildes hiwe*, *GD* 306. 22 *sum arwyrþa wita* (cf. *Bede* 198. 21 *sum arwyrðe mæssepreost*), and *Bede* 70. 3, where MS *T* has *sum eorðlic æ*, MS *O* *sum eorðlice æ*. A good many examples show the possibly indeterminate *-an* for *-um* in dative singular masculine or dative singular neuter, e.g. *ÆCHom* ii. 104. 13 *be sumon rican menn* and *ÆCHom* ii. 178. 21 *on anum lytlan glæsenan fæte*. (So

---

[44] The remaining examples are *Beo* 255, *Beo* 1180, and *GenA* 2330 (in these three the possessive is in a different line, separated from adjective + noun by a verb, and may originally have been appositive), and *GenA* 2182, 2425, and 2466 (in these three the possessive follows the noun and the elements are again in different lines).

also *ÆCHom* i. 340. 18, 582. 24 (but cf. *ÆCHom* ii. 106. 15), *ÆLS* 6. 275, and *ÆHomM* 8. 24.) The adjectives in examples like *ÆLS* 3. 82 *to anre widgyllan byrig*, *ÆLS* 7. 346 *on anre lytlan byrig*, and *ÆCHom* ii. 438. 9 *into sumere eaðelican byrig*, may be weak or may show late analogical extension of -*an* (for -*um*) to dative singular feminine of the strong declension of the adjective. When a demonstrative or a possessive precedes *an*, the attributive adjective is declined weak, e.g. *Bo* 136. 26 *se an gestæþþega cyning*, *ÆLS* 12. 89 *se an goda dæg*, and *ÆCHom* i. 500. 24 *ðurh his ænne ancennedan Sunu*.[45]

§124. Funke, citing some of these examples, describes them as being 'after the indefinite article' and remarks that 'these cases show that the feeling for the "definite" function of the weak adj. seems to be on the decline' (p. 153). But it is difficult for us to be certain that in such examples *an* and *sum* have completely lost the strong individualizing force they so often have; see §388.

(8) *Adjectives denoting quantity or number + adjective + noun*

§125. After words like *ægðer, ælc, ænig, eall, (ge)hwilc, manig,* and *genog*,[46] the attributive adjective is usually declined strong unless a demonstrative or possessive intervenes, as in *Bede* 100. 17 *ealle þa gelæredestan men* and (cited after Carlton[47]) *ealle his leofan halgan*. (With some of these words, of course, such intervention cannot occur.) Examples of the strong form include *ÆCHom* ii. 6. 7 *buton ælcum eorðlicum fæder*, *ÆCHom* i. 224. 33 *gehwilce wise lareowas*, *CP* 157. 11 *ymb hwelc eorðlic ðing*, *CP* 157. 16 *hwelc dieglu scond*, *ÆCHom* i. 4. 2 *manega lease Cristas*, and *BlHom* 223. 27 *nænigum woruldricum men*. There are exceptions, e.g. *GD* 276. 5 *ælces lichamlican gemanan*. Similarly we find the strong form after numerals as well as *an* (§123), e.g. *ÆCHom* i. 216. 24 *twegen gelyfede men*; see further §136.

b. Adjective after noun

§126. The rules set out in the preceding sections apply when the adjective follows its noun. Thus we find that an adjective standing alone in post-position has a strong form when it is the only qualifier,

---

[45] On this construction, see Rissanen, pp. 14–15. I am grateful to Rissanen (private communication) for confirming the findings in this section and for supplying some of the examples cited. For further examples see Schrader, pp. 27–8 and 32; Krohn, pp. 18 and 57; and Wülfing, i. 298–302 and 432–3.

[46] These words, of course, sometimes function as pronouns. On their classification and use see §241.

[47] Carlton 1958, p. 236, and *JEGP* 62 (1963), 780—in both places without reference.

e.g. *BlHom* 35. 27 *Nu is þearf mycel*, *ÆLS* 26. 225 *gebeoras bliðe*, *WHom* 20(*EI*). 141 *And eac her syn on earde apostatan abroþene*; when a genitive expression precedes the noun, e.g. *CP* 175. 6 *sumere hearpan strengas aðenede*; when an adjective of quantity or number precedes it, e.g. *Or* 19. 5 *7 þær sint swiðe micle meras fersce*, *ChronA* 68. 11 (865) *alle Cent eastewearde*, and *Ch* 1200 *enig meghond neor*; and even when a demonstrative or possessive precedes the noun, e.g. *Ch* 1508 *in þissum life ondwardum*, *ÆCHom* i. 426. 20 *ure godas geyrsode* (cf. in the same line *ða asmeadan tintregan*), and *ÆCHom* ii. 516. 25 *ðine meda gewisse*. But the weak form of the adjective is found when it is accompanied by a demonstrative and/or a possessive, e.g. *BlHom* 61. 34 *þær he hæfþ weallendene leg 7 hwilum cyle þone grimmestan*, the vocative *ÆCHom* i. 28. 20 *men ða leofestan*, *LS* 3 (*St. Chad*) 178 *his monunge þere heofonlican*, and *ÆLS* 7. 314 *Iohannem and Paulum mine ða getreowostan*. The distinction is clearly demonstrated in *BlHom* 179. 13 *ungelæredne fiscere þone leasostan*.

§127. In the poetry we find the same fluctuations after the noun as we find before it (see above), e.g. *El* 1067 *frea mihtig* and *JDay* ii 294 *meowle seo clæne*, but *Beo* 1801 *hrefn blaca*. Examples such as *Beo* 3028 *se secg hwata* and *Mald* 240 *on wlancan þam wicge* reflect the general tendency of the poetry to vary the element order and to use weak forms of the adjective more freely; see §§114 and 3944-6.

3. PREDICATIVE USE

§128. When used predicatively in the nominative the adjective/ participle is declined strong in the positive and superlative.[48] It is usually found with no inflexional ending in the singular and with -*e* in the plural, e.g. *ÆCHom* ii. 20. 34 *þu eart mære and micel*, and *ÆCHom* ii. 484. 29 *ge sind ælðeodige*, and (with the superlative) *ÆCHom* i. 50. 4 *se . . . wearð fyrmest on ðrowunge* and *ÆCHom* ii. 80. 31 *þus beoð þa endenextan fyrmeste*. The necessary qualifications for prose and poetry are set out in §§33-8.

§129. In the accusative the predicative adjective/participle is also declined strong when it is declined, e.g. *ÆCHom* i. 10. 18 *God hi gesceop ealle gode*, *ÆCHom* i. 260. 28 *we sceolon . . . healdan þone broðerlican bend unforedne*, and *ÆCHom* ii. 124. 4 *Godes swingle*,

---

[48] *WHom* 6. 29 . . . *he mihte beon þæs efengelica ðe hine gescop*, cited by Mohrbutter (p. 63), is not an exception; see BTS, s.v., where *efengelica* is taken as a noun. The comparative is of course weak; Flamme gives examples at pp. 80-1.

þe we on ær towearde ondrædan sceoldon. But it need not be declined, e.g. *ÆCHom* ii. 28. 29 [*heo*] *micclum truwode hire hæle
toweard*; on this point see further §§1434 and 1437-9. All the examples in the accusative from *Beowulf* quoted by Scheinert (*PBB* 30
(1905), 416-17) are declined strong with the exception of *Beo* 372
Ic hine cuðe cnihtwesende (and, of course, comparatives). On the
non-agreement of this participle, which might be better regarded as
appositive, since the sense is 'I knew him as a boy', not 'I knew him
to be a boy', see again §§1434 and 1437-9.

4. APPOSITIVE USE

§130. On apposition in general, see §§1428-63. The adjective/par-
ticiple in apposition follows the rules set out above—without a
demonstrative it is declined strong, e.g. *ÆCHom* i. 336. 5 *sum arwurðe munuc wæs on ðam earde Licaonia, swiðe eawfæst*, *ÆCHom*
i. 66. 12 . . . *gewitt he of ðissere worulde, nacod and forscyldigod* (or
predicative?), and *ÆCHom* ii. 390. 26 *We strange sceolon beran ðæra
unstrengra byrðene*; with a demonstrative it is declined weak, e.g.
ÆCHom i. 392. 1 *Saulus se arleasa* (which may be a stylistic variant
of the attributive found in the next line, *se arfæsta Paulus*). On non-
inflexion of the appositive adjective/participle in the accusative, see
§1439. This rule holds for the poetry. For examples from *Beowulf*,
see Scheinert's collections in *PBB* 30 (1905), 410-12.

§131. In *GD(C)* 17. 15 we read *sum wif bær hire sunu deadne*. MS
H has 17. 13 *sum wif bær hire deadan sunu*. Here a stylistic variation
necessarily produces a change of inflexion. Whether *deadne* in MS *C*
is to be explained as appositive or an emphatic attributive adjective
could, I suppose, be argued. The same is true of *Bede* 152. 22 *ond
[Cadwalla]* . . . *on ungearone þone Osric mid his fyrd becwom*.

5. ADJECTIVES USED AS NOUNS

§132. The following examples will serve to illustrate this dishonoured
term (see Collinson, *TPS* 1941, pp. 70 and 125)—which I use because
alternatives such as Jespersen's 'adjective primary' and 'adjective secondary' have not been universally accepted:[49] *ÆCHom* i. 46. 32 *Iudei
ða . . . heoldon heora earan* (noun), *ÆCHom* i. 106. 6 *þa Iudeiscan
hyrdas* (adjective), and *ÆCHom* i. 106. 19 *þa Iudeiscan ðe on Crist
gelyfdon* (adjective used as noun).

[49] *TPS* 1941, pp. 72-3. The term 'nominalized adjective' used by Closs (pp. 75-7) does
not seem a great improvement.

§133. The rules set out above generally apply. Thus we find *ÆCHom* i. 6. 31 *se Ælmihtiga, ÆCHom* i. 16. 22 *þone unwaran, Luke(WSCp)* 10. 27 *þinne nehstan, ÆCHom* ii. 512. 7 *Manega eac wurdon met-trume gehælede,* and *ÆCHom* ii. 442. 14 *we sceolon ða hungrian fedan, nacode scrydan, . . . ða ungeðwæran gesibbian, untrume geneosian, deade bebyrian.* In *CP* 271. 9 *ða suiðe suigean* we find an adverb intervening and in *ÆCHom* ii. 374. 34 *ða modigan synfullan . . . ða eadmodan synfullan* weak forms of the adjective are qualified by weak forms.[50] There is fluctuation after words like *an* and *sum,* e.g. *ÆCHom* ii. 26. 20 *twegen landes menn and an ælðeodig* but *ÆCHom* ii. 470. 22 *sum wælhreowa;* cf. §123. These rules also hold for the poetry.[51] The strong form *lufigendne* is noteworthy in *ÆCHom* ii. 88. 29 *. . . and heora lufigendne gemaciað weligne ecelice.*

§134. Occasional examples occur in the prose of a weak form used alone with no preceding noun which it can be said to qualify, e.g. *ÆCHom* i. 64. 21 *ge gehældon untruman.* According to K. Brunner (ii. 73), 'die Verwendung von Adjektiven als Substantiva ist ae. allgemein und ohne Einschränkung möglich. . . . doch kommen in der Poesie auch noch schwach flektierte Formen ohne Artikel vor, wie beim attributiven Gebrauch' ['adjectives can be used as nouns universally and without restriction in OE. . . . however, in poetry there also occur forms like that of the attributive adjective, with the weak inflexion and no article']. He gives no examples of the last usage. Lichtenheld claims that this is so rare in the poetry that the examples should be regarded as exceptions or scribal errors (*ZfdA* 16 (1873), 329-31). This is a little extreme. Lichtenheld certainly manages to dispose fairly successfully of most of those he cites. Neither he nor Phoenix (with his very wide definition of *Substantivierung*) manages to produce anything quite like *ÆCHom* i. 64. 21 above. But there remain from their collections sentences in which a weak form of the adjective occurs alone but can be referred to a noun in the previous few lines, e.g. *GenA* 2523 *þæt fæsten . . .* ‖ *steape, Beo* 2928 *. . . se froda fæder Ohtheres . . .* [2931] *gomela,* and *Beo* 2961 *þær wearð Ongenðiow ecgum sweorda,* ‖ *blondenfexa on*

---

[50] For further examples from the prose, see Flamme, pp. 13-14; Philipsen, pp. 32-4; Wülfing, i. 291-5; Shannon, p. 25; and Brown 1963, p. 42 fn. 1. Some of the German dissertations referred to in this and the next note spread their net very wide; thus Brown (ibid.) justly objects to the inclusion here of examples like *CP* 161. 1 *ðylæs he sie scyldig ealra hira scylda.*

[51] See Scheinert in *PBB* 30 (1905), 412-13 (examples from *Beowulf*), and among 'the eighteen German dissertations', those by Ahrens, Conradi, Dethloff, Fritsche, Kempf, Lange, Madert, Mahn, Meyer, Oldenburg, Pingel, Schürmann, and Stieger.

bid wrecen. Whether we call *blondenfexa* an adjective or an adjective used as a noun is a question of terminology.

§135. The comparative and superlative of adjectives can be used as nouns. So also can participles. Examples include *BlHom* 45. 17 *Godes gingra*, *BlHom* 169. 21 *se læsta . . . 7 se heanosta*, and *BlHom* 61. 10 *þæm rihtdondum*. For further examples see Wülfing, i. 297–8, and Flamme, pp. 13–14 and 54.

6. THE USES OF THE STRONG AND WEAK FORMS: CONCLUSION

§136. The weak form of the adjective is used after a demonstrative, possessive, or noun genitive (group)—no matter whether the adjective is before the noun, after it, or without a noun. When the adjective is not so accompanied, or is preceded by an adjective of quantity or number, it is declined strong. After *an* and *sum* the strong form is preferred. Exceptions to these rules have been set out in the preceding sections.

§137. The significance of the two uses may now be considered. Funke (p. 151) writes:

As to the historical background it is the generally accepted opinion that in the articleless stage the group **jungaz sunuz* (the strong adj.) might signify a definite or indefinite conception (i.e. 'the' young son or 'a' young son), whereas the group **sunuz jungō* (the weak adj.) would have referred to a definite idea alone (i.e. 'the' young son). The rise of the def. article then went parallel with the development of the weak adjective and the combination [def. art. + weak adj. + noun] thus became a means for definite reference, the strong adjective (without the article) being restricted to the indefinite use.

Examples can be adduced to demonstrate this distinction, e.g. *ÆCHom* i. 4. 8 *gif he bið þurh boclice lare getrymmed* and *ÆCHom* i. 2. 20 *ungelærede menn*, but *ÆCHom* ii. 8. 22 *se frumsceapena mann Adam* and *ÆCHom* ii. 2. 23 *swilce he gebringe ða soðan lare to leasum gedwylde*. But it should not, I think, be too readily assumed that the form of the adjective (still) had any significance in itself; the distinction could have been conveyed by the presence or absence of the demonstrative, as it is in MnE. The fluctuation between the two forms of the adjective in the vocative perhaps points in this direction. Indeed it is not always easy to see a distinction of meaning between the two patterns; cf. *ÆCHom* i. 58. 32 *se Ælmihtiga Hælend* with *ÆCHom* i. 90. 21 *Ælmihtig Drihten*, *ÆCHom* i. 4. 5 *se Ælmihtiga God* with *ÆCHom* i. 6. 8 *God Ælmihtig* (it must be admitted that there is a strong presumption of Latin influence in this particular example (§172)), and *ÆCHom* ii. 276. 2 *he hæfð þæt ece lif* with *ÆCHom* ii. 274. 32 *he hæfð ece lif.* On the other hand, a distinction sometimes seems to exist between two expressions having the same form, e.g. *ÆCHom* i. 64. 27 *þa heofenlican æhta sind us eallum gemæne* (where 'all heavenly possessions' seems to be the meaning) but *ÆCHom* i. 346. 29 *Nabbað ealle menn gelice gife æt Gode, for-ðan ðe he forgifð ða gastlican geðincðu ælcum be his gecneordnys-sum* (where, as *ÆCHom* i. 446. 2–5 confirms, 'all spiritual honours' is precisely what is not meant).

§138. Andrew (*Postscript*, p. 79) claims that in *Beowulf* there is a difference of meaning between the combinations weak form of adjective + noun and strong form of adjective + noun. Examples like *Beo* 2290 *dyrnan cræfte* and *Beo* 2168 *dyrnum cræfte*, however, led him to restrict this: 'only in the nominative are the forms distinct in sense, e.g. geong guma "*a* young man", geonga garwiga "*the* young warrior" '. That such a distinction could be restricted to the nominative is theoretically unlikely, though it could have arisen from the situation visualized by Funke; see my §137. But it does not hold. For we find strong forms of the adjective when the reference is to a definite individual, e.g. *Beo* 31 *leof landfruma* (Scyld), *Beo* 54 *leof leodcyning* (Beowulf I), and *Beo* 61 *Halga til*, and weak forms when the reference is to any one member of a class or species, e.g. *Beo* 1245 *heaþosteapa helm*, *Beo* 1343 *hreþerbealo hearde*, and *Beo* 1801 *hrefn blaca*. It would have been neat if *geong guma* had always meant 'a young man' and *geonga guma* 'the young man'. But use of the weak form without a demonstrative inevitably led to ambiguity, e.g. in

Beo 1432   Sumne Geata leod
         of flanbogan   feores getwæfde,
         yðgewinnes,   þæt him on aldre stod
         herestræl hearda,

where we can translate 'the hard war-arrow' or 'a hard war-arrow'; Andrew's observation (*Postscript*, p. 79) that '*se* . . . may be understood in this attributive construction, e.g. gamela Scylding, mæran cynnes' merely begs the question.

§139. Funke (p. 153) says that the group strong form of adjective + noun without demonstrative and with definite reference 'historically seen, is clearly an archaism'. In addition to three instances noted by Krohn (p. 37), viz. *CP* 87. 1 *mæstne demm and mæste scande*, *CP* 185. 3 *eaðmodlic lif haligra monna*, and *CP* 9. 8 *ofer sealtne sæ*, he cites examples from *Maldon*, e.g. 91 *ofer cald wæter*. Those from the early prose need not surprise us if his theory is right and those from the later poetry can be viewed as imitations or survivals for metrical convenience. But Funke (rather more surprisingly) then claims to 'have come across a few instances in Aelfric, esp. with adjectives having the force of proper names' (p. 154). But those he adduces are (to say the least) dubious. They both occur in *ÆCHom* i. 30. 5 *þa ferde Ioseph, Cristes fosterfæder, fram Galileiscum earde, of ðære byrig Nazareð, to Iudeiscre byrig, seo wæs Dauides, and wæs geciged Bethleem* and can be translated respectively 'from a Galilean home (dwelling)' and 'to a Jewish city'; both are indefinite until made definite by a following phrase or clause. Other apparent examples can also be explained away, e.g. *ÆCHom* ii. 2. 5 *of Ledenum bocum to Engliscum gereorde* and *ÆCHom* i. 2. 18 *of Ledenum gereorde to Engliscre spræce*, where the reference is general rather than specific.

§140. Other exceptions to the rules here set out have already been discussed. The patterns weak form of adjective + noun (§§114–17) and possessive + strong form of adjective + noun (§§121–2) occur and may be archaisms. But Christophersen has not substantiated his claim that demonstrative + strong form of adjective + noun survived as an archaism in later OE prose (§§118–20) or that the strong form of adjective + noun is found in Ælfric with a definite reference (see §139).

§141. Closs (p. 116) claims that 'failure to observe the weak–strong distinctions consistently throughout is actually evidenced in most texts'. Neither of her two examples from *Orosius* is quite to the point—*Or(C)* 124. 27 has the expected *micelne* for *L*'s *micel*—and *Or* 274. 10 *þara cristenra monna*, though rare in eW-S (*OEG*, §656), can easily be paralleled elsewhere. For the rest, Closs refers us to Krohn's evidence, which is discussed above (§§116 and 119). But these sporadic exceptions scarcely justify her remark; apart from them and subject to the qualifications made above in the formulation of the 'rule', the weak–strong distinction in the declension of adjectives is consistently observed in the prose.

7. THE POSITION OF ADJECTIVES

a. Introductory remarks

§142. Two considerations arise—the position of the adjectives relative to one another and to the other qualifying elements with which they are associated, and their position with regard to the noun.

b. The relative position of the qualifying elements

§143. The basic rules for the prose when all the elements precede the noun are usefully summarized in the table by Carlton reproduced below from an article which shows a happy application of the techniques of descriptive linguistics—without its jargon—to OE syntax.[52] This study is based on fifty 'original charters or copies contemporary with the events described in them [his italics] . . . dated from AD 805 to 1066' (p. 778). Carlton writes:

By placing all the noun headwords in one column and then spacing the modifiers in front of the noun column so that all forms of the same word or all words of the same part of speech fall in the same column according to position in front of the noun and other modifiers (maintaining the same relative position to the other modifiers), we obtain a six-position arrangement of the modifiers as shown below:

6th Position (eall, sum, manig)	5th Position (pron.)	4th Position (numeral)	3rd Position (oþer)	2nd Position (adj. and part.)	1st Position (noun in gen. case)	Head word (noun)
	þære			geættredan	deofles	lare
		an	oþer	healf		gear
		ænne		blacne		stedan
	þæm	þriim				dælum
	min	twa				wergeld
	þa		oþoro			lond
mænig			oþer	god		man
allum	þæm					halgum
ealle	his			leofan		halgan
sum	þæt					lond
ealle	mine					freondum
			oþrum	sue miclum		lande

§144. The table requires some qualification. The rules need not apply when the qualifying group contains *and*, e.g. *ÆCHom* ii. 290. 21 *micele and manega fixas*. Two attributive adjectives may occupy position 2, either with or without *and*; see §167. As examples like

---

[52] *JEGP* 62 (1963), 778–83. The table appears on p. 780. Lists of examples which conform to the table will be found in Shannon, pp. 26–7, and Zuck, pp. 8–10. Their other examples will be discussed below.

Some interesting comparisons between the position of some of these elements in OE and that of their equivalents in ON are made by Heltveit (1977, pp. 85–93).

ChronA 48. 17 (755) *hiera agenne dom* and *Bo* 80. 25 *pæs wæteres agnu cyð* show, *agen* 'own' can be added to the possessive in position 5 or to the noun genitive in position 1. In the light of the examples discussed in §§103-12—Carlton's example *Birch* 452. 23 (*Ch* 204) *his ðære haligran unlu[st]* is suspect—it can be said that, when both demonstrative and possessive occur in position 5, each element can precede or follow the other.

§145. According to Carlton 'position 6 includes a special group of adjectives—*sum, eall, manig, ælc, nænig, æghwilc*—which always precede all other modifiers of the headword and which are not preceded by other modifiers' (p. 781). There are exceptions to this. *PPs* 118. 86 *pine ealle gebann*, Latin *omnia mandata tua*, may be a special case; cf. *Or* 1. 1 *ealne pisne middangeard*. In examples like *Solil* 42. 11 *se æalra betsta cræft* and *Solil* 67. 24 *pa ealra wissestan on pisse weorulde*, *ealra* is used almost adverbially—'the very best . . .' and 'the very wisest . . .'. Both *manig* and *feawe* (the latter not represented in Carlton's table) can be used after a demonstrative, e.g. *Or* 3.25 *pa monegan yflan wundor*, *Or* 214. 15 *pa monegan cyningas*, and *Or* 218. 20 *para monegena gewinna*, and *BlHom* 37. 11 *pas feawan dagas*. They can therefore function in position 4 (as numerals) as well as in position 6; see Schwartz, *Lang.* 44 (1968), 751. Conversely, the numeral can appear in position 6, e.g. *ÆLS* 4. 65 *twegen his halgan*, *ÆLS* 26. 10 *twegen his æftergengan*, and Carlton's example *twægen mine mægas*, of which he writes (p. 782) 'it is possible that the genitive pronoun has been drawn into position 1 with the genitive nouns by analogy and therefore tends to fluctuate between position 5 and position 1'. Another possible analogy would be with *begen*, which is found in position 6 rather than position 4, e.g. *Or* 186. 30 *begen pa consulas*. However, I am inclined to see these as examples of 'partitive apposition' (§1455); cf. *Or* 244. 6 *wið monige his mægas*,[53] *ApT* 8. 21 *mid feawum pam getrywestum mannum*, and *ÆCHom* i. 44. 25 *sume ða ungeleaffullan Iudei*.

§146. *Oðer* is not restricted to position 3, e.g. *Bede* 54. 30 *oðre monige munecas* (but *ChronA* 87. 28 (894) *monige opre cyninges pegnas*) and *ÆLS* 3. 631 *oðre fela bisceopas* (but *ÆCHom* ii. 112. 31

---

[53] Cf. *ÆLS* 7. 293 *pa Romaniscan mædenu manega eac ðurhwunodon on clænum mægðhade*, where the opening expression is clearly partitive, and the examples with *twegen* in post-position discussed in §164. These two examples with *monig* cast doubt on Marckwardt's conclusions (*Meritt Essays*, p. 53) about the unambiguity of the constructions with *monig*. On his remarks about those with *fela*, see §427.

fela oðre gecorene halgan). We find it in position 6 twice in *Bede* 140. 2 . . . *oðer his bearn, of Æðelberge þære cwene acende, Æþelhun 7 Æðelfrið his dohtor 7 oðer his sunu, Wuscfrea wæs haten* and before rather than after a numeral in *Or* 17. 13 *on þæm oþrum þrim dagum* and *ChronA* 91. 7 (897) *from þæm þrim scipum to þæm oðrum þrim* (but cf. MnE 'in the next three days' and 'in the three following days').

§147. We may note here the fundamental similarity between the patterns set out in Carlton's table (as far as it goes) and those of MnE; important exceptions include the combination possessive + demonstrative (§§103-12) and the position of the noun genitive (§1305).

§148. Unfortunately the dangers of working from a limited corpus become apparent, not only in the exceptions noted above and in the fact that the idiom seen in *ÆCHom* i. 144. 26 *anum gehwilcum gelyfedum men* was apparently not represented in Carlton's material —see §469 and Rissanen, pp. 239-44, for examples from prose and verse—but also with special reference to elements of position 2, 'the attributive adjective'. Here we can distinguish three separate types. First we have *ilca*, which is always weak and is always preceded by a demonstrative, as in *se ilca* 'the same'. Second there are the adjectives proper like *blæc, leof,* and *god,* which are used without a demonstrative or after one; exceptions like *Bede* 152. 22 *ond . . . on ungearone þone Osric mid his fyrd becwom* and *Mald* 240 *on wlancan þam wicge* are rare. But see §131. The third group (represented in Carlton's material (p. 782) by *in þissum life ondwardum*) consists of adjectives such as *eastweard, foreweard, hindeweard, middeweard,* and *midd,* which appear in varying positions with noun alone or with demonstrative or possessive + noun. Thus we find *CP* 297. 11 *mid forewearde orde, Or* 252. 1 *on foreweardre þisse seofeþan bec, ÆCHom* ii. 266. 11 *ure forewearde heafod,* and *Bede* 386. 27 *in ðæs cyninges rice forewordum.* An even richer variety of examples with *midd* includes weak forms without a demonstrative and strong forms with one—*ChronE* 136. 23 (1006) *to ðam middan wintran* but *ChronE* 136. 11 (1006) *ofer þone midne sumor; ÆCHom* i. 312. 4 *on middan ðære sæ* but *Bede* 384. 19 *on midre ðære sæ; CP* 431. 30 *on midre sæ* but *ÆCHom* i. 12. 35 *on middan neorxnawange;* and (with *midd* following the noun) *ÆCHom* ii. 142. 30 *on sæ middan, ÆCHom* ii. 350. 20 *on ðam þeostrum middum,* and *ÆCHom* ii. 336. 2 *on ðære þriddan nihte middan.*

§149. A table similar to Carlton's can be drawn up for the poetry.[54]

6th Position (eall, sum, manig)	5th Position (dem. and/or poss.)	4th Position (numeral)	3rd Position (oþer)	2nd Position (adj./ptc.)	1st Position (noun in gen. case)	Head word (noun)
1	min			yldra		fæder
2	þin agen					bearn
3					godes agen	bearn
4	se			halga |	heahengla	god
5	min se			swetesta |	sunnan	scima
6		twelfe . . . |		tireadige		hæleð
7	þa	þry				naman
8	be þissum || feawum					forðspellum
9	þa		oðre			fynd
10 manigu			oðru			gesceaft
11 sum						woðbora
12 eall	þæt					maþþumgesteald
13 ealne |				yrmenne		grund

§150. Most of the qualifications made in §§144-8 to Carlton's table apply to this one too. Some are included in the table; see also GK, s.vv. *foreweard* and *mid, midd*.[55] There is, however, a striking difference between the prose and the poetry—in the poetry the qualifying elements are very often separated from one another and/or from the governing word. This separation may be by 'speech material(s)' (this term is discussed below), by the medial or end caesura, or by both speech material and caesura. It may take place when all elements precede the noun or when some or all follow it; for the latter see §§175-7.

§151. The earlier writers of 'the eighteen German dissertations' concentrated on whether the noun preceded or followed and on the grammatical classification of the speech material which did the separation. Schürmann, the first, wrote in 1884 that 'eine Trennung des Adjektivs vom Substantiv durch andere Satzglieder oder durch Bestimmungen ist dem Dichter sehr geläufig' ['it is very common for a poet to divide the adjective from the noun by another phrase or qualifying word'] and gave examples from *Elene* (pp. 373-4).

[54] The examples quoted are, in order, *El* 436, *GenA* 2189, *ChristB* 572, *El* 750, *Jul* 166, *And* 2, *Creed* 46, *Vain* 46, *GenB* 322, *Met* 11. 44, *ChristA* 302, *Jul* 36, and *Jul* 10. They occupy the same half-line unless the symbols \| or \|\| appear.

[55] There are no examples yet noted of the combination demonstrative + possessive (pattern (b) in §107), of *monig* in position 4, or of numerals in partitive apposition before the noun.

Conradi (1886) classified his examples according to the separating element, e.g. demonstrative (*Jul* 36), genitive of noun (*Jul* 166), prepositional phrase (*Jul* 97-8), and so on (pp. 21-2), and was followed by others.[56]

§152. It was left to later writers, including Slay and Fakundiny,[57] to deal with the more important question—the effect of separation (and post-position; see §§175-7) on the stressing of position 5 and 6 elements. However, they failed to realize that the earlier writers' interest in what grammatical element(s) did the separation was not completely misplaced. Slay (p. 6) speaks of separation 'by the end of a half-line or by other speech material ("interception")', and Fakundiny (p. 133) of separation 'by the metrical caesura or by speech materials'. But the term 'speech material(s)' is too loose; we need to know whether the intervening material consists only of elements shown in the table or whether it includes other words (such as personal pronouns, verbs, or adverbs other than intensifiers (§178)) and/or phrases, before we can decide whether such intervention alone is decisive. One has only to look at examples 1 and 2, and at *Phoen* 3 *se foldan sceat* and *Phoen* 20 *þæt æþele lond*, to see that Fakundiny's observation (p. 139) that 'when the preceding demonstrative is separated from the noun it is always in the lift in OE. verse' requires qualification; this will be made below.

§153. When an indefinite, a demonstrative, or a possessive, precedes its noun, it can be in any one of the following six situations:

(1) in the same half-line immediately before the noun;

(2) in the same half-line separated by one of the elements shown in the table;

(3) in the same half-line separated by other speech material;

(4) in a different half-line immediately before the noun;

(5) in a different half-line separated by one of the elements shown in the table;

(6) in a different half-line separated by other speech material.

---

[56] They include Ahrens, Dethloff, Fritsche, Höser, Kempf, Lange, Mahn, and Meyer. See also A. Bohlen, *Zusammengehörige Wortgruppen getrennt durch Cäsur oder Versschluss, in der angelsächsischen Epik* (Berlin diss., 1908).

[57] Slay in *TPS* 1952, pp. 1-14, and Fakundiny in *RES* 21 (1970), 129-42 and 257-66. The latter criticizes the former for his 'reliance upon an undefined notion of "normal" usage' or 'practice' (pp. 131-2 and 258). But the norm she supplies—based as it is on the limited corpus of the prose texts in Sweet's *Anglo-Saxon Reader*—is of dubious validity as a *prose* norm and of dubious relevance to *verse*. Indeed, most of her sensitive critical comment about the art of the OE poets was produced without it by comparing the patterns of verse with and without displacement.

Both Slay and Fakundiny fail to distinguish these six possibilities and thus (it seems to me) confuse the issue. Each must be considered in turn.

§154. In situation (1) the three elements under discussion can have varying metrical values.[58] But in situation (2) they will occupy the dip; this is in accordance with the rules of OE versification and is illustrated by examples 1, 2, 7, 9, 10, 12 in my table.[59] The only examples I know of any of these words in situation (3) are *Beo* 929b *Fela ic laþes gebad* and *Wid* 10a *Fela ic monna gefrægn*. In both *fela* is the first word in a 'verse clause' and stands in the dip, and in both the intercepting word is *ic*; cf. *Wulf* 9, discussed in §176. There may be other examples. But these two suggest that even separation by an element other than those shown in the table was by itself insufficient to cause stressing of a separated indefinite or (we might add) of a separated demonstrative or possessive. *Max i* 167 *Swa monige beoþ men ofer eorþan* | is an extended half-line and does not contradict this; for the stressing of *monige* here, cf. *Mald* 188 *þe him mænigne oft* | *mear gesealde*.

§155. We turn now to situations (4), (5), and (6), in all of which the separated element is in a different half-line from its noun. In situation (4) the three elements under discussion carry stress, e.g. *Beo* 627 *þæt heo on ænigne* | *eorl gelyfde*, *GenA* 1219 *se on lichoman* | *lengest þissa* || *worulddreama breac*, and *Beo* 2481 *þeah ðe oðer his* | *ealdre gebohte* (Fakundiny, pp. 134, 139, and 137). The same is true in situation (5), e.g. *Beo* 689 *ond hine ymb monig* || *snellic særinc*, *GenA* 1211 *of þyssum lænan* | *life feran*, and *Jul* 166 *min se swetesta* | *sunnan scima* (Fakundiny, pp. 134-5, 139, and 137). In situation (6) the indefinite is stressed, whether it stands as the first word in its verse-clause or later; the only two exceptions seem to be *Beo* 2814 *ealle wyrd forsweop* || *mine magas* and *ChristA* 39 *Nænig efenlic þam* | . . . || . . . | *wifes gearnung*, where the indefinite is the first word in the clause and occupies the dip (Slay, p. 8, and Fakundiny, pp. 134-5). The demonstrative and the possessive are stressed, e.g. *Beo* 1248 *ge gehwæþer þara* || *efne swylce mæla* and *Beo* 251 *Nu ic eower sceal* || *frumcyn witan* (Fakundiny, pp. 138-9 and pp. 137-8).

---

[58] See Slay, pp. 2-10, *OEG*, §98, and Fakundiny, pp. 132-3; id., pp. 138-9; and id., pp. 136-8.

[59] Fakundiny, p. 138, refers non-committally to *GuthB* 1076b *min þæt leofe bearn* and two similar examples (*GuthB* 1080b and *GuthA* 381b). All belong here.

§156. To summarize. On the evidence so far available, we may say that

(a) the indefinite, the demonstrative, and the possessive, can be stressed when they appear immediately before the noun in the same half-line; this is one particular case of Campbell's 'any rule for sentence stress may be broken owing to special rhetorical emphasis' (*OEG*, §99);

(b) examples seem to fail in which these words are stressed when they appear before and in the same half-line as the noun, but separated from it by any other word—whether that word belongs to one of the classes noted in the tables, or not;

(c) with the exception of *Beo* 2814b and *ChristA* 39a (see above), where the indefinite is unstressed when in first position in its clause, these words seem always to carry stress if separated from the following noun by a caesura, whether or not any speech material intervenes.

§157. It would seem therefore that (with the exception noted in (a) above) separation by a metrical caesura is essential if one of these words is to carry stress when it precedes the noun, though even that does not ensure it in the last two examples cited. The intervention of other speech material is not essential and does not cause stressing unless the metrical caesura also intervenes. Further investigation will be necessary to establish the validity of these observations. But they are in accord with Campbell's formulation: 'Proclitic words receive a full stress if they are removed from their *natural* [my italics] position immediately before the governed word. . . . An intervening line-end is sufficient to cause a proclitic to be stressed, even if it immediately precedes the governed word. . . .'[60] However, at the moment I would be inclined to make the last sentence read 'An indefinite, a demonstrative, or a possessive, which precedes its noun will be stressed only if a (half-)line end intervenes, unless there is special rhetorical emphasis.'

§158. Guest (*TPS* 5 (1851), 97–101) offers the suggestion that in the poetry an adjective sometimes intervenes between two elements of a compound. So he translates *Beo* 1896 *sæ geap naca* as 'the curved sea-boat' and *Dan* 378 *winter biter weder* as 'the bitter winter-weather'. Later editors have seen *sægeap* and *winterbiter* as compounds.

---

[60] *OEG*, §97. We may feel inclined to accept Fakundiny's objection to the word 'proclitics' (p. 131).

c. *The position of the qualifying elements in regard to*
the noun

(1) *with no or one attributive adjective*

§159. So far we have quoted only examples in which all the qualifying elements precede the noun. This, the MnE arrangement, is the commonest pattern in OE prose. But in prose and (more frequently) in poetry, all or some may follow the noun. When all follow, says Carlton, 'position 6 is closest to the noun head-word rather than farthest from it' (*JEGP* 62 (1963), 783). In other words, the elements remain in the same order relative to one another, e.g. *BlHom* 61. 35 *cyle þone grimmestan, Phoen* 613 *hungor se hata,* and *And* 478 *freondscipe... ‖ ... þinne... ‖ godne.*

§160. The attributive adjective in post-position is declined strong or weak as appropriate; for examples see §§126-7.[61] Here it is not always clear whether we have to do with an attributive, predicative, or appositional, use, e.g. *Or* 21. 16 *twegen fætels full ealað oððe wæteres, ChronA* 70. 26 (871) *Sidroc eorl se gioncga, ÆCHom* ii. 516. 2 *Martinus se eadiga* (see Müllner, pp. 38-40), and (an arrangement common in the poetry) *Phoen* 266 *fugel feþrum deal* and *Mald* 107 *earn æses georn.* The same difficulty seems to arise in three of the examples of unusual separation cited by Flamme (p. 89)— *BlHom* 71. 17 *of cilda muþe meolcsucendra, BlHom* 151. 30 *Godes Sunu þæs lyfgendan,* and *BlHom* 181. 15 *þone hlaf . . . berenne.* (This is also true of some of the examples with two preceding attributive adjectives, e.g. *BlHom* 169. 16 *þus healices 7 ðus foremæres ures mundboran.*)

§161. Several writers have commented on the chiastic combinations which occur in the poetry because the poet is free to vary the position of the adjective, e.g. *Ex* 89 *halige seglas,* ‖ *lyftwundor leoht* and *Phoen* 613 *hungor se hata ne se hearda þurst;* see, *inter al.,* Schürmann, p. 373, and Kempf, p. 13.

§162. Most of the other qualifiers shown in the tables can follow their noun, sometimes as the only qualifier, sometimes with another preceding the noun. Examples of indefinites include: *WHom* 20(*EI*). 72 *hlafordswican manege, CP* 29. 17 *to hefegum byrðenum manegum, Beo* 1341 *þegne monegum, Beo* 908 *snotor ceorl monig, ChronA* 78. 17 (885) *þa scipo alle, ChronA* 88. 26 (895) *hira scipu*

---

[61] It is the result of chance that Shannon could write (p. 28) that 'the few instances of descriptive adjectives following the noun are accompanied by demonstratives'.

sumu, and *Mald* 196 *þa geearnunga ealle*. For further examples see Shannon, p. 27.

§163. The demonstrative sometimes follows its noun in the poetry, e.g. *Beo* 2007 *uhthlem þone* and *Mald* 52 *eþel þysne*. So too does the possessive, e.g. *Beo* 2479 *mægwine mine* and *JDay ii* 49 *mid swiðran his*. On the metrical effects of this post-position, see §§175-7. I have found no examples of a demonstrative after its noun in the prose, but the possessive is sometimes so found in the vocative, e.g. *CP* 37. 16 *sunu min*, Latin *fili*, *CP* 273. 8 *sunu min*, Latin *fili mi*, and *ÆCHom* i. 566. 21 *modor min*; see further §1243.

§164. Post-position of the numeral occurs in the poetry, e.g. *El* 868 *þa roda þreo*, *GenA* 1545 *mid his eaforum þrim*, and *GenA* 1477 *ymb wucan þriddan* (but *GenA* 1546 *and heora feower wif*). *ChronA* 66. 31 (855) *Æþelwulfes suna twegen* is quoted as an example by Palm (p. 140)—if I understand him aright—and by Shannon (p. 27). But *twegen* is probably not an adjective here: 'two of Æ.'s sons' is the sense required. Zuck (p. 10) translates *ChronA* 86. 26 (894) *his suna twegen* as 'his two sons'. But do we know how many sons Hæsten had? The two examples with *begen* cited by Shannon (p. 27) are also dubious: in both *ChronA* 68. 25 (867) *7 þa cyningas begen ofslægene* and *ChronA* 70. 27 (871) *7 þa hergas begen gefliemde* the verb *wæron* needs to be supplied somewhere and *begen* may be appositional.

§165. *Oþer* is occasionally found after its noun, e.g. *Bede* 148. 7 *Osfrið his sunu oðer* (but 148. 8 *oðer his sunu ... Eadfrið*—breaking Carlton's 'rules'; so also *Bede* 140. 2) and *Beo* 1353 *ænig man oðer*. Further examples of adjectives in post-position will be found in Carlton 1958, pp. 63-4; Shannon, p. 27; Zuck, pp. 8-10; and (for the poetry) in the references given at §151 fn. On the position of the noun genitive, see §§1304-30.

(2) *with two or more attributive adjectives*

§166. With two adjectives these patterns occur: both may either precede or follow the noun, one may precede and one follow, or the noun may be repeated with the second adjective.[62] Strong or weak forms occur as appropriate and the second adjective may be preceded by a conjunction such as *ond*, *ac*, *ne*, or *oððe*; in such cases a demonstrative, preposition, or adverb, is repeated with the second adjective.

---

[62] See Müllner, p. 42. Flamme, pp. 89-90, gives some good examples. For the poetry see the dissertations of Ahrens, Conradi, Dethloff, Höser, Kempf, Meyer, and Schürmann.

Examples follow. There are, of course, more arrangements possible when there are three attributive adjectives. Some of these are exemplified below.

§167. Both adjectives before the noun. Examples include *Or* 158. 5 *monige scearpe isene næglas*, *ÆCHom* i. 156. 28 *mid godum and mid clænum geðohtum*, and *ÆCHom* ii. 290. 21 *micele and manega fixas*; *BlHom* 129. 12 *of his þæm hean heofonlican setle*, *ÆCHom* i. 252. 34 *se goda Heofonlica Fæder*, and *ÆCHom* ii. 178. 21 *on anum lytlan glæsenan fæte*; *ÆCHom* ii. 126. 4 *se arfæsta and se mildheorta God* and *ÆCHom* ii. 352. 31 *þeos wynsume and ðeos blostmbære stow*. In the poetry we find *Phoen* 652 *swetum* . . . ‖ *ond wynsumum wyrtum*, *Jul* 339 *þa heardestan* ‖ *ond þa wyrrestan witu*, *JDay ii* 199 *betwyx forsworcenum sweartum nihtum*, and *JDay ii* 296 *þurh þa scenan scinendan ricu*.

§168. Both adjectives after the noun. All the examples so far recorded have strong forms of the adjective and may seem predicative to some readers: *ÆCHom* i. 10. 15 *ac hi sindon ealle gastas swiðe strange and mihtige and wlitige*, *ÆCHom* ii. 270. 8 *hit is gesceaft brosniendlic and awendedlic*, *ÆCHom* ii. 432. 25 *Ða genam he ða maðmfatu, gyldene and sylfrene*, and (from the poetry) *Phoen* 153 *haswigfeðra*, ‖ *gomol, gearum frod* and *Jul* 25 *ealdordom* ‖ *micelne ond mærne*. There is an *apo koinou* construction in *El* 798 *sawla nergend*, ‖ *ece ælmihtig, Israhela cining*.

§169. One adjective before, one (or more) after the noun. A second adjective is occasionally found after the noun without a conjunction, e.g. *CP* 83. 23 *of twispunnenum twine linenum*, *Or* 18. 10 *tamra deora unbebohtra syx hund*, *BlHom* 91. 32 *blodig wolcen mycel*, *ÆCHom* i. 106. 24 *niwne steorran beorhtne*, and, with one strong form and one weak, *BlHom* 179. 13 *ungelæredne fiscere þone leasostan*. In the poetry we find *Phoen* 476 *halge lare* ‖ *hate æt heortan* (possibly predicative), *Phoen* 98 *seo deorce niht* ‖ *won gewiteð*, and *Phoen* 528 *þa æpelan* . . . ‖ *wyrta wynsume* (but see §3971).

§170. But the pattern in which the second adjective is preceded by the appropriate conjunction seems to be more common; it is used both when the two adjectives supplement one another and when they exclude one another, e.g. *ÆCHom* i. 482. 12 *liflice onsægednysse and halige and Gode andfenge*, *ÆCHom* i. 64. 8 *swa clæne gold ne swa read*, *ÆCHom* i. 162. 13 *He nolde his heafod befon mid gyldenum cynehelme, ac mid þyrnenum*, and *Or* 18. 21 *berenne kyrtel oððe yterenne*; *Bo* 129. 15 *eall ðios unstille gesceaft 7 þios hwearfiende, Or* 21. 1 *to þæm ærestan dæle 7 to þæm mæstan*, and *ÆCHom* i. 190. 9 *ægðer ge ðære ealdan æ ge ðære niwan*. Here too, we note, the demonstrative and/or the preposition is repeated after the conjunction. Examples from the poetry include *Dan* 519 *ærenum clammum and isernum* and (with two following adjectives joined by *and*) *Dan* 553 *þa halgan word*, ‖ *yrre and egeslicu* and *Pan* 64 *swete stenc*, ‖ *wlitig ond wynsum* (predicative?).

§171. Further on the so-called *Erweiterungsgruppen* or 'split constructions' exemplified above, see §§1464-72; in these, other elements can intervene between the noun and the second adjective, e.g. *BlHom* 117. 8 *þa halwendan men cwædon, and þa geleafsuman, . . . and ÆCHom* ii. 354. 21 *Maran cyle ic geseah, and wyrsan*. According to Sørensen 'it is tempting to assume that the widespread use of the construction adjective + substantive + adjective in OE was supported by, if not a direct outcome of, this general tendency towards looseness in construction' (*EStudies*, 37 (1956), 262-3).

§172. The reasons for post-position are various; they include Latin influence—Carlton compares the common calque *God Ælmihtig* with *Ch(B)* ii. 36. 3 *ðæs ælmaehtigan godes unhlis . . .*[63]—a desire for emphasis, rhythmic and stylistic variation, and in poetry the demands of metre; see §§175-7. But in OE, as in MnE, the order adjective + noun is the norm. On this topic, see further Palm, pp. 1-9; Scheinert in *PBB* 30 (1905), 408-10; Müllner, p. 41; and Franz in *Zeitschrift für französischen und englischen Unterricht*, 20 (1921), 121-2.

§173. There is room for more work on the arrangements when two attributive adjectives qualify the same noun. As far as I have observed, the pattern in which both precede the noun without a linking conjunction, as in MnE 'such pure red gold', is less common in OE than it is now. But, as some of the examples quoted in §167 testify, it does occur—despite Spamer's claim (*Glossa*, 13 (1979), 243) that 'in Old English, the adjectives were non-recursive: each head noun could have at most only one adjective preceding it'.

---

[63] *JEGP* 62 (1963), 782. On the latter construction, see §1312. For various OE renderings of Latin *omnipotens Deus* and *Deus omnipotens* see Mustanoja 'Almighty' in Early English: a Study in Positional Syntax', in *Festschrift Prof. Dr. Herbert Koziol zum siebzigsten Geburtstag* (Wiener Beiträge zur englischen Philologie, 75) (1973), 204-12.

§174. The noun may be repeated with the second of two parallel adjectives; see §95.

d. The effect of post-position in the poetry

§175. Slay (p. 7) and Fakundiny (pp. 135–6) agree that when an indefinite is placed immediately after its noun in the same half-line it occupies a lift or a half-lift. According to the latter (p. 136), it is always in a lift when 'interception either by the caesura or by speech materials' occurs. But all the examples provided again show interception by the caesura; cf. §157. Here too then it seems that a more accurate phrasing would be 'interception by caesura or by caesura and speech materials'.

§176. The situation with the possessive is much the same. Fakundiny (p. 138) notes only three examples in which a directly post-posited possessive does not carry full stress—all *wine min* in *Beo* 457b, 530b, and 1704b. The possessive is also stressed when the metrical caesura intervenes, whether or not other speech materials are present. That interception by speech materials alone is insufficient here too is suggested by the fact that the possessive is unstressed in the only example cited where a caesura does not intervene, but speech materials do. This is *Wulf* 9 *Wulfes ic mines widlastum* | *wenum dogode*; cf. *Beo* 929b and *Wid* 10a, where similar interception by *ic* in the same half-line left pre-posited *fela* unstressed (§154).

§177. As for the demonstrative, Fakundiny (p. 139) notes only examples of direct post-position in the same half-line. Here the demonstrative occupies the second lift.

e. The position of intensifying adverbs in adjective groups

§178. Except in such conversational uses as 'Great goal—very'— a pattern I have not found in Old English—intensifying adverbs precede the adjective they modify. But not all of them always precede the demonstrative. Thus in MnE we have 'almost all the men' (adv. + adj.) and 'almost the greatest men' (adv. + pron. + adj.), but 'the very greatest men' (pron. + adv. + adj.). It is perhaps unnecessary to erect two classes, but we must note the difference in usage between 'ever the pure virgin', where 'ever' modifies the whole phrase, and 'the ever-pure virgin', where it modifies the adjective 'pure'.

§179. The same distinction can be made in OE. Thus we have adverb + adjective in *Or* 19. 5 *swiðe micle meras fersce*, *Or* 36. 9

forneah eall þæt folc, Or 200. 16 *mæst ealle þe þærbinnan wæron,*
Bede 252. 21 *lytestne alle his geferan* (MS *Ca* has *mæst* for *T*'s
lytestne), *ChronA* 100. 12 (919) *mæst ealle þa burgware,*[64] and
BlHom 217. 15 *dagas wel manige*; adverb + pronoun + adjective in
Or 88. 29 *forneah þa mæstan 7 þa pleolecestan* and *Lch* iii. 432. 18
fornean þ ytemeste iglond; and pronoun + adverb + adjective in *CP*
175. 24 *ða suiðe suigean, ÆLS* 32. 1 *sum swyðe gelæred munuc,*
and (with an intensifying use of an adverb of time) *BlHom* 5. 19
þære a clænan fæmnan.

§180. So in both OE and MnE the intensifying adverb usually
immediately precedes the adjective or the adjective group it qualifies;
we find it before a preposition in *Or* 112. 28 *forneah buton ælcon
gewinne.* But there are exceptions in OE, e.g. *Or* 210. 10 *Seo dæd
wearð forneah Romanum to ðæm mæstan hearme, ÆGram* 38. 16
swa swa ealle mæst þissere declinunge, ÆGram 46. 16 *þa oðre synd
ealle mæst mascvlini generis,* and *ÆGram* 215. 10 *ealle mæst ðas
word synd ðære forman geðeodnysse.*

8. COMPARISON

a. Introductory remarks

§181. The comparative adjective ends in *-ra* in the nominative singular masculine and is declined weak. It is used attributively with the
demonstrative, e.g. *CP* 387. 23 *mid ðære lufan ðæs beteran lifes* and
CP 429. 18 *on ðæm anbide ðæs maran wites,* and without it, e.g.
CP 411. 33 *on beteran hade* and *CP* 429. 19 *mare wite.* Whether a
distinction was always intended is hard to say.[65] The superlative,
normally ending in *-ost,* is declined both strong and weak, according
to the rules set out in §102, e.g. *ÆCHom* i. 50. 4 *se . . . wearð
fyrmest on ðrowunge* and *ÆCHom* i. 384. 3 *ðes wyrresta cyning.*
The weak form of the superlative without a demonstrative is common in the poetry, e.g. *Beo* 2182 *ginfæstan gife*; cf. §§114–17. On
examples like *Or* 224. 2 *Romana ieldesta biscep* see §113.[66] Both

---

[64] In *ChronA* 100.7 (918) *þa holdas ealle 7 þa ieldstan men ealle mæste ðe to Bedan
forda hierdon* the form *mæste* suggests that we have an adjective rather than an adverb.

[65] See Closs, pp. 124–8, for examples in *Orosius.* Krohn, p. 32, reports that the form
with the article is less frequent in the 'Alfredian' texts.

[66] On the forms see *OEG,* §§657–60, and F. Seelig in AF 70 (1930). Krohn gives lists of
examples at pp. 19–20, 31–2, 43, 58–9, and 72–3; see also Closs, pp. 128–30. For examples
in *Beowulf* see *PBB* 30 (1905), 405–6 and R. Wagner in *Palaestra,* 91 (1910), *passim.* Bauch
(p. 67) draws our attention to two examples of lack of concord—*swærra . . . rod* in *ChristC*
1489 (he might also have mentioned *þeos heardra* in 1488) and *se selesta* in *Met* 20. 203,
which is scarcely an example, for (as he points out) it takes its gender from the immediately
following gen. pl. *sundorcræfta.*

the comparative and the superlative can be used as nouns; see §135.

b. The comparative

§182. The comparative adjective is used attributively, as in the examples given above, and predicatively, either alone, e.g. *Or* 18. 30 *Eastewerd hit mæg bion syxtig mila brad oþþe hwene bradre; 7 middeweard þritig oððe bradre*, or with a noun, e.g. *Beo* 980 *Ða wæs swigra secg sunu Ecglafes*. It may also be used in conjunction with the dative/instrumental case (§3261) and with conjunctions and prepositions, including *þonne* (§§3205-38), *þon ma (þe)* (§§3243-50), *ac* (§3251), *be* (§3256), *butan* (§3631), and *nefne* (§3650). On the proportional comparative with *swa* and *þy*, see §§3287-9 and 3334-46. A comparative adjective may take a case, e.g. *Brun* 48 . . . *þæt heo beaduweorca beteran wurdun*. See further the General Index.

§183. When a comparative is used without any real comparison being intended, as in Spenser's oft-quoted 'Her looser golden lockes he rudely rent', where 'looser' means something like 'too loose' or 'very loose', we have what is called 'the comparative absolute'. Borst (*AF* 10 (1902), 9) says that this construction is unknown in OE— 'dem Ae eigentlich völlig fremd'. 'This Latinism', says Kellner (p. 160), 'was imitated by Elizabethan writers, but seems to have been a stranger to English both before and after that period.' Editors and critics usually follow Klaeber (*Ang. B.* 17 (1906), 102) in explaining *syllicre* in

Dream 4   þuhte me þæt ic gesawe   syllicre treow
               on lyft lædan,   leohte bewunden,
               beama beorhtost

as an absolute comparative—'the most wonderful, very wonderful'. Some have added *ne* after *ic*; see Swanton's note. But the negative scarcely fits with *beama beorhtost*. So, unless we emend *syllicre* to *syllice*, this does seem an example. Could it be an imitation of a phrase in a Latin hymn now lost? Or are we to link it with

Dream 90   Hwæt, me þa geweorðode   wuldres ealdor
               ofer holmwudu,   heofonrices weard . . .

and to understand it as meaning 'a more wonderful tree [than any other]'?

§184. Scheinert (*PBB* 30 (1905), 406) and Klaeber (3, p. xcii and fn. 3) give different lists of examples from *Beowulf*; the two common to both are

Beo 2651   . . .
        þæt me is micle leofre,   þæt minne lichaman
        mid minne goldgyfan   gled fæðmie

and *Beo* 1702 *þæt ðes eorl wære* || *geboren betera*. Klaeber speaks of these two as contexts 'where, according to our ideas, no real comparison takes place', distinguishing them from examples like *Beo* 980 *Ða wæs swigra secg sunu Ecglafes*, where 'the missing member of the comparison is easily supplied . . . ("more reticent", sc. "than before")'. The distinction seems a fine one; it is not difficult to supply 'than that I should run away' for the first example and 'than anyone else' for the second.

§185. In her thesis (pp. 99–101), Most added more alleged examples from the poetry. In my view, a comparison is either expressly made or clearly implied in all except one, where there is no comparative; see Mitchell 1976a, pp. 27–8. In a subsequent article,[67] she analyses more examples—including those which Klaeber cited in *MP* 3 (1905), 251–2, but omitted from his edition of *Beowulf*—in an attempt 'to establish the existence of the comparative absolute in OE' (p. 177). She herself eliminates many of these because 'it may be that some actual comparison is intended, however remote' (p. 187). This is true of most of these examples, including *Beo* 980 (§184). But in some the comparison is so far from being remote that it is actually explicit, e.g. *CP* 5. 24 *7 woldon ðæt her ðy mara wisdom on londe wære ðy we ma geðeoda cuðon*. Here '[than before]' is also implied.

§186. There remain the thirteen which she describes as 'the more certain occurrences of the comparative absolute' (p. 177). I have discussed *Dream* 4 in §183. In *Beo* 83 *lenge* need not be taken as a comparative; see Klaeber's note. In

Beo 134   Næs hit lengra fyrst,
        ac ymb ane niht   eft gefremede
        morðbeala mare,

the comparison is explicit. The remainder, in my opinion, belong in the same category as *Beo* 980, e.g. *Beo* 450 *no ðu ymb mines ne þearft* || *lices feorme leng sorgian* '. . . no longer [than now]', *Beo*

---

[67] Sheila Most Ingersoll, 'The Comparative Absolute in Old English', *NM* 77 (1976), 177–89. My article and hers were at press together. But see §1146.

2651 (§184), *Beo* 3038 *Ær hi þær gesegan syllicran wiht,* ‖ *wyrm on wonge . . .* 'a more wondrous creature [than Beowulf]' (see Mitchell, at press (b), 22 fn. 11), and *CP* 7. 6, where the implication is that it is better to translate the books which it is most necessary for all men to know than to leave them untranslated as previous generations had done. So at the moment I am reluctant to accept her claim (p. 189) that 'it now seems quite clear that the comparative absolute did exist in Old English, that it was not a rare occurrence, and that it functioned as a means of intensification'. In my opinion, *Dream* 4 remains the most likely example. But even it is not certain; see §183. *ÆCHom* i. 50. 2 *Witodlice Stephanus wæs to diacone gehadod æt ðæra apostola handum; ac he hi forestop on heofenan rice mid sigefæstum deaðe; and swa se ðe wæs neoðor on endebyrdnysse, wearð fyrmest on ðrowunge* is a salutary warning against over-zealousness in detecting comparative absolutes in OE.

c. The superlative

§187. The superlative may agree with its noun in case, e.g. *ÆCHom* i. 50. 23 *his leofostan frynd,* or be followed by a partitive genitive, especially when used predicatively, e.g. *ÆCHom* i. 34. 11 *ne eart ðu wacost burga, ÆCHom* i. 134. 1 *Geleafa is ealra mægena fyrmest,* and *ÆCHom* ii. 542. 28 *seo bið ealra biterost.* But other qualifications are possible—a noun in the appropriate case (§192), e.g. *ÆCHom* ii. 462. 33 *Gode leofost,* or a prepositional phrase, e.g. *ÆCHom* i. 50. 5 *fyrmest on ðrowunge.* A partitive genitive and a prepositional phrase are found together, e.g. *Or* 66. 32 *ðeh þe hie Romana bremuste wæron to ðæm cyninge* and *ÆLS* 6. 51 *he wæs fyrmest muneca to ðam mæran benedicte.* On this use of *to,* see §1214; on the superlative with an adjective clause, §2403. The idea of the superlative may be expressed in other ways, e.g. *ÆCHom* i. 84. 13 *martyra blostman, ÆCHom* ii. 14. 28 *Crist is soðlice ealra biscopa Biscop and ealra cyninga Cyning,* and *Met* 24. 19 *æt ðæm ælcealdan anum steorran.*

§188. In *Exod* 32. 21, the Laud MS reads *Hit hæfð geworht ane þa mæstan synne ⁊ Gode þa laþustan.* Other manuscripts lack *ane.* The Laud reading is cited by Rissanen (1967, p. 191) as the one recorded example in OE of the type 'one the best man'.[68] *ÆCHom*

---

[68] There are various theories on the origin of the construction. Stoffel (*EStudien,* 27 (1900), 256) felt 'little hesitation' in regarding it as a Latinism; Visser (i. 225-6) offers some comments on this. Holthausen (*EStudien,* 35 (1905), 186-7) argued that, since it was a Common Gmc. construction as well as Latin, it was also IE. Mustanoja (pp. 298-9) glances

ii. 438. 29 *Swa hwæt swa ge doð on minum naman anum ðam læstum, þæt ge doð me sylfum* comes close to being another. But Thorpe's translation 'Whatsoever ye do in my name for one of the least . . .' is true to the Gospel passage Ælfric probably had in mind —*Matt(WSCp)* 25. 40 *swa lange swa ge dydon anum of ðysum minum læstum gebroðorum* . . . , Latin *uni ex his fratribus meis minimis*. Similar examples with the plural have been cited by Kellner (p. 110) and Mustanoja (p. 299), e.g. *BlHom* 73. 21 *þær wæron þreo þa betstan ele, ApT* 8. 21 *mid feawum þam getrywestum mannum*, and (with possessive as well as demonstrative) *Alex* 45. 3 *mine þrie ða getreowestan frynd*. There is also *Gen* 27. 9 *twa ða betstan ticcenu*, Latin *duos haedos optimos* and (without a noun) *ChronE* 226. 17 (1091) *Ðas forewarde gesworan xii þa betste of þes cynges healfe*. In both the singular and plural examples we are clearly dealing with some sort of apposition. Whether it is partitive or not (§409) cannot be determined. Here I differ slightly in emphasis from Mustanoja (p. 300): 'Most of the instances—perhaps all—can be explained without presuming an implication of partitivity.' Kellner's versions of *BlHom* 73. 21 above illustrate the point: 'there were three of the best ointments, or rather, the very best of all'.

d. Other means of comparison

§189. The beginnings of periphrastic comparison are probably to be seen in OE examples like *GD* 111. 1 *bet . . . gelærede, Bede* 260. 17 *ma . . . gelæred*, and *Bede* 2. 17 *betst gelæred*; cf. *Bede* 142. 16 *se gelæredesta*.[69] Knüpfer gives a list of similar constructions (with Latin equivalents where possible) from *Or, CP, Bede, GD, Chron, BlHom*, Ælfric, and other texts—they include both present and second participles, with the modifiers *swiþor, swiþost, bet, betst, ma*, but not *mæst*. There are occasional examples with adjectives; they include *CP* 33. 17 *bet wyrðe* and *GD(C)* 151. 27 *ma gode* where MS *H* has *beteran*. The variation between the comparative adjective and *suiður* + the positive form of the participle in *CP* 305. 8 . . . *he sceolde bion him micle ðy eaðmodra 7 his larum ðe suiður under- ðied* is instructive. Ælfric prefers the modifiers *swiþor* and *swiþost*,

---

at the possibility of borrowing from one Gmc. language to another, but concludes that the construction is a native one. On his comparison with the type *min se leofesta freond*, see Samuels, *MÆ* 29 (1960), 147. The scarcity of OE instances needs to be borne in mind in such discussions. Rissanen (1967a, p. 192) records one example each from OE of two other combinations of *an* with a superlative, viz. *GD* 277. 18 *seo an hefigeste mettrumnes* and *Mark(WSCp)* 12. 6 *ænne leofostne sunu*.

[69] Mustanoja, pp. 278-80, discusses the possible influence of Latin and French on the development of this construction. See also F. Seelig, *AF* 70 (1930), 78-9.

e.g. *ÆCHom* i. 484. 21 *swyðor gehalgod* and 558. 24 *swiðost gelufod*; this perhaps lends point to E. Borst's remark that in the OE ['ae.'] period, *swithe* (adv. OE ['ae.'] *swiðe*, more rarely *swiðlice*) was the intensifying word *par excellence* (AF 10 (1902), 116).

§190. Inferiority is spasmodically expressed by means of the formula 'less' + adjective, e.g. *GD* 209. 27 *myccle læs gehyred* and *Bede* 424. 25 *nohte þon læs unaarefndlice*, Latin *non minus intolerabile*. The possibility exists that this is due to Latin influence.[70]

e. Multiple comparison

§191. According to Mustanoja (p. 281), multiple comparison 'occurs sporadically in OE (*ma wyrse*)'. This example is presumably that cited by Knüpfer (p. 335) from *LibSc* 109. 7 *micele ma wyrse*, in direct imitation of Latin *quanto magis peius*. The only other known to me is *ÆCHom* i. 514. 1 *he bið swa micele wlitegra ætforan Godes gesihðe, swa he swiðor ætforan him sylfum eadmodra bið*.[71]

9. ADJECTIVAL RECTION

a. Introductory remarks

§192. An alphabetical list of adjectives which take a case is given in §219. Details of its arrangement and of other lists given below are discussed in the sections which follow. Useful collections of examples will be found in Wülfing, i, with an Index at pp. 471-2, and Shipley, pp. 69-85. Hofer gives the adjectives which take the dative and instrumental in *Ang.* 7 (1884), 374-8 and 402-4. Some of the theses give lists of examples in individual texts, e.g. Tilley, pp. 10-20; Brown 1963, pp. 95-100 (though on p. 98 he wrongly construes *CP* 431. 31, where the EETS edition had it right); and Closs, pp. 120-3.

§193. The lists given below were in manuscript before 1963, when those in Visser, i. 327-40, became available. Inevitably our collections supplement one another here and there, and I have silently added a few adjectives from his collection. As will become clear, our classifications differ somewhat. But I acknowledge my debt gratefully.

---

[70] Cf. the comparative adverb in *PPs* 118. 87 *lytle læs laþe*, Latin *paulo minus*, with a different construction following.

[71] In *Jul* 413 we find *ma* ‖ *geornor*, where the two adverbs are taken by Knüpfer (p. 335) and by Gehse, p. 37, as forming a double comparative. They may be parallel.

§194. Many OE adjectives can be limited in some way or another by the genitive or dative of a noun or pronoun, e.g. *Or* 122. 21 *þæs gefeohtes georn, ÆCHom* ii. 78. 23 *beo min gemyndig*, and *BlHom* 69. 33 *neh Oliuetes dune*; by a prepositional phrase, e.g. *Or* 18. 8 *swyðe spedig man on þæm æhtum . . .* ; or by an infinitive (see §§928-31). The same adjective may take more than one of these constructions, e.g. *Beo* 579 *siþes werig, Beo* 2937 *wundum werge, And* 593 *werige æfter waðe*, and *Beo* 1603 *modes seoce, Beo* 2740 *feorhbennum seoc, GuthB* 1077 *on sefan to seoc*.

§195. The various types of genitive and dative which occur with nouns are distinguished in §§197-217. Most of them can be recognized here. But, as is shown in §196, they merge into one another; thus *Or* 21. 16 *twegen fætels full ealað oððe wæteres* could exemplify the descriptive or the instrumental genitive and *Beo* 579 *siþes werig* the subjective or the objective genitive—'weary of the journey' or 'wearied by the journey'. To classify adjectives by such criteria would be repetitive and futile. It will perhaps be more serviceable to divide them according to meaning into those which prefer the genitive and those which prefer the dative, and to note exceptions where appropriate. An alphabetical list of adjectives which take a case is given in §219.

§196. But rigid divisions according to case cannot always be made and are liable to produce artificial results. The most obvious difference between the two cases is seen when the genitive shows the thing and the dative the person involved, e.g. *Sea* 40 *his gifena þæs god* but *PPs* 118. 103 *Me is on gomum god*. But this does not always work, e.g. *Max i* 83 *geofum god* and *Jud* 231 *ecgum gecoste*, where we find the dative for the thing, not the person. We may perhaps be able to detect a difference between *Beo* 1475 *siðes fus, Beo* 3119 *fæðergearwum fus*, and *Beo* 3025 *fus ofer fægum*. But how real is it? Shipley (pp. 69 and 74), following Wülfing (i, §6), distinguishes *fremde* 'strange, foreign, to someone or something' (with dative) from *fremde* 'devoid of someone, something' (with genitive). But this probably rests on the MnE preps. 'to' and 'of' rather than on any real semantic difference; BTS (s.v. *fremede* 6) glosses *fremede* in one sense as 'free from, not participating in, deprived of', with either a case or the prep. *fram*. In the lists below (which do not contain all the words given in the *List of adjectival rections*), adjectives like *fus* and *fremde* are placed in the most appropriate group, but are marked with a following asterisk to denote that they are found with at least two of the genitive, the dative, and a preposition, in more or less parallel constructions. On the gradual triumph of the preposition, see Visser, i. 327-8, and my §§1220-8.

b. The genitive with adjectives

§197. Adjectives with the meanings given below generally seem to prefer the genitive. Those followed by an asterisk (*) are sometimes found with the dative and/or a preposition in more or less parallel constructions, e.g. *seoc* and *werig* (examples in §194) and *ungeleafful*, e.g. *ÆCHom* i. 234. 20 *he ungeleafful wæs Cristes æristes*, but *ÆCHom* i. 202. 5 *ungeleafful þæs engles bodungum*. BTS errs in citing *LS* 23. 16 as an example of *ungeleafful* + preposition; *be þam þingum* depends on *writende*.

§198. Many adjectives may also take a dative of the indirect object or of the person interested, e.g. *HomS* 40. 259. 1 *þu man, to hwan eart þu me swa ungeþancfull minra gifena?* and (with an apparent instrumental) *BlHom* 169. 15 *ac wesað þancfulle þon Hælende eoweres andleofan*. These adjectives have not been distinguished in the lists which follow; it is after all largely a matter of chance whether a particular adjective happens to have been so used in the surviving literature.

§199. Shipley (p. 69) rightly tells us that 'compared with the prose . . . Anglo-Saxon poetry is rich in the genitive with adjectives'. However, he goes on: 'This is to be expected by reason of the greater flexibility of the poetical language, as well as on account of its highly imaginative character.' I do not immediately see why this construction is more imaginative than the alternatives and, while agreeing that poets are more free in their handling of syntax, I would argue that the demands of metre give them less rather than more flexibility in comparison with prose writers. This last fact, allied with the natural conservatism of poetry, might explain why the genitive construction is more common than that with prepositions.

§200. Adjectives of happiness and despair and of gratitude and ingratitude which take the genitive include: *bliþe**, *eadig**, *(ge)fægen**, *geomor**, *glæd**, *hremig**, *ormod*, *gesund*, *ortriewe**, *(un)(ge)þancfull**, *unþancol*, *orwena*, and *unwene*. See Visser, i, §334, for more adjectives with these meanings used with the dative of the person interested.

§201. Adjectives meaning 'generous' or 'mean' take the genitive of the thing and (where appropriate) the dative of the person, e.g. *este,*

gneað, fæsthafol, gehealdsum*, hnah, (un)hneaw*, liðe, and *rummod.*
See again Visser, i, §334.

§202. Adjectives denoting guilt or unworthiness and their opposites
take the genitive, e.g. *(un)scyldig*, untæle,* and *(un)weorþ** (see the
List of adjectival rections).

§203. Adjectives denoting agreement and admission which take the
genitive include: *geandwyrde, gecnæwe, oncyðig, geþafa*, geþæf,*
and *gewyrde.*

§204. Adjectives denoting remembering and forgetting which take
the genitive include: *giemeleas, unforgitende, ofergitol, gemun, (un)-
gemyndig*,*[72] and *geþancol*.* See also §§209 and 214.

§205. Adjectives denoting fullness, such as the following, take the
genitive: *oferdruncen, este, full*, genyhtsum*, sæd, æhtspedig, tiða,*
and *trum*.* I have found the simplex *spedig* with dative and preposition *on,* but not with the genitive.

§206. Adjectives denoting emptiness, lack, or want, take the genitive of the thing lacked and (where appropriate) the dative of the
person interested. They include: *æmtig*, clæne, earm, fealog,
feasceaft, fremde*, freo*, geasne*, hal*, orhlytte, idel*, leas, dælleas,
beliden*, ormod, nacod, sceard, orsorg, orsorglic, untilod, tom,
þearfa, þurstig, ofþyrsted, wædla, wan, wana,* and *weste. Orfeorme*
takes the dative.

§207. Adjectives meaning 'bold', 'brave', 'distinguished', 'useful',
etc., are found with the genitive, e.g. *cene, deormod, dyrstig, eacen*,
frec, from*, god*, heard, anhydig, (un)nytt*, anræd, rof*, strang*,
trum*, þriste*,* and *wlanc*. Geþungen* has the dative or a preposition.
Visser (i, §341) gives more adjectives which express necessity, usefulness, and uselessness, used with the dative of the person interested.

§208. Adjectives of measure or extent like *brad, deop, eald, heah,
lang, þicce,* and *wid,* take the genitive. On this see §1331.

§209. Adjectives of knowledge and ignorance and of (un)belief with
the genitive include: *cræftig*, searucræftig, uncyðig, giffæst, frod*,*

---

[72] This word is found with the dative; see, e.g., *ÆCHom* i. 312. 34. It is tempting to see
hryre in *Wan* 7 as an example of *gemyndig* + dative. But the genitives which precede it seem
to rule this out. See further §65, but consider the possible relevance of the variations of
case after *þurh* (§1207) and *ymb(e)* (§1218).

gleaw*, (un)geleafful*, ungeleaffullic 'unbelieving' (for the sense 'un-believable', see §214), gerad, snottor*, gearosnottor, getæl (gen. or dat.?), gewær, (ge)wis*, andwis, and unwis. In *Beo* 626 wisfæst has dative. See also §§204 and 214.

§210. Adjectives meaning 'desirous' and 'ready', and their opposites, take the genitive, e.g. *frec, frimdig, fus*, gearu*, georn*, geornfull, gifre, grædig, ofergrædig, hræd*, anhydig, lata, (un)læt, oflyst(ed), recen, sæne, seoc*, þurstig, ofþyrsted, wær*,* and *werig*.*

c. The dative with adjectives

§211. Adjectives with the meanings given below generally prefer the dative. Those which I have noted with a preposition or prepositions are asterisked. But I am conscious of the possibility of omissions here. Some of those found only with the dative of the person affected have not been recorded; see §§196 and 198. Visser (i. 327–40) gives a useful collection of examples of this sort.

§212. Adjectives meaning 'fit', 'proper', 'natural', and the opposite, have the dative, e.g. *agen, (un)gebyrde, gecope, (un)gecynde(lic), gedefe, geheme* (see BTS, s.v. *gehæme*), *gemæne, gemæte, gemet, (un)gerisene, (un)gerisenlic, swice, (un)geþeawe, geþywe, (un)weorþ** (see the *List of adjectival rections*), and *(un)gewunelic.*

§213. Adjectives denoting (in)equality, (dis)similarity, or compari-son, with the dative include: *efeneald, efenece, emngod, emleof, anlic, edwistlic, efenlic, gelic, ungelic, onlic, wiþmeten, unwiþmeten-lic, efenmicel, efenmihtig, emnneah, efensarig, efenswiþ, efenweorþ,* and *efenwierþe.* There are, of course, numerous spelling variants, e.g. *efensarig, emnsarig,* and *emsarig.*

§214. Adjectives denoting (un)familiarity and the like which take the dative include: *cuþ, hiwcuþ, namcuþ, uncuþ, deagol, (un)dyrne, gefræge, ungeleaffulic* 'unbelievable' (for the sense 'unbelieving', see §209), *gelenge, mære, ingemynde, gemyndelic, open, ungesewenlic, gesiene, seldsiene, sweotol,* and *(un)gewuna.* See also §§204 and 209.

§215. Adjectives meaning 'easy' or 'difficult' take the dative, e.g. *earfoþe, earfoþlic, earfoþrime, (un)eaþe(lic),* and *yþdæde.*

§216. Adjectives denoting nearness and distance, e.g. *(un)feor**, *neahgangol, an-/onhende, gehende, ofhende, neah*, getenge, and-weard, fromweard*, and *toweard*, are found with the dative. *(Un)-feor* and *neah* are sometimes glossed as adverbs and prepositions rather than adjectives in the constructions referred to in the alphabetical list below; see BT(S), s.vv. and Wülfing, ii. 674-5.

§217. Adjectives meaning 'pleasing', 'friendly', 'obedient', 'loyal', to someone (thing), or the opposite, take the dative. They include: *(un-)bliþe*, (un)gecweme, deore, deriendlic, underigende, an-/ondrysne, andfenge, arfæst, egefull, (un)(ge)hiersum, oferhire, (un)hold, laþ, (un)leof, gemede, eaþmod, ungesibb, swice, swicol, (un)(ge)treowe, (un)(ge)triewe, undergeþeoded, (un)geþwære*, weorþ*, unþanc-weorþ, wiþerræde, wiþerweard*, wraþ, (un)gewylde*, and *yrre**. Visser (i, §§334-5 and 337-8) includes many more adjectives with one of these meanings used with the dative of the person interested.

d. List of adjectival rections

(1) *Notes*

§218. Compound adjectives are grouped together in the alphabetical position of the second element; thus *cuþ, hiw-cuþ*, and *un-cuþ*, will be found together under *c*. The list does not include all compounds of adjectives such as *fæst, grædig, scyldig*, and *spedig*.

All the adjectives in the lists in §§197-217 appear here, except those with the genitive of measure or extent given in §208.

Adjectives which are followed only by prepositions are not given. For combinations of adjective + preposition, see Wülfing, ii, §§607a-1106, *passim*, and the references given in my §§192-3.

Not all adjectives which take only a dative of personal interest (or dative of advantage or disadvantage; see §1355) are included. In this respect, the lists given by Visser (i, §§334-5, 337-8, and 341) supplement mine; see §193 above.

Apart from these exceptions, the lists aim at completeness. But there are (I fear) bound to be omissions, especially of adjectives which occur only with the descriptive or defining genitive or dative; see §§195 and 1331.

So far, time has not permitted a study of the comparative frequency of the various constructions or of such questions as whether one particular usage occurs in prose, poetry, and glosses, or is limited to one or two of these. This can, I suppose, be said to be the job of the lexicographer.

(2) *Alphabetical list*

§219. Here s.o. = 'someone', s.t. = 'something'.

æmanne, see Wülfing, i. 3

æmtig empty of, free from, s.t. (gen., prep. *fram*)

agen peculiar to s.o. (dat.)

ge-anwyrde confessed of s.t. (gen.)

beliden p.p., deprived of s.t. (gen., dat.)

bliþe glad at, with, s.t. (gen., dat., prep, for, wiþ); graceful, mild, to s.o. (dat., prep. *to*)

un-bliþe unkind to s.o. (dat.)

un-bleo, see Wülfing, i. 71

ge-byrde inborn, natural, to s.o. (dat.)

un-ge-byrde not natural to s.o. (dat.)

cene bold in s.t. (gen.)

clæne clean from, free from, s.t. (gen.)

ge-cnæwe acknowledging, confessing, being conscious of, s.t. (gen.)

ge-cope fit, proper, for s.o. (dat.)

ge-cost tried, proved, in s.t. (dat.)

cræftig skilled in, with, s.t. (gen., dat.)

searu-cræftig skilled in, cunning in, s.t. (gen.)

cuþ known to s.o. (dat.)

hiw-cuþ well known to s.o. (dat.)

nam-cuþ well known to s.o. (dat.)

un-cuþ unknown, uncertain, to s.o. (dat.)

ge-cweme pleasing, acceptable, to s.o. (dat.), fit for the use of s.o. (dat.)

un-ge-cweme unpleasing to s.o. (dat.)

ge-cwemedlic pleasing, agreeable, to s.o. (dat.)

ge-cwemlic pleasing, agreeable, to s.o. (dat.)

cystig liberal, generous, to s.o., in s.t. (dat.)

ge-cynde natural to s.o. (dat.)

ge-cyndelic natural to s.o. (dat.)

un-ge-cyndelic unnatural to s.o. (dat.)

on-cyþig revealing s.t. (gen.); see P. O. E. Gradon, *Cynewulf's Elene*, line 724 n.

un-cyþig ignorant of, devoid of, s.t. (gen.)

yþ-dæde easy for s.o. (dat.) to do

deagol, *digol* secret from, hidden from, unknown to, s.o. (dat.)

ge-defe fitting, seemly, to s.o. (dat.)

deore dear to s.o. (dat.)

deriendlic injurious to s.o. (dat.)

un-derigende harmless, innocent, in respect of s.t. (dat.)

ofer-druncen intoxicated with s.t. (gen.)

on-, *an-drysne* terrifying to s.o. (dat.)

dyrne hidden, secret, from s.t. (dat.)

un-dyrne revealed to s.o. (dat.)

dyrstig daring, bold, in s.t. (gen.)

eacen powerful, excellent, in s.t. (gen., dat.)

eadig happy, rich, in s.t. (gen., prep. *on*)

efen-eald of equal age with s.o. (dat.)

earfeþe, *earfoþe* difficult, troublesome, for s.o. (dat.)

earfoþlic difficult, troublesome, for s.o. (dat.)

earfoþ-rime difficult for s.o. (dat.) to count

earm poor in s.t. (gen.)

eaþe(lic) easy for s.o. (dat.)

un-eaþe(lic) difficult for s.o. (dat.)

efen-ece co-eternal with s.o. (dat.)

este gracious, bountiful, in s.t. (gen.)

fægen, *ge-fægen* rejoicing in, glad at, s.t. (gen., dat., prep. *in*, *on*)

ar-fæst gracious to s.o. (dat.)

gif-fæst gifted in, capable of, s.t. (gen.)

wis-fæst wise, discreet, in s.t. (dat.)

and-fenge acceptable to s.o. (dat.)

feor far from s.t. (dat., prep. *fram*, *of*)

un-feor near to s.t. (dat., prep. *fram*)

or-feorme destitute of s.t. (dat.)

ge-fræge renowned to s.o. (dat.)

frec desirous of, bold in, s.t. (gen.)

fremde strange to, devoid of, s.o. or s.t. (gen., dat., prep. *fram*)

freo free from s.t. (gen., prep. *fram*)

frimdig asking for, desirous of, s.t. (gen.)

frod advanced in years (dat.); wise, experienced, in s.t. (gen., dat., prep. *on*)

from bold, strenuous, abundant, in s.t. (gen., dat., prep. *in*, *on*, *to*)

full full of s.t. (gen., dat., prep. *mid*)

ege-full terrifying to s.o. (dat.)

fus eager, ready, for s.t. (gen., dat., prep. *on*)

gearu ready, equipped, with s.t. (dat); ready for s.t. (gen., dat., prep. *in, on, to, wið*)

neah-gangol in attendance on s.o. (dat.)

gæsne, geasne deprived of, void of, s.t. (gen., prep. *on*)

geomor sad in, for, s.t. (gen., dat.)

georn eager for s.t. (gen., dat.)

geornfull eager for s.t. (gen.)

gifeþe given, granted, to s.o. (dat.)

gifre greedy for, desirous of, s.t. (gen.)

un-for-gitende forgetful of s.t. (gen.)

ofer-gitol forgetful of s.o. or s.t. (gen.)

glæd glad in, well-disposed to, s.t. (gen., dat., prep. *fore, in, mid, on, wið*)

gleaw clever, skilled, in s.t. (gen., dat., prep. *in, on, to*)

gneaþ mean, frugal, in s.t. (gen.)

god good in or for s.t. (gen., dat., prep. *on, to*); beneficial to s.o. (dat.)

emn-god equally good as s.o. (dat.)

grædig greedy for s.t. (gen.)

ofer-grædig over-greedy for s.t. (gen.)

fæst-hafol mean about s.t. (gen.)

hal cured of, safe from, s.t. (gen., dat., prep. *from, of*)

ge-healdsum protective of, sparing, s.o. or s.t. (gen., prep. *on*)

heard severe to s.o. (dat.); bold in s.t. (gen.)

ge-heme, see BTS, s.v. *gehæme*

an-, on-hende on hand to, demanding attention from, s.o. (dat.)

ge-hende near to s.o. or s.t. (dat.)

of-hende taken away, lost to s.o. (dat.)

(ge-)hiersum obedient to s.o. or s.t. (dat.)

un-ge-hiersum inattentive, disobedient, to s.o. or s.t. (dat.)

ofer-hire disobedient to s.o. (dat.)

or-hlyt(t)e free from s.t. (gen.)

hnah mean in s.t. (gen.)

hneaw niggard in s.t. (gen.)

un-hneaw liberal, bounteous, in s.t. (gen., dat.)

hold gracious, loyal, to s.o. (dat.)

un-hold unfriendly, hostile, to s.o. (dat.)

hræd prompt in s.t. (gen., prep. *mid, on, to*)

hremig exulting in, boasting of, s.t. (gen., dat.)

an-hydig resolute in s.t. (gen.)

idel devoid, destitute, of s.t. (gen., dat.)

læt, lata sluggish in s.t. (gen.)

un-læt not sluggish in s.t. (gen.)

ge-lang dependent on s.o. or s.t. (prep. *æt, on*) for s.t. (gen.); ready for s.o. (dat.)

ge-lastfull helpful to s.o. (dat.)

laþ hateful to s.o. (dat.)

ge-leafful believing s.t. (dat.)

un-ge-leafful unbelieving of s.t. (gen., dat., prep. *be*)

un-ge-leaffullic, un-ge-leaflic unbelievable to s.o. (dat.); unbelieving of s.t. (dat.)

leas free from, lacking in, s.t. (gen.)

dæl-leas destitute of s.t. (gen.)

gewit-leas, Rössger (*Ang.* 8 (1885), 368) is wrong: *þæs* is part of conj. *þæs . . . þæt* in *ChristC* 1472

gieme-leas careless of s.t. (gen.)

ge-lenge belonging to, related to, s.o. (dat.)

leof dear to s.o. (dat.)

em-leof equally pleasing to s.o. (dat.)

un-leof hateful to s.o. (dat.)

an-, on-lic like, similar to, s.o. or s.t. (dat.)

edwist-lic co-substantial with s.o. (dat.)

efen-lic equal to s.o. or s.t. (dat.)

ge-lic like, equal, to, s.o. or s.t. (dat.); see Wülfing, i. 10–11

un-ge-lic dissimilar to s.o. or s.t. (dat.)

liþe gracious in s.t. (gen.). Despite Thorpe, *heortan* in *ÆCHom* ii. 470. 25 is an example

fea-log destitute of s.t. (gen.)

of-lyst, -lysted very desirous of s.t. (gen.)

ge-mæne common to, mutual to, shared with or between, s.o. (dat.)

mære famous, widely known, to s.o. (dat.)

ge-mæte meet, suitable, fit, for s.o. or s.t. (dat.)

ge-mede agreeable, pleasing, to s.o. (dat.)

ge-met fit, meet, proper, to s.o. (dat.) (but see BTS)

wiþ-meten compared, comparable, to s.t. (dat.)

un-wiþ-meten-lic incomparable, not to be compared, with s.o. (dat.)

efen-micel equally great with s.o. (dat.)

efen-mihtig equally mighty with s.o. (dat.)

deor-mod bold in s.t. (gen.)

eaþ-mod humble, obedient, to s.o. (dat.)

or-mod hopeless, despairing of s.t. (gen.)

rum-mod liberal to s.o. (dat.) with s.t. (gen.)

ge-mun mindful of s.t. (gen.)

in-ge-mynde present to the mind of s.o. (dat.)

ge-myndelic memorable to s.o. (dat.)

ge-myndig mindful of s.o. or s.t. (gen., dat., prep. *ymb*)

un-ge-myndig unmindful of s.o. or s.t. (gen.)

nacod naked, destitute of s.t. (gen.)

neah near to s.o. or s.t. (dat., prep. *to*)

emn-neah equally near to s.o. or s.t. (dat.)

ge-nyhtsum abounding in s.t. (gen., prep. *on*); satisfied with s.t. (gen.)

nytt useful, profitable, to s.o. (dat., prep. *æt*) in s.t. (gen., prep. *on, to*)

un-nytt useless to s.o. (dat.) in s.t. (gen.)

nyt-weorþ useful, advantageous, profitable, to s.o. (dat.)

open open, revealed, to s.o. (dat.)

an-ræd resolute in s.t. (gen.)

wiþer-ræde hostile, rebellious, offensive, disadvantageous, of contrary nature, to s.o. or s.t. (dat., prep. *wiþ*)

ge-rad expert, skilful, in s.t. (gen.)

recen ready, prompt, in s.t. (gen.)

ge-risene fit, convenient, proper, to s.o. (dat., ? prep. *to* in *Bede* 296.29)

un-ge-risene unsuitable, unseemly, to s.o. (dat.)

ge-risenlic convenient, suitable, befitting, to s.o. (dat.)

un-ge-risenlic unseemly, dishonourable, to s.o. (dat.)

rof strong, valiant, in s.t. (gen., dat.)

sæd sated with, having had one's fill of, s.t. (gen.)

sæne slow, sluggish, in s.t. (gen.)

efen-sarig, em-sarig equally sorry for or in s.t. (dat.); equally sorry with s.o. (dat.)

efen-scearp equally sharp to s.t. (dat.)

fea-sceaft destitute of s.t. (gen.)

sceard deprived of s.t. (gen.)

scyldig guilty of s.t. (gen., dat.) against s.o. (prep. *wiþ*); responsible for, liable for, s.t. (gen., dat.); liable to forfeit s.t. (gen., dat.); liable to punishment (gen., dat., prep. *to*)

un-scyldig innocent of, not responsible for, s.t. (gen., prep. *æt, wiþ*)

seoc sick of s.t. (gen., dat., prep. *on*)

un-ge-sewen(lic) invisible to s.o. (dat.)

un-ge-sibb not related to, not at peace with, s.o. (dat.)

ge-siene visible in or on s.o. or s.t. (dat.); apparent to s.o. (dat.)

seld-siene unfamiliar to s.o. (dat.)

snottor wise in s.t. (gen., dat., prep. *on*)

gearo-snottor very wise in s.t. (gen.)

or-sorg secure from s.t. (gen.)

or-sorg-lic secure from s.t. (gen.)

spedig rich, powerful, in s.t. (dat., prep. *on*)

æht-spedig rich in s.t. (gen.)

strang strong in s.t. (gen., dat., prep. *on*)

ge-sund safe in s.t. (gen.)

sweotol clear to s.o. (dat.)

swice false to the expectation of s.o. (dat.). See BT s.v. *swice* II

swicol false to s.o. (dat.)

efen-swiþ equally strong to s.o. (dat.)

ge-tæl competent in, eager for, s.t. (gen. or dat.: *PPs* 56. 5)

un-tæle blameless about s.t. (gen.)

ge-tenge near to, pressing upon, s.o. or s.t. (dat.)

un-tilod unprovided for (refl. gen.)

tiþa possessing s.t. (gen.); with *beon, weorþan* to obtain one's request (gen.)

tom empty of s.t. (gen.)

ge-treow(e) true, faithful, to s.o. (dat.)

un-treow(e), un-ge-treow(e) untrue, unfaithful, to s.o. (dat.)

ge-triewe true, faithful, to s.o. (dat.)

or-triewe despairing, hopeless, about s.t. (gen., prep. *be*); faithless to s.o. (dat.)

un-triewe, un-ge-triewe untrue, unfaithful, to s.o. (dat.)

trum strong in s.t. (gen., dat., prep. *in, on*); strong against s.t. (dat., prep. *wiþ*)

ge-þæf agreeing, consenting, to s.t. (gen.)

ge-þafa agreeing, consenting, to s.t. (gen., dat.)

þanc-full thankful to s.o. (dat., prep. *to*) for s.t. (gen.); contented with s.t. (dat.)

un-þanc-full, un-ge-þanc-full unthankful, ungrateful to s.o. (dat.) for s.t. (gen.)

ge-þancol mindful of s.t. (gen.); thoughtful in s.t. (dat.)

un-þancol ungrateful to s.o. (dat.) for s.t. (gen.)

un-þanc-weorþ not agreeable, unacceptable, to s.o. (dat.)

þearfa destitute of, needing, s.t. (gen.)

ge-þeawe customary, usual, to s.o. (dat.)

un-ge-þeawe not customary to s.o. or s.t. (dat.)

under-(ge-)þeod(ed) subject to s.o. (dat.)

þriste bold in s.t. (gen., dat., prep. *on*)

ge-þungen perfect, excellent, in or for s.t. (dat., prep. *on, to*)

þurstig thirsty for s.t. (gen.)

ge-þwære agreeing, concordant, to s.t. (dat.); agreeable to s.o. (dat.); in agreement with s.o. (dat.)

un-ge-þwære discordant among themselves (prep. *betwux*); discordant to s.o. (dat.)

of-þyrsted thirsting for s.t. (gen.)

ge-þywe customary, usual, to s.o. (dat.)

wædla poor in, wanting, s.t. (gen.)

wær prepared for s.t. (gen., prep. *wiþ*); on guard against s.t. (gen., prep. *æt*)

ge-wær aware of s.o. or s.t. (gen.)

wan lacking s.t. (gen.); lacking to s.o. (dat.)

wana lacking s.t. (gen.)

and-weard near, close at hand, to s.o. (dat.)

from-weard about to depart from s.o. (dat.)

to-weard approaching s.o. or s.t. (dat.)

wiþer-weard contrary, hostile, obstinate, opposed, opposite, to s.o. (dat., prep. *wiþ*)

or-wena, or-wene hopeless, despairing, about s.t. (gen.)

un-wene hopeless, despairing, about s.t. (gen.)

weorþ honoured by, dear to, s.o. (dat.); worthy of, fit for, having a right to, subject to, liable to, s.t. (gen., dat., ? prep. *into* in *ÆCHom* i. 532. 25). *Note*: on *weorþ, wyrþe*, + gen. and dat., see Wülfing, *EStudien*, 15 (1891), 159–60, and Pearce, *MLN* 6 (1891), 1–4

efen-weorþ of equal dignity with s.o. (dat.)

nyt-weorþ useful, advantageous, profitable, to s.o. (dat.) in s.t. (prep. *on*)

un-þanc-weorþ ungrateful to s.o. (dat.)

un-weorþ unworthy of s.t. (gen.); worthless to s.o. (dat.)

weorþ-full honourable, glorious, to s.o. (dat.)

werig weary of s.o. or s.t., exhausted by s.t. (gen., dat., prep. *for*)

weste devoid of s.t. (gen.)

wierþe, see *weorþ*

efen-wierþe, see *efen-weorþ*

un-wierþe, see *un-weorþ*

wis skilled in s.t. (gen., dat., prep. *in*)

and-wis expert in s.t. (gen.)

ge-wis certain about, acquainted with, s.t. (gen., prep. *be*)

un-wis, un-ge-wis(s) uncertain, ignorant, of s.t. (gen.)

wlanc splendid, proud, in s.t. (gen., dat.)

wraþ angry with s.o. (dat.)

ge-wuna accustomed to s.t. (dat.)

un-ge-wuna unaccustomed to s.t. (dat.)

ge-wunelic usual, customary, to s.o. (dat.); suitable for s.o. or s.t. (dat.)

un-ge-wunelic unusual to s.o. (dat.)

ge-wylde subject to, at the disposal of, s.o. (dat.)

un-ge-wylde not under control of, not in subjection to, s.o. (dat.)

ge-wyrde in agreement with s.t. (gen.)

yrre 'angry with s.o.' (dat., prep. *wiþ*)

D. THE ARTICLES

1. *AN* AS THE 'INDEFINITE ARTICLE'

a. *Introductory remarks*

§220. Rissanen states the situation succinctly:

English *a*, *an*, of course, go back to OE *an*. In OE, there is no indefinite article which differs in form from the numeral *an*, but there are several hundred instances of the use of *an* in a function more or less resembling that of the indefinite article. It seems that this *an* is not yet totally unstressed—it retains the full case endings and probably some of its original numerical or individualizing force —but it no doubt represents one stage in the development from the stressed numeral 'one' to the present-day indefinite article *a, an.*[73]

Or, as Quirk and Wrenn put it (QW, p. 71), '*an* is usually a numeral, and when it is not it shares for the most part with *sum* a "strong indefiniteness" akin to Mod. E. "a certain" rather than the "weak indefiniteness" of Mod. E. "a(n)" '.

§221. It is futile (as Rissanen, p. 272, points out) to try to determine the exact point at which *an* can be called an article. I therefore follow him in putting the term in inverted commas when the OE use is referred to; this, he says (p. 261 fn. 3), may serve 'to remind the reader that the function of *an* is not necessarily identical with that of the present-day indefinite article'. But the remarks already quoted and the various examples with and without *an* given below suggest the omission of the word 'necessarily'; it is quite clear that OE *an* is often not used where MnE would have the indefinite article and that where it does occur it usually carries some sense stronger than MnE 'a, an'. The difficulty of determining its exact significance and the impossibility of laying down rules are underlined by the presence in both early and late prose of examples like the following, where *an* is present and then absent in what otherwise appear to be identical contexts: *Or* 278. 16 *Raþe þæs hiene ofslog an þunor*, Latin *fulmine ictus interiit*, but *Or* 160. 18 *þunor toslog heora hiehstan godes hus Iofeses*, Latin *ædes . . . ictu fulminis dissoluta*; *ÆCHom* i. 320. 1 *on anre culfran anlicnysse* but *ÆCHom* i. 320. 12 *on culfran anlicnysse*; and *ÆCHom* i. 126. 10 *Ic eom an man geset under anwealde* but *ÆCHom* i. 130. 7 *Ic eom man under anwealde gesett*. Many more such examples can be culled from those

---

[73] Rissanen, p. 261. For reasons for believing that in lOE *an* was weaker in stress in this use than in others, see ibid., p. 263.

quoted by Wülfing, Süsskand, and Rissanen, in the places referred to below.

§222. Süsskand attempts an ambitious scheme of classification based on Behaghel's; see the former's end-paper for details. But I find the system itself confused (his groups I and II seem to depend on semantic criteria, his groups III–V on syntactic) and his confident assignment of examples to this or that category unjustified. Thus *Or* 19. 9 *Ohthere sæde þæt sio scir hatte Halgoland þe he on bude. He cwæð þæt nan man ne bude be norðan him. þonne is an port on suðeweardum þæm lande, þone man hæt Sciringes heal* (I quote the passage from which Süsskand, p. 100, quotes only the last sentence) could well mean that there is only one port in Ohthere's district and not that *Sciringes heal* is one of a fixed but not stated number, as Süsskand suggests. Moreover, it seems a dubious procedure to distinguish this example from *Or* 142. 12 *Hit is, cwæð he, þæm gelicost, þonne ic his geþencean sceal, þe ic sitte on anre heare dune, 7 geseo þonne on smeðum felda fela fyra byrnan* on the grounds that in the latter the particular hill mentioned is one of an unfixed number (p. 100). There were probably fewer ports in Ohthere's district than there were hills in the world known to Orosius, but there is a limit to both. There is no limit to the number of hypothetical hills on which Orosius might imagine he was sitting, but I cannot see that this is relevant to the problem under discussion. And lastly we have no means of checking Süsskand's figures. *An port* is said to be one of seventy-six similar examples. The phrase *on anre heare dune* is included in his *Orosius* examples with the 'indefinite article' (p. 100) but the phrase *on smeðum felda* in the same example—which seems to be parallel—is not quoted in the corresponding category without article (p. 102), though it may be the one example not quoted of the eight he says exist. Again he claims (p. 35) that there are only four chance examples in the prose of Alfred's time in which *an* or *sum* is not used with a noun denoting a particular person or thing known to the speaker, but not to the hearer. Christophersen (pp. 101–2) and Rissanen (p. 270) accept Süsskand's assurance. But these four examples are not quoted and I have not succeeded in identifying them. Thus I cannot compare them with the many examples cited from the same texts by Wülfing (i. 290–1) and Süsskand himself (pp. 100–9) in which the 'indefinite article' is not used with nouns which seem to perform this function, e.g. *Bede* 24. 29 *Breoton is garsecges ealond*, *Or* 20. 5 *Seo Wisle is swyðe mycel ea*, *Or* 21. 10 *7 þæt is mid Estum þeaw . . .* , *Or* 162. 31 *. . . Caperronie wæs hatenu heora goda nunne*, and *CP* 155. 3 *ða geseah ic duru*.

§223. The history of the development of the indefinite article in English lies outside the scope of this work.[74] But the examples set out below (largely after Rissanen, pp. 270-4) give some idea of the main stages. The idiom seems to go back to the dependent individualizing use in which *an* is placed before a noun denoting a particular thing or person (§535), e.g. *Or* 184. 21 *on Piceno þæm wuda an wielle weol blode* and *ÆLS* 4. 143 *þa bærst sum sagol into anes beateres eagan*. Then we have examples in which 'the interest seems to be centred round the generic qualities of the person or thing rather than round its individual characteristics' (Rissanen, p. 271), e.g. *Or* 134. 22 *Ðær wearð Alexander þurhscoten mid anre flan* and *ÆCHom* ii. 452. 27 *Iob . . . ascræp ðone wyrms of his lice mid anum crocscearde*; examples in which the noun refers to any one person or thing in a species or class, e.g. *Bo* 97. 12 *forðæm he riht 7 ræt eallum gesceaftum, swa swa good stiora anum scipe* and *ÆLS* 12. 116 *Gif man læt nu ænne þeof to slege . . .* ; and distributive expressions in which the noun with *an* seems to have lost its individualizing force and refers to several objects, e.g. *CP* 9. 1 *7 on ælcre bið an æstel* and *an* (in contrast with *anre*) in *ÆCHom* ii. 194. 7 *on ælcum huse ealre ðære ðeode, on anre nihte, læg an dead mann*. In these we can detect forerunners of MnE usages. But the use of the article with a noun referring to a whole species or class, as in 'A cat loves comfort' does not seem to be reached in OE (according to Rissanen, pp. 273-4), with the possible exception of *Bo* 114. 4 *Swa swa an mon bið man þa hwile ðe sio saul 7 se lichama ætsomne bioð. . . .* However, this could easily be included in more than one of the groups differentiated above.

§224. But it is important to realize that, as the exceptions cited by Wülfing, Süsskand, and Rissanen, testify, the use of *an* is by no means the established or regular thing in any of the contexts mentioned above. Schrader (p. 10) remarks that the numeral *an* is already widely used as the indefinite article by Ælfric, although the noun on

---

[74] Rissanen discusses its origin and history and gives references to other discussions and lists of examples (pp. 261-303). See also Hüllweck, pp. 46-51; Wülfing, i. 287-91; Süsskand, pp. 3-49, 97-132; Christophersen, pp. 97-108, and Heltveit 1977, pp. 88-90; and (for the poetry) 'the eighteen German dissertations' (less Reussner and Rose), *passim*; Wack, *Ang.* 15 (1893), 209-20; and Sorg, pp. 79-82.

Note also the important suggestion made by Samuels in his review of Rissanen's book (*NQ* 213 (1968), 396); he speaks of 'the evolution of a new system of determiners in which, firstly, the various forms of the Old English demonstratives *se* and *þes* were re-aligned to the pattern *the/this/that*, and secondly, as a result of systemic pressure to complete that pattern, the use of nouns without determiners decreased, the indefinite article *a* was differentiated from *one*, and the uses of both *a* and *one* were extended. Such extension would be favoured because *sum*, which already had greater currency in plural contexts than *an*, was increasingly selected in quantitative and partitive functions, and avoided in its older uses.'

its own is still quite sufficient, and is more common. So we find many examples in late OE prose where the 'indefinite article' is not expressed where MnE would have it, e.g. *ÆCHom* i. 86. 3 *Hine gelæhte unasecgendlic adl*, *ÆCHom* i. 128. 19 *Wel wat gehwa þæt cyning hæfð maran mihte, ÆCHom* i. 134. 14 *ælc wif ðe cild gebære*, *ÆCHom* i. 364. 21 *Eadig eart ðu, Simon, culfran bearn*, and *ÆCHom* i. 146. 1 *he wæs of mædene acenned*. So the absence of *an* in *ÆCHom* i. 212. 25 *Menig man is cristen geteald* . . . does not certify that *cristen* is an adjective.

§225. Süsskand (pp. 43-4 and 48-9) finds that the *Blickling Homilies* and the West-Saxon Gospels use the 'indefinite article' less frequently. He characterizes the language of the former as archaic—*'eine tote Sprache'*—and suggests archaic language and the original Latin as possible explanations in the latter. Time does not permit further examination of this subject, and the law of diminishing returns would seem to apply. The apparently random presence or absence of *an* in contexts where MnE would always use an indefinite article gives room for speculation, but compels us to the obvious and well-known conclusion that the modern use of the indefinite article was not established in OE times.

b. The syntactic patterns in the prose

§226. When the 'indefinite article' is used, the basic pattern is *an* + (adjective +) singular noun; see the examples quoted above and (with an abstract noun; see Rissanen, pp. 274-5) *ÆCHom* ii. 432. 27 . . . *þæt he on swefne ane gesihðe be him sylfum geseah*. The adjective may be preceded by *swa*, e.g. *LS* 34. 415 *ænne swa geradne mann*. (The type 'so prudent a man' is not found till the thirteenth century, according to Rissanen, p. 266.) *An oþer* may be used dependently or independently, e.g. *ÆLS* 31. 813 *anum oþrum munece* and *ÆCHom* ii. 358. 6 *ænne oðerne him swiðe gelicne* (see Rissanen, pp. 284-6). There are spasmodic examples of *an* + *lytel*, e.g. *CP* 399. 22 *Her is an lytele burg swiðe neah, ðær ic mæg min feorh on generian. Hio is an lytel, 7 ðeah ic mæg ðæron libban* (see Rissanen, p. 294 and pp. 286-9), and of *an* + *healf*, e.g. *ÆTemp* 48. 11 *on ðam iglande hæfð se lengsta dæg on geare twelf tida 7 lytle mare ðonne ane healfe tide* (see Rissanen, pp. 26 and 267-8).

§227. The pattern 'indefinite article' + adjective occurs in *CP* 399. 24 *an lytel* (§226). Rissanen (p. 294 fn. 1) says that this is the only such example in OE except for *Mark(WSCp)* 7. 32 *7 hi læddon him*

ænne deafne 7 dumbne 7 hine bædon þ he his hand him on sette.
MS *A* adds *man* after *dumbne*, but without it *ænne* may carry stress
rather than be the 'indefinite article'.

§228. Apart from these, departures from the basic pattern are rare.
Rissanen discusses *GD* 183. 20 . . . *biddendum anum blindum
gesyhðe he sealde* (pp. 264-5). Schrader (p. 10) detects a plural 'indefinite article' with a singular meaning in *ÆCHom* ii. 354. 31 *þa
betwux ðam oðrum geseah he hwær man bytlode ane gebytlu, eal
mid smætum golde, and ða wyrhtan worhton ða gebytlu on ðam
Sæternes dæge, and wæs ða fornean geendod. He befran ða hwam ða
gebytlu gemynte wæron, swa mærlice getimbrode.* But the whole
passage (which he does not quote) shows that *gebytlu* starts as an
indeclinable feminine singular—note *wæs*—but is made plural in
the second sentence because of the formal ambiguity of *ða gebytlu*.

c. The syntactic contexts in the prose

§229. Examples of *an* 'indefinite article' with a noun which is subject, object, in the genitive or dative case, and in a prepositional
phrase, will all be found above. On the form of an accompanying
adjective see §§123-4. It can also be used with a noun which serves
as the predicate complement (see below); as the second element in
a comparison (e.g. *ÆCHom* ii. 232. 2 *he aras of ðære byrgene ðaða
he wolde, swilce of anum bedde*); in apposition (e.g. *LS* 34. 710 *nu
stentst þu her an geong man*); and as the so-called 'object of result'
(e.g. *ÆCHom* ii. 84. 22 *Sum wis lareow hatte Amalarius, se awrat
ane boc be cyrclicum ðeawum*). Rissanen (pp. 275-6) observes that
with these last four constructions 'there is often little need for individualization even with nouns referring to a particular individual'.
He suggests the same explanation for the more irregular use of *an*
with abstract nouns (pp. 274-5). For further discussion and examples
of these uses see Süsskand, *passim*, and Rissanen, pp. 275-84.

§230. Visser (i. 227 and 230-1) distinguishes two types of construction in which the verb 'to be' has a noun complement. The first is
that in which the noun denotes a rank, post, or title, that can be held
by only one person at one time. Here (Visser claims) the indefinite
article has been absent from OE to the present day. The OE examples
he quotes include *Bede* 252. 18 *þa wæs in þa tid Uitalius papa þæs
apostolican seðles aldorbiscop* (could *Uitalius papa* be subject?) and
ÆCHom i. 168. 7 *Deofol is ealra unrihtwisra manna heafod.* One
cannot deny that there is no 'indefinite article' in these examples.

But my own feeling is that if any article were to be inserted in these and in all the examples he quotes from all periods it would be the definite; cf. *ÆCHom* i. 364. 19 *Petrus him andwyrde, þu eart Crist, ðæs lifigendan Godes Sunu* with A.V. *Matt* 16. 16 'And Simon Peter answered and said, Thou art the Christ, the Son of the Living God.'

§231. The second is the type 'He is (a) lawyer', where (says Visser) in OE and ME up to about 1250 'the predicate noun is not preceded by *an* or *a*, and such collocations as "Ic eom mundbora", "þæt wæs god cyning", "hie was riche woman" are normal'. It is true that in OE *an* is not normally used in such contexts; thus we find *Or* 18. 8 *He wæs swyðe spedig man on þæm æhtum þe heora speda on beoð*, *CP* 49. 7 *ic eom cnioht; hwæt conn ic sprecan?*, and *ÆCHom* i. 134. 18 *þæt is feowertig daga, gif hit hysecild wære: gif hit þonne mædencild wære, þonne sceolde heo forhabban fram ingange Godes huses hundehtatig daga.* Although Visser noted one example with *an*— *HomU* 37. 241. 1 *ac ðu hæfdest deofles geþanc æt þinre heortan, and þu wære an licetere, and þe þuhte æfre to lytel ure ælmesse*— he left blank his column of examples with the indefinite article up to 1250. Schrader (p. 10) and Rissanen (pp. 276–8) have added over thirty more examples. In most of them the noun complement is qualified by a phrase or clause, e.g. *Or* 234. 8 *7 mon geseah swelce hit wære an gylden hring on heofonum brædre þonne sunne*, *BlHom* 43. 33 *Hit is an biscop se dyde mare yfel þonne god*, and *ÆGram* 222. 14 *Adverbium is an dæl ledenspræce undeclinigendlic.* According to Rissanen (p. 277) *ÆGram* 75. 9 *Tigris ys an ea and anes cynnes deor* is the only example not so qualified. But we may add from his own list *Mart2* 174. 6 *forðæm þe he ne moste ane godes fæmnan, þæt wæs an nunne, him to wife onfon* and from Schrader's *ÆCHom* i. 210. 21 *Sion is an dun, and heo is gecweden sceawungstow*, as well as some from the group in the second paragraph on Rissanen's p. 277 in which (he says) 'the need for individualization is perhaps less evident'; these include *ÆCHom* i. 170. 24 *forðon þe se gylp is an heafodleahter* and the example from *HomU* 37. 241. 1 noted by Visser. All these and the ME example noted by Davis (*RES* 17 (1966), 74) from *ChronE* 267. 31 (1140) *for he was an yuel man* should be added to Visser's table (i. 231).

d. In the poetry

§232. Rissanen, p. 295, states:

The 'indefinite article' is uncommon in OE poetry. This must be attributed to the archaic character of the alliterative poetry—perhaps also to the demands of the poetic style. Yet, in some fifteen OE poetic passages *an* is used dependently in a function which seems to correspond roughly with that of the 'indefinite article' in OE prose. It refers either to a particular individual or to any person or thing.

Rissanen goes on to discuss and to quote these examples (pp. 295-9).

§233. In those in which *an* refers to a particular individual, it may be unstressed, e.g.

GenA 2018   Him þa secg hraðe   gewat siðian,
             an gara laf,   se ða guðe genæs,
             Abraham secan,

or stressed, e.g. *Met* 25. 1 *Geher nu an spell be ðæm ofermodum.* There are some dubious examples in which *an* may or may not alliterate, e.g. *Met* 16. 12 *an iglond ligð ut on garsecg.* There are four examples which refer to any person or thing; in these, *an* is stressed, as in

MSol 391   Hwæt! Him mæg eadig eorl   eaðe geceosan
            on his modsefan   mildne hlaford,
            anne æðeling.

§234. There are also examples in which *an* is separated from a following noun or adjective by a verb, adverb, or another speech-group, e.g.

Mald 225   þa he forð eode,   fæhðe gemunde,
            þæt he mid orde   anne geræhte
            flotan on þam folce . . .

and *El* 417 *þa þær for eorlum an reordode,* ‖ *gidda gearosnotor.* In these, Rissanen argues, *an* has an individualizing function (pp. 297-8 and 291-2). On other uses of *an* in the poetry, see §§523 and 543.

§235. As with the prose, there is room for difference of opinion about the function and character of *an* in many examples in the poetry. Rissanen (pp. 295-9) takes issue with some of the suggestions advanced by Süsskand (pp. 9-18). These points cannot be pursued here: some at any rate seem to depend on metre—a tool too blunt to be decisive in many instances.

2. *SUM* AS THE 'INDEFINITE ARTICLE'

§236. *Sum* is sometimes used where MnE would require an indefinite article; see §387.

3. THE 'DEFINITE ARTICLE'

§237. The dem. *se seo þæt* can often be translated by MnE 'the'. Whether native speakers distinguished this from an accented use of dependent *se* (MnE 'that'/'those') cannot be determined. But it seems unlikely; see §§328-9.

§238. A few examples of *þe* 'the' are recorded, e.g. *Matt(Li)* 2. 3 *Herodes ðe cynig* and *ApT* 28. 4 *Ða soðlice geendode þe gebeorscipe.*[75] In *Dan* 22 *þa geseah ic þe gedriht* and similar examples, emendation to the appropriate form of *se* seems inescapable.

E. PRONOUNS AND 'PRONOUN/ADJECTIVES'[76]

1. CLASSIFICATION

§239. Pronouns are traditionally classified thus: personal, reflexive, reciprocal, possessive, demonstrative, interrogative, indefinite, and relative. In OE (as in other stages of the language) a problem of terminology arises. Words like *ic, þu, he*, are used independently in place of a noun (group) and can therefore be called pronouns. The question of a dependent use does not arise with them except in the genitive, which is used as a possessive both independently and dependently. The genitive forms of the third person are not declined, e.g. *ÆCHom* i. 62. 35 *Hi dydon be his hæse* and *ÆCHom* i. 2. 23 *on heora gewritum*. But the singular, dual, and plural, of the first and second person can be, e.g. *John(WSCp)* 17. 6 *Hig wæron þine* and *ÆCHom* i. 62. 32 *eowre speda . . . mines Drihtnes lare . . . incre byrðene gyrda*, but need not be, e.g. *ÆCHom* i. 174. 28 *we sceolon wendan ure mod to Godes lare* and *ÆGram* 105. 1 *eower domas ic herige*. Sometimes, of course, we cannot tell whether a form is inflected or uninflected because the forms coincide, e.g. *Exod* 19. 5 *eal eorðe is min* and *ÆCHom* i. 62. 31 *eower mod . . . and eower andwlita*. Whether we call these words possessive pronouns or possessive adjectives, or both, will depend on our criteria—formal (i.e. inflected or uninflected) or functional (i.e. dependent or independent). We can, I hope, avoid being trapped for ever in the revolving doors of this argument by describing these words as possessives which may

---

[75] See further *OED*, s.v. *the* A. I, and Wülfing, i, §147(4). Sedgefield does not support the two examples Wülfing cites from *Boethius*; see *Bo* 102. 18 and 132. 26.

[76] I use this term only to reject it; see §240.

be used dependently or independently. Where necessary, the general term 'possessives' may be subdivided into:

(1) genitives of the personal pronoun (all persons);

(2) inflected forms of *min, þin, ure, eower, uncer, incer*;

(3) ambiguous forms, i.e. those which may equally well be classified as (1) or (2).

§240. The demonstratives *se* and *þes* and some interrogatives (e.g. *hwelc*) can be used both dependently and independently. Other interrogatives (e.g. *hwa, hwæt*) can be used only independently. The former could be called 'pronoun/adjectives' (since they may function now as one, now as the other) and the latter pronouns. But it should suffice to speak of dependent and independent use and of inflected and uninflected forms.

§241. 'Indefinite' is a blanket term for many words, some of which can be used dependently and independently, some independently only. Scholars differ about which words to include and which to exclude; the lists in §§361–519 aim at including all those with a reasonable claim. Closs distinguishes 'the only truly indefinite pronouns . . . indeclinable *man* "one" . . . *hwa* "someone" and . . . *hwæt* "something" ' (p. 110) from 'general pronouns', which include (in different sub-classes according to their individual patterns of behaviour) *fela; eall, sum; ænig, ælc, an, feawa, genog, manig; oðer* (pp. 96 ff.; this function of *an* and *sum* she distinguishes from others). Commenting on Campbell's use of the term 'common indefinite pronouns (adjs.)' (*OEG*, §725) and on the fact that Wülfing classifies *eall, monig, fela*, and *feawa*, as both adjectives and pronouns (i, §§366–75), she claims that 'the disagreement in classification points to certain confusion in analysis' (this and the next two quotations are all on Closs, p. 96) and then proceeds to point out that these 'general pronouns' are like adjectives in that they can be used attributively (though with less freedom), but differ in that they can be used pronominally, can take a partitive genitive, and cannot be compared. There are other differences—some can be accompanied by a demonstrative, some can be modified by intensifying adverbs, some may occupy more than one position in a noun group (see §145). However, it is strange that this analysis leads Closs to conclude that 'the set is therefore established as the category of general pronouns'. Since (in her own words) 'they occur more often attributively than independently as indisputable subjects for NP [noun phrases]', one might have expected her to call them 'general adjectives'. Her terminology has little to commend it; here too we can conveniently speak of dependent and independent use. The term 'indefinite' is further discussed in §361.

§242. For details of the forms see *OEG*, chap. XV. It should be noted that *hie, þa, þas,* may be accusative singular feminine and nominative and accusative plural all genders. Ambiguity sometimes arises as a result; see §77.

2. THE PERSONAL PRONOUNS

a. General

§243. The first and second person pronouns are inflected for number (singular, dual, and plural) and case, the third for number (singular and plural), case, and (in the singular) gender; see *OEG*, §§ 702–4. Before *we* and *ge*, plural endings of verbs can be reduced, e.g. *ÆCHom* i. 220. 14 *ne beo ge na afyrhte*, but need not be, e.g. *ApT* 28. 8 *beon ge gesunde, Matt(WSCp)* 25. 34 *cumað ge gebletsode mines fæder*, and *And* 1609 *Ne beoð ge to forhte*; see *OEG,* §730. The form *nic* 'not I' occurs in *John(WSCp)* 1. 21 *Ða cwædon hi. eart ðu witega. 7 he andwyrde and cwæð nic.*

§244. The personal pronoun is normally expressed when it is the subject of a verb, even when the verb form is unambiguous for person and a Latin original without a pronoun is being closely glossed, e.g. *Ps(A)* 15. 2 *ic cweð,* Latin *dixi,* and *Gen* 1. 4 *he todælde,* Latin *divisit.* It is most frequently absent with an un-negated second person singular imperative, but even here is sometimes expressed; see §§887–91. On its absence in other circumstances see §§1503–16.

§245. On the non-expression of the pronoun object see §§1572–9 and on its position in the sentence §3907.

§246. The personal pronoun may stand in lieu of an already-expressed noun, e.g. *ÆCHom* i. 6. 20 *Ure Drihten bebead his discipulum þæt hi sceoldon læran and tæcan eallum þeodum ða ðing þe he sylf him tæhte, ÆCHom* i. 470. 7 . . . *and urnon hi and he to his byrgene,* and (with an independent use of the genitive) *ÆCHom* i. 168. 5 [*se Hælend*] . . . *he geðafode ðam deofle þæt he his fandode,* or in apposition with a noun, adjective, or participle, e.g. *ÆCHom* i. 2. 12 *Ic Ælfric, ÆCHom* ii. 388. 34 *on him manegum, ÆCHom* i. 254. 9 *us yfele, ÆCHom* i. 286. 8 *We sprecað ymbe God, deaðlice be Undeað-licum,* and *ÆCHom* i. 2. 26 . . . *ic gedyrstlæhte, on Gode truwiende,* or with *self* (see §§275-7). A form of apposition which seems to us tautologic but which may have been emphatic is seen in sentences like *ÆCHom* ii. 18. 19 *Swa gelice eac se hæðena cyning Nabuchodonosor, he geseah ehsynes þæs lifigendan Godes Sunu* and (with the appositional elements separated) *ÆCHom* i. 146. 33 *He cwæð, se apostol Paulus.* Wülfing gives numerous examples of this sort (i, §235). Further on these and on examples like *Or* 12. 19 *Nilus seo ea hire æwielme, Or* 8. 28 *Affrica 7 Asia hiera landgemircu,* and *Or* 28. 21 *Balearis þa tu igland him is be norðan Affrica,* see §298.

§247. O'Neil (p. 205 fn. 8) says that 'there is no backwards pronominalization in Old English'. There is room for work here. I have so far noted no examples of the pattern 'When he heard this, the King became angry'. So this may be one of the rocks on which Friend's interpretation of *Beo* 1142 ff. founders, for he takes *he* in *Beo* 1142 as referring to 'postcedent Fin' in *Beo* 1146 (*MLN* 69 (1954), 385-7). But we do find a form of 'backwards pronominalization' with vocatives, e.g. *Dream* 78 *Nu ðu miht gehyran, hæleð min se leofa*; with noun clauses (§1487); and with clauses in which a pronoun anticipates a noun subject, e.g. *Bede* 26. 2 (§1486), *LS* 34. 429 (§1503), and *ÆCHom* i. 146. 33 (§246).

§248. The personal pronoun may be used without an antecedent when the reference is obvious, e.g. *ÆCHom* i. 4. 20 *Crist ure Drihten* and *ÆCHom* i. 8. 5 [*God*] . . . *na swylce he behofige ures fultumes, ac þæt we geearnion þæt ece lif þurh his weorces fremminge.* See also §§260-4.

§249. Waterhouse has some interesting observations on pronouns in her discussion of 'Ælfric's Use of Modes of Address in *LS* Homilies' (1978, pp. 381-416) and in an article based thereon; see *SN* 54 (1982), 3-24.

§250. W. Bliemel's somewhat repetitive thesis *Die Umschreibung des Personalpronomens im Englischen* (Breslau, 1933) starts from the dubious proposition that in a sentence like *Beo* 730 *þa his mod ahlog, his mod* can profitably be viewed as a circumlocution for the pers. pron. *he*. On this basis Bliemel attempts to lay down the conditions under which such circumlocutions occur in all periods of English and gives the commoner patterns and their frequency. He claims that there are four main conditions which produce these substitutes —linguistic (the 'phonetic poverty' or *Lautarmut* of the personal pronoun and the demands of alliteration and rhythm), e.g. *Beo* 255 *minne gehyraþ* || *anfealdne geþoht* instead of *gehyraþ me*; emotional, e.g. *LS* 7. 193 *wa me mine sweteste bearn. wa me mira eagena leoht and mines lifes frofor, hwa bereafode me minra speda . . . hwa forcearf minne wingeard. . . . Hwa bescirede me mines hihtes. oþþe hwa gewemde þone wlite mire dohtor*; social, e.g. 'Your Excellency' (no OE examples given); and cultural, e.g. *Beo* 730 above, where the influence of a 'primitive Weltanschauung' leads the poet to write *his mod* for *he*. It is clear from the examples cited that many will fulfil more than one of these conditions, as Bliemel himself recognizes (p. 3). The commonest types of circumlocution are (not surprisingly) those involving parts of the body, e.g. *Beo* 445 *minne . . .* || *hafalan*, and spiritual or moral attributes, e.g. *Beo* 573 *his ellen*. The commonest patterns (again not surprisingly) are those involving possessive + [adjective +] noun, demonstrative + noun, and dative of personal pronoun + noun. Bliemel throughout stresses the point that these substitutes make for vividness and imaginative writing. But to view them primarily as circumlocutions for personal pronouns results in a limited and mechanical approach which is ill-equipped to deal with what are basically artistic problems and often produces the impression of triviality.

b. First person

§251. Occasional examples of what may be the 'plural of authorship' occur alongside the singular. Thus we find in the prose *Or* 14. 5 *Nu hæbbe we awriten þære Asian supdæl,*[77] *ÆCHom* i. 28. 26 *We wyllað to trymminge eowres geleafan eow gereccan þæs Hælendes acennednysse,* and *ÆCHom* i. 556. 13 *We mihton ðas halgan rædinge menigfealdlicor trahtnian . . . ac us twynað . . .* , but *Or* 10. 3 *Scortlice ic hæbbe nu gesæd ymbe þa þrie dælas* and *ÆCHom* i. 2. 26 *For þisum antimbre ic gedyrstlæhte . . . þæt ic ðas gesetnysse undergann.* Both can appear in the same sentence, e.g. *ÆCHom* i. 8. 9 *Nu bidde ic and halsige . . . þylæs þe we þurh gymelease writeras geleahtrode beon* (where *we* could include the congregation) and *ÆCHom* i. 580. 26 *Ic wene þæt þas word ne sind eow full cuðe, gif we hi openlicor eow ne onwreoð.* Examples from the poetry include *GenA* 939 *we nu gehyrað, Ex* 1 *We feor and neah gefrigen habað,* and *GenA* 1121 *Us gewritu secgað,* but *El* 240 *Ne hyrde ic, GenA* 2244 *þa ic . . . gefrægn,* and *Dan* 22 *þa geseah ic.* Cynewulf uses the singular, e.g. *Fates* 88 *Nu ic þonne bidde* and *El* 1254 *swa ic on*

---

[77] This is described by Fröhlich, p. 67, as the 'Plural der Bescheidenheit [modesty]'. Krebs attempts to distinguish between *pluralis modestatis* and *pluralis majestatis* in *NQ* 10 (1914), 337. Which we have depends, no doubt, on who is using it.

bocum fand; the reference in *Fates* 115 *Ah utu we þe geornor to gode cleopigan* is clearly plural. *Menologium* uses first person plural consistently, e.g. *Men* 68 *Sculan we hwæðere gyt* ‖ *martira gemynd ma areccan* and *Men* 189 *We þa æþelingas* ‖ *fyrn gefrunan . . .* , except in the formulaic *Men* 101 *Ne hyrde ic. . . .* It is clear from these and from other examples given by Sorg (pp. 30-4) that OE poets used both *ic* and *we*. In most of those with *we*, the poet could be including his audience; there are similar examples in the prose. But we are left with a few sentences in both prose and poetry where we may have the 'plural of authorship'.

§252. There are also places where a single individual other than an author seems to use the first person plural. But in some of these at any rate the reference may be to more than one. Thus GK and *OED* take *we* in *Beo* 958 *We þæt ellenweorc estum miclum,* ‖ *feohtan fremedon* as referring to Beowulf alone—the so-called 'plural of majesty'. But it is more probably a genuine plural; as Klaeber has it 'Beowulf generously includes his men.' Such examples as *ÆCHom* i. 418. 31 *Witodlice we beorgað ðinre ylde: gehyrsuma urum bebodum . . .* and *ÆCHom* i. 428. 20 *Awurp ðone truwan ðines drycræftes, and gerece us ðine mægðe* (where the Emperor Decius addresses Sixtus and St. Laurence respectively) may perhaps also have a plural reference;[78] note that Decius uses the singular in *ÆCHom* i. 426. 4 *Ic geseo . . . me . . . ic swerige . . . ic* and that in *ÆCHom* ii. 128. 6 *Gehyrsumiað eadmodlice on eallum ðingum Augustine, þone ðe we eow to ealdre gesetton. . . . Se Ælmihtiga God þurh his gife eow gescylde and geunne me þæt ic mote eoweres geswinces wæstm on ðam ecan eðele geseon . . .* , where Pope Gregory changes from *we* to *ic, we* may include his advisers. If any of these are accepted as examples of the 'plural of majesty', they pre-date that from the proclamation of Henry II quoted by Bøgholm (*Jespersen Gram. Misc.*, p. 219). But in this too *we* may include advisers: *þæt witen ge wel alle, þæt we willen and unnen þæt þæt ure rædesmen alle, oþer þe moare dæl of heom þæt beoþ ichosen þurg us and þurg þæt loandes folk, on ure kuneriche, habbeþ idon . . . beo stedefæst.*

c. Second person

(1) The plural of address

§253. We must, I think, agree with Miller (*RES* 15 (1964), 410), when he confirms Finkenstaedt's findings with the remark 'The

[78] See T. Finkenstaedt, *You und Thou* (Berlin, 1963), 35. He gives other examples at pp. 30-47.

plural of address to a single person, *you* for *thou*, does not occur in
Old English.' For Finkenstaedt (ibid.), after examining many possible
examples of the plural of majesty, reverence, or rank ('Standespl.'),
concludes that all can be otherwise explained—as references to mankind in general or to a king or leader along with warriors, counsellors,
or people ('soziativ'): 'die Forschung hat bisher noch keinen einzigen
Fall eines Pl. reverentiae oder gar Standespl. im ae. Schrifttum ent-
decken können' ['Research has still not succeeded in uncovering a
single example of a *pluralis reverentiae* or even a plural of rank in OE
literature'] (p. 30). An instructive example is *ÆCHom* ii. 308. 9
'*Alexander papa, ic sece ærest æt þe, þæt þu me ardlice secge hwæt
se intinga sy þæt ge wyllað sweltan sylfwilles for Criste, ærðan ðe ge
æfre his geleafan wiðsacan*', where the Emperor Aurelian is addressing
Pope Alexander (*þu*), but *ge* includes his two priests, Eventius and
Theodulus. The negative argument of explaining away the plurals is
buttressed by examples in which Beowulf, Hrothgar, Byrhtnoth,
bishops, Roman Emperors, and English kings, are addressed as *ðu* or
speak of themselves as *ic*; cf. §252. Kisbye, in *Archiv*, 201 (1964-5),
432-5, offers alternative explanations for the plural in some of
Finkenstaedt's examples without attempting to upset his conclusions.
Nevertheless, it is difficult to understand why Beowulf would use the
imperative plurals *fremmað* and *hatað* in addressing Wiglaf in

Beo 2799   Nu ic on maðma hord   mine bebohte
                frode feorhlege,   fremmað gena
                leoda þearfe;   ne mæg ic her leng wesan.
                Hatað heaðomære   hlæw gewyrcean. . . .

The two are alone as Beowulf dies and Wiglaf is addressed as *ðu* in
Beo 2743 and *þu* in 2813. The form *fremmað* could be a present
indicative plural with ['treasures'] as the subject ('. . . will supply . . .').
So too *hatað*; we could translate 'The war-veterans will command the
building of a barrow . . .'.

(2) *The pronoun subject and the imperative*

§254. On the presence or absence of a second person pronoun subject with an imperative, see §§887-91.

d. *Third person*

§255. Problems concerning the third person pronoun are discussed
as they become relevant; see the General Index. There is, however,
one general point. BTS (s.v. *he* A) speaks of 'the want of clearness
that results from the pronoun material being so limited in Old English'.

Ambiguities certainly do arise because *hie* can be accusative singular feminine and nominative and accusative plural and because dat. *him* can be singular or plural; see §77. But others, perhaps more serious, are the result of careless use of the pronoun without proper reference to an antecedent or of the absence of a pronoun. A well-known instance is the story of Cynewulf and Cyneheard, where close analysis is required to determine the referents of *hi, hiera,* and *him,* in parts of the reported speech. (Unthinking transposition from non-dependent speech may be the cause.)

§256. Sometimes, of course, gender gives the clue to a change of subject, e.g. *ÆCHom* i. 16. 15 *and se man is ece on anum dæle, þæt is on ðære sawle; heo ne geendað næfre*; cf. *ÆCHom* i. 552. 13. But not always. *He* refers to the subject of the preceding clauses in *ÆCHom* i. 304. 15 *Se ðe rihtlice gelyfð . . . se bið gehealden, and he hæfð ece lif . . .* , but to the object in *ÆCHom* i. 62. 18 *Se apostol hine fullode mid eallum his hirede, and he ongann Godes geleafan openlice bodian.* The referent of *he* and *hi* respectively is not clear in *ÆCHom* i. 86. 4 *his lichama barn wiðutan mid langsumere hætan, and he eal innan samod forswæled wæs* and *ÆCHom* i. 520. 20 *Eornostlice haligra manna gelaðung is heofonan rice, forðan ðe heora heortan ne beoð begripene on eorðlicum gewilnungum, ac hi geomriað to ðam upplican.* In these the ambiguity is of less moment than that in *ÆCHom* i. 376. 11 *Simon bræd his hiw ætforan ðam casere . . . þa Nero þæt geseah, ða wende he þæt he [Simon] Godes sunu wære. Petrus cwæð þæt he [Simon] Godes wiðersaca wære.* The fact that a pronoun subject need not be expressed, e.g. *ÆCHom* i. 336. 10 *þa ofhreow ðam munece þæs hreoflian mægenleast, and bewand hine mid his cæppan and bær to mynstreweard,* and that a personal pronoun may be used reflexively alone (§266) makes it uncertain whether Paul (as in *Acts* 9. 4) or the great light (as in Thorpe's translation) is the subject of *astrehte* in *ÆCHom* i. 386. 6 *. . . þæt him com færlice to micel leoht, and hine astrehte to eorðan, and he gehyrde stemne.* On this problem, see further §§1509-10.

e. The dual

§257. The dual pronouns *wit* 'we two' and *git* 'you two' (*OEG,* §703) are found alone, e.g. *ÆLS* 4. 45 *and wit* ('I and thou') *ne beoð totwæmede, ÆCHom* i. 362. 15 *and wit* ('I and he') *cumað to him,* and *ÆCHom* i. 374. 23 *and gyt* ('thou and he') *siððan samod to minum rice becumað*; with *twegen* or *begen,* e.g. *GenA* 2255 *dema mid unc twih* ('between me and her'), *Gen* 41. 11 *þa mætte unc begen swefen on anre nihte* ('Then he and I both dreamt'), *Solil* 25. 15 [*Se*] *hlaford is incer beigra wealdend* ('of you and of him'),

GenB 562   Gehyge on þinum breostum   þæt þu inc bam twam meaht
                wite bewarigan,

('from both you two [Adam and Eve]'; for further examples see Wülfing, i, §§176 and 222); or with the proper name of the second individual, e.g. *Ch* 1507 *wyt Æþered, Ch* 495 *uncer Brentinges*, and (from the poetry) *Wid* 103 *wit Scilling, Beo* 2002 *uncer Grendles, Hell* 135 *git Iohannis* (but see §1313 fn.), and *Sat* 409 *wit Adam twa.*

§258. But the plural may be used of two, e.g. *Gen* 22. 5 *ic 7 þæt cild gað unc to gebiddenne, 7 we syððan cumað sona eft to eow* and *ÆCHom* i. 316. 31 *Ða cwæð Petrus, Sege me, beceapode ge ðus micel landes? . . . Hwi gewearð inc swa, þæt gyt dorston fandian Godes?*

§259. There is, of course, no special form of the dual for the third person; the plural is regularly used, either alone, e.g. *ÆCHom* i. 316. 21 *þa wæs sum ðegen, Annanias gehaten, and his wif Saphira: hi cwædon him betweonan . . .* , or with *twegen* or *begen*, e.g. *Or* 262. 24 *Æfter þæm mon dyde him twæm þone triumphan, Uespasiane 7 Tituse* and *Or* 146. 10 *þa geascade þæt Umenis, 7 forsætade hie . . . 7 hie begen ofslog.* In *Bede* 256. 17 *þa ðæt þa cuðe ærendwrecan sægdon Ecgberhte þæm cyninge, þætte se biscop wære in Froncna rice, þone þe hy Osweo bædon from þam Romaniscan biscope . . .* , the phrase *hy Osweo* appears to mean 'King Ecgberht and King Osweo'. This example and

GenA 2216   þa wæs Sarran   sar on mode,
                þæt him Abrahame   ænig ne wearð
                þurh gebedscipe   bearn gemæne,
                freolic to frofre

lend some support to Sweet's preference for the reading of the Hatton MS *him Arone* against the Cotton *him 7 Arone* in *CP* 201. 3 *Be ðæm ilcan cuæð Moyses; ða he gehierde ðæt ðæt folc mænde to him Arone ymb hiera earfeðo, ða cuæð he: Hwæt is eower murcung wið unc? Hwæt sint wit?* Both Sweet (EETS edition of *Cura Pastoralis*, p. 484) and Klaeber (*Ang.* 27 (1903), 402) compare the Old Norse idiom *þeir Kari, þeir þorsteinn.*

f. The personal pronoun as a synonym for indefinite man

§260. Fröhlich has pointed out that the personal pronouns are sometimes used in contexts where indefinite *man* might have appeared (pp. 63-7 and 96-8). But an analysis of his examples confirms his cautious remark that in none of them does the personal pronoun indisputably have an indefinite sense. Einenkel, in *Ang.* 27 (1903), 144, observes that the use of the personal pronoun alone as an indefinite is a foreign idiom; he gives no OE examples.

§261. Fröhlich's examples with *we* include (with his alternative explanations in brackets) *Or* 134. 23 *Nyte we nu hwæðer sie swiþor to wundrianne* . . . ('Plural der Bescheidenheit [modesty]'), *Or* 58. 21 *Nu we witan þæt ure Dryhten us gesceop* ('wir Menschen'), and *Or* 14. 24 . . . *Albani hi sint genemde in Latina, 7 we hie hataþ nu Liubene* ('wir Heutigen oder wir Briten' [!] ['we today, or we Britons']). In these, as in the example from the Laws of Canute where *we*, *man*, and *hwa*, are used—*IICn* 68 (Liebermann, i. 354)— *we* retains a strong personal element. We need not wonder why no one has proposed an indefinite use of *ic*.

§262. Fröhlich quotes no examples with *þu* or *ge* and concludes that such a usage was not idiomatic (pp. 66 and 140). This is not surprising in view of the strong personal element these pronouns carry.

§263. Indefinite *he* is not mentioned by Fröhlich and it is hard to find convincing OE examples. In *ÆCHom* i. 394. 9 *Nis na fulfremedlic fela æhta to forlætenne, buton he Gode folgige, he* has an indefinite reference. But it may be referred back to *ÆCHom* i. 394. 5 *þeah hwa forlæte micele æhta, and ne forlæt ða gitsunge, ne forlæt he ealle ðing*; the change of tense probably gives the clue, for a verb in the preterite accompanies *he* on the three occasions it refers to *Petrus* in the intervening lines. In *LawIIAs* 3.4 *ond we cwædon be hlafordsearwe, ðæt he beo his feores scyldig, he* means 'anyone who commits it'. But this is an anacoluthon rather than idiomatic use of *he* as an indefinite. The same is probably true of *HomU* 35. 223. 34- 224. 8, where we have changes of number from pl. *ealle þa þe* to sg. *he* . . . *he* . . . *he hine* . . . back to pl. *þa þe* . . . *hie*, and of *HomU* 35. 212. 25-32, where there are similar changes; cf. those discussed in §77. Pogatscher (*Ang.* 23 (1900), 297) is, I think, wrong to take such examples as evidence for an indefinite use of *he*. In the remaining examples of *he* referring to 'the persons indefinite' given in BTS, s.v. *he* A I(2), *he* has an antecedent.

§264. It is 3rd pers. pl. *hie* which comes closest to being used as a substitute for indefinite *man*, e.g. *John(WSCp)* 12. 3 *Maria nam an*

pund deorwyðre sealfe mid þam wyrtgemange þe hig nardus hatað[79]
and *Or* 40. 23 *Ic wolde nu, cwæð Orosius, þæt me ða geandwyrdan
þa þe secgað þæt þeos world sy nu wyrse on ðysan cristendome
þonne hio ær on þæm hæþenscype wære, þonne hi swylc geblot 7
swylc morð donde wæron.* . . . But the latter at any rate gives a
strong impression of individuals committing their several crimes. And
some of Fröhlich's other examples are even more dubious, e.g. *Or*
18. 10 *þa deor hi hatað hranas*, where *hi* could refer to the Lapps.
On *he* and *hie* referring back to an antecedent *man*, see §377.

3. THE REFLEXIVES

a. General

§265. The personal pronoun serves as a reflexive, either alone or
emphasized by *self*, which is usually declined to agree with the pronoun in number, gender, and case. On *self* alone, see §278.[80] On the
classification of verbs which govern reflexives, see §§1052-9.

b. The personal pronoun alone

(1) *Accusative*

§266. The accusative of the personal pronoun is used reflexively
with transitive verbs, with verbs which can be transitive or intransitive, with otherwise intransitive verbs, and with prepositions. The
subject is usually a person, but need not be. With transitive verbs we
find *ÆCHom* ii. 600. 22 *Ic bletsige me* (but *ÆCHom* ii. 598. 23
Ælmihtig God, gebletsa us) and *ÆCHom* ii. 494. 25 . . . *þæt hi
sceoldon hi gebiddan to ðære sunnan anlicnysse* (but *ÆCHom* ii.
598. 20 *We biddað þe, Drihten,* . . .).

§267. With verbs which can be transitive or intransitive we find (for
example) *Bede* 118. 6 *Ða for se wallenda leg 7 hine brædde to þam
biscope* and *HomS* 40. 262. 5 *þæt treow þonne* . . . *hlifað up ofer
eall þa oðre treowu and brædeð hit* (but *Or* 166. 18 *7 he se cyning*

[79] Hatton MS omits *hig*. There is no equivalent in the Latin. But in the two examples
cited by BTS (s.v. *he* A I(2)(*b*)(β)), the OE plural pronoun is directly due to Latin influence. In *Exod* 21. 29 *hi . . . cyddon* corresponds to *contestati sunt* and in *Matt(WSCp)* 5. 11
hi wyriað to *maledixerint*. (I now note that the latter is the sole such example quoted by
Visser (i. 52).)

[80] For examples of the personal pronoun used alone as a reflexive, see (in addition to
those quoted below) Penning, pp. 8–13; Bock 1887, pp. 14–19; Voges, *Ang.* 6 (1883), 317–
74; Farr, pp. 8–18; Ropers, pp. 30–2; Hermodsson, pp. 193–210; Visser, i, §§426–38; and
(for the poetry) 'the eighteen German dissertations', *passim*. Further on the reflexive and
other uses of *self*, see §§472–500.

his handa wæs uppweardes brædende wið þæs heofenes and *WHom* 5. 50 *Nu ða yfelan 7 ða swicelan swa oferlice swyðe brædað on worulde.*) Visser (i. 145-7) gives examples of the 'absolute use of verbs that are often found construed with a reflexive object' without distinguishing this group from the next.

§268. A reflexive accusative, described by Ropers (p. 30) as more or less pleonastic, is also found after verbs which are otherwise intransitive, e.g. *BlHom* 147. 1 *on þære halgan Marian hus on þæt þe heo hie inne reste* and *ÆCHom* i. 372. 17 *Simon to ðisum wordum hine gebealh* (but *BlHom* 47. 18 *on niht ær he ræste* and *ÆLS* 2. 223 *þa wearð se geræfa þearle gebolgen*).

§269. Prepositions may govern a reflexive accusative, e.g. *CP* 373. 1 *ðeah ðe he do God behindan hine* and *Bede* 108. 16 *7 [Mellitus] þa mid hine . . . brohte.*

(2) Genitive
§270. A reflexive genitive can occur with a verb, e.g. *CP* 23. 10 *forðon ic min mað* and *ÆLS* 19. 172 *Yfele deð him sylfum þe mid swicdome his tilað*; with a noun, e.g. *Or* 174. 30 *7 he siþþan þa folc gelædde . . . 7 gesette twa folc diegellice on twa healfa his, 7 þridde beæftan him*; or with a preposition, e.g. *Bede* 128. 15 *þa geseah he semninga on midre niht sumne mon wið his gongan*, Latin . . . *uidit subito intempesta nocte silentio adpropinquantem sibi hominem.* On the reflexive use of possessives (which may be exemplified in *Or* 174. 30 above), see §297 (possessive alone) and §§483-6 (with *self*).

(3) Dative
§271. Here Farr (pp. 8-9) makes a distinction between the 'necessary' and the 'pleonastic' reflexive dative. This has some validity for the modern reader at least. The former can be said to appear as the direct object of verbs which take a dative, e.g. *ÆCHom* i. 416. 19 *Gebeorh ðe and ðinum preostum*; as the indirect object of other verbs, e.g. *Or* 224. 3 . . . *ongean Aristonocuse þæm cyninge, se wolde geagnian him þa læssan Asiam, þeh þe hie ær Attalis his agen broðor hæfde Romanum to boclande geseald* ('wished to gain for himself'); and with prepositions, e.g. *Or* 30. 29 *swa þæt ælcne þara þe hio geacsian myhte þæt kynekynnes wæs, hio to hyre gespon for hyre geligernesse*, *ÆCHom* i. 278. 27 *Fyr acenð of him beorhtnysse*, and *ÆCHom* ii. 528. 25 *Se Hælend . . . sende hi twam and twam ætforan him.*

§272. Reflexive datives which it seems to us reasonable to regard as 'pleonastic' are found both with transitive verbs, e.g. *ÆCHom* i. 596. 35 *Egeas him ondred ða menigu* and *ÆSpir* 57. 20 *þonne he . . . can him gescead betwux soð and leas*, and with intransitive ones, especially those implying motion or rest, e.g. *ÆCHom* ii. 394. 22 *Gang ðe nu on sibbe, ÆCHom* ii. 518. 29 *Ða wurdon ða oðre awrehte mid þam sange, and gecyrdon him ham*, and *ÆLS* 6. 160 *Hwæt ða on sumum dæge sæton him ætgædere Florus and Maurus.*

§273. But the distinction cannot always be made with certainty by a modern reader, e.g. *Or* 3. 9 *ond he him geceas Bizantium þa burg, ÆCHom* ii. 230. 31 *Soðlice Crist . . . geceas him mæden to meder*, and *ÆCHom* ii. 266. 18 *þone timan hi heoldon him to Eastertide*. (Indeed some of the examples I give above with apparent assurance may well seem dubious to others.) Visser (i. 322) admits that 'the classification . . . remains arbitrary' when he makes what seems to me essentially the same distinction by separating the dative reflexive object from the *he him gewat* type. He assumes that he has the latter 'when there do not seem to be any examples in which the verb in question is construed with an object consisting of pronoun + *self*'. But it is hard to accept that this is a sound criterion when we consider the examples quoted in §§276 and 487, when we remember that OE *self* is not exclusively reflexive (§275), and when Visser, while accepting an example from Sir Thomas More with 'themself' as decisive, rejects *ÆLS* 7. 213 *and ferde him sylf aweg* because *sylf* is nominative (i. 321-2). However, the existence of the 'pleonastic' reflexive dative is important in considering the origin of MnE 'himself' and the like (see §475). For examples from the poetry, see Sorg, pp. 34-7.

§274. Exactly what nuance it conveyed to the Anglo-Saxons cannot be determined. It is indeed possible, as Visser (i. 321) suggests, that it was used 'when circumstances prompted them to give linguistic expression to the notion that the person denoted by the subject was particularly affected by the result of the action or event'. This might account for the difference between *Bede* 124. 12 *7 he sigefæst swa eft ham ferde* and *Or* 74. 32 *he him hamweard ferde to his agnum rice.*

c. The personal pronoun + self

§275. The personal pronoun, of course, is not exclusively reflexive. This fact opens the way for the two interpretations of *ChronA* 48. 16

(755) *7 þa gatu him to belocen hæfdon*—'they had locked the gates against the others' *or* (as Wrenn suggests) 'on themselves'[81]—and helps to add to the confusion in other parts of that notorious annal. Modern readers looking at *hine sylfne* and *hine*—both reflexive—in *ÆCHom* i. 332. 31 *Ne lufað se hine sylfne seðe hine mid synnum bebint* may think it a pity that Ælfric did not remove all possible ambiguity by adding *sylfne* to the second *hine* as well. Again, they may take it for granted that the use of *sylfne* in *BlHom* 65. 4 *Se mon se þe operne acwelþ, 7 instæpes hine sylfne ongyteþ, þæt he mycel man 7 myccle synne gedon hæbbe* . . . removes the possibility of momentary ambiguity which *hine* alone might have left in their minds. Such thoughts would be quite without foundation, for OE *self* often emphasizes a non-reflexive personal pronoun (sometimes, perhaps, to the confusion of a modern reader), e.g. *Or* 192. 10 . . . *Claudius Marcellus* . . . *for dearnenga mid gewealdene fultume on þone ende Hannibales folces þe he self on wæs, 7 fela þæs folces ofslog, 7 hiene selfne gefliemde* and *CP* 131. 11 . . . *Moyses, se ðe wæs Gode sua weorð ðæt he oft wið hine selfne spræc* . . . ; see also *Or* 146. 9, *Or* 172. 11, *Beo* 961, and Penning (pp. 20-4).

§276. But it is doubtful whether the fact that (for example) both *hine* and *hine selfne* can be used reflexively and non-reflexively presented much of a problem to the Anglo-Saxons. The context usually makes it clear. There is no doubt that *him* is reflexive in *ÆCHom* ii. 186. 9 *Hwilc wundor wæs, ðeah se halga wer ealne middaneard ætforan him gesawe, ðaða he wæs ahafen on his modes leohte ofer middanearde?* There is no ambiguity in

ÆCHom ii. 156. 21   On sumum dæge, þaða he ana wæs, þa com him to se costere. Witodlice an blac þrostle flicorode ymbe his neb swa gemahlice, þæt he hi mid his handa gefon mihte, gif he swa wolde; ac he hine bletsode mid þære halgan rode tacne, and se fugol sona aweg gewat. þa gestod hine swa micel lichamlic costung, þæt he uneaðe þære lichamlican ontendnysse wiðstandan mihte; þa beðohte he hine sylfne, and unscrydde hine ealne, and wylode hine sylfne on ðam þiccum bremlum and þornum and netelum. . . .

In *Or* 58. 15 *Ond for þon þe he þæt god forlet þe him geseald wæs, 7 wyrse geceas, hit God siþþan longsumlice wrecende wæs, ærest on him selfum, 7 siþþan on his bearnum* . . . and *Bede* 56. 17 *7 he ælmihtigne God bæd þæt he hi mid his gife gescylde: 7 þæt he him seolfum forgeafe þæt* . . . , we can argue whether *self* is used emphatically or with reflexive reference to a noun or pronoun which is

---

[81] *History*, 25 (1940-1), 212. But one example from a fourteenth-century romance and one from Coverdale's Bible do not support the notion that we have here an otherwise unrecorded OE colloquial idiom.

not the subject of the clause in which it appears. But again there is no real ambiguity.

§277. The combination personal pronoun + *self* can of course (like the personal pronoun alone) be used reflexively in the accusative, e.g. *ÆCHom* ii. 156. 21 (§276), the genitive, e.g. *ÆLS* 12. 122 *Bið nu micel ræd þæm þe his sylfes recð*, and the dative, e.g. *LS* 34. 523 *and he . . . bearh him sylfum swiðe georne*. For further examples of reflexive *self* with a personal pronoun see Penning, pp. 13–19 (these are mostly from the poetry) and Visser, i, §§426–38.

d. Self *alone*

§278. *Self* alone in an oblique case is sometimes (not always) reflexive; see §§499–500.

4. THE RECIPROCAL RELATIONSHIP

a. *The personal pronoun*

§279. Reciprocity between two individuals or groups combined in one plural subject may be expressed by the personal pronoun alone in the appropriate case, e.g. *Or* 128. 1 *Of þære stowe for Alexander þriddan siþe ongean Darius, 7 hie æt Tharse þære byrig hie gemetton*, *LS* 8. 369 . . . *God unc geuþe þæt wit unc gemetton*, *Mald* 34 *Ne þurfe we us spillan*, *CP* 349. 21 *hu ða fuglas, ðe him gelice beoð, 7 anes cynnes beoð*, and (with a preceding *ægðer*) *Bo* 63. 9 *ægðer hiora bið þy forcuðra gif hi hi gemetað*.

§280. As in MnE, a preposition meaning 'between, among' may govern the personal pronoun, e.g. *CP* 93. 22 *Habbað ge sealt on ieow 7 sibbe habbað betweoh iow*, *Or* 1. 8 *Hu Thelesci 7 Ciarsæthi þa leode him betweonum wunnon*, and *CP* 197. 7 *ðonne don hie ðæt suiðe diegellice betweoxn him*. Visser (i, §483) toys with the notion that an example like *CP* 99. 14 *Ne untreowsige ge no eow betweoxn* can be analysed 'as a combination of subject + verb + reciprocal object' with *betweoxn* as an adverbial adjunct, but rejects it because dat. *him* rather than acc. *hie* regularly occurs in the third person, e.g. *Exod* 2. 13 . . . *he geseah twegen Ebreisce him betwynan sacan*. I think he is right, although occasional examples of *betweoh* with the accusative do occur; see BT(S), s.v.

§281. The reciprocal pronoun is reinforced by an adverb under Latin influence in *John(WSCp)* 15. 12 *þ ge lufion eow gemænelice*,

Latin *ut diligatis inuicem* (Visser, i, §482) and in *BenR* 59. 4 *elles þa opre ealle heom gemænelice betwyh on þisse þenunge þeowian*, Latin *ceteri sibi invicem serviant* (Visser, i, §490). In the other example quoted by Visser (i, §482)—*LibSc* 30. 12 *gebiddaþ eow gemænelice*, Latin *orate pro inuicem*—*eow* could be reflexive rather than reciprocal. If so, the example belongs in §287.

b. The personal pronoun + self

§282. In this combination, *self* usually agrees with the reciprocal pronoun, e.g. *Or* 142. 10 *Alexandres æfterfylgendas . . . hu hie hie selfe mid missellican gefeohtum fordydon*, Latin *inter se bella gesserint Macedonum duces*, *Or* 64. 16 *ge eac him selfum betweonum*, and *ÆCHom* ii. 292. 35 *and fracodlice him betwynan sacian*. In *ÆCHom* ii. 356. 12 *and we magon us sylfe betwux us on life ælc oðrum fultumian to ðam upplican life*, *sylfe* probably agrees with the subject *we* (see §478), with the first *us* a 'pleonastic' dative reflexive (see §271). It is perhaps just possible that *us sylfe* is accusative governed by *betwux* and that the second *us* goes with *fultumian*, *ælc oðrum* then being parenthetical. But I reject both this and the third (theoretically possible) explanation that *sylfe* goes with *we*, the first *us* with *betwux*, and the second with *fultumian*.

c. Oþer

§283. Reciprocity may be expressed by *oþer* preceded by a word other than a pronoun meaning 'either' or 'each', e.g. *WHom* 20(C). 69 *Ne bearh nu foroft gesib gesibban . . . ne broðor oðrum*.

d. Ægþer, naþer, oþer (. . .) oþer

§284. These combinations, with the first element in the nominative and *oþer* in an oblique case, express reciprocity between two persons, e.g. *Or* 52. 21 *for þon ðe se cyning ne gemunde þara monigra teonena þe hiora ægðer oþrum on ærdagum gedyde*, *Or* 96. 32 . . . *þæt naðer ne mehte on oþrum sige geræcan*, *ÆCHom* i. 142. 13 *hi sind swa geworhte, gif hyra oðer oðerne forlyst, þonne ne secð seo cucu næfre hire oðerne gemacan*, and *Mald* 132 *Eode swa anræd eorl to þam ceorle,* || *ægþer hyra oðrum yfeles hogode*.

e. Æghwylc, ælc, gehwa, gehwylc, ænig, (. . .) oþer

§285. These combinations are used in the same way, but express reciprocity between more than two, e.g. *ÆCHom* ii. 330. 13 . . .

we sceolon andettan ure synna gelome, and ælc for oðerne gebiddan,
Mald 234 *þæt ure æghwylc oþerne bylde, Mark(WSCp)* 4. 41 *7*
cwædon ælc to oðrum, Latin *et dicebant ad alterutrum* (*L* has
7 hia cuedon him bitwien), *Coll* 235 *7 framige anra gehwylc oþron,*
Latin *et prosit unusquisque alteri, ÆGram* 125. 8 *forþan ðe gehwa*
hæt oðerne, na hyne sylfne, and *WHom* 20(C). 73 *ne ænig wið*
oðerne getrywlice þohte. For further examples of the combinations
discussed in this and the preceding section see Wülfing, i, §§358-9.
For other uses of these pronouns, see the Index of Words and Phrases.

f. An (. . .) oþer, ☆sum (. . .) oþer

§286. Rissanen (p. 97) reports three examples of *an (. . .) oþer* in
OE, all under direct Latin influence, viz. *Mem* 124. 11 *þæt an to*
oðran ne si geþeod, Latin *et ne unus ad alium coniungatur, Mem*
127. 29 *þæt an oðerne na derie,* Latin *ut unus alium non noceat,*
and *ChrodR* 99. 31 *amancg þam þe hi him an oðer betwynan spræ-*
con, Latin *cumque uicissim aliqua confabularentur.* No examples of
reciprocal *sum (. . .) oþer* have as yet come to my notice.

g. Subject + adverb

§287. This combination too may express reciprocity, e.g. *ChronE*
5. 8 (-) *7 þa hi ærost togedore geræsdon, Or* 96. 31 *Hie siþþan on*
ðæm sæ togædere foran, GenB 788 *þa hie fela spræcon* ‖ *sorhworda*
somed, sinhiwan twa, and *Mald* 67 *hwænne hi togædere garas beron.*

h. The verb alone

§288. In MnE reciprocity may be expressed by the verb alone, e.g.
'They met, they kissed, they loved.' *Or* 242. 11 . . . *þæt hiora nan*
oðerne on þone andwlitan ne sloge, þær þær hie æt gefeohtum
gemette seems a convincing OE example, as does *GuthA* 1 *Se bið*
gefeana fægrast þonne hy æt frymðe gemetað, ‖ *engel ond seo eadge*
sawl; it would be perverse to claim that *hie* and *hy* were accusative.
The third OE sentence quoted by Visser (i, §158) *LS* 8. 335 *þa aras*
he and gelæhte hine be þam swuran and cyste and clypte is not an
example, for we have merely non-repetition of the object with a
divided group of verbs; see §§1464-7. Further on reciprocity, see
Potter, 'The Expression of Reciprocity', *EStudies,* 34 (1953), 252-7,
and Visser, i, §§486-91.

5. THE POSSESSIVES

a. General

§289. On the forms and declension of the possessives see *OEG*, §§705-7. Examples from the poetry will be found in Sorg (pp. 37–50) and in 'the eighteen German dissertations' (*passim*). The possessives of the first and second persons—*min, þin, uncer, incer, ure, eower*—and the third person *sin* (see §§290-3) can be inflected like strong adjectives for number, case, and gender. The third person *his, hire, hira*, are uninflected and, of course, denote the sex of the possessor, not the gender of the accompanying noun.

b. Sin

§290. The poss. *sin* 'his, her, their' had been largely replaced in OE by the genitive forms of *he*. But it occurs spasmodically in poetry of all periods, being found as late as the *Chronicle* entry (MSS *C* and *D*) for 1065, where *ChronC* 194. 17 reads:

```
7 se froda swa þeah    befæste þ rice
heahþungenum menn    Harolde sylfum
æþelum eorle    se in ealle tid
hyrde holdlice    hærran sinum.
```

There are no examples in 'Alfredian' prose, in Ælfric, or in Wulfstan. Ælfric in his *Grammar* (103. 19) glosses *suus, his*: *suus ager, his æcer, sui agri, his æceres, and swa forð*. A solitary example occurs in *BlHom* 125. 21 *sin hwyrfel* in a passage of almost 'poetic' description. There are examples in the early Kentish Laws and in other glosses or close translations; see BT and BTS, s.v. *sin*, and Bauer's collection in *Ang.* 81 (1963), 323-34. Bauer (p. 333) suggests that 'eine Art poetischer Sprachcharakter' ['a poetical kind of style'] may lie behind these.

§291. The almost complete absence of *sin* in the prose suggests that it was archaic and was preserved in the poetry, very often for metrical convenience. Bauer (pp. 332-3) rightly prefers this to the alternative possibility that *sin* was originally used in the extant prose as well as in the poetry, and was then eliminated from the prose by later scribes who felt it archaic, but left it in the poetry when it was metrically essential and sometimes when it was not. The frequency of *sin* varies from poem to poem; see Bauer, pp. 326-32.

§292. There is no syntactical distinction between *sin* and the possessive forms of *he*. *Sin* is usually reflexive, referring to the subject of the same or of a previous sentence and so equalling Lat. *suus*, e.g. *Jud* 29, *And* 813, and *And* 663. But it sometimes refers to an object and so equals Lat. *eius*, e.g. *GenA* 1049 and *Jud* 99. Its antecedent is usually a masculine singular nominative, but can be a feminine singular, e.g. *BlHom* 125. 21 and *Beo* 1506. Bauer (pp. 323–4) cites *GenA* 913 *mid fotum sinum*, referring to *þæt wif*, as his only example of *sin* referring to a neuter singular. But it may be a triumph of sex over gender, as BT (s.v. *sin*) suggests. The emendation of *þinne* to *sinne* in *Dan* 392 provides the only example in the poetry in which *sin* refers to a plural antecedent. Bauer quotes *Ps(I)* 17. 46, where *claudicauerunt a semitis suis* is glossed by *luncodon fram stigum synum ł fram heora paðum*.

§293. *Sin* is found before and after its noun. There are marked variations in the percentages of the two positions in different poems. Bauer (p. 334) discusses these and other syntactical and metrical peculiarities of *sin* and concludes that 'sin eben im normalen, nicht-poetischen Sprachgebrauch nicht mehr usuell und sein Vorkommen in der Dichtung traditionsgebunden, archaisierend war' ['it was simply that *sin* was no longer current in normal, non-poetic usage, and that its appearance in poetry was archaizing and determined by tradition'].

c. The dependent possessive

§294. The dependent possessive is normally found before the noun and its qualifying elements, e.g. *BlHom* 21. 1 *Eower Fæder*, *ÆCHom* i. 30. 12 *hyre frumcennedan sunu*, *BlHom* 117. 12 *his þam halgum*, and *BlHom* 5. 15 *of his þæm fæderlican sceate*. (On the use of both demonstrative and possessive before a noun—especially common in the *Blickling Homilies*—see §§103–12.) It may be repeated before a second noun, e.g. *BlHom* 99. 17 *heora bliss 7 heora plegan*, but need not be, e.g. *BlHom* 99. 20 *heora fyrenlustas 7 wiste 7 plegan 7 oforgedrync 7 dyslice 7 unrædlice halsunga* and *BlHom* 13. 10 *ure se trumesta staþol, 7 se selosta scyld*.

§295. Post-position is rare in the prose, but is found in the vocative, e.g. *CP* 37. 16 *sunu min* and *ÆCHom* i. 566. 21 *modor min*; see further Wülfing, i, §247. Examples from the glosses are, of course, of no syntactical significance. There are occasional prose examples in which the possessive is separated from its noun by something other than a demonstrative or adjective, e.g. *CP* 9. 12 (§296), *BlHom* 177. 8 *þonne witodlice þa hie heora hæfdan witgan*, and *BlHom* 243. 18 *he ure wæs wealdend*. Separation and post-position are more common in the poetry, e.g. *Men* 171 *gast onsende* || *Matheus his*. On this and on the position of the possessive in relation to other qualifying elements in prose and poetry, see §§142–77. Breitkreuz (pp. 8–14) gives examples from poetry and the glosses of the dependent possessive before and after the noun.

§296. The pronominal origin of the possessive is emphasized by sentences in which it serves as antecedent to an adjective clause, e.g. *Bede* 132. 27 . . . *þæt þu onfo his geleafan 7 his bebodu healde, se ðe þe from wilwendlecum earfeðum generede* and *Bede* 290. 17 . . . *swa swa heo bidende wære his ondsware, þone þe heo geseah 7 þæm þe heo tosprecende wæs* (for further examples see Wülfing, i, §278) and by occasional examples in which the genitive of the first and second person pronouns is used instead of inflected forms of the possessive, e.g. *CP* 9. 12 *Siððan min on Englisc Ælfred kyning awende worda gehwelc*, *ÆCHom* i. 518. 9 *eower gebedu*, *ÆCHom* i. 242. 20 *to eower agenre ðearfe*, and *Rid* 35. 4 *hygeþoncum min*.

§297. All the possessives, including *sin*, can be used reflexively of the subject of the sentence, or non-reflexively of someone or something else, e.g. *CP* 45. 9 *Sceawiað iowre fet* and *ÆCHom* i. 78. 27 *Hi geopenodon heora hordfatu* but *ÆCHom* i. 18. 13 *Forðan ðe ðu . . . min bebod forsawe*, and *ÆCHom* i. 24. 21 *þa asende he his engel Gabrihel* but *ÆCHom* i. 34. 6 . . . *þæt we us gegadrian to his halgan gelaðunge*. Both usages can, of course, occur in the same sentence, e.g. *ÆCHom* i. 22. 10 *Ic wylle settan min wedd betwux me and eow*. All except *sin* may be reinforced or emphasized by *self*; see §§483–6.

§298. There are a few much-quoted sentences in which an uninflected form of a foreign name is followed by the genitive of a personal pronoun, the two in combination making a genitive. They include *Or* 8. 10 *Asia 7 Europe hiera landgemircu*, *Or* 8. 28 *Affrica 7 Asia hiera landgemircu*, and *Or* 12. 19 *Nilus seo ea hire æwielme*.[82] These are best regarded as isolated phenomena, related to similar examples in later periods of English only in so far as the difficulty of inflecting proper names lies at the root of them. They may be

---

[82] *Num(L)* 13. 29 *Enac his cynryn* is usually cited too (e.g. by Kellner, p. 193, and Mustanoja, p. 160) but a comparison with the reading of MS *B Enachus cynryn* and with *Deut* 1. 28 *Enachis suna* and *Josh* 11. 21 *Enachim* (acc.) suggests that BTS (s.v. *he*) is right in reading *Enachis*.

compared with examples in which the nominative of a personal pronoun is used tautologically with a foreign name, e.g. *Or* 8. 14 *Europe hio onginð*, and with examples in which the dative of a personal pronoun indicates that an uninflected foreign name is to be taken as dative, e.g. *Or* 28. 21 *Balearis þa tu igland him is be norðan Affrica* and *Or* 12. 16 *Seo Ægyptus . . . be norþan hire . . . be eastan hiere . . . be westan hire . . . be suþan hire*, and may be contrasted with examples in which uninflected forms of foreign names serve as genitive or dative, e.g. *Or* 8. 23 *Se westsuþende Europe landgemirce*, *Or* 8. 31 *þære Affrica norþwestgemere*, *Or* 10. 15 *India gemæro*, and *Or* 10. 19 *Of þære ie Indus*. See further §§ 1442 and 3880-1.

d. The independent possessive

§ 299. The possessive may be used independently, or (perhaps more accurately) without repetition of its governing noun, as the subject, e.g. *Or* 182. 14 . . . *nu we sindon cumen to þæm godan tidun þe us Romane opwitað, 7 to ðære genihtsumnisse þe hie us ealneg foregielpað þæt ure ne sien ðæm gelican;*[83] as the predicate, e.g. *CP* 139. 1 *Se ðe ne gimð ðara ðe his beoð, 7 huru Godes ðeowa, . . .* and *ÆCHom* ii. 292. 25 *Witodlice se ðe Cristes Gast on him næfð, nis se his*; as the object, e.g. *Bo* 84. 26 . . . *þonne scealt þu nede gelefan þ sum anwald sie mara þonne his, þ þonne his swa gesomnige swa he þone urne deð*; as a partitive genitive, e.g. *Ch* 1527 *and Wlwine habbe þat lond þe he mines hafde* (see further § 1921a); or in a sentence with no verb expressed, e.g. *ÆCHom* i. 222. 19 . . . *he bodade þa blisse þisre freolstide, and ure mærða. Hwæðer cweðe we, ðe ure ðe ðæra engla? We cweðað soðlice, ægðer ge ure ge heora.* Breitkreuz (pp. 14-15) gives further examples.

§ 300. That the inflected forms of the possessive of the first and second person were used independently can be demonstrated, e.g. *Gen* 48. 5 *hi beoþ mine* and *Bo* 84. 27 *swa he þone urne deð* (quoted in full in § 299). That the genitive of the first and second person pronouns was so used is (I suppose) certain, but cannot be demonstrated; in *Deut* 32. 35 *Seo wracu is min, min* is ambiguous since the forms coincide and in the Rushworth version of *John* 16. 15 *alle ðaðe swa hwæt hæfeð ðe fæder min sint* (where the others have *mine* or *mino*), *min* may be genitive singular of *ic*, nominative plural neuter of the possessive, or an uninflected form in the predicate (see § 34).

[83] The variation between *his* and *hig/hy* for *sui* in the different versions of *John* 1. 11 *hig hyne ne underfengon*, Latin *sui eum non receperunt*, may be noted.

§301. The genitive of the personal pronoun is used to form independent combinations with *begen, twegen,* and *self,* e.g. *Sol* 25. 15 *se hlaford is incer beigra wealdend, CP* 45. 11 . . . *gieman urra niehstena sua sua ure selfra, CP* 220. 7 *ðone anwald ure selfra,* and *Beo* 2530 *hwæðer . . . uncer twega.* But inflected forms of the possessive are occasionally found where one would expect the genitive of the personal pronoun, e.g. with *self* (which presents a special problem discussed in §486) *CP* 220. 5 *ðæt we sceoldon urra selfra waldan,* and, with other pronouns, *CP* 63. 1 *Hwæt wenstu nu, gif hwelc forworht monn cymð, 7 bitt urne hwelcne ðæt we hine læden to sumum ricum menn . . . , CP* 211. 13 *Forðæmðe on eowerre towesnesse ge habbað gecyðed ðæt ge ures nanes ne siendon, CP* 379. 13 . . . *ic eom clæne 7 unscildig nu giet to dæg eowres ælces blodes, GD* 243. 5 *gelyfað ge me nu þyses, þæt in næniges eowres muð nu todæge ne cymþ hlaf* (Latin *nullius vestrum ore), BlHom* 151. 29 *Nis þæt soþlice min miht ne næniges ures,* and *ApT* 30. 22 *þonne asænde ic þa gewrita minre dohtor þæt heo sylf geceose hwilcne eowerne heo wille,* where Goolden—rightly, I think, in view of the other examples —keeps the manuscript *eowerne* instead of following Thorpe's emendation to *eower.* But Goolden's observation that '*eowerne* is adjectival' does not go far enough. It should not be; the inflected possessive in these examples is grammatically wrong. An example from the poetry is *Beo* 2659 *urum sceal sweord ond helm, ‖ byrne ond beaduscrud bam gemæne.* I quote more from the prose in *NM* 73 (1972), 229.

§302. Visser (i, §283) observes that the pattern 'It is not mine to give' occurs in all periods but 'today it seems to be restricted to "literary" English'. The pattern has perhaps never been really 'popular'. There is, of course, no surviving 'non-literary' Old English, but all the examples Visser quotes from OE and ME are versions of *Matt* 20. 23 *sedere autem ad dexteram meam vel sinistram, non est meum dare vobis* and *Mark* 10. 40, where the wording is the same except for *ad* after *vel.* To these examples Visser adds *BlHom* 117. 23 *Nis þæt eower . . . þæt ge witan þa þrage 7 þa tide,* Latin *non est vestrum nosse tempora,* where we have a *þæt* clause instead of an infinitive.

*e. The possessive, the demonstrative, and the
'dative of possession'*

§303. With the so-called 'nouns of possession'—'nouns denoting parts of the body, mental faculties, articles of clothing and other personal belongings'[84]—MnE may have a possessive or a definite article when the possessor is the subject of the clause, e.g. 'He's got a nasty wound on his/the head'. The article is preferred when the possessor is not the subject, but is otherwise specified, e.g. 'She hit him a savage blow on the head' and 'She hit him on the head' (where historically speaking 'him' may be accusative or dative; see §308). The possessive is, of course, essential in sentences like 'There was a nasty look in his eye' and 'A grimace of pain passed over his face'. The situation was more complicated in OE, and I number the patterns for ease of reference. But it should be noted that the modern ones—numbers (2) or (3) and (8) or (9) below—are well established in OE.

§304. In OE clauses in which the possessor is the subject, these nouns can occur (1) alone, e.g. ÆCHom i. 508. 18 *Se hrof eac swylce hæfde mislice heahnysse: on sumere stowe hine man mihte mid heafde geræcan, on sumere mid handa earfoðlice*; (2) with a demonstrative, e.g. *Deut* 28. 35 . . . *ðæt ðu næbbe nan ðincg hales fram ðam fotwolmun of ðone hneccan*; and (3) with a possessive, e.g. *ÆCHom* i. 150. 30 *hi beron þeahhwæðere þæt leoht on heora handum*. We find both (1) and (3) in *BlHom* 207. 21 *Eac swylce se hrof wæs on mislicre heanesse; on sumre stowe he wæs þæt man mid his handa nealice geræcean mihte, in sumre eaþelice mid heafde gehrinan*. To patterns (1) and (3), however, there can be added a dative of the personal pronoun—the so-called 'dative of possession' (see §1357) or 'dativus sympatheticus', defined by Ahlgren (pp. 196-7) as 'the dative of a personal pronoun, or less frequently of a noun, denoting the person affected by, or involved in, the action of the verb'. So we find (4) *ÆCHom* ii. 60. 26 *and Abraham hæfde him on handa fyr and swurd* and (6) *ÆCHom* ii. 544. 4 *On eowerum geðylde ge geahniað eow eowere sawla*. There seems no reason why pattern (5) ✶*he hæfde him on þære handa fyr and swurd* should not occur too. But no examples have come to my notice.

§305. We can next distinguish clauses in which the possessor is the object. Here we find the equivalents of patterns (1)-(3) above, viz. (7) with 'noun of possession' alone, e.g. *Beo* 813 *ac hine se modega mæg Hygelaces* ‖ *hæfde be honda* (no examples yet noted in the prose); (8) with demonstrative, e.g. *ÆCHom* i. 496. 10 *ða genam he hi be ðære handa*; and (9) with possessive, e.g. *ÆLS* 18. 335 *and Hieu hine scet bæftan his bæce*. Patterns (8) and (9) occur together

---

[84] This term of Kruisinga's is used by A. Ahlgren, *On the Use of the Definite Article with 'Nouns of Possession' in English* (Uppsala, 1946). I owe some of my examples to Ahlgren.

alongside a clause with no expressed object in *HomU* 26. 141. 4
*stingað stranglic sar on his eagan . . . stingað hine scearplice on þone
muð . . . stingað hine mid sorhlicum sare on his heortan.*

§306. Then there are clauses in which the possessor is neither the
subject nor the object, but is specified by the dative of the personal
pronoun. The patterns vary. Some are acceptable in MnE, others are
not. The 'noun of possession' may be the subject or object, or a genitive, but is most often governed by a preposition. But again the same
three basic patterns can be distinguished, the 'noun of possession'
being found (10) alone, e.g. *Beo* 755 *Hyge wæs him hinfus, ÆLS*
9. 100 *þa cnitton hi rapas . . . hire to handum and fotum*, and
ÆCHom i. 186. 30 *Mid þam ðe he tobræc ða hlafas, þa wæron hi
gemenigfylde, and weoxon him on handum*; (11) with a demonstrative, e.g. *BlHom* 173. 3 *Petrus wæs on rode gefæstnod, 7 him þæt
heafod wæs adune gewended 7 þa fet up, Or* 290. 14 *7 him self leat
forþ þæt him mon aslog þæt heafod of, Mart5* 28. 3 *ond hire man
bestang sweord on þa hracan, Lch* ii. 62. 12 *stinge him gelome on þa
hracan*, and *ÆCHom* i. 86. 13 *Him stod stincende steam of ðam
muðe*; and (12) with a possessive, e.g. *BlHom* 135. 20 *þa wæs him
micel langung 7 sorh on heora heortan, ChronF* 56. 24 (796) *Her on
ðyson gearæ Ceolwulf Myrcna cing ouerhergode Cent 7 gefeng Ead-
berht Præn heora cing 7 gebundene lædde on Myrce 7 let him pytan
ut his eagan 7 ceorfan of his handa*, and *ÆCHom* i. 514. 16 *selre
him wære þæt him wære getiged an ormæte cwyrnstan to his swuran.*
In *Or* 178. 23 *þa forcurfon hie him þa twa ædran on twa healfa þara
eagena* we find two 'nouns of possession' in pattern (11)—one as
object, the other in the genitive. Two different patterns are sometimes found in the same sentence, e.g. *Bede* 40. 9 *ac him ða eagan of
his heafde ascuton* (patterns (11) and (12)) and *Lch* ii. 202. 2
7 þonne þu him þine hand setest on þa lifre . . . (patterns (3) and
(11)). Ahlgren gives more OE examples of some of these patterns at
pp. 12-14 and 196-201, and examples of later survivals of the 'dative
of possession' at pp. 216-21.

§307. The 'dative of possession' is most common with pronouns, as
in the examples given above. But it is found with numerals, e.g.
ÆCHom ii. 246. 21 *Ða abræd Petrus bealdlice his swurd, and gesloh
heora anum þæt swiðre eare of* (pattern (11)), and with nouns, e.g.
Or 64. 34 *ær þara Romana wif mid heora cildum iernende wæron
gemong ðæm gefeohtum 7 heora fæderum wæron to fotum feallende*
(pattern (10)), *Or* 76. 31 *Seo cwen het þa ðæm cyninge þæt heafod of
aceorfan* (pattern (11)), and *ChronA* 56. 10 (797) *Her Romane Leone*

þæm papan his tungon forcurfon 7 his eagan astungon (pattern (12)). This situation can scarcely arise in patterns (1)-(9), where (by definition) the noun or numeral will occur as subject or object if it is expressed.

§308. Visser (i, §351 fn. 1) cites *Or* 168. 4 *þa sticode him mon þa eagan ut* (one variety of pattern (11)) and remarks that between this and ☆*þa sticode man his eagan ut*—a MnE pattern which does, of course, occur in OE, e.g. *Or* 68. 10 *for þæm he hie het gebindan . . . 7 siþþan mid æxsum heora heafda of aceorfan* and *ÆCHom* i. 428. 31 *þa het se wælhreowa mid stanum ðæs halgan muð cnucian*—'there is about the same difference as in Pres. D. English between "she kissed *me* on the cheek" and "she kissed *my* cheek" '. This seems dubious. *Or* 168. 4 is the equivalent of ☆'she kissed me the cheek', whereas 'she kissed me on the cheek' can be paralleled by both *HomU* 26. 141. 6 *stingað hine scearplice on þone muð* (pattern (8)) and by *Lch* ii. 62. 12 *stinge him gelome on þa hracan* (another variety of pattern (11)). So 'me' in 'she kissed me on the cheek' might historically be either accusative or dative—as Visser (i, §706) himself recognizes—and the manuscript *hi* in *BlHom* 47. 12 *forþon him biþ mara broga þonne ænigum men sy, þeah hi mon slea mid sweorde wiþ þæs heafdes* could be replaced by *hine* or *him*.

§309. The most common patterns in the poetry are those without demonstrative or possessive, viz. (1) e.g. *Beo* 495 . . . *se þe on handa bær hroden ealowæge*; (4) e.g. *Beo* 1242 *Setton him to heafdon hilderandas*; (7) e.g. *Beo* 813 *ac hine se modega mæg Hygelaces* ‖ *hæfde be honda*; and (10) e.g. *Beo* 726 *him of eagum stod* ‖ *ligge gelicost leoht unfæger*. As Klaeber (3, p. xciii) remarks: 'That the possessive pronoun is dispensed with in many places where a modern English translation would use it, and that the personal pronoun in the dative may be found instead, need hardly be mentioned.' He gives further examples. But the demonstrative and possessive do occur, e.g. *ChristC* 1362 . . . *to þam yflum . . .* ‖ . . . *þe him bið on þa wynstran hond*, *PPs* 108. 5 *stande him on þa swyþeran hand*, *Dream* 63 *gestodon him æt his lices heafdum*, and *Jud* 98 *genam ða þone hæðenan mannan* ‖ *fæste be feaxe sinum*.

§310. Ahlgren shows that the 'dativus sympatheticus' becomes less frequent and the possessive more common throughout the OE period, though (as one would expect from the MnE fluctuations) the latter never completely supersedes the demonstrative; see further §§338-9. Among the factors called in by Ahlgren to account for this change are the levelling of the dative and accusative (pp. 14 and 201-2); fluctuation in the use of the dative and accusative, either with OE verbs which take both cases, e.g. *belgan* and *fylgan* (pp. 203-6) or under foreign influence (pp. 206-10); and the preference for the possessive in the Latin of the Vulgate and the Fathers, which (he argues) led to the disuse of the dative in direct translations and in works based on Latin sources (pp. 210-16).

6. THE DEMONSTRATIVES

a. General

§311. OE has two demonstratives—*se* and *þes*; for the forms see *OEG*, §§708-11, and T. Heltveit, *Studies in English Demonstrative Pronouns. A Contribution to the History of English Morphology* (Oslo, 1953). *þes* is much less frequent than *se*; thus Shannon (p. 32) counted approximately 280 examples of *se*, and four of *þes*, in the Parker Chronicle from 734 to 891.

§312. *Geon* 'yon' occurs in *CP* 443. 24 *Ða ondwyrde him Dryhten: Aris, 7 gong to geonre byrg*. According to Trnka (p. 161), the fact that it is in non-dependent speech suggests that it was a colloquial usage.

§313. *þes* can contrast with *se* by pointing to something near as opposed to something far, e.g. *ÆHomM* 8. 29. 119 *of þisum sceortan life up to þam ecan* and *ChronA* 38. 11 (682) *on þissum geare*[85] against *ChronA* 1. 1 (–) *þy geare þe wæs agan fram Cristes acennesse cccc wintra 7 xciiii wintra* and *CP* 39. 16 *Hu ne is ðis sio micle Babilon ðe ic self atimbrede to kynestole*, or by identifying something which has already been pointed out by *se*, e.g. *ÆCHom* i. 476. 26 . . . *be ðam mæran Fulluhtere Iohanne . . . se wælhreowa cyning Herodes . . . þes Iohannes . . . þes Herodes.* . . . Further on *þes* see §§340-5.

§314. A full treatment of the OE uses of the demonstratives must be left to the lexicographer. Some of them are obsolete, e.g. the combination of demonstrative and genitive seen in *And* 885 *Ðam bið hæleða well* || *þe þara blissa brucan moton*. Others are still current

---

[85] With this exception, *her* introduces the annals of the Parker Chronicle up to 888. Thereafter the formula varies: 889 *on þissum geare*, 890 *her*, 893 *her on þysum geare*, 894 *on þys geare*, and so on. According to QW (p. 69) *þes* in examples like *ChronA* 38. 11 'points to and singles out a part of a series, the whole of which may already be specific'.

with the elements differently arranged, e.g. *CP* 191. 6 *ða ofer oðre gesettan* 'those set over others'. The use of *ðæt . . . hit* in *CP* 121. 17 *. . . he wolde habban ða ðenunga ðeawas 7 ðeodscipe to læranne; ond ða he ðæt hæfde, ða wolde he hit habban him to agnum anwalde . . .* to refer to sg. *ða ðenunga* is noteworthy; for *hit* referring to masculine or feminine antecedents, see §69. Further similarities and differences between OE and MnE are discussed below.

b. Se

(1) *The problem of stress*

§315. The dem. *se* can be used independently, e.g. *ÆCHom* i. 490. 11 *hundeahtatig geara . . . swa hwæt swa he ofer ðam leofað . . .* , and dependently, e.g. *ÆCHom* i. 492. 1 *se deada cniht*. Sometimes it clearly carries some emphasis, e.g. (independent) *ÆCHom* i. 6. 22 *ac þæra is nu to lyt ðe wile wel tæcan* and *ÆCHom* i. 34. 6 *þæt we us gegadrian to his halgan gelaðunge, and on ðære ures geleafan gafol . . . him agifan*, and (dependent) *ÆCHom* i. 28. 30 *. . . on ðam timan se Romanisca casere Octauianus sette gebann . . .* ('. . . at that time . . .'). But in both uses our inability to determine with any certainty the intonation patterns and degree of stress gives rise to difficulties which would not have troubled native speakers.

(2) *Independent* se

(a) *Its uses*

§316. *Se* is used independently in a second and subsequent sentence to avoid repetition of a preceding noun, e.g. *ChronC* 96. 31 (912) *. . . and þær ða burh getimbrede, 7 þæs ilcan geares þa æt Bricge,* *ChronC* 96. 34 (913–915) *. . . þa burh þær getimbrede . . . þa æt Stæfforda . . . þa æt Eadesbyrig . . . þa æt Wæringwicum . . . þa æt Cyricbyrig . . . þa æt Weardbyrig . . . þa æt Rumcofan, ÆCHom* i. 234. 2 *þam mannum . . . and þam*, and *ÆCHom* i. 234. 26 *ac to ði he heold þa dolhswaðu, þæt he wolde mid þam þa twynigendan getrymman*. In these examples the antecedent is a person or thing. But *se* is also found referring to a preceding or to a following clause, e.g. *ÆCHom* i. 234. 23 *ðaða he wæs gebroht to geleafan mid ðære grapunge, þa wearð seo twynung þurh þæt us ætbroden* and *ÆCHom* i. 112. 4 *þæt is rihtwisnys þæt gehwylcum sy his agen cyre geðafod*; see further §2125.

§317. *Se* may also sum up what has gone before. In this function, which is very common in 'Alfredian' texts, it is frequently tautologic, e.g. *Or* 26. 35 *Ðara iglanda þe man hæt Ciclades þara sindon þreo 7 fiftig* and *Or* 74. 22 *Seo ilce burg Babylonia, seo ðe mæst wæs 7 ærest ealra burga, seo is nu læst 7 westast*, and sometimes to modern readers anacoluthic as well, e.g. *Or* 22. 22 *þa land þe man hæt Gallia Bellica, be eastan þæm is sio ea þe man hæt Rin*. Sentences like this can be easily paralleled—Wülfing (i. 372-4) quotes more—and may give the impression that the writer is not completely in control. This can only be a matter of opinion; see §§3878-81. But, as in MnE, the device can be rhetorically effective in the hands of the conscious stylist, e.g. *ÆCHom* i. 232. 31 *þæra manna synna þe ge forgyfað, þæra beoð forgifene; and ðam ðe ge ofteoð þa forgifenysse, ðam bið oftogen* and *ÆCHom* ii. 564. 2 *Ælc ðæra manna ðe hine forhæfð fram unalyfedlicere gesihðe, fram unalyfedlicere heorcnunge, fram unalyfedlicum swæcce, fram unalyfedlicum stence, fram unalyfedlic-ere hrepunge, se hæfð mædenes naman for ðære anwalhnysse.*

§318. The oblique cases of the neut. dem. *þæt* can be used as ad-verbs and conjunctions, either alone, e.g. *þæs, þy*, or with preposi-tions, e.g. *to þæs* and *forþon*. The particle *þe* may be added to the conjunctions, e.g. *þæs þe* and *forþon þe*. See further §§2418-20, 2422, and 1232-3.

§319. On the use of *se* in relative combinations—*seþe, se'þe, se . . . se, se . . . seþe*, and so on—see §§2109-21 and 2153-79. Its subject-changing function deserves a separate section.

(b) The subject-changing function of se

§320. It seems likely that the demonstrative carried stress in examples like *ÆCHom* i. 240. 15 *Se is hyra and na hyrde, seðe bið begripen on woruldðingum* and that this stressed use lies behind the develop-ment by *se* of a subject-changing function. Thus in *ÆCHom* i. 82. 12 [*Herodes*] *ðohte gif he hi ealle ofsloge, þæt se an ne ætburste þe he sohte, se an* indicates that the subject is no longer Herod, but the Infant Christ. Similarly *se* in *BlHom* 9. 14 *Wel þæt wæs gecweden, forþon þe se hæfde mægen ofer ealle gesceafta þe he toweard[n]e* [cf. *BlHom* 81. 31 and 87. 11] *sægde and bodode* distinguishes the Infant Christ from the herald angel *he*. (*BlHom* 81. 31 and 87. 11 have the expected *toweardne* in similar contexts.) But we also find independent *se* used without a following adjective clause to mark a change of subject, as in *ÆCHom* ii. 488. 14 *Hi habbað mid him awyriendne engel, mancynnes feond, and se hæfð andweald on ðam mannum ðe heora Scyppend forseoð* (where *he* would not be am-biguous) and *ÆCHom* ii. 480. 5 *Hwæt ða Drihten arærde micelne wind, and se gelæhte ealne þone lig, and abær hine to ðæs cyninges botle* (where *he* might have caused momentary ambiguity—compare *hine* referring back to *þone lig*; see further §§255-6). The same idiom is found in the poetry, e.g. *Mald* 149 *Forlet þa drenga sum daroð of handa* || . . . *þæt se to forð gewat.* I give more examples in *RES* 15 (1964), 132-3.

§321. It is no surprise to find the demonstrative in this function, for its use avoids the momentary ambiguity which the personal pronoun has in examples like *BlHom* 15. 12 *Hi þa þa Cristes þegnas þeossa worda nan ongeotan ne mehton; ac hie wæron him bediglede* and *Mald* 285 *þa æt guðe sloh* || *Offa þone sælidan, þæt he on eorðan feoll.* But there are times when it is not easy to see a difference between the demonstrative and the personal pronoun, e.g. *ÆCHom* i. 34. 6 *to his halgan gelaðunge* . . . *on ðære* but *ÆCHom* i. 34. 14 *Bethleem* . . . *on hire, ÆCHom* i. 304. 5 *se man ðe* . . . *he* but *ÆCHom* i. 304. 6 *se ðe* . . . *se,* and sequences like *ÆCHom* i. 540. 21-5 and *ÆCHom* i. 184. 6 *Ealle þa ðe him to cumað . . . þa gesihð se Hælend, and þam he gemiltsað, and hyra mod onliht mid his gife, þæt hi magon him to cuman . . . and ðam he forgifð ðone gastlican fodan, þæt hi ne ateorian be wege.* One can only speculate.

(c) The ambiguous demonstrative/relative

§322. In examples like *ÆCHom* ii. 96. 19 . . . *sumne man on Romebyrig, his nama wæs Seruulus, ðearfa on æhtum, and welig on geearnungum. Se læg bedryda fram cildhade oð his geendunge. He læg singallice* . . . and *ÆCHom* ii. 58. 25 . . . *Abel, Adames sunu, rihtwis and Gode andfenge, þone ofsloh Cain his broðor . . .,* se and *þone* can be taken as demonstrative or relative. On this ambiguity see §§327 and 2109-21.

(d) þæt is . . . , þæt sind . . . , þa sind . . .

§323. The demonstrative also appears in the OE equivalent of the MnE parenthetic and explanatory 'that is'. But the OE idiom takes different forms. *þæt is/þæt wæs* is used with a singular noun complement irrespective of its gender, e.g. *Bede* 52. 4 . . . *Wihtsætan; þæt is seo ðeod þe Wiht þæt ealond oneardað* and *ÆCHom* i. 8. 24 *An angin is ealra þinga, þæt is God Ælmihtig,* and with a complement consisting of two or more singular nouns joined by *and,* e.g. *ÆCHom* i. 498. 33 *he is heora begra Gast, þæt is heora begra Lufu and Willa* and *ÆCHom* i. 288. 18 *heo hæfð on hire ðreo ðing, þæt is gemynd, and andgit, and willa.*

§324. With a plural complement we find either *þæt sind (wæron),* e.g. *ÆCHom* i. 142. 33 *Crist, seðe com to gehælenne ura wunda, þæt sindon ure synna, ÆCHom* i. 244. 11 *Ðas dagas synd gehatene Letaniae, þæt sint, Gebeddagas* and *ÆCHom* i. 450. 1 . . . *swylce lac swa he sylf breac, þæt wæron ðry berene hlafas*—compare French *ce sont*—or *þa sind*, e.g. *ÆCHom* i. 276. 1 *Englas he worhte, þa sind gastas*, where, however, *þa* may be a relative (see §327); contrast *ÆCHom* i. 132. 5 *Ða sind Godes bearn gecigede, þe hine lufiað swiðor þonne þisne middangeard*, where *ða* is the antecedent of *þe*.

§325. With a noun complement, then, the number of the verb is governed by the number of the complement, not by *þæt*. With numerals, the verb may be singular, e.g. *Or* 38. 25 *swa fela manna . . . swa mid Moyse wæron: þæt wæs syx hund þusenda manna*, or plural, e.g. *Or* 128. 22 *þæt wæron fieftiene hund þusend monna*; see §563.

§326. Other complements may follow *þæt is*, e.g. a prepositional phrase in *Or* 18. 8 . . . *on þæm æhtum þe heora speda on beoð, þæt is, on wildrum*; a participial phrase in *ÆCHom* i. 32. 20 *and he wæs forði Augustus geciged, þæt is geycende his rice*; a clause in *ÆCHom* i. 188. 26 . . . *þæt is, þæt he sceal ða flæsclican lustas gewyldan*; and a sentence in *CP* 279. 16 *Ac se se ðe ðone wer bricð, 7 ðæt wæter utforlæt, se bið fruma ðæs geflites. Ðæt is ðonne se ðe his tungan ne gemidlað, se towierpð anmodnesse.* Wülfing (i. 374–8) and Jost (1909, pp. 51–2) give examples of all the patterns mentioned.

§327. The problem of the ambiguous demonstrative/relative arises here too, e.g. in *ÆCHom* i. 276. 1 (§324) and *ÆCHom* i. 40. 10 *þæt word, þæt is se wisdom, is acenned of ðam Ælmihtigum Fæder.* But examples like *ÆCHom* i. 26. 5 *Siþþan he geceas twa and hund-seofontig, þa sind genemnede discipuli, þæt sind leorningcnihtas* and *ÆCHom* i. 324. 16 *An God is gecyndelice on ðrim hadum, Fæder, and his Sunu, þæt is his Wisdom, and se Halga Gast, seðe is heora begra Lufu and Willa* suggest that *þa sind* is probably relative, while the *þæt is/þæt sind* formulae are demonstrative. So do the nominatives *deofol* and *seo cyrce* in *ÆCHom* ii. 226. 27 *geeuenlæcende heora fæder, þæt is deofol* and *ÆCHom* ii. 592. 21 *þæt he Godes bryde, þæt is seo cyrce, wið feo sylle.* In these *þæt is* clearly removes the noun from the sentence, putting it (as it were) in inverted commas.

(3) *Dependent use*

(a) The 'definite article'

§328. Here modern scholars have created for themselves the unreal problem of the OE 'definite article'. Some of the early writers such as Flamme (p. 25) were content to remark that the dem. *se* was used as the 'definite article'. Hüllweck (p. 1) distinguished the demonstrative 'in fast ungeschwächter Kraft' from the 'definite article', and Philipsen (pp. 6, 10, and 14) speaks of the article 'mit starker Demonstration', 'mit schwächerer Demonstration', and 'ohne demonstrative Kraft'.[86] Others, like Wülfing (i. 277-87 and 371-2), were more aware of the difficulty of distinguishing the 'definite article' from other uses of dependent *se* and grouped all examples except a few which obviously carry stress under the title 'der bestimmte Artikel'. But, as Quirk and Wrenn (QW, p. 70) rightly point out,

the existence of a 'definite article' in OE is a vexed question, but it seems to be one which has been raised largely by our desire to impose upon OE a terminology familiar in and suitable for Mod.E.: where today we have three contrastive and formally distinct defining words, *the*, *that*, *this*, each with a name, in OE there were but two, *se* and *þes*, and we are left as it were with a name to spare. The problem partly disappears when we reflect that in many instances of their use today, *the* and *that* are interchangeable ('Do you remember the/that man I was speaking to last night?'); in OE *se* (*þæt*, *seo*) embraced practically the whole range of functions performed today, jointly or separately, by *the* and *that*.

There are also contexts in which *se* is used where we would either omit it or translate it 'this' rather than 'that', e.g. *ChronA* 46. 27 (755) *7 se Cyneheard wæs þæs Sigebryhtes broþur* (see QW, p. 71), *ÆCHom* i. 14. 15 *Adam . . . And God þa geswefode þone Adam . . . Adam*, and *ÆCHom* i. 134. 30 *Symeon . . . Se Halga Gast wæs wunigende on ðæm Symeone . . . ðes man*.

§329. The problem is further complicated by the fact that, while we must concede that dependent *se* sometimes carried stress, we have no certain means of deciding when it does in any but the most obvious examples. Thus sentences such as *ChronA* 90. 13 (897) *ealra swiþust mid ðæm æscum þe hie fela geara ær getimbredon* have sometimes been taken as exemplifying the stressed dependent dem. 'with thóse ships which . . .'; see Ropers, pp. 35-6 and Conradi, pp. 54-5. But we could just as easily take *þa* as unstressed 'with the shíps which . . .', as Christophersen (p. 92) does in the analysis of part of the annal for 897 in which he attempts to support his claim that 'I can think of no better way of briefly illustrating the fact that the language of that time possessed a real definite article than by simply quoting a piece of prose sufficient in length to prevent the use of the article being merely accidental.' Such quoting, of course, proves nothing; most of the dependent demonstratives in the passage can be

[86] 'with its demonstrative force almost undiminished' . . . 'with strong demonstrative force', 'with lesser demonstrative force', 'without demonstrative force'.

taken in at least two ways, e.g. *ChronA* 90. 11 (897) *þy ilcan geare* 'in the same year/in that same year' and *ChronA* 90. 14 (897) *þa het Ælfred cyng timbran lang scipu ongen ða æscas*, where (depending on the degree of contrast present in the words *scipu* and *æscas*) *ða* could mean 'the/those/these'. Even in sentences where MnE requires 'that/those', e.g. *Or* 42. 22 *on þæm dagum* 'in those days' and *ÆCHom* i. 28. 30 *on ðam timan* 'at that time', we cannot be sure what degree of stress the demonstrative carried. The point need not be laboured, for it is clear that there is little to be gained by pursuing this terminological will-o'-the-wisp.[87] We must be content with a brief catalogue of the contexts in which dependent *se* is found.

(b) The uses of dependent se

§330. By definition dependent *se* is accompanied by a noun or noun equivalent. It shows the same variety of uses as MnE 'the/that'. Thus it may point forward, e.g. *CP* 41. 17 *hie habbað ða arodnesse 7 ða bieldo ðæt hie magon anweald habban*, or back, e.g. *CP* 163. 22 *Genim ðe ane iserne hierstepannan . . . Đurh ða pannan is getacnod se wielm ðæs modes*. It may refer to something which has already been indirectly introduced, e.g. *Or* 40. 31 *Perseus se cyningc . . . in Asiam mid fyrde for, 7 on ða ðeode winnende wæs*, or to something for which the reader must rely on outside knowledge, e.g. *CP* 29. 8 *se sealmscop cuæð. . . .* For further examples see Hüllweck, pp. 1–14.

§331. The simple pattern *se* + noun may be augmented by the addition of an adjective and/or a possessive; on the various combinations see §§103–12. With cardinal numerals *se* is present or absent as the sense demands; cf. *Or* 1. 7 *þa twa byrig . . . Sodome 7 Gomorre* with *Or* 8. 5 *twegen dælas* and *Or* 10. 27 *twa micla ea*. The usage with ordinal numerals fluctuates; see §567.

§332. On the possible influence of the presence or absence of a demonstrative on the form of a following relative pronoun, see §§2253–5.

(c) Presence or absence of se with nouns

§333. The writers of the German dissertations on prose and verse

---

[87] Cf. Wülfing, i. 371–2, and Shannon, p. 32 fn. 5. Christophersen (pp. 84–7) attempts to account for the rise of the definite article.

I agree with Purdy (*York Papers in Linguistics*, 2 (1972), 121–4) that OE did not have a definite article. His suggestion that OE 'nevertheless had a semantic/grammatical void which was very susceptible to being filled by a definite article' is no doubt supported by the fact that English did develop the definite article. But it gets no support from Purdy's article, which in my opinion contains misstatements about both OE and MnE usage.

texts devoted much space to listing the occurrence or non-occurrence of the demonstrative with nouns of different classes. We may take Schrader as typical—he deals in turn with 'der Artikel bei Gattungs-namen', 'Eigennamen', 'Stoffnamen', 'Collectiven', and 'Abstracten', and then goes on to deal with other nouns under such headings as 'Namen von göttlichen Wesen', 'die Himmelsgegenden', 'die Namen der Feste', and 'Zeitbestimmungen' (pp. 3-10).[88] Wülfing arranges things slightly differently but the results are the same.[89] No consistent rules can be deduced; even God appears as *se God* in *ÆCHom* i. 276. 23. What Closs (p. 91) says of Wülfing is generally applicable: 'in the final analysis the distinctions are very small and only of a statistical nature. Only a few individual examples seem to be distinctive, e.g. *hel* "hell", *middaneard* "earth", *weorold* "world", *eorþe* "earth", *heofon* "heaven", etc. all of which are rarely preceded by *Da* [for the uninitiated this means *se*].' Thus the most that can be said is that some OE nouns are more often found with the dem. *se* than other OE nouns.

§334. Hence there are numerous inconsistencies. Some can be explained by comparison with MnE, e.g. *ÆCHom* i. 350. 12 *Behreowsi-gendum mannum he miltsað, ac he ne behet þam elcigendum gewiss lif oð merigen* 'to repentant men . . . to the procrastinating'. But not all; consider, for instance, *ÆCHom* i. 132. 24 *ða forsworenan mid forsworenum*, *ÆCHom* i. 16. 11 *man . . . mannan . . . þone man . . . se man*, where MnE would have 'man' or 'mankind' in all places, and *ÆCHom* i. 214. 32 *se dead . . . oð dead*. Most interesting of these is perhaps the fluctuating use with *deofol* 'The Devil' seen in Ælfric, e.g. *ÆCHom* i. 172. 21 *he deofle gecwemð* but *ÆCHom* i. 172. 32 *he cwæð to ðam deofle*.[90] This must cast doubt on what seems to be a generally accepted view, that 'in contrast to Ælfric Wulfstan uses . . . *deofol* without an article' (Bethurum, p. 54). Even if this were true, it is a test of dubious value; it is not hard to see how a 'Wulfstan imitator' could imitate it.

§335. So there is no regular correspondence between OE and MnE usage. *Se* is found where we would not use 'the/that', e.g. *ÆCHom*

[88] 'the article with common nouns', 'proper nouns', 'names of materials', 'collective nouns', 'abstract nouns', . . . 'names of deities', 'the points of the compass', 'the names of feasts', 'divisions of time'.

[89] Wülfing, i. 278-85 and 286-7. See further Flamme, pp. 25-7, Hüllweck, pp. 18-31, Mohrbutter, pp. 2-5, Philipsen, pp. 17-32 and 38-44, and (for the poetry) 'the eighteen German dissertations', *passim*. Christophersen attempts a summary—see pp. 94-5, 136, 147, 170, 173, 177-8, and 190.

[90] For further examples of fluctuation in addition to those quoted by Schrader, p. 9, see *ÆCHom* i. 172. 18, 20, and 33, 192. 10 ff., 268. 11, and *ÆCHom* ii. 226. 27.

i. 312. 3 *se Pharao*, where Pharaoh has not yet been mentioned in the Homily, *ÆCHom* i. 254. 18 *Se man hæfð gold, þæt is god be his mæðe . . . Ac ne bið se man god þurh ðas ðing* 'a man . . . the/that man', and *ÆCHom* i. 394. 13 *seo gitsung ðæra æhta* 'desire for possessions'. It can be absent where we would use 'the/that', e.g. *ÆCHom* i. 262. 1 *God Fæder* and *ÆCHom* i. 554. 24 *geleaffullum gedafenað . . .* 'to the faithful'.

§336. The early poetry tends to do without dependent *se* more often than the prose and later poetry—this is reflected in the editorial omission of manuscript *þara* in *Beo* 9—and so has more examples of the combination weak form of adjective + noun; see §§114-17. This absence of *se* may be due in part to archaism or archaizing tendencies—the difference in usage between the conservative *Brunanburh* (seven demonstratives in seventy-three lines) against *Maldon* (where Lichtenheld records eighty-five in 325 lines) is instructive. But examples like

Beo 1151   Ða wæs heal roden
              feonda feorum,   swilce Fin slægen,
              cyning on corþre,   ond seo cwen numen

suggest that metrical convenience was also an important factor. See further Klaeber (3, p. xcii), Christophersen, pp. 86-7, and §2287.

(d) *Repetition of* se

§337. The demonstrative is usually repeated with the second of two nouns joined by *and*, whether they express the same idea or not, e.g. *CP* 15. 11 *ða ofermodan 7 ða upahafenan on hira mode* and *CP* 183. 9 *se welega 7 se wædla*. But it need not be. Thus we find, not only *CP* 171. 20 *from ðære geornfulnesse ðære rædinge 7 leornunge haligra gewrita* and *Bede* 120. 19 *þone geleafan 7 bigong hire æfestnisse* (where the two nouns have the same gender), but also *CP* 39. 14 . . . *he fægnode ðæs miclan weorces 7 fægernesse ðærre ceastre* and *Bede(T, O)* 140. 9 *mid þone cyning 7 cwene* (where the nouns are of different gender). But the possibility of scribal omission certainly arises in *Bede* 140. 9 (where the form *cwene* may be accusative or dative; MS *Ca* has *ðære* before *cwene* and MS *B* reads *ðam kyninge 7 þære cwene*). If the first of a series of adjectives joined by *and* and qualifying the same noun is accompanied by the demonstrative, this is repeated with the rest of the series, e.g. *ÆCHom* ii. 598. 10 *Ic andette ða anan halgan and ða geleaffullan and ða apostolican gelaðunge* and *ÆCHom* i. 190. 9 *ge ðære ealdan æ ge ðære niwan*; cf. (without *and*) *ÆCHom* i. 252. 34 *se goda Heofonlica Fæder*.

(e) The demonstrative or the possessive

§338. The demonstrative is often found in OE where MnE would require the possessive, e.g. *ÆCHom* i. 290. 7 *hu ælc sunu bið gingra þonne se fæder on ðisum life* and *ÆCHom* ii. 474. 2 *And to swa hwilcere leode swa we cumað, we cunnon ðære gereord.* When so used, the demonstrative is often accompanied by a dative of possession, e.g. *ÆCHom* ii. 246. 22 *Petrus . . . gesloh heora anum þæt swiðre eare of* and *ÆLS* 32. 124 *. . . þa hæþenan . . . mid anum swencge slogon him of þæt heafod.* On this, see §§303-10.

§339. Ahlgren (pp. 2-6) makes a distinction between what may be called the 'individualizing' article, e.g. 'She hit him in the face' and *Bede* 178. 19 7 *his heafod on eorðan hylde; 7 þa faam of þæm muðe eode,* and the 'generalizing' article, e.g. 'On the throat they have a small pouch of naked skin' and *Lch* ii. 232. 12 *þa wambseocan men þrowiað on þam bæcþearme 7 on þam niþerran hrife.* The real point is that in the second MnE example the OE idiom seen in the second OE example and discussed in §338 is retained.

c. þes

§340. Like its MnE descendant, *þes* refers to a person or thing present, near, or just mentioned, e.g. *ÆCHom* i. 290. 25 *Oðer gedwolman . . . He cwæð . . . þes gedwola* and *ÆCHom* ii. 274. 14 *þis is min lichama and min blod.* So it is often used in contrast with *se*; see §313. Like *se*, *þes* can be used dependently or independently, e.g. the two sentences already quoted and *ÆCHom* i. 380. 6 *Ðu goda cyning, ne understenst ðu ðisra twegra manna gereonunge ongean me . . . ðas ðweorigað wið me.*

§341. The problem of stress arises here, as it did with *se* (§315), but is less serious because independent *þes* is not used as a relative pronoun and because dependent *þes* seems to have a narrower range of stress than *se*. The question of the 'definite article', of course, does not arise.

§342. In the neuter, *þes* can refer to clauses or sentences, e.g. *ÆCHom* i. 2. 26 *For þisum antimbre ic gedyrstlæhte . . . , ÆCHom* i. 134. 23 *þis wæs geset be wifum,* and *ÆCHom* i. 58. 14 *þis is þæt forme tacn. . . .* As with the *þæt is* formula, a plural complement requires a plural verb, e.g. *Or* 100. 13 *þiss wæron ealle Creca leode* and *CP* 453. 8 *Ðis sint nu ða lara . . . ;* cf. *ÆCHom* ii. 274. 14 *þis is min lichama and min blod.* Carlton regards *þis* in examples like these as 'a type of expletive which causes the subject to follow the verb' (1970, p. 31) and so classifies their element order as VS (1970, p. 37). I can see no reason against taking them as SVC patterns.

§343. *þes* is found as antecedent to a relative pronoun, e.g. *BlHom* 85. 14 *hwæt is þes þe þus unforht gæþ . . . ?*

§344. As in MnE, there are certain contexts in which there is no one 'right' use. Thus *se* and *þes* seem equally possible in *ÆCHom* ii. 58. 1 *þa six wæterfatu* and *ÆCHom* ii. 218. 23 *þas eahta heafodleahtras*; in *Bo* 80. 33 *Ælc þara gesceafta þe we gefyrn ær ymbe spræcon* and *ÆCHom* i. 148. 10 *ðeos Anna þe we gefyrn ær embe spræcon*; and (in the independent use) in *ÆCHom* i. 342. 9 *Sind ðeahhwæðere forwel mænige rihtwise . . . þam ne mæg nan dædbeta beon geefenlæht, forðan ðe hi sind rihtwise and behreowsigende. Be ðam is to smeagenne hu micclum se rihtwisa mid eadmodre heofunge God gegladige, ÆCHom* i. 346. 17 *Sume Godes ðeowan sind onælede . . . Hu magon ðas beon gecigede buton seraphim . . . ?,* and *ÆCHom* i. 344. 18 *Menige geleaffulle men . . . þas beoð geendebyrde to englum.* For further examples see Wülfing, i. 383-4, and (from the poetry) Wack, *Ang.* 15 (1892), 219. Like *se*, *þes* sometimes seems interchangeable with the personal pronoun, e.g. *ÆCHom* i. 396. 19 *hi . . . him* but *ÆCHom* i. 396. 26 *ðas . . . þisum.*

§345. The use of *þes* in reference to something possibly not otherwise referred to produces ambiguity for the modern reader in *ChronA* 78. 30 (885) *þy ilcan geare feng Carl to þam west rice, 7 to allum þam west rice behienan Wendelsæ, 7 begeondan þisse sæ,* where *þisse* may refer back to *Wendelsæ* 'the Mediterranean' or may refer to the English Channel; see the notes on this passage in the various editions.

7. THE INTERROGATIVES

a. General

§346. These include *hwa, hwæt,* and *hulic* (which are used independently, either alone or with a partitive genitive) and *hwæþer* and *hwelc* (which are used both independently and dependently). They are found (in the appropriate case) in both non-dependent and dependent questions, e.g. *ÆGram* 113. 15 *quis hoc fecit?, hwa dyde ðis?, ÆGram* 113. 16 *nescio, quis hoc fecit, nat ic, hwa ðis dyde, BlHom* 59. 33 *Hwylc man is þæt mæge ariman ealle þa sar . . . ?,* and

BlHom 175. 31 *me þynceþ wundor mid hwylcere yldo þu sceole be-foran cininge gylpan.* The usage in the poetry is similar; for examples see GK, svv., and 'the eighteen German dissertations'. Karlberg deals with the uses and development of 'who', 'what', and 'which', in all periods of English; for his general conclusions, see his pp. 289–93. For declension and forms, see *OEG*, §§716–17. On *hulic* see Wülfing, i, §319, BT(S), s.v., and Karlberg, pp. 171–5. On *loc(a) hwa, loc(a) hwæt, loc hwæþer, loc hwelc,* see §2383.

§347. Wülfing (i, §§317–18) quotes an apparently interrogative use of *gehwylc* in *Bede(Ca)* 4. 7 *Swyðe fela hi me sædon fram gehwyl-cum biscopum, 7 hwylcum cyninga tidum Eastseaxe 7 Westseaxe 7 Eastengle 7 Norðanhumbre þære gife onfengon Cristes geleafan* (MS B has *gehwylcum* in both places) and of *æghwylc* in *Bo* 74. 2 *7 hi witon eac on hwelcum wæterum 7 on æghwelcra ea muþum hi sculon secan fiscas.* Karlberg (p. 155) glosses *hu* in examples like *Phoen* 355 *God ana wat* ‖ *. . . hu his gecynde bið* as 'what . . . like', which implies the translation 'God alone knows . . . what his nature is like.' Rissanen notes that 'one' is not found with an interrogative until eME (pp. 238 and 251–2).

b. Hwa, hwæt

§348. These are used independently only, in non-dependent and dependent questions, both alone, e.g. *ÆGram* 113. 15 (§346), *CP* 443. 22 *Hwæt eart ðu, Drihten?*, *ÆCHom* i. 278. 15 *Hwæt is se Fæder?*—in sentences like these the interrogative 'from a logical point of view, . . . can be either subject or predicative' (Karlberg, pp. 86 ff.)—*Coll* 53 *Hunta ic eom. Hwæs?*, and *ÆGram* 113. 16 (§346), and with a partitive genitive, e.g. *Bo* 125. 31 *Hwa unlæredra ne wundrað þæs roderes færeldes . . . ?*, *Met* 28. 5 *Hwa is moncynnes* ‖ *þæt ne wundrie ymb þas wlitegan tungl. . . ?*, *ÆLS* 10. 191 *Hwæt eom ic manna þæt ic mihte god forbeodan?*, *ÆCHom* ii. 242. 14 *Hwæt ða se deofol . . . openlice befran, hwæt hi him feos geuðon,* and *ÆCHom* ii. 502. 26 *Ða befran se sceaða . . . hwæt he manna wære. . . .*[91] As the examples show, the genitive may follow immediately, or be separated from, *hwa* or *hwæt.* The combination *hwæt . . . æfre* appears, e.g. *LS* 34. 532 *La hwæt þis æfre beon scyle þæt ic her wundres gehyre . . . ?* and *ÆLS* 34. 516 *hwæt þis æfre beon sceole*

---

[91] Karlberg (pp. 205–6) quotes some examples from the glosses in which *hwæt* comes close to being used dependently and discusses the rise of attributive 'what' and the restriction of 'which' (pp. 197–284). In view of the examples he cites at p. 82, he is guilty only of lax expression when he writes (p. 175): 'OE *hwæt* is only found connected with a genitive.' He gives further examples of *hwæt* in its various uses at pp. 175–96.

færlices þæt ic her geseo swa wunderlices . . . ? On *hwæt* clauses which shade into dependent exclamation, see §2063.

§349. Flamme (p. 31) attempts to import into OE the modern distinction of 'who' for persons and 'what' for things or with reference to nature, character, and function. But this does not seem to hold even for all his own examples; *hwæt* in *BlHom* 43. 32 *Hwæt is þes ealda man . . . Hit is an biscop se dyde mare yfel þonne god* is better translated 'who' than 'what' or 'what kind of'. In his *Beowulf* glossary (s.v. *hwa*) Klaeber distinguishes between *hwæt* 'who' in *Beo* 232 *hine fyrwyt bræc* ‖ *modgehygdum, hwæt þa men wæron*—where *hwæt* is used alone—and *hwæt* 'what sort of' in *Beo* 237 *Hwæt syndon ge searohæbbendra . . . ?*—where it is accompanied by a partitive genitive. Only a native informant could pronounce on this; Wrenn follows Klaeber and translates 'who' and 'what kind of armed men' respectively, but Donaldson has 'what' and 'what are you, bearers of armor'. Again, Schrader's equation (pp. 48-9) of *hwæt* (both with and without a genitive plural) with *qualis* does not demand acceptance. One of his examples is *ÆCHom* ii. 502. 26 *Ða befran se sceaða . . . hwæt he manna wære . . . Martinus him to cwæð, þæt he cristen wære*, where Thorpe plausibly translates 'who he was', despite the obvious attraction of 'what sort of man he was'.

§350. *OED* (s.v. *what* A. 2) rightly avoids such rigidity, remarking that *hwæt* was used 'formerly generally, in reference to name or identity, and thus equivalent to "who" '. So we find *Ps(P)* 23. 10 *Hwæt is se gewuldroda kyning?, Quis est iste rex gloriae?, Bo* 36. 21 *7 he hine het secgan hwæt his geferan wæron ðe mid him ymbe sieredon . . .* , and *ÆCHom* i. 386. 10 *Hwæt eart ðu, leof Hlaford? . . . Ic eom se Hælend þe ðu ehst.* Sweet (*NEG*, §2119) points out that 'in Old-English the neuter *hwæt* is always used (conjunctively as well as relatively) instead of *hwa* when there is an accompanying pronoun to show that persons are meant: *hwæt sind ge?* "who are ye?"/*he nyste hwæt hie wæron* "he did not know who they were", that is, "he did not know what their nationality was".' Such examples stand in contrast to others like *Or* 42. 6 *Hwa is þæt þe eall ða yfel . . . asecgean mæge . . . ?* But *hwa* meaning 'who' is not restricted to such contexts. So we find e.g. *Ps(P)* 34. 11 *Eala Drihten, hwa is ðin gelica?, Domine, quis similis tibi?, Bo* 60. 7 *Hwær is þonne seo gemetgung, oððe hwa hæfð hi?*, and *ÆCHom* ii. 318. 1 *Hwa is ure nexta?*

§351. This overlap of *hwa* and *hwæt* inevitably means that ambiguity will arise. We can perhaps see the modern distinction in examples like

ÆCHom i. 254. 5 *Ac hwa is ure Fæder? Se Ælmihtiga God* (identity) and in *ÆCHom* i. 278. 15 *Hwæt is se Fæder? Ælmihtig Scyppend, na geworht ne acenned* . . . and *ÆCHom* i. 278. 17 *Hwæt is se Sunu? He is ðæs Fæder Wisdom, and his Word* (where the nature of the Father and the Son may be in question; cf., however, *ÆCHom* i. 254. 7 *And hwilc is se Fæder?* . . . *Se ðe æfre is god, he brincð us yfele to godum mannum*). But does *hwæt* mean 'who' or 'of what sort' in *ÆCHom* ii. 390. 22 *Hwæt sind ða strangan, hwæt ða unstrangan? Đa beoð strange and trume, ðe þurh geleafan and godum geearnungum wel ðeonde beoð. Đa sind unstrange þe slawe beoð to godum weorcum?* Does it mean 'who' or 'what' in *ÆCHom* i. 168. 10 *þam deofle wæs micel twynung, hwæt Crist wære* . . . *þa smeade se deofol hwæt he wære; hwæðer he wære Godes sunu, seðe manncynne behaten wæs* and *ÆCHom* i. 14. 4 *Gyse hu mihte Adam tocnawan hwæt he wære, buton he wære gehyrsum on sumum þince his Hlaforde?*

§352. The verb after *hwa* or *hwæt* (which have no number—or no plural) is regularly plural when it refers to a plural subject or predicate, e.g. *Or* 232. 17 *þeh ic hit nu scortlice secgan scyle* . . . *hwa þæs ordfruman wæron, ÆHomM* 8. 179 *La, hwa is min modor oððe hwa synd mine gebroðru, ÆCHom* ii. 390. 22 *Hwæt sind ða strangan, hwæt ða unstrangan?* and *ÆCHom* ii. 352. 16 *Hwæt þa min latteow* . . . *me befran hwæðer ic wiste, hwæt ða þing wæron.* . . . For further examples see *ÆCHom* i. 252. 23, 256. 1, 346. 11, and 412. 23.

§353. On oblique cases of *hwæt* used as interrogatives, e.g. *hu, to hwæs, hwi, for hwi, for hwan,* and so on, see §§1148-9, 1661, and 2062.

§354. The sequence *hwæt* . . . *hwæt* occurs in examples like *CP* 329. 13 *Hwæt wene ge hwæt sio ðurhtogene unryhtwisnes geearnige* . . . *?,* Latin (Migne, 77. 86A) *Perpendant quid mereatur injustitia illata*—the EETS translation reads 'What do ye think that unrighteousness carried out deserves?'—(where the element order after the second *hwæt* seems to rule out the possibility that we have two non-dependent questions), and *Bede* 462. 21 *oð ðæt ic wite hwæt God wylle, hwæt be me gewurðe,* Latin *donec sciam quid de me fieri uelit Deus*; Miller's rendering is 'till I know what it is God's will to do with me'. A variant with *hwæt* . . . *þæt* occurs, e.g. *GD(H)* 321. 9 *hwæt is þæt la, ic þe acsige, hwæt in ðam fægrum stowum wæs gesewen, þæt sumes mannes hus wæs getimbrod mid gyldenum stafum* . . . *?,* Latin (Migne, 77. 385D) *Quid est hoc, quæso te, quod* *in amœnis locis cujusdam domus laterculis aureis ædificari vide-batur?* (where MS *C* has *hwæt . . . þæt . . . hwæt*, MS *O hwæt . . . þæt . . . þæt*), and *ÆCHom* i. 152. 21 *Hwæt wylt ðu þæt ic þe do?* Karlberg (pp. 294–7), who describes these as 'concatenations', quotes examples of other sequences, e.g. *GD* 209. 1 *hwæt cweðað we, hwylces mægnes 7 hwylcre geearnunge þæt wære . . . ?*, Latin (Migne, 77. 253D) *quid virtutis, quid fuisse meriti dicimus*, and *Or* 50. 1 *Hu wene ge hwelce sibbe þa weras hæfden . . . ?* (no Latin equivalent); here again the element order is against the notion that we have two non-dependent questions.

c. Hwæþer

§355. *Hwæþer*—often glossed as 'which of two', but note *Or* 134. 23 below—is used dependently, e.g. *Or* 100. 8 . . . *bið gecyþed hwæðer healf hæfð þonne sige*, and independently, e.g. (alone) *Or* 17. 13 *þa beag þæt land þær eastryhte, oþþe seo sæ in on ðæt lond, he nysse hwæðer*; (with partitive genitive) *Or* 156. 1 *þa he hie ascade his godas hwæþer heora sceolde on oþrum sige habban, þe he on Romanum, þe Romane on him*; and (with three possibilities spelt out) *Or* 134. 23 *Nyte we nu hwæðer sie swiþor to wundrianne, þe þæt, hu he ana . . . hiene awerede, þe eft . . . hu he þurh þæt folc geþrang . . . , þe eft þara þegna angin þa hie untweogendlice wendon þæt heora hlaford wære on heora feonda gewealde. . . .*

d. Hwelc

§356. *Hwelc* is used both independently and dependently. Basically it implies 'what sort of', e.g. *ÆGram* 116. 11 *qualis est rex?, hwylc ys se cyning?*, *ÆGram* 116. 13 *nescio, qualis est rex, nat ic, hwylc se cyning is*, *ÆCHom* i. 254. 6 *And hwilcera manna Fæder is he?*, *ÆCHom* i. 324. 26 *Ælces mannes weorc cyðað hwilc gast hine wissað*, and, with correlative *swilc*, *Or* 48. 4 *Hit is scondlic . . . ymb swelc to sprecanne hwelc hit þa wæs. . . .* But it also appears in an 'identifying' rather than a 'selective' sense[92]—'which', sometimes al-most 'who'—e.g. *PPs* 76. 11 *hwylc is mihtig god butan ure se mæra god?*, Latin *quis Deus magnus sicut Deus noster?*, *BlHom* 169. 8 *Ge næddrena cynn, hwylc æteowde eow to fleonne . . . ?*, *ÆCHom* i. 338. 14 *Hwilc eower hæfð hundteontig sceapa . . . ?*, *BlHom* 147. 18 *Hwylc is of us Drihten þæt hæbbe swa hwite saule swa þeos halige*

---

[92] The terms are those used by Karlberg. He comments in some detail on the differences between *hwa* and *hwelc* (pp. 7–9 and 70–82) and between *hwæt* and *hwelc* (pp. 7–9 and 82–6).

Marie?, *ÆCHom* i. 288. 15 *On hwilcum dæle hæfð se man Godes anlicnysse on him?*, and *ÆCHom* i. 128. 11 *He ða befran on hwilcere tide he gewyrpte.*

§357. *Hwelc* is also used in what are (almost) exclamations, e.g. *Bo* 35. 32 *hu wunderlic wolde eow ðæt þincan; hwelce cehhettunge ge woldan þæs habban, 7 mid hwelce hleahtre ge woldon bion astered*; see further §1671.

§358. As in MnE, the noun need not be repeated with *hwelc*, e.g. *GD* 223. 12 *gif ic of ðisum ceorle ut ga, in hwylcne gange ic eft?* and *Coll* 51 *Ænne cræft ic cann. Hwylcne?* Further on the dependent ('attributive') use of *hwelc*, see Karlberg, pp. 158-70.

e. Hwa, hwæt, *and* hwelc, *as relatives?*

§359. That the distinction between interrogative and relative was still a real one in OE is clear from a comparison of

El 859   Ne meahte hire Iudas,   ne ful gere wiste
             sweotole gecyþan   be ðam sigebeame,
             on hwylcne se hælend   ahafen wære,

where *hwylcne* is an interrogative introducing a noun clause object of *gecyþan*, with

El 443   ...ond geflitu ræran
             be ðam sigebeame   on þam soðcyning
             ahangen wæs,

where we have the relative construction; the difference in the mood of the verbs is instructive. It is also clear that the use of interrogatives as relatives is merely a matter of time. But I agree with *OED* (s.vv.) and with Karlberg that unambiguous examples of this use of *hwa*, *hwæt*, and *hwelc*, do not occur until eME. On other interrogatives see the Index of Words and Phrases, and Mitchell 1965*c*, pp. 157-60.

§360. A suggested exception is *eall hwæt*. Karlberg (p. 68) writes:

As appears from this critical survey there are no instances of the *wh*- pronouns as clearly relative earlier than the 12th century, with one exception: *eall hwæt*. . . . On the other hand there are certainly quite a few cases which are suggestive of a relative interpretation, and it is seen that conditions existed for the cognitive pronouns to become relative, not only independent but also dependent relative pronouns.

Some examples of the alleged relative use of *eall hwæt* are noted by Wülfing (i, §310) and Bødtker (1910, pp. 17-18). All can (in my view) be otherwise explained. They are *Bo* 140. 28 (see below); *Solil* 57. 9 *æall hwæt* (double objects or *eall* adv.?); *Ps(P)* 37. 9 *þu wast nu eall hwæs ic wilnie* (*eall* adv. or *hwæs* gen. on *eall*?); and *HomU* 23. 122. 8 *eal hwæt* (double subjects or *eall* adv.?). Bødtker also speculates (ibid., p. 18) on the possibility of a temporal meaning for *hwæt* in lOE. Karlberg (pp. 62-4) quotes some of these and adds more. According to him '*eall hwæt* must be regarded as a relative complex' in two—*Bo(B)* 140. 28 *7 eall hwæt hi wilniað hi begitað* (where *eall* and the *hwæt* clause could be described as double objects but where the Cotton MS has the expected *eall þ*) and *Ps(F)* 115. 3 *hwæt ic selle drihtne for eallum hwæt he sealde me*, Vulgate *Ps* 115. 12 *Quid retribuam Domino pro omnibus quae retribuit mihi* (where *Ps(J)* also has *hwæt* but the other manuscripts have a regular OE relative construction, e.g. *Ps(K) for eallum þa* and *PPs* 115. 3 *for eallum þam godum þe*). Both therefore have variants which display the patterns we should expect and both are in late manuscripts—in Karlberg's words 'clearly relative *eall hwæt* occurs first in the glossed psalters F, 11th c., and J, 1050-1100, and in Boethius, MS B, *c.* 1100' (p. 64). That these two readings are signs of what is to come is certain; Karlberg refers to examples up to Shakespeare's *Timon* and Mabbe's 1631 translation of *Celestina* (pp. 62-4). Whether *hwæt* was really felt as a relative in either of them is dubious. But even if it was, they can scarcely be used as evidence for *eall hwæt* as a relative combination in OE proper.

8. THE INDEFINITES

a. Classification

§361. The best sub-division of this blanket term (§241) seems to be that used by Sandfeld for the French indefinites.[93] He distinguishes six classes—(1) *on*; (2) *quelqu'un, quelque, quelque chose*, and (3) their equivalents and synonyms; (4) negatives like *personne, aucun, nul, rien*, and their equivalents; (5) words which mark totality, like *chacun, chaque, n'importe qui, tous, tout*; (6) words marking identity and the contrary, like *même* and *autre*. I follow this classification, except that I combine (2) and (3) and add another group— words meaning 'either of two, one or the other'.[94]

---

[93] K. Sandfeld, *Syntaxe du français contemporain*, i. *Les pronoms* (Paris, 1928), 329-454.

[94] The long series of articles by Einenkel on *Das englische Indefinitum* (*Ang.* 21-4, 26-7, 29-31, and 33-6) contains examples of the various indefinites in all periods of English; for fuller references see *Ang.* 24 (1901), 343; ibid. 27 (1903), 204; and ibid. 36 (1912), 139. Specific reference is made when necessary. As I note below, *passim*, there is a surprising

§362. The indefinites behave in the same way in prose and poetry if one allows for the general differences between the two discussed in §§3944-7 and 3959-71. Examples from the poetry are therefore not usually quoted in the sections which follow. They can be found in GK, in 'the eighteen German dissertations' (excluding those of Reussner and Rose), *passim*, and in Sorg, pp. 67–79. On problems of verbal agreement involving indefinites, see §32(3).

b. Man

(1) *Senses*

§363. *Man, mann,* is frequently used—in the nominative singular only—as an indefinite. According to Fröhlich five senses can be distinguished.[95] They are set out here, with one of his examples by way of illustration.

§364. *Man* 1 denotes 'der Mensch oder ein Mensch' ['mankind or a man'] (as opposed to God or other living creatures), e.g. *Matt (WSCp)* 12. 12 *Witodlice micle ma mann ys sceape betera* (Fröhlich, pp. 15–17). *Man* 2 means 'ein Mensch, ein Individuum, eine Person, (irgend-)jemand oder (irgend-)einer' ['anyone, whatever individual is chosen'], e.g. *Or* 20. 19 *7 þær is mid Estum ðeaw, þonne þær bið man dead, þæt he lið inne* . . . (Fröhlich, pp. 17–45).

§365. In the remaining senses 3–5 *man* is a 'generell-indefinites Pronomen' (Fröhlich, pp. 45, 70, and 102). *Man* 3 is 'allgemein', denoting 'a number of people, everyone [who knows about it, who was there]', e.g. *Or* 10. 28 *On ðæm londe is xxxii þeoda. Nu hæt hit mon eall Parthia* and *Or* 126. 24 . . . *he wolde beladian his modor Nectanebuses þæs drys, þe mon sæde þæt heo hie wið forlege* (Fröhlich, pp. 45–70). *Man* 4–5 means broadly 'someone'. The distinction seems to depend on the degree to which the 'someone' can be identified and/or the extent to which the writer was interested in identifying him.

---

amount of almost verbatim repetition in the course of these articles. See *Ang.* 28 (1905), 127 ff. Collections of 'Alfredian' examples will be found in Wülfing, i, §§321–75.

[95] Fröhlich summarizes his findings (which include lists of synonymous constructions) at pp. 111–15. Gray, in *Word*, 1 (1945), 19–32, distinguishes twelve different uses of indefinite *man* to suit his interest in the origin of the use of *man = on*. His criteria are sometimes semantic, sometimes syntactic, sometimes based on the Latin original, and sometimes on other considerations, such as whether *man* appears in a quotation, in a paraphrase, in an addition to the original text, or in a mistranslation.

§366. *Man* 4 is described as 'speziell' in that it denotes a particular agent. Fröhlich further distinguishes *man* 4(*a*), where this agent is unknown and cannot be identified, e.g. *Or* 60. 32 . . . *æfter þæm ðe mon heora cyning ofslog Sardanopolum*, from *man* 4(*b*), where the agent can be deduced and *man* replaced by a noun, e.g. *Or* 80. 19 *Ac gesette þa men on ænne truman þe mon hiora mægas ær on ðæm londe slog*, where it is clear that it was the Greeks who slew the relatives of the Persians (Fröhlich, pp. 70-101). *Man* 5 is 'definierbar'; *mon* refers back to a definite antecedent, as in *Or* 174. 3 *þa com of ðæm wætre an nædre . . . þa gegaderade Regulus ealle þa scyttan þe on ðæm færelte wæron, þæt hie mon mid flanum ofercome*, where *mon* refers to *ealle þa scyttan* (Fröhlich, pp. 102-10).

§367. That *man* in these senses 3-5 can refer to more than one person is emphasized by sentences in which there is a change of number in a second verb, e.g. *Or* 88. 11 *7 ælce dæg mon com unarimedlice oft to þæm senatum 7 him sædon* and *Judg* 16. 25 *7 hine man sona gefette mid swiðlicre wafunge 7 heton hine standan betwux twam stænenum swerum*, or in a second parallel subject, e.g. *Or* 226. 17 *Ac þære ilcan niht þe mon on dæg hæfde þa burg mid stacum gemearcod, swa swa hie hie þa wyrcean woldon . . .* and *Matt(WSCp)* 23. 6-8 *Hig lufigeað þa fyrmystan setl on gebeorscypum 7 þa fyrmystan lareowsetl on gesomnungum 7 þ hig man grete on strætum 7 þ menn hig lareowas nemnon. Ne gyrne ge þ eow man lareowas nemne*, Latin *Amant enim primos recubitos in cenis et primas cathedras in synagogis et salutationes in foro et uocari ab hominibus rabbi. Uos autem nolite uocari rabbi*. In these (as with collective nouns) the sense of different individuals is strong. But the few sentences in which *man* is immediately followed by a plural verb are to be regarded with suspicion as possible scribal errors. They include *ChronA* 18. 15 (565) *þæt igland þe man Ii nemnað* (a late addition), *CP* 2 (heading) *ðas boc . . . þe man Pastoralem nemnað*, and *LS* 34. 599 *and man mid witum ofgan willað æt me . . .* (where Skeat records a variant *ofgan wile*).

§368. As Fröhlich himself recognizes (e.g. p. 112), these five senses inevitably shade into one another. I have discussed this problem in Mitchell, at press (*a*), where, after suggesting that Fröhlich might have done well to eliminate 4(*b*)—the most elusive of his types— and to call 4(*a*) 4, I conclude that, while Fröhlich's distinctions can sometimes be made, they must not be pressed too far.

§369. The same article dismisses, as terminological, objections to Campbell's statement (*OEG,* §723) that *man* + an active verb form is often used as 'a periphrasis for the passive voice' and discusses Gray's article (*Word*, 1 (1945), 19–32; see my §363 fn.) on the use and origin of indefinite *man*.

(2) *Indefinite* man *not expressed*

§370. According to Pogatscher (pp. 294–9), the possibility that indefinite *man* is not expressed arises in two types of construction. However, if anything is to be supplied, it could as easily be *hit* in the first type and *he* in some of the examples of the second. But there remain some difficult sentences with forms of *magan*; see §374.

§371. Pogatscher's first group comprises examples in which verbs like *cweðan, cyðan, secgan,* and *onginnan*—which usually have a personal subject—are used in the third person singular present indicative, in what appears to be an impersonal construction, e.g. *BlHom* 133. 36 *We leornedon, 7 on þæm godspelle cwið, þæt se Drihtnes Gast ofer hiene astige . . . , BlHom* 45. 3 *7 her sægþ on þyssum bocum, þæt . . . , BlHom* 23. 12 *Her us cyþ þæt se godspellere sæde . . . ,* and (with a past tense) *Or* 40. 26 *. . . swylc morð . . . swylc her ær beforan sæde.* For further examples, see Pogatscher, pp. 294–6. Visser (i. 7) says that 'the usage hardly outlived Old English'.

§372. It is difficult to establish the exact grammatical status of these; there are in OE active and passive variants, both personal and impersonal (on these terms see §§749 and 1025), e.g. *ÆTest* 24. 212 *Nu segð us seo boc be Noes ofspringe, þæt . . . , Bede* 2. 7 *Forðon þis gewrit oððe hit god sagað be godum mannum . . . oððe hit yfel sagaþ be yfelum mannum, Or* 128. 24 *swa hit her beforan sægð, Bede* 360. 1 *Se man wæs se gelærdesta in gewreotum; se wæs sægd, þæt he his broðor wære Osweos sunu þæs cyninges, Bede* 154. 23 *Is þæt sægd, þæt he þæt Cristæs mæl hraðe weorce geworhte,* and *BlHom* 61. 16 *Sægd is þæt se ilca wiþerwearda. . . .* The presence of the last pattern in *ÆCHom* ii. 356. 1 *Him wæs gesæd þæt hi wæron gemynte anum sutere on Romanabyrig, and hine eac namode* suggests that the *and* clause may be an anacoluthon rather than an example of 'idiomatic' non-expression of *man*. On the basis of ON constructions similar to those under discussion, Pogatscher argues that we have here remains of a Pr. Gmc. construction; to him *hit* in examples like *Or* 128. 24 above is an easily understandable but none the less later insertion. Somehow, this notion of supplying *hit* seems more acceptable than that of supplying *mon*, for the idiom seen in *Or* 124. 23 *þa sægde him mon þæt Darius hæfde eft fird gegaderod,* in *LawCn* 1020 [5] *þa cydde man me, þæt us mara hearm to fundode*, and in similar examples cited by Fröhlich (pp. 45–8 and 71–3), seems a different thing.

§373. Pogatscher's second group falls into two divisions. First, I quote his two examples with full verbs, viz. *Beo* 1290 *helm ne gemunde, ‖ byrnan side, þa hine se broga angeat* and *Charm* 2. 25 *þæt næfre for gefloge feorh ne gesealde ‖ syþðan him mon mægðan to mete gegyrede*. In these, *he* can reasonably be understood from *hine* and *him* respectively and it is quite unnecessary to postulate the omission of *man*.

§374. Then there are three examples with *magan*, viz. *Beo* 1365 *þær mæg nihta gehwæm niðwundor seon, ‖ fyr on flode*, *Mald* 215 *nu mæg cunnian hwa cene sy*, and *Alex* 37. 12 *ða ondsworadon hie mec 7 sægdon þ nære mara weg þonne meahte on tyn dagum geferan*. In the last example, Rypins suggests, 'the suppression . . . of the pronoun . . . may, of course, be but a scribal slip'. This explanation will hardly do for the verse examples. An apparently obvious solution is to explain *seon, cunnian*, and *geferan*, as passive infinitives, but (for the reasons given in §§3762–5) I have no hesitation in rejecting this. The presence of *unbyrnende*, which must be nominative referring to an unexpressed subject since it cannot be taken with *deop*, rules out this explanation in

Beo 2542   Geseah ða be wealle   se ðe worna fela
            gumcystum god   guða gedigde,
            hildehlemma,   þonne hnitan feðan,
            stondan stanbogan,   stream ut þonan
            brecan of beorge;   wæs þære burnan wælm
            heaðofyrum hat,   ne meahte horde neah
            unbyrnende   ænige hwile
            deop gedygan   for dracan lege,

where Klaeber postulates unexpressed *man* in one place (3, p. xciii), but also admits the possibility of unexpressed *he* (ibid., p. 215, note to line 2547). But this last explanation does not seem possible for *Beo* 1365, and to understand *ic* in *Mald* 215 and *Alex* 37. 12 seems far-fetched. (See further Pogatscher, p. 296.) So it is tempting to accept Klaeber's suggestion (3, p. xciii) that 'the indefinite pronoun *man* is left unexpressed' for these last three examples at any rate. But we may have a special use of *magan*. This idea seems to lie behind Wahlén's observation (p. 107) that 'it is hardly necessary to assume with Pogatscher . . . that a subject, whether definite or indefinite (OE *man*), is omitted. The phrases as they stand may be quite as original, it seems, as e.g. *hit rinþ, hine hyngreð*. The notion of a subject is kept entirely in the background.' Wahlén (p. 106) adds to these examples

And 951   Is þe guð weotod,
    heardum heoruswengum   scel þin hra dælan
    wundum weorðan,   wættre geliccost
    faran flode blod,

which he conveniently truncates at *dælan*. However Krapp, ASPR, and Brooks, reasonably emend to *dæled*.

§375. Another example of a different kind is *LRid* 11 *Uil mec huethrae suae ðeh uidæ ofaer eorðu* ‖ *hatan mith heliðum hyhtlic giuæde*, where the Exeter Book version inserts *mon* after *mec*. That the absence of *mon* is the result of scribal omission is suggested by the absence of other examples of *hatan* without *mon*; the usual idiom is that seen in *Or* 12. 18 *7 be suþan hire se beorg þe mon hæt Climax* and similar examples quoted by Fröhlich (pp. 45-6). But the existence of the examples with *magan* above does leave a nagging doubt in one's mind that *LRid* 11 may be another example of a dying idiom which was not recognized by whoever inserted *mon* in the W-S version.

§376. The remaining examples in which Pogatscher (pp. 298-9) saw a possible need for the insertion of *man* can, I think, be dismissed. The inf. *dælan* in *And* 951 (§374) is probably due (as Brooks suggested in his edition) 'to a scribe who expected an inf. after *scel*'. In *And* 1082 *gemette* can be taken as a preterite subjunctive plural after *sægdon*. The two examples from the Laws—*LawAbt* 54 *Gif þuman ofaslæhð, xx scill.* and *LawIne* 2 *gif hit swa ne sie, xxx scill. gebete* —can easily be paralleled in the two codes. They arise either from the mechanical repetition of a (truncated) formula which, when properly used, has an unexpressed subject which is to be understood from that of the accompanying *gif* clause, e.g. *LawAbt* 10 *Gif man wið cyninges mægdenman geligeþ, L scillinga gebete* and *LawIne* 7 *Gif hwa stalie swa his wif nyte 7 his bearn, geselle LX scill. to wite*, or (in the Laws of Ine at any rate) from scribal omission of *he*—cf. *LawIne* 2. 1 *Gif hit ðonne sie dead butan fulwihte, gebete he hit mid eallum ðam ðe he age*—or possibly *man*—cf. *LawIne* 34. 1 . . . *7 ðy ilcan ryhte do man be ðam deorborenran*. There is no need to suppose that *man* is the unexpressed subject in Pogatscher's examples or others like them. Other formulae can be used unthinkingly, e.g. *LawAbt* 48 *Gif nasu ælcor sceard weorð, gehwylc vi scill. gebete*.

Schibsbye's attempt in *EStudies*, 50 (1969), 380–1, to explain the refrain in *Deor* as an instance of unexpressed subject [*man*] by citing examples of the two types discussed above and the plural verbs with unexpressed subject in *Beo* 1251 and *Cæd* 1 does not convince; none of the alleged parallels can really be said to be parallel.

(3) Man . . . *anaphoric pronoun*

§377. Although *man* can be repeated in a following clause, as in *Or* 52. 35 . . . *þæt hine mon sloge swa raðe swa mon hiora fiend wolde*, it is more often picked up by a third person pronoun, which may be singular, e.g. *Or* 40. 28 . . . *þæt mon him þurfe swilc ondrædan, þæt hine mon ænigum godum blote*, *ÆCHom* ii. 340. 12 *Nis na genoh þæt man his nextan god do, buton he hine lufige swa swa hine sylfne*, and (in the same clause) *Beo* 3175 . . . *þæt mon his winedryhten wordum herge*, or plural, e.g. *Or* 226. 17 *Ac þære ilcan niht þe mon on dæg hæfde þa burg mid stacum gemearcod, swa swa hie hie þa wyrcean woldon* . . . and *ThCap1* 14. 1 *Ne spane nan mæssepreost nanne mon of oðre cyrcean hyrnysse to his cyrcan ne of oðre preost- scyre lære þ mon hys cyrcan gesece 7 him heora teoðinge syllan 7 þa geryhtu þe hig þam oðrum syllan sceoldan*. The translation of *CP* 145. 20 *Forðæm eac ða godan recceras, ðonne hie ne recceað hwæðer mon hie selfe synderlice 7 ungemetlice lufige* . . . given in Sweet's edition: 'Therefore also good rulers, while they do not care whether men love themselves specially and excessively . . .' seems to suggest that the pl. *hie selfe* goes with the sg. *mon*. This is wrong, for it refers back to *ða godan recceras*; see §§275–6.

c. *Words meaning 'any, some'*

(1) *List*

§378. In the list which follows, those asterisked are used indepen- dently only (in other words as pronouns, but not as adjectives):

ænig 'any', *sum* 'some';

hwa*, *ahwa** 'anyone, someone'; *hwæt**, *ahwæt** 'anything, some- thing'; *hwæthwugu* 'something, some' (see BTS, s.v.); *nathwa** 'someone (I know not who)', *nathwæt** 'something';

hwilc 'any'; *hwilchwugu* 'some'; *nathwelc, samhwelc* 'some, any'; *awiht**, *awuht** 'something, anything'.

On variant forms and spellings see *OEG*, §§718 and 721–3. On the use of some of these words with *elles* and *weald* see BTS, s.vv. *elles* and *weald*, and §§1232 fn. and 2938–9. *Awiht* is used indepen- dently, not dependently, in the three examples cited by Wülfing (i, §362). The following words taken by some authorities, but not by Campbell, *OEG*, as indefinites are discussed below: *feawe* (adj. *OEG*, §653(2))); *fela, gewiss, lytel*, and *micel* (adjs. with comp., *OEG*, §§643(5) and 659); *manig* (adj. *OEG*, §643(5)); and combinations of *þing* (other than *nanþing, OEG*, §725). For references, see the Index of Words and Phrases.

(2) *General characteristics*

§379. The words given above can be declined and used in all cases, but unlike adjectives they cannot be compared and cannot be modified by intensifying adverbs such as *swiþe*. Those asterisked can be used independently only, the remainder can be used both dependently (usually before a noun) and independently. They can appear in the predicate and as antecedent to a relative pronoun. Some can be used with *an*, some with *oþer*, some with a partitive genitive. Some can be used correlatively, some serve also as interrogatives. The oblique cases of some can be used adverbially. For references, see the Index of Words and Phrases.

§380. To give examples of all these words in all these functions would be superfluous; they can be found in BT(S) (s.vv.) and in Wülfing (i. 432-62). Further on the following, which need no special comment here, see the references in brackets: *ahwa, ahwæþer* (*OEG*, §718); *nathwa* (*OEG*, §723); *nathwelc, samhwelc* (*OEG*, §723); *awiht, awuht* (*OEG*, §723, and Einenkel, *Ang.* 27 (1903), 151-63). Wülfing (i, §365) records *ænig wuht*. But certain points about the rest need separate consideration.

(3) Ænig

§381. Unlike *nænig*, which is chiefly Anglian (§440), *ænig* 'any-(one)' is frequent in both W-S and Anglian texts. It is used in the singular and (less frequently) in the plural, both dependently, e.g. *Or* 58. 22 *ænig mon* and *Or* 96. 35 *ænige twegen latteowas*, and independently without a partitive genitive, e.g. *Or* 150. 24 *Ne wene ic . . . þæt ænig wære þe þæt atellan mehte* and *Bede* 414. 18 . . . *gif wen wære þæt hi þær ænige þurh heora lare Criste begytan mihte*. The singular is common with a partitive genitive, e.g. *Bede* 164. 22 *ænig his eldrena*, but no unambiguous examples of *ænig* plural + partitive genitive have come to my notice; the same is true of *nænig* (§438). So *ængum* in *Sol* 55. 6 *be ængum þissa þinga* is probably singular. Like Ropers (p. 61) I have found no examples in Ælfric of independent *ænig* used alone. This may be a reason for preferring the *ænigum menn* of MSS *M* and *N* to that accepted by Pope in *ÆHom* 9. 45 *hwilc fremu is ænigum on aðrum þæra?*

§382. How is *ænig* to be explained in *Bede* 192. 4 *ænige his reliquias* (MS *Ca ænig his reliquias*), *LawAf* 43 *on ænegum hiora hwilsticcum*—these two are quoted by Einenkel in identical paragraphs in *Ang.* 22 (1899), 497, and *Ang.* 26 (1903), 559—*ChronE* 219. 20 (1086) *Se cyng Willelm . . . wæs . . . wurðfulre and strengere þonne ænig his foregenga wære*, and *ÆCHom* i. 474. 19 *Se cristena mann ðe on ænigre þissere gelicnysse bið gebrocod . . . ?* Is it to be taken as dependent—'any relics of him', 'any moments of them', 'any predecessor of him', 'in any manner like this'—or as independent— 'any of his relics' (*Ca*'s version could be translated 'anything [which might be] his relics'), 'any of their moments', 'any of his predecessors', and (following Thorpe) 'any of this like'? This problem arises in connection with other words, especially *sum*, and is further discussed in §§409-16.

§383. Some familiar combinations are recorded in OE, e.g. *ChristB* 683 *Nyle he ængum anum ealle gesyllan, Or* 80. 33 *ænig ma folca, Or* 58. 22 *ænig mon, CP* 113. 15 *ænig oðer*, and *Luke(WSCp)* 4. 41 *æni þing*.

§384. Schrader (p. 58) has drawn our attention to the fact that *ænig* tends to occur in negative sentences and clauses, e.g. *ÆCHom* i. 414. 16 *næs ic ðe derigende on ænigum ðingum*, in rhetorical questions implying negation, e.g. *ÆCHom* i. 336. 25 *Hu mihte he gefredan æniges hefes swærnysse, ðaða he ðone ferode ðe hine bær?*, in questions where the answer is in doubt, e.g. *ÆCHom* i. 510. 29 *Wyle eower lareow Crist ænig toll syllan?*, and in other types of clause where some condition or doubt is implied, e.g. *ÆCHom* i. 404. 3 *Gif hwa hwæt lytles æniges bigwistes him sylfum gearcode* and *ÆCHom* i. 474. 19 *Se cristena mann ðe on ænigre þissere gelicnysse bið gebrocod.*[96] To this list, Fröhlich (pp. 25-6) adds the comparative clause in *Or* 19. 18 . . . *swyðe mycel sæ . . . seo is bradre þonne ænig man ofer seon mæge.* The same tendency is apparent in MnE; see Jespersen, *Ess.*, §§17. 91-2. But (as both Jespersen and Einenkel point out) there are examples of the word in positive clauses in both MnE, e.g. 'Anyone can do it' and 'He can do anything', and

---

[96] Einenkel makes much the same points as Schrader in *Ang.* 22 (1899), 489, and—in almost identical paragraphs—*Ang.* 26 (1903), 550. In the paragraphs which follow these— many of them again (almost) identical—Einenkel gives examples of 'any' in all periods of English. More will be found in Wülfing, i, §§354-5, and Ropers, pp. 60-1.

OE. Thus Wülfing's examples contain both comparative clauses and other clauses in which no negation or doubt is implied, e.g. *Or* 72. 25 . . . *to Babylonia, þe þa welegre wæs þonne ænigu oþeru burg, CP* 3. 18 *Gode ælmihtegum sie ðonc ðæt[te] we nu ænigne on stal habbað lareowa*, and *Or* 74. 7 *Swa ungeliefedlic is ænigum menn.* . . .

(4) Sum

(a) Declension and uses

§385. *Sum* is declined *strong* (*OEG*, §§642 and 724) and in general differs from *ænig* as MnE 'some' differs from 'any'; see Einenkel in *Ang.* 26 (1903), 550, and Jespersen, *Ess.*, §§17. 91-3. It is used in the same way in poetry as in prose, if allowance is made for the differences in element order and other things discussed in §§3944-7 and 3959-71; see further Süsskand, pp. 19-29. It is found in the singular and plural, both dependently, usually before the noun but occasionally after it, e.g. *Bede* 284. 30 *cneohtcild sum* and *Whale* 12 *on ealond sum*, and independently.

(b) Dependent sum

§386. Despite the absence of intonation patterns, we can reasonably distinguish the two nuances set out below. First, *sum* may refer to a particular referent specified by name, e.g. *ÆCHom* i. 322. 34 *Amos hatte sum hryðerhyrde*, *ÆCHom* i. 386. 17 *Wæs ða sum Godes ðegen . . . his nama wæs Annanias*, and *ÆCHom* i. 2. 15 . . . *to sumum mynstre þe is Cernel gehaten*. Then we have examples in which the reference is not specific, e.g. (in the singular) *ÆCHom* i. 224. 26 *Nu cwyð sum man on his geðance* 'some man or other', *GD* 339. 23 *mid sumre anre leasunge*, *ÆCHom* i. 336. 7 *to sumum oðrum mynstre*, *ÆCHom* i. 62. 24 *æt sumum sæle*, and *ÆCHom* i. 380. 27 *sume hwile*; (in the singular with a partitive genitive) *ÆCHom* i. 92. 34 *sumne dæl þæs felles* and *ÆCHom* i. 138. 22 *sum ðing godes*; and (in the plural) *GD* 151. 15 *sume twa nunnan*, Latin *duae quaedam sanctimoniales feminae*, and *ÆCHom* i. 328. 24 *sume men*.

§387. The indefiniteness apparent in examples like *ÆCHom* i. 224. 26 (§386) and the fact that *sum man* can there be translated 'a man' has led some authorities to argue that *sum* serves as an 'indefinite article'. Wülfing (i, §149) so classifies many examples like *Or* 98. 4 *Pissandor hatte sum Læcedemonia latteow* and *CP* 31. 17 . . . *him wære betere ðæt him wære sumu esulcweorn to ðæm suiran getiged*. Süsskand (*passim*) and Ropers (pp. 55-7) discuss the differences between the 'indefinite articles' *an* and *sum*. However, Rissanen (p. 299) is probably right when he remarks that 'this *sum* cannot be regarded

as a true indefinite article any more than the dependent individualizing *an*'; on the latter, see §535. But it must be admitted that here
(as elsewhere) certainty cannot be reached. It is not immediately
clear how *Bo* 7. 11 *þa wæs sum consul, þ we heretoha hataδ, Boetius
wæs gehaten* differs from *Or* 98. 4 and *CP* 31. 17 above. Yet to
Wülfing (i, §321) *sum* in *Bo* 7. 11 meant 'a certain, some' rather
than 'a'. Again, Thorpe translates *ÆCHom* i. 400. 19 *asend him twa
scrud and sum pund* 'send him two garments and a pound'. Naaman's
reply *ÆCHom* i. 400. 20 *Waclic biδ him swa lytel to sendenne; ac
genim feower scrud and twa pund* suggests that Thorpe is more likely
to be right than Schrader (pp. 54-5), who says it means 'about
a pound'. But an example like *BlHom* 93. 1 *7 heofon biþ open on
sumum ende on þæm eastdæle; 7 mycel mægen forþcymeþ þurh
þone openan dæl* makes it very hard for us to be sure that *sum pund*
is not the OE equivalent of 'one pound' rather than of 'a pound'.

§388. *An* and *sum* appear to have been used more or less side by
side throughout the OE period in the individualizing function. Both
are common in Ælfric. Süsskand (pp. 49-50) believes that this use
of *an* was characteristic of the spoken language, whereas *sum* was
literary. But Rissanen (pp. 299-302) advances the possibility that
the difference may originally have been dialectal—*an* having been
preferred in W-S, *sum* in Anglian, in earlier stages of OE. See also
Christophersen, pp. 102-3, and (for examples from the poetry) Sorg,
pp. 79-82.

§389. The indefiniteness associated with *sum* led to its use to express approximation. Examples like *ChronA* 89. 7 (896) *sume feower
cyninges þegnas* and *ÆCHom* i. 254. 13 *Se δe synful biδ, he biδ yfel,
and nan man nis on life butan sumere synne* may show how this use
arose rather than exemplify it—the sense may be 'four King's thanes
I could name' and 'some particular sin' rather than 'four or five
thanes' and 'a certain amount of sin'. Rissanen (p. 234) suggests the
first explanation for two examples from the Chronicle—*ChronA*
88. 8 (894) *besæton þeah þæt geweorc utan sume twegen dagas* (on
this see §392) and *ChronA* 98. 27 (918) . . . *æt sumum twam cirron,
æt oþrum cierre . . . 7 æt oþrum cierre . . . þa slog hie mon æt
ægþrum cirre.* In this last example the translation 'on about two
occasions' is obviously impossible. There seems to be more feeling of
approximation in examples like *Bo* 115. 18 *þa hæfde he sume hundred scipa; þa wæron hi sume ten gear on þam gewinne, ChronA*
86. 7 (894) *þa gegaderodon þa þe in Norþhymbrum bugeaδ . . . sum
hund scipa, 7 foron suδ ymbutan, 7 sum feowertig scipa norþ*

ymbutan, *ÆCHom* i. 386. 32 *Wunode ða sume feawa daga*, *ÆLS* 25. 357 *þær wurdon ofslagene sume þreo þusend*, and *ÆHom* 17. 238 (§390a).

§390. Tempted no doubt by the gen. plur. *scipa*, Sedgefield translates *Bo* 115. 18 (§389) 'he had several hundred ships, and they were fighting about ten years'. In MnE there is a distinction between 'some hundreds of ships' and 'some hundred ships' (though I may be on dangerous ground, as I do not find the former construction mentioned in *OED*, s.v. 'some'). But it can scarcely be imported into OE on the available evidence. The *Boethius* passage is a prose rendering of Latin *Metre* iv. 3, which does not give a number. The corresponding OE *Metre* has

Met 26. 13   For wiges heard
                Creca drihten   campsted secan,
                Aulixes mid,   an hund scipa
                lædde ofer lagustream,   sæt longe ðær
                tyn winter full.

This obviously does not support Sedgefield's 'several hundred ships', though (since *an* carries alliteration) it is not conclusive against it. Does the fact that *scipa* is genitive plural prove Sedgefield right?

§390a. The syntactical patterns vary and are illustrated by reference to examples in §389:

(1) *sum* singular + numeral + genitive plural of noun (examples: *ChronA* 86. 7 (both clauses)[97]);

(2) *sum* plural + numeral + noun in same case as *sum* (examples: *Bo* 115. 18 (second sentence), *ÆLS* 25. 357);

(3) *sum* plural (but not genitive plural) + numeral + noun in genitive plural (examples: *Bo* 115. 18 (first sentence), *ÆCHom* i. 386. 32).

To these can be added *ÆHom(CDEFKM)* 17. 238 *þa swyn ða ealle endemes scuton into þære sæ, sume twa þusend* where, Pope reports, 'H has traces of another letter, probably *o*, *a*, or *e*'; this therefore can be said to exemplify either (2) or—MS *H*—(3).

§391. One can perhaps see why Sedgefield thought the two constructions in *Bo* 115. 18 (§389) differed in meaning—the plural of *sum* + gen. pl. *scipa* 'several hundred ships' against the plural of *sum* + acc. pl. *gear* 'some ten years'. But the presence of a genitive plural

[97] I have found no examples of the pattern *sum* singular + numeral + noun in the same case as *sum*. That quoted by Einenkel in *Ang.* 26 (1903), 544—*Bede* 172. 6 *feower 7 twentig wintra 7 sumne monað*, Latin *XXIIII annis et aliquot mensibus*—is irrelevant, since there is no numeral after *sumne*. Miller reports *sumne* in all extant manuscripts. It is odd. The Latin demands *sume*, unless we have something on the lines of the Modern Swedish singular usage *Han var där någon månad* 'He was there some months'.

does not seem decisive. In *ChronA* 86. 8 *sum feowertig scipa* has the genitive plural but can scarcely mean 'several forty ships', and the fluctuation between nom. *þusend* and gen. *þusenda* (*-o, -e*) in *ÆHom* 17. 238 (§390a) is against the notion that the construction with a genitive plural was different. The same example disproves the proposition that the plural of *sume* must mean 'several'. All manuscripts have the plural *sume*, yet the meaning must be 'some two thousand' —'several two thousand(s)' seems impossible and Mark's account of the incident (*Mark* 5. 13) gives the number as *ad duo milia*. (It is unfortunate that none of the OE versions of Mark uses *sum*, for the positive argument therefore fails.) The other example of pattern (3) —*ÆCHom* i. 386. 32 (§389)—also argues against Sedgefield, for *sume feawa daga* can scarcely mean 'several few days'.

§392. So we can, I think, rule out Sedgefield's interpretation of the first sentence in *Bo* 115. 18. But it seems impossible to decide whether *sum* in examples like *ÆLS* 4. 324 *sume þreo niht* is individualizing or approximating, though I think that a martyr-elect is more likely to ask for 'three clear nights' of conversation with his mother than for 'about three nights'. Rissanen's first example— *ChronA* 88. 9 (894) *sume twegen dagas* is perhaps ambiguous in the same way; see §389.

§393. We find dependent *sum* used correlatively with independent *sum* both in the singular and plural, e.g. *ÆCHom* i. 322. 25 *Sumum men he forgifð wisdom and spræce, sumum god ingehyd, sumum micelne geleafan, sumum . . . and ÆCHom* ii. 48. 16 *Sume lareowas sindon beteran ðonne sume, swa swa wæron þa apostoli; sume sind waccran, swa swa we beoð.*

(c) *Independent* sum

§394. *Sum* can be used independently in the singular and plural, either alone, e.g. *MSol* 345 *Sum to lyt hafað, Bede* 22. 34 *Ðæt sum on Norðanhymbra mægðe of deaðe arisende sume swiðe ondryslicu . . . secgende wæs*, and *ÆCHom* i. 192. 27 *Sume wæron eac be ðære eadigan Marian gewitegode*, or correlatively, e.g. *Bo* 76. 15 *þonne lufað sum ðæt, sum elles hwæt, CP* 210. 3 *sume cwædon . . . , sume cwædon . . . , sume . . . , sum cwæð . . . , ÆCHom* ii. 302. 19 *þa wearð þæt earme mennisc for heora mandædum, sum mid hungre acweald, sum mid heardum isene* (note the singular forms), *ÆCHom* ii. 48. 16 *Sume lareowas sindon beteran ðonne sume*, and *ÆCHom* i. 126. 34 *Manega oðre men . . . sume . . . sume . . . sume. Sume . . . sume* is the most usual OE equivalent of MnE 'some . . . others'. But we find at least the beginnings of an opposition between *sum* and *oþer* in examples like *Or* 248. 15–23 *Sum . . . Oþer . . . þridde, Or* 206. 16 . . . *þa bebead he sumum þæm folce þæt hie from þæm fæstenne aforen, and þa oþre he het þæt hie wið þara oþerra flugen, Solil* 9. 21 *ealle gescæafta wrixleað: sume þeah on oððer wyssan, swa þat þa ylcan eft ne cumæð þær ðær hy er weron . . . Ac cumað oðre for hy, swa swa leaf on treowum, ÆCHom* ii. 160. 2 . . . *heora cild . . . of ðam wæs sum gehaten Placidus and sum oðer Maurus, ÆCHom* i. 542. 26–33 *Sume hi . . . sume . . . oðre . . . oþre . . . sume . . . sume . . . oðre . . . oðre . . . sume . . . sume . . . sume . . . sume . . . , ÆCHom* i. 238. 16 *and se wulf sum gelæcð and ða oðre tostencð,* and *Mark(Li)* 12. 5 *And eft he him sumne sende 7 hi þæne ofslogon 7 manega oþre. . . .*

§395. *Sum* singular is frequently used with a partitive genitive plural, e.g. *Bede* 428. 1 *þara monna sum wæs . . . bescoren preost, sum wes læwde, sum wæs wifmon, ÆCHom* i. 580. 5 *eower sum*, and *ÆHom* 8. 151 *sum his þegna*; this is Rissanen's 'individualizing *sum*' (p. 61). In

Beo 1240	Beorscealca sum
	fus ond fæge fletræste gebeag.
	Setton him to heafdon hilderandas,

the plural *setton* is due rather to *beorscealca* than to a collective use of *sum*, as Andrew (*Postscript*, p. 61) argues. With *sum* plural, partitive apposition (see §409) seems to be the rule. The partitive genitive is rare. But I have noted the following examples: *Matt(Ru)* 28. 11 *sume þara wearda*, Latin *quidam de custodibus*, where *Li* has *summe of ðæm haldendum* and the W-S version *sume þa weardas* (partitive apposition); *Luke(WSCp)* 20. 39 *sume þara bocera*, Latin *quidam scribarum*; *ÆCHom* i. 540. 6 *sume ðæra haligra gasta* (but note that Ælfric continues with a three-fold partitive apposition *Sume hi . . . Sume hi . . . Sume hi*); *BlHom* 213. 26 *þara arfæstra dæda sume*; *ÆCHom* ii. 356. 29 *sume þæs Norðernan folces* (note the collective genitive singular); *ÆLS* 6. 50 *sume þæra*; and (with the genitive of a numeral) *Law(Ot)IIAs* 11 *7 hie gan siððan twelfa sume*, where MS *H* has *xii sume* and MS *Ld twelfa sum*.[98] In view of examples like *ÆCHom* ii. 222. 28 *sume ða hæðenan* (where *ða* rules out the possibility that *hæðenan* is genitive) it would, I think, be perverse to claim that *geferan* is a late genitive plural form in *ÆCHom* i. 560. 14 *sume his geferan* and the like.

---

[98] It may be noted that in the same section MS *So* wrongly has *þreora sume* where the other manuscripts correctly have sg. *sum*.

§396. The construction with *of* occurs spasmodically—with both singular and plural forms of *sum*—under Latin influence in *Bede*, e.g. *Bede* 286. 10 *sumu of þæm ilcan Godes þeowum*, and in the Gospels, e.g. *Mark(WSCp)* 8. 28 *sumne of þam witegum*, Latin *unum de prophetis*, and *Luke(WSCp)* 24. 24 *sume of urum*, Latin *quidam ex nostris*.[99] There are occasional instances in Ælfric, e.g. *ÆCHom* ii. 160. 2 . . . *heora cild* . . . , *of ðam wæs sum gehaten Placidus and sum oðer Maurus* and *ÆCHom* ii. 274. 24 *sume of ðam folce*. For more examples, see Heltveit 1977, p. 54. But the glossators did not always follow their original slavishly. Thus in *Matt(WSCp)* 12. 38 *sume þa boceras* represents Latin *quidam de scribis* (where the OE is probably the native idiom; see §410) and in *Luke(WSCp)* 20. 27 *sume of Saduceum* represents Latin *quidam Saducaeorum* (where the partitive genitive is avoided in the OE in favour of what seems to be an accepted construction in glosses).[100]

§397. Independent *sum* is often found in the singular with the genitive of a numeral. Wülfing (*EStudien*, 17 (1892), 285-91; 24 (1898), 463; and 26 (1899), 455) rightly divides his sixteen examples into three groups. In the first, the literal meaning stands and the main person mentioned is included in the count, e.g.

Beo 3120   Huru se snotra   sunu Wihstanes
                   acigde of corðre   cyniges þegnas
                   syfone (to)somne, þa selestan,
                   eode eahta sum   under inwithrof
                   hilderinca

(where it is clear from the context that *eahta sum* means 'one of eight, with seven others') and

GuthA 708   Ic eom meotudes þegn.
                   Eom ic þara twelfa sum   þe he getreoweste
                   under monnes hiw   mode gelufade

(where we know from external sources that there were twelve and not thirteen Apostles). Another likely example is

Beo 2401   Gewat þa twelfa sum   torne gebolgen
                   dryhten Geata   dracan sceawian;
                   hæfde þa gefrunen,   hwanan sio fæhð aras,
                   bealonið biorna;   him to bearme cwom

---

[99] 'The unique example *sume wif of urum* (*Luke* 24. 24)' referred to by Heltveit (1969, p. 227) is to be found in *Luke(WSCp)* 24. 22. It represents Latin *mulieres quaedam ex nostris*. That such constructions are not native is suggested by the fact that both here and in *Luke* 24. 24 *Li* and *Ru2* have gen. pl. *us(e)ra*.

[100] With *sum of* + dative, cf. *an of* + dative; see Rissanen, p. 57; Heltveit, 1969, p. 228; and §1201.

maðþumfæt mære   þurh ðæs meldan hond.
Se wæs on ðam ðreate   þreotteoða secg,
se ðæs orleges   or onstealde

(where Beowulf, Wiglaf, and the *tydre treowlogan tyne ætsomne* of *Beo* 2847, presumably make up the twelve and the messenger is a thirteenth). To these may be added examples like *Solil* 34. 8 *Ðara fif þinga þu ondredst þæt þu scyle sum forleosan* and

Sea 68   Simle þreora sum   þinga gehwylce
              ær his tiddege   to tweon weorþeð

(in both of which the author spells out all the possibilities).

§398. In the second group, the main person mentioned is clearly excluded from the count, e.g. *Or* 202. 15 *7 Hannibal opfleah feowera sum to Aprametum þæm fæstenne*, Latin *Annibal cum quatuor equitibus Adrumetum confugit*, *LawIIAtr* 4 . . . *oððon gange feowra sum to 7 oðsace—7 beo him sylf fifta*, and *Law(Ld)IIAs* 11 *7 hio gan syððan twelfa sum* [*(So) sume*], Latin *et eant alii cum xii.*

§399. The third group consists of examples which are more or less ambiguous, e.g. *Or* 18. 7 *þara he sæde þæt he syxa sum ofsloge syxtig on twam dagum* and

Beo 207   fiftyna sum
              sundwudu sohte,   secg wisade,
              lagucræftig mon   landgemyrcu.

In these, neither external knowledge nor the context gives any help and the idiom may be used either literally or loosely. The odds are that the latter is the case in examples involving a round number such as *ChronA* 76. 16 (878) *þæs ymb iii wiecan com se cyning to him Godrum þritiga sum þara monna þe in þam here weorþuste wæron æt Alre*, where the meaning is probably 'with thirty of the most important men in the army', and *Bede* 58. 1 *On þyssum ealande com upp se Godes þeow Agustinus 7 his geferan; wæs he feowertiga sum*, Latin *In hac ergo adplicuit seruus Domini Augustinus et socü eius, uiri ut ferunt ferme XL.*

§400. It is generally—and probably rightly—supposed that the literal meaning preserved in MnE 'foursome' is the original one. The confusion which arose may have stemmed in part from the use of the construction with round numbers, as in the last two examples cited, and in part from its use with words or phrases expressing an indefinite number, e.g. *Beo* 1412 *he feara sum beforan gengde* ‖ *wisra monna*, *ÆCHom* i. 580. 5 *eower sum*, and *ÆHom* 8. 151 *sum his*

þegna. For further examples of the construction, see Wülfing, i,
§196 Anm. 2; BT, s.v. *sum* I(1)(*b*); and Brooks's note to *And* 1311.

§401. This usage shades into what Wrenn (*Beowulf*, Glossary, s.v.
sum) describes as 'a remarkable almost demonstr. use'. He detects
this in examples from the poetry like *Beo* 248 *eower sum* 'a notable
one among you' and *Beo* 1312 *eorla sum* 'the notable warrior'—
both references to Beowulf—and in *MRune* 48 *Tir biþ tacna sum*,
which he translates 'Tir is a most important symbol'. We can accept
this sense of *sum*. His extension of it to examples in which *sum* is
used absolutely, e.g. *Beo* 1113 *sume on wæle crungon!* 'notable men
had fallen in the slaughter' and *Wan* 80 *sume wig fornom*, is attractive. Whether or not the usage is to be detected in particular examples
must, however, remain a matter of individual judgement.

(*d*) Sum *in apposition*

i. *With a pronoun*

§402. In the singular, *sum* is regularly found with the partitive genitive of a personal pronoun, e.g. *ÆCHom* i. 580. 5 *eower sum*; see
§410. But the absence of examples of the type ☆*eower sume* suggests
that when a plural form of *sum* is in apposition with a personal pronoun we have what might be called partitive apposition. In other
words *ÆHom* 18. 62 *ge sume* is the plural equivalent of *ÆCHom* i.
580. 5 *eower sum* and means 'some of you'. *Sum* is so used with pronouns of all three persons, immediately before or after the pronoun,
or separated from it, e.g. *Bede* 4. 19 *sume we* and *ÆCHom* i. 212. 21
sume hi; *Or* 88. 22 *hie sume* and *ÆCHom* ii. 546. 22 *hi sume*; *CP*
9. 15 *hi . . . sume* and *ÆCHom* i. 348. 16 *hi . . . sume*. For more such
examples see Heltveit 1977, pp. 52–3.

§403. The type ☆*sum ic (þu)* is, of course, impossible. But we find
sum singular in apposition with a singular third person pronoun
where the reference is to part of a singular collective. The relative
position of the two elements varies as noted above, e.g. *Or* 196. 29
*Binnan ðære byrig wæs micel li[c]ggende feoh funden. Sum hit
Scipia to Rome sende, sum he hit het ðæm folce dælan* and *ChronE*
75. 23 (877) *7 þa on herfeste gefor se here on Myrcena land 7 hit
gedældon sum and sum Ceolwulfe sealdon*. The correlative *sum . . .
sum* clinches the partitive interpretation in both these examples. The
context seems to me similarly decisive in *WHom* 6. 23 *Nu wille ic
þeah be suman dæle scortlice hit eow sum asecgan*.

§404. *Sum* can also be used in partitive apposition with nom. and acc. pl. *þa* 'the, those', in contrast to *ÆLS* 6. 50 *sume þæra*, which is unparalleled in my collections. A few examples will suffice: (with independent *þa*) *Bede* 378. 6 . . . *heofenlicu mægen 7 hælo tacen untrumra* . . . *Ða sume we geara for gemynde awriton in ðære bec* and *Bede* 4. 18 *þa þing þe on Eastenglum gewordene wæron, sume we þa of ealdra manna gewritum oððe sægene metton, sume we mid Isses gesægene . . . geleornodon*; (with dependent *þa*) *Or* 104. 9 *7 Titus Cuintius þa oðre sume gefliemde sume ofslog*; and (with what may be taken as relative *þa*) *Bede* 282. 20 *monig tacn gastlicra mægena . . . þa sumu woe nu gemdon geþeodan in þis user ciriclice stær*, which Miller translates 'many signs of spiritual power . . . some of which we have taken care to insert in this our ecclesiastical history'. But we could have a stop before *þa sumu* and translate 'Some of these . . .', as Miller does in *Bede* 378. 6 above. Alternatively, we could have commas in both. The ambiguity of *þa* is of course notorious. Indeed, it may be the adverb 'then' in some of the examples cited here. Heltveit (1977, p. 52) cites more examples of *þa (. . .) sume* and *sume (. . .) þa*. Neither of us has noted any examples with singular forms of *se*. But since we find *Or* 196. 30 *sum hit* and *Or* 126. 15 *þæt folc sum*, the absence of ☆*þæt sum* and ☆*sum þæt* may be the result of chance.

ii. *With a demonstrative or possessive and a singular noun*

§405. *Sum* in the singular is regularly found with a partitive genitive plural, e.g. *Bede* 156. 20 *sumne þara broðra* and *ÆHom* 8. 151 *sum his þegna*; cf. *eower sum* and the like (§402). Einenkel, however, has drawn our attention to a few examples in which a singular form of *sum* agrees or seems to agree in number, gender, and case, with a noun accompanied by a possessive; see *Ang.* 26 (1903), 545. In one of them—*Bede* 218. 21 *in portice his cirican sumre*, Latin *in porticu quodam ecclesiae*—*sum* is clearly dependent and (as the Latin suggests) goes with *portice* and not with *his cirican*. In *Bede(T)* 418. 7 *sumum hiora geferan, þæs nama wæs Tilmon*, Latin *cuidam de sociis suis, cui nomen erat Tilmon*, MSS *O* and *Ca* agree with *T* in reading *geferan*. But MS *B* has *geferena*, which would give the regular partitive genitive. In *ÆCHom* ii. 520. 10 *ac swa ðeah se wisa Augustinus sæde on sumere his trahtnunge*, Heltveit (1977, pp. 75-6) argues, Thorpe 'would seem to be justified in choosing the rendering "some treatise of his" . . . rather than "one of his treatises", . . . the meaning "part of his treatise" being out of the question'. I do not quite see why, if *LS* 23. 793 *sumne hire lichaman* can mean 'part of her body' (Heltveit 1977, p. 75). Perhaps *trahtnung* and *lichama* were thought of as collective nouns; see §406. *ÆCHom* ii. 520. 10 above could also be regularized by reading *trahtnunge* as genitive plural. But this is a desperate and (I think) scarcely tenable explanation. It could hardly apply to *Bede* 38. 30 . . . *bæd Scs Albanus fram Gode him wæter seald beon to sumre his þenunge*, Latin . . . *Albanus dari sibi a Deo aquam rogauit*,[101] and its shakiness becomes apparent from *GD* 282. 23 *soþlice þære wisan ure munuc sum wæs þær betweoh, se leofað nu gyt*—unless we read *munuca*. But here we must note the different readings in *Bede* 308. 1 *sumum his preosta, þæs noma wæs Berhtwini*, Latin *cuidam de clericis suis*—MSS *O* and *Ca* have *sumum his preoste*—and *Bede* 166. 2 *his þegna sum*, Latin *ministrum ipsius*—where MSS *O* and *Ca* have *his þeng sum*. One can scarcely explain away all these to avoid recognizing that there is an OE idiom in which *sum* singular is in agreement with a (not collective) noun accompanied by a possessive, though we can perhaps agree that it is a rare one; hence I am inclined to support the MS alteration of *lande* to *landa* in *ÆLS* 22. 187 *to sumum his landa* 'to one of his estates'. The translation 'some of his land' is impossible here. I take *ÆCHom* ii. 288. 4 *sume his geswutelunge . . . sume* (cited by Heltveit 1977, p. 51) as plural. In the sermon which follows, Ælfric refers to two appearances by Christ after his Resurrection: first, *John* 21. 1-14, and second, *Luke* 24. 36-51. Whether *sum* here is dependent rather than appositional is a terminological problem; cf. §382. But it is not easy to see how the construction differs from the more usual one with the partitive genitive. In *Bede* 308. 1 above (for example) there seems no significant difference between 'a certain [one] his priest' and 'a certain [one] of his priests'; the context shows what we can readily surmise—that the bishop has more than one priest.

§406. *Sum* is found in the singular with a collective noun in what is clearly a partitive construction; cf. *sum hit* and the like in §403. The pattern ☆*sum his folces* does not, to the best of my knowledge, occur. So I am reluctant to agree with Heltveit (1977, p. 51) that *LS* 23. 793 *sumne hire lichaman* 'may be partitive genitive construction', but prefer to construe *lichaman* as accusative; see §405. Examples of the singular partitive appositive construction, which are found with either the pers. pron. *his* or with the appropriate gender and case of the dem. *se*, include *Or* 188. 10 *sum his folc, Or* 140. 20 *mid sumum þæm fultume, Or* 126. 15 *7 þæt folc sum þær sittan let, sum þonan adræfde, sume on elðiode him wið feo gesealde* (where

---

[101] In fact it is hard to explain this in any way. Perhaps the translator became confused and imported *þenunge* from the phrase in the Latin *martyri obsequium* = *Bede* 38. 33 *to his þenunge*.

the collective singular gives way to the plural), *Or* 206. 16 *þa bebead he sumum þæm folce þæt hie from þæm fæstenne aforen, 7 þa oþre he het þæt hie wið þara oþerra flugen, ChronA* 96. 27 (913) *sum his fultum,* and *ÆCHom* ii. 66. 18 *Nabochodonosor, þe þæt synfulle Godes folc sum acwealde and sum gehæft to his rice gelædde.* For more such examples see Heltveit 1977, pp. 51–2. The second person in *ÆLS* 17. 170 *sum eowre orf* is noteworthy.

iii. *With a demonstrative or possessive and a plural noun*

§407. In the plural, *sum* is used in agreement with the noun, e.g. *ÆCHom* i. 112. 8 *sume þa englas, ÆCHom* i. 98. 26 *sume ure ðeningbec, ÆCHom* ii. 222. 28 *sume ða hæðenan,* and *ÆCHom* i. 560. 14 *sume his geferan*; cf. *sume hi* and the like (§402). That this pattern sometimes at least expresses a partitive relationship can be seen from the context in examples like *ÆCHom* i. 112. 7 *Ða miswendon sume þa englas heora agenne cyre, and þurh modignysse hy sylfe to awyrigedum deoflum geworhton* and from the correlative *sume . . . sume (oðre)* in examples like *ÆCHom* i. 608. 23 *Sume ðas tacna we gesawon gefremmede, sume we ondrædað us towearde* and *ÆCHom* ii. 186. 23 *he cyðde his forðsið on ær sumum his leorning-cnihtum mid him drohtnigendum and sumum oðrum on fyrlenum stowum wunigendum.*

§408. As with the pronoun (§402), *sum* can immediately precede or follow the noun combination, or can be separated from it, e.g. *Or* 162. 14 *sume heora þeowas, ChronE* 57. 13 (794) *heora scipu sume, CP* 433. 7 *sume ða yða, Bede* 388. 2 *ða wundur sumu,* Latin *e quibus aliqua,* and *Or* 18. 1 *þa teð . . . sume*; for further examples see Wülf-ing, i, §322(*b*); Einenkel, *Ang.* 26 (1903), 544; and Heltveit 1977, pp. 51–2. This variation in position adds to the difficulty of deciding whether *sum* is used dependently or independently in such sentences. It would be possible to argue that in *Or* 162. 14 above it was depen-dent (cf. *ÆCHom* i. 386. 17 *sum Godes ðegen*) and that in *Bede* 388. 2 and *Or* 18. 1 above it was independent. Variations like MS *O*'s *sume þa broþor* for *Bede(T)* 320. 3 *sume broðor* might support this. But MS *B* has *þa gebroðor sume*! The problem is terminological; we cannot say and I doubt if it matters.

iv. *Partitive apposition*

§409. But a question which does matter is whether the patterns *ÆCHom* i. 112. 8 *sume þa englas, ÆCHom* ii. 448. 13 *sume his ðeawas,* and *ÆCHom* ii. 350. 32 *þa awerigedan gastas sume,* always express a partitive relationship. There is no doubt in examples like

ÆCHom ii. 56. 23 *Nis gecweden on ðam godspelle, þæt ða wæter-fatu, sume heoldon twyfealde gemetu, sume þryfealde* and *ÆCHom* ii. 264. 23 *Sume ðas race we habbað getrahtnod on oðre stowe, sume we willað nu geopenian, þæt þe belimpð to ðam halgan husle.*[102] Wülfing (i, §322) preceded a collection of examples of *sum* singular and plural used in agreement with nouns and pronouns with the following observation: 'dem Sinne nach sollte man erwarten, daß das Hauptwort oder das Fürwort im (partitiven) Genitive stände, denn *sum* bezeichnet beim Hauptwort ein einzelnes Stück oder einzelne Stücke der durch dieses bezeichneten Gattung, beim Fürworte einen Teil des durch dieses ausgedrückten Begriffes.'[103] Heltveit, however, disagrees.[104] He claims that 'scholars seem to have been reluctant to recognize the appositional construction as a construction in its own right, and thus different from the partitive construction' (1969, p. 231) and, after quoting part of Wülfing's remark above, goes on (1969, p. 232):

A priori, however, it would seem highly unreasonable to think that the appositional construction had no other function than that of expressing partitiveness, the more so as there were two other constructions available, the partitive genitive construction and the *of*-construction. The fact that these constructions and the appositional constructions are all found in Old English with the same pronominal adjectives gives us a right to assume that the appositional construction was only partly similar in meaning to the partitive genitive and *of*-constructions.

He repeats the accusation of reluctance (1977, pp. 72-3) and the claim that the existence of three constructions with *sum* justifies his assumption that there is a semantic (not merely a syntactic) difference between them (1977, pp. 73, 74, 76-7, and 79). In his view, the construction which I call partitive apposition is the equivalent and

---

[102] Heltveit (1977, pp. 74-5) takes *sume ðas race* in this example as singular and follows Thorpe's translation, 'some of this narrative'. The translation 'some of these narratives' is acceptable in the context, and is more plausible syntactically, for it makes the phrase regular rather than exceptional, unless we assume that *racu* was thought of as a collective noun; cf. §406. The fact that *þæt þe* is singular does not certify that *sume ðas race* and *sume* are singular. That would require the nominative singular feminine of the '*sepe* relative, viz. *seo þe*. (The *se'þe* form would be *þa þe*, which could be accusative singular feminine or nominative accusative plural.) I believe that *þæt þe* is used here emphatically, in the sense 'thát which' or 'what'; see §2130.

[103] 'according to the sense, one should expect the noun or pronoun to be in the (partitive) genitive, for *sum* denotes in the case of the noun an individual member or members of the class denoted by the noun, in the case of the pronoun a part of the concept expressed by the pronoun'.

[104] Here I permit myself the rare luxury of explaining the genesis of one of my discussions (or of a discussion of mine). I had reached the conclusions set out here before I read Heltveit's article in *EStudies*, 50 (1969), 225-35. I then rebutted (to my own satisfaction) the views he expressed there. But, although in my opinion he had really nothing new to say on the use of *sum*, he returned to the topic in *NJL* 31 (1977), 47-94, at such length that I felt compelled to scrap what I had written and to rewrite these sections.

forerunner of the MnE construction seen in phrases like 'some companions of his' and 'a friend of mine' (1969, pp. 225-35, and 1977, pp. 72-82). As I hope to show by examining both the assumption[105] and the conclusion, the scholars Heltveit criticizes had good reasons for being 'reluctant'.

§410. The table which follows is based on Heltveit's figures (1977, pp. 51-72). It gives the number of examples of the three constructions in Old English; I have excluded ME examples[106] and have made some necessary, but silent, corrections.

TABLE 1

Code Letter	Construction		*Sum* singular	*Sum* plural
(*a*)	*Sum* in partitive apposition (Heltveit's 'concatenative construction')	singular of a collective noun	18	107
		singular of a non-collective noun	2[107]	0
(*b*)	*Sum* + partitive genitive		31	5[108]
(*c*)	*Sum* + *of* + dative		6	11

This table suggests to me that we do not have 'a right to assume that the appositional construction was only partly similar in meaning to the partitive genitive and *of*-constructions' (Heltveit 1969, p. 232). Before reading Heltveit's 1969 article, I had considered the possibility that the appositive and partitive constructions were originally different, that the same sort of confusion or conflation might have taken place as befell the English equivalent of the *unus maximus* construction, and that one could therefore translate *ÆCHom* i. 44. 25 *sume ða ungeleaffullan Iudei* as 'certain men, the unbelieving Jews', *ÆCHom* i. 206. 16 *sume ða ungeleaffullan* as 'certain men, the unbelievers', and *ÆCHom* ii. 516. 4 *sumum his gebroðrum* as 'to certain men, his

[105] For what it is worth, it can be said that the fact that *fela* is used in three different constructions (§426) has not led to the assumption that they differed semantically.
[106] Heltveit (1977, p. 79) gives these figures for his ME texts: (*a*) 7, (*b*) 25, and (*c*) 45. (Heltveit's figures are not complete. Nor are mine. There is room for more work here.)
[107] These are *ÆCHom* ii. 264. 23, which can be taken as plural (§409), and *ÆCHom* ii. 520. 10(11) (§§405 and 411). I have excluded *ÆCHom* ii. 288. 4 (§405) and *ÆLS* 22. 187 (§405).
[108] These are *BlHom* 213. 26, *ÆCHom* i. 540. 6, *ÆCHom* ii. 356. 29, *Luke(WSCp)* 20. 39, and *ÆLS* 6. 50. None of these is of the type *ꞩeower sume*; see §402. All involve a noun in the genitive except *ÆLS* 6. 50 *sume þæra*. There are more; see §395.

brothers'. This would have meant that the appositive construction could sometimes be all-embracing, as in these examples, sometimes partitive, as in *ÆCHom* ii. 56. 23 and *ÆCHom* ii. 264. 23 (both in §409). I was forced to reject this idea. My initial reason was that the context in all three examples (and, as far as I could see, in all similar ones) suggested that a partitive relationship existed. But the following facts confirmed me in my judgement: first, all three constructions are used to render *Matt* 28. 11 (§395), while for *Matt* 9. 3 *quidam de scribis* the W-S version has *sume þa boceras, Li sum oðer from uðuutum*, and *Rul sume þara bocera*; second, this *of* construction is in my opinion essentially of Latin, not native, origin, as Heltveit almost concedes (1977, pp. 78 and 79), and is therefore an addition to—not a competitor of—the other two constructions; and third, as the table shows, there is no real overlap between the other two constructions, the general rule being *sum* singular + partitive genitive—except with a collective noun or pronoun, when we have partitive apposition—and *sum* plural + partitive apposition. There is thus a syntactical difference between them, as Heltveit almost realized (1977, pp. 74-5) and as another table based on the same figures shows.

TABLE 2

Construction	Partitive apposition	Partitive genitive
Appositive *sum* with singular of collective noun or pronoun	18	0
Appositive *sum* with plural	107	5
Singular *sum* and non-collective noun	2	31
Totals	127	36

The seven exceptions are all in late texts (fnn. 107 and 108 to Table 1 above) and can be explained as the result of analogical confusion—an assumption justified by a comparison of the figures for OE given in Table 1 above with those for ME given in fn. 106 to the same table.

§411. Having established that there is a syntactical difference between the two constructions, I conclude that Heltveit's search for a semantic one was unnecessary. It is now time to ask whether the one he produced does in fact exist. Before I read his second article,

I had written as follows of his suggestion that the MnE idiom 'a friend of mine' may derive from the construction seen in *sume his geferan*:

I do not yet see how *his* can mean 'of his' in two of the examples on which he pins his argument in 1969, pp. 232-3, viz. *ÆCHom* ii. 520. 11 *on sumere his trahtnunge* and *ChronE* 53. 4 (777) *his ane mynstre* (quoted correctly in 1969, p. 231, wrongly in 1969, p. 232). It is rather to be translated 'of him, belonging to him', which is not quite the same thing as far as his argument is concerned. There is something odd about the morphology of the latter (a Peterborough addition). For different ways of interpreting it, see the idioms discussed by Rissanen, pp. 15-16, 80-2, and 157-8.

Despite Heltveit's reiterated claims (1977, pp. 75 and 89), I persist in the belief that the gen. *his* in *ÆCHom* ii. 520. 11 *on sumere his trahtnunge* or in *ChronE* 53. 4 (777) *his ane mynstre* is not the equivalent of 'of his' in 'some treatise of his' or in 'a church of his', no matter whether we say that the MnE phrases are 'unmarked for partitiveness', as Heltveit (1977, p. 75) asserts, or that in them 'the partitive idea . . . mingles with that of possession' (Curme 1931, p. 76). Attempts to equate the two constructions must, I believe, founder on this rock. Heltveit seems to me to concede this when he says (1977, p. 77) that in *ÆCHom* ii. 356. 24 . . . *ða æt sumon gefeohte wearð an ðegen Æþelredes cyninges mid oðrum cempum afylled* 'Thorpe's translation . . . *a thane of King Æthelred* would seem to be more adequate than would have been *one of King Æthelred's thanes*', although in my opinion the second translation is impossible rather than less 'adequate'; it would require *ðegna*. For similar reasons, *Or* 216. 20 *On þæm fleame wearð an Ueriatuses þegn þæm oþrum to longe æfterfylgende* . . . (Heltveit 1977, pp. 54-5) must be translated 'a thane of Veriatus', not 'one of Veriatus's thanes'.

§412. In his 1977 article, Heltveit brings to his support examples with a demonstrative—in addition to those with a genitive or possessive to which he restricted himself in 1969—examples such as *Or* 290. 5 *sume þa munecas, Or* 18. 1 *þa teð hie brohton sume þæm cyninge, Matt(WSCp)* 12. 38 *sume þa boceras*, Latin *quidam de scribis, ÆCHom* i. 44. 25 *sume ða ungeleaffullan Iudei, ÆCHom* ii. 350. 32 *þa awerigedan gastas sume, WHom* 12. 73 *sume þa Denisce men*, and *ChronE* 179. 7 (1052) *sume þa scipu.* Now it is obvious that these have nothing to do with 'a friend of mine'. What do they mean? Heltveit (1977, p. 78) says that in *Or* 18. 1 above '*sume* may be characterized as a detached adjunct giving additional information about the headword, viz. the information that only a limited number of members of the class in question are involved'. Could one have a better definition of partitive apposition? He admits (1977,

p. 82) that *Matt(WSCp)* 12. 38 is partitive in meaning. It is beyond dispute that *ÆCHom* i. 112. 7 *Ða miswendon sume þa englas heora agenne cyre and þurh modignysse hy sylfe to awyrigedum deoflum geworhton* is partitive. It does not refer to a certain group, viz. the angels as opposed to God or to Adam and Eve, but means 'some of the angels'. As I have already said, this is in my opinion true of all examples with plural *sum* and an appositive element. Heltveit's claim (1977, p. 80) that *WHom* 12. 21-4 contains two exceptions with *sume hy* cannot stand. In his previous paragraph, Wulfstan twice says (*WHom* 12. 4 and 12. 11) that *mancyn(n)* was deceived. Here he is explaining the various heresies into which different groups fell.

§413. If we now return to *ÆCHom* i. 560. 14 *and he eac sume his geferan to Ispanian gesende, þæt hi ðam leodscipe lifes word gecyddon*, we see that it would be perverse to claim that Dionysius sent all his companions to Spain. There is no possible ambiguity in *ÆCHom* ii. 186. 22 *þæs geares ðe he gewat he cyðde his forðsið on ær sumum his leorningcnihtum mid him drohtnigendum and sumum oðrum on fyrlenum stowum wunigendum*. In examples like these too we have partitive apposition.

§414. Heltveit (1977, p. 85) believes that 'possessives were not on a par with the definite article as determiners in Old English times'. The evidence for this belief is slender—seven examples of the combination possessive + strong form of adjective other than dat. sg. masc./neut. *-um* + noun out of 435, i.e. 1.6 per cent (1977, pp. 83-4)—and the belief is not necessary for the acceptance of 'the *possibility* [my italics] that the concept of "belonging" ("some men who are his") . . . is in focus in both the Old English and the Old Norse concatenative constructions containing a possessive or a genitive' (1977, p. 77) and 'that the concatenative construction containing a demonstrative (or the definite article) . . . may have been preferred . . . in cases where interest centres round a group as an entity' (1977, p. 77). The difference between a possessive or genitive and a demonstrative in itself establishes the *possibility*. But even if we accept this difference as real, both constructions exemplify partitive apposition, for in each the group is part of a larger group. So Heltveit was guilty of a false dichotomy when he wrote 'rather than that of partitiveness' before the phrase 'is in focus' in the first of the two statements just cited and 'to the latter' [the partitive genitive construction] after the word 'preferred' in the second. The vital point is that—with a few exceptions which I regard as analogical—the only way of combining the plural of *sum*, a possessive or genitive or a demonstrative, and a plural noun, in OE was to use the idiom seen in ✩*sume Godes/*

his/þa men. I cannot say whether *se mann on þæm Cloppames wæne* would have taken *ÆLS* 7. 385 *mid sumum his mannum* to mean 'with some men who were his' or 'with some of his men', or whether he would have been unconscious of the delicate difference. But I remain persuaded that such an OE phrase is not the syntactic or semantic equivalent of 'some men of his' and that the difference between partitive apposition and the partitive genitive is syntactic, and not semantic, as Heltveit would have us believe.[109]

§415. In the course of his second article, Heltveit cites numerous examples from OE involving 'quantifiers' other than *sum* and from MnE. But their relevance may be questioned. I cannot, for example, see how the fact that *ChronE* 142. 25 (1012) *his þa haligan sawle* and MnE 'that holy soul of his' are not partitive (1977, pp. 79-80) throws any light on OE constructions with *sum*. The same can be said of many other examples. The invalidity of many of the comparisons he makes and the obscuration caused by the blanket figures he produces (1977, pp. 72-82) can be demonstrated by the tendencies apparent in the table below for 'quantifiers' other than *sum*, which are based on Heltveit's figures (1977, pp. 51-72) but never clearly emerge in his work.

TABLE 3

Quantifier	Number of Old English examples			
	Appositive construction		Partitive genitive	*Of* + dative
An	6		95	35
Other numerals (excluding exx. with *sum*)	32	(including 20 with pers. pron. in pre-position)	28	7
Nan	0		85	0
Manig	11		16	7
Ælc	1		95	1
Ænig	2		14	1
Nænig	0		6	0
Ægðer	0		25	0
Naðer	0		4	0
Feawe	3	(2 partitive, 1 predicative)	8	0

[109] It is only fair to remark here that Schrader (p. 55) and Einenkel (*Ang.* 26 (1903), 544-5, repeating much of *Ang.* 21 (1889), 516-18) had the root of the matter. See further Einenkel in *Ang.* 28 (1905), 504-8. In *Language*, 44 (1968), 750-3, Schwartz briefly mentions variations between appositional and partitive constructions with *sum* and other OE words in the course of discussing MnE usages.

Notes on Table 3:

1. Of the three constructions under discussion, the partitive genitive is the only one Heltveit recorded for OE with *nan, nænig* (but see §437), *ægðer,* and *naðer,* and is markedly preponderant with *ælc* (ninety-five of ninety-seven examples) and *ænig* (fourteen of seventeen examples).

2. Of the six examples with *an, hiera* in *ChronA* 14. 1 (465) *hiera þegn an* may be a partitive genitive; *ChronE* 15. 1 (465) has *heora an þegn* and *ChronB* and *C* omit *þegn.* Partitive apposition is possible, though not obligatory, in *Or* 216. 21, and seems the most likely explanation in the remaining four.

3. Of the thirty-two examples with numerals other than *an*—I omit *Luke(WSCp)* 10. 1 . . . *and sende hig twam,* where *hig* is accusative and *twam* distributive dative—the twelve in pre-position all involve an adjective and/or a noun and all seem to me to exemplify partitive apposition. The remaining twenty all have a personal pronoun followed by a numeral. In most of them the numeral is probably predicative, e.g. *Or* 152. 14 *betux him twæm,* where the reference is to Seleucus and Lisimachus and the translator would have used the third person dual pronoun had there been one, and *Mark(WSCp)* 3. 14 *hi twelfe,* Latin *duodecim* (not 'zero', as Heltveit reports). *Mark(WSCp)* 16. 12 *him twam* represents Latin *duobus ex eis,* but is hardly evidence for a native partitive use of such combinations. Indeed, the distribution of the twenty examples—*Orosius* four, *Gospels* nine, and *ÆCHom* and *ÆLS* seven—suggests that the combination may have been an alien one, whatever its function.

4. Of Heltveit's twelve examples with *manig,* I exclude *ÆCHom* i. 266. 28. In *Mark(WSCp)* 2. 15 and *BlHom* 79. 31, *þa þe* may equal 'who' rather than 'those who', as Heltveit (1977, pp. 81–2) points out. In *ÆCHom* ii. 276. 23 *manega* is predicative. The remaining eight seem to me to exemplify partitive apposition.

§416. The examples of partitive apposition with *an,* with numerals other than *an,* and with *manig,* set out in Table 3, added to those with *sum,* establish partitive apposition as an OE idiom. That is where my brief ends. To prolong this discussion by attempting to determine the origin of the MnE idiom 'a friend of mine' lies outside the scope of this work.

(5) Hwa, hwæt

§417. These are used independently, either alone, e.g. *ÆCHom* i. 8. 9 *Nu bidde ic . . . gif hwa þas boc awritan wylle, þæt he hi geornlice gerihte . . . ,* or with a partitive genitive, e.g. *ÆCHom* i. 404. 3

Gif hwa hwæt lytles æniges bigwistes him sylfum gearcode; Wülfing is wrong when he describes *hwa* in *Bo* 109. 13 as an adjective (i, §326). Again, it is clearly a slip on Closs's part when she states that the indefinites *hwa* and *hwæt* are indeclinable (pp. 110-11); we find *Bo* 118. 12 *Ac gif dysegra hwone tweoge æniges þara spella þe we ær ymb spræacon*, *ÆCHom* ii. 588. 28 *Gif hwæs getimbrung ðurhwunað and ðam fyre wiðstent*. . . . *Gif hwæs weorc forbyrnð* . . . , and *ÆCHom* i. 132. 27 *Gif hwam twynige be ðam gemænelicum æriste*. . . .

§418. By virtue of their meaning, *hwa* and *hwæt* appear most frequently in clauses introduced by conjunctions implying condition or doubt, e.g. *gif* (see §417 and, for further examples, Fröhlich, pp. 27-8), *buton* (*CP* 9. 6), *þeah* (*Or* 34. 35), *ðonne* (*CP* 39. 6), *ðylæs* (*CP* 23. 13), or *þæt* (*ÆCHom* i. 256. 20; cf. *ÆCHom* i. 256. 21 *gif hwa*). But there are naturally some exceptions, e.g. *CP* 347. 5 *7 on ðæm chore beoð manige menn gegadrode anes hwæt to singanne* and *Mald* 2 *Het þa hyssa hwæne hors forlætan*. Further on *anes hwæt* 'anything, something', see Wülfing, i, §328, and Rissanen, pp. 244-5. On the interrogative use of *hwa* and *hwæt*, see §§348-54.

(6) Hwæthwugu

§419. In the sense of 'something (small)', *hwæthwugu* appears independently, both alone, e.g. *Bede* 342. 29 *Cedmon, sing me hwæthwugu* and *ÆCHom* ii. 90. 29 *þæt sæd þe bufon ðam stænigum lande feol sprytte hwæt hwega*, and with a partitive genitive, e.g. *CP* 147. 1 . . . *ðætte ðonne ðæt mod ðara underðiedra hwæthwugu ryhtlices ongitan mæg*. . . . It may also occur dependently, e.g. *Bede* 6. 19 *Ðæt, ða seo ehtnysse blan, seo cyrice on Breotene hwæthwugu fæc sibbe hæfde*. . . . According to Bately (*Ang.* 88 (1970), 448), it does not occur in *Orosius*.

(7) Hwilc, hwilchwugu

§420. *Hwilc* is used both dependently, e.g. *BlHom* 239. 29 *Wen is þæt hwilc wundor ineode on þæt carcern*, and independently, e.g. (alone) *BlHom* 153. 19 *7 þonne gif hwylc gelyfe on God* . . . and (with a partitive genitive) *BlHom* 125. 12 . . . *þonne ure Drihten ure hwylces neosian wille*. On the construction *urne hwelcne* in *CP* 63. 1 and examples like it, see §301.

§421. Like *hwa* and *hwæt*, *hwilc* is usually found in clauses introduced by conjunctions implying condition or doubt. Thus, in addition to the examples in §420, we find clauses introduced by *gif* (*ÆCHom* i. 140. 2), *se ðe* (*Bo* 12. 8), *swelce* 'as if' (*Alex* 26. 18), *þeah* (*Bo* 77. 18), and *þy læs* (*Bede* 58. 20). But there are exceptions, e.g. *ThCap1* 28. 14 *Sona swa sacerda hwylc hwone on won gesyhð* and *Bede* 66. 19 *Ac me nu þynceð 7 bet licað, þætte swa hwæt swa þu oðþo in Romana cirican oðþo in Gallia oðþo in hwylcre oðerre hwæt þæs gemætte, þætte ælmeahtegum Gode ma licie, þæt þu bihygdelice þæt geceose.* . . . Fröhlich's limited corpus led him to express himself too strongly on this point (p. 27). For further examples of *hwilc oþer* see BTS, s.v. *hwilc* IV(1)(*b*).

§422. As Rissanen notes (p. 239), *hwilc* is sometimes found with *an*, either in agreement with it, e.g. *CP* 413. 24 *for anre hwelcre* and *Bo* 86. 28 *hwylc an þara fif goda*, or in the combination *anra hwilc*, e.g. *Bo* 77. 23 *ure anra hwelc*. Of his eight examples, six are in 'Alfredian' prose and two in verse. He glosses *hwilc* as 'every', 'each', 'any'. The first two senses, though supported by some of the translators and by GK for one of the verse examples (*Met* 20. 65), are not well attested. In some of the examples given by Rissanen and BT(S), the sense 'any one' is possible and perhaps preferable. But 'every' or 'each' seems right in *CP* 435. 26 . . . *ðætte he fullfremme hwelc yfel huru ðurh geðeaht* 'every evil', *LawAfEl(E)* 49. 7 *æt mæstra hwelcre misdæde* [MS *So hwelcra*, MS *Ld hwylcra*, but MS *H gehwylcre* 'ge- änd. in -cere' (Liebermann)] (BT, s.v. *hwilc* III, 'for almost every misdeed'), *BlHom* 125. 12 . . . *þonne ure Drihten ure hwylces neosian wille*, Morris 'when our Lord will visit each of us', and (with *an*, following Rissanen) *CP* 413. 23 . . . *ðonne hie for anre hwelcre* [*synne*] *hreowsiað, ðonne hreowsiað hie for ealle*, where the Latin has *unumquodque erroris*. The lexicographers have some work to do here.

§423. *Hwilchwugu* is used in the same way as *hwilc*; for examples see Wülfing, i, §341; BT(S), s.v.; *OEG*, §722; and Rissanen, pp. 238 and 239. Bately notes that it occurs only once in *Orosius*—*Or* 110. 13—and twice in *Boethius* (*Ang.* 88 (1970), 448 fn. 105).

(8) Feawe

§424. *Feawe* 'few' can be declined strong and weak, is found in the superlative (see *OEG*, §§653(2) and 657), and can be accompanied by an intensifying adverb. It is used dependently, e.g. *Or* 17. 4 *on feawum stowum*, *BlHom* 37. 11 *þas feawan dagas*, and *ÆGram* 30. 3 *ane feawa naman*, and independently—both alone, e.g. *Or* 32. 19 *butan swiðe feawum*, *CP* 3. 13 *swiðe feawa*, *Or* 92. 20 *þa feawan þe þær to lafe wurdon*, *ÆCHom* i. 70. 21 *Feawa he awrat be his menniscnysse*, and *ÆCHom* ii. 158. 33 *ane feawe*, and with a partitive

genitive, e.g. *Or* 56. 9 . . . *hiera feawe to lafe wurdon, ÆCHom* ii.
396. 7 *seofon hlafas and feawa fixa, ÆCHom* i. 386. 32 *sume feawa
daga*, and *ÆCHom* ii. 444. 26 *and feawa is ðæra manna ðe mage
ealle ða halgan bec* . . . *þurhsmeagan* (where the singular verb suggests
that Ælfric was thinking collectively). For further examples, see
Schrader, p. 55, and Wülfing, i, §§374-5.

§425. *Feawe* is also found in partitive apposition (§409), e.g. *CP*
5. 7 7 *swiðe feawe ða ðeawas, Bede* 332. 21 *mid feawum hire
geferum* (cf. *Bede* 358. 25 *mid feawa his geferena* and *Bede* 388. 7
mid feaum broðrum his geferum), and *ApT* 8. 21 *and swa mid
feawum þam getrywestum mannum.*

(9) Fela *and* unrim

§426. *Fela* 'much, many' is indeclinable and cannot be compared,
but can be accompanied by an intensifying adverb. It can be used
dependently, e.g. *Bede* 448. 19 *fela gear, ÆCHom* i. 358. 6 *fela
witegan, ÆGram* 84. 7 *fela win*, and *ÆCHom* ii. 112. 31 *fela oðre
gecorene halgan*, and independently—both alone, e.g. *Bede* 4. 7
Swyðe fela hi me sædon . . . , *ÆHom* 2. 246 *to fela*, and *ÆCHom* i.
386. 25 *and he sceal fela ðrowian*, and with a partitive genitive,
which may be singular, e.g. *Or* 24. 25 *þæs landes swa fela, BlHom*
21. 7 *feala fægeres*, and *Mald* 90 *landes to fela*, or plural, e.g. *Or*
17. 31 *fela spella, ÆCHom* i. 4. 3 *fela tacna and wundra*, and *Beo*
311 *ofer landa fela*. It can also occur in partitive apposition (§409),
e.g. *ÆHomM* 4. 32 *forþam ðe þa Iudeiscan fela gelyfdon on urne
hælend Crist*. In view of this variety of usage, the observation by
Marckwardt (*Meritt Essays*, p. 54) that '*fela* became obsolete, possibly because the distinctive genitive plural case construction it originally demanded did not survive the Middle English breakdown of the
Old English inflectional system' seems dubious. For further examples
of all patterns, see Schrader, pp. 55-6; Wülfing, i, §§372-3; and
Einenkel, *Ang.* 27 (1903), 89-90.

§427. Marckwardt (*Meritt Essays*, p. 53) remarks that 'the construction *fela oðerra muneca* could have been interpreted either as "many
of the other monks", or "many other monks" '. I have not been able
to trace this example (which he may have manufactured, for elsewhere he cites author and text, though not always page and line—
a lapse in which he has too many companions). But it seems to me
that in the absence of *þara* the latter is what it would mean; cf. *Or*
280. 19 7 *for þon gebode gewurdon fela martyra on X wintra firste*
'. . . many martyrs' with *Or* 268. 28 7 *fela þara senatorum he het*

ofslean þe þær betste wæron '. . . many of the senators . . .'. So we cannot be certain that he is right in suggesting (loc. cit.) that 'the resolution of the ambiguity through the use of *monig* may well bear some relationship to the increase, in Middle English, in the frequency of *many* at the expense of *fela*'.

§428. Closs (p. 97) tells us that '*fela* "many" always determines singular number in the following verb'. This is not true either for her particular text, *Orosius*, or for OE in general, and may not even be true of the example she cites to illustrate her 'rule', viz. *Or* 68. 25 *þa acsedon hie hine hu fela þær swelcerra manna wære*, where *wære* might be preterite subjunctive plural; see §19 and below. It is hard to see why Closs made this statement, for Wülfing (i, §§372-3) long ago cited examples from 'Alfredian' texts (including *Orosius*) of *fela* with both singular and plural verbs, especially drawing attention to *Or* 38. 23 *Se kyningc Pharon hæfde syx hund wigwægna, 7 swa fela þæs oðres heres wæs þæt man mæg þanon oncnawan, þa him swa fela manna ondredon swa mid Moyse wæron*, and BTS (s.v. *fela* I(2)(*b*)) quotes similar examples from both prose (including *Orosius*) and poetry.

§429. According to Wülfing the verb is in the singular when *fela* means 'much' (*viel*) and in the plural when it means 'many' (*viele*). This seems to involve circular argument and would lead to some un-natural translations in MnE—*fela* in *Or* 182. 34 *7 fela ofslagen wearð on ægðere healfe* and in *Or* 82. 26 *7 hiora þær wearð fela ofslægen 7 adruncen 7 gefangen* can hardly be translated 'much', though this may be possible in *Bo* 144. 25 *Fela is þara þinga þe God ær wat ær hit geweorðe*. The situation seems to be this in *Orosius*: *fela* alone (as in *Or* 182. 34 above) or with a genitive singular (as in *Or* 148. 16 . . . *þæs folces wæs swa fela to him gecirred*) has a singular verb, but with *fela* + genitive plural the verb can be singular (as in *Or* 82. 26 above) or plural (e.g. *Or* 188. 1 . . . *þara horsa fela for-wurdon* and *Or* 280. 19 *7 for þon gebode gewurdon fela martyra on X wintra firste*). The translation will depend on the context and on the meaning of the noun in the genitive; it may be helpful to recall here Marckwardt's observation (*Meritt Essays*, pp. 50-1) that *fela* is used with the singular of 'mass nouns' (cf. MnE 'much water') and with the plural of 'count nouns' (cf. MnE 'many books' and 'many waters'). If the situation is as described above, the ambiguous *wære* would be singular in *Or* 24. 25 *næs na for ðam þe þæs landes swa fela wære* and either singular or plural in *Or* 68. 25 (Closs's example quoted in §428). Similarly, *mægge* in *Bede* 234. 22 *ma þonne fela monna gelyfan mægge* could be singular or plural. This would be in accordance with the fluctuation of number after collectives and genitive plurals discussed in §§78–86 and 2343–50. As far as I have observed, the same distinction seems to hold for *unrim*; for examples, see BT, s.v.

§430. In Ælfric the verb after *fela* is usually plural, e.g. *ÆCHom* ii. 82. 5 *fela cumað, ÆHom* 1. 47 *swa fela swa hine underfengon, ÆHom* 2. 246 *to fela forfarap*, and *ÆCHom* i. 22. 23 *pa wæron pær swa fela gereord swa ðær manna wæron*. But it can be singular, e.g. *ÆCHom* i. 318. 22 *and wæron siððan swa fela gereord swa ðæra wyrhtena wæs* (cf. the previous example) and *ÆHom* 18. 63 *ac eower fela nat hu hyt wæs be Loðe*.

§431. In Wulfstan, however, *fela* has a singular verb, even when accompanied by a genitive plural, e.g. *WHom* 20(*C*). 105 *7 fela ungelumpa gelumpð pisse peode.*[110]

(10) Lytel *and* micel, manig

§432. Einenkel includes these words, which are usually classified as adjectives, in his list of indefinites.[111] They can be declined, compared,[112] and preceded by intensifying adverbs. They can be used dependently, e.g. *Or* 20. 14 *7 pær bið swyðe manig burh, 7 on ælcere byrig bið cyningc* (where *manig*—with a singular verb—is distributive, 'many a city') and *ChronA* 98. 33 (918) *monige men*, and independently, either alone, e.g. *ChronA* 62. 35 (838) *7 monige mid him* and *Or* 218. 3 *swa pa monegan ær dydan*, or with a partitive genitive, e.g. *Lch* i. 86. 7 *do lytel sealtes to, Bo* 99. 16 *hiora monigne, Bede* 174. 14 *monige para broðra*, and *ÆCHom* i. 316. 32 *micel landes*,[113]

---

[110] See Mohrbutter, p. 54, and Bethurum, p. 360, note to line 54 (where 'Dunkhase' should be 'Mohrbutter').

[111] In *Ang.* 26 (1902), 546, he adds *gewis* on the strength of examples like *GD* 98. 29 *on gewissum dagum*, Latin *certis diebus*; cf. BTS, s.v. *gewis* III. It seems to me possible that in these *gewis* may mean something different from *sum* and may not be indefinite; the idea that it is may arise through an ambiguity in MnE 'certain', which could perhaps translate both. But the problem is semantic rather than syntactic; the ambiguity of words meaning 'certain' is not restricted to MnE.

[112] The grammars do not seem to provide comparative and superlative forms for *manig*. But it is open to argument that in examples like *ChronA* 84. 29 (894) *mæstra daga ælce, mæst* is the superlative of *manig* rather than of *micel*. Cf. Curme 1931, p. 501. Marckwardt (*Merrit Essays*, p. 53) observes that *monig word, monig leoð, monig sædeor* can be construed as nominative/accusative singular or nominative/accusative plural. But the standard grammars show the preferred neuter plural form of *monig* as *monigu*.

[113] It seems superfluous to quote further examples. They can be found as follows: *lytel*, Einenkel, *Ang.* 27 (1903), 131–4; *læs* and *læst*, ibid., pp. 135–6; *manig*, Schrader, p. 56, Wülfing, i, §§370–1, and Einenkel, *Ang.* 27 (1903), 81–8; *micel*, Schrader, pp. 56–7, and Einenkel, *Ang.* 27 (1903), 96–7; *mara* and *mæst*, ibid., pp. 98–128 and 129–30. See also BT(S), s.vv.

Marckwardt (*Meritt Essays*, pp. 53–4) sees the use of *mycel* in 'absolute constructions' as or with *of* + the dative, e.g. *ÆLS* 31. 183 *manega of þam folce*. For more examples of these last two constructions and of *manig* in partitive apposition, see §§415–16.

§433. Distributive *manig* is usually accompanied by a singular verb, e.g. *ChronA* 66. 1 (853) *7 þær wearþ monig mon ofslægen* and *Beo* 918 *Eode scealc monig*, but the plural is found in *El* 231 *þær wlanc manig æt Wendelsæ* ‖ *on stæðe stodon. Visser*, i. 79, seems to overlook the significance of this example. Andrew (*Postscript*, pp. 60–1) draws our attention to several examples like

Beo 171   Monig oft gesæt
              rice to rune;   ræd eahtedon . . . ,

where distributive *monig* is followed first by a singular, then by a plural, verb. Again, we may compare the usage after collectives; see §§78–86.

(11) þing

§434. The noun *þing* is often found in combination with some of the words discussed in these sections. Thus we find *ænig þing, sum þing; æghwilc þing, ælc þing, gehwilc þing; nan þing, nænig þing*; and *oþer þing*. Such combinations as *ænige þinga* and *nænige þinga* are used adverbially, the former usually in negative clauses or clauses expressing condition or doubt; on these see Arngart, *NM* 80 (1979), 46, and 82 (1981), 368–9, who also lists prepositional phrases such as *þurh ænig/ælc þing* 'by any/every means' and *mid nanum þingum* 'by no means'. Einenkel detects indefiniteness in combinations like *soð þing* and *wundorlic þing*, which he glosses as *(etwas) wahres* and *(etwas) wunderbares*. See further *Ang.* 27 (1903), 178.

d. Words meaning 'either of two, one or the other'

§435. *Hwæþer* seems to occur only independently with a partitive genitive, e.g. *Bo* 106. 9 *Twa ðing sindon . . . gif ðonne hwæm ðara twega hwæðres wana bið. . . .*[114] That this is probably the result of

in *ÆCHom* i. 316. 32 *micel landes*, where 'the reference is clearly to extent or quantity' as one factor in the change by which *mycel* came to imply quantity 'much' rather than size 'big, great'. He sees another as its use 'with non-countables and abstractions, where the notions of size and quantity tend to merge'; he cites examples like *mycel mod*. Examples involving a collective noun, e.g. *ChronA* 102. 3 (921) *micel folc*, are probably important too.

[114] For further examples, see Wülfing, i, §342. According to BT, s.v. *hwæþer* III, and BTS, s.v. *hwæþer* IV, *hwæþer* means 'each of two, both' in *Sat* 131 *Hwæþer hat and ceald . . .* and in *ChronE* 73. 2 (871) *on hwæðre hand* (a dependent use). But ASPR and Clubb both read *Hwæt! her* in the first example and in the second the variant reading *ChronA* 72. 2 *on gehwæþere hond* may be correct.

chance or faulty observation is suggested by the fact that *ahwæþer* and its contractions *awþer, owþer, aþer* (*OEG*, §718 fn. 3) are used both dependently, e.g. *Or* 58. 2 *(Heora) þeh wurdon feawa to lafe on aðre hand*, and independently, alone, e.g. *Or* 290. 21 *þa ofer-ho(go)de he þæt he him aðer dyde, oþþe wiernde, oþþe tigþade . . .*, or with a partitive genitive, e.g. *Or* 134. 7 . . . *ær heora aðer mehte on oþrum sige geræcan*; see Wülfing, i, §§344–6. The correlative is *oþer*, as in the last example and *CP* 189. 9 *Ðonne is micel ðearf, ðonne him mon ðissa tuega hwæðer ondrætt suiður ðonne oðer. . . .*

e. Negative indefinites

(1) *List*

§436. These include *nænig, ne . . . ænig*, 'no, none'; *nan* 'no, none'; *nahwæðer, nawðer, naðor*, 'neither' (also a conjunction; see §1847); *naht, nawiht, nanwuht*, 'nothing'.[115] All can be used dependently— with the possible exception of *naht* (see below)—and independently, either alone or with a 'partitive' genitive, which may precede or follow; on this term see §1297. On the use of *ænig* in negative sentences, see §§1607 and 1610–12.

(2) Nænig *and* nan

§437. *Nænig* singular is used dependently, e.g. *Bede* 28. 32 *nænig mann*, and independently, both alone, e.g. *Bede* 52. 25 *7 him nænig wiðstod*, and with a partitive genitive, e.g. *Bede* 64. 23 *nænig heora*. Note also *Bede* 354. 16 *7 nænigne of eallum butan þe*, Latin *neminem ex omnibus praeter te*; see §415.

§438. It is found in the plural as well as the singular when used dependently, e.g. *BlHom* 13. 28 *nænig ende* and *BlHom* 181. 27 *. . . þæt he næfre nænige godcunde englas næfde buton hundlice englas*. In the independent use the idea of plurality is expressed by the singular and a partitive genitive (or, perhaps under Latin influence, *of* + dative) as in §437; see §381.

§439. Like *nænig, nan* is used dependently in both singular and plural, e.g. *Bo* 61. 20 . . . *þær nane oðre an ne sæton buton þa weorðestan*, *ÆCHom* i. 52. 33 *nan man*, *ÆCHom* ii. 192. 29 *nan orf*, *ÆCHom* i. 344. 8 *nane oðre englas ne sind . . .*, *ÆCHom* i. 76. 19 *nan ðing elles*, and *ÆCHom* i. 574. 16 *ðæs ættres nan ðing*. Independently it is found in the singular, both alone, e.g. *Bo* 79. 16 *forþam*

---

[115] For further variations in the form of this word, and for *nænig wuht*, see Wülfing, i, §§363–5a.

ðe nan mihtigra þe nis, ne nan þin gelica and ÆHom 13. 99 Ne for-
deme ge nænne, and with a partitive genitive, e.g. ÆHom 7. 10
eower nan, ÆCHom i. 284. 4 heora nan . . . ne nan . . . ne nan . . . ne
nan, ÆCHom i. 284. 1 ne nan heora an nis . . . 'nor is one of them
alone . . .', ÆCHom ii. 42. 27 Ne trucað heora nan ana ðurh unmihte,
and ÆCHom ii. 212. 33 nan . . . ðæra ungelyfedra. Ropers (pp. 62-3)
gives further examples from Ælfric. On combinations with an, see
Rissanen, p. 238.

§440. An important question here is the distribution of nænig and
nan. Jost produces figures to show that, while ænig occurs in both
W-S and Anglian, nænig is chiefly an Anglian form, avoided by most
W-S writers, including Alfred, Ælfric, and Wulfstan; see Jost 1950,
pp. 159-62, and also Pope, Ælfric, i. 100 and fn. 2. Nan is the
equivalent preferred except in the works of Wulfstan, who (according
to Jost) shows a pronounced preference for ænig in negated sentences, as in WHom 20(C). 71 ne ure ænig his lif ne fadode swa swa
he scolde. Jost found only two examples of nænig in Wulfstan, one
suspect (1950, p. 159 fn. 8).

§441. Two of the three examples known to me of nænig in the
Chronicle occur in the annal for 755—ChronA 48. 8 hiera nænig
and 48. 20 nænig mæg and the corresponding passages. The third is
ChronA 10. 17 (418) nænig mon, where MS E has nan man. Wülfing (i, §§356-7) found independent nænig in Bede only. Bede contained most of his dependent examples too, the only exceptions
being Or 20. 18 nænig ealo (in Wulfstan's narrative),[116] one from
the Laws, and nanege munde from Solil, where both Endter (68. 8)
and Carnicelli (95. 7) accept Wülker's reading nane gemunde, which
Wülfing himself quotes. According to Bately (Ang. 88 (1970), 458
fn. 205) nænig occurs twelve times in the Metres, but only once 'in
the whole of Alfred's prose'—a phrase which, as her work and that
of Raith and Liggins has clearly demonstrated, must now be used
with great caution. This is CP(H) 107. 11 on næn[eg]um ðingum.
The Cotton MSS have on nanum ðingum. Inspection of MS H confirms that [eg] is an addition above the line, but its date is uncertain;
see Sweet (ed.), CP, p. viii but p. 481, and Ker, p. 385.

§442. According to Ropers (p. 62), nan is not used in the plural in
Ælfric. This is true only of the independent or pronominal use of
nan (with which he was concerned). The position seems to be that

---

[116] Bately points out other Anglian elements in this narrative; see Ang. 88 (1970), 439
fn. 31.

in Ælfric, as elsewhere, *nan* is used in singular and plural when dependent, but in the singular when independent, both alone and with a partitive genitive. So in *ÆCHom* ii. 602. 19 *and ic ne gemune nanra his synna* we have probably a dependent use, *nanra* agreeing with *synna*. Both Schrader (p. 58) and Ropers (pp. 60-1) remark that Ælfric, in spite of his liking for doubled negatives, never uses *nænig*. No examples have yet come to my notice. But finality on this and the other points of distribution discussed above must await full collections.

(3) Naðor

§443. *Naðor* 'neither of two (individuals or groups)' is used dependently, e.g. *ÆCHom* ii. 608. 9 *naðrum werode*, independently, alone e.g. *ÆCHom* i. 112. 3 *to naðrum*, or with a partitive genitive, e.g. *ÆCHom* i. 20. 13 *of heora naðrum* and *ÆCHom* ii. 390. 28 . . . *ægðer ge ða truman ge ða untruman, forðan ðe Godes gelaðung nis buton naðrum ðæra*. The combination *naðor . . . oðer* occurs, e.g. *Or* 96. 32 . . . *þæt naðer ne mehte on oþrum sige geræcan*. For further examples, see Wülfing, i, §359. 5.

§444. In combinations of the type *naðor . . . ne . . . ne*, two or more things may be involved, e.g. *Bo* 16. 12 *ða ðing ða ðe nawðer ne sint ne getrewe to habbanne, ne eac ieðe to forlætanne* and *CP* 401. 26 *Nawðer ne ða wohhæmendan, ne ða ðe diofulgieldum ðiowiað, ne ða unfæsðradan, ðe ne magon hira unryhthæmdes geswican, ne ða ðiofas, ne ða gietseras, ne ða druncenwillnan, ne ða wiergendan, ne ða reaferas Godes rice ne gesittað*. Here *naðor* should be regarded as a conjunction, though, as Wülfing points out (i, §§347-8), the line is sometimes hard to draw.

(4) Naht, nawiht, nanwuht

§445. This is used independently in the sense 'nothing', either alone, e.g. *Or* 184. 14 *þæt him þa geþuhte swelc þæt mæste wæl swelc hie oft ær for noht hæfdon* and *ÆCHom* ii. 608. 23 *Nis ðæs mannes fæsten naht*, or with a partitive genitive, e.g. *Or* 178. 14 . . . *þæt hie nanuht þara ærenda ne underfenge* and *ÆCHom* i. 342. 5 *ne ðeah on nanum gecampe naht ðegenlices ne gefremode*.

§446. Wülfing (i. 460-1) quotes three examples from *Boethius* in which he suggests that *naht* is used dependently. In the first (*Bo* 25. 21) *nauht* is clearly independent; in the third (*Bo* 37. 17) it is (as Wülfing himself suggests) an adverb. The only one in which it could possibly be dependent is *Bo* 32. 14 *nu ge wenað þ eowre nauht welan send eowre gesælþa*, Latin *cum uilissima rerum uestra bona esse iudicatis*. In his glossary, Sedgefield describes *nauht* as being 'used as indecl. adj.', translating 'worthless wealth'. This is probably right; *nauht* is unlikely to be an adverb 'your not-wealth', since it qualifies the noun. But see §§1100 and 1630.

f. Words conveying totality[117]

(1) List and general characteristics

§447. These include *eall* 'all'; *ælc* 'each'; *æghwa** 'everyone' [words asterisked are used independently only], *æghwæt** 'everything'; *æghwæþer, ægþer* 'each of two, every'; *æghwilc* 'each, every'; *æthwa** 'each'; *gehwa* 'every(one)', *gehwæt* 'every(thing)'; *gehwæþer* 'each of two'; *gehwilc* 'each'; *welhwylc, gewelhwylc* 'every'.

§448. Campbell's observation (*OEG*, §719) that the prefix *ge-* gives 'a general inclusive sense' to *hwa* and *hwilc* does not always hold; *gehwa* can mean 'anyone' and 'someone', *gehwæt* can mean 'anything' and 'something' (see BTS, s.v. *gehwa* A II and A III), and *gehwilc* in the plural can mean 'many' or 'certain', e.g. *ÆCHom* ii. 444. 21 *ac ða geleaffullan lareowas, Augustinus, Hieronimus, Gregorius, and gehwilce oðre* and *ÆCHom* ii. 518. 8 *Hwæt ða gehyrdon gehwilce on life halige englas singan* (see BTS, s.v. *gehwilc* II; Schrader, p. 59; and Jost 1950, p. 164).

§449. All the words given above can be declined, some in the singular only (e.g. *æghwa, gehwa*), others in the singular and plural (e.g. *æghwilc, gehwilc*). They can be used in all cases. (The adverbial uses of the oblique cases are discussed in §§1135-7.) They cannot be compared or modified by an intensifying adverb such as *swiðe*; note however examples like *Or* 36. 9 . . . *þæt forneah eall þæt folc forwearð* and like *ÆGram* 215. 10 *ealle mæst ðas word synd ðære forman geðeodnysse* and *ÆCHom* ii. 466. 21 . . . *þæs dæges godspel . . . is eal mæst mid haligra manna naman geset*.

---

[117] A licentiate thesis for the University of Helsinki on the syntactic uses and the shades of meaning of the Old English pronouns for 'every' and 'each' by Leena Kahlas-Tarkka is nearing completion under the supervision of Professor M. Rissanen. I acknowledge gratefully the help I have received from them. It will include the suggestion that *æghwa* and *gehwa* may be to some extent archaic and will discuss Latin influence (*omnis* and *quisque* are usually represented by a simple indefinite, *unusquisque* by an indefinite + *an/anra*), the possibility of dialectal variations (the Lindisfarne Gospels consistently use *æghwilc*), and the preferences of individual texts and authors. Kahlas has distilled some of her findings in *Stockholm Studies in English*, 52 (1980), 125-32, and in an as yet unpublished paper given at Odense at the 2nd International Conference of English Historical Linguistics in April 1981 entitled 'On the Variation of the Words Meaning "Every" and "Each" in Old English'.

§450. As noted in §447, the words asterisked are used independently only; the rest can be used independently (some with a partitive genitive) and dependently (usually before the noun, but occasionally after it, e.g. *Bede* 66. 25 *of syndrigum ciricum gehwylcum*, Latin *ex singulis ergo quibusque ecclesiis*). Those meaning 'each' can be used in combination with *an* (see §§518-19) and *oþer*. They can serve as antecedent of a relative pronoun or as predicate.

§451. To give examples of all these in all functions would be superfluous; they can be found in BT(S) and Wülfing, i, §§321-75, s.vv. The following need no further comment: *æghwa, æghwæt, æthwa, gehwæþer*, and *(ge)welhwylc*. The rest require special consideration.

§452. In general the rules of concord set out in §§25-47 apply to these words. But the plural verbs with the genitive plural in *Met* 26. 43 *þæt on ða tide þeoda æghwilc || hæfdon heora hlaford . . .* and *PPs* 118. 161 *Min earwunga ehtan ongunnon || ealdurmanna gehwylc* may be compared with the similar examples with a singular collective + genitive plural in §84. The closeness of meaning between 'each, every' and 'all' produces fluctuations of number such as those seen in

Met 21. 28   Forðæm æghwilc ðing   þe on þys andweardan
                 life licað   lænu sindon,
                 eorðlicu þing   a fleondu,

Jud 166   Æghwylcum wearð
                 men on ðære medobyrig   mod areted,
                 syððan hie ongeaton   þæt wæs Iudith cumen . . . ,

and *Lch* i. 280. 18 *Wiþ lungen adle 7 wið gehwylce yfelu þe on þam innoðe dereþ.* . . . In

Met 20. 63   Habbað þeah þa feower   frumstol hiora,
                 æghwilc hiora   agenne stede,

we have an appositional construction acceptable today. See further Bauch, pp. 49-51, and Sorg, pp. 67-82.

(2) Eall

§453. *Eall* is used dependently in the singular and plural, e.g. *ÆCHom* i. 114. 14 *ealle ðing, ÆCHom* ii. 594. 14 *mid ealre heortan, ÆCHom* i. 272. 21 *be eallum cristenum mannum, ÆCHom* i. 272. 20 *ealle ða word*, and *ÆCHom* i. 22. 14 *on eallum his life. Eall* may follow its noun, but usually precedes it, though its position in relation to other qualifying elements may vary; see §§143-58.[118]

§454. *Eall* occurs independently alone in the singular, e.g. *CP* 155. 12 *him bið eall cuð*, *ChronA* 90. 1 (897) *ealles swiþost*, and *ÆCHom* i. 12. 21 *mid ealle*, and in the plural, e.g. *Bede* 106. 31 *ealra swiðust*, *ÆGram* 16. 1 *iustissimus ealra rihtwisost*, *ChronC* 171. 21 (1049) *syððan hine forleton ealle butan ii*, and *Beo* 145 *ana wið eallum*.

§455. Shipley (p. 91) says that 'strictly speaking, gen. with *eall* is not partitive, though it may be accounted for by the working of analogy with the part. gen. after other indefinite pronominal words'; in this it may be compared with the genitive after such negatives as *naht*, e.g. *ÆCHom* ii. 158. 1 *naht ðyllices*. There is obviously some truth in this remark; what is the difference between *PPs* 69. 3 *ealle hiora* and examples of *eall* in apposition (see §458) like *Bede* 134. 5 *hi ealle*? But it may need some qualification; see §457. *Eall* + genitive is more common in the poetry, e.g. (in the singular)

Beo 743   sona hæfde
             unlyfigendes   eal gefeormod,
             fet ond folma,

(in the plural) *PPs* 69. 3 *ealle hiora scamien, þe me yfel hogedon*, and (singular or plural?) *Beo* 1057 *Metod eallum weold ‖ gumena cynnes*; Shipley (pp. 91-2) gives more examples. But the combination does occur in the prose in both singular, e.g. *ÆHom* 17. 5 *Ða ferde he geond eall þære foresædan scire*, and plural, e.g. *ÆCHom* i. 398. 15 *ealle heora æhta samod*.

§456. There are also examples of *eall* + genitive of a relative pronoun, e.g.

ChristC 1032   Hafað eall on him
             þæs þe he on foldan   in fyrndagum,
             godes oþþe gales,   on his gæste gehlod

---

[118] Schrader (p. 53) claims that *eall* sometimes means 'every' (*jeder*). But see Einenkel in *Ang.* 27 (1903), 9-13, and *OED*, s.v. *all* A. I. 3. Ropers (pp. 59-60) sides with Schrader, citing as examples *Exod(L)* 18. 22 *on ealle tid* (MS *B on eallum tidum*), *Bede* 230. 29 *alle tid* (Miller 'all the time'), *ÆCHom* i. 300. 27 and *ÆCHom* i. 302. 8 ff. *eall gesceaft* or oblique cases thereof; here 'all creation' would do as well as Thorpe's 'every creature' and is supported by *ÆCHom* i. 302. 19 *ealra gesceafta* 'of all creatures'. Without further evidence, we must accept the verdict of *OED* that *eall* 'every' is 'unknown to OE'. Einenkel discusses examples like *Jul* 644 *eal engla cynn* and *KtPs* 50: 59 *ealra synna cynn* in *Ang.* 27 (1903), 23-33. For fuller discussion of *eall* and 'all' in all periods and functions see *Ang.* 27 (1903), 1-41, which repeats (with minor additions and variations) *Ang.* 24 (1901), 343-80.

(on this passage see §2228) and

Beo 1122   Lig ealle forswealg,
            gæsta gifrost,   þara ðe þær guð fornam
            bega folces.

Andrew (*SS*, pp. 106-7) is doubtful whether *ealle . . . þara* 'all of those' was 'good OE usage'. But, while I have as yet noted no prose parallels, I see no reason for rejecting it when there are examples like *PPs* 69. 3 (§455), *ChristC* 1032 above,

PPs 89. 11   Gif on mihtigum   mannum geweorðeð,
            þæt hi hundehtatig   ylda gebiden,
            ealle þe þær ofer beoð   æfre getealde
            wintra on worulde,   þa beoð gewinn and sar,

and

ChristA 46   . . . þa se waldend cwom,
            se þe reorda gehwæs   ryne gemiclað
            ðara þe geneahhe   noman scyppendes
            þurh horscne had   hergan willað.

§457. The combination of *eall þæt* (relative pronoun) with a genitive is not uncommon. The genitive usually appears in the adjective clause, either immediately after *þæt*, e.g. *Or* 18. 25 *Eal þæt his man aþer oððe ettan oððe erian mæg þæt lið wið ða sæ*, or separated from it, e.g. *Or* 76. 13 *7 þær beæftan forlet eall þæt þær liðes wæs 7 swetes, Or* 38. 9 *ge eall þæt on þæm lande wæs weaxendes 7 growendes*,

Jud 338   ond eal þæt se rinca baldor
            swiðmod sinces ahte   oððe syndoryrfes,
            beaga ond beorhtra maðma,

and

Exhort 22   And þeah þu æfter þinum ende   eall gesylle
            þæt þu on eorðan   ær gestryndes
            goda gehwylces. . . .

Constructions like *Or* 88. 5 . . . *mid ðæm þe hie gegaderedon eal moncynnes þæt þær læfed wæs*, where the genitive occupies its MnE position in the principal clause, are rare. There has been argument whether the genitive is dependent on *eall* or on *eall þæt*; see Wülfing, i. 408-9 and 465, Kock, pp. 27-8, and Shipley, p. 92. The element order in *Or* 88. 5 above suggests that the *þæt* clause refers to *moncynnes* and that the genitive is dependent on *eall* and is not in the strict sense partitive. But with the examples in which the genitive is in the adjective clause, both the above views seem tenable. If we take the former and translate *Jud* 338 above 'all of the treasure that the leader owned', the genitive is (strictly speaking) not partitive; if

we take the latter and translate 'all that the leader owned of the treasure' the genitive is (I suppose) partitive. Those who hold the former
view are therefore saying that the adjective clause limits *eall* + genitive, the others that it limits *eall* alone. Wülfing's observation (i.
465) seems misleading if it implies that the presence of a limiting adjective
clause certifies that the genitive is partitive: 'Mit einem partitiven
Genitiv steht *eall*: Or 88, 6 *hie gegaderedon eal moncynnes þæt þær
læfed wæs*; was natürlich nur möglich ist wegen des folgenden ein-
schränkenden Relativsatzes.'[119] However, the argument seems a bar-
ren one. For we could take the opposite grammatical view of the
examples discussed above and could argue that in *Or* 88. 5 we have
separation of antecedent and rel. pron. *eal . . . þæt* and in *Or* 38. 9
separation of *eall* and part. gen. *weaxendes 7 growendes*, since both
these constructions are idiomatic in OE. And since in normal MnE
(one suspects) 'all of the treasure that the leader owned' could mean
either 'all the leader's treasure' or 'all the leader's share of the treasure', it would not be startling to find a similar ambiguity in OE—
if indeed this is an example of a distinction with a difference. See
further §§ 2226–30.

§458. *Eall* is found in apposition with both nouns and pronouns.
As the following examples show, its position varies: *ÆCHom* i. 402.
19 *Seo Godes gelaðung . . . ferde eal samod of ðære byrig*, *ÆCHom*
ii. 318. 2 *Ge ealle sind gebroðra*, *ÆCHom* i. 260. 19 . . . *ealle cristene men . . . ealle hi sind gebroðra*, *ÆCHom* i. 54. 8 *Ealle we sind
gebroðra . . . and we ealle cweðað*, *Bede* 304. 3 *ealra heora heortan*,
ÆCHom i. 88. 30 *þæt hi mid heora arleasan hlaforde ealle forwur-
don*, *ÆCHom* ii. 512. 11 *swa þæt he fornean eal wearð tocwysed*
(or adverb?), and (with the verb rather than *eall* negated) *ÆCHom*
ii. 288. 6 *We wenað þæt ge ealle on andwerdnysse her ne beon to
ðam dæge þe we þæt godspel rædan sceolon*, where the meaning is
'not all of you' and not 'none of you'.

(3) Ælc
§459. *Ælc* is used dependently in sg. 'each, every' and in pl. 'all',
e.g. *ÆCHom* i. 234. 11 *ælc synful man* and *ÆCHom* ii. 212. 4
on ælcum lacum. It is singular when used independently, e.g. (alone)
Bo 62. 20 *ac ælces me ðincð þ he sie wyrðe* and (with a partitive
genitive) *ÆCHom* i. 182. 10 *hyra ælc*. Appositional *ælc* is distributive in examples like *ÆCHom* i. 446. 2 *Godes gecorenan scinað on*

[119] '*Eall* takes a partitive genitive: Or 88. 6 *hie gegaderedon eal moncynnes þæt þær læfed
wæs*; which of course is only possible because of the limiting adjective clause that follows.'

heofonlicum wuldre ælc be his geðingcðum and *ÆCHom* ii. 582. 18
þa geleaffullan ælc hylt his æftergengan up. *Ælc an* can similarly be
used dependently and independently, e.g. *Or* 170. 27 *on ælcre anre
talentan* and *ÆCHom* ii. 604. 33 *ælc heora an*; for further examples
see Einenkel, *Ang*. 27 (1903), 54, and Rissanen, pp. 246-51. *Ælc
. . . oþer* expresses a reciprocal relationship, e.g. *Or* 21. 2 *7 swa ælc
æfter oðrum* and *ÆCHom* ii. 582. 18 *ælc berð oðerne*. According to
Ropers (pp. 57-9), Ælfric uses *ælc* more often than *gehwilc* and
prefers these to *gehwa, æghwa,* and *æghwilc*. Jost (1950, pp. 165-6)
tells us that *ælc* is the word most used by Wulfstan for 'every'.

§460. *Æfre ælc* (> MnE 'every') first appears about AD 1000, e.g.
WHom 4. 34 *ne cymð ure æfre ænig to Godes rice ær we beon æfre
ælcere synne swa clæne amerede . . .* ; see *OEG*, §725 fn. 6, and
Einenkel, *Ang*. 27 (1903), 52-3. Einenkel explains examples like
Or 294. 27 . . . *þæt his fultum mehte mæstra ælcne heora flana on
hiora feondum afæstnian* and *ChronA* 84. 28 (894) *7 him mon eac
mid oþrum floccum sohte mæstra daga ælce* as the result of attraction; in his view *mæst* is properly adverbial, as in *WHom* 4. 44 *7 mid
his gedwimerum mæst ælcne man beswicð*; see *Ang*. 27 (1903), 55,
and (for further examples of the various uses noted above) ibid.,
pp. 52-61.

(4) Ægþer, æghwæþer
§461. The meaning is 'each (of two), both' (but see Nusser, p. 39). The
obvious uses occur here—dependent, e.g. *Or* 50. 14 *on ægðere hand*
and *Bede* 58. 1 *7 æghwæþer ende lið on sæ*; independent, e.g. (alone)
ÆCHom i. 106. 17 *He is ure sibb, seðe dyde ægðer to anum, towur-
pende ða ærran feondscipas on him sylfum* and (with a partitive genitive) *ÆCHom* i. 52. 11 *on heora ægðrum*; and with *oþer*, e.g. *ChronA*
80. 28 (887) *7 æghwæþer oþerne oftrædlice ut dræfde*. *Ægþer* is
uninflected in *ÆCHom* ii. 2. 13 *On ægðer þæra boca sind feowertig
cwyda* and is used in the plural referring to two groups in *Bede* 272.
22 *æghwæðre þara wæron in drohtunge munuclifes geornlice 7 wel
gelærde*. The difference between *ægþer* pron. and *ægþer* conj. (see
§§1813-17) is sometimes hard to draw, e.g. *Or* 238. 13 *se wæs
ægþer ge heora cyning ge heora biscop* and *ÆCHom* ii. 390. 27 *On
Petres gange soðlice wæron getacnode . . . ægðer ge ða truman ge ða
untruman*. The difference in number may be decisive in the latter,
but compare *ÆCHom* ii. 2. 13 above. For further examples of the
various uses, see Einenkel, *Ang*. 27 (1903), 62-71.

(5) Æghwilc

§462. *Æghwilc* is used dependently in sg. 'each', e.g. *ÆCHom* i.
436. 28 *geond æghwylces geares ymbryne*, and in pl. 'all', e.g. *HomU*
29. 170. 8 *ælce wigwæpna and æghwylce woruldsaca læte man stille*,
and independently, e.g. (alone) *Bede* 66. 3 *swa æghwylcum þearf
wæs* and (with a partitive genitive) *WHom* 13. 80 *an tima cymð ure
æghwylcum*. All these usages except the plural independent one are
recorded in the poetry; see BT(S) and GK.

§463. Jost (1950, pp. 164 and 166) notes that Ælfric prefers *gehwilc*
to *æghwilc* and that Wulfstan uses *æghwilc* more often, but prefers
ælc. He found *æghwilc* only three times in Ælfric. Pope's Glossary to
ÆHom does not list it. Wülfing (i. 441-3) cites thirty-five examples
of *æghwilc* and some twenty of *gehwylc*. Bately (*Ang.* 88 (1970),
448) notes that *æghwylc* occurs only once in *Orosius*—*Or* 18. 19, in
the account of Ohthere's voyages—but is more common in *Boethius*.

§464. *Æghwilc* is found in combination with *an*, which may agree
with *æghwilc*, e.g. *BlHom* 91. 29 *æghwylce ane dæge*, or be genitive
plural dependent on it, e.g. *BlHom* 121. 8 *æghwylc anra heora*.
According to Rissanen (p. 247) the former is more common in the
prose, but only the latter occurs in the poetry, e.g. *Dream* 86
æghwylcne anra, þara þe him bið egesa to me. See further Rissanen,
pp. 246-51.

(6) Gehwa, gehwæt

§465. Here we find the independent use in both prose and poetry,
e.g. (alone) *ÆLet1* 98 *7 hy gebetton gehwæt þe tobrocen wæs*
('everything'), *ÆCHom* i. 8. 14 *forþi sceal gehwa gerihtlæcan þæt*
('everyone'), and *Ex* 371 *frumcneow gehwæs*, and (with partitive
genitive) *Bo* 40. 22 *7 mete, 7 ealo, 7 claþas, 7 gehwæt þæs ðe þa
þre geferscipas behofiað*, *ÆCHom* i. 164. 26 *gehwa cristenra manna*,
and *Ex* 6 *lifigendra gehwam*. *Gehwa* appears to be more common in
Ælfric than in the 'Alfredian' translations; see Wülfing, i, §§329-30,
and Jost 1950, p. 162. The phrase *and gehwæt* seems to mean almost
et cetera in *ÆGram* 278. 5 *he* [the interjection] *getacnað hwilon ðæs
modes blisse, hwilon sarnysse, hwilon wundrunge and gehwæt*, though
it may retain the meaning 'and everything' in *ÆCHom* ii. 372. 32 . . .
*we magon gefredan hwæt bið heard, hwæt hnesce, hwæt smeðe,
hwæt unsmeðe, and swa gehwæt*.

§466. In the prose the nominative is the most common case—according to Jost (1950, p. 165), it is the only form found in Wulfstan—

but there are occasional examples of the accusative (see §465) and the dative, e.g. *Or* 102. 24 *7 ic gehwam wille þærto tæcan* and *ÆCHom* ii. 52. 17 *Is nu forði micel neod gehwam.* . . . But the oblique cases are common in the poetry; for further examples see GK s.v. The idiom *anra gehwa* 'each one'—e.g. *Phoen* 598 *weorc anra gehwæs*—is restricted to the poetry, according to Rissanen (pp. 239-40). (Kahlas (my §447 fn.) notes *Matt(Ru)* 16. 27 *anra gehwæm.*) So too are the occasional examples of a dependent use of *gehwa*, e.g. *Dan* 114 *rices gehwæs* . . . *ende, Dan* 423 *be naman gehwam*, and *Cæd(Ca)* 3 *wuldres gehwæs* . . . *ord*, where MS *T* has *wundra gehwæs* . . . *or*. Several other apparent examples have been cited; see Rose, p. 18 fn. 1, GK, p. 365, s.v. *gehwa* (though here they are not distinguished from independent uses), and BTS, s.v. *gehwa* B. All are shown with a noun ending in *-e*. In three—*El* 972, *ChristB* 490, and *Phoen* 206—ASPR and recent editors agree in reading a genitive plural in *-a*; my inspection of the facsimiles confirms *-a*. In the others —*Prec* 74, *PPs* 56. 5, 62. 1, and 108. 6—*-e* may be a weakened form of genitive plural.

(7) Gehwilc

§467. *Gehwilc* is found in the sg. 'every' and in the pl. 'all' when used dependently, e.g. *ÆCHom* i. 454. 6 *gehwilc man, ÆCHom* i. 408. 3 *to gehwilcum þwyrlicum mannum*, and *ÆCHom* i. 54. 27 *gehwilce oðre lac*. In the independent use, it can be singular or plural when alone, e.g. *ÆCHom* i. 348. 18 *and þæt þæt gehwilc on him sylfum be dæle hæfð* and *ÆCHom* ii. 518. 8 *Hwæt ða gehyrdon gehwilce* . . . *halige englas singan* (where, however, *gehwilce* may mean 'many' or 'certain'; on this weakened sense of the plural forms, see BTS, s.v. *gehwilc* II). But it is singular with the partitive genitive, e.g. *ÆCHom* i. 310. 15 *heora gehwilc* and *ÆCHom* i. 348. 30 *gehwilc ðæra weroda*, and plural when used in apposition, e.g. *ÆCHom* i. 564. 35 *and gehwilce gedrehte þær beoð geblissode, ÆCHom* i. 38. 20 *gehwilce oðre þe englas gesawon*, and *ÆCHom* ii. 124. 9 *gehwilce ænlipige sind* . . . *aweste*; on this distinction see §§409-16.

§468. For further examples see BT(S), s.v., Wülfing, i, §§334-6, and Jost 1950, pp. 163-5. According to Jost, Wulfstan uses *gehwilc* only in the combination genitive plural + *gehwylc*, e.g. *WHom* 6. 4 *manna gehwylc*. He found only one example of this pattern in Ælfric—*ÆLS* 26. 238 *heora freonda gehwilcum*. The fact that we find *manna gehwylcum* in *ÆHom* 27. 109 might therefore support Pope's view that these lines are 'probably not by Ælfric' (ii. 779).

But the following additional examples recorded from Ælfric by Kahlas (my §447 fn.) destroy this argument: *ÆCHom* i. 40. 19, 208. 3, and 348. 30; *ÆCHom* ii. 524. 29 and 558. 15.

§469. *Gehwilc* is often found in combination with *an*. The two may be used dependently in agreement with a noun, e.g. *ÆCHom* ii. 588. 25 *anes gehwilces mannes weorc*, in apposition and agreement with one another, e.g. *ÆCHom* ii. 316. 11 *seðe ænne gehwilcne þurh his Gast geneosað*, or in the combination *anra gehwilc* (which, says Trnka (p. 161), is the result of analogy with *ealra gehwilc*[120]) e.g. *ÆCHom* i. 208. 3 *anra gehwilc manna* and *ÆCHom* i. 602. 27 . . . *on ðam underfehð anra gehwilc be ðam ðe he geearnode on lichaman.* According to Rissanen (pp. 239-44), this last pattern becomes less popular and the type *an gehwilc* becomes more popular as OE prose develops: he gives examples.

g. Words marking identity and the contrary

(1) List and general characteristics

§470. These include: *se (þes) ilca* 'the same', *self* 'self, the same' (cf. *ÆGram* 99. 17 *ipse he sylf oþþe se ylca*), *agen* 'own, proper', *swylc* 'such', *þyllic* 'of that sort, such', and *oðer* 'other, another, second'. Like most other indefinites, they can be declined, but not compared, and can be used both dependently and independently.

(2) Se/þes ilca

§471. *Ilca* differs from other indefinites in that it is always declined weak and always used with *se* and *þes*. Closs's decision (pp. 96-7) to include it with adjectives takes this into account but (on the grounds that the same is also true of 'some adjectives, e.g. those ending in *weard*') disregards the fact that *ilca*—unlike adjectives—is not compared. The combination is found both with and without a noun, and may refer forwards or backwards. Examples follow: *CP* 37. 3 *Se ilca Dauid ðe forbær ðæt he ðone kyning ne yfelode . . . Se ilca Dauid . . . , CP* 137. 25 *Ðas ilcan geornfulnesse ðara hierda sanctus Paulus aweahte, CP* 29. 2 *Ðæt ilce cuæð sanctus Paulus*, and *CP* 253. 11 *Be ðys ilcan is gecueden on kyninga bocum. . . .* For further examples see Wülfing, i, §§263-4. BTS records *ge-ilca* in a charter dated by Thorpe after 1066 but not recorded in Sawyer, viz. *Ch(Th)* 433. 24 *7 eall þe geilcan gerihta* and 433. 36 *7 eall þæ geylcan gerihta.*

---

[120] For other possible explanations, see Rissanen, pp. 240-1. Trnka (p. 161) remarks that the pattern *anra gehwilc* occurs only in OE. Rissanen (p. 239) notes *Rood Tree* 22. 14 *anre gehwilc.*

(3) Self

(a) Declension and functions

§472. *Self* is used as an adjective and as a pronoun or (as Visser, i, §427, has it) an 'adjective adjunct'. As an adjective, it is declined strong or weak according to the usual rules. As a pronoun, it is usually declined strong, e.g. *ÆCHom* i. 430. 7 *me sylfne*, *ÆCHom* i. 242. 1 *his sylfes*, and *ÆCHom* i. 244. 13 *us sylfum*, but weak forms are occasionally found in the nominative singular, e.g. *BlHom* 13. 26 *he sylfa*, *ÆCHom* ii. 332. 23 *he sylfe*, *WHom* 11. 107 *God sylfa*, and *Beo* 29 *he selfa*; cf. the more usual *BlHom* 13. 13 *heo sylf*, *ÆCHom* ii. 118. 28 *he sylf*, *WHom* 6. 63 *Godd sylf*, and *Beo* 594 *þu self*. Farr (pp. 20–2) gives further examples and notes (p. 22 fn. 1)—agreeing with Wülfing (i. 353)—that in the 'Alfredian' texts *selfa* occurs only in *Bede*. In *Bede* 242. 10 *Se ærra wæs Æðelwines broðor Gode þæs leofan weres, se seolfa eac swilce þære æfterfylgendan eldo Hiberniam gesohte*, it is possible to take *se* as a relative pronoun with *seolfa* in apposition. But *se* may be demonstrative, with *se seolfa* meaning 'the same'; see §494. On patterns like *he him sylf* in *ÆCHom* i. 514. 14 *swilce he him sylf witega wære*, see §488.

§473. Wülfing records uninflected *self* in apposition with a nominative plural in *Or* 42. 23 *þa men sylf* (i. 393) and *Or* 96. 6 *hie self* (i. 353). *Or* 20. 1 *7 þa habbað him sylf cyning* almost belongs here too; but see §488. So the variations in *Bede(Ca)* 4. 17 *hi sylf* (MS *B hi sylfe*), in *Or(L)* 144. 32 *þa burgware self* (MS *C þa burgware selfe*), and in *Or(L)* 116. 24 *þeh þe Sciþþie hæfdon maran monmenie, 7 self hwætran wæron* (MS *C 7 hy selfe*), may be genuine rather than the result of scribal error. On the absolute use of *self*, as in *Or(L)* 116. 24 above, see §§495–9. I have found no certain examples in which uninflected *self* is in apposition with an accusative, genitive, or dative. But see Mitchell 1979*a*, pp. 39–40.

§474. *Self* occasionally glosses Latin *solus*; BTS (s.v. *self* C) quotes three examples from *Defensoris Liber Scintillarum* including *LibSc* 183. 11 *7 willa on him sylf oferprut ys*, Latin *et uoluntas in eis sola superba est*. Pope (*ASE* 3 (1974), 78–9) adds more from the same text and elsewhere in support of the proposition that *sylf* in *Sea* 35 should be translated 'alone'. There are, however, lexicographical difficulties which lie outside my terms of reference; see *ASE* 9 (1980), 199–211, where Greenfield argues that *self* cannot mean 'unaccompanied, without companions' and, for *Sea* 35 *sylf*, rejects his own 'of my own accord' (*JEGP* 68 (1969), 217–19) in favour of 'by and for the speaker's self'. However, *self* more usually means 'self', 'the same', 'very'. These meanings merge into one another; see especially §494.

§475. As has already been noted in §265, the personal pronoun can function as a reflexive either alone or emphasized by *self*. We can probably agree with Visser when he writes (i, §438 n.):

> Although it is natural to assume that *self* was originally only added to the reflexive pronoun-object with the purpose of emphasizing the identity of the person or thing denoted by the object and the subject, and that consequently the stress was on *self* (just as today in such sentences as 'she washed first her children and then herself'), there are already among the later Old English instances a few (e.g. 'he het me syððan gan, and me sylfne aðwean'; 'gemyne þe sylfne'; 'he geeaðmode hine selfne'; 'heo wolde hi selfe baðian') from which one might infer a tendency for reflexive pronoun + *self* to be used in the same non-emphatic way as it is in Pres. Day English when no contrast is to be expressed, as e.g. in 'He prided himself on his knowledge'; 'he didn't exert himself much'.

But there seems little point in following Closs (pp. 106–9) when she distinguishes emphatic from reflexive *self*. The distinction is valid for MnE—cf. 'He himself did it' and 'He killed himself' (where 'self' is essential for the reflexive idea)—but, as Penning (p. 20) in 1875, Wülfing (i, §§239 and 242) in 1890, and Farr (pp. 22 and 25) in 1905, all realized, not for OE, where *self* can emphasize a personal pronoun whether it is used reflexively or not (§§275–6). It is easy to see the beginnings of the MnE distinction in examples like *ÆCHom* ii. 432. 31 *Hu ne is þis seo miccle Babilon ðe ic sylf getimbrode to cynestole and to ðrymme me sylfum*. But to import it into OE is to follow a false native informant. As I see it, Quirk and Wrenn are on the right track when they say (p. 72): 'For the most part, *self* was used in OE simply to emphasise and was not, as in Mod.E., associated with being a reflexive sign or a pronoun-enclitic.' Two points illustrate this: Ropers's comment (p. 64) on Ælfric's liking for an emphasizing *self* with a personal pronoun used reflexively, and the use of *self* to emphasize a personal pronoun functioning reciprocally (§282).

§476. Visser (i, §426) notes that emphatic *self* is found in the earliest texts in the nominative, e.g. *Beo* 594 *swa þu self talast* and *GenA* 2149 *ac þu selfa most heonon* ‖ *huðe lædan*, and after prepositions, e.g. *GenB* 885 *Nu ic þæs tacen wege* ‖ *sweotol on me selfum*, but that its use with an accusative reflexive pronoun appears to come later. It is not found in *Beowulf, Genesis, Exodus, Christ and Satan, Deor*, or even *Juliana*, though it is evident in the prose of King Alfred's time, e.g. *GD* 293. 14 *þa befleah he . . . 7 hine sylfne ahydde*. Visser (i, §§426–38) gives further examples of the various types.

§477. Whether *self* was actually used as a noun in OE is a terminological question. See Mitchell 1979*a*, pp. 40–1.

(*b*) Self *in apposition*

§478. *Self* may be used as a pronoun in apposition with a noun, personal pronoun (reflexive or non-reflexive), or with a relative pronoun. Its function is to emphasize. The examples which follow show that in the nominative—where, I suppose, it is by definition not reflexive—*self* follows the noun or pronoun, either immediately, e.g. *Or* 220. 20 *Romane selfe, ÆCHom* i. 292. 9 *Crist sylf, ÆCHom* ii. 366. 18 *þæt Bearn sylf, ÆCHom* i. 124. 19 *he sylf, WHom* 7. 152 *Nis æfre ænig man þe sylf geþencan cunne*, and *GenA* 2761 *swa he self gecwæð*, or separated from it, e.g. *CP* 31. 14 *Ac hie woldon selfe fleon, ÆCHom* ii. 452. 3 *Ac wite gehwa, þæt se ne mæg nan fyr of heofenum asendan, seðe on heofenum sylf cuman ne mot, GenA* 937 *adl unliðe þe þu on æple ær* ‖ *selfa forswulge*, and *ÆCHom* i. 514. 14 . . . *swilce he him sylf witega wære* (on examples like this, where the intervening element is the dative of a personal pronoun used reflexively, see §488). In *ÆLS* 3. 591 *Se ebreisca cwæð: sylf ic swelte þonne, sylf* precedes the pronoun. But this example—the only one of its kind known to me in the prose—may be a deliberate departure from the norm for emphasis and rhythm and (since it is in one of Ælfric's later homilies) may reflect the freer element order of poetry. The fact that the two elements can be together or separated means that the referent of *self* cannot be determined grammatically in examples like *Bo* 47. 5 *forðæm ic hit no self nauht ne ondræde* and *Or* 17. 32 *ac he nyste hwæt þæs soþes wæs, for þæm he hit self ne geseah*. But the appearance of *sylf ic* in *ÆLS* 3. 591 above—cf. *Beo* 920 *self cyning* and *PPs* 121. 3 *þær syndon dælas on sylfre hire* (?*metri causa*)—scarcely raises the possibility that *sylf* goes with *wisdom* in *ÆCHom* ii. 586. 28 *forðan þe he is sylf soð wisdom* and still less (despite examples like *Or* 96. 6 *hie self*) the possibility that *sylf* goes with *domas* in *BlHom* 43. 11 . . . *gif he wille sylf Godes domas gedegan*.

§479. The use of *self* with a personal pronoun and an ordinal numeral seen in *LawICn* 5. 1a *nime vi his gehadan . . . 7 beo he sylf seofoþa* and *And* 664 *nemne ellefne . . .* ‖ *He wæs twelfta sylf* provides an alternative to the idiom discussed in §§397–400.

§480. In the accusative, genitive, and dative, appositive *self* usually immediately follows the noun or pronoun, e.g. *Or* 52. 7 *hiene selfne,* *CP* 95. 10 *ðurh hie selfe,* *CP* 35. 7 *his selfes,* *Or* 62. 29 *heora selfra,* and *Or* 58. 17 *on him selfum.* But there are a few instances in which other elements intervene, e.g. *Bo* 100. 27 *ac me ðincð selfum,* *CP* 113. 10 *Æresð him ðuhte selfum,* and *Or* 170. 10 *swa him eac selfum siþþan æfter lamp* (all with the dative governed by impersonal verbs), *Bo* 5. 33 *Hu se Wisdom hæfde getæht þam Mode þa anlic-nessa þara soðena sælþa; wolde hi þa selfe getæcan,* *CP* 463. 33 . . . *ðæt mod . . . gæderað him ðonne selfum to lofe eall ðæt god,* and *WHom* 9. 146 . . . *hwa folgie eallinge his luste 7 his lust him to lage sylfum gesette,* and occasional examples of an oblique form of *self* before the pronoun in the poetry, e.g. *GenA* 2714 *sylfum þe, ChristA* 108 *of sylfum þe, PPs* 121. 3 *on sylfre hire.*

§481. The combination personal pronoun + *self* is frequently re-flexive in the accusative, genitive, and dative, e.g. *ÆCHom* i. 120. 17 *geswutela ðe sylfne ðam sacerde, ÆCHom* i. 240. 34 . . . *ac tylað his sylfes, ÆCHom* i. 244. 12 *On ðisum dagum we sceolon gebiddan . . . us sylfum gesundfulnysse, ÆCHom* ii. 142. 10 . . . *Cuðberhtus . . . wolde þurh hine sylfne sona hi geneosian, ÆCHom* i. 340. 35 . . . *be ðam asolcenum þe truwað be him sylfum þæt . . . ,* and (with the elements separated) *CP* 463. 33 and *WHom* 9. 146 (both in §480). But, as already noted in §475, it can be emphatic but not reflexive, as in *Or* 54. 4 *Hi þa hrædlice . . . gewendan eft ongean þone cyning, 7 ealne his here gefliemdon, 7 hiene selfne gefengon* and *Or* 58. 16 . . . *hit God siþþan longsumlice wrecende wæs, ærest on him selfum, 7 siþþan on his bearnum.* OED (s.v. *self* pron. A. 3. b) notes five examples of this non-reflexive use of *self* with pronouns in oblique cases—from *Orosius* to Coverdale; Wülfing (i, §239) offers more, but I have found none in Ælfric. There is work for lexicographers here. Examples with the genitive are hard to come by. Three appar-ent examples are

Or 48. 17 Hu ungemetlice ge Romware bemurciað 7 besprecað þæt eow nu wyrs (s)ie on þiosan cristendome þonne þæm þeodum þa wære, for þon þa Gotan eow hwon oferhergedon, 7 iowre burg abræcon, 7 iower feawe ofslogon; 7 for hiora cræftum 7 for hiora hwætscipe iowra selfra anwaldes eoweres unþonces habban mehton . . . ,

GenA 2920
þe wile gasta weard
lissum gyldan þæt þe wæs leofre his
sibb and hyldo þonne þin sylfes bearn,

and

Jud 285
Her ys geswutelod ure sylfra forwyrd,
toweard getacnod þæt þære tide ys

> mid niðum neah geðrungen,   þe we sculon nyde losian,
> somod æt sæcce forweorðan.

But in these three examples *self* is at least to some extent reflexive—
note respectively *ge Romware, þe* after an impersonal verb, and *we*
—and comes close to having the sense of MnE 'own'; see further
§§483-6. Similar examples with the dative are discussed in §487.

§482. The subject of a sentence containing a reflexive need not, of
course, be a person, e.g. *CP* 242. 6 *forðæm ðæt yfelwillende mod
gefielt hit self twyfeald oninnan him selfum, 7 sio twyfealdnes ðæs
yflan willan hiene selfne twyfealdne gefielt oninnan him selfum*
(where *hiene selfne* apparently takes its gender from *willan*, which is
logically the subject) and *BlHom* 187. 15 *Nu mæg soð hit sylf gecyþan*; *hit self* in these two examples is the forerunner of MnE *itself*,
though *self* may be nominative rather than accusative.

(c) The genitive of a personal pronoun, or the possessive, + self

§483. *Self* is often used to emphasize a personal pronoun in the
genitive or a possessive. These combinations are found most often in
the poetry and are commoner in the early than the late prose, where
agen (§§501-2) is preferred before a noun. They take several different forms. (Here I disregard the (to me unlikely) possibility that *self*
is a noun; see §477.)

§484. The genitive of a personal pronoun with *self* in agreement is
found in two contexts. In the first, the combination is used quite
independently, e.g. *Bo* 30. 12 *ne magon ne þin gehelpan, ne heora
selfra* and *ÆCHom* i. 240. 34 . . . *ac tylað his selfes*. In the second, it
is dependent in the sense that it is the equivalent of an inflected form
of a possessive. Thus in *GenA* 791 *Hwæt, þu Eue, hæfst yfele
gemearcod* || *uncer sylfra sið*, we could have had (metre apart) ✩*un-
cerne sið* (cf. *GenA* 796 *þurh uncres hearran þanc*) and in *ChristA*
254 *þurh þin sylfes gong*, we could have had ✩*þurh þinne gong* (cf.
ChristA 250 *þurh ðinne hercyme*). Other possible examples of the
second type include *GenA* 2922 *þin sylfes bearn* (*bearn* nom. sg.
neut.) and *ChristA* 9 *þin sylfes weorc* (*weorc* acc. sg. neut.). But in
these last two, it is impossible to say whether we have the genitive of
the personal pronoun agreeing with *self* or a form of the possessive
agreeing with the noun. This difficulty does not arise with examples
involving the third person pronouns *his*, *hire*, and *hira*, since they
cannot be inflected as possessives. In *Beo* 2040 *ond hyra sylfra
feorh*, *hyra* and *sylfra* obviously agree with one another. In *Bede*
262. 3 *mid his seolfes hondum* and *Beo* 1115 *hire selfre sunu*, self

agrees with the personal pronoun and takes, not the gender of the noun, but the sex (natural gender) of the person concerned.

§485. But we also find a possessive inflected to agree with *self*. Here too the combination may be used quite independently, e.g. *CP* 220. 5 *we sceoldon urra selfra waldan*, *Bo* 25. 22 *fulne anweald þines selfes*, *LS* 35. 109 *begym þines sylfes*, and

Met 16. 1   Se þe wille anwald agon,   ðonne sceal he ærest tilian
               þæt he his selfes   on sefan age
               anwald innan,

or with a noun (which must be of different gender and/or case if we are to prove that we do not have the genitive of a personal pronoun), e.g. *BlHom* 185. 1 *þin rice 7 þines sylfes feorh*, *And* 1417 *on þines sylfes hand*, *ChristA* 339 *þinre sylfre sunu* (in these three examples *sylf* is masculine or feminine according to the sex of the referent of the personal pronoun), and *Or* 48. 21 *iowra selfra anwaldes*. For more examples, all from the poetry, see Penning, p. 18(3), and Bauch, p. 23. Farr, pp. 22-3, includes some of those from the prose already quoted.

§486. This is clearly odd. An even odder pattern occurs, represented in the prose by two examples, but not in the poetry.[121] The two examples are *Bede* 480. 21 *of minre sylfre cyþeþe*, Latin *ex mea ipse cognitione*, and *Alex* 14. 1 *be minre seolfre nedþearfe*, Latin *de proprio meo . . . periculo*. In these, the possessive and *self* agree with one another and with the related noun as well, i.e. all three elements show grammatical gender and have nothing to do with the sex of the speaker, which is in both instances male. I believe that the pattern seen in *ChristA* 254 *þurh þin sylfes gong* is the original form of the idiom. I discuss it and the other patterns cited here in Mitchell 1979a, pp. 41-4.

(d) The dative of the personal pronoun + self

§487. This combination is found with pronouns of all three persons and takes two forms. The first is the dative equivalent of (say) *he self, hine selfne, his selfes*, i.e. both personal pronoun and *self* are in the dative. This is used both reflexively, e.g. *Bede* 84. 9 *þa wiif . . . in*

---

[121] For my objections to an attempt to turn *Wife* 2 *minre sylfre sið* into one and thereby to establish the possibility that *The Wife's Lament* was spoken by a man, see Mitchell 1972. This phenomenon is not restricted to *self*. Thus in *CP* 379. 13 . . . *ic eom clæne 7 unscildig nu giet to dæg eowres ælces blodes*, we should have *eower*, '. . . of the blood of each of you'.

him seolfum sculon lichoman clænnisse healdan, Or 40. 33 7 [*Perseus*] *þære þeode operne naman ascop be him syluum, swa hi mon syððan het Persi, ÆCHom* i. 262. 2 *Ic gefylle mid me sylfum heofonas and eorðan, ÆCHom* i. 578. 17 *Ne scealt ðu on ðe silfum wuldrian,* and *ÆCHom* ii. 366. 18 *and þæt Bearn sylf . . . forgeaf us him sylfum,* and non-reflexively, e.g. *Or* 40. 27 *Hwær is nu on ænigan cristendome betuh him sylfum þæt mon him þurfe swilc ondrædan . . . ?, Or* 58. 15 *Ond for þon þe he þæt god forlet . . . 7 wyrse geceas, hit God siþþan longsumlice wrecende wæs, ærest on him selfum 7 siþþan on his bearnum, Or* 152. 26 *sume he self ofslog, sume an gefeohtum beforan him selfum mon afslog,* and *ÆCHom* i. 336. 28 *þæt þæt ge doð þearfum on minum naman, þæt ge doð me sylfum.* In *Bede* 2. 2 7 *ic ðe sende þæt spell . . . ðe sylfum to rædanne, ðe sylfum* is in a sense reflexive, even though it does not refer to the grammatical subject of the clause; there is a concealed accusative and infinitive or purpose clause with the subject [*ðe*] or [*ðu*]. Again, *him seolfum* in *Bede* 56. 17 7 *he* [*Gregorius*] *ælmihtigne God bæd þæt he hi mid his gife gescylde: 7 þæt he him seolfum forgeafe þæt he moste ðone wæstm heora gewinnes in heofona rices wuldre geseon* refers to *Gregorius,* the subject of the main clause, and not to *God,* the subject of the clause in which it stands. So it is not strictly reflexive; Miller's 'he prayed to Almighty God to . . . grant to himself' is exactly what Bede does not mean. A similar example is *ÆCHom* i. 140. 29 *Gif ðu oncnæwst ðinne Drihten . . . hit fremeð þe sylfum to ðam ecan life: gif ðu hine forgitst, hit hearmað þe sylfum,* where *þe sylfum* is in effect reflexive, though not grammatically so. For further examples, see Wülfing, i, §§239 and 242; Farr, pp. 23–5; and Visser, i, §428.

§488. In the second form of the combination, we have the dative of a personal pronoun used more or less reflexively (see below) and followed immediately by the nominative of *self,* singular or plural in agreement with the subject of the sentence, e.g. *Or* 260. 29 *he het æt sumum cierre onbærnan Romeburg . . . 7 gestod him self on þæm hiehstan torre þe þærbinnan wæs, Bo* 11. 7 *Ic wiste þ̄ þu ut afaren wære, ac ic nysste hu feor, ær ðu þe self hit me gerehtest mid þinum sarcwidum, Bede* 52. 22 . . . *þæt hi woldan him sylfe niman 7 hergian, þær hi hit findan mihton, ÆCHom* i. 514. 14 *swilce he him sylf witega wære, ÆCHom* i. 150. 8 *He wæs mid wisdome afylled, forþan ðe he is him sylf wisdom,* and *ÆCHom* ii. 542. 21 *Sume eac burgon heora feore . . . and ferdon him sylfe to helle wite* (cf. *ÆLS* 7. 211). The uninflected form *self* occasionally occurs for the plural, e.g. *Or* 19. 36 7 *þonne Burgenda land wæs us on bæcbord, 7 þa habbað him sylf cyning, Or* 164. 3 . . . *nu Romane him self þyllic writon 7 setton for heora agnum gielpe,* and *Or* 236. 24 *Marius 7 Silla geforan him self, 7 Cinna wæs ofslagen;* cf. the examples cited in §473. The weak form *selfa* is sometimes found in the poetry, e.g.

GenA 1562   Đa þæt geeode,   þæt se eadega wer
                 on his wicum wearð   wine druncen,
                 swæf symbelwerig,   and him selfa sceaf
                 reaf of lice,

GuthA 468 . . . *þu þe sylfa gesawe þæt we þec soð onstældun,* and (with nominative personal pronoun unexpressed after an imperative; see §889) *And* 1348 *Ga þe sylfa to!* For further examples, see Penning, pp. 22-4, Wülfing, i, §239, and Farr, pp. 26-8.

§489. It is perhaps less easy for the modern reader to distinguish the 'necessary' and the 'pleonastic' reflexive dative here than it was with the personal pronoun alone (§§271-4). *Self* of course is 'necessary' in the sense that the writer inserted it to give emphasis. In the first pattern (§487), e.g. *ÆCHom* i. 244. 12 *On ðisum dagum we sceolon gebiddan ure eorðlicra wæstma genihtsumnysse, and us sylfum gesundfulnysse and sibbe* . . . and *ÆCHom* i. 408. 12 *Witodlice seo ðwyre sawul is on sibbe wunigende* . . . *ac bedygelað hire sylfre ða æfterfiligendan yrmða,* the dative of the personal pronoun conveys the reflexive idea and probably cannot be omitted because that would leave *self* used absolutely in an oblique case—a construction normally avoided in the prose; see §498.

§490. For the second pattern (§488) we can say that *self* is again 'necessary' in that it gives emphasis, and that the personal pronoun is essential in examples like *Or* 42. 10 *7 hu he his agenne sunu his godum to blote acwealde, 7 hine him sylf siððan to mete gegyrede* and *Exod* 5. 7 *ac gan 7 gaderian him sylf healm* (the preparing and the gathering could have been for someone else). But there are others where the presence or absence of a dative personal pronoun may seem to us to make little difference. Possible examples include some of those quoted in §488, *Bo* 28. 23 *7 þonne þu ealle gedælde hæfst þonne bist þu ðe self wædla, Solil* 45. 23 *gyf he hale eagan hæfð, he mæg hym self hawian on ða sunnan,* and sentences like *ÆHex* 316 *ac wolde beon him sylf on his sylfes anwealde, ÆLS* 7. 211 *þa ne dorste se heahgerefa naht ongean þa hæðen gyldan ac forlet his gingran togeanes þære ceaste and ferde him sylf aweg sorhful on mode,* and *ÆCHom* ii. 62. 22 *swa eac Crist wæs gehyrsum his Fæder oð dead, and him sylf his rode abær,* in which the personal pronoun seems to add little and *self* could stand alone in the co-ordinate clause; see §496.

§491. This combination of dative of personal pronoun + nominative of *self* is, of course, the source of some uses of MnE 'himself', 'herself', and 'themselves'; see *OED*, s.v. *self* A. 4. The difficulty of determining its exact status in OE can be demonstrated by a comparison of the examples within the three following groups: first, *Or* 3. 8 *7 hu Philippus, þæs maran Alexandres fæder, feng to Mæcedonia rice, Or* 284. 17 *Æfter þæm Magnentius ofslog Constans, 7 feng him to þæm rice, Or* 134. 12 *þa wundrade Alexander hwy hit swa æmenne wære; 7 hrædlice þone weall self oferclom*, and *Or* 66. 6 . . . *Numetores, þone he eac ofslog, ða he cyning wæs, 7 him self siþþan to ðæm rice feng*; second, *GenA* 906 *þu scealt . . . faran feðeleas, GenB* 543 *ac þu meaht þe forð faran, GenB* 556 *Nu sceal he sylf faran*, and *LPr* ii. 37 *and þu þe silf eart soðfæst dema*; and third, *GenB* 666 *Ic mæg heonon geseon, GenA* 2168 *Ne læt þu þe þin mod asealcan, PPs* 118. 159 *Swylce ic sylf geseah*, and *GenB* 611 *þu meaht nu þe self geseon . . . ‖ þæt.* . . . (Note that in the verse examples *self* carries stress and alliteration.) I discuss these questions further in Mitchell 1979*a*, pp. 44–5.

(*e*) Self *as an adjective*

§492. When used with a noun *self* is declined strong or weak, according to the usual rules (§102). Examples with no demonstrative and the strong form of *self* are rare, but do occur, e.g. *Lch* ii. 72. 17 *on selfe wisan* 'in the same fashion', *PPs* 54. 15 *to sylfum drihtne*, and *Beo* 920 *self cyning* (where *self* may be appositive, as in *Or* 166. 15 *se cyning self* and *CP* 51. 21 *God selfa*; see §§478 and 472). A strong form with a demonstrative appears in *Bede(Ca)* 26. 20 *under þam sylfum norðdæle middangeardes* (where, however, MS *B* has the expected *sylfan*).

§493. The more common examples with a demonstrative and the weak form of *self* before a noun can be divided into two groups— those in which *self* points backwards, e.g. *Bede* 76. 18 *þæt seolfe sar* and *ÆCHom* i. 588. 34 *þæt sylfe wite*, and those in which *self* points forward to a limiting adjective clause, e.g. *CP* 77. 15 *On ðæm selfan hrægle, ðe he on his breostum wæg . . .* and *ÆCHom* ii. 104. 3 *Witodlice þæt sylfe land þe ðu ðe geagnast nis ðin.* The combination demonstrative + weak form of *self* also occurs without a noun, with the same references backwards and forwards, e.g. *CP* 327. 14 *ðylæs*

hie eft scilen don ðæt selfe[122] and *Bede* 202. 18 *7 se leg 7 seo hætu*
ræsde on þa seolfan, þe þæt fyr ældon. . . . The fact that *self* adj.
obeys the normal rules must cast serious doubt on the reading of MS
T in *Bede* 346. 4 *seolfan þa his lareowas*, where one would expect
seolfe; cf. *Lch* i. 322. 2 *genim þas wyrte sylfe gecnucude*, but *Lch*
i. 322. 5 *genim þas ylcan wyrte swa we ær cwædon gecnucude*, and
CP 25. 11 *from ðære dura selfre ðisse bec, ðæt is from onginne ðisse*
spræce (where *selfre* probably goes with *ðære dura*). *Bede(B)* 346. 4
has *þa sylfan lareowas*, MS *C þa seolfan his lareowas*. Both offer
good syntax. See further Mitchell 1974*b*, pp. 126–8.

§494. *Self* adj. points both backwards and forwards in the poetry
too, e.g. *ChristC* 1208 *se sylfa cyning* and *PPs* 107. 10 *Hwæt, þu*
eart se sylfa god, þe us synnige iu ‖ adrife fram dome. This difference
of reference may lie behind the distinction made by BT and GK,
which both take *sylfa* in *ChristC* 1208 as 'self' and *se sylfa* in *PPs*
107. 10 as 'the same' (BT, s.v. *self* A. I(δ) and B.(α), and GK, s.v. *self*
2. and 3., respectively). This distinction is unreal; we could easily
translate the first as 'That same king' and the second as 'The very
God who . . .' or 'That God himself who . . .'. Similarly, *Lch* ii. 72. 17
on selfe wisan quoted in §492 casts doubt on the notion apparently
held by GK that the strong form of *self* cannot mean 'the same', for
we find there, s.v. *self*, only three divisions—'1. *starke Flexion, ipse*
. . . 2. *schwache Flexion, ipse* . . . 3. *schwache Flexion, derselbe,*
idem . . .' ['1. *strong declension, ipse* . . . 2. *weak declension, ipse*
. . . 3. *weak declension, the same, idem* . . .']. As I have suggested
elsewhere (Mitchell 1974*b*, p. 128), a rethinking of the basic divisions in these articles on *self* is needed.

(f) The absolute use of self

§495. We need to distinguish examples in the nominative from
those in the oblique cases. Ælfric in his *Grammar* (100. 3) observes:
ipse, gif he stent ana, þonne byð hit he sylf oððe se ylca · eft ego
ipse, ic sylf, tu ipse, ðu sylf, ille ipse, he sylf ET CETERA. So it is
perhaps no surprise that there are few examples like *CP* 105. 19 *Oft*
eac gebyreð ðonne se scrift ongit ðæs costunga ðe he him ondetteð
ðæt eac self bið mid ðæm ilcum gecostod,

---

[122] This phrase also occurs where it cannot be the object of a verb, e.g. *ChristC* 937.
Penning (p. 14) takes this (and similar uses) as adverbial. Cook, in the Glossary to his edition (1900), s.v. *ðæt sylfe*, describes it as a conjunction 'also, likewise'. For further examples
of *self* adj., see Wülfing, i, §§273–4. He includes examples with a noun + the strong form
of *self* in post-position which I have treated as appositives (§478).

Beo 418   forþan hie mægenes cræft   minne cuþon;
                   selfe ofersawon,   ða ic of searwum cwom,
                   fah from freondum,

and

Beo 1465   Huru ne gemunde   mago Ecglafes
                   eafoþes cræftig,   þæt he ær gespræc
                   wine druncen,   þa he þæs wæpnes onlah
                   selran sweordfrecan;   selfa ne dorste
                   under yða gewin   aldre geneþan.

Indeed, Andrew (*Postscript*, p. 82) observes that in *Beowulf*

self and its weak form *selfa* are used indifferently to qualify either nouns or pronouns . . . ; neither, however, can stand alone as a pronoun in the nominative, and sentences like 419 selfe ofersawon, 1468 selfa ne dorste, should be construed as co-ordinate clauses to the sentences before which supply their noun- or pronoun-subjects.

§496. This is certainly a tenable view, for *self* does occur alone in the nominative in the second of two co-ordinate clauses joined by *ond*, reinforcing (as it were) an unexpressed pronoun subject, e.g. *Or* 106. 32 *ac he ægðer fleah ge þa dæd ge þa sægene, 7 eac self sæde þæt seo dæd his nære, Or* 134. 12 *þa wundrade Alexander hwy hit swa æmenne wære; 7 hrædlice þone weall self oferclom,* and

GenA 2370   Abraham fremede   swa him se eca bebead,
                   . . .   . . .
                   . . .   and þa seolf onfeng
                   torhtum tacne.

§497. Whether we regard a nominative form of *self* as absolute when it is accompanied by the dative of a personal pronoun used reflexively in a clause or sentence with no expressed subject depends on our attitude to the construction discussed in §495. Such examples occur in co-ordinate clauses, e.g. *ÆCHom* ii. 542. 21 *Sume eac burgon heora feore . . . and ferdon him sylfe to helle wite* and

GenA 1562   Ða þæt geeode,   þæt se eadega wer
                   on his wicum wearð   wine druncen,
                   swæf symbelwerig,   and him selfa sceaf
                   reaf of lice,

and in sentences in which the pronoun subject of an imperative verb is not expressed (§889), e.g. *Or* 100. 27 *sece him þonne self þæt* and *GenA* 1916 *Leorna þe seolfa.* In *ChristA* 59 *Sioh nu sylfa þe geond þas sidan gesceaft, sylfa* precedes the dative pronoun.

§498. The absolute use of *self* in oblique cases is rare in the prose—again perhaps not surprisingly in view of the quotation from Ælfric's *Grammar* given in §495. Penning (pp. 19–20) cites examples only from the poetry and Farr specifically states (p. 25) that 'this omission is a poetic license'. However, BT (s.v. *self* III) quotes three examples from the Laws—*LawWi* 18 *Preost hine clænsie sylfæs soþe*, *LawWi* 20 *Gest hine clænsie sylfes aþe*, and *LawGeþyncðo* 4 *And se ðe swa geþogene forwyrhtan næfde swore for silfne*. All three are reflexive.

§499. Absolute *self* is more common in the poetry, but is not always reflexive, as Farr (pp. 25–6) implies; some of his own examples are clearly non-reflexive. Examples in which *self* is reflexive include *El* 488 *soð sigora frea, seolfne geywde*, *Beo* 2638 *Ðe he usic on herge geceas ‖ to ðyssum siðfate sylfes willum*, *Jul* 99 *Wiðsæcest þu to swiþe sylfre rædes ‖ þinum brydguman*, *El* 1206 *ond sybbe swa same sylfra betweonum*, and *MSol* 374 *Oft heo to bealwe bearn afedeð, ‖ seolfre to sorge*. But *self* is not reflexive in *Beo* 1977 *Gesæt þa wið sylfne se ða sæcce genæs, ‖ mæg wið mæge*, *GenA* 1915 *Ic þe selfes dom ‖ life, leofa*, *And* 1300 *Sleað synnigne ofer seolfes muð, ‖ folces gewinnan!*, and *ChristC* 1240 *Him on scinað ærgewyrhtu, ‖ on sylfra gehwam sunnan beorhtran*.

§500. Penning remarks (p. 20) that if *hie* goes with *sylfe* in

El 998

	Hie se casere heht
ofstum myclum	eft gearwian
sylfe to siðe,	

then *sylfe* 'is used without any reflective relation at all'. His reason is his claim that in *And* 795 *Het hie to þam siðe gyrwan*, *gyrwan* is used without a reflexive pronoun. My own view is that *hie . . . sylfe* and *hie* are the reflexive objects (not the subjects) of the infinitives. Such separation of personal pronoun and appositive *self* occurs; see §478. In *Rid* 57. 6 *Nemnað hy sylfe* the editors argue which of two translations to accept—'They name themselves' or 'Name them [your] selves'. I have not yet found a parallel to support the latter; on the analogy of examples like *GenA* 1916 *Leorna þe seolfa* one would expect ☆*Nemnað eow hy sylfe/sylfan*.

(4) Agen

§501. *Agen* may be used independently, e.g. *ÆHom* 1. 46 *on his agenum he com, 7 his age(ne) ne underfengon hine*, and may refer back to a noun which is not repeated, e.g. *ÆCHom* i. 414. 26 *for oðra manna beterunge, na for his agenre*. But normally it is used dependently in agreement with a following noun, e.g. *BlHom* 45. 2 *þa wæs him forgolden æfter his agenum gewyrhtum*; in this, it naturally differs from *an*, e.g. *BlHom* 105. 12 *7 him ealle þas cynericu on his anes æht geagnian*, and *self*, e.g. *BlHom* 59. 1 *þurh his sylfes muþ* (but see §484). It is regularly declined strong even when preceded by a possessive, but weak forms do occur, e.g. *WHom* 14. 54 *for heora agenan þearfe*, where *agenan* cannot be for *agenum*, since *þearf* is feminine. The grammars remain silent on this point. All Wülfing's examples (Wülfing, i, §253) are declined strong. Ropers (pp. 33–4 and 64) comments on the comparative frequency of *agen* in his selection from Ælfric.

§502. As in MnE, *agen* is usually preceded by the genitive of a noun, e.g. *Bo* 80. 25 *þæs wæteres agnu cyð is on eorþan* and *ÆHom* 7. 6 *þæs Hælendes agene word*, or by a possessive, e.g. *Or* 100. 19 *on urum agnum tidum*, *CP* 27. 15 *of hira agnum dome*, *ÆCHom* i. 212. 20 . . . *þa martyras, þe for Cristes geleafan sealdon heora agenne lichaman* (on the number, see §§87–91), and *WHom* 6. 19 *þinre agenre sawle*. The genitive of the noun is occasionally found after *agen*, e.g. *ÆLet5* 8 *þæt me is lað to tælenne agenne Godes freond* (see §1318). The genitive or possessive is sometimes not expressed when the dative of a noun or personal pronoun makes the reference clear, e.g. *ÆCHom* i. 112. 4 *ac forgeaf him agenne cyre* (but *ÆCHom* i. 112. 5 . . . *þæt gehwylcum sy his agen cyre geðafod*), *ÆCHom* i. 112. 11 *þa forgeaf he Adame and Euan agenne cyre*, *WHom* 20(*EI*). 100 *hu mæg mare scamu þurh Godes yrre mannum gelimpan þonne us deð gelome for agenum gewyrhtum*, and (without a following noun) *LawIVEg* 1. 5a *þæt he him to agenum teleð*. Sometimes we find simply *agen* + a noun, e.g. *ÆHom* 9. 34 *for ðan þe manega magon maran ræd findan þonne ænlypige magon mid agenum gewille* and *ÆGram* 25. 14 *On as geendiað agene naman* 'proper names' and *ÆGram* 25. 16 *hit is agen nama* 'a proper name'.

(5) Swelc

§503. *Swelc, swilc, swylc* (on the forms see *OEG*, §725) may refer back, as in the examples below, or may refer forward as antecedent to clauses of different kinds; on the types of clause and the combinations see the Index of Words and Phrases, s.v. *swelc*. It may be used dependently, e.g. *ÆCHom* i. 516. 9 *swilc freond* and *ÆCHom* i. 408. 5 *swilcera manna*, or independently, e.g. (alone) *Coll* 106 *Hærincgas 7 leaxas . . . 7 fela swylces*, *ÆCHom* i. 84. 16 *ða breost þe swylce gesihton*, and (with a partitive genitive) *Lch* ii. 130. 2 *7 hwites sealtes swilc swa mæge mid feower fingrum geniman* and

CP 203. 19 *suelc eower*. Dependent *swilc* regularly precedes its noun, but may follow it when it refers forward to a clause, e.g. *Solil* 53. 18 . . . *þam he sealde sumne dæl ecra gyfa, swilcra swilce nu wisdom is* . . . and *ÆLS* 29. 262 *þa com þær heofonlic leoht . . . swilc swa hi ær ne gesawon*.

§504. Ropers (pp. 40-1) remarks that in Ælfric *swelc* is always declined strong and is never found with a demonstrative. As far as I have observed, this rule holds for Ælfric and indeed is generally true. But examples of a demonstrative + a weak form of *swelc* appear in 'Alfredian' prose, e.g. *CP* 159. 10 *ge ðonne . . . gelærað ða suelcan*, *CP* 265. 17 *Oft eac ða swelcan monn sceal forsion*, *CP* 293. 21 *Ða suelcan we magon ealra betest geryhtan*, and *Solil* 54. 2 *Ða swilcan gifa hi ne þurfon næfre forlætan*. There is even an example of demonstrative + strong form in *GD* 247. 13 *þone swylcne seocne læcas nemniað gewitleasne*. Full collections of variations like these may well throw light on problems of authorship; the articles on the *Orosius* by Bately and Liggins in *Ang*. 88 (1970) point the way.

§505. Einenkel notes some early examples of the pattern 'such and such', e.g. *Bo* 116. 30 *Be swilcum 7 be swylcum þu miht ongitan þ se cræft þæs lichoman bið on þam mode*.[123] On correlative *swelc* . . . *swelc* see §2375. *Swelc* may be used in combination with other words, including numerals, e.g. *ÆCHom* i. 514. 3 *ænne swilcne lyttling* (see Rissanan, p. 238) and *Beo* 1347 *swylce twegen* ‖ *micle mearcstapan*; *oþer* in the sense 'second' or 'another' and in the sense 'other', e.g. *Or* 194. 20 *7 eft wearð oþer swelc ren*, *Beo* 1582 *fyftyne men,* ‖ *ond oðer swylc*, *Lch* ii. 256. 6 *7 medmicel pipores oþer swilc cymenes oððe ma*, and *ÆCHom* i. 164. 5 *ac ðas undeawas and oðre swilce*; and *manig*, e.g. *Bo* 87. 8 *manege swelce cræftas*.

(6) þyllic

§506. *þyllic* is used with or without a demonstrative, both dependently, e.g. *ÆCHom* i. 406. 21 *ðillic orf*, *ÆCHom* i. 406. 24 *ðillice cypan*, *ÆCHom* i. 480. 20 *þyllice wundra*,[124] and *ÆCHom* ii. 590. 28 *ðas þyllice gyltas*,[125] and independently, e.g. *ÆCHom* ii. 398. 6 *þas ðyllice* 'such as these', *ÆCHom* ii. 590. 26 *ðas and ðyllice* 'these

---

[123] *Ang*. 26 (1903), 571; see also p. 569. Einenkel discusses *swelc* and its descendants in *Ang*. 26 (1903), 561-72. This repeats (with minor variations) *Ang*. 23 (1900), 109-22.

[124] Ropers, p. 43, explains *wundra* as a partitive genitive. The absence of unambiguous genitives argues against this view.

[125] The absence of such examples from Ropers's material (or his failure to observe them) led him to a false conclusion (pp. 42-3).

and the like', *ÆCHom* ii. 592. 7 *Ðas synna and oðre ðyllice*, and *ÆCHom* i. 412. 23 *Hwæt sind ðyllice buton sceaðan?*

§507. *þyllic* is usually declined strong—always so in Ælfric, according to Schrader (p. 47) and Ropers (p. 42)—even when used with a demonstrative; see the examples in §506. Occasional weak forms occur in 'Alfredian' texts, e.g. *CP* 227. 23 *Ac hwam beoð ðonne ðas ðyllecan* [both manuscripts] *geliccran ðonne ðæm folce ðe* . . . and *GD* 263. 2 *ac þas þyslican syndon to rihtanne.* . . . On the forms of *þyllic*, see *OEG*, §725. See also Christophersen, pp. 117–20, and, for examples, Wülfing, i, §§265–6.

(7) Oþer

§508. *Oþer* 'other, another, second' is always declined strong, even after a demonstrative, and can be used both dependently and independently, either with or without a demonstrative.[126] Thus, we find *ÆCHom* i. 154. 9 *oðer ðing digle* 'another thing hidden' and *ÆCHom* i. 170. 31 *oðere siðe* 'a second time' (cf. *ÆCHom* i. 168. 35 *æne* 'once') but *ÆCHom* ii. 520. 25 *se oðer Iacobus* 'the other James' and *ÆCHom* i. 374. 27 *on ðone oðerne dæg* 'on the next day', and (with the plural) *Bo* 14. 9 *Loca nu be þære sunnan 7 eac be oðrum tunglum* but *Or* 5. 18 *Craccus se consul wonn wið þa oðre consulas.* From these and from examples of independent *oþer* like *Or* 148. 29 *Ac Antigones, se mid ungemete girnde anwalda ofer opre* but *Or* 56. 24 *þa þe ær æt þæm aþum næren, þæt þa ham gelendon... 7 þa oðere* . . . , one might argue that the demonstrative was used when the reference was definite, but not when it was indefinite. But examples like *Or* 112. 14 *7 him ðær wearþ oþer eage mid anre flan ut ascoten* (where MS *C* has *þæt oðer eage*) and *Or* 180. 6 *þær wearð Lutatia wund þurh oþer cneow* (where MS *C* has *þæt oðer cneow*) suggest that the usage varied; see further §567 and Rissanen, pp. 91–2 and 98–100. Similar variations can be found when *oþer* is used correlatively: e.g. (independent *oþer*) *Or* 46. 16 *tu . . . oþer . . . oðer*, *Or* 96. 14 *wið þa twegen heras . . . wið oþerne . . . þone oðerne*, *CP* 291. 15 *Oðer hira wæs haten Timotheus, oðer Titus . . .* , *CP* 291. 20 *ðone oðerne . . . oðerne*, *CP* 131. 10 *on ðæm oðrum . . . on ðæm oðrum*, and (*oþer* dependent at least once) *Or* 218. 26 *æt oþrum cirre . . . et oþrum*, *Bo* 106. 8 *oðre hwile . . . oðre hwile*, *Bo* 43. 23 *on oðrum lande . . . on ðæm oðrum*, *Or* 138. 12 *7 Fauius se oðer consul æfter þæs oðres fielle sige hæfde*, and *Bede(Ca)* 148. 7 *his oðer sunu . . . Eadfrið se oðer* (on this reading see §517).

---

[126] Further on *oþer* 'second' see §§567–8. Einenkel gives examples of *oþer* in various functions in OE, and later, in *Ang.* 26 (1903), 521–35. This repeats with variations *Ang.* 21 (1899), 289–99.

§509. In examples like *CP* 29. 21 *Monige eac wise lareowas winnað mid hira ðeawum wið ða gæsðlecan bebodu ðe hi mid wordum lærað, ðonne hie on oðre wisan libbað, on oðre hi lærað, Or* 288. 15 *for þon he wiste þæt he hit on him wrecan wolde, gif he anfunde þæt he on oþran geleafan wære, on oþran he self wæs,* and *ÆCHom* ii. 574. 1 *Drihten ne oncnæwð hi, forðan ðe hi sind oðre, oþre hi wæron,* 'other than' sometimes offers a convenient translation in MnE (as Wülfing, i. 455-6, Einenkel in *Ang.* 26 (1903), 522, and BT, s.v. *oðer* II 2(*a*), all quoting more examples, suggest). But we still have to do with correlative *oþer . . . oþer*; thus Sweet translates the first example 'when they live in one way and teach in another'.

§510. Correlative pairs apart from *oþer . . . oþer* (as exemplified in §§508-9) are found both dependently and independently, e.g. *ÆCHom* i. 276. 8 *. . . twa ðing syndon: an is Scyppend, oðer is gesceaft, ÆCHom* ii. 2. 12 *ane boc . . . ða oðre, ÆCHom* ii. 480. 20 *Se . . . sette his ænne sunu to ealdormen, and oðerne to cyninge, Or* 238. 9 *simle an legie æfter oþerre* (on this construction see Rissanen, pp. 103-4), *ÆCHom* ii. 170. 13 *twegen butrucas . . . þone oðerne . . . ænne, ÆCHom* i. 126. 11 *to ðisum . . . to oðrum, ÆCHom* ii. 356. 13 *ælc oðrum, Or* 90. 16 *oþ hiora ægþer þæt mæste folc ongean oþerne geteah,* and *ÆCHom* i. 318. 20 *and heora nan ne cuðe oðres spræce tocnawan.* On correlative *sum . . . oþer* see §394. On other correlative combinations involving *oþer* see §§1863-4.

§511. *Oþer* may be used in conjunction with other words, e.g. *ÆLet2* 84 *sume þa oðre, ÆCHom* i. 364. 18 *sum oðer witega, ÆCHom* i. 540. 12 *nane oðre, ÆCHom* i. 344. 8 *nane oðre englas, ÆCHom* i. 38. 20 *gehwilce oðre, ÆCHom* i. 54. 27 *gehwilce oðre lac, Or* 194. 20 *7 eft wearð oþer swelc ren, Bede* 276. 28 *monig oðer, ÆCHom* i. 126. 34 *manega oðre men* (but note the variant order in *Bede* 40. 31 *oðre monige* and *BlHom* 79. 31 *oþor manig*), *BlHom* 79. 10 *ænigu oþru, BlHom* 113. 10 *ænig oþor man, ÆCHom* ii. 358. 6 *ænne oðerne,* and *Or* 80. 29 *on an oþer fæstre land* (on this last combination, see Rissanen, pp. 284-5).

§512. In the pattern *oþer . . . (oþþe) . . . oþþe,* e.g. *Or* 44. 20 *7 him sædon þæt hie oðer dyden, oðþe ham comen, oðða hie him woldon oðerra wera ceosan* and

Mald 207   hi woldon þa ealle   oðer twega,
                  lif forlætan   oðða leofne gewrecan,

we have *oþer* 'one of two', as in *Or* 196. 11 *buton þara consula oþres sunu, Scipia wæs haten.* See further Wülfing, i, §359a.

§513. A special use of *oþer* after *swa/swilce* 'as, like' demands attention. Einenkel (*Ang.* 26 (1903), 526-7) cites two examples—*ÆCHom* ii. 194. 21 *and þæt wæter stod him on twa healfa swilce oðer stanweall* and *ÆCHom* ii. 488. 26 *hi ðærrihte ongunnon to ceowenne heora lichaman, swa þæt hi* [*ða drymen*] *ðotorodon swilce oðre wulfas*—and describes *oðer* as pleonastic. Tengstrand (*SN* 37 (1965), 382-92) adds four more: *LS* 34. 73 *swilce oðer wæterflod swa fleow heora blod, LS* 34. 75 *and man sette heora heafda swilce oþra ðeofa buton ðam portweallon on ðam heafodstoccum, ÆHex* 289 *Ða ylpas beoð swa mycele swylce oðre muntas*, and (an example supplied by J. Søderlind) Cotton MS Vit. D xvii, f. 48ᵛ, line 5 *se stan . . . ongan fleotan ofer þæm wætere swa oþer leaf.* Søderlind (private communication) has kindly supplied me with two further examples from the same manuscript and indeed from the same text—the Passion of Saint Pantaleon (Ker 222 art. 14)—f. 43, line 24 *7 þær rihte wearð þæt sweord forbegid swa oðer wex* and f. 48, line 12 *forðan men nu scærpað heora tungan wið me swa oðer sweord.* There is also *ÆHom* 20. 164 *we synd wið hi* [*entas*] *geðuhte swylce oðre gærstapan.*

§514. Two points should be noted about these examples: first, the items compared are either both singular or both plural (contrary to Pope's observation quoted in §515, they are almost evenly balanced—five singular, four plural), and second, MnE 'other' does not seem an appropriate translation for OE *oþer* because no other stone wall, wolves, or the like, are involved. Tengstrand (p. 383) draws our attention to the second point when he writes of *ÆCHom* ii. 194. 21 above:

Thorpe's 'another' makes no sense in the context. Einenkel translates: 'wie ein (zweiter) steinwall'. However, as no first stone wall has been mentioned or alluded to, it is difficult to see how it is possible to speak of a second one. Unless we prefer to leave *oðer* untranslated, the only idiomatic rendering of *swilce oðer stanweall* seems to be 'like any stone wall'.

But he overlooks the first when he translates the plural *swilce oðre wulfas* in *ÆCHom* ii. 488. 26 above 'like any wolf' and *swa mycele swylce oðre muntas* in *ÆHex* 289 'as big as any mountain'. This will hardly do in the light of examples like *Ps(P)* 44. 4 *scearpre þonne æni sweord* and *Or* 72. 25 *to Babylonia, þe þa welegre wæs þonne ænigu oþeru burg*, where *ænig* is used (as it is in ME and MnE) in just the way Tengstrand explains *oðer/oðre*. It is true that these examples involve *þonne* and that neither I nor Rissanen (private communication) have found any like ☆*scearp swilce/swa ænig sweord*, though both Mustanoja (p. 263) and Rissanen (pp. 302-3) quote ME examples. But this scarcely constitutes an argument in favour of

Tengstrand's translation. Skeat's rendering of *LS* 34. 75—'and set their heads, like those of others who were thieves, outside the town-walls upon head-stakes'—merely evades the problem.

§515. As always, Pope is illuminating. Without referring to Teng-strand, he writes (*Ælfric*, ii. 663):

The word *oðre*, 'other', has the force of such modern substitutes as 'so many', 'veritable'. The purpose of such expressions is to insist upon a likeness between obviously, even grotesquely dissimilar members of a comparison. Translate, 'we seem, in comparison with them, like so many grasshoppers'. The same idiom in the singular is a little less unfamiliar: cf. *CH* II. 194, 21 sq., *þæt wæter stod him on twa healfa swilce oðer stanweall*, 'the water stood on both sides of them like another (a veritable) stone wall'. At the corresponding place in the translation of *Numbers* Ælfric has, *ðam we ne synd ðe gelicran ðe lytle gærstapan* (Craw-ford, p. 317).

In view of examples like

ChristB 862   hwær we sælan sceolon   sundhengestas,
               ealde yðmearas,   ancrum fæste

and

Whale 13   ond þonne gehydað   heahstefn scipu
               to þam unlonde   oncyrrapum,
               setlaþ sæmearas   sundes æt ende,

where the identification of the things compared is so complete that it may appear absurd to modern readers, it is tempting to go further than Pope and to suggest that the idea is to insist upon identity rather than likeness; we could then translate literally 'like other wolves' or 'as big as other mountains' or 'like another stone wall'. But it is dangerous to press this in the light of the examples quoted by Tengstrand from other languages, such as OFr, MHG, and the Scandinavian, including 'a quite current Swedish idiom, which is, however, more exclusively contemptuous' (Søderlind, private com-munication). But, as Tengstrand (*passim*) points out and the examples show, the OE idiom can be pejorative or non-pejorative.

§516. Einenkel (*Ang.* 26 (1903), 527) suggests that Latin is a prob-able source of this usage. But the fact that the phenomenon is well evidenced in MHG and the Scandinavian languages, but less so in Greek and OFr, and the absence of firm parallels in Latin, leads Tengstrand (p. 392 and elsewhere) to view this notion with grave suspicion; indeed, at p. 391 he quotes Löfstedt's opinion that 'con-structions of this kind can arise at any time and in any language'. One last point of interest—all the OE examples so far noted have associations with Ælfric, being either in works by him (among which, Søderlind informs me, the Passion of St. Pantaleon is not to be numbered) or in manuscripts containing works agreed to be by him.

§517. The partitive genitive is found with singular forms of *oþer*, e.g. *CP* 239. 8 *Oðer is ðara gesuinca ðæt hi simle seceað endelease ladunga* and *ÆCHom* i. 576. 3 *þa twegen sceaðan . . . heora oðer*. But when *oþer* is plural, a form of partitive apposition seems to be the rule,[127] e.g. *CP* 407. 36 *oðrum minum sunum oððe dohtrum, ÆLet2* 84 *sume þa oðre*, and *ÆCHom* i. 220. 10 *Crist wearð æteowed on ðam ylcan dæge Petre, and oðrum twam his leorningcnihtum*. Another example is *oðer his bearn* in *Bede* 138. 32 *In þæm wæron Osfrið 7 Eatfrið Eadwines suna cyninges, þa begen him wæron cende . . . of Cwenburghe . . . Wæron eac gefulwade æfterfylgendre tiide oðer his bearn, of Æðelberge þære cwene acende, Æþelhun 7 Æðelfrið his dohtor 7 oðer his sunu, Wuscfrea wæs haten*, where the fact that *oðer his bearn* means 'other children of him' rather than 'his other children' (as Miller translates it) seems to be proved by the mention of another child Eanflæd in *Bede* 150. 5 *Hæfdon heo [se biscop Paulinus 7 seo cwen Æðelburg] swylce mid him Eanflæde Eadwines dohtor 7 Wuscfrean his sunu . . . , ða eft seo modor æfter þon onsende . . . in Gallia rice*. These last sentences also remove a possible ambiguity in *Bede(T)* 148. 7 . . . *Osfrið his sunu oðer ær him gefeoll . . . Oðer his sunu . . . to Pendan þæm cyninge gebeag* (where *Ca* has—wrongly, it seems likely—*his oðer sunu . . . Eadfrið se oðer*); the implication is 'one son of him . . . another son of him' and not, as *Ca* seems to suggest, 'his one son . . . Eadfrith the second [son]'. Here (as in *oðer his sunu Wuscfrea* above) the position of *oðer* seems vital; whether we have to do with a form of partitive apposition in the singular or a special use of dependent *oðer* is a terminological problem.

h. The indefinites + an: summary

§518. *An* is found with certain indefinites when they are used dependently or independently. The various combinations are listed below, with appropriate references. For a full treatment see Rissanen, pp. 238-60; I lean heavily on his discussion. It is his opinion (p. 244) that 'in the language reflected by the extant OE texts, the primary function of *an* was probably to make the pronoun more emphatic'.

---

[127] The same variation is found with *ænig* (§381), *nænig* (§§437-8), and (with some modification) *sum* (§§409-16).

§519. The following combinations have been recorded:

(1) *ænig an*: e.g. *ChristB* 683 *ængum anum* (Rissanen, pp. 258-9);

(2) *sum an*: e.g. *GD* 339. 23 *mid sumre anre leasunge* (Rissanen, p. 259);

(3) *anra hwa*: Rissanen (p. 240) notes one example—*Met* 16. 16;

(4) *anes hwæt*: Rissanen (pp. 244-5) notes five examples, including *CP* 346. 6 and *Beo* 3010;

(5) *an hwelc* and *anra hwelc*: Rissanen (p. 239) notes eight examples. See §422;

(6) *hwilchwugu an*: Rissanen (p. 239) notes one example—*GD(C)* 41. 17;

(7) *nan . . . an*: e.g. *ÆCHom* i. 284. 1 *ne nan heora an* (Rissanen, p. 259);

(8) *ælc an* and *ælc anra*: Rissanen (p. 246) notes 'half a dozen' examples. See §459;

(9) *æghwilc an* and *æghwilc anra*: Rissanen (p. 246) notes 'a dozen OE instances'. See §464;

(10) *anra gehwa*: Rissanen (pp. 239-40) found nine examples in the poetry. See §466;

(11) *an gehwilc* and *anra gehwilc*: Rissanen (pp. 239 ff.) found over one hundred OE examples. See §469;

(12) *swelc . . . an*: Rissanen (p. 251) notes one example—*Lch* ii. 42. 20 *swilc þara an*.

9. THE RELATIVES

a. List and references forward

§520. The following words serve as relatives:

se, þe, and combinations of the two;

þe + personal pronoun;

swelc;

loc(a) hwa, loc(a) hwæt, loc(a) hwæþer, loc(a) hwelc;

swa hwa swa, swa hwæt swa, swa hwæþer swa, swa hwelc swa.

For references see the Index of Words and Phrases. On the alleged use of *swa* as a relative, see §§2379-82; on the ambiguous demonstrative relative, see §§2109-21.

§521. Unambiguous examples of *hwa, hwæt*, and *hwelc*, used alone as relatives, do not occur; see §2385.

F. NUMERALS

1. CLASSIFICATION AND INFLEXION

§522. The traditional classification set out on the Contents pages has been followed. Details of the inflexions will be found in *OEG*, §§682-700. It should be noted that some of the cardinal numerals may have inflexions or may be indeclinable; examples are given below. Heltveit (1977, pp. 54-9) gives references to examples of numerals used in partitive apposition, with the partitive genitive, and with *of* + the dative. See further §550.

2. *AN*

a. *Introductory remarks*

§523. The authority on this subject is M. Rissanen, *The Uses of 'One' in Old and Early Middle English* (Helsinki, 1967). Alston, reviewing this book in *MÆ* 37 (1968), 245-6, begins thus: 'The temptation, in considering works of this sort, is often to be unkind: to deplore the expenditure of such energy and effort on a problem so apparently trivial as the use of the cardinal numeral *one*.' It is a temptation better resisted. First, it would be no great task to find a hundred recent articles on OE literature more deserving of the epithet 'trivial'. Second, if all morphological, syntactic, and semantic, problems in OE had been investigated with the same care and with the same concern for literary considerations, OE studies would be in a better position today. Rissanen gives a summary of his findings (pp. 309-17) and a bibliography. Items which he lists are not repeated here unless specific reference is made to their contents. Collections of examples will be found in the works by Fricke (pp. 9-12) and Wülfing (i. 298-302). Other topics discussed by Rissanen include compounds and derivatives of *an* (pp. 304-8), emphasis by position (pp. 7, 208-12, and 312), the strengthening of *an* by *anlipig* and *furþum* (pp. 18-19 and 41), the possibility of Latin influence (pp. 13 and 316), and some special uses in the poetry (pp. 12, 151, and 312).

b. *The main senses of* an

§524. Süsskand (pp. 9-18) is content to distinguish three uses of *an* in the poetry: (1) the stressed numeral, e.g. *Beo* 705 *ealle buton anum*; (2) the emphatic pronoun, e.g. *Beo* 2210 *oð ðæt an ongan* ‖ *deorcum nihtum draca ricsian*; and (3) *an* immediately before a noun in a usage close to the 'indefinite article' (see §§220-35), e.g. *Beo* 2774 *anne mannan.* Rissanen distinguishes ten 'functions or shades of meaning' (p. 4) of *an,* but is careful to point out the dangers of rigidity in classification (pp. 14 and 39). These 'functions or shades of meaning' are briefly summarized and exemplified in the sections which follow; since I adhere to Rissanen's order, page references to his work are not given.

§525. (1) The strictly numerical sense is found indicating 'the abstract concept of unity', e.g. *ÆGram* 83. 5 *anfeald getel ys on anum,* and (with varying degrees of contrast) 'one in contrast to a higher number', e.g. *Coll* 25. 71 *twegen heortas 7 ænne bar.* It can refer to a particular person, e.g. *ÆCHom* i. 258. 25 *God Fæder Ælmihtig hæfð ænne Sunu gecyndelice and menige gewiscendlice,* or to a representative of a species or class, e.g. *ÆGram* 7. 7 *hwilon byð þæt stæfgefeg on anum stæfe, hwilon on twam.*

§526. (2) In the sense 'a single, (not) even one', *an* occurs mainly but not exclusively in negative expressions. It may indicate total absence of something, e.g. *ÆLS* 17. 262 . . . *ne beo furðon an frig man,* or its insignificance, e.g. *Matt(WSCp)* 10. 42 *And swa hwylc swa sylþ anne drinc cealdes wæteres anum þyssa lytylra manna.* . . .

§527. (3) The individualizing use either distinguishes a particular individual in a group, e.g. *GD* 42. 25 *þa munecas . . . an þara muneca,* or refers to anyone in a group, e.g. *ÆCHom* i. 274. 10 *gif bið an ure geferena on sumre earfoðnysse.* Christophersen (pp. 101-2) offers some comments on this use, including: 'Several writings, such as the Blickling Homilies and the West Saxon Gospels, show a less frequent use of *an,* either from a conscious or unconscious archaicness of style or under the influence of the foreign original (see Süsskand pp. 43-4, 48-9).' I have, however, observed little difference between the language of Alfred and Ælfric in this respect. But the point requires further investigation. (The 'pronominal' uses discussed by Rissanen in this section of his book probably go back to this individualizing use but seem to develop in eME.)

§528. (4) *An* can also denote identity or union. The most important subdivisions for OE are perhaps continuity, e.g. *ÆCHom* i. 456. 25 *Æfre he bið anes modes,* identity, e.g. *Or* 256. 26 . . . *he oft wyscte þæt ealle Romane hæfden ænne sweoran, þæt he hiene raþost forceorfan mehte,* or union, e.g. *ÆCHom* i. 244. 1 *and hi gehyrað mine stemne, and sceal beon an eowd, and an hyrde.*

§529. (5) In the exclusive use *an* may denote isolation, e.g. *ÆCHom* i. 224. 29 *Crist forðferde ana on ðam timan, ac he ne aras na ana of deaðe, ac aras mid micclum werede*, separateness, e.g. *ÆCHom* i. 302. 25 *ealle eorðlice þing sind gesceapene for ðam men anum*, or singleness, uniqueness, e.g. *Bo* 89. 10 *þ is seo an friðstow 7 sio an frofer*. The form *ana* is common in post-position; see §537.

§530. (6) In the intensifying function *an* 'is used mainly to empha-size, to intensify, the quality expressed by the governing word or phrase'. There are not many examples of this type in OE. Those cited by Rissanen include (with a superlative) *Exod(L)* 32. 21 *þis folc . . . hæfð geworht ane þa mæstan synne* (but the earlier MS *B* does not have *ane*) and *GD* 277. 18 *seo an hefigeste mettrumnes*, and (without a superlative) *Beo* 1885 *þæt wæs an cyning* and *GD* 313. 15 *se an broðor*.

§531. Rissanen's next four divisions do not need illustration here. They are:

(7) adverbial uses (see *OEG,* §§668 and 700);

(8) *an* before cardinal numerals or before 'few' (see §545);

(9) *an* with indefinite and interrogative pronouns (see Rissanen, pp. 238-60; Kahlas, *Stockholm Studies in English*, 52 (1980), 128-9 and 131-2; and my §§518-19);

(10) *an* as the indefinite article (see §§220-35).

Two of these—(8) and (9)—seem to rest on syntactic rather than semantic distinctions; in both, *an* has varying senses among those already mentioned. Simon offers further criticism of Rissanen's classification in *Éa* 22 (1969), 302-3.

c. The syntactic uses of an related to its various meanings

§532. Alston (*MÆ* 37 (1968), 246) comments: 'It would also have been useful if the author could have indicated more clearly the gram-matical functions of *one* as the basis for semantic analysis.' This task is attempted here, though its value as 'the basis for semantic analysis' is questionable. No simple table of correspondences can be produced; see Rissanen, p. 309.

§533. The first distinction to be made is a syntactic one noted by Rissanen (p. 6)—*an* can be adjectival or 'dependent', e.g. *Coll* 25. 71 *ænne bar*, or substantival or 'independent', e.g. *ÆGram* 83. 5 *anfeald getel ys on anum*. We may also note that *an* is sometimes present, sometimes absent, in what seem to be identical contexts; for examples, see Rissanen, pp. 23, 26, 28-9, and 30, and my §221.

§534. Some syntactic patterns seem to be more or less completely identified with one of the meanings of *an* distinguished by Rissanen. Used with superlatives, *an* is mostly intensifying (Rissanen, pp. 189-200 and 45-6). The combinations *an* + possessive/genitive of noun + noun and *an* + noun + genitive of noun are individualizing (Rissanen, pp. 82-4). Forms such as *æne, ane*, and *anes*, are adverbs, 'once', though this can also be expressed by *an* + noun or *an* + a partitive genitive (Rissanen, pp. 217-27). Used as the 'indefinite article', *an* by definition has one basic pattern—*an* + noun—to which an adjective can be added (Rissanen, pp. 261-303). For a few minor qualifications, see §§226-8. But this pattern is not restricted to this sense; see below.

§535. Indeed, such identification is the exception rather than the rule. Most senses of *an* are found in more than one syntactic pattern, and in most syntactic patterns *an* can have more than one sense. (I give in brackets the references to Rissanen's discussions.) Thus *an* in *an* [+ adjective] + noun can be strictly numerical (pp. 16 ff.); can mean 'each' or 'a single' (pp. 34-8 and 41 ff.); can be individualizing (pp. 78-9), identifying (pp. 106 ff.), or intensifying (pp. 200 ff.); can indicate totality (pp. 212-16); or can be used adverbially (pp. 217 ff.) or as the 'indefinite article' (pp. 261-303). On *an* with a noun of time or measure, see Rissanen, pp. 22 ff., 29-30, 49-50, 84-8, and 228-37. With demonstrative + *an* [+ noun] *an* is numerical (pp. 14-15), individualizing (pp. 80 and 91 ff.), exclusive (pp. 152-3), or intensifying (pp. 201 ff.). *An* in the combination possessive/genitive of noun + *an* [+ noun] may be strictly numerical (pp. 15-16), individualizing (pp. 80 ff.), exclusive (pp. 135 and 157-8), or may mean 'a single' (p. 40). See also the first and second paragraphs on Rissanen, p. 313. Appositive *an* can mean 'a single' (pp. 40-1); can identify (pp. 107 ff.), exclude (pp. 140-1 and 313-14), or intensify (pp. 202 ff.); and can express totality (p. 213); with indefinite or interrogative pronouns it is primarily emphasizing (p. 244). With a partitive genitive *an* can mean 'a single' (p. 42), or can be individualizing (pp. 54 ff.) or adverbial (p. 217). Independent *an* can be strictly numerical (p. 14), individualizing (pp. 54-61), or adverbial (pp. 217-26 and 314); it can express identity (pp. 106 ff.) or union (pp. 118-33); when used in the genitive plural with pronouns, it is primarily emphasizing (p. 244).

d. Strong and weak forms of an

§536. *An* is usually declined strong, even when preceded by a demonstrative, e.g. *Bo* 89. 10 *seo an friðstow and sio an frofer* and *ÆHom* 18. 33 *And twa grindað þonne on anre cwyrne ætgædere; seo an bið genumen, and seo oðer bið forlæten.* Here it follows *blind* (*OEG,* §639). It is naturally more common in the singular, but can be used in the plural; see §§545-7.

§537. Whether *an* is declined weak is a matter of dispute. The form *ana*—common in post-position in the sense 'alone'—is often described as the nominative singular masculine of the weak declension; see *OEG,* §683. The form *ane,* which appears spasmodically in the same function as *ana* and could be called nominative singular feminine weak, is more likely to be a weakened form of *ana.* I discuss these below. The form *anan* also occurs. But, as *ÆGram* 115. 1 *solus, sola, solum, ana and heora ealra, solius, anes; soli, anum* suggests, it is rather a weakening of *anum* than a true weak form; consider *LS* 34. 594 *syllice is me anan gelumpen* (Skeat indeed substitutes *anum*) and compare *WHom* 5. 93 *to þam anan* with *WHom* 9. 142 *to ðam anum.* (Similar examples will be found in *LS* 34. 525, *LS* 34. 598, and *Ch* 1275, dat. sg. *anan man.*) This explanation can even hold for *Bo* 32. 18 *þy anan*; see Rissanen, p. 138. On *ÆCHom* ii. 598. 10 *Ic andette ða anan halgan and ða geleaffullan and ða apostolican gelaðunge,* see §544. Rissanen (pp. 7-9 and 138-42) gives further details on these points.

§538. If for the time being we accept the notion that *an* can be declined weak when used in post-position meaning 'alone', we find that the nom. sg. masc. *ana* is usual when one would expect other cases of the masculine singular, e.g. *ÆCHom* ii. 350. 20 *min latteow me þær ana forlet* and *ÆCHom* ii. 340. 20 *Ne lufode he woruldlice æhta for his neode ana, ac to dælenne eallum wædliendum,* and even when one would expect a feminine singular, a neuter singular, or a plural, form, e.g. *ÆCHom* ii. 62. 26 *and seo menniscnys ana deað and sar for us ðrowade,* *ÆLS* 1. 148 *ðuruh þæt gescead ana,* and *ÆCHom* i. 66. 13 *synna ana* (acc. pl. fem.), *LS* 34. 376 *ða sawla ana* (nom. pl. fem.), and *ÆCHom* ii. 130. 2 *ða þing ana* (acc. pl. neut.). As my examples suggest, this is more common in the later prose. Of the early examples, we must dismiss *Bede* 28. 3 *On fruman ærest wæron þysses ealondes bigengan Bryttas ane* (cited by Rissanen, p. 139, but hardly an example, since *ane* (not *ana*) may be plural; see §§545-7. *GD* 211. 15 *seo nædre ongan slincan in þæt scræf 7 com þider ana, 7 þær heo hi astrehte beforan þam halgan were, þe hine þær gebæd ana* seems more certain, but the first *ana* may be an anticipation of the second. In *GD(H)* 53. 32 *ac hit wæs openlice geswutelod, þæt his forðfore begeat seo þingung ana þæs arwurðan weres Anastasies, ana* is the reviser's; MS *C* lacks *ana* and MS *O* reads *an*.

§539. Rissanen has kindly supplemented the remarks made in his book (p. 134) by a private communication in which he gives more examples of *ana* as nom. sg. fem. 'alone'; details will be found in Mitchell 1972, p. 223 fn. 6. To these may be added instances from the poetry such as *ChristA* 287 *þu . . . ana* (of the Virgin Mary) and *Soul ii* 52 *ic ana* (where *seo sawl* is speaking). In the same communication, he adds four examples of *ane* as nom. sg. fem. 'alone' to *LS* 7. 107, where St. Euphrosyne says *ealle þas niht witodlice ic ane wunode* (Rissanen, p. 134). He admits himself that three of these are suspect. In the first, *GD(C)* 96. 20 *his fostormoder ane wæs him fylgende*, MSS *H* and *O* both have *ana*. The second and third are both remarks addressed by the devil to St. Margaret—*LS* 14. 235 *þu ane* and *LS* 14. 249 *þu ane*. That Rissanen is right in suggesting that these 'perhaps show the EME levelling of the ending' is strongly supported by the devil's own remark *LS* 14. 247 *eal þis ic me ane wat* (which he does not quote). Rissanen's last example must strengthen our doubts. It too comes from the *Life of St. Euphrosyne*, but is addressed to a man: *LS* 7. 149 *Se abbod him to cwæð. þu eart geong . ne miht þu ane wunian*. In the absence of firm examples, I must withdraw my statement (*NM* 73 (1972), 223-4) that *ane* is an 'established' usage for the nominative singular feminine of 'alone'.

§540. We are left then with a so-called weak declension consisting of a nominative singular masculine which occurs only in post-position in the sense 'alone' but can be used with nouns or pronouns of any gender, number, or case. Is the category justified? Schrader (pp. 33-4) adds further examples of *ana* referring to something other than a nominative singular masculine and sees it as a fossilized form— 'eine erstarrte Form'. But, as d'Ardenne (p. 76) points out, it may be adverbial; she derives ME '*ane, adv*, alone, only' from 'OE *ana* usually said to be a weak adj. but apparently indeclinable and an adv. cognate with OHG. *eino*, ON. *eina*'. Pope (*Ælfric*, ii, Glossary, s.v. *ana*) has 'orig. nsm. wk. of *an*?' and speaks of the adverbial character of *ana* in the three functions he detects. An especially telling point is his observation (s.v. *an*) that strong plural forms meaning 'alone' occur in post-position as alternatives to *ana*; cf. *ÆHom* 6. 320 *þa ane* and *ÆHom* 20. 200 *hi ane twegen* with *ÆHom* 3. 59 *hi ana* and *ÆHom* 11. 353 *ða godan ana*, and see §541. (Erickson's incomplete statements and sweeping comments (*Arch.L.* 4 (1973), 75-7) are made in apparent ignorance of Rissanen's work.)

§541. Whatever we call *ana*, we must agree that it regularly means 'alone', e.g. *ÆCHom* i. 224. 29 *Crist forðferde ana on ðam timan* 'Christ departed alone at that time'. But strong forms too are common in this sense 'alone', both in the nominative singular, e.g. *Verc Hom* 7. 14 *he an aræfnede betweoh arleasum*, and in oblique cases, e.g. *BlHom* 237. 22 *he geseah þone eadigan Mattheus ænne sitton singende*, *ÆCHom* ii. 304. 30 *for his anes deaðe*, *ÆCHom* i. 588. 13 *oðþæt hi gewitað of heora lichaman . . . , naht mid him ferigende buton synna anum* (cf. *ÆCHom* i. 66. 12 *þonne færlice gewitt he of ðissere worulde, . . . synna ana mid him ferigende*), and *ÆCHom* i. 24. 35 *hit* [*Crist*] *weox swa swa oðre cild doð, buton synne anum.* Schrader (pp. 32-3) rightly notes the use of *anum* with accusative plural feminine in *ÆCHom* i. 588. 13 and accusative singular feminine in *ÆCHom* i. 24. 35, and, rightly objecting to Thorpe's translation 'without any sin' for *ÆCHom* i. 24. 35, translates 'only without sin'. But he does not specifically state that Thorpe's 'but sins alone' is right for *ÆCHom* i. 588. 13 and so fails to draw our attention to the almost adverbial, but different, uses of *anum* in these two sentences. Further on the expression of 'alone' in OE, see Wülfing, i, §§164-5, and Rissanen, pp. 134-41.

§542. As Rissanen observes, 'OE exclusive *an* denoting isolation or separateness is generally placed in apposition to the governing noun or pronoun' (p. 146; for examples, see Rissanen, pp. 146-50; see also Rissanen, pp. 168-73 and 184-8). But it can have other senses and other functions. Used dependently before a noun, it occasionally denotes singleness ('the only man'), e.g. *ÆCHom* i. 500. 24 *ðurh his ænne ancennedan Sunu . . . his anum Bearne*, and—a little more frequently—separateness, e.g. *ÆCHom* ii. 8. 26 *Seo ðridde gesceapennys . . . þeos an gesceapennys*. The strong form is usual. Rissanen (pp. 154 and 156) notes that when the 'weak' form *ana* is used attributively in the singular, it always refers to *God* or its synonyms when it denotes singleness, e.g. *ÆCHom* i. 466. 7 *ðu eart ana God* 'the only God', or separateness, e.g. *ÆHex* 382 *Ælc ðing hæfð anginn and ordfruman ðurh God, buton se ana Scyppend ðe ealle ðing gesceop* 'except the Creator alone'. For further examples and discussion, see Rissanen, pp. 152-9.

§543. An important negative point made by Rissanen (pp. 152-3 and 317) is that there are no examples of attributive *an* denoting isolation—the type '(the) one man', 'the solitary man'—or of the independent pronominal use of exclusive *an*—the type '(the lonely) one'. Rissanen accordingly rejects the notion that the Ruthwell Cross reading of *Dream* 58—*æþþilæ til anum*—can mean 'noble ones to the lonely one', preferring the attested 'noble ones together'; see *NM* 68 (1967), 283-7, and my discussion in *ASE* 4 (1975), 24-5.

§544. Rissanen seems to hint at pp. 8 and 314 that there are examples in which the 'weak' form is used in other than the exclusive function. The only example I have found in his book is *ChronE* 119. 8 (972) *he wæs þa ana wana xxx wintra*. Three things combine to make this dubious: first, all similar examples have *anes* (Rissanen, pp. 32-3); second, MS *D* has *ane* (all others have a variant version of MnE 'twenty-nine'); third, the sequence *þa . . . wana . . . wintra* could be a source of scribal error. He has, however, privately drawn my attention to *ÆCHom* ii. 598. 10 *Ic andette ða anan halgan and ða geleaffullan and ða apostolican gelaðunge* (where, as he suggests, the possibility of attraction arises) and *ÆGram* 91. 4 *o une, eala ðu ana* (where the vocative use is sufficient to account for the 'weak' form; see §1247). These examples scarcely upset the proposition that the 'weak' form of *an* is restricted to the exclusive use. Indeed, in the remaining senses, strong forms, not 'weak', are the rule even when *an* is preceded by a demonstrative or a possessive, e.g. *Solil* 63. 21 *be þisse anre bysena* and *GD(H)* 16. 1 *his an hors*, where MS *C* has *his agen hors*. Like *ÆCHom* ii. 598. 10 above, *ÆLS* 1. 32 *se ana ælmihtiga god* can be explained by attraction; see Schrader, p. 32.

e. Plural uses of an

§545. *An* is sometimes used in a strong plural form before a cardinal numeral or before *feawa*, e.g. *ÆGram* 158. 9 *ane twa word*, *ÆLS* 32. 244 *ane seofon menn ætgædere*, and *ÆCHom* ii. 158. 33 . . . *he gesette twelf munecas, and ane feawa he geheold mid him sylfum*. Some scholars have argued that when so used *an* always imparts a notion of approximation or indefiniteness. Good reasons for rejecting this in favour of Campbell's view that '*an* may be used in pl. before collective expressions, e.g. *ane nigon naman* "a batch of nine names" ' (*OEG*, §683) are given by Rissanen (pp. 228-37). He does quote (p. 230) two examples in which a strong plural form of *an* appears before a cardinal numeral in 'a phrase containing an implication of approximity', viz. *BenR* 97. 9 *embe ane feower dagas oþþe fife*, Latin *post quattuor aut quinque dies*, where *embe* renders *post* (§1219), and *GD(C)* 79. 11 *for anum xii nihtum huhugu swa*, where the Latin reads *ante dies fere duodecim* and *GD(H)* has *nealice for twelf dagum*. Campbell's statement is also applicable to these, for in both of them the idea of approximity is expressed by other means, not by *ane/anum*. On the use of singular *an* with a plural and a collective, see Rissanen, pp. 107 and 229.

§546. *An* may also be used in the plural to denote identity, e.g. *BenR* 139. 16 *Ane þeawas, an lif and ane gesceadwisne hi healdaþ muneca mynstra on eallum þingum* (Rissanen, p. 106), and exclusiveness, e.g. *GD(H)* 44. 5 *forþam þe se ylca wer eallunga forseah þas eorðlican þing 7 þa heofonlican ane lufode* (Rissanen, pp. 146 fn. 1, and 315) and, preceded by a definite article and followed by an adjective clause, *BlHom* 75. 35 *þa ane men habbaþ Crist on heora heortan þe geteode beoþ to þon ecean life* (Rissanen, pp. 155-9). On *ana* alone with plurals, see §538, and on genitive plural forms of *an* with indefinites, §§518-19. It is an interesting question whether *anum* in

Met 17. 3   hi of anum twæm   ealle comon,
               were and wife   on woruld innan

is singular or plural; see Rissanen, p. 111.

§547. Further on the use of 'one' and the indefinite article with plural nouns in English, see Rissanen, *NM* 73 (1972), 340-52.

3. OTHER CARDINAL NUMBERS

§548. The cardinal numbers may be used independently as nouns or dependently as adjectives (the terminology is that used by Mustanoja).[128] When used alone, they are of course independent, e.g. *ÆGram* 283. 9 *fram tyn to tynum*; see further §550. When a noun precedes or follows, the distinction depends on its form in relation to that of the numeral. Thus we have the independent use with the partitive genitive in *Or* 190. 9 *þara consula twegen* and *ÆCHom* i. 236. 24 *embe þreo and ðritig geara* and the dependent use in *Bede* 22. 30 *his geferan twegen* 'his two companions', *Bede* 414. 3 *halige*

---

[128] Examples of the constructions discussed here will be found in the following works: Bock 1887, pp. 39-43; Flamme, pp. 14-16; Fricke, pp. 12-38 and 56-8; Mohrbutter, pp. 19-20; Schrader, pp. 35-8; Wülfing, i. 302-23; Palm, pp. 139 ff. (his examples should not be accepted without checking); and Heltveit 1977, pp. 57-9.

weoras 7 geornfulle tuelfe, and *ÆCHom* i. 92. 12 *mid fif stafum*.
When both numeral and noun are in the genitive plural this test of
course fails, whether the numeral is declined or not, e.g. *ÆGram*
288. 1 *triduum þreora daga fæc, quatriduum feower daga fæc*. Both
uses may occur in the same sentence, e.g. *ÆCHom* i. 184. 28 *he þa
gefylde fif ðusend manna mid fif hlafum*. This last sentence conveniently illustrates the fact that when used with a noun the cardinal
numbers up to nineteen are more often used dependently; thereafter
the situation is reversed and the preference is for the independent use
with the partitive genitive.

§549. These remarks apply to the prose and poetry, although—as
might be expected (see §§3944–6)—the poetry shows more freedom in the position of the partitive genitive, and post-position (as in
El 879 *þara roda twa*) is more common; see Shipley, p. 97 and
pp. 99–103.

§550. Cardinal numbers may be used independently in different
ways, e.g.
    (1) alone, either declined or undeclined, e.g. *ÆCHom* ii. 246. 28
to six ðusendum . . . twa and hundseofontig ðusend, ÆGram 283. 9
fram tyn to tynum, and *ÆCHom* i. 402. 34 *fela ðusenda* (cf. *ÆCHom*
ii. 246. 29 *swa fela ðusend engla*);
    (2) with an adjective, e.g. *Or* 110. 33 *heora monig ðusend*;
    (3) with a demonstrative, e.g. *ÆCHom* i. 82. 12 *se an*;
    (4) with *an*, e.g. *ÆLS* 5. 221 *of anum þusende anne*;
    (5) with *sum*, e.g. *Bo* 115. 18 *þa hæfde he sume hundred scipa; þa
wæron hi sume ten gear on þam gewinne*. On these usages see further
§§389–92;
    (6) with *oþer*, e.g. *ÆCHom* ii. 338. 20 *ða oðre twegen*;
    (7) in apposition with a noun, e.g. *ÆLS* 4. 65 *twegen his halgan*
'two (of) his saints' (see §§409–16), or with a pronoun, e.g. *ÆCHom*
i. 326. 19 *heora begra*;
    (8) with a partitive genitive. In the early texts, the genitive is
found both before and after the numeral, e.g. *Or* 110. 33 *heora
monig ðusend, Or* 190. 9 *þara consula twegen*, and *Or* 188. 16 *þæs
opres folces XXV M*, but *Or* 50. 10 *M scipa, Bo* 115. 18 *sume hundred scipa*, and *Or* 182. 11 *X hiera ieldstena wietena*. But the order
numeral + genitive seems more common in these texts. My impression is that it became the rule as time went by, perhaps through the
analogy of the dependent and appositive uses of the numeral, where
examples like *Bede* 22. 30 *his geferan twegen* are the exception. So
we find *ÆCHom* ii. 246. 29 *swa fela ðusend engla, ÆCHom* i. 348. 2

þusend ðusenda, and *ÆCHom* i. 422. 23 *nigontyne wera and wifa his hiwisces*. I have not noted any exceptions in Ælfric, but my collections both for him and for other writers are far from complete. However, the development I outline is what we should expect;

(9) with the prep. *of*, e.g. *ChronF* 130. 21 (995) *hi naman twegen of heom* and *ÆLS* 5. 221 *of anum þusende anne*. On the relation between (8) and (9), see §415.

§551. The dependent use of the cardinal numbers calls for some comment. Apart from *an* (see §§536–41), they have no weak forms; the same forms occur with and without a demonstrative, e.g. *Or* 128. 25 *binnan þæm þrim gearum* and *Bede* 52. 2 *of þrim folcum*. *Twegen, begen*, and *þrie*, are regularly declined in agreement with the noun, e.g. *ÆCHom* i. 376. 30 *on his twam slyfum*, *ÆGram* 36. 5 *bam ðam wifum*, and *ÆCHom* ii. 334. 9 *ða ðry englas*. As Schrader (p. 35) points out, Ælfric describes *butu* as the feminine and neuter equivalent of *begen* (*ÆGram* 35. 13, 36. 3, and 36. 7). So *ÆCHom* ii. 484. 9 *ða apostoli begen* and *ÆCHom* ii. 438. 17 *hi . . . butu* (for Martha and Mary) are to be expected. The use of *hie butu* for Adam and Eve in *ÆCHom* i. 18. 10 is to be explained as a generalization of *butu* (see *OEG*, §683) rather than the result of an alleged tendency to use feminine or neuter forms when male and female are referred to. Cf. §38. For examples from the poetry, see Bauch, p. 25.

§552. In *OEG*, §683, Campbell writes: 'When not immediately before the qualified noun the numerals 4–12 may be declined, e.g. *niceras nigene, syxa sum, mid nigonum ðara niwena scipa*.' It is true that these numerals are regularly uninflected when they immediately precede a noun, e.g. *ÆCHom* i. 202. 2 *syx monðum*, *CP* 77. 16 *ða naman ðara twelf heahfædera*, and *ÆGram* 12. 5 *aries ys an ðara twelf tacna*. But declined forms do occur in this position in contexts which suggest that analogy is at work, e.g. *ÆCHom* i. 586. 8 *ða getacnunge ðæra feowera apostola namena* and *ÆCHom* i. 26. 23 *an ðæra twelfa Cristes geferena*.[129] *Bede* 262. 14 *mid feawum broðrum, þæt is seofonum oðþo eahtum* presumably exemplifies Campbell's statement. The contrast between *GD(C)* 96. 3 *æt feowrum his gingrum* and *GD(H)* 96. 3 *æt his feower gingrum* certainly does.

§553. When used dependently, the numerals in *-tiene* are usually uninflected, e.g. *Bede* 422. 4 *æfter feowertene dagum*, but inflected

---

[129] These exceptions are in addition to those in Mercian and Northumbrian mentioned by Campbell (*OEG*, §683). Fricke, p. 57, quotes '*butan fifum mannum* Sx. Chr. 897'. None of MSS *A, B, C*, or *D*, has *mannum*; see *ChronA* 90. 29 (897) and the apparatus. *ChronE* lacks this annal.

forms do occur, e.g. *HomU* 35. 217. 3 *syxtinan fædman hegre*. Those
in *-tig* can be declined, e.g. *ÆCHom* i. 66. 16 *þritigum nihtum ær*
and *HomU* 35. 216. 21 *hundteontigum wintrum*, but cf. *ÆCHom* i.
402. 12 *feowertig geara fyrst* and see further *OEG*, §686. *Hund* and
þusend can be used as uninflected adjectives, e.g. *ÆCHom* i. 456. 21
hund siðon and *WHom* 5. 43 *æfter þusend gearum*, but the independent uses illustrated in §550 are the norm.

§554. Roman numerals are sometimes used for the cardinals, e.g. in
the *Chronicle* and in *Orosius*. That they were capable of causing the
same difficulty for Anglo-Saxon scribes as they do for modern bibliographers is clear from the fate of what was presumably XXIX in the
Chronicle annal for 755 and became XXXI (MSS *A*, *B*, *C*), XXI (MS
D), and XVI (MS *E*). The roman numeral usually appears without
inflexion, e.g. *Or* 172. 9 *mid XXX scipun . . . his XXX scipa genom.*
But the dat. pl. ending *-gum*, *-tigum* is sometimes added where appropriate, e.g. *Or* 240. 23 *mid XXXgum cyningum* and *Or* 164. 10
LXXIItigum wintra, and once at least, as Bock (1887, p. 41) points
out, where it is not—*Or* 176. 34 *mid XXX M gehorsedra, 7 mid XXX
elpenda 7 Cgum*. The Anglo-Saxon and the Roman form may be
used in combination, e.g. *ÆCHom* i. 24. 10 *feower hund geara and
XXXIII*. Roman numerals are also used in the poetic codices; see
Shipley, pp. 99–103, for examples. On the use of subtraction and
multiplication to express cardinal numerals, see §§573 and 572–7.

4. THE ORDER OF THE COMPOUND NUMERALS

a. With two components

§555. In the prose, the units precede the tens, to which they are
joined by *and*, e.g. *Or* 28. 13 *twa 7 twentig mila*, and usually remain
undeclined, e.g. *Or* 256. 1 *þara twa 7 twentigra monna*. A preposition may be repeated with the second element, e.g. *Or* 14. 22 *on twa
7 on þritig þeoda*. Occasional exceptions occur in the glosses under
Latin influence, e.g. *MattPref* 8. 2 *tuoentig feuer aldra*, Latin *uiginti
quattuor seniorum* and *John(Li)* 2. 20 *feortig 7 sex*, Latin *quadra-
ginta et sex*. Rissanen (p. 31) notes *ByrM* 60. 27 *Nim þæt þrittig
getæl 7 þæt an* and *ByrM* 90. 3 *Se monð þe hæfð þrittig daga 7 anne
dæg . . .* , and remarks that here 'the splitting of the numeral is perhaps caused by the wish to emphasize the difference between the
months having thirty days and those having thirty-one'.

§556. The hundreds usually precede both units and tens in the
prose, e.g. *Or* 68. 4 *II hunde wintrum 7 IIII* and *Or* 108. 32 *III hund*

7 hundeahtatig. A noun may accompany either element or be re-peated, e.g. *Or* 40. 11 *syx hund wintran 7 fif, Or* 86. 21 *III hund 7 siex men, Or* 36. 22 *eahta hund wintra 7 fif wintrum,* and (with a different noun) *Or* 36. 3 *eahta hund wintra 7 tyn gearan.* But there are occasional exceptions like *Bede* 94. 1 *fif winter 7 syx hund wintra, Or* 182. 19 *æfter L wintra 7 feower hundum, Or* 176. 13 *IIII 7 an hund,* and *Or* 172. 5 *XXX 7 C.*

§557. The thousands usually precede the hundreds, e.g. *ChronE* 7. 1 (11) *v þusend wintra 7 cc wintra,* but not always, e.g. *Or* 28. 25 *þrim hund wintra 7 þusend wintra.* For further examples of regular and exceptional uses in the prose, see Bock 1887, pp. 42–3, and Wülfing, i. 316–23.

§558. The usual order in the poetry is units + tens, e.g. *GenA* 1169 *fif and sixtig,* units + hundreds, e.g. *GenA* 1131 *fif and hundteontig,* and tens + hundreds, e.g. *GenA* 1120 *XXX and C.* This order may obtain when other matter intervenes, e.g. *GenA* 1139 *seofon winter her | . . . || and eahtahund.* But the larger number then often precedes, e.g. *Jul* 678 *þær XXX wæs || ond feowere eac, Men* 187 *ymb twen-tig þæs . . . || and seofon nihtum, GenA* 1740 *wintra hæfde || twa hundteontig | . . . || and fife eac* (Shipley (p. 97) notes that *wintra hæfde* 'generally stands at the beginning of the sentence'), and *GenA* 1600 *ðreohund wintra | . . . || . . . | and fiftig eac.* In these circum-stances the detached part carries stress and alliteration.

b. With three components

§559. In the prose the hundreds again precede the units and tens, e.g. *Or* 26. 31 *an hund mila brad 7 twa 7 twentig* and (with the tens unusually before the units) *Bede* 32. 1 *hundteontig 7 fiftig 7 six gear.* According to Wülfing (i. 321–3), the thousands occupy no regu-lar position. But there seems a tendency for them to come first, e.g. *Or* 32. 1 *þusend wintra 7 an hund 7 syxtig, Or* 58. 9 *feower þusend wintra 7 feower hund 7 twa 7 hundeahtatig,* and (with units last) *Or* 62. 16 *M wintra 7 C 7 LX 7 folnæh feower,* more often than last, as in *Or* 42. 3 *LX wintra 7 an hund 7 an þusend.* They do not seem to occupy a middle position.

§560. The situation in the poetry is different. Shipley (pp. 97–8) writes:

Strictly speaking, compound numbers above 120 do not occur in Anglo-Saxon poetry. When the necessity of expressing them arises, their parts are held together so loosely as to have the value of separate numbers, units and tens being held together and hundreds following (except And 1037, El 2, Gen 1184). This separation is demanded by the limitations of the poetic line. The detached part always bears the alliteration and is usually connected in thought with what precedes by the addition of a conjunctive particle, *eac, to*. Compound numbers take gen.

The usual situation is seen in *GenA* 1215 *V and syxtig* || . . . || *and eac III hund*. The exceptions he cites are *GenA* 1184 *fif and hundteontig* || . . . || *and syxtig eac, And* 1035 *tu ond hundteontig* | . . . || *swylce feowertig*, and *El* 2 *tu hund ond þreo* | . . . || *swylce XXX eac*. Compound numbers above a thousand do not occur in the poetry (Shipley, p. 98), though there are of course several examples like *And* 591 *fif ðusendo*.

5. THE NUMBER OF THE VERB WHEN A NUMERAL IS SUBJECT

§561. When a numeral other than *an* is (part of) a subject which precedes its verb, the verb is (not surprisingly) plural, e.g. (with a numeral alone) *Bede* 232. 29 *Twegen wæron biscopas*, (with a numeral used adjectivally) *Or* 100. 18 *7 twa byrig, Ebora 7 Elice, on eorþan besuncon*, and (with a numeral and a partitive genitive) *Or* 120. 23 *þa þara Somnita XX M ofslagen wurdon*. Similar examples can of course be cited from the poetry; see Bauch, pp. 51-2.

§562. In both prose and poetry the singular may be found when the collective idea is uppermost, e.g. *BlHom* 119. 5 . . . *hu lange he ure Drihten þas gedon wille, hwæþer þis þusend sceole beon scytre* . . . and *Wid* 91 *on þam siex hund wæs smætes goldes*, || *gescyred sceatta scillingrime*. In *Beo* 2163 *Hyrde ic þæt þam frætwum feower mearas* || . . . *last weardode, weardode* is plural; see §19.

§563. When the verb precedes the subject, it may be singular or plural; compare *Or* 14. 4 *7 on þæm twæm Ægyptum sindon XXIIII þeoda* (where MS *C* has *is*) with *Or* 10. 17 *On Indea londe is XLIIII þeoda*, and *Or* 10. 27 *7 on ðæm londe sindon twa micla ea* with *Or* 10. 28 *On ðæm londe is XXXII þeoda*. The singular is most common with numbers denoting multiples of ten (including hundreds and thousands), where the collective sense is strong. But even here the plural may occur. Thus we find *Or* 172. 23 *7 þær wearð þæt III hund monna ofslagen* and *Or* 40. 13 *in Egypt wearð on anre niht fiftig manna ofslegen*, but *Or* 172. 4 *þær wæron XXX 7 C gearora* and *Or* 196. 34 *siþþan him eodon on hand feowertig burga*. Most of

the examples of this sort have a plural partitive genitive, whether the
verb is singular or plural; see Stoelke, pp. 13–16 (he quotes most of
these sentences at pp. 33–5), and Wülfing, i, §§197–207. But the
verb can be plural even when there is no such genitive, e.g. *Or* 124. 11
On his feðehere wæron XXXII M. All the examples from the poetry
quoted by Bauch have singular verbs except *Sat* 300 *Us ongean
cumað ‖ þusend engla*.

§564. Where the subject following the verb is a number other than
a multiple of ten, and the idea of collectivity is less likely to be
present, the verb is more often plural, e.g. *Or* 194. 33 . . . *wæron
twegen consulas, Bede* 440. 11 *Ond þa wæron arisende twegen
ðara atolra gasta, BlHom* 239. 13 *And þær wæron on þæm carcerne
twa hund and eahta and feowertig wera, and nigon and feowertig
wifa*, and *GuthB* 1134 *Wæron feowere ða forð gewitene ‖ dagas on
rime*. But the singular does occur both in prose and poetry, e.g. *Or*
10. 17 *On Indea londe is XLIIII þeoda, Bede* 32. 1 *Ða wæs fram
Cristes hidercyme hundteontig 7 fiftig 7 six gear*, and *ChristC* 1234
þær bið on eadgum eðgesyne ‖ þreo tacen somod. Further examples
of this fluctuation have already been quoted at the beginning of §563.

§565. The fluctuation already noted in §47(3) is apparent when
the numeral is complement, e.g. *Or* 70. 36 *ðæt wæs, an hund monna*
and *Or* 128. 22 *þæt wæron fieftiene hund þusend monna*. For further examples, see Bock 1887, p. 43, Fricke, pp. 59–60, and Flamme,
p. 75.

6. ORDINAL NUMBERS

§566. Like the cardinals, the ordinals can be used independently or
dependently. There is no need to spell out all the grammatical combinations involving ordinals—such as apposition (e.g. *ÆCHom* i.
396. 4 *seo ðreotteoðe mæigð, Leui*)—but examples of the more
common ones are given.

§567. The ordinal may occur independently with or without a
demonstrative, e.g. *ÆCHom* ii. 8. 31 *and seo ðridde wæs on hryre
acenned* and *ÆCHom* i. 44. 16 *Stephanus wæs se fyrmesta, oðer
Philippus, þridda Procorus*. . . . It also occurs with a partitive genitive, e.g. *ÆCHom* ii. 520. 30 *Paulus is se ðreotteoða ðyses heapes*
(cf. *Matt(WSCp)* 8. 21 *oþer of hys leornungcnihtum*). Dependently
too it is found with or without a partitive genitive, e.g. *ÆCHom* i.
310. 25 *se fifteogoða dæg ðære easterlican tide* and *ÆCHom* ii.

8. 26 *seo ðridde gesceapennys*. The demonstrative need not be present, e.g. *Or* 52. 32 *he . . . hæfde þriddan dæl his firde beæftan him* (where the translation 'a third part' is possible) and *Or* 36. 29 *þridde yfel wæs æfter þam þæt gnættas comon ofer eall þæt land* (where '*the* third plague' is clearly meant; all the others—from *Or* 36. 25 *þæt forme* to *Or* 38. 15 *þæt teoðe*—have the demonstrative). Ordinals may also be used with *an*, e.g. *ÆCHom* ii. 334. 6 *twegen englas . . . an ðridda engel.*[130] As in MnE, the noun need not be repeated with the second and later ordinals in a series, e.g. *ÆCHom* i. 454. 13 *seo forme India . . . seo oðer . . . seo ðridde . . . ; þeos ðridde India.*

§568. The ordinal numerals are declined weak, except for forms in *-st* for 'first' (which can be strong or weak, e.g. *ÆCHom* i. 100. 27 *fyrmest daga* and *ÆCHom* i. 44. 16 *se fyrmesta*) and *oþer* 'second' (which is always strong; see §508). *An* and *sum* may appear for 'first' in a series, e.g. *Or* 58. 28 *an . . . þæt oðer . . . þridda . . . se feorða* and *Or* 248. 13 *monig tacen . . . sum . . . oþer . . . þridde*. On combinations of the ordinal with *self*, see §479.

§569. Compound ordinals usually consist of an uninflected cardinal and an ordinal ten which can be inflected, e.g. *ÆGram* 283. 7 *se an and twenteogoða* and *ÆCHom* i. 382. 26 *on þam syx and þrittegoðan geare*. But the cardinal element too may be declined, e.g. *Or* 250. 22 *on þæm twæm 7 feowerteoþan wintra* and (with the preposition, but not the demonstrative, repeated) *Or* 252. 31 *on þæm twæm 7 on feowerteoþan wintra*. Another arrangement not uncommon in *Bede* is ordinal unit + prep. *eac* + dative of cardinal ten, e.g. *Bede* 48. 1 *his rices þy ðriddan geare eac twentigum*; Fricke, p. 45, cites more examples. Roman numerals may be used, either alone, e.g. *ChronA* 46. 12 (752) *þy xii geare his rices*, or with an ordinal suffix, e.g. *Ch* 1342 *on ðy XXteoðan geare*. Ælfric gives no forms for ordinals over 100, but resorts to circumlocution—*ÆGram* 283. 15 *ducentesimus, se ðe byð on ðam twam hundredum æftemyst* and *ÆGram* 284. 3 *millesimus, se ðe bið æftemyst on ðusendgetele*. Fricke (p. 46) quotes a late example from a dubious charter of Cnut—*Ch* 959 *on ðan þusende 7 ðri 7 twentehte gære fram ures*

---

[130] For further examples of the ordinals in these various functions, see Fricke, pp. 39–46 and 61–2; Wülfing, i. 323–30; Bock 1887, pp. 44–5; Shannon, pp. 31–2; Flamme, pp. 16–17; Schrader, pp. 38–9; Hüllweck, pp. 38–42; and Philipsen, pp. 34–5. For more examples with and without a demonstrative, see the last two, Wülfing, i. 285–6, and Rissanen, pp. 91–2 and 98–100.

Rissanen rejects Hüllweck's theory that the OE 'definite article' is used in these contexts only when the order of persons or things is determined beforehand (Hüllweck, p. 38, and Rissanen, p. 92).

hlauordes hælendes xpes akennednesse. For further details of the declension and arrangement of ordinals, see *OEG*, §§692-5.

7. OTHER METHODS OF FORMING NUMERALS

a. Addition

§570. *The Menologium* shows an unusual method of forming numerals by addition, e.g. *Men* 95 *þæs emb eahta and nigon* ‖ *dogera rimes, Men* 221 *swylce emb eahta and twelf* ‖ *nihtgerimes,* and *Men* 116 *ymb þreotyne . . .* ‖ *. . .* ‖ *tyn nihtum eac;* see further Fritsche, p. 77.

§571. BT, quoting *Men* 210 *þænne embe eahta niht* ‖ *and feowerum* and *Men* 187 *ymb twentig þæs . . .* ‖ *and fif* [ASPR *seofon*] *nihtum,* glosses *and* as a preposition with the dative.[131] But in both these, and in *Men* 116 (§570) and *Men* 133 *ymb feower niht . . .* ‖ *ond twentigum,* the dative ending *-um* is metrically essential. Further, if *and* is a preposition + dative in these examples, it ought to be a preposition + accusative in *Men* 54 *swylce emb feower and þreo* (not *þrim*) and *Men* 107 *ymb twa and feower* (not *feowerum,* as in *Men* 210 above). It seems preferable to explain *and* as the conjunction 'and' and the variation between the accusative and dative (both of which are found after *ymb*) as one of metrical convenience. The fact that the forms in the different cases are separated (not by much in *Men* 210!) may have helped to make the variation possible, but is not likely to be the reason for it, despite Jacobsen (1908, p. 80). Campbell is in basic agreement. His comment in BTC reads: '*and* prep.: the word probably does not exist, in all citations we have *and,* conj., or an error for *an, on.*'

b. Multiplication

§572. The following examples will serve: *Or* 252. 6 *tuwa seofon hund wintra, Or(C)* 262. 23 *endlufon siþon hund M,* where MS *L* has *XI hund M, MSol* 272 *ðria XXX ðusend wintra,* and *MSol* 291 *ðria ðreoteno ðusendgerimes.*

c. Subtraction

§573. In the pattern 'one less than twenty', 'less than' can be expressed by *læs* (*Æ Gram* 287. 6 *undeuiginti, an læs twentig, duodeui-*

---

[131] BT, s.v. *and* prep. I. This suggestion is not withdrawn in BTS, though that made under II is modified in that *and* preposition + accusative is explained as a variant of *an, on.*

ginti, twam læs twentig); *læs þe* (*Bede(B)*) 252. 9 *an læs ðe twentig wintra*); *læs þonne* (*Solil* 36. 5 *anne læs þen*[*n*]*e XX*); *wana* (*Bede (Ca)* 252. 9 *anes wona XX wintra*); *wan þe* (*Bede(T)*) 252. 9 *anes wonðe twentig wintra*); and *wana þe* (*Bede(O)*) 252. 9 *anes wana þe XX wintra*).

§574. The subtraction method is, of course, an alternative to the addition method; thus we find *ChronA* 92. 1 (901) *oþrum healfum læs þe XXX wintra* but *ChronE* 93. 1 (901) *XXVIII wintra ᵹ healf gear*. But it is much less common. In my opinion, *þe* does not mean 'than' in any of the examples quoted in this and the previous section. See §§3239-42.

§575. Rissanen (pp. 32-4) gives more examples and points out that when *an* appears in those with *læs*, it is usually uninflected—his material contains two exceptions (one with independent *an*, one with dependent)—and that with *wan(a)* the form is, with one exception, *anes*.

§576. The subtraction method is occasionally used with the hundreds and the thousands, e.g. *Mart1* 2. 9 *fif þusend geara ond ane geare læs þonne twa hund* and *Ch* 1383 *wana þreo ᵹ þritig hida of ðam þrim hund hidun þe oðre bisceopas ær hæfdon*.

§577. Like Wülfing (i. 310), I have searched in vain for Fricke's example (p. 27) from *Bede* V. 19, *ymb twentig wintra butan an*. It may be a contracted version of *Bede(O)* 446. 2 . . . *Ealdfrið . . . forð-ferde ymb twentig wintra his rices, butan an ne wæs þa gena gefylled*, where all extant manuscripts have *his rices* and *butan* is a conjunction. However, we may note *ÆGram* 285. 10 *millenarius, þusendfeald getel oððe se ðe leofað þusend geara, swaswa dyde Matvsalam buton an and þrittig geara*. On the status of *butan* see §§3629-31.

d. Fractions

§578. A half is expressed by prepositional phrases, e.g. *ÆCHom* ii. 250. 25 *Iudas . . . tobærst on emtwa* (cf. *ÆCHom* i. 388. 19 *þæt hi on twa ferdon* 'that they should separate'), or by the word *healf*, which can be used either independently, e.g. *ÆCHom* i. 130. 36 *Zacheus, seðe healfe his æhta þearfum dælde*, or dependently, either with *dæl*, e.g. *Or* 76. 29 *se healfa dæl, ÆCHom* i. 582. 7 *þa hæfde Zacheus beceapod heofonan rice mid healfum dæle his æhta*, and *ÆCHom* ii. 584. 22 *be healfan dæle* (cf. 'by half'), or with an ordinal numeral.

§579. Examples with an ordinal numeral fall into two patterns—
those in which the base numeral is expressed, e.g. *Bede* 262. 18 *tu
ger 7 þridda healf* and *Bede* 474. 27 *feower 7 þritig wintra ond þæt
fifte healf*, and (more common) those in which it is unexpressed, e.g.
ChronA 82. 22 (891) *of þriddan healfre hyde* 'from two and a half
hides' (lit. 'the third hide a half' or 'half the third hide'), *Or* 222. 30
fifte healf hund, and *Or* 124. 12 *fifte healf M*. An interesting variant
of this last pattern, with a cardinal numeral replacing *healf*, occurs in
Bede 44. 3 *feower hund wintra 7 þæs fiftan hundseofontig*.

§580. There are special words for two-thirds, *twæde*; for a quarter,
feorþling, feorþung; and for a tenth, *teoþung*; for examples, see BT,
s.vv. The word *dæl* is also used, e.g. *Or* 76. 20 *mid þæm twæm
dælum . . . þone ðriddan dæl*, *Or* 74. 16 *seofeða dæl anre mile*, and
BlHom 35. 20 *þone teoþan dæl*. For further discussion and examples
of fractions see *OEG*, §696, Wülfing, i. 330-1, and Fricke, pp. 47-9.

e. Multiplicatives

§581. These are expressed by compounds of cardinals + *-feald*, e.g.
ÆGram 284. 16 *singularis, anfeald, dualis, twyfeald . . .* and *ÆGram*
286. 17 *simplum be anfealdum ic forgylde, duplum be twyfealdum,
triplum be þrimfealdum*. Note the double dative declension in *þrimfealdum* (for further examples see *OEG*, §697 fn. 1) and the combination of methods in *ÆCHom* i. 348. 3 *ten ðusend siðan hundfealde
ðusenda*.

§582. *Swa* and *swylce* may serve as multiplicatives in combination
with cardinal numbers, e.g. *LawMirce Inscr(Ha)* 1. 1 *syx swa micel*
(MS *Lda* has *syxfeald*), *ÆCHom* ii. 458. 20 *He hæfde seofon suna
and ðreo dohtra ær, and siððan eft eal swa fela*, *Lch* i. 400. 17 *selle
him twa swylc swylce man æt him nime*, and *Beo* 1582 *fiftyne men,
|| ond oðer swylc*.

§583. On adverbs answering the question 'How often?', see §591.
For further examples of the multiplicatives, see *OEG*, §697; Mohrbutter, p. 20; Wülfing, i. 331-2; and Fricke, pp. 49-51.

f. Distributives

§584. Ælfric has *ÆGram* 284. 5 *singuli homines, ænlipige men,
bini, getwynne oððe twam and twam, terni, þrim and þrim, quaterni,
feower and feower. ealswa quini, seni, . . . similiter ceteri . . . milleni,*

þusendfealde oðþe ðusendum and þusendum. For further examples, see Fricke, pp. 51–3.

§585. The modern 'one by one' does not seem to appear, but we find *ÆCHom* ii. 32. 6 *hi urnon to me, an æfter anum, CP* 7. 19 *hwilum word be worde*, and *ChronE* 230. 28 (1095) *mænifealdlice steorran of heofenan feollan. naht be anan oððe twam. ac swa þiclice þ hit nan mann ateallan ne mihte*. Se further Rissanen, pp. 101–5.

§586. Rissanen (pp. 34–8) points out that the term 'distributive' is also used of 'expressions indicating a quantity per person, thing, unit etc., ModE *a hundred a year* . . .', and quotes examples of *an* in this function, e.g. *Or* 68. 3 *an gear an monn* and (with a preposition) *Or* 46. 33 *on an scip . . . an þusend manna*. But *ælc*, as in *Or* 170. 27 *on ælcre anre talentan* and *ByrM* 134. 13 *of ælcum huse an lamb* is more common in this function. The same notion can be expressed by *syndrig* or *anlipig*, e.g. *Matt(WSCp)* 20. 10 *þa onfengon hig syndrige penegas* and *BenRGl* 54. 11 *ænlepige geond ænlepige bedd hi slapan*.

g. Sundry compounds and phrases

§587. See *ÆGram* 287. 9–289. 6 for Ælfric's list.

8. THE USE OF NUMERALS IN AN INDEFINITE SENSE

§588. Mustanoja (pp. 307–8) discusses the use in ME of round numbers (tens, hundreds, and thousands) in an indefinite sense. The numerals in such phrases as *Beo* 2209 *fiftig wintra* (the length of Beowulf's reign) and *Beo* 3050 *þusend wintra* (the period the dragon's treasures had lain in the earth) may have the same function.

§589. Words like *fea, fela, manig, micel, sum*, and the like, are described as 'indefinite numerals' by the authors of some of the early German dissertations on both prose and verse texts, e.g. Bock 1887 (pp. 35–8) and Ahrens (pp. 26–7). On their uses see the Index of Words and Phrases.

§590. Whether *sum* before a numeral is used to express approximation is discussed in §§389–92. This idea can be expressed by adverbs, as in *Or* 48. 11 *folneah C wintra* and *BlHom* 207. 14 *hu hwego fif hund manna*. The preposition *ymb(e)* is sometimes taken to mean 'about, approximately' in expressions of time. The notion seems to me weakly based; see §1219.

9. ADVERBS

§591. The question 'How often?' is answered by *æne, tuwa*, and *þriwa* (note *Or* 6. 2 *7 hu Iulius gefeaht wið Ptholomeus IIIa*, where *Or* 242. 25 has *þriwa*), or by phrases with *sið*, e.g. *BlHom* 47. 15 *seofon siþum.* [132] Morris translates Andrew's remark *BlHom* 243. 27 *Min Drihten Hælend Crist, ane tid on rode þu þrowodest* as '. . . once thou didst suffer on the cross'. But the accusative and the fact that Andrew next complains that it is *nu III dagas* that he has been dragged through the streets suggest that *ane tid* means 'for a time'. So I would dismiss this—presumably the solitary example referred to by Rissanen (p. 217 fn. 1). But we do find *Bede(T)* 278. 18 *æne siða* 'once' (other manuscripts have *æne siðe*) and *Beo* 1579 *oftor micle ðonne on ænne sið*.

§592. 'Which time?' is answered by phrases with *sið*, e.g. *Beo* 2286 *forman siðe* and *BlHom* 27. 14 *þriddan siþe*. Fricke (pp. 55-6) quotes examples with *cyrr* and *sæl*. The phrase *BlHom* 127. 20 *on forman* 'first' should also be noted. See further §§1425-6.

§593. For miscellaneous phrases and compounds referring to time see *ÆGram* 287. 11-19. On the uses of cases to express duration and point of time, see §§1383-4, 1387-8, 1400-3, and 1421-4.

G. VERBS

1. TECHNICAL TERMS AND BIBLIOGRAPHICAL NOTES

§594. I follow recommendation XXIV of the Joint Committee's Report: 'That the term *Auxiliary Verb* be retained in its ordinary sense, and that Verbs that are not auxiliary be described as *Verbs with full meaning.*' So I distinguish 'is' in 'He is a group-captain' (verb with full meaning) from 'is' in 'He is called Bill' (auxiliary verb). On the terms 'second participle', 'transitive and intransitive verbs', and 'modal' auxiliaries, see respectively §23, §§602-6, and §§990-1. Other necessary explanations are given where appropriate. But most of the technical terms used are the accepted ones.

§595. The verbs seem to have attracted more attention than any other syntactical topic in Old English, except perhaps element order.

---

[132] For further examples, see *ÆGram* 285. 13-286. 15; Wülfing, i, §219; and Fricke, pp. 53-5. For a full treatment of OE forms meaning 'once', see Rissanen, pp. 217-27.

Here I have cleared the decks by silently eliminating those works which might appear from the title to be concerned with OE syntax but are not and those which have nothing of any moment to offer students of it, in the hope of listing them and justifying their present omission in *A Critical Bibliography of Writings on Old English Syntax*. Works of interest which concern themselves with one topic— such as tense, mood, or aspect—are treated in the appropriate place below. But a few necessary comments on general studies follow.

§596. The dissertations given in this and the next two sections contain little beyond examples of various verbal phenomena in the text concerned, usually (but not always) including verbal rection, but are of course useful for them. Readers who wish to get some idea of the scope of the ones written in German might well in the first instance glance at those of Schürmann (1884) and Reussner (1889). Schürmann's treatment of words, sentences, and periods, served as a model for later writers on both prose, e.g. Flamme (1885),[133] and poetry, e.g. Conradi (1886) and Kempf (1888)—though the last two flagged a little. So too (in various ways) did the authors of the rest of 'the eighteen German dissertations' on OE poems. Indeed, not all of them dealt with verbs. Ahrens, Dethloff, and Meyer, were able to refer to the dissertations of Planer, Spaeth, and Walter, respectively. (For details of these see §597.) But Rose published only that portion dealing with number and case, including verbal rection, and failed to mention in his bibliography M. Prollius, *Ueber den syntactischen Gebrauch des Conjunctivs in den Cynewulfschen Dichtungen Elene, Juliana und Crist* (Marburg, 1888). Oldenburg was silent about verbs, except for a few remarks on concord.

§597. In that part of his dissertation which was published, Reussner dealt only with verbs. His method was, however, based on that of Schürmann and was used by the writers of seven dissertations on OE poems:

M. Furkert, *Der syntaktische Gebrauch des Verbums in dem angelsächsischen Gedichte vom heiligen Guthlac* (Leipzig, 1889).
B. Hertel, *Der syntaktische Gebrauch des Verbums in dem angelsächsischen Gedichte 'Crist'* (Leipzig, 1891).

---

[133] Mohrbutter (1885) follows the same pattern. Unlike the others, he acknowledges no debt to Schürmann, though he does quote him. The original source of the scheme may have been Körting, who sponsored the publication of Schürmann's work and is thanked by Mohrbutter.

Schrader (1887) acknowledges a debt to Napier and Wagner, but makes no mention of Schürmann and covers less ground—chapters 1-5 of Schürmann's Part I, differently arranged and with some omissions and some additions.

H. Seyfarth, *Der syntaktische Gebrauch des Verbums in dem Cæd-mon beigelegten angelsächsischen Gedicht von der Genesis* (Leipzig, 1891).

A. Müller, *Der syntaktische Gebrauch des Verbums in dem angel-sächsischen Gedichte von der Judith* (Leipzig, 1892).

J. D. Spaeth, *Die Syntax des Verbums in dem angelsächsischen Gedicht Daniel* (Leipzig, 1893).

(J. O.) L. Walter, *Der syntaktische Gebrauch des Verbums in dem angelsächsischen Gedichte 'Christ und Satan'* (Rostock, 1907).

J. Planer, *Untersuchungen über den syntaktischen Gebrauch des Verbums in dem angelsächsischen Gedicht vom Phoenix* (Leipzig, n.d.).

§598. The following (in addition of course to Wülfing, ii) offer collections of examples from prose texts:

Th. Wohlfahrt, *Die Syntax des Verbums in Ælfric's Uebersetzung des Heptateuch und des Buches Hiob* (Munich, 1885).

P. T. Kühn, *Die Syntax des Verbums in Ælfrics 'Heiligenleben'* (Leipzig, 1889) [Kühn followed Wohlfahrt's plan].

H. M. Blain, *The Syntax of the Verb in the Anglo-Saxon Chronicle from 787 A.D. to 1001 A. D.* (University of Virginia diss., 1901).

W. A. Robertson, *Tempus und Modus in der altenglischen Chronik* (Marburg, 1906).

§599. In his article 'Auxiliary and verbal in "Beowulf" ' (*ASE* 9 (1981), 157-82), where 'verbal' covers infinitives and past or second participles, Bliss suggests that 'there are a number of constraints controlling the word order in clauses containing an auxiliary and a verbal; there are also a number of tendencies which, while they cannot be said to control the word order, none the less make one word order preferable to another' (p. 178) and points out various ways in which his lines and methods of research might be extended to other OE poems.

2. INTRODUCTORY REMARKS

a. Inflexion

§600. The OE verbs are divided according to their inflexion into four groups—strong, weak, preterite-present, and 'anomalous' (*willan, don, gan,* and *beon*); see *OEG*, §726. Full details of the inflexions will be found in *OEG*, §§726-68. But the basic features are these:

(1) Apart from *hatte* 'is/was called', pl. *hatton*, the passive voice occurs only in the second participle of transitive verbs (§§728 and 734-5), which is used with *weorþan* or *beon/wesan* to form a passive

equivalent; see §§786–801. The remaining forms of the verb, including the infinitives (§923) and the present participle (§976), are active.

(2) The indicative and subjunctive moods distinguish two tenses—present and past. The three persons are differentiated in the singular of the present indicative. The first and third person singular of the past indicative have the same form, which differs from that of the second person. The subjunctive and the plural indicative make no distinction of person in either tense.

(3) The imperative has only the second person singular and plural of the present tense. But see Mitchell 1979*b*, pp. 538–9.

(4) Plural verb forms are used with the nominative of the dual of the first and second person pronouns.

§601. That certain distinctions could not be made within the OE verb system and that some forms were ambiguous has already been mentioned in §§16–22. In *EStudies*, 36 (1955), 206–8, Visser proposed the terms 'modally zero' or 'modally non-marked form' and 'modally marked form', the latter being in practice a substitute for both 'imperative' and 'subjunctive'. I give my reasons for rejecting these terms in Mitchell 1979*b*, pp. 537–8. But we must recognize that in practice there are in OE four, not three, formal categories—indicative forms, imperative forms, subjunctive forms, and ambiguous forms such as *woldest*. (On the word 'ambiguous', see §1223.) For, as *ÆGram* 262. 10 *ni uelles, non uenisses, buton þu woldest, ne come ðu* and manuscript variations like *þu . . . cuðe/cuðest* at *Bo* 15. 14 certify, the ending *-est* in the preterite may be either indicative or subjunctive. These forms must be distinguished carefully (Visser's claim (*ii*, §834) that the forms *we lufodon/we lufoden* are in 'opposition' is as misleading as any of the remarks which he condemns other grammarians of Old English for making) and those which are ambiguous must not be used to establish the prevailing mood of any particular construction. The possibility that scribal imprecision may have led to the use of an unexpected mood must also be borne in mind.

§601a. Most of the forms which are ambiguous can be either indicative or subjunctive. They are:

(1) first person singular present of strong and weak verbs;

(2) present indicative plural forms like *binde we, binde ge* (see *OEG,* §730);

(3) second person singular preterite of strong verbs;

(4) all three persons of the singular preterite of weak verbs (on *-est*, see *OEG,* §752);

(5) preterite plural of strong and weak verbs, where the endings
-on/-en are notoriously unreliable and -e is also ambiguous (see §19).
We may also note

(6) the endings aþ, -iaþ, which are found in both the present indicative plural and the imperative plural;

(7) the forms beo, do, and ga, which can be either imperative singular or second person singular present subjunctive.

The futility of Visser's system for OE is clearly demonstrated by
his classification of ne ritst (þu) as modally non-marked and of both
ne rid (þu) and ne ride (þu) as modally marked (ii, §842). It is an
inevitable consequence of all this that his identification of OE
examples must always be checked.

b. 'Transitive' and 'intransitive' uses

§602. The traditional syntactical classification adopted, for example,
by Wülfing (ii, §376), distinguishes Begriffszeitwörter (Nesfield's
'notional' or 'principal' verbs)—which embrace 'transitive' and 'reflexive' verbs and also 'intransitive' and 'impersonal'—from Hülfszeitwörter ('auxiliaries'). According to PG, transitive verbs are capable
of governing a direct object while intransitive verbs do not require
(and often cannot take) a direct object. One difficulty—the fact
that there sometimes exist side by side an intransitive verb and 'an
etymologically related transitive homonym', e.g. byrnan 'to burn'
—has been well discussed by Visser (i. 97) in a passage quoted in
§605. A second is that some verbs regarded as transitive today take
an accusative in OE, e.g. ofslean 'to kill', while others take a dative,
e.g. derian 'to harm' and helpan 'to help'. QW (§107) says of the
latter that 'the dative was used for the sole "object" of many intransitive verbs, the cognates of which in Mod.E. are regarded as transitive'
and Ardern (§26c) speaks of the dative 'as QUASI-OBJECT to intransitive Verbs'. How then are we to classify verbs like abelgan 'to
anger', which are found with both accusative and dative?

§603. The fact that many OE verbs can take more than one case
leads us into other terminological difficulties. Thus Ardern (§25d)
speaks of the genitive being used as the 'PARTITIVE OBJECT of
certain Verbs: primarily, where the action affects less than the totality
of a thing: e.g. "taste" (abyrige þæs haligwæteres . . .)'. But he is
forced to make an artificial distinction between ÆCHom i. 80. 6
to þam Romaniscan casere, þe ealne middangeard on þam timan
geweold and ÆCHom i. 82. 4 and se ælfremeda Herodes þæs rices
geweold by translating the first as 'held control, ruled', the second as

'*seized* control', and by claiming that the latter is an example of a normally transitive verb used in a special sense. How would he have distinguished *Bede* 332. 15 . . . *hire sweostor Hereswið* . . . *baad þone ecan sige*, Latin . . . *soror ipsius Heresuid* . . . *coronam expectabat æternam*, from *Bede* 348. 15 *wuton we wel þære tide bidan*, Latin *ergo exspectemus horam illam?*[134] And how would he have coped with *brucan*, which is found with accusative, genitive, and dative? Case syncretism can probably be invoked to explain some at least of these variations. See (in addition to the references given in §8 fnn.) Sarrazin (*EStudien*, 16 (1891), 84); Wülfing (*EStudien*, 17 (1892), 291-2); and QW, §107. For a brief attempt to explain why some verbs take both accusative and genitive and others both genitive and dative, and for references to other discussions, see Shipley, pp. 11-13.

§604. Fortunately we can cut short this terminological discussion by adapting the classification used by Visser in his *An Historical Syntax of the English Language*. He distinguishes 'verbs without complement' from 'verbs with complement' and divides the latter into two groups (Visser, i. 189, and (for the examples quoted) ibid., pp. 190 and 412): (A) those involving distinct subordination ('copulas'), where the main stress is on the 'complement' (traditionally called the 'complement') and the preceding verb is merely a link, e.g. the *and* clause in *ÆTest* 26. 257 *(God þa hine gebletsode) 7 his bearn wæs gesund*; and (B) those involving no distinct subordination, where there is hardly any difference of stress between the verb and the 'complement' (traditionally called the 'object'), e.g. *Bede* 354. 23 . . . *hio smaelo hrægel weofað*. These are not the exact equivalent of so-called 'transitive' verbs, for they may take other kinds of object than an accusative; see §1565.

§605. To explain the term 'Verb without Complement' as he applies it to OE, I take the liberty of quoting Visser at length (i. 97):

Syntactical units in Old English that consist of subject + verb and, without further complement, form complete, intelligible utterances, may be divided into four groups:

(1) the type *heo fordwineþ; we slapað*[135]
(2) the type *heofoncandel barn; hi cwylmiaþ*

---

[134] I suppose that, notwithstanding *Bede* 348. 15, it is possible to argue that Latin influence may be responsible for the accusative in *Bede* 332. 15 and for other irregularities such as the dative after *brucan* in *Bede* 318. 14 . . . *þæt heo næfre linnum hræglum brucan wolde ac wyllenum*, Latin *quia . . . nunquam lineis sed solum laneis uestimentis uti uoluerit*. But the problem of classification remains.

[135] [*My note*] See, however, *Ps(A)* 75. 6 *hneapedun slep heara*, Latin *dormierunt somnum suum*, where the original glossator or a contemporary has inserted *vel slypton*.

(3) the types *hit ne deraþ*; *ic gehyrsume*; *he giornade*; *ic miltsige*
(4) the type *ic bryttie*; *ic befrine*; *he getimbrode*.

In type (1) the verb is of the self-sufficient intransitive kind, i.e. it is never found construed with either a direct, an indirect, a prepositional or a causative object.

In type (2) the verb is an intransitive verb alongside of which there exists an etymologically related transitive homonym. *Beornan* (= to burn) and *cwylman* [*sic*] (= to suffer) in the above instances are intransitive; their homonyms, in e.g. 'Swa fyr *wudu byrneð*' and 'We *ða flæsclican lustas cwylmiað*' are transitive. Conventionally the verbs of this group are marked 'Intrans. + trans.' in our grammars and dictionaries, without heeding the contradiction in terms. For, if *intransitive* means 'does not take a direct object', and *transitive* 'requires a direct object', a verb can never have these contradictory qualities at the same time. It should be borne in mind that *burn* intr. is a different verb from *burn* tr., although they are given only one entry in the dictionaries, *burn* intr. meaning 'to be on fire', and *burn* tr. 'to cause to be consumed by fire'. Similarly *swim* intr. = 'to move along in water', and *swim* tr. = 'to traverse by swimming'; *sit* intr. = 'to be seated', and *sit* tr. (= e.g. in *to sit a horse*) = 'to know how to ride'. For lack of a better term, and for the sake of convenient reference further on in the discussion, these verbs will be called double-functioned or amphibious verbs.

In type (3) the verb belongs to that kind of intransitive verbs that are usually construed with an indirect object (in the dative) or with a causative object (in the genitive), as e.g. in 'hit ne deraþ *þæm*'; 'ic gehyrsume *þæm*'; 'miltsa *eallum ðinum wiðerwinnum*'; 'he giornade *friðes*'; 'miltsa *min*'. (In later English the causative objects were gradually replaced by prepositional objects.) Type (3) illustrates the *absolute* use of verbs.

In type (4) the verb, though transitive, is used without the direct object it normally requires, and is, just as that in type (3), used *absolutely*. (Cf. Genesis 1181, '(he) . . . *gold brittade*' and: O.E. Gosp., Mt. II, 7, 'Herodes *befran hi*'; Lindisf. Gosp., Mt. VII, 26, 'he *getrimberde* [*sic*] *hus his*'.) This 'suppression' of the direct object occurs wherever it is so clear from the context or situation that the utterance is intelligible without it.

§606. One point in particular demands criticism here—that is Visser's use of the term 'intransitive' in his definition of the verbs in his type (3); the remarks I have made above suggest that it would be better omitted. And so I propose to adopt Visser's classification —or rather adapt it—by avoiding as far as possible the terms 'transitive' and 'intransitive' and by preserving the traditional distinction between 'object' and 'complement' noted above. But the term '(in)transitive verb' is sometimes used as a convenient shorthand for the phrase 'verb used (in)transitively'. A discussion of simple sentences along these lines will be found in my chapter III; note particularly §1565, where I follow Visser in listing and exemplifying the various kinds of 'object'. I supply a list of verbal rections in §1092.

c. Reflexive and impersonal verbs

§607. Verbs which often take a reflexive object are sometimes used absolutely (§267); Visser (i. 145) rightly draws our attention to the danger of careless use of the term 'reflexive'. Similarly, while many of the so-called 'impersonal verbs' take a noun or a personal pronoun as 'object', there are exceptions. For these and for the terminological problems involved, see §§1025–30.

d. Independent and periphrastic forms

§608. Wülfing (ii. 48 ff.) distinguishes *die selbständigen Zeitformen*, e.g. *Or* 8. 14 *Europe hio onginð . . . of Danai þære ie* and *Or* 10. 4 *swa ic ær gehet* from *die Umschreibungsformen*, a term which embraces the various combinations of auxiliaries with participles or infinitives. Campbell (*OEG,* §§727–8) speaks of independent and periphrastic forms, Brown (1963, pp. 23–4) of the 'simple finite verb' as opposed to the 'verb phrase', which he defines as

one of two constructions: a) finite verb and non-finite verb (infinitive, participle, or gerund), i.e., a complex verb; or b) finite verb (or complex verb) and adjective, i.e., a predicate adjective construction.

As an example of the latter, he cites *CP* 437. 12 *Swiðe lytle beoð ða dropan ðæs smalan renes.* But it is hard to see why he fails to mention the other kinds of 'complement' admitted by Visser, especially the traditional 'object'.

§609. A classification which at first sight seems simple and satisfying is Visser's basic division of syntactical units into those with one, two, and three or more, verbs. But difficulties arise in practice. It is perhaps possible to accept 'he will do it tomorrow', 'he has done his duty', and 'he was writing letters', as syntactical units containing two verbs, and 'he may have misunderstood you' and 'he has been writing letters' as ones containing three (Visser, i. 2). But to treat as 'syntactical units' sentences containing the so-called 'indirect consecution', e.g. 'I saw him go/going', 'I want it done', and 'I have seen him go' (Visser, i, pp. vi–vii), seems a dubious procedure and one likely to lead to confusion if adopted here. See further Davis in *RES* 17 (1966), 73.

§610. Twaddell, in his consideration of the English of 'many educated adult Americans, with some bias toward linguistic conservatism but without marked affectation' distinguishes

two sets of auxiliaries: the primary auxiliaries with subject-agreement -s and full 'Past' syntax (*have, be; do*) and the modal auxiliaries without -s and without full

'Past' syntax (can, could, dare, may, might, must, need, ought, shall, should, will, would). In verb constructions containing members of both sets, the modal precedes the primary auxiliaries, not vice versa.

(We may note here that, according to Wülfing (ii, §§381-7), the OE equivalents of these 'primary auxiliaries' can be used as both Begriffs- and Hülfszeitwörter; see further below.) Twaddell then points out that

along with 'Past'-inflection, have and be participate in a four-element system of constructions, which is a formal system, not a semantic one. The four elements are:
  I. 'Past' (-ed, -t, alternative form of stem, zero)
  II. Current relevance (have + participle)
  III. Limited duration (be + -ing)
  IV. Passive (be + participle).

Some use is made of this classification in the sections which follow. (The three quotations are from pages 1, 2, and 2, respectively of Twaddell.)

3. THE INDEPENDENT TENSES

a. Introductory

§611. It is, of course, a commonplace that the independent (or simple) tenses perform many more functions in OE than they do in Greek, Latin, or MnE; the periphrastic forms are present only in embryo (see below). The exact meaning must often be deduced from the context, though adverbs are sometimes used. Ælfric's remarks on the tenses and his OE examples underline these points:

ÆGram 123.12   TEMPVS ACCIDIT VERBO, tid gelimpð worde for getacnunge mislicra dæda. æfter gecynde synd þreo tida on ælcum worde, þe fulfremed byð: PRAESENS TEMPVS ys andwerd tid: sto, ic stande; PRAETERITVM TEMPVS ys forðgewiten tid: steti, ic stod; FVTVRVM TEMPVS is towerd tid: stabo, ic stande nu rihte oððe on sumne timan. ac swa ðeah wise lareowas todældon þone PRAETERITVM TEMPVS, þæt is, ðone forðgewitenan timan, on þreo: on PRAETERITVM INPERFECTVM, þæt is unfulfremed forðgewiten, swilce þæt ðing beo ongunnen and ne beo fuldon: stabam, ic stod. PRAETERITVM PERFECTVM ys forðgewiten fulfremed: steti, ic stod fullice. PRAETERITVM PLVSQVAMPERFECTVM is forðgewiten mare, þonne fulfremed, forðan ðe hit wæs gefyrn gedon: steteram, ic stod gefyrn. forði is se forðgewitena tima on ðreo todæled, forðan ðe naht ne byð swa gemyndelic on gecynde, swa þæt ys, þæt gedon byð.

§612. Visser (ii. 661 and 745) has discussed the inappropriateness of the terms 'present tense' and 'past tense', but the absence of satisfactory substitutes led him to retain them. I follow him in this and in his subdivisions of the 'present tense forms' (my 'present indicative') into those referring to neither the past nor the future,[136] to the future, and to the past. For my reasons for retaining the term 'subjunctive' as opposed to his 'modally marked form', see §601.

b. The present indicative

(1) *Time sphere neither past nor future*

§613. First we may have a reference to the actual present, the 'now', e.g. *Bede* 2. 1 *Ic Beda . . . sende gretan ðone leofastan cyning Ceolwulf. 7 ic ðe sende þæt spell, ÆCHom* i. 78. 6 *Hwær is Iudeiscra leoda Cyning . . . ?*, and *Beo* 2794 *ðara frætwa . . . ǁ . . . þe ic her on starie*. It can be contrasted with a past tense when so used, e.g. *ÆCHom* i. 224. 1 *Ge secað þone Hælend: he aras: nis he her* and *ÆCHom* i. 182. 29 *forðon ðe he astah up to heofenum, and þær sitt nuða mid his halgum*.

§614. However, despite the adverb *nuða*, this last example could perhaps equally well be grouped with those which express a permanent condition or a general truth, e.g. *CP* 327. 18 *Mare is ðæt mod ðonne se mete*, *Or* 8. 15 *of Riffeng þæm beorgum, þa sindon neh þæm garsecge þe mon hateð Sarmondisc, ÆCHom* i. 134. 3 *and se rihtwisa leofað be his geleafan*, and *Max i* 69 *Gifre biþ se þam golde onfehð*. Here too we find a contrast between tenses, e.g. *ÆCHom* i. 216. 4 *We habbað oft gesæd, and git secgað, þæt Cristes rihtwisnys is swa micel, þæt he nolde niman mancyn neadunga of ðam deofle, buton he hit forwyrhte*, where *forwyrhte* is pluperfect, and *ÆCHom* i. 42. 9 *and heo acende butan sare, and þurhwunað on mægðhade*, where *acende* refers to a single completed act in the past. The idea of permanency or general truth can be reinforced by an adverb, e.g. *ÆLS* 16. 370 *forðan seðe wis byð, ne wurð he næfre modig* and *El* 746 [Cherubim] *singallice singaþ in wuldre ǁ . . . heofoncininges lof*.

§615. The reference may also be to a regular or habitual action. The line between this and the previous type is again hard to draw. Thus Carlton (1970, p. 111) cites *Ch* 1501 *. . . buton anre hide ic gean into þære cyrcean þam preoste þe þar gode þeowaþ*, but the reference could be to a continuing state; contrast another of his examples —*Rec* 6. 5 *7 ðæm godcundan geferscipe . . . ðe in Cristes circan*

---

[136] A bad misprint in his Contents (ii, p. v) makes him speak there of 'neither past nor present'. But see ii. 661. For a suggestive attempt to harness tense-usage as a criterion for the criticism of OE poetry, see Fanagan, *Neophil.* 62 (1978), 290-3.

dæghwæmlice Godes lof rærað. The really unambiguous examples
are perhaps those with an adverb. So we find *CP* 435. 2 *Ac hi beoð
ðæs ðe lator ðe hi oftor ymbðeahtiað, WHom* 20(*EI*). 49 *And þæs
we habbað ealle þurh Godes yrre bysmor gelome, Wan* 1 *Oft him
anhaga are gebideð, Fort* 1 *Ful oft þæt gegongeð . . . ‖ þætte wer
ond wif in woruld cennað ‖ bearn*, and (with a contrast in tense)
ÆCHom i. 184. 24 *Fela wundra worhte God, and dæghwamlice
wyrcð*.

§616. Visser (ii, §§711-16) gives examples of these types in all
periods of English. But some defy classification, e.g. *ÆCHom* ii. 168.
29 *Fela yfela ðu wyrcst, and fela ðu worhtest*, in which *wyrcst* could
refer to the actual present, to a continuing action, or to a habitual
one.

(2) *Time sphere the future*

§617. The time reference is clearly to the future in *Bede* 76. 16 *In
dolore paries: in saare þu cennest bearn, ÆCHom* i. 552. 8 *Eadige
beoð þa mildheortan, forðan þe hi begytað mildheortnysse*, and
And 859 *We ðe, Andreas, eaðe gecyðað ‖ sið userne*. The same is
also true of those examples in which Visser (ii, §§733-5) detects
strong determination, sometimes amounting to a threat, e.g. *John
(WSCp)* 13. 8 *Petrus cwæð to him, ne þwyhst þu næfre mine fet* and
ÆLS 3. 223 *þonne ic eft gecyrre sigefæste fram fyrde, ic aweste
þinne buruh and gewyrce to yrðlande*, or a hypothetical utterance
whose 'apodosis mentions the inevitable, quasi-automatic, consequence of the fulfilment of the action expressed in the protasis', e.g.
ÆLS 3. 559 *Ac far þe to westene and þu fintst anne wer haliges lifes
se hatte Effrem*. An adverb or adverb phrase or clause sometimes
certifies the future time-reference, e.g. *Bede* 186. 28 *þonne cume ic
to ðe* 7 *þec þonon ham lædo, Bede* 462. 29 *Ac westu gearo; forðon
æfter feower gearum ic eft hwyrfe* 7 *þe neosige, ÆCHom* ii. 244. 35
Æfter ðan ðe ic arise of deaðe gesund (= future perfect; see §618),
ic eow eft gemete on Galileiscum earde, ÆLS 3. 223 above, and
(with a contrast in tense as well), *ÆCHom* ii. 600. 25 *þu ðe æfre
wære, and nu eart, and æfre bist an Ælmihtig God*. (On the use of
beon with a future reference, see §§652-64.) Carlton (1970, pp. 110-
11) draws our attention to the fact that the present indicative with
an adverbial expression of time may denote, not only the simple
future, but also 'a present action which is to take effect in the future',
e.g. *Ch* 1533 7 *ic an þæs landes æt Ingepenne ofer minne dæg Æffan*.
Schrader (p. 65) and Visser (ii, §719) have pointed out that in the
second person these tense forms may approximate to commands, e.g.

Exod 31. 15 *Syx dagas ðu wyrcst; on þam seofoðan þu rest* and
ÆCHom ii. 544. 4 *On eowerum geðylde ge geahniað eow eowere
sawla.*

§618. Like MnE, OE often has the present indicative where Latin
would have the future or the future perfect (see GL, §§565, 571,
and 595) in certain conditional and temporal clauses, e.g. *ÆCHom*
ii. 244. 35 (§617), *BlHom* 21. 28 *ac sona he molsnaþ, 7 wyrþ to
þære ilcan eorþan þe he ær of gesceapen wæs, oþþæt Drihten cymeþ
on domes dæg,*

Beo 296   . . .   oþ ðæt eft byreð
       ofer lagustreamas   leofne mannan
       wudu wundenhals   to Wedermearce,

ÆCHom i. 52. 27 *Gif ge forgyfað þam mannum þe wið eow agyltað,
þonne forgyfð eow eower Fæder eowere synna, ÆLS* 3. 590 *Hwæt
destu gif ic to mergen middeges gebide,* and *Beo* 446 *ac he me habban wile* ‖ *dreore fahne, gif mec deað nimeð;* on similar examples involving adjective clauses, e.g. *Beo* 440 *ðær gelyfan sceal* ‖ *Dryhtnes
dome se þe hine deað nimeð,* see §§2201–5.

§619. Visser makes two groups of these conditional and temporal
clauses (ii, §§722 and 755). Most of his OE examples are placed in
§722, the criterion being that 'there is reference to the future', while
those in §755 are temporal clauses in which 'the action denoted by
the verb must be understood as past at the moment in the future referred to'. But some at least of the temporal clauses in §722 could
equally well have been put in §755, e.g. *John(WSCp)* 4. 25 *þonne he
cymð he cyð us ealle ðing,* Latin *cum ergo venerit ille, nobis annuntiabit omnia,* and

ChristB 789   Huru ic wene me
       ond eac ondræde   dom ðy reþran,
       ðonne eft cymeð   engla þeoden.

So too could some of the conditional clauses, e.g. *Bede* 28. 16 *oððe
gif hwylc eow wiðstondeð, þonne gefultumiað we eow,* Latin *uel, si
qui restiterit, nobis auxiliariis utimini,* and

El 531   Nu ge geare cunnon
      hwæt eow þæs on sefan   selest þince
      to gecyðanne,   gif ðeos cwen usic
      frigneð ymb ðæt treo. . . .

Visser, it seems to me, complicates the issue by attempting an arbitrary division. It is hard to be sure where to put some examples, e.g.

ÆLS 3. 590 (§618), and the point is of grammatical rather than of practical importance.

§620. Other difficulties of classification, if not meaning, arise. Visser includes *CP* 324. 1 *Ga, 7 cum to morgen, ðonne selle ic ðe hwæthwugu*, Latin *Vade et revertere, et cras dabo tibi, Bede* 462. 29 *Ac westu gearo; forðon æfter feower gearum ic eft hwyrfe 7 þe neosige*, Latin *Sed paratus esto; quia post quadriennium reuertens uisitabo te*, and *And* 1218 *Ic þe mid wunige*, among his examples with a future reference (ii, §717) but notes (ii, §730) that they might be interpreted as 'dispositional presents', i.e. utterances which 'refer to an action for which arrangements or dispositions have been made at a time previous to the moment of speaking'. But the two Latin futures argue against such an interpretation in the prose examples, and it is possible that *wunige* in *And* 1218 and in *And* 99 *Ic þe mid wunige || ond þe alyse of þyssum leoðubendum* refers to a permanent state rather than to the future; cf. *Matt(WSCp)* 28. 20 *7 ic beo mid eow ealle dagas oð worulde geendunge*, Latin *Et ecce ego vobiscum sum omnibus diebus*. . . . An interesting switch of reference occurs in *ÆCHom* i. 362. 14 *Se ðe me lufað, he hylt min bebod, and min Fæder hine lufað and wit cumað to him, and mid him wuniað*; cf. *John(WSCp)* 14. 21 *Se þe hæfð mine bebodu 7 gehylt þa, he ys þe me lufað; Min fæder lufað þæne þe me lufað 7 ic lufige hyne 7 geswutelige him me sylfne*, Latin *Qui habet mandata mea, et servat ea, ille est qui diligit me. Qui autem diligit me, diligetur a Patre meo; et ego diligam eum, et manifestabo ei meipsum.*

§621. Another possibility of ambiguity arises when the present indicative is accompanied by the adverb *giet*. The reference is sometimes to the present, e.g. *CP* 261. 24 *se ðe butan ælcre synne wæs 7 giet is* (where the future might require *bið*; but see §§652–64), *ÆCHom* i. 458. 18 *Ic hæbbe gebunden ðone feond þe hi drehte, and ge gyt hi ondrædað*, and *Beo* 944 *gyf heo gyt lyfað*, sometimes to the future, e.g. *Ps(P)* 26. 9 *Ic sohte þine ansyne, ic sece gyt symle*, Latin *Quesiui uultum tuum uultum tuum dn̄e requiram, ÆGram* 140. 15 TEMPORE FVTVRO *amabor, ic beo gelufod gyt . . . amabimur, we beoð gelufode gyt*, and *GenB* 618 *Gif giet þurh cuscne siodo || læst mina lara, þonne gife ic him þæs leohtes genog*. So we can understand the fluctuations in Thorpe's renderings of *ÆCHom* i. 216. 4 *We habbað oft gesæd, and git secgað, þæt Cristes rihtwisnys is swa micel* . . . 'We have often said, and yet say, that the justice of Christ is so great . . .' but *ÆCHom* i. 416. 16 *Ic symle geoffrode, and gyt offrige mine lac ðam Ælmihtigan Gode* . . . 'I have ever offered and will yet offer my gift to the Almighty God . . .'.

§622. The adverb *ær* is occasionally used with the present tense to indicate what is strictly the future perfect relationship. The example cited by BTS (s.v. *ær* adv. II(1a))—*Lch* ii. 110. 9 *Uið ælcum attre redic 7 clate ete ær ne mæg þe nan man attre awyrdan*—can be compared with *Rid* 11. 10, *Dream* 118,

Fort 48	Sumum meces ecg on meodubence yrrum ealowosan ealdor oþþringeð, were winsadum; bið ær his worda to hræd,

Rid 95. 1	Ic eom indryhten ond eorlum cuð, ond reste oft; ricum ond heanum, folcum gefræge fereð wide, ond me fremdes ær freondum stondeð hiþendra hyht, gif ic habban sceal blæd in burgum oþþe beorhtne god

(where the absence of *ær* with *fereð* may be a small argument in favour of the emendation *fere*), and

Dream 107	... þæt þe þonne wile deman, se ah domes geweald anra gehwylcum swa he him ærur her on þyssum lænum life geearnaþ.

One of the examples which troubled Visser (ii. 738) can be similarly explained:

Max ii 10	Soð bið switolost, sinc byð deorost, gold gumena gehwam, and gomol snoterost, fyrngearum frod, se þe ær feala gebideð.

In the other we have *iu* rather than *ær*:

Men 210	þænne embe eahta niht and feowerum þætte fan gode besenctun on sægrund sigefæstne wer, on brime haran, þe iu beorna fela Clementes oft clypiað to þearfe.

Here the present tense *clypiað* probably certifies that the writer is viewing the appeal to Clement as something which is to precede the coming of his feast day rather than as something which preceded his death, as Visser's suggested *clypodon* would imply.

(3) *Time sphere the past*

§623. The verbs in such sentences as *BlHom* 27. 1 *her sagaþ Matheus se godspellere þætte Hælend wære læded on westen* and *ChristB* 785 *Us secgað bec* ‖ *hu . . .* , which Visser classifies here, can equally well be taken as referring to a timeless present, even though similar examples are found with the past tense, e.g. *BlHom* 75. 16 *Swa Paulus se apostol cwæþ . . .* (Visser, ii, §§781-3). *ChronF* 7. 31 (47) *Marcus se godspellere in Egipta aginþ writan þ godspell* is a unique example in the Chronicle but is not to be explained as a 'historical present' (Steadman, p. 11).

§624. The present tense can also be used of the past 'when one refers to or quotes a statement made by the person with whom one is speaking' (Visser, ii, §786), e.g.

And 417   Gif ðu þegn sie   þrymsittendes,
                wuldorcyninges,   swa ðu worde becwist,
                rece þa gerynu,   hu . . . ;

when an action completed in the past is felt as belonging to the present moment, e.g. *ÆCHom* ii. 394. 6 *Deorwurðe wæron ða fnædu þe swa eaðelice þa untrumnyssa aflygdon, swa swa we rædað be sumon wife . . .* and *Beo* 290 *Ic þæt gehyre, þæt þis is hold weorod* —this is most common with a first person pronoun as subject (Visser, ii, §791); or when continuity of an action up to the present time is implied, e.g. *ÆLS* 22. 43 *Efne min wif is for manegum wintrum untrum* (Visser, ii, §792, and Steadman, p. 4).

§625. As Steadman (p. 5) points out, these presents and those in which the present tense of non-dependent speech is used in dependent speech (§§1941-3) 'should be carefully differentiated from the historical present; in all of them there is an element of real present time. The historical present, on the other hand, is a real preterit tense. In meaning it is the exact equivalent of a past tense. The action is looked upon as beginning and ending in the time sphere of the past.' He analyses possible OE examples of the historic present from both poetry (pp. 5-10) and prose (pp. 10-12), and dismisses them all with the exception of

Sat 34   Cleopað ðonne se alda   ut of helle,
                wriceð wordcwedas   weregan reorde,
                eisegan stefne: 'Hwær com engla ðrym . . . ?'

where, he says (p. 6), *cleopað* and *wriceð* are clear cases of the historic present. Clubb, however, in his 1935 edition of the poem, put forward the not unreasonable suggestion that here the present tense is, 'with ðonne, a means of introducing an action of indefinite date (or possibly even an action many times repeated), at any time between the fall and the New Testament period'.

§626. In ii, §760, Visser cites all Steadman's verse examples except *Ex* 359 *reccað* and *Beo* 381 *hæbbe* and adds three more—*Beo* 1928 *gebiden hæbbe* (not an easy example to explain away, though, like several others, it should not have been in §760, where Visser was not concerned with subjunctives),[137] *Beo* 2719 *healde* (another present subjunctive which might, however, be for *heolde*; cf. *fea* for *feo* in *Beo* 156), and the verbs in *Seasons* 35 (which refer to the continuing promises of God).[138] As Visser (ibid.) rightly remarks, 'it deserves notice that in most of them the present tenses occur in subordinate clauses, so that what they refer to is not to be seen as a detached item in the stream of happenings recounted by the nar-rator'. In *And* 1309 *sceal*, emended by Grein and others to *sceolde* but explained by Brooks as 'historic present', could be said to be in a 'semi-subordinate' clause of result and therefore to conform to Visser's description.

§627. Neither Steadman nor Visser mentions *ChronA* 86. 7 (894) *þa gegaderedon þa þe in Norþhymbrum bugeað, 7 on East Englum, sum hund scipa*, but *bugeað* can be described as the present indicative of habitual action or as part of a cliché which is the equivalent of *ChronA* 84. 18 (894) *Norþhymbre 7 East Engle hæfdon Ælfrede cyninge aþas geseald.*

§628. The absence of really convincing OE examples of the historic present, added to the fact that the OE *Bede, Gospels*, and *Blickling Homilies*, studiously represent Latin historic presents by a past tense —for the evidence see Steadman, pp. 12-14—leads Steadman to the following conclusions (p. 21, repeated with slight variations in wording at p. 44):

1. The historical present does not occur in Old English. The two examples in *Christ and Satan* are exceptions to this general statement. [But see my comments on *Sat* 34 (§625).]
2. It is, however, very common in the Latin writings written in England during the Old English period.
3. The Old English translators consistently and repeatedly avoided translating a historical present of the Latin by an English historical present.
4. The historical present appeared first in English at the beginning of the thirteenth century; it became fairly common before the end of the century; and by the end of the fourteenth century it was used with the greatest freedom.

We can, I think, accept findings 1-3. Visser (ii, §761) amplifies and qualifies the last. See also Dobson, *RES* 17 (1966), 71-2.

---

[137] Hoops compares *hæbbe* in *Beo* 381. Both are in subordinate clauses, *Beo* 381 in a noun clause, *Beo* 1928 in a concessive clause. See further §863.

[138] Visser rightly dismisses the present tenses in *Beo* 2041 ff. (the Heathobard Episode), which Wattie (p. 125) had suggested were historic presents. See further Brodeur, pp. 157 ff.

§629. Steadman (pp. 21-44) examined six different theories about the origin of the historic present in English. Part of his discussion was based on Streitberg's now-discredited discussion of *Aktionsart* (see §865) and he reached the conclusion that 'it is impossible to establish any theory with absolute certainty' (p. 44). However, Visser's more comprehensive investigation (ii. 705 ff.) led him to explain the absence of the historic present from OE thus (§774):

the foregoing scrutiny of this usage in Middle English has made it clear that rhyme and metre were the determinative factors. Neither of these played a part in the [sc. Old English] prose, nor did rhyme in the [sc. Old English] poetry, while the metre in the poetry did not make it necessary to avoid a preterite, since Old English alliterative verse did not have a fixed number of syllables. The absence of the usage in Middle English prose can be similarly accounted for.

§630. On the present indicative with the adverb *ær* expressing what we may take as a perfect relationship, see §1114.

c. The present subjunctive

§631. When the syntax of the sentence demands its use (see §876), the present subjunctive can express the same time relationships as the present indicative. A few examples will suffice. We find (with reference to neither the past nor the future) *Or* 17. 3 *He sæde þeah þæt land sie swiþe lang norþ þonan*, *ÆLS* 5. 216 *Do þin mod hluttor þæt þu leornian mæge þurh soðfæst gescead hwa þin scyppend sy*, and *Beo* 411 *secgað sæliðend, þæt þæs sele stande* ‖ . . . ‖ *idel ond unnyt*; (with reference to the future) *Bede* 166. 10 *Ne forealdige þeos hond æfre*, *ÆLS* 21. 375 *gif ðinum fynd hingrige fed hine mid mettum oððe gif him þyrste ðu do him drincan*, and *Beo* 452 *Onsend Higelace, gif mec hild nime*, ‖ *beaduscruda betst*; and (with what seems to be a reference to the immediate present)

Beo 377   Ðonne sægdon þæt   sæliþende,
              þa ðe gifsceattas   Geata fyredon
              þyder to þance,   þæt he þritiges
              manna mægencræft   on his mundgripe
              heaþorof hæbbe.

In examples like *ÆLS* 5. 332 *Ure hælend lyfde þæt mann his life gebeorge*, the present subjunctive is used because the reference is to an eternal truth. But the second *gescyrte* in *ÆCHom* i. 4. 5 *and butan se Ælmihtiga God ða dagas gescyrte, eall mennisc forwurde; ac for his gecorenum he gescyrte þa dagas* is probably pret. 'has shortened' after *Mark* 13. 20 *breviavit*. Thorpe translates 'will shorten', probably with *Matt* 24. 22 *breviabuntur* in mind. But one would expect the present indicative if that were right, and would have to explain the second *gescyrte* as a present subjunctive erroneously repeated from the first.

d. The past indicative

§632. Visser concludes that the past indicative is not only used with reference to past time, but is 'also employed in units with a non-past time situation' (ii, §797). In my opinion, this last proposition is untenable for OE at least; my reasons are given in §§647–50.

§633. The past indicative is the tense of ordinary narrative in sentences like *ChronA* 74. 7 (876) *Her hiene bestæl se here into Werham . . . 7 wiþ þone here se cyning friþ nam*, *Bede* 266. 11 *Se leofa cuma . . . cwom swelce to dæge to me* (on this use of the past tense with 'today' and 'tonight', see Visser, ii, §800), *ÆCHom* i. 82. 3 *Ða com Crist*, and *Beo* 702 *Com on wanre niht* ‖ *scriðan sceadugenga*. This shades into the imperfect use as seen (according to Visser, ii, §799) in *ChronA* 84. 1 (893) *se micla here þe we gefyrn ymbe spræcon* and (perhaps more convincingly) in *ChronA* 84. 11 (893) *inne on þæm fæstenne sæton feawa cirlisce men on*, *ChronA* 89. 9 (896) *þa hwile þe hie hira corn gerypon*, *ÆCHom* i. 60. 11 *Mid þam ðe se apostol Iohannes stop into ðære byrig Ephesum*, and *Beo* 703 *Sceotend swæfon*. A good example (quoted in part by Wattie, p. 126, and Visser, ii, §799) is *ApT* 18. 26 . . . *þa geseah he ænne nacodne cnapan geond þa stræte yrnan se wæs mid ele gesmerod and mid scitan begird and bær iungra manna plegan on handa to ðam bæð-stede belimpende and cliopode micelre stæfne and cwæð . . .* , where the OE verbs *bær, cliopode,* and *cwæð*, represent the Latin participles *ferentem, clamantem,* and *dicentem*. This in its turn shades into the habitual sense in examples like *ÆCHom* i. 82. 3 *on ðam timan þe . . . se ælfremeda Herodes þæs rices geweold* and *ÆCHom* ii. 382. 22 *Petrus cnucode forð, oðþæt hi hine inn leton*. But there are more certain examples of the habitual use, e.g. *Bede* 342. 20 *Ond he for-þon oft in gebeorscipe . . . þonne he geseah þa hearpan him nealecan, þonne aras he* (where *þonne* means 'whenever'; see §2562), *ÆCHom* i. 26. 10 *and he forgeaf blindum mannum gesihðe . . . dumbum he forgeaf getingnysse . . . and ælce untrumnysse he gehælde*, and (with *þonne* again certifying that the action was repeated)

Beo 1579   oftor micle   ðonne on ænne sið,
    þonne he Hroðgares   heorðgeneatas
    sloh on sweofote.

§634. The simple past often stands for the not-yet-developed perfect in both principal and subordinate clauses. Visser (ii, §805) distinguishes two groups—those without adverbial adjuncts and those with them. I find some of Visser's OE examples unconvincing in that, when translated, they do not seem to demand a MnE perfect rather than a simple past, e.g. *Bo* 79. 27 *Ac þu ealle þing geworhtest swiðe gode 7 swiðe fægere*, *WHom* 13. 6 *And syððan is eac þearf þæt gehwa understande hwanan he sylf com*, and *Dan* 608 *Ðu eart seo micle and min seo mære burh* ‖ *þe ic geworhte*. *Wan* 92 *Hwær cwom mearg?* is usually translated 'Where has the horse gone?' But is 'Where did the horse go?' out of the question? Such difficulties are perhaps inevitable. Wattie writes (p. 127):

The special force of the perfect tense is not so much to indicate a completed action as to imply that this particular happening of the past has a bearing on the present. . . . This bearing of the past on the present is frequently indicated in Old English, as in Modern English, by the resolved perfect tense; but the older usage, the simple past, lacking in this delicacy of suggestion, is also of frequent occurrence

and Visser himself notes examples of fluctuation between perfect and simple past in the same sentence (ii. 750) or construction (ii. 755).

§635. There are, however, more convincing examples of both his types than those given above, e.g. (without adverb) *Bede* 4. 28 *þæt ic be ðam halgan fæder Cuðbyrhte wrat*, Latin . . . *quae de sanctissimo patre . . . Cudbercto . . . conscripsi*, *ÆCHom* i. 224. 1 *Ge secað þone Hælend: he aras: nis he her*, *ÆCHom* ii. 360. 8 *Fæder min, se tima com*, *Wan* 36 *Wyn eal gedreas*,

Beo 426

                        Ic þe nu ða,
brego Beorht-Dena,   biddan wille,
eodor Scyldinga,   anre bene,
þæt ðu me ne forwyrne,   wigendra hleo,
freowine folca,   nu ic þus feorran com,

and (with an adverb or adverbial phrase) *Bede* 60. 4 . . . *þa wisan, þe we longre tide mid ealle Ongolþeode heoldon*, Latin . . . *eis quae tanto tempore cum omni Anglorum gente seruaui*, *BlHom* 175. 10 *ic eom Godes Sunu . . . ac ic adreah mycel broc oþ þis mid Petre*, *ÆCHom* i. 18. 23 . . . *Adam ne eal mancynn þe him siððan of acom*, *ÆCHom* i. 4. 26 *ac he ne mæg nænne gehælan þe God sylf ær geuntrumode*, *ÆCHom* i. 378. 1 *Simon me mid his englum geðiwde, nu sende he hundas to me*, which Thorpe mistranslates 'now he sends dogs to me',

Beo 1337 He æt wige gecrang
ealdres scyldig, ond nu oþer cwom
mihtig manscaða,

and *Sat* 252 *þis is idel gylp* ‖ *þæt we ær drugon ealle hwile.* The adv. *nu* with the simple past sometimes has the sense 'just', e.g. *ÆCHom* i. 152. 3 ... *on þissum godspelle, þe we nu gehyrdon of ðæs diacones muðe.*

§636. On the use of a past indicative to express a future perfect see §2768.

§637. No displacement in time of the events described is involved by taking a past tense as a perfect; as we have seen (§634), it does not affect the time-relationship if we translate *Wan* 92 *Hwær cwom mearg* as 'Where did the horse go?' or 'Where has the horse gone?' This is not true when we take a past tense as a pluperfect. There are, of course, occasions when the simple past can be *translated* as either a past or a pluperfect, e.g. *ÆCHom* i. 186. 29 *and hi ferdon geond ealne middangeard, and bodedon, swa swa him Crist sylf tæhte* '... as Christ himself (had) taught' and *GenA* 1314 *Noe fremede swa hine nergend heht* 'as the Saviour (had) ordered him'; see further Visser, ii, §808. There are examples in which the actual time reference is not clear-cut, e.g. *ÆLS* 3. 496 *Ða gehyrde he be þam wundrum þe Basilius worhte* 'Then he heard of the wonders which Basil performed/had performed/was performing'. However, the existence of these possibilities does not alter the fact that the action of the two *swa (swa)* clauses just quoted preceded the action of the principal clause. But no one is likely to argue that in

Sea 31 Nap nihtscua, norþan sniwde,
hrim hrusan bond, hægl feol on eorþan
corna caldast,

bond means 'had bound', for the four past tense forms obviously go together and there is no hint that any displacement in time is involved. The most common hint in both prose and poetry is, of course, an adverb or an adverbial expression, which may occur in principal clauses, e.g. *ÆLS* 21. 156 *On þam dagum wæron on Wiht-lande þreo wif. þa twa wæron blinde geond nigon geara fec* and *Beo* 1615 *sweord ær gemealt,* ‖ *forbarn brodenmæl*; in clauses which are introduced by *ond* or *ac* or are parenthetical, e.g. *ÆLS* 5. 90 *and þæs þægnes gebedda . . . wæs for six gearum for swiðlicre untrumnysse hire spræce benæmed,*

Beo 2971   Ne meahte se snella   sunu Wonredes
                ealdum ceorle   ondslyht giofan,
                ac he him on heafde   helm ær gescer,
                þæt he blode fah   bugan sceolde,
                feoll on foldan,

and

Beo 898   Se wæs wreccena   wide mærost
                ofer werþeode,   wigendra hleo,
                ellendædum   —he þæs ær onðah—,
                siððan Heremodes   hild sweðrode,
                eafoð ond ellen;

in subordinate clauses of time, e.g. *Bede* 262. 17 *þa he ða in þære mægðe tu ger 7 þridda healf þa cirican wuldorlice heold 7 rehte,* Latin *Qui cum in illa prouincia duobus annis ac dimidio ecclesiam gloriosissime rexisset,* and

GuthB 932   Wæs gewinnes þa
                yrmþa for eorðan   endedogor
                þurh nydgedal   neah geþrungen,
                siþþan he on westenne   wiceard geceas
                fiftynu gear;

or some other kind of subordinate clause, e.g. *Bede* 42. 4 *þa cristenan men 7 ða geleafsuman, þa þe hi ær on ða frecnan tid þære ehtnysse on wudum 7 on westenum 7 scræfum hi hyddon 7 digledon,* Latin *fideles Christi, qui se tempore discriminis siluis ac desertis abditisue speluncis occulerant, ÆLS* 4. 210 . . . *þær manna lic lagon þe wæran ær acwealde on ðam cwearterne gefyrn,*

Beo 1355   no hie fæder cunnon,
                hwæþer him ænig wæs   ær acenned
                dyrnra gasta,

Beo 1465   Huru ne gemunde   mago Ecglafes
                eafoþes cræftig,   þæt he ær gespræc
                wine druncen,

and *Deor* 40 . . . *londryht . . . ‖ þæt me eorla hleo ær gesealde.*

§638. However, in view of the way some elementary OE grammars express themselves, it must be stressed that the past indicative + *ær* does not always imply a MnE pluperfect. Thus, in *ÆCHom* i. 4. 26 and *Sat* 252 (both in §635) the perfect seems more suitable, and in *ÆCHom* i. 148. 32 *Uton fon nu on þæt godspel ðær we hit ær forleton, ær* seems to have its adverbial meaning 'let us now resume the gospel where we previously left it'. Similarly *ær* can sometimes reinforce the pluperfect periphrasis, e.g. *Or* 144. 14 *ealle þa wræccan*

. . . *þe on ðæm londum wæron þe he ær self gehergad hæfde*; cf. *Or* 80. 19 *þa men . . . þe mon hiora mægas ær on ðæm londe slog* (simple past tense + *ær*) and the examples given in §723 and Mitchell 1975*a*, p. 21, in which the *hæfde* periphrasis has the sense of the simple past. When we add to these variations the use of *ær* as a tense indicator with the present, it becomes clear that there are no particular rules about the use of *ær*. So, despite Sweet (*CP* (ed.), p. xli), I am not sure that we have 'pleonastic *ær*' in *CP* 297. 19 . . . *ðæt hit sceal suiðe hrædlice afeallan of ðære weamodnesse ðe hit ær on ahæfen wæs*.

§639. But an adverb or an adverb phrase is not the only way of detecting a pluperfect reference in a simple past tense. In certain temporal clauses the subordinating conjunction itself certifies that the action of the temporal clause preceded that of the subordinate clause, e.g. *ChronA* 78. 16 (885) *sona swa hie comon on Stufemuþan, þa metton hie xvi scipu wicenga*, *ÆCHom* i. 26. 2 . . . *ærðan ðe he wæs þritig wintre on þære menniscnysse*, and *Beo* 115 *Gewat ða neosian, syþðan niht becom,* ‖ *hean huses*. With other subordinate clauses the context is often decisive, e.g. *Bede* 218. 20 *7 his lichoman se ilca ealdormon Eorconwald onfeng, 7 in portice his cirican sumre geheold, þa he in his tune getimbrode* 'which he had built', *BlHom* 53. 25 . . . *buton þæt hi on heofona heanessum gebrohton eal þæt hi on eorþan begeaton þurh Godes fultum* 'all that they had gained', the *swa (swa)* clauses in *ÆCHom* i. 186. 29 and *GenA* 1314 (both in §637),

Beo 841	No his lifgedal
	sarlic þuhte secga ænegum
	þara þe tirleases trode sceawode,
	hu he werigmod on weg þanon,
	niða ofercumen, on nicera mere
	fæge ond geflymed feorhlastas bær,

Beo 1397	Ahleop ða se gomela, Gode þancode,
	mihtigan Drihtne, þæs se man gespræc,

Beo 142	heold hyne syðþan
	fyr ond fæstor se þæm feonde ætwand,

and

Beo 1333	Heo þa fæhðe wræc,
	þe þu gystran niht Grendel cwealdest
	þurh hæstne had heardum clammum,
	forþan he to lange leode mine
	wanode ond wyrde

(where *bær* means 'had borne', *gespræc* 'had spoken', *ætwand* 'had escaped', and *wanode ond wyrde* 'had reduced and killed').[139] The context too can make it clear that a pluperfect relationship is involved in a parenthesis, e.g. *Or* 44. 29 *þa wurdon hiora wif swa sarige on hiora mode, 7 swa swiðlice gedrefed—ægþær ge þara æþelinga wif ge þara oþerra monna þe mid him ofslægene wæron— þætte hie wæpna naman, Or* 72. 30 *Ða gebeotode Cirus ðæt he his ðegn on hire* [the River Euphrates] *swa gewrecan wolde—þa he swa grom wearð on his mode 7 wið þa ea gebolgen—þæt hie mehte wifmon be hiere cneowe oferwadan . . .* , and

Beo 53   Ða wæs on burgum   Beowulf Scyldinga,
               leof leodcyning   longe þrage
               folcum gefræge   —fæder ellor hwearf,
               aldor of earde—,   oþ þæt him eft onwoc
               heah Healfdene,

and (in the poetry at any rate) in an *ac* clause, e.g.

Beo 2826   Beahhordum leng
       wyrm wohbogen   wealdan ne moste,
       ac him irenna   ecga fornamon,
       hearde heaðoscearþe   homera lafe,
       þæt se widfloga   wundum stille
       hreas on hrusan   hordærne neah.

§640. But all the examples so far quoted in which a simple past tense with no accompanying adverbial element is the equivalent of the pluperfect are in subordinate clauses where 'the pluperfect time-relation is often implicit by reason of the type of clause' (QW, §127), in parentheses, or in *ac* clauses. What is the position in principal clauses? Under what circumstances is it clear that a simple past tense with no accompanying adverbial element functions as a pluperfect?

§641. Glosses and the Latin original may of course be evidence for a pluperfect in a principal clause, e.g. *Luke(WSCp)* 2. 36 *And Anna wæs witegystre Fanueles dohtor . . . þeos wunude manigne dæg 7 heo leofode mid hyre were seofan ger of hyre fæmnhade*, Latin *et erat Anna prophetissa filia Phanuel . . . hæc processerat in diebus multis et uixerat cum uiro suo annis septem a uirginitate sua*; see further Visser, ii, §808. But these are for scholars and can in no way be described as contextual hints available for the ordinary reader of OE prose or poetry. The context can, however, be decisive when an accompanying clause—subordinate or co-ordinate—provides the

[139] On the past subjunctive with a pluperfect time reference in conditional clauses expressing impossibility in the past, see §§3606-8.

clue, e.g. *Or* 32. 24 *Ær ðam ðe Romeburh getimbred wære eahta hund wintra, mid Egyptum wearð syfan gear se ungemetlica eorðwela* 'there had been . . .', *ÆCHom* i. 94. 24 *ac hi ne dorston nænne oðerne naman Criste gescyppan þonne se heahengel him gesette, ærðan þe he on his modor innoðe geeacnod wære, þæt is, IESUS, and on urum gereorde, HÆLEND, forðan ðe he gehælð his folc fram heora synnum* 'had fixed . . .' (*þonne* clause governs *ær* clause),

Beo 262   Wæs min fæder   folcum gecyþed,
             æþele ordfruma,   Ecgþeow haten;
             gebad wintra worn, ær he on weg hwurfe,
             gamol of geardum,

and—note the parallel *habban* periphrasis—

Beo 828   Hæfde East-Denum
        Geatmecga leod   gilp gelæsted,
        swylce oncyþðe   ealle gebette,
        inwidsorge,   þe hie ær drugon. . . .

§642. However, critics and translators of poetry—I have not yet come across a similar instance in the prose—have sometimes been prepared to take as pluperfect a simple past tense in a principal clause which occurs in a sequence of such clauses with no specific indication of a change in the time relationship. Two examples are *ongunnon* and *het* in

Wife 6   Ærest min hlaford gewat   heonan of leodum
          ofer yþa gelac;   hæfde ic uhtceare
          hwær min leodfruma   londes wære.
          Ða ic me feran gewat   folgað secan,
          wineleas wræcca,   for minre weaþearfe.
          Ongunnon þæt þæs monnes   magas hycgan
          þurh dyrne geþoht,   þæt hy todælden unc,
          þæt wit gewidost   in woruldrice
          lifdon laðlicost,   ond mec longade.
          Het mec hlaford min   herheard niman,
          ahte ic leofra lyt   on þissum londstede,
          holdra freonda.   Forþon is min hyge geomor,
          ða ic me ful gemæcne   monnan funde,
          heardsæligne,   hygegeomorne,
          mod miþendne,   morþor hycgendne.

Both of these have been taken as pluperfect; see initially the translations by Crossley-Holland (*BM*, p. 83)—'had laid careful plans | And schemed' for *ongunnon . . . hycgan*—and Hamer (p. 73)—'had ordered' for *het*. Such renderings obviously suit—indeed are essential to—their author's interpretation of the poem. Can such isolated forms be taken as pluperfect?

§643. Ælfric's *Grammar* offers us no encouragement to say 'Yes'. There we find *ÆGram* 123. 15 *PRAETERITVM TEMPVS ys forðgewiten tid: steti, ic stod* and *ÆGram* 124. 5 *PRAETERITVM PERFEC-TVM ys forðgewiten fulfremed: steti, ic stod fullice. PRAETERITVM PLVSQVAMPERFECTVM is forðgewiten mare, þonne fulfremed, forðan ðe hit wæs gefyrn gedon: steteram, ic stod gefyrn.* The phrases *ic stod fullice* and *ic stod gefyrn* seem to be pedagogic formulae rather than living idioms. But the fact that Ælfric found it necessary to use *fullice* and *gefyrn* demonstrates for me at any rate—if demonstration is necessary—that for him *ic stod* was neither specifically perfect nor pluperfect.

§644. As far as I am aware, Short (*NM* 71 (1970), 588-9) was the first to object seriously to the notion that *ongunnon* in *Wife* 11 could be pluperfect. He has clearly done us a service by showing that critics have too easily taken for granted the proposition that one simple past tense in a series of past tenses can—with no contextual or grammatical hint—interrupt the narrative flow and disrupt the obvious time sequence by referring further back in time. He has, however, not succeeded in demonstrating that they are wrong to do so. Is such demonstration possible? I doubt it. But I have given my reasons for supporting Short in *ASE* 4 (1975), 16-23. As I see it, the onus is not on Short or me to demonstrate that it is impossible for *ongunnon* and *het* to be taken as pluperfect. It is for those who wish to do so to demonstrate that it is possible. I see little likelihood of their being able to do that—their only way out, it seems to me, is to suggest that the poet knew or assumed his hearers to have previous knowledge of a story of two lovers now lost to us, knowledge which would make them understand *ongunnon* and/or *het* as pluperfect, knowledge such as that which enables Wentersdorf (*Speculum*, 56 (1981), 494) to claim—with some plausibility, but not with absolute certainty, for the poet may be following the logic of his own vision—that in *Dream* 46 '*þurhdrifon* [*sic*] clearly denotes "had pierced" '. But that will not be proof. I am in no position to lay down rules. But my present impression is that writers of both prose and poetry used the *hæfde* periphrasis whenever they were departing from the narrative sequence in a principal clause in which this departure was not made clear by an adverb, an accompanying clause, the context, or the like.

e. The past subjunctive

§645. The syntax of the sentence may demand the past subjunctive instead of the past indicative; see §876. A few examples from the

poetry will suffice to demonstrate that the same temporal relationships can be expressed: *Mald* 117 *Gehyrde ic þæt Eadweard anne
sloge* (narrative),

Finn 22   ac he frægn ofer eal   undearninga
                   deormod hæleþ,   hwa ða duru heolde (*imperfect*),

GenA 2710   Ne wæs me on mode cuð,
                   hwæðer on þyssum folce   frean ælmihtiges
                   egesa wære,   þa ic her ærest com (*habitual*),

Wald i 12   Nalles ic ðe, wine min,   wordum cide,
                   ðy ic ðe gesawe   æt ðam sweordplegan
                   ðurh edwitscype   æniges monnes
                   wig forbugan   (*perfect*),

and *Beo* 1319 *frægn gif him wære* || *æfter neodlaðum niht getæse*
(pluperfect). There is, of course, the same possibility of overlap in
these categories as that already noted with the past indicative. In
Wald i 12 above, *gesawe* could be translated 'I saw' as well as 'I have
seen', the pres. *cide* notwithstanding, and *Wife* 7 *hæfde ic uhtceare* ||
hwær min leodfruma londes wære could refer to one point of time or
to an habitual state.

§646. The past subjunctive can also refer to the future-in-the-past,
e.g.

Beo 1596   . . . þæt hig þæs æðelinges   eft ne wendon,
                    þæt he sigehreðig   secean come

and *GenB* 500 *het þæt þu þisses ofætes æte* (see the General Index),
and can express impossibility in the past in conditional clauses, e.g.

Beo 590   Secge ic þe to soðe,   sunu Ecglafes,
                   þæt næfre Grendel swa fela   gryra gefremede,
                   atol æglæca   ealdre þinum,
                   hynðo on Heorote,   gif þin hige wære,
                   sefa swa searogrim,   swa þu self talast

(see §§3606–8).

f. F. Th. Visser and the 'modal preterite'

§647. According to Visser (ii, §812), the types 'O! that I *had* wings',
'Yf hyt were myne, þen *did* y ill', 'It is time we *moved* on', and 'I
wish he *came*', are

examples of the modal or, as Jespersen (NEG IV, 112) calls it, the imaginative use
of the preterite. There is no relation to any particular time-sphere. The sentences
have the modality of non-reality: they express wish, supposition, contingency,

probability, suggestion, hypothesis, open and rejected condition, non-fulfilment, etc. In Old English this modality inherent in the utterance was often expressed by means of a special form of the preterite (the modally marked form, or, traditionally, the subjunctive, as e.g. in Beowulf 676 'ær he on bed *stige*'; 1096 'Fin Hengeste . . . aðum benemde þæt he þa wealafe weotena dome arum *heolde*'), whereas here the preterite is modally non-marked, or modally zero.

He gives OE examples of this 'modal preterite' (ii, §§803 and 812–20). In most of them, the verb-form in question is ambiguous, but is to be taken as a subjunctive (see §§601–1a), e.g. *John(WSCp)* 8. 42 *Gif god wære eowre fæder, witodlice ge lufedon me*, Latin *Si Deus pater vester esset, diligeretis utique me*, and *Li gif god faeder iuer uoere gie ualde lufiga uutudlice mec* (ii, §815), *Alex* 17. 1 *mid þy we æfter ferscum wætre hie frunon, þa ondswaredon hie us 7 sædon hwær we hit findan mehton in hiora gereorde 7 cwædon þ we fundon sumne swiðe micelne mere in þæm wære fersc wæter 7 swete genog 7 þ we genog raðe to þæm becwoman gif we geornfulle wæron*, of which Visser (ii, §803) makes the Alice in Wonderland-ish remark that '*fundon* seems to stand for *mehton findan*'[140] —what of *becwoman* and *wæron?*—and *ÆLS* 8. 149 *þa tihton þa hæftlingas þæt halige mæden þæt heo awæg eode*. This, says Visser (ii, §803), is the equivalent of 'that she should go away'. That is right; it cannot mean 'so that she went away', for Agatha replies . . . *ac ic þurhwunige her*. In *Gen* 42. 38 Visser (ii, §815) wrongly reads *ic wurde* for *ic wurþe*.

§648. Some of the ambiguous verb-forms could be taken as indicative, e.g. *Or* 204. 3 *7 Quintius Flaminius geniedde begen þa cyningas þæt hie sealdon hiera suna to gislum* (quoted by Visser, ii, §817), for the passage continues directly *Philippus, Mæcedonia cyning, sealde Demetrias his sunu, 7 Nauiða sealde, Læcedemonia cyning, Armenan his sunu.* (Further on the interpretation of ambiguous verb-forms in such contexts, see §601.) But only five of Visser's OE examples have a verb-form which is unambiguously indicative or (as we might put it here) non-subjunctive. We are not bound to detect 'modality of non-reality' in any of them.

§649. In *Bede* 140. 27 . . . *þæt he eac swylce Eorpwald Eastengla cyning Rædwaldes sunu to þon gespeon, þæt he forlet þa idelnesse deofolgilda 7 þæm gerynum onfeng Cristes geleafan mid his mægðe Eastenglum*, Latin . . . *ut etiam regi Orientalium Anglorum Earpualdo filio Redualdi persuaderet relictis idolorum superstitionibus fidem et sacramenta Christi cum sua prouincia suscipere* (Visser, ii, §820), the

---

[140] On a somewhat similar and equally unacceptable interpretation of *Ruin* 6–9, see Mitchell 1965a, pp. 44–6.

OE indicatives emphasize the actual result and do not imply contingency. The same is true in *ChronE* 127. 2 (991) *7 on þam geare man gerædde þ man geald ærest gafol Deniscan mannum* (ii, §817). They gave tribute, for the annal states *þ wæs ærest X þusend punda.* (On such result clauses see further §2969.) The third example (ii, §819) also implies no contingency. It is from *Ps(B)* 7.5 and *geald* is merely a close gloss of Latin *reddidi*;*Ps(P)* 7. 4 has *gulde.* The fourth example —the only one of this type cited by Visser (ii, §818) before 1400 —is

GenB 468   þæt wæs lifes beam;
          moste on ecnisse   æfter lybban,
          wesan on worulde,   se þæs wæstmes onbat
          swa him æfter þy   yldo ne derede. . . .

Here too we may have to do with a straight statement, as in

Beo 142   heold hyne syðþan
          fyr ond fæstor   se þæm feonde ætwand.

Some did escape Grendel, and the *Genesis* poet may have visualized the angels, who possess eternal life, as having eaten of the fruit. If this explanation is accepted, the adjective clauses in these examples approximate to open conditions and not to rejected or imaginary conditions; see §3544. The fifth too can perhaps be otherwise explained. In

GenB 641   ac he þeoda gehwam
          hefonrice forgeaf,   halig drihten,
          widbradne welan,   gif hie þone wæstm an
          lætan wolden   þe þæt laðe treow
          on his bogum bær

(ii, §815), the ind. *forgeaf* implies that God actually gave mankind the kingdom, provided that they of their own volition left the fruit alone: cf. *Gen*(AV) 2. 15–17 'And the Lord God took the man, and put him into the garden of Eden to dress it and to keep it. . . . But of the tree of the knowledge of good and evil, thou shalt not eat of it; for in the day that thou eatest thereof thou shalt surely die.'

§650. The examples of a 'timeless' ('zeitlos') use of the preterite— cf. Mustanoja's 'preterite of unlimited time' (p. 498)—quoted by Caro (1899, p. 84) hardly warrant the term 'modal preterite'. They are *ÆCHom* ii. 566. 4 *'Amen dico uobis, receperunt mercedem suam', 'Soð ic eow secge, hi underfengon heora mede';BenR* 52. 11 *gif he sweðunga gegearwode . . . and æt nyhstan amansumunge bærnet and swingella wita þurhteah—and ongyt, þæt eal his hogu . . . naht framað, he þonne gegearwige . . . his agen gebed and ealra broðra for hine*; and *BenR* 119. 17 *Ðænce se abbod siðþan he gehadod sy, hu micele byrðene and hu hefigtyme he underfeng mid þam hade.* These are (as Caro points out) examples of an OE preterite used where MnE would prefer a perfect. So I remain to be convinced that the term 'modal preterite' has any place in a syntax of Old English.

4. INDIVIDUAL VERBS

a. Beon *and* wesan

§651. On the inflexions, see *OEG,* §768(*d*). One point needs to be made: in lW-S at any rate the forms *sindon, syndon, sind, sint,* are not necessarily contrasted with *syn.* Thus Ælfric manuscripts occasionally use *syndon* where a subjunctive is required, e.g. *ÆCHom* i. 284. 15 *Ne bepæce nan man hine sylfne, swa þæt he secge oððe gelyfe þæt ðry Godas syndon; oððe ænig had on þære Halgan þrynnysse sy unmihtigra þonne oðer* (see Pope, *Ælfric,* i. 101–2), and some Wulfstan manuscripts have *syn* where others have *sind* or *beoð* and an indicative is required, e.g. *WHom* 20(*EI*). 71 *Forþam her syn on lande ungetrywþa micle for Gode 7 for worolde, 7 eac her syn on earde on mistlice wisan hlafordswican manege* (see my comments in *NM* 70 (1969), 74–5).

§652. The use of *beon* and *wesan* in conjunction with present and second participles is discussed in §§681–858. For references to discussions of these and their other uses, e.g. as copulas and with infinitives, see the Indexes. Some other problems are of lexicographical rather than syntactic interest; note here the difference of opinion between *OED* (s.v. *be, v.*) and Jost (1909, pp. 5–6) about the exact senses of the two verbs in OE.[141] One aspect of this problem must, however, be pursued here: the respective functions of *is/sind* and *bið/beoð.* The difference between these 'present indicative' forms was said by the earliest scholars to be temporal—*is/sind* present, *bið/beoð* future, though the existence of exceptions was recognized in varying degrees; see Jost 1909, pp. 1–4.

§653. These exceptions (some of which are quoted below) led Jost to produce a theory based on the distinction between 'konkret' and 'abstrakt' sentences which Paul explained thus (I quote from Jost 1909, p. 12):

[141] For examples of their use as an independent verb, see Wülfing, ii, §381; Schrader, pp. 70–1; Visser, i, §170; and (for the poetry) 'the eighteen German dissertations'.

Ich verstehe hier und im folgenden unter einem Konkretum immer etwas, was als real existierend gesetzt wird, an bestimmte Schranken des Raumes und der Zeit gebunden; unter einem Abstraktum einen allgemeinen Begriff, bloßen Vorstellungsinhalt an sich, losgelöst von räumlicher und zeitlicher Begrenzung. . . . Normalerweise ist es das Subjekt, welches dem Satze konkrete Natur gibt. . . . Ist das Subjekt konkret, so kann der Satz nicht abstrakt sein.[142]

Jost illustrates the distinction by quoting (1909, p. 13) as 'konkret'

Beo 2529   Gebide ge on beorge   . . .

              . . .   . . .

              . . .   Nis þæt eower sið

              ne gemet mannes,   nefne min anes,

              þæt he wið aglæcean   eofoðo dæle

and as 'abstrakt'

Beo 2541   ne bið swylc earges sið!

His basic theory is that *beon* is limited to future and abstract sentences, while *wesan* is used only in concrete (1909, p. 17).

§654. But, though his work won the approval of Borst, Exter, and Flasdieck,[143] his theory was no more successful in eliminating exceptions than those he criticized. The basic rule required complicated qualifications; see Jost's own summary (1909, pp. 138-41) and that of Flasdieck. The fact that the fundamental distinction between 'concrete' and 'abstract' is not at all clear-cut—in Flasdieck's words (p. 337) 'Doch ist natürlich dieser Unterschied zwischen konkret und abstrakt nicht streng logisch durchgeführt' ['However, this distinction between concrete and abstract is not adhered to in a strictly logical manner']—meant that Jost had to admit the existence of 'formalkonkreten Sätzen' (1909, p. 28) and of 'konkret-abstrakte', though he was able to do without the 'abstrakt-konkrete' which Paul also distinguished (1909, p. 13).

§655. Moreover, there are difficulties in practice. One is hard-pressed to understand why there is a distinction between *CP* 95. 5 *Sua se*

---

[142] 'Here and in the following pages I always mean by "concrete" something that is stated to be physically existent, tied to fixed limits of space and time; and by "abstract" a general idea, which has only conceptual content, free from spatial and temporal restrictions. . . . Normally it is the subject which imparts a concrete quality to the sentence. . . . If the subject is concrete, then the sentence cannot be abstract.'

[143] Borst, in his review in *EStudien*, 41 (1910), 79-83, said that Jost's theory worked for the prose *Life of St. Guthlac* (*LS* 10), with the exception of two sentences which both represent Latin *quia Dominus adjutor tuus est*—160. 17 *forþon drihten þe bið on fultume*, but 171. 24 *forþon god þe ys on fultume*. O. Exter, in his *Beon und wesan in Alfreds Übersetzung des Boethius, der Metra und der Soliloquien* (Kiel, 1911), said it worked in these three texts too, though with exceptions. Flasdieck's article 'Das altgermanische Verbum Substantivum unter besonderer Berücksichtigung des Altenglischen' (*EStudien*, 71 (1936-7), 321-49) summarizes Jost's findings at pp. 336-9.

æppel bið betogen mid anfealdre rinde, where we are said to have *beon* in an abstract sentence (Jost 1909, p. 19), and *CP* 65. 21 *forðam is sio nosu gereaht to gesceadwisnesse*, where we are said to have *wesan* with an abstract subject in a personal construction (Jost 1909, pp. 33–4). One is perhaps less certain that *beoð* in *ÆCHom* i. 12. 33 *Ealra þæra þinga þe on neorxnawange sindon þu most brucan, and hi ealle beoð þe betæhte, buton anum treowe* must be regarded as future (cf. Jost 1909, p. 107) when one looks at sentences like *ÆCHom* i. 210. 6 *þonne we sind geladode, þonne sind we untigede; and ðonne we beoð forlætene to urum agenum cyre, þonne bið hit swilce we beon ongean asende* (Jost 1909, p. 103). The suspicion inevitably arises that sometimes at any rate the form of the verb dictates the explanation and that Jost's rules work only because he believes them.[144]

§656. Throughout Jost's book, there are examples which confirm the impression that the rules involve circular argument and really do not work. Consider *Or* 20. 14 *þæt Estland is swyðe mycel, 7 þær bið swyðe manig burh, 7 on ælcere byrig bið cyningc* and the other examples on Jost 1909, p. 88; *CP* 45. 14 *Monige menn siendon . . . ðe beoð geweorðode mid miclum 7 mid monegum Godes giefum* but *CP* 67. 2 *Ac monige menn beoð ðe noldon ðone hlisan habban ðæt hie unwiese sien* (Jost 1909, pp. 23 and 24); *CP* 249. 17 . . . *buton ðæt we sint gesceapene æfter ðære biesene ures Scippendes* but *CP* 117. 22 *Forðam we beoð mid Gode sua micle suiðor gebundne . . .* (Jost 1909, p. 29); *CP* 383. 16 *Nu se is ðonne gehaten Godes ðegn se ðe mid ðæm andan onæled bið godcundre lufan . . .* but *CP* 97. 4 *Se ðonne se ðe ðolað flowednesse his sædes he bið unclæne gecueden* (Jost 1909, pp. 33 and 34); and *CP* 249. 16 *Oððe hwæt is ure weorðscipe on ðissum eorðlicum lichoman buton ðæt . . . ?* but *CP* 343. 10 *Hwæt bið ðonne unaberendlicre to gesionne ðonne . . . ?* (Jost 1909, pp. 29 and 38). Indeed, Jost comes close to admitting that his failure was inevitable (1909, p. 55): 'Es hat sich im Verlaufe dieser Untersuchung ergeben, daß die zu Anfang aufgestellte Hauptregel, wonach konkrete Sätze *wesan*, abstrakte *beon* verwenden, mancherlei Einschränkungen erfährt. Der Unterschied zwischen konkret und abstrakt

---

[144] A striking demonstration of how fallible such observations about any particular OE example must be presented itself to me in tutorials while I was actually drafting this section. We were reading the *New English Bible* version of 1 Cor. 15. 51–2 'Listen! I will unfold a mystery: we shall not all die, but we shall all be changed in a flash, in the twinkling of an eye, at the last trumpet-call. For the trumpet will sound, and the dead will rise immortal, and we shall be changed.' Most of my undergraduates saw here an indiscriminate use of *will* and *shall*. One or two suggested that 'I will unfold . . .' might imply something stronger than mere futurity. To me, brought up on Nesfield's rules (§ 115), the existence of a regular pattern seemed possible (on the evidence of this passage alone). And this with native speakers!

ist, wie dies überhaupt nicht anders zu erwarten steht, nicht streng logisch durchgeführt.'[145]

§657. Jost's table 3 and table 5 (1909, pp. 64 and 97) show how far from satisfying his conclusions are, and must raise the question whether these distinctions ever existed. One feels that the concept of concrete and abstract sentences is too theoretical to be something which weighed with speakers of Anglo-Saxon; is not the old idea that the distinction is temporal more plausible? Jost (1909, pp. 133 ff.) feels compelled to meet this challenge. Borst (*EStudien*, 41 (1910), 81-3) seems satisfied with his reply. I must be content with the brief comment that I am not, and that I find it hard to understand how 'der ursprünglich rein zeitliche Unterschied zwischen *beon* und *wesan* ergab einen Unterschied der Satzart, den Unterschied zwischen konkreten und abstrakten Sätzen',[145a] a distinction which began to disappear at the end of the OE period (Jost 1909, p. 135). The examples cited above and below seem to agree better with the hypothesis that the intermediate stage postulated by Jost never occurred.

§658. Visser (ii, §723) claims that 'when in Old English the existential verb *beon* was the predicate and the reference was with future time, the present tense forms from the *bheu*-root (*beo, bist, biþ, beoþ*) were used with the exclusion of the other forms (*eom, eart, is, sindon, sint*)', suggesting that 'a notion of futurity may also have been present in such generic and gnomic statements as: *Beow.* 186, "Wel biþ þæm þe mot æfter deaðdæge Drihten secean" ("Well it will be for him"?)' and *Beo* 1940, quoted by Campbell (my §659) as an example of 'an invariable fact'. This point is, I think, neatly illustrated by a comparison of the sequence *wære . . . eart . . . bist* in *ÆCHom* ii. 600. 24 *Eala ðu Halige Ðrynnys, Fæder and Sunu and Halig Gast, þu ðe æfre wære, and nu eart, and æfre bist an Ælmihtig God untodæledlic . . .* with *ÆCHom* i. 262. 33 *Æfre wæs Godes rice, and æfre bið*, where (in the absence of *and nu is*) *bið* must carry a reference to both the now and the future; cf. *ÆCHom* i. 374. 20 *ic beo mid þe, and ic sende minne ðeowan Paulum ðe to frofre*. This suggestion of Visser's is in a sense a step back from Jost, almost a return to the old simple view that the distinction is temporal, seen (for example) in Clemoes's statement (*CB*, p. 201) that Ælfric's

---

[145] 'It has transpired in the course of this investigation that the main rule laid down at the beginning, according to which concrete sentences use *wesan* and abstract ones *beon*, is subject to a variety of qualifications. The distinction between concrete and abstract, as was entirely to be expected, is not adhered to in a strictly logical manner.'

[145a] 'The original, purely temporal, distinction between *beon* and *wesan* gave rise to a distinction in the type of sentence, the distinction between concrete and abstract sentences.'

'distinction between the *is, sind* forms of the verb "to be" to denote present time and the *biδ, beoδ* forms to denote future illustrates his regard for fine points of grammar'. But there is more to it than that.

§659. Mustanoja and Campbell both introduce elements other than the purely temporal. Mustanoja (p. 583) says that 'while the principal function of *wesan* is to express a state prevailing generally or at the time of speaking, that of *beon* is to express future or iterative activity'. Campbell's more cautious formulation (*OEG*, pp. 350-1) puts it somewhat differently:

The distinction of the pres. indic. tenses *eom* and *beo* is fairly well preserved in OE: *beo* expresses what is (*a*) an invariable fact, e.g. *ne biδ swylc cwenlic þeaw* 'such is not a queenly custom' [*Beow*. 1940], or (*b*) the future, e.g. *ne biδ þe wilna gad* 'you will have no lack of pleasures' [id. 660], or (*c*) iterative extension into the future, e.g. *biþ storma gehwylc aswefed* 'every storm is always allayed' (i.e. on all occasions of the flight of the Phoenix, past and to come) [*Phoen*. 185-6]; *eom* expresses a present state provided its continuance is not especially regarded, e.g. *wlitig is se wong* 'the plain is beautiful'.

There is no difficulty in finding examples which illustrate the usages mentioned by Campbell, even in later texts like those of Ælfric. (For examples from 'Alfredian' texts the reader is referred to Jost 1909 and Exter.) Thus we have the immediate present in *ÆCHom* i. 224. 1 *Ge secaδ þone Hælend: he aras: nis he her*; the continuing present in *ÆCHom* i. 34. 9 . . . *on þære byrig δe is gehaten Bethleem*; invariable fact in *ÆCHom* ii. 230. 29 *We menn beoδ mid synnum acennede: ne we beoδ be agenum dihte acennede*; future in *ÆCHom* ii. 590. 32 *and hwæt biδ þonne eal se lichama and seo sawul samod δrowiaδ . . . ?*; and, shading into iterative extension into the future, *ÆCHom* i. 2. 28 *and beoδ fela frecednyssa on mancynne ærδan þe se ende becume*, *ÆCHom* i. 20. 17 *se ylca forgyfδ cildum sawle and lif on heora modor innoδe, þonne hi gesceapene beoδ*, *ÆCHom* ii. 524. 1 . . . *se δe synnum þeowaδ, biδ ascyred fram Godes ræde*, and *ÆHom* 6. 224 *Đeah δe hwa secge be me tal oδδe hosp, hit byδ him forgyfen, gif he hit behreowsaδ*.

§660. But, as the following examples suggest, attempts to adjudicate between Campbell's formulation and that of Mustanoja seem pointless; there is too much No Man's Land. (I shall content myself here with quoting examples from Ælfric; earlier ones are given in §663.) Ælfric himself says in *ÆGram* 201. 8 *Sum ic eom is edwistlic word and gebyraδ to gode anum synderlice, forδan þe god is æfre unbegunnen and ungeendod*, a point he reiterates at *ÆCHom* ii. 236. 4-20. This is pretty striking evidence against the notion that the

invariable fact is reserved for *bið/beoð*. There are other examples
with *is/sind* referring to what seem to be invariable facts, e.g. *ÆCHom*
i. 224. 27 *forðan ðe he is God*, *ÆCHom* i. 276. 24 . . . *soðlice oðer is
se Fæder, oðer is se Sunu, oðer is se Halga Gast; ac þeahhwæðere
ðæra ðreora is an Godcundnys*, and two sentences in which the *bið*
can plausibly be explained as referring to the future, viz. *ÆCHom* i.
150. 23 *He þrowade, ac he ne ðrowað heononforð næfre eft, ac bið
æfre butan ende, eallswa ece on þære menniscnysse swa he is on
þære godcundnysse* and *ÆCHom* i. 280. 4 *Nu habbað ge gehyred
þæt se Sunu is of ðam Fæder butan ælcum anginne; forðan ðe he is
þæs Fæder Wisdom, and he wæs æfre mid þam Fæder, and æfre bið*.
And there are examples in which *is/sind* and *bið/beoð* seem to be
used indiscriminately, e.g. *ÆCHom* i. 182. 33 *Swa is þeos woruld;
hwiltidum heo is gesundful and myrige on to wunigenne, hwilon heo
is eac swiðe styrnlic, and mid mislicum þingum gemenged, swa þæt
heo for oft bið swiðe unwynsum on to eardigenne. Hwilon we beoð
hale, hwilon untrume* and *ÆCHom* i. 96. 33 *Gif we ðas gastlican
ymbsnidennysse on urum ðeawum healdað, þonne sind we Abrahames
cynnes* but *ÆCHom* i. 210. 35 . . . *forðan ðe we beoð tempel and
fætels þæs Halgan Gastes, gif we us wið fule leahtras gescyldað*.

§661. Nor am I yet convinced that Ælfric saw the distinction between present and future quite as sharply as the statement by
Clemoes (my §658) seems to suggest. There are not many examples
anywhere in OE of *is/sind* with a future reference. Those with *toweard* cited by Visser (ii, §723) scarcely qualify, since *toweard*
means 'approaching, to come'. *Mark(WSCp)* 13. 33 *ge nyton hwænne
seo tid ys*, Latin *nescitis enim quando tempus sit*, is one, for what it
is worth, and *ÆCHom* i. 68. 28 *Berað ða gyrda to wuda, and þa
stanas to sæstrande: hi synd gecyrrede to heora gecynde* may be
another, though Jost's suggestion (1909, p. 102 fn. 1) that they have
already returned to their original state attractively saves the 'rule'.
But it is not easy to press for a future interpretation of every *bið* in
ÆCHom ii. 10. 34 *Hu bið se mann tuwa acenned? Ælc man bið
acenned lichamlice of fæder and of meder, ac he ne bið Godes bearn,
buton he beo eft acenned of ðære gastlican meder* or of *beoð* in
ÆCHom ii. 230. 29 *We menn beoð mid synnum acennede: ne we
ne beoð be agenum dihte acennede* or of *bið* in *ÆCHom* i. 212. 8
*ac siððan he to cyninge gehalgod bið, þonne hæfð he anweald ofer
þæt folc*; cf. *ÆGram* 125. 7 *forþan ðe nan man ne hæt don, þæt
ðe gedon byð*. Indeed, Schrader quoted this last example (p. 71) just
after observing—in 1887—'Zu beachten ist aber, dass Ælfric
durchaus nicht bestrebt ist, dem *beon* ausschliesslich diese Bedeutung

[des Futurs] zu vindicieren und demgemäss für das Präsens mehr *wesan* zu gebrauchen.'[146]

§662. Unbiased examination of the variations in the following sequences must cast doubt on the view that Ælfric rigidly observed the various distinctions set out above: *ÆCHom* i. 4. 14 *þonne cymð se Antecrist, se bið mennisc mann and soð deofol, swa swa ure Hælend is soðlice mann and God on anum hade, ÆCHom* i. 8. 25 *he is ordfruma, forði þe he wæs æfre; he is ende butan ælcere geendunge, forðan þe he bið æfre ungeendod, ÆCHom* i. 210. 6 *þonne we sind gelaðode, þonne sind we untigede; and ðonne we beoð forlætene to urum agenum cyre, þonne bið hit swilce we beon ongean asende,* and *ÆCHom* i. 276. 27 *Ælmihtig God is se Fæder, Ælmihtig God is se Sunu, Ælmihtig God is se Halga Gast; ac þeahhwæðere ne sind ðry Ælmihtige Godas, ac an Ælmihtig God. Ðry hi sind on hadum and on naman, and an on Godcundnysse. þry, forði þe se Fæder bið æfre Fæder, and se Sunu bið æfre Sunu, and se Halga Gast bið æfre Halig Gast; and hyra nan ne awent næfre of ðam ðe he is.* It is not easy to see why we have *bið* in *ÆCHom* i. 212. 3 *Se ðe ne bið Godes tempel, he bið deofles tempel,* but *is* in *ÆCHom* i. 212. 28 *Ac ðæs mannes cristendom is herigendlic, seðe nele, for nanre ehtnysse, bugan fram Criste.* We could apply Campbell's distinction of 'invariable fact' against 'a present state provided its continuance is not especially regarded'. But taken together the examples cited here suggest that whatever distinctions once existed between *is/sind* and *bið/beoð* had begun to break down by Ælfric's time at any rate.

§663. Examples like *LawAGuProl Ðis is ðæt frið, ðæt Ælfred cyninc 7 Gyðrum cyning 7 ealles Angelcynnes witan 7 eal seo ðeod ðe on Eastænglum beoð ealle gecweden habbað,* and those already quoted above as testing Jost's rules—(§656) *Or* 20. 14 and the pairs given in §§655-6—suggest that even in the earlier phase the distinctions being discussed were not binding. This is confirmed by Jost's table 3 (1909, p. 64), where he says that in *Cura Pastoralis* 13.7 per cent of abstract sentences have *wesan,* not *beon.* Similar exceptions occur in the poetry: compare the use of *bið* and *sind* in

Phoen 355
>
> God ana wat,
> cyning ælmihtig,   hu his gecynde bið,
> wifhades þe weres;   þæt ne wat ænig
> monna cynnes,   butan meotod ana,
> hu þa wisan sind   wundorlice,
> fæger fyrngesceap,   ymb þæs fugles gebyrd;

---

[146] 'But it must be noted that Ælfric is by no means trying to claim this meaning (of the future tense) exclusively for *beon* and consequently to use *wesan* more for the present.'

contrast *Jul* 645 *þær is help gelong* || *ece to ealdre* and

Jul 182   meotud moncynnes,   in þæs meahtum sind
                 a butan ende   ealle gesceafta,

where *is* and *sind* appear in sentences in which the continuance of a present state seems to be 'regarded', with

El 605   þe synt tu gearu,
          swa lif swa deað,   swa þe leofre bið
          to geceosanne,

where we find *bið* with what seems close to a reference to the immediate future; and note the variation of *is* and *bið* in two apparently identical constructions in

Gifts 97   Nis nu ofer eorþan   ænig monna
                mode þæs cræftig,   ne þæs mægeneacen,
                þæt hi æfre anum   ealle weorþen
                gegearwade . . .

and

Gifts 8   Ne bið ænig þæs   earfoðsælig
                mon on moldan,   ne þæs medspedig,
                lytelhydig,   ne þæs læthydig,
                þæt hine se argifa   ealles biscyrge
                modes cræfta   oþþe mægendæda. . . .

But the presence of *nu* in *Gifts* 97 may provide the explanation here.

§664. Since exceptions like these exist at all periods, one may perhaps wonder whether there were ever any firm rules and despair at establishing them. But the fact that Jost's table 5 (1909, p. 97) shows *wesan* in 49.5 per cent of abstract sentences in the *Catholic Homilies* against the 13.7 per cent already quoted for the *Cura Pastoralis* confirms that the departure from what 'rules' did exist was a gradual movement, part of the continuing process of change. That this should be so is scarcely surprising in light of the general confusion of forms in ME described in *OED*, s.v. *be v.*; of Mustanoja's statement (p. 583) that '*traces* of this old use of the *b*- forms to express futurity occur in early ME and *to some extent* even later in the period' [my italics]; and of the subsequent disappearance of even these traces. The most practical solution to this problem is to accept Campbell's statement (§659) as a working hypothesis, but to bear in mind that the use of *is/sind* rather than *bið/beoð* or vice versa cannot be used to *prove* anything about the implications of a particular example.[147]

[147] The problem is complicated by the interesting riddle why the distinction in the indicative forms is syntactical while that in the subjunctive forms is dialectal (*OEG*, p. 351). Jost

b. Don

§665. The element orders vSV(?) and SvV were, of course, common enough in OE with the so-called modal verbs, e.g. *ÆCHom* i. 14. 4 *Gyse hu mihte Adam tocnawan hwæt he wære . . . ?* and *ÆCHom* i. 20. 27 *Ic wylle fordon eal mancynn mid wætere . . .* , and with the verbs *habban* and *beon/wesan*, e.g. *ÆCHom* ii. 184. 8 *hwæt hæfst þu gedon?*, *ÆCHom* i. 28. 12 *He hæfð gerymed rihtwisum mannum infær to his rice*, *BlHom* 5. 2 *forþon wæs se engel sprecende to ures Drihtnes meder*, *ÆCHom* i. 276. 17 *and æfre he bið þurhwunigende*, *ÆCHom* i. 280. 13 *Nis he geworht*, and *ÆCHom* i. 224. 10 *Galilea is gecweden 'Oferfæreld'*. One of the most important developments in the English verb system has been the extension of these patterns to the verb 'do' in the types 'Did he (not) come?', 'He did (not) come after all!', and the like. All the evidence points to the belief that these uses of 'do' developed in ME times. But the OE syntactician must ask whether they grew from any seeds apparent in OE, where *don* is used as a full verb in various senses, or vicariously to avoid repetition of a preceding verb, or as a causative. Examples of all three are given by Ellegård (see initially pp. 213–14) and Visser (i. 509–11; i. 167–82 and 511–17; and iii. 1345–6). A few comments are necessary.

§666. Ellegård (p. 16) remarks that, when the full verb was used (in apposition) with another verb,

it will appear that all through OE and ME, the explanatory verb practically always appeared in the same form as *do*: finite if *do* was finite, infinite if *do* was infinite. No unambiguous example of the infinitive after finite *do* in this type of expression—except the instance from Ælfred above [*Bo* 14. 17; see below]—is to be found until the 15th century.

Thus we find imperative of *don* + imperative in the familiar *John (WSCp)* 8. 11 *Do ga 7 ne synga þu næfre ma* (Millward (pp. 45–6) offers some more examples); present tense of *don* + present tense in *CP* 375. 8 *Ac ðonne we doð ægðer, ge we ða wætru todælað æfter kyninga herestrætum, ge eac us selfe habbað . . .* ; and past tense of *don* + past tense in *Or* 290. 21 *þa oferhogode he þæt he him aðer dyde, oþþe wiernde oþþe tigþade*. Further on this explanatory or anticipatory use, see Royster 1922, pp. 348–50. Ellegård's exception from Alfred, which is accepted by Visser (iii. 1491 and 1525), is

is not content with the latter statement. He finds no certain syntactical difference in the subjunctive in *Cura Pastoralis* (1909, p. 122) or in the plural subjunctive in Ælfric, but erects an unconvincing distinction in Ælfric's use of the singular subjunctive of the two verbs (1909, pp. 123–4). There will be an important discussion on Jost's theory in the forthcoming work by Kilpiö (my §744).

Bo 14. 17 *Swa doð nu ða þeostro þinre gedrefednesse wiðstondan minum leohtum larum.* The Latin (Book i, Metre 7) casts no light. *Met* 5. 21 reads *Swa nu þa þiostro þinre heortan ‖ willað minre leohtan lare wiðstandan.* But the context of the prose passage is such that it is reasonable to interpret *doð* as causative, with idiomatic absence of acc. *þe.* However, Visser (iii, §§1413 and 1414a)—anxious to deny the truth of the statement by Ellegård quoted above and to support his own claim that 'since infinitives . . . were frequently used as objects . . . , it is only natural to assume that they were also used in Old English after factitive *don*'—accuses Ellegård of apparent omission and cites two OE examples in which (he says) we have 'finite *don* preceding the infinitive', viz. *WPol* 123, §§173-4 *Riht is þæt munecas . . . don, swa heom ðearf is: carian æfre, hu hi swyðost magan Gode gecweman* and *WPol* 200, §55 *And we lærað, þæt preostas swa dælan folces ælmessan, þæt hig ægðer don, ge God gegladian ge folc to ælmessan gewænian.* But here *carian, gegladian,* and *gewænian,* can be explained as present subjunctive exemplifying the sequence 'finite form of *don* + finite verb', for (as Whitelock, p. 43, says of *Sermo Lupi*) 'in common with most texts of this period, *-an* can represent earlier *-on, -en,* and *-um*'. Visser also claims that eight more examples, all from Wulfstan, exemplify 'anticipative *do* + explanatory infinitive' (iii, §1413). They are essentially identical and in all of them two explanations other than Visser's present themselves. The first can be taken as typical (Visser's attribution of *Sermo Lupi* to Ælfric is just another slip): *WHom* 20(*EI*). 190 *And utan don swa us þearf is, gebugan to rihte 7 be suman dæle unriht forlætan 7 betan swyþe georne þæt we ær bræcan.* Here *gebugan, forlætan,* and *betan,* can be taken as either infinitives on *utan* parallel to the inf. *don* or (less likely) as present subjunctives parallel to *utan don.* To take them as infinitives on *don* seems to me impossible. Ellegård, not Visser, is right as far as the OE examples are concerned. Even the latter's ME examples must be viewed with suspicion; some can be taken as explanatory or anticipatory, others as causative.

§667. Royster (1922, p. 346) gives a list of alleged examples cited by Grein of '*don* . . . with a following infinitive' and says of them: 'It may be that all of these are examples of a fully developed *don* tense auxiliary. It cannot be proved that they were not felt as auxiliaries by their Old English users.' Unfortunately, I cannot find an infinitive in any of the examples in this list. (Dietze's addition, *Or* 126. 31, has *don* + an inflected infinitive.) His statement is certainly not true of the seventeen examples of *don* + simple infinitive (three from *PPs,* the rest from prose texts) or of the three prose examples of *don* + inflected infinitive he gives elsewhere (1922, pp. 337-9). There is no possibility that *Do us lufian* (which he cites thus) can mean 'Do love us' in *ÆCHom* ii. 600. 12 . . . *and do us lufian þæt þæt ðu bebytst* and I interpret *don* as causative in all twenty examples. The most likely exception is an example rejected by Ellegård (p. 16) and Visser (iii. 1517 fn. 1), viz. *PPs* 118. 25 *do me æfter þinum wordum wel gecwician*, Latin *vivifica me secundum verbum tuum*, where, Royster (1922, pp. 347-8) argues, our interpretation must depend on whether we take *gecwician* to mean 'be alive, come to life' or 'make alive, animate'. But it seems to me perverse to adopt the latter here. However, the reasons Royster (1922, pp. 345-51) gives for his belief that there were in OE 'surrounding language conditions' the existence of which 'creates a favorable attitude toward accepting auxiliary interpretation' of *don* deserve consideration.

§668. Causative *don* is found in OE with an infinitive, e.g. *PsCa6* 7. 58 *ic ofslea 7 lifgan gedom* [sic], Latin *ego occidam et uiuere faciam*; with an accusative and infinitive, e.g. *ÆCHom* i. 468. 20 *Swa swa ðu dydest minne broðor his god forlætan, and on ðinne god gelyfan, swa do ic eac ðe forlætan ðinne god, and on minne gelyfan*; and with a clause, e.g. *ÆCHom* i. 184. 16 *Doð þæt þæt folc sitte*. Ellegård (pp. 16-20, 39, and 47-56) discusses other possible examples, but does not deviate from his initial position (p. 16) that 'causative *do* + infinitive was rare indeed in Old English. Before Ælfric and Wulfstan it occurs only in slavish translations from the Latin, and it does not become a common phrase until Middle English times.' Visser (iii, §1212) agrees that 'the number of examples in Old English is very small' but objects to the notion that they should 'be looked upon as slavish translations of Latin idiom' on the strength of a few examples from Gothic and Modern Dutch. One would like stronger evidence. But future workers should note that Royster (1922, pp. 339-45), objecting to Callaway's claim (1913, p. 205) that Latin influence is 'highly probable' in the use of the infinitive after causative *don* in preference to the idiomatic *þæt* clause, prefers to view it as another manifestation of the general tendency to replace *þæt* clauses by infinitive constructions and goes on to suggest that the increase in the use of the simple infinitive after both causative and auxiliary *don* in ME can be explained by the fact that both uses were gradually developed in colloquial OE but found little written expression in OE. They should also note his later caveat (pp. 350-1):

I still hold that extensive causative use of *don* very probably preceded wide use of the verb as a tense auxiliary. And if we are willing to assume a large causative use of *don* in colloquial Old English, we may then assume auxiliary use in the same language sphere. But causative use appears liberally in early Middle English in all sorts of writing, while extensive auxiliary use does not get into the preserved record for a century and a half or two centuries later.

§669. The relative part played by these three uses of *don* in the development of the MnE periphrases lies outside the scope of this work; see Mustanoja, pp. 600-10, and Visser, iii, §§1411-76, for summaries of different views and references to wider discussions. But we must ask whether there are any OE examples. The time has come to dismiss *Or* 48. 8 *7 æfter ðæm hie dydon ægþer ge cyninga ricu settan ge niwu ceastra timbredon*, where *settan* is a past tense (*OED*, s.v. *do* III 25a; Ellegård, p. 16; and Visser, iii. 1490 fn. 2). I cannot follow Visser (ii, §731) in seeing sentences like *Mark(WSCp)* 10. 17 *hwæt do ic þ ic ece lif age* as OE prototypes of the pattern 'Do I leave this fellow tied like that?', for *do* in the four OE examples quoted by Visser is a full verb. We must, I think, agree with Ellegård (p. 20): 'I conclude that the existence of purely periphrastic auxiliary *do* in OE has not been proved.'

c. Habban

§670. For the use of *habban* + second participle to form perfect and pluperfect tenses, see §§705-33. On *habban* + infinitive, see §§950-3. Visser (i, §§649-51) gives some OE examples of special uses of *habban* of the types seen in *Bede* 74. 21 *All þas þing þære neowan ðeode Ongolcynnes in Godes geleafan gedafenað cuð habban* and *ÆCHom* ii. 310. 12 . . . *and befran ðone papan hwæt hi wæron gehæfde. þa sæde se biscop, þæt hi soðlice wæron halige mæssepreostas. Habban* is also found with the auxiliary *weorþan*, e.g. *ÆCHom* ii. 148. 1 *Æfter ðisum wordum wearð gemot gehæfd.*

d. Weorþan

§671. *Weorþan* is used as an independent verb, e.g. *ChronA* 70. 1 (868) *7 þær nan hefelic gefeoht ne wearþ* and *ChronE* 181. 8 (1052) *7 wearð him þær on anon unwræste scipe*; as a copula with nouns, adjectives, or *to* phrases, e.g. *ChronA* 28. 13 (655) *7 Mierce wurdon Cristne, ChronA* 98. 32 (918) *oþ þone first þe hie wurdon swiþe metelease*, and *Or* 56. 8 *7 hie to ðon swiðe forslagene wurdon on agþere hand, þæt hiera feawa to lafe wurdon*; and as an auxiliary— of the 'perfect/pluperfect' with second participles of intransitive verbs (see §§734-42) and of the passive with those of transitive verbs (see §§786-801). The BT(S) articles are now supplemented by Visser (i. 161, 201, and 208).

§672. Visser (ii. 673) argues that 'the present tense forms of the verb *weorðan* rivalled with the *beo, bist, við* and *beoð* forms in this [the future] function', citing in support of his view examples like *And* 1382 . . . *ende næfre* ǁ *þines wræces weorðeð*. He goes on to remark:

Sentences with the *bið* forms far outnumber those with the forms of *weorðan*; the reason for this is hard to discover, especially since the following two quotations by one and the same writer show that there was not much to choose between the two possibilities: Ælfred, Boeth. (Fox) 256. 28, 'ge þætte ær wæs, ge þætte nu is, ge þætte æfter us *bið*, eall hit is him andweard'/Ælfred, Boeth. (Fox) 20. 24 'Hwa wæs æfre, oþþe is nu, oððe hwa *wyrþ* get æfter us?'[148]

This seems a case of not seeing the wood for the trees. The reason is not far to seek; it lies in the fact that when used absolutely *weorþan* usually means something like 'to come to be, to be made, to arise, come, be' (so BT, s.v. I(1)), whereas the primary meaning of *beon* and *wesan* is rather 'to be'. The point is neatly illustrated by *ÆCHom* ii. 526. 1 *and he wæs Godes Bearn swa hraðe swa he mannes Bearn wearð*. Of course, it must not be pressed too far; BT's gloss of *weorþan* as 'be' and examples like *ÆLS* 6. 272 . . . *on ðam þrytteoðan geare æfter þam þe he munuc wæs* underline this.

§673. But the distinction is at least partly responsible for the growth of the notion that, when used with the second participle of a transitive verb to form a passive (equivalent), *beon* and *wesan* denote the resulting state and *weorþan* the process. Thus Frary tells us (pp. 15–16) 'that the same distinction between *wearð* and *wæs* occurs whether used absolutely, with a predicate noun or adjective, with a prepositional phrase, or with a past participle. *Wearð* introduces a new element or change of state; *wæs* stresses the existing state or predicates a fact or result.' I will show that this rule cannot be applied rigidly to periphrases with the second participle (see §§786–801) and am more than doubtful about its universal validity when the auxiliaries are used in the other combinations mentioned above. However, it can (I think) be reasonably claimed that closer definition of the meanings of *beon, wesan,* and *weorþan,* is a matter for the lexicographer.

§674. The ptc. *geworden* is usually found with *beon/wesan* when the sense is 'happened, came to pass', e.g. *Bede* 4. 5 . . . *under hwilcum cyninge þæt ðonne geworden wæs* and *Beo* 3078 . . . *swa us geworden is*. But it occurs with *weorþan* in *Luke(WSCp)* 1. 65 *Đa*

---

[148] Other examples (not cited by Visser) include *CP* 299. 14, *WHom* 10c. 116, *Phoen* 47, and *Phoen* 140. See further Wülfing, ii, §407, and Frary, pp. 26, 48, and elsewhere.

wearð ege geworden ofer ealle hyra nehcheburas. When it means 'agreed', it can of course be used with *habban*, e.g. *Or* 208. 28 *þeh þe Romane hæfde geworden hwene ær þæt he on Asiam faran sceolde* and

Beo 2026 hafað þæs geworden wine Scyldinga,
       rices hyrde, ond þæt ræd talað,
       . . . .

e. Onginnan, aginnan, *and* beginnan

§675. There is no doubt that OE *onginnan* and its less common variants *aginnan* and *beginnan*[149] can have the meaning 'to begin', e.g. *ÆGram* 137. 3 *inchoo, ic ongynne, ÆGram* 212. 3 *calesco, ic onginne to wearmigenne, Judg* 13. 5 *for þam þe he onginð to alysenne his folc*, Latin *et ipse incipiet liberare Israel*, and *CP* 7. 17 *ða ongan ic . . . ða boc wendan on Englisc*. It is of course a commonplace that the aphetic form *ginnen* can be used in ME with infinitives as an auxiliary of the present, e.g. *so Crist vs gynneþ lere* 'as Christ teaches us', and of the past, e.g. *he gon æten* 'he ate'. Can we detect signs of the transition in OE?

§676. According to Mustanoja (p. 611) 'OE *onginnan*, when it occurs as an auxiliary with an infinitive, can be said to carry out two principal functions: (1) it brings out the ingressive and perfective aspects of the action represented by the infinitive, and (2) it intensifies the descriptive force of the infinitive.' I do not quite understand how the same verb can bring out both the 'ingressive' and 'perfective' aspects of an action and in any case I do not consider 'aspect' a valid category for OE; see §§865–73. Nor do I understand what is meant by the statement 'it intensifies the descriptive force of the infinitive'; cf. Visser, iii, §1477. So I shall content myself with asking whether there are clear examples in OE in which *onginnan* and its variants have a weakened sense approaching the ME auxiliary use.

§677. This is a very subjective question. Mustanoja (p. 610) quotes *ongann sprecan* as an example in which 'OE *onginnan* . . . retains its original full meaning "to begin" '. Yet Terasawa (*Poetica* (Tokyo), 1 (1974), 90) quotes *Dream* 27 *Ongan þa word sprecan wudu selesta* and the similar examples in *Dream* 65, 67, and 73, in defence of his claim that 'it is a fairly well-attested fact that OE *onginnan* is

---

[149] The aphetic form first appears in ME 'c1230 (?a1200)', according to *MED*, s.v. *ginnen* v. But see BTS and BTC, s.v. *ginnan*.

sometimes used in functions similar to those of ME *gan'*. Mustanoja (p. 611) finds 'a sense approaching that of the periphrastic *do'* in

GenA 2717   þa ongan Abimæleh   Abraham swiðan
                woruldgestreonum   and him his wif ageaf.

BTS flirts with the notion of an auxiliary use by observing (s.v. *on-ginnan* I): 'with almost the sense of the auxiliary *do*. Cf. later *gan* with infinitive:—*Ongan ic steppan forð, Sat.* 248.' Terasawa (*Poetica* (Tokyo), 1 (1974), 90-2) adds *Husb* 26 *Ongin mere secan* and *Beo* 244 *No her cuðlicor cuman ongunnon* ‖ *lindhæbbende* (where Wrenn takes *cuman . . . ongunnon* as a periphrastic preterite) and cites examples from the Gospels in which *onginnan* and *beginnan* represent Greek ἄρχομαι where it 'is more or less losing its full meaning of "begin" '. But these latter, he admits, cannot be conclusive, for they depend on what the OE translator thought ἄρχομαι meant.

§678. Of the examples from the poetry quoted in §677, I can only say that it seems to me quite reasonable to argue that the poet intended the idea of 'beginning' in all of them. Thus in *Beo* 244 the fact that Wrenn translates his alleged periphrastic preterite as a perfect 'have . . . come' is not significant, since 'Never did warriors come here more openly' would have done as well; see §§634-5. But his interpretation seems to run contrary to expectation; the point (it could be argued) is that the visit to Denmark is just beginning and the coastguard is uncertain whether to allow it to continue. Here I can, I think, reasonably hand over this problem to the lexicographers (see BT(S), s.vv.) and to the syntacticians of Middle English (see Mustanoja, pp. 610-15).

f. Hatan *and* lætan?

§679. Royster (1922, p. 351) suggests that '*hatan* is used, also, as a mere tense-auxiliary', citing in support *ChronE* 146. 2 (1015) *7 se cyng þa genam eall heora æhta 7 het nimon Sigeferðes lafe 7 gebringon binnon Mealdelmes byrig*, where he detects—but I hesitate to accept—'convertible use of the simple preterite and *hatan* plus infinitive', and examples from *Genesis* and *Exodus* such as *Gen* 12. 18 *Farao ða het clypian Abram*, Latin *Vocauitque Pharao Abram*, where he comments that '*het* plus infinitive is, furthermore, used frequently to translate a simple Latin past tense', but where some of his other examples suggest that the equation is too simple. Thus in *Exod* 4. 22 *þonne cweð ðu to him: Drihten het þe secgan þas þing, Israhel is min frumcenneda sunu*, Latin *Dicesque ad eum: Haec dicit*

Dominus: Filius meus primogenitus Israel, the presence of *þe* gives a different twist, and in *Gen* 40. 22 *þone operne he het hon on gealgan*, Latin *Alterum suspendit in patibulo*, Pharaoh is unlikely to have carried out the execution personally. Here perhaps we can detect the translator's desire to remove the possibility of misconception rather than exact equivalence between the original and the translation.

§680. Royster (1922, pp. 351-3) also detects 'synonimity [*sic*] of *hatan* and *lætan* . . . convertible use of the two verbs' in examples like *ChronA* 26. 15 (643) *ꝼ se Cenwalh het atimbran þa ciricean on Wintunceastre* and *ChronF* 28. 16 (648) *Her wearð getimbrod ð mynster on Winceastre þ Cynwalh cing let macian* and goes on to quote examples like *ChronE* 195. 3 (1066) *On þissum geare man halgode þet mynster æt Westmynster on Cildamæssedæg* in support of the proposition that sometimes—as in examples like *ChronC* 192. 20 (1065) *And Eadweard kingc . . . þ mynster þar let halgian . . . on Cildamæssedæig*—'let' is merely a form element in an analytical expression of past action . . . has lost its causative signification . . . [is] scarcely more than a periphrasis for the passive voice'. I am reluctant to lose the nuances which I detect in these examples. (The important article by Nagucka on 'The grammar of *hatan*' (*SAP* 11 (1980), 27-39), which includes a discussion of the causative use of *hatan*, came to my attention when this book was at press.)

5. PERIPHRASTIC FORMS

a. Terminology

§681. This term is often used with special reference to examples of the pattern *beon/wesan* + present participle, which have been variously described as periphrastic tenses (Pessels), progressive forms (Püttmann and Curme), and periphrastic forms (various writers). Åkerlund contrasted the indefinite (or simple) with the definite (or progressive) forms, Raith spoke of 'einfache und umschriebene Verbalformen', and Nickel of simple and expanded forms (SF(F) and EF(F) respectively). E. Buyssens *Les Deux Aspectifs de la conjugaison anglaise au XXe siècle* (Paris, 1968) finds the various names for simple and expanded tenses unsatisfactory and calls them the first and second aspects. This seems even more unsatisfactory: see §865. I follow Campbell (*OEG*, §728) in using 'periphrastic form' as a general term in opposition to 'simple (independent) form'. The term is made specific for OE by the following qualifications: periphrastic

forms with the present participle (§§682-701); periphrastic forms
with the infinitive (§§996-9); the periphrastic perfect and pluperfect (§§702-43); the periphrastic passive (§§744-858).

b. Periphrastic forms with the present participle

(1) Bibliographical notes

§682. The main contributions to this much-discussed subject are
listed in Mitchell 1976*b*, p. 478 fn. 1. The remarks which follow
were already in type when Part III, Second Half, of F. Th. Visser's
An Historical Syntax of the English Language appeared in 1973.
Visser's discussion (§§1798-889) does not affect my conclusions,
but is a convenient source of further examples. Matsunami, whose
articles did not come to my notice until 1980, also discusses these
periphrases (1958, pp. 171-2, and 1966*b*, pp. 37-49). He did not
have access to Nickel's work.

(2) The patterns

§683. In MnE the combination verb + present participle is felt as
a verbal periphrasis only when the verb is a form of 'to be'. Whether
such combinations with *beon/wesan* are truly verbal in OE is doubtful but is discussed below. Examples with *weorþan* appear occasionally, as Mossé (1938, §§263-6), Raith (pp. 115-16), and Matsunami (1966*b*, pp. 48-9), noted. Visser (iii, §§1798-9), while missing
some of their examples, added a few more but not enough to justify
for OE his observation that

the type 'he wearþ gesionde', 'he wearþ cweþende' so frequently occurs in Old
and early Middle English that one wonders how it is that in none of the existing
historical grammars of English—apart from F. Mossé's *Histoire de la Forme
Périphrastique* Être + *Participe Présent*—adequate attention is paid to it, especially so since it may have played an important rôle in the development, and
even the proliferation of the 'progressive' or 'expanded' form.

The verbal character of these combinations is even more doubtful.
The variety of patterns—naturally less in OE than in ME—is exemplified below.

Present indicative and subjunctive with present reference

ÆCHom i. 386. 19 *and gecum to minum ðeowan Saulum, se is biddende minre miltsunge mid eornestum mode*, *ÆCHom* ii. 500. 34
*Martinus me bewæfde efne mid ðyssere wæde, þeah ðe he ungefullod
gyt farende sy*, and *ChronE* 36. 33 (675) . . . *þa wurðe he efre
wuniende mid God Ælmihti on heuenrice*.

Present indicative and subjunctive with future reference

ÆCHom i. 160. 15 *ac heo . . . bið gehealden to ðam ecan deaðe, þær þær heo æfre bið on pinungum wunigende* and *ÆCHom* ii. 74. 12 *. . . þæt hi symle þa misweaxendan bogas of ascreadian, þæt ða toweardan ðeonde beon.*

Past indicative and subjunctive with past reference

ÆCHom i. 66. 15 *Efne ðaða se apostol þas lare sprecende wæs, ða bær sum wuduwe hira suna lic to bebyrgenne, ÆCHom* i. 374. 5 *Petrus wearð æfterweard þus cweðende . . . , ÆLS* 1. 6 *. . . hi cwædon þæt Crist godes sunu nære æfre mid þam halgan fæder wuniende* (there is room for argument about the exact time-reference of this example), and *ÆCHom* ii. 152. 32 *þa wearð þæt halige lic hal on eorðan gemet, gesundful licgende, swilce he slapende wære.*

Past subjunctive referring to the future-in-the-past

ÆCHom i. 124. 25 *ac he demde þæt he sceolde beon ascyred fram manna neawiste, gif his hreofla wyrsigende wære* and *ÆCHom* ii. 252. 32 *. . . hi cwædon be Cristes blode, þæt seo wracu wære on him wunigende, and on heora bearnum.* The preterite indicative in *ÆCHom* i. 246. 16 is noteworthy; see §3612.

Imperative

ÆCHom i. 64. 15 *Beoð blowende and welige hwilwendlice, þæt ge ecelice wædlion* and *ÆCHom* ii. 564. 24 *Beon eower lendena ymbgyrde, and eower leohtfatu byrnende.*

Modal verb + beon/weorþan

ÆCHom ii. 44. 30 *. . . to ði þæt hi sceoldon beon byrnende and caue to Godes willan, ÆCHom* ii. 324. 34 *. . . þæt se wisdom mage on him wunigende beon*, and *WHom* 20(*EI*). 22 *gif hit sceal heonanforð godiende weorðan.* Wülfing (ii. 39-43) and Visser (iii, §2143) give further examples of these patterns.

§684. I have found no examples of either the (plu)perfect 'has (had) been taking' or of the passive 'is (was) being taken' or of combinations involving them. This is not surprising in view of the late appearance of the equivalents of the participles 'been' and 'being'; see §1099.

(3) *Functions*

§685. The obvious question 'What are the functions of this periphrasis in OE?' cannot be answered with any certainty by modern grammarians, who cannot assume that any combination of *beon/ wesan* + present participle is purely verbal merely because it can be so taken—the participle may be adjectival, appositive, or an agent noun; see Mitchell 1976*b*, pp. 479-83. And even those who do assume this find themselves unable to decide exactly what nuance any particular OE periphrasis conveys. Sometimes, in both the present and the past, it seems to refer to a specific moment, sometimes to a continuing process,[150] either serving as the frame for another action or being contrasted with a general truth, with an action presented as finished, or with a 'point action'; see ibid., pp. 483-4.

§686. Such examples suggest that the periphrasis had a significance of its own—one perhaps not so far removed from that of the modern equivalent. But other examples suggest the opposite. These include the not uncommon ones in which a periphrasis and a simple verb appear in parallel clauses or sentences, in some of which at any rate a modern translator could not possibly use the periphrasis, e.g. *Or* 8. 14 *Europe hio onginð, swa ic ær cwæþ, of Danai þære ie, seo is irnende of norþdæle, of Riffeng þæm beorgum, þa sindon neh þæm garsecge þe mon hateð Sarmondisc; 7 seo ea Danai irnð þonan suðryhte on westhealfe Alexandres herga*; see further Mitchell 1976*b*, pp. 484-7. These suggest that the two forms were sometimes at any rate mere stylistic variants. The fact that the eleventh-century reviser of Gregory's *Dialogues* greatly reduces the number of periphrases— of fifty-six noted by Scheler (pp. 55-6) in MS *C*, only fifteen remain in MS *H*—and never uses one where MSS *C* and *O* have a simple verb form (Yerkes, pp. 215-18) obviously reflects a personal preference. But it also tells against the view that the periphrasis had full and unambiguous verbal value even in late OE.

§687. However, there is fairly general agreement that OE periphrases sometimes express limited or perpetual duration, e.g. *ÆLS* 20. 125 *and hi siððan buta ðrittig geara wæron wunigende butan hæmede* and *LS* 34. 620 *and he Malchus ealle þa word gehyrde and æfre wæs his uneaðnys wexende*. As in MnE, the periphrasis expressing duration shades into that expressing habitual action when an adverb (expression or element) is used, e.g. *LS* 34. 620 above, *LS* 34. 220, and *ÆCHom* i. 406. 26 *and he hi gehælde and wæs lærende þæt folc dæghwomlice binnan ðam temple*. In such examples the so-called 'characterizing' function can often be detected (Nickel 1966, p. 265); a popular OE example is *Or* 130. 31 *he wæs sinþyrstende monnes*

---

[150] Samuels (*MÆ* 31 (1962), 147-8) has rightly pointed out the dangers of pressing this distinction too far.

blodes.[151] *ÆLS* 5. 417 . . . *to ðam gode þe bið eardigende on heo-fonum*—with *bið* implying 'always'—and *ÆLS* 1. 41 *þæs an scyp-pend wat ealle þing . . . Symble he bið gyfende*—where we have *symble*—might belong here too. But duration can also be expressed by a simple verb form, either alone or with an adverb, e.g. *ÆCHom* i. 184. 5 *þa se Hælend gesæt up on ðære dune . . .* and *ÆCHom* i. 58. 17 *and [he] symle syððan Drihtne folgode.* So these distinctions are not grammatical; they depend on context and/or adverbs or adverb expressions.

§688. There are examples without an adverbial element into which it is possible to read the idea of habitual and recurrent action, e.g. *ChronA* 76. 2 (878) *7 þæs on Eastron worhte Ælfred cyning lytle werede geweorc æt Æþelinga eigge, 7 of þam geweorce was winnende wiþ þone here,* quoted by Mossé (1938, §233) and *ÆCHom* ii. 316. 19 *Ge beoð mine frynd, gif ge wyrcende beoð ða ðincg ðe ic bebeode eow to gehealdenne.* But these are at best dubious; the idea could well be that of a continuing state of warfare or good deeds rather than a recurring series.

§689. The periphrasis is often used under Latin influence in the glosses and in closely translated texts. But even here the equivalence is far from exact and the use far from consistent. For details see Mitchell 1976*b*, pp. 487-9. Nor was consistency a characteristic of texts which were less influenced by the Latin original or of texts which are native prose. As Nickel has shown (1966, pp. 83-207), the nature of the subject-matter and the preferences of the translator or writer are among the factors which cause variations. Perhaps the most striking are to be seen in the *Blickling Homilies*—Nickel's figures (1966, pp. 201 and 206) show no periphrases in homilies 3, 9, 15, and 16; eighty-seven in homily 13; and sixty-nine in the remaining fourteen homilies. But this text is not alone; see Mitchell 1976*b*, p. 489.

§690. It is clear then that OE shows no uniformity in the use of the periphrases with the present participle; as in MnE there are variations from author to author[152] and within the same text. And if modern

---

[151] Another is *ÆLS* 1. 52, discussed by Åkerlund (p. 11), Aronstein (pp. 11-12), Nickel (1966, p. 266 fn. 822), and Curme (1913, pp. 162-3). But there is no adverb in this example —or indeed in several others quoted by Nickel (1966, p. 266). So *creopende* is perhaps better regarded as nominal or adjectival rather than verbal in function.

[152] The most complete statistics on this point have been given by Nickel, whose 'K-Wert' compares the number of periphrases with the total number of verbal expressions and is obtained by the formula $EF/(EF + SF) \times 10,000$ (Nickel 1966, pp. 17-23). So, for the

scholars, who have the benefit of native informants and intonation patterns, cannot reach agreement about the exact functions of the periphrasis in MnE, it is not to be expected that agreement will be reached for OE, where these aids are lacking; where (as Campbell puts it in *RES* 18 (1967), 443) 'what is there in the Latin is not always what the translator chooses to say'; where it is dangerous to assume that a periphrasis is identical in function with its MnE verbal equivalent; where what seems to be a present participle may be adjectival or an agent noun rather than verbal—in short, where many examples cannot be interpreted with certainty.

§691. More important than statistics is a consideration of certain tendencies which are apparent in all texts, though naturally with variations.[153] First the verbs which on Nickel's evidence display periphrastic forms tend to be 'imperfective' (defined by Mustanoja (p. 445) as verbs expressing an activity 'durative in character, i.e. . . . . conceived as a continuous line in time, the beginning and end of which we do not see or think about') and to belong to certain semantic groups—verbs of rest, e.g. *wunian*; of movement, e.g. *faran*; of speaking, e.g. *cweþan*; and of physical action, e.g. *feohtan*; and verbs which express a state or a change of state, e.g. *libban* and *growan*, or a mood, e.g. *sorgian*. A special favourite with Ælfric is *wunian*— twenty-seven per cent of his periphrases have it (Nickel 1966, p. 190) —while *cweþan*, *gangan*, and *sprecan*, are common in the *Blickling Homilies* (1966, p. 201). Second, they tend to be intransitive; even in *Bede*, where an accusative object is more frequent, the majority of periphrases have no object or a prepositional one (1966, p. 173). Third, there are some grammatical tendencies. The periphrases are more often found in the third person singular or plural; this is true even in the *Boethius* where one might have expected examples in the first or second person in the frequent passages of dialogue (Nickel 1966, p. 104). They are often accompanied by temporal, local, or modal, adverb modifiers (1966, *passim* and p. 328); this is less

Chronicle, where there are fifty-two periphrases in a total of 7,658 verbal expressions, simple and periphrastic, the K-value is (52 × 10,000)/7658 = 68 (Nickel 1966, p. 207). This can also be expressed in terms of the percentage of periphrases in the total number of verbal expressions; a K-value of 68 is 0.68 per cent. But his figures are not always complete and not always sufficiently analysed. In view of this and of the fact that any figures can be only approximate because of the difficulties of classification discussed above, we should not perhaps take the statistics too seriously. But the general tendencies are clear: apart from the aberrant *BlHom* 13, the periphrasis is most common in certain narrative parts of *Orosius* and *Bede* and least common in the more meditative or more prosaic texts and in the poetry.

[153] Except where otherwise acknowledged, the information given in this section is based on Nickel's discussions, especially 1966, pp. 99-107, 120-5, 135, 159-61, 171-4, 190-5, and 199-204. We would have been even more in his debt had he been able to make his summaries more adequate and to provide Indexes.

frequent in the *Blickling Homilies* and in the genuine and pseudo-Wulfstan (1966, p. 202). A periphrasis may occur in principal clauses and in subordinate clauses of all types, especially in adjective clauses (1966, pp. 327-8). Liggins (1970, pp. 310-11) tells us that in the three narratives—*Bede, Orosius*, and the *Dialogues*—'past tenses far outnumber present forms, while it is the present periphrastics which prevail in *CP, Bo* and *Sol*. Neither of these things is surprising.'

§692. Other tendencies have already been discussed. The periphrasis may refer to a specific moment[154] or to a continuing process which serves as a frame for another action or is contrasted with a general truth, with an action presented as finished, or with a 'point action'; it may express duration or habitual or recurring action.

§693. But these are only tendencies. For, as Nickel remarks in his English summary (1966, p. 391): 'Within the Old English verbal system the *EF* is a locution still in process of development. Consequently it is subject to many fluctuations in use. Its use, however, shows clear tendencies which are not dissimilar to those apparent in modern English.'[155] Even Nickel has not completely avoided the danger of stressing these tendencies at the expense of the fluctuations; we must agree with Campbell (*RES* 18 (1967), 443) that 'while there is no reason to doubt the continuous history of the English expanded form, Dr. Nickel tends to exaggerate the similarity of its use in Old and Modern English'. Stylistic nuances are, of course, apparent. But they cannot be further systematized.

§694. This has not prevented the expenditure of scholarly ingenuity in attempts to do so. I have discussed—only to reject—the elaborate system proposed by Mossé (1938, §§201-80 and p. 126) and the suggestions that the OE periphrasis was used with passive, intensive, and inchoative, functions; see Mitchell 1976*b*, pp. 490-1. Yet, despite this and despite our inability to decide whether the participle is adjectival, appositive, or an agent noun, or whether it combines with *beon/wesan* in a truly verbal periphrasis, there can be no doubt that we have in these combinations the genesis of the MnE continuous tenses. How did they originate?

---

[154] See Nickel 1966, p. 257. The reservations expressed by Wattie (pp. 135-6) illustrate the dangers of working with too few examples.

[155] For the same statement in German see Nickel 1966, p. 266; for comments on previous discussions about the uses of the OE periphrasis see Nickel 1966, pp. 233-8.

(4) *Origin*

§695. The fact that the periphrasis is most common in texts translated from or based on Latin not unnaturally led to the notion that it
was of Latin origin. Thus Raith (p. 109) says: 'Die Umschreibung ist
das Ergebnis einer in den Klöstern aufgekommenen Übersetzungs-
technik, die um eine möglichst wortgetreue Wiedergabe der lat. Vorlage bemüht war. Sie hat sich dann von der lat. Vorlage abgelöst und
wird unabhängig davon gebraucht. . . .'[156] But some earlier writers
had seen in the OE usage a certain independence of Latin—Pessels
(p. 57) speaks of 'the Anglo Saxon significance of this tense' and
Püttmann (p. 451) of the 'Bedeutung der angelsächsischen Konstruk-
tion'—or had even admitted the possibility that it might have been
native. Thus Pessels (p. 74) remarks: 'If the periphrasis is not native,
the freedom and frequency of its use shows that it was early naturalized and thoroughly', and Mossé (1938, §281) speaks of it as 'tour
importé du latin ou simplement vivifié par l'usage latin'. Scheler
(pp. 66-7) saw two factors at work—'der lateinische Einfluß' and
'die innersprachlichen, heimischen Kräfte'.

§696. Nickel—somewhat harshly, it seems to me—dismisses
Scheler in three lines on the ground that he introduces hardly any
new ideas (1966, p. 15) and, like King Alfred in his preface to the
Cura Pastoralis, seems to exaggerate the faults of his predecessors
(1966, p. 205):

Man hat bisher den Einfluß der Glossen und Interlinearversionen auf die Entstehung der *EF* weit überschätzt. Umgekehrt hat man die Möglichkeit gewisser
innersprachlicher altenglischer Tendenzen in der Verwendung dieser Konstruktionen in den außerhalb der Glossen liegenden weniger wörtlichen Übersetzun-
gen unterschätzt bzw. manchmal sogar ganz außer acht gelassen.[157]

But his discussions—see Nickel 1966, pp. 268-300, and id. 1967—
are decisive in demonstrating that the OE periphrasis with the
present participle is not of purely Latin origin. In his English summary (1966, p. 390) he writes: 'Hence in verbal [? literal] translations the use of the *EF* is strongly influenced by the system of Latin
whereas in other cases it represents an idiomatic, native grammatical
category. This ambivalence is one of the most striking characteristics
of the Old English *EF*.' In the course of this attack he produced

---

[156] 'The periphrasis is the result of a translation technique which developed in the mona-
steries, whose aim was to produce a version which adhered as closely as possible to the Latin
original. It then became separated from the Latin original, and was used independently of it.'
[157] 'The influence of glosses and interlinear versions on the origin of the *EF* has hitherto
been greatly exaggerated. Conversely, the possibility that certain tendencies inherent in the
OE language are at work in the examples of this construction in the less literal translations,
outside the glosses, has been underestimated or in some cases even totally ignored.'

three main arguments 'against regarding it as a mere artificial device for facilitating translations from Latin into OE' (1967, p. 262). These are (i) 'there are a number of EFF which do not render any of the Latin constructions in question'; (ii) 'the vast majority of the relevant Latin constructions are rendered by SFF or other constructions and not by EFF'; (iii) 'the EF already has quite clearly defined functions within the OE verbal system' (1967, p. 262). So he concludes (1967, p. 262): 'Since on the one hand EFF occur only sporadically in the other Germanic dialects, and since on the other hand OE EFF are more or less independent of Latin, we must assume that the EF developed independently in OE.'

§697. Nickel—perceptively and, I believe, rightly—sees the OE periphrasis as the product of a syntactic blend of three constructions which (as I have pointed out in §685) are often difficult to distinguish. This blend was assisted by several factors—'the tendency to re-establish the system of aspectual relations, which had broken down in primitive OE'; 'the general trend in OE to build up a so called analytic form system using free instead of bound forms'; and 'Latin periphrastic constructions, particularly appositive and absolute participle constructions, [which] favoured the development of the OE EF' (Nickel 1967, p. 263).

§698. The first construction is the verb 'to be' + a predicative adjective. Sweet wrote (*NEG*, §2204): 'They were no doubt originally formed on the analogy of the combination of the verb "be" with adjectives, so that such a paraphrase as *hie wæron blissiende* "they were rejoicing" was felt to be intermediate between *hie blissodon* "they rejoiced" and *hie wæron bliþe* "they were glad".' Both Åkerlund (p. 9) and Curme (1913, p. 159) spoke of the adjectival function of the predicative participle. Thus (to use Nickel's examples) we have patterns like *hyge is bliþe* and alongside them those like *hyge is blissiende*. 'The next step was the integration of these structures into the verbal system, where they are opposed to simple forms such as *blissaþ*' (Nickel 1967, p. 270).

§699. The second construction is the appositive participle seen in *he wæs on temple lærende his discipulas* and perhaps in *þa he on temple wæs lærende his discipulas*. But the latter is ambiguous—*wæs lærende* need not be divided by a pause (*wæs, lærende*), but can be taken as a verbal periphrasis (*wæs lærende*). 'It is possible', says Nickel (1967, p. 271), 'that this ambiguity reflects a historical transition:

appositive participle → predicative participle.' However, he concludes cautiously (1967, p. 272):

If EFF in OE do not actually owe their existence to [OE] appositive participle constructions they were at least strongly supported by them. There can be no doubt about that. A similar supporting influence can also be ascribed to constructions of the type *he sæt lærende, he cwom ridende*, i.e. first participles with verbs of state or motion.

§700. The third construction is the verb 'to be' + an agent noun in *-end*. Nickel believes 'that this is in fact the most likely source for the EF' and gives seven different reasons for this (1967, pp. 272-4). Briefly the point is this. Since *ehtan* may govern the genitive, we may have either an agent noun or a participle in *hie wæron ehtende cristenra monna*. This ambiguity too may reflect a historical transition. Visser (i, §372) has the same idea:

It is clear that there was an important difference between 'he wæs *ehtend* cristenra manna' and 'he wæs *ehtende* cristenra manna', the first sentence meaning 'he was a persecutor of Christians', the second 'he was persecuting Christians'. [But see my §974.] But, since the total meaning of the sentences is practically equivalent, and perhaps also, because with a plural subject the ending *-end* of the nomina agentis appeared as *-ende* and was consequently not formally distinguished from the *-ende* of the present participle, . . . confusion may have set in. . . .

§701. Nickel concludes (1967, p. 274): 'However, the EF in OE does not owe its existence to any single one of the constructions discussed, i.e. predicative adjectives, appositive participles, the type *he sæt lærende*, and agent nouns, but rather to a blending of all of them.' We can, I think, accept this gratefully.[158]

c. The periphrastic perfect and pluperfect

(1) General

§702. There are three auxiliaries in common use—*habban, beon/wesan*, and *weorþan*. (On *agan*, see §743.) With transitive verbs, with which only *habban* is used, we have to do with four elements—subject, *habban*, second participle, and object—as in MnE 'He has hit the boy'. With intransitive verbs there are of course only three—subject, *habban/wesan/weorþan*, and second participle—as in MnE 'He has come' and 'He is come'. As the basic paradigms set out in §§1094-8 show, the MnE pattern 'He will have hit the boy' occasionally occurs, but 'He will have been hitting the boy' is not represented in OE. *Habban* + second participle can express the future perfect; see §723.

---

[158] At iii, §§1852-60, Visser comes down in favour of the view that the periphrasis is of native, not Latin, origin. But his failure to take cognizance of Nickel 1967 means that his discussion is outdated.

§ 703. These combinations are found in principal and subordinate clauses in the poetry and in all kinds of prose—narration, description, conversation, argument, and so on; essential qualifications are discussed below where appropriate. The relative order of the elements to one another and their position in the sentence varies with the type of clause and with the demands of emphasis, style, and (in poetry) metre.[159] The main discussion on element order will be found in chapter IX. But the position of the second participle in relation to the verb and to the direct object (when it occurs) is dealt with here because it is important for a consideration of the function of these periphrases in OE and for their subsequent history. The presence of an adverb or adverb phrase between the verb and the participle—as in *ÆCHom* i. 340. 23 *We habbað gelomlice gesewen þæt* . . . and *ÆCHom* i. 292. 10 *and ðone geleafan God hæfð mid manegum wundrum getrymmed and gefæstnod*—has, however, been disregarded here since it can occur in all periods of English. Other elements too may intervene, as will be clear from the examples quoted below. Sometimes the result is a pattern which is possible in MnE, sometimes one which is not. A full treatment of the development of the periphrastic perfect and pluperfect in OE would demand consideration of these patterns and of their relative frequency in different kinds of clauses in texts of the different periods of OE; cf. the methods I adopted in 'Syntax and Word-Order in *The Peterborough Chronicle* 1122-1154', *NM* 65 (1964), 113-44. This is not possible here. So all intervening elements have been disregarded in the table in § 706. None the less, some significant results do emerge.

§ 704. Future workers will also need to bear in mind the distinction made by Visser (iii, §§ 2116-22) between 'I had him cornered'—type (*a*)—and 'I have had an eye-tooth extracted [by my dentist]'—type (*b*): 'Type (*b*) can be told from type (*a*) by the fact that the activity referred to by the infinitive of the past participle is not performed by the person denoted by the subject of the sentence, but by a different person.' He records no OE examples of type (*b*) in § 2118. The three OE examples in §§ 2119-20 are or could be type (*a*). In *Luke(Ru)* 14. 19 *hæfe mec gilefenne*, Latin *habe me excusatum*, only the giver of the feast can excuse. In *LS* 34. 402 *and*

---

[159] Trnka (p. 159) observes that 'in the Anglo-Saxon poetry the periphrastic perfect is almost exclusively found in direct speech'. If by this is meant that combinations of a present tense of *habban* and a second participle are almost exclusively found within inverted commas in modern editions, the figures for *Beowulf* support the statement—thirteen examples out of fifteen conform, the exceptions being *Beo* 1196 and 1928. But of the thirty-three combinations of a past tense of *habban* and a second participle, only two (*Beo* 2104 and 2145) conform. Four (*Beo* 117, 1599, 2301, 2726) are in dependent speech.

[*ælmihtig god se milda*] *hine þa na lengc ahwænedne habban nolde* and *WHom* 5. 109 (§718), God is in my opinion both the wisher and the doer.

(2) *The periphrases with* habban

§705. These are found in both principal and subordinate clauses. The principal clauses may be affirmative (examples in §711), negative, e.g. *CP* 447. 12 *næfð he no forlæten ðone truwan 7 ðone tohopan his gehwearfnesse*, interrogative, e.g. *Bo* 17. 17 *Habbe ic þe awer benumen þinra gifena . . . ?*, or exclamatory, e.g. *Bo* 50. 13 *hu þu me hæfst afrefredne*. . . . Caro gives further examples in his table I (1896, pp. 412–21), but is in error when he classifies *GenB* 791 *Hwæt, þu Eue, hæfst y fele gemearcod uncer sylfra sið* as imperative. In his table II (1896, pp. 422–30) Caro records examples in all types of subordinate clause except those of purpose. This is not surprising. The periphrasis can occur in a clause of result, e.g. *ÆCHom* i. 170. 9 *Swa hold is God mancynne, þæt he hæfð geset his englas us to hyrdum*, but not in one of purpose.

§706. Caro gives fifteen combinations of the four elements subject-*habban*-object-second participle, with lists of the types of clause in which they occur (1896, pp. 406–8) and with examples (table VI at 1896, pp. 444–9). But his classification is haphazard and fails to consider some important distinctions. The system used below is my own, but I acknowledge gratefully the basis supplied by G. Hoffmann in his 1934 Breslau dissertation. I distinguish patterns (1)–(8) as shown in the tables which follow.[160]

TABLE 1

Basic order	Accusative object		Gen./dat. object	Prep. phrase object	Noun clause object
	Ptc. inflected	Ptc. uninflected	Ptc. uninflected	Ptc. uninflected	Ptc. uninflected
1. *hæfþ* + ptc. + obj.	Yes	Yes	Yes	Yes	Yes
2. ptc. + *hæfþ* + obj.	No	Yes	Yes	No	Yes
3. ptc. + obj. + *hæfþ*	No	No	No	No	No

---

[160] BTS (s.v. *habban* B. II(2a)) quotes *Or* 294. 15 *þa gelædde Theodosius eft fird wið him twæm to þære ilcan clusan þe he ær hæfde wið Maximus* as an example in which 'the participle has to be supplied from the context'; 'had [led an army]' is the suggested translation. The account seems confused, for Theodosius here appears to march against a *cluse* which has already been destroyed at *Or* 294. 2. However, some such sense as 'had at his disposal, got, took' for *hæfde* would suit.

The examples given in the sections which follow can be supplemented from Wülfing (ii, §§412–13) and from Caro 1896, pp. 392–403 and 410–11, from tables I and II in Caro 1896, and from Caro 1899, pp. 67, 69, 74–5, 77–8, and 84.

TABLE 2

Basic order	Accusative object		Gen./dat. object	Prep. phrase object	Noun clause object
	Ptc. inflected	Ptc. uninflected	Ptc. uninflected	Ptc. uninflected	Ptc. uninflected
4. _hæfþ_ + obj. + ptc.	Yes	Yes	Yes	Yes	No
5. obj. + _hæfþ_ + ptc.	Yes	Yes	Yes	Yes	No
6. obj. + ptc. + _hæfþ_	Yes	Yes	Yes	No	No

TABLE 3

Basic order	No object
7. _hæfþ_ + participle	Yes
8. participle + _hæfþ_	Yes

§ 707. These tables show all the possible arrangements of the three elements concerned; _hæfþ_ stands for any finite form of _habban_. The word 'Yes' indicates that the pattern in question occurs and is exemplified below, the word 'No' that no examples have yet been found. For reasons of space, however, it is not possible to quote examples of all patterns from all periods of the prose and from poetry.

§ 708. The position of the subject must of course be considered in the full treatment referred to above. It will vary according to the principles set out in chapter IX. But we may note here that in patterns 1, 4, and 7, both SV and VS are common. So, while these patterns have _hæfþ_ as their first element—the regular pattern in MnE—the clauses which have it do not necessarily conform in all respects to MnE idiom.

§ 709. Only an accusative object is accompanied by an inflected participle. In the only other contexts in which it is possible for the participle to carry inflexion—i.e. when the object is genitive or dative—it does not do so.[161] And even with an accusative object, the participle is more often without an inflexional ending. In some examples we can say that it is definitely uninflected, e.g. _ÆCHom_

---

[161] The only example I have come across in which the participle may be inflected in agreement with an object in an oblique case is _Exod(L)_ 32. 29 _Todæg ge habbað Gode gecwemede 7 eowere handa gehalgode_. But MS _B_ has _gecwemed_, and _gecwemede_ is more likely to be a scribal error than an inflected form; it would be instrumental and we should expect dat. _gecwemedum._

i. 10. 28 *Ðaða hi ealle hæfdon þysne ræd betwux him gefæstnod*, while in others we cannot be sure because the uninflected and inflected forms coincide, e.g. *ÆCHom* ii. 184. 8 *Hwæt hæfst þu gedon?* This point was clearly overlooked by Harrison (1887) and by Caro, whose statistics (presented below) contrast merely 'inflected' and 'uninflected' forms, without introducing this third category—the 'zero'-inflexion of modern linguists. I do not think their failure reprehensible. There is little (if any) point in making detailed distinctions here and the term 'uninflected' is used below of examples like both *ÆCHom* i. 10. 28 and *ÆCHom* ii. 184. 8. We can however see this third group as an analogical factor in the ultimate disappearance of the inflected forms. The same three possibilities, of course, occur with *wesan/weorþan*, whether the periphrasis is the equivalent of a perfect (§§737-8) or of a passive (§759).

§710. Examples with an inflected participle become less common with the passing of time; Pope (*Ælfric*, i. 184) observes that 'the past participle with *habban* is normally uninflected, the only exception in these homilies being at xxi. 466 *abedene*, where it follows the object and seems to be felt as an adjective'. But they are not predominant in any OE text, either prose or verse. In Hoffmann's table II (p. 52), all the texts have more uninflected than inflected forms. According to Harrison (1887, pp. 134-5), 18 out of 114 participles are inflected in the *Cura Pastoralis*, 30 out of 230 in the *Chronicle* (according to Sprockel, pp. 206-7, only accusative singular masculine forms are inflected in *ChronA*), 8 out of 70 in Napier's *Wulfstan*, and 2 out of 39 in *Beowulf*. His percentage of inflected forms is fourteen per cent.[162] Caro (1896, p. 406) found twenty-five per cent in his texts. So the three agree that inflected forms are in a clear minority. Caro (1896, pp. 404-6, and table V—which is not to be trusted completely) gives figures which confirm the reasonable expectation that the order object–participle produces a higher percentage of inflected forms (twenty-seven per cent) than the order participle-object (fifteen per cent).

§711. There are, however, examples in which the same object is accompanied by two participles, one inflected, one uninflected, e.g. *ÆCHom* i. 578. 24 *Fela Godes wundra we habbað gehyred and eac gesewene, GenB* 392 *he hæfð us þeah þæs leohtes bescyrede,* ‖ *beworpen on ealra wita mæste,* and

---

[162] These and the other figures Harrison gives caused him to doubt whether the form of the periphrasis with accusative object and inflected participle was the original.

Ex 30   Hæfde he þa geswiðed   soðum cræftum
                and gewurðodne   werodes aldor,
                Faraones feond,   on forðwegas,

or in which we find two parallel objects, accompanied in one clause
by an inflected participle and in the other by one without inflexion,
e.g. (with *habban* repeated) *Or* 96. 3 *for ðon þa feawan þe þær ut
opflugon hæfdon eft þa burg gebune, 7 hæfdon Thebane, Creca
leode, him on fultum asponon* and *GenB* 301 *Hete hæfde he æt his
hearran gewunnen, hyldo hæfde his ferlorene,* and (with *habban* not
repeated) *BlHom* 87. 22 *Astig nu, Drihten Hælend Crist, up, nu þu
hafast helle bereafod, 7 þæs deaþes aldor on þyssum witum gebundenne, Exod(B)* 32. 29 *Todæg ge habbað Gode gecwemed, 7 eowre
handa gehalgode* (MS *L*'s *gecwemede* has been discussed in §709
fn.), and *GenB* 726 *Nu hæbbe ic þine hyldo me ‖ witode geworhte,
and þinne willan gelæst.*[163]

§712. Examples of pattern (1) include: (with inflected participle,
accusative object, and SV) *Bede* 54. 7 *7 heo hæfdon utamærede þa
bigengan þisses ealondes, ÆCHom* i. 516. 31 . . . *þæt gehwilc hæbbe
fram his acennednysse him betæhtne engel to hyrdrædene, Dream* 16
gimmas hæfdon ‖ bewrigene weorðlice wealdendes treow (a dubious
example[164]), and (with VS) *Bo* 49. 5 *Swa hæfð se ælmihtiga God
geheaðorade ealle his gescefta . . .* and *WHom* 6. 49 *þa hæfdon hy
forworhte hy sylfe*; (with uninflected participle, accusative object,

[163] Hoffmann, p. 30, fails to distinguish these two types and wrongly remarks that,
except for *GenB* 727, it is the second of the participles which is inflected. I cannot follow
why he claims that these examples prove his theory that most examples of the OE periphrasis denote the action ('die Handlung').

Lussky (p. 53) sees similar variations in the *Heliand* as 'sudden shifts in point of view
[which] must not cause us too much surprise. They are characteristic of the old writers',
due (he says, quoting Kellner, §9) to their naïvety. I see rather the sophistication of a
modern scholar desperately buttressing a theory which cannot stand.

[164] Dickins and Ross, following Kemble, emend to *bewrigen*, observing that 'the MS
form *bewrigene* appears to be impossible on grounds of syntax'. This is true as far as the
normal agreement is concerned since *treow* is neuter; it is unlikely to be a *weak* neuter
singular form. The dubious *ametene* in *Sat* 705, with a clause as object, presents a similar
problem; see my next footnote.

In his 1970 edition of *The Dream of the Rood*, Swanton compares *Dream* 14 *Geseah ic
wuldres treow, ‖ wædum geweorðode*, which—while not strictly parallel, since the verb
involved is [*wesan*], not *habban*—raises the same question: is *geweorðode* a *weak* neuter
singular or an error, perhaps by the scribe? I incline to the latter explanation for this and
the two examples cited above; it is worth noting that in all three the participles are preceded by a plural.

Two similar examples with different element order may also involve scribal error. On
gecwemede in *Exod(L)* 32. 29 *Todæg ge habbað Gode gecwemede 7 eowere handa gehalgode*, where MS *B* has *gecwemed*, see §709 fn. *ChronE* 63. 18 (836) has *aflymde* where
ChronA 62. 20 (quoted in §717 as an example of pattern (5)) has *afliemed*, which must
be right—unless we read *aflymdne*.

and SV) *Or* 94. 33 *æfter þæm þe Læcedemonie hæfdon oferwunnen Ahtene þa burg, CP* 5. 16 *forðæm we habbað nu ægðer forlæten ge ðone welan ge ðone wisdom, ÆCHom* i. 28. 12 *He hæfð gerymed rihtwisum mannum infær to his rice, ÆCHom* i. 458. 18 *Ic hæbbe gebunden ðone feond þe hi drehte,* and *GenB* 395 *He hæfð nu gemearcod anne middangeard,* and (with VS) *Or* 14. 5 *Nu hæbbe we awriten þære Asian supdæl, ChronA* 86. 19 (894) *hæfde Hæsten ær geworht þæt geweorc æt Beamfleote,* and *ÆCHom* i. 276. 33 *Nu habbað ge gehyred þa Halgan þrynnysse;* (with a dative object) *CP* 183. 9 *Forðæm oft se welega 7 se wædla habbað sua gehweorfed hira ðeawum . . .* and *ÆCHom* ii. 52. 8 *þonne hæfð he wiðsacen . . . deofle and eallum leahtrum;* (with a prepositional phrase as object) *Or* 10. 3 *Scortlice ic hæbbe nu gesæd ymb þa þrie dælas ealles þises middangeardes* and *ÆCHom* i. 478. 1 *Nu hæbbe ge oft gehyred be his mæran drohtnunge;* and (with a noun clause) *Or* 108. 16 *Seo hæfde gehaten heora gydenne Dianan þæt heo wolde hiere lif on fæmnhade alibban, ÆCHom* i. 280. 4 *Nu habbað ge gehyred þæt se Sunu is of ðam Fæder, Or* 250. 26 *Nu ic hæbbe gesæd . . . hu eall moncyn angeald þæs ærestan monnes synna,* and *ÆCHom* i. 464. 9 *Efne nu ge habbað gehyred hwilc ðes god is.*[165] As the examples show, pattern (1) is more common in principal clauses, but is not restricted to them; see chapter IX.

§713. Pattern (2) is not common. I have noted none with an in-flected participle, but examples include: (with an accusative object) *CP* 469. 7 *Ac hladað iow nu drincan, nu iow Dryhten geaf ðæt iow Gregorius gegiered hafað to durum iowrum Dryhtnes welle, WHom* 6. 190 *7 he mid þam werede to heofonum ferde, 7 ðærto gerymed hæfð us eallum rihtne weg,* and *GenB* 252 *Gesett hæfde he hie swa gesæliglice;* (with a genitive object) *CP* 407. 19 *Ongean ðæt sint to manigenne ða ðe ðonne giet ungefandod habbað flæsclicra scylda;*[166] and (with a noun clause) *CP* 285. 2 *7 ðonne he wenð ðæt he funden hæbbe hwæt he ryhtlice ondræde* and *LS* 34. 686 *Nu þurh þinre leasan tale ic her ongyten hæbbe þæt þu eart an forswiðe leas man.* I have found no examples of pattern (3).

---

[165] The inflected form *ametene* in

Sat 705   seoððan þu þonne hafast   handum ametene
             hu heh and deop   hell inneweard seo,
             grim græfhus

is allowed to stand without comment by Clubb and by ASPR. In view of the sg. subject *þu* and the dependent question object *hu . . .* , I can find no justification for the *-e*. Cf. *ameten hæbbe* in *Sat* 709.

[166] This example—which occurs again with variations at *CP* 409. 16 and 409. 22—tests Khomiakov's assertion in *JEGP* 63 (1964), 675-6, that all the forms with the prefix *un-* must be considered as adjectives rather than participles.

§714. Table 1 contains those patterns in which the participle precedes the object, as it does in the modern (plu)perfect tense, viz. 'I have finished the job'. The absence of examples of pattern (3) and the scarcity of those of pattern (2) suggest that already in OE there was a marked tendency for *hæfþ* to precede the second participle when that participle preceded the object. In other words, the modern arrangement of these three elements was already well established in principal clauses in OE.

§715. Table 2 contains those patterns in which the object precedes the participle, as in MnE 'I have the job finished'. But here there is no marked tendency for *hæfþ* to precede the other two elements. On the analogy of the patterns with independent verb forms (see chapter IX), one would expect pattern (4) (SVO or VSO) to be more common in principal clauses and pattern (6) (SOV) to be the norm in *ond, ac*, and subordinate, clauses. This seems to be the situation. But, as the examples show, pattern (4)—like pattern (1)—is not restricted to principal clauses. I have found occasional examples of pattern (6) in principal clauses in the poetry; see §719.

§716. Examples of pattern (4) include: (with accusative object, inflected participle, and SV) *CP* 441. 30 *Ic hæbbe ðe nu todæg gesetne ofer rice*, *ChronA* 85. 23 (894) *Ac hie hæfdon þa heora stemn gesetenne, 7 hiora mete genotudne*, *Or* 132. 21 *7 he hæfde Poros monegum wundum gewundodne*, *ÆCHom* ii. 500. 23 *and hæfde ær his ðing þearfum gedælede*, *ÆCHom* i. 266. 36 *oðþæt ge habban ealle eowre gyltas geðrowade*, and *Beo* 939 *Nu scealc hafað* ‖ *þurh Drihtnes miht dæd gefremede*, and (with VS) *Beo* 205 *Hæfde se goda Geata leoda* ‖ *cempan gecorone* and *GenB* 254 *hæfde he hine swa hwitne geworhtne*; (with accusative object, uninflected participle, and SV) *CP* 155. 3 *Ða ic hæfde ðone weall ðurhðyrelod* (but note pattern (6) in *CP* 153. 18 *Ða ic ða ðone wah ðurhðyreludne hæfde*), *BlHom* 87. 22 *nu þu hafast helle bereafod*, *Gen* 44. 4 *7 hi . . . hæfdon sumne dæl weges gefaren*, and *El* 907 *Nu cwom elþeodig*, ‖ *. . .* ‖ *hafað mec bereafod*, and (with VS) *Bo* 13. 3 *ac me hæfð þios gnornung ðære gemynde benumen*, *ChronA* 84. 31 (894) *hæfde se cyning his fierd on tu tonumen*, and *GenB* 390 *Hafað us god sylfa* ‖ *forswapen on þas sweartan mistas*; (with genitive or dative object) *WHom* 15. 59 *gyf hwa hæfð his hlaforde sare abolgen* and *Beo* 2300 *he þæt sona onfand*, ‖ *ðæt hæfde gumena sum goldes gefandod*; and (with a prepositional phrase as object) *Or* 26. 26 *Nu hæbbe we ymb Affrica landgemæro gesæd*. This pattern is not to be expected with a noun clause object.

§717. Pattern (5), like pattern (2), is not common. Most of the examples are in principal clauses and involve a personal pronoun object occupying its idiomatic position before the verb; in these instances and in those in *ond, ac,* and subordinate, clauses, pattern (5) is a variation of pattern (4), just as S pron. OV is a variation of SV noun O; see §3907. Examples include: (with accusative object and inflected participle) *Bo* 50. 13 *hu þu me hæfst afrefredne, BlHom* 15. 24 *þin agen geleafa þe hæfþ gehæledne, WHom* 3. 27 *ac we hi habbað syððan afylede swyðe,* and *Mald* 237 *Us Godric hæfð,* ‖ *earh Oddan bearn, ealle beswicene;* (with accusative object and uninflected participle) *ChronA* 62. 20 (836) *7 hine hæfde ær Offa . . . 7 Beorhtric . . . afliemed* (see §712 fn. 164), *Or* 24. 25 *ac for ðam þe se Wendelsæ hit hæfð swa todæled . . .* , and *ÆLS* 2. 419 *me hæfð gebroht min hælend crist to his halgena blysse;* and (with a genitive object) *Bo* 145. 1 *Swiðe wel þu min hæfst geholpen æt þære spræce.*

✕§718. Examples with an object other than a personal pronoun include: (with accusative object and inflected participle) *ChronE* 221. 22 (1086) *Đas þing we habbað be him gewritene, ægðer ge gode ge yfele* and *GenB* 252 *ænne hæfde he swa swiðne geworhtne;* (with accusative object and uninflected participle) *ChronF* 67. 25 (855) *Ælfred his þriddan sune he hæfde gesend to Rome, ÆCHom* ii. 184. 8 *Hwæt hæfst þu gedon?, WHom* 8c. 19 *And syððan se man þæt can 7 rihtne geleafan hæfð ariht understanden, Met* 8. 1 *Sona swa se wisdom þas word hæfde* ‖ *swetole areahte,* and *Beo* 1294 *hraðe heo æþelinga anne hæfde* ‖ *fæste befangen;* (with relative pronoun object and uninflected participles) *WHom* 5. 109 *Ac for þæra gebeorge þe him syn gecorene 7 ðe he habban wyle gehealden 7 geholpen . . . ;* (with a dative object) *Res* 78 *Gode ic hæbbe* ‖ *abolgen, brego moncynnes;* and (with a prepositional phrase) *ÆCHom* ii. 604. 20 *Be ðisum we habbað on oðre stowe awriten.* This pattern is not to be expected with a noun clause object.

§719. I have noted a few examples of pattern (6) in principal clauses in the poetry, e.g. *Beo* 2397 *Swa he niða gehwane genesen hæfde* and *Dream* 50 *Feala ic on þam beorge gebiden hæbbe* ‖ *wraðra wyrda.* Examples in other clauses include: (with accusative object and inflected participle) *Bede* 328. 6 *Ond hine ascode hwæðer he ða alysendlecan rune cuðe 7 þa stafas mid him awritene hæfde, ChronA* 48. 4 (755) *oþ þæt hie hine ofslægenne hæfdon,* and *ÆCHom* i. 14. 15 *ðaða he hi gesceapene hæfde;* (with accusative object and uninflected participle) *ChronA* 84. 17 (894) *On þys geare, þæt wæs ymb twelf monað þæs þe hie on þæm eastrice geweorc geworht hæfdon* and *WHom* 4. 56 *Ac syððan he þæne mann gebrocod hæfð*;[167] and (with genitive or dative object) *Or* 32. 21 . . . *wilniende þæt hi ælcum gewinne oðflogen hæfdon, HomU* 35. 211. 22 *gif heo æfre fulluhtes onfangen hæfdon*, and *Beo* 106 *siþðan him Scyppend forscrifen hæfde*. . . .

§720. Table 3 includes those examples in which the verb has no object and in which the participle cannot possibly be inflected. The verbs involved may be transitive, intransitive, or capable of functioning as either. Pattern (7)—*hæfþ* + participle—is found in principle clauses, e.g. *GD(C)* 21. 17 *ic hæfde gyrstandæge gecweden* . . . , *Exod* 32. 7 *þin folc hæfð gesyngod, LS* 34. 575 *Wella, min drihten, hwæt, ic her nu hreowlice hæbbe gefaren*, and *Sat* 61 *Habbað we alle swa* ‖ *for ðinum leasungum lyðre gefered*, and occasionally in other clauses, e.g. *Or* 186. 22 *þa he hæfde on þæm emnete gefaren oþ he com to Ticenan þære ie, Or* 196. 23 *þa Scipia hæfde gefaren to ðære niwan byrig Cartaina*, and *Gen* 27. 25-6 *þa he hæfde gedruncen, ða cwæð he to him.*

§721. My own examples of pattern (8)—participle + *hæfþ*—are (perhaps not surprisingly) restricted to co-ordinate clauses introduced by *ond, ac*, and the like, and to subordinate clauses, although there may be a few in principal clauses which have escaped my net. Examples include *ChronA* 89. 14 (896) *þa hie ða þæt geweorc furþum ongunnen hæfdon 7 þær to gewicod hæfdon, Or* 122. 28 *swa he gecweden hæfde, Bo* 129. 17 *7 he welt eallra gesceafta swa swa he æt fruman getiohhod hæfde 7 get hæfð, CP* 405. 22 *æfter ðæmðe hie gesyngod habbað, Gen* 31. 54 *þa hi eten hæfdon, hi wunedon ðær, Exod* 14. 5 . . . *hwær þæt Israhelisce folc gewicod hæfde wið ða Readan Sæ* (cf. *Exod* 14. 9 *7 beferde ðæt Israhelise folc ðær hi gewicode wæron be ðære Readan Sæ*), *ÆCHom* i. 80. 27 *and wæs ða, þurh his langsume fær, þæra cildra slege geuferod swiðor þonne he gemynt hæfde, WHom* 6. 136 *swa ic eow nu areht hæbbe, Beo* 2104 *ond we to symble geseten hæfdon, Jul* 677 *ær þon hy to lande geliden hæfdon*, and *GenB* 688 *wæs se feond full neah* ‖ *þe on þa frecnan fyrd gefaren hæfde* (cf. examples with *wesan* such as *Or* 132. 11 . . . *Ercol se ent þær wæs to gefaren* and *ÆLS* 6. 132 *forðan þe his gebedda gefaren wæs of life*, and the transitive use seen in *LS* 34. 19 *Ða he ða þreo burga gefaren hæfde*).

§722. It will be noted that the intransitive verbs quoted above include examples from the earliest prose and verse. Hoffmann

---

[167] *CP* 385. 2 *siððan he his cnihtas gelæred hæfde ðone cræft ðæs lareowdomes*, with the participle and verb between two accusative objects, may belong here.

(pp. 34-9) says—with characteristic repetition—that the only intransitive verbs used with *habban* up to the time of Ælfric are 'perfectives' whose second participles can also be used attributively, that these verbs are found more frequently with *wesan*, that with *habban* they denote the action or the completion of the action ('die Handlung' or 'die Vollendung der Handlung')—on the ambiguity involved here see below—e.g. *Exod* 14. 5 *Ða cydde man Pharaone, hwær þæt Israhelisce folc gewicod hæfde wið ða Readan Sæ*, but with *wesan* the state ('der Zustand') e.g. *Exod* 14. 9 *7 beferde ðæt Israhelise folc ðær hi gewicode wæron be ðære Readan Sæ*. Then (from the time of Ælfric) verbs whose second participles cannot be used attributively or with *wesan* appear with *habban*, viz. 'perfectives' such as *agyltan*, e.g. *ÆLS* 12. 21 *swa swa se ælmihtiga god to Adame cwæð siððan he agylt hæfde ongean godes bebod*, and 'imperfectives' like *standan*, e.g. *ChronE* 207. 24 (1070) . . . *in þære cyrce þ ær hæfde standen fulle seofeniht forutan ælces cynnes riht*, and *þegnian* (cited at his p. 38 fn. 10 without reference to a text).[168] However, there seems little point—and indeed little validity—in distinguishing 'perfectives' or 'mutatives' (Hoffmann, pp. 16 ff., and Mustanoja, p. 500) from 'imperfectives' or 'duratives' (Lussky, p. 63). For general objections to importing the notion of aspect into OE, see §§865-73. The main objection here is that it does not work. Why is *faran* classed as 'perfective' in an example which must be identified as *Or* 196. 23 *þa Scipia hæfde gefaren to ðære niwan byrig Cartaina* (Hoffmann, p. 35) but as 'imperfective' in *Or* 186. 22 *þa he hæfde on þæm emnete gefaren oþ he com to Ticenan þære ie*, which is described as the only example before Ælfric of an 'imperfective' with *habban* (Hoffmann, pp. 35 and 38)? Why is *Beo* 2103 *syððan mergen com, || ond we to symble geseten hæfdon* listed as 'perfective' and *ChronE* 207. 24 above as 'imperfective' (Hoffmann, pp. 35-6)? How can we reconcile Mustanoja's observation (p. 500 fn. 2) that 'to go' and 'to come' are 'mutative' ('perfective') with Lussky's classification of *cuman* (which, he says, takes *wesan*) as 'perfective' and *gan* (which, he says, takes *habban*) as 'durative' (p. 63)? I find the alleged distinction confusing rather than helpful. The important thing is that intransitive verbs are used with *habban* throughout the OE period—a point which eluded *OED*; see below.[169]

---

[168] In his list of 'perfectives' and 'imperfectives', Hoffmann usually gives only the verb and the text in which it is found. So some of the examples quoted above are supplied from my own collections in the hope that they represent what Hoffmann had in mind.

[169] Of course not all intransitive verbs which survive to use the auxiliary 'have' today are found with *habban* in OE. Visser (who introduces the term 'Resultative Form' (iii, §1898) for the pattern 'He is come' to distinguish it from the perfect 'He has come' and from the passive) gives some useful information on this point (iii, §§1898-904). He found no

§723. That all these different patterns occur in 'Alfredian' prose, in the prose of Ælfric and his (near-)contemporaries, and in the poetry, establishes that the periphrasis had no one fixed form. It had no one fixed function either. It served as a future perfect, e.g. *CP* 23. 6 *Ðonne hwa ðis eall gefylled hæbbe, hu he ðonne sceal hine selfne geðencean 7 ongietan*, *LS* 14. 164 *Gif ic minne lichaman to þe geeadmede, þonne scealt þu inne þæt wallende pic into helle wite; þær þu scealt wunian æfre. Þonne miht þu habban minne lichaman þe to gæmene, and god hæfð mine sawle fram þe generod*, and

GenA 2882   Wit eft cumað,
    siððan wit ærende   uncer twega
    gastcyninge   agifen habbað.[170]

The well-known overlap between the past tense and the periphrasis is attested by their use in parallel or connected sentences—compare *Bo* 118. 29 *For hwylcum oðrum ðingum woldes þu þ sprecan buton for ðæm þe þu nu sædes?* with *Bo* 74. 16 *Genog ic þe hæbbe nu gereaht, Or* 80. 19 *Ac gesette þa men on ænne truman þe mon hiora mægas ær on ðæm londe slog . . .* with *Or* 144. 14 *for þon þe he þæron bebead þæt mon ealle þa wræccan an cyþþe forlete þe on ðæm londum wæron þe he ær self gehergad hæfde, ÆCHom* i. 158. 32 *þin geleafa ðe gehælde* with *ÆCHom* i. 152. 23 *þin geleafa hæfð ðe gehæled*, and the two verbs in

Beo 1195   . . .   healsbeaga mæst
    þara þe ic on foldan   gefrægen hæbbe.
    Nænigne ic under swegle   selran hyrde
    hordmaðum hæleþa . . .—

and in the same sentences, e.g. *Bede* 132. 24 *Ono hwæt þu nu hafast þurh Godes gife þinra feonda hond beswicade . . . 7 þu þurh his sylene 7 gife þæm rice onfenge . . . , ÆCHom* i. 316. 26 *Annania, deofol bepæhte ðine heortan, and ðu hæfst alogen þam Halgan Gaste,*

El 907   Nu cwom elþeodig,
    þone ic ær on firenum   fæstne talde,

examples in any period of *habban* 'have' + *ætlicgan, ætlimpan, belifan* (iii, §1899), *limpan* (iii, §1901), *cyrran, dreosan, fysan, hweorfan, oðfeallan, gewitan* (iii, §1902), and so on (iii, §1904). Verbs which survive in MnE but are not recorded with *habban* in OE include— according to Visser—*abidan, bidan, clifian, clingan, dwellan* 'to remain', *læstan* 'to continue', *licgan* (iii, §1899), and so on (iii, §§1900-4). Verbs already found with *habban* in OE include *restan, sittan, gewician* (Visser, iii, §1899), *onginnan* (iii, §1900), and so on (iii, §§1901-4). But even Visser's collections—which compel admiration—are not complete. Thus *standan* does not appear in iii, §1899. His valuable treatment of the uses of the participles *geworden* (iii. 2050-2 and 2094) and *gehæfd* (iii, §1928) should be noted.

[170] For further examples see Caro 1896, pp. 397-8 and 411, Caro 1899, p. 84, and Visser, iii, §2010. On the three examples of the ' "zeitlose" Gebrauch' of the preterite quoted at Caro 1899, p. 84, see §650.

> hafað mec bereafod   rihta gehwylces,
> feohgestreona,

and

Beo 694   ac hie hæfdon gefrunen,   þæt hie ær to fela micles
in þæm winsele   wældeað fornam,
Denigea leode.[171]

§724. We have already seen that the periphrasis with *habban* was well established in the earliest OE prose and poetry and that even there the majority of participles were uninflected. It appears to be clearly of native origin (as Zadorožny (1974, p. 387) tells us) and to owe nothing to the Latin *urbem captam habet* 'He has captured the city and is keeping it captured' (see GL, §238). But we need, I think, have little hesitation in accepting the orthodox view that in the original form of the periphrasis the participle was inflected and adjectival.[172] That it is verbal in MnE sentences like 'I have seen it again' is certain. Between the two there is, inevitably, a plethora of disputed examples.

§725. The adjectival function of the inflected participle is clearly seen, as Hoffmann (pp. 26–7) points out, in examples in which the object is actually in the possession of the subject. These were already in a minority in OE. Indeed, according to Hoffmann (pp. 27–8), there were only seven such examples in OE and in them the function of the periphrasis is 'Zustandsbezeichnung', denoting the state arising from the action. These examples are *CP* 45. 12 *ðonne hæbbe we begen fet gescode suiðe untællice*, *CP* 61. 2 *Se læce . . . hæfð on his agnum nebbe opene wunde unlacnode*, *CP* 217. 19 . . . *ðæt he scolde ðone Godes alter habban uppan aholodne*, *Bede* 328. 6 . . . *hwæðer*

---

[171] Visser (ii, §808) gives more OE examples of a preterite where MnE might use the periphrasis and cites sentences such as *John(Li)* 11. 28 *⁊ miððy ðas cuoeð ɫ cuoeden hæfde*, Latin *et cum hæc dixisset*, in which the glossator offers both forms.

[172] So Schrader, p. 69; Caro 1896, pp. 404–5; *OED*, s.v. 'have' II; QW, §123; and others. Even Lussky accepts it (p. 38). But his theory that in OS 'the Circumscriptions formed with the perfect participle . . . arose from an effort to circumscribe the perfective "Aktionsart" (perfective–inchoative resultative)' (p. 48) and that 'the circumscribed verb forms in Anglo-Saxon originated in the same way as those in Old-Saxon, namely from an effort to circumscribe the perfective "Aktionsart" ' (p. 64) does not convince. Lussky bases it on the now-discredited notion that aspect is a meaningful category in the Germanic languages (see §865) and on an unacceptably rigid distinction between inflected and uninflected participles (see §709); he appears to work on the unlikely hypothesis that the language of the *Heliand* represents a state of the circumlocution close to the original, that what holds for the *Heliand* holds for *Beowulf*, and that what holds for *Beowulf* holds for OE in general; he is forced to neglect element order because he chooses to work with poems (pp. 35 and 67); and he does not avoid the special pleading to which his method exposes him—'*we must interpret rather than count instances*' [his italics] (p. 33).

he . . . þa stafas mid him awritene hæfde, Bede 428. 6 . . . *ic ðone sweg ða gena gemengedne in earum hæfde, ÆCHom* i. 516. 31 . . . *þæt gehwilc hæbbe fram his acennednysse him betæhtne engel to hyrdrædene,* and *GenA* 60 *Hæfde styrne mod* ‖ *gegremed grymme.* Here, and in other examples where the participle is clearly adjectival, 'the tense of these circumscriptions was determined by the tense of the auxiliary. They were as a consequence either present or preterit', says Lussky (p. 39). This is dubious; see §§723 and 727-33.

§726. Hoffmann (pp. 28-31 and 47) distinguishes these seven examples from others in which the object is not actually in the possession of the subject, i.e. in which *habban* is used in a weakened sense. This stage had already been reached in OE, e.g. (from Hoffmann) *BlHom* 15. 26 *þin agen geleafa þe hæfþ gehæledne*[173] and *Beo* 939 *Nu scealc hafað* ‖ *þurh Drihtnes miht dæd gefremede,* and (from my own collections) *ChronA* 85. 23 (894) *Ac hie hæfdon þa . . . hiora mete genotudne, ÆCHom* ii. 500. 21 *Ða næfde Martinus nan ðing to syllenne þam nacodan ðearfan . . . buton his gewædum . . . and hæfde ær his ðing þearfum gedælede,* and *Mald* 237 *Us Godric hæfð,* ‖ *earh Oddan bearn, ealle beswicene.* But some examples are less clear-cut, e.g. (from Hoffmann) *Or* 132. 21 *7 he hæfde Poros monegum wundum gewundodne, 7 hiene eac gewildne gedyde,* Latin *Porus multis vulneribus confossus et captus est* (Poros was in the power of Alexander), and

Beo 205   Hæfde se goda Geata leoda
       cempan gecorone þara þe he cenoste
       findan mihte

---

[173] The original of this—*fides tua te saluum fecit* (*Mark* 10. 52, *Luke* 17. 19, *Luke* 18. 42)—and the variant *fides tua te saluam fecit* (*Matt* 9. 22, *Mark* 5. 34, *Luke* 7. 50, *Luke* 8. 48) have produced various translations (all from the *Corpus* version): *þin geleafa þe gehælde* (*Matt* 9. 22 and *Luke* 18. 42); *þin geleafa þe halne gedyde* (*Mark* 10. 52 and *Luke* 17. 19); *þin geleafa þe hale gedyde* (*Mark* 5. 34 and *Luke* 8. 48); and *þin geleafa þe dyde hale* (*Luke* 7. 50). Those with *gehælde* perhaps further illustrate the overlap between the preterite and the periphrasis in OE already noted in §723; the examples given there include *ÆCHom* i. 158. 32 *þin geleafa ðe gehælde* and *ÆCHom* i. 152. 23 *þin geleafa hæfð ðe gehæled.* On the other hand, those with *(ge)dyde* suggest the possibility that *hæfþ* in *BlHom* 15. 26 carries the almost causal implication of Latin *fecit.* Hoffmann ought to have noticed this, for he detects (pp. 26-7) a third group in which the object is possessed by someone other than the subject; his examples are 'Ich habe ihm die Haare geschnitten' 'I have his hair cut' as opposed to 'Ich habe die Haare geschnitten' 'I have my hair cut'. This third pattern with *habban* does not play an important part in OE. Indeed *OED* (s.v. *have* 17) records no OE examples. BTS (s.v. *habban* XVII)—followed by Visser (i, §651)—cites examples with adjectives in which *habban* means 'to get something into a specified condition', e.g. *BlHom* 107. 15 *þonne magon we us God ælmihtigne mildne habban,* and says that in *Or* 112. 34 *þa hie to ðæm gemære comon mid heora firde, þa hæfdon hie hiera clusan belocene, habban* with the second participle means 'to get something done, *cause* to be done'. This is (I suppose) possible. But it is not immediately clear to me that the last example differs radically from (say) *Or* 132. 21 (quoted below).

(the chosen warriors were in Beowulf's company: Visser (iii, §2029) calls this a 'resultative pluperfect'), and (from my own collections) *ChronA* 48. 4 (755) *7 hie alle on þone Cyning wærun feohtende oþ þæt hie hine ofslægenne hæfdon* (the King's body remained in the *burg* with Cyneheard and his thanes) and *CP* 441. 30 *Ic hæbbe ðe nu todæg gesetne ofer rice 7 ofer ðioda* (Jeremiah was in the hands of God). One must admire, but not share, the confidence with which Hoffmann isolates the seven sentences in his first group from all other OE examples. But his basic division, though not of course original, is sound. So too is his observation (p. 28) that when the object is not actually in the possession of the subject we can begin to get a feeling for the action ('die Handlung') as opposed to the resulting state ('der Zustand').

§727. The use of *habban* in this weakened sense is an essential preliminary to the use of the periphrasis with first, verbs which take an object which is not accusative—for typical examples of patterns (1)-(2) and (4)-(6) see §§712-19—and second, with verbs which take no object—for typical examples of patterns (7)-(8) see §§720-1. With verbs taking a genitive or dative object, inflexion of the participle is possible, but rare; see §709 fn. 161. With verbs taking a prepositional phrase or a noun clause object and with verbs taking no object, inflexion of the participle—essential (it could be argued) when it was felt as adjectival but cf. §§735 and 762—is not only superfluous but, as far as I can judge, impossible. One must, however, beware of making rigid distinctions about the functions either of the participle or of the periphrasis as a whole. It is tempting to produce the simple equations 'inflected participle = adjectival use', 'uninflected participle = verbal use'. Indeed Lussky does just this: '. . . when the perfect participle is inflected it has adjective force, and when it is uninflected it has lost its adjective force. . . . We accept this . . . view' (p. 39). From this he concludes (p. 62) that

wherever the participle is inflected it is felt as an adjective belonging to the noun and the circumscribed form denotes state or condition and is *present* or *preterit*; wherever it is uninflected it is felt as belonging to the verb and the circumscribed form denotes completed action and is *perfect* or *pluperfect* in the case of habban and wesan; and present in the case of weorðan.

This is to ignore (as Lussky does) the element order within the group. One might with equal justification be tempted to say 'When the participle follows the object (patterns (4), (5), and (6)), the participle is adjectival. When the participle precedes the object (patterns (1) and (2)), the participle is verbal.' Both temptations must be resisted. There is no room for such rigidity. It is clear from the examples quoted in §711 that there was a period of transition. One would have thought the point hardly needed demonstrating. But it would be instructive to hear Lussky explaining the difference between the inflected and uninflected forms of the participle in those examples and in others like *CP* 153. 18 *Ða ic ða ðone wah ðurhðyreludne hæfde . . . ða iewde he me ane duru beinnan ðæm wealle* and *CP* 155. 3 *Ða ic hæfde ðone weall ðurhðyrelod, ða geseah ic duru.*

§728. That the common description of the change in the function of the participle from adjectival to verbal or in the function of the periphrasis from denoting a state to denoting an action is somewhat superficial has not (to the best of my knowledge) been pointed out. What is actually involved with transitive verbs is a change from an *adjectival* use of a *passive* participle to an *active verbal* use of the same participle. We may therefore agree that in examples like *ChronA* 68. 18 (867) *7 hie hæfdun hiera cyning aworpenne Osbryht* the original sense of the construction was 'They had (= held) their king Osbryht (having been) rejected'. But in *ÆCHom* i. 458. 18 *Ic hæbbe gebunden ðone feond* we can pose the question in two ways: 'Is *gebunden* adjectival or verbal?' or 'Is *gebunden* passive or active?'[174] Here the analogy of intransitive verbs must have played an important part, for—in Mustanoja's words (p. 500 fn. 3)—'while the past participles of intransitive verbs are active in meaning, those of transitive verbs are passive'.

§729. Hoffmann's theory about the function of the periphrasis in OE shows rigidity, repetition, and perhaps even some confusion. Thus he writes 'Wie steht es im Ae.? Hier drücken die Verbindungen mit *habban* stets die Handlung aus' (p. 27) and again '. . . die *wesan*-Verbindungen den Zustand, die *habban*-Verbindungen die Handlung bezeichneten' (p. 36). But he also writes '*habban* war nur ein Mittel, die Vollendung der Handlung auszudrücken' (p. 39), '*habban* . . . wurde Hilfszeitwort und ein bloßes Mittel, die Vollendung der Handlung auszudrücken' (p. 47), and again '*habban* war im Ae. nur ein Mittel, die Vollendung der Handlung zu bezeichnen' (pp. 48-9).[175] I am not sure that denoting the action is the same thing as denoting

---

[174] Whether the passive participle indicated pure passivity—as opposed to passivity in past time—is discussed in §§768–81, but does not seem to be important here. Visser (iii, §1890) seems unaware of the problem.

[175] 'What is the position in OE? Here the compounds with *habban* always denote the action' (p. 27) . . . '. . . the *wesan*-compounds denoted the state, the *habban*-compounds the action' (p. 36) . . . '*habban* was simply a means of expressing the completion of the action' (p. 39) . . . '*habban* . . . became an auxiliary verb and merely a means of denoting the completion of the action' (p. 47) . . . '*habban* was in OE simply a means of expressing the completion of the action' (pp. 48-9).

the completion of the action. However, as Mustanoja says (p. 499): 'Hoffmann . . . thinks that it is not until early ME that the participial constructions with *be* and *have* can be regarded as true perfects and pluperfects expressing action rather than a state resulting from an action.' Hoffmann's argument (pp. 39-40 and 46-50) is that OE did not possess a periphrastic perfect—'ein umschriebenes Perfektum gibt es im Ae. nicht'—since the perfect is a temporal gradation ['Zeitstufe'] which stands in relationship to the present and preterite tenses; only when this relationship exists and we have a series like 'ich schreibe', 'ich schrieb', 'ich habe geschrieben', can we properly speak of a perfect. That this was not so in OE, Hoffmann claims, is attested by the fact that Ælfric has

ÆGram 123. 15 PRAETERITVM TEMPVS ys forðgewiten tid: *steti*, ic stod
. . . (124. 5) PRAETERITVM PERFEKTVM ys forðgewiten fulfremed: *steti*, ic stod fullice. PRAETERITVM PLVSQVAMPERFEKTVM is forðgewiten mare, þonne fulfremed, forðan ðe hit wæs gefyrn gedon: *steteram*, ic stod gefyrn,

thereby demonstrating that he understood the Latin perfect but did not regard the periphrasis as an adequate means of expressing it.

§730. As Mustanoja says (p. 499), Hoffmann's 'view has not been universally accepted, however, and there are many who believe that in numerous OE instances the combinations of *be* and *have* with past participles are real perfects and pluperfects'. The argument must eventually come down to a matter of personal interpretation. *OED* (s.v. *have* II) says that 'with transitive verbs the developed use was already frequent in OE'. Many native speakers of English will find it hard to disagree over examples in both early and late texts such as *CP* 273. 15 *Ðin ðeow hæfð nu funden his wisdom* and *ÆCHom* i. 458. 18 *Ic hæbbe gebunden ðone feond þe hi drehte.* Some may even feel inclined to go further than *OED* (loc. cit.)—'In early ME. the usage is found with verbs of action without an object, whence it was extended to intransitive verbs'—and to see at least some of those examples in which the participle is uninflected and where the object is not accusative or of those in which there is no object, as true perfects, again in both early and late texts, e.g. *Or* 108. 16 *Seo hæfde gehaten heora gydenne Dianan þæt heo wolde hiere lif on fæmnhade alibban* and *ÆCHom* i. 316. 27 *ðu hæfst alogen þam Halgan Gaste.*

§731. A characteristic of the modern perfect is that of 'current relevance' (Gleason, p. 236) or, as Sweet put it (*NEG*, §275):

the perfect therefore expresses an occurrence which began in the past and is connected with the present, either by actual continuance up to the present time . . .

or in its results, . . . where although the action . . . is completed, its result . . . is felt to belong to the present. The simple preterite, on the other hand, expresses a past occurrence without any reference to the present.

Some OE examples display this. We may compare *Bo* 74. 16 *Genog ic þe hæbbe nu gereaht ymb ða anlicnessa* with *Bo* 73. 13 *Forðæm ic þe recce eall þ ic þe ær reahte*, the two verbs in *Bo* 73. 21 *Ða se Wisdom ða þis spell areaht hæfde, þa ongon he eft gieddigan 7 þus singinde cwæð* . . . and in *ÆCHom* i. 216. 4 *We habbað oft gesæd, and git secgað, þæt* . . .—Hoffmann (p. 40) concedes that this example shows that the last phase in the development of the perfect had begun—and the last two verbs in

GenA 2819 . . . þæt þu wille me
wesan fæle freond fremena to leane,
þara þe ic to duguðum ðe gedon hæbbe,
siððan ðu feasceaft feorran come. . . .

The idea of continuance up to the present time appears also in two examples noted by Visser (ii. 750) in which the *habban* periphrasis is accompanied by *ær*. They are *WPol* 222, §18 . . . *þæt he wite* . . . *hu he hine ærþam gehealden wið God and wið men hæbbe* and

Max i 18 þing sceal gehegan
frod wiþ frodne; biþ hyra ferð gelic,
hi a sace semaþ, sibbe gelærað,
þa ær wonsælge awegen habbað.

These two are perhaps less remarkable than Visser seems to think— *ær* can be translated 'previously' to give a perfectly acceptable MnE sentence. The existence in late OE of sentences like *LS* 34. 398 *Ac ælmihtig god* . . . *þa he ðæs caseres mycclan hreowsunga geseah, him eac sona þæt hreow* . . . *and hine þa ne lengc ahwænedne habban nolde*, where *habban* has the sense 'keep, cause to be', do not argue against the recognition of the perfect in OE, since they exist in all periods of English; see Visser, iii, §§ 2001 and 2120.

§ 732. A new consideration has now been introduced by Visser, who writes (iii, § 2004):

In discussing this opposition one should not lose sight of the fact that in the course of time the character of this opposition has undergone a fundamental change: In Old English the time-sphere of e.g. 'he hæfð begen fet gescode' is decidedly the present, expressing as it does what 'now', 'at the present moment' is a fact, whereas in the Old English statement *'he gesceode begen his fet' the time-sphere is clearly the past. Consequently the opposition preterite/perfect was at the time of a temporal character. When in later English the sentence with a perfect had adopted the modern word-order, it referred to something happening or occurring in the past.

If this were true, it would seem to certify that some at least of the OE examples just quoted are true perfects. But is it not too simple? On the test of 'current relevance', the MnE perfect still has reference to the present and to the past, just as did the OE *He hæfð begen fet gescode*, where the 'having' is in the present, the 'shoeing' in the past.

§733. Each reader will no doubt have his own favourite examples in which the OE *habban* periphrasis seems to be the equivalent of the MnE perfect. Thus Visser seems pretty confident about *Gen* 27. 25-6 *þa he hæfde gedruncen, ða cwæð he to him*, Latin *quo hausto, dixit ad eum* (iii, §2002), and even about *Mark(WSCp)* 8. 17 *gyt ge habbað eowre heortan geblende*, Latin *adhuc caecatum habetis cor uestrum* (iii, §2001). But from the inconsistencies already noted in the use of the periphrasis and from the mere fact that we are reduced to arguing about individual examples, it must be clear that, while the formal distinction *ic binde—ic band—ic hæbbe gebunden* existed in OE, the modern functional distinction was not established; it cannot yet be said, as Twaddell (p. 8) says of the modern periphrasis, that it 'explicitly links an earlier event or state with the current situation. It signals a significant persistence of results, a continued truth value, a valid present relevance of the effects of earlier events, the continued reliability of conclusions based on earlier behavior.' This situation was not reached until much later: 'In ME and early Mod.E the functional distinction between the preterite and the compound tenses of the past is not, however, nearly so clear-cut as it is today' (Mustanoja, p. 504) and 'It is only after the time of Shakespeare that the preterite and the *have* + past participle construction are used as they are used nowadays. . . . Occasionally there are still deviations' (Visser, ii. 751). To this extent Hoffmann is right. Similar problems arise, of course, in the Romance languages and elsewhere. But they cannot be considered here.[176]

(3) *The periphrases with* beon/wesan *and with* weorþan

§734. In the 'perfect/pluperfect' periphrases, *beon/wesan* and (less frequently) *weorþan* occur with both personal and impersonal intransitive verbs—whose second participles are active. With transitive verbs—whose second participles are passive—*beon/wesan* and *weorþan* formed the passive (see §§786-801) and *habban* formed

---

[176] In *Littérature, linguistique, civilisation, pédagogie* (Actes du [13ème] Congrès [de la Société des Anglicistes de l'Enseignement supérieur] de Grenoble) (Paris, 1973), 'Études anglaises', 65 (1976), 193-201, Jean-Louis Duchet offers 'Considérations historiques et théoriques sur le parfait anglais', including *inter alia* a discussion of the relationship between 'have' and 'be' as auxiliaries and bibliographical references on the development of the English perfect. But he has nothing new to say about OE usage.

the 'perfect/pluperfect', its object being expressed. The gradual extension of the sphere of *habban* to intransitive verbs already outlined in §§705–33 points to the ultimate disappearance of *beon/wesan* and *weorþan* as auxiliaries of the 'perfect/pluperfect'—if they ever were truly auxiliaries; see below.[177]

§735. Another factor in this disappearance of *beon/wesan* and *weorþan* is, of course, their use with the passive—'it is perhaps not without significance that while *be* is becoming an auxiliary *par excellence* of the passive voice, it is losing ground as an auxiliary of the perfect and pluperfect tenses' (Mustanoja, p. 501). There was in fact a more than theoretical possibility of confusion between the two; this is perhaps implicit in another observation by Mustanoja (p. 500) in his discussion of the 'Auxiliaries of the Perfect and Pluperfect'— 'Yet unlike *habban* it [*beon/wesan*] never loses its capacity to express a state (cf. present-day *we could not go in because the door was closed*).' For here 'was closed' could be a passive, or a verb + adjective equivalent; cf. *ÆCHom* i. 280. 13 *Nis he geworht, ne gesceapen, ne acenned*. Sweet (*R.8*, §348) remarks that in the verb-forms in *ÆCHom* i. 58. 11 *þa gelamp hit þæt æt ðam gyftum win wearð ateorod* and *ÆLS* 26. 205 *þa wearð his hors gesicclod*

which are exceptionally formed by *wearþ* instead of *wæs* with an intransitive past participle, it is simplest to take *wearþ* in the literal sense of 'became' and regard the participle as an adjective—'became wanting', 'became sickened'. There is evidently some confusion with the passive construction, where the participle often has the same half-adjectival meaning.

Wattie (p. 142) quotes these two examples, adds *CP* 169. 22 . . . *of ðæm treowe, ðe is haten sethim, ðæt ne wyrð næfre forrotad*, and explains them in the same way. Lussky (p. 57) feels that *Beo* 823 *Denum eallum wearð* ‖ *æfter þam wælræse willa gelumpen* is 'perhaps passive', but it is hard to see how this could be so when *gelimpan* is recorded only in intransitive uses. However, *ChronE* 221. 28 (1086) . . . *þa Dænescan . . . wurdon awende to þære meste untriwðe* is genuinely ambiguous and can be either active or passive, because *awendan* can be either intransitive or transitive. The same is true of an example with *beon/wesan*, viz. *Beo* 476 *is min fletwerod,* ‖ *wigheap gewanod*, as Jost (1909, §27) rightly points out. Again the ambiguity is due to the fact that the verb involved may be either intransitive, as in *Beo* 1605 *þa þæt sweord ongan* ‖ . . . *wigbil wanian*, or transitive, as in *Beo* 1336 *forþan he to lange leode mine* ‖ *wanode ond wyrde*. That we have *is* rather than *wæs* might support the notion that

---

[177] *Mutatis mutandis*, the criticisms of Lussky's work made in §§724–7 concerning the periphrases with *habban* apply here.

gewanod is intransitive rather than transitive if we accepted Campbell's distinction (*OEG*, §727). But the fact that the time reference of second participles of transitive and intransitive verbs is in my opinion uncertain (see §§768–81) makes me more than reluctant to use the alleged time-distinction in this argument. Another difficulty arises with *beon/wesan* in *Beo* 361 *Her syndon geferede, feorran cumene* ‖ . . . *Geata leode*, where *geferede* is the past participle of a transitive verb and therefore passive (so Klaeber 3, Glossary) and *cumene*—intransitive and active—may be taken as parallel to *geferede* or in apposition to *leode*. (This problem is complicated by the possibility suggested by Kilpiö (my §744) that *geferede* could be for *geferde* < *feran* 'to go' and could therefore be intransitive; see *OEG*, §751(3).) A similar example with *weorþan*—except that the two participles are joined by *ond* and the possibility of apposition cannot therefore arise—is *GD* 152. 19 *þa binnan feawum dagum hi wurdon forðferde butu 7 bebyrgde in þære cyrcan.* The same combination occurs in *ÆCHom* ii. 174. 13 *Hi . . . wurdon ða færlice forðferede, and binnon ðære cyrcan bebyrigede.* Hoffmann (p. 21) quotes two similar examples with *beon/wesan*—*Bede* 48. 7 *betwih him twam we þus tweofealdne deað þrowiað, oððe sticode beoð oððe on sæ adruncene* and *ChronE* 67. 1 (852) *7 þær wæron feala ofslægene 7 adruncen on ægðre hand.* These, he argues, point to an adjectival function for the second participle—the absence of inflexion in *adruncen* is not (I believe) conclusive for a verbal use; cf. §727— and form his main reason for rejecting the theory that *ic eom cumen* could mean either 'I am come' (state) or 'I have come' (action). For him *cumen* is an adjective. I take this point up in §741.[178]

§736. Hoffmann claims that with both auxiliaries the reference is to state—with *beon/wesan* the periphrasis denotes 'der Zustand', with *weorþan* 'das Geraten in einen Zustand, den Beginn oder das Eintreten eines Zustandes' (p. 46) ['the state' . . . 'the action of becoming in a certain state, the beginning or coming into existence of a state']. This distinction seems reasonable today. That it existed for native speakers at one stage in the development of the language is plausible in view of the general senses of *beon/wesan* and *weorþan*. But the fact that there are comparatively few OE examples with *weorþan* and its early disappearance in ME must be noted; see further §739. On the distinction between *wesan* and *weorþan* in the passive periphrases, see §§786–801.

---

[178] Kuntz (pp. 187–91) sees Hoffmann's two examples as containing two passives and cites 'des exemples mieux assurés'. My uncertainty remains.

§737. After *beon/wesan* and *weorþan* the participle is nominative. In general it is uninflected in the singular and has -*e* in the plural, e.g. singular with *beon/wesan Or* 74. 26 *Nu ic þuss gehroren eam 7 aweg gewiten, ÆCHom* ii. 472. 18 *An þæs cynges cnihta wæs ær afaren to Hierusalem, Beo* 375 *is his eafora nu ‖ heard her cumen,* and (possibly, as Jost (1909, §152) suggests) with a future reference *CP* 351. 14 *Gif ðonne ðæs monnes mod 7 his lufu bið behleapen eallunga on ða lænan sibbe* . . . ; plural with *beon/wesan Or* 224. 5 *Craccuse wæron monege cyningas of monegum landum to fultume cumene, ÆCHom* i. 88. 17 *soðlice hi sind forðfarene, ðaðe ymbe þæs cildes feorh syrwdon,* and *PPs* 106. 24 *beoð heora yþa up astigene* (here again the reference may be future);[179] singular with *weorþan* (in addition to the examples cited in §735) *ÆCHom* i. 86. 24 *þa wearð se lichama eal toslopen, ÆCHom* i. 258. 9 *Se Hælend Crist, syððan he to ðisum life com, and man wearð geweaxen,* and *Mald* 202 *þa wearð afeallen þæs folces ealdor;* and plural with *weorþan Or* 88. 14 . . . *on þære ondrædinge hwonne hie on þa eorþan besuncene wurden* (where the passive would be *besencte;* cf. *BlHom* 49. 8 *7 þa wurdon on helle besencte*) and *PPs* 91. 6 . . . *þæt hi forwordene weorðen syþþan on worulda woruld.*

§738. These rules for inflexion always obtain in Ælfric. There are occasional exceptions elsewhere, e.g. (with an inflected form in the feminine singular) *CP* 3. 13 *Swa clæne hio wæs oðfeallenu on Angelcynne,* an uninflected plural in *Or* 82. 13 *Hie wæron cumen Leoniðan to fultume,* and (with an uninflected plural alongside an inflected one)

El 1266 Nu synt geardagas
 æfter fyrstmearce forð gewitene,
 lifwynne geliden.

See further §§33-7.

§739. *Weorþan* is much less common in this periphrasis than *beon/wesan* in OE. Neither *OED* (s.v. *worth v.*[1]) nor Mustanoja provides any ME examples. It could therefore be argued that it never became a true auxiliary in this function. I have to admit that the point cannot be proven. Yet I cannot see on what grounds Wattie (p. 142) so confidently avers that in

Beo 1233 Wyrd ne cuþon,
 geosceaft grimme, swa hit agangen wearð
 eorla manegum

'the tense is a genuine pluperfect'.

---

[179] Jost (1909, pp. 83-6) discusses more examples from *Cura Pastoralis.*

§740. What is the position with *beon/wesan*? With *habban* periphrases we have the evidence of MnE usage to show that a perfect/pluperfect tense did develop. There is no such evidence from MnE with the *beon/wesan* periphrases. *OED* (s.v. *be* v., IV. 14. b.) says that 'be' appears with

intransitive verbs, forming perfect tenses, in which use it is now largely displaced by *have* after the pattern of transitive verbs: *be* being retained only with *come, go, rise, set, fall, arrive, depart, grow*, and the like, when we express the condition or state now attained, rather than the action of reaching it, as 'the sun is set,' 'our guests are gone,' 'Babylon is fallen,' 'the children are all grown up.'

Mustanoja (pp. 500-1) accepts the notion implicit in *OED* that 'be' did become an auxiliary of the perfect and pluperfect tenses, but that 'have' gradually took over:

Wesan/beon with a past participle is originally also used to indicate a state and then comes to indicate the effect or result of an action (i.e., it becomes a true auxiliary of the perfect and pluperfect). . . .[180] Throughout the ME period a steady increase is noticeable in the use of *have* as an auxiliary of the perfect and pluperfect tenses.

Mustanoja (p. 500) also remarks: '*Wesan/beon* occurs with intransitive verbs. Originally this auxiliary is used only with perfective, "mutative" intransitives (e.g. *nu is se dæg cumen, Beow.* 2646; cf. also *hie beoþ adruncene* and *se halga fæder wæs inn agan*)', defining mutative verbs as verbs 'indicating a transition from one place or condition to another (*to go, come, return, become, grow, fade, disappear*, etc.)' (p. 500 fn. 2). As I am reluctant to press too far the distinction between 'perfective' ('mutative') and 'imperfective' verbs (see §722), I do not pursue this point. But it should be noted that *habban* is found in the earliest prose and poetry with so-called 'mutative' verbs, e.g. *Or* 186. 22 *þa he hæfde on þæm emnete gefaren oþ he com to Ticenan þære ie* and *Beo* 2103 *syððan mergen com,* ǁ *and we to symble geseten hæfdon*; see further §§722-33, Zadorožny 1974, pp. 385-6, and (for more contrasting examples) Kuntz, pp. 192-232.

§741. If it is accepted that the development did occur, the question arises: when did the combination *beon/wesan* + second participle of an intransitive verb become a 'true' perfect/pluperfect? Lussky (*passim* and p. 67) claims that this stage was reached in OE when the participle was uninflected. I have already given my reasons for reject-

---

[180] It has already been pointed out (§729 above) that there is an inconsistency between this definition of the function of the perfect/pluperfect and that given by Mustanoja on p. 499, where he speaks of 'true perfects and pluperfects expressing action rather than a state resulting from an action'.

ing this argument in §727. Jost, after citing examples like *Beo* 375 *is his eafora nu* || *heard her cumen*, observes (1909, §28) 'Alle diese zusammengesetzten Formen bezeichnen nach Nader [*Anglia*, 10] (S. 561 u. 556) ein Perfektum, oder wie ich mich lieber ausdrücke: sie bezeichnen den aus einer abgeschlossenen (vollendeten) Handlung resultierenden präsentischen Zustand.'[181] Hoffmann (pp. 15-16), faced with the difficulty of deciding when the participle is adjectival and when it is verbal, decides that it is clearly adjectival in three situations:

(1) when only the participle occurs in OE, e.g. *ÆCHom* i. 204. 1 *Eadige beoð þa þe sind ofhingrode*;

(2) when the participle corresponds to a Latin adjective, e.g. *Gen* 18. 12 *Syððan ic ealdode 7 min hlaford geripod ys*, Latin *Postquam consenui et dominus meus uetulus est*;[182]

(3) when the participle is co-ordinate with an adjective, e.g. *ÆCHom* i. 456. 20 *næs his reaf horig ne tosigen*.

To these we can add 'when the participle is modified by an adverb', e.g. *ChronA* 48. 10 (755) *7 se swiþe gewundad wæs*. But even after eliminating all these, he still concludes (pp. 24 and 46-7) that *beon/wesan* and *weorþan* do not serve as auxiliaries in these periphrases and that the participle remains adjectival.[183] This is consistent with his general thesis that 'ein umschriebenes Perfektum gibt es im Ae. nicht' (p. 46); see §729. Is he right? Or are those right who (as already noted) believe there was a periphrastic perfect with *beon/ wesan* in OE? I do not know the answer, and do not know how it can be found.

§742. Hoffmann, however, is confident that the development did take place, for he says that in Laȝamon we find a perfect formed with *wesan* (pp. 25-6) and observes that, in ME *heo beoþ icumene*, *wesan* became an auxiliary verb (p. 49). Yet in pointing out that the adjectival function of the participle is demonstrable in MnE examples of this periphrasis and in agreeing with *OED* that it now expresses state or condition, he makes the significant observation that *wesan* never becomes an auxiliary to the same extent as *habban* (p. 26). This must provoke the question: Did *beon/wesan* ever become a true auxiliary of the perfect/pluperfect? The original function of these periphrases seems to have been (in the words of *OED* already quoted)

---

[181] 'All these compound forms denote, according to Nader [*Anglia*, 10] (pp. 561 and 556), a perfect, or, as I prefer to express it, they denote the present state resulting from a finished (completed) action.'

[182] Some of his examples in this group (pp. 15-16) are unhappy because the Latin equivalent too may be a participle or an adjective, e.g. *offensus* or *iratus* translated by *gebolgen*.

[183] This question crops up again in the passive periphrasis; see §762.

to 'express the condition or state now attained, rather than the act of reaching it'. Did they ever move beyond it? I am not sure that the evidence provided by Hoffmann or by Mustanoja (pp. 499 ff.) establishes that they did. However, the problem lies outside the scope of this work.

(4) *The periphrases with* agan

§ 743. In her note on

Sea 27   Forþon him gelyfeð lyt,   se þe ah lifes wyn
              gebiden in burgum,   bealosiþa hwon,
              wlonc ond wingal,

Kershaw wrote: 'For the use of *agan* (in the sense of *habban*) with the p.p. cf. Wulfstan's *Sermo ad Anglos* [*WHom* 20. 51 *Ne prælas ne moton habban þæt hi agon on agenan hwilan mid earfeðan gewunnen*].' Gordon in her edition accepts this and adds: 'Probably the construction retained a more literal force than with *hafað*, and we may translate "he who has a pleasant life, lived in dwellings of men . . .".' One cannot generalize from two examples—I have noted no more. Zadorožny (1974, pp. 384–5) discusses some OHG examples.

d. The periphrastic passive

(1) *Introductory remarks*

§ 744. The discussion which follows was ready for typing when Part III, Second Half, of F. Th. Visser's *An Historical Syntax of the English Language* (Leiden, 1973) came into my hands. His discussion of the passive (§§ 1905–2000) is confused and misleading as far as Old English is concerned and I have made no alterations of any substance as a result of reading it. But I have included references to Visser's discussions and examples where necessary. I have, however, benefited from my reading of a 1979 Licentiate Thesis for the University of Helsinki by Matti Kilpiö entitled 'Passive Constructions in the Old English Bede and the *Pastoral Care*: a Comparative Study with Special Reference to Translation Technique' and from discussion with the author. I hope that this general acknowledgement will be acceptable to him in lieu of detailed reference to a work which will soon be superseded by his doctoral thesis. Future workers, especially those interested in the methods of Anglo-Saxon translators of Latin, should take cognizance of Kilpiö's work.

§ 745. In view of Lieber's assertion (*Linguistic Inquiry*, 10 (1979), 667–8) that 'under the analysis to be presented below, nothing more need be said: the rules which relate passive to active sentences remain stable throughout the history of English', I must now express the hope that the sections which follow will not be thought supererogatory. That Lieber is unlikely to have said the last word emerges from the fact that, while she spots the flaw in Visser, iii, §1959, she fails to spot those in Visser, iii, §§1934 and 1967-8 (her pp. 681-6, but Mitchell 1979*b*, pp. 539-42, and my §836 fn.); that, on the evidence of her statements (p. 685) about *agitan, æmtian,* and *forgifan,* she appears not to have understood BT(S); and that, in her treatment of *Bede* 392. 2 (p. 687), she makes two mistakes in transcribing and three elementary errors in translating a short sentence which is correctly translated by Miller, but gives no sense in her translation.

§746. Only one OE verb had a synthetic passive, viz. *hatte* 'is/was called', e.g. *ÆLS* 32. 3 *and se munuc hatte Abbo.* But, as QW notes (p. 81), 'despite its distinctive passive inflection, *hatan.* was often used with the periphrastic construction and also with *man: hi sind gehatene* 'they are called', *to þæm porte þe mon hæt æt Hæþum* 'to the trading place which is called Hedeby'. Visser (iii, §1914) offers further examples.

§747. Impersonal *man* was often used in the nominative singular with an active verb form as an equivalent of the passive voice (§§363-9). It expresses the agent with varying degrees of indefiniteness. Other passive equivalents noted by Kilpiö (my §744) include a qualifier + *man,* e.g. *CP* 457. 20 *forðæmðe nan mon ne mæg nauðer ðissa swa forlætan ðæt ðæt oðer ne weaxe,* Latin *in quo nimirum unum vitium nullatenus extinguitur;* pl. *men(n),* e.g. *Bede(T)* 386. 18 . . . *þætte men sweotolice ongeaton meahton . . . ,* Latin . . . *ut palam daretur intellegi . . . ;* indefinite *we,* e.g. *CP* 343. 12 *Be ðæm we magon ongietan . . . ,* Latin . . . *ostenditur;* indefinite *þu,* e.g. *CP* 241. 14 *ðu meahtes geseon . . . ,* Latin *videbatur;* a reflexive construction, e.g. *CP* 435. 25 . . . *se ðe hine upahefeð,* Latin . . . *qui . . . attollitur . . .* (contrast *CP* 463. 22 . . . *ðu wurde upahæfen,* Latin . . . *te elevas*); and an OE intransitive verb, e.g. *Bede(Ca)* 46. 7 . . . *þanon ðe hi* [MS *B him*] *sciphere on becom,* Latin . . . *quo naues eorum habebantur.*

§748. But the ancestor of the modern passive—in which the direct (OE accusative) object of the active verb becomes the subject of the passive—was also common, i.e. *beon/wesan* + the second participle of a transitive verb, e.g. *ÆLS* 32. 64 *Eala þu bisceop to bysmore synd getawode þas earman landleoda.* Alongside this periphrasis was that with *weorþan*—described by Wattie (p. 143) as 'the unnecessary duplication of passive auxiliaries' and 'the only false start' in the OE tense-system—e.g. *ÆLS* 32. 10 *Se munuc þa Abbo . . . wearð sona to abbode geset.* Second participles are also found with other verbs, e.g. *ChronA* 48. 15 (755) . . . *þær se cyning ofslægen læg, ÆLS* 32. 68 *þin folc lið ofslagen, ÆLS* 7. 336 *þa com Gallicanus eac to gode gebogen,* and *ÆCHom* i. 348. 9 *Soðlice ða ðe to us asende becumað. . . .* But while these demonstrate how natural it was for the construction to arise, they need not be classed as periphrastic passives.

§749. Certain formal distinctions made by various writers need to be mentioned here because they are sometimes invoked in the discussions which follow. First we have the distinction between the 'personal' passive, e.g. *Solil* 2. 14 *þa bec sint gehatene Soliloquiorum,* and the 'impersonal', which in OE may occur either with or without the subject *hit,* e.g. *Solil* 19. 14 *Hyt is gecwæden on þære æ þæt man sceole lufian hys nehstan* and *CP* 65. 23 *Be ðæm is gecueden on ðære bryde lofe: Ðin nosu is suelc se torr on Liuano ðæm munte.* The use of these terms is open to the objection that a book is no more a person than is a saying. I use the terms differently: 'personal' means that the accusative object of the active verb form becomes the subject of the passive form and 'impersonal' covers all other situations, a typical example being *ÆCHom* ii. 510. 10 *and wæs ða geholpen ðam unscyldigum huse.* (I have to admit that this use is also open to objection and now regret that I did not use some other terms such as 'direct' and 'indirect'.) Then we have the passive which expresses an action (*eine Handlung*) opposed to that which expresses a state (*ein Zustand*); on this distinction in OE see §§786-801 below. Fröhlich (pp. 10-12) distinguishes seven categories in pursuance of his interest in the expression of the indefinite agent. For our purposes, these can (I think) be reasonably reduced to two—those involving a personal agent (his groups 1 and 4-7) and those involving an impersonal agent (his group 3); in either case, the agent can of course be expressed or unexpressed (see §§802-33). Since *geendian* can be intransitive as well as transitive, Fröhlich's only example in group 2—*Or* 60. 16 *þa wearð Babylonia ⁊ Asiria anwald geendad, ⁊ gehwearf on Meðas*—is better taken as active than passive; there is no need to erect a separate category to cover examples like this.

(2) *Basic paradigms of verbs which govern only one accusative object*
§750. As we consider the passive forms of OE verbs whose only object is in the accusative case, it will be useful to have before us a purely formal or, to use F. R. Palmer's term (*A Linguistic Study of the English Verb* (Longman, 1965), 55-7), basic paradigm of the

periphrastic personal passive as it occurs in 'Alfredian' texts and in
Ælfric. Meaning and function are considered below. Only one example of each form is given, person, number, negation, relative position of verb and participle (§§757-8), inflexion or non-inflexion of
participle (§§759-61), and intervention of other elements, not being
taken into account; in situations such as these we can perhaps agree
with Greenfield's dictum that 'statistically there is very little difference between one example and none' (p. 118). But see Mitchell
1975a, pp. 26-8. The passive of verbs which govern something other
than one accusative object is discussed in §§834-58.

§751.   'ALFREDIAN' TEXTS

Form	*beon/wesan* + second (passive) ptc. of trans. verb	*weorþan* + second (passive) ptc. of trans. verb
pres. ind.	*Or* 72. 10 *is* . . . *sungen* *Or* 14. 24 *sint genemde* *Or* 20. 18 *bið* . . . *gebrowen* *Or* 18. 18 *beoð* . . . *geworht*	*Or* 248. 29 *wyrþ aworpen*
pres. subj.	*Or* 18. 22 *sy* . . . *geworht* *CP* 87. 4 *beon gewlitegode*	*CP* 191. 15 *wyrðen* . . . *gedemede*
imp.	*CP* 169. 17 *beo ðu abisgad*	*CP* 443. 16 *weorðað* . . . *gefullwade*
past ind.	*Or* 126. 5 *wæs* . . . *funden*	*Or* 186. 24 *gewundod wearð*
past subj.	*Or* 186. 24 *ofslagen wære*	*Or* 264. 13 *geboren* . . . *wurde*
uninflected inf.[184]		
(a) after adj.	—	—
(b) with 'modal' verbs[185]	*Bede* 20. 14 *gewemmed beon* . . . *mihte* *Bede* 72. 11 *mot* . . . *halgad beon*	*CP* 399. 17 *magon* . . . *weorðan gehælede* —

[184] As far as I have observed, only the uninflected infinitives *beon, wesan,* and *weorþan,* occur in the periphrastic passive infinitive; the *to* form does not. Callaway (1913, p. 6) and van der Gaaf (*EStudies,* 10 (1928), 109) agree. According to Scheler (p. 101), the periphrastic passive infinitive owes its existence to Latin influence. Riggert (pp. 75-6), who gives some twenty examples from OE poetry, says it is avoided in OHG, except in translations. On the uses of this infinitive, see §922. On the inflected infinitive with 'a passive sense', see §§934-43.

[185] 'Modal' is a dangerous word, as *ÆGram* 143. 19 *amari uolo, ic wylle beon gelufod* shows. See further §991. Tense and mood are disregarded here. For further examples with these and other verbs such as **durran, ðurfan,* and *gewilnian,* see Callaway 1913, pp. 83-8, and Visser, iii, §1921.

'ALFREDIAN' TEXTS (*cont.*)

Form	beon/wesan + second (passive) ptc. of trans. verb	weorþan + second (passive) ptc. of trans. verb
uninflected inf. (*cont.*)		
(*b*) with 'modal' verbs (*cont.*)	*Or* 21. 11 *sceal . . . beon forbærned*	*Bede* 38. 29 *sceolde . . . gehalgod weorþan*
	Or 128. 5 *oferwunnen beon wolde*	*CP* 387. 26 *wolden weorðan forlorene*
(*c*) in acc. and inf. construction	*Bede* 34. 15 *he hine þa geseah . . . beon abysgadne*	—[186]
	Bede(Ca) 402. 23 *ic wiste . . . me aðwegenne beon*	
	Bede 330. 13 . . . *feola . . . he oncneow . . . him forgifen weosan*	

§752.   ÆLFRIC

Form	beon/wesan + second (passive) ptc. of trans. verb	weorþan + second (passive) ptc. of trans. verb
pres. ind.	*ÆCHom* i. 346. 27 *bedæled is*	*ÆHom* 16. 285 *wurð . . . geendod*
	ÆCHom i. 346. 4 *sind . . . getealde*	
	ÆCHom i. 270. 11 *bið forwyrned*	
	ÆCHom ii. 294. 25 *beoð arærede*	
pres. subj.	*ÆCHom* i. 268. 9 *sy afandod*	*ÆCHom* ii. 268. 10 *weorðe awend*
	ÆCHom i. 170. 15 *beon afandode*	
imp.	*ÆCHom* i. 92. 3 *beo ðu geciged*	*ÆLS* 34. 260 *wurðað ymbscrydde*
past ind.	*ÆCHom* ii. 510. 12 *wæs . . . gehalgod*	*ÆCHom* ii. 548. 17 *ætbroden wearð*
past subj.	*ÆCHom* ii. 512. 1 *alyfed wære*	*ÆCHom* i. 112. 17 *wurde . . . gemiltsod*

[186] I cannot add to the solitary example given by Callaway (1913, pp. 120-4 and 125) —*GuthB* 1259-62. Even this is very dubious, for *soden* may be adjectival, parallel to *unrotne . . . meðne modseocne*, despite the absence of inflexion; see §42(8).

Form	*beon/wesan* + second (passive) ptc. of trans. verb	*weorþan* + second (passive) ptc. of trans. verb
uninflected inf.		
(*a*) after adj.	*ÆCHom* ii. 316. 22 *we ðe næron wurðe beon his wealas gecigde*[187]	—
(*b*) with 'modal' verbs	*ÆCHom* ii. 344. 33 *mage . . . beon geclænsod*	
	ÆCHom i. 56. 12 *moste . . . geteald beon*	
	ÆCHom i. 262. 12 *sceal . . . beon gemyngod*	*ÆHomM* 15. 147 *wurþan scealt . . . ofslagen*
	ÆCHom i. 598. 5 *nelle . . . beon alysed*	
	ÆCHom i. 602. 2 *uton . . . beon ymbscrydde*	
(*c*) in acc. and inf. construction	*ÆLS* 11. 215 *læt me beon geteald*	—

§753. A comparison of the basic OE paradigm with its MnE equivalent shows that the former lacked the continuous tenses, e.g. 'he is/was being loved', the perfect, e.g. 'he has/had been loved',[188] and combinations of the latter with the 'modal' auxiliaries, e.g. 'He shall/should (may/might, will/would) have been loved'. OE also lacks patterns like 'He might be being interrogated right now' and 'He had been being scolded for a long time'; on these, see Visser, iii, §2182. These differences between the OE and the MnE paradigms are not surprising; the continuous tenses were not established in OE (§§685-90) and there were no OE participles equivalent to MnE 'being' and 'been' until very late (§1099).

§754. Visser offers us OE examples of other constructions involving the passive. They include sentences in which the cognate object becomes the subject in the passive construction, e.g. *Bede* 236. 16 *þa ðis gefeoht neah Winwede streame wæs gefohten* (iii, §1929); passives introduced by expletive *þær*, e.g. *ChronA* 60. 11 (823)

---

[187] Callaway (1913, p. 158) records only this example. Neither van der Gaaf (*EStudies*, 10 (1928), 130) nor I have found another. Nor Visser (iii, §1921).

[188] The best support Visser (iii, §2161) can muster for his statement that 'in Old English the idiom ['an explicit perfect passive'], though rare, was not unknown' is *Luke(WSCp)* 12. 50 *Ic hæbbe on fulluhte beon gefullod,* Latin *baptisma autem habeo baptizari* where *beon* is an infinitive, not a participle, and the ME *Lambeth Hom, feren it is þat we and ure heldrene habbæð ben turnd fro him* (quoted after Visser).

7 þær wæs micel wæl geslægen (iii, §1931, but see my §1493); examples of beon/wesan accompanied by two participles, e.g. GD(H) 164. 7 7 sona eac beseah on þone ceorl, þe þær gebunden wæs gehæft and (Visser argues) the manuscript reading of Beo 991 Ða wæs haten hreþe Heort innanweard || folmum gefrætwod (iii, §2166); and the 'double passive group' seen in Bede 78. 2 þa þe þonne in gewunan monaðaðle numene beoð, butan beorðres intingan, heo wæron bewered heora weorum gemengde beon, Latin quippe quia et sine partus causa, cum in suetis menstruis detinentur, uiris suis misceri prohibentur (iii, §2183). On examples like Max i 93 Scip sceal genægled, see §1007.

§755. As we might expect from §§617–18, the future passive is expressed not by the periphrases with willan and sculan, but by combinations of the present tense of beon or weorþan with the second participle, e.g. ÆCHom i. 270. 11 ac him bið forwyrned þurh Godes gescyldnysse, ÆCHom i. 270. 19 ac hi beoð a ungeendode on þære toweardan worulde, and ÆHom 16. 284 Lytel þing is geteald þises lifes ryne wið ða ecan worulde, þe ne wurð na geendod. For further examples, mostly from the poetry, see Visser, iii, §§1915 and 1918. But I cannot quite see why Visser should describe 'the existence of a passive construction with reference to the future containing the present tense of the verb weorðan' as 'a remarkable phenomenon' (iii, §1918).

§756. Both Åkerlund (EStudien, 47 (1913–14), 324) and Visser (iii, §§1872–87) suggest that the equivalent of the idiom 'The house is building' occurred in OE. I give my reasons for rejecting this view in EStudies, 57 (1976), 385–9.

(3) Order of elements

§757. The examples given in the basic paradigms illustrate the obvious truth that the verb may precede or follow the participle in phrases consisting of these two elements only. This, the position of the subject, and the intervention or non-intervention of other elements, are all governed by the principles set out in chapter IX. Visser (iii, §1745) draws our attention to ÆGenPref 78. 64 Eft is seo halige ðrynnys geswutelod on ðisre bec, swa swa is on ðam worde, ðe God cwæð, where the participle is not repeated with the second is.[189]

[189] Minkoff, Neophil. 61 (1977), 127–42, discusses the order of these elements in the Heptateuch, in the corresponding Biblical quotations in ÆCHom, and in the Vulgate, with a view to establishing that Ælfric's practices differed in 'literal translation' and in 'close paraphrase'. He does not, however, restrict himself to the portion of the Heptateuch attributed to Ælfric (see Plan, p. 84) and fails to make such fundamental distinctions as that between examples in principal clauses and those in subordinate clauses.

§758. When the periphrastic passive infinitive contains three elements, six arrangements are theoretically possible if we consider only these three—auxiliary verb, active infinitive, and second (passive) participle—and disregard the other factors mentioned in §757. Three of these are of common occurrence:

(1) verb–infinitive–participle (the modern order), e.g. *Or* 248. 17 *þæt tacnade þæt on his dagum* sceolde beon geboren *se se þe us ealle to anum mæggemote gelaþaþ* and *ÆCHom* ii. 38. 32 *La leof, ic* sceal beon gefullod *æt ðinum handum*;

(2) verb–participle–infinitive, e.g. *Bede* 72. 11 . . . *hwæðer mot biscop* halgad beon *buton oðera biscopa ondweardnesse?* and *ÆCHom* i. 56. 11 . . . *wið þan þæt he* moste *sumum rican men to bearne* geteald beon;

(3) participle–infinitive–verb, e.g. *Or* 128. 5 *þa Darius geseah þæt he* oferwunnen beon wolde . . . (I have found no such examples in the later prose).

The next two combinations have so far been observed (by Callaway 1913, p. 86) only sporadically and only with *weorþan*, not with *beon/wesan*:

(4) participle–verb–infinitive, e.g. *And* 757 *þæt of his cynne* cenned sceolde ‖ weorðan *wuldres god* and *HomU* 26. 140. 20 *wa me earmre, þæt ic æfre* geboren sceolde wurðan . . . ;

(5) infinitive–verb–participle, e.g. *Met* 29. 87 *æghwilc hiora ealle to nauhte* ‖ weorðan sceoldon *wraðe* toslopena and *ÆHomM* 15. 147 *Wite ðu nu, Achior, þæt ðu* wurþan scealt *mid urum swurdum* ofslagen *mid him*. I have, however, noticed one example of this pattern with *beon*, viz. *Bede* 366. 17 *Wæs seo eorðe to ðæs heard 7 to ðæs stanihte, þæt ðær nænig wiht wyllsprynges* beon mihte *on* gesewen.

No examples of the last pattern have come to my attention:

(6) infinitive–participle–verb, viz. ☆*þæt þu* beon/weorþan ofslægen scealt.

(4) *The participle–inflexion, agreement, function, and time-reference*

§759. When the second (passive) participle in the periphrases with *wesan/weorþan* is declined, it is declined strong. As noted in §§33–7, we can distinguish three situations exemplified respectively by *Or* 188. 22 . . . *seo sunne wæs swelce heo wære eall gelytladu* and *Or* 106. 18 . . . *þonne wæron ealle þa dura betyneda*, where the participle is inflected in agreement with the subject; by *Or* 102. 1 *Æfter þæm þe Romeburg getimbred wæs* . . . , *Or* 106. 7 . . . *ænig mon* . . . *þe on gewritun findan mæge þæt Ianas dura siþþan belocen wurde buton anum geare* (where *wurde* is subjunctive plural; cf. Latin *clausas Iani portas*), and *Or* 18. 17 . . . *on þæm sciprapum, þe beoð of hwæles hyde geworht*, where the participle could have an inflexional ending but does not; and by *Or* 60. 11 *Se æresta cyning wæs Ninus haten* and *Or* 126. 4 *7 þær wæs ungemetlic micel licgende feoh funden on ðæm wicstowun*, where it is impossible to say definitely either that the participle is inflected or that it is uninflected—or (to put it another way) whether the 'zero-morpheme' is present or absent! This last situation always arises when the subject is masculine singular or neuter singular and may exist when the subject is feminine singular or neuter plural and the participle did not have a long syllable + a short syllable, with medial *i* or *u*; see *OEG,* §643(5).

§760. Details of the inflexional endings have been given in §§33-7. In brief, they are usually sg. −, the generalized pl. *-e*. I have noted no exceptions to this in Ælfric[190] or in Wulfstan, but there are a few plurals with − in *BlHom*; see §34. In the earlier prose, there are sporadic examples of fem. sg. *-u*, fem. pl. *-a*, neut. pl. *-u*, and pl. all genders −. So too in the poetry. In general, then, it can be said that throughout the OE period the participle agrees with its referent as far as the inflexional system allows, except when it is feminine singular. The absence of *-u* in the feminine singular forms is apparent early and can be explained by the working of analogy, for the majority of participles properly had the nominative singular ending −; but see further §33 fn. The sporadic early examples of pl. − can be similarly explained by reference to the existence of both feminine and neuter nouns which had − in the nominative plural.

§761. If a participle in an accusative and passive infinitive construction is inflected, it will of course be accusative, e.g. acc. sg. masc. *-ne* in *Bede* 34. 15 (§751) and acc. sg. fem. *-e* in *Bede* 24. 3 ... *geseah him fram deoflum tobrohte beon ða boc his agenra synna.*

§762. Mustanoja remarks (p. 440) that

the past participle accompanying OE *beon* (*wesan, weorðan*) is originally a predicate adjective (cf. present-day *I am pleased*, etc.). In the course of time the combination comes to be regarded as an integral verbal unit, and the participle tends

---

[190] An apparent exception after *cuman* is *aræred* in *ÆHom* 11A. 162 *And he ... cymð eft to demende on ðam micclan dæge eallum manncynne, ælcum be his dædum, 7 we ealle menn cumað cuce him togeanes of urum deaðe aræred ðurh his drihtenlican mihte, ælc mann ðe ær cucu wæs on his moder innoðe, þæt ure ælc ðær onfo edlean æt Gode. . . .* But here we can claim that *aræred* is singular under the influence of *ælcum ... his ... ælc mann ... his ... ure ælc* and especially of the idiomatic singular *deaðe* (see §87), that the plural *cuce* goes with *cumað*, and that the phrase *of urum deaðe aræred* is dependent on *ælc mann.* The fact that MS *P* has *arærde* seems to me testimony of the strength of the feeling that a participle referring to a plural antecedent should be inflected.

to lose its predicative, adjectival, character. One result of this is that although the great majority of participles in OE passive periphrases retain their adjectival flectional endings, there are also participles without endings. In ME, along with the breaking up of the OE inflections, all participles lose their flectional endings. They are still seen, for example, in *Poema Morale (fewe beoþ icorene*, 104).

His third sentence has been qualified in §760. Were the changes he spells out in his second sentence occurring in OE? The fact that in most of the singular forms in — the 'zero-morpheme' could, as it were, be present and that -*e* occurs in the plural without exception in Ælfric and Wulfstan makes it possible to argue that the participle was still adjectival in the sense that it carried inflexion. (But see §§727 and 735.) This led scholars such as Kurtz (pp. 56-7) and Hoffmann (p. 6) to express the view endorsed by Mustanoja in the first sentence above—that in the periphrases the participle was originally an adjective. But, as Green has pointed out (1913, pp. 91 and 117-18), the fact that these participles can be accompanied by an expression of agency or instrumentality (either dative/instrumental alone or a preposition + the appropriate case) reinforces the common-sense argument that, since they are after all derived from verbs, they were at least partly verbal and not purely adjectival.[191]

§763. Closs and Lussky suggest that the presence or absence of inflexion is the deciding factor. Closs writes (p. 33) 'Constructions which resemble passives abound. They differ from the regular passive only in that . . . [the] past participle . . . is inflected like an adjective . . . whereas the regular passive is uninflected.' She gives as an example *Or* 156. 15 *⁊ þeh þe Romane gefliemed wæren, hie wæron þeh gebielde mid þæm þæt hie wiston hu hie to ðæm elpendon sceoldon*, which she translates 'Although the Romans were put to flight, yet they were encouraged in that they knew how . . .'. She goes on: 'these inflected passive participles may be treated as adjectivalizations'.

[191] The combined implication of the first sentence in Visser, iii, §1909, and of iii, §1908, seems to be that 'originally' the agent was never expressed. Such a view has received specific expression: 'Since in the author's [Pilch's] opinion—which is certainly correct—Old English "agents" in passive sentences are to be regarded as Latin loan-syntax (with *fram* = Latin *a*, and *þurh* = *per*), what is transformed is the predicate, i.e. verb plus object' (Hallander, *SN* 48 (1950), 140 fn. 20). I have no doubt that the influence of the Latin ablative played a part in the use of the dative/instrumental with 'passive periphrases' and elsewhere (see Dančev 1969, §29)—though here dialect too may be relevant (but see ibid., §30)—and that the Latin preposition affected the translator's choice of preposition; cf. van Dam's observation (p. xii) that 'Latin influence is highly probable in the case of *fram* + the dative, *mid* + the dative, the instrumental, or the accusative, and *þurh* + the accusative, when these prepositions introduce an agent in the passive.' But I am not yet convinced that sentences such as *Or* 40. 13 . . . *in Egyptum wearð on anre niht fiftig manna ofslegen, ealle fram hiora agnum sunum*, where *a/ab* does not occur in the Latin printed by Sweet, have no native basis and would not have developed without the help of Latin. There is room for more work here.

This seems to be Lussky's view too, for—generalizing from *Beowulf* —he claims (p. 62) that 'in Anglo-Saxon . . . wherever the participle is inflected it is felt as an adjective belonging to the noun . . . ; wherever it is uninflected, it is felt as belonging to the verb . . .'.

§764. I cannot accept this. I cannot even see that Closs's example illustrates it unambiguously. (She would have been on even shakier ground if she had cited those I quote in the next footnote.) However, it is easy enough to find examples which seem to do so; cf. *Or* 1. 18 *Hu on Egyptum wurdon on anre niht L monna ofslagen from hiora agnum sunum* with *Or* 32. 18 *7 þæt drugon oþ hi mid ealle ofslegene wæron butan swiðe feawum*. (This pair of examples also seems to illustrate the alleged distinction between *weorþan* and *beon/wesan* discussed in §§786–801. But see §799.) However, the distinction does not hold even for Closs's own text, *Orosius*, as the following series demonstrates, at least to the satisfaction of this non-native informant: *Or* 106. 8 . . . *þæt Ianas dura siþþan belocen wurde buton anum geare* (see §759), *Or* 106. 18 *7 þonne hie frið hæfdon, þonne wæron ealle þa dura betyneda*, and *Or* 106. 20 *Ac þa þa Octauianus se casere to rice feng, þa wurdon Ianas dura betyneda*. Lussky's case is no stronger. But we can envy the ease with which he disposes of examples which do not suit him: they are 'determined by the subjective point of view of the author' (p. 68); 'such sudden shifts in point of view must not cause us too much surprise. They are characteristic of the old writers' (p. 53).

§765. I hope it will not cause the reader too much surprise if I state categorically that the material presented above is enough to show that the alleged distinction is untenable for OE. Even if it has any meaning in view of the large number of ' "zero-morpheme" situations', it requires us to believe that a 'regular passive' with the participle uninflected sprang like Cadmus' soldiers into full being alongside the construction with an inflected participle, then existed spasmodically in singular and plural in the 'Alfredian' texts, but subsequently disappeared in Ælfric and Wulfstan in the plural and perhaps even in the singular. That such a distinction could have existed in the language before the OE period, or that speakers of Old English felt it, seems more than unlikely. It is easier to believe this than to believe that the Lindisfarne and Rushworth glossators had different ideas about the interpretation of *Matt* 9. 1 *remittuntur tibi peccata tua* because we find *Li forgefen biðon ł sie forgefen ðe synno ðina* but *Ru þe sindun forletne synnae þine*.[192]

---

[192] For what it is worth, it may also be observed that this theory runs counter to the commonly held distinction between periphrases with *beon/wesan* and those with *weorþan*

§766. Lieber (*Linguistic Inquiry*, 10 (1979), 675–7) proposed two other tests. First, she argues that such 'typical examples' as *Bede* 236. 16 . . . *þa ðis gefeoht neah Winwede streame wæs gefohten* 'are most naturally interpreted as dynamic [passives] because of the locative or directional prepositional phrases'. This would presumably hold if we substituted *gesegen* 'seen' for *gefohten*. But consider the effect of reading *gesene* 'visible'. Second, she says that sentences like *Dream* 44 *Rod wæs ic aræred*—which she renders 'rood was I raised up "I was raised up a cross" '—'indicate that OE must have had a verbal passive'. But we could translate 'I raised up was a cross' or 'I was a cross raised up'. A better test here, one would have thought, is the presence of an expressed agent, as in *Or* 1. 18 (§764).

§767. The position of the participle does not affect either inflexion or sense and cannot throw any light on whether it is adjectival or verbal. A limited study of the adverbial expressions with which the periphrases are used suggested that the method was unlikely to produce firm results. Ambiguity often exists. The same is true in MnE. The contrast between 'The window has been cracked all this week' and 'The window was cracked yesterday' seems at first glance to illustrate neatly the distinction between a 'statal passive' and an 'actional passive' (Mustanoja, p. 438). But 'The window was cracked yesterday' could contrast with 'The window was not cracked the day before yesterday', the inference being 'It must have been cracked by the heavy frost during the night'. None the less, the argument might be better continued in terms of whether the passive expresses an action or a state than in terms of whether the participle is adjectival or verbal—the latter seems to me another of those insoluble pseudo-problems which it is easier to become involved in than to escape from, for we must agree with Hoffmann (p. 9) that, if we look around for criteria, we will find none.

§768. But here we must consider the time-reference of the OE second participle. First, transitive verbs. On these, Campbell remarks (*OEG*, §727 and fn. 2): 'The passive voice has only a verbal adjective, the passive participle: it expresses pure passivity, not necessarily passivity in past time. Note that therefore Lat. *amatus est* is OE *he wæs gelufod*.' Ælfric's *Grammar* (on which Campbell's example is based) conforms to this rule; we read *ÆGram* 139. 17 *amor*, ic eom

which is discussed and (I hope) justifiably dismissed in §§786–801. Thus Klaeber in *EStudien*, 57 (1923), 188, classifies as passives examples with inflected participles such as *Or* 180. 10 *7 gefliemde wurdon* and *Or* 174. 23 *þa æfter þæm þe Cartainiense gefliemde wæron*. . . .

gelufod ys PASSIVUM . . . PRAETERITO INPERFECTO *amabar*, ic
wæs gelufod . . . PRAETERITO PERFECTO *amatus sum* VEL
amatus fui, ic wæs fulfremedlice gelufod . . . PRAETERITO PLVS-
QVAMPERFECTO *amatus eram* VEL *amatus fueram*, ic wæs gefyrn
gelufod . . . and again (a fuller explanation of the passive)

ÆGram 120. 1   SIGNIFICATIO ys getacnung, hwæt þæt word getacnige. ælc
fulfremed word geendað on *o* oððe on *or*. on *o* geendiað ACTIVA VERBA, þæt
synd dædlice word, þa ðe geswuteliað, hwæt men doð. *amo* ic lufige geswutelað
min weorc; ealswa *doceo*, ic tæce, *lego*, ic ræde, *audio*, ic gehyre: on eallum
þisum wordum ys min weorc geswutelod. þas and ðyllice synd ACTIVA gehatene, þæt synd dædlice, forðan ðe hi geswuteliað dæda: do ænne *r* to ðisum
wordum, þonne beoð hi PASSIVA, þæt synd ðrowiendlice; na swylce hi æfre
pinunge getacnion, ac, þonne oðres mannes dæd befylð on me oððe on ðe,
þonne byþ þæt on ledenspræce PASSIVVM VERBVM. ic cweðe nu: *amo*, ic
lufige, þonne cwyst ðu: *quem amas?*, hwæne lufast ðu? ic cweþe: *te amo*, þe
ic lufige; þonne befylð min lufu on ðe, and ðu miht cweðan: *amor a te*, ic eom
gelufod fram ðe. *doceo te*, ic tæce ðe, and ðu cwyst: *doceor a te* ic eom gelæred
fram ðe; ET CETERA.[193]

§769. But Ælfric does not tell the whole truth; the limitations of
the OE verb system did not permit it. There is no doubt that *beon/
wesan* + the second participle can refer to the present; note *ÆGram*
139. 17 *amor, ic eom gelufod* 'I am (being) loved' and *ÆGram*
127. 1 *PASSIVVM: amatur; amatur a me, ic lufige; legitur a me, ic
ræde*. But Latin *amatus est* was not always OE *he wæs gelufod*. For,
as GL (§122) notes, *amatus est* can mean 'has been loved'—completed action and continued state in the present—or 'was loved'—
action completed in the past; compare respectively the 'Pure Perfect'
amavi 'I have loved' and the 'Historical Perfect' *amavi* 'I loved' (GL,
§112). So, in the absence of a second participle for *beon/wesan*, it
would seem likely in theory that Anglo-Saxon translators would be
forced to use *is gelufod* for both *amatur* and *amatus est* 'has been
loved' and *wæs gelufod* for *amatus est* 'was loved' and *amatus eram*.
Such a state of affairs would be consistent with the first of the two
sentences from Campbell quoted above. But it would lead us to expect exceptions to the 'rule' expressed in his second sentence. And
they do exist.

§770. The glossators sometimes vary in their renderings of the Latin
passive. Mossé (1938, §139) contrasts *Ps(A)* 113. 3 *conuersus est*,

---

[193] Hoffmann (pp. 12–13) quotes this passage as proof of his contention that the OE
periphrasis expressed a state, not an action. I do not see how this position can be maintained.
Indeed, one might argue the contrary on the evidence of *dædlice word . . . hwæt men doð
. . . min weorc . . . dæda . . . oðres mannes dæd* and of the repeated phrase *fram ðe*, for
Ælfric uses *fram* as well as *þurh* to express the agent.

gecerred wes with *Ps(A)* 113. 5 *conuersus es, gecerred earðu*, but fails
to point out that the Cambridge, Junius, Lambeth, Royal, Stowe,
and Trinity, Psalters all have *is/ys* in *Ps* 113. 3. Such instances as
these are usually (and not unreasonably) explained as the result of
literal glossing—as Mossé (1938, §139) has it, 'soit ignorance, soit
étourderie'.

§771. But the presence of similar examples in *Cura Pastoralis* is
more significant. Wattie (p. 140) cites *CP* 339. 14 *Nu is ðonne sio
æxs aset on ðane wyrttruman ðæs treowes* as a 'perfect passive with
"is" '—a not unreasonable verdict, one might think, in view of Latin
Iam securis ad radicem arboris posita est, but one which runs directly
counter to Campbell's 'rule'. The doubt raised by this example is not
dispelled by a consideration of those from the same text discussed by
Jost, for not all conform to the 'rule'. Ten exceptions appear in Jost
1909, §149. Seven are presented as quotations from scripture, e.g.
CP 425. 31 *Ge wæron ær on yflum weorcum, ac ge sint nu geclænsode 7 gehalgode, 1 Cor. 6. 11 Et hæc quidam fuistis, sed abluti
estis, sed sanctificati estis . . .* , one—*CP* 119. 22 *To ealdormenn ðu
eart gesett, ne beo ðu ðeah to upahafen,* Latin *Ducem te constituer-
unt, noli extolli*—is a variant of *Ecclus* 32. 1, and the remaining two
are direct renderings of Gregory's own Latin—*CP* 249. 15 . . . *ða
ðe . . . adrifene sindon . . . we sint gesceapene,* Latin *. . . qui . . . sunt
. . . separati . . . sumus . . . creati* (in non-dependent speech), and
CP 365. 13 . . . *ðæt ða halgan gewritu sint us to leohtfatum gesald,*
Latin *. . . quod Scriptura Sancta in nocte vitae praesentis quasi quaedam nobis lucerna sit posita* (in dependent speech). Jost (1909, §151)
adds an eleventh—*CP* 399. 26 *Nis hit [þæt lif] naht feor ascaden
from ðisse worulde,* Latin *quia coniugalis vita nec a mundo longe
divisa est.*[194]

§772. Jost, who sees all these as expressing a state resulting from a
completed action, is so impressed by them that he complains (1909,
§149) that *CP* 411. 11 *Hire sint forgifena swiðe manega synna* does
not properly represent the Latin *Remittuntur ei peccata multa* and
claims (1909, §151) that *CP* 41. 11 *Ac monige siendun mid miclum
giefum monegra cræfta 7 mægene geweorðode* must be taken as perfect despite the present tense in the Latin *Nam sunt nonnulli, qui
eximia virtutem dona percipiunt, et pro exercitatione ceterorum
magnis muneribus exaltantur.* Yet both of these conform to Campbell's 'rule'. Wülfing (ii, §405) reacted in the same way, for, after

---

[194] This is the only one of the eleven examples not in either non-dependent or dependent speech. At the moment, I do not know whether there is any significance in this. But
I doubt it.

quoting *CP* 132. 12 *Toworpne sint ða stanas ðæs temples*, Latin *dispersi sunt lapides sanctuarii* (this is one of Jost's seven scriptural quotations), he goes on to quote *CP* '304. 14 *to ðæm londe ðe ic on geboren wæs* (= *natus sum!*)'. The exclamation mark suggests that he was not conscious of the 'rule' later formulated by Campbell. This is confirmed by a sentence later in the same section: '*Vgl. Ælfric Gramm.* 140, 9 amati sunt = hi wæron(!) gelufode'. Visser (ii, §798) displays a similar 'ignorance' when he writes: 'Perhaps on the analogy of *sprecend wæs*, as a much used translation of *locutus sum*, the Lindisfarne Gospel uses a preterite instead of a present tense in Mt. ix. 30 "Untynde *weron* ego hiera." (aperti sunt oculi illorum).' But all other versions of *Matt* 9. 30 also have *weron* or variant. This is what we should expect in view of Campbell's 'rule', which holds throughout *Matt* 9. But the eleven exceptions from *Cura Pastoralis* (§771) remain.

§773. These are not alone. Other passive constructions also provide exceptions. Thus, while *CP* 409. 3 *is gecyðed*, *CP* 109. 4 *hit is gesæd*, and *CP* 53. 23 *hit is gecweden*, represent Latin *ostenditur, memorantur*, and *dicitur*, we find *wæs* (. . .) *gecweden* in *CP* 69. 9 and 139. 11 representing Latin *dicitur, cwæð* in *CP* 203. 19 representing Latin *dicitur, wæs* (. . .) *beboden* in *CP* 77. 8 and *CP* 93. 3 representing Latin *præcipitur*, and *hit is awriten* in *CP* 93. 6 representing Latin *scriptum est*. (For further examples, see Jost 1909, pp. 32–3 and 76.) But such fluctuations may represent merely the whim of the translator, for one can quite naturally say 'The book said . . .' or 'The book says . . . '. Kilpiö (my §744) notes that *narrantur* is rendered by *earon sægd* in *Bede(T)* 178. 14 (MS *B earan sægde*) but by *wæron sæde* in MSS *O* and *Ca*, and blames the scribes of MSS *O* and *Ca* for failing to recognize the Mercian form *earon*. This leads him to list some twelve examples in which a similar substitution might have occurred.

§774. Other examples which test Campbell's 'rule' are those in which an OE second (passive) participle + a present tense of *wesan/weorþan* represents a Latin perfect passive participle without a verb, e.g. *CP* 39. 7 *ða ðe him underðiedde bioð*, Latin *subiecti*, and *CP* 177. 20 *ða ðe beoð mid synscipe gebundene*, Latin *coniugiis obligati*. Of course the old argument whether the participle is adjectival or verbal reappears here and it can readily be seen from the context why we have the OE present tense in these examples. But one would, I think, expect an OE past tense *according to the 'rule'*.

§775. Let me continue my doubt-sowing by asking two questions. First, why does a translator who has—correctly according to the 'rule'—written *CP* 267. 10 *bið . . . gelacnad . . . gehæled* for Latin *curatur . . . ad sanitatem reducitur, CP* 267. 10 *ne wearð gehæled* for Latin *non est sanata*, and *CP* 267. 20 *wurdon gehwierfde* for Latin *versi sunt*, produce *CP* 267. 6 *nis no gewend* for Latin *non est reversus*?[195] Second, why does Ælfric write *ÆGram* 248. 3 *osculatus sum, ic cyste oððe ic eom gecyssed*?[196]

§776. It is hard to see how all these exceptions can be explained as the result of error or over-literalness. We have our variations today; cf. 'I was pleased by your kind words [yesterday]' with 'I am [remain] pleased that you spoke so kindly'. That the situation was more complicated for the Anglo-Saxons can be seen from these examples: *Bede* 480. 25 *Mid þy ic wæs seofanwintre, þa wæs ic mid gimene minra maga seald to fedanne 7 to lærenne þam arwyrþan abbude Benedicte*, Latin *cum essem annorum vii, cura propinquorum datus sum educandus reuerentissimo abbati Benedicto, CP* 335. 9 *ðios eorðe . . . eallum mannum is to gemanan geseald*, Latin *cunctis hominibus terra communis est*, and *CP* 351. 15 *to ðære ðe him geseald is*, Latin *ad illam quae danda est*. So perhaps we are foolish to expect complete consistency. Indeed, it may be that Campbell is not implying that we have it, for he writes of the transitive verb (*OEG*, §727): 'the passive participle . . . expresses pure passivity, not *necessarily* [my italics] passivity in past time'. There is room for more work here.

§777. So much then for the transitive verb. The participle of the intransitive verb is a different matter, according to Campbell (*OEG*,

[195] It could be argued that *gewendan* is used intransitively and that *is* is therefore 'correct'; see §§777–81. I think this unlikely. But if it is right, we are left with *CP* 267. 20, which, if intransitive, breaks the 'rule'.

[196] Jost (1909, p. 109) claims that in this example *ge-* expresses the perfect. In support he cites *ÆGram(O)* 122. 3 *osculor a te . . . ic eom fram ðe cyssed*. But at least three manuscripts have *gecyssed*. And MS *O* itself has *ÆGram* 120. 16 *amor a te, ic eom gelufod fram ðe . . . doceor a te, ic eom gelæred fram ðe*. So Jost's claim must fail. However, I am indebted to Kilpiö (my §744; private communication) for the following suggestion: 'I think the two translations, differing as they do both in voice and tense, reflect Ælfric's knowledge of both Classical and Post-Classical Latin. The first translation, *ic cyste*, is the expected translation of the perfect of the classical deponent *osculari*; the second is a translation of the archaic or post-classical *osculare*, of which *osculatus sum* is a passive form. The fact that the translation is in the present tense, *ic eom gecyssed*, may simply reflect the fact that Ælfric was acquainted with the tense systems of both Classical and Late Latin. In the latter, there was a great deal of confusion and shifting in the tense system of the passive, so that the original perfect *amatus sum* acquired the present tense force of *amor*, and the original perfect was replaced by a new formation *amatus fui*; see Veikko Väänänen, *Introduction au latin vulgaire* (Paris, 1963), 135 ff.' This has important implications for future workers.

§727 fn. 2): 'from intransitive verbs the part. is past: *ða wæs geworden* "then it had come to pass"'. Strictly speaking, this is irrelevant here, since the participle of an intransitive verb is not passive. But this very fact might provide us with a theoretical explanation for the alleged (and at first glance apparently odd) distinction: that with a transitive verb we have a *passive* participle, with an intransitive verb a *past* participle. However, we must ask whether Campbell's statement is true.

§778. It is not clear to me that the phrase *ða wæs geworden* demonstrates that the ptc. *geworden* refers to the past. If *he is gelufod* means 'he is [now] loved', cannot *hit is geworden* mean 'it is [now] come to pass' and *he is cumen* 'he is [now] come', with all the participles referring to a state in the present? Similarly could not *hit wæs geworden* mean 'it was come to pass, it came to pass' (not necessarily 'it had come to pass'[197]) and *he wæs cumen* 'he was come, he came' (not necessarily 'he had come')? It does not seem to distort the time reference if we translate

Beo 3077   Oft sceall eorl monig   anes willan
                wræc adreogan,   swa us geworden is

'as is come to pass with us',

Beo 823   Denum eallum wearð
                æfter þam wælræse   willa gelumpen

'the desire of all the Danes was come to pass', and *Beo* 1303 *cearu wæs geniwod,* ‖ *geworden in wicun* (with transitive and intransitive verbs parallel) 'sorrow was renewed, was come to pass in the building'. The same is true of *Beo* 375 *is his eafora nu* ‖ *heard her cumen* 'is come', *Jud* 146 *Wæs ða eft cumen* ‖ *leof to leodum* 'was come', and (with a future reference) *GenA* 2197 *Gien þe sunu weorðeð,* ‖ *bearn of bryde þurh gebyrd cumen* 'shall be come'.

§779. Ælfric's *Grammar* offers little help here. His main concern (pp. 120-3, 139-44, 158-61, 182-5, and 194-7) is with the passive of transitive verbs. But he does write *ÆGram* 218. 6 *uenio, ic cume is nevtrvm and of ðam conuenio, ic samod cume activvm and conuenior passivvm, ic eom samod cumen oððe me gewearð.* This is inconclusive for our purpose. The equation *conuenior, ic eom samod cumen* seems to support the notion that *cumen* does not refer to the past. But the introduction of *gewearð* casts doubt on this, even though

___

[197] It can of course mean this, e.g. *Luke(Li)* 24. 12 *þte aworden wæs,* Latin *quod factum fuerat.* Or is this merely the best the glossator could do in the absence of the ptc. *(ge)beon* (§1099)?

it is hard to see any way in which *gewearð* can be the temporal equivalent of *conuenior*. A similar contradiction seems to exist between *ÆGram* 246. 6 *Praeteritvm is forðgewiten: factus, geworht* and *ÆGram* 247. 8 *factus, geworden oððe geworht* on the one hand and *ÆGram* 204. 14 *fio, ic eom geworden oððe geworht* and *ÆGram* 247. 7 *fio, ic eom geworht oððe geworden* on the other. To Jost (1909, §212) the equation in the last two sentences is unintelligible and can only be explained as an unsuccessful attempt at translation which has nothing to do with living idiom. But the fact that Ælfric twice gives *ic eom geworden* (rather than *ic (ge)weorþe*) as the equivalent of *fio* cannot be so easily dismissed in the light of the usage in some of the continuous glosses.

§780. For the most common rendering in the OE Gospels for Latin *(et) factum est,* AV 'and it came to pass', is a combination of *geworden* and *wæs* (not *is*). The following variants occur: *7 hyt wæs geworden* in *Matt(WSCp)* 11. 1, *þa wæs geworden* in *Matt(WSCp)* 7. 28, *7 geworden wæs* in *Mark(Li)* 2. 15, and *7 aworden wæs* in *Mark(Li)* 1. 9.[198] But there is sometimes doubt; thus we find in *Matt(Li)* 7. 28 *7 geworden is ł uæs,* in *Matt(Li)* 11. 1 *7 geworden is ł wæs,* and in *Luke(Li)* 2. 15 *aworden is . . . aworden wæs*—all glossing *factum est.* Similar variations occur in the *Psalms*: in *Ps* 32. 9 *facta sunt* appears as both *wæron gewordyne (Ps(C))* and *gedone synd (Ps(K))* and in *Ps* 113. 2 *facta est* is represented by both *gewordyn ys (Ps(C))* and *geworden wes (Ps(A))*. And we have the already quoted *Luke(Li)* 24. 12 *þte aworden wæs,* Latin *quod factum fuerat.*

§781. The situation then is confused—and must remain so, at least for the time being. But there is clearly room for doubt whether Campbell's briefly formulated 'rule' does in fact hold good throughout OE. Let me ask three final questions. First, what is the time-reference of *gewanod* (which can be active or passive) in *Beo* 476 *is min fletwerod, ‖ wigheap gewanod?* Second, does the time-reference of *geferede* (passive or active?) differ from that of *cumene* (active) in *Beo* 361 *Her syndon geferede, feorran cumene ‖ ofer geofenes begang Geata leode?* (On these two, see §735.) And third, is the time-reference of *gefaren* different in *Or* 186. 22 *þa he hæfde on þæm emnete gefaren oþ he com to Ticenan þære ie* (intransitive) and *LS* 34. 19 *Ða he ða þreo burga gefaren hæfde . . .* (transitive?)?

---

[198] There are other versions, e.g. *7 gelamp* in *Matt(Ru)* 13. 53, *7 hit gewearð* in *Mark (WSCp)* 2. 15, and no equivalent in *Mark(WSCp)* 1. 9.

(5) *Time-reference of the periphrasis*

§782. Differing attitudes to the question whether the participle is adjectival or verbal and doubts about the time-reference of the participle lead to different opinions about the time-reference of the periphrasis. However, the question 'Is there a perfect/pluperfect passive in OE?' is largely, if not completely, a modern academic one. For, as already noted (§753), the pattern 'he has/had been loved' is not found in OE, where there is no participle equivalent to MnE 'been' until very late (§1099). So formally there is no perfect/pluperfect passive in OE. That ought to be the end of the matter. But it is perhaps a little cavalier to dismiss the 'literature' of the subject so.

§783. From the first, the writers of German dissertations confidently distinguished a present, past, perfect, pluperfect, and future, passive, in both poetry (e.g. Schürmann 1884 and Kempf 1888) and prose (e.g. Flamme 1885 and Mohrbutter 1885). Differing interpretations similar to those noted in the preceding paragraphs occur. Thus Schürmann (p. 320) and Flamme (p. 39) classify as perfect only examples with the present tense of the auxiliary, whereas Wülfing (ii, §§405-6) takes *Or* 1. 6 *Hu þæt heofenisce fyr forbærnde þæt lond on þæm wæron þa twa byrig on getimbred, Sodome 7 Gomorre* as perfect, but *Bede* 26. 17 . . . *mid þam æðelestum ceastrum . . . ða þe wæron mid weallum 7 torrum 7 geatum 7 þam trumestum locum getimbrade* as pluperfect. But all these early German writers were prepared to attempt these distinctions. In this, they were anticipated by March (1873), and doubtless by other German writers. But they were not followed by men like Sweet, Ardern, Brook, and Quirk and Wrenn, who wrote introductory grammars of OE in English; indeed Sweet (*Pr. 8*, p. 47) observed that the passive periphrases 'are very vague in meaning' and both Ardern (p. xliii) and QW (p. 81) note the absence of an OE participle meaning 'been', the latter adding the necessary rider 'until very late'. Nor were they followed by Jost (1909, *passim* and pp. 74-82). But his elaborate system—based on distinctions between perfective and imperfective verbs, concrete and abstract sentences, and *beon, wesan,* and *weorþan*—fails in my opinion, for reasons already given in §§652-7.

§784. Wattie (1930), however, went further (pp. 139-41) and distinguished a 'progressive present passive with "is" ', e.g.

GenB 755   Swa hwæt swa wit her morðres þoliað,
          hit is nu Adame   eall forgolden,

which he translated '. . . it is now being requited on Adam', from a 'perfect passive with "is" ', e.g. *CP* 339. 14 *Nu is ðonne sio æxs aset*

on ðane wyrttruman ðæs treowes, where the Latin has *posita est*.
The latter, he says, 'may be described as a resultant present'.[199] Unfortunately neither *GenB* 755—which is better translated (with
Kennedy) 'Whatever death we suffer here is now repaid on Adam'—
nor Wattie's other three examples—*Rid* 2. 3, *Wan* 49, and *Phoen*
544—unambiguously illustrate the 'progressive present passive'; they
all come from verse, they can all be translated without the word
'being', and none has a Latin original by which the time-reference
can be tested, though Wattie observes that 'the corresponding tense
in Latin *is* the present passive' [my italics]. According to Campbell's
'rule' (§768), it *would be*; *CP* 339. 14 has already been cited in
§771 as an exception to this, whereas examples like *CP* 59. 3 *Hwæt
is ðonne ðæt rice 7 se ealdordoom butan ðæs modes storm, se simle
bið cnyssende ðæt scip ðære heortan mid ðara geðohta ystum, 7 bið
drifen hider 7 ðider on swiðe nearwe bygeas worda 7 weorca, swelce
hit sie ongemong miclum 7 monigum stancludum tobrocen?*, Latin
*Quid namque est potestas culminis, nisi tempestas mentis? in qua
semper cogitationum procellis navis cordis quatitur, huc illucque in-
cessanter impellitur, ut per repentinos excessus oris et operis quasi
per obviantia saxa frangatur*, and *CP* 119. 13 *Ða ðe ofer oðre bioð
giemen hie geornlice ðætte sua micle sua hira onwald bið mara gesewen ofer oðre menn ðæt hie sua micle ma sien innan geðryccede mid
eaðmodnesse* . . . , Latin *Studeant igitur sine intermissione, qui prae-
sunt, ut eorum potentia quanto magna exterius cernitur, tanto apud
eos interius deprimatur* . . . illustrate the correspondence it demands.[200] But even these can hardly be called progressive. Wattie's
distinction, like so many others, depends on the subjective criteria
of a modern scholar. It is only fair to point out that Wülfing (ii,
§403) saw that this was true of the OE passive: 'In manchen dieser
Fälle ist nicht deutlich zu erkennen und zu bestimmen, ob Praesens
oder Perfekt oder auch Futur vorliegt' ['In many of these cases it is
not clear whether we are dealing with a present, a perfect, or even
a future'].

§785. But in 1934 Hoffmann posed the question (p. 14): 'Hat es
also im Ae. bereits ein Perfektum Passivi gegeben?' and replied succinctly 'Antwort: nein.' This conclusion—that OE did not have a
perfect passive—must be right, for it is in accord with the basic fact
that formally the perfect/pluperfect did not exist in OE. I am content

---

[199] At least, that is the way I read the ambiguous paragraph at the top of p. 141.

[200] These sentences, with *bið* . . . *sie* and *bið* . . . *sien*, show that the distinction between
combinations of *wesan* and *beon* with the second participle made by Jost (1909, §§148 and
153) is an unreal one—on the evidence of his own examples.

to leave it like that, with the observation that the MnE perfect/pluperfect passive will often be a convenient translation for the OE periphrasis with the present and past tenses of *wesan/weorþan*.

(6) *The auxiliaries* beon/wesan *and* weorþan

§786. Students of OE frequently find what they want to find. This is probably nowhere more true than here. Mention has already been made in §§672-3 of the possibility that modern scholars have been led by the simple opposition between *beon/wesan* 'to be' and *weorþan* 'to become' and (for native speakers at least) by modern German idiom to postulate that the combination *beon/wesan* + second participle denotes the state resulting from an action whereas *weorþan* + second participle denotes the action or process. Thus Klaeber (1923, p. 190) spoke of MSS *C* and *O* of Gregory's *Dialogues* showing a correct feeling for the original distinction between *wæs* and *wearð* and made this difference the basis for the 'rule' which he detected in *Orosius* and elsewhere but not, he had to admit, in *Bede*, where he found only six examples of the past passive with *wearð* (1923, p. 187). (Kilpiö's figures (my §744) show twenty-four examples with *weorþan* (twenty-three preterite) out of *c.*1344 in *Bede* against 105 out of 992 in *Cura Pastoralis*.) His 'rule' for *Orosius* reads (1923, p. 188):

Hier finden wir durchgehends *wearð* sowohl wie *wæs* gebraucht, und zwar scheint der begriffliche Unterschied zwischen den beiden Konstruktionen dieser zu sein: *wearð*, das naturgemäß eine durch eine Handlung bewirkte Veränderung ausdrückt, dient dazu, ein augenfälliges Ereignis, einen Fortschritt der Erzählung, ein 'novum' zu bezeichnen: *wæs* konstatiert eine vorliegende Tatsache, ohne auf den Werdegang Rücksicht zu nehmen. Temporal gefaßt, neigt *wearð* dazu, die Vergangenheit zu bezeichnen, *wæs* die Vorvergangenheit.[201]

Klaeber's pupil Frary accepted this uncritically and in 1929 wrote (pp. 16 and 17): '*Wearð* introduces a new element or change of state; *wæs* stresses the existing state or predicates a fact or result. . . . From the standpoint of time, *wearð* is close to the preterite; *wæs* approaches a pluperfect.'[202] Kurtz (1931) was in the unhappy position

---

[201] 'Here we find both *wæs* and *wearð* used throughout, and the conceptual distinction between the two constructions seems to be the following: *wearð*, which by its nature expresses a change brought about by an action, serves to denote a significant event, a step forward in the narrative, something 'new': *wæs* denotes a state, without regard for how it came into being. From a temporal point of view, *wearð* tends to denote the past, *wæs* the pluperfect.'

[202] Frary's book is pure Klaeber—note her dedication. Curme's capital review of it in *JEGP* 29 (1930), 271-2 (I use the word 'capital' deliberately in two senses, for he executed the book) spared Klaeber—except perhaps by implication in the first paragraph—from the unhappily well-founded charge that he made her his mouthpiece. Yet Frary is still regarded by some as authoritative; Zadorožny (1974, pp. 367-8) is among them.

I have to confess that I have not accepted in full the advice of several scholars whose

—he says—of finding himself forestalled by Frary in that part of his investigation which dealt with OE, but agreed with her findings —'durchaus richtig' they are! (pp. 11-12)—and made extensive use of them. Timmer (1934, p. 102) also accepted the 'rule' postulated by Klaeber and Frary.[203]

§787. I cannot claim to have made a complete study of the history of this 'rule'. It is not to be found in the first of 'the eighteen German dissertations' on the syntax of the poetry—that of Schürmann (1884)—or in the early dissertations on the prose by Flamme (1885), Mohrbutter (1885), or Schrader (1887). Wülfing (1901) makes no mention of it. But what are perhaps—but ought not to have been—the seeds of it occur in the remarks made by Sweet in the first (1882) edition of his *Anglo-Saxon Primer* (p. 47) and in the subsequent editions for which he was responsible: 'The passive is formed with *wesan* or *weorþan* with the past participle. These forms are very vague in meaning, and the distinction between the two auxiliaries is not clearly marked, but *wesan* appears to indicate a state, *weorþan* an action.' One's admiration for Sweet can only increase as one compares this careful statement with the rigid ones of Klaeber and Frary. When Davis revised the *Primer* (9th edn., 1953), he allowed Sweet's paragraph to stand almost unchanged (p. 52): 'Except for the form *hatte* . . . , the passive is formed periphrastically with *wesan* or *weorþan* and the past participle. These forms are very vague in meaning, and the distinction between the two auxiliaries is not clearly marked. Generally *wesan* appears to indicate a state, *weorþan* an action.' Apart from printing the words 'appears to' in

judgement I respect to tone down the criticisms in the discussion which follows. I have made some changes but found that I could not do more without losing the immediacy of the argument.

[203] Visser tells us (iii, §1909) that 'the *wearþ* + past participle construction . . . on account of the meaning of the notional verb *weorþan* = "to come to be", "to get to be" was essentially dynamic: "wearþ killed" = "was being killed" '. It would seem that he is introducing a third distinction, for he also says (iii, §1916) that 'by the side of the ambiguous passive with *wæs* Old and Early Middle English also frequently used the non-ambiguous pattern with *wearþ* in prose and poetry'. I should like to have seen him classify the 186 examples in the table in §799 into those meaning respectively 'was/were being killed', 'was/were (became) killed', and 'was/were killed (dead)'. But he then goes on to contradict the notion that the construction with *wearþ* was 'non-ambiguous' by remarking (iii, §1916): 'Frary (1929, p. 72) has made an elaborate attempt to find out and describe the differences in meaning between the passives with *wearð* and those with *wæs*, but, apparently owing to their subtlety and elusiveness, no clear picture of the differences has emerged [I agree!]. That there must have been a great deal of free variation appears from a comparison of the parallel texts in MS C . . . and MS H . . . of a number of passages from Wærferth's translation of Pope Gregory's *Dialogues*. . . .' I fail to see how 'non-ambiguity' and 'free variation' are compatible. Other possible explanations for these and other variations are discussed in the sections which follow.

bold type, I would accept this statement. One or two comments, however, will not be out of place. First, the subsequent disappearance of *weorþan* (see Mustanoja, pp. 616-19) would lead us to expect that if the distinction ever existed, it would already have been blurred in OE. Second, I do not believe that the distinction ever did exist as something consistently applied or understood in either the conscious or subconscious mind of the generality of speakers, hearers, or writers.

§788. Here we need to remind ourselves that in MnE the verb 'to be' expresses both action and state. So when the translator of Bede uses *wæs* almost without exception and when Ælfric in his *Grammar* uses *beon/wesan*—not *weorþan*—to represent the Latin passive, they were using the auxiliary which was to become the standard one in English. As Curme puts it in *JEGP* 29 (1930), 272, Frary 'ought to have seen that Bede appropriately chose the auxiliary that the English people later adopted as its normal form of expression' and 'it ought not to have seemed unnatural to her that Ælfric should recognize as English what later was universally recognized as English'. And again, 'that the author of *Beowulf* employed in his English poem a common English auxiliary should not call forth a learned discussion to explain its use' (ibid.).

§789. If Sweet's statement had been heeded and proper respect had been paid to MnE usage, we would have been spared the labour of following the Protean excesses which Klaeber inspired in Frary, and their often unheeded dismissal by Curme and Klingebiel would have been unnecessary. Unlike some writers from his own and other countries, Klingebiel eschews theory after a page of curt and telling criticism of his predecessors and gets down to the texts, demonstrating that *beon/wesan* + second participle denoted action (or process) as well as state (pp. 1-32) and giving twelve criteria—with examples— by which it is possible to recognize the former use. Inevitably there is room for difference of opinion about details, but basically his position is sound. It is a pity we cannot leave it at that.

§790. But some consideration of particular examples is necessary. There is no doubt that there are many sentences in which the 'rule' *seems* to operate—or *can be made* to operate. They include: (in the present tense) *CP* 35. 4 *On ðæm gesundfulnessum ðæt mod wierð upahafen 7 on ðæm earfeðum, ðeah hit ær upahafen wære, hit bið geeaðmedd* (see Frary, pp. 23-4); *WHom* 10c. 116 *Doð dædbote eowra synna 7 eow sona wyrð heofona rices duru raðe untyned* but

HomU 37. 239. 1 *Wa ðæs mannes sawle, þe betynð his duru ongean godes þearfan for ðam þingon, þæt hine lærð se deofol; swa him bið betyned heofona rices duru ongean on domes dæge* (see Frary, p. 48);

Dan 274   ac wæs þær inne   ealles gelicost
                 efne þonne on sumera   sunne scineð,
                 and deaw dryge   on dæge weorðeð,
                 winde geondsawen

but

GenB 377   Me habbað hringa gespong,
              sliðhearda sal   siðes amyrred,
              afyrred me mine feðe;   fet synt gebundene,
              handa gehæfte.   Synt þissa heldora
              wegas forworhte,   swa ic mid wihte ne mæg
              of þissum lioðobendum;

and (in the past tense) *Or* 64. 20 *Ymb feower hunde wintra 7 ymb feowertig þæs þe Troia Creca burg awested wæs, wearð Romeburg getimbred from twam gebroðrum, Remuse 7 Romuluse* but *Or* 74. 11 *Seo burg wæs getimbred an fildum lande 7 on swiþe emnum, 7 heo wæs swiþe fæger an to locianne; ÆCHom* i. 292. 2 *and he wolde eft þurh ðone ylcan us alysan fram helle wite, ðaða we forwyrhte wæron* but *ÆCHom* i. 292. 7 *and we wurdon alysede, þurh his unscyldigan deað, fram ðam ecan deaðe; ÆCHom* ii. 166. 3 *þa wurpon hi ða anlicnysse inn to heora kycenan, and færlice ða wearð him eallum geðuht swilce fyr eode of ðære anlicnysse, swa þæt seo kycene eal forburne; ac hit næs swa him geðuht wæs, ac wæs deofles dydrung; Beo* 2692 *he geblodegod wearð ‖ sawuldriore, swat yðum weoll,* but *Beo* 36 *þær wæs madma fela ‖ of feorwegum frætwa gelæded; Jud* 97 *þa wearð hyre rume on mode, ‖ haligre hyht geniwod* but

Jud 55   eodon ða stercedferhðe,
         hæleð heora hearran cyðan   þæt wæs seo halige meowle
         gebroht on his burgetelde.

§791. So far, so good? But as one reads Klaeber 1923, Frary, Kurtz, and Timmer 1934, doubts rise ever more strongly. I hope I will not be accused of undue flippancy if I express my own reaction thus: Whenever a plausible explanation for the particular example under discussion can be dreamt up, the 'rule' is said to operate. When the 'rule' obviously does not work, either the writer is inconsistent or confused[204] or a plausible explanation presents itself for the non-operation

---

[204] Klaeber's remarks about the poetry (1923, p. 191) seem to imply this. It is definitely stated by Frary (pp. 16 fn. 3, 40, 41, 42, 48, and so on), by Kurtz (p. 40) following Frary, and by Timmer (1934, p. 108).

of the 'rule'. The fact that it is very often a different explanation does not worry Klaeber or Frary, for (as the latter says on p. 49) 'there is usually some explanation'. The truth is that both believe the 'rule' and are determined to make the facts fit; Frary's words (p. 60) typify their attitude: 'It seems quite safe to assume that the [*Beowulf*] poet had a distinct feeling for the difference in the use of *weorðan* and *wesan*.' A brief catalogue of these explanations will not be out of place.

§792. Latin influence is, of course, the main culprit. This is responsible for the almost total absence of *weorðan* in *Bede* (Klaeber 1923, p. 193, quoted by Frary, pp. 30-1, but see Klingebiel, pp. 102-3, and (for a general discussion) Zieglschmid, *JEGP* 28 (1929), 360-5) and for Ælfric's use of *beon/wesan* in his *Grammar* to represent the Latin passive (Klaeber 1923, pp. 193-4, and Frary, p. 11);[205] see also Kurtz (p. 54) and Timmer (1934, *passim*). But while in 'Ælfric's translation of the *Heptateuch and Job* . . . accuracy is the translator's chief aim, apparently, and the rendering is as literal as it could be without being slavish' (Frary, p. 43), 'there are plenty of evidences that the translator is following his instinct, and is not being held back by the Latin original from making his choice of *wearð* and *wæs*' (Frary, p. 45); see also Kurtz (pp. 42 and 45-6) and Timmer (1934, p. 105). This is double-dealing in a big way; in the vernacular phrase, the exponents of the 'rule' 'can't lose'. This double-dealing is not restricted to the discussions about the influence of Latin, for, while in the poetry in general 'the more frequent use of *wesan*' than in the prose is due to the fact that the poet is 'more subtle' (Frary, p. 58), we find that in *Maldon* 'the use of *weorðan* is in some respects like that in *Daniel* and *Judith* and marks a successful attempt to take over the prose usage of Ælfred and Ælfric into poetry' (Frary, p. 67). Again *weorðan* 'probably' appears in the Kentish Laws because it is 'the old form' (Frary, p. 33 and fn. 37), but its presence in some examples in Ælfric's *Lives* is probably the result of 'an extension of the use of *weorðan*' (Frary, p. 35 fn. 1). This must be the late resurgence of *weorðan* referred to by Klaeber (1923, pp. 194-5) and Frary (*passim*).

[205] On this point, Curme writes in *JEGP* 29 (1930), 271-2: 'Ælfric in his Latin Grammar, written about 1000 A.D., translates *amor* by *eom gelufod*, i.e. *am loved*, thus representing *be* as the normal actional passive auxiliary. Dr Frary, who believes that *weorðan* was the usual passive auxiliary at this time, explains Ælfric's attitude by claiming he was under Latin influence. . . . It seems remarkable to the reviewer that Dr Frary can see in *be* a latinism. No two forms could be more unlike than Latin *amor* and English *am loved*.' It might have been fairer if he had also quoted *amatus sum* = *ic wæs gelufod*, where the parallel is obviously closer. But all the same, his point still stands, in my opinion; the change of tense (see §§768-81) demonstrates that the OE is not a slavish imitation of the Latin.

§793. Other factors called in to explain breaches of the 'rule' include analogy (Frary, p. 17 fn. 6 and p. 36 fn. 4), 'a matter of emphasis' (Frary, p. 25), differing attitudes to native subject-matter (Frary, p. 33), possible foreign influence other than Latin (Frary, pp. 54-7), and the demands of metre (Frary, p. 62). One almost gets the feeling that writers of OE prose and poetry were an unstable lot; prose writers broke the 'rule' because of pleasure in variation or desire for variety (Klaeber 1923, p. 189, and Frary, pp. 32 and 51) and poets broke it under the influence of their stylistic preferences (Klaeber 1923, p. 190, and Frary, pp. 45 and 51; see also Kurtz, pp. 53-4). Multiple authorship is also invoked (Frary, pp. 49-50). But the authors are not always to blame—there is scribal interference (Frary, p. 30 fn. 31) and variety of manuscripts (Klaeber 1923, p. 190).

§794. That such variety and inconsistency of explanation is possible reflects great credit on the ingenuity of the scholars and something close to ridicule on the 'rule'. It is never clear what determines the point at which they break into this circle of explanations. Why, for instance, is the scarcity of *weorðan* in *Bede* the result of Latin influence rather than of the translator's stylistic preference? Indeed, Frary herself once admits that she does not know which one to plump for (p. 36 fn. 4):.'This is a clear slip on the part of the translator. Shall we say that he made a mistake, or attribute the instance to analogy? As this is unquestionably a preterite, we might take it as evidence that *wearð* was beginning to be felt as the logical auxiliary of the preterite passive.' And when she comes to Wulfstan, she has to give up the unequal struggle (p. 48): '*Wulfstan's Homilies* do not show as clear-cut a distinction between *weorðan* and *wesan* as do the works of Ælfric.'

§795. Faced with all this, one does not know which to wonder at more—the persistency of scholars who could continue to believe in a 'rule' with so many exceptions and explanations or the volatility they were willing to attribute to the Anglo-Saxon writers who broke the 'rule' with such frequency and (one might almost say) panache. Time would fail me to tell of all the exceptions. The reader of the works in question will have no difficulty in finding more than enough, but could with advantage consult Klingebiel (pp. 1-32). However, a few typical examples in which the 'rule' does not work must be cited. Thus we might compare *Or* 180. 9 *Raðe þæs coman eft Pene mid firde to him, 7 gefliemde wurdon, 7 ofslagen II M* with *Or* 192. 24 *Æfter þæm Sempronius Craccus se consul for eft mid fierde angean Hannibal, 7 gefliemed wearð, 7 his heres wæs micel wæl geslagen* and *Or* 186. 26 *þær wearð Romana micel wæl geslagen. Hiora ðæt æfterre gefeoht wæs æt Trefia ðære ie, 7 eft wæron Romane forslægen 7 gefliemed* (see Klaeber 1923, pp. 188-9); *Or* 174. 20 *On ðæm gefeohte wæs Cartainiensa VII M ofslagen, 7 VX M gefangen* with *Or* 176. 3 *þær wearð Romana XXX M ofslagen, 7 Regulus gefangen* (see Frary, p. 20); *Or* 248. 10 *On þæm hringe wes getacnad þæt on his dagum sceolde weorþan geboren se se þe leohtra is 7 scinendra þonne sio sunne þa wære* with *Or* 248. 17 *þæt tacnade þæt on his dagum sceolde beon geboren se se þe us ealle to anum mæggemote gelaþaþ* (see Frary, pp. 18-19); *CP* 299. 12 *Ælc ðara ðe bið geeaðmed, he bið upahæfen*, Latin *Omnis qui se humiliat, exaltabitur*, with *CP* 299. 14 *Ælc ðara ðe hine selfne upahefeð, he wierð gehined*, Latin *Omnis qui se exalat, humiliabitur* (see Wülfing, ii, §407, and Frary, p. 24); *LS* 23. 408 *and ic sona wæs ut aprungen fram eallum þam folce* and *LS* 23. 414 *þa wæs ic ana ut asceofen* with *ÆLS* 35. 244 *þæt cweartern wearð afylled mid fulum adelan and butan ælcum leohte atelice stincende* (see Frary, pp. 36 and 37); *ÆLS* 20. 113 *þær wæron gehælede þurh ða halgan femnan fela adlige menn* and *ÆLS* 21. 128 *He wæs ða gehæled þurh ðone halgan Swyðun* with *ÆLS* 21. 132 *þær wurdon gehælede æt ðære halgan byrgene eahta untrume menn* (see Frary, p. 35); *ÆCHom* i. 186. 30 *Mid þam ðe he tobræc ða hlafas, þa wæron hi gemenigfylde* with *ÆCHom* i. 402. 33 *and hi wurdon ða utan ymbsette mid Romaniscum here swa lange þæt ðær fela ðusenda mid hungre wurdon acwealde* (see Frary, p. 41); *Beo* 1072 *unsynnum wearð* ‖ *beloren leofum* (not mentioned by Frary, p. 62) with *Beo* 1399 *þa wæs Hroðgare hors gebæted* (Frary, p. 61); *Beo* 2961 *þær wearð Ongenðiow . . .* ‖ *. . . on bid wrecen* with *Beo* 1288 *Ða wæs on healle heardecg togen* (see Frary, pp. 61 and 62); and *Dan* 261 *Freobearn wurdon* ‖ *alæten liges gange* with *Dan* 434 *Wæron þa bende forburnene þe him on banum lagon* (see Frary, p. 63). To these I now add *ApT* 36. 12 *þæt haliern wearð ða geopenod and þa lac wæron in gebrohte*, of which Visser (iii, §1917) remarks in Delphic terms 'Note the juxtaposition of *wearþ* and *wæron*.' The riddle is not resolved by the Latin *Et aperto sacrario oblatisque muneribus. . . .*

§796. So I have no hesitation in claiming that it is clear that *beon/ wesan* could express an action or process as well as a state. What was the function of *weorþan*? According to Curme (*JEGP* 29 (1930), 271)

. . . our passive auxiliary *be* expresses both action and state. *Be* has always performed this double function. Just as we today often employ *get* instead of *be* to make clear the idea of action, *weorðan* was often used in Old English instead of *beon* (*be*). *Weorðan* had the force that *get* now has. At that time *get* was not in use in this meaning, and hence was not available.

I think this 'rule' also too rigid and not borne out by the facts.

§797. Klingebiel's figures (pp. 101–4) in general support Wattie's remark (p. 141) that 'the use of *weorðan* to form the present passive is not common'. On Klingebiel's evidence, the most striking exception is Wulfstan; see also Frary, p. 48. Whether Wattie's further observation (p. 141) that 'in this tense the sense of "becoming" is still prominent' is true can only be a matter of opinion. It contrasts strangely with his sound observation (pp. 141–2) that in the past tense *weorþan* is 'practically an alternative to "be"'' and it is, after all, undue insistence on the validity of the distinction which is the basis for both the 'rule' postulated by Klaeber and Frary which I have so vigorously condemned and for Curme's suggestion that *weorþan* equals MnE 'get', which (as we shall see) I am also unable to accept. On the use of the periphrasis with the present tense of *weorþan* to express the future, see §755.

§798. The periphrasis with *weorþan* is much more frequent in the past. As I have already said, I agree with Wattie's remark (pp. 141–2) that *weorþan* in the past 'is practically an alternative to "be"''— which I understand to mean that *weorþan* could express state as well as action. Examples which demonstrate this include the principal clause in *Or* 32. 24 *Ær ðam ðe Romeburh getimbred wære eahta hund wintra, mid Egyptum wearð syfan gear se ungemetlica eorð-wela*, where *wearð* occurs without a second participle expressing duration of time (see Frary, p. 16), *Or* 106. 7 *Siþþan þæt gewin angunnen wæs, gif ænig mon* [*sie*], *cwæð Orosius, þe on gewritun findan mæge þæt Ianas dura siþþan belocen wurde buton anum geare*, where *wære* would be at least as acceptable as *wurde* (Frary brushes this example aside rather lightly at p. 18), *ÆLS* 35. 244 *þæt cweart-ern wearð afylled mid fulum adelan and butan ælcum leohte atelice stincende*, the principal clause in *ÆCHom* i. 402. 33 *and hi wurdon ða utan ymbsette mid Romaniscum here swa lange þæt ðær fela ðusenda mid hungre wurdon acwealde*, *Beo* 227 *Gode þancedon ‖ þæs þe him yþlade eaðe wurdon* (with adjective instead of second participle),

Beo 1071   Ne huru Hildeburh   herian þorfte
                 Eotena treowe;   unsynnum wearð

> beloren leofum   æt þam lindplegan
> bearnum ond broðrum;   hie on gebyrd hruron
> gare wunde;   þæt wæs geomuru ides!

where the sequence of events suggests reference to a state 'had been deprived' rather than to an action 'was deprived', and

Beo 2982   Ða wæron monige,   þe his mæg wriðon,
ricone aræerdon,   ða him gerymed wearð,
þæt hie wælstowe   wealdan moston,

where the Wrenn-Clark Hall translation reads '. . . when victory in the battle-field had been granted them'.

§799. Some readers may object that—even with those given in §795—this is a very small corpus of examples. I concede this, but would urge in reply the point that I made in the opening sections of this discussion: that we are so used to the idea that *weorþan* means 'become' that we automatically take *weorþan* examples as referring to an action unless this is manifestly impossible. But the idea that *wesan* and *weorþan* are interchangeable in the work of some writers at least is supported by some of the examples quoted in §790. Another and particular case in point is the variation between the two auxiliaries with *ofslægen* in *Orosius* and the *Chronicle*, where the situation can be shown by means of a table based on Hoffmann's figures (p. 12):

Text	*wæs/wæron ofslægen/-e*	*wearð/wurdon ofslægen/-e*
Orosius	50	66
ChronA	12	20
ChronE	17	21

Frary (p. 32) says that 'only a desire for variety' can explain this. But if that is true, it is hard to escape the conclusion that there was no significant difference between them and that they were interchangeable. And this is exactly what the subsequent disappearance of *weorðan* would lead us to expect.

§800. If we accept this idea of interchangeability, we have a situation in which some writers might use *wesan* and *weorþan* more or less indifferently, some might use one rather than the other with reference to both states and actions (cf. QW, pp. 80–1), and some might make the distinctions postulated by Klaeber and Frary and by

Curme.[206] This is a perfectly credible situation, perhaps not altogether unlike that which obtains today for MnE 'shall' and 'will' as auxiliaries of the future. It would account for the great variety of usage and would admit some of the explanations for it put forward by Klaeber, Frary, Kurtz, and Timmer.

§801. From this it can be seen that the relative percentages of *beon/ wesan* and *weorþan* in individual texts such as those given by Klingebiel (pp. 101-4) are likely to be less significant than some writers have thought. The fact that *weorþan* is more frequent than *beon/ wesan* in MS *H* than in MS *C* of Gregory's *Dialogues* (see Timmer 1934, pp. 102-20, and Visser, iii, §1916), in Ælfric's *Homilies* and *Lives of the Saints* than in the *Blickling Homilies* (see Klingebiel, pp. 101-4), and in Wulfstan than in *Bede* (ibid.) has led to the theory that *weorþan* was destined to replace *beon/wesan* as the auxiliary of the periphrastic passive in English and that only foreign influence saved the day for the latter—Scandinavian, according to Klaeber (1923, pp. 194-5) and others, French, according to Klingebiel (pp. 105-8) and others. The evidence given above all combines to suggest that such simplistic views grossly underrate the cut and thrust of the native language. Mustanoja's emphasis (p. 618) is, I believe, sounder: 'The disappearance of *wurthe* is no doubt a complicated process, due in all probability to the convergence of several factors, mainly native, it seems, though foreign models—French in the first place—must also be considered as contributory influences.' However, the broad outline of the history of the passive in OE is clear: combinations of a second participle with both *beon/wesan* and *weorþan* could denote both a process or action and a state in all periods of OE. But since the former auxiliary gradually prevailed over the latter, it is idle to expect consistency. Those wishing to pursue further the disappearance of *weorþan* should see in the first instance Mustanoja, pp. 615-19.

[206] The fact that we use 'lie', 'remain', 'stand', 'stay', as well as 'be', to express the idea of 'being in a state', and 'become', 'fall', 'go', 'grow', 'rise', 'run', 'turn', 'wax', as well as 'get' to express the idea of 'becoming', suggests that Wattie was wrong when he wrote (p. 143) of the OE tense system that 'the only false start . . . is the unnecessary duplication of passive auxiliaries, and the rarity of *weorðan* in Middle English proves that this mistake was soon recognized and rectified.' The process is unlikely to have been as conscious as his wording suggests and the distinction was a useful one sometimes exploited by some OE writers.

Klaeber's interesting comparison (1923, p. 194) between the stories of the lives of St. Gregory and St. Oswald in *Bede* and in Ælfric's *Lives* might well be worth following up.

(7) *The expression of the agent or instrument*

(a) *Introductory remarks*

§802. A person or a thing serving as the subject of a verb in the active voice, e.g. *he* in *ChronA* 46. 21 (755) . . . *oþ he ofslog þone aldormon* or *sweord* in

Beo 1285   þonne heoru bunden,   hamere geþruen,
              sweord swate fah   swin ofer helme
              ecgum dyhtig   andweard scireð,

becomes respectively the agent or the instrument when the verb is used passively.

§803. The instrument can be expressed by a case-form alone, e.g. *Beo* 679 *forþan ic hine sweorde swebban nelle* (on dative/instrumental syncretism see §8) or by a preposition with a case-form, e.g. *Beo* 574 *Hwæþere me gesælde, þæt ic mid sweorde ofsloh || niceras nigene.* (On the gradual triumph of the preposition see §§1365-70.) But the instrument can remain unknown, e.g. *Mald* 288 *Raðe wearð æt hilde Offa forheawen*, or can be otherwise expressed, either by giving the sentence a different twist, e.g.

Mald 134   Sende ða se særinc   suþerne gar,
              þæt gewundod wearð   wigena hlaford,

or (as Knispel, pp. 60-1, points out) by means of compounds, e.g. *Mark(WSCp)* 14. 58 *ic towurpe þis handworhte tempel 7 æfter þrim dagum ic oðer unhandworht getimbrie.* Knispel (ibid.) would add prefixes, e.g. *ÆCHom* ii. 272. 26 *swilce ðær læge . . . anes fingres lið eal geblodgod.* But the idea of 'to cover with blood' is implicit in the verb *blodegian*, despite *Beo* 2692 *he geblodegod wearð || sawuldriore*; cf. *GD(C)* 15. 1 *þa hors . . . mid þam spurum geblodgode wæron*, where the instrument is expressed.

§804. The agent too can be expressed by a preposition + a case-form, e.g. *Or* 100. 23 *ac heo wearð gescild þurh þone cristnan casere Arcadiusan, 7 þurh þæt cristene folc* and *Or* 64. 21 . . . *wearð Romeburg getimbred from twam gebroðrum, Remuse 7 Romuluse* (but see §833), or by other constructions, e.g. those involving impersonal *man* or another pronoun and an active verb form discussed in §§260-4. It can also be expressed by implication, e.g. *ChronA* 72. 3 (871). . . *7 þa Deniscan ahton wælstowe gewald, 7 þær wearþ Heahmund bisc ofslægen 7 fela godra monna*, or can remain unknown, e.g. *ChronE* 29. 21 (656) *Her wæs Peada ofslagan.*

§805. Whether there are clear examples of the expression of the personal agent by a case-form alone is a disputed question; see §§1371-8. But there can be no doubt that in OE a preposition is the norm. Indeed, Green (1914, p. 515) has written that 'the Agent, i.e. the person functioning as the logical subject of passive expressions, seems to have been one of the first categories in Germanic to require the elucidative services of propositions', and remarks (1913, §§140-1) that 'after Cædmon the tendency in poetry is entirely towards the analytical' in the expression of agency.[207] But he uses the terms 'agency' and 'personal agency' very broadly, including examples which I regard as expressing instrumentality. In view of this and of the inevitable overlap between the two, it is convenient to consider together the expression of the agent and the instrument by means of individual prepositions. On whether the prepositions became more frequent in these constructions during the OE period, see §§1365-79.

§806. Visser (iii, §1987) quotes an amusing observation by L. M. Myers to the effect that the frequency of the passive construction 'owes something also to the fact that passive statements can be made without indicating exactly who is responsible. The passing of the buck is thereby greatly facilitated. ("Your request is denied").' But I cannot quite see how he can also say (iii, §1908) that the 'dynamic' passive (as opposed to the 'statal') is 'obvious when there is a prepositional agentive adjunct or another adjunct denoting particulars of the action'. The only OE example he cites to prove his point is *Bede* 240. 27 *þy wiite eac swylce Tuda Cristes þeow, se wæs æfter Colmane Norþanhymbra biscop, wæs of middangearde genumen 7 wæs arweorðlice bebyrged in þæm mynstre*, where he fails to quote the first two words, which express the real instrument or agent by an instrumental form without a preposition. Does he really think *of middangearde* is the agent? He contrasts this 'dynamic' passive with the 'statal' one in *Or* 12. 11 *Seo Asia on ælce healfe heo is befangen mid sealtum wætre*, where by an unhappy—but convenient—oversight, he fails to quote the last three words.

§807. Van Dam (pp. 1-39) gives some valuable information about the early prose; note especially the following table (p. 23) which 'shows the frequencies with which (*a*) personal agents, (*b*) animals

---

[207] In his two works on the expression of the agent, Green offers a useful collection of examples and analyses them in a way which is interesting, though not always acceptable to me. His examples and views are discussed below as they become relevant.

and natural forces, (c) non-personal agents were found to be introduced by the various prepositions':

	Personal agents	Animals or natural forces	Non-personal agents
for + dative (p. 7)	1	—	48
for + instrumental (p. 15)	—	—	2
fram + dative (p. 21)	305	10	14
in + dative (p. 32)	—	—	1
mid + dative (p. 25)	8	5	394
mid + instrumental (p. 27)	1	1	67
mid + accusative (p. 28)	1	—	24
of + dative (p. 29)	7	6	15
on + dative (p. 32)	—	—	1
þurh + accusative (p. 36)	57	—	76
ymb + accusative (p. 39)	1	—	—

Most noteworthy, of course, is the preponderance of *fram* to express the personal agent (but see §§813-17) and of *mid* to express the 'non-personal agent' or the instrument.

(b) Æt

§808. Green (1914, pp. 528-9) notes that *æt*—like *be* (§810)—is a preposition in which the notion of locality or rest can develop into the sense of the personal agent; consider *ÆCHom* ii. 48. 1 . . . *swa eac he forgeaf þæt fulluht Iohanne, and wæs eft gefullod æt Iohanne* and *ÆCHom* i. 50. 2 *Witodlice Stephanus wæs to diacone gehadod æt ðæra apostola handum* 'at the hands of . . .'. But the idea of 'motion from' or of 'receiving something from' is still the predominant one in these examples. See also Visser, iii, §1990.

§809. It could, I suppose, be somewhat pedantically argued that in *ÆCHom* i. 50. 2 (§808) the idea of agency merges into that of instrumentality. Indeed, according to Green (1914, p. 547), *Beo* 557 *heaþoræs fornam ‖ mihtig meredeor þurh mine hand* expresses the instrument of the action. But since the actual instrument has already been expressed in

Beo 555   hwæþre me gyfeþe wearð,
        þæt ic aglæcan   orde geræhte
        hildebille,

þurh mine hand means little more than *þurh me*; cf. *CP* 117. 20 *ðurh us scylen bion hiora scylda gestiered* and *GuthA* 315 *he mec þurh engel oft afrefeð.* Here Bliemel's 1930 thesis (my §250) might have helped Green if it had been written in 1914. But the point is little more than terminological—'through my agency' and 'through my instrumentality' both seem possible renderings of *þurh mine hand* in *Beo* 557. In *CP* 377. 22 . . . *nu is to ongietanne æt hu micelre scylde ða beoð befangne* . . . the *æt* phrase represents the ablative of Latin *Quanta ergo culpa involvantur aspiciant.* . . .

(c) Be

§810. *Be*—originally, says Green (1914, p. 525) 'a local preposition denoting proximity'—is sometimes used to express the means or instrument, e.g. *ÆLS* 3. 478 *Se messepreost leofode be hlafe and be wætere* and *GenB* 598 *forlædd be þam lygenum.*[208] Examples like *Beo* 1647 *þa wæs be feaxe on flet boren* ‖ *Grendles heafod* are sometimes cited here, but are not on all fours, since the active form would be something like 'They carried Grendel's head into the hall by the hair', not 'The hair carried Grendel's head into the hall', whereas one could say 'Bread and water sustained the priest' and 'Lies deceived so many a thane'.

§811. *OED* does not recognize the dative of agency with *be* in OE. It distinguishes the immediate or subordinate agent (first quotation *c.*1300, *K. Alis.* 4304 *Darie hit wot by a spye*; s.v. *by* A. V. 32) from the principal agent, on which use it remarks 'This, which has now become a main use of *by*, is hardly found before 15th c.; OE. used *of, fram*' (s.v. *by* A. V. 33). There are some examples with *sendan be* which come close to the first use, e.g. *ÆCHom* ii. 170. 13 *Sum eawfæst man sende ðam halgan were twegen butrucas mid wine to lace, be anum cnapan.*[209] Green (1914, pp. 526–7) adds examples with verbs of begetting 'which border on personal agency', e.g. *Or* 56. 25 *7 bi eallum heora wifum bearna striendon* and *GenA* 2327 *þu scealt sunu agan,* ‖ *bearn be bryde þinre.* But I have found no real evidence that the principal agent was expressed by *be* in native OE. GK is silent. BTS (s.v. *be* A. III. 20) has 'marking agent:—*þa ðing þe be him wærun gewordene quae fiebant ab eo*, Lk. 9. 7'. Wülfing (ii, §643) and Gottweis (p. 49) cite *Bede* 450. 18 (= Smith 637. 3), the latter adding *BlHom* 163. 27. But Bødtker (1908, pp. 37–8) offers plausible alternative explanations. The *DOE* collections may produce

---

[208] For further examples, see BTS, s.v. *be* A. III. 19, and Dusenschön, pp. 32–4. Green (1914, p. 526) adds more, but mistakenly cites *GenB* 598 and similar examples as offering 'sufficient, though not ample, evidence of the *personal agent* with passive verbs' [my italics] (1914, pp. 526–7).

[209] See Gottweis, pp. 48–9, Bødtker 1908, p. 37, and Green 1914, p. 526.

more convincing examples, but the possibility seems remote. However, those already quoted support Green's suggestion (1914, pp.
525-6) that Einenkel made too much of the influence of OFr. *par* in
his discussions of the origin of the modern use of 'by' to express personal agent.[210]

(*d*) For

§812. Van Dam (pp. 7-9 and 15) notes that when a prepositional
phrase introduced by *for* is used with a passive verb, its primary function is still to express cause, but goes on to point out that with abstract nouns this may shade into the expression of 'non-personal
agency', e.g. *GD(C)* 133. 28 *ne byð næfre Romeburuh toworpen
fram hæþenum þeodum, ac for hreonessum 7 ligetslehtum, for
þodenum 7 eorðstyrenum heo byð geswenced*, where MS *H* has *mid*
instead of *for* in both places. But even in *Or* 260. 5 . . . *þæt þæt
angin nære gestilled for þæs cristendomes Gode*, where *for* comes
close to expressing the personal agent, and in *GD(C)* 213. 3 . . . *ac
þæt he sceolde beon eall tosliten for þam clifstanum, þe þær gehwær
ut sceorodon of þam munte*, where *for* comes close to expressing the
instrument, but where MS *O* has *from*, *for* retains its primary causal
function. Cf. Visser, iii, §1993, but note that some element of cause,
'because of', is present in all his examples.

(*e*) Fram

§813. *Fram* shares with *of* the idea of 'motion from', 'separation
from', 'coming from a place'. This idea 'yields to that of causality as
soon as the place stands no more for the origin of the action but becomes identical with the causer and doer thereof' (Green 1914,
p. 531). The same point is made by Fischer (pp. 86-7), who compares *BlHom* 247. 19 *Soðlice fram Gode he is send, and he is Godes
þeowa* (expressing the starting-point or source) with *ÆLS* 26. 7
*Betwux þam wearð ofslagen Eadwine his eam Norðhymbra cyningc
on Crist gelyfed fram Brytta cyninge Ceadwalla geciged* (expressing
the actual agent? See §815). See also van Dam, pp. 20-3.

§814. Many of the examples cited by Wullen (p. 21), Green (1913,
§141, and 1914, pp. 520-1 and 531-3), BTS (s.v. *fram* I. 13), Wülfing (ii, §682), and van Dam, pp. 21-2, can still be regarded as containing at least some element of 'motion or separation from' or of

---

[210] The only example given by Visser (iii, §1992) which is not quoted here is the unconvincing *PPs* 140. 9 . . . *be helwarena hæfteneodum*, Latin *secus infernum*. I have not seen
O. S. Akhmanova's 1941 dissertation for the Moscow Institute of Foreign Languages on the
origin and the development of the use of the preposition *by* to express the agent.

'sending' or 'giving'. One cannot even dismiss it from those sentences which Green (1914, p. 520) confidently thinks express agency, e.g. *Bede* 194. 35 . . . *he wæs from eallum monnum lufod* and

Met 20. 243　　　　　　　　Wunedon ætsomne
　　　　　efen swa lange　　swa him lyfed wæs
　　　　　from þæm ælmihtigan,[211]

or from *BlHom* 45. 33 *þonne onfoþ hi from Gode maran mede þonne hi from ænigum oþrum lacum don*, the second of two examples cited by *OED* (s.v. *from* A. 11) of *from* 'in OE. also indicating the agent = by'. And it is very hard to see how Green (1914, p. 532) can be so sure that *Bede* 30. 24 *Fram þam ylcan casere Claudie wæs sended Uespassianus on Breotone* is 'plainly locative', while including among 'outspoken examples of agency' *ChronE* 25. 22 (627) *Her wes Eadwine cining gefullod fram Pauline* and *CP* 107. 22 *ac wile ðæt simle se oðer beo aræred from ðæm oðrum*; the fact that this latter example represents Latin *alter regatur ab altero* is interesting, but irrelevant or at best inconclusive. For since Latin *a, ab* often has some idea of separation or departure, it is not the fact that (as Fischer, pp. 86-7, has it) the Latin equivalent of *BlHom* 27. 3 *7 þæt he [Hælend] wære costod from deofle* is *ut tentaretur a diabolo* which might incline us to accept the verdict of the *OED* (s.v. *from* A. 11) that *from* here means 'by'. It is our knowledge that, unlike Adam and Eve in *GenesisB*, Christ was tempted in the wilderness by the Devil himself. But how confident can we be that the distinction between origin (MnE 'from') and agency (MnE 'by') in 'so that He might be tempted from/ by the Devil' was a real one for the Anglo-Saxons? This doubt must indeed hang over many of the seemingly convincing examples of *fram* expressing agency.

§815. Another doubt not always resolvable from our linguistic feeling, the context, or outside information, is whether *fram* expresses the actual agent or whether an intermediary was involved, as may be the case in Fischer's example, *ÆLS* 26. 7 (§813). None the less it must be conceded that most modern readers will agree that the actual agent is expressed in examples like *Or* 1. 18 *Hu on Egyptum wurdon on anre niht L monna ofslagen from hiora agnum sunum* (cf. *Or* 40. 13 and *Or* 270. 18), *Or* 64. 21 . . . *wearð Romeburg getimbred from twam gebroðrum, Remuse 7 Romuluse, Bede* 90. 28 *7 from þære stowe bigengum in uncymre byrgenne geseted wæs, ChronA* 4. 31 (3) *Her swealt Herodus from him selfum ofsticod,*

---

[211] But I must admit that the more I read what he says about this last example, the less sure I am about what he means.

ÆHom 1. 192 *Gode wæron þa englas fram Gode gesceapene, HomU* 26. 146. 15 *þær beoð þa sawla forgytene fram eallum þam ðe hi ær cuðon on eorðan*, and (despite the mess made of the preceding Latin by the translator) *PPs* 67. 23 *fram þam þine gangas wæron gesewene*, Latin *Viderunt ingressus tuos, Deus*. However, Pope in his Glossary (s.v. *fram* (*a*)) rightly observes that in examples like *ÆHom* 1. 37 *Sum man wæs asend fram Gode sylfum, fram* can be taken as 'from' or 'by', and adds more examples (s.v. *fram* (*h*)), with this definition: 'of agency, indicating the person or thing whence action proceeds, now usually *by*'. This emphasizes the dangers of attempting too rigid a distinction between 'origin' and 'agency'.

§816. The inclusion of the words 'or thing' in Pope's definition raises the question of the use of *fram* to express instrumentality. The dictionaries and collections of examples have little to offer on this point and Pope gives only two examples (both quoted below) which do not refer to a person. But there are occasional sentences in which *fram* comes close to expressing the instrument as opposed to the agent, though in some at least the idea of origin is still present. Thus we find *Or* 12. 33 *þonne on þæm wintregum tidum wyrþ se muþa fordrifen foran from þæm norþernum windum, Or* 32. 2 . . . *þæt wæstmbære land . . . wearð fram heofonlicum fyre forbærned*, and *ÆHom* 12. 227 *Moyses se heretoga on þam micclum westene worhte be Godes hæse ane ærene næddran þa þa þæt folc wæs fram ðam næddrum tosliten*; for several more, see Visser, iii, §1994. Pope points out that *fram* in *ÆHom* 2. 22 *se wearþ sona hal fram swa hwilcere untrumnysse swa he wære gehæfd* means 'from' if taken with *hal*, 'by' if taken with *gehæfd*. But the construction is a slightly awkward one (see Pope's note) and the sense 'by' is only incidental.

§817. Van Dam (pp. 22-3) offers two examples in which the 'non-personal ·agents' are animals (cf. *ÆHom* 12. 227 in §816), eight in which they are living natural forces (cf. *Or* 12. 33 and 32. 2 in §816), and fourteen others. In most of these *fram* governs an abstract noun and expresses cause. In some, there are manuscript variations, e.g. *GD(C)* 38. 23 *7 þa swa se Godes þeowa wæs genyded fram werignysse his geferan* . . . , where MS *O* has *for* and MS *H* mid. In others *fram* clearly expresses origin, e.g. *GD* 279. 4 *þa godcundun gyfta beoð symble ongunnene fram heafe*. The nearest we come to finding *fram* with an inanimate object as instrument is in *Bede(Ca)* 14. 26 *Ðætte on Hibernia sum man fram his reliquium fram deaðes liðe wæs gehæled*, where MS *B* has *æt his reliquium*, and *GD* 322. 23 . . . *eac he geseah þæt sumra manna hus gehran se mist þæs fulan stences, sumra ne mihton fram þam beon gehrinene*.

(f) Mid

§818. 'The sociative-comitative preposition par excellence of the Germanic dialects' (Green 1914, p. 545), *mid* is clearly used in OE to express the instrument or means, both with things, e.g. *ÆTemp* 4. 53 *7 heora orcyrdas mid æpplum afyllede* and *Jul* 580 . . . *ad onælan, se wæs æghwonan* || *ymbboren mid brondum,* and with abstractions, e.g. *Or* 256. 22 *He wæs swiþe gefylled mid unþeawum 7 mid firenlustum* and

GuthA 651
                        Eom ic soðlice
        leohte geleafan   ond mid lufan dryhtnes
        fægre gefylled. . . .

Further on this, see Hittle, pp. 66–93, and Green 1913, §141. Van Dam (p. 25) detects 'a strong causal character' in *mid* 'when the grammatical agent is an abstract noun and at the same time the psychological agent', as in *CP* 257. 6 . . . *sua gælð se lichoma ðæt mod oððæt he gebrocad wierð mid sumre mettrymnesse.* 'The idea of causality gives way to that of instrumentality' when the two are not identical, as in *CP* 271. 1 *Sua beoð eac ful oft ða wunda mid ele gehælda* and *Or* 144. 26 *þær wearð Leostenas . . . mid anre flan ofscoten.*

§819. With persons, *mid* is often comitative. Thus, despite Haarstrick (p. 49), *Or* 110. 20 *Philippus þa he cniht wæs, wæs Thebanum to gisle geseald, Paminunde, þæm strongan cyninge 7 þæm gelæredestan philosophe, from his agnum breþer Alexandre, þe Læcedemonia rice þa hæfde, 7 mid him gelæred wearð on þam þrim gearum þa he ðær wæs,* Latin *apud Epaminondam . . . eruditus est* 'in the house of' (but cf. *Bede* 3. 18 *Swyðost he me sæde of þeodores gemynde, se wæs biscop on Cantwara byrig, 7 Adrianus abbud, forðon he swyðost wæs mid him gelæred,* Latin . . . *qui in ecclesia Cantuariorum a beatae memoriae Theodoro archiepiscopo et Hadriano abbate, uiris uenerabilibus atque eruditissimis, institutus . . .*), and *Bede* 424. 32 *Mid þy heo ða þæs ungesælgan wrixles feor 7 wide, swa geseon meahton, butan fyrstmearce ænigre ræste mid þa unriman mængo sweartra gasta þreste wæron . . . ,* Latin *innumerabilis spirituum deformium multitudo torqueretur,* probably express a comitative idea rather than that of agency. Whether *mid* is ever used to express personal agency is a question sometimes of personal opinion, sometimes of terminology. Thus different views are possible about *CP* 415. 17 *7 ða wæs his mod gehæft mid ðæm mædene,* 'occupied with', 'attached to' (Sweet), or 'made captive by'; *Or* 134. 19 *7 swa eall þæt folc wearð mid him anum agæled þæt hie þæs wealles nane gieman ne dydon*, 'occupied with/by'; *ÆHom* 1. 24 . . . *he wearð swa afylled mid þam Halgan Gaste þæt he ongann to writenne þa halgan Cristes boc*, 'filled with/by'; and *GenB* 319 . . . *fylde helle* ‖ *mid þam andsacum*, 'filled with/by'; while it does not much matter whether we regard the human beings in the following examples as instruments with which, or agents by which, the action was accomplished: *Bede(B)* 316. 3 *⁊ his lichama mid his freondum . . . wæs to Turnum gelæded*, where other manuscripts read *fram*, *ÆCHom* i. 404. 17 *Seo burh wearð syððan on oðre stowe getimbrod and mid ðam Sarasceniscum gesett*, and

Met 25. 1   Geher nu an spell   be ðæm ofermodum
              unrihtwisum   eorðan cyningum,
              ða her nu manegum   and mislicum
              wædum wlitebeorhtum   wundrum scinað
              . . .
              utan ymbestandne   mid unrime
              ðegna and eorla.

§820. But *mid* is more common when the instrument is a thing or an abstraction than when it is a person, and even in lOE the distinction *mid* instrument, *þurh* or *fram* agent, remains a real one, e.g. *ÆLS* 32. 75 . . . *æfter minum leofum þegnum þe on heora bedde wurdon . . . færlice ofslægene fram þysum flotmannum* but *ÆLS* 32. 117 . . . *oð þæt he eall wæs besæt mid heora scotungum*, and *WHom* 9. 110 *And to fela manna wyrð þeah mid þyllican wrencan þurh deofol forlæred*. For further examples of *mid* expressing the agent and instrument, see van Dam, pp. 25–8, and Visser, iii, §1995.

(g) Of

§821. Like *fram, of* is a preposition expressing the idea of origin or separation, into which the notion of instrumentality or agency can easily enter. The two overlap to some extent in these, as in some other uses; see further §813 and van Dam, pp. 29–30.

§822. Most of the examples in which *of* is said to express agency still retain some element of origin or separation, e.g. *Or* 154. 28 *for þon þe Tarente seo burg wæs getimbred of Læcedemonium, þe his rice þa wæs*, *ÆHom* 1. 334 *for þan þe ælc wisdom is of Gode sylfum ⁊ we nan god nabbað buton of Godes gyfe*, and *Beo* 1432 *Sumne Geata leod* ‖ *of flanbogan feores getwæfde*. To a modern reader the idea of agency may seem established in examples like *ChronA* 26. 11 (640) *⁊ Ermenred gestrynde twegen sunu, þa syððan wurðan gemartirode of Ðunore* and *Luke(WSCp)* 8. 43 . . . *sum wif . . . seo fordælde*

on lǽcas eall þ heo ahte 7 ne mihte þeah of ænegum beon gehǽlyd;
these and others are quoted by Wülfing (ii, §747). None the less, it
is significant that Pope, whose Glossary supplements BT(S) and *OED*
on the OE uses of *of*, makes no mention of its expressing the agent
and that some idea of origin or separation remains in at least two of
the three examples of *of* indicating the agent or doer cited by *OED*
(s.v. *of* V. 15), viz. *Or* 1. 25 *7 hu II æþelingas wurdon afliemed of
Scippium* and *ChronD* 105. 15 (924) *7 Æþelstan wæs gecoren to
cynge of Myrcum.* The third is *ChronC* 157. 35 (1030) *Her wæs Olaf
cing ofslagen on Norwegon of his agenum folce,* where the idea of
agency does seem stronger. But the idea of origin can still be detected
even here.

§823. A similar situation occurs when we consider the expression of
instrumentality. BT(S) (s.v. *of* V) describe *of* as 'denoting the instrument'. Future lexicographers should, I think, note that the examples
given are not conclusive, since the idea of 'from, out of' seems
present in all, to some degree at least. Bødtker remarks: 'OE *of* introduced the agent in the passive, but its instrumental use was apparently limited [he cites two transitional examples]. . . . But *Beow*
1432 *Sumne Geata leod of flanbogan feores getwæfde* leaves no
doubt of the thoroughly instrumental meaning' (*EStudien*, 45 (1912),
465). This is too strong, for the idea of 'from a bow' is present; see
Klaeber's Glossary. Wülfing (ii, §750) was on firmer ground when he
remarked of his examples, 'Auch hier bleibt die Urbedeutung "von
—her" leicht erkennbar' ['Here too the original meaning "(direction)
from—towards (the speaker)" remains easily discernible']; they
include *Or* 34. 7 *7 he sǽde þæt he of þǽm drycræfte geleornode
godcundne wisdom* and (slightly more convincing as an example of
instrumentality?) *Or* 34. 3 *þa sǽde he Sompeius þæt he þær dry-
cræftas geleornode, 7 of þǽm drycræftum þæt he gewunode monige
wundor to wyrcenne.* Similarly *BlHom* 233. 25 *Ic geseo þæt þas
broþor synd geswencede of ðisse sǽwe hreonesse* (Green 1914,
p. 521) and the three examples which, according to *OED* (s.v. *of*
VI. 18), indicate means or instrument—*CP* 249. 11 *ðylæs fremde
menn weorðen gefylled of ðinum gesuince, Bede* 76. 1 *Ono þætte
þǽre menniscan gecynde of ælmehteges Godes gefe gehealden wæs
. . . ,* and *VSal* 49 *And he of V hlafon and of twam fixum fif þusend
manna gefylde*—are not entirely free of the idea of origin or source.
The same notion can be detected in the examples quoted by Bødtker
1908, pp. 7–8, and Fischer, pp. 87–9. *ÆCHom* ii. 526. 10 *Næfð nan
man geleafan buton of Cristes gife, ne nan man ne ðurhwunað on
geleafan buton þurh Cristes gife,* with the fluctuation of *of* and *þurh,*

is interesting, but again hardly conclusive. Even in *LS* 34. 249 *ealle him wæron gehefgode ða eagan of ðam menigfealdum biterlicum tearum*, we have not really to do with an instrument. Visser (iii, §1996) adds a few more examples. Some of them come close to expressing instrumentality, but once one gets the idea that some element of origin or source is present, it is hard to dismiss it.

(h) þurh

§824. Green (1914, pp. 547–8) sees *þurh* as a 'directive preposition' denoting 'at first simple entrance, passing, piercing through a resisting space or object' which 'once conceived causally . . . comes to express not only the instrument of the action, . . . but the intermediate person responsible for the action, as well as the actual agent with passives'.

§825. There can be no doubt that *þurh* expresses the instrument in 'Alfredian' prose, e.g. *CP* 87. 20 *Hwæt mæg ðonne elles beon getacnod ðurh ðæt fleax butan lichoman clænnes . . . ?* (for further examples see Wülfing, ii, §832d and e); in later prose, e.g. *ÆCHom* i. 52. 7 *þær nis Paulus gescynd þurh Stephanes slege* and *WHom* 20(*EI*). 131 . . . *ac wearð þes þeodscipe . . . swyþe forsyngod þurh mænigfealde synna 7 þurh fela misdæda*; and in both early and later poetry, e.g. *GenA* 11 *þurh geweald godes*, *Dan* 4 *þurh metodes mægen*, *Beo* 1695 *þurh runstafas rihte gemearcod*, *And* 725 *þurh handmægen*, and *El* 341 *þurh weres frige*.

§826. Similarly *þurh* expresses the intermediate agent in prose and poetry of all periods, e.g. *CP* 81. 11 *Bi ðæm wæs gecueden ðurh ðone witgan*, *BlHom* 9. 1 *Iu geara heofonrices duru, þe ic wæs þurh hider onsended, belocen standeþ þurh þa ærestan men, nu heo sceal þonne þurh þe ontened beon*, *ÆHom* 1. 44 *On middanearde he wæs, 7 þes middaneard wæs geworht eall þurh hine*, Latin *et mundus per ipsum factus est*—confirmed as intermediate agent by *ÆHom* 1. 72 *God geworhte on anginne heofonan 7 eorðan, 7 þæt anginn is his ancenneda Sunu, þurh þone he gesceop ealle gesceafta*—

Soul i 44   . . . *þæt ðu wære þurh flæsc   ond þurh fyrenlustas*
               strange gestryned   ond gestaðolod þurh me,
               ond ic wæs gast on ðe   fram gode sended,

El 921   *Ic þurh Iudas ær*
               hyhtful gewearð,   ond nu gehyned eom,
               goda geasne,   þurh Iudas eft,
               fah ond freondleas,

and

MSol 364   Gode oððe yfle,
                    ðonne hie beoð ðurh ane   idese acende,
                    twegen getwinnas,   ne bið hira tir gelic.[212]

§827. Whether *þurh* expresses the personal agent is another terminological question. Wülfing (ii, §832d) offers several examples from
'Alfredian' prose which look fairly convincing, e.g. *Bede* 42. 27 *Seo
hergung wæs þurh Alaricum Gotena cyning geworden*, Latin . . . *ante
biennium Romanae inruptionis, quae per Halaricum regem Gothorum
facta est*, *Or* 62. 24 *þeh þe ægþer þissa burga þurh Godes diegelnessa
þus getacnod wurde: ærest Babylonia þurh hiere agenne ealdormon,
þa he hiere cyning beswac*, Latin . . . *ut et ibi praefectus* . . . *hujus
Attalus regnare tentaverit*, and *Or* 100. 23 *ac heo wearð gescild þurh
þone cristnan casere Arcadiusan, 7 þurh þæt cristene folc*, Latin . . .
*donec orationibus Arcadii principis et populi Christiani, praesentem
perditionem Deus exoratus averteret*. But note that the Latin original
of the first example has *per*; on this see §830.

§828. It is also tempting to regard examples involving the Deity or
the devil as personal agent: *ÆHom* 3. 34 *þys ys þurh God gedon,
ÆCHom* i. 22. 27 *Ða siððan wearð mancynn þurh deofol beswicen,
HomU* 21. 5. 7 *ac þa beoð adwealde and þurh deofol beswicene,
WHom* 9. 110 *And to fela manna wyrð þeah mid þyllican wrencan
þurh deofol forlæred* (where *mid* expresses the instrument, *þurh* the
agent, in contrast to *ÆCHom* i. 52. 5 *þider ðe Stephanus forestop,
mid Saules stanum oftorfod, ðider folgode Paulus, gefultumod þurh
Stephanes gebedu*),

And 435   Wæteregesa sceal,
                    geðyd ond geðreatod   þurh þryðcining,
                    lagu lacende,   liðra wyrðan,

ChristA 43   þær wisna fela   wearð inlihted
                    lare longsume   þurh lifes fruman,

and

ChristC 1039   Ðonne biþ geyced   ond geedniwad
                    moncyn þurh meotud.

But we shall perhaps be less certain even about this when we read
ÆHom 2. 17 *On þam wæterscipe wurdon wundra gelome þurh þone*

---

[212] Good examples from the poetry of *þurh* expressing the intermediate agent, but not
with a passive verb form, include *GenA* 1759 *þurh þe*, *El* 963 *þurh bearn godes*, and *GuthA*
315 *þurh engel*. Phrases like *Ex* 262 *þurh mine hand* can be taken as instrument or intermediate agent; cf. §809.

ælmihtigan God, swa þæt he his engel asende of heofonlicum þrymme, and he þæt wæter styrode. . . .

§829. For the rest, my own impression is that *þurh* + a person tends to express the intermediate agent rather than 'the person immediately operative' (Green 1914, p. 519)—with both active and passive verbs, e.g. (from the early prose) *Bede* 2. 22 *on ealdra manna sægenum . . . þa he me . . . þurh Noðhelm ðone æfestan mæssepreost . . . to me sende*, Latin *per religiosum Lundoniensis ecclesiae presbyterum Nothelmum*, and *CP* 69. 9 *Be ðæm wæs wel gecweden ðurh ðone ængel*, Latin *Cui bene per Angelum dicitur* (see further Wülfing, ii, §832d, e); (from the later prose) *ÆHom* 4. 150 *Godes hand soðlice is ure Hælend Crist, þurh ðone he gesceop ealle gesceafta, and Godes finger is witodlice se Halga Gast, þurh ðone adræfde ure Drihten ða deofla, and þurh ðone syndon geliffæste ealle lybbende gesceaftu* and *ÆCHom* i. 34. 19 *forðan þe þæt halige husel is gastlice Cristes lichama; and þurh ðone we beoð alysede fram ðam ecan deaðe* (where *ðone* can refer to either *lichama* or *Cristes*); and (from the poetry) examples such as

El 1152   Wæs se witedom
    þurh fyrnwitan   beforan sungen
    eall æfter orde

and others like it quoted by Wullen in *Ang.* 34 (1911), 484–5. Green's own example (1914, p. 519) of *þurh* expressing the personal agent is

El 773   . . .   se ðe on rode wæs,
    ond þurh Marian   in middangeard
    acenned wearð   in cildes had,
    þeoden engla,

but this is perhaps better regarded as expressing intermediate agent; cf. *MSol* 364 (§826) and

GenA 2231   and afanda hwæðer   frea wille
    ænigne þe   yrfewearda
    on woruld lætan   þurh þæt wif cuman.[213]

§830. Green, after citing *El* 773 above as an example of *þurh* expressing the personal agent, observes (1914, p. 519): 'This use of *þurh*, certainly a derivative of its function of denoting the intermediate person—the sole one to-day—is at this time distinct as yet from the latter, and expresses the person immediately operative, in

---

[213] This example seems to be on all fours with *El* 773. So Green (1913, §140, and 1914, p. 519) must have overlooked it when, having classified *El* 773 as personal agency, he asserts that *þurh* does not express personal agency in the 'Cædmonian' poems.

the same manner as *by* to-day introduces the logical bearer of the passive action.' This remark reflects the thinking of a twentieth-century scholar rather than the linguistic consciousness of an Anglo-Saxon. In Wülfing's collections *þurh* often represents Latin *per*, *fram* Latin *a, ab*, and *of* Latin *de* or *ex*. That this is a general rule here or elsewhere in OE remains to be established. But these equivalences suggest that we may be too ingenious in equating *þurh, fram*, or *of*, with the expression of the personal agent; it may well be that the personal agent in the sense in which we mean it today was not expressed in English until the usage with 'by' became established. Green's notion that *þurh* originally expressed intermediate agent, came to express personal agency as well, and then lost this new sense while retaining the original one, somehow seems less likely than that *þurh* in the OE examples under discussion meant what we mean by 'through' (rather than 'by') in similar contexts today. For *Bede* 42. 27 *Seo hergung wæs þurh Alaricum Gotena cyning geworden* gives good sense if translated 'The devastation came to pass through Alaric, the King of the Goths'. Visser's examples (iii, §1999) do not compel me to change my mind on this point. Cf. van Dam, pp. 36–7. However, as Kilpiö (my §744; private communication) points out, 'one thing that complicates our interpretation of examples of *þurh* corresponding to Latin *per* is the fact that in Latin, especially in later Latin, *per* can represent personal agent; see J. B. Hoffmann and Anton Szantyr, *Lateinische Syntax und Stilistik* (München, 1965), §130, p. 240'.

(*j*) Wið

§831. MnE 'with' is often used to express the instrument. There are occasional examples of OE *wið* which anticipate this use, e.g. *Lch* ii. 162. 22 *Læcedomas wiþ þon þe monnes þ uferre hrif sie gefylled wið yfelre wætan* (Hittle errs in saying at p. 161 that this is the only such example in OE), *Gen* 38. 20 *Iudas sende an ticcen wið hys Odolamatiscean hyrde*, Latin *per pastorem suum*, *Beo* 2599 *Hiora in anum weoll ‖ sefa wið sorgum*, and *PPs* 77. 49 *and þæt wið yfele englas sende*, Latin *per angelos malos*.

§832. According to Green (1914, p. 522) '*with* assumes the force of agency in Middle English'. I have noted no OE examples. Nor has Visser (iii, §2000).

(*k*) *Conclusion*

§833. Green detects a gradual movement by which *þurh* was replaced as the preposition expressing the dative of agency by *fram* (1914, pp. 519-20), which in turn gave way to *of* (1914, pp. 520-2 and 536), *of* finally being replaced by 'by' (1914, pp. 525-8); see also Green 1914, pp. 550-2. I would want to see much more evidence than he supplies before accepting this theory. Two things, however, lead me to surmise that it is untenable: first, the great overlap in the use of those prepositions in apparently similar functions in the same texts suggests that the Anglo-Saxons made distinctions at whose significance we can only guess, and second, the fact that my own investigations described above have led me to doubt whether any of the OE prepositions *þurh*, *fram*, and *of*, ever expressed personal agency in the sense in which we understand it. On this see §830.

§833a. In the course of his treatment of the agent in the passive construction, Visser (iii, §§1987-2000) discusses all the prepositions listed above and adds *betux* (§1991)—his sole OE example is

Men 160	Be him wealdend cwæð
þæt nan mærra man	geond middangeard
betux wife and were	wurde acenned—

and *in/on* (§1997)—it 'is occasionally used, especially in translations from Latin. It expresses cause, reason, or motive.' But the local sense remains detectable. van Dam discusses *in/on* (p. 32) and *ymb* (p. 39). Kilpiö (my §744) notes that, although *ongemong* in *CP* 59. 6 translates Latin *per*, it retains its local sense, and rightly hesitates to regard the phrase *abisgod ymb* in *CP* 103. 1 and 169. 1 as representing 'a real agent'.

(8) *The passive of verbs which govern something other than one*
    accusative object[214]

(a) *Introductory remarks*

§834. As noted in §748, the norm for OE is that the accusative object of the active verb becomes the subject of the passive, e.g. *He ofslog þone cyning* but *Se cyning wæs ofslægen (fram him)*. MnE, however, while not in a position to do anything about *Se Fæder him tiðað þæs* and *þa healp he þæm cyninge*, does not scruple to turn 'The whole audience laughed at him' into 'He was laughed at by the whole audience' and 'They gave him the book' into 'He was given the

---

[214] We must of course not confuse true passives with constructions involving the second participle of 'intransitive' verbs, either impersonal, e.g. *ÆCHom* i. 316. 30 *þa com his wif Saphira, and nyste hu hire were gelumpen wæs*, or personal, e.g. *ÆCHom* ii. 278. 29 *Næs þæt Israhela folc gewunod to hreawum flæsce* (on these see §§734-42) or with sentences like *ÆCHom* i. 204. 1 *Eadige beoð þa þe sind ofhingrode and oflyste rihtwisnysse*, where we can follow BT in taking the participles as adjectives. Visser (i. 103 fn. 2) makes this last error, as well as citing an incorrect reading; see BTC, s.vv. *acreopian* and *acreowed*.

book' as well as the expected 'The book was given to him'. Such constructions do not occur in OE, where the personal passive is used only when the subject would have been the accusative object in the active voice. Otherwise the impersonal passive was the rule, as in *ÆCHom* i. 330. 29 *ac him næs getiðod ðære lytlan lisse* and *ÆCHom* ii. 510. 10 *and wæs ða geholpen ðam unscyldigum huse*. The verb *fultumian* may provide exceptions (see §851), but no others have yet come to my notice.[215] In the discussion which follows, I use verb divisions (ii)–(vii) as set out in §1090.

(b) *Verbs with the double accusative or an accusative and a noun clause or infinitive*

§835. Here we would expect one of the accusatives to become the subject of the passive verb. With verbs of teaching and similar verbs —as opposed to those with 'predicative adjuncts' (§1083)—the personal object of the active verb regularly becomes the subject of the passive verb, e.g. *Bede* 208. 10 *ond he scole gesette, in þære cneohtas 7 geonge menn tydde 7 lærde wæron*, *ÆGram* 158. 12 *doceor, ic eom gelæred*, and *El* 172 *þa þæt gefrugnon þa þurh fulwihte* ‖ *lærde wæron*. The absence from my collections of examples with a retained accusative of what is taught (MnE 'He was taught singing') must be the result of either chance or faulty observation, for we find a noun clause in *BlHom* 19. 13 and an infinitive in *Gifts* 44; see §836. I have not yet found an example in which the accusative of person appears when what is taught is the subject of the passive verb, though the dative of the person taught appears in *Conf* 3. 1 11. 12; see §838. Visser (iii, §1962)has none either.

§836. When what is taught is expressed by a noun clause or an infinitive, the accusative personal object again becomes the subject of the passive verb, e.g. *BlHom* 19. 13 *þæt is þonne þæt we sceolan beon gelærede mid þysse bysene, þonne we beoþ mid mycclum hungre yfelra geþohta abisgode, þonne sceolan we geornlice biddan*

---

[215] None of the OE examples cited by Visser in his discussion of the passive (iii, §§1905–2000) breaks the general rule that only verbs which can take an accusative object in the active voice are used personally in the passive. Visser seemed to have grasped this in iii, §§1933–5, but had lost his hold on it by the time he got to iii, §1959, and had not regained it by iii, §§1964, 1968, and 1981–3; see Mitchell 1979*b*, pp. 539–42.

Lieber (*Linguistic Inquiry*, 10 (1979), 680) tells us that 'impersonal passives with accusatives do exist' but does not give examples. I do not remember encountering the type *⁕Hine wæs ofslægen* 'He was slain'. It is, I suppose, arguable that *Solil* 19. 14 *Hyt is gecwæden on þære æ þæt man sceole lufian hys nehstan* represents an active form *⁕Man cwiþ/cwæþ hyt on þære æ þæt man sceole lufian hys nehstan* and that in *CP* 409. 2 *Ðæm monnum is gecyðed hwelce stowe hi moton habban* . . . the *hwelce* clause is the subject of *is gecyðed*. But these are susceptible to other analyses and are special cases.

þæt he us gescylde wiþ þa þusendlican cræftas deofles costunga,
BlHom 173. 18 *Đa wearþ Simon se dry eallunga aweht wiþ ðam*
apostolum 7 gelæred þæt he feala yfla sægde, 7 þæt Petrus bigswica
wære, Bede 388. 27 *Đa he ða hio gesegnad hæfde, ða heht he tion eft*
in muð, 7 heht hine spreocan; 7 ðus cwæð: Cweð hwelc hwugu word;
cweð nu gee. Đa sona instæpe was se bend onlesed his tungan, 7 he
cuæð ðæt he haten wæs, Latin *Dixit ille statim, soluto uinculo linguae,*
quod iussus erat—the active form of the last OE sentence would
probably be ☆*He heht hine cweðan þæt* or ☆*He heht þæt cwepan,*
rather than (as Visser, i. 636, has it) ☆*hie hine hataþ þæt*[216]—and

Gifts 44	Sum mæg wrætlice	weorc ahycgan
	heahtimbra gehwæs;	hond bið gelæred,
	wis ond gewealden,	swa bið wyrhtan ryht
	sele asettan. . . .	

§837. With verbs which take an accusative object and a predicative
adjunct, the accusative object becomes—as we should expect—the
subject of the passive verb, with the second accusative in the nominative, e.g. *Bede* 62. 26 . . . *se halga wer Agustinus . . . wæs gehalgod*
ercebiscop Ongolþeode, GD(H) 26. 5 . . . *Æquitius se for his lifes*
geearnunge wæs gehæfd micelre halinysse man, ÆCHom ii. 136. 22
and he . . . wearð geset cumena ðen, ÆCHom i. 498. 29 *Nis se Fæder*
gehæfd gemænelice Fæder fram ðam Suna and þam Halgan Gaste,
LS 23. 436 *þu wære symle fæmne oncnawan,* and *LS* 23. 439 . . .
forþan ðe ic gehyrde þæt god wære mann . . . gefremod. . . . We can
compare these with examples like *ÆLS* 32. 10 *Se munuc þa Abbo*
. . . wearð sona to abbode geset on þam ylcan mynstre, where the
predicative nominative is replaced by a *to* phrase. The two idioms
occur in the passive in *The Coronation of Edgar*—

CEdg 17	And him Eadmundes	eafora hæfde
	nigon and XX,	niðweorca heard,
	wintra on worulde,	ða þis geworden wæs,
	and þa on ðam XXX wæs	ðeoden gehalgod

but

CEdg 1	Her Eadgar wæs,	Engla waldend,
	corðre miclum	to cyninge gehalgod
	on ðære ealdan byrig,	Acemannesceastre.

[216] Visser includes this example among those in which 'the indirect object of the active
construction has been converted into the subject of the passive construction, while
the direct object of the active construction is retained as such' (iii, §1967). He gives a collection
of alleged OE examples in iii, §1968. Apart from *Bede* 100. 27, which I discuss in §845,
the subject of the passive construction in all of them would be accusative (not dative) in the
active form after the verbs *biddan, forgiefan, hatan,* and *forlætan.* So these are not exceptions to the general statement set out in §834.

Visser gives more examples of these two patterns (iii, §§1936-8) and adds two OE examples with *for*, one of which is *WHom* 12. 50 *þas manfullan men . . . wæron getealde for ða mærostan godas* (iii, §1939). Similar constructions are found when the adjunct is an adjective or a prepositional phrase, as in *Bede* 458. 27 *7 ealra heora dome he unscyldig 7 butan leahtrum wæs clæne gemeted þara þinga . . .* ; see further Visser, iii, §§1942 and 1946.

(c) *Verbs with an* accusative *and a genitive, dative, or preposition*

§838. Verbs which take a direct object in the accusative and a second element in the genitive, dative, or with a preposition, follow the usual rule (§834): the accusative object of the active verb becomes the subject of the passive. But the second element, if expressed, remains unaltered. Examples include: *Or* 76. 32 . . . *on anne cylle se wæs afylled monnes blodes, Bede* 222. 16 . . . *ge æðele ge unæðele . . . mid fulwihte bæðe from synnum aðwegene wæron, GD(C)* 150. 31 *uneaðe, Petrus, his seo gemæne spræc wæs æmetegod þære mycelnysse his godan mægnes, GD(C)* 76. 15 . . . *þæt þes wer wære mid arfæstnysse mode gelustfullod, GD* 290. 16 . . . *þæt he wære geæmtigod to his gebede, Conf* 3. 1 11. 12 *7 mid hwylcere ful-fremednesse se dædbeta gebet hæbbe þæt him getæht wæs, LS* 35. 244 *And ic wæs gelustfullod minre hæftnyde, ÆCHom* ii. 548. 15 *and swa hi ufor ferdon, swa mihton ða licmen læs þæs sanges ge-hyran, oðþæt he mid ealle heora earum ætbroden wearð, ÆCHom* ii. 440. 23 *Maria geceas þone selestan dæl, se ðe ne bið hire næfre ætbroden, ÆCHom* i. 472. 4 *he bið ðonne aðwogen fram his synn-um, ÆHom* 12. 130 *ac seo halige modor, þe is Godes gelaþung, wat þæt þæt cild . . . bið up abroden fram synnum aðwogen, þurh þæt halige fulluht, Beo* 1677 *Ða wæs gylden hilt gamelum rince* ‖ . . . *on hand gyfen,* and *JDay i* 12 *bið eal þes ginna grund gleda gefylled,* ‖ *reþra bronda.*

§839. The type 'The girl was given the book' does not occur in OE; as we have seen, *ÆLS* 9. 130 *Ic secge eow to soþan þæt sib is for-gifen godes gelaðunge* 'peace is given to God's congregation' is the OE idiom. It is scarcely surprising that the conversion of the indirect personal object into the subject of a passive construction did not occur in OE times, for the process depends on the disappearance of the distinction in case endings; see van der Gaaf in *EStudies*, 11 (1929), 1-11 and 58-67, and Ahlgren, pp. 202-3. An interesting example quoted by van der Gaaf is *ÆLS* 9. 134 *Swa swa seo cata-nenscisce burh binnan hire weallum hæfð minre swyster agathen miccle foreþingunga swa ic eom forgifen fram þam ælmihtigan gode*

. . . *eow to geþingienne*, which he translates (p. 62) 'Even as the city of Catana within its walls has the powerful intercession of my sister Agatha, so *am I allowed* by Almighty God . . . *to intercede for you*.' Despite Marchand (*Ang.* 70 (1951), 71-2), we must agree with van der Gaaf when he writes: 'It would be unjustifiable to conclude from this quotation that the initial stage of the shift by which the personal object was converted into the subject may be dated as far back as Ælfric's time' (p. 62). In the active form of this construction *ic* would be *me* accusative, not dative, and the sense 'God has given me', not 'God has allowed to me'. The comparison is with *Matt (WSCp)* 27. 26 *Ða forgeaf he hym Barabban*, not with *Matt(WSCp)* 19. 8 *Moyses for eower heortan heardnesse lyfde eow eower wif to forlætenne*. *ChronA* 42. 18 (718) . . . *7 hio wæs forgifen Norþan-hymbra cyninge Aldferþe* demonstrates the possibility of my inter-pretation—and (I believe) its correctness.

§840. Visser's treatment of these constructions—which I discuss in Mitchell 1979*b*, pp. 539-42—has nothing to make me alter my position: with the possible exception of *fultumian* (see §851), I have found no OE verb used personally in the passive which could not take an accusative in the active form, and no personal passive con-struction with a subject which could not be the direct accusative object in the active form.

(*d*) *Verbs with a noun clause or infinitive* and/or *a genitive, dative, or preposition*

§841. Some of these verbs also belong to the previous group. When so used, they naturally take the personal passive, e.g. *CP* 31. 18 *Ðurh ða cweorne is getacnod se ymbhwyrft ðisse worolde*, *Or* 202. 18 *þa . . . wearð Cartainum frið aliefed from Scipian*, *Max i* 109 *þonne him biþ wic alyfed*, *Beo* 1688 *on ðæm wæs or writen || fyrngewinnes*, and *BlHom* 55. 29 *forþon þe þæt halige sæd . . . þæt him ær of þæs lareowes muþe wæs bodad 7 sægd*. When they are used in the passive with a noun clause, we find either a pronoun subject, e.g. *CP* 93. 6 *Hit is awriten ðæt . . .* , *CP* 109. 4 *Hwæt hit is gesæd ðæt . . .* , and *ÆHom* 13. 120 *þis mæg beon gecweden . . . þæt*, or no expressed subject other than the clause, e.g. *CP* 79. 1 *Be ðam is awriten ðæt . . .* and *BlHom* 61. 16 *Sægd is þæt. . . .*[217] Similarly, with an infinitive we find either *hit*, e.g. *Matt(WSH)* 12. 12 *witodlice hyt ys alyfed on restedagen wel to donne*, or no expressed subject other than the infinitive, e.g. *Matt(WSCp)* 12. 12 *witodlice ys alyfed on restedagum*

---

[217] *Secgan* is also used in the active, e.g. *BlHom* 41. 3 *þonne sægþ on þissum bocum þæt.* . . . Jost (1909, p. 30) notes that verbs of saying prefer *wesan* when used passively.

wel to donne; see Grünberg (my §110), §49, pp. 302-3, but my §§1537-9.

§842. As with verbs which take a direct object in the accusative, the second element, if expressed, remains unaltered, e.g. *CP* 201. 20 *Ðæm ðeowan is beboden, 7 ðus to cueden: Beoð ge underðeodde eowrum woroldhlafordum, ÆHom* 20. 376 *Ðam folce wæs behaten . . . þæt hi sceoldon habban soðlice renscuras, GD(H)* 156. 2 . . . *þæt him wære alyfed ut to farenne, BlHom* 137. 14 *eac us is alefed . . . heofena rice to gesittenne*, and *ÆCHom* ii. 510. 34 *þa bestang se halga his hand him on muð, het hine ceowan mid scearpum toðum his liðegan fingras, gif him alyfed wære*. In so far as the direct object of the active verb—the noun clause or infinitive—is (or is in apposition with) the subject of the passive verb, we have the so-called personal passive. But there are no OE examples of the type 'He was said to be *x*' (the earliest *OED* citation (s.v. *say* B. 2. f. (*c*)) is from Shakespeare) and none in which a person is the subject of a verb of saying or the like in the passive. In *CP* 171. 14 *Ða saglas is beboden ðæt scoldon beon mid golde befongne* the sg. *is* shows that *ða saglas* is the subject of *scoldon*. In *Bede* 358. 33 *Ða feng Ealdfrið æfter Ecgfriðe to rice. Se man wæs se gelærdesta in gewreotum; se wæs sægd, þæt he his broðor wære Osweos sunu þæs cyninges* we have a passive example of the confused construction sometimes encountered when an adjective clause and a verb of saying appear together; see further §1980. (This comparison holds even if, like Miller, we take the third *se* as demonstrative, not relative.) The subject of *wæs sægd* is the *þæt* clause. We can obtain acceptable translations by omitting *se* 'it was said that he was his brother and the son of King Oswio' or *þæt he* 'who, it was said, was his brother . . .'.

(e) *Verbs which take* either *an accusative* or *a genitive, dative, or preposition*

§843. We turn now to those verbs which are sometimes called 'transitive' in the sense that they take a 'direct' object which is in the genitive or dative, or is governed by a preposition; on the use of the term see van der Gaaf 1930, pp. 1 and 19, and QW, pp. 61-3 and 65. They can conveniently be divided into two main groups, which are respectively discussed here and in §§848-54. First there are those verbs which take a direct object which may be in the accusative or in the genitive or dative, e.g. *afandian* in *ÆCHom* i. 268. 14 *Swa swa man afandað gold on fyre, swa afandað God þæs mannes mod* but *ÆCHom* i. 268. 11 *Deofol mot ælces mannes afandigan*. But we find the regular 'personal' passive in *ÆCHom* i. 268. 8 *ac hwæðere nan*

man ne cymð to Godes rice, buton he sy afandod. Similarly we find
ÆCHom i. 170. 14 *We ne beoð na fulfremede buton we beon afand-
ode*—this in the midst of the series *ÆCHom* i. 170. 12 *Hi moton
ure afandian, ÆCHom* i. 170. 26 *Ne sceal man his Drihtnes fandian*,
and *ÆCHom* i. 170. 27 *Se man fandiað his Drihtnes . . .* , all of
which have the genitive. We must conclude that these two passive
expressions are based on the use of *afandian* with the accusative.
The same will be true of *ÆCHom* i. 262. 12 *þonne sceal ure mod
beon . . . gemyngod*, for *gemyndgian* too can take either accusative
or genitive. Again Ælfric, who can write both *ÆHom* 11. 118 *Ælc
man him ondræt þæs lichaman deað* and *ÆLS* 34. 139 *þonne mihte
we ondrædan us deaðes rihtlice*, has *ÆGram* 123. 3 *timeo deum, ic
me ondræde god. timeor, ic eom ondræd.*

§844. Similarly, the verb *blissian* 'to gladden', which takes either
the accusative, e.g. *And* 1607 *þa se halga ongann hæleð blissigean*,
or the dative, e.g. *LPr ii* 34 *swa þu, engla god, eallum blissast*, has the
personal passive in *ChristC* 1162 *Hyge wearð mongum blissad* and
GuthA 722 *Ða wæs Guðlaces gæst geblissad* (on this example see
Mitchell 1979*b*, pp. 541-2).

§845. Another example of the personal passive with a retained noun
clause presents difficulties—*Bede* 100. 27 *7 nu gif Agustinus is
milde 7 eaðmodre heortan, þonne is he gelyfed þæt he Cristes geoc
bere 7 eow lære to beorenne*, Latin *Si ergo Augustinus ille mitis est
et humilis corde, credibile est quia iugum Christi et ipse portet et
uobis portandum offerat*, translated by Miller 'and now if Augustine
is meek and of lowly heart, then it is credible that he bears the yoke
of Christ and teaches you to bear it'. This construction might be possible if *gelyfed* were taken as a form of *geliefan* 'to allow s.o. (acc.)
that he do s.t. (noun clause)'—the two constructions are recorded
separately, though I have not yet found them together. But I cannot
see how it could occur with *geliefan* 'to believe' except *apo koinou*
'I believe him (accusative; see *PPs* 118. 66) that he bears the yoke'.
We cannot solve the difficulty by taking *gelyfed* as an adjectival
second participle, for then it would mean 'believing, faithful'; see
BT. This is not unlike the confusion seen in *Bede* 358. 33 (§842);
cf. the neater impersonal construction which follows—*Bede* 100. 29
*Gif he þonne is unmilde 7 oferhygdig, þonne is þæt cuð þæt he nis
of Gode*, Latin . . . *constat quia non est de Deo.*

§846. Van der Gaaf (*EStudies*, 11 (1929), 7) quotes a passive construction with *biddan*, which can take a dative or an accusative of

the person addressed—*Bede* 162. 31 *7 heo wilnadon, þæt heo þære þeode hælo beon meahten, þe heo bedene wæron*—and remarks 'When construed with an accusative, it [the verb] could, of course, be used in the passive voice.' The use of the personal passive—which is what he means—is interesting in view of the fact that *biddan* appears with *of* + the dative a few lines earlier in *Bede* 162. 21 . . . *þa Oswald se cyning of Scotta ealonde biscopes bede.*

§847. The examples quoted above, along with those of the impersonal passive in §§849 and 853 and those with *forwyrnan* and *ofteon* in §857, make it clear that the idea that the choice between the personal and impersonal passive must sometimes have presented itself is no mere theoretical possibility, but a fact of living speech. They also suggest that the personal passive was preferred when it was possible and that the impersonal passive was used only when it had to be. Such a conclusion is not surprising in view of the subsequent disappearance of the latter.

(f) Verbs with a genitive and/or a dative

§848. The second main group (§843) is made up of those verbs which do not take the accusative, but do take the genitive and/or the dative. When these are used passively, the 'impersonal' passive is the rule, whether the verb has one object or two.

§849. Let us consider first the impersonal passive with verbs which take either the genitive or the dative. A good example of this will be found in *Bo* 67. 11 *Forðæm se ðe his ær tide ne tiolað, þonne bið his on tid untilad*, where *tilian* takes the genitive and is then used impersonally in the passive—'then it will be unprovided in respect of him when the time comes'. The genitive object *his* remains unchanged in the passive form. *Helpan* is used with the genitive, e.g. *ÆCHom* ii. 442. 13 . . . *we sceolon earmra manna helpan*, or the dative, e.g. *ÆCHom* ii. 356. 11 *We . . . magon helpan þam forðfarenum*, but not with the accusative. The passive is impersonal, e.g. *ÆCHom* ii. 510. 7 *ac Martinus astah on ðam sticelan hrofe . . . and wæs ða geholpen ðam unscyldigum huse.* Similarly *ðenian*, which is found with the dative in Ælfric, e.g. *ÆHom* 25a. 9 *he þenað Criste; and Crist þenað hym* . . . (though Wülfing (i. 250) records a few 'Alfredian' examples with the accusative), has the impersonal passive in *ÆCHom* i. 514. 6 *forðam him bið geðenod mid his ðearfena þenunge, and he sylf bið underfangen on heora anfenge.* In these examples *wæs geholpen* and *bið geðenod* are used impersonally and the dative object of the active verb remains dative; we may contrast *he . . . bið underfangen* in

ÆCHom i. 514. 6 above, or *læran*, which governs the accusative in Ælfric, e.g. *ÆHom* 2. 85 *þær he lærde þæt folc*, and therefore has the regular personal passive, e.g. *ÆCHom* i. 440. 3 *þeah ðe þa apostoli . . . on ealre soðfæstnysse gelærede wurdon*. An example of this sort of impersonal passive from the poetry is

Beo 1102   . . . ðeah hie hira beaggyfan   banan folgedon
ðeodenlease,   þa him swa geþearfod wæs.

The examples with the dative given by Visser (iii, §1933) belong here.

§850. In his discussion of verbs which take an 'indirect object as sole object'—his examples are *he Gode þancode* and *ic forgiefe ðam þeowum*—Visser (i, §323) classifies seven clauses or sentences as 'passive constructions proving completed shift from indirect to direct object'. I dismiss these in Mitchell 1979*b*, pp. 541-2.

×§851. However, there is at least one verb where he might have made out a case for such a shift—though not a 'completed' one. The verb *(ge)fultumian* 'to help someone or something' is recorded in BT(S) and GK with the dative of the person or thing helped or with ambiguous forms such as *me* and *us*. No examples with an unambiguous accusative are cited.[218] So Visser (i, §323) is on good ground in recording it with the dative only. However, he fails to quote examples like *OccGl* 49. 657 *ðe is gefultumad, qui adiuvatur, Bede* 342. 14 *ac he wæs godcundlice gefultumed, Bede* 390. 14 *7 he swa dyde 7 wæs gefultumad . . . , ÆLS* 11. 84 *Æfre we wæron gefultumode on ælcum gefeohte*, and *ÆCHom* i. 52. 6 *ðider folgode Paulus, gefultumod þurh Stephanes gebedu*—all personal passives, although later (iii, §1934) he does cite two of these, viz. *Bede* 342. 14 and *ÆLS* 11. 84, and adds *LS* 3(*H*) 184. 240 *þet we . . . seon gefultumade*. As we can scarcely argue that accusative/dative syncretism had been completed in OE times, we are left to conclude either that *(ge)fultumian* could take the accusative as well as the dative or that these are examples of a verb which took only the dative being used personally in the passive. But perhaps these are only different ways of saying the same thing.[219]

[218] *ÆCHom* ii. 106. 19 *ac þæt we ða wædligendan gefultumedon* is not one. Malcolm Godden tells me that the other ten copies all read *ðam* for *ða* and that six have *wædliendum*, four *wædliendan*. So the scribe's *ða* is more likely to be wrong than to be an early example of *(ge)fultumian* with the accusative.

[219] Despite Thorpe's translation 'He will be ready to support our good will', *ÆCHom* ii. 84. 15 *He gearcað urne godan willan to fultumigenne, and he fylst ðam willan gegearcodne* is not an example of *(ge)fultumian* with an accusative; BTS had it right (s.v. *gegearcian* I. (3a)): 'he prepares our good will for helping/to be helped'; see §§959 and 2952. Since, as Malcolm Godden has kindly told me, all nine manuscripts (representing three or four

§852. There may well be more such verbs. This suggests another respect in which my List of verbal rections may be incomplete and warns lexicographers that they will have to look out for examples of verbs which are recorded only with the genitive and/or dative in the active form being used personally in the passive.

§853. Typical examples of verbs which take both the genitive and the dative and are used impersonally in the passive are *gestieran*, e.g. *GD* 243. 4 *7 him woldon þæs heafes gestyran* and *CP* 341. 11 *Swa wyrð eac gestiered ðæm gitsere ðæs reaflaces*, and *(ge)tiðian*, e.g. *ÆHom* 8. 65 *and se Fæder þe tiðað untwylice þæs*, *ÆCHom* i. 330. 28 *He bæd þa Abraham mid earmlicre stemne þæt Lazarus moste his tungan drypan; ac him næs getiðod ðære lytlan lisse*, *ÆCHom* ii. 528. 5 *Paulus se apostol bæd æt Gode þæt he afyrsode ðæs deofles ehtnysse him fram, ac him næs þære bene getiðod*, and

Beo 2283   Ða wæs hord rasod,
       onboren beaga hord,   bene getiðad
       feasceaftum men.

For further such examples, see Visser, iii, §1959(1).

§854. Such verbs can be contrasted with verbs like *bedælan*, which takes the accusative and the genitive, e.g. *CP* 333. 3 . . . *se hine wile selfne bedælan ðære bledsunge 7 ðæs weolan on ðæm ytemestan dæge*, and therefore regularly has the personal passive (indeed, *bedælan* seems to occur much more frequently in the passive than in the active voice), e.g. *CP* 333. 5 . . . *ðonne weorðað hie bedælede ðæs ecean eðles ures Fæder* and *ÆCHom* i. 346. 27 *Ac seo [sawol] ðe bedæled is þam godnyssum, heo geomrige*.

(g) Verbs which can take only a preposition

§855. Included here are not only verbs like *flitan*, which are used only absolutely or with a preposition, e.g. *ÆCHom* i. 592. 4 *Ure Hælend . . . ne flat ne ne hrymde* and *ÆCHom* i. 290. 3 *Arrius hatte an gedwolman, se flat wið ænne biscop*, but also verbs which can govern the accusative and/or other cases, as well as noun clauses or infinitives, but are also found with only a preposition—as, for example, *Or* 278. 10 *þa gierndon eac æfter þæm onwalde*, *Or* 160. 2

independent witnesses) have acc. sg. masc. *gegearcodne* in the *and* clause, it must be right. Thorpe's 'and he will aid the ready will' will not do. BTS (ibid.) had the root of the matter 'and he helps that will when it is prepared'. The point is that *gegearcodne* is accusative singular masculine agreeing with *urne godan willan* and so acquires strong emphasis. A change in the MnE order brings out the point: 'and—when it is prepared—he helps that will'.

þa sendon hie on Affrice to Cartaginenses æfter fultume, CP 355. 21
. . . *wið ðone to cidanne ðe yfel deð, Bede* 162. 32 *ond swiðe on þon sargedon, þæt heo þam lareowe onfon ne woldon, ÆCHom* i. 68. 35
. . . *and awrat ða feorðan Cristes boc, seo hrepað swyðost ymbe Cristes godcundnysse, ÆCHom* i. 82. 20 *þearflæs he syrwde ymbe Crist,* and *ÆLS* 5. 151 . . . *caflice to campienne for Cristes geleafan.*
On the analogy of verbs which take only the genitive and/or dative and therefore have the impersonal passive, we might expect to find with these prepositional verbs impersonal passives such as ☆*þa wæs wið ænne biscop gefliten,* ☆*þa wæs æfter þæm onwalde girned,* and ☆*þa wæs for Gode gecampod.* But I have found no such examples. In MnE, of course, the case-form gives way entirely to the preposition and we find the passive of 'prepositional verbs' such as 'the bishop was fought against', 'Peace was yearned for', and 'England was fought for'. But the OE equivalents—☆*An biscop wæs ymbe gefliten* or ☆*An biscop wæs gefliten ymbe,* ☆*þa wæs se onweald girned æfter,* and ☆*þa wæs God gecampod for*—do not occur. According to van der Gaaf (pp. 19-20), examples 'first crop up in texts dating from about 1300'; see also Mustanoja, p. 441,[220] and Visser, iii, §§ 1947-58.

(h) Conclusion

§856. The basic situation, then, is that when the active verb can have an accusative object, that object becomes the subject of the passive verb and that when the active verb is not found with an accusative object we have the impersonal passive. The only exception I have noted is *fultumian*; see §851. When a verb which can take a direct object is used without one, the passive will be impersonal; cf. *BlHom* 197. 22 *þonne syndon from þære burge weallum twelf mila ametene up* (this is not an example of the type 'He was laughed at', since *up* is not essential) with *ÆHom* 13. 119 *On ðam gemete þe ge ametað, eow bið eft ameten.*

§857. But there are verbs which have a variety of meanings and constructions, so that they straddle the patterns discussed above. Some, e.g. *aliefan* and *writan*, have already been mentioned in §841. More interesting are those which are found with both the impersonal and the personal passive, e.g. *forwyrnan* and *ofteon.* The verb *forwyrnan* takes the accusative in the sense 'withhold' in *ÆHom* 8. 81 . . . *þæt*

---

[220] It is not clear why Mustanoja quotes *ÆLS* 20. 94 *þa gewæda þe heo bewunden wæs mid* in connection with 'He was laughed at'. The two are not on all fours. The respective active forms in MnE would be 'They bound her [direct object] with a cloth [instrument]' —not 'They bound-with her'—but 'They laughed-at him'. Another of his examples, *ÆGram* 127. 7 *se oðer had is, þe se forma sprecð to,* is more to the point. Further on examples like *ÆLS* 20. 94, see Mitchell 1978a, p. 251.

he renscuras forwyrnde to feorðan healfan geare and even in the sense 'hinder, prevent' in *HomU* 44. 285. 13 . . . *buton hine þæra þreora þinga hwylc forwyrne, yld oððe iuguð oððe unhæl.* But the regular constructions when it means 'deny, refuse, restrain, prevent' are dative + genitive, e.g. *ÆHom* 8. 147 *for ðan þe se munuc, mid his micclum gebedum, forwyrnde me þæs weges* and *ÆHom* 26. 46 *ac se biscop . . . forwyrnde hym innganges,* or dative + a clause which, according to Pope, may be expressed, e.g. *ÆHom* 26. 53 . . . *oððe hwæþer þin miht þe mæge forwyrnan þæt ðu þas synne ne sceole oncnawan?,* or 'omitted', e.g. *ÆHom* 4. 139 *þes finger oferswiðde soðlice þa drymen on Egipta lande ætforan Farao, þa ða hi wunnon wið Moysen and God, woldon wyrcan gnættas, ac God him forwyrnde.* (But one could just as easily postulate 'omission' of *þæs* in the last example.) So it is no surprise to find the impersonal passive when *forwyrnan* has these meanings, e.g. *CP* 387. 6 . . . *ða ðe . . . wilna 7 welena wilniað, 7 swaðeah . . . hiora him bið færwirned,* *ÆCHom* i. 270. 10 *and deofol us wile ofslean, gif he mot; ac him bið forwyrned þurh Godes gescyldnysse, HomU* 26. 134. 22 . . . *þe læs þe him beo forwyrned his sawle reste on domes dæg,* and *Jul* 440 . . . *me hwilum biþ ‖ forwyrned þurh wiþersteall willan mines.* But *forwyrnan* is used personally in the passive in the sense 'denied, deprived of' in

Exhort 25   ne mihtu mid þæm eallum   sauwle þine
                 ut alysan,   gif heo inne wyrð
                 feondum befangen,   frofre bedæled,
                 welena forwyrned.

One can see how it happened. The ptc. *forwyrned* is the third on *wyrð* and so may be more adjectival than verbal. The participle which precedes it is from *bedælan,* which takes accusative (not dative) + genitive; see §838. But this remains an interesting transitional example.

§858. With *ofteon* the situation is similar. It can mean 'to take/deny something (acc.) from/to someone (dat.)', e.g. *ÆCHom* ii. 102. 32 *Efne nu ic ðe ofteo minne fultum,* or 'to deprive someone (dat.) of something (gen.)', e.g.

Met 25. 24   and him þonne oftion   ðara ðegnunga
                 and þæs anwaldes   ðe he ær hæfde.

In the first sense it belongs in §838 and has the personal passive, e.g. *ÆCHom* ii. 96. 4 . . . *þæt ðam godum þe hit gehealdan willað, ne sy oftogen seo gastlice deopnyss* and *ÆCHom* ii. 530. 30 *Ðe bið seo bodung oftogen.* But in the second sense, it belongs in §848 and has the impersonal passive, e.g. *ÆCHom* i. 570. 30 . . . *ac him wæs ða oftogen ælces fodan six dagas, Max i 39 Blind sceal his eagna þolian, ‖ oftigen biþ him torhtre gesihþe*, and

Met 25. 30   Gif him þonne æfre   unmendlinga
                weas geberede   þæt him wurde oftogen
                þrymmes and wæda   and þegnunga
                and ðæs anwaldes   þe we ymbe sprecað. . . .

As the case system progressively collapsed, such verbs would obviously serve as a bridge between verbs which took the accusative and so had a personal passive and those which took a genitive or dative and so had the doomed impersonal passive.

6. THE SEQUENCE OF TENSES

§859. This topic need not detain us long. The rule 'primary tenses follow primary tenses; historic tenses historic' is, of course, basically a logical rather than a grammatical conception: the words of Kluge, quoted by Hale in *AJP* 8 (1887), 77—'a mechanical dependence of the tenses of the subordinate sentence upon those of the main sentence does not exist, and . . . the choice of the tense in each sentence depends upon the conception lying at the bottom of it'—and of Gildersleeve and Lodge (GL, §509. 2)—'tense means time, not merely tense-form'—are as valid for OE as for Latin.

§860. Most of the early writers on OE syntax realized this truth, e.g. Adams (p. 159) and Benham (pp. 237-9). But there are others who do not appear to have grasped it fully. Thus Henk (p. 39) regarded as departures from the *consecutio temporum* such examples as *ofgeafon* in

Wan 60   þonne ic eorla lif   eal geondþence,
            hu hi færlice   flet ofgeafon

and *is* in *Soul i 25 Hwæt, ðu on worulde ær ‖ lyt geþohtest hu þis is þus lang hider*, and Bauch (pp. 80-1), after stating the 'rule', quotes as exceptions sentences like *Sat 191 þa hig god bedraf ‖ in þæt hate hof þam is hel nama* (*Sat 189 Hwearf þa to helle þa he gehened wæs* follows the 'rule'!) and *GenB 816 Nu me mæg hreowan þæt ic bæd heofnes god.* . . . Many of the examples of 'irregular sequence' given by Shearin for the prose (1903, pp. 123-8) and for the poetry (1909, pp. 250-1) are of the same pattern.

§861. It is obviously quite wrong to think of such logical sequences as 'irregular'. Combinations of a present tense in a principal clause with a past tense in a subordinate clause are common in English of all periods; OE examples include sentences expressing a universal truth, e.g. *ÆCHom* ii. 236. 6 *ærðan ðe Abraham gewurde ic eom* and

PPs 89. 2 Ærðon munta gesceaft ofer middangeard
      oððe ymbhwyrft eorðan wære
      oþþe world wære, þu eart, wuldres god,

and sentences making an ordinary statement, e.g. *ÆCHom* ii. 486. 29 *Nu sind ge ðurh deofl bepæhte, þæt ge . . . forlætað eowerne scyppend þe eow geworhte* and

Beo 1323   Dead is Æschere,
    Yrmenlafes yldra broþor,
    min runwita ond min rædbora,
    eaxlgestealla, ðonne we on orlege
    hafelan weredon. . . .

Similar examples are to be found in dependent speech, e.g. *ÆCHom* i. 518. 26 *Is nu geleaflic þæt se heahengel Michahel hæbbe gymene cristenra manna, seðe wæs ðæs Ebreiscan folces ealdor, þa hwile ðe hi on God belyfdon* and *Wan* 60 (§860). Another is *Instr* 229–34, discussed by Torkar in *Ang.* 89 (1971), 170–2.

§862. The opposite pattern—past tense in a principal clause with a present tense in a subordinate clause—is also common. Some examples do not contravene even the ludicrously strict interpretation of the 'rule', inasmuch as the OE past tense sometimes functions as a perfect (see §§634–5) and can therefore be described as a primary tense, e.g. *ÆCHom* i. 112. 19 *Ac eft seo miccle mildheortnys ures Drihtnes us alysde þurh his menniscnysse, gif we his bebodum mid ealre heortan gehyrsumiað, ÆCHom* ii. 482. 19 *We sind Ebreisce, Hælendes Cristes þeowan, and we comon hider for eowere hæle, þæt ge eowere deofolgild forlæton . . . , ChristA* 383 . . . *nu us hælend god ‖ wærfæst onwrah þæt we hine witan moton,* and

PPs 59. 4   þu becnunge beorhte sealdest
     þam þe ege ðinne elne healdað,
     þæt hi him gebeorgen bogan and stræle
     and wæron alysede leofe þine,

Latin *Dedisti metuentibus te significationem, ut fugiant a facie arcus; ut liberentur dilecti tui.*

GuthB 865   Nænig monna wæs
    of þam sigetudre siþþan æfre
    godes willan þæs georn, ne gynnwised,
    þæt he bibugan mæge þone bitran drync

> þone Eue fyrn   Adame geaf,
> byrelade bryd geong

may be another example, but even if *wæs* is taken as a perfect, *meahte* would perhaps seem more logical than *mæge*. This ambivalence of the OE past tense—primary or historic—accounts for many apparent failures of sequence in both prose and poetry and is of special importance in connection with the wavering use of tense and mood in the expression of universal truths in dependent speech (see § 1942) and with causal clauses introduced by *nu* (see § § 3099-100).

§ 863. Other examples in which we have a principal clause with a past tense and a subordinate clause with a present tense are found in non-dependent speech, e.g. (expressing a universal truth) *ÆCHom* i. 216. 9 *þa getimode ðam reðan deofle swa swa deð þam grædigan fisce,*

> *Beo* 1282   Wæs se gryre læssa
> efne swa micle   swa bið mægþa cræft,
> wiggryre wifes   be wæpnedmen,

and

> *Sea* 6   . . .   þær mec oft bigeat
> nearo nihtwaco   æt nacan stefnan,
> þonne he be clifum cnossað,

and (making an ordinary statement) *ChronA* 86. 7 (894) *þa gegaderedon þa þe in Norþhymbrum bugeað* (see § 627 and cf. *Beo* 1921 and 2484), *ÆCHom* i. 228. 17 *And ða heardheortan Iudei ðeah þurh ealle ða tacna noldon gebugan mid geleafan to ðam mildheortan Hælende, seðe wile eallum mannum gehelpan on hine gelyfendum, Beo* 1925, and

> *Men* 40   Swylce Benedictus
> embe nigon niht þæs   nergend sohte,
> heard and higestrang,   þæne heriað wel
> in gewritum wise,   wealdendes þeow
> rincas regolfæste.

They occur in dependent speech too, e.g. *ÆCHom* i. 224. 33 *and þæt sædon gehwilce wise lareowas, þæt hi habbað gefremod heora ærist to ðam ecan life, swa swa we ealle don sceolon on ende þisre worulde, ÆCHom* i. 564. 22 *þa wearð him geswutelod þæt he æt Gode abæde, þæt on ælces geares ymbryne, ymbe his ðrowungtide, seo sæ seofan dagas drigne grund þam folce gegearcige, þæt hi binnan ðam fyrste his halgan lichaman gesecan magon* (with *magon* cf. *mæge* in *GuthB* 865 in §862),

Beo 377   Ðonne sægdon þæt   sæliþende,
                 þa ðe gifsceattas   Geata fyredon
                 þyder to þance,   þæt he þritiges
                 manna mægencræft   on his mundgripe
                 heaþorof hæbbe,

Beo 1313, *Beo* 2493, possibly *Beo* 2717, and

Mald 29   Me sendon to þe   sæmen snelle,
                 heton ðe secgan   þæt þu most sendan raðe
                 beagas wið gebeorge.

There are also examples of non-dependent speech in the present tense after a verb of saying in the past, e.g. *ÆCHom* i. 18. 1 *Ða cwæð se deofol 'Nis hit na swa ðu segst . . .'* and *Beo* 1321 *Hroðgar maþelode, helm Scyldinga:* || *'Ne frin þu æfter sælum! . . .'*. The problems associated with 'represented speech' are discussed in §1945.

§864. A few difficult examples remain. Most have been discussed as possible instances of the historic present; see §§625-9. The last to be considered is *Ps(P)* 25. 6 *Ac ic wilnode symle þæt ic aðwoge mine handa betwuh þam unscæððigum; [þæt is þæt ic wære unscyldig betwuh him] þæt ic meahte hweorfan ymb þinne þone halgan alter, Drihten. [7.] And þær gehyran þa stemne þines lofes, and þæt ic mæge cyþan eall þin wundru,* Latin *Lavabo inter innocentes manus meas, et circumdabo altare tuum, Domine;* [7.] *Ut audiam vocem laudis tuae, et enarrem universa mirabilia tua.* Shearin (1903, p. 128, and 1909, p. 251) offers a plausible explanation for this failure on logical grounds. But comparison with the Latin and with other OE versions suggests that the preterites in *Ps(P)* 25. 6 are errors by the translator; they do not appear, for example, in *Ps(A)* or *Ps(K)*. For further examples and discussion see (for the poetry) Shearin 1909, pp. 250-1; Bauch, pp. 80-1; Henk, p. 39; Behre, pp. 78-80, 124, and 215-16; and (for the prose) Adams, p. 159; Shearin 1903, pp. 123-8; Benham, pp. 237-9; Burnham, pp. 124-5; and Liggins 1955, pp. 237-8.

7. ASPECT

§865. 'The term *aspect*', J. Lyons tells us (*Introduction to Theoretical Linguistics* (Cambridge, 1968), 313) '. . . is a translation of the Russian word *vid*.' According to A. H. Semeonoff (*A New Russian Grammar* (Dent, 1934), §124),

the aspects [in Russian] *are different forms of one and the same verb, differentiating between the* DURATION *and the* COMPLETION *of an action.*

There are two aspects: the *imperfective* which expresses an action in its *duration* without indicating its beginning or its end, and the *perfective* which expresses an action in its *completion* in either the past or the future, with its beginning and its end; or, at least, the beginning must be complete. . . .

We cannot quarrel with these remarks. But we can quarrel with those who apply the term to the Germanic languages. There can be no doubt that it is possible to give a coherent account of the OE verb without using the term 'aspect'. (The same is, of course, true of the MnE verb. The Subject Index to F. R. Palmer's *A Linguistic Study of the English Verb* (Longmans, 1965) has one reference to 'aspect'. This is on p. 59, where the author, speaking of perfect and non-perfect forms, makes the unenthusiastic comment that 'the term "aspect" could be used to designate this category'.) There can also be no doubt that Scherer succeeded in carrying out his proposal to demonstrate that 'verbal forms are indifferent to aspect' in the Corpus MS of the West-Saxon Gospels (*Language*, 34 (1958), 245–51); he had previously demonstrated this for Gothic (see *Language*, 30 (1954), 211–23) and for ninth-century East-Franconian (see *Language*, 32 (1956), 423–34). So I have no hesitation in agreeing with Zandvoort that

the attempt to transfer the category of 'aspect' from Slavonic to Germanic, and from there to Modern English grammar, strikes one as an instance of misplaced ingenuity. Streitberg's application of the notion to Gothic, which was the beginning of the trouble, is now completely discredited, and with it the endeavours of his imitators in the fields of other Germanic dialects, including Old English. But even those who admit defeat on the rest of the Germanic front still cling to the Modern English progressive . . . whichever way we look at it, the conclusion seems inescapable that the question asked in the title of this paper should be answered in the negative.[221]

§866. This seems to me the appropriate place to leave aspect. But to do so may savour to some of running away from the problem. In reality, it is a question, not of running away, but of facing another problem. Mustanoja remarks (p. 445 fn. 1)

One must bear in mind, however, that in the Germanic and Romance languages the term 'aspect' means something entirely different from what it means in the Slavonic languages, where the contrast between the imperfective and perfective aspects is a feature running through the whole verbal system. . . . The idea of aspect in the non-Slavonic languages is largely incommensurable with the idea behind the Slavonic term.

I do not think that this ought to be so. But since it is so for some writers on OE, I must briefly raise my head from the sand.

---

[221] R. W. Zandvoort, 'Is Aspect an English Verbal Category?', *Contributions to English Syntax and Philology*, ed. F. Behre (Gothenburg Studies in English, 14) (1962), 19–20.

§867. The aspects which have been detected in OE include 'perfective' and 'durative' (see Ardern, §42, and QW, §130), 'inchoative' (see Visser, iii. 1372-82), 'terminative' (see Visser, iii. 1384-91), 'iterative' (see Raith, p. 21, and Mustanoja, p. 446), 'intensive' (see Raith, pp. 21 ff.), and 'causative' (see Raith, pp. 22 ff.). (Some of these have alternative names. But a rose. . . .) I have already attacked the 'inchoative' and the 'intensive' (see §694). A few swings at one or two of the others will not be out of place.

§868. Quirk and Wrenn make the distinction between the 'perfective' and 'durative' aspects in these words (QW, §129):

In speaking of the present tense of 'have' (*habban*, rarely *agan*) and 'be' with a past participle, we pass from the consideration of tense (the expression of the *time* of an action) to the consideration of aspect (the expression of the *manner* or *quality* of an action). For ordinary purposes, we need distinguish only 'perfective' aspect (relating to momentary actions, such as inception or completion) and 'durative' aspect (relating to both habitual and continuous actions).

They then discuss 'perfective' aspect:

The perfect of transitive verbs expressed with 'have' (*he hafað onfunden* 'he has found') and the perfect of intransitive verbs expressed with 'be' (*is nu geworden* '(it) has now happened') do not refer to a different time from the simple preterites (*he onfand, nu geweard*) but to the same time regarded more specifically as perfective.

Here they do what Palmer has already been quoted as saying we *could* do (perhaps implying that we *should not*) and fall into the error of equating the expression of completion with perfective aspect —a not uncommon mistake rightly condemned by Davis in *RES* 23 (1972), 66. They go on to reduce the whole notion to absurdity by the suggestions that 'in OE the perfective aspect could equally well be expressed with the simple preterite form: *Hine halig God . . . us onsende* 'Holy God has despatched him to us' (which opens up the possibility of perfective aspect expressed by the periphrasis with the present participle; see §686 and the MnE examples quoted below); that 'in other cases, the function was assisted by adverbs' (their example could equally well be translated by a MnE past tense); and that 'some verbs (such as *cuman* "come", *feallan* "fall", *weorðan* "become") are, as it were, inherently perfective and need no formal indication of aspect' (a statement dubious in itself—if we had looked over the writer's shoulder as he was penning these words, we could have said 'He's coming to a new point. He's falling into error. He's becoming muddled'—and one which confuses grammatical and lexical means of conveying aspect). Consider too the following MnE sentences in the light of Mustanoja's remark (p. 445) that 'the difference between the imperfective and perfective aspects is strikingly illustrated by verb-pairs like *sit* (imperfective)–*sit down* (perfective) and *stand–stand up*':

He was sitting in the chair for hours.
He was [in the act of] sitting when I arrived.
He was [already] sitting down when I arrived.
He was [just] sitting down when I arrived.

§869. Quirk and Wrenn are not alone in this error. Visser (iii, §§1255-1311) refers to three kinds of 'verbs of aspect' which respectively express 'ingressive', 'durative', and 'terminative', aspect. (This is what he means; he is confused in §1255.) The folly of this is amusingly revealed in an observation by Bodelsen:

. . . there is no more reason why we should establish special categories of verbs according as they denote completeness or incompleteness, beginning or end, etc., than why we should establish categories according as they denote something hard or soft, or something pleasant or unpleasant (*he patted her cheek*: soft aspect; *he smacked her face*: hard aspect!). Once we leave the ground of inflectional *form*, we are lost in a chaos of infinite possibilities of distinction.[222]

However, Quirk and Wrenn go on to say that 'the durative aspect is inherent in the meaning of most verbs ("be", "live", for example)' (QW, §130), thereby repeating the error. The sentence continues:

and it is therefore not surprising that special forms and constructions were used only to a minor extent in OE to express it: *ðeos woruld . . . nealæcð þam ende* 'this world is approaching the end', *we forhealdað æghwær Godes gerihta ealles to gelome* 'we (repeatedly) withhold God's dues everywhere all too frequently', *wæs se cyng . . . on fære mid þære scire þe mid him fierdedon* 'the king was on his way with the shire-men that were campaigning with him'.

It is hard to see any 'special forms and constructions' for the expression of aspect in these examples or in the others which follow them.

---

[222] *EStudies*, 32 (1951), 259-60. Further on this point see Goedsche in *JEGP* 39 (1940), 189-96, and Carlton (1970, p. 124).

None the less, K. A. Tandy's 'Aspect and Ælfric' (Ph.D. diss., University of California, Berkeley, 1976) 'examines patterns of aspectual features of verbs in Ælfric's *Lives of Saints*' (*DAI* 37A (1977), 5812A). See also the same author's 'Verbal Aspect as a Narrative Structure in Ælfric's *Lives of Saints*', *The Old English Homily and its Backgrounds*, edd. Paul E. Szarmach and Bernard F. Huppé (Albany, 1978), 181-202. Here Tandy tells us that 'in English aspect is not expressed overtly, in a morphological system, but covertly, in modifiers, periphrastic verb structures, and lexical meaning, and consequently aspect is accessible largely through the semantic analysis that was forbidden by formal grammarians' (p. 181). This involves the study of 'special verbal phrasings', of 'lexical embedding', of 'adverbial modification', of 'the phonesthemic clusters in English', and of 'the marking of aspect by syntactical units larger than single adverbs' (ibid., pp. 182-3). I have never 'forbidden' anyone to undertake such analysis. But I believe, with Bodelsen, that anyone doing so runs the risk of being 'lost in a chaos of infinite possibilities of distinction'.

§870. Prefixes such as '*a-, be-, for-, ge-, of-, to-*' (QW, §129) are often described as means of expressing perfective aspect. Even if we substitute 'completion of an action' for 'perfective aspect' (see §868), it is clear that this is not the sole function of any of these prefixes. It is the function of the lexicographer to deal fully with them, but brief mention may be made of *be-* and *ge-*. The *locus classicus* for the ambiguity of *be-* is, of course, the now infamous crux *ealuscerwen* in *Beo* 769. The prefix *ge-* is equally ambiguous, as Lindemann decisively shows:

> Now, if OE simplexes, as we have just seen, are capable of expressing *perfective* aspect as well as imperfective, and if *ge-* compounds are capable of expressing *imperfective* aspect as well as perfective, then *ge-* cannot be a 'formal', preverbal tag indicating perfective aspect. We find for OE what Scherer found for Goth. and OHG, namely, that *form*—always excepting the expanded form [but see my §865]—does not determine aspect, but that aspect is a *connotation* inherent in specific verbal meaning *and* syntactic context. *Ge-* has no immediate bearing on aspect at all, and the doctrine is untenable.[223]

On the relevance of this to literary criticism, see my comments on *Wan* 1 *Oft him anhaga are gebideð* in *NM* 69 (1968), 172-5.

§871. The OE 'aspects' not so far discussed are the 'iterative', the 'causative', and the 'terminative'. Mention has been made in §§687-8 and 692 of examples in which the periphrasis with the present participle may express habitual or recurrent action. Neither these nor such things as the use of *þonne* to introduce clauses expressing repeated action (§§2562-3) justify the importation of 'iterative' or 'frequentative' aspect into OE. Both 'causative' aspect as described by Raith (p. 22) and 'terminative' aspect as described by Visser (iii, §§1289-311) are a matter of particular verbs, not of verb-forms, and are therefore lexical, not grammatical; see §868. This 'terminative' aspect is different from what Goedsche, encouraged by Curme, called 'terminate' aspect in *JEGP* 31 (1932), 469-77. In his view,

> the progressive form [the periphrasis with the present participle] may express under certain circumstances also the *action as a whole*, thus having *terminate*

---

[223] J. W. R. Lindemann, *Old English Preverbal Ge-: Its Meaning* (University Press of Virginia, 1970), 17-18. Part I of this book is a reprint of Lindemann's article in *JEGP* 64 (1965), 64-83. The book contains an almost complete bibliography of the numerous writings on the prefix *ge-* (pp. 67-71). To it may be added the items listed in Mitchell 1978*a* and 1980*b* and a discussion in the forthcoming work by Kilpiö (my §744). Zadorožny (1973, pp. 56-66) fails to mention Lindemann.

Lindemann has set an example worthy of emulation by any writer of a Ph.D. thesis planning publication: he revised his thesis before publishing it. The last paragraph of 'Part III. Conclusions' in his thesis 'Ge- as a Preverb in Late Old English Prose. Its Meaning and Function as suggested by a Collation of West-Saxon, Mercian, and Northumbrian Versions of *The Gospel according to St Matthew*' (University of Wisconsin diss., 1957) begins (p. 412): 'The data of this study appear to substantiate the observation that has prevailed for well on to four hundred years, namely that the preverb ge- perfectivated. . . .' The reader should, however, consult Stanley's review of Lindemann 1970 in *Ang.* 91 (1973), 493-4.

aspect [p. 469]. . . . The expanded form with terminate aspect is a survival from the Old English [p. 471] . . . which has been overlooked by modern scholars [p. 477]. . . . It is used to indicate the speaker's opinion or emotional feeling, or stress a characteristic trait as a whole [p. 475].

I have already mentioned the last usage in §685. But the concept of 'terminate' aspect as defined is too wide to be of any value and cannot qualify as an 'aspect' in the absence of a distinct grammatical form of the verb to express it.

×§872. Klaeber (3, pp. 186 and 221) detects an ' "imperfective" function' in the verbs *bræc* in

Beo 1509   ac hine wundra þæs fela
            swencte on sunde,   sædeor monig
            hildetuxum   heresyrcan bræc,
            ehton aglæcan

and *wehte* in

Beo 2852   He gewergad sæt,
            feðecempa   frean eaxlum neah,
            wehte hyne wætre;   him wiht ne speow,

which he translates respectively 'was in the act of breaking', or 'tried to pierce', and 'tried to rouse'. This is a rather violent extension of the idea of 'imperfective' as opposed to 'perfective' so that it embraces the notion of 'non-perfection' in the sense of failure. On these two verbs in particular, see Mitchell 1975a, p. 16, but see also Stanley, *Archiv*, 214 (1977), 136. However, despite Klaeber, there is in my opinion no such thing as an 'imperfective aspect' in OE. Schücking's attempt to find an example by taking *seah* as 'tried to look' in

Beo 2717   seah on enta geweorc,
            hu ða stanbogan   stapulum fæste
            ece eorðreced   innan healde

is reported by Penttilä in a somewhat confused note (p. 25 fn. 1). It need not detain us. Again, Thorpe translates *ÆCHom* i. 564. 4 *þa forlet he þæt folc, and ðone biscop ænne to þam hæðengylde genydde; ac ðaða he geseah þæt he nateshwon hine gebigan ne mihte . . . '. . . and would compel the bishop alone to idolatry'. But we have here testimony, not to the existence of an 'imperfective' aspect in OE, but to the fact that OE *niedan* did not necessarily carry the idea of *successful* pressure on someone; see again Mitchell 1975a, p. 16.

§873. I do not propose to pursue aspect further into the philological fens. For those who wish to do so, I offer in a footnote a more than adequate supply of landmarks—or will-o'-the-wisps.[224]

8. MOOD

a. Introductory remarks

§874. OE distinguished indicative, subjunctive, and imperative moods, two infinitives, and two participles. The infinitives and the participles are treated separately; see the Contents. On the forms see *OEG,* chap. xvi.

b. The indicative and the subjunctive

(1) *Forms and uses*

§875. The necessity for recognizing the existence of three *formal* categories—indicative, subjunctive, and ambiguous forms—has been explained in §601. A convenient illustration of the importance of this will be found in my note on *wenede* in *Wan* 36; see *NM* 68 (1967), 139–49.

§876. The indicative and the subjunctive occur in both principal and subordinate clauses, and in clauses introduced by *ond, ac, ne,* and the like. The mood in these last depends on the mood in the clause with which the particular example is co-ordinate; there is in this sense a 'sequence of moods'. The occasional exceptions are discussed as they arise. The mood in principal clauses depends in general on the nature of the clause. That in subordinate clauses may be influenced by various factors, including the type of clause, the attitude of the speaker, and the mood of the principal clause. Detailed discussions on the uses of these two moods and on the factors affecting them will be found in later chapters. For references, see the General Index.

---

[224] Lindemann gives in part I of the book cited in §870 a review of some previous writings on aspect and *Aktionsart* and at pp. 67–71 of the same work a very comprehensive bibliography. Others who have touched on these topics include Lussky in *JEGP* 21 (1922), 32–69; F. Mossé, 'Le renouvellement de l'aspect en germanique', *Mélanges linguistiques offerts à M. J. Vendryes* (Paris, 1925), 287–99; A. Mirowicz in *Die Aspektfrage im Gotischen* (Wilno, 1935); Scherer in the three articles cited in §865; and Isadore Barrett (not 'Barratt' as Collinson has it in *TPS* 1941, pp. 101–2, where he offers a short summary of the thesis) in 'On Aspect in Germanic', an unpublished thesis presented in 1938 for the Degree of Master of Arts in the University of Liverpool.

(2) *The moods of fact and fancy?*

§877. Although full treatment of these moods has been postponed, it will be as well to rid our minds here and now of one false notion. In general terms, we can agree that the *indicative* is used to present something as a fact, as certain, as true, or as a result which has followed or will follow and that when the *subjunctive* is found, some mental attitude to what is being said is usually implied—condition, desire, obligation, supposition, perplexity, doubt, uncertainty, or unreality. But to say this is not to agree with Cook (p. 104) that 'certainty is rendered by the indicative' or with Mossé (1945, p. 159) that 'toutes les fois qu'il s'agit d'un fait, d'une constatation, d'une réalité, on emploie l'indicatif . . .'. The indicative does not always state a fact, e.g. *Matt(WSCp)* 18. 13 *7 gyf hyt gelimpþ þ he hyt fint*, nor does the subjunctive always imply uncertainty, doubt, or the like, e.g. *ÆCHom* i. 116. 22 *Mine gebroðra, uton we geoffrian urum Drihtne gold, þæt we andettan þæt he soð Cyning sy, and æghwær rixige* (they all believe that he *is* the true God) and *ÆCHom* i. 48. 9 *Se wisa Augustinus spræc ymbe ðas rædinge, and smeade hwi se halga cyðere Stephanus cwæde þæt he gesawe mannes bearn standan æt Godes swyðran* (Augustine is not casting doubt on Stephen's statement). I drew attention to this error in *NQ* 208 (1963), 327–8, *NM* 68 (1967), 146, and *Guide,* §156. But it persists. Visser (ii, §834) enshrines it in a discussion which I criticize in §601. So too does Carlton (1970, p. 122) when he translates *Ch* 1445 *ða cwæð he ðæt he wære ðeof* as 'Then he said that he *might be* [his italics] a thief'. Helmstan *was* a thief, for he had stolen both Æthelred's belt and then—as his bramble-scratched face proved—stray oxen. It is more than time that we dismissed the simplistic notion encapsulated in my heading.

(3) *Bibliographical notes*

§878. I propose to eschew here discussion of the nature of the subjunctive. I shall deal (as briefly as possible) with the question as it arises in connection with individual constructions. Writers who have treated it include Callaway (1931, pp. 1-10), Delbrück, Glunz, Hotz, Vogt, Wilde, and (with special reference to the poetry) Behre and Cobb. Works restricted to the study of mood in individual texts or writers include those by Fleischhauer (*Cura Pastoralis*), Faulkner (*Bede*), Robertson (*ASC*), Henshaw (The Gospels), Mourek and Nader (*Beowulf*), Steche (*Genesis*), and Prollius (the works of Cynewulf). I shall refer to these works when it seems necessary or profitable. See also Mitchell 1959, pp. 640–4 and *passim*.

c. The imperative and the subjunctive

(1) Introductory remarks

§879. Three problems require our attention here: first, the form of the verb which expresses the command, wish, exhortation, or suggestion; second, whether the subject is expressed or not; and third, the relative order of the subject and verb. The last two will be taken together.

§880. There are three works which deal with these topics. We do not need to accept all the elaborate distinctions made by Suter, who offers examples from a limited corpus, some without pronouns. Yamakawa, who acknowledges his debt to Suter and to Voges (1966, pp. 6-25), has observations of interest, but is more concerned with the later history of the construction. Millward offers a useful collection of examples, again from a limited corpus. But some are not quoted in full and her classification and comments must be viewed with extreme caution; see my review in *EStudies*, 55 (1974), 387-9. Visser (i, §§13-14 and 23-6, and ii, §§841-9) also gives examples. They cannot be accepted without checking. I have detected him omitting even such vital words as *ond, oðða, þæt*, and *uton*. On the expression of commands and the like by other grammatical means, see §§916-19.

§880a. Bacquet (pp. 232-73) offers a valuable collection of positive and negative examples with the imperative and the subjunctive and discusses at length the order of the various elements. *Mutatis mutandis*, most of his findings apply to other types of sentences and clauses; see my chapter IX and my review of his book in *NM* 67 (1966), 86-97. But here too his anxiety to establish an 'ordre de base' to contrast with an 'ordre marqué' leads him astray; see §915.

(2) Imperatives, subjunctives, and ambiguous forms

§881. Wülfing (i, §§228-33) grouped together as imperatives forms such as *gemyne* in *Bede* 132. 26 *Ac gemyne nu þæt þu þæt þridde gelæstest, sing* in *Bede* 344. 2 *Sing me frumsceaft*, and *fullian* in *Bede(B)* 76. 19 *fullian we þ cennede wif*. He was not followed in this by Suter (§§6-7) or by Visser (ii, §842). Millward, however, whose bibliography contains none of these works, makes enthusiastic and successful attempts to confuse imperative and subjunctive forms; for details see my review of her book already cited. There seems to me no point in describing unambiguously *subjunctive* forms as *imperatives*. So I begin by setting out briefly in §883 the *formal* position in

OE. Naturally most of the examples cited below involve simple verb-forms. But examples do occur of periphrases with the present participle, e.g. *ÆCHom* i. 64. 15 *Beoð blowende* and *ÆCHom* ii. 252. 19 *Beo his blodes gyte ofer urum bearnum, and eal seo wracu on us wunigende*, and of the passive, usually with *beon/wesan*, e.g. *CP* 201. 21 *Beoð ge underðeodde eowrum woroldhlafordum, ApT* 4. 20 *sy he beheafdod, ÆCHom* i. 92. 3 *Ne beo ðu geciged heononforð Abram*, and *ÆCHom* i. 92. 4 *ne ðin wif ne beo gehaten Sarai ac beo gehaten Sarra* (where Thorpe wrongly has *Ne* before *ðin*), but occasionally with *weorþan*, e.g. *CP* 425. 35 *Hreowsiað 7 weorðað gefulwade, eower ælc* and *ÆLS* 34. 259 *awurpað caflice eow fram þæra þeostra weorc and wurðað ymbscrydde mid leohtes wæpnum.*[225] The dual pronoun is sometimes found with an imperative verb-form, e.g. *GenA* 2881 *Rincas mine, restað incit ‖ her on þissum wicum.*

§882. An imperative or subjunctive simple sentence or principal clause sometimes performs the function of a conditional clause, e.g. *ÆCHom* i. 178. 23 *do þonne ða six sunnandagas of ðam getele, þonne beoð þa six and ðritig þæs geares teoðingdagas us to forhæfednysse getealde* and *ÆCHom* ii. 294. 31 *Wurde ure miht geedniwod, þonne towurpe we ðis deofolgild*. For further examples, see Visser, i, §26, and my §3678.

(3) *Imperatives and subjunctives in simple sentences and principal clauses beginning with the subject, the verb, or* ne + *the verb*

(a) *The basic syntactical paradigm*

§883. This paradigm of the strong verb *helpan* is applicable (*mutatis mutandis*) to strong contracted verbs and to weak verbs of all classes. On the preterite-present and the anomalous verbs, see *OEG*, §§767-8; such forms as *wite, ga, beo*, and the like, are ambiguous in that when used as second person singulars they can be either imperative or subjunctive.

Person and Number	Imperative	Present Subjunctive	Ambiguous
1st pers. sg.	—	[*helpe*][226]	—
2nd pers. sg.	*help* *help þu* *þu (. . .) help*	*helpe* *helpe þu*	—
3rd pers. sg.	—	*helpe he* *he (. . .) helpe*	—

---

[225] See Visser, iii, §1836, and §§1918, 1923, and 1924, for further examples of periphrases with the present participle and of the passive.   [226] See §884.

Person and Number	Imperative	Present Subjunctive	Ambiguous
1st pers. pl.	—	*helpen* *helpen we*	*helpe we*
2nd pers. pl.	*helpaþ*	*helpen ge*	*helpe ge*[227] *helpaþ ge*[228] *ge(. . .)helpaþ*[228]
3rd pers. pl.	—	*helpen hie* *hie (. . .) helpe(n)*	—

I discuss this paradigm in the sections which follow. My main concern is with the circumstances under which the subject is absent, and with the relative position of the subject and verb when the subject is present. A lot more could be said about the relative position of elements other than subject and verb in these clauses with imperatives and what I unrepentantly call 'jussive subjunctives'. But what is said about element order in general in chapter IX (including order in clauses which do not begin with the subject, the verb, or *ne* + the verb) applies here. Millward offers some useful *examples* at pp. 34-40, but see again my review in *EStudies*, 55 (1974), 387-9.

(b) First person present subjunctives

§884. 'In OE., as in other Germanic languages', says Behre (p. 18 fn. 1), 'the adhortative subjunctive (= IE. conjunctivus) does not occur in the 1st pers. sing. In this respect Germanic languages contrast with Aryan, Greek, and O. Lat. . . .'. I have found no examples in OE.

§885. But in the plural, the subjunctive may exhort, command, encourage, or warn, a group which includes the speaker. The nom. pron. *we* is usually found after the verb, e.g. *BlHom* 13. 6 *Lufian we hine nu*, *HomU* 27. 151. 15 *ne yldon we na fram dæge to dæge*, *Sat* 201 *Gemunan we þone halgan drihten*, and (with a verb in *-e*) *Mark (WSCp)* 1. 38 *fare we on gehende tunas*. But it may be unexpressed when a reflexive personal pronoun is used, e.g. *LS* 34. 202 *faran us into þam mycclan scræfe* and *Sat* 203 *ceosan us eard in wuldre*. The only examples without either *we* or reflexive *us* which have come to my notice are from the poetry—

Sat 205 beoran on breostum bliðe geþohtas
      sibbe and snytero; gemunan soð and riht,

---

[227] See *OEG*, §730. Visser (ii, §843) wrongly regards these forms as 'modally marked' —'subjunctive' for the uninitiated.

[228] In these patterns, *helpaþ* could be either imperative or indicative, and is therefore ambiguous. But see §888.

where we have the sequence *gemunan we* (*Sat* 201, quoted above)
. . . *ceosan us* (*Sat* 203, quoted above). . . *beoran* . . . *gemunan*, and

Sat 285   Gemunan symle on mode   meotodes strengðo;
              gearwian us togenes   grene stræte
              up to englum,

which represents an abrupt transition to the first person plural but
where *us* at least gives a clue.[229] I have found no clauses in prose or
poetry in which initial *we* is followed by a subjunctive of this sort.

§886. Alternative constructions are discussed in §§916-19. They
include *uton* + infinitive, which Ælfric tends to prefer, though the
point requires further investigation. Visser (ii, §844) seems to be saying that in *BlHom* 19. 19 *Gehyraþ we nu* . . . we have a first person
plural imperative. He was probably misled by Morris's translation.
A reading of *BlHom* 17. 9-25. 36 will, I think, persuade readers that
gehyraþ can reasonably be taken as an unromantic indicative. It is
Visser too (iii. 2207 fn. 1) who discovers an 'imperative of the perfect' in *habbað* . . . *getrahtod* in

And 1356   Utan gangan eft
              þæt we bysmrigen   bendum fæstne
              oðwitan him his wræcsið.   Habbað word gearu
              wið þam æglæcan   eall getrahtod!

He presumably means that *habbað* is first person plural imperative,
not second person. Even if it were imperative, it would not be perfect, for *getrahtod* would be adjectival rather than verbal. But
habbað is present indicative; as Brooks pointed out in his edition of
Andreas (p. 110), 'the subject *we* is omitted, cf. 1364, 1487'.

(c) Second person imperatives in positive clauses

§887. In positive clauses we have three possibilities. Most commonly there is no subject pronoun—I disagree with Zernov's conclusion (*IAF* 4 (1971), 127) that 'the second person pronoun in . . .
the Old English imperative sentence . . . cannot be treated as the subject of the sentence'—either in the singular, as in *ÆCHom* i. 38. 25
Beheald þæt ðu ðas dæde ne do, ÆCHom i. 480. 10 *oððe gif ic
sceole cyðan ðinne tocyme hellwarum, swa swa ic middangearde þe
toweardne bodade, geswutela,* and

---

[229] That there was a first person plural imperative in *-an/-on* as opposed to the first
person plural present subjunctive in *-en* is suggested by Wright (*Old English Grammar*, 3rd
edn. (Oxford, 1925), §478), SB (§362. 2), and Millward (p. 17). I find no trace of this distinction in *OEG*, §§731(*b*), 735(*f*), 752, 756, or elsewhere. So we may have to do with
vowel reduction and scribal confusion; see SB, §361 Anm. 1. See Behre, pp. 18-19 and
22-3, for further examples of the subjunctive under discussion.

Dan 325   Fyl nu frumspræce,   ðeah heora fea lifigen!
            Wlitiga þinne wordcwyde   and þin wuldor on us!
            Gecyð cræft and miht . . . ,

or in the plural, as in *ÆCHom* i. 64. 15 *Beoð blowende and welige hwilwendlice*, *ÆCHom* i. 64. 6 *Gað to smiððan, and fandiað þises goldes* (a common enough OE construction condemned in MnE by some grammatical purists), and *Dan* 472 *Onhicgað nu halige mihte, || wise wundor godes!* Less often we find examples with subject pronoun after the verb, e.g. *ÆCHom* i. 14. 9 *ic ðe secge, forgang ðu anes treowes wæstm, Dan* 427 *Aban þu þa beornas, brego Caldea, || ut of ofne, BlHom* 39. 26 *Bringaþ ge on min beren eowerne teoðan sceat*, and *PPs* 113. 23 *Wesað ge fram gode geara gebletsade*. In the last two examples, the element order, (for native speakers) intonation, and context, would remove any notion that *bringaþ* and *wesað* were indicatives.

§888. The third possibility is for the subject pronoun to precede the verb. No ambiguity can arise in the singular, for the singular imperative form is distinctive, e.g. *ChristA* 249 *þu þisne middangeard milde geblissa || . . . hælende Crist* and *GuthB* 1192 *Ðu hyre eac saga.* . . . There is a theoretical possibility of ambiguity in the plural, where *-aþ* may be indicative or imperative. But as in the previous section, element order, context, and intonation, would presumably prevent this in practice, e.g. *El* 406 *Ge nu hraðe gangað* and

Jul 652   Ge mid lufan sibbe,
            leohte geleafan,   to þam lifgendan
            stane stiðhydge   staþol fæstniað.

One can hardly explain *ge* as a vocative in examples like these last two, despite

Beo 254   Nu ge feorbuend,
            mereliðende,   minne gehyrað
            anfealdne geþoht.

For further examples see Suter, pp. 62–75, and Visser, i, §25. All those I have noted *in clauses of the type under discussion* are from the poetry; such ambiguity might have been intolerable in the prose. But see §§909–10.

§889. The subject pronoun is unexpressed in sentences where the imperative governs a reflexive pronoun, e.g. *ÆCHom* i. 126. 21 *Far ðe ham, Sat* 697 *Cer ðe on bæcling!*, *ÆCHom* i. 258. 17 *Gebiddað eow mid þisum wordum*, and *GenA* 2881 *restað incit || her on þissum wicum.* When we compare *ÆCHom* i. 126. 21 *Far ðe ham* with

ÆCHom i. 126. 11 *and ic cweðe to ðisum, Far ðu, and he færð; to oðrum, Cum ðu, and he cymð; to minum ðeowan, Do ðis, and he deð*, we see that *ðe, ðu*, and *ðis*, while differing in syntax, play the same rhythmical part in their sentences.

(d) Second person imperatives in negative clauses

§890. Here the position is the reverse of that in positive clauses: the pronoun is usually expressed, as in *ÆCHom* ii. 560. 13 *Ne hera ðu nænne man on his life, Wald i* 24 *Ne murn ðu for ði mece, BlHom* 191. 21 *Ne beoð ge nu unrote*, and *And* 1609 *Ne beoð ge to forhte*. The contrast is neatly illustrated in the Ten Commandments (*Exod* 20. 4-17 and *Deut* 5. 7-21) and in the Lord's Prayer (*Matt* 6. 9-13, *Luke* 11. 2-4, *ÆCHom* i. 258. 19-24, and *ÆCHom* ii. 596. 5-10), where the prohibitions always have the pronoun (except in *Exod* 20. 5, where the clause begins with the conj. *ne*; see §907) and the positive injunctions are always without it. Whether this was the original idiom is discussed in §913. I have noted no examples in prose or poetry of the pattern initial subject pronoun + *ne* + imperative.

§891. According to Millward (p. 24), 'the use of *þu* with second-person singular negative imperatives is obligatory'. This is too strong. She herself speaks (p. 24 fn. 3) of eight exceptions in the clauses under discussion, 'all from earlier texts and mostly from poetry', without giving references. Examples include *Solil* 49. 1 *Ne drece me*, *CP* 115. 11 *Aris, ne do sua, CP* 294. 15 *Gecier la, 7 geswic, ne folga me, Beo* 1384 *Ne sorga, snotor guma, GenA* 2914 *Abraham leofa, ne sleah þin agen bearn, Wald i* 6 *Ætlan ordwyga, ne læt ðin ellen nu gyt* || *gedreosan to dæge*, and two in

ChristA 155   ne læt þe behindan,   þonne þu heonan cyrre,
                   mænigo þus micle,   ac þu miltse on us
                   gecyð cynelice,   Crist nergende,
                   wuldres æþeling,   ne læt awyrgde ofer us
                   onwald agan.

In the three prose examples, *me, sua*, and *me*, respectively play the rhythmical role of the absent subject, while metrical considerations can be called in to account for those in the poetry. More exceptions with the singular are discussed in §889. In the plural too, examples without a subject pronoun are uncommon. I have noted none from the poetry. Those from the prose include (with a reflexive pronoun) *ÆCHom* i. 30. 18 *Ne ondredað eow*—but cf. *BlHom* 247. 20 *Mine bearn, ne ondrædaþ ge eow*—and (with no pronoun) *Exod* 22. 22 *Ne deriaþ wudewum ne steopcildum*, where the Latin *Viduae et pupillo non nocebitis* may be responsible. The same may be true of *Lev* 25. 17 *Ne swenceað eowre magas*, Latin *Nolite affligere contribules uestros*.

(e) Second person present subjunctives

§892. It is tempting to dismiss apparent examples in which the second person subjunctive expresses a wish or exhortation as scribal errors or as genuine forms showing late confusion of endings. Thus *CP* 291. 16 *Lære hie* can be compared with *CP* 291. 18 *Lær ðæt folc*, *Gen(L)* 27. 8 *hlyste minre lare* with *Gen(B)* 27. 8 *hlyst minre lare*, and *CP(H)* 105. 7 *Ne forbinden ge na ðæm ðyrstendum oxum ðone muð* with *CP(C)* 104. 8 *Ne forbinde ge . . .* , which could be taken as the equivalent of *Ne forbindaþ ge*; see §895. The question is, are there sufficient examples to establish the usage as an OE idiom?

§893. The examples with no expressed subject include two in §892 —*CP* 291. 16 and *Gen(L)* 27. 8—*Or* 242. 6 *gefera, gefera, gemyne þæt ðu ure gecwedrædenne . . . ne oferbrec*, and *BlHom* 237. 13 *Gehiere me, Andreas*. They are all singular and all in positive sentences, as far as I have observed.

× §894. Examples with the verb followed by a subject pronoun include *PPs* 136. 7 *Gemune þu, drihten, manigra bearna . . .* , *Exod* 34. 14 *Ne geeadmede þu þe to heora unrihtum godum, ApT* 28. 8 *beon ge gesunde*, and *CP(H)* 189. 23 *Ne gremigen ge eowru bearn* (*CP(C)* 188. 23 has *Ne gremige ge . . .*). Suter (p. 55), Behre (pp. 16–17 and 21), and Visser (ii, §§842–3), give more like these, though Visser has numerous errors. There are no examples in my collections of subject + subjunctive in the clauses under discussion, except *MCharm* 6. 19 *Ic hit bebicge, ge hit bebicgan*, where the two half-lines are syntactically and metrically identical, except for the mood of the verbs; see §§884 and 909.

§895. In examples like *CP* 99. 14 *Ne untreowsige ge no eow betweoxn . . . 7 eft sona cirrað to eowrum ryhthæmede, ÆCHom* i. 146. 30 *Behealde ge wif and understandað hu he hire awriten is*, and *Beo* 2529 *Gebide ge on beorge*, the verbal ending *-e* can stand for *-en* or *-aþ*; see *OEG*, §730. So, despite Visser (ii, §843), examples of this sort are ambiguous, not certain subjunctives. Even those in *-en* such as *CP(H)* 105. 7 *Ne forbinden ge . . .* (§892) and *CP(H)* 189. 23 *Ne gremigen ge . . .* (§894) could be explained as the result of wrongful addition of *n* to forms in *-e* which really stood for *-aþ*: The examples with *-e* in the singular could also be explained away as errors or the result of late confusion; see, for example, Campbell's remarks on *gemun/gemune* (*OEG*, p. 345 and fn. 1).

§896. So the evidence so far presented for 'hortative' use of the second person present subjunctive is not strong. But it is difficult to dismiss it completely and to deny that it was an OE idiom in view of the examples discussed in §§908-10.

(f) Third person present subjunctives

§897. As Visser (ii, §846) reminds us, the accomplishment of wishes expressed by the third person present subjunctive may sometimes be in the speaker's power or control and sometimes beyond it. We need not attempt to distinguish the two usages; Visser, who does, has to admit that there is 'no sharp line of demarcation' and that the classification is often 'merely arbitrary' (ibid.). Nor is the existence of the distinction an argument for recognizing the third person imperative on which Millward insists (pp. 20 and 28). Morphologically speaking, the forms are subjunctive. Common sense demands that we call them that.

§898. The subject must of course be expressed in simple sentences and principal clauses of the type being discussed, except when the verb is impersonal; then it can be absent, as in *BlHom* 9. 20 *geweorþe me æfter þinum wordum*, or present, as in *ÆCHom* i. 612. 19 *Ne gewurðe hit la* (see §§1031-5). When they are positive, the verb often occupies first position, e.g. *ÆCHom* i. 14. 24 *beo hire name Uirago*, *ÆCHom* i. 446. 32 *habbon hi hoge*, *ÆCHom* ii. 416. 6 *unbinde eow Godes engel*, and *Dream* 144 *Si me dryhten freond*. But the order SV does occur, e.g. *ÆCHom* i. 90. 30 *þæt tacn sy betwux me and eow*. *Ælc hysecild . . . sy ymbsniden*, *ÆCHom* ii. 466. 10 *God us gerihtlæce*, *Luke(WSCp)* 16. 29 *hig hlyston him*, and *Beo* 955 *Alwalda þec* || *gode forgylde*. See further Bacquet, p. 252 fn. 3.

§899. In the corresponding negative construction, the adverb *ne* is in first position immediately followed by the verb, e.g. *ÆCHom* i. 52. 33 *Ne bepæce nan man hine sylfne*, *WHom* 10a. 11 *Ne beon hi æfre manslagan ne manswican*, and *GuthA* 698 *Ne sy him banes bryce*. According to Millward (p. 28), 'the subject always follows the verb' in what she calls 'third-person negative imperatives'. This is of course true when the negative in question is the adverb which must be immediately followed by the verb. (I have so far found no examples of the type ☆*Banes bryce ne sy him*.) But there are numerous examples in which the co-ordinating conjunction *ne* has initial position and is followed by the order SV; see §§907-9.

§900. We need not speak of an unexpressed subject in examples like *ÆCHom* i. 254. 17 *Se ðe god beon wile, clypige to ðam þe æfre is god*, for we have two possible subjects for *clypige*—the dem. *se* or the adjective clause. The same possibilities exist in *ÆCHom* i. 446. 33 *þa ðe on clænan wudewanhade sind, herion hi and arwurðion*, where the acc. sg. fem. *hi* refers to the Virgin Mary. But the appropriate personal pronoun may appear in the principal clause in such patterns, e.g. *ÆCHom* i. 484. 21 *Se ðe halig is, beo he gyt swyðor gehalgod*. In *ÆHom* 5. 143 *Ælcum þe þyrst[e], cume to and drince*, *ælcum* has the case of the adjective clause; see Pope's note. But the variation in case merits comparison with that in the immediately following *ÆHom* 5. 144 *Se ðe gelyfð on me, . . . of his innoðe flowað liflices wæteres flod*.

§901. The possibility of a third person plural imperative in *-(i)aþ* arises from what Visser (ii, §846) rightly calls 'a remarkable medley of forms in *-aþ* and forms in *-ige*' in *Dan* 362-400. He classifies them all as 'modally marked'. But a comparison with the corresponding passage in *Az* 73-157 suggests rather scribal confusion; see Mitchell 1979*b*, pp. 538-9.

(4) *Imperatives and subjunctives in sentences beginning with some other element*

(a) *Those beginning with the object, an adverb (phrase), or a clause*

§902. The order VS is often preserved in sentences which begin with an object or objects, e.g. *ÆCHom* i. 546. 33 *þæs us getiðige se mildheorta Drihten* and *Beo* 1778 *þæs sig Metode þanc*, or with an adverb (phrase), e.g. *ÆCHom* ii. 52. 30 *To ðyssere eadignysse and to ðære ecan eadignysse gebringe us se Ælmihtiga God*, *BlHom* 235. 10 *Nu þonne, min bearn, ne ondrædaþ ge eow*, and *ChristA* 230 *Nu sie geworden forþ a to widan feore* || *leoht, lixende gefea*. But the order SV sometimes occurs, e.g. *Lch* iii. 60. 14 *swa þyos dæd for monnum mære gewurþe* (cf. *MCharm* 10. 5 *swa ðeos dæd wyrþe for monnum mære*), *WHom* 10c. 54 *swa hit geweorðe*, *Az* 146 *Meotud monna bearn miltsum hergen*, *GenA* 1116 *Him þæs þanc sie*, *Az* 108 *A þin dom sy*, *ChristA* 149 *Nu þu sylfa cum*, || *heofones heahcyning*, and *El* 372 *Nu ge raþe gangaþ*. The order SV seems to be preferred after *nu* in the poetry; for further examples see Suter, pp. 62-75. But note *ChristA* 230 above.

§903. The order VS is also common in principal clauses which form part of two patterns in which the imperative or the jussive subjunctive commonly occurs, i.e. conditional clause + principal clause, e.g.

LawIICn 44 *Gif deaðscyldig man scriftspæce gyrne, ne wyrne him man æfre,* and adjective clause + principal clause, e.g. *ÆCHom* i. 160. 29 *Se ðe me þenige, fylige he me.* But we also find examples with no expressed subject, e.g. *ÆLS* 12. 138 *Gif he hwæt tobrece ongean godes willan, bete þæt georne,* and with SV, e.g. *ÆCHom* i. 448. 3 *Gif hwa synful sy, he andette.* On sentences like *Luke(WSCp)* 8. 8 *Gehyre se ðe earan hæbbe,* where *se* may belong to either clause, see §2218.

(*b*) *Those introduced by the conjunctions* ond, ac, *or* ne

§904. The sentences cited in the last two sections are merely particular examples of patterns already discussed. But the conjunctions *ond, ac,* and *ne,* must be treated separately because of their still-not-understood-by-some tendency to affect the position of the verb; see §§1731 and 1845. To avoid undue repetition, I restrict myself in the sections which follow to examples from the prose. Millward (pp. 29–33) offers a collection of interesting examples, in some of which the co-ordinate clause has the same subject as the main clause, in some a different one. But her comments are better disregarded.

§905. The characteristic effect of initial *ond* can be seen by comparing the element order in the two clauses in *BlHom* 13. 6 *Lufian we hine nu 7 his noman mycclian, ÆCHom* i. 164. 26 *cume forði gehwa cristenra manna to his scrifte, and his diglan gyltas geandette, LS* 34. 202 *faran us into þam mycclan scræfe . . . and we us ðær georne to gode gebiddan, ÆCHom* ii. 124. 6 *Geopenige ure sarnys us infær soðre gecyrrednysse, and þæt wite ðe we ðrowiað tobrece ure heortan heardnysse,* and *ÆCHom* i. 560. 3 *Si ðe forgyfen miht to gebindenne . . . and þu far to ðæra Francena rice;* see also *ÆCHom* i. 606. 13–22. To these we may add (with a negative) *ÆCHom* ii. 48. 13 *and swa gefullod mann ne beo na eft oðre siðe gefullod* and *ÆCHom* i. 182. 20 *Gaderiað þa lafe, and hi ne losion.* In all the *ond* clauses, we find either the subject or the object, or both, *before* the verb. The element orders in the examples quoted may be characterized (in the order in which they appear above) as OV, OV, SOV, SVO, SV, SV, and SV. These are typical orders after *ond;* see §§1719–32. But the order VS sometimes triumphs even after *ond,* e.g. *BlHom* 225. 21 *7 gemyne þu ure þearfa, Deut* 23. 25 *7 ne rip ðu na mid sicele,* and *HomU* 32. 189. 10 *and ondrædon we us symle þæne toweardan dom.*

§906. The most common pattern with *ac* seems to be that in which there is no expressed subject, e.g. *ÆCHom* i. 92. 4 *ne ðin wif ne beo gehaten Sarai, ac beo gehaten Sarra, ÆCHom* i. 114. 18 *Ne talige nan*

man his yfelan dæda to Gode, ac talige ærest to þam deofle, and *Gen
37. 22 Ne ofslea we hyne . . . ac wurpað hyne on ðone pytt*. The absence of a subject from these examples is scarcely surprising, for the
ac clause expresses a positive exhortation after a negative one which
has a subject; see §890. But we find SV in *Ps(P)* 36. 3 *Ac þu hopa
to Drihtne*, Latin *Spera in Domino*, OVS in *Ch* 1110 *ac Godes grið
7 min habben heo* (not SVO, as the Latin *sed pacem Dei 7 meam
habeant ipsi* attests), and VS in *BlHom* 225. 20 *Ah miltsa þu hweþre
us* and *HomU* 32. 189. 9 *ac lufian we georne þæne hehstan cyning.*

§907. The contrast between the influence of the adverb *ne*, which
is always followed immediately by the verb, and the conjunction *ne*
is conveniently illustrated in the sentences which follow (I give in
square brackets the element order of the clauses introduced by the
conjunction): *ÆCHom* i. 92. 3 *Ne beo ðu geciged heononforð
Abram, ac Abraham . . . ne ðin wif ne beo gehaten Sarai* [SVC],
Gen 37. 22 *Ne ofslea we hyne, ne we hys blod ne ageoton* [SOV],
Exod 23. 2 *Ne filig ðu þam folce þe yfel wille don: ne beforan
manegon soþes ne wanda* [OV], and *Lev* 25. 4 *ne saw ðu þonne, ne
ne rip* [V], *ne ðinne wingeard ne wyrc* [OV]. In Millward's book
'strings of imperatives with but a single *ne* between the verbs are
treated as entirely separate clauses' (p. 31 fn. 3). This must not be
pressed too far. It might seem that the OE syntax would be more
justly represented if examples like *Lev* 19. 11 *Ne stel ðu, ne leoh ðu,
ne beswic ðu ðinne nextan* were printed *Ne stel ðu. Ne leoh ðu. Ne
beswic ðu ðinne nextan*. But *Exod* 22. 28 *Ne tæl ðu ne wirig ðu
þines folces ealdor* reveals the danger of this simplistic suggestion, for
the Latin has *Non detrahes, et principi populi tui non maledices*. On
this problem see further §1845.

§908. The second person subjunctive expressing a wish or exhortation also occurs after *ond, ac*, and *ne*. Most of my examples are from
the poetry. In the singular we have *GenB* 518 *nim þe þis ofæt on
hand, ‖ bit his and byrige, GenA* 2282 *ac þu sece eft, ‖ earna þe ara,*

ChristA 243
               Cum nu, sigores weard,
    meotod moncynnes,   ond þine miltse her
    arfæst ywe!,

PPs 118. 10 *ne þu huru me ‖ fram þinum bebodum feor adrife*, and
PPs 127. 6 *and þu bruce eac ‖ on Hierusalem goda gehwylces*. In
some of these, the *-e* is metrically essential. We can if we wish explain
away the remainder as examples of scribal confusion or late falling-
together; cf. §883. Indeed *byrige* in *GenB* 518 above is described as

imperative by GK and by Behre (p. 21), but as subjunctive—the word is clearly implied—by Visser (ii, §842).

§909. The examples in the plural are at first sight less tractable. They include *Exod 5. 8 7 asettaþ him þæt illce tigolgeweorc þe hi ær worhton, ne ge nan þing ne gewanion, Deut 31. 6 ne ondrædað eow ne ge ne forhtion,*

PPs 74. 5   Ne ahebbað ge to hea   eowre hygeþancas,
              ne ge wið gode æfre   gramword sprecan,

and *PPs* 99. 1 *and blisse gode bealde þeowie.* The verbs in all the clauses introduced by the conjunctions *ne* and *ond* are unambiguous subjunctives. We cannot explain these away by suggesting confusion, as we did with *Ne forbinden ge . . .* in §895. But one thing is obvious: if we replaced the subjunctives by imperative forms in *-(i)aþ*, these could easily be read as indicatives. This is clear with the first three examples and becomes clear for the fourth when we quote the verse in full:

PPs 99. 1   Nu ge mycle gefean   mihtigum drihtne
              eall þeos eorðe   elne hyre
              and blisse gode   bealde þeowie,

Latin *Iubilate Deo, omnis terra; servite Domino in laetitia.* The first clause here underlines the point, for there too a form in *-aþ* (*hyraþ*) would be taken as indicative. The reason is that all these clauses have the order SVO except the second one in *PPs* 99. 1, where the subject is not expressed. The same is true of all the examples cited by Visser (ii, §§842-3) and by Behre (pp. 16–17 and 21) which do not follow the pattern *Ne forbinden ge . . .* , whether they are introduced by *ne*, by *and*, by *nu*, e.g. *PPs* 99. 1 above, by *næfre*, e.g.

MCharm 8. 9   Sitte ge, sigewif,   sigað to eorþan!
                Næfre ge wilde   to wuda fleogan,

or even by the subject, e.g.

MCharm 6. 19   Ic hit bebicge,   ge hit bebicgan
                 þas sweartan wulle   and þysse sorge corn,

on which see §894.

§910. So we are forced to the conclusion that to avoid ambiguity the second person plural subjunctive could be used to express a wish or exhortation in clauses or sentences with the order SV. This provides some sort of foundation for the proposition that in the patterns

Gehiere me
Ne geeadmede þu

Ne þu . . . adrife[230]
Ne forbinden ge

we have to do with genuine subjunctives. But it remains a fact that imperative examples do occur (in the poetry at any rate) with the pattern *ge . . . gangaþ*; see §888.

(5) *Two dilemmas for the Anglo-Saxon*

(a) *Imperative or subjunctive?*

§911. Two reasons have already been advanced for the use of a second person subjunctive rather than an imperative—for the singular a metrical one (§908), for the plural the need to avoid ambiguity (§910). Another may be a desire to soften a blunt command or prohibition into something milder; as Visser puts it (ii, §842) 'In both cases we have to do with a wish to see an action performed by the person spoken to. It seems a fair assumption that in case (*b*) [the imperative] the wish had more the character of a command, whereas in (*c*) [the subjunctive] it was more like a mild exhortation, an advice or a suggestion. . . .' Dalbey extends this idea by including among the devices by which the Blickling homilist attempts 'to ameliorate the tone of his source' the use of first person plural subjunctives and third person singular subjunctives rather than the second person imperatives found in the sources; see *NM* 70 (1969), 641–58.

§912. If it is true that originally the imperative was found in positive clauses and the subjunctive in negative clauses (see §913), analogy must have played its part in producing subjunctives in positive clauses and imperatives in negative ones.

(b) *Pronoun subject or not?*

§913. As has been noted, the general tendency is for the 2nd pers. prons. *þu* and *ge* to be expressed in negative clauses but not in positive ones, e.g. *ÆCHom* ii. 596. 9 *And ne læd þu na us on costnunge, ac alys us fram yfele*. The possibility that this represents the original state of affairs and that examples like *ÆCHom* i. 126. 11 *Far ðu* and *Beo* 1384 *Ne sorga* are the result of analogy (see Sweet, *NEG* ii, §1806) would perhaps be strengthened if Behaghel is right when he says (*DS* ii, §677) that 'der Imperativ steht wie idg. so auch germanisch ursprünglich nur bei positiver Aufforderung; die negative Aufforderung wird durch den Konj. ausgedrückt' ['in Gmc., as in

---

[230] On the absence of the adverb *ne* in this example (*PPs* 118. 10) and in *Num* 23. 25 *Ne ðu hine wyrige, ne ðu hine bletsa*, see §1627. On initial conj. *ne*, see §1841.

IE, the imperative was originally used only for positive commands; negative commands were expressed by the subjunctive']. On this point, which cannot be pursued here, see further Suter, §§37 and 43.

§914. It is, however, clear from the preceding discussion that analogy had already produced many 'exceptions' in OE to the 'original rule', and so had opened the way for individual variations which may be conscious or unconscious on the writer's part. Various reasons for the presence or absence of a pronoun subject have been discussed by Ropers (pp. 6-8), Yamakawa (1966, pp. 9 and 11), and in particular by Suter (throughout his work). But it is not always possible to give any particular reason why a pronoun subject is absent in any particular example. Thus in *Bo* 35. 18 *Leorniað forðæm wisdom, 7 þonne ge hine geleornod hæbben, ne forhycgað hine þonne*, we may suggest the influence of *ond* (but cf. *Matt(WSCp)* 5. 42 *Syle þam ðe þe bidde, 7 þam ðe wylle æt þe borgian ne wyrn þu him*), analogy with the opening command, the writer's desire for stylistic parallel or for some special emphasis, or the presence of a pronoun object *hine* which would play the same rhythmic role as the pronoun subject *þu* in *Matt* 5. 42.

§915. Bacquet's concern to establish an 'ordre de base' and an 'ordre marqué' leads him astray here, as it does in other kinds of sentences and clauses; see my review in *NM* 67 (1966), 86-97. For him the imperative sentence with the pronoun is emphatic both when it is positive (pp. 232-4) and—in the teeth of his own statistics— when it is negative (pp. 267-9). I believe this to be wrong; in my opinion the 'remarquable symétrie' which Bacquet (p. 273) finds between positive and negative imperative sentences exists only in his own mind.

(6) *Other constructions expressing a command or wish*

§916. In first person plural clauses, we find the construction *uton* (*wuton/witon*) (+ *we*) + the uninflected infinitive 'let us . . .'. 'The word was originally a tense of the verb witan, and its verbal character is occasionally still marked by the use of the pronoun' (BT, s.v. *witon, wuton*); see further *OEG,* §§219 and 471. Examples with a negative like *Solil* 50. 14 *næse, la nese; uton ne forlætan gyet ðas boc*, representing Latin *non sinam omnino concludi hunc libellum*, are rare. The most common patterns are seen in *ÆCHom* i. 16. 12 *Uton gewyrcan mannan to ure anlicnysse, ÆCHom* i. 216. 35 *ac uton nu sprecan be ðyses dæges wurðmynte, ÆHom* 27. 8 *7 uton geswican æfre ælces yfeles, ÆCHom* i. 414. 29 *Ac uton we beon carfulle*, and *ÆCHom* i. 228. 20 *Ac uton we gelyfan þæt God fæder wæs æfre butan anginne.* Behre gives examples from the poetry (pp. 19 and 23). The passive infinitive is occasionally found, e.g. *ÆLS* 11. 68 *uton beon gehyrte.* See further Callaway 1913, chap. vi.

§916a. Meyer (p. 35) was presumably following BT—'*witon, wuton* . . . interjectional form with an infinitive, the combination being the equivalent of a subjunctive, = *let us* . . .'—when he described *uton* as an interjection. *Pace* the observation by BT already cited, I would argue that the fact that *uton* is followed by an infinitive is decisive for 'its verbal character', unless it can be demonstrated that all the forms in -*an* are first person present subjunctive either without *we* or reflexive *us* or with preceding *we*. Both of these are unlikely; see §885. The only argument I can see in favour of the view expressed by BT and Meyer is the intervention of what must be the adv. *ne* between *uton* and the infinitive, which occurs in *Solil* 50. 14 (§916) and *HomS* 24. 282 *Uton la ne toslitan þa tunecan*, Latin *Non scindamus eam*; see §1602. We cannot claim that these are mechanical glosses, although we may note that in both the *sense* (but not the *mood*) of the negated Latin verb is conveyed by the OE infinitive. There are more such examples, including *HomU* 7. 240 . . . *7 uton ne lætan* . . . but not *HomS* 45. 149 *And uton na forgytan*, where we have the more natural *na*; see §1614. The scarcity of examples with an intervening negative adverb may suggest that the use of *uton* to express prohibitions was not a natural one. The possibility of twofold analogy presents itself. First, as I show in §1602, there are occasional examples in which adv. *ne* precedes an infinitive. Second, *uton* is frequently separated from its infinitive not only by subjects, but also by other elements, including clauses, phrases, reflexive pronouns, e.g. *Num* 14. 4 *Vton us gesettan efne nu heretogan*, Latin *Constituamus nobis ducem*, and other adverbs, e.g. *ÆCHom* i. 216. 35 (§916), *ÆCHom* ii. 84. 9 *Uton forði ealle clypian* . . . , and *Beo* 3101 *Uton nu efstan.* . . .

§917. As an alternative in second person negative commands and wishes, we find the forms *nelle þu* + infinitive, e.g. *Matt(WSCp)* 1. 20 *nelle þu ondrædan Marian þine gemæccean to onfonne*, Latin *noli timere accipere Mariam coniugem tuam*; *nelle(n) ge* + infinitive, e.g. *Matt(WSCp)* 5. 17 *Nelle ge wenan þ ic come towurpan þa æ*, Latin *Nolite putare quoniam ueni soluere legem*, and *Matt(WSCp)* 6. 19 *Nellen ge goldhordian eow goldhordas on eorþan*, Latin *nolite thesaurizare uobis thesauros in terra*; and *nellað ge* + infinitive, e.g. *PPs* 61. 10 *Nellað ge gewenan welan unrihte*, Latin *Nolite sperare in iniquitatem.* In *Luke(WSCp)* 2. 10 *Nelle ge eow adrædan*, Latin *nolite timere*, we have a reflexive pronoun as well as a subject pronoun. For further examples (all from the Gospels and the Psalms), see Suter, §14, and Millward, pp. 26-7. The existence of this construction seems a clear case of Latin influence; Scheler, p. 101, agrees. Even *Bede* 424. 2 *Ne welle þu ðe ondrædan*—with the negative separate—represents Latin *Noli . . . timere*, while the similar *Ex* 266 *Ne willað eow andrædan deade feðan* could well have been influenced by the Latin *Nolite timere. . . .* The fact that the subject pronoun is expressed in all these examples suggests that Thorpe was wrong to read *nelle geortruwian* rather than *nelle ge ortruwian* in *ÆCHom* ii. 420. 28 *Mine gebroðra, nelle geortruwian, gelyfað on Crist, and beoð gefullode.* In discussing this construction, Visser (iii, §1578) irrelevantly observes that 'Ælfric denies the existence of an "imperative" *willan*' in *ÆGram* 200. 1. What is relevant is *ÆGram* 200. 10 *ðis word* [*ne + willan*] *hæfð imperativum noli, nelle ðu, nolite, nelle ge.*

§918. Other 'modal' verbs also serve to express commands or wishes. **Sculan* is found in positive and negative clauses in all persons, e.g. *ÆHom* 8. 12 *Nu sceole we gehyran þæt halige godspell, ÆHom* 6. 195 *and on þære þu scealt geþeon, ÆHom* 12. 106 *Nu ne scyle ge healdan eowre cild to plihte*, and *ÆHom* 1. 369 *7 þin broðor Aaron sceal beon þin witega. þurfan* occurs in negative clauses in all persons, e.g. *ÆHom* 5. 174 *Nu ne þurfe we astigan to sticolum muntum, ÆHom* 11. 125 *Ne ðearft ðu na hogian hu ðu sceole sweltan*, and *BlHom* 101. 13 *Ne þearf þæs nan mon wenan þæt hine oþer mon mæge from ecum witum alesan.* For a discussion and examples from the poetry of both **sculan* and *þurfan*, see Behre, pp. 19-21 and 23-5.

§919. Further on the use of *beon/wesan* in imperative constructions, see Suter (pp. 35-41), Bacquet (pp. 264-7 and 272-3), and Millward (pp. 46-7). Suter also discusses *willan* and *witan* (pp. 32-5), Millward *lætan, gewitan*, and *don* (pp. 43-6).

9. THE INFINITIVES

a. Bibliographical notes

§920. Morgan Callaway, Jr.'s *The Infinitive in Anglo-Saxon* (Washington, D.C., 1913) remains the main work; it deals with both prose and poetry, and discusses the infinitive in other Germanic languages and the origins of the OE constructions. He added further material in pp. 90-198 and 203-15 of his *Studies in the Syntax of the Lindisfarne Gospels* (Baltimore, 1918) and drew 'tentative conclusions' about which uses of the infinitive were native and which were Latinate (pp. 209-14). Other works will be cited as they become relevant.

b. Forms

§921. With the minor qualifications set out below, we can accept Callaway's statement (1913, p. 2):

> As to form, then, the Anglo-Saxon had two infinitives: (1) the uninflected, or simple, infinitive in -*an* (occasionally written -*on*, -*un*, -*en*, and in Northumbrian -*a*, with loss of *n*), which in origin is the petrified nominative-accusative case of a neuter verbal noun; and (2) the inflected, or gerundial, or prepositional, infinitive, made up of the preposition *to* plus the dative case of a verbal noun ending in -*anne* (-*enne*, occasionally -*onne*; and, with simplification of the double consonant, -*ane*, -*ene*), though occasionally the *to* is followed by an infinitive in -*an* and occasionally by an infinitive in -*ende* (by confusion with the form of the present participle), both of which forms are counted as inflected in this study. Very rarely, too, we have the -*anne* infinitive not preceded by *to*; and twice preceded by *for to*.

These need not be exemplified here. But Callaway's examples of the inflected infinitive without *to* are suspect. *Licgenne* in *ÆLS* 31. 980 *þa comon his geferan and fundon hine licgenne on blodigum limum* could be an error for *licgend(n)e* (see §101); cf. *ÆLS(J)* 10. 38 *Eft æt sumon sæle þa Petrus siþode neosigenne þa geleaffullan*, where MSS *B* and *U* have *neosigende* (Callaway 1913, p. 148 n. 5), and the examples of 'the prepositional infinitive in -*ende*' quoted by Shearin (1903, pp. 20-1), which include *Ps(A)* 69. 2 *dryhten to gefultumiende me oefesta*, Latin *domine ad adiuuandum me festina*, and *John (WSCp)* 7. 25 *hu nis ðis se ðe hi seceaþ to ofsleande*, Latin *nonne hic est quem querunt interficere*, where *WSH* has *to ofsleanne*, *Li to acuellanne*, and *Ru to acwellanne*. MS *B* inserts the *to* missing from *Law(H)WifInscr* 2 *Æfter ðam is witanne, hwam ðæt fosterlean gebyrige*. *For to* is late; no one has been able to ante-date the two examples cited by Shearin (1903, p. 18): *Ch* 1163 *And ich bidde eou alle þ ge bien hym on fultume at þys cristendome Godes yerichtten for to setten 7 to driuen* (AD 1066) and the ME *ChronE* 256. 34 (1127) *oc se kyng hit dide for to hauene sibbe of se eorl of Angeow 7 for helpe to hauene togænes his neue Willelm*. *Bede* 408. 16 must be dismissed; see Bock 1931, pp. 186-7, and Ono, 'The Infinitive with *for to* in Early Middle English', *Essays and Studies presented to Professor Fumio Nakajima on his Sixtieth Birthday* (Tokyo, 1965), 265-6. The suggestion by T. J. Farrar, *The Gerund in Old English* (Baltimore, 1902), that the inflected infinitive is sometimes introduced by 'the preposition *a*' (p. 11) is based on his misreading of examples like *BenR* 116. 11 *beon hig a behealdene mid steore* (pp. 22-3).

§922. That the Anglo-Saxons did not recognize a perfect or passive infinitive is clear from Ælfric's remarks in

ÆGram 134. 2   INFINITIVO MODO ungeendigendlicum gemete NVMERIS ET PERSONIS on getelum and on hadum TEMPORE PRAESENTI ET PRAE-TERITO INPERFECTO *amare*, lufian, PRAETERITO PERFECTO ET PLVS-QVAMPERFECTO *amasse* VEL *amauisse*, lufian. INFINITIVVS ys ungeendigend-lic, ac do ðær to getel and had and tide, þonne byð hit geendod spræc: *amare uolo*, ic wylle nu lufian; *amare uolebam*, ic wolde lufian; *sciui te aliquando amasse deum*, ic wiste, þæt ðu hwilon lufodest god. FVTVRO *amatum ire* VEL *amaturum esse*, lufian; *uis amatum ire*, wylt ðu faran lufian; *uenatum pergo*, ic fare huntian; *uis doctum ire*, wylt ðu gan leornian; *lectum pergit*, he gæð rædan; *bibitum pergo*, ic gange drincan; ET CETERA. þæt syxte gemet gæð ofer ealle þa oðre fif gemetu and nimð æfre þone þriddan had of ðam PASSIVVM: *amatur; amatur a me*, ic lufige, *amabatur a me*, ic lufode, and swa forð, ac hit nis na swiðe gewunelic on ledenspræce ne huru on englisc.

But occasional examples of what were to become the perfect and passive infinitives do occur, e.g. (perfect) *CP* 217. 19 . . . *ðæt he scolde ðone Godes alter habban uppan aholodne*, where we have an inflected participle, MS *CCCC* 162, p. 408 . . . *ne geþristlæce he þis fæsten to abrecenne be þam þe he wille him for Gode geborgen habban*, where I take *him* to be governed by *habban* in the case appropriate to *(ge)beorgan* 'by which he is willing/wishes to have himself protected', *GD(H)* 60. 17 *þaþa he wolde habban forsuwod þæt þæt na forholen beon ne mihte, Bo* 48. 14 *mid hu micelan feo woldest þu þa habban geboht þ ðu switole mihtest tocnawan þine frind 7 ðine fynd*—the same expression recurs at *Bo* 48. 16 and *Bo* 89. 27—*LS* 34. 254 *for his micclan wundrum þe eft he gedon habban wolde*, and *ChronD* 201. 26 (1067) *Se forewitola Scyppend wiste on ær hwæt he of hyre gedon habban wolde*, and (passive) *GD* 269. 15 *ac witodlice þæt gesegen beon mæg, ne þearf þæt beon gelyfed, Or* 21. 10 *7 þæt is mid Estum þeaw þæt þær sceal ælces geðeodes man beon forbærned*, and *ÆCHom* i. 56. 11 *wið þan þæt he moste sumum rican men to bearne geteald beon*. In these patterns the simple infs. *habban* and *beon* are the rule. The passive infinitive is occasionally found with *wesan*, e.g. *Lch* iii. 74. 24 *þy mæg seo wund wesan gehæled*, and with *weorþan*, e.g. *CP* 399. 17 . . . *ðonne magon hie ðeah weorðan gehælede*, where the participle is inflected. For other such examples see *Bede* 424. 28 . . . *worpene beon* and *ÆCHom* ii. 28. 13 *and ðeah hi ne magon beon ealle gegaderode*. So far, I have found no examples to contradict van der Gaaf's statement (*EStudies*, 10 (1928), 109) that 'the Old English passive infinitive is never preceded by *to*'. Callaway (1913, pp. 271-2) and Scheler (p. 101) both state that the OE passive infinitive is due to Latin influence. This may well be so of many individual instances. But it would, I think, have evolved—and indeed in some examples probably did evolve—independently.

§923. Both the simple and inflected infinitives are basically active in form and sense. It is sometimes convenient to translate them as passive when they are used after nouns (§927) and adjectives (§930), in the accusative and infinitive construction (§§3762-5), and with *beon/wesan* to express futurity or obligation (§§934-44). Both Callaway (1913, pp. 6 and 173, and 1918, p. 92) and van der Gaaf (*EStudies*, 10 (1928), 108) speak guardedly of the infinitives being 'passive in sense' or being 'used in a passive sense'. Others have been less guarded; thus QW (§131) remarks that 'a passive infinitive was usually expressed with the active form'. The argument, which is largely terminological, is pursued in the sections already referred to.

§924. The pattern inflected infinitive + *ond* + uninflected infinitive, as in *ÆCHom* ii. 372. 18 quoted in the next section, is common, though not of course obligatory, as *WHom* 18. 49, below, shows. But an inflected infinitive does not give place to an uninflected one after *ðonne* 'than' or *butan* (conj.) 'except'; thus we find *Or* 44. 13 . . . *þæt him leofre wære wið hiene to feohtanne þonne gafol to gieldanne* and *WHom* 18. 49 *Ne gebyreð æt cyrican ænig þing to donne butan God to herianne 7 hine to gebiddanne*; for further examples see Callaway (1913, p. 78)—he takes *butan* as a conjunctive adverb rather than a preposition in such sentences—and Visser, ii, §§968, 971, and 973.

c. The infinitives with nouns or pronouns

§925. Here the inflected infinitive is almost *de rigueur*; the periphrastic passive infinitive is not recorded and Callaway (1913, p. 181) notes only four simple infinitives in his total of 246 examples— And 1537 *Wæs him ut myne* ‖ *fleon fealone stream, woldon feore beorgan* (where the lack of inflexion may be due to the 'peculiar sense' of *myne* or to metrical demands); *Luke* 12. 5 (where *WSCp*'s *anweald . . . on helle asendan* represents Latin *potestatem . . . mittere in gehennam* and *Li* has *gesenda ł to gesendanne*); and two very similar sentences in which an inflected infinitive is followed by *and*

+ a simple infinitive, e.g. *ÆCHom* ii. 372. 18 *Ic bohte ænne tun, and me is neod to farenne and ðone geseon* (where—according to Callaway (1913, p. 181)—the separation of noun and infinitive may be responsible). Visser (ii, §967) adds another example of this 'non-repetition of *to* after *and*' with a noun, viz. *ÆLS* 6. 126 *and se hæfde gemynt mynster to aræerenne and mid munecum gesettan*. Similar instances occur with adjectives (§929) and verbs (§§933, 935, and 956).

§926. Typical examples of the pattern noun/pronoun + inflected infinitive include *CP* 237. 12 *Fela ic hæbbe eow to secganne*, *Bede* 230. 17 *7 him stowe geceas mynster to getimbrigenne in heawum morum uppe*, *Or* 142. 24 . . . *þonne seo leo bringð his hungregum hwelpum hwæt to etanne* (contrast *LawIICn* 84 . . . *7 oft 7 gelome smeage swyðe georne hwæt him sig to donne 7 hwæt to forganne*, where the infinitives could be described as complements 'what is for doing' rather than as directly dependent on *hwæt* 'what for doing is'), *ÆCHom* ii. 360. 22 *He geceas him timan to acennenne on menniscnysse, to ðrowigenne, to arisenne of deaðe, to astigenne up to heofenan* . . . , *ÆCHom* i. 560. 3 *Si ðe forgyfen miht to gebindenne and to alysenne*, *GD(C)* 20. 26 *7 þa forþon þe he næfde gyrde hine mid to sleanne*, and *John(WSCp)* 4. 11 *leof ne ðu næfst nan þing mid to hladene*. The position of *mid* in the last two examples can be contrasted with that of *bi* in *ChronE* 266. 12 (1140) *me lihtede candles to æten bi*, which Visser (ii, §930) cites as the earliest example of a 'preposition after the infinitive'. But note that the adverb *up* follows the infinitive in the phrase *timan . . . to astigenne up to heofenan* in *ÆCHom* ii. 360. 22 above. (This question is pursued in §§1060-80.)

§927. For further examples of this pattern, see Wülfing, ii, §§504 and 939; Callaway 1913, chapter xiii; and Visser, ii, §§926-32, where Visser notes (§926) the syntactic ambiguity of examples like *Luke(Li)* 23. 26 . . . *7 geseton him þ rod to bearanne*—'set on him that cross to bear' or 'set on him to bear that cross'? I believe that in OE the infinitive with nouns is active in form and sense, as in MnE 'He had nothing to eat and not even water to drink'; see further Callaway 1913, p. 173, and Visser, ii, §926. I hesitate to admit as exceptions even sentences like *Lev* 11. 6 *Hara* [7] *7 swyn* [8] *synd forbodene to æthrinene* (Visser, iii, §2137) and *Bede(T)* 98. 31 *ond þurh swa hwelces bene swa he gehæled sy, þisses geleafa 7 wyrcnis seo lefed God onfenge 7 allum to fylgenne* [other manuscripts have *Gode*], Latin *et per cuius preces fuerit curatus, huius fides et operatio*

Deo deuota atque omnibus sequenda credatur. Wülfing (ii. 225) saw the inflected infinitive in such sentences as almost adjectival—the same, of course, could be said of most of the examples cited above—but Callaway (1913, p. 180) remarks that 'in these examples, as usually in the predicative infinitive with *beon* (*wesan*), the infinitive is passive in sense, and translates a Latin gerundive'. I am not so sure. How significant is it that the Colgrave and Mynors translation of the Latin reads 'and let the faith and practice of him by whose prayers he is healed be considered as in accordance with God's will and proper for us all to follow'? But see further §930.

d. The infinitives with adjectives

§928. The inflected infinitive is regularly found (not necessarily immediately) after the adjective it qualifies, e.g. *Bo* 107. 32 *ðu eart gearo to ongitanne mina lara, ÆCHom* i. 128. 18 *and he wæs gearo ungelaðod to siðigenne lichamlice mid þam hundredes ealdre, Or* 32. 13 *7 ða syndon swyþe fægere 7 lustsumlice on to seonne,* and *ÆCHom* i. 184. 1 *swa þæt heo for oft bið swiðe unwynsum on to eardigenne* (on the position of the prepositional adverbs, see §1073). The only example of the inflected infinitive preceding the adjective cited by Callaway (1913, p. 150) is *Gen* 2. 9 ... *ælces cynnes treow, fæger on gesyhðe 7 to brucenne wynsum,* where the influence of the Latin is clear: *omne lignum pulchrum uisu, et ad uescendum suaue.*

§929. The uninflected infinitive is rare—only six examples out of Callaway's 247. The adjective always came first. The inf. *beon* is of course uninflected in the only example of the pattern adjective + passive infinitive so far noted in OE: *ÆCHom* ii. 316. 22 *we ðe næron wurðe beon his wealas gecigde;* see §§752 fn. 187 and 922. The only possible example of an uninflected infinitive with an adjective in the poetry seems to be

GuthB 1077   Ic eom siþes fus
       upeard niman   edleana georn
       in þam ecan gefean,   ærgewyrhtum
       geseon sigora frean,   min þæt swæse bearn;

on this see Callaway 1913, p. 149. The best recorded example from the prose in which an uninflected infinitive depends directly on an adjective is *Bede* 56. 20 *forðon he gearo wære in þam ylcan gewinne mid him beon,* which probably represents Latin . . . *quia laborare scilicet uolo.* Visser (ii, §938) adds more. But all depend on Latin originals, e.g. *Coll* 74 *Hu wære þu dyrstig ofstikian bar?,* Latin *Quomodo*

fuisti ausus iugulare aprum? In the remainder, an inflected infinitive
and the conjunction *and* intervene, as in *ÆCHom* ii. 130. 3 *and for
ðære soðfæstnysse ðe hi bodedon gearowe wæron ehtnysse to
ðoligenne, and deaðe sweltan.* According to Callaway (1913, p. 158)
'the lack of inflection in both poetry and prose appears to be due
chiefly to the remoteness of the infinitive from the adjective that it
modifies'.

§930. Further examples of this combination will be found in
Wülfing, ii, §826 (cf. ii, §938); Callaway 1913, chapter xi; and Visser, ii, §§938-45, and iii, §1921. Visser distinguishes examples such
as *Bo* 107. 32 (my §928), in which the subject of the sentence is the
same as that of the infinitive, from those in which the action of the
infinitive is to be performed by someone else, e.g. *Or* 32. 13 (my
§928)—where the performer is not named—and *BlHom* 225. 25
. . . *gif ic nugit sie þinum folce nedþearflic her on worlde to hæbbenne* . . . and *BlHom* 59. 14 *7 he þonne se deada byð uneaþe ælcon
men on neaweste to hæbbenne*—where the performer appears in
the dative before and after the adjective respectively. It seems to me
that the infinitive is active in both form and sense when used with
adjectives. The doubtful cases were discussed and (I think) rightly
dismissed by Callaway (1913, pp. 149-50). Van der Gaaf (*EStudies*,
10 (1928), 129-31) 'cannot endorse Callaway's views unreservedly'
and cites twelve examples in which he 'consider[s] the infinitives to
have a passive meaning'. In the MnE equivalents, an active construction is at least as natural as a passive one and in some the latter
would be impossible, e.g. *ÆCHom* ii. 542. 27 *Ælc ehtnys bið earfoðe
to þolienne* and *Alex* 12. 13 *þa ic þ wæter bergde ða wæs hit biterre
7 grimre to drincanne þonne ic æfre ænig oðer bergde.* See further
Bock 1931, pp. 201-4.

§931. In *ÆCHom* ii. 386. 3 *Ðis fers is swiðe deoplic eow to understandenne, ðis fers* can be the nominative subject of *is* or the accusative object of the inflected infinitive which would then be the subject
of *is*. The latter is not possible in *ÆCHom* ii. 542. 27 (§930), for
ælc ehtnys is nominative. See further §937.

e. The infinitives with verbs

(1) Agan

§932. Callaway (1918, pp. 118-19) cites five examples from *Li* in
which, he says, *agan* means 'owe, ought'. In three of them—*Matt(Li)*
18. 24, *Matt(Li)* 18. 28, and *Luke(Li)* 7. 41 *an ahte to geldanne*

penningas fif hund, Latin *unus debebat denarios quingentos*—the phrase *ahte to geldanne/geldanna* glosses Latin *debebat*. In the other two—*Matt(Li)* 18. 28 again and *Luke(Li)* 16. 5 *huu micel aht ðu to geldanne hlaferde minum*, Latin *quantum debes domino meo*—*ðu aht/aht ðu to geldanne* glosses Latin *debes*. I do not believe that *agan* means either 'owe' or 'ought' in these examples, despite Visser (i, §567, and iii, §§1711-13). The whole combination *agan to geldanne* is the equivalent of Latin *debere* 'to owe' and the sense of *agan* is 'to have, to possess', the idea of obligation being contained in the inflected infinitive, as it is in *ÆLS* 4. 176 *Se god is to gelyfanne* . . . and *ÆLS* 17. 181 *Us is to secenne* . . . *þa bote æt Gode*. . . . We should compare MnE 'I have my house to let' rather than 'I have to let my house'. As Visser (iii, §1401) remarks cryptically after quoting two of these examples '(Different in meaning from Modern English *ought to*)'.

§933. Elsewhere (1913, pp. 80-1) Callaway gives twenty-eight more examples of '*agan (nagan), owe (not), ought (not)*'. In the four which do not belong to the late tenth or to the eleventh century, *agan* in my opinion again has the sense of possession; *LawAf* 2 *age he þreora nihta fierst him to gebeorganne* is typical. But some of the others suggest that *OED* is in error in noting no examples before *c.*1175 of *agan* + infinitive meaning 'to have it as a duty or obligation', e.g. *HomU* 46. 291. 26 *Leofan men, us bisceopum and eallum mæsse-preostum is swiðe deope beboden, þæt we æfre sculon mynegian and tyhtan eow* . . . *hu ge agan her on life rihtlice to libbanne* and *ChronA* 204. 9 (1070) *Ða ða Landfranc crafede fæstnunge his gehersumnesse mid aðswerunge. þa forsoc he 7 sæde þ he hit nahte to donne*. So Ono may have some justification for his claim that 'it was towards the end of the eleventh century that the meanings "to have to pay" and "to have as a duty (*to do*)" became prevalent. In the earlier period these meanings were usually expressed by *sculan*' (*Hitotsu-bashi Journal of Arts and Sciences*, 1 (1960), 48). I have developed my argument at greater length in *NM* 70 (1969), 369-80, where I attempt to show that the reading *Hwæðre þu me aht singan* for the angel's reply to Cædmon in Sweet's *Reader* (1967 edn., p. 46, line 33) is unjustified. The fact that *agan* is recorded only with the inflected, and not with the simple or passive, infinitive—except for the not uncommon variation after *ond* in *HomU* 46. 294. 24 *ac man ah cyrican and haligdom to secanne and þær hine georne inne to gebiddanne and mid eadmodnysse hlystan*—constitutes an additional argument against this reading.

(2) Beon/wesan

(*a*) *Expressing necessity or obligation*

§934. We can perhaps start by quoting

ÆGram 134. 19   QVINQVE PARTICIPALIA VERBA VENIVNT A VERBO
ACTIVO fif dælnymendlice word cumað of ðam dædlicum worde: *amandi*, to
lufigenne, *amando*, lufigende, *amandum*, to lufigenne, *amatum* we sædon ær,
amatu, mid lufe. we secgað þas word gewislicor: *tempus est arandi*, hit ys tima to
erigenne, *arando proficio*, erigende ic geðeo, *legendo doceo*, rædende ic tæce,
arandum est mihi me ys to erigenne, *legendum est nobis*, us ys to rædenne, *habes
agros ad arandum* hæfst ðu æceras to erigenne, *commoda mihi librum ad legendum*, læne me ða boc to rædenne. *amatum* we sædon ær.

The fact that the Latin gerund is here represented by the inflected
infinitive is not surprising in view of the fact that in Latin 'the other
cases of the Infinitive are supplied by the Gerund' (*GL*, §425). But
the equivalence is not necessarily exact—the inflected infinitive may
rather be the best they could do *faute de mieux*—and by comparing
the examples which follow we can see the dangers of the frequent
assumption that, if the Latin has a passive, the OE infinitive which
represents it must also be passive: *Bede* 208. 31 *bi ðon her æfter in
heora tiid is to secgenne*, Latin *de quibus in sequentibus suo tempore
dicendum est*, but *Bede* 334. 30 *Bi þæm midlestan is nu to secgenne*,
Latin *De medio nunc dicamus*, and *Bede* 68. 6 *þonne is hit of lufan
to donne*, Latin *ex caritate agendum est*, but *Bede* 128. 12 *7 ne wiste
. . . hwæt him selest to donne wære*, Latin *quid ageret . . . nescius*.
The different constructions in *CP* 201. 15 *Ðam hlafordum is eac to
cyðanne ðætte . . .* , Latin *domini quoque admonendi sunt quia . . .* ,
and *CP* 301. 14 *Ðæm eaðmodum is to cyðanne ðætte . . .* , Latin
Dicatur ergo humilibus quia . . . , are also worth noting. Callaway
sometimes leans too heavily on the Latin; see especially Callaway
1918, pp. 92–3.

§935. The infinitive with *to* is the rule with *beon/wesan*. The only
exceptions are the now-familiar ones after *ond*, e.g. *ÆCHom* i. 400.
30 *Is nu forði munuchades mannum mid micelre gecnyrdnysse to
forbugenne ðas yfelan gebysnunga, and geefenlæcan þam apostolum
. . .* ; cf. *Bede* 78. 23 *Ond hwæt elles is to secenne wið þæm hungre
nemne ondlifen, wið þurst drync, wið hæto celnis, wið cyle hrægl,
wið werignesse reste, wið untrymnesse lacedom secan*, where a series
of phrases in asyndetic parataxis separates the two infinitives, the
first with *to*, the second without it.

§936. Those on whom the obligation or necessity falls may be specified by a noun or pronoun in the dative, e.g. *CP* 215. 6 *Ðæm unge-*

ðyldegum is to secganne ðæt . . . and ÆCHom i. 110. 6 Us is eac to witenne þæt . . . , or may be implied, e.g. Bede 334. 30 Bi þæm midlestan is nu to secgenne . . . , Latin De medio nunc dicamus . . . , and ÆGram 153. 15 Sciendum est . . . is to witenne. The verb involved may be intransitive—this is rare—e.g. WHom 8b. 37 þonne is æfter eallum þisum mid rihtum geleafan to efstanne wið þæs fontbæðes georne (where the prepositional phrase could in a sense be seen as an object; see §937, E. (3))—transitive with object unexpressed, e.g. ÆGram 135. 5 arandum est mihi me ys to erigenne, or transitive with what may be the object of the infinitive expressed, e.g. ÆCHom i. 254. 3 Us is to smeagenne þæt word þe he cwæð and ÆCHom i. 308. 19 Us is to smeagenne hu seo clænnys wæs ðeonde geond þa geferedan ðenas. . . . There are also examples in which a pronoun appears as the grammatical subject of beon/wesan, e.g. Bede 372. 27 Is ðæt to gelyfenne þætte . . . , GD(C) 146. 2 hwæþer hit to gelyfenne sy þæt . . . , and ÆCHom i. 314. 33 La leof, hwæt is us to donne? For further examples see Callaway 1913, pp. 97–104, and 1918, 123–6; Wahlén, pp. 123–4; Jost 1909, §§116–20, and 1950, p. 167; van der Gaaf, EStudies, 10 (1928), 107–8, and 13 (1931), 180; and Visser, i, §§367–9, and iii, §§1373–4 and 1384. As will become apparent, I do not always accept their classification of examples.

§937. The italicized phrase 'what may be the object' was used advisedly, for reasons which will become apparent. So too is the blanket-term 'subject/object' in the classified list of patterns which follows.

A. Singular subject before is + infinitive, e.g. (1) Bede 70. 10 forþon seo æftere cneoris . . . alle gemete is to forbeorenne 7 to forlætenne and (2) ÆLS 4. 176 Se god is to gelyfanne þe ða cristenan on gelyfað.

B. Singular subject/object before infinitive, e.g. (1) Bede 224. 22 ond þæs seðel wære ece to gelyfenne in heofonum, Latin cuius sedes aeterna . . . in caelis esset credenda [setl, according to BT, is neut., masc.(?)], (2) GD(C) 146. 2 hwæþer hit to gelyfenne sy þæt . . . , (3) Bede 372. 27 Is ðæt to gelyfenne, þætte . . . , and (4) ÆCHom i. 314. 33 hwæt is us to donne?

C. Singular subject/object after infinitive, e.g. (1) Bede 228. 23 Ac to gelyfanne is þæt swylc deað þæs æfestan monnes . . . swylce synne adilgode and (2) LS 23. 108 and fram þysum weorcum is to gelyfanne þæt God Zosimus on þæt mynster gelædde.

D. Singular accusative object after infinitive, e.g. (1) GD 340. 28 forþan him is to warnianne þone rihtan dom þam þe ær ne beoþ his *synna forlætene* and (2) *ÆCHom* ii. 494. 33 *Us is to biddenne Drihtnes mildheortnysse.*

E. Singular or plural genitive, dative, or prepositional, object, e.g. (1) *Bo* 90. 12 *Gif hi on ecnesse næren, þonne nære hiora swa swiðe to girnanne*, (2) *Conf 3. 1 7. 2 Nis þam bisceope ne þam sacerde þam men to forwyrnenne scriftes*, and (3) *HomU* 27. 147. 9 *mycelum ys to warnigenne us eallum wið swylce eardungstowe.*

F. Plural subject before *syndon* + infinitive, e.g. (1) *Bede* 70. 26 *ac heo seondon to monienne . . . þæt heo ahebban heo from swylcum unrihtum*, (2) the second clause in *Bede* 66. 24 *Forðon ne seondon to lufienne þa wiisan fore stowum, ac fore godum wisum stowe seondon to lufienne*, (3) *GD(C)* 67. 30 *7 þa weorc us syndon swyðor to wundrianne þa þe us se ealda preost cyþde*, and (4) *ÆLS* 15. 222 *an þas feower ana syndon to underfonne.*

G. Plural subject/object after infinitive, e.g. (1) *CP* 13. 20 *Ðætte on oðre wisan sint to manianne weras, on oðre wiif*, (2) the first clause in example F(2), and (3) *ÆLS* 24. 21 *þysum is to gearcigenne þa reþestan wita.*

§938. All these examples A–G are from Callaway 1913, pp. 97–104, taken indifferently from his group 1 'The Infinitive Passive in Sense' and his group 2 'The Infinitive Active in Sense'. I will not waste time saying which he thought was which, but will try to discuss *de novo* the question of the voice of these infinitives. Disregarding comparison with the Latin original, which (as I have shown in §934) cannot be decisive, four possible criteria present themselves—the case of the subject/object, its position relative to the infinitive, the number of the verb *beon/wesan*, and the presence or absence of a dative expressing the person obliged or compelled.

§939. It seems certain that the infinitive is active in the examples in group D, where *dom* and *mildheortnysse* are accusative and so must be its objects. It is probably also active in group E, where it would (I think) be stretching it to describe the infinitive as an 'impersonal passive' of the type described in §§848–9. The fact that in group A *seo æftere cneoris* and *se god* are nominative tells us that they are the subjects of *is*, but does not prove anything about the voice of the infinitive. We tend to translate those in A(1) as active and that in A(2) as passive, but A(2) could be translated 'That god whom the Christians believe, is (for us) to believe'. In all the other groups, the case form alone is ambiguous.

§940. So we turn to element order. If we take example A(2) as passive 'to be believed' and compare it with D(1) and D(2), we might think element order a possible guide. But a comparison of A(1) with A(2), of the two clauses in F(2), and of G(1) and G(3), denies this. So too do the following pair quoted after Callaway 1913, p. 102: '*Pr. Gu.* v. 58 [= AF 27]: ac on seofon nihta fyrstes fæste ne *bið to clænsienne* ðone man (Vercelli MS: ac on seofon nihta fyrsten fæsten *bið to clænsigeanne* se man) = sed septenarum dierum valida castigatio jejunium est', and a comparison of the examples in B and C. The order of the elements can tell us nothing about the voice of the infinitive.

§941. Similarly the number of the verb and the presence or absence of a dative prove broken reeds. At first glance the singular *is* seems to tells us that *to gearcigenne* is active with an accusative object following it in G(3). Conversely, the plural elements which precede *seondon/syndon* in F(1)-(4) seem to be subjects of the verb, not objects of the infinitive. The same may be true of *weras* and *þa wiisan* in G(1) and G(2). But the change of number in *CP* 187. 15 *Ðæm oferbliðum is to cyðanne ða unrotnessa ðe ðæræfter cumað, 7 ðam unbliðum sint to cyðanne ða gefean ðe him gehatene sindon* makes me hesitate and wonder whether these variations in the number of the verb may merely reflect the fluctuating influence of the singular infinitive and the plural noun or pronoun; cf. *ÆCHom* i. 530. 22 *þa inran þeostru sind þære heortan blindnys. þa yttran þeostru is seo swearte niht þære ecan geniðerunge.* However, even if we accept the apparently obvious deductions about the case and function of the plural nouns or pronouns in F(1)-(4) and G(1)-(3), we cannot deduce anything about the voice of the infinitive and are not bound to agree with Callaway (1913, p. 102) that in *CP* 187. 15 above 'the second *to cyðanne* is probably passive in sense'. One would like to know to whom. If the change of number in the verb is significant, the implication to an Anglo-Saxon reader or hearer may well have been 'To the overcheerful, it is [for you *or* those in authority] to make known the sadness which follows, and to the sad the joys which are promised them are [for you *or* those in authority] to make known.' For while the presence of *us* in F(3) suggests that the literal translation may be 'Those works are for us to wonder at . . . ',[231] the fact that *us* is absent from the corresponding passage in *GD(H)* 67. 29 *þonne þa weorc syndon swyðor to wundrianne, þe her se ealda preost sæde* means, not that the immediate audience are not to wonder, but merely that the reviser is widening his audience; we understand this from the context. So the absence of a dative of the person obliged or

---

[231] Similarly, example B(4) means 'What is [there] for us to do?', not—as van der Gaaf has it in *E Studies*, 10 (1928), 112—'What is [there] for us to be done?'

compelled does not prove that the infinitive is passive any more than the fact that it represents a Latin passive.

§942. So all we can prove from our four criteria is the unremarkable fact that in some of the examples discussed the infinitive must be active. We have not been able to prove that it must be passive in even one example. There is no doubt that it often represents a Latin passive and can frequently be translated into MnE as such. But in all the examples in which it can be taken as passive, it can equally well be taken as active. Is it likely that the OE inflected infinitive could have had two such different (one might say contradictory) functions? Can we really believe with Callaway (quoted in §941) that the same form could be both active and passive in the same sentence? Can we agree with van der Gaaf (*EStudies*, 13 (1931), 117) that 'the circumstance that late Old English had two constructions, *ðas ðing sint to donne*, and *ðas ðing sint to cumenne*, identical in form, but different in meaning, did not lead to misunderstanding, as in the older one the subject was passive, while in the later one it was active'? Or do we rather feel with the same writer (*EStudies*, 10 (1928), 108) that 'it is peculiar that the inflected infinitive, which otherwise is generally, if not always, active in meaning, should have come to be used in a passive sense in Old English, Old High German, and Old Scandinavian, in spite of the fact that these languages had a genuine passive infinitive as well'? It certainly seems peculiar to me. In my opinion, it is more likely that in *ðas ðing sint to donne* the infinitive was active and that when the dative of the person involved was not expressed it was for the very same reason that the accusative in the accusative and (active) infinitive construction (see §3757) was not expressed—because it was clear or immaterial who was to perform the task ordered or advised. We may compare *BlHom* 15. 28 *Hwæt we nu gehyrdon þis halige godspel beforan us rædan* (whether the reader was an anonymous monk or a familiar priest, he was sitting there for everyone to see) with *BlHom* 19. 31 *Eac is to geþencenne hwæt Drihten spræc* (which Morris translates 'We must also think of what our Lord spake'). If there was a time when speakers of English could conceive of the infinitive with *to* as active or passive, why did the periphrastic passive infinitive ever develop? And would not the fact that this last infinitive is only embryonic in OE account for the use of the inflected infinitive with *to* to translate both active and passive Latin constructions?

§943. In the event, then, I find myself less in sympathy with Callaway, and his (it seems to me) arbitrary divisions into active and passive, than with Bock, who speaks (1931, p. 201) of 'die

Wahrscheinlichkeit, daß in solchen Fällen das Englische den Infinitiv auf ein unbestimmtes Subjekt bezog und dadurch den Infinitiv activ auffaßte' ['the probability that in such cases English related the infinitive to an unspecified subject, and thus regarded the infinitive as active'], and with Visser, who remarks (i. 352) that 'modern grammarians, however, are apt to call the construction [*þæt þing is to donne, þa þing synt to donne*] passive, apparently on the ground that in later English "it is to be done" was almost universally substituted for "it is to do", analyzing, in so doing, a variant instead of the actual construction'. So the question is ultimately terminological. The hopeless ambiguity of the recurrent sentence 'Here the infinitive is passive in sense' demonstrates this. If it means that the Anglo-Saxons thought of the inflected infinitive as both active and passive, I disagree. If it means that it can sometimes be translated as active, sometimes as passive, I must agree. See further §3764.

§944. On the evidence provided by Callaway and from my own observation, it seems that the inflected infinitive with *beon/wesan* expressing necessity or obligation is rare in the poetry—Callaway (1913, p. 98) notes only ten examples against some 900 in the prose —and is more common in translated texts or texts based on Latin than in original texts. This leads Callaway to suggest that it is of Latin origin (1913, pp. 200-2 and 239-40). Scheler (p. 101) qualifies Callaway's views and Visser (i, §367) dissents: 'It seems more plausible to assume descent from Indo-European for both the English and Latin construction.' I do not propose to enter this arena.

(b) Expressing futurity

§945. The inflected infinitive of transitive and intransitive verbs is also used with *beon/wesan* to express futurity—according to Visser (iii, §1379), 'a special kind of futurity: a connotation, perhaps first of predestination or fore-ordaining, later of destiny was inherent in it, though growing weaker and weaker'. When so used, the infinitive is active in form and sense. There are occasional examples in the early prose, e.g. *Bede* 224. 24 *þætte ealle þa ðe his willan leornode 7 worhte, from þæm þe hy gescepene wæron, þæt heo þonne wæren from him ece mede to onfonne*, Latin *quia omnes, qui uoluntatem eius a quo creati sunt discerent et facerent, aeterna ab illo praemia essent percepturi*. But it is most common in the translation of the Old Testament and the Gospels, e.g. *Exod* 4. 13 *Ic bidde þe, Drihten, send þone þe ðu to sendene eart*, Latin *At ille: obsecro, inquit, Domine, mitte quem missurus es*, and *Matt(WSCp)* 11. 3 *7 cwæð eart þu þe to cumenne eart*, Latin *ait illi tu es qui uenturus es*. As far as I have observed, *beon/wesan* is never used impersonally in this idiom. Visser (ii, §758) is wrong to take here *Bede* 298. 11 *7 to Rome ferde 7 þær his lif geendade, swa swa heræfter is swutolecor to secgenne*, Latin *ac Roman abiens ibi uitam finiuit, ut in sequentibus latius dicendum est*; this expresses obligation rather than mere futurity, as he himself *in sequentibus* (iii, §1384) admits. For further examples, see Callaway 1913, pp. 104–5, and Visser, iii, §1379.

§946. Callaway (1913, p. 203) concludes that the usage 'is due to Latin influence'. Van der Gaaf (*EStudies*, 13 (1931), 176) concurs. But Visser (iii, §1379) refuses to accept this explanation or the alternative one that the infinitive originally expressed purpose. To him

it seems somewhat more probable to assume that the idiom arose from a tendency to replace the form in *-ende* by a form in *-enne* in the group 'is tocumende', which occurs as a translation of *venturus est* in e.g. Lindisf. Gosp., Mt. 11, 3, 'arð ðu seðe tocymende is' and Mt. 3, 11, 'ðe ðe soðlice æfter mec to cumende . . . is', and which form was probably already in use in early Old English. Similarly perhaps with such combinations as *to-gefyllende wæs* in O. E. Gosp., Luke 9, 31, 'his gewitendnesse þe he to-gefyllende wæs on hierusalem'.

On the interchange of the endings *-ende* and *-enne*, see Visser, ii, §§1018 ff., and my §921.

§947. Alongside this we have the use of **sculan/willan* + a simple infinitive as a translation of the Latin periphrastic future, e.g. *ÆGram* 246. 11 *lecturus sum cras, ic sceal rædan to merigen*, and *ÆGram* 152. 10 *docturus sum cras pueros, ic wylle tæcan to merigen þam cildum*. See further §§1023–4.

§948. Both Callaway (1913, p. 105) and Visser (iii, §1379) record the occasional use of *beon/wesan* + *toweard* + an inflected infinitive to express futurity, e.g. *Bede* 268. 34 *hwonne he, heofonum 7 eorðan byrnendum, toweard sy in heofones wolcnum in micelre meahte 7 þrymme to demanne cwice 7 deade*, Latin *quando ipse caelis ac terris ardentibus uenturus est in nubibus, in potestate magna et maiestate, ad iudicandos uiuos et mortuos*.

(c) *Expressing purpose?*

§949. Callaway (1913, pp. 105–6) erects this category for a few examples of *beon/wesan* with the inflected infinitive. Analysis of them suggests to me that it is unnecessary to do so; they can all be otherwise explained. See §2940.

(3) Habban

§950. *Habban* is found only with the inflected infinitive (Callaway 1913, p. 43). As with *agan*, the main problem is semantic: does *habban* + inflected infinitive mean 'to be under obligation, to be obliged; to be necessitated *to do something* . . . a kind of Future of obligation or duty' (*OED*, s.v. *have* B. I. 7. c)? *OED* does not recognize this usage in OE. For the editors, examples like *BlHom* 91. 13 *Uton we forþon geþencean hwylc handlean we him forþ to berenne habban* show *habban* in the sense 'to possess as a duty or thing to be done. With object and dative infinitive expressing what is to be done by the subject' (*OED*, s.v. *have* B. I. 7). This, they say, 'is in origin a particular case of 2b'—which they exemplify by *Matt(WSCp)* 3. 9 *We habbað Abraham us to fæder.* I see no reason for departing from this, despite van der Gaaf and Visser.

§951. The former, writing in *EStudies*, 13 (1931), 180–8, distinguishes three stages in OE: first, that already noted in which the infinitive was an adjunct to the object of *habban*, e.g. *Or* 116. 14 *þa ofþuhte him þæt he þæt feoh to sellanne næfde his here swa hie bewuna wæron*; second, that in which *habban* denoted both possession and some kind of duty, e.g. *Or* 94. 16 *nu ic longe spell hæbbe to secgenne*; and, third, the stage which, he says, was reached in late OE in which *habban* + inflected infinitive is synonymous with *agan* + inflected infinitive and expresses the idea of duty. His first example is *BlHom* 91. 13 (§950). The other two—*Exod* 16. 23 and *Matt(WSCp)* 20. 22 *mage gyt drincan þone calic ðe ic to drincenne hæbbe*, Latin *potestis bibere calicem quem ego bibiturus sum*— seem to me on all fours with the first and with the five examples of *agan* + inflected infinitive from *Li* discussed in §932. I cannot accept van der Gaaf's judgement on the examples in his last two groups or his assertion that *habban* in *ÆCHom* ii. 78. 12 *Gif ge noldon Gode lybban on cildhade, ne on geogoðe, gecyrrað nu huruðinga on ylde to lifes wege, nu ge habbað hwonlice to swincenne* 'undoubtedly denotes duty, obligation', for here the implication is not 'you ought to work for a short time' but 'you have a short time [to live and] to work'; if *hwonlice* is not grammatically the object of *habban*, it is logically, despite Visser, iii, §1408. In iii, §1400, Visser quotes three sentences which allegedly belong to van der Gaaf's second group. In my opinion, however, all three—including the ubiquitous *BlHom* 91. 13—are examples of the first stage. The same is true of his two examples 'in which *have* expresses nothing but obligation, duty, compulsion or necessity' (iii, §1403)—viz. *Luke(WSCp)* 14. 28 (where, as I read it, the object of *hæbbe* is to be understood from the previous clause) and the oft-quoted *Luke(Li)* 7. 40 *ic hafo ðe huothuoego to cuoeðanne*, Latin *habeo tibi aliquid dicere*—and of all the OE examples he cites in iii, §§1402-10, for (as he rightly says in §1402) 'the fact that the object is not placed between *to have* and the infinitive cannot always be viewed as an indication . . . that *have* expresses nothing but obligation, compulsion or necessity'. Bock too (1931, pp. 164-5) makes this point in his criticism of Callaway's handling of the construction (1913, p. 43, and *passim*).

§952. BTS is similarly confused. It puts the veteran examples *Luke* 7. 40 and *BlHom* 91. 13 s.v. *habban* 'VII. with object and dat. infin. expressing what is to be done by the subject, *to have* as a duty or thing to be done'. But *Matt* 20. 22 appears under 'VIII. with dat. infin., *to have, be obliged* to do something'. The other two examples it gives under VIII are equally unconvincing. In *LawIne* 60 the idea of possession or of ability (to pay) is paramount—*hæbbe* appears as *habeat* in the *Quadripartitus*—and in *Bo* 52. 26 *Nære hit no þ hehste god gif him ænig butan wære, forþæm hit þonne hæfde to wilnianne sumes goodes þe hit self næfde*—a superficially convincing example—the subj. *hæfde* represents *posset* of the Latin . . . *quoniam relinqueretur extrinsecus quod posset optari.*

§953. In the event, then, I would extend to all the OE examples of *habban* + inflected infinitive the observation made by Bock (1931, p. 165) about those he discussed: 'In allen Beispielen ist in gleicher Weise der *to*-Infinitiv abhängig von dem Akkusativobjekt' ['In all the examples the *to* infinitive is dependent in the same way on the direct object']. Since the only two instances known to me in which *habban* seems not to have a direct object are *ÆCHom* ii. 78. 12 and *Luke(WSCp)* 14. 28—both discussed in §951—I feel justified in agreeing with *OED* and Bock. As always, *we* can see the writing on the wall. I do not think that it was visible to the Anglo-Saxons in this particular instance.

(4) *Other verbs*

§954. As in MnE, many verbs can be accompanied by an infinitive, e.g. *ÆCHom* ii. 146. 4 *and þæt flod hi awearp ðær ðær he sylf smeade þæt hus to aræenne* ('the objective infinitive', according to Callaway (1913, p. 39)); *ÆCHom* i. 52. 23 *Uton lufian ure gebroðra* (Callaway's 'predicative infinitive' (1913, p. 95)); and *ÆCHom* ii. 130. 16 *Ongunnon ða dæghwomlice forwel menige efstan to gehyrenne ða halgan bodunge* (which Callaway (1913, p. 137) describes as a 'final infinitive'). The line of demarcation is often a tenuous one; see

Bock (1931, *passim*, especially pp. 124 ff., 157-60, and 164-5) and §§1552-4.

§955. Some verbs, such as *hatan* 'to command', *lætan* 'to allow, cause', and *wuton* 'let us . . .', have not been recorded with the inflected infinitive; see Callaway 1913, pp. 31 and 93. Others, such as *læran* and *tæcan* 'to teach' and *giernan* 'to yearn for', have not been found with the uninflected infinitive; see Callaway 1913, p. 37.[232] But many are used with both, e.g. *wilnian* in *ÆCHom* i. 432. 25 *We wilniað mid urum hlaforde clænlice sweltan, swiðor ðonne unclænlice mid eow lybban* and *Alex* 15. 5 *ða wilnade ic þara monna onsyne to geseonne*; *onginnan* in *ÆCHom* i. 50. 5 *and se ðe wæs leorningcniht on hade, ongann wesan lareow on martyrdome* and *ÆCHom* i. 314. 9 *and hi . . . ongunnon to sprecenne mid mislicum gereordum*; *þencan* (see van der Gaaf in *EStudien*, 34 (1904), 52-3); and *gan*, e.g. *ÆCHom* ii. 242. 35 *He eode eft sittan siððan mid his ðegnum* and *ÆCHom* ii. 428. 17 *He eode into Godes temple hine to gebiddenne*. It would be possible to list here all the OE verbs which are used with simple and/or inflected infinitives and to attempt to state their preference, if any. Space must be my excuse for not doing so. The material will be found in Callaway 1913, where the author sets out his examples under the following headings: the objective infinitive with verbs of commanding, of causing and permitting, of sense perception, of mental perception, of beginning, delaying, and ceasing (on these, see Bock 1931, pp. 170-2), of inclination and will, and with other verbs (chapter ii); the predicative infinitive with auxiliary verbs, including the 'modal' verbs (see my §§996-9) and *agan*, **durran*, and *þurfan* (chapter iv), with verbs of motion and rest (chapter v), and with *(w)uton* (chapter vi); and the final infinitive (chapter x). Visser (iii, §§1174-371) offers a valuable collection of examples from all periods of English and Jost (1950, pp. 166-8) has something to say about inflected infinitives in Wulfstan.

§956. It is not unusual to find that, when two infinitives are joined by *and*, the first is inflected but the second is not, e.g. *Bede* 250. 18 *þa sende he Gearaman þone biscop . . . to gereccenne þone gedwolan 7 heo to soðfæstnesse geleafan eft gecegan*, *Or* 282. 9 *7 þohte his sunu* [*to*] *beswicanne 7 him siþþan fon to þæm onwalde*, *ÆCHom* ii. 488. 34 *Ða ongunnon ealle ða næddran to ceowenne heora flæsc and heora blod sucan*, and *ÆCHom* ii. 588. 11 *swa eac nu of eallum*

---

[232] Visser (iii, §1231) notes *Matt(Li)* Contents, p. 17, line 4, of Skeat's edition, *gesueriga laeres*, Latin *iurare docet*. But such a direct gloss does not constitute an exception.

þeodum gewilniað men to geseonne . . . Crist . . . , and ðone god-spellican wisdom gehyran. Schrader (p. 70) and Visser (ii, §967) offer further examples.

(5) *Combinations of active and passive verb-forms and infinitives*

§957. The active infinitive with an active verb-form is, of course, a commonplace which need not be exemplified here. There are occasional examples of the active infinitive with a passive verb-form, e.g. *Bede* 68. 13 *7 heora weoruldgod, þa heo agan, him healdað þa ðe heo geare gesegene beoð eahtan 7 witnian,* Latin . . . *insequi uidentur,* and *Bede* 68. 19 *þætte Godes cirice mid æteacnesse onfo, þæt heo gesegen bið of eorðlicum þingum anforlæten,* Latin . . . *uideatur amittere.* Scheler (p. 101) describes these as examples of the nominative with the infinitive.

§958. The passive infinitive is found with both active verb-forms, e.g. *GD* 204. 4 *þonne hi gewilniað fullfremede beon,* Latin *dum appetunt perfecti esse,* and *ÆCHom* i. 602. 2 *Uton awurpan ðeostra weorc, and beon ymbscrydde mid leohtes wæpnum,* and with passive verb-forms in imitation of Latin, e.g. *GD* 203. 22 *þæt he nane þinga næs gelyfed beon gefylled,* Latin *ut illis tot virtutibus nisi sciretur plenus nullo modo crederetur,* and *Bede* 78. 2 *þa þe þonne in gewunan monaðaðle numene beoð, butan beorðres intingan, heo wæron bewered heora weorum gemengde beon,* Latin *quippe quia et sine partus causa, cum in suetis menstruis detinentur, uiris suis misceri prohibentur.* For further examples see Callaway 1913, pp. 71–2, and Scheler (p. 101), who also lists *Bede* 78. 2 and the like among his examples of the nominative with the infinitive.

f. The infinitives used adverbially

§959. The main adverbial use of the infinitives is to express purpose; on this see §§ 2940–51. Callaway (1913, chapter xii, and 1918, p. 206) proposes other categories. But they are scarcely needed. There is nothing special about his 'causal infinitives' except that they follow verbs of emotion, e.g. *ÆCHom* i. 538. 26 *Be þam we forhtiað fela to sprecenne.* He admits (1913, p. 162) that all his examples of 'the infinitive of specification with verbs' are doubtful except *GD* 180. 25 . . . *þa þa he gehyrde, þæt he gelæred wæs wyrta to begangenne,* which scarcely deserves a separate category. The same is true of his examples of the 'consecutive infinitive', which follows adjectives, e.g. *ÆCHom* i. 340. 24 *þæt hi ne beoð ealles swa carfulle to beganne ða earfoðlican drohtnunge,* or verbs meaning 'to incite', 'to persuade', 'to compel', 'to prepare', 'to suffice', and the like, e.g. *ÆCHom* ii.

84. 15 *He gearcað urne godan willan to fultumigenne*; see §2952. Callaway himself dismisses the 'conditional infinitive' and the 'modal infinitive'. Bock (1931, pp. 157-60) discusses particular examples of inconsistency in Callaway's classifications.

g. The absolute infinitive

§960. This is the name given by Callaway (1913, p. 169) and Visser (ii, §987) to examples like *Bo* 41. 3 *þ is nu hraðost to secganne, (þ ic wilnode weorðfullice to libbanne þa hwile þe ic lifde)* and *WHom* 20(C). 56 *forðam unriht is to wide mannum gemæne 7 unlaga leofe, 7, raðost is to cweðenne, Godes laga laðe 7 lara forsawene.*

h. Other uses of the infinitives

§961. The following constructions are discussed elsewhere: the use of the infinitive as subject, object, or complement, of a simple sentence or clause; the infinitive in apposition; the infinitive with modal auxiliaries; the infinitive with verbs used impersonally; and the accusative and infinitive. For references, see the General Index.

j. Element order

§962. The position of the infinitive in its clause depends in part on its function (see the preceding discussions and, further, §§1535-54), in part on the general principles of element order discussed in chapter IX, and in part on the stylistic intentions of the writer, e.g. *ÆCHom* ii. 320. 3 *Biscop sceal læran his leoda symle, mid boclicere lare, and him bysnian wel, ðreagan ða ðwyran and ða ðeawfæstan lufian, beon heora hyrde.* . . . But the position of the infinitive does not help us to determine whether it is active or passive; see §940.

§963. Using as a basis a corpus selected from non-Ælfrician homilies and the work of Ælfric, Fujiwara discusses the relative frequency of examples in which the *to* infinitive follows the object it governs or the adverbial element which accompanies it (X + *to* infinitive) against those in which the infinitive precedes these elements (*to* infinitive + X).[233] He decides that in these works the former is 'the fundamental neutral order' and the latter 'the stylistic one', and goes on (p. 75)

Freedom in the word order was freedom of selecting either of them. In this we could say that OE had a principle of its own. In rhythmical prose (and in verse)

[233] 'On the word order in the phrase of the *to*-infinitive during the transitional period from OE to ME', *The Annual Collection of Critical Studies* (The Department of Literature, Gakushuin University), 13 (1966), 61-81.

we see another principle of prosodic demand. These two principles determined the actual word order in Ælfric's works. But the actual complicated word order, it seems, came to lose its original significance, and led people to think that they had liberty in the word order as to the *to*-inf.

I would agree that the existence of these two orders is merely a special case of the general tendency by which the order SOV gives way to SVO, but would suggest that, if a choice between the two could be made on stylistic grounds, then both could claim to be 'stylistic'. As Fujiwara puts it in his later conclusion (pp. 79-80):

in the *Peterborough Chronicle* 1070-1154, the modifier still precedes the *to*-inf. often. But these two orders are indiscriminately used. In *Ancrene Riwle to*-I + X is normal and X + *to*-I is stylistic. As far as the word-order is concerned, the revolving table of English turned half round with the *Peterborough Chronicle* 1070-1154 as its pivot.

We cannot escape the fact that all these works were written in a period of transition and that some 'indiscriminate use' at least will be present in all. Fujiwara's article contains a valuable collection of material which illustrates the change in question.

§964. On Visser's statement (i, §404) that 'a preposition accompanying an inflected infinitive always precedes it in Old English', see §§1073 and 1075 fn.

k. Alternative constructions

§965. The inflected infinitive can be used in parallel with *to* + a noun phrase, e.g. *ÆCHom* ii. 430. 33 *Efne þes sunderhalga . . . hæfde opene eagan to forhæfednysse, to ælmesdædum to ðancigenne Gode . . .* , or as an alternative to one, e.g. *GD(C)* 32. 18 *þa leafe . . . þære bodunge* but *GD(H)* 32. 17 *leafe to bodianne* and *ÆCHom* ii. 454. 24 *To ðreagenne ge logiað eowere spræce* but *ÆCHom* i. 360. 29 *Us gelustfullað gyt furður to sprecenne be ðan halgan were Iohanne, him to wurðmynte and us to beterunge.* See further Visser, ii, §§897 and 976.

§966. Like infinitives, clauses can be used with nouns or with adjectives, can serve as subject, object, and so on, of verbs, and can express purpose; see the General Index. Generally speaking, OE uses clauses more widely in such functions than does MnE.

§967. When a finite form of an intransitive verb of rest or motion is used with another verb, we find four constructions (for convenience, I label them A, B, C, and D, after van der Gaaf in *EStudies*, 16 (1934), 81-99):

A. finite verb + *ond* + finite verb, e.g. *BlHom* 123. 21 *hwæt stondaþ ge her 7 þyses wundriað, 7 up on þysne heofon lociaþ?*, *ÆCHom* i. 246. 2 *and se witega læg and slep*, and *ÆCHom* i. 246. 15 *Aris nu, and ga to ðære mycelan byrig Niniuen, and boda swa swa ic ðe ær sæde*;

B. finite verb + present participle, e.g. *ÆCHom* i. 296. 5 *hwi stande ge ðus starigende wið heofenas weard?*, *ÆCHom* i. 156. 6 *he sitt be ðam wege biddende*, and *ÆCHom* i. 338. 25 . . . *ðonne forlæt he ða nigon and hundnigontig on westene, and gæð secende þæt an ðe him losode*;

C. finite verb + inflected infinitive, e.g. (with accusative and infinitive) *ÆCHom* i. 48. 17 *forði gemunde swiðe gedafenlice þæt godcunde gewrit, mannes Sunu standan æt Godes swiðran to gescyndenne þæra Iudeiscra ungeleaffulnysse*, *ÆCHom* i. 542. 19 . . . *þæt hi on ðam micclum dome ofer twelf domsetl sittende beoð, to demenne eallum mannum*, and *ÆCHom* i. 142. 33 . . . *ure Hælend Crist, seðe com to gehælenne ure wunda*;

D. finite verb + simple infinitive, e.g. *LS* 34. 416 *þar þæt scræf wæs tomiddes þe ða seofon halgan lagon inne slapan*, *LS* 14. 328 *And þa ure drihten him self com of heofonum to eorþan astigan*, *LS* 14. 292 *And þa þær com fleogan drihtnes ængel*, *ÆCHom* ii. 242. 35 *He eode eft sittan siððan mid his ðegnum*, and *ÆCHom* ii. 372. 23 *Ic bohte fif getymu oxena, and ic wille faran fandian ðæra.*

For further examples of C and D, see Callaway 1913, chapters v and x, and of B, Visser, iii, §§1793–4.

§968. With verbs of rest, says van der Gaaf (loc. cit., p. 82), 'the A, B, and D constructions evidently had pretty much the same function. In all of them the second verb denoted what the agent was doing while lying, sitting, or standing . . . the C construction, too, was already in Old English sometimes used to express simultaneousness of the two "actions".' The examples he quotes in support of this last proposition are *ÆCHom* i. 48. 17 and *ÆCHom* i. 542. 19 (both under C above), *Mark(WSCp)* 11. 25 *And þonne ge standað eow to gebiddenne*, Latin *Et cum stabitis ad orandum*, and—'if any doubt should be left' (p. 84)—*Deut* 27. 12 *Ðis synd ða ðe sculon standan 7 bletsian Drihten uppan Gazarim dune*, Latin *Hi stabunt ad benedicendum populo super montem Garizim* . . . [*sic*, but actually not C], *Deut* 27. 13 *7 ðas sceolon standan on Hebal dune to wyrgenne* . . . , Latin . . . *isti stabunt ad maledicendum in monte Hebal.* I detect an element of purpose in all these and so remain unconvinced that the C type necessarily implies 'simultaneousness', despite the Dutch and ME evidence adduced by van der Gaaf.

§969. Van der Gaaf also discusses the possible origins of these four constructions and their subsequent history, pointing out (p. 88) that 'the D construction . . . fell into disuse in Middle English' and that 'the C construction is now seldom, if ever, used in the same function as the A and B constructions'. Pattern D has also disappeared with verbs of motion. Callaway (1913, pp. 221-4) discusses possible reasons for this.

l. Summary of the uses of the simple and inflected infinitives

§970. Callaway (1913, chapter xvii) offers a more detailed summary of the uses of both the active infinitives and of the periphrastic passive infinitive. The latter is not included in my table because the paucity of examples may make its presence or absence a matter of chance rather than of principle or rule. Exceptional uses of the simple infinitive after *ond* are not infrequent. Examples have been quoted in the preceding sections. It is clear from the summary that, while one or other of the active infinitives was (almost) obligatory in some situations, there was room for variation in others. Liggins (1970, pp. 313-14) offers some comparative figures on the way the 'Alfredian' translations (including *Bede*) use the two infinitives. Klaeber (3, p. 466) after comparing the three half-lines· *Beo* 473a *Sorh is me to secganne*, *Beo* 316a *Mæl is me to feran*, and *Beo* 174b *to gefremmanne*, remarks that 'there are three nicely discriminated sets of metrical grades answering to three sets of textual context. The systematic distinction may be considered a Beowulfian peculiarity.' Perhaps it would be less remarkable if we had more poetry.

§971.

Function	Simple infinitive	Inflected infinitive
With nouns/pronouns	Very rare, except after *ond*	The norm
With adjectives	Very rare, except after *ond*	The norm
With *agan*	Only after *ond*	The norm
With *beon/wesan*	Occasionally after *ond* or in asyndetic parataxis	The norm
With *habban*	No examples noted	The norm
With other verbs	See §§954-6	See §§954-6
With 'modal' auxiliaries (except *agan*)	The norm	See §§996-9
With verbs used impersonally	See §1029	See §1029

Function	Simple infinitive	Inflected infinitive
As subject	See §§1537-9	See §§1537-9
As object	See §§1548-51	See §§1548-51
As predicate	See §1543	See §1543
As complement	See §§1540-2	See §§1540-2
In apposition	See §§1544-7	See §§1544-7
Expressing purpose	See §§1552-4 and 2940-51	See §§1552-4 and 2940-51
The absolute infinitive	No examples noted	The norm
The acc. and inf. construction	See §§3722-88	See §§3722-88

10. THE PARTICIPLES

a. Introductory remarks

§972. There are two participles in Old English—the present participle and that which is variously described as past—usually with reference to intransitive verbs—or passive—with reference to transitive verbs. For reasons given in §23, I call the latter the 'second participle'. On its time-reference, see §§768-81.

§973. There is no work which gives a complete treatment of the OE participles. Reference is made as appropriate to studies which deal with individual uses. There are many items which deal with the development of 'the English gerund' and the verbal noun -*ing* in ME and MnE, sometimes with reference to OE constructions as their (possible) origin. They are referred to only if they have some particular relevance to OE usage. The use of the participles in the Germanic languages also lies outside my brief. The works by Zadorožny (1973 and 1974) display bibliographical gaps and should be approached with caution. Matsunami (1958, pp. 161-9, and 1966*a*, pp. 326-48) offers useful discussions of this topic in the context of OE usage. In his view (1958, p. 162), 'the shrinking of the prs. participle is a peculiar characteristic of Gmc.'. On this see Matsunami 1958, pp. 162-3, 170, and 175; 1966*a*, pp. 326-8; and 1958, pp. 176 and 178, where Matsunami attributes an increase in the use of the participles, especially the present, in the OE period to Latin influence. (His ideas of eOE and lOE require modification.) See further Callaway 1901, pp. 348-52, and Wedel, *JEGP* 77 (1978), 383-97.

b. Present participles

§974. Present participles in -*ende*, like adjectives, can be declined strong—after *wilde* (*OEG*, §644)—or weak (*OEG*, §656). For further details, including occasional examples of comparison and the results of a mixture of substantival and adjectival endings in the strong declension, see §§101 and 1556. These forms in -*ende* are often distinguished from those in -*end* (*OEG*, §632). Visser describes the former as having 'clearly verbal character' (ii, §1010) and the latter as nouns (ii, §1009). But the confusion of endings is greater than he allows and the distinction cannot be generally maintained; see Mitchell 1976*b*, p. 481, and §690.

§975. A consideration of the functions of the present participle in OE inevitably involves adopting a system of classification. This problem has been tackled by Callaway (1901, pp. 141-9); Matsunami (1966*a*, pp. 315-24, where he criticizes Callaway, and 1966*b*, pp. 1-2, where he goes on to give a collection of examples from OE poetry at pp. 3-58); Visser, who offers a system which I find confused (ii, §§1009-18); and Zadorožny (1974, *passim*). I have discussed some of the difficulties in Mitchell 1976*b*, pp. 478-87, where I stress the fact that 'the function of the [present] participle cannot always be accurately determined'. As will become apparent here and in §1556, I distinguish the following uses: independent ('noun'), attributive ('adjective'), predicative, and appositional or appositive. To distinguish these last two is sometimes particularly difficult. The former embraces the combinations with *beon/wesan* which form what can be regarded as verbal periphrases; see §§682-701. With Callaway (1901, p. 149), I use the latter to include 'the participle that is equivalent to an adjectival clause as well as that which is equal to an adverbial clause'. The present participle is usually defined as a 'verbal adjective'. It has more the function of an adjective when used attributively before a noun, e.g. *ÆCHom* ii. 26. 25 *under anum yrnendum hweole* and *ÆCHom* ii. 274. 19 *þæt flowende wæter*, or independently without one, e.g. *BlHom* 5. 8 *þa hingrigendan he gefylleþ mid godum* and *ÆCHom* ii. 88. 28 . . . *þæs heofenlican wisdomes goldhordas þe . . . heora lufigendne gemaciað weligne ecelice*. In general the observations made about adjectives in §§97-219 apply to participles used adjectivally.

§976. The present participle has more the function of an active form of a verb when used predicatively, e.g. *ÆCHom* ii. 188. 14 *Witodlice sum gemyndleas wif ferde worigende geond wudas and feldas* and *ÆCHom* ii. 382. 29 *Ða mid þam ðe he swiðost motode, on his domsetle sittende . . .* , or appositively, e.g. *ÆCHom* i. 370. 27 *Syððan, ymbe tyn geara fyrst, he gewende to Romebyrig, bodigende godspel, ÆCHom* ii. 498. 29 *ða arn he to cyrcan . . . , fulluhtes biddende, ÆCHom* ii. 352. 10 *Ic þa, betwux ðam weorodum þam engle fylgende, þohte þæt hit wære heofonan rice,* and *ÆCHom* i. 372. 28 *þæt folc ða mid anre stemne clypigende cwæð, 'An God is ðe Petrus bodað'.* The presence of accusative, genitive, or dative, objects in some of these examples emphasizes the verbal force of the participle.

§977. But the boundary between these uses must not be drawn too rigidly, if indeed it is to be drawn at all. Thus we may compare *ÆCHom* ii. 382. 5 *Efne ða com Godes engel scinende* with *ÆLS* 5. 101 *þone scinendan æncgel* and *ÆCHom* ii. 150. 4 *Eft on ðære ylcan tide he mid ele gesmyrode an licgende mæden on langsumum sare* with *BlHom* 171. 11 *swa him Drihten Crist eallum rihtgelyfdum mannum wunigendum for his noman . . . geheht 7 cwæþ . . .* ; we may try to decide whether *ðancigende* is predicative or appositive in *ÆCHom* ii. 578. 28 *and þæt folc syððan mid bliðre heortan, on ðam eahteoðan dæge ham gewende, ðancigende þam Ælmihtigan ealra his goda;* and we can note that we would probably reverse the classifications of *ÆCHom* ii. 188. 14 and *ÆCHom* i. 370. 27 if they read respectively ✭*. . . ferde geond wudas and feldas worigende* and ✭*. . . to Romebyrig gewende, bodigende godspel.*

§978. The problem of deciding whether the present participle is to be taken as adjectival or as verbal, i.e. as forming a periphrastic tense with the verb, arises particularly when the verb is *beon/wesan* or *weorþan.* The examples in which the appositive participle takes a direct object preclude us from drawing the apparently obvious conclusion that in *ÆCHom* i. 66. 15 *Efne ðaða se apostol þas lare sprecende wæs* and *ÆCHom* i. 386. 19 *and gecum to minum ðeowan Saulum, se is biddende minre miltsunge mid eornestum mode* the participle must be purely verbal because it takes an object. On this question, see §§685-94.

§979. On the analogy of MnE, it is reasonable to assert that it is possible (as opposed to essential) to argue that OE combinations of a verb + a present participle are periphrastic verb forms only when the verb is *beon/wesan* and possibly *weorþan;* see §683. Visser (iii, §§1789-889) adopts this position by placing these verbs under the heading 'Distinct Subordination [of the First Verb to the Second]' and by citing under the heading 'Slight Subordination' examples of such combinations with verbs of beginning, continuing, and ending, e.g. *GD* 337. 2 *heo byþ deadlic, þonne heo anforlæt syngiende* (these are not common in OE) and with verbs of motion and of rest, e.g. *ÆCHom* ii. 134. 2 . . . *se eadiga Cuðberhtus . . . arn, swa swa him his nytenlice yld tihte, plegende mid his efenealdum* and *ÆCHom* ii. 312. 24 *Ða læg se earming, his yrmðe bemænende*; see further my §§965-9.

§980. The accusative + present participle is found in a construction similar to the accusative + infinitive, e.g. *Or* 92. 9 *þa gesawan hie Romana ærendracan on hie feohtende mid þæm burgwarum* and *ÆCHom* i. 48. 31 *and se eadiga cyðere Stephanus hine geseah standende*; cf. *ÆCHom* i. 48. 26 *Se eadiga Stephanus geseah Crist standan.* (For *standende* as an accusative form, see §101.) This construction—said by Callaway (1913, pp. 225-30) to be the result of Latin influence—is discussed in §§3766-76.

§981. The accusative + present participle is one of the four situations noted by Dal (*NTS* 16 (1952), 101-2) in which OE could use either a present participle or a preposition + an *-ung, -ing* noun. They are (with his examples) appositively—*spræc wepende* : *spræc on wepinge*; with a verb of rest or movement—*com ridende* : *com on ridinge*; with *beon/wesan*—*wæs feohtende* : *wæs on feohtinge*;[234] and with verbs of causing or perception—*geseah hine ridendne* : *geseah hine on ridinge*. See also Visser, ii, chapter ix, and iii, §§2083-110.

§982. On the use of the present participle in absolute phrases, see §§3804-46, and further on the appositive participle, §§1434-6. More examples of (some of) the patterns discussed above will be found in Callaway 1901 (all texts), Callaway 1918 (*Li*), and K. Köhler (*Beowulf*; Klaeber 3, p. clxvi). Visser (iii, §§1773-4, 1786, and 2145-7) gives what he thinks are OE examples of certain MnE constructions. Most of them are from the New Testament, the Psalters, or other translated texts, and do not always seem convincing ancestors for their putative offspring.

c. Second participles

§983. The second participles of strong verbs end in *-en, -in, -æn* (*OEG*, §735(k)), those of weak verbs in *-(e)d, -t, -od*. They can

---

[234] The construction seen in *ChronA* 70. 28 (871) *7 on feohtende wæron oþ niht* may be a confused blend of these two types. But it is, I think, more likely that we have to do with an embryo compound *on-feohtan*; see §§1072-3.

be declined strong (*OEG,* §643(5)(*c*)) or weak (*OEG,* §656), and are occasionally found in the comparative or superlative (see §101). On the time-reference of the second participles of transitive and intransitive verbs, see §§768-81. I have not noted the equivalent of MnE 'having taken'.

§984. As Callaway (1901, p. 142) observes, 'the preterite [= second] participle . . . is more adjectival than the present; as the present participle with an object is more verbal than one without an object'. Second participles alone could not take objects—those of intransitive verbs by definition and those of transitive verbs because they were passive. The four exceptions noted by Callaway (1901, p. 314, and 1918, pp. 71-2) are all in the Gospels and, as he points out, are all the result of Latin influence. On the change by which the second participles of transitive verbs used with *habban* in the perfect/pluperfect periphrasis acquired an active verbal force rather than the original passive adjectival and appositional one, see §728. As noted there, opinions differ as to whether this stage had been reached in OE. On the so-called 'passive participles with active meaning', see §24.

§985. The use of second participles with *beon/wesan* and *weorþan* to form the periphrastic passive has been discussed in §§786-801. But alongside these combinations we find the second participle used predicatively (or appositively?) with verbs of resting, e.g. *CP* 135. 11 . . . *hira ðære halegestan halignesse gimmas . . . licggeað toworpne æfter strætum* and *ÆCHom* ii. 356. 26 *Se læg dæg and niht geswogen betwux ðam ofslegenum*, or of movement, e.g. *ÆLS* 7. 336 *þa com Gallicanus eac to gode gebogen*, and with other verbs, such as those of seeming or continuing, e.g. *Bede* 324. 3 *Swelce eac seo heafodstow wundorcræftiglice geworht 7 gescrepelice geheowod æteowde to þam gemete hire heafdes* and *ÆLS* 14. 47 *ac se halga wer wunode ungederod*. For further examples see Visser, iii, §§1891-4.

§986. The second participle can also be used attributively, usually before a noun, as in *CP* 257. 21 *ða gedonan synna, Bede* 34. 22 *se foresprecena Godes man, ÆCHom* ii. 186. 30 *astrehtum handum*, and *ÆCHom* ii. 564. 25 *on ðam ymbgyrdum lendenum*. Visser (ii, §§1128-9, 1132-3, 1137, and 1139) offers a classification and more examples. The same writer (ii, §1140) notes occasional examples of second participles after the noun. *ÆLS* 5. 357 *Tiburtius gemette ænne mann afeallene* belongs, not here, but with the examples discussed in §988 and with those cited s.v. *(ge)metan* by Visser (iii, §2114). Most of Visser's examples are from the poetry, e.g.

Dan 469   . . . and þa on þam meðle   ofer menigo bebead
                   wyrd gewordene   and wundor godes,
                   þætte on þam cnihtum   gecyðed wæs,

where one can scarcely supply *beon* with *gewordene*, or from the glosses, or show idiomatic post-position of the second of two adjectives, as in *Bede* 216. 24 *sum swiðe æfest monn 7 geþungen*. He also gives examples (ii, §§1141-3) of various arrangements of the combinations of a second participle and a modifier, e.g. *Bede* 210. 23 *Wæs fæger mynster getimbred in wuda neah sæ in sumre ceastre . . .* , Latin *Erat autem monasterium siluarum et maris uicinitate amoenum, constructum in castro quodam . . .* , and *ÆLS* 21. 351 *to sumum ænlicum felda fægre geblowen* (participle after noun) but *Bede* 362. 15 *þæt sende wite from Gode Sceppende* and *ÆCHom* ii. 290. 14 *and se æftra fixnoð . . . getacnode þa towerdan gelaðunge gecorenra manna to ðam ecan life* (participle before noun). Visser also attempts (ii, §§1147-8) to distinguish examples like these from those in which a second participle or participial phrase expresses an adverbial relationship. But the distinction is not to be pressed, for the participles remain basically adjectival. His examples include *Bede* 260. 7 *Ac for intingan hersumnesse ic haten geþafode þæt ic þone had underhnah* (where 'having been ordered' or Miller's 'when ordered' would do as well as Visser's 'because ordered') and *Bede* 278. 18 *Gif he, æne siða onfongen, haten ham hweorfan, ne wille* (where the adverbial element is supplied by *gif*).

§987. Like adjectives and present participles, second participles can also be used independently, e.g. *BlHom* 85. 7 *ealle his þa gecorenan*, *BlHom* 85. 26 *ealle his gecorene*, and *ChronA* 132. 23 (1001) *7 ðær wearð fela ofslegenra*. See Visser, ii, §§1158-67.

§988. We find alongside the accusative + passive infinitive construction a pattern without the inf. *beon* in which the participle might be called predicative or appositive; cf. *GD(C)* 67. 6 *þa gemette he þone wyrttun oferwrigene mid unasecgendlicre mænige emela* with *GD(H)* 67. 6 *þa gemette he þone wyrttun beon oferwrigenne mid micelre menieo emela*. Visser, who quotes this pair (iii, §2112), gives examples of the construction from all periods of English (iii, §§2111-15). When one looks at these two examples and at *GD* 250. 3 *se bodode me þone ylcan wer forðferedne*, Latin *quia eundem virum obisse nuntiauit*, it is tempting to suggest that *beon* is merely 'omitted' or unexpressed. But the existence of a construction with accusative + present participle parallel to the accusative + active infinitive (see §3769) and the fact that one cannot supply *beon* in constructions involving *habban*—e.g. *ChronA* 48. 4 (755) *oþ þæt hie hine ofslægenne hæfdon*—suggests that the two may have originated independently. See further §§3766-76.

§989. On adjectives in *-lic* and adverbs in *-lice* formed on second participles, see Visser, ii, §§1166-7. On second participles in absolute constructions, see §§3804-46, and further on appositive participles, §§1434-6.

11. THE 'MODAL' AUXILIARIES

a. *Introductory remarks*

§990. The OE verbs covered by this term are *agan, cunnan, *durran, magan, *motan, *sculan, þurfan,* and *willan*. (On the asterisks see §993.) This list includes the OE forms of all the verbs in Twaddell's list of MnE 'modal auxiliaries' (p. 2) except 'need', which has replaced the now-obsolete *þurfan*; OE *neodian* is not used personally in the sense 'to need', though it has the impersonal sense 'to be necessary' in *BenR* 89. 6 *on cealdum eardum neodað, þæt þæs reafes mare sy, on hleowfæstum læs. Ðæs abbodes foresceawunge sceal beon be þysum, hu ðæs neodige.*

§991. I call these ' "modal" auxiliaries' for want of a better name. Palmer (p. 8) and Twaddell (ibid.) speak of the 'modal auxiliaries' of MnE. But we ought not to use the term 'auxiliary' of OE verbs which can be used independently (see §§1000-1) or which have full meaning, as *willan* has in *ÆGram* 143. 19 *amari uolo, ic wylle beon gelufod.* And the term 'modal' is dangerously proleptic with reference to OE, because generally speaking none of these verbs expresses mood in OE—for a few possible examples see §1014—and some of them do not do so in MnE. Gleason's term 'verbal auxiliary' (p. 104) is no better, because it might well include OE *beon/wesan, weorþan,* and *habban,* and MnE 'be', 'have', and 'do'. So I take refuge in a combination of tradition and inverted commas.[235]

---

[235] See further Tellier, pp. 7-10. The term 'preterite-present'—or, as he has it, 'perfecto-présent'—embraces the verbs already mentioned (except for *willan*) and others not generally considered 'modal', viz. *witan* (see Tellier, pp. 96-100), and *dugan, gemunan, *be-/ge-nugan,* and *unnan* (on these and on *durran* and *þurfan,* see Campbell *OEG,* §767, and Tellier, pp. 102-4, 114, and 118-19).

§992. The verbs which demand special consideration in the sections which follow are *agan, cunnan, magan, *motan, *sculan*, and *willan*. For the rest, see the dictionaries and the references given in the last footnote.

b. Conjugation

§993. On the conjugation of the verbs under consideration see *OEG*, §767, and (for *willan*) §768. As far as I have observed, an infinitive form is not recorded for those asterisked. The recorded participles are the forms *-cunnen* (only from *oncunnan* 'to accuse') and *willende*; see Visser, iii, §1839. So these verbs do not appear as the participial element in the periphrastic combinations discussed in §§681–858. For a basic paradigm setting out the patterns in which they do occur in OE, see §1095.

§994. As with other verbs, the preterite can serve as a perfect or pluperfect, e.g. *Bede* 354. 28 *Forhwon ne woldes ðu sona hraðe ða deagolnisse me cyðan 7 secgan?*, Latin *Et quare non citius hoc conpertum mihi reuelare uoluisti?*, and *ÆCHom* ii. 120. 3 *Swa fulfremedlice he drohtnode on anginne his gecyrrednysse swa þæt he mihte ða gyu beon geteald on fulfremedra halgena getele.* The preterite subjunctive can express impossibility, e.g. *ÆCHom* i. 18. 23 *Ne þorfte Adam ne eal mancynn þe him siððan of acom næfre deaðes onbyrian, gif þæt treow moste standan ungehrepod, and his nan man ne onbyrigde; ac sceolde Adam and his ofspring tyman on asettum tyman.* . . .

§995. In his review of Standop, Campbell says (*RES* 10 (1959), 187) that 'equivalents to such tenses [perfect and pluperfect tenses from modal verbs] can be formed by use of the adverb *furðum*, e.g. *ðonne hi furðum gan magon* "when they have become able to walk", *siððan he . . . furðum meahte his waldendes willan fremman* "after he had been able to perform his ruler's wish" '. But the time-reference of a subordinate *þonne* clause without *furþum* with the present tense can often be taken as anterior to that of the principal clause, e.g. *CP* 245. 10 *Wið ða speru ðære soðfæstnesse hie hie scildað, ðonne hi mon tælan wile 7 arasian for hira unðeawum, BlHom* 19. 14 *þonne we beoþ mid mycclum hungre yfelra geþohta abisgode, þonne sceolan we geornlice biddan . . .*, and *BlHom* 19. 28 *þonne we ure synna ondettaþ 7 us forgifnessa biddaþ, þonne bið he sona us efenþrowiende . . .*; cf. *BlHom* 35. 2 *On þisse bysene is gecyþed þæt eallum geleaffullum mannum englas þegniaþ, þonne hi habbaþ deofol oferswiþed*. I cannot see how the time-reference in the three examples with *þonne* + present tense differs from that in the full version of Campbell's first example *Bo* 108. 8 *Hwæt, þa cild, ðonne hi furðum gan magon, 7 eac ða ealdan ceorlas, þa hwile þe hi gan magon, wilniað sumes weorðscipes 7 sumre mærðe*; in all of them the state or action described in the *þonne* clause must be existing or performed before the action of the principal clause takes place. When we compare *Bo* 108. 8 with *Bo* 103. 12 *Ða he furðum on ðæt leoht com, ða beseah he hine underbæc wið ðæs wifes*, we see that the *þonne* clause in the former could be translated 'as soon as they can walk'. As for the second of Campbell's examples (*GenA* 2380), the time-reference of a subordinate *siþþan* clause with a past tense is always anterior to that of the principal clause, e.g. *ÆCHom* i. 6. 15 *forðan þe he sylf næs on heofonum, syððan he for his modignysse of aworpen wæs* and *ÆCHom* i. 232. 27 *ac syððan hi wæron gefyllede mid þam Halgum Gaste, hi wurdon swa gehyrte* . . . ; cf. *Or* 178. 2 *Ac siþþan Metellus þa elpendas ofercom, siþþan he hæfde eac raðe þæt oþer folc gefliemed* and see §§2666-78. (I would not regard *Beo* 648 *siððan hie sunnan leoht geseon meahton* as an exception.) So *meahte* in Campbell's example would carry a pluperfect implication even without *furðum*; with it we should perhaps translate 'as soon as he had been (was) able to perform his ruler's work'. So *furþum* does not seem to be an essential element for the perfect/pluperfect time reference in either of these examples. They merely reflect the fact that, as pointed out in §611, the OE simple tenses had to be more flexible than their MnE counterparts.

c. Which infinitive?

§996. Of the eight verbs mentioned in §990, *agan* alone prefers— or better, demands—the inflected infinitive. The only exceptions are with the second of two infinitives joined by *ond*; see §933. The remaining seven take only the simple infinitive. No exceptions to this have come to my notice with *magan, *motan*, or *þurfan*. For the rest, I know of six very dubious examples. I shall content myself with giving references to them and to discussions on them: *cunnan* (*Ex* 436 and *Rid* 36. 12; see Callaway 1913, pp. 81-2, and Bock 1931, pp. 156-7); **durran* (*BenR* 135. 11 *gegremianne* without *to*; see Callaway 1913, p. 82); **sculan* (*ChronE* 30. 8 (656)—*cumene* without *to* in a late addition—and *GD(H)* 37. 8 *ic sende þe, þæt þu sceoldest man to me gelædan 7 na gærs to beranne*—an example which disappears immediately we insert a comma after *gelædan*; see Callaway 1913, p. 82, and Visser, iii, §1731); and *willan* (*Matt(Li)*

5. 40 *geflitta 7 . . . to niomanne*, Latin *contendere et . . . tollere—*
in a gloss and after *ond*; see Visser, iii, §1729). So let us say that
agan has the inflected infinitive; the rest the simple (uninflected)
infinitive.

§997. As noted in §922, the periphrastic passive infinitive is found
only with simple forms of *beon, wesan*, and *weorþan*. So, as we
might expect, we do not find it after *agan*; see §996. But it does
occur after the other verbs, e.g. *CP* 387. 26 *ðæt hie wolden weorðan
forlorene 7 oferwunnene* (Callaway (1913, p. 87) missed this one),
Or 128. 5 *þa Darius geseah þæt he oferwunnen beon wolde*,
ÆCHom i. 292. 22 *. . . þæt nan man ne mot beon tuwa gefullod*,
WHom 4. 35 *swa æfre ænig gold mæg clænost amerod weorðan*, and
GenA 2287 *þæt se magorinc sceal || mid yldum wesan Ismahel haten*.
According to Visser (iii, §2150), '*wesan* was common besides *beon*'.
My own observations suggest that this overstates the frequency of
wesan.

§998. Examples in the poetry like *Beo* 2255 *Sceal se hearda helm
hyrstedgolde || fætum befeallen* and *Max i* 93 *Scip sceal genægled,
scyld gebunden*, where *beon* can be understood after *sceal*, probably
reflect the demands of metre. Visser (iii, §1895) adds from the prose
ChronE 19. 16 (565) *7 þam sculon underþædde ealle Scotta biscopes*
—without observing that Blain's *beon* after *sculon* comes from MS
F—and *Coll* 7 *Wille beswungen on leornunge*, which is merely a
word-for-word gloss of the Latin *Uultis flagellari in discendo*.

§999. Visser observes (i, §548) that 'since infinitives were nouns,
the relation between them and the verbs *shall, can*, etc. to which
they were joined must originally have been the same as that between
a direct object and a full verb, so that there was structurally no difference in this respect between "he can manigfealdan spræce" and
"he can sprecan" '. This leads us conveniently into our next section.
Callaway (1913, pp. 79-88) offers more examples of the sort discussed above.

d. Uses without an infinitive

(1) *Independent*

§1000. These verbs sometimes appear without an infinitive. We can
distinguish first those examples in which they serve as full or independent verbs, either intransitive, e.g. *Bede* 30. 3 *Eac neah þan ealle
þa ðing, þe ðanon cumað, wið ælcum attre magon*, Latin *quin potius*

omnia pene quae de eadem insula sunt contra uenenum ualent, or
transitive with an object which may be a noun, e.g. *Or* 96. 18 . . .
þæt he geornor wolde sibbe wið hiene þonne gewinn; a pronoun, e.g.
Bede 174. 7 *ond þæt heo þa hy frugne, hwæt heo sohten oððe hwæt
heo þider wolden*; or a clause, e.g. *Or* 136. 30 *Ac þæt hie magon þæt
hie þas tida leahtrien*. I give below some of the main meanings for
each verb. Examples and more details can readily be found in the
dictionaries and in the sources given in brackets after each verb.

§1001. The main meanings of these verbs when used independently
are: *agan* 'to have, to possess' (Visser, i, §§563-72, and Tellier, pp.
102, 114-15, 119). Despite Visser (i, §§567-8), *agan* alone does not
mean 'to owe'. His examples have *to gieldanne*. See §§932-3; *cunnan*
'to know, to be acquainted with' (Visser, i, §§551 and 555, and
Tellier, pp. 95-100); *magan* 'to be strong, sufficient, in good health'
(Visser, i, §177); **motan* (not used independently, but does occur
with 'ellipsis' of infinitive; see §§1003-5); **sculan* 'to owe' (Lüttgens, pp. 1-4, and Visser, i, §§549-50); *willan* 'to will, to wish, to
desire' (Lüttgens, pp. 56 and 60-1, and Visser, i, §§558-61).

(2) 'Ellipsis' or non-expression of infinitive

§1002. Opposed to these independent uses are examples in which
an infinitive is not repeated with one of two 'modal' auxiliaries or in
which an infinitive is clearly to be supplied from a preceding finite
verb or participle. Visser (iii, §§1735-70) discusses these patterns
and others which do not occur in OE in the course of his treatment
of 'two or more auxiliaries with a common verbal complement'. I am
indebted to him for the basic classification and for some examples.

§1003. Examples in which the infinitive is not repeated with one of
two auxiliaries—which may have the same or different subjects—
include first, those with the infinitive after the second auxiliary, e.g.
ÆCHom i. 12. 8 . . . *swa þæt hi næfre ne mihton ne noldon syððan
fram his willan gebugan; ne hi ne magon nu, ne hi nellað nane synne
gewyrcan*, *ÆLS* 12. 177 *Eft ne mot nan mann ne ne sceal secgan
. . .* , and *Az* 164 . . . *þæt hi ne meahtan, ne meotod wolde, ‖ acwellan
cnyhta æ*; second, those with the infinitive after the first auxiliary,
e.g. *BlHom* 237. 6 *To deaðe hie þe willaþ gelædan, ac hi ne magon*
and *ÆCHom* i. 12. 12 *Swa mihton eac þa oðre þe ðær feollon don,
gif hi woldon*; and third, those with the infinitive before both auxiliaries, e.g. *CP* 405. 29 *7 him getæhte hwæt hi on ðæm don sceoldon,
hwæt ne scolden*, *Or* 194. 11 *7 cwædon þæt hie þa burg werian
wolden, gif þa wæpnedmen ne dorsten*, and *ÆCHom* i. 86. 15 *cwæð
þæt hi hine gehælan mihton and noldon*.

§1004. Those in which an infinitive has to be supplied from a preceding finite verb are exemplified in Visser, iii, §§1746-55. Examples include (with a present tense of the finite verb) *WHom* 5. 29 *Ne man God ne lufað swa swa man scolde*, (with a preterite tense) *Or* 272. 18 *He wearð diegellice cristen, for þon he eawenga ne dorste*, and (with a jussive subjunctive) *ÆLS* 5. 333 *fara nu se þe wille*. Visser (iii, §1753) misconstrues *Or* 294. 15, which he does not quote in full. *Hæfde* means 'had, held'. It is not an auxiliary.

§1005. To these must be added examples in which an infinitive has to be supplied from a participle, which may form part of a periphrasis, e.g. *CP* 165. 20 . . . *ðæt he his hieremonna mod suiður gedrefed hæfð ðonne he scolde*, or may be used appositively, e.g. *ÆTest* 67. 1135 *biddende miltsunge þe þam ðe he mihte*.

(3) *Independent use or 'ellipsis' (non-expression) of the infinitive?*

§1006. There are many examples which fall between these two constructions. *CP* 7. 10 *ðæt*[*te*] *eall sio gioguð ðe nu is on Angelcynne friora monna, ðara ðe ða speda hæbben ðæt hie ðæm befeolan mægen, sien to liornunga oðfæste, ða hwile ðe hie to nanre oðerre note ne mægen, oð ðone first ðe hie wel cunnen Englisc gewrit arædan* will serve to introduce the problem. BT (s.v. *magan* I) glosses *mægen* as a full verb, 'to be strong, efficacious, to avail, prevail, be sufficient'. But Whitelock, in her revision of Sweet's *Reader* (1967), gives this sense only for *MCharm* 8. 4. So presumably she is taking *mægen* as an auxiliary, with *beon oðfæste* inferred from *sien . . . oðfæste*. Are we to understand some such infinitive as *fylgean* or *libban* after *woldon* in *CP* 407. 12 *Ðonne we gehirað under bæc ðæs maniendes stemne, ðonne we to him gecierrað, ðonne ðonne he us ciegeð huru æfter urum scyldum, ðonne he us æfter cliopað, ðeah we ær nolden æfter his lare?* Are we to postulate 'ellipsis' of the infinitive of a verb of motion in examples like *Or* 160. 27 *þa mid þæm þe hi hie getrymed hæfdon, 7 togædere woldon . . .* , *Or* 86. 3 *þeh ic ær sæde þæt we to helle sceolden . . .* , *Or* 170. 21 *þæt hie wið Pena folce mehte*, *LS* 7. 85 *Loca nu þin fæder sceal mid me to mynstre*, *Beo* 2816 *ic him æfter sceal*, and similar examples quoted in BT (s.v. *sculan* III)? See §1007. Is *beon, wesan*, or *weorþan*, to be understood either alone or with the ptc. *gedon* in

Beo 2089	He mec þær on innan unsynnigne,
	dior dædfruma gedon wolde
	manigra sumne; hyt ne mihte swa,
	syððan ic on yrre uppriht astod

and alone in

Wan 65

Wita sceal geþyldig,

ne sceal no to hatheort   ne to hrædwyrde,

ne to wac wiga   ne to wanhydig,

ne to forht ne to fægen,   ne to feohgifre

ne næfre gielpes to georn,   ær he geare cunne,

Mald 312   Hige sceal þe heardra,   heorte þe cenre,

                     mod sceal þe mare,   þe ure mægen lytlað,

and *WHom* 20(*C*). 24 *La hwæt, we witan ful georne þæt to micelan bryce sceal micel bot nide?* More such examples will be found in BT (s.v. *sculan* III) and in Visser (i, §§557 and 573).

§1007. Examples with 'ellipsis' (non-expression)—or apparent 'ellipsis'—of the infinitive of a verb of motion are common enough in OE. They include *Or* 286. 20 *. . . þæt he nyste hwær he ut sceolde, BlHom* 127. 8 *is þonne on westan medmycel duru þæt mannes heafod ge þa sculdro magan in, ChronE* 139. 20 (1009) *. . . þa hi to scipan woldon,* and *Beo* 754 *no þy ær fram meahte.* I tend to agree with Visser (i, §178) that 'to call this idiom elliptical, as OED does, is misleading'.

§1008. Each reader will have his opinion whether a particular example shows an independent use of *magan, *sculan,* or *willan,* or 'ellipsis' of an infinitive. Many indeed will be in the same position as Visser, who sees *Mald* 312 (§1006) as exemplifying first 'independent *shall*' (i, §176) and then 'omission' of the 'copula *to be*' (i, §231). We can leave it there. Anyone wishing to pursue the point will find material in Lüttgens (pp. 51–5 and 86–8), Wülfing (ii, §§389–95), BT(S) (s.vv.), and Visser (in the places already referred to).

e. The meaning of the individual verbs

(1) *Introductory remarks*

✕ §1009. In my review of Standop (*NQ* 205 (1960), 273–4), I expressed regret that he did not systematically distinguish the extent to which the verbs are used in OE in these three ways: independently; with an infinitive to give a finer shade of meaning than the simplex verb can express in any mood; and with an infinitive as a mere circumlocution for a mood or tense. This task still remains; Tellier has not succeeded in disposing of it. It is, of course, a difficult one, as Lüttgens—who was concerned with the meaning as well as the use of *sculan and willan—recognized in 1888 when he wrote (p. iii): 'Nicht immer mag es mir gelungen sein, alle hier vorhandenen Erscheinungen richtig zu charakterisieren, die oft in einander verschwimmenden Grenzen genau festzustellen und jeden einzelnen Fall seiner Gruppe richtig zuzuweisen.'[236] Standop's summing-up (pp. 167-71) underlines the difficulties. For my part, I feel justified in passing to the lexicographers the complex semantic problems involved in determining the various functions of the six verbs under discussion. To attempt such a task would be to involve myself in the study of these verbs not only in OE but also in earlier periods (on these see Tellier, pp. 25-59) and in later periods (on these see Visser, iii, §§1483-725). So I shall content myself in the sections which follow with making some scattered observations and offering some references for those who wish to pursue these verbs beyond the entries in the standard dictionaries.

(2) Agan

§1010. I have already discussed in §§932-3 whether *agan* with an infinitive ever expresses obligation in OE. On the later history of *agan*, see Ono, 'The Early Development of the Auxiliary *Ought*', *Hitotsubashi Journal of Arts and Sciences*, 1 (1960), 41-61, and Visser, iii, §§1711-25.

(3) Cunnan

§1011. *Cunnan* + infinitive is glossed by BT as 'to know how to do, to have power, to be able, can', e.g. *Bede* 234. 29 *Nu se hæðna ne con usse gife onfon* (I cannot see why Visser (iii, §1480) is so troubled by this example). That it is not entirely synonymous with *magan* is attested by examples like *ÆCHom* ii. 576. 17 *Forgif me wisdom, þæt ic mage þin miccle folc gewissian, and ic cunne tocnawan betwux god and yfel*; it is doubtful whether Visser's suggestion (iii, §§1622 and 1657) that *magan* denoted physical capability, *cunnan* mental or intellectual capability, will explain this and similar sentences, though admittedly it sometimes can be made to work, e.g. *WHom* 7. 152 *Nis æfre ænig man þe sylf geþencan cunne oðþon oðrum areccan mæge. . . .* Visser (iii, §§1477-82 and 1622-52) offers examples of, and discussions on, the use of this verb in ME and MnE. Some important differences in the use of *witan* and *cunnan* have been brought out by Ono, 'The Old English Verbs of Knowing', *Studies in English Literature* (English Literary Society of Japan),

---

[236] 'I may not always have succeeded in characterizing correctly all the examples that appear here, in determining the often blurred dividing-lines, and in assigning each individual case to its correct group.'

English Number (1975), 33-60. On the basis of these, he concludes that 'we may deduce that *cunnan* was on the way to becoming an auxiliary verb already in Old English' (p. 60).

(4) Magan

§1012. BT recognizes a range of meanings for *magan* + infinitive from 'to be able, may (because a thing is possible)' to 'may (because a thing is permissible or lawful, because there is sufficient cause)'. The OE meanings of *magan* are further explored by Standop, pp. 18-66, Tellier, pp. 85-124, and myself, *NM* 66 (1965), 107-11.

§1013. *Magan* + infinitive does not express a wish in OE. As Campbell says in his review of Standop (*RES* 10 (1959), 186), 'E. V. Gordon's downright "the use of *mæg* in an optative sense is unknown in OE" (note on *Maldon* 315) remains unshaken by all Standop can say to the contrary (cf. p. 40 and footnote).' Visser accepts this for the present tense (iii, §1680), but quotes two OE examples in which 'exclamatory *might* is used to express an idle wish' (iii, §1681). His doubts about *BlHom* 69. 6 *To hwon sceolde þeos smyrenes þus beon to lore gedon? eaþe heo mehte beon geseald to þrim hunde penega* . . . are justified. It is a statement; cf. *Matt(WSCp)* 26. 9 *þis mihte beon geseald to myclum wurþe.* The second is *Bo* 34. 6 *Eala þ ure tida nu ne mihtan weorþan swilce*, which could be taken as a despairing exclamation, 'Alas! that our times were not able to become like those.' The negative seems out of place in a wish.

§1014. BT (s.v. *magan* V) notes the use of *magan* in the Northumbrian Gospels as an auxiliary in the translation of the Latin subjunctive, e.g. *Matt(Li)* 12. 14 *huu hine mæhtes to lose gedoa*, Latin *quomodo eum perderent*. It would seem that sentences in which an indicative form of *magan* + infinitive may be equivalent to a subjunctive are not restricted to the Gospel glosses; consider *Bo* 132. 4 *Ic þe mæg eac reccan sum bispell be þæm þ þu hit meaht þe sweotolor ongitan* (final 'you may recognize . . .' or consecutive 'you will (be able to) recognize'; see §1015) and

And 544   Nænig manna is
         under heofonhwealfe,   hæleða cynnes,
         ðætte areccan mæg   oððe rim wite . . . ,

an example whose significance is overlooked by Standop; see *NQ* 205 (1960), 273. Alongside these, we have examples with a subjunctive form of *magan* + infinitive parallel to the subjunctive of an independent verb, e.g. *ÆCHom* ii. 268. 7 *Nu smeadon gehwilce men oft, and gyt gelome smeagað, hu se hlaf, þe bið of corne gegearcod, and ðurh fyres hætan abacen, mage beon awend to Cristes lichaman; oððe þæt win, ðe bið of manegum berium awrungen, weorðe awend, þurh ænigre bletsunge to Drihtnes blode* and *ÆCHom* ii. 344. 32 *ac beo him gesæd, ær he gewite, ða teartan witu, þæt his heorte mid ðære biternysee beo gehrepod, þæt he eft mage æt sumon sæle beon geclænsod, gif he his unrihtwisnysse huru on his forðsiðe behreowsað, and genihtsumlice ælmessan dælð.* Did the translator take *discam* as a subjunctive rather than a future in

PPs 118. 73   syle me nu andgyt,   þæt ic eall mæge
                  þine bliðe bebodu   beorhte leornian,

Latin *da mihi intellectum, et discam mandata tua?* I take up this question in §§2971-80. But it demands the close attention of the lexicographers, as does Standop's observation (p. 45) 'Es wird beim Studium der ae. Hv. Völlig klar, daß in keiner Weise der Formenverlust für die Einführung der Hv. verantwortlich gemacht werden kann' ['It becomes quite evident in studying the OE auxiliary verbs that the loss of grammatical forms cannot under any circumstances be held responsible for the introduction of the auxiliary verbs']. See also Tellier, p. 112.

§1015. BT (s.v. *magan* V) also notes its use in the Northumbrian and W-S Gospels as an auxiliary in the translation of the Latin future, e.g. *Matt(Li)* 18. 21 *synngiga mæge*, Latin *peccabit*, and *Matt(WSCp)* 26. 54 *magon beon gefyllede*, Latin *implebuntur*. Elsewhere, we have the present tense of *magan* used with future reference, just as that of any other verb can be, e.g. (full verb) *ÆCHom* i. 364. 23 ... *þu eart stænen, and ofer ðysne stan ic timbrige mine cyrcan, and helle gatu naht ne magon ongean hi* and (auxiliary) *ÆCHom* i. 4. 7 *Gehwa mæg þe eaðelicor ða toweardan costnunge acuman* and

ChristC 1310   ond nænig bihelan mæg   on þam heardan dæge
                   wom unbeted,   ðær hit þa weorud geseoð.

Visser (iii, §§1653-87) illustrates the meanings of *magan* and its descendants in all periods of English.

(5) *Motan

§1016. BT gives two senses for **motan* + infinitive—'to be allowed to' (the main and earlier sense in OE) and 'to be obliged to, must'. It is not always possible to tell which we have. Thus

Mald 29   Me sendon to þe   sæmen snelle,
              heton ðe secgan   þæt þu most sendan raðe
              beagas wið gebeorge

—at first sight a clear example of *motan = 'must'—may in view of
the context be ironical—'you have our gracious permission to'; see
further Standop, pp. 76-7; Visser, iii, §1694; and Solo, *NM* 78
(1977), 215-32. The present tense is used because the reference is to
the immediate now. It is used in

GuthA 784   Him wæs lean geseald
        setl on swegle,   þær he symle mot
        awo to ealdre   eardfæst wesan

—described by Visser (iii, §1691) as an example of what 'looks like
an infringement of the rule of sequence of tenses'—because the
reference is to the eternal now of Heaven.

§1017. The growth of the sense 'must' and the other nuances of
meaning found in OE are well treated (with examples) by Standop
(pp. 67-93). See also Tellier (pp. 85-124). The subsequent history of
*motan is discussed and exemplified by Ono, 'Some Notes on the
Auxiliary *motan', *Anglica*, 3 (1958), 64-80; Tellier (see his Table
des Matières); and Visser (§§1688-710).

(6) Cunnan, magan, *and* *motan

§1018. The extent to which these three are in opposition and to
which they overlap is another difficult problem for the lexicographer.
Standop (pp. 66 and 92-3) summarizes briefly the views he sets out
at pp. 7-17 and *passim*. Tellier also discusses it, bringing in *witan* as
well (pp. 85-101, 110-13, 117-18, and 121-4). I cannot accept all
his conclusions, but this is not the place for a discussion of this topic.

(7) *Sculan

§1019. BT (s.v. *sculan* II) glosses *sculan* + infinitive as 'denoting
obligation or constraint of various kinds, *shall, must, ought, (I) have*
or *am* (with infin.), *am bound*'. This is a blunt heading for the thirteen sub-divisions which follow and embrace such varying examples
as *BlHom* 19. 35 *Gelimplice he us lærde 7 monade, hu we us gebiddan
sceoldan*, *BlHom* 23. 14 *þu scealt fylgean me*, *BlHom* 123. 9 *þu eart
eorþe . . . 7 þu scealt on eorþan gangan 7 eft to eorðan weorðan*,
BlHom 37. 17 *7 se þe wille Drihtne bringan gecweme lac fæsten,
þonne sceal he þæt mid ælmessan 7 mid mildheortum weorcum
fullian*, *BlHom* 169. 22 *Hwæt sceal ic ðonne ma secgean . . . ?*,
BlHom 77. 29 . . . *þæt seo burh sceolde abrocen weorþan 7 bereafod*,
BlHom 41. 31 *forþon be þære ælmessan 7 be þæm fæstenne heo
lifian sceal abuton ende*, *BlHom* 183. 31 *Wenstu þæt ic sceole sprecan
to þissum treowleasan men*, and *ÆLS* 12. 181 *He cwæð þæt sum*

wer wære þe his wif forsæde swa þæt heo sceolde hi sceandlice for-licgan.

§1020. The reader will get valuable aid from Standop (pp. 94–132), who distinguishes six senses—*sollen, müssen,* das *sculan* der Bestimmung ['the qualifying *sculan*'], das 'ethische' *sculan, pflegen,* and *dicitur*—and from Visser (iii, §§1483–561). Lüttgens (pp. 4–55) offers more material than Standop, but his classification is less satisfactory. See also Tellier, pp. 61–124.

(8) Willan

§1021. In contrast to its blanket gloss for *sculan,* BT has some dozen main senses for *willan* + infinitive. Standop (pp. 133–55) makes the following divisions: (*a*) 'generelle und aktuelle Handlung', (*b*) '*willan* zur Bezeichnung der vollendeten Handlung', (*c*) '*willan* zum Ausdruck einer Haltung', (*d*) '*willan* = *pflegen* usw.', (*e*) '*willan* bei Sachen' [(*a*) 'general and present action', (*b*) '*willan* to denote a completed action', (*c*) '*willan* to express an attitude', (*d*) '*willan* = *to do habitually* etc.', (*e*) '*willan* with things']. See also Lüttgens, pp. 55–88, Tellier, pp. 61–124, and Visser, iii, §§1562–621.

§1022. On examples like *Matt(WSCp)* 1. 20 *Iosep Dauides sunu nelle þu ondrædan Marian þine gemæccean to onfonne,* Latin *noli timere . . .* , see §917. On the use of *willan* in examples like *Dream* 33 *Geseah ic þa frean mancynnes* || *efstan elne mycle þæt he me wolde on gestigan,* see §§2976–80. The use of *wolde* 'would' to express a polite wish for the present or future begins in OE, e.g. *Bo* 140. 19 *ac ic þe wolde acsian hwæðer we ænigne freodom hæbben . . .* and *ÆCHom* i. 412. 34 *Mine gebroðru, ic wolde eow ane lytle race gereccan, seo mæig ðearle eower mod getimbrian, gif ge mid gymene hi gehyran wyllað.*

(9) *Sculan *and* willan *as auxiliaries of the future tense?*

§1023. Examples like the following (some from Standop, some from my own collections) suggest that **sculan* and *willan* at times come pretty close to expressing futurity with no undertone of compulsion or volition: (with **sculan*) *Matt(Li)* 20. 18 *we stiges ł we scilon stige,* Latin *ascendimus, Matt(Li)* 13. 14 *ge sciolon gesea ł ge geseas,* Latin *uidebitis, Matt(WSCp)* 20. 10 *7 þa þe þær ærest comon wendon þ hig sceoldon mare onfon,* Latin *essent accepturi, ÆGram* 246. 11 *lecturus sum cras, ic sceal rædan to merigen,* and *ÆCHom* ii. 18. 6 *þa deadan sceolon arisan, and þa ðe licgað on byrgenum, hi geedcuciað*; and (with *willan*) *CP* 63. 4 *ic wille him suiðe ræðe* *andwyrdan*, Latin *protinus respondemus, Bo* 105. 21 *þonne wilt ðu cweþan*, Latin *dices, CP* 231. 20 *ðonne ðyncð him ðæt hie wiellen acuelan* . . . , Latin *moriuntur, Or* 128. 5 *þa Darius geseah þæt he oferwunnen beon wolde*, Latin *Sed Darius cum vinci suos videret, ÆGram* 152. 10 *docturus sum cras pueros, ic wylle tæcan to merigen þam cildum, ÆCHom* i. 4. 14 *þonne cymð se Antecrist . . . And se gesewenlica deofol . . . wile neadian mancynn to his gedwylde, ÆC Hom* ii. 582. 24 *Gif we deoplicor ymbe þis sprecað. þonne wene we þæt hit wile ðincan ðam ungelæredum to menigfeald*, and

PPs 59. 8   Hwylc gelædeð me   leofran on ceastre
                     weallum beworhte?   Hwa wyle swylce me
                     in Idumea   eac gelædan?,

Latin *Quis deducet . . . ? Quis deducet . . . ?*

§ 1024. Those who wish to pursue this question further should heed Visser's warning (iii. 1582 fn. 1): 'A good deal of labour has been spent by numerous grammarians on the question when it was that the combination *shall* + infinitive reached the status of a "future tense", without their first saying what a "future tense" really is.' But anyone attempting the task should refer to Schrader (pp. 72-5); Lüttgens (pp. 42-51 and 79-86); Gorrell, pp. 451-2; Wattie (pp. 128-30); Standop (pp. 118-32 and 156-66); Campbell (*RES* 10 (1959), 186-7); Tellier (pp. 64-84, 116, and 120-1); and Visser (ii, §§ 717 and 725, and iii, § 1483).

12. IMPERSONAL CONSTRUCTIONS

a. Introductory remarks

§ 1025. There has been much discussion on how to define and how to account for impersonal constructions in the IE languages; for a brief summary, see Wahlén, pp. 1-12. I propose to adopt what is (I hope) a simple definition: an impersonal construction is one which has only the formal subject *hit*, e.g. *ÆGram* 128. 17 *ningit hit sniwð*, or which has no expressed subject and for which no subject other than the formal *hit* can be supplied, e.g. *ÆGram* 76. 2 *Gif hwam twynað be ðam menigfealdan GENITIVO.* . . . This excludes constructions with *man*; on these see §§ 363-77. I eschew the term 'quasi-impersonal' used by various scholars for sentences in which an infinitive or noun clause serves as subject of a verb; see Wahlén, pp. 108-9. One might just as well call *Beo* 639 *Đam wife þa word wel licodon* 'quasi-impersonal' in contrast to *ChristC* 1333 *þæt he on þa grimman tid gode licie*—'personal'—and *PPs* 146. 11 *ne þe on þinum selegescotum swiðe licað*—'impersonal'. Where would one then put *Beo* 1853 *Me þin modsefa* ‖ *licað leng swa wel*? It seems enough to me to distinguish the impersonal use in *PPs* 146. 11 from the personal use in the other three examples, even though it involves stretching the sense of 'personal'. But see further Wahlén, pp. 3–8, and my §749.

§1026. The threefold syntactical classification adopted by Wahlén (pp. 11–12) is simple and satisfying and will be adopted here, with the omission of his term 'verb of material import', which is often used, never defined, and conveys nothing to me, and with some extension of his group III:

    I. Impersonal constructions containing verbs in the active voice;
   II. Impersonal constructions containing verbs in the passive voice;
  III. Impersonal constructions containing *beon* (*wesan*) or (*ge*)-*weorþan*, as copulas, + an adnominal element.

As we shall see, further subdivision—syntactic and semantic—is possible. But before we discuss these major divisions, two points of general interest demand treatment—verbal rection and the presence or absence of the formal subject *hit*.

b. Verbal rection

§1027. Verbs in the active voice in impersonal constructions can, of course, be used absolutely, as in *Bo* 49. 18 *Swa nu lencten 7 hærfest: on lencten hit grewð, 7 on hærfest hit wealwað. 7 eft sumer 7 winter: on sumera hit bið wearm, 7 on wintra ceald.* But reference can be made in the accusative or dative to the person affected by the action or event—here we can sympathize with Visser's remark (i, §29) that for constructions like these the term 'impersonal' is a misnomer. Some verbs, such as *langian*, are found only with the accusative or with ambiguous forms like *me, us, þe*, and *eow*, which can be accusative, e.g. *Or* 84. 26 . . . *þæt us nu æfter swelcum longian mæge* and *BlHom* 113. 14 *þa ongan hine eft langian on his cyþþe*. Others, such as *þyncan*, are found only with the dative or with the ambiguous forms mentioned above, which can also be dative, e.g. *GD(C)* 25. 24 *swa me þinceð* and *ÆCHom* ii. 382. 10 *and ðuhte him swilce hit swefen wære*. Others, such as *hyngrian*, are found with the accusative, the dative, and the ambiguous forms, e.g. *BlHom* 27. 4 *þa hingrede hine*, *ÆCHom* i. 166. 11 *ac siððan him hingrode*, and *BlHom* 39. 30 *þonne ne hingreþ us næfre on ecnesse*. (On *hyngrian* and similar verbs used personally, see §1038.) No examples have come to my notice in which the person affected is expressed in the genitive case.

§1028. The cause of the emotion, or the person or thing towards which the feeling is directed—Visser's 'causative object' (i, §30)—may be expressed in the genitive case, by a prepositional phrase, by an infinitive, or by a noun clause. Examples with the genitive include *CP* 227. 19 . . . *ðætte oft ðone geðyldegestan scamað ðæs siges, GD* 181. 2 *7 hine ongan wel his worda lystan, ÆCHom* i. 18. 11 *and him ðæs sceamode*, and *ÆCHom* i. 238. 3 *Ne him ne lyst nanre galnysse.* Prepositional phrases with *æfter* and *on* respectively will be found in *Or* 84. 26 and *BlHom* 113. 14 (both in §1027). On sentences with infinitives and with noun clauses, see §§1039-40. Wahlén (pp. 13-141) gives numerous examples of all patterns.

§1029. A study of Wahlén's examples with the infinitive (pp. 113-26) will show that, while some verbs, e.g. *onhagian* (pp. 113 and 121), prefer the inflected infinitive, others, e.g. *gelystan* (p. 116), prefer the simple form. There seems no point in attempting to lay down rules.

§1030. On impersonal passive constructions with verbs not taking a direct object in the accusative, e.g. *ÆCHom* i. 330. 29 *ac him næs getiðod ðære lytlan lisse*, see §834.

c. The presence or absence of the formal subject hit

§1031. Wahlén (pp. 8-11) discusses the origin and use of the so-called 'sham-subject' which occurs in the Germanic and Romance languages. He accepts Brugmann's conclusion that it is a comparatively recent innovation, wanting in many of the ancient languages. In OE, he rightly observes, its presence or absence in impersonal phrases is of no consequence; it has no real semantic function and is not of constant occurrence.

§1032. It is true that certain tendencies can be detected. Thus Wahlén points out (p. 10)

that whole categories of Impersonalia, with but few exceptions, never occur with this *hit*. This rule holds good for instance with the fairly numerous impersonal sentences belonging to the semantic group implying *physical* and *mental affections*. In these cases, as a rule, an oblique form of a personal pronoun initiates the sentence. As examples: *Hine þyrste hwylum and hwilum hingrode.* (*Wulfstan* 17: 4)—*Him sceal sceamian ætforan gode ælmihtigum.* (*Saints* I 272: 169).

One or both of two factors may be relevant to the absence of *hit*. The first is the fact that it is not needed rhythmically or (as it were) psychologically because a noun or personal pronoun in an oblique case precedes the verb. The second is the fact (already noted in §1028) that the cause of the emotion or the person or thing towards which the feeling is directed is often otherwise expressed. So, as Penhallurick (*Lingua*, 36 (1975), 20-1) observes, it is difficult to see how it can be said that [*hit*] is the subject in examples like *ÆCHom* i. 18. 11 *and hi wæron ða nacode, and him ðæs sceamode.* (There is room for further work here. Penhallurick promises some.) The rare examples with *hit* cited by Wahlén (pp. 41, 46, 50(2), and 57) either do not have such a noun or personal pronoun or can be explained as personal rather than impersonal, e.g. *ÆCHom* ii. 122. 7 *Gregorius . . . cwæð, þæt he sylf gearo wære þæt weorc to gefremmenne mid Godes fultume, gif hit ðam papan swa gelicode*, where *hit* could refer to *þæt weorc.* On the other hand, my observations and Wahlén's examples (pp. 16-30) suggest that expressions for natural phenomena, which usually occur without mention of the person or persons involved, tend to prefer *hit*, e.g. *Bede* 134. 28 *7 hit rine 7 sniwe 7 styrme ute, Bede* 154. 34 *7 sona on morne swa hit dagian ongan, GD* 234. 21 *þa þa hit ærest leohtode, Bo* 49. 18 (§1027), and *ÆLS* 21. 172 *Mid þam þe hit dagode.* . . . Apart from *ÆGram* 128. 16 *tinnit, swegð*, which is immediately followed by *pluit, hit rinþ* and five similar examples with *hit*—including *ningit, hit sniwð*—the most convincing exceptions are two with *sniwan*, viz. *Alex* 34. 20 *ða cwom þær micel snaw 7 swa miclum sniwde swelce micel flys feolle* and *Sea* 31 *Nap nihtscua, norþan sniwde.* Here *snaw* and *nihtscua* might be the respective subjects of *sniwde*. But an impersonal use seems more likely.

§1033. Elsewhere, however, the usage with the same verb frequently fluctuates. Thus we find *Or* 40. 26 *swylc her ær beforan sæde* but *Or* 128. 24 *swa hit her beforan sægð, CP* 214. 11 . . . *him eft gehreoweð . . .* but *CP* 220. 15 . . . *ðæt hit him gehreowe, ÆCHom* i. 64. 33 *ac se ungesæliga gytsere wile mare habban þonne him genihtsumað* but *ÆCHom* ii. 570. 13 *þi læs ðe hit ne genihtsumige us and eow, farað to ðam syllendum, and bicgað eow ele*, and (with *beon/wesan*) *ÆLS* 11. 142 *On þam timan wæs swiþe hefigtime wynter* but *LS* 7. 121 *hit is nu hreowsunga tid.*

§1034. Similar fluctuations occur with patterns involving infinitives and noun clauses (§§1039-40). Wahlén (p. 9) reminds us of Brugmann's theory that the formal subject was taken from sentences in which *hit* served as a 'real subject' anticipating an infinitive (phrase) or a noun clause, e.g. *Bede* 1. 10 *Forþon hit is god godne to herianne* and *Or* 108. 24 *þa gewearð hit . . . þætte sume Romana wif on swelcum scinlace wurdon. . . .*

§1035. Wahlén concludes (pp. 10-11) with the observation that 'on the whole, there seem to be no fixed rules for the addition of this secondary formal subject in OE. As far as I can see, the state of things in this respect is next to chaotic. Nor shall I attempt in this treatise to trace any rules for the application or omission of *hit*.' I shall not attempt to rectify this omission here. But my own impression is that 'next to chaotic' overstates the case and that full collections may reveal that certain verbs and certain authors prefer one or the other construction. Certainly, *hit* seems less frequent in the poetry than in the prose. For further examples see Wahlén (*passim*); Wülfing (i, §§76, 227, and 237); Sorg (pp. 3-9); Ropers (pp. 12-21); and Visser (i, §§3, 10, 29-43, and 44-50).

d. *Impersonal constructions containing verbs in the active voice*

§1036. This is Wahlén's group I and is the only one he discusses in detail. He adopts a syntactic division—simple sentences and 'complex sentences' consisting of 'finite verbs + infinitives' or 'finite verbs + dependent clauses'. Each of these groups is subdivided according to the meaning of the verb, but the inevitability of some overlapping is admitted (p. 13). Each of these is treated descriptively in his chapter I, historically in his chapter II.

§1037. The eight semantic groups are (1) expressions for natural phenomena, e.g. *ÆGram* 128. 18 *gelat, hit fryst*; (2) expressions for various specifications of time, e.g. *ÆLS* 13. 27 *oþþæt hit æfnode*; (3) expressions denoting some specification of locality, e.g. *Law VIIIAtr* 3 *And gif hit þonne to bote gega* (Wahlén admits (p. 38) that 'these may be personal constructions'; the category is dubious); (4) expressions denoting physical and mental affections, e.g. *ÆCHom* i. 168. 21 *Hwi hingrað þe?* and *ÆCHom* ii. 122. 10 *gif hit ðam papan swa gelicode*; (5) expressions denoting some manifestation of mental activity, e.g. *LS* 34. 513 *and þa he wundrigende þohte swilce hine on niht mætte*; (6) expressions denoting different aspects of the course of events, the state of things, e.g. *ÆCHom* i. 82. 9 *swa swa hit ge-lamp*;[237] (7) expressions implying a statement, an explanation; an

---

[237] Bately offers some comments on the different words meaning 'to happen' used in the various 'Alfredian' texts; see *Ang.* 88 (1970), 445-6.

exhortation, an admonition; a permission, e.g. *BlHom* 161. 1 *Men þa leofestan, her us manaþ 7 mynegaþ on þissum bocum . . . be þisse halgan tide weorþunga*; and (8) the *mæg cunnian* group, i.e. *Beo* 1365 *þær mæg nihta gehwæm niðwundor seon*, || *fyr on flode* and three similar examples involving a modal verb + an infinitive with no expressed subject which I discuss in §374.

§1038. A noteworthy feature of Wahlén's discussion of these eight groups is the frequency with which he points out that the verb in a particular example may be used personally rather than impersonally. Such ambiguity must arise when a verb which can be used in both these ways appears with a noun or pronoun which could be nominative or accusative. Thus,

PPs 82. 12   Gedo þæt hiora ansyn   awa sceamige,
                þonne hi naman þinne   neode seceað

is ambiguous when compared with *GD* 185. 13 *se awyrgda gast his sceamode* and *GD* 190. 8 *þa scamode þone biscop*, and *BlHom* 143. 12 *7 ne tweoge þis folc be hire untrumnesse* is ambiguous when compared with *BlHom* 41. 19 *gif ge þonne tweogaþ be þæm ælmessum . . .* and *BlHom* 41. 36 *Forþon ne þearf þæs nanne man tweogean. . . .* These examples show how inevitable it was for the personal construction to triumph over the impersonal as the case distinctions progressively disappeared. One more example must suffice. As we have already noted, *hyngrian* is used impersonally with the accusative, e.g. *BlHom* 27. 4 *þa hingrede hine*, and with the dative, which Ælfric uses in *ÆCHom* i. 166. 11 *ac siððan him hingrode* and in the first example in *ÆCHom* i. 168. 16 *Ða fæste Crist feowertig daga and feowertig nihta on an, ða on eallum þam fyrste ne cwæð se deofol to him þæt he etan sceolde, forðan þe he geseh þæt him nan ðing ne hingrode. Eft, ðaða Crist hingrode æfter swa langum fyrste. . . .* What case is *Crist* in this last clause? It could be nominative, for *hyngrian* is used personally in passages from the Scriptures or based on them, e.g. *Matt(WSCp)* 5. 6 *Eadige synt þa ðe rihtwisnesse hingriað 7 þyrstað*, Latin *Beati qui esuriunt et sitiunt iustitiam*, and *ÆCHom* i. 202. 35 *God gefylð þa hingrigendan mid his godum*. But the possibility exists that it is accusative. In view of the fluctuations in Ælfric's use of cases after other verbs discussed in §§843 and 1089, the argument that *Crist* could not be accusative here because Ælfric here and elsewhere uses the dative after *hyngrian* is not as conclusive as it might seem. Moreover, the possibility remains that the personal construction was Latin rather than native idiom.

§1039. We turn now to constructions involving combinations of the active form of a verb which can be used impersonally and an infinitive or a noun clause. Such combinations present no difficulty in themselves. But what to call them seems to: are the verbs used personally with the infinitive or clause as subject or impersonally with the infinitive or clause as the 'causative object'? (I have already given in §1025 my reasons for avoiding the term 'quasi-impersonal'.) According to my definition (§1025), such constructions are impersonal only if we can show that the infinitive or the clause is not the subject of the verb. It is difficult—indeed, impossible—to assert this when we have a formal *hit* with which the infinitive or clause is in apposition, as in *ÆCHom* i. 394. 15 *ac hit ne fremede him swa gedon* and *ÆCHom* i. 58. 11 *þa gelamp hit þæt æt ðam gyftum win wearð ateorod*. Wahlén takes this point (pp. 108–9) and excludes examples with the formal subject *hit* from his lists of impersonal constructions in chapter I, section B. The verb is, I suppose, used impersonally in examples like *ApT* 32. 2 *Lareow, ne ofþingð hit ðe gif ic þus wer geceose*, where the conditional clause can scarcely be in apposition with *hit*. If so, it is a fine distinction—or a terminological one. See also §2059.

§1040. But the absence of the formal subject *hit* does not certify that the verb is used impersonally. The status of *gelustfullian* as an impersonal verb is uncertain, but it occurs in two personal constructions (Wahlén, pp. 47–8). One of these is exemplified in *ÆCHom* ii. 130. 8 *Ða æt nextan gelustfullode ðam cyninge Æðelbrihte heora clæne lif and heora wynsume behat*, where a singular verb is followed by two subjects joined by *and* which occupy last position in their clause; on the analogy of *ÆCHom* i. 238. 3 *Ne him ne lyst nanre galnysse*, one would expect ☆*heora clænan lifes and heora wynsuman behates* if the verb were used impersonally. Hence *to sprecenne* is probably the subject rather than the 'causative object' in *ÆCHom* i. 360. 29 *Us gelustfullað gyt furður to sprecenne be ðan halgan were Iohanne*. So also, since *gedafenian* can be used personally as well as impersonally (Wahlén, pp. 95–6), the *þæt* clause in *ÆCHom* i. 580. 33 *Zachee, stih ardlice adun, forðan ðe me gedafenað þæt ic nu todæg þe gecyrre*.

§1041. These last two examples also show that, despite Visser (i, §§31–3), element order cannot help us to determine whether the verb is used personally or impersonally. Nor can the form of the infinitive, as Wahlén shows (pp. 109–10).

§1042. We must agree with Wahlén (pp. 110–13) that the only criterion likely to be decisive is the way in which the verb in question is used elsewhere in OE. But, as we have already seen, even this test is of dubious value, since it cannot be conclusive unless we can show that the verb is used only impersonally or only personally. And there are few verbs like that. Even *(ge)lystan*, singled out for special attention by Wahlén (pp. 111 and 112), is in fact a dubious case. It is normally used impersonally, as in *GD* 181. 2 *7 hine ongan wel his worda lystan*. It is used personally meaning 'to desire' in *GD(C)* 45. 21 *manige men hine geornlice lystan geseon of manigum boldgetalum*, *GD(H)* 45. 21 *fela manna of manegum scirum geornlice lyston hine geseon*, and *GD* 244. 27 *þonne seo sawl þyrsteð 7 lysteð Godes rice*; the existence of the first two examples rules out Wahlén's suggestion (p. 49) that the last 'is an abnormal construction and a blending, due to the juxtaposition of the personal phrase preceding'. But even if, on the strength of *Met* 1. 9 *guðe gelysted*, we attribute to *lystan* in these examples the sense 'to be pleased', this will not permit us to make the infinitive the subject of *lystan* in *Bede* 398. 7 *7 cwæð þæt hine lyste mid him etan 7 drincan* or in *ÆCHom* ii. 220. 22 *Se leahtor deð þæt ðam men ne lyst nan ðing to gode gedon*. However, Wahlén overlooks examples like *Bo* 76. 33 *Ne him eac næfre genog ne þincð ær he hæbbe eal þ hine lyst* and *CP* 459. 1 *for ðæm ðæt he ðy ieð meahte ðæt oðer forlætan ðe he on ðæm oðrum hæfde ðæt hine lyste*, where the relative pronouns seem to serve as the subjects of *lyst(e)*.[238] So the possibility exists that the infinitives could be the subjects of *lyst(e)* in *Bede* 398. 7 and *ÆCHom* ii. 220. 22 above.

§1043. More work from the lexicographers is needed here, with reference to later periods of English as well as to OE. I must confess that I find much of Wahlén's discussion muddling. One masterpiece of fence-sitting (p. 109) suggests that he was muddled too:

. . . the term *quasi-Impersonale, quasi-impersonal construction*, etc., is used in this treatise to denote those complex sentences only, in which the infinitive, or the subordinate clause, has the function of a subject. All other complex sentences in which the principal verb is void of any (pro)nominal subject, as in the two examples mentioned, are here taken as constituting impersonal constructions. But it should be kept in mind that the latter often may also admit of a quasi-impersonal interpretation. On the other hand, sentences with a predominant quasi-impersonal aspect may sometimes tend towards an impersonal import.

---

[238] *Bo* 32. 2 *7 se gesceadwislica willa þ hine þara twega lyste* is not, I think, another such example. The lack of concord in gender and the pres. subj. *lyste* combine to suggest that the *þ* clause is consecutive; see §2139. This avoids the necessity of postulating a reflexive use of *lystan*!

It seems pointless to me to argue whether the *þæt* clause in examples like *BlHom* 23. 12 *Her us cyþ þæt se godspellere sæde hu Drihten cwæþ to Petre* is the object of *cyþ* used actively or the subject of *cyþ* used passively (Wahlén, p. 141) or to attempt to prove or disprove such assertions as 'OE. sentences of the types: *hine (him) lyst faran, hine (him) lyst + a þæt-clause,* and *cwið on bocum þæt* . . . , where the infinitive or the dependent clause, judging from the construction or the import of the principal verb, cannot, at least not from the outset, be the subject' and 'doubtless, we may consider the type: *hine lyst(eð) þæt* . . . , to have originated in the dropping out of an originally extant pronoun such as *þæs*, which was perhaps felt to be unwieldy', made by Wahlén at pp. 109 and 129 respectively. So I do not propose to continue such arguments. But Wahlén's collection of examples should not be overlooked by lexicographers. His chapter II (pp. 142-216) discusses the origin of the OE impersonalia, reviewing previous writings on the subject and giving lists of cognate expressions in other IE languages. On the loss of these impersonal constructions in ME, see W. van der Gaaf, *The Transition from the Impersonal to the Personal Construction in Middle English* (AF 14), (1904); Wahlén, *passim*; Mustanoja, pp. 112-13 and 434-6; and Visser, i, §§29-43 and 324.

e. Impersonal constructions containing verbs in the passive voice

§1044. These are discussed in §§834-58.

f. Impersonal constructions containing beon/wesan or (ge)weorþan

§1045. Wahlén's third division (p. 12) comprises 'impersonal phrases containing *beon (wesan)* or *(ge-)weorðan*, as copulas, + an adnominal element', e.g. *Bo* 49. 19 *on sumera hit bið wearm, 7 on wintra ceald* and *HomU* 38. 243. 18 *ne wyrð hit æfre ful god ær on þisse ðeode.* . . . These need not detain us.

§1046. But these verbs can be used in other 'impersonal' constructions. *Beon/wesan* occurs with infinitives in various functions (see §§934-49) and with noun clauses, e.g. *Bede* 40. 24 *Ða wæs sona æfter þon þæt smyltnes com cristenra tida* and *Bo* 64. 11 *Hit wæs gio giond ealle Romana mearce þ heretogan 7 domeras . . . 7 þa wisestan witan hæfdon mæstne weorðscipe.*

§1047. *(Ge)weorþan* appears with noun clauses in meanings ranging from 'it happened', e.g. *Or* 36. 23 *gewearð þæt Moyses lædde Israhela folc of Egyptum* and *Or* 108. 24 *þa gewearð hit . . . þætte sume Romana wif on swelcum scinlace wurdon . . .*, to something like 'the thought struck them' = 'they agreed' (so Wahlén, p. 137), e.g. *Or* 178. 6 *ac hie gewearð þæt hie wolden to Romanum friþes wilnian.* But, in view of the formal subject *hit* in *Or* 108. 24 and of the personal uses of the verb in *Or(C)* 176. 4 *þes sige gewearþ Punicum on þæm teoðan geare hiora gewinnes 7 Romana* and *Or* 234. 1 *7 eac on þæm geare gewurdon monega wundor on monegum londum*, examples like *Or* 36. 23 and *Or* 178. 6 are not unambiguously impersonal.

§1048. Further on the wide variety of senses and constructions in which *(ge)weorþan* is found, see (in addition to the dictionaries) Hubbard in *JEGP* 17 (1918), 119–24, and Klaeber in *JEGP* 18 (1919), 250–71.

§1049. The auxiliaries *beon/wesan* and *weorþan* are unexpectedly found with the second participle of *(ge)þyncan* 'to seem'. My examples are from the *Catholic Homilies*, where the participle is uninflected in the singular, but has *-e* in the plural. They occur with a nominative subject describing a person or thing, e.g. *ÆCHom* ii. 82. 18 *and we earfoðlice him filiað to merigen, seðe nu todæg is ure folgere geðuht*, *ÆCHom* i. 334. 30 *Ðeah ðe hi syn waclice geðuhte . . .*, *ÆCHom* i. 356. 34 *. . . þæt he soð God wæs, seðe wæs ærðan witega geðuht*, *ÆCHom* i. 376. 12 *. . . swa þæt he wearð færlice geðuht cnapa*, and *ÆCHom* ii. 186. 14 *. . . hu nearowe ealle ða niðerlican gesceafta him wæron geðuhte*; with a *swilce* 'as if' clause, e.g. *ÆCHom* ii. 166. 4 *. . . and færlice ða wearð him eallum geðuht swilce fyr eode of ðære anlicnysse*; or with a noun clause, e.g. *ÆCHom* i. 236. 11 *Nu is geðuht þæt him sy sumera ðinga eaðelicor to arærenne ðone deadan of ðam duste . . .* and *ÆCHom* i. 6. 33 *For swylcum bebodum wearð me geðuht þæt ic nære unscyldig wið God. . . .* In view of the first group of examples and of the fact that active finite forms of *(ge)-þyncan* are used personally, e.g. *ÆCHom* ii. 570. 15 *Soðlice on ðam micclum dome ælcum ænlipium men ðincð to lytel his agen ingehyd him to gewitnysse*, we are justified in taking the *þæt* clauses in *ÆCHom* i. 236. 11 and *ÆCHom* i. 6. 33 as subjects. The fact that we have a *swilce* clause in *ÆCHom* ii. 166. 4 above demonstrates the inadequacy of our terminology rather than the inaccuracy of our analysis; cf. §1039.

§1050. Thorpe translates *ÆCHom* i. 356. 33 *and his hlisa weox geond ealne middangeard, þæt he soð God wæs, seðe wæs ærðan witega geðuht* as '. . . that he was true God, who before that had seemed a prophet'. This seems to offer a possible solution: that *geþyncan* is a verb whose perfect and pluperfect is formed with *beon/wesan* or with *weorþan*. But the preceding sentence seems to rule this out: *ÆCHom* i. 356. 31 *þa wæs he geðuht ðam folce þæt he witega wære, and Iohannes Crist* 'Then it seemed to the people that he was a prophet and that John was Christ'.

§1051. It is hard to see why *þyncan* should behave in this way. Perhaps (as Norman Davis has suggested to me privately) we have here an early stage in the confusion of the verbs *þyncan* and *þencan*. In this connection, it is noteworthy that all manuscripts read *þincan* in *ÆCHom* ii. 40. 23 *ac he wolde mid his eadmodnysse astellan ða bysne, þæt nan cyning ne nan rice man ne sceolde þincan to huxlic þæt he gebuge to Cristes fulluhte*, where the sense demands 'think', not 'seem'. But it is clear from Pope's note on *ÆHom* 20. 164 *we synd wið hi geðuhte swylce oðre gærstapan* that there is more to it:

The passive expression, *beon geþuht*, 'to seem', is well attested. With the active, impersonal *þyncan*, accompanied by a dative of person, the seeming is said to occur in the mind of one or more specified observers. With the passive form the seeming is attributed to whatever is named as the subject, regardless of who does the observing. Here the seeming is contingent on the comparison introduced by *wið hi.*

As far as I have observed, Ælfric uses the 'passive' *is/bið/wæs/wearþ geþuht* and *beon/sind/wæron geþuhte* 'personally' in the way Pope describes, the 'active' form being used in the sense 'seem good', e.g. *ÆCHom* i. 582. 18 *Hi ealle sealdon þone dæl heora speda þe him geðuhte*, and with reference to ideas expressed in a co-ordinate clause, e.g. *ÆCHom* i. 292. 4 *Buton ælcere ðrowunge he mihte us habban, ac him ðuhte þæt unrihtlic*, or in a clause introduced by *swylce*, e.g. *ÆHom* 29. 16 *7 eallum þam þuhte þe hire on locodan swylce heo myre wære*, or *þæt*, e.g. *ÆHom* 19. 156 *Him þuhte þæt he spræce þegenlice word*. These last two usages have been exemplified above with the 'passive' form in *ÆCHom* i. 356. 31 and *ÆCHom* ii. 166. 4. So there is an overlap in Ælfric. But the 'active' form is occasionally used 'personally' elsewhere in OE, e.g. (from the poetry) *Beo* 866 *ðær him foldwegas fægere þuhton* and *ChristA* 1488 *Hwæt, me þeos [rod] heardra þynceð!* and (from 'Alfredian' texts) *CP* 23. 11 *Ðara byrðenna hefignesse, eall ðæt ic his geman, ic awrite on ðisse andweardan bec, ðylæs hi hwæm leohte ðyncen to underfonne* and (with both 'impersonal' and 'personal' 'active' uses) *CP* 113. 10 *Æresð him ðuhte selfum ðæt ðæt he wære suiðe unmedeme, ac siððan he understungen 7 awreðed wæs mid ðys hwilendlican onwalde, he ðuhte him selfum suiðe unlytel 7 suiðe medeme.* As far as I have observed, the 'passive' use does not occur in the poetry. But it is recorded in 'Alfredian' texts, e.g. *CP* 113. 15 *Ðæt wæs wunderlicu gemetgung ðætte ða ða he him selfum wæs lytel geðuht, ða wæs he Gode micel geðuht, ond ða ða he wæs him selfum micel geðuht, ða wæs he Gode lytel geðuht.* There is room for more work here.

13. VERBS USED REFLEXIVELY

§1052. Verbs used reflexively obviously include those found with a reflexive object—the personal pronoun alone, *self* alone, or combinations of the two, in the accusative, genitive, and dative. These are discussed in §§265-78 and 472-500, where examples will be found. The subject is usually a person, but need not be. Thus we find *se wallenda leg* in *Bede* 118. 6 and *þæt treow* in *HomS* 40. 262. 5 (both in §267), and *CP* 242. 6 *forðæm ðæt yfelwillende mod gefielt hit self twyfeald oninnan him selfum.*

§1053. Wülfing (ii, §§377-80) was content to classify his 'reflexive Zeitwörter' along these lines. So he distinguished those taking the accusative—sub-divided into two groups: those which are otherwise transitive and those which are otherwise intransitive—those taking the genitive, and those taking the dative. These last were divided by Voges into four groups—verbs of rest, verbs of bodily movement, verbs of emotion, and other verbs. Farr (pp. 9-10) made it three— verbs whose activity contains the idea of construction or possession, verbs which express the transitive or intransitive exercise of a bodily or mental function, and verbs which express an intransitive state of bodily motion or quiescence. For him the combination of verb and pronoun formed a kind of medial voice in the last two groups; his examples were *ÆSpir* 57. 20 *ponne he . . . can him gescead betwux soð and leas* and *ChronA* 66. 9 (855) *7 þa him hamweard for.* Hermodsson (p. 194) also uses 'medial', applying it to combinations like *hine ahebban, hine behealdan,* and the like—which (he says) contain 'keine Objektsbeziehung' ['no relation to an object']—as opposed to *hine acwellan, hine begyrdan,* and so on. We can do without the term.

§1054. But Wülfing's classification requires refinement. For there are verbs which can be used absolutely and (we might say) reflexively with no object expressed—though absolute uses are not necessarily reflexive; see Visser, i, §§152-5 and 165. Nader (1880, §28) had noted some verbs which are reflexive in NHG, but are used without a reflexive pronoun in *Beowulf*. His list requires some qualification for OE in general. Thus *windan* can be used transitively—note *Beo* 1193 *wunden gold*—and appears with what may be a repeated subject or a reflexive acc. *hit* in *Bede* 178. 23 *þa wæs hit [his hors] longe mid hefige sare swiðe swenced 7 in missenlice dælas hit wond 7 þræste.* But others, like *gebæran* and *bugan*, seem always to be used intransitively and without a reflexive pronoun, as in

Beo 1011   Ne gefrægen ic þa mægþe   maran weorode
              ymb hyra sincgyfan   sel gebæran.
              Bugon þa to bence   blædagande,
              fylle gefægon.

Wülfing failed to take cognizance of this. His omission was partially rectified by Hermodsson (pp. 193–210), who distinguished A., reflexive verbs, from B., verbs with double function, i.e. transitive and intransitive; the latter include B. a., denominative verbs, and B. b., non-denominative verbs. He further sub-divides B. b. according to meaning, distinguishing verbs of movement, of mixing and scattering, of appearing, of destroying, of changing, and of opening and shutting.[239] Visser (i, §§159–60) also speaks of an 'absolute use of verbs that are often found construed with a reflexive object'. But both Hermodsson and Visser fail to make the distinction between transitive verbs used absolutely and intransitive verbs which sometimes appear used with a reflexive accusative described by Ropers (p. 30) as more or less pleonastic.

§1055. The dangers of rigid classification naturally arise here too. The case after some verbs fluctuates. Thus *gebiddan* 'to pray' is found with both accusative, e.g. *ÆCHom* i. 166. 28 *Gehwa sceal hine gebiddan to his Drihtne anum*, and dative, e.g. *LS* 8. 424 . . . *þæt hi him to gode gebædon.* It must be purely fortuitous whether examples survive or not of the reflexive use of a particular verb. It is a reasonable assumption that those who washed themselves in Anglo-Saxon England also dried themselves. But I have so far found no reflexive use of *drygan* to parallel that of *þwean* in *CP* 421. 16 *ealne weg hi hi ðweað, 7 ne beoð hie næfre clæne.* So we need not accept Visser's claim (i, §159) that 'one can only speak of "omission" [a word which I avoid] of the reflexive complement in those cases where the verb in question is also found used *with* the reflexive complement during the same period'. None the less, we can attempt a broad threefold

---

[239] K. F. Sunden in his *Essay II. A Category of Predicational Change in English* (Uppsala, 1916), 250–3, claims that, when these verbs with double function are used intransitively, a reflexive pronoun has been lost. Hermodsson (pp. 195–6, 200–1, and 208–10) argues that both uses were original in many of these verbs, but agrees that there is room for doubt with some, especially the non-denominative verbs.

division of OE verbs which are used reflexively. Sub-divisions according to the case of the reflexive object and the meaning of the verb can of course be made.

§1056. First, there are transitive verbs which are used with a reflexive object, but not absolutely, e.g. *ahebban* (*Bede* 38. 13 *Scs Albanus . . . eode . . . 7 his eagan ahof upp to heofonum* and *CP* 144. 7 *Hie ðonne ahebbað hie ofer hiera hieremenn*) and *bletsian* (*ÆCHom* ii. 598. 23 *Ælmihtig Fæder, gebletsa us* and *ÆCHom* ii. 600. 22 *Ic bletsige me*).

§1057. Second, there are transitive verbs which are used both with a reflexive object and absolutely, e.g. *biddan* (*ÆCHom* ii. 598. 20 *We biddað þe, Drihten*, *ÆCHom* ii. 494. 25 . . . *þæt hi sceoldon hi gebiddan to ðære sunnan anlicnysse*, and *LS* 23. 718 *gebide for me*) and *bræddan* (for examples, see §267).

§1058. Third, there are intransitive verbs which can be used in a reflexive sense either absolutely or with a pronoun object, e.g. *bestelan* (*Or* 198. 11 *þæs on þæm æfterran geare Hannibal bestæl on Marcellus Claudius þone consul* and *Or* 218. 29 *Æfter þæm Mantius se consul for on Numentine . . . 7 hiene siþþan aweg bestæl*), *belgan*, and *restan* (for examples of these see §268). We could perhaps add here *weorðan* and *wesan*, both of which, as QW (§107) observes, 'appear on occasion with dative pronouns, usually classed as reflexive: *he wearð him on anon scipe* "he got aboard a ship", *he wearð him aweg* "he went away", *Adam sceal . . . wesan him on wynne* "Adam shall live in joy" '.

§1059. Further examples will be found in Schrader (pp. 63–4); Wülfing (ii, §§377–80); Penttilä (p. 28 and *passim*); Visser (i, §§426–38); and in my own discussions referred to in §1052.

14. PREPOSITIONS, ADVERBS, PREPOSITIONAL ADVERBS, POSTPOSITIONS, SEPARABLE PREFIXES, OR INSEPARABLE PREFIXES?

a. Introductory remarks

§1060. The unwieldy heading to this sub-chapter emphasizes the fact that the question under consideration is in part terminological. That it is also a practical problem is neatly illustrated by Thorpe's use of hyphens in *ÆCHom* i. 120. 20 *Se lareow Hægmon cweð on ðissere trahtnunge þæt seo dun þe se Hælend of-astah getacnode heofenan rice, of ðam niðer-astah se Ælmihtiga Godes Sunu. . . .* It has been much discussed; see Mitchell and Kingsmill, *NM* 81 (1980), 313–17.

b. Prepositions and adverbs

§1061. That there are in OE prepositions and adverbs and that some words can be used in both functions is an acknowledged commonplace. The presence of an immediately following noun, demonstrative, personal pronoun, or other, object, is, of course, decisive for the preposition in its literal sense 'pre-position', e.g. *ÆHom* 1. 207 *on dæge, ÆHom* 1. 276 *on him sylfum, ÆHom* 1. 18 *hu he to mannum com*, and (with an intervening genitive) *ÆHom* 1. 447 *ær Cristes þrowunge*. So too is the presence of a following declined relative; see §2231. A list of these prepositions is given and their use discussed in §§1177–1219. On the position in their clause of such prepositional phrases—Visser's type (*a*) (i, §401)—see §§1158 and 1593.

✗ §1062. But we also have sentences like *ÆHom* 20. 232 . . . *þæt hi comon him to*. Fakundiny (p. 139 fn. 1) writes: 'For obvious reasons of logic, prepositional words when they are post-posited are here referred to simply as "postpositions".' As we shall see, it is not as simple as that. So for the time being I shall speak of words used in pre-position and post-position. Most of the words usually called prepositions can be used in both; cf. *GD(C)* 142. 4 *ne drinc ðu of þære* with *GD(H)* 142. 4 . . . *þæt þu þær of ne drince*. We will have to await the full concordances being prepared for the new *Dictionary of Old English* before laying down 'rules'. But the general position can be set out thus:

pre-position before nouns and demonstratives (a few exceptions are referred to in *NM* 79 (1978), 242; see also Wende, pp. 136–8), interrogatives (Wende, p. 136, records no exceptions and I have found none), and the relatives *se* and *'seþe* (see §2231);

post-position after adverbs like *her* and *þær*—Visser's type (*e*) (i, §405)—and the relatives *þe* and *se'þe*;

both pre-position before and post-position after personal pronouns used alone (see *NM* 79 (1978), 242).

Wende, who argues that this represents an original state of affairs (pp. 266–9), is a mine of information and examples here. I discuss some problems associated with these usages in *NM* 79 (1978), 240–57.

§1063. If the presence of an immediately following object is decisive for the preposition, the absence of any possible object is decisive for the adverb as traditionally defined, e.g. *on* in *ÆHom* 1. 275 *We secgað nu forð on embe þis soðe godspell*, *to* in *ÆHom* 5. 143 *cume to and drince*, and *ær* in *ÆHom* 1. 442 *swa swa we sædon ær*.

§1064. Harrison (1892, p. 58) includes *up* and *ut* in his list of words which are never used as prepositions in OE. However, Wülfing (ii, §967) cites *Bo* 53. 7 *oð he eft cymð to ðæm ilcan æwelme þe he ær ut fleow* as a solitary example of the prepositional use of *ut*. We could compare this with examples like *Bo* 6. 16 *7 hu mon sceolde ælcne mon hatan be þam deore þe he gelicost wære* and say that *þe* serves as a dative dependent on the verb *fleow* and not on *ut*. But since *ut/out* was used as a preposition in ME, Wülfing may be right. Wende includes *ut(e)* and *up(pe)* among 'eine Reihe von Adverbien, die sich ganz wie nachgestellte Präpositionen an ein vorausgehendes Beziehungswort anlehnen können' ['a list of adverbs which can refer back to a word which precedes them, just as if they were prepositions in post-position'] (p. 14). Examples like *Bede* 384. 26 *ðæt ealond . . . ðæt we ær ut of gongende wæron* (which he quotes on p. 56) do not support him. But *CP* 101. 24 *Forðæm Moyses oft eode inn 7 ut on ðæt templ, forðæm he wæs ðærinne getogen to ðære godcundan sceawunga, 7 ðærut he wæs abisgod ymb ðæs folces ðearfe* (Wende, p. 31), with its contrasting *ðærinne* and *ðærut*, cannot be so easily dismissed. In view of such difficulties, I propose to use Campbell's term 'prepositional adverb' (*OEG*, §72) to describe words like *on*, *to*, *ær*, *inne*, *up(pe)*, and *ut(e)*, which serve or may serve in both functions. But I return to the terminological problems in my conclusion (§1080).

§1065. One of Campbell's comments, however, demands clarification. He remarks (*OEG*, §72 fn. 1) that the term 'prepositional adverb'

denotes words which can be readily used in both a prepositional and an adverbial function. As verbal prefixes, they have an adverbial function when combined with intransitive verbs; in combination with transitive verbs, they have a function approximating to that of prepositions, the object being under their government.[240]

The important thing is not whether the prefixes are combined with an intransitive or transitive verb;[241] it is what sort of verb results

---

[240] As the examples in *OEG*, §73, show, Campbell's term 'prepositional adverb' covers not only words but also bound forms like *æ-* and *or-*.

[241] I use '(in)trans. verb' as a convenient shorthand for the phrase 'verb used (in)transitively'.

from the combining of the two elements. We can agree that (*a*) when a compound verb consisting of a prefix and an intransitive verb remains intransitive, the prefix has an adverbial function; cf. *Beo* 760 *fingras burston* with *Mald* 136 . . . *se sceaft tobærst.* But (*b*) when a compound consisting of a prefix and an intransitive verb becomes transitive, the prefix has a prepositional function, e.g. *Beo* 1408 *Ofereode þa æþelinga bearn* ‖ *steap stanhliðo,* the object being under its government. And (*c*) when a compound consisting of a prefix and a transitive verb remains transitive, the prefix has an adverbial function; cf. *Beo* 1510 *sædeor monig* ‖ *hildetuxum heresyrcan bræc* with

Beo 779 . . . þæt hit a mid gemete   manna ænig
            betlic ond banfag   tobrecan meahte.

(I cannot think of examples in which a prefix and a transitive verb combine to form an intransitive verb.)

§1066. The same is true of combinations of a prepositional adverb and verb which are not or need not be compounds. Thus we have *Beo* 1650 *weras on sawon* (corresponding to (*a*) above), *Beo* 513 *þær git . . .* ‖ *. . .* ‖ *glidon ofer garsecg* (corresponding to (*b*) above), and *Beo* 2152 *Het ða in beran eafor heafodsegn* (corresponding to (*c*) above).

c. *Prepositional adverbs used with transitive verbs*

§1067. When used in combination with a transitive verb, the prepositional adverb has (as we have seen above) an adverbial function. There are four positions in which it can occur in OE. First, it can immediately follow the object in clauses with the element order SVO, as in MnE 'He cut the meat up', or VSO. This arrangement is naturally more common in principal clauses, e.g. *Or* 168. 4 *þa sticode him mon þa eagan ut, BlHom* 183. 24 *Adyde þa leomu 7 þæt heafod on weg þæs sceapes, ÆGram* 174. 11 *ðas oðre lætað ðone n aweg on sopinum,* and *Exod* 1. 22 *wurpaþ hit ut on þæt wæter.* But it occurs occasionally in subordinate clauses, e.g. *ÆLS* 21. 66 *getiða me synfullum þæt ic ateo þas hringan up of ðysum hlyde* and *ÆCHom* i. 138. 15 *. . . þæt hi sceoldon him offrian ælc frumcenned hysecild, oþþe alysan hit ut mid fif scillingum* (an exception to the 'rule' that prepositional adverbs normally precede an infinitive or a participle). The prepositional adverb may have final position in the sentence, but— despite Visser, i, §668(*c*)—this is not obligatory, as is shown by some of the examples above and by others he quotes.

§1068. Second, it can immediately follow the finite verb, as in MnE 'He cut up the meat'. This order occurs in both principal and subordinate clauses, with the element orders SVO, SOV, and V(S), e.g. *ÆLS* 31. 469 *Se bisceop him togeanes bræd of his ceppan*, *BlHom* 187. 35 *þa ahof Paulus up his heafod*, *ÆCHom* i. 516. 4 *ceorf of þæt lim*, *ÆLS* 25. 381 *and hi ferdon ða to and þa fylðe adydon ut of ðam godes huse*, *ÆCHom* ii. 178. 25 *Se halga wer ða wearð astyred on mode and het oðerne munuc awurpan ut þæt glæsene fæt* (another example with the prepositional adverb not immediately preceding an infinitive), and *ÆCHom* ii. 178. 35 *swa þæt hi brudon of ðone clað*. According to Harrison (1892, p. 57), the prepositional adverb regularly follows the verb in sentences with the element order V(S) and prefers this position when the element order is SVO. Another adverb may intervene, as in *ÆHom* 14. 118 *and hy hit awurpon þa ut* and *ChronE* 145. 23 (1014) *7 let þær up þa gislas*. For further examples, see Visser, i, §668(*b*).

§1069. The third position for the prepositional adverb in OE when used in combination with a transitive verb is immediately before the verb. This arrangement, impossible in MnE—for we cannot have 'He upcut/up cut the meat'[242]—is found in both principal and subordinate clauses, e.g. *BlHom* 71. 17 *He þa . . . ut awearp þa sceomolas þara cypemanna*, *BlHom* 221. 21 *Ða wiðstodan him ða hæþenan man 7 hine mid teonan aweg adrifon*, *ÆLS* 1. 214 *Nis seo orþung þe we ut blawaþ and in ateoð*, *ÆCHom* ii. 382. 23 *oðþæt hi hine inn leton*, *ÆCHom* ii. 520. 13 *and be ðam hunde ðe his hand eft inn abær*, *ÆLS* 26. 162 *þa het se hæþena cynincg his heafod of aslean*, *ÆC Hom* ii. 74. 12 *þæt hi symle þa misweaxandan bogas of ascreadian*, and *Lch* i. 326. 14 *ic þe ofslea 7 þe þine teþ of abeate*. According to Harrison (1892, p. 57), the prepositional adverb prefers this position when the sentence has the order SOV or when the verb with which it is linked is an infinitive or a participle. For further examples see Visser, i, §668(*a*).

§1070. These three positions are also represented in the poetry, e.g.

Rid 54. 1   Hyse cwom gangan   . . .
           . . .   . . .
           . . . ,   hof his agen
           hrægl hondum up,

---

[242] There are patterns like 'He overlooked this book'. But this does not mean 'He looked over this book'. If one can say 'The ivy overgrew the tree', that is not quite the same as 'The ivy grew over the tree'. There may, however, be better examples of the third type in MnE.

GenA 148 *þæt se rica ahof* ‖ *up from eorðan*, and *Beo* 2152 *Het ða in beran eafor heafodsegn.*

§1071. The fourth position for the prepositional adverb in OE when used with a transitive verb is before both object and verb. The only example of this I have noted so far is

Sat 479   Ic on neorxnawonge   niwe asette
             treow mid telgum,   þæt ða tanas up
             æpla bæron.[243]

d. Inseparable and separable prefixes?

§1072. There is no doubt that some of these prepositional adverbs sometimes serve as inseparable prefixes. This is most obviously demonstrated by the existence of compounds of prepositional adverb + verb for which there is no corresponding use of the simple verb + the same prepositional adverb, e.g. *utlagian* 'to outlaw' and combinations of *to-* = Latin *dis-* (*OED*, s.v. *to-* prefix, 2) such as *tocweðan* 'to forbid' and *tosendan* 'to disperse',[244] or which differ in meaning from combinations involving the simple verb and the same prepositional adverb, e.g. *ChronA* 70. 7 (870) *7 þa Deniscan sige namon 7 þone cyning ofslogon* but *ÆLS* 32. 124 *þa tugon þa hæþenan þone halgan to slæge and mid anum swencge slogon him of þæt heafod.*

§1073. Supporting evidence is at first glance supplied by the position of the negative *ne* or the *to* of the inflected infinitive in relation to the prepositional adverb. Normally it immediately precedes them. So Harrison (1892, p. 58) writes: 'Therefore, whenever a particle is placed between *to* and the dat. inf. or between *ne* and the verb, or is combined in the imperative or in inverted order, there is a tendency towards composition.' Often—indeed (it seems to me) in a majority of cases—the presence of a prepositional adverb between *ne* and the verb or between *to* and the inflected infinitive is decisive evidence that the combination is an inseparable compound; compare *CP* 337. 10 *Swa se fiicbeam ofersceadað ðæt lond ðæt hit under him ne mæg gegrowan, forðæm hit sio sunne ne mot gescinan, ne he self nanne*

---

[243] A fifth possibility is seen in examples like MnE 'Up he threw the ball' and 'Up the ball went'. Like Roberts (*JEGP* 35 (1936), 476), I have not noticed this pattern in OE. But we do of course find other adverbs in an initial position followed by SV(O), e.g. *ÆCHom* i. 56. 34 *nu todæg hi underfengon Stephanum . . .* and *ÆCHom* i. 56. 30 *nu todæg se æðela cempa Stephanus . . . to heofenum ferde.*

[244] I do not understand why *ÆHomM* 14. 61 *. . . þæt ealle Medas cweðað . . . to þisre dæde* appears in BTC, s.v. *tocweþan*, with the observation 'with tmesis'; the meaning is 'agree to . . .'.

wæsðm ðærofer ne bireð . . . with *Or* 242. 6 *gefera, gefera, gemyne
þæt ðu ure gecwedrædenne 7 geferrædenne to longe ne oferbrec*
and *CP* 277. 24 *7 hio bið micle ðe ieðre to oferfeohtanne*, where the
combinations in the second and third examples seem clearly inseparable when compared with *ðærofer ne bireð* in the first. But very
occasional examples in which such intervention occurs in what cannot be described as inseparable compounds suggest that Harrison's
caution was justified. They include *Bo(B)* 20. 17 *Wenstu nu þ þe
anum þellecu hwearfung 7 þillecu unrotnes on becume 7 nanum
oðrum mode swelc ne on become, ne ær þe ne æfter þe?* (cf. *Bo*
61. 19 *forðæm hit wæs ða swiðe micel sido mid Romwarum þ þær
nane oðre an ne sæton buton þa weorðestan*). However, this problem too is largely terminological. I have discussed it at greater length
in *NM* 79 (1978), 246-7.

e. Prepositional adverbs for which an object can be understood

§1074. I turn now to those sentences in which an object for the
prepositional adverb can be understood from a preceding phrase,
clause, or sentence, e.g. *BlHom* 111. 31 *hwæt biþ hit la elles buton
flæsc seoððan se ecea dæl of biþ, þæt is seo sawl?* Such prepositional
adverbs are sometimes called postpositions, sometimes separable prefixes. I avoid the former term here for reasons given below (§1076)
and do not find it necessary to use the latter.

§1075. Once we eliminate the object from the four orders discussed
in §§1067-71, we are left with two possibilities—the prepositional
adverb may precede or follow the intransitive verb with which it is
used. Both arrangements are found in principal clauses, in clauses
introduced by *ond, ne,* and the like, and in subordinate clauses. Thus
we find the prepositional adverb preceding the verb in the second
clause in *ÆHom* 20. 232 *þæt hi comon him to, and cuðlice to
spræcon,* in *ÆHom* 21. 471 (an example in a *ne* clause), in *BlHom*
111. 31 (§1074), and in *ÆHom* 1. 204 *Ac æfter Adames gylte us
wæs seo eorðe betæht on to wunigenne on þissere worulde.*[245] With
the prepositional adverb following the verb—not necessarily imme-

---

[245] The prepositional adverb normally precedes the inflected infinitive in OE—as in this
example—whereas it follows in its MnE equivalent, e.g. 'to dwell on'. Van der Gaaf
(*EStudies*, 12 (1930), 6) gives more examples. Visser (i, §404(*d*)) gives five. In four of these
a possible object for the prepositional adverb can be understood from the context. In the
fifth it is the particle *þe.* For exceptions in what may be taken as inseparable compounds,
see §1073. Examples like *ÆCHom* ii. 158. 13 *þa begunnon hi to cidenne ærest him betwynan,* where the object of the prepositional adverb is expressed, belong to the type B
discussed in §§1077-8.

diately—we have the second sentence in *ÆHom* 3. 15 *Eft se hlaford
syððan sende oðre þeowan, micele ma him to . . . He sende þa æt
nextan his sunu to, and cwæð . . .* , *ÆHom* 5. 143 *cume to and
drince*, *ÆLS* 32. 116 *Hi scuton þa mid gafelucum—swilce him to
gamenes—to*, *LS* 8. 149 *þa ferdon hi to*, *ÆLS* 25. 381 *and hi ferdon
ða to*, and *BlHom* 33. 27 *þeah we beotiaþ to.*

f. Postpositions: prepositional adverbs which follow
a possible object

§1076. A second situation in which the terminological difficulties
discussed in §1074 arise is in sentences in which a possible object—
a noun, a demonstrative, a personal pronoun, or the relative particle *þe*—occurs in the same clause or sentence *before* the prepositional adverb, e.g. *ÆHom* 20. 232 . . . *þæt hi comon him to*, where
to has been variously called a 'preposition' (objected to on etymologi-
cal grounds, though no one now objects to the appearance of 'subjunctives' in principal clauses), a 'postposition', or a 'separable prefix';
cf. *tocumendum* in *Mart2* 168. 25 . . . *þæt he for godes lufon eode to
reordum mid þam tocumendum mannum.* The last two prejudge the
issue. But I propose to use the term 'postposition' here, restricting it
to those prepositional adverbs which follow (directly or not, as the
case may be) a word which they may govern and using it without the
implication that, if they do govern it, they govern it directly rather
than as part of the verb. The 'governed' word may be a noun, a pronoun, or an adverb such as *her, þær*, and the like.

§1077. As Wende (pp. 82-103) notes, such postpositions can occur
in one of three positions in relation to the word they may govern and
to the verb with which they may be associated. These can be characterized as follows (with *him* representing any governed word):

A. . . . *him (. . .) to (. . .) com* (Wende's type A; see also Visser, i,
§402(*b*));

B. . . . *com (. . .) him (. . .) to* (Wende's type B; Visser (i. 396 fn.
1) quotes one example);

C. . . . *him (. . .) com (. . .) to* (Wende's type C;[246] Visser (i,
§402) mentions it in passing).

For convenience, I adopt Wende's system. So too does Timmer (1934,
pp. 93-8), who gives more examples from *Gregory's Dialogues.*

---

[246] Wende actually characterizes this as *him (. . .) com to* (p. 82). But there are in the
prose examples in which a complement or an object intervenes between the verb and the
postposition, and in the poetry examples of intervention of nouns and/or adverbs between
the same two elements; for details see *NM* 79 (1978), 248 fn. 12. So *him (. . .) com (. . .) to*
seems better as a general shorthand.

§1078. None of these patterns is acceptable in MnE, where we can say only 'He looked at her', not 'He her at looked', 'He looked her at', or 'He her looked at'.[247] But they occur in OE prose and poetry, both without other elements intervening—e.g. (type A) *ÆCHom* i. 12. 33 *and him to cwæð* and *Beo* 671 *Ða he him of dyde isern-byrnan*; (type B) *ÆCHom* ii. 314. 26 *and wit cumað him to* and *Wan* 46 *gesihð him biforan fealwe wegas*; (type C) *ÆCHom* i. 332. 1 *Se heahfæder Abraham him cwæð to* and *Beo* 1396 *swa ic þe wene to* —and with other elements intervening—e.g. (type A) *ÆCHom* i. 32. 19 *to ðan swiðe þæt him eal middangeard to beah* and *Beo* 909 *se þe him bealwa to bote gelyfde*; (type B) *ÆCHom* ii. 414. 27 *Hwæt ða Hermogenes se dry clypode him deoflu to* and *Beo* 1626 *Eodon him þa togeanes*; and (type C) *ÆCHom* ii. 134. 26 *him com ða ridende to sum arwurðe ridda* and *JDay i* 18 *Him biþ fyr ongean*. I discuss and exemplify these patterns at greater length in *NM* 79 (1978), 248-55. But it may be said here that in the prose the three types tend to occur in the kinds of clause we should expect:

type A—*him (. . .) to (. . .) com*—(which seems to be most common) in clauses introduced by *ond* or *ac* and in subordinate clauses;

type B—*com (. . .) him (. . .) to*—in independent commands, prohibitions, and exclamations, not introduced by *ond* or *ac*;

and type C—*him (. . .) com (. . .) to* (which occurs least often) in principal clauses.

g. Conclusion

§1079. To sum up, we may note the following general tendencies:

prepositions before nouns, demonstratives, interrogatives, the relatives *se* and *'seþe*;

postpositions after *her* and *þær*; the relatives *þe* and *se'þe*;

prepositions before and postpositions after personal pronouns.

Exceptions and qualifications have been noted in the appropriate sections above or in *NM* 79 (1978), 240-57. The basic contrast is neatly illustrated in the following sentences: *ÆCHom* i. 118. 29 *to urum eðele . . . , þe we to gesceapene wæron*, *ÆCHom* i. 162. 19 *to urum eðele, þær we to gesceapene wæron*, and *ÆCHom* ii. 58. 21 *Crist gewat on ðære rode, and his side wearð mid spere geopenad, and of ðære fleowon þa gerynu þe his gelaðung wearð mid gesceapen him to clænre bryde*.

---

[247] 'He read it through' could perhaps be described as a MnE example of type B; cf. 'He read through it'. But 'He saw it through' does not mean 'He saw through it'.

§1080. As I point out in *NM* 79 (1978), 255-7, no resolution is possible of the terminological problem posed in the clumsy heading I felt forced to adopt. We have reached the boundaries where the kingdoms of the preposition, the adverb, the separable prefix, and the inseparable prefix, meet and melt into one another. We had better be *micle mearcstapan* here, not insisting on any one of the four terms for any particular example or pattern, but recognizing that, as Campbell puts it (*OEG*, §78), 'we have in fact a system of separable verbs like those of Dutch and German'—in embryo, at any rate. How best to deal with these problems in future dictionaries and glossaries remains a difficulty; see again *NM* 79 (1978), 255-7.

15. VERBAL RECTION

a. Introductory remarks

§1081. Even in a well-conducted language like classical Latin, the rules governing verbal rection were not completely consistent; for examples see GL, §§339, 346, and 376. They are much less so in OE. No doubt the fact that the case-endings in many nouns were no longer distinctive (see §§9 and 12) has something to do with this. Both phenomena, indeed, herald the lessening importance of case and the increasing reliance on element order and prepositions in English.

§1082. Certain broad tendencies—some of them, of course, apparent in Latin too—may, however, be noted. The accusative is primarily the case of the direct object; on this, see §§1255-9 and Visser, i, §§418-666. Verbs expressing emotion or mental state, desiring or needing, giving or refusing, gaining or losing, touching and testing, possessing and ruling, enjoying and using, caring or neglecting, remembering or forgetting, often take the genitive.[248] The dative frequently appears—with reference to the person affected or interested—as the sole object of verbs of helping or harming, serving or resisting, pleasing or displeasing, liking or disliking, and believing or disbelieving. It also occurs after verbs of addressing and answering, and after certain impersonal verbs. Visser (i, §§316-24) discusses

---

[248] Shipley (pp. 14-20) attempts an elaborate classification of verbs which take the genitive. But he has to admit that there are exceptions. Visser, who uses the term 'causative object' in preference to 'genitive object' (i, §§370-1), divides his list of verbs which take the genitive into fourteen groups (i, §§378-92). His discussion of the later disappearance of 'the "causative object" in the genitive' (i, §§373-7) is marred by an unhappy use of evidence from the Paris and Junius Psalters; see Davis, *RES* 17 (1966), 73-4.

these verbs and gives an alphabetical list of them.[249] Prepositional phrases may replace case forms, e.g. *Beo* 450 *no ðu ymb mines ne þearft* || *lices feorme leng sorgian* and

GenA 2424   ac him to sende
        stiðmod cyning   strange twegen
        aras sine.

Phrases of similar meaning to simple verbs may, of course, take the same case, e.g. *Beo* 201 *þa him wæs manna þearf, Beo* 562 *Næs hie ðære fylle gefean hæfdon,* and *Beo* 2682 *Him þæt gifeðe ne wæs....* Further examples can readily be found by consulting Visser, i, pp. ix-xxii.

§1083. We turn now to verbs of double rection. A few verbs may take a double accusative. Visser's list (i, §§698-9) supplements that given by Wülfing (i, §117). Examples include *CP* 291. 21 ... *oðerne he lærde geðyld, CP* 385. 2 *siððan he his cnihtas gelæred hæfde ðone cræft ðæs lareowdomes ... , BlHom* 131. 29 *Se Halga Gast hie æghwylc god lærde ... , ÆCHom* ii. 178. 16 *An subdiacon bæd þone halgan wer sumne dæl eles ... ,* and

Beo 3079   Ne meahton we gelæran   leofne þeoden,
        rices hyrde   ræd ænigne,
        þæt he ne grette   goldweard þone,
        lete hyne licgean,   þær he longe wæs,
        wicum wunian   oð woruldende.

To be distinguished from these are sentences in which the second accusative serves as a 'predicative adjunct', e.g. *ChronA* 106. 1 (931) *Her mon hadode Byrnstan bisceop to Wintanceastre, Gen* 17. 5 ... *for þam ðe ic þe gesette manegra þeoda fæder, ÆCHom* ii. 102. 27 *God gesette ðone welegan dælere on his godum,* and

And 1647   þær se ar godes   anne gesette,
        wisfæstne wer,   wordes gleawne,
        in þære beorhtan byrig   bisceop þam leodum,
        ond gehalgode   fore þam heremægene
        þurh apostolhad,   Platan nemned,
        þeodum on þearfe.

Visser (i, §§645-59) gives more examples including those with an adjectival second element, e.g. *Josh(L)* 8. 23 *ðone cyning hi brohton cucenne to Iosue.* (The treatment promised by Wülfing (i, §117) never appeared.) In *ÆCHom* ii. 108. 24 ... *La leof, hwænne gesawe*

[249] Visser also discusses what he calls the 'transitivation' in later English of verbs which in OE take the genitive or dative; see Visser, i. 97 ff., 127 ff., 280 ff., and 411 ff.

*we ðe hungrine, oððe ðurstine, oððe cuman, oþþe nacodne, oððe
geuntrumodne* . . . *?*, we have a noun *cuman* in the midst of a series
of adjectives. But examples with two nouns are not numerous and
some are doubtful—*ChronA* 106. 1 above may be an example of
apposition ('Bishop Byrnstan was consecrated to Winchester' rather
than 'Byrnstan was consecrated Bishop of Winchester') and

GenA 1719   þa þæs mæles wæs   mearc agongen
                 þæt him Abraham   idese brohte,
                 wif to hame,   þær he wic ahte,
                 fæger and freolic

may be an example of poetic variation. On the predicative accusative,
see further §3767. There are, of course, alternative constructions
with *for*, e.g. *WHom* 12. 17 . . . *þæt hy wurðedon him for godas þa
sunnan 7 ðone monan*, with *for* and *swa*, e.g.

Met 26. 42   Cuð is wide
                 þæt on ða tide   þeoda æghwilc
                 hæfdon heora hlaford   for ðone hehstan god,
                 and weorðodon   swa swa wuldres cining,
                 gif he to ðæm rice wæs   on rihte boren,

with *swa (swa)*, e.g. *Luke(WSCp)* 15. 19 *do me swa anne of þinum
yrðlingum* and *Ps(P)* 43. 13 *þu us geþafodest him to metsianne, swa
swa sceap*, and—a characteristic OE construction—with *to*, e.g. *Or*
88. 7 *7 genamon anne earmne mon him to consule, ChronA* 64. 29
(853) *7 he hine to cyninge gehalgode, Bede* 166. 27 *þa het se papa
hine to biscope gehalgian* (MS *B* has *hadigean to bysceope*),

PPs 104. 16   Sende him soð cyning   sweotule are,
                 alysde hine lungre   and hine þam leodum þa
                 to ealdormen   eallum sette,

PPs 104. 17 *He sette hine on his huse to hlafwearde*, and (with a
double accusative followed by a *to*- phrase) *ÆCHom* i. 390. 23 *þæt
bilewite scep ða gefullode ðone arleasan Saulum, and worhte hine
arfæstne Paulum. He gefullode ðone wulf and geworhte to lambe.*
(Here *hine* is not expressed after *geworhte*; see §1577.) According to
QW (pp. 60–1) ' "double objects", as in Mod.E. "they crowned her
queen", are expressed in OE as an accus. and a *to*-phrase'. But the
examples with *for* and *swa* and those with a double accusative already
quoted—to which can be added passive examples like *Bede* 62. 26
. . . *se halga wer Agustinus* . . . *wæs gehalgod ærcebiscop Ongolþeode*
and *ÆCHom* ii. 136. 22 *and he* . . . *wearð geset cumena ðen*, which
must be based on active forms with double accusatives (see §837)—
show that the idiom with *to* had rivals in OE. See further Visser, i,
§§660–6.

§1084. The most common verbs of double rection are those which take the accusative of the direct object and the dative of the indirect. These need not be exemplified here; the first clause in *ÆCHom* i. 250. 7 (§1085) will serve. Visser (i, §§682-95) gives a list of them.

§1085. Verbs of accusing and the like, of asking, and of depriving, often take the accusative of the person and the genitive of the thing, e.g. *Bede* 168. 20 *7 hine his rices benom*, *ÆCHom* i. 250. 7 *Hwilc fæder wile syllan his cilde stan, gif hit hine hlafes bitt?*, and *GenB* 581 *Tyhð me untryowða*. See Visser, i, §§678-9, for further examples. Alongside this construction we sometimes find the accusative of the person and the dative of the thing with verbs of depriving, e.g. *GD* 254. 10 . . . *þæt hi hine sceoldon þy heafde beheawan*, *LS* 23. 216 *He þa fæstlice swa dyde swa heo bebead hine þam scyccelse ongyrede*, and *Beo* 679 *forþan ic hine sweorde swebban nelle, ‖ aldre beneotan*; see further Visser, i, §§680-1.

§1086. Verbs of thanking, giving, refusing, and taking from, may take the genitive of the thing and the dative of the person, e.g. *Or* 98. 30 . . . *næs na for þæm þe hie him ænigra goda uþen*, *ÆCHom* i. 400. 13 *ðanca Gode ðinre gesundfulnysse*, and *Beo* 1225 *Ic þe an tela ‖ sincgestreona*. Visser (i, §§676-7) gives more examples. An alternative after verbs of taking away is the accusative of the thing and the dative of the person, e.g. *GD(C)* 69. 25 . . . *þæt heo hæfde henna . . . ac þa hire afyrrde 7 bereafode an fox*, *BlHom* 131. 29 *Se Halga Gast . . . him æghwylc yfel bewerede*, and *Jul* 499 *ond þa forman men, ‖ Adam ond Aeue, þam ic ealdor oðþrong*. Visser (i, §§696-7) makes rather heavy weather of explaining this and his alleged examples do not all conform.

§1087. To these we may add verbs which take the dative + a preposition, e.g. *CP* 143. 22 *Ac ða recceras ðe hira agnes gilpes giernað, ðæm hie geðafigað ðyllic ðe hie ondrædað ðæt him derian mæge æt ðæm gielpe* and *WHom* 13. 105 *þonne beorge we us sylfum wið ece wite*; the accusative + a preposition, e.g. *Or* 34. 32 . . . *þæs þe he hi æt hungre ahredde*, *Or* 156. 1 *þa he hie ascade his godas hwæþer heora sceolde on oþrum sige habban . . .*, *BlHom* 65. 12 *forþon þe hie næfre forgifenesse æt Gode ne biddaþ*, and *BlHom* 177. 23 *7 wiþ heora folc rihte feala worhte*; or two prepositions, e.g. *Bede* 4. 16 *7 eac ymb þara biscopa lif 7 forþfore we geacsodan fram þam broðrum þæs mynstres*. Visser (i, §§700-9) has examples and discussion of these verbs.

§1088. Phrases of similar meaning to verbs of double rection may govern the same cases, e.g. *Bo* 142. 9 *þæm he geaf micle gife freo-domes* and *ChristC* 1212 *Hy þæs eðles þonc* || *hyra waldende wita ne cuþon.* Triple rections are, of course, possible, e.g. *Bo* 126. 25 *gif him God abrit of þam mode þ dysig þ hit ær mid oferwrigen was,* *ÆCHom* i. 88. 32 *Nelle we ðas race na leng teon . . . ac biddað eow þingunge æt þysum unscæððigum martyrum,* and

Jud 83   Ic ðe, frymða god   ond frofre gæst,
           bearn alwaldan,   biddan wylle
           miltse þinre   me þearfendre,
           ðrynesse ðrym.

§1089. However, as a glance at my List of verbal rections (§1092) will show, anyone who tries to erect these tendencies into elaborate and rigid schemes of classification will not get far; even Visser's lists sometimes make things seem more regular than they really are. For the fact is that the same verb can take different constructions not only in the works of different writers or in different places in the works of the same writers, but even in the same sentence. Thus Ælfric—admittedly before he translated the *Grammar* and learnt better habits—could write *ÆCHom* i. 66. 10 *he gymð grædelice his teolunge, his gafoles, his gebytlu* (but perhaps we should read *ge-bytla?*) and *ÆCHom* i. 158. 20 *Ne bæd se blinda naðor ne goldes ne seolfres ne nane woruldlice ðing, ac bæd his gesihðe,* and we find in the non-Ælfrician 'Seven Sleepers' *LS* 34. 110 *se fæder wiðsoc his bearne and þæt bearn wiðsoc þone fæder and æt nextan ælc freond wiðsoc oðres.* Schabram (pp. 42-3) quotes more examples.

§1090. Nevertheless, the proper treatment of the passive (§§744-858) demands that we distinguish the following types of verbs:
    (1) those which take a direct object in the accusative only;
    (2) those with the double accusative *or* an accusative and a noun clause or infinitive;
    (3) those with an accusative *and* a genitive, dative or preposition;
    (4) those with a noun clause or infinitive *and* a genitive, dative, or preposition;
    (5) those which take *either* an accusative *or* a genitive, dative, or preposition;
    (6) those with a genitive and/or a dative;
    (7) those which can take only a preposition.
But it must not be forgotten that some verbs will straddle even these groups. Examples are *forwyrnan* and *ofteon,* discussed in §857. Even so, I think it neither necessary nor wise to scrap this purely

syntactical classification in favour of that proposed by Visser (i, §315), which hovers uneasily between division on syntactical and on semantic grounds. It is quite clear, for example, that what he calls the 'causative object' could be expressed in OE by the dative or by a preposition, as well as by the genitive, to which he seems to restrict it (i, §370). He tacitly admits the inadequacy of his own classification by introducing the so-called 'ablative object' (i, §680).

b. *List of verbal rections*

(1) *Notes*

§1091. Compound verbs are grouped together in the alphabetical position of the second element; thus *ge-hieran, hieran, mis-hieran*, and *ofer-hieran*, will be found together under *h*. The following are not included:

(1) verbs which take the accusative only (on these see Wülfing, i, §§97–118);

(2) the purely accusative senses of verbs which take the accusative in some senses, but the genitive, dative, or instrumental, in others;

(3) verbs taking the accusative of 'direct object' and the dative of 'indirect object', agent or instrument, accompaniment, or the like, e.g. *betæcan, opiewan* 'to show', and *slean*. Visser (i, §682) gives a list of 'the principal verbs which take this . . . construction';

(4) verbs taking the dative of 'indirect object' or 'advantage', e.g. *oncweðan* and *opiewan* 'to appear'. Visser (i, §323) gives 'a fairly comprehensive list' of verbs which take the dative;

(5) verbs taking the accusative of 'direct object' and a prepositional phrase, e.g. *adælan*. Visser (i, §701) gives a list of such verbs;

(6) verbs which take only a prepositional phrase (or prepositional phrases) and/or a noun clause and/or an infinitive, e.g. *higian*.

Apart from these exceptions, and from the point discussed in §1080, the list aims at completeness. I hope the inevitable omissions will not greatly impair its usefulness. So far, time has not permitted a study of the comparative frequency of the various constructions or of such questions as whether one particular usage occurs in prose, poetry, and glosses, or is limited to one or two of these. This can, I suppose, be said to be the job of the lexicographer. An important article for that purpose is the one on types of object in OE by V. N. Žigadlo in *Učenye zapiski Leningradskogo gosudarstvennogo universiteta*, 233, vyp. 36 (Germanskoe jazykoznanie) (Leningrad, 1958), 68–87. The evidence is cited only when it does not appear in BT(S, C), GK, Wülfing (i, §§11–42, 66–79, 97–118, and 124), or Shipley. This list was in manuscript form before Visser, i, appeared.

I have made some additions with its help and gratefully acknowledge my debt here. But he is not always right, e.g. on his p. 375
misgiman governs *sceare*, which could be accusative.

(2) *Alphabetical List*

§1092. Here s.o. = 'someone', s.t. = 'something'.

agan possess s.t. (acc., gen., e.g. *HomU*
46. 294. 32)

æmtian devote oneself (acc.) to s.t.
(dat.)

ge-æmtian free oneself (acc.) of s.t.
(gen.)

ærendian, ge-ærendian go on an errand
(acc., gen.) for s.o. (dat.) to s.o.
(prep. *to*)

andwyrdan (i) answer s.o. (dat.); (ii)
answer s.t. (acc.) to s.o. (dat.)

anþracian lament s.t. (gen.)

arian, ge-arian honour, show mercy to,
s.o. or s.t. (acc., dat.)

ascian ask s.o. (acc., dat., prep. *æt*) for
s.t. (acc., gen., prep. *æfter, be*)

be-ascian ask s.o. (acc.) for advice
(dat.)

bacan bake s.t. (acc., gen. in *HomU*
35. 224. 2)

bædan, a-bædan, ge-bædan (i) urge,
compel, s.o. (acc.); (ii) require, demand, s.t. (gen.)

for-bærnan burn up s.t. (acc., gen. in
GD 219. 16)

basnian wait for s.t. (gen.)

beatan (i) beat s.o. or s.t. (acc.); (ii)
beat on (dat., e.g. *Dan* 265)

belgan, a-belgan, ge-belgan anger s.o.
(acc., dat.)

bensian pray to s.o. (acc.) for s.t.
(gen.)

*beodan, a-beodan, be-beodan, ge-
beodan* command, announce, offer,
give, commit, s.t. (acc.) to s.o.
(dat.)

for-beodan forbid s.t. (acc.) to s.o.
(dat.)

mis-beodan do wrong to, offend, s.o.
(dat.)

beorgan, be-beorgan, ge-beorgan save,
protect, defend, s.o. or s.t. (dat.)
against s.t. (acc., prep. *wiþ*)

for-beran bear patiently s.t. (acc.)
from s.o. (dat.)

æt-berstan escape from s.o. or s.t.
(acc., dat.)

bicnan, bicnian make a sign to s.o.
(dat., prep. *to*)

bidan, a-bidan, ge-bidan wait for s.t.
(acc., gen.)

on-bidan wait for s.t. (gen.)

biddan, a-biddan, ge-biddan ask, pray,
s.o. (acc., prep. *æt, of* (*Bede* 162.
21; see § 2564), *to*) for s.t. (gen.,
acc.: note *ÆCHom* i. 158. 20) for
s.o. (dat., prep. *for*)

a-biddan get by asking (same constructions)

ge-biddan say one's prayers (refl. acc.,
dat.) to s.o. (prep. *to*)

an(d)bidian, ge-an(d)bidian wait for
s.t. (acc., gen.)

bisenian, bysnian, ge-bysnian give an
example to s.o. (dat.) of s.t. (prep.
to)

bismerian reproach, revile, s.o. (usually acc., sometimes dat.)

a-bitan, on-bitan taste, partake of, s.t.
(gen.)

blinnan, a-blinnan, ge-blinnan cease
from s.t. (gen.)

blissian (i) rejoice at s.t. (gen., prep.
on); (ii) gladden s.o. (acc., dat.)

efen-blissian rejoice at s.t. (gen.)

boeta acquire s.t. (gen.): see *Matt(Li)*
18. 15

bon boast of s.t. (gen. in *Vain* 28)

bregdan change s.t. (usually acc., occasionally dat., e.g. *PPs* 138. 9 and
Met 13. 47)

a-bregdan move s.t. (acc., dat.) quickly

æt-bregdan take s.o. or s.t. (acc.) from
s.o. or s.t. (dat., prep. *fram, of*)

ge-bregdan unsheath s.t. (acc., dat.,
instr.)

on-bregdan move s.t. (acc. or dat.)
quickly

to-bregdan start from sleep (dat.). See
also *Max i* 190

wiþ-bregdan restrain s.o. or s.t. (dat.)
from s.t. (gen., prep. *fram*)

brucan, ge-brucan enjoy, use, s.t. or
s.o. (gen., acc., dat.)

brycian, brycsian do good to s.o. or
s.t. (dat.)

ge-buan dwell (intr. or with refl. dat.)

a-bugan bow to s.o. (dat., prep. *to*)

for-bugan avoid s.o. or s.t. (acc., dat.)

on-bugan submit to s.o. (dat., prep. *to*)

byrgan, a-byrgan, ge-byrgan, on-byrgan
eat, taste, s.t. (acc., gen.). *Note*: (i)
simplex *byrgan* prefers acc.; (ii) *ge-
byrgan* is recorded with prep. *of, to*

ge-byrian (i) happen to s.o. (dat.); (ii)
for s.o. (dat.) to be concerned with
s.t. (prep. *to*); (iii) belong to, be
appropriate to, behove, s.o. (dat.)

bysgian, a-bysgian, ge-bysgian occupy,
trouble, s.o. (acc.) with s.t. (gen.,
prep. *betwix, mid, on, ymbe*)

campian, ge-campian fight for s.o. or
s.t. (dat. or prep. *for*)

ceapian buy, pay for, s.t. (gen., acc.,
e.g. *Or* 228. 20)

be-ceorfan deprive s.o. (acc.) of s.t.
(dat.) by cutting

ceosan choose s.o. or s.t. (acc., gen.)
for s.o. (dat.)

cepan, be-cepan, ge-cepan be heedful
of, attend to, desire, look out for,
take, s.o. or s.t. (gen., acc. (see
ÆCHom i. 580. 28))

cidan, ge-cidan rebuke s.o. (dat., prep.
ongean, wið)

ge-cigan summon s.o. (acc., but dat.
found in *Li*)

ge-clifian stick to s.t. (dat., prep. *to*)

costian, ge-costian, costnian, ge-costnian
tempt, test, s.o. or s.t. (acc., gen.)

cuman (+ dat., see BTS, s.v. *cuman*
VIII)

be-cuman happen to s.o. (pers. and impers.: dat., prep. *ofer, on, to*)

be-cuman behove s.o. (acc. See BTS,
s.v. *becuman* III)

for-cuman overcome s.t. (acc., dat. in
PPs 73. 13)

ofer-cuman overcome s.o. or s.t. (acc.
only; see §1406)

cunnan have knowledge of s.t. (acc.,
gen., prep. *on*)

on-cunnan accuse s.o. (acc.) of s.t.
(gen., prep. *be, for*)

cunnian, ge-cunnian make trial of s.o.
or s.t. (acc., gen.)

cweman, ge-cweman please, satisfy,
s.o. (dat.)

mis-cweman displease s.o. (dat.?)

mis-cweþan curse s.o. (dat.)

wiþ-cweþan (i) reply to s.o. (dat.); (ii)
contradict s.o. (dat.); (iii) refuse s.t.
(acc., gen.) to s.o. (dat.); (iv) oppose, refuse, forbid, s.t. (dat.)

be-dælan (i) deprive s.o. (acc.) of s.t.
(gen., dat., prep. *be*); (ii) free s.o.
(acc.) from s.t. (gen., dat., prep. *be*)

ge-dafenian be becoming to, behove,
s.o. or s.t. (pers. and impers.: dat.)

deman, ge-deman (i) judge s.o. (acc.,
dat.); (ii) celebrate s.t. (dat.)

derian, ge-derian hurt, damage, s.o. or
s.t. (dat.: for late acc., see BTS, s.v.
derian)

be-diglian hide s.o. or s.t. (acc.) from
s.o. (dat.)

don make s.o. (dat., e.g. *PPs* 82. 8) as
s.t. (dat.)

wel-don satisfy s.o. (dat.)

on-drædan (i) fear s.t. (acc., gen., prep.
from); (ii) be afraid. Found in both
meanings with and without refl. dat.

dreccan afflict, torment, s.o. (acc., dat.)

drincan drink s.t. (acc., gen.)

ofer-drincan overdrink oneself (refl.
acc.) of s.t. (gen., prep. *fram*)

on-drincan drink of s.t. (gen.)

dryman rejoice in s.o. (dat.)

dugan, dygan be of use to, benefit, s.o.
(dat.)

a-dumbian remain silent about s.t. (?
gen.; see Visser, i, §390)

dwelian, ge-dwelian, dwellan, ge-dwellan
(i) go astray from s.t. (gen., prep.
fram, mid, of); (ii) lead s.o. (acc.)
astray from s.t. (gen., prep. *of*)

dyrnan, be-dyrnan conceal s.t. (acc.)
from s.o. (dat.)

eahtan, ehtan, ehtian persecute, pursue,
s.o. (acc., gen.)

earmian cause pity in s.o. (pers. and impers.: dat.)

earnian, ge-earnian labour for, strive after, deserve, earn, s.t. (acc., gen., prep. *æfter*) of s.o. (prep. *to*)

ge-eaþmedan worship, adore, s.o. (acc., occasionally dat.)

efestan strive after, undertake, s.t. (gen.)

efnetan eat as much as s.o.?, imitate? (dat. in *Rid* 40. 63)

eglan, æt-eglan, ge-eglan, eglian, ge-eglian trouble, pain, grieve, s.o. (pers. or impers.: dat.)

elcian delay s.t. (gen., prep. *ongean, to*)

etan eat s.t. (acc., gen.)

fægnian, ge-fægnian, fagnian, ge-fagnian rejoice at s.t. (gen., dat., prep. *for, on*). See Stanley, *NM* 72 (1971), 405, and my §1339 fn.

fæstan abstain from s.t. (gen., prep. *from*)

fandian, a-fandian, ge-fandian try, tempt, examine, seek for, s.o. or s.t. (acc., gen., dat.)

oð-feallan fall away from, fail, s.o. (dat.)

feligean follow s.o. or s.t. (dat.)

felan, ge-felan feel, perceive, touch, s.o. or s.t. (gen.)

æt-felgan adhere to, cling to, s.o. or s.t. (dat.)

æt-feolan adhere to, stick to, s.o. or s.t. (dat.)

be-feolan (i) apply oneself to s.t. (dat.); (ii) press, be urgent with, s.o. (dat.)

ge-feolan (i) stick to, adhere to, s.o. or s.t. (dat.); (ii) continue in s.t. (dat.)

wiþ-feolan apply oneself to s.t. (dat.)

ge-feon rejoice at s.t. (gen., dat., instr., prep. *æfter, for, in, on*)

efen-ge-feon rejoice together at s.t. (gen.)

æt-fleon escape from s.t. (dat.) to s.t. (prep. *to*)

be-fleon flee from s.t. (acc., dat., prep. *fram*)

oð-fleon flee from s.o. or s.t. (dat.)

folgian follow, obey, s.o. or s.t. (acc., dat.)

fon get, gain, grasp, attack, s.o. or s.t. (acc., gen., dat., prep. *on, to*, etc.)

a-fon receive s.t. (acc., gen.)

mis-fon fail to take, mistake, s.t. (gen., instr.)

on-fon take, receive, accept, s.o. or s.t. (acc., gen., dat.)

under-fon receive s.t. (acc., gen.)

wiþ-fon lay hold on s.o. (dat.)

forhtian fear s.o. or s.t. (acc., gen., prep. *for, on*)

framian, fremian, fromian profit, avail, s.o. or s.t. (dat., prep. *to*)

frasian tempt s.o. (gen.)

fremman do s.t. (acc., gen., in *Or* 168. 17; on *HomU* 45. 291. 18, see §2316)

ge-freogan free s.o. (acc.) from s.t. (gen., prep. *fram, of*)

ge-freolsian free s.o. (acc.) from s.t. (?gen. or dat. in *Bo* 144. 9, prep. *of*)

freoþian, ge-freoþian, friþian, ge-friþian protect s.o. or s.t. (acc., dat.) from s.t. (gen.)

friclan desire s.t. (gen.)

frignan, be-frignan, ge-frignan (i) ask s.o. (acc.) about s.t. (gen., prep. *æfter, be, fram, of, ymb*); (ii) ask s.t. (acc.) of s.o. (gen., prep. *æt, fram*)

frodian make s.o. wise (dat. in *Rim* 32)

lust-fullian, ge-lust-fullian: see under the letter *l*

fultuman, -ian, ge-fultuman, -ian help, support, s.o. or s.t. (dat.). But see §851

fylgan, æfter-fylgan, full-fylgan, ge-fylgan, ofer-fylgan follow, pursue, s.o. or s.t. (acc., dat.)

fyllan, a-fyllan, ge-fyllan fill s.t. (acc.) with s.t. (gen., dat., instr., prep. *mid, of*. In *GenA* 1613 and 2161 ?acc.)

fylstan, ge-fylstan help s.o. (dat.)

ge-fysan make s.o. (acc.) ready for s.t. (gen., dat.)

gælan, a-gælan hinder, delay, s.o. (acc.) from s.t. (gen.)

ful(l)-gan, ful(l)-gangan, ful-ge-gan perform, fulfil, follow, s.o. or s.t. (dat., gen.)

ge-gan, ge-gangan get into the keeping or power of s.o. (dat.)

geocian preserve, save, s.o. or s.t. (gen. or dat.)

geornian: see *giernan*

for-giefan (i) forgive s.t. (acc.) to s.o. (dat.); (ii) forgive s.o. (dat.)

gieman take care of s.o. or s.t. (acc., gen., prep. *in, ymb*)

be-gieman care for s.o. or s.t. (acc., gen.)

for-gieman neglect s.t. (acc., ?gen. in *Beo* 1751)

giernan ask for, desire, s.t. (gen., prep. *æfter, to*)

on-gierwan strip s.o. (acc.) of s.t. (gen., dat., instr.)

be-gietan acquire, obtain, s.t. (acc., gen.)

for-gietan, ofer-gietan forget, neglect, s.o. or s.t. (acc., gen.)

on-gietan perceive, understand, s.t. (acc., gen.)

on-gildan (i) pay for, be punished for, s.t. (acc., gen.); (ii) pay with s.t. (gen.)

gilpan boast of, glory in, s.t. (gen., instr., prep. *for*)

un-girwan divest s.o. (acc.) of s.t. (gen.)

ofer-gitolian overlook, forget, s.t. (acc., ?gen.; see Visser, i. 376)

gitsian covet, desire, s.t. (gen., dat.)

ge-gladian reconcile s.o. (acc.) to s.o. (dat.)

godian enrich s.o. (dat. in *Rim* 32)

gramian be offensive to, vex, s.o. (dat.)

be-grindan deprive s.o. (acc.) of s.t. (dat.)

for-grindan destroy, crush, s.o. (acc., dat.)

for-gripan destroy s.o. or s.t. (dat.)

wiþ-gripan grapple with s.o. (dat.)

habban (i) have, etc. s.t. (acc., gen.: see §1342 and Schabram, p. 42); (ii) consider as of s.t. (gen.: see BTS, s.v. *habban* XII(1))

for-habban abstain from s.t. (dat., prep. *from*)

wiþ-habban hold out against, withstand, resist, s.t. (dat., prep. *fram*)

ge-hælan heal s.o. (acc.) from s.t. (gen., prep. *fram*)

hatan command s.o. (acc., dat.) to do s.t.

ge-hatan promise s.o. (dat.) s.t. (acc., gen.)

hawian look at, observe, s.t. (acc., gen., prep. *on, to*)

healdan do s.t. (dat.) for s.o. (dat.)

hearmian harm s.o. or s.t. (dat.)

be-heawan deprive s.o. (acc.) of s.t. (dat.)

hedan care for, pay attention to, s.t. (gen., acc.)

helan conceal s.t. (acc.) from s.o. (dat., prep. *fram, wiþ*)

for-helan conceal s.t. (acc.) from s.o. (dat.)

helpan, a-helpan, ge-helpan help s.o. (gen., dat.)

hentan pursue, follow, s.o. or s.t. (gen., prep. *æfter*)

heofan lament, be sorry for, s.t. (acc., gen.)

heorcnian listen to s.o. or s.t. (acc., gen., dat.)

hieran, ge-hieran (i) obey s.o. or s.t. (dat.); (ii) hear s.t. (acc.)

mis-hieran disobey s.o. or s.t. (dat.)

ofer-hieran neglect, disobey, s.o. or s.t. (acc., dat.)

hiersumian, ge-hiersumian obey, serve, s.o. or s.t. (dat.)

hleotan obtain s.t. (acc., gen., dat.) by lot

hliehhan (i) laugh at s.o. or s.t. (acc., gen., prep. *ofer, on*); (ii) smile at s.o. (dat.)

hligan give s.o. (acc.) a reputation for s.t. (gen.)

hlosnian listen to, wait for, s.o. or s.t. (gen., prep. *be*)

hlystan, ge-hlystan listen to, obey, s.o. (gen., dat.)

under-hnigan submit to s.o. or s.t. (acc., dat.)

be-hofian (i) to have need of s.t. (gen.); (ii) (impers.) behove, concern, s.o. (dat.)

hogian: see *hycgan*

hopian have confidence in, watch for, s.o. or s.t. (acc., gen., prep. *on, to*)

hreddan, a-hreddan rescue s.o. (acc.) from s.t. (gen., dat., prep. *æt, fram, of, on, wiþ*) *hreman* exult in s.t. (gen. or dat. in *Brun* 39)

ge-hreofan strip s.o. (acc.) of a garment (gen. in *Mark(Li)* 15. 20)

hreowan, ge-hreowan affect s.o. (acc., dat.) with sorrow, pity, at s.t. (acc., gen.)

of-hreowan (i) cause pity, regret, to s.o. (dat.); (ii) (impers.) cause grief to s.o. (dat.) in respect of s.t. (gen.)

hreowsian, be-hreowsian grieve for, lament for, s.o. or s.t. (acc., gen., prep. *for*)

hrinan, ge-hrinan touch, reach, strike, s.o. or s.t. (acc., gen., dat.)

æt-hrinan touch s.o. or s.t. (acc., gen., dat.)

on-hrinan touch s.o. or s.t. (gen., dat.)

oþ-hrinan touch s.o. or s.t. (gen., dat., ?acc.)

hwopan threaten s.o. (dat.) with s.t. (dat., instr.)

hycgan, ge-hycgan, hogian think of, about, s.o. or s.t. (gen., prep. *on, to, ymb*, etc.)

ofer-hycgan despise s.o. or s.t. (acc., dat. in *ÆCHom* i. 502. 12)

wiþ-hycgan be hostile to s.o. or s.t. (dat.)

hyngrian cause hunger to s.o. (acc., dat.)

hyrian imitate s.o. or s.t. (dat.)

on-hyrian imitate s.o. or s.t. (acc., dat.)

a-idlian deprive of s.t. (gen.)

for-ildan delay, put off, s.t. (acc., dat.)

ildian delay s.t. (acc., ?dat. in *ÆCHom* i. 350. 14)

ladian clear oneself (acc.) of a charge (gen.)

efen-læcan, ge-efen-læcan be like or equal to, imitate, s.o. or s.t. (acc., dat.)

ed-læcan, ge-ed-læcan renew, repeat, s.t. (acc., dat.)

nea(h)-læcan, ge-nea(h)-læcan draw near to, approach, adhere to, s.o. or s.t. (acc., dat., prep. *to*)

on-lænan lend s.t. (acc., gen.) to s.o. (dat.)

læran, ge-læran teach s.o. (acc., dat.) s.t. (acc., prep. *to*)

læstan, ge-læstan follow, be of service to, s.o. (acc., dat.)

ful-læstan help s.o. (dat.)

læswian feed s.o. or s.t. (acc., dat.)

of-lætan give up s.t. (acc., gen.)

to-lætan release s.t. (gen.) to s.o. (dat.); see *ÆCHom* i. 560 1

læþan cause s.o. (dat.) to shun s.t. (acc.)

laþettan make s.o. (acc.) hateful to s.o. (dat.)

laþian, a-laþian be hateful to s.o. (dat.)

latian delay from s.t. (gen.)

leanian, ge-leanian reward s.o. (dat.) for s.t. (acc., gen.)

leogan, a-leogan, ge-leogan deceive s.o. (dat.)

on-leon loan s.t. (gen.) to s.o. (dat.)

be-leosan lose, be deprived of, s.t. (gen., dat.)

for-leosan lose s.t. (acc., dat.)

lettan, ge-lettan hinder s.o. (acc.) from s.t. (gen.)

libban live to s.o. (dat.)

licettan pretend s.t. (acc., dat.)

under-licgan be subject to, submit to, s.o. or s.t. (dat.)

lician, ge-lician please s.o. (dat.)

mis-lician, of-lician, un-ge-lician displease s.o. (dat.)

liefan, a-liefan, ge-liefan allow, grant, s.t. (acc.) to s.o. (dat., acc.)

liefan, ge-liefan believe, believe in, s.o. or s.t. (acc., gen., dat., prep. *in, on*)

a-liesan release s.o. (acc.) from s.t. (gen., dat., prep. *æt, fram, of*)

on-lihtan give light to s.o. (acc., dat.)

limpan, a-limpan, be-limpan, ge-limpan happen to, befall, s.o. (dat.)

mis-limpan turn out badly for s.o. (dat.)

linnan cease from, part from, s.t. (gen., dat.)

of-linnan desist from s.t. (gen.)

be-liþan: see *beliden* in §219

locian gaze on, examine, have regard to, take care of, s.o. or s.t. (gen., prep. *ofer, on, to*)

losian be lost to, escape from, s.o. or s.t. (dat., prep. *of*)

lustfullian, ge-lustfullian (i) rejoice in s.o. or s.t. (dat., acc., gen., prep.

ofer, on); (ii) give delight to s.o. (dat.)

æt-lutian hide from s.o. (dat.)

lyffettan flatter s.o. (dat.)

lystan, ge-lystan (i) cause pleasure, desire, to s.o. (acc., dat.) in or for s.o. or s.t. (gen.); (ii) desire s.t. (gen.)

mætan, ge-mætan dream (impers.: acc., dat. of person, acc. of dream)

magan prevail over s.o. or s.t. (dat., prep. *wiþ*)

manian, ge-manian claim s.t. (gen.) of s.o. (acc.)

be-metan measure oneself (acc.) in respect of s.t. (gen.)

wiþ-metan compare s.t. (acc.) to s.o. (dat.)

metgian, ge-metgian assign due measure to s.o. (dat.)

migan pass, discharge, s.t. (dat.) in one's water

miltsian, ge-miltsian pity, pardon, s.o. or s.t. (gen., dat.)

missan (i) miss, fail to hit, s.t. (gen.); (ii) escape the notice of s.o. (dat.)

miþan (i) conceal, dissemble, s.t. (acc., gen.); (ii) refrain from s.t. (dat., instr.)

munan, ge-munan, ge-mynan recollect, bear in mind, s.t. (acc., gen.)

on-munan consider s.o. (acc.) worthy of s.t. (gen.)

be-murnan care for s.t. (acc., dat.)

myndgian, mynegian, ge-myndgian (i) remind s.o. (acc.) of s.t. (gen.); (ii) recollect, be mindful of, s.t. (acc., gen., prep. *æfter*); (iii) make mention of s.o. (acc., gen.); (iv) ask payment of s.t. (gen.)

a-myrran hinder s.o. (acc.) from s.t. (gen., prep. *æt*)

nabban not to have etc. s.t. (acc., gen.; see *habban*)

nagan not to have s.t. (acc., gen.)

nægan, ge-nægan address, approach, assail, s.o. (acc.) with s.t. (gen., dat.)

be-næman deprive s.o. (acc., dat.) of s.t. (gen., dat.)

neosan, neosian, ge-neosian (i) search out, find out, s.t. (acc., gen.); (ii) seek, visit, s.o. or s.t. (acc., gen.)

neotan use, enjoy, s.t. (acc., gen., dat.)

be-neotan deprive s.o. (acc.) of s.t. (gen., dat.)

nerian, ge-nerian (i) deliver s.o. (acc.) from s.o. or s.t. (gen., prep. *fram, of*); (ii) defend s.o. (acc.) from s.t. (prep. *wiþ*); (iii) save s.o. (acc.) in respect of his life (dat., prep. *æt*)

neþan, ge-neþan risk one's life (dat.)

be-niman (i) take s.t. (acc., gen.) from s.o. (dat.); (ii) deprive s.o. (acc.) of s.o. or s.t. (gen., dat., instr.)

dæl-nimend a sharer of, sharing in, s.t. (gen.)

for-niman carry, destroy, s.o. (acc., dat. in *Beo* 2828)

ge-niman take, receive, accept, obtain, s.o. or s.t. (acc., gen.)

notian make use of, employ, enjoy, s.t. (acc., gen., dat.)

be-nugan need, enjoy, s.t. (gen.)

ge-nugan have abundance of s.t. (gen.)

nyhtsumian, ge-nyhtsumian be sufficient (pers. and impers.) for s.o. (dat.)

nytan be ignorant of s.t. (acc., gen.)

nyttian make use of, enjoy, s.t. (gen.)

oleccan, ge-oleccan flatter, propitiate, be submissive to, charm, please, s.o. (dat., ?acc. in *ÆCHom* i. 494. 4)

ge-ortreowan (i) despair of s.t. (gen., prep. *be*); (ii) not to trust to s.o. (dat.) for s.t. (clause)

ge-ortruwian despair of s.t. (gen., prep. *be*)

for-pæran lose s.t. (acc., dat.)

pleon (i) risk s.t. (gen.); (ii) expose s.t. (gen.) to danger

plihtan bring danger upon s.o. or s.t. (dat.)

racian rule s.o. or s.t. (dat.)

ge-ræcan offer s.t. (dat.) to s.o. (prep. *to*); see *Max i* 90

rædan, ge-rædan (i) give advice to s.o. (dat.); (ii) rule, govern, direct, s.o. (dat., instr.); (iii) possess s.t. (dat.)

be-rædan deprive s.o. (acc.) of s.t. (gen., dat., prep. *æt*)

reafian rob s.o. (acc.) of s.t. (gen., prep. *æt*)

be-reafian, be-rebban, be-reofan deprive, bespoil, s.o. (acc.) of s.t. (gen., dat., prep. *æt*) *on-reafian* despoil s.o. (acc.) of s.t. (gen.)

recan, reccan, ge-reccan (i) care for s.o. or s.t. (gen., prep. *be*); (ii) charge s.o. (dat., prep. *on*) with s.t. (acc.)

ge-restan rest from s.t. (gen.)

ricsian rule (intrans., gen. in *Matt(Li)* 20. 25; see also Visser, i, §387)

risan, ge-risan be fitting to s.o. (pers. and impers.)

romian strive after s.t. (gen.)

ryman, ge-ryman (i) make way for s.o. or s.t. (dat., gen. in *ÆCHom* i. 222. 9); (ii) make s.t. (acc.) clear for s.o. (dat.)

be-rypan strip s.o. (acc.) of s.t. (gen., prep. *æt*)

æt-sacan (i) deny s.t. (gen.); (ii) deny, disown, s.o. or s.t. (gen., acc.)

oþ-sacan deny s.t. (gen.)

wiþ-sacan (i) refuse, reject, resist, decline, deny, s.t. (dat., acc., gen.); (ii) deny, refuse to acknowledge, s.o. (gen., acc.)

sælan, ge-sælan befall, happen to, s.o. (dat.)

to-sælan (impers.) (i) happen amiss to s.o. (dat.) in respect of s.t. (gen.); (ii) be lacking to s.o. (dat.) of s.t. (gen.)

sætan, sætian, sætnian lie in wait for s.o. (gen.)

ge-sætnian lie in wait for s.o. (dat.)

be-sargian be sorry for, bewail, s.o. (acc., dat., gen. in *ÆCHom* i. 408. 5)

sceadan part from s.t. (dat. in *Ruin* 30)

a-sceadan separate s.o. (acc.) from s.t. (gen., prep. *fram, of*)

sceamian, ge-sceamian (i) feel ashamed of s.t. (gen.); (ii) cause shame (impers.) to s.o. (acc., dat.) for s.t. (gen., prep. *for*)

of-sceamian put s.o. (dat., ?acc.: see Mitchell 1979*b*, p. 541) to shame for s.t. (gen.)

sceaþan, ge-sceaþan, sceþþan, ge-sceþþan (i) hurt s.o. (dat., acc.) in respect of his life (dat.); (ii) damage s.t. (acc.) to s.o.'s disadvantage (dat.)

scendan shame s.o. (acc., dat. in *ChristC* 1548)

ge-sceon happen to, come upon, s.o. (dat.)

under-sceotan intercept s.t. (acc., dat.)

be-scierian, be-scierwan (i) deprive s.o. (acc.) of s.t. (gen., dat., prep. *fram, of*); (ii) separate s.o. (acc.) from s.t. (gen., dat., prep. *fram, of*)

scildan, ge-scildan protect s.o. (usually acc., occasionally dat.)

sciran get clear of, get rid of, s.t. (gen.)

a-scirian separate s.o. (acc.) from s.t. (gen., prep. *fram*)

wiþ-scorian refuse s.t. (dat.)

scrifan care for s.t. (gen., dat.)

for-scrifan proscribe s.o. (acc., dat.)

un-scrydan (i) strip s.o. (acc.) of a garment (dat.); (ii) take off a garment (dat.)

secan seek s.o. (acc., dat. in *ChronA* 84. 29 (894))

on-secan require s.t. (gen.) of s.o. (acc.)

secgan say s.t. (acc., ?gen. in *Beo* 3028 (see Mitchell 1976*b*, pp. 482-3) and *Dan* 482 (with MS reading)) to s.o. (dat.)

on-seon ?look on s.o. (?acc. in *Ex* 178, ?gen. in *Or* 186. 7). See Mitchell 1979*a*, p. 40

fore-settan set s.o. or s.t. (acc., ?gen.; see Visser, i. 374) before s.o. (dat.)

wiþ-settan oppose, resist, s.o. (dat.)

sinnan care for, heed, s.o. or s.t. (gen.)

a-sittan fear s.t. (gen.)

fore-sittan preside at or over a meeting (acc., dat.)

for-sittan be absent from, neglect, delay, s.t. (acc., instr.)

a-slacian become slack in, hold back from, s.t. (gen., prep. *fram, to*)

slæpan be asleep to, not to be alert to, s.t. (gen.)

a-slawian become sluggish in s.t. (gen.)

be-slean deprive s.o. (acc.) of s.t. (gen., dat.)

be-slitan deprive s.o. or s.t. (acc.) of s.t. (dat.) by tearing

be-snædan deprive s.t. (acc.) of s.t. (dat.) by cutting

be-snyþian deprive s.o. (acc.) of s.t. (dat.)

be-spanan (i) allure, entice, incite, s.o. (acc.) to s.t. (prep. *on, to*); (ii) incite s.o. (?dat. in *Jul* 294: see Woolf's note)

sparian spare, show mercy to, s.o. or s.t. (acc., dat.)

spiwan, spiwian spit up, vomit, s.t. (dat.)

spowan, ge-spowan (i) (pers.) be successful in s.t. (dat.); (ii) (impers.) turn out well for s.o. (dat.) in respect of s.t. (gen., prep. *æt, mid, on*)

mis-spowan (impers.) turn out badly for s.o. (dat.)

sprecan say s.t. (acc., ?dat., ?gen. in *Ps(P)* 40. 8) to s.o. (dat., prep. *to, wiþ*, in *Or* 206. 29)

a-springan be lacking to s.o. (dat.)

spyrian ask for s.t. (acc., gen., prep. *æfter*)

for-standan (i) stand in the way of s.o. (dat.); (ii) block s.t. (acc.) for s.o. (dat.); (iii) stop s.o. (dat.) doing s.t. (acc.); (iv) protect s.o. (acc.) from s.o. or s.t. (dat.); (v) avail s.o. (dat.)

wiþ-standan (i) withstand, resist, s.o. or s.t. (dat.); (ii) succeed in opposing, be a match for, s.o. (dat.); (iii) be a hindrance to, prevent, s.o. or s.t. (dat.) in respect of s.t. (gen.)

fore-stapan, for-stapan go before s.o. (acc., dat.)

stefnian summon, cite, s.o. (dat.)

stelan steal from s.o. (dat.)

be-stelan (i) steal away from s.o. (dat.); (ii) (in passive only) deprive s.o. of s.t. (dat.)

stepan, stipan exalt, elevate, s.o. (acc., dat.) by or in s.t. (dat.)

ofer-stigan rise over s.t. (acc., gen. in *ÆCHom* i. 262. 11)

stillan, ge-stillan make calm, appease, assuage, s.t. (acc., dat.)

stipan: see *stepan*

a-stipan (in passive only) deprive s.o. (acc.) of s.t. (gen.)

streonan, strynan (i) gain, acquire, s.t. (acc., gen.); (ii) beget a child (acc., gen., ?dat.: see BTS)

strudan pillage s.t. (acc., ?gen. in *Dan* 61)

ge-strydan steal s.t. (acc.) from s.o. (dat.)

be-strypan strip s.o. (acc.) of s.t. (gen.)

styran, ge-styran (i) prohibit, restrain, s.o. or s.t. (acc., dat.) from s.t. (gen., prep. *fram*); (ii) rebuke, punish, s.o. or s.t. (dat.)

on-styrian stir s.o. (acc.) with a feeling (dat., prep. *mid*)

for-suwian keep silent about s.t. (acc., gen.)

be-swapan incite, persuade, s.o. (dat.)

swelgan swallow s.t. (acc., dat.)

sweltan (i) die to s.t. (gen.); (ii) be no longer conscious of s.t. (gen.); (iii) die of s.t. (dat., prep. *for, mid*); (iv) die a death (dat.)

swican, ge-swican (i) depart from s.o. (dat., prep. *from*); (ii) cease from s.t. (dat., gen., prep. *from*); (iii) betray, deceive, s.o. (dat.)

a-swican betray s.o. (dat.)

be-swican fail, deceive, s.o. (acc., dat.)

from-swican desert s.o. (dat.)

swigian, ge-swigian (i) be silent about s.t. (gen., acc.); (ii) refrain from saying s.t. (gen., acc.)

for-swigian: see *for-suwian*

ge-syngian sin against s.o. (dat.)

tæcan, ge-tæcan (i) show, teach, s.t. (acc.) to s.o. (dat.); (ii) persuade s.o. (dat.); (iii) show s.o. (acc., dat.) a direction (prep. *to, fram*)

be-tæcan show, deliver, entrust, s.o. or s.t. (acc.) to s.o. (dat.)

tellan impute s.t. (acc.) to s.o. (dat., prep. *to, uppon*)

teon accuse s.o. (acc.) of s.t. (gen.)

be-teon accuse s.o. (acc.) of s.t. (gen., dat.)

of-teon (i) deprive s.o. (dat., acc.) of s.t. (gen.); (ii) take, withhold, s.t. (acc.) from s.o. (dat.); (iii) withdraw s.o. (acc.) from s.t. (gen.)

wiþ-teon restrain, hold back, s.o. or s.t. (dat.)

tidan happen to s.o. (dat.)

tilian, ge-tilian (i) strive after, acquire, s.t. (acc., gen., dat.) for oneself (dat.); (ii) labour for s.o. (dat.); (iii) care for, provide for, s.o. or s.t. (gen., acc.); (iv) attend, treat, cure, s.o. (gen., dat., acc.)

ge-timian happen, befall, s.o. (dat.)

mis-timian happen to s.o. (dat.)

tiþian, ge-tiþian grant s.t. (acc., gen., dat.) to s.o. (dat., acc.)

ge-treowan (i) trust s.o. or s.t. (dat., acc., gen., prep. *in, on*); (ii) persuade s.o. (dat.); (iii) clear oneself (acc.) of s.t. (gen.)

on-treowan trust in, believe in, s.t. (acc., ?dat. in *Dan* 268)

ge-treowsian clear oneself (acc.) of s.t. (gen.)

trucian fail s.o. (dat.)

truwian, ge-truwian (i) trust, trust in, rely on, s.o. or s.t. (dat., gen., prep. *be, in, on, to*); (ii) be faithful to s.o. (dat.); (iii) trust s.t. (acc.) to s.o. (dat.); (iv) clear s.o. (dat., acc.; see BTS, s.v. III) of s.t. (gen.)

or-truwian, or-trywan, ge-ortruwian despair of s.t. (gen., prep. *be*)

ge-twæfan (i) hinder, prevent, separate, deprive, s.o. (acc.) from or of s.t. (gen.); (ii) take s.t. (acc.) from s.o. (dat.)

ge-twæman separate s.o. (acc.) from s.o. or s.t. (gen., prep. *from*)

tweogan, ge-tweogan (i) (pers.) doubt s.o. or s.t. (gen., dat.); (ii) (impers.) inspire doubt in s.o. (acc.) about s.t. (gen., prep. *ymb*); (iii) (impers.) hesitate about, doubt, s.t. (gen., prep. *be, ymb*)

tweonian, ge-tweonian (i) (impers.) cause doubt to s.o. (acc., dat.) about s.t. (gen., prep. *be*); (ii) (impers.) seem doubtful to s.o. (acc.); (iii) (pers.) feel doubt about s.t. (gen., prep. *be*)

þafian, ge-þafian (i) allow, permit, assent to, s.t. (acc., dat.); (ii) permit s.t. (acc., gen. in *Or* 88. 21) to s.o. (dat.)

þancian, ge-þancian thank s.o. (dat.) for s.t. (gen.)

þegan acquire s.t. (dat.)

þegnian serve, attend upon, s.o. (dat.)

þencan, ge-þencan (i) think about s.t. (acc., gen., prep. *be, on, ymb*); (ii) intend s.t. (acc., gen.); (iii) remember s.o. or s.t. (acc., gen.)

under-þeodan subject s.o. (acc.) to s.t. (dat., prep. *under*)

ge-þeon prosper to s.o. (dat. ?acc. in *Jul* 605)

þeowan, þeowian serve s.o. or s.t. (dat.)

þicgan partake of s.t. (gen.)

oþ-þicgan take s.t. (acc.) from s.o. (dat.)

þingian, ge-þingian (i) plead for s.o. (dat.); (ii) make terms for s.o. (dat., prep. *for*) with s.o. (prep. *wiþ*)

ge-þoftian league together (refl. dat. or acc.)

þolian, ge-þolian (i) suffer, bear with, tolerate, s.o. or s.t. (acc.); (ii) suffer lack of s.o. or s.t. (gen.); (iii) lose s.t. (gen.)

a-þolian: see GK, p. 3

for-þolian be deprived of, lack, s.t. (dat.)

þorfnian (?)suffer lack of s.t. (gen.: see BTS)

þreotan weary s.o. (acc. or dat.?)

a-þreotan (i) (impers.) weary s.o. (acc.) of s.t. (gen.); (ii) (pers.) be weary of s.t. (gen.?: see *Bede* 170. 1)

oþ-þringan take s.t. (acc.) from s.o. (dat.)

efen-þrowian suffer with, sympathize with, s.o. or s.t. (dat.)

*þurfan need s.t. (gen., acc.)

be-þurfan (i) (pers.) need s.t. (gen.); (ii) (impers.) be lacking in s.t. (gen.) to s.o. (dat.)

ge-þwærian (i) consent to, conform to, agree to, s.t. (dat.); (ii) agree with s.o. (dat., prep. *mid*)

a-þwean cleanse s.o. (acc.) of s.t. (gen.)

þyncan, ge-þyncan (pers. and impers.) (i) seem, appear to, s.o. (dat.); (ii) seem good to s.o. (dat.)

mis-þyncan (impers.) give a wrong idea to s.o. (dat.)

of-þyncan (i) (impers.) cause regret, sorrow, displeasure, to s.o. (dat.) about s.t. (gen.); (ii) (pers.) displease s.o. (dat.)

þyrstan (i) (impers.) afflict s.o. (acc., dat.) with thirst for s.t. (gen.); (ii) (pers.) thirst for s.t. (gen., acc.)

sin-þyrstan thirst always for s.t. (gen. in *Or* 130. 31)

unnan, ge-unnan (i) grant s.o. (dat.) s.t. (gen., acc.); (ii) wish s.o. (dat.) s.t. (gen.)

of-unnan begrudge, refuse to grant, s.o. (dat.) s.t. (gen.)

wædlian lack s.t. (gen.)

a-wægan fail to perform s.t. (acc., gen.)

wafian wonder at s.t. (gen.)

wandian (i) turn aside from s.t. (gen.); (ii) spare s.o. or s.t. (dat.)

wealdan, ge-wealdan (i) wield a weapon etc. (gen., dat./instr.); (ii) gain control of, have power over, s.o. or s.t. (gen., acc., dat./instr.)

weardian guard s.t. (acc., gen.)

wiþer-weardian oppose s.o. (acc. or dat.?)

weddian engage to do s.t. (gen.)

be-weddian betroth s.o. (acc.) to s.o. (dat.)

wenan, ge-wenan (i) think, suppose, s.t. (acc., gen., prep. *to*); (ii) hope for s.t. (acc., gen.) for s.o. (dat.) from s.o. (prep. *on, to*)

wendan, ge-wendan go, proceed, depart (absolute or with refl. dat.)

weorþan, ge-weorþan (i) come (absolute or with refl. dat.); (ii) (pers. and impers.) happen to s.o. (acc., dat.)

ge-weorþan (i) (impers.) suit s.o. (acc.) in respect of s.t. (gen.); (ii) (impers.) please s.o. (dat.); (iii) (pers.) agree about s.t. (gen.)

mis-weorþan (impers.) turn out badly for s.o. (dat.)

ge-weorþian (i) honour s.o. (acc.) with s.t. (dat.); (ii) (passive) be made worthy of s.t. (gen.)

werian (i) keep s.t. (acc.) from s.o. (dat.); (ii) defend s.t. (acc.) from s.o. (dat., prep. *wiþ*)

be-werian restrain s.o. or s.t. (acc.) from s.t. (gen., prep. *fram*)

wesan be (sometimes with predicative gen.: see §1339)

ge-wifian marry (absolute or with refl. dat.)

wilnian, ge-wilnian (i) desire, ask for, s.t. (gen., acc., dat., prep. *to*); (ii) tend to an end (gen.)

æt-windan escape from s.o. or s.t. (dat., acc.)

winnan suffer s.t. (acc., gen.)

ge-winnan win, get by fighting, s.t. (acc., gen., dat.)

wiþ-winnan strive against s.o. or s.t. (acc. or dat.?)

wisian, ge-wisian (i) guide, direct, s.o. (dat., acc.); (ii) show s.t. (acc.) to s.o. (dat.)

wissian, ge-wissian (i) show a way (acc.) to s.o. (dat.); (ii) guide s.o. (acc., dat.) to s.t. (prep. *to*)

witan, ge-witan know s.t. (acc., gen.)

witan lay a charge (acc.) against s.o. (dat.)

æt-witan reproach s.o. (dat.) with s.t. (acc.)

oþ-witan charge s.o. (dat.) with s.t. (acc.)

fore-wregan accuse s.o. (acc.) of s.t. (gen.)

æt-wrencan cheat s.o. (acc.) of s.t. (gen.)

wrixlan (i) change s.t. (dat.); (ii) exchange s.t. (dat.)

wundrian wonder at s.t. (gen., acc., prep. *æfter, be, fram, on, ymb*)

þurh-wunian persevere with s.t. (dat., prep. *on*)

wyldan, ge-wyldan control s.t. (acc., gen., dat. in *GD(C)* 36. 6)

wyrcan, ge-wyrcan (i) do, make, s.t. (acc., gen., dat.); (ii) attain an end (acc., gen.)

and-wyrdan answer s.o. (dat.)

wyrnan refuse, prohibit, withhold, s.t. (gen., acc.) to or from s.o. (dat.)

for-wyrnan (i) prevent s.t. (gen.) to s.o. (dat.); (ii) refuse s.t. (gen.) to s.o. (dat.); (iii) restrain s.o. (dat.) from s.t. (gen.)

wyscan, ge-wyscan wish for s.t. (acc., gen.) for s.o. (dat.)

æt-ycan add s.t. (acc.) to s.t. (dat.)

ge-yflian (impers.) cause illness to s.o. (acc., dat.)

fore-yrnan run in front of s.o. (dat.)

16. THE OLD ENGLISH VERB: BASIC PARADIGMS

a. Introduction

§1093. Using as a standard of comparison the basic paradigms of the MnE verb 'take' supplied by Palmer (pp. 56, 58, and 105), I offer basic paradigms of the OE verb *niman*, together with references to my discussions of them. The corresponding *forms* do not necessarily correspond in *function*, and there is no guarantee that all the OE patterns actually occur with the verb *niman*. But they all occur. More detailed paradigms of the periphrastic combinations will be found in §§682-701 (present participles), §§702-43 (perfect and pluperfect), and §§744-858 (passive). I cannot spare space to correct the numerous misstatements which have been made about the OE verbal paradigms. Thus Traugott is cited by Yoshino (p. 287), as his authority for the misleading statement that neither 'perfects' nor 'progressives' occur 'with modals'.

b. Primary pattern: third person singular[250]

§1094.

	MnE	OE	Reference
(1)	takes	nimþ	§§613-31
(2)	took	nam	§§632-50
(3)	is taking	is nimende	§§682-701
(4)	was taking	wæs nimende	§§682-701
(5)	has taken	hæfþ genumen	§§702-43
(6)	had taken	hæfde genumen	§§702-43
(7)	has been taking	No	§684
(8)	had been taking	No	§684
(9)	is taken	is genumen, wierþ genumen	§§751-2
(10)	was taken	wæs genumen, wearþ genumen	§§751-2
(11)	is being taken	No	§§684 and 753
(12)	was being taken	No	§§684 and 753
(13)	has been taken	No	§753
(14)	had been taken	No	§753
(15)	has been being taken (?)	No	§753
(16)	had been being taken (?)	No	§753

[250] I supply here the OE indicative forms. If allowance is made for ambiguous forms such as *hæfde* (see §601a), a full paradigm can be supplied for the subjunctive in OE.

c. Secondary pattern: third person singular[250a]

§1095.

MnE	OE	Reference
(1) *will take*	*wil(l)e niman*	§996
(2) *would take*	*wolde niman*	§996
(3) *will be taking*	*wil(l)e beon nimende*	§683
(4) *would be taking*	*wolde beon nimende*	§683
(5) *will have taken*	*wil(l)e habban genumen*	§922
(6) *would have taken*	*wolde habban genumen*	§922
(7) *will have been taking*	No	§753
(8) *would have been taking*	No	§753
(9) *will be taken*	*wil(l)e beon/weorþan genumen*	§§751-2 and 997
(10) *would be taken*	*wolde beon/weorþan genumen*	§§751-2 and 997
(11) *will be being taken*	No	§684
(12) *would be being taken*	No	§684
(13) *will have been taken*	No	§753
(14) *would have been taken*	No	§753
(15) *will have been being taken*(?)	No	§684
(16) *would have been being taken*(?)	No	§684

d. Imperatives[251]

§1096.

MnE	OE	Reference
Take	*Nim*	§883
Be taking	*Beo nimende*	§§683 and 881
Be taken	*Beo/weorþ genumen*[251]	§§751-2 and 881
Be being taken	No	§684

[250a] The previous footnote applies here.

[251] See Palmer, p. 58. On the use of OE subjunctive forms as imperative equivalents, see §§879-919.

e. Infinitives

§1097.

	MnE	OE	References
(1/2)	to take	niman, to nimenne	§921
(3/4)	to be taking	beon nimende	§683
(5/6)	to have taken	habban genumen	§922
(7/8)	to have been taking	No	§§684 and 753
(9/10)	to be taken	beon/weorþan genumen	§§751-2 and 922
(11/12)	to be being taken	No	§§684 and 753
(13/14)	to have been taken	No	§§684 and 753
(15/16)	to have been being taken (?)	No	§§684 and 753

f. Participles

§1098.

	MnE	OE	References
(1/2)	taking	nimende	§974
(3/4)	[No being taking]	No	§753
(5/6)	having taken	No[252]	§983
(7/8)	having been taken	No[252]	§753
(9/10)	being taken	No	§§684 and 753
(11/12)	[No being being taken]	No	§753
(13/14)	having been taken	No	§753
(15/16)	having been being taken (?)	No	§753

g. Summary

§1099. The main differences between the OE paradigms and their MnE counterparts are:

1. a reduction in the number of inflexions;

2. the almost complete absence from MnE of the subjunctive forms found in OE;

3. the OE use of weorþan as well as beon/wesan as an auxiliary of the passive;

[252] On the voice and the time reference of genumen—the second participle of the transitive verb niman, which corresponds to MnE 'taken'—see §§768-81.

4. the absence from OE of any forms with the present participles
wesende or *beonde,* such as MnE 'He is being taken'. These participles do not appear until late—*wesende* in lW-S and *beonde* in
eleventh-century texts (*OEG,* §768);

5. the absence from OE of any forms with the second participles
of *beon* or *wesan,* such as MnE 'He has been taking' or 'He has been
taken'. As far as I know, this participle first appears in *ChronE* 232.
19 (1096) . . . *he heafde gebeon on þes cynges swicdome*;

6. and, of course, the absence from OE of the *do* periphrases.

H. ADVERBS

1. INTRODUCTORY REMARKS

§1100. As in MnE, an adverb may modify a verb, e.g. *Or* 192. 11
He for dearnenga mid gewealdene fultume; another adverb, e.g. *CP*
3. 2 *swiðe oft* and *Bede* 410. 32 *Forhwon segdes ðu Æcgbrihte swa
gemeleaslice 7 swa wlæclice þa ðing . . . ?*; an adjective, e.g. *Or* 124.
30 *þa ongan he hine baðian þæron swa swatigne, Or* 10. 25 *7 þær
sint swiþe scearpe wegas,* and *BlHom* 5. 19 *þære a clænan fæmnan*
(see §§178-80); a participle used adjectivally, e.g. *GD(H)* 90. 9
for his ær gefremodum gyltum; a numeral, e.g. *Or* 48. 11 *folneah c
wintra*; a noun, e.g. *Bede* 410. 13 *þa æteaude me min giu magister
7 festerfæder min se leofesta Bosel* (see §§446 and 1108);[253] a pronoun, e.g. *Bede* 342. 16 *Ond he forðon næfre noht leasunge . . .
wyrcan meahte, ac efne þa an þa ðe to æfæstnesse belumpon*; a
prepositional phrase, e.g. *Or* 234. 24 *. . . þæt he ealles buton arunge
to Rome ne com*; a conjunction (or clause), e.g. *BlHom* 75. 7 *Efne
swa seo hefige byrþen siteþ on þæm deadan lichoman þære byrgenne
7 þæs deaþes . . . swa sæt þonne seo unaræfnedlice byrþen synna on
eallum þysum menniscan cynne . . .* ; or a sentence, e.g. *Matt(WSCp)*
14. 33 *Soþlice þu eart godes sunu.* An adverb may also be used predicatively, e.g. *Bede* 148. 12 *Ne wæs þæt holinga* and *Gen* 12. 13
þæt me wel sy for ðe. Some of these functions can of course be
performed by prepositional phrases (§1167), noun phrases (§1589),
or adverb clauses (§2416).

---

[253] It is tempting to cite *Solil* 64. 32 *Ne wene ic na þæt þæt lyf þær beo butan gewitte*
as an example—'that life there'. But it is more likely that *þær* modifies *beo*; cf. *Solil* 64. 30
Ic wat nu þæt þæt lyf a byð and þæt gewit, where *a* cannot modify *þæt lyf,* and *CP* 153. 20
. . . ða wierrestan ðing ðe ðas menn her doð, Latin *abominationes pessimas quas isti faciunt
hic,* where Brown (1970, p. 66) rightly objects to the EETS translation 'the . . . most wicked
things which the men here do'. We can see in all three sentences an adverb idiomatically
preceding the verb which it modifies. But such examples are straws in the wind.

§1101. As Onions (pp. 15-18) points out, a distinction can be made between co-ordinating conjunctions (e.g. 'and', 'but', 'or') and 'sentence adverbs' (e.g. 'however', 'so', 'therefore'). But while the latter 'qualify the sentence as a whole', they also can, I believe (*pace* Onions), be said to 'link together'. This, and the fact that in OE many words which could be called 'sentence adverbs' are also subordinating conjunctions (e.g. *forþon, swa, þeah*), will, I hope, justify their inclusion in the List of Conjunctions given in §1232. (In this, I note, I agree with Curme 1931, pp. 161-9.)

§1102. There is, however, another group of words taken by Onions (p. 18) as 'sentence adverbs' which cannot properly be called conjunctions; they include MnE 'truly' and 'certainly'. An OE example may be *gewisslice* as in *ÆCHom* ii. 132. 1 *þu miht blissigan gewisslice þæt.* . . . But the dangers of rigid classification become apparent when we note that words like *eornostlice, huru*, and *soþlice*, seem to be used in both ways, e.g. *Matt(WSCp)* 14. 33 *Soþlice þa þe on þam scype wæron comon 7 to him gebædon 7 þus cwædon. Soþlice þu eart godes sunu*, where *soþlice* translates first *autem* and then *vere*.

§1103. Brown (1963, pp. 102-14 and 1970, pp. 65-70) uses the term 'clause modifier' (which he distinguishes from 'adjective modifiers' and 'verb modifiers'). But he is very confused—his examples include 'verb modifiers' belonging to the clause he quotes (e.g. *CP* 153. 21 *ðær*) or to a different one (e.g. *CP* 29. 23 *oft*), co-ordinating conjunctions (e.g. *CP* 435. 7 *forðæm*), and even a subordinating conjunction (e.g. *CP* 431. 4 *ær*). He claims that eighty-one per cent of his 'verb modifiers' immediately precede the verb, whereas forty-six per cent of adverbs or adverb phrases used as 'clause modifiers' occur initially. But I suspect that he has involved himself in a circular argument, for the criterion for distinguishing the two frequently seems to be their position in the sentence. Thus he describes *simle* in *CP* 171. 17 *Be ðam saglum is suiðe gesceadlice gecueden ðæt hie sculon simle stician on ðam hringum* as a 'verb modifier', whereas in *CP* 171. 21 *Forðæm is eac gecueden ðætte simle ða ofergyldan saglas sceolden stician on ðæm gyldnum hringum* it is said to be a 'clause modifier'. But the difference is one of emphasis rather than of function.

§1104. I follow here a traditional classification which is basically semantic and distinguishes adverbs of time, of place, of affirmation and denial, of manner (or description), of quantity, extent, and degree, and of interrogation. The penultimate group embraces, I suppose, numeral adverbs (§§591-3) and the use of interrogative or exclamatory *hu* seen in *Matt(WSCp)* 17. 17 *hu lange beo ic mid eow?* and *PPs* 72. 1 *Hu god is ece god mid Israhelum . . . !*

§1105. According to Curme (1931, p. 135), some adverbs—including the negative (as in 'He did it, not I') and words like 'merely', 'just', and 'particularly'—are often used as 'distinguishing adverbs', that is, 'as belonging to some particular word, phrase, or clause which is prominent in the situation as a whole'. But it seems scarcely necessary to erect a separate class; a good many of the examples quoted in §1100 display this not unusual function.

§1106. Exner tells us that there are in *Beowulf* two kinds of adverbial modification.[254] The first he describes as the indispensable ('unentbehrliche oder einfach determinierende'); these express time, place, and manner. Examples are *Beo* 1 *in geardagum* 'in days of old' —i.e. (he observes) not in the poet's time—*Beo* 28 *to brimes faroðe*, and *Beo* 1724 *wintrum (frod)*. The second is the dispensable, but not pleonastic ('entbehrliche, aber keineswegs pleonastische'); these can portray a new feature ('einen neuen Zug ausmalen'), e.g. *Beo* 158 *to banan folmum*, *Beo* 163 *hwyrftum (scripað)*, and *Beo* 1162 *of wunderfatum*, or add emphasis, e.g. *Beo* 150 *undyrne cuð*, *Beo* 248 *ofer eorþan*, and *Beo* 310 *under roderum*. But, he goes on, there are expressions which belong to neither group, such as *Beo* 7-8 *(he . . . weox) under wolcnum* and *Beo* 52 *(hæleð) under heofenum*. The phrase *under wolcnum* is not completely dispensable, he argues; but, while it paints ('ausmalt'), it disturbs the sense or sphere of reference ('stört es die Begriffssphäre') of the verb in the sentence. The son grows whether there are clouds in the sky or not. He does not always live in the open air nor is there any hyperbolical suggestion that he grew tall, almost up to the clouds. We are given a static picture of the hero under the clouds, without further narrative. Similarly, the heroes of *Beo* 52 could sometimes be found in their hall. 'Solche A.B. [adverbiale Bestimmungen] nenne ich typisch ausmalende oder kurz typische' ['I term this kind of adverbial modification "typically descriptive" or simply "typical" ']—abbreviated T.A.B. A second kind of T.A.B. works not 'veranschaulichend' or 'sinnlich'—not objectively or by appealing to the senses—but 'verinnerlichend' or 'geistig'—subjectively, by appealing to the mind[255]—e.g.

---

[254] See pp. 1-5 of P. Exner, *Typische Adverbialbestimmungen in Frühenglischer Poesie* (Berlin, 1912)—a strange title for a work which discusses poems not only in OE, but also in ME, eMnE (ballads), ON, OFr, and High German of all periods.

[255] He tries to explain the difference in this footnote (p. 4): 'Wenn ich mich im Verlaufe der Darstellung zur Unterscheidung der beiden Arten von T.A.B. der Ausdrücke veranschaulichend und verinnerlichend, resp. sinnlich und geistig, bediene, so meine ich damit nur, daß

GuthA 590   Him se eadga wer   ondswarode
                   Guðlac in gæste   mid godes mægne.

The expression *in gæste*, says Exner, means something quite different
from phrases like 'to have love in the heart' or 'to have fear in the
soul'; Guthlac speaks, not only in spirit, but also aloud. These divisions are far from convincing. It is hard to see why *wintrum* in *Beo*
1724 *wintrum frod* is any more 'indispensable' than *hwyrftum* in
Beo 163 *hwyrftum scripað*, and one could argue that Beowulf was
wise in the summer as well as in the winter. And the example from
GuthA can be otherwise explained. C. W. Kennedy (*The Poems of
Cynewulf* (New York, 1949), 281) quite reasonably translates it 'But
the blessed man Guthlac gave them answer with God's power in his
soul.' Alternatively, it might be another instance of the OE preference for *on/in* where MnE uses 'from' (§1205); we read that *God
wæs Guðlac! He in gæste bær* || *heofoncundne hyt* (*GuthA* 170-1)
and in *GuthA* 592 ff. he was no doubt speaking *from* a heart inspired
by that heavenly hope. Exner goes on to extend these concepts to
other poetry, including *Genesis* and various OE secular and Christian
poems. I did not find the results particularly illuminating.

§1107. The formation of adverbs has been treated by Nicolai and
Campbell.[256] The same authorities have dealt with the adverbial use
of case forms; on this see §§1380-427. F. Seelig (*Die Komparation
der Adjektiva und Adverbien im Altenglischen* (AF 70) (1930)) and
Campbell (*OEG*, §§670-6) discuss the comparison of adverbs. On
verbs compounded with an adverb, see §§1060-80, and on the position of adverbs, §3942.

§1108. As in MnE, there is a certain amount of overlap in the functions of adjectives and adverbs. Uhler (AF 62 (1926), 9) draws our
attention to a variant reading *sarilice* for *sarige* in *ÆLS* 31. 212 *Ða*

die von den Dichtern zwecks längeren Verweilens auf dem Begriffe verwendeten T.A.B. für
uns bei näherer Betrachtung veranschaulichenden oder verinnerlichenden Charakter haben;
nicht aber, daß diese T.A.B. damas von den Hörern oder Lesern als veranschaulichend oder
verinnerlichend empfunden worden sind. Vielmehr lasse ich diese Frage gänzlich offen.'
['When in the course of this discussion I use the terms "objective" and "subjective", or
"appealing to the senses" and "appealing to the mind", to distinguish between the two
kinds of typical adverbial modification, I simply mean that the adverbial phrases the poets
used in order to dwell longer on an idea seem to us, on closer examination, to have objective
or subjective quality; I do not mean that the hearers or the readers of the time felt them to
be objective or subjective. I prefer to leave that question open.']

[256] Nicolai, *passim*—he gives a table of contents at pp. 53-6, a luxury denied us by a
good many of his contemporaries—and *OEG*, chapter xiii. See also K. Uhler, *Die Bedeutungsgleichheit der altenglischen Adjektiva und Adverbia mit und ohne* -lic (-lice) (AF 62)
(1926), 1-4. On compound adverbs generally, see Nicolai, pp. 38-41; on those with prepositions, e.g. *tomiddes*, see Wülfing, ii. 251, *OEG*, §§82 and 669, and Mustanoja, p. 424.

gebroþra sarige þa sæton ofer þæt lic and speaks elsewhere in his work of similar variations. When the forms are similar (*OEG*, §661), we cannot always be sure which we have, e.g. *milde* in *ChristA* 249 *þu þisne middangeard milde geblissa*, *hearde* in *Mald* 33 . . . *þon we swa hearde hilde dælon*, and *þicce* in *ÆCHom* ii. 156. 28 *on ðam þiccum bremlum and þornum and netelum, ðe þær on ðam westene þicce stodon*. There are, however, times when OE writers use one where we should prefer the other, e.g. *Beo* 496 *Scop hwilum sang* ‖ *hador on Heorote*—Klaeber speaks of 'the employment of the (more concrete) adjective in cases where our modern linguistic feeling inclines toward the (abstract) adverb'[257]—*Jud* 93 . . . *þæt me ys þus torne on mode*, ‖ *hate on hreðre minum*, and *Bede* 436. 28 *mid ofercyme sæmninga deaðes*. (Cf. MnE 'the then King' and 'in after years', and, for similar OE examples, see §1100 and Wülfing, ii. 300.) But to speak of these as examples of 'adjectives used as adverbs' or vice versa would be imperceptive.

§1109. Brown (1963, p. 112) prefers to consider present participles such as that in *CP* 151. 24 *he hit him ðeah suigende gesæde* as adverbial rather than adjectival in function. The translation 'silently' is certainly convenient. But formally *suigende* remains a present participle. *ÆCHom* i. 52. 19 *and he for ðam stænendum welwillende gebæd* presents a similar instance.

§1110. It seems unnecessary to attempt here a full alphabetical list of OE adverbs. Lists of various types and degrees of completeness will be found in *OEG*, §§661-81 and 720-2, Wülfing, ii. 251-300, and Nicolai, pp. 42-52.[258] Those words which serve as both adverbs and conjunctions are discussed in chapters V-VII. The sections which follow treat points of special interest in connection with the different types of adverbs.

2. ADVERBS OF TIME

§1111. As Wülfing (ii. 265) points out, adverbs of time may refer to time when, e.g. *þa* 'then', time how long, e.g. *symle* 'always', and time from when, e.g. *nu* and *þæs* (see below). But he wisely refuses

---

[257] Klaeber, 3, p. xcii. But it is not clear to me how he *knows* that *unbliðe* in *Beo* 129 *Mære þeoden* . . . ‖ *unbliðe sæt* is an adjective and not an adverb.

[258] For examples from individual texts see Haddock's thesis, part iii; Mohrbutter, pp. 45-50; Tilley, pp. 71-9; and for the poetry 'the eighteen German dissertations', less those of Kempf, Reussner, and Rose. *Boethius* and *Cura Pastoralis* agree in certain adverbial usages against *Orosius*; see Bately in *Ang.* 88 (1970), 447-8 and 451-2.

to divide his list (ii. 265-73) into three groups because of the over-
laps of meaning which exist. These are not restricted to temporal
senses. Thus *þanon* can have, not only a temporal, but also a local,
meaning; cf. *Bede* 142. 12 *Ono hwæt Eorpwald þa se cyning nales
æfter micelre tide wæs ofslegen from sumum hæðnum men, Ricberht
hatte. þonon þa seo mægð þreo gear ful in gedwolan wæs lifiende
. . .* (there may even be some element of result here) and *Or* 8. 16
*. . . neh þæm garsecge þe mon hateð Sarmondisc; 7 seo ea Danai
irnð þonan suðryhte.* A few points of interest about particular adverbs of time are discussed in the sections which follow.

§1112. As an adverb, *ær* sometimes indicates or emphasizes a temporal relationship. But the strength of this function must not be
exaggerated. Its use as 'a sign of the pluperfect' (*Guide,* §168) is not
exemplified by Ælfric (*ÆGram* 124. 7-11 or elsewhere)—naturally
enough, because this is merely another way of saying that when an
adverb which means 'before, previously' is used with an independent
past tense, it can often be *translated* by a MnE pluperfect. But the
examples given below are sufficient to show that this pluperfect
function is only one of its OE uses and that the idea of it is unlikely
to have struck speakers or writers of OE.

§1113. Like other adverbs, *ær* tends to precede rather than follow
the verb and can be used in both principal and other clauses. With
both present and past independent tenses it can mean simply 'before',
'previously', 'earlier', 'first', e.g. (present) *BlHom* 19. 7, *BlHom* 101.
11, and *BlHom* 139. 32 *Broðor Pawlus, aris þu 7 gebide þe ær,
forðon þu eart leohtes swer,* and (past), e.g. *BlHom* 85. 12, *BlHom*
17. 12 *We nestan ær hwæt se blinda wæs,* and *BlHom* 123. 18 . . .
swa ic ær sægde. It can also be used with other adverbs, e.g. *BlHom*
123. 36 . . . *ealle deofles men þe nu ær her on worlde synt* and
BlHom 95. 2 *swa Antecrist ær beforan dyde.*

§1114. With the present tense, *ær* is found where MnE could have
a perfect or future perfect, e.g. *BlHom* 51. 35 *7 us is swiþe uncuþ
hwæt ure yrfeweardas 7 lastweardas getreowlices don willon æfter
urum life, gif we hit sylfe ær agimeleasiaþ* and *Fort* 48 (§622) (cf.
Dream 107 (§622), where *ærur* is used); for further examples see
§622.

§1115. With the past tense, *ær* may represent a MnE perfect or
future perfect, e.g. *BlHom* 9. 11 *7 he forgifeþ eall swa hwæt swa
þes middangeard ær wiþ hine æbyligða geworhte, BlHom* 15. 32 *Nu*

ær we gehyrdon þæt Hælend his þegnum sæde his prowunga . . . ,
BlHom 43. 7 *þa mæssepreostas* . . . *sceolan heora scriftbec mid rihte
tæcan* . . . *swa swa hie ure fæderas ær demdon,* and

Beo 655   Næfre ic ænegum men   ær alyfde,
siþðan ic hond ond rond   hebban mihte,

or a MnE pluperfect, e.g. *BlHom* 23. 24, *BlHom* 29. 18 . . . *he eode
on westen þær ær Adam forwearþ,* (with the passive) *BlHom* 9. 25
. . . *on ða uplican ricu, þonon þe he ær sended wæs* and *ÆLS* 32. 178
and his swura wæs gehalod þe ær wæs forslagen, Beo 778 *þæs ne
wendon ær witan Scyldinga,* and *Beo* 825 *se þe ær feorran com;* see
further §§637-8. But examples like *BlHom* 19. 1 *buton he gebete
þæt he ær forgiten hæfde, BlHom* 19. 34 *Drihten . . . se þe ær geteod
hæfde þæt he þon biddendan ece lif forgeafe,* and *BlHom* 95. 14
þeah þe hie ær eorþe bewrigen hæfde—in which *ær* is used with the
hæfde periphrasis— show clearly that *ær* was more than just 'a sign
of the pluperfect'. On *no þy ær,* see §§1800-1.

§1116. The distinction between the conjunctions *þa* and *þonne* set
out in §2562 seems to hold generally for the adverbs when they are
used in a purely temporal sense. Thus, in

ChronA 84. 20 (894)   . . . 7 þeh ofer þa treowa, swa oft swa þa oþre hergas
mid ealle herige ut foron, þonne foron hie, oþþe mid, oþþe on heora healfe on.
þa gegaderade Ælfred cyning his fierd, 7 for þæt he gewicode betwuh þæm
twam hergum, þær þær he niehst rymet hæfde for wudufæstenne, ond for
wæterfæstenne, swa þæt he mehte ægþerne geræcan gif hie ænigne feld secan
wolden. þa foron hie siþþan æfter þæm wealda hloþum 7 flocradum. bi swa
hwaþerre efes swa hit þonne fierdleas wæs,

both *þa* and *þonne* appear twice. In both places *þa* refers to a single
completed act in the past. The first *þonne* refers to a repeated act in
the past, the second to a single act at some indefinite time in the past
—'whenever that was'. These should be compared with *ChronE*
135. 15 (1003) *Ðonne se heretoga wacað þonne bið eall se here
swiðe gehindred.* All the examples cited in BT(S) of *þa* adv. have the
past tense. The only example given by Klaeber (3, p. 413) of *þonne*
adv. 'then' (time) with the past tense is

Beo 1104   gyf þonne Frysna hwylc   frecnan spræce
ðæs morþorhetes   myndgiend wære,
þonne hit sweordes ecg   seðan sceolde.

Here we have an open condition in reported or represented speech
(see §§3612-14), where *þonne* is carried over from the non-dependent
speech while the original present tense becomes past; cf. *BlHom* 17. 2

. . . *7, ðonne me*[*n*] *hine gesawon sweltendne, þæt hie þonne wæron afrefrede*, where the time-reference is again to the future-in-the-past. See §646.

§1117. When used in other than purely temporal senses, *þonne* adv. can be accompanied by a past tense, e.g.

Beo 484   Ðonne wæs þeos medoheal   on morgentid,
                    drihtsele dreorfah,   þonne dæg lixte,

where it is not only correlative with frequentative *þonne*, but also marks a stage in the narrative, and *ÆCHom* i. 134. 18 *þæt is feowertig daga, gif hit hysecild wære: gif hit þonne mædencild wære, þonne sceolde heo forhabban fram ingange Godes huses hundehtatig daga*, where it implies a qualification or contrast. In view of the subsequent disappearance of the reflexes of *þa*, we might expect to find occasional OE examples of *þonne* adv. in a purely temporal sense referring to a single act in the past. So far I have not found any. That the distinction was well preserved in later OE is clear from the fact that in Ælfric's homily *Dominica III in Quadragesima* (*ÆHom* 4) *þonne* occurs nineteen times as an adverb, always with a present tense, and *þa* fifteen times, always with a past tense. But the full concordances will probably reveal exceptions I have missed.

§1118. On correlative *þa . . . þa, þonne . . . þonne*, and *gif . . . þonne*, see §§2576, 2584–5, and 2571–2, and on *þa . . . furþum* and possibly *þa . . . ærest* = Latin *cum . . . primum*, see §§2704 and 2706.

§1119. Ericson (1932, pp. 74–6) remarks that 'from the practice of using *swa*-modal as a transitional link, develops easily a *swa*-type used with an implication of time'. His examples—all from Bede—include *Bede* 8. 25 *Ðæt þa ylcan biscopas Bryttum on gefeohte godcundne fultum forgeafon; 7 swa ham wæron eft hweorfende*.

§1120. *Nu* and *þæs* are sometimes used with a prepositional phrase to express the time from which a reckoning is to be made. Examples include *ÆHom* 6. 22 *nu for feawum dagum* 'a few days ago', *ÆLS* 2. 422 *nu on sunnandæg* 'next Sunday', *ÆLS* 10. 260 *nu æfter ðrym dagum* 'three days from now', *ÆCHom* i. 214. 27 *of ðisum dæge oð nu on ðunresdæg* 'from today until next Thursday', *ÆLS* 2. 72 *þæs on mergen* 'the next morning', and *ÆHom* 11. 54 *ðæs ymbe tyn niht* 'ten nights after that'. Schrader (pp. 75–6) gives some of these examples and also quotes *ÆLS* 9. 64 *Ne dreah ic nu þrym gearum nane oþre dæda.* But this does not seem to belong exactly, either in form (there is no preposition) or in meaning (the sense is 'for these three years'). On *nu* + past tense = perfect, as here, see §635.

3. ADVERBS OF PLACE

§1121. The traditional division of local adverbs into place where, e.g. *her* and *þær*, place to which, e.g. *hider* and *þider*, and place from which, e.g. *heonan* and *þonan*, is given by Campbell (*OEG*, §677), with the necessary proviso that 'generally the senses of rest and movement towards tend to be confused, and *her* is often used for *hider, þær* for *þider*, etc.' The ideas of rest and movement from were also sometimes viewed differently; see the discussion on the uses of the preps. *of* and *on* in §1205. Burkhart offers a somewhat more elaborate division—immediacy, semi-immediacy, non-immediacy, change of position, indefinite position (all of which he subdivides), and miscellaneous (direction and 'as far as')—and exemplifies all the adverbs and adverb phrases which denote place; see his table of contents.

§1122. Klaeber (3, p. xciii) sums up the position in *Beowulf* thus (I insert three of his footnotes in square brackets):

The peculiar use of such adverbs of place as *hider, þonan, nean, feor, ufan, suþan* [Thus, in 394, 2408, 528, 1701, 1805, 330, 606] and of certain prepositions, like *ofer, under*, and *on* with acc., *to, of* furnishes numerous instructive instances of the characteristic fact that in the old Germanic languages the vivid idea of 'motion' (considered literally or figuratively) was predominant in many verbs [including, e.g., such as *(ge)seon, sceawian, (ge)hyran, . . . bidan, secan, . . . sprecan, scinan, standan*] which are now more commonly felt to be verbs of 'rest'. Sometimes, it should be added, motion was conceived in a different direction from the ordinary modern use [See some examples under *to*], and sometimes, contrary to our expectations, the idea of rest rather than motion determined the use (or regimen) of the preposition (see *æt, on* with dat.).

§1123. All the adverbs of place from which given by Campbell end in *-an*, which can of course be spelt *-on*. So we find *ÆGram* 231. 11 *unde hwanon, ÆCHom* i. 314. 26 *and ic sylle mine forebeacn ufan of heofonum, GenA* 1321 *geofonhusa mæst . . . || innan and utan eorðan lime || gefæstnod wið flode*, and *PPs* 70. 19 *of neowelnesse . . . neoðan.* But the ending *-an* in these adverbs does not always imply motion from, e.g. *BlHom* 197. 8 *Heo is eac on onsyne utan yfeles heowes, ac heo is innan mid ece mægene geweorþod,*[259] *JDay* i

---

[259] As far as I am aware, the work on *innan* and *utan* promised by Meroney in the quotation given in §1124 did not appear. But this example and some of those in BT(S) suggest that these words did not always imply 'from'.

22 *Ufan hit is enge ond hit is innan hat,* and *PPs* 103. 7 *He nywol-nessa neoðan swa swa ryfte* ‖ *him to gewæde woruhte swylce.* (The phrases with a preposition + adverb in *-an*, as in *Or* 16. 18 *Be norþan eastan Maroara sindon Dalamentsan 7 be eastan Dalamentsan sindon Horigti*, are a special case; see *OEG,* §669.) There seems to be some-thing in R. T. Farrell's suggestion (private communication) that *-an* kept the sense 'from' longer with points of the compass than else-where, e.g. *Or* 8. 7 *Asia is befangen mid Oceano þæm garsecge suþan 7 norþan 7 eastan.* I have not found any examples in which they do not imply 'from'. Wülfing (ii. 259) says that *norþan* once means 'to the north'. The example he seems to have in mind is *Bede* 118. 12. But whatever the difficulties of translating, the point is that the wind which had been *suþan* 'from the south' turned and blew *norþan* 'from the north'. Wülfing is wrong.

§1124. Meroney's article 'The Early History of "down" as an Ad-verb' (*JEGP* 44 (1945), 378-86) documents the gradual assumption by the northern *ofdune* of the functions of *niðer, niðere, neoðan, niðor,* and *ufan,* and reveals some interesting differences in the spheres of reference of these words, e.g. '*ufan* does great service only for motion from high overhead, whereas *niðer* and *ofdune* function alike within all limits' (p. 383). It also makes the following general observation (p. 386)

By and large, English reveals a decay in the twofold scheme of directional par-ticles. The block of oppositions *upp* : *ufan* :: *niðer* : *neoðan* degenerates into *up* and *down,* even as *inn* : *innan* :: *ut* : *utan* becomes simply *in* and *out.* Other Modern English pairs, e.g. *far* and *near, fore* and *aft,* have a kindred history. I doubt that the corruption was altogether subsequent to the Norman Conquest. Already deferred for proof elsewhere is the claim that OE. *innan* and *utan* soon lost the force of 'from within' and 'from without'. Until each set of analogous particles, including OE. *hwonan* and *hwider,* has been investigated on its own merits, the Old English system will remain obscure. It presents, I judge, a stage of compromise between Germanic and Modern English: some OE. *-an* adverbs (e.g. *hwonan*) are used correctly, some incorrectly (e.g. *innan*), by Germanic standards. It seems that *ufan* was used correctly, though sparingly. But its weak-ness should not be attributed to the success of *ofdune,* since *niðer* just as often means 'down from above' in texts where *ofdune* has not gained acceptance.

Lexicographers may find these suggestions useful and should not neglect this article. (There is also Meroney's unpublished Ph.D. dis-sertation (University of Chicago, 1943) on Old English *upp, uppe, uppan,* and *upon,* which I have not seen.)

§1125. Further examples of, and observations on, adverbs of place will be found in *OEG,* §§678-81. Wülfing (ii. 251-64) gives an alphabetical list. Markey discusses the etymology of, and dialectal distinctions in the use of, some adverbs of place in 'A Note on Germanic Directional and Place Adverbs' (*Studia Linguistica*, 24 (1970), 73–86).

4. ADVERBS OF AFFIRMATION, DENIAL, AND NEGATION

§1126. Wülfing (ii. 290) includes *gea, giese, gise*, and *nese (nese)*, but observes (ii. 695) that the addition of *la* makes *gea la gea, gise la gise*, and *nese la nese*, into interjections. The *OED* describes MnE 'yes' and 'no' as adverbs and I suppose we could argue that in *gea la gea* we have adverb + interjection + adverb. But the point is terminological and I have included *gea, giese*, and *nese*, in the list of Interjections (§1239).

§1127. We may reasonably follow Flamme (§114) in listing here ˙*soþlice* (*BlHom* 31. 1), *witodlice* (*BlHom* 65. 9), *mid soðe* (*BlHom* 17. 4), and the like. The same writer draws our attention to the use of phrases with *for* and *þurh* in connection with prayers or oaths, e.g. *BlHom* 89. 17 *Ic þe halsige nu, Drihten, for þinre þeowene, Sancta Marian . . .* and *BlHom* 189. 7 *Ic eow halsige scucna englas . . . þurh God Ælmihtigne. . . .*

§1128. The adverbs of negation are: *ne*; *na, no (ni + a, o)*; *næfre (ni + æfre)*; *næs, nalles, nealles (ni + ealles)*; and *naht, noht, nawiht (ni + awiht)*. Negative phrases include *Bede* 82. 7 *nænge þinga*, Latin *nullatenus*, *GD(C)* 155. 30 *nanum gemete*, Latin *nullo modo*, and their variants.[260] For the syntax of these when used alone or in combination, see §§1595–632.

§1129. It is a commonplace that negative contraction—the loss of unaccented *i* in *ni* in pretonic syllables (*OEG*, §354)—affects not only adverbs (see §1128) and pronouns (see §§243 and 436), but also verbs, e.g. *nahte, næbbe, næs, nat*, and *nolde*.[261] Levin discusses this phenomenon in Indo-European generally, and in the Germanic languages. Among these, Levin tells us, OE and OFris. show the

---

[260] See further Einenkel in *Ang.* 22 (1899), 495, repeated in *Ang.* 26 (1903), 556–7, and *Ang.* 35 (1912), 203. BTS notes an adverbial use of *nan* s.v. *nan* (last entry). *Deut(L)* 1. 37 *Næs ðæt nan þing wundor*, quoted by Einenkel, *Ang.* 27 (1903–4), 173, is dubious —MS *B* omits *þing*. The example from *Bede* he gives on p. 183—*Bede* 130. 31—does not, according to Miller, show *nænig þing* in any of the manuscripts.

[261] On a (possible) distinction between word and sentence negation in OE, see §§1133 and 1596–7.

highest degree of contraction, the latter going one better by producing *nertha* <*ni wertha* 'not to become'.[262] Several points of interest arise.

§1130. Using a limited selection of texts of all periods, Levin suggests that 'West Saxon usage is almost entirely in favor of contraction whereas, in Anglian usage, uncontracted forms are freely employed'. His chart for the distribution of forms in the early OE texts he read will give an idea of the strength of these tendencies in one period:

	Contracted	Uncontracted
West-Saxon	306	9
Mercian	127	56
Northumbrian	66	43

His figures for lW-S show a similarly striking preference for contracted forms; in his selections from Ælfric he finds 477 contracted and only four definitely uncontracted, in those from Wulfstan 281 contracted and 14 uncontracted—all of the latter in homilies not admitted to the canon by Bethurum (*JEGP* 57 (1958), 496-7; so we have an additional test for the Wulfstan canon, though it cannot decide between Ælfric and Wulfstan). On the basis of these and similar figures for eME Levin concludes (ibid., p. 498 and fn. 22):

In Middle English the area of contraction comprises the Southern and West Midland dialects (these two dialects in Middle English carry on the West Saxon literary and linguistic traditions); on the other side of this isogloss are texts of East Midland and Northern provenience. . . . Kentish agrees with East Midland and Northern rather than with Southern and West Midland.

§1131. Levin's examination of the distribution of these forms in OE poetry (thesis, pp. 29-40) raises a question of interest to students of OE metre. Many variations between uncontracted and contracted forms, he says, can be explained on metrical grounds—there is no contraction in *GenB* 352 *þæt he ne wolde | wereda drihtnes*, where *wolde* alliterates, or in *GenA* 1590b *Cham ne wolde*, where contraction would leave only three syllables. But why do we have contraction in *GenA* 1448 *salwigfeðera | secan nolde* and not in *GenA* 2571 *hyran ne wolde. | Nu sceal heard and steap*? The existence of this last

---

[262] See initially his article 'Negative Contraction: An Old and Middle English Dialect Criterion' in *JEGP* 57 (1958), 492-501; he describes the texts he used at pp. 494-8. The quotation appears at p. 498 and the chart at p. 495. This article distils the conclusions on this point which he reached in his thesis—'Negative Contraction with Old English Verbs' (unpublished Ph.D. dissertation, University of Pennsylvania, 1956).

and other such examples in 'the longer poems', which made up his corpus (thesis, p. 31), leads him to this comment (ibid., p. 37):

In the face of the heavy preference for contracted forms and considering the fact that many uncontracted forms can be explained in the light of what we do understand about Old English prosodic practice, we may be justified in suppos- ing that these and the other remaining uncontracted forms could also be ex- plained if we knew some additional facts about the Old English prosodic system. In my opinion these deviations may be attributed to a principle governing larger prosodic contours; i.e., contours extending over the whole line, or even over more than one line.

This suggestion might repay investigation. We can, however, no longer accept Klaeber's confident assertion (3, p. xciv) that Einen- kel's work in *Ang.* 35 (1911), 187-248 and 401-24, had 'the gratify- ing result of establishing *Beowulf* as an Anglian poem of about 725 A.D.' See further Levin's thesis, pp. 38-9.

§1132. On negative disjunction see §§1832-57. Special difficulties are treated as they arise; on these see the General Index, s.v. *Negation.*

§1133. A study of negative prefixes cannot be undertaken here. For this the reader is referred to the standard works on word-formation. But attention may be drawn to the article by Shuman and Hutchings entitled 'The *un-* Prefix: A Means of Germanic Irony in *Beowulf*' in *MP* 57 (1959-60), 217-22, and to the references there given. Schu- chardt, who also discusses *un-* (pp. 11-15), describes it as a form of direct negation, but adds a section on indirect negation (pp. 54-66). Here he distinguishes first, word negation (by means of *leas, -leas, fra-* (as in *fracod*), *or-, won-, idel, ofer* (as in *Beo* 685 *wig ofer wæpen*), and second participles such as that in *Beo* 721 *dreamum bedæled*); second, sentence negation (by means of *lyt, lytle, lythwon, læs,* and *butan*); and third, the use in a positive expression of a verb which is in effect negative (e.g., *Beo* 804 *ac he sigewæpnum for- sworen hæfde*). But the distinction between *un-* (direct negation) and affixes like *won-* and *-leas* (indirect negation) seems a fine one, and it is hard to see how *forsworen* in *Beo* 804 above differs from *be- dæled* in *Beo* 721 above as an expression of negation.

5. ADVERBS OF MANNER

§1134. Wülfing's collection of 'Adverbien der Art und Weise' (ii. 273-89) embraces both adverbs of manner (or description), e.g. *Or* 192. 11 *dearnenga* and *Or* 272. 18 *eawenga*, and the adverbs of degree and the like which are discussed in the sections which follow.

He does not give all the examples of the former in the 'Alfredian' texts; thus *Or* 272. 18 *diegellice* does not appear in its own right and *Or* 142. 9 *bismerlice* is omitted. But that is no cause for criticism. This is the largest class, embracing as it does most of the 'adjectival adverbs' (*OEG*, §§661-5), which can of course be formed at will. There would be little point in compiling a complete list. On the position of these adverbs in the sentence, see §3942.

6. ADVERBS OF QUANTITY, EXTENT, AND DEGREE

§1135. There is no point in attempting the threefold division suggested by this traditional, clumsy, but useful, term, which embraces numeral adverbs, e.g. *Or* 252. 6 *Babylonia . . . Sio gestod tuwa seofon hund wintra* (§§591-3); *æror*, e.g. *ÆCHom* i. 70. 2 *Ða oðre þry godspelleras . . . awriton æror be Cristes menniscnysse*; *micle*, e.g. *Or* 18. 3 *Se hwæl bið micle læssa þonne oðre hwalas*; *ealles*, e.g. *Or* 234. 24 . . . *þæt he ealles buton arunge to Rome ne com*; *genoh*, e.g. *Or* 126. 31 *genoh sweotollice*; *swa*, e.g. *Or* 48. 5 *swa earme wif 7 swa elðeodge* and *ÆCHom* ii. 78. 30 *and rihtlice swa*; *to*, e.g. *Or* 56. 21 *to raðe*; *wel*, e.g. *ÆCHom* ii. 84. 14 *Nu we wel willað . . .* ; and the like. (*Swa* and *to* are discussed below.) A semantic distinction is often made between 'intensifying' (or 'intensive'), and 'weakening' (or 'restrictive') adverbs (the latter are sometimes called 'downtoners'), e.g. *micle* in *Or* 18. 3 *micle læssa* and *hwene* in *Or* 18. 30 *syxtig mila brad, oþþe hwene bradre*, respectively. Peltola (*NM* 72 (1971), 667-8), noting that the most common intensifying adverbs in prose and poetry are *swiþe* and *full*, points to 'a marked difference between these two intensives . . . in alliterative poetry. *Swiþe* is emphatic and can enter into alliteration. . . . On the other hand there are no instances of obligatory alliteration with *full*. It is placed in the "dip" . . . and bears no stress.'

§1136. Wülfing's collection of 'Adverbien der Art und Weise' (ii. 273-89) contains some adverbs of quantity, extent, and degree. It is naturally not complete for OE. The following can be added from the poetry and the later prose without any claim to completeness: *æghwæs, æthwega, aninga, clæne* (*WHom* 20(*BH*). 28 *clæne berypte*), *eall, fela, feor* (see Wülfing ii. 253), *firnum, gegninga, gewisslice, þearle, ungefræglice, ungemet(e, -es), ungemetlice, ungescead*, and *wundrum*.[263] There are also, of course, compounds such as

---

[263] Most (pp. 272-3) adds *þænne = adhuc* in *ÆColl* 32. She gives alphabetical lists of intensive adverbs (pp. 231-81) and restrictive adverbs (pp. 296-300) from a restricted corpus of prose and poetry. She marks those she thinks no one else has noticed with (*). But

forswiðe, nateshwon, and *oferswiðe*, and phrases such as *ænige þinga* and *þinga gehwylce, be ænigum (sumum) dæle*, and *to soðe*. To these Most (pp. 231-81 and 296-300) and Peltola (*NM* 72 (1971), 674-81) add (mostly from the poetry) words such as *deope, bittre, hearde*, and *sare*. It would be superfluous to quote examples of all these here (they can be found in BT(S), Wülfing, Most, and Peltola, s.vv.) or to attempt a complete list; inclusion or omission is so much a matter of opinion.[264]

§1137. According to Most (p. 231) many adverbs of degree

are restricted in the part or parts of speech they may modify. Some, like *æghwæs*, modify only adjectives; a few, like *gyt*, are associated only with adjectives and adverbs in the comparative degree; *ealra* modifies superlatives; another group, like *anunga*, is restricted to verbs; others, like *ealles*, may modify adjectives and adverbs in the positive degree; while still others, like *wel*, are capable of modifying all the above parts of speech, plus comparative and superlative forms.

There is room for further work here. It has already been pointed out in §§1101-3 that it is often very difficult to distinguish 'word modifiers' from 'sentence modifiers' in OE. Most (p. 229) suggests that adverbs like *huru, soðlice*, and *gewisslice*, are adverbs of manner when they modify words, but act as sentence modifiers when used intensively.

§1138. An adverb of degree usually, of course, precedes the word or phrase it modifies; see §§178-80. But it sometimes follows it, e.g. *Bede* 142. 14 *þreo gear ful* and perhaps *ÆCHom* ii. 508. 34 *hetelice swiðe* 'very violently' (cf. *ÆCHom* i. 452. 14 *hetelice* 'violently'). It

as her bibliography does not include Wülfing, her asterisks are of little significance. Some of the asterisked ones are also given by Peltola, whose articles were not available to her. These lists are now more accessible in Ingersoll, pp. 162-203 and 218-21. On Ælfric's use of *forwel*, see Godden, *EStudies*, 61 (1980), 209.

[264] Most (pp. 222-9) discusses the formation of adverbs of degree and points out that they include words which were originally adverbs of quantity and size, e.g. *fullice* and *lytle*, of place and direction, e.g. *neah* and *gegnunga*, of time, e.g. *æfre*, and of quality and manner, e.g. *clæne* and *hearde*. She cites as an example in which the adverb *þearle* has almost completely lost its original meaning *ÆLS* 32. 195 *þa wurðode þæt landfolc mid geleafan þone sanct and þeodred bisceop þearle mid gifum on golde and on seolfre þam sancte to wurðmynte*. The demands of alliteration are perhaps responsible for a forced use of *þearle*.

This discussion is now available in Ingersoll, pp. 153-61. She claims (p. 155) that *swa, þæs, to þæs, to þam, to þon*, and *þus*, 'at first . . . were followed by a clause which specified the extent, degree, or point. Later the explanatory clause was omitted, and these adverbs of extent became adverbs of degree, meaning "so, very".' The alleged process is more readily understandable for the *to* groups than for *swa, þæs*, and *þus*. But it implies that the reference of these words was always forward, never back, and remains a possibility rather than a certainty, even for the *to* groups.

is usually repeated with each of a series of adjectives or adverbs joined by *and*, e.g. *Bo* 24. 7 *Manege beoð þeah ægðer ge full æðele ge full welige, Solil* 32. 13 *swiðe wundorlice and swiðe soðlice, BlHom* 139. 7 *swiþe gefeonde 7 swiþe blissigende, ÆCHom* i. 64. 8 *swa clæne gold, ne swa read*, and *Sat* 348 *Nis nænig swa snotor ne swa cræftig,* ‖ *ne þæs swa gleaw . . .* , where both the alliteration on *swa* and the doubled *þæs swa* are unusual. There are exceptions, e.g. *Bede* 424. 1 *þeh ðe hio swiðe forht were 7 beofiende* and *Bede* 462. 22 *Com me to 7 ætstod sum swiðe beorht mon 7 scinende on hwitum gegyrelan*, but in these it is not certain that *swiðe* is to be taken with the participles.

§1139. *Swa* is common as an intensifying adverb; Peltola (*NM* 72 (1971), 670) sees this as an extension of the deictic use. But *swa* presents terminological problems. Ericson (1932, pp. 23-7) speaks of 'pseudo constructions of *swa*' and points out that in sentences like *Bede* 286. 15 *Ic wat þæt ge wenað, þæt ic ungewitge mode sprece. Ac hwæðre witað ge þæt hit swa nis* 'the *swa* is equivalent to New English *so* = "true" '. This he calls 'pseudo-adjectival'. Of the alleged use of *swa* as a pronoun he writes 'Careful investigation must convince any scholar that examples of indisputable pronominal *swa* are seldom met with. Old English lexicographers and translators have been too ready to render these pseudo-substantives as pronouns.' Seeing that we can transpose 'He did that' into 'That was done (by him)' but not 'He did so' into 'So was done (by him)', we must, I think, agree that *swa* in *Gen* 12. 18 *Hwæt la, hwi dydest ðu swa wið me?* is no more a pronoun than *wel* in *Luke(WSCp)* 6. 33 *And gyf ge wel doð þam ðe eow wel deð. . . .* But the notion dies hard. See my comments in *Ang.* 81 (1963), 300; *RES* 15 (1964), 140; and *NM* 70 (1969), 75-8. This problem has been discussed by Visser for sentences containing 'do' + 'so' (i. 177-82) and other verbs + 'so' (i. 483-6). He seems to share my view of the function of OE *swa* in these sentences, but goes on (i. 483) 'it seems safest to say that in the course of time *so* in the collocations of the type "I think so" gradually assumed the function of a quasi-object, almost passing into the sense "that" '.

§1140. On *swa* as a co-ordinating conjunction, alone and in combinations like *swa eac*, see §§1740, 1748, and 1825-6. On *swa* as a subordinating conjunction, alone or in combinations like *swa . . . swa, swa . . . swylce, swa þæt*, and *swa . . . þæt*, see the Index of Words and Phrases.

§1141. *þæs* sometimes appears in the poetry as an adverb marking degree or proportion where *swa* would be used in the prose; BT (s.v.

se V. 2(*b*)) compares the 'colloquial use of *that* = *so* with adjectives'. A typical example is

Pan 4   þæs wide sind   geond world innan
                  fugla ond deora   foldhrerendra
                  wornas widsceope. . . .[265]

To þæs occasionally serves the same function in the early prose, e.g. *Bede* 366. 17 *Wæs seo eorðe to ðæs heard 7 to ðæs stanihte, þæt ðær nænig wiht wyllsprynges beon mihte on gesewen*, and in the poetry, e.g.

Sea 39   Forþon nis þæs modwlonc   mon ofer eorþan,
                  ne his gifena þæs god,   ne in geoguþe to þæs hwæt,
                  ne in his dædum to þæs deor,   ne him his dryhten to þæs hold,
                  þæt he a his sæfore   sorge næbbe,
                  to hwon hine dryhten ˈ gedon wille,

where we have *þæs* twice and *to þæs* thrice. The various uses of adv. *þæs* and *to þæs* to form conjunctions are discussed as they become relevant; see the Index of Words and Phrases.

§1142. As in MnE, *to* indicates excess, e.g. *ÆCHom* ii. 138. 26 *ðylæs ðe ðeos racu eow to lang ðince* and *ÆCHom* ii. 340. 2 *Ne tæle ge to dyrstelice*. But (as I have suggested elsewhere) it seems to me that it did not always have this connotation. Instances in point are

And 97   Ic þe, Matheus,   mine sylle
                  sybbe under swegle.   Ne beo ðu on sefan to forht,
                  ne on mode ne murn,

where God is more likely to be saying 'Don't be at all afraid' than 'Don't be too afraid', and *WHom* 20(*C*). 14 *7 unrihta to fela ricsode on lande*, where it is hard to accept that Wulfstan is urging the value of sin in moderation. The *locus classicus* in OE for this use—a sort of meiosis or understatement—is (I believe)

Wan 65   Wita sceal geþyldig,
                  ne sceal no to hatheort   ne to hrædwyrde,
                  ne to wac wiga   ne to wanhydig,
                  ne to forht ne to fægen,   ne to feohgifre
                  ne næfre gielpes to georn, ær he geare cunne.
                  Beorn sceal gebidan,   þonne he beot spriceð,
                  oþþæt collenferð   cunne gearwe
                  hwider hreþra gehygd   hweorfan wille.

§1143. For the full development of my argument, the reader is referred to *NM* 69 (1968), 191–8. After the appearance of that article,

---

[265] On *þæs . . . þæt* in *Bo(C)* 75. 4 where MS *B* has *swa . . . þæt*, and in two other prose examples, see §2878.

and after the drafting of the above paragraph (Jan. 1972), Downs's 'Notes on the Intensive Use of Germanic *te, *to, "to : too"' (*JEGP* 38 (1939), 64-8) came to my notice. In this, Downs dismissed earlier explanations of the origin of the intensifying use of *to* and advanced this theory (p. 68):

To recapitulate: OE *to*, OS *te*, OHG *zi, ze*, OFr *to, te*, ON *til* are used in the prepositional function and with the original meaning to indicate the point to which an action extends. From negative understatements which imply absolute negation, the positive comes to suggest an activity which is in excess of what is right and proper. This semantic change is then supported by the use with adjectives or adverbs which in themselves suggest high degree or great quantity [he cited *And* 1301 *to feala* and *Jul* 99 *to swiþe*], and further strengthened by the addition to the construction of intensifying adverbs which also indicate a high degree or completeness [he cited *Beo* 694 *to fela micles*].

The OE examples in which he found *to* implying absolute negation are *And* 97 (§1142), *And* 1431 *Ne wep þone wræcsið, wine leofesta,* ‖ *nis þe to frecne, Jul* 573 *Næs se feond to læt, Soul i* 38 *Nis nu huru se ende to god* (which has a modern ring), and *ChristA* 372 *Cym nu, hæleþa cyning,* ‖ *ne lata to lange* which (he said) 'obviously means "do not tarry at all, come now, at once"'. He thus anticipated my conclusion without extending it to *Wan* 65b-72 or to OE prose.

§1144. On *(ne) þæt an (þæt)* '(not) only', see §§1777-99.

§1145. Rissanen notes nine examples of *for an*—four directly translating *tantum(modo)*, *Lch* i. 286. 10, and four from *The Seven Sleepers* (*LS* 34, not—it is generally agreed—by Ælfric). It is exclusive and means 'only' in all but one of these; in the exception (*LS* 34. 701) it is intensifying. (I follow Rissanen rather than Skeat on *LS* 34. 112; see Rissanen 1967a, pp. 183-4).

§1146. Three scholars—Borst, Most, and Peltola—have concerned themselves with other ways in which English can express variations in extent or degree. Between them they provide eleven possibilities:

(i) 'intensifying' adjectives;
(ii) and (iii) compounds of various sorts;
(iv) comparison;
(v) repetition;
(vi) understatement;
(vii) negation;
(viii) 'stylistic interpretation';
(ix) variations in element order and sentence structure, including parataxis;
(x) stress, intonation, and vowel or consonant lengthening;
(xi) the use of interjections, exclamations, and rhetorical questions.

I give the bibliographical details and discuss these possibilities in *NM* 77 (1976), 25–31. On the comparative absolute, see further §§183–6. Most adds a few observations on some of these devices in *NM* 77 (1976), 178–89. She took no cognizance of my work in her 1978 'greatly revised version' of her thesis (Ingersoll, p. vii). I have not made a detailed comparison of her two versions. But a comparative study of my 1976 article and her 1978 version suggests that no changes of great moment were made in the treatment of the topics in question.

7. INTERROGATIVE ADVERBS

§1147. As in MnE, interrogative adverbs can introduce both non-dependent and dependent questions, e.g. *ÆLS* 32. 150 *Hwær eart þu nu, gefera?* and *ÆLS* 32. 211 *Men þa þæs wundrodon hu þa weargas hangodon.*

§1148. Those most common in OE are *hwær* 'where?', 'whither?', *hwider* 'whither?', and *hwanon* 'whence?'; *hwonne* 'when?'; *hwy* and *hwæt* 'why?'; and *hu* and *humeta* 'how?'. Some of these may be used in combinations involving adverbs, prepositions, and/or adjectives (+ nouns), e.g. *Matt(WSCp)* 17. 17 *Hu lange beo ic mid eow? Hu lange forbere ic eow?*, *ÆCHom* i. 344. 29 *Hwærto beoð þas geendebyrde . . . ?*, *Luke(WSCp)* 16. 5 *Hu mycel scealt þu minum hlaforde?*, and *ÆIntSig* 91 *On hu manegum wisum is Godes weorc?*

§1149. Some combinations of a preposition and an oblique case of *hwæt* 'what?' also serve as interrogative adverbs, e.g. *to hwæs* 'whither?', *of hwam* 'whence?', and *for hwæm* (*hwan, hwy*) 'why?', e.g. *CP* 241. 16 *ðonne mon mæg ongietan of hwam hit æresð com, 7 for hwæm*, where the EETS translation reads 'then we can understand whence it arose, and wherefore'.

§1150. In MnE, most interrogative adverbs can also be used as relatives and as conjunctions, e.g. 'I know (the place) where it happened'. *Hwonne* had (I believe) advanced further along this road than the other OE interrogatives; see §§2507 and 2775–83.

J. PREPOSITIONS

1. INTRODUCTORY REMARKS

§1151. Just as I use 'subjunctive mood' without regard to whether the verb concerned appears in a principal or subordinate clause, so

I use 'preposition' irrespective of whether the word in question precedes or follows the word it 'governs' or with which it is used;[266] on this see §§1060-2. Where necessary 'pre-position' and 'post-position' are distinguished. Here (as with adverbs) the difficulty is to determine where a syntax ends and a dictionary begins. It is clearly impossible for me to give a full treatment of the subtle nuances which can be implied by many OE prepositions. I have tried to do three things: first, to discuss syntactical points of interest about OE prepositions in general, with references forward where necessary; second, to provide a list of OE prepositions, giving the cases with which they are used, their main MnE equivalents, and comments on any points of interest or controversy peculiar to each one; and third, to give a brief outline of developments in the OE period.

§1152. In addition to the dictionaries, the following works can be consulted for lists of examples: (for the prose) Harstrick, Wülfing, ii, Flamme, and Mohrbutter; (for the poetry) Taubert and 'the eighteen German dissertations' less those of Reussner and Rose; for prepositions denoting place in both prose and poetry Burkhart; and for prepositions expressing cause in prose, van Dam, pp. 1-39, and Liggins 1955, pp. 479-509. Reference is made to these when they have more than lists to offer. Part I of Haddock's thesis gives full lists of examples of the prepositions in the *Lindisfarne Gospels*. Studies of individual prepositions are cited when appropriate. Timmer (1934, pp. 46-101) contains much information of value to the lexicographer. Brorström's first concern is not with OE in his studies on English prepositions. But he too has some points of interest to the lexicographer in his article entitled 'A Historical Survey of Prepositions Expressing the Sense "for the duration of" ' in *EStudies*, 52 (1971), 105-16, and in the two works mentioned in the bibliography to that article. Brorström's work stimulated Yamakawa, who offers some important observations on the semantic development of the various OE prepositions which express duration of time; he lists *binnan, for, geond, on, þurh*, and *to* (1980, pp. 14-19). See §1384.

§1153. I am informed by Dr Arthur Sandved of Oslo University that two of his students—Helge Arnljot Lund and Sylvi Ferning—have written Cand.Phil. theses in which they have examined the regimen of some OE prepositions. Ferning studied *for(e), innan, mid, ofer, þurh, under, wiþ*, and *ymb*, in Thorpe's edition of the Second Series of Ælfric's *Catholic Homilies*. Lund, working on the First

---

[266] This use of 'governs' has respectable antecedents; see *OED*, s.v. *govern* 11. But a historical objection to its use is succinctly put by Ardern, p. xxvi.

Series, studied the corrections carried out in MS Royal 7C.xii after *ofer, ongean, þurh, wiþ*, and *ymb*, using the facsimile edition edited by Eliason and Clemoes. After all these prepositions except *ymb*, they noted a *tendency* to prefer the accusative with singular and plural pronouns and with singular nouns, but the dative with plural nouns. However, their work did not permit the drawing of firm conclusions either about the extent of this tendency or the reason(s) for it. One possible theory—that Ælfric was avoiding ambiguous inflexional forms—did not seem to hold. More work here might prove rewarding. (For more details and for a discussion of the difficulties and possibilities, see now Sandved, 'Some Notes on the Syntax of Prepositions in Ælfric's Homilies', *Studies in English Language and Early Literature in Honour of Paul Christophersen* (Occasional Papers in Linguistics and Language Teaching, The New University of Ulster, 8 (1981), 117-35).)

2. THE FUNCTIONS OF PREPOSITIONS AND PREPOSITIONAL PHRASES

a. General remarks

§1154. It is not always easy to decide on the exact function of a word which is normally regarded as a preposition. Thus *æt* in *Bede* 342. 27 *þa stod him sum mon æt þurh swefn* might be described as a preposition, an adverb, or a separable prefix. On this terminological problem, which is linked with the question of the origin of prepositions, see §§1060-80.

§1155. As in MnE, prepositions may govern nouns and noun equivalents (examples will readily be found in the sections which follow); pronouns, e.g. *Bede* 326. 26 *nu oð þis* and *ÆLS* 4. 265 *on þære hwile oðþæt*; adverbs and adverbial expressions, e.g. *ChronA* 48. 16 (755) *7 þa þær to eodon*,[267] *GD* 234. 9 *oð nu iv gear, ÆCHom* ii. 186. 23 *on ær* 'beforehand', and *ÆCHom* ii. 184. 27 *oð forð nihtes*; and even a prepositional phrase, e.g. *Bede* 52. 10 *oð to dæge* and *ÆCHom* i. 214. 28 *oð nu on ðunresdæg*. Two prepositions may govern one noun, e.g. *Ch* 939 *ægþer ge on life ge æfter*.

[267] In *EStudien*, 73 (1938-9), 334-5, Ellinger gives further OE examples of such combinations of an adverb and a preposition as a preliminary to a study of them in later periods of English. His examples include *heræfter, þærinne, þær into, þær of, þær on*, and *þær to*. As BT remarks (s.v. *þær* IV), *þær* 'in combination with suffixed prepositions . . . has the force of a pronoun'. But we need not follow those who, like Nagashima (p. 150), claim that it 'has turned into' one.

§1156. A preposition may also govern a clause, e.g. *Lch* iii. 86. 11 *Eft sona wið gyf þeo ylca adle cilde egelic on geogeþe, nim garluces heafud . . .* , *Matt(WSCp)* 5. 13 *Gyf þ̄ sealt awyrð on þam þe hit gesylt bið, hit ne mæg syððan to nahte buton þ̄ hit sy utaworpen...* , Latin *... ad nihilum ualet ultra nisi ut mittatur foras ...* ,

Sat 387
  Him beforan fereð   fægere leoht
  þonne we æfre ær   eagum gesawon,
  buton þa we mid englum   uppe wæron,

and

Men 29
        Swylce eac is wide cuð
  ymb III and twa   þeodum gewelhwær
  his cyme kalend   ceorlum and eorlum
  (butan þænne bises   geboden weorðe
  feorðan geare;   þænne he furðor cymeð
  ufor anre niht   us to tune),

or the accusative and infinitive construction, e.g. *Sea* 18 *þær ic ne gehyrde butan hlimman sæ,* || *iscaldne wæg.* However, the status of *butan* in such examples is arguable; see §§3628-33.

§1157. Some prepositions double as adverbs and/or conjunctions, e.g. *ær*; see the Index of Words and Phrases. On adverbs and conjunctions formed with prepositions, e.g. *to þæs (þe)*, see §§1230, 1233, and 2420.

§1158. Prepositional phrases may be used in combination with nouns and noun equivalents, adjectives, verbs—these three are discussed in §§1159-69; adverbs (e.g. *Bede* 326. 26 (§1155), *BlHom* 209. 32 *norð of ðæm stane,* and *ÆCHom* i. 100. 8 *ær on þam feorðan dæge* 'before the fourth day'); and other prepositional phrases (e.g. *LS* 4. 265 (§1155)). They are often the equivalent of a simple case form (see §§1223-8) and can be used in parallel with other prepositional phrases, with participial phrases—*ÆCHom* ii. 516. 29 *Æfter ðisum gebede, he abad on ðam legere ane feawa dagas, mid fefore gewæht, þurh wacolon gebedum, on flore licgende, bestreowod mid axum, on stiðre hæran, up ahafenum eagum and handum to heofenum, and ne geswac his gebeda oðþæt he sawlode* is a convenient illustration of these two—and with inflected infinitives, e.g. *ÆCHom* ii. 340. 20 *Ne lufode he woruldlice æhta for his neode ana, ac to dælenne eallum wædliendum.* They can also serve as a complement, e.g. *ÆCHom* ii. 58. 2 *Seo forme yld wæs fram Adame oð Noe.*

§1158a. The prepositions *æt, for, from, mid, on,* and *to*, were sometimes used by Anglo-Saxon glossators to mark the case of the noun
or adjective over which they were placed; see Robinson in *Festschrift
Prof. Dr. Herbert Koziol zum siebzigsten Geburtstag* (Wiener Beiträge
zur englischen Philologie, 75 (1973), 267-8) and the references
given there.

b. Nouns, numerals, or pronouns, + prepositional phrase

§1159. It could be said that, when used with a noun, a prepositional
phrase, like the genitive case (§100), sometimes comes close to being
the equivalent of an adjective, e.g. *Bede* 246. 18 *twegen biscopas of
Bretta ðeode*—cf. *ChronA* 48. 10 (755) *butan anum Bryttiscum
gisle*—and *Dan* 175 *gyld of golde*—cf. *Dan* 204 *to þam gyldnan
gylde*. Further on the partitive use in the first example, see §415.

§1160. But the function of the prepositional phrase with a noun is
often wider than this: it may not only describe, but may express
place, purpose, personal relationship, and so on, e.g. *Or* 262. 1
scopleoð be þæm bryne, Bede 256. 26 *he hæfde caseres ærendo
sumo to Breotone cyningum wið Froncna rice, Bo* 102. 8 *nænne ege
to oðrum, Or* 154. 30 *he hæfde xx elpenda to þæm gefeohte, CP*
142. 9 *ðylæs hiera lufu wið hiene aslacige*, and *ÆCHom* ii. 84. 22
. . . *Amalarius, se awrat ane boc be cyrclicum ðeawum*. Sometimes
a phrase may be taken with the noun or with the verb, e.g. *Bede*
46. 6 *Swylce eac on þæs sæs waroþe to suðdæle, þanon ðe hisciphere
on becom, torras timbredon to gebeorghe ðæs sæs* and *ÆCHom* ii.
44. 23 *We rædað on bocum be ðære culfran gecynde.* . . .

§1161. Examples of what appears to be an independent use of
phrases with no governing noun are given in §1201.

§1162. Numerals and words like *ænig, feala, nan,* and *sum,* can be
followed by *of* + dative of a noun or pronoun; see again §1201. So
also *monig,* e.g. *Bede* 240. 31 *monige of Ongelþeode ge æðelinga ge
oðerra.*

§1163. I have as yet noted no OE examples of the type 'Those from
London' or 'For those in peril on the sea', unless we admit those
from *ChronC* in §316, which have an expressed antecedent. In sentences like *ÆCHom* i. 332. 34 *forðan ðe se ðearfa nære fullice ge-
wrecen on ðam rican, gif he on his wite hine ne oncneowe* 'if he
[the rich man] in his punishment had not recognized him [the poor

man]' and *ÆCHom* ii. 552. 26 . . . *þonne he on ðam ecum eðele, betwux engla heapum, be his edleane blissað wiðutan*, the prepositional phrases can equally well be taken with the verb as with the personal pronoun. The earliest unambiguous English examples of these patterns seem to be *ChronE* 260. 20 (1129) *mid him helden ða of Rome* and *ChronE* 267. 25 (1140) *hi of Normandi*. The Gothic parallels spoken of by Bødtker (1910, §44) are presumably the translations or transliterations of the Greek cited by Mätzner (iii. 351).

§1164. But there are examples with a relative pronoun, e.g. *Bede* 68. 19 *Ac feor þæt la sy, þætte Godes cirice mid æteacnesse onfo, þæt heo gesegen bið of eorðlicum þingum anforlæten* (lit. 'what of earthly things') and perhaps *Or* 200. 34 *7 he ealle ofslog þe of þæm landum his men wæron, 7 mid him ofer sæ nolden*, though here *of þæm landum* may depend on *ealle* rather than *þe*; on this point see §§2227-8 and compare *ÆCHom* i. 216. 30 *and ealle ða ðe of heora cynne Gode ær gecwemdon*. Wülfing (ii, §754) has other somewhat similar examples.

c. Adjectives or participles + prepositional phrase

§1165. This combination is familiar in all periods of English; *ÆCHom* i. 50. 4 *and swa se ðe wæs neoðor on endebyrdnesse, wearð fyrmest on ðrowunge*, *ÆCHom* ii. 516. 31 *on flore licgende*, and *ÆCHom* ii. 586. 16 *ymbscryd mid menigfealdre fahnysse*, will suffice to exemplify it.

§1166. Adjectives which can be followed by the genitive and/or dative and by a prepositional phrase are given in the List of adjectival rections in §§218-19. I have not thought it necessary to list adjectives which are used with prepositions but not with oblique cases; there can be very few (if there are any) adjectives which cannot be so used. On constructions like *Or* 32. 13 *7 ða syndon swyþe fægere 7 lustsumlice on to seonne*, see §§928-31.

d. Verbs + preposition or prepositional phrase

§1167. A prepositional phrase with a verb is often the equivalent of an adverb. A few examples of this common use must suffice: *Or* 1. 16 *Hu Moyses lædde Israhela folc from Egyptum ofer þone Readan Sæ*, *Or* 156. 33 *þæt wearð eac Romanum an yfelum tacne opiewed ær þæm gefeohte, þa hie on firde wæron*, and *Or* 104. 2 *Gallie oferhergedan Romana lond oð iiii mila to ðære byrig*. Arngart (*NM* 80 (1979), 46) gives a list of such phrases containing the noun *þing*.

§1168. The following topics are discussed elsewhere: the use of *to* + dative rather than the simple dative as the indirect objects of verbs; prepositional phrases as the complement of verbs like *wesan* and *weorþan*; verbs constructed with a preposition, e.g. *geleornian æt/ þurh*; verbs compounded with a preposition; the so-called 'separable prefixes'; and the expression of instrumentality or agency by prepositions. For references see the General Index.

§1169. Using a corpus of 1,820 phrases with *mid, be,* or *wið,* L. V. Danyljuk, 'Pro strukturu pryjmennykovoho slovospolučennja staroanhlijs'koji movy', *Inozemna Filolohija,* 42 (1976), 51-7, divides prepositional phrases consisting of 'v[erb] → prep[osition] ⇄ L[exeme]$_{case}$' into those with obligatory elements only, e.g. verb + preposition + noun or pronoun, and those with further optional elements, e.g. verb + preposition + demonstrative + noun or numeral + noun or noun + dependent noun. He distinguishes six types of element order in such phrases and attempts an elaborate analysis on the basis of what is in my opinion an insufficient corpus.

e. Repetition and non-repetition of prepositions

§1170. Prepositions are often repeated in the prose when they govern more than one noun or noun equivalent which are joined by a conjunction such as *ond,* e.g. *CP* 101. 3 *for arfæsðnesse 7 for niedðearfe, Or* 4. 4 *mid þrim hunde scipa 7 mid xxx,* and *Or* 254. 3 *on þæm twæm 7 on feowerteogþan geare.* But they need not be, e.g. *CP* 135. 20 *for ða betstan 7 ða halgestan, Or* 20. 29 *on fif oððe syx, hwylum on ma,* and *Or* 18. 17 *on deora fellum, 7 on fugela feðerum, 7 hwales bane, 7 on þæm sciprapum.* The same fluctuation is apparent with a second adjective, whether it precedes or follows the noun, e.g. *CP* 45. 15 *mid miclum 7 mid monegum Godes giefum* and *Or* 21. 1 *to þæm ærestan dæle 7 to þæm mæstan* but *CP* 301. 13 *betwiux ðæm læsðum 7 ðæm gingestum monnum* and *Bede* 248. 20 *to þam soðan geleafan 7 þæm apostolican.* So also with a genitive, e.g. *Or* 18. 18 *of hwæles hyde geworht, 7 of seoles,* but *Bede* 150. 7 *for Eadbaldes ege 7 Oswaldes.* For further examples, see Wülfing, ii, §§1101-3, and Gottweis, pp. 79-83.

§1171. As in MnE, the preposition is not repeated with the second of two expressions in apposition, e.g. *Or* 14. 28 *From þære ie Danais west oþ Rin þa ea* and *Bede* 2. 24 *þurh Noðhelm ðone æfestan mæssepreost.* In these constructions there is, of course, no conjunction.

§ 1172. The same situations obtain in the poetry. The preposition is often repeated, e.g. *GenB* 482 *mid swate and mid sorgum* and *Sea* 44 *Ne biþ him to hearpan hyge ne to hringþege*, but need not be, e.g.

Wid 84   Mid Moidum ic wæs ond mid Persum   ond mid Myrgingum,
                  ond Mofdingum   ond ongend Myrgingum,
                  ond mid Amothingum.   Mid Eastþyringum ic wæs
                  ond mid Eolum ond mid Istum   ond Idumingum.

However, my observation is that the exigencies of the metrical line mean that, if the preposition is not dispensed with—as it is in *Beo* 40 *billum ond byrnum*—it is more often repeated than not, especially when the two expressions are in different half-lines. None the less, the absence of *to* before *meoto* in *Beo* 489 *Site nu to symle ond onsæl meoto* (Klaeber's reading) would seem to rule out Robinson's notion that *meoto* is for *meodo* 'mead' and his translation 'Sit now to the feast and, in time, [to] the mead' (*EStudies*, 49 (1968), 513-15). In my view, the intervention of *on sæl* would demand ☆*to meoto* if his interpretation were right.

§ 1173. But the preposition is not repeated with the second of two expressions in apposition, e.g. *Pan* 33 *butan þam attorsceaþan* ‖ *his fyrngeflitan*, *Wid* 5 *mid Ealhhilde, fælre freoþuwebban*, and (with an intervening verb) *Dream* 151 *þa he mid manigeo com,* ‖ *gasta weorode*. On the lack of agreement in *Beo* 1830 *Ic on Higelace wat,* ‖ *Geata dryhten . . .* , see § 1441.

§ 1174. The fact that the line between apposition and variation is hard to draw in poetry must be called in to explain some apparent inconsistencies or exceptions. In

Mald 96   Wodon þa wælwulfas   (for wætere ne murnon),
                   wicinga werod,   west ofer Pantan,
                   ofer scir wæter   scyldas wegon,
                   lidmen to lande   linde bæron,

the repetition of *ofer* either gives added emphasis—cf. MnE 'over Everest, over the highest mountain in the world'—or suggests that *ofer scir wæter* is used *apo koinou* with both *wodon* and *wegon* rather than simply in apposition with *ofer Pantan*. In

Mald 122   Swa stemnetton   stiðhicgende
                    hysas æt hilde,   hogodon georne
                    hwa þær mid orde   ærost mihte
                    on fægean men   feorh gewinnan,
                    wigan mid wæpnum;   wæl feol on eorðan,

the absence of *on* before *wigan* supports the natural feeling that *wigan* is in apposition with *hysas* and not with *on fægean men*. In

Sea 58   Forþon nu min hyge hweorfeð   ofer hreþerlocan,
             min modsefa   mid mereflode
             ofer hwæles eþel   hweorfeð wide,
             eorþan sceatas,   cymeð eft to me
             gifre ond grædig,   gielleð anfloga,
             hweteð on hwælweg   hreþer unwearnum
             ofer holma gelagu,

the absence of *ofer* before *eorþan sceatas* emphasizes the fact that the latter is (as Christopher Ball put it in a private communication) 'a gloss on *hwæles eþel*'. The repetition of *of* in

El 293   Hwæt, ge ealle snyttro   unwislice,
             wraðe wiðweorpon,   þa ge wergdon þane
             þe eow of wergðe   þurh his wuldres miht,
             fram ligcwale,   lysan þohte,
             of hæftnede

is dictated by the separation of the two nouns, whereas the repetition of *be* in

Mald 317   Ic eom frod feores;   fram ic ne wille,
             ac ic me be healfe   minum hlaforde,
             be swa leofan men,   licgan þence

shows that *leofan men* is not in apposition with *minum hlaforde*. The poet has achieved greater emphasis by varying not only his words but also his syntax. We could indeed say that he had to repeat *be* because the phrases are not syntactically parallel in the sense that *men* cannot be in apposition with *healfe*.

§1175. So I am now prepared to go further than I did in *NM* 73 (1972), 233-4. I now believe that this last example deals the final death-blow to Stevens's suggestion that in

Wife 1   Ic þis giedd wrece   bi me ful geomorre,
             minre sylfre sið

we read *siðe* for *sið*, understand *bi* before *minre*, and take line 2a as parallel to *me*. It will not do to say that we can understand *bi* in this way. The fact is that ☆*siðe* could not be in apposition with *me* but would have to be a variant of it. So (I would argue) the repetition of *bi* would be obligatory. For the same reason I reject Wrenn's suggestion that in

Beo 874   welhwylc gecwæð,
             þæt he fram Sigemunde   secgan hyrde,
             ellendædum,   uncuþes fela . . .

ellendædum 'is in apposition to the dat. *Sigemunde*, and there is no need to emend to gen. *Sigemundes*, as Klaeber and some others have done'; for similar separation of a preposition from the noun it governs, compare *Beo* 450 *no ðu ymb mines ne þearft* || *lices feorme leng sorgian*.

Jul 652

	Ge mid lufan sibbe,
leohte geleafan,	to þam lifgendan
stane stiðhydge	staþol fæstniað,

would not, in my opinion, justify the failure to repeat *bi* and *for*, for 'love of peace' comes from 'true belief' and the second is a parenthetic, almost appositional, variation of the first; cf. *Sea* 58 (§1174).

§1176. As far as I have observed then, OE is like MnE. One can say 'over hill and over dale', 'over hill and dale', 'over hill, over dale', 'over Everest, the highest mountain in the world', and 'over Everest, over the highest mountain in the world' (where the repetition of 'over' is for stylistic effect). But one cannot say 'over hill, dale'. The absence from my collections of examples like 'over hill, dale, and fen' may be the result of chance or faulty observation.

3. LIST OF PREPOSITIONS

a. Notes

§1177. (1) The prepositions are arranged alphabetically. No attempt has been made to distinguish *eigentlich* from *uneigentlich* or simple from compound prepositions, or to divide compound prepositions into those formed from nouns, adjectives, or adverbs; see Wülfing, ii, pp. viiia–viiim. It is sometimes difficult to separate compound prepositions and prepositional phrases, and I have perhaps erred in excluding groups like *be eastan, be suþaneastan, to norþdæle*, and *wiþ eastan* (Wülfing, ii. 677–9, and Hittle, p. 164), *for lufan* and *for naman* (Flamme, pp. 58 and 71), *on laste* (Ahrens, p. 46, and others of 'the eighteen German dissertations'), and *to willan* (Höser, p. 43), while including *tomiddes* + genitive, where (as BT, s.v. II, remarks) 'perhaps, *middes* should rather be taken as noun governing the following word in the genitive'; see also Flamme, p. 58, and Wülfing, ii. 676. But one must draw a line somewhere.

(2) Traditionally prepositions do not 'govern' the nominative case. Carlton (1970, pp. 84–5) remarks that a noun after *ongean* 'is either nominative or accusative' and (perhaps more sensibly) that after *ymb* 'forms are either nominative or accusative'. The testimony of

unambiguous contexts suggests that we are justified in taking these nouns or pronouns as accusative rather than in erecting an otherwise unsupported 'rule' that prepositions can be used with the nominative. (See further my review of Carlton 1970 in *MÆ* 40 (1971), 181-4.) So we can say that in OE prepositions may be followed by the accusative, genitive, dative, and instrumental. Since there is no significance in variations between the dative and instrumental (see §8), the latter has not been included in the list. Prepositions are sometimes found with more than one case in the same sentence, e.g. *ÆCHom* ii. 358. 10 *ðurh drycræft oððe ðurh runstafum* and—more oddly, since the preposition is not repeated—*LS* 34. 241 *wið þam awyrgedan strangan and þone ealdan wiðerwinnan.* We find another variation in *El* 703 *to ðan strang . . . þæs þearl . . . to ðæs heard*, where *to ðan*, *þæs*, and *to ðæs*, all mean 'so' (not 'too', as in Kennedy's prose translation). Such variations presumably played a part in the breakdown of the inflexional system; see §1222.

(3) ? before a word indicates that its use as a preposition in OE is doubtful, and before an abbreviation for a case that the use of that case with the preposition in question is doubtful.

(4) Prepositions marked with a dagger (†) are used with both accusative and dative, the distinction often being accusative of motion towards, and dative of rest in, a place. However, there seems to have been a different conception of motion and rest (cf. §1205) and the distinction is not always observed, either with the prepositions marked †—e.g., *ofer* (*GenA* 1493 *He . . . ǁ stah ofer streamweall* but *GenA* 1433 *hwonne hie . . . ofer nægledbord* [acc.] ǁ *ofer streamstaðe* [dat.] *stæppan mosten* and *Beo* 982 *siþðan æþelingas . . . ǁ ofer heanne hrof hand sceawedon*—the demands of metre are obvious in these examples) and *on* (*Or* 17. 4 *buton on feawum stowum styccemælum wiciað Finnas* but *Or* 264. 9 *And he bebead þæt mon Iohannes þone apostol gebrohte on Bothmose þæm iglande* and *Or* 17. 24 *Ac him wæs ealne weg weste land on þæt steorbord*) —or with other prepositions which may seem to us on all fours with them—e.g., *geond* (*Or* 38. 2 *7 hy crupon þæm mannum betuh þa þeoh ge geond eall þa limu* but *Or* 19. 5 *7 þær sint swiðe micle meras fersce geond þa moras*) and *into* (e.g. *ChronA* 74. 10 (876) *7 hie þa under þam hie nihtes bestælon þære fierde se gehorsoda here into Escan ceaster* but *Or* 138. 28 *7 þæs ymb an gear Somnite gefuhton wið Romanum . . . 7 hie bedrifon into Romebyrg*).[268]

---

[268] Wülfing, ii, gives numerous examples of such variations; thus, for more with *on*, see his §§784, 801, and 821. Marcq, however, in his 'Structure du système des prépositions spatiales dans le *Beowulf*', *Études germaniques*, 28 (1973), 1-19, constantly speaks of the dative as 'marque de relation locative' and of the accusative as 'marque de relation directive'.

Similarly, the distinction between the accusative indicating duration and the dative indicating the point of time does not always hold, either with or without prepositions; see §§1207, 1387-8, and 1421-4.

(5) On the use of prepositions to express agency or instrumentality, see §§802-33a. References to the use of individual prepositions in these functions are given in the appropriate section below.

b. Alphabetical list

§1178.

abutan (dat., acc.) about, around
æfter (dat., acc.). See §§1179-82.
ær (dat., acc. (see Wülfing, ii. 668, and BTS, s.v.)) before (time)
æt (dat.) at, etc.; (acc.) as far as, until. (See Flamme, p. 59; Wülfing, ii. 311; Belden, pp. 73-8; Gottweis, pp. 4-28; and Dusenschön, pp. 15-26.) On *æt* expressing agency, see §§808-9.
ætforan (dat., acc. (see Wülfing, ii. 636)) before
?*ætsamne* (dat.) together with. (See Wülfing, ii. 668.)
agen, see *ongean*
an, see *on*
?*and*, see §1739
angean, see *ongean*
andlang (gen., acc.) along
andlanges (gen.) along
be (dat., acc. (*ÆCHom* i. 486. 17)). See §§1183-4.
bæftan, *beæftan* (dat.) behind, without. See also *wiþæftan*.
beforan (†dat., acc.) before, in front of. (See Timmer 1934, pp. 51-2.)
begeondan (dat., ?acc. (*Matt(WSCp)* 19. 1)) beyond
beheonan (dat.) on this side of
behindan (†dat., acc.) behind. See also *wiþhindan*.
beinnan, see *binnan*
beneoþan (dat.) beneath
beutan (dat.) outside
betweoh, *betweonum*, *betweox* (dat., acc.) between, among. (The two alleged examples with the genitive from *Bede* are best explained otherwise; see Wülfing, ii. 670. *Or* prefers *betweonum*, *Bo betwuh* and its variants; see Bately, *Ang.* 88 (1970), 449.)
binnan (†dat., acc.) within
bufan (†dat., acc.) above. See also *ofer-, on-, wiþ-, ufan*.
butan (dat., acc.) without, out of, except. (Bale, p. 39, notes *butan* + genitive in *Matt(Li)* 5. 32 and *Mark(Li)* 7. 15. Both these are direct glosses of Latin genitives. In *ÆHex* 434 *anes treowes* probably depends on *geweald* in line 430.) See also *a-, on-, butan*.
*ce (dat.) (*ÆCHom* i. 124. 31) concerning, should read *be*
eac (dat.) in addition to
emb, emban, embe, see *ymb, ymbe*
emnlange (dat.) along. (See Wülfing, ii. 674.)
?*feor* (dat.) far from. (See Wülfing, ii. 674.) See also ?*unfeor*.
for, fore (dat., acc., ?gen.). See §§1185-7.
foran (dat.) before. (On its use as an adverb with other prepositions, see BTS, s.v. *foran* II(2).) See also *æt-, be-, on-, to-, wiþ-, foran*.
?*forþ*, see *Bo* 122. 4 and *OED*, s.v. *forth* B. prep. 1. But we may have *forþ* adv. + accusative of duration of time.
fram (dat.). See §§1188-9.
gean, see *ongean*
gehende (dat.) near
gemang (†dat., acc.) among. See also *ongemang, onmang*.

geond (acc., dat. (in prose only?; see GK and Jacobsen 1908, pp. 36-7)) through, over, among. See also *be-*, *wiþ-*, *geondan*.

in (†dat., acc.). See §§1190-3.

innan (†dat., acc., gen.) in, within. See also *be-*, *on-*, *wiþ-*, *innan*.

?inne (case doubtful) in. (See my discussion in *Neophil.* 52 (1968) 294-7.)

into (dat., acc.) into. (See Wülfing, ii. 649-50, and *OED*, s.v.)

mid (dat., acc.). See §§1194-8.

?neah (dat.) near to. (See Wülfing, ii. 674-5.)

of (dat.). See §§1199-203.

ofer (†dat., acc.) over, across, through; on, upon; after; contrary to. (See Wullen, pp. 424-62.)

oferufan(dat., acc.) on, above

on (†dat., acc., ?gen.). See §§1204-6.

onbutan (dat., acc.) about

onefn, onemn (dat., acc.) near. See also *toefnes*.

onforan(acc.) before, in front of

onforeweardan (dat.) in front of

ongean (dat., acc.) opposite, against. See also *togean*.

ongemang (dat., acc.) among

oninnan (dat.) within

onlang, see *andlang*

onmang (dat.) among

onmiddan (dat.) in the middle of. See also *tomiddes*.

onufan (dat., acc.) on, upon, after (time)

onuppan (dat.) upon, on, over and above

oþ (dat., acc.) up to, as far as, until

samod (dat.) with, at

?siþþan, see *ÆCHom* ii. 298. 6 and §3832

te, til, see *to*

to (dat., gen., acc.). See §§1209-16.

toeacan (dat.) in addition to, besides

toefnes, toemnes (dat.) on a level with, beside

toforan (dat., gen.) in front of, before, beyond, etc.

togean, togeanes (dat.) towards, against

tomiddes (dat., ?gen. (see §1177(1))) in the midst of

toweard, to . . . weard (dat., gen.) towards.[269] See also *wiþ . . . weard*.

toweardes (dat.) towards

towiþre (dat., ?acc. (*Max i* 128)) in reply to, against

þurh (acc., dat., ?gen.). See §§1207-8.

þurhut (dat., acc.) throughout, quite through

ufan (acc.) upon in *LS* 7. 312.[270]

ufenan (acc.) above, besides

under (†dat., acc.) under. (See Wullen, pp. 25-51.)

underneoþan (acc.) underneath

?unfeor (dat.) not far from. (See Wülfing, ii. 676-7.)

?unneah (dat.) far from. (See BT, s.v.)

uppan (†dat., acc.) upon, on, on to

?up(pe), see §1064

?ut (case doubtful) out of. See §1064. See also *þurhut*.

utan (gen.) outside of. (See Shipley, p. 120.) See also *butan, be-, wiþ-, ymb-, utan*.

?wana (gen.) wanting in. (See Wülfing, ii. 677.)

wiþ (gen.) towards, against; (dat., acc.) towards, against, near, beside, by, at, etc. (See Hittle, pp. 105-65.) On *wiþ* expressing the instrument, see §§831-2.

wiþæftan (dat., ?acc. (see BT, s.v.)) behind

wiþer (acc.) against

wiþforan, wiþ . . . foran (dat., acc.) before

wiþgeondan (case doubtful (see BT, s.v.)) beyond

---

[269] Belden, p. 60, cites *Or* 202. 2 *þæt land . . . þæt hie toweard wæron* as an example of *toweard* + acc. But *þæt* may be used without regard to case; see §§2238-43.

[270] The reader should not accept the examples cited by Meroney in *JEGP* 44 (1945), 382 fn. 22, without examination. In some, e.g. *BlHom* 51. 12, *ufan* is clearly an adverb.

wiþhindan (dat.) behind
wiþinnan (dat. (see BTS, s.v.)) within
wiþufan (acc. (see BT, s.v.)) above
wiþutan (†dat., acc.) outside, without

wiþ . . . weard, weardes (gen., ?acc.).
  See §1217.
ymb, ymbe (acc., dat.). See §§1218–19.
ymbutan (dat., acc.) about, around,
  without

4. NOTES ON INDIVIDUAL PREPOSITIONS

a. Æfter

§1179. (1) *Æfter* 'after, along, according to' usually takes the dative. BTS (s.v. II) observes that the accusative is 'rare except in Northumbrian Glosses'. Page ('Northumbrian *æfter* (= in memory of) + accusative', *SN* 30 (1958), 145–52) has shown that the accusative is more common in *Li* and *DurRitGl* than in *Ru2*. He argues that this suggests a dialectal difference between North and South Northumbrian and that this view is supported by the fact that the Mercian glosses (*Ru1, PsCa(Kuhn)*, and *Ps(A)*) show a strong preference for the dative. Thus, he remarks, 'at least there must remain the possibility that within Northumbria local dialects existed in which the accusative usage with *æfter* was common' (p. 148). He then considers *æfter* 'in memory of' in memorial inscriptions and concludes that 'the evidence given above does not certainly prove a Northumbrian use of *æfter* (= in memory of) + accusative. It does, however, suggest that the possibility of such a usage is too great to be rejected out of hand, and that in certain texts *æfter* should be glossed as "with accusative or dative" ' (p. 152). Examples of *æfter* + accusative from other texts include *Or* 44. 28 *æfter hrædlice tide* and *Wan* 50 *sare æfter swæsne*.

§1180. (2) Wülfing (ii. 311) cites several examples like *CP* 331. 24 *Ðæt ierfe ðæt ge ærest æfter hiegiað* and suggests that the relative construction was used without thought for what was to follow. We could explain these as early examples of relative pronoun *þæt* used without regard to case, number, or gender (§§2134–5 and 2137), or (perhaps better) take *æfter hiegiað* and the other verbs as compounds (§§1065–6). But they may be genuine examples of *æfter* + accusative.

§1181. (3) Lehmann (p. 40) adds *æfter* to the list of prepositions which take the genitive, citing as his authority *Or* 86. 24 . . . *mid þæm miclan wolbryne monncwealmes, þe him rað ðæs æfter com.* It seems better to explain *ðæs* and *æfter* as adverbs.

§1182. (4) In his note on the last half-line of

ChristA 234   leoma leohtade   leoda mægþum,
    torht mid tunglum,   æfter þon tida bigong,

J. J. Campbell writes:

æfterþon. Grein, Gollancz, and Cook print this as *æfter þon*, apparently not disturbed that *þon*, as an article, is in the instrumental case but modifies a noun in the accusative. K–D suggest that *æfterþon* is a compound word and perhaps should be considered analogous to *ærþon*. Unfortunately, the *ærþon* they use for analogy (l. 25 of this poem) [= *ChristA* 238] is obviously a conjunction rather than a preposition. It does seem likely that this compound preposition did exist in Old English, however, although Sweet's *Student's Anglo-Saxon Dictionary* is the only dictionary which lists it.[271]

In the absence of other examples of such a preposition, an alternative (and perhaps more likely) solution is to read *þone* for *þon*, in the belief that the scribe had *æfter þone* . . . and carelessly substituted the formulaic *æfter þon*.

b. Be

§1183. (1) The reader must consult the dictionaries for the various meanings of *be*; to attempt a summary would be merely confusing.[272] *Be* takes the dative/instrumental. Neither BT(S) nor Wülfing offers examples with any other case. Dusenschön (pp. 26–35) found none in the poetry; GK's tentative citing of *Deor* 1 *be wurman* as an example of *be* + accusative (p. 36, top right) need not stand. Gottweis (p. 63) draws our attention to *ÆCHom* i. 486. 17 *Nu is to besceawigenne humeta se Ælmihtiga God, be his gecorenan and ða gelufedan ðenas . . . geðafað þæt hi mid swa micclum witum beon fornumene . . .* , where *be* may take the dative and then the accusative. This probably testifies to a weakening of case distinctions rather than to a genuine usage of *be* + accusative; it was perhaps encouraged by examples like those mentioned in §1177(2), where such variations represent genuine dative/accusative fluctuation after other prepositions.

§1184. (2) The most interesting point about *be* is probably whether it is used to express the means or agent by which something is done. On this see §§810–11.

[271] J. J. Campbell, *The Advent Lyrics of the Exeter Book* (Princeton, 1959), 94, note to line 22. I must confess that I cannot find *æfterþon* listed by Sweet as a preposition. Dusenschön (pp. 7–15) discusses *æfter* in OE poetry.
[272] *Be* is glossed by BT (s.v. I) as (among other things) 'at'. But this does not justify Thorpe's translation 'at this present tide' in *ÆCHom* ii. 84. 19; cf. *ÆCHom* ii. 84. 23 and note that the BTS discussion (s.v. II) of temporal *be* makes no mention of the meaning 'at'. Bødtker 1908, pp. 38–9, comments on several uses of *be*. Gottweis (pp. 28–64) gives examples.

c. For, fore

§ 1185. (1) Here too the reader must consult the dictionaries on the various meanings and functions of *for* and *fore*. On *for* = 'before' (temporal) in *Gregory's Dialogues*, see Timmer 1934, pp. 52–3. *OED* (s.v. *for*) remarks that 'in OE. *for* and *fore* seem to have been used indiscriminately as preps.' and Wülfing (ii. 339 and 354) observes that, while *fore* is less frequent than *for* in 'Alfredian' texts, it does not differ from it in meaning or use; note the manuscript variations in (for example) *CP* 55. 14 and 107. 24. One tendency, however, should be noted: a general preference for *for* immediately before its case and the use of *fore* in other positions. Belden (p. 61) puts it thus:

> *For* and *fore*, distinct in Gothic . . . are confused in Ags., especially in *Bede*. In the other texts read for this work [*CP, Or, Bo, Chron, ÆCHom* i, *ÆGram*], though distinction of meaning is not firmly held to, there is a distinction in syntactical function: *for* is the preferred form, in most of the categories, for the preposition proper, immediately preceding its case, while *fore* is always used when the particle is removed from its case and more closely united with the verb.

The root of the matter is here, but it is slackly expressed. The points are these. First, *for* is preferred to *fore* before its case, though both occur. It does not matter whether the pre-position is immediate, e.g. *ÆCHom* i. 10. 23 *for þære fægernysse* and *ÆCHom* i. 16. 26 *for urum synnum*, or not, e.g. *ÆCHom* i. 578. 11 *for heora æhtum* and *ÆCHom* i. 132. 35 *for ðæs hundredes ealdres geleafan*. Second, both *for* and *fore* appear in compound verbs, but it seems likely that only *fore* is used in loose syntactic combinations of prepositional adverbs before verbs (see §§ 1069–70 and 1075 and *OEG,* § 78). This is true of Harrison's examples (1892, pp. 16–18), but the point must await full collections. The third and really important point is this. *For* does not (as far as I have yet observed) occur in post-position. *Fore* is regular, both immediately after its case, e.g. *CP* 103. 19 *ða ðe oðrum fore beoð, ÆCHom* ii. 140. 23 *him fore*, and *El* 637 *þe us fore wæron*, and when separated from it, e.g. *Bede* 228. 5 *seo syn, þe se cyning fore ofslegen wæs*, *BlHom* 119. 15 *⁊ hie seoþþan . . . him nowiht fore ne ondredon*, and *Pan* 34 *his fyrngeflitan, þe ic ær fore sægde*. This is spelt out by Wende, who lists only *fore* in post-position in all the different categories he distinguishes in prose and poetry. See §§ 1060–80 and Wende, pp. 51–2, 111, 136–41, 151–3, 188, and 209–16, and note also Flamme, p. 61: '*fore* ist Postposition'. Whether *for* is *ever* used in post-position must also await the full collections. But there is no doubt that the word 'indiscriminately' in the *OED* observation quoted above should be dropped, for OE at least. Belden (pp. 61–73) and Jacobsen (1908, pp. 32–5) give more examples of *for* and *fore*.

§1186. (2) *For* is not usually said to take the genitive. Lehmann (p. 40) and BTS (s.v. *for* D) quote as an example *Or* 62. 28 *hit þeh God for heora cristendome ne geþafode, naþer ne for heora caseras ne for heora selfra, ac hie nugiet ricsiende sindon ægþer ge mid hiera cristendome ge mid hiora anwalde ge mid hiera caserum.* The presence of *for* + dative, *for* + accusative, and *for* + genitive, in one sentence seems suspicious. Yet, though *for* + dative is the norm in *Or*, Wülfing (ii, §§654-6) gives some examples of *for* + accusative and we have seen elsewhere (§1177(2)) sentences in which the same preposition takes different cases. So *caseras* is syntactically possible. But it does not make sense. We must, I think, accept Wülfing's suggestion (ii. 346) that *caseras* is for gen. sg. *caseres* and explain the two genitive phrases as expansions of *heora* in *for heora cristendome.* As Father L. K. Shook has suggested to me privately, the sg. *caseres* is probably a reference to Honorius—cf. *Or* 64. 12 *hiora cyninges*—while the pl. *caserum* in *Or* 62. 31 refers to the two emperors of Orosius' own day. Van Dam (pp. 18-20) offers some further comments on *for* + accusative, but is in my opinion wrong to accept acc. pl. *caseras* in *Or* 62. 28. For causal *for* see also Liggins 1955, pp. 479-87. BTS (s.v. *for* D) adds an example from MS Hatton 76 (ed. H. W. Norman (1849) and reproduced here with Napier's corrections—which I have checked against the manuscript—from the copy in the English Faculty Library, Oxford): *ÆAdmon1* 36. 20 *He underfehð gife eorðlices gestreones for his eorðlices geswinces · ac þu scealt underfon þa heofonlican gife for þam gastlican gewinne.* BTS stops at *geswinces*, but the rest of the quotation suggests that the genitive after the first *for* is more likely to be the result of scribal confusion than testimony for the use of *for* + genitive.

§1187. (3) Van Dam (pp. 4-23) has some valuable notes on *for* in early prose. It 'is the most common preposition in Old English to express cause or reason' (p. 4); in 'a concrete situation' like *GD* 168. 13 *soþlice he ne mihte na gan ut of þam huse for þam ungewydere* it 'may, *in addition*, [my italics; see §§3081-4] express hindrance' (p. 5); '*for* with the dative is also found to denote purpose' (pp. 6 and 14), e.g. *GD* 217. 26 . . . *þæt he sylfa naht ne cuðe ne nyste buton þone hælendan Crist 7 þysne hangiendne 7 þrowiendne for ealles mancynnes hæle*; and it may express 'non-personal agency' (pp. 7-9 and 15; see my §812).

d. Fram

§1188. (1) The senses of OE *fram* can be divided into two groups —those which can be more or less represented by MnE 'from, out of' and its use to express the agent, MnE 'by'; on the latter see §§813-17. *Fram* is found only with the dative/instrumental. Wullen (p. 9) uses the equivalent of 'preferably' instead of 'only' but fails to supply any convincing examples of *fram* with any other case; *Beo* 194 *fram ham* (endingless locative) and *Met* 1. 14 *from Muntgiop* (foreign name) will not do. *ÆLS* 30. 211 *þi læs þe ic beo aworpen fram þine ansyne* seems an exception; Fischer (p. 42) is probably right in suggesting *þinre*. Fischer (pp. 42-103) and Wullen (pp. 9-24) give examples (from prose and poetry respectively) of *fram* + dative. Bale (pp. 12 and 40-5) gives examples from *Li* of *fram* (as well as *of*) with nouns, pronouns, and numerals, as a substitute for the genitive. But, according to Curme (*MP* 11 (1913-14), 160-1), *fram* is much less frequent.

§1189. (2) Bødtker (1908, p. 6) says that *of* means essentially 'out of' and *fram* 'away from'. According to Timmer (1934, pp. 46-9), this fundamental distinction is generally preserved in MS *H* of *GD*. It may be reasonably claimed that the point is lexicographical.

e. In

§1190. (1) Basically *in* with dative means 'in', with accusative 'into, to'; but see §1177(4). However, OE *in* cannot be considered without reference to the prep. *on*. Of these Belden (p. 1) writes: 'Originally distinct in form and meaning, they became in course of time so confused in meaning that *in* was dropped, *on* being felt to have the same value.' To elaborate and qualify this statement is the task of the lexicographer rather than of the syntactician. But a few points must be made.

§1191. (2) The general preference for *on* in OE is clear from a comparison of the length of the articles on *in* and *on* in BT(S) and GK. The situation in *Bede* is discussed in §1192. MS *C* of *GD* has *in* 112 times and *on* 88 times, whereas MS *O* has *in* 104 times and *on* 96 times. But, according to Yerkes (*Manuscripta*, 21 (1977), 40), these occurrences are 'not completely at random. Their common ancestor or archetype apparently already had both words.' The revision (MS *H*) has only *on*. The other 'Alfredian' texts prefer *on* (Wülfing, ii. 383, and Belden, pp. 45-7). So do *Blickling Homilies* and Wulfstan (Dodd's glossary gives the figures as *in* + accusative 21, + dative 14, against *on* + accusative 385, + dative 956). Belden (pp. 1 and 46) cites *ÆCHom* i. 618. 35 *in ealra worulda woruld* as the sole example of *in* in *ÆCHom*. Pope (i. 82 and ii. 812) adds a few more examples from *ÆHom* and attributes them to the scribes. Neither he nor Belden notes *ÆCHom(K)* ii. 438. 23 *in ðam huse*, where (Godden reports) MSS *B, G, H*, and *I*, have *on*. But it is quite clear that Ælfric too avoids *in* in favour of *on*, though we occasionally find *innan* (*ÆCHom* i. 526. 24 *innon þam hellicum fyre*), *into* (*ÆCHom* i. 20. 34 *in to þe*), and *inn oð* (*ÆCHom* ii. 300. 24 *inn oð þæt bragen*). The poetry too shows a general, though not so overwhelming, preference for *on*. Klaeber notes some forty-six examples of *in* against 373 of *on* in *Beowulf*; figures for other poems are given by Taubert (pp. 28-9) and Krohmer (pp. 11-13). *OED* (s.v. *in* prep.) sums up thus:

In OE. (as in OS. and to some extent in OFris.) the prep. *in* was displaced by the prep. *on* . . . , so that in classical and late WSaxon, and to some extent in other OE. dialects, *on* was used for both *on* and *in*, an emphatic or distinctive sense of 'in' being however expressed by *innan*. . . . In Anglian, esp. in the north and west, *in* remained (though, under WSax. influence, often displaced by *on* in documents); and in ME. the distinction of *in* and *on* was gradually restored, though many traces of their former blending still remain.

For examples, including those showing fluctuation between *in* and *on*, see Belden, pp. 1-47, and Krohmer, pp. 15-45.

§1192. (3) Details of this displacement of *in* by *on* in various texts are given by Miller (i, pp. xxxiii-xliv); some of his figures are corrected by Wülfing (ii. 383). Miller says that *in* predominates in *Bede* (i, p. xlii), but there is something in Wülfing's claim (ii. 383) that the figures are not as significant as Miller believes. Final conclusions here must await full examination of the manuscripts. Another point of difference must also await investigation. Belden (p. vi) says that from a study of *Bede* 'little was found . . . to show dependence of the Ags. prepositional idiom on the Latin'. Wülfing (ii. 383) argues that there was at least some dependence. Miller (i, p. xliii) is inconclusive.

§1193. (4) Krohmer (pp. 3-5 and *passim*) detects three periods of dialectal influence in the course of the *in/on* variation. In the first (the period of Anglian intellectual supremacy), Anglian influenced W-S; according to Krohmer, who argues in part from the absence of prep. *in* in the *Heliand*, every *on = auf* and probably every *in* in W-S is of Anglian origin. (Note, however, that Sehrt glosses OS *an* as meaning other things as well as *auf*, s.v. *an* B, präp. I.) The second is the period documented by Miller, when under the influence of W-S scribal practice *in* gradually disappeared from Anglian documents, but not from the spoken language. The third period is after the Norman Conquest, when the Anglian spoken dialects reassert themselves, both *in* and *on* being found, and again influence W-S. In this period, the influence of French *en* and Latin *in* was also important, according to Mustanoja (pp. 386-7). Krohmer's theory will need to be tested when full collections are available.

f. Mid

§1194. (1) The main sense of *mid* is MnE 'with' (excluding the idea of opposition) or, as BT puts it, 'at the root of the various meanings lies the idea of association, of being together'. Hittle (pp. 5-104) gives discussions and examples from prose and poetry. Among other things, *mid* can express the instrument; on the question of agency, see §§818-20. The prevailing case with *mid* is the dative; this is true of the 'Alfredian' prose texts, of *Bede* (see below), of the *Blickling Homilies*, Ælfric, and Wulfstan, and of the poetry (see below).

§1195. (2) *Mid* with the accusative is generally agreed to be Anglian. See Miller, i, pp. xliv–xlix, and Napier, *Ang.* 10 (1887-8), 138-9. It occurs with any regularity in only *Bede* and the poetry. But even in these, the dative is more common; Wülfing (ii. 390-418) cites more than twice as many unambiguous examples with the dative as with the accusative (in seven of the latter, MS *B* replaces the accusative by the dative; cf. Miller, i, pp. xlvii–xlviii) and a glance at the GK entry s.v. *mid* will show that the dative is even more prevalent in the poetry. Klaeber speaks of *mid* + accusative as an Anglianism (3, p. xciv), but his Glossary records only six examples in *Beowulf* with the accusative against over sixty with the dative/instrumental. Only sporadic examples of *mid* + accusative are found outside *Bede* and the poetry. Wülfing (ii. 415-18) has some from the 'Alfredian' texts. Timmer (1934, pp. 53-4) says that *mid* + accusative is not found in MS *H* of *GD*. Morris notes *BlHom* 145. 35 and 155. 10. Others are found in *Li* (Haddock, Part I). There are also *Alex* 45. 2 *mid mec* and *WHom* 9. 144 *mid eal swylcan laran*. We may note that most of the examples of *mid* + accusative refer to individuals (with nouns in the singular and plural, with pronouns generally in the singular, but note *Or* 48. 16 *þæt hi hie mid gefeohten*) or to collective nouns meaning a group of individuals. See further Miller, i, pp. xliv–xlix, and Hittle, pp. 6-7.

§1196. (3) Lehmann (p. 40) proposes *Or* 56. 15 . . . *for þon Mesiane noldon ðæt Læcedemonia mægdenmenn mid heora ofreden 7 heora godum onsægden* as an example of *mid* with the genitive. He adds 'NB. bei Haarstrick nicht angegeben.' Haarstrick had good reason. We must understand *mægdenmannum* after *heora* and translate (as Thorpe did in the Bohn edition, p. 289) 'because the Messenians would not permit the Spartan virgins to make offerings with theirs and sacrifice to their gods'.

§1197. (4) For a detailed study of *mid*, see Dančev 1967. (It is described as Part I, but as yet I have not found Part II. However, there is another article by Dančev on prepositions, viz. Dančev 1969.) After an introduction (pp. 55–60) and a comparison of the systems of classification used by previous writers (pp. 61–72), Dančev distinguishes three 'basic patterns' (pp. 72–6)—'association', e.g. *Bede 394. 25 Bæd ic eac ætgædre mid hiene*; 'adverbiality', e.g. *BenR 82. 12 and Crist sig swa mid eadmodnysse gebeden*; and 'instrumentality', e.g. *GD(C) 81. 6 7 þa bæd se biscop hine eft þæs mid þam ylcum wordum*. The rest of the article is devoted to an analysis of basic pattern 1, which Dančev subdivides into four 'sub-patterns'— 'reference to place', e.g. *Or 54. 12 Ac Cirus mid Perseum to ðæm anwalde feng*; 'joint action', e.g. *ChronA 92. 5 (901) þa rad se cyning mid firde*; 'subordination', e.g. *Or 21. 4 7 þonne rideð ælc hys weges mid ðan feo*; and 'attributive function', e.g. *Bede 196. 12 þa lihte he sona 7 heht þam þearfan þæt hors syllan mid þæm cynelicum gebætum þe him onstodon*. The article is not without errors and contradictions, and not everybody will be willing to accept the system of classification adopted. But it offers many examples and some valuable observations.

§1198. (5) *Mid* and *wið* are used interchangeably in *Deut* 27. 20 *Sy se awyrged se ðe hæme mid his fæder wife* and *Deut* 27. 21 *Beo se man awyrged ðe hæme wið nyten*.

g. Of

§1199. (1) OE *of* can usually be translated by MnE 'of, out of, from' (see §1189), except when it seems to express the agent or the instrument; on these see §§821–3. The combination *ut of* does occur; for examples see Wülfing, ii. 655–6, and *Jud* 70 and 135.

§1200. (2) The prevailing case with *of* in both prose and poetry is the dative; for examples see Fischer, pp. 42–103, and Jacobsen 1908, pp. 45–68. Wülfing (ii. 448) adds a few examples with the instrumental and offers alternative explanations for the apparent instances of *of* with accusative or genitive, including *Bede 320. 3 þa heht heo sume broðor faran 7 þone stan secan, þæt mon meahte þa ðruh of geheawan 7 gewyrcan*, where—he implies (ii. 440)—*þæt* introduces a purpose clause, 'dass man daraus . . .'. This is certainly possible. But the Latin *iussitque quosdam e fratribus quaerere lapidem, de quo locellum in hoc facere possent* suggests that the clause ought to be adjectival. If so, MS *B*'s *þe* is right, in my opinion, since *þe* . . *of* could represent *de quo*, but with the declined relative we should expect *of þæm*; see §2231. MS *Ca*'s *þ* may represent an intermediate stage in the error. Bødtker's article 'Of and the genitive Case in Late Old English' (*EStudien*, 45 (1912), 465-7) does not contain (as the title may seem to suggest) examples of *of* with the genitive, but adds more examples to those given in Bødtker 1908, pp. 5-33, of how *of* became a substitute for the genitive.

§1201. (3) Most of the examples given by BT(S) (s.v. *of* IX) of the partitive use of *of* come from texts in which Latin influence is at least a strong possibility; the only one from the poetry is *GuthB* 865 *Nænig monna wæs ‖ of þam sigetudre*, where I should be inclined to describe *monna* as partitive genitive and *of* as meaning 'out of'. Two questions arise. First, what syntactical distinctions exist in the use of partitive *of*? Second, are these constructions native or due to Latin influence? BT(S) confuses different syntactical patterns. There are first the examples in which a noun, a numeral, or a word like *ænig, an, feala, ma,* or *sum,* is followed by *of* + dative of a noun or pronoun, e.g. *Matt(Li)* 6. 29 *an of ðisum*, Latin *unum ex istis*, and *Mark(WSCp)* 14. 20 *an of eow twelfum*, Latin *unus ex duodecim*. All these are exemplified in BT(S) or by Johnsen.[273] The latter rightly points out that the *of* phrase (like the inflected genitive) may precede the word on which it depends, e.g. *ÆLS* 5. 221 *of anum þusende anne*. But in the examples he cites, metrical or rhetorical considerations seem to prevail. Similar to, but to be distinguished from, this first group are those examples with *sum* + *of* + dative of a possessive, e.g. *Luke(WSCp)* 24. 24 *sume of urum*, Latin *quidam ex nostris*, and *Luke(WSCp)* 24. 22 *sume wif of urum*, Latin *mulieres quædam ex nostris*; further on these see §§409-16.[274] Neither Rissanen nor I have noted any such examples with *an* + a possessive. Thirdly, we have the examples in which the *of* phrase appears

---

[273] 'Remarks on the Use of Partitive "of" in Anglo-Saxon' (*Ang.* 36 (1912), 283-4). (I must confess that I do not always see the distinction between partitive *of* and *of* 'out of, from, among' quite as clearly as Johnsen seems to.) Rissanen (p. 57) gives more examples with *an*.

[274] Examples like these, along with similar ones with an inflected genitive, e.g. *GenA* 2177 . . . *eaforan* . . . *‖ ænegum minra* and *Ch* 1527 *þat lond þe he mines hafde*, have been used in discussions on the origin of the construction 'a friend of mine'; see, in addition to Hatcher (*Word*, 6 (1950), 1-25) and Heltveit (1969 and 1977), my §§108 fn., 409, and 416.

independently, with no governing noun or the like; the *of* phrase may stand in lieu of the subject, e.g. *ÆLS* 6. 186 *Æfter þysum ongunnon of ðam gegaderwyrhtum tælan ðone halgan*, or of the object, e.g. *ChronE* 224. 16 (1087) *7 he sende of his mannan to þisum lande*, or may form the complement, e.g. *Bede* 246. 26 *Wæs he of discipulum Aidanes þæs godan biscopes*. The exact status of *of* in the examples given here is discussed by Bødtker (1908, p. 19), Johnsen (ibid.), and Curme (*MP* 11 (1913-14), 149-50).

§1202. (4) The question of the origin of this partitive use of *of* can scarcely be separated from a consideration of the development of the *of* phrase as a genitive equivalent in English. This vexed topic cannot be fully treated here. Bødtker (1908, p. 33) remarked 'Thus, about the middle of the 12th century, *of* had made its appearance in English literature. We can hardly believe that French was able to effect this important syntactical change scarcely a hundred years after the Conquest. . . . French influence more probably came later on.' Curme, writing in 1913, recorded how he 'recently read with a feeling of pain' the *OED* observation (s.v. *of*) that 'the great intrusion of "of" upon the old domain of the genitive . . . was mainly due to the influence of French *de*'. He was anxious to deny French influence and does not mention the possibility in his *Syntax* (1931, pp. 74-5). To him the main factors are 'the graphic force of the preposition "of" . . . and . . . the lack of clear genitive forms in the later period of the decay of the old declensions'.[275] But he goes too far. The possibility exists that he may at times have overestimated the 'nativeness' of the *of* construction in OE. Much of his evidence comes from the Glosses and some of his remarks are revealing, e.g. 'If "of" is used a large number of times in this translation it was surely used much more in natural spoken language' and 'A few such examples are the only ones that the writer has been able to find. They are all confined to the Lindisfarne MS. They all follow the Latin closely and yet the writer has absolute confidence in the idiomatic quality of the English' (*MP* 11 (1913-14), 163 and 290; see also pp. 151 and 160-3). Heltveit, however, has recently remarked that 'a generally accepted view seems to be that it is a highly doubtful procedure to quote the examples from the Gospels of *of* + possessive pronoun as evidence that this phrase was in use in the Old English period. In fact, the relatively high frequency in the Gospels of the *of*-phrase as a genitive equivalent is in itself very suspicious' (*EStudies*, 50 (1969), 228. Thomas, whose conclusion is quoted below, similarly rejected as

---

[275] The quotations are from Curme's articles in *MP* 11 (1913-14), 313 and 159 respectively. He further denies French influence at pp. 165 ff., 174 ff., and 293.

evidence examples from *Li, Ru1*, and *Ru2* (p. 59).) Indeed, it is possible that *of* + dative might be a glossator's idiom which sometimes triumphs over the genitive in a gloss even when the Latin had the genitive. Full collections may throw further light on this problem. But Mustanoja, in a balanced summing-up (pp. 77-8), rightly allows room for the native development and for French influence, along with other factors, including that stressed by Thomas (p. 177):

Other factors were probably at work, such as analogy, imitation of French idiom, the gradually increasing preference of the periphrastic form for partitive expressions, etc. But one fact stands out in our investigation: *A significant advance in the use of the adnominal periphrastic genitive did not take place until loss of inflection in the definite article and strong adjective had set in.*

This seems to be the vital point. Curme's 'law of immediate contact' (*MP* 11 (1913-14), 164-5) states that 'inflection was demanded only at the point where the two components of the adnominal group touched each other'. Thus, in his two examples *þis childes witige gost* and *seinte poul hegest alre lorþew*, the genitive forms *childes* and *alre* carry the uninflected *þis* and *lorþew*. But when articles and adjectives ceased to carry inflexion, the synthetic genitive could not function after a governing noun and so disappeared entirely, since such combinations as 'the eyes the girl' were meaningless and the phrase 'the gnashing teeth' meant something entirely different from 'the gnashing of teeth'. For further discussions, see the references given by Mustanoja, pp. 92-3. For further examples, see Wülfing, ii. 437-9 and 445-7; Shipley, pp. 88-9; and Bale, pp. 12 and 40-4.

§1203. (5) The genitive and *of* + dative were of course sometimes used in what appear to be similar functions, e.g. *Bede* 222. 33 *Ceolloh, se wæs eac Scotta cynnes* but *Bede* 210. 26 *Wæs þes wer Furseus of þæm æþelestan cynne Scotta*; *Matt(WSCp)* 25. 2 *hyra fif* but *Matt(WSCp)* 6. 29 *an of ðyson* (on this partitive usage see §415); and *Beo* 1694 *on ðæm scennum sciran goldes* but *Dan* 175 *gyld of golde*. We might also compare *ChronA* 68. 30 (868) *Burgræd Miercna cyning* with *ChronD* 105. 15 (924) *7 Æþelstan wæs gecoren to cynge of Myrcum*, where possession and agency respectively seem to be involved. See further Curme in *MP* 11 (1913-14), 152-3, 156-8, 291, and 297. There is no doubt that the genitive and *of* + the dative overlapped in some functions, e.g. origin and material. The question is: Does *of* + the dative denote pure possession in OE? I am not sure whether Wülfing, Flamme, and Mustanoja, believe that it does, because I do not know whether the words 'genitivischen', 'Genetiv', and 'genitival', in the following quotations are really meant to imply 'possessive': '*of* im partitiven oder überhaupt genitivischen Sinne von

einem Hauptworte abhängig' (Wülfing, ii. 445); 'of . . . bezeichnet
. . . den reinen Genetiv' (Flamme, pp. 64–5) ['of in the partitive, or
simply genitive sense, dependent on a noun' . . . 'of denotes the pure
genitive']; and 'the preposition [of] is not uncommon in genitival
function in Ælfric's writings' (Mustanoja, p. 74). Personally I believe
—with Bødtker (1908, p. 20)—that none of the examples cited by
Wülfing (ii. 445) and Flamme (p. 65) has to be taken as possessive.
However, the decision must be a personal one.[276] But when I read
ÆCHom i. 282. 7 *Seo sunne ðe ofer us scinð is lichamlic gesceaft,*
and hæfð swaðeah ðreo agennyssa on hire: an is seo lichamlice
edwist, þæt is ðære sunnan trendel; oðer is se leoma oððe beorhtnys
æfre of ðære sunnan, seoðe onliht ealne middangeard; þridde is seo
hætu, þe mid þam leoman cymð to us and compare *ðære sunnan*
trendel with *se leoma oððe beorhtnys æfre of ðære sunnan*, I find it
difficult to resist the conclusion that, when Ælfric penned those
phrases, they did not imply the same relationship.

h. On

§1204. (1) For the meanings and functions of *on*, see the dictionaries; the general preference for *on* rather than *in* is discussed in
§§1190–3.

§1205. (2) Some earlier editions of Sweet's *Reader* (revised by
Onions) emended *on* to *of* in *Dream* 138, where we read

Dream 135   ond ic wene me
            daga gehwylce   hwænne me dryhtnes rod,
            þe ic her on eorðan   ær sceawode,
            on þysson lænan   life gefetige. . . .

Whitelock, in her revision (Sweet, *R*. 15), has rightly restored *on*,
which is supported by examples like *Or* 146. 29 *7 hiene bædon þæt*
he him ageafe þæt he ær on him gereafade, *BlHom* 51. 2 *gif Drihten*
on þe genimþ þa nigan dælas, and *Beo* 122 *ond on ræste genam* ǁ
þritig þegna, but failed to do so in *Max ii* 40 (Sweet, *R*. 15, p. 175).
However, the modern idiom with *of* is found in OE too, e.g. *ÆCHom*
i. 178. 13 *Elias . . . siððan wæs genumen butan deaðe of ðisum life*
and *GenA* 177 *and him listum ateah* ǁ *rib of sidan*. It is interesting
that the examples cited by Fischer (pp. 7–10) to show that in general
the use of prepositions in the *Blickling Homilies* and *Lives of the*

---

[276] Curme (pp. 295–6) assures us that 'the subjective genitive . . . is the only genitive
category which did not in Old English develop the analytic form'. But his 'subjective' genitive differs from his 'possessive' genitive (p. 296) and he says (p. 291) that in OE *of* was
'also employed instead of the synthetic form in the categories of material, composition,
origin, source, and *possession* . . .' [my italics]. I cannot follow his distinction.

Saints is idiomatic and unaffected by the Latin original include *LS* 23. 429 *Ða geseah ic of þære stowe*, Latin *et prospexi in loco*, and *ÆLS* 31. 1016 *of þære wic*, Latin *in illo uico*; cf. the variations between *of*, *on*, and *in*, in the three manuscripts of Gregory's *Dialogues* given by Timmer (1934, pp. 58-62). For a further note on the use of *of/on*, see Meroney, *JEGP* 44 (1945), 385 fn. 27.

§1206. (3) On *Marv* 57. 13 and *ÆIntSig* 38. 360, where *on* seems to take the genitive, see Mitchell 1979*a*, p. 40 fn. 2.

j. þurh

§1207. (1) The basic meaning of *þurh* is 'through'—local, temporal, causal, instrumental, and expressing agency (§§824-30). An interesting example of the temporal use is *ÆCHom* i. 228. 17 *And ða heardheortan Iudei ðeah þurh ealle ða tacna noldon gebugan mid geleafan to ðam mildheortan Hælende*, where *þurh* carries almost the opposite implication to the one it has in the previous sentence *ÆCHom* i. 228. 16 *Hell oncneow Crist . . . þurh ðæs Hælendes hergunge. þurh* takes the accusative and (less often) the dative. The dative seems to be a late analogical usage. Only the accusative has been recorded in the 'Alfredian' texts (Wülfing, ii. 512; Haarstrick is silent) and (apart from *ChristA* 185 (§1208)) in the poetry (Wullen, p. 462). Morris records one example of the dative in *BlHom* 145. 35 and Dodd gives one in *HomU* 36. 230. 3—not by Wulfstan—against 308 with the accusative. The dative is most common in certain manuscripts of the *Catholic Homilies*; see Sisam, pp. 180-5. Sisam's conclusion (pp. 183-4) is this: 'Clearly, on this evidence, Ælfric is responsible for the abnormal use of the dative in both the First and Second Series as originally issued; and he regularized his usage with prepositions after the Second Series had been published, revising at least the First Series minutely to bring it into line.' Sisam further suggests (p. 184) that, since the dative after *þurh* practically disappears from the works of Ælfric which follow his *Latin Grammar*, 'the task of explaining Latin usage and translating the examples would bring home to him the anomalies of his own practice in English, and the advantages of regularity'. As a result of this revision, there are sentences in some manuscripts of both series of the *Catholic Homilies* in which *þurh* is followed by both the accusative and the dative, e.g. *ÆCHom* ii. 358. 10 . . . *hwæðer he ðurh drycræft oððe ðurh runstafum his bendas tobræce*. Further on these and similar variations, see §1218.

§1208. (2) A clear example of *þurh* + genitive occurs in *ÆCHom* ii. 266. 23 *and we beoð geclænsode þurh ðæs halgan huselganges*. So J. J. Campbell was not strictly accurate when he wrote of the last half-line in

ChristA 185   Is þæt wide cuð
                        þæt ic of þam torhtan   temple dryhtnes
                        onfeng freolice   fæmnan clæne,
                        womma lease,   ond nu gehwyrfed is
                        þurh nathwylces

that 'the MS gives no indication of it, but there is something definitely wrong with this half line, in that *þurh* cannot take a genitive object'.[277] (The same idea probably lies behind the typically laconic ASPR note 'This seems to be syntactically incomplete.') Whether the Ælfric example justifies the reading in *Christ* is a moot point; J. J. Campbell (in the same note) quotes Gollancz's suggestion that the genitive is an error for the accusative and is due to the influence of *nat*, which can take the genitive, as in *Beo* 681 *nat he þara goda*.

k. To

§1209. (1) The main senses of *to* are 'to, at, alongside, for'; see further the dictionaries. The most common case is the dative, but the genitive is found and occasionally the accusative. J. Albers devotes his thesis (Kiel, 1907) to the use of *to* in OE poetry.

§1210. (2) According to QW (p. 65), 'in late OE, *to* came to be used with the indirect object just as in Mod.E.; thus *gyfan (to) ænigum* "give (to) anyone"'. With a few verbs, notably *cweðan* and *sprecan*, *to* was normal OE practice: *he cwæþ to me (mihi dixit)* "he said to me".' But I have as yet found no examples of the type ☆*giefan to ænigum* 'give to anyone'. That such a usage is on its way is clear; that it had arrived remains to be established. The use of *to* + dative of a person is established with verbs of speaking like *cweþan, sprecan*, and *cleopian*,[278] and is found with verbs like *bringan, lætan, niman*, and *sendan*.[279] But it does not seem to occur with *tæcan* or verbs

---

[277] J. J. Campbell, *The Advent Lyrics of the Exeter Book* (Princeton, 1959), 93.

[278] See Wendt, *EStudien*, 15 (1891), 83; Belden, p. 50; and Carlton 1970, pp. 57-8. Belden (p. 50) reports that *secgan to* + dative occurs only once in his corpus, in a late addition to *Chron*; see *ChronF* (Thorpe) 136. 24 (870).

[279] For examples with *bringan*, see Belden, p. 49 (he reports *bringan to* + dative as an emphatic alternative) and Carlton 1970, p. 58.

For examples with *lætan* see *Ch* 1283, *Ch* 385, *Ch* 1391, and Lebow, pp. 634-5; with *niman ChronE* 31. 10 (656).

Belden (p. 51) says that 'the verb *sendan* shows a distinction between *ind. obj.* and *to* + *dat*. In the simple sense of "send", with object expressed, *sendan* is followed by *ind. obj.*

meaning 'to give'. One can *agifan to* a monastery—*LawIIEg* 1. 1 and *HomU* 36. 231. 1—or to a place—*LawIAs* 4. One can *(ge)sellan (in)to* a church—*LawIIEg* 2 and *Ch* 1188 (two examples)—or shame—*LS* 7. 78. Bødtker (1908, p. 40) quotes two sentences which at first glance seem to contain clear examples of verbs of giving with *to* + dative of person. But neither stands examination. In *ChronE* 75. 8 (876) *7 him þa gislas sealdon þe on þam here weorþuste wæron to þam cyninge, him* goes with *sealdon* and *to þam cyninge* with *weorþuste*; for the latter idiom see (6) below. Bødtker quotes the second from Thorpe's edition of the Charters 563. 27 *7 ic gean to Wolkytele 7 Kytele minum sunum þæs londes æt Wælsingaham*, but Whitelock (*Will* 32 = *Ch* 1535) does not print *to* and Miss Anne M. Oakley of the Cathedral Archives and Library, Canterbury, has kindly verified its absence for me. My findings therefore coincide with those expressed by Quirk in a private communication: 'in no instance does the indirect object happen to be a personal noun (the classical indirect object) but rather a noun that could be interpreted as locative'. The reader can confirm this contrast—verb of giving with dative of person but with *to* + dative of a place—by an examination of *Ch* 1188 or *Ch* 1494. The sentence in *Ch* 1494 (quoted from Whitelock, *Will* 14) *7 ic gean þæs landæs æt Dictunæ into Ylig to sc̄æ Æþælðryð 7 to hire geswustran* is not an exception; the gift is to the shrine.

§1211. (3) Wrenn (*History*, 25 (1940-1), 212) claims that *him to* in the well-known clause in *ChronA* 48. 16 (755) *7 þa gatu him to belocen hæfdon* is a colloquial usage meaning 'on themselves', paralleled only in a fourteenth-century romance and in Coverdale's Bible. It is hard to see any justification for the word 'colloquial'. The idiom does, however, occur in *LS* 35. 196. 31 *and he sylf into þære inran eode and ða duru him to beclysde*; cf. *LS* 35. 196. 38 . . . *and hy in let to him sylfum*. But *him to* in the Chronicle passage could also mean 'against the others'; see BT, s.v. *to* 4(*f*).

§1212. (4) Green (1914, pp. 548-50), in pursuance of the distinction already noted in §8 fn. 2, attempts to distinguish some ME constructions with *to* which (he argues) derive from 'the older synthetic dative of interest in the function of the agent' from others which exemplify 'those datives of agency which derive their origin from the

of personal pronouns, and sometimes of nouns; while in the sense of "send (to some one for something)" it is always followed by *to*. In the latter case, the object is commonly not expressed.' He illustrates his point with examples like *Or* 162. 7 . . . *Cartaginenses sendon fultum Tarentinum* but *Or* 114. 16 *þa sendan hie to Philippuse, 7 bædon.* . . .
Bødtker 1908, pp. 39-42, analyses some of the examples quoted or referred to here.

lost instrumental'. This is ingenious, but perhaps open to the same criticism (*mutatis mutandis*) which Green himself (1914, p. 549) levels against Einenkel: 'Einenkel evidently is still on the working basis of the old dative of interest, hence in the danger of gathering too much under that category.' Green's enthusiasm seems to me to have coloured his interpretation of his OE examples with the simple dative.

§1213. (5) *To* with genitive expresses time, the object of motion, and degree; for examples see the dictionaries. A point of interest is that so far no examples appear to have been recorded of *to* + genitive expressing motion in the prose or of *to* + genitive expressing time in the poetry. The evidence is of course purely negative; see Belden, p. 58, and Shipley, p. 119. (The prose *Ps* 36. 6 *to middes dæges* (cited by GK, s.v. *to* II) is of course no exception.) Dobbie writes of *Beo* 1585 that 'one is tempted to believe that some of the text, containing a verb of motion, has been lost before l. 1585b'. I defend the integrity of the text in *ASE* 4 (1975), 22-3.

§1214. (6) On the idiom seen in *ChronE* 75. 8 (876) (§1210), and in *GenB* 254 *hehstne to him on heofona rice*, see Sisam, p. 76. A similar use of *heah* not noted by BT or Sisam occurs in *Bo* 99. 11 . . . *hi woldon witan hu heah hit wære to ðæm heofone*.

§1215. (7) Belden (p. 48), quoting *Bede* 402. 13 *to mec spræcende*, Latin *ad me*, and '*Bede* 382. 29' (this reference is wrong and I have not been able to trace the example) *to hie eode*, Latin *ad eam*, speaks of *to* + accusative as 'quite abnormal . . . doubtless un-English . . . too close dependence on the Latin'. BT(S) (s.v. *to* III) cites other examples, including two from the poetry—*ChristA* 32 and the manuscript reading of *GuthA* 549 *to deað*, emended in BASP and ASPR to *to deaðe*.[280] In *ÆCHom* i. 376. 28 *He ða leat to ðæs caseres eare, eare* may be for *earan* (see §65) and in *ÆCHom* ii. 174. 11 *Se halga wer asende ða to, ða* may be an adverb. A good many of the other examples can also be explained away. But a hard core remains.

§1216. (8) On the construction seen in *ÆLS* 32. 10 *Se munuc . . . wearð sona to abbode geset*, see §§837 and 1083.

---

[280] See also GK, s.v. *to* III. Lange, p. 10, speaks of *to* in *Maldon* with dative and accusative, but on p. 15 rightly says it has only the dative.

l. Wiþ . . . weard

§1217. *Wiþ . . . weard(es)* is normally found with the genitive, e.g. *ÆCHom* i. 376. 33 *micele hundas . . . ræsdon wið Petres weard* and *Jud* 99 *. . . teah hyne folmum wið hyre weard.*[281] If we exclude the six *Orosius* examples like *Or* 5. 10 *wið Rome weard*, where the case of *Rome* is indeterminate,[282] the genitive is in fact the rule in all the instances I have noted except in the formula *wið heofonas weard*, which occurs in *ÆCHom* i. 46. 29; 296. 5; 382. 9; 464. 29; and in *ÆCHom* ii. 182. 16; 186. 30; 304. 8. Wülfing (ii. 657) prints two of these thus: *ÆCHom* i. 46. 29 *and beheold wið heofonas (!) weard* and *ÆCHom* ii. 182. 16 *his handbredu astrehte wið heofenas (!) weard*. Wülfing (ii. 657) adds 'Holy Rood 3, 13 *gelome beheold wiþ heofenas (!) weard*'. In view of examples like *ÆCHom* i. 376. 33 above and *ÆCHom* ii. 168. 24 *wið his weard*, he is right to be suspicious. We are probably justified in taking *heofonas* in all these examples as genitive singular. Indeed, on the evidence of *ÆLS* 26. 117 *he wurðode æfre god upawendum handbredum wiþ þæs heofones weard* (where, according to Skeat, MS *U* omits *þæs*) and *ÆCHom* i. 6. 8 *geweald heofenas and eorþan*, we can strike out the 'probably'.

m. Ymb, ymbe

§1218. (1) The main meanings are 'about, around' (of place), 'at, after' (of time), and 'about' (as in 'to speak (be busy) about' and the like). On the sense 'about' expressing approximate time, see §1219. The predominant case with this preposition is the accusative. Gottweis gives examples from the prose (pp. 66–76). Wülfing (ii. 635–6) notes a few examples of the dative with *ymb* in post-position. The only dative example given by Flamme in the *Blickling Homilies* (99. 25) is of this sort.[283] Gottweis (pp. 76–8) records twelve examples of the dative in Ælfric, all with *ymb* in pre-position. They include *ÆCHom* ii. 70. 13 *. . . ymbe ðas wæterfatu and heora getacnungum*, with both accusative and dative; cf. *ÆHom* 18. 116 *. . . ymbe fela geþohtas and mislicum dædum*; such examples may be the result of the partial correction discussed in §1207. Dodd has only *HomU* 36. 226. 12 *. . . ymb ures drihtnes ærendgewrite*. The only datives

---

[281] Dobbie (ASPR iv. 284) says of *Jud* 99: 'No other example is recorded of this word order with *wið*.' It is in fact the only order I have found with *wið . . . weard(es)* in prose and poetry, with nouns and pronouns. See BT, s.vv. *weard* adv., *weardes* adv., *wiþ* prep. IX, and N. D[avis], *RES* 6 (1955), 301.

[282] See Wülfing, ii. 657, for the rest of these, and for other examples with the genitive.

[283] Flamme, p. 70. (In §142, I (p. 69) 'Dativ' is an error by Flamme; as his examples show, he should have said 'Akkusativ'.)

in the poetry cited by GK (s.vv. *ymb* and *ymbe*) show *ymb* in post-position. They include *Sat* 567 *Him ymbflugon engla þreatas* (so ASPR). To these can be added *Met* 20. 207 *hire utan ymb*. Jacobsen (1908, p. 80) says that the dative is more common in the prose than in the poetry. The real difference lies in the absence of *ymb* with the dative in pre-position in the poetry, except in *Men* 116–18, 133–4, 187–8, and 210–11, where the second element of compound numerals is involved and the dative plural ending *-um* is metrically essential; see §558.

✕ §1219. (2) According to Flamme (p. 70) and Gottweis (p. 69), *ymb* in *BlHom* 133. 13 . . . *se dæg þe is nemned Pentecosten ymb fiftig nihta æfter þære gecyþdan æriste* means 'about': indeed Morris so translates it. As the etymology of the word 'Pentecost' (Greek πεντηκοστή the 'fiftieth day') and a glance at the calendar of the Christian Church will show, Pentecost is not *about* fifty days after Easter. It *is* fifty days after it. Gottweis (p. 69) takes a similar view of *ÆCHom* ii. 432. 28 *Æfter ðison ymbe twelf monað*, which Thorpe translates 'about a twelvemonth after this', and *WHom* 6. 122 *Ac eft æfter þam ymbe lxx geara, þæs ðe seo hergung wæs*. Simi-larly one sometimes hears passages like *ChronA* 70. 11 (871) *7 þæs ymb iii niht* translated 'and about three nights after that'. I am ex-tremely dubious about such translations, and suspect that they arise from careless reading of dictionaries or glossaries. One can *rædan ymbe* . . . 'read about . . .' (*ÆCHom* ii. 188. 25). One can *faran ymb* . . . 'go about . . .' (*ÆCHom* i. 524. 11). One can use *ymb* of a point of time, as in *ÆCHom* ii. 256. 33 *Hwæt ða, ymb midne dæg wearð middaneard aðeostrod*, where *ymb* might mean 'about' though I am inclined to prefer 'at', but must in fairness point to examples like *Mark(Li)* 6. 48 *ymb ða fearða wacan*, Latin *circa quartam uigiliam*. However, the use of *ymb* 'about' to indicate that something happens at or near a particular point of time does not justify the translation 'about' of a period of time. No such sense is recognized by BT(S). It is clearly wrong in examples like *BlHom* 133. 13 above and in

Men 15   Swylce emb feower wucan
                   þætte Solmonað   sigeð to tune
                   butan twam nihtum,   swa hit getealdon geo,
                   Februarius fær,   frode gesiþas,
                   ealde ægleawe.   And þæs embe ane niht
                   þæt we Marian   mæssan healdað,
                   cyninges modor,   forþan heo Crist on þam dæge,
                   bearn wealdendes,   brohte to temple

(one is unlikely to say 'about four weeks less two days' and the Presentation of Christ in the Temple is one day, not *about* one day, after 1 February). So I would translate *ÆCHom* i. 236. 23 *Se apostol Paulus cwæð, þæt we sceolon arisan of deaðe on ðære ylde þe Crist wæs þaða he ðrowade, þæt is embe þreo and ðritig geara*, not (as Thorpe does) 'about three and thirty years' but 'after thirty-three years'; cf. *ÆCHom* ii. 184. 15 *Eft siððan ymbe ðry dagas stod se halga wer on his gebedum, and beseah ut*, where Thorpe is content with 'three days after'. All the examples in which Gottweis (pp. 69–70) thinks *ymb* means 'about' of time refer to either a point of time or a period of time 'after'. All Wülfing's examples (ii, §1013) are point of time. *Sat* 424 remains a difficulty; see Clubb's note. But at the moment I do not see the justification for taking *ymb* to mean 'before'. (*Sat* 570 has been otherwise explained.) There is something suspicious about *Sat* 424. Is there an omission?

5. DEVELOPMENTS IN THE OE PERIOD

§1220. In view of the subsequent history of English, three questions arise: How often is it impossible to tell which case an OE preposition governs because the form of the noun or pronoun is ambiguous? Are there OE prepositions which begin by taking one case and end by taking more than one? Can any increase in the use of prepositions be detected in the OE period?

§1221. The first question can be answered only by pointing to the ambiguities of form discussed in §§8–15. Percentages here would obviously be a matter of chance, depending on which nouns or pronouns happened to be used, e.g. *to londe* is unambiguous whereas in *to giefe* we might have to do with an accusative, genitive, or dative, as far as the form is concerned. And percentages would very likely be misleading as a reflection of the feeling of the original speaker or writer. For example, Lebow (pp. 45–6) says that in his text (3) *Laws Hl* Inscr.–3 there are 18.2 per cent of examples in which the function is conveyed neither by preposition nor by case-form, but by some other means such as element order or context.[284] This is because the expression *Cantwara cyningas* appears twice. Even if we agree that *Cantwara* can be nominative or accusative as well as genitive (but see *OEG*, §610(7)), it is by no means certain that the case-form really gave no clue to a native speaker (or indeed gives none to a modern reader) of OE. Similarly Lebow (pp. 47–9) says that the preposition

[284] This 1954 thesis is based on a selection of 122 English texts which he dates from 602 to 1531 (but see §1223) and on thirty-five French and fourteen German texts.

alone conveys the function in *LawWi* 3 *oþþe of ciricean gemanan ascadene sien*, 'the case form being absent' (his p. 34). This is, I suppose, true from the viewpoint of a modern theoretician. But was it really true for the man who also used such expressions as *LawWi* Prol. 3 *mid ealra gemedum* and *LawWi* 5 *ofer cyngæs bebod*, and could have said ☆*oþþe of Godes þeowum ascadene sien*?

§1222. But the existence of ambiguous forms, of prepositions which took more than one case, and of overlap in functions between prepositions which took different cases (e.g. the various prepositions expressing agency discussed in §§802-33a), must have resulted in analogical confusion and helped to bring about changes in the cases used with certain prepositions. For the answer to the second question—Are there OE prepositions which begin by taking one case and end by taking more than one?—is 'Yes'. With some prepositions two originally dialectal usages seem to have been confused; see for example §1179 (*æfter*) and §1195 (*mid*). With others the analogies already mentioned led to the use of two cases where one had been the rule; note the fluctuations after *wið* in *Beo* 424-5 and 1977-8, and see (for example) §1183 (*be*) and §1207, where Ælfric's use of *þurh* + dative and his subsequent correction of this is discussed. Sisam (p. 181 fn. 3) points out that there are similar corrections with other prepositions in some manuscripts of the *Catholic Homilies* (a possible example is given in §1218 (*ymb*)) and rightly suggests that 'the questions of syntax involved deserve a dissertation'.[285] Lebow does not seem to have been concerned with this problem and his choice of material was such that it was unlikely to force itself upon his notice.

§1223. Lebow did, however, aim at answering the third question—Can any increase in the use of prepositions be detected in the OE period?—as part of the general investigation implied in his title.[286] But he can scarcely be said to have succeeded, for there are several fundamental weaknesses in his method which should have been apparent at least to his 'Sponsoring Committee'. First, as I have already hinted, there is what seems to me a too easy acceptance of the proposition that forms which are ambiguous to a modern scholar were necessarily so for the original speaker or writer.[287] Second,

---

[285] The writer of such a dissertation would do well to absorb thoroughly the methods and findings of both Sisam and of Timmer (1934, pp. 46-91).

[286] It lay outside Mustanoja's terms of reference. But see pp. 67-70 and 345-427 of his book.

[287] I realize that this is a time-honoured assumption which becomes increasingly valid as the inflexions become increasingly blurred. But (as I have tried to show above) I am uneasy

Lebow fails to separate the accusative, genitive, and dative, cases. Instead he lumps them all together as examples in which the case-form alone denotes the function (p. 34). This is important because (as §1203 suggests) the replacement of the genitive by *of* seems not to have proceeded *pari passu* with the replacement of the dative/instrumental relationship by the various prepositions and because accusative/dative syncretism is more common in OE than syncretism involving the genitive. So a small but significant variation in the proportion of prepositions + dative to simple datives could easily escape notice because it would be swamped under the high percentage of inflected genitives likely to occur in any passage. This did dawn on Lebow (p. 570). But he failed to appreciate its fundamental importance. To demonstrate the point let us take his text (2), *Cædmon's Hymn.* Here he finds seven genitives + *wuldurfadur* (which he takes as an ambiguous form) against one preposition *til hrofe* (pp. 43-4). You could say what he says—that there are only 11.1 per cent of prepositions. You could also say that 100 per cent of the genitives have inflexion only, while 100 per cent of the datives have prepositions. All remarks are equally misleading and illustrate, not only the bluntness of his distinctions, but also the third weakness—that his selected texts, ranging as they do from about five to thirty or so lines in length, are far too short to be statistically significant. The spasmodic but violent variations on the various graphs at all periods—which he is often forced to disregard, e.g. pp. 573-4—demonstrate this clearly; see further §1225. Fourth, though he is aware of the difficulty of dating OE texts (pp. 13-14), his solutions cannot always be accepted. The clearest case in point is the material which he adduces for the seventh century. This comprises four texts—*Cædmon's Hymn*—his (2), which he dates 657-80—and three short extracts from the *Textus Roffensis*, dated by Ker (p. 443) as 'almost certainly in the time of Bishop Ernulf (1115-24)'. These texts are (1) *LawsAbt* Inscr.-5, which Lebow dates 602-3; (3) *LawsHl* Inscr.-3, which he dates 673-85; and (4) *LawsWi* Inscr.-3, which he dates *c.*696. We can scarcely admit these texts as valid evidence for the seventh century. So we are left with *Cædmon's Hymn.* For the eighth century Lebow offers (5) the Franks Casket (which he dates between 700 and 749); (6) *Bede's Death Song* (which he dates before 735); and (7) the Ruthwell Cross (which he dates *c.*750). We can appreciate his difficulty, but must agree that these provide a weak

about some aspects of Lebow's use of it, not only with words like *Cantwara* where there is doubt about the actual ambiguity of the form when it was originally used, but even with such things as the *-an* endings of weak nouns, where no formal distinction existed between certain cases.

foundation for graphs of seventh- and eighth-century usages, or for any serious conclusions.

§1224. Yet one of Lebow's most striking findings is that 'the frequency of prepositions increased considerably before the middle of the eighth century' (p. 625; the same idea is expressed in different forms at pp. 588, 591, 616, 619, and 645). This must be dismissed, for it is based entirely on the fact that, whereas text (1)—which we must reject as seventh-century evidence (§1223)—has only four prepositions against twenty-three inflected forms (three said to be ambiguous) and text (2)—*Cædmon's Hymn*, already analysed in §1223—has only one preposition against eight inflected forms (one said to be ambiguous), texts (3) and (4)—which we must also reject as evidence for the seventh century (§1223)—have respectively four prepositions (including *hyrefter, þær . . . to,* and *þærto*!) against seven inflexions (two said to be ambiguous) and ten prepositions (including *hyrefter*) against twenty-eight inflexions (twelve said to be ambiguous or 'historically incorrect').

§1225. In fairness to Lebow, it must be admitted that his study shows that, up to the early sixteenth century (when his material stops), the percentage of prepositions used with words which are uninflected increases, the percentage of words which are inflected and without prepositions decreases, and the percentage of examples in which both preposition and inflexion occur first rises, then falls. But it would have been surprising indeed if he had reached any other conclusions. He says (p. 568) that 'the graphs must not be considered to represent lines of development but rather bands with variable upper and lower extremes, disclosing a pattern of growth'. In my opinion these variations reflect the smallness of his samples and the bluntness of his distinctions, and the variable bands are so broad that (as I have suggested) they are more likely to hide than to disclose what is of real significance. I must therefore conclude that, for OE at any rate, Lebow's conclusions are of little value.[288] It still remains

---

[288] Anyone who after this still wishes to look at Lebow's findings for OE should consult in the first instance graph I, p. 577, and the comments on pp. 588-9 (the employment of case-form without preposition was fairly constant during the eighth and ninth centuries, but showed a small drop during the tenth and eleventh); graph II, p. 578, and the comments on p. 593 (the graph for the employment of preposition + case-form from the mid-ninth century shows a wide band with great peaks and depressions and an axis at about fifty per cent); graph III, p. 579, and the comments on p. 597 (the graph for the use of preposition without case form—i.e. with ambiguous forms as well as endingless locatives and the like —shows up to 1100 a band with a level axis at about fifteen per cent); and pp. 619-21 and 645-7, where general summaries of the findings of the whole thesis are given. Lebow's failure to mention the impact of the Danish invasions on the English language when comparing the external influences which affected English and German (pp. 1-2) is noteworthy.

to be determined whether the use of prepositions increased significantly during the OE period. Time does not permit me to attempt an
answer at the moment: I hope that full concordances will eventually
provide the mass of material necessary. But, for what it is worth, my
own impression is that—perhaps contrary to what we might expect
—little significant change in the comparative percentages of case-
forms alone and of prepositions + case-forms in those contexts
where both are possible can be detected in the extant OE monuments.[289] See further §1227.

§1226. Timmer's studies of prepositions in Gregory's *Dialogues* support this impression. In a chapter full of valuable material for the
lexicographer (Timmer 1934, chapter II), he first deals with those
examples in which a Latin preposition is represented by an OE
preposition (1934, pp. 46-79). He then turns to sentences in which
an OE preposition renders, not a Latin preposition, but one of the
three cases: genitive, dative, or ablative (1934, pp. 79-91). 'In the
majority of these examples C also has a preposition, but one differing from H; there are, however, a few instances of Latin genitive or
dative corresponding with a case in C' (1934, p. 79). Typical of the
latter are *GD(H)* 22. 3 . . . *þæt hit wære for his agenum gylte* but
GD(C) 22. 3 . . . *þæt hit his sylfes gylt wære*, Latin *suae culpae . . .*
fuisse, and *GD(H)* 95. 2 . . . *ne sealde his mod to nanum unrihtum*
luste but *GD(C)* 95. 2 . . . *ne sealde he his mod nænigum unrihtum*,
Latin *nulli animum voluptati dedit*. Timmer quotes or refers to some
eighteen such examples. On the other hand, there are four examples
in which MS *H* and the Latin lack a preposition where MS *C* has
one: *GD* 56. 11, *GD* 83. 2, *GD(H)* 27. 21 *se wæs bisceop Amiternine*
þære ceastre but *GD(C)* 27. 22 *se wæs biscop on Amiternine þære*
ceastre, Latin *Amiterninae civitatis episcopum*, and *GD(H)* 35. 25
. . . *bisceop Sabinensi þære cyrcean* but *GD(C)* 35. 23 . . . *biscop on*
Sabinense þære cyrcan, Latin *qui Sabinensi aecclesiae . . . praefuit*.
So the evidence would not support a claim that prepositions were
significantly more frequent in MS *H* than in MS *C*. We see the reviser

[289] The examples given in §1210, in which some verbs have only the dative, while others
are already used with *to*, are of interest here.

  Visser (i. 327-8) touches on this subject in a brief discussion on the replacement of the
type *Ic wæs him leof* (case-form) by the modern idiom 'I was dear to him' (preposition). As
I have already said in §1166, there are many OE adjectives which can take either a case-
form or a preposition + a case-form. Visser's inclusion of examples from Alfred among
those 'already to be noted in later Old English' seems strange and (as he admits himself) his
collections—like mine—are incomplete. Thus we find *god to* in *Or* 18. 1 *7 hiora hyd bið*
swiðe god to sciprapum, long before the ME citation he offers as the first: '1225 *good to*
freonde'.

choosing a different idiom—not always consistently—not rejecting an archaic one.[290] Timmer's work strengthens the feeling that any reader of OE must get: that prepositions already played an important part in the expression of both adnominal and adverbial relationships in the earliest texts.

§1227. My tentative conclusion in §1225 that there was little evidence in OE for a decrease in the percentage of constructions without prepositions against those with prepositions has received independent confirmation from Dančev (1969).[291] The gist of it is contained in his own summing-up (1969, p. 90):

1. In prose the prepositional phrase was already firmly established by the time of the first bulkier written records, i.e. the 9th century.
2. Contrary to expectation, no decrease in the frequency of prepositionless instances is observable over the period encompassed by the corpus, i.e. from the 9th to the 11th century.
3. A limited number of synthetic constructions were still current, and their preservation up to a certain stage in the development of Old English syntax is due to several factors, which we shall mention anew:
(a) Obvious (direct) Latin influence.
(b) Consciously archaic use for stylistic reasons, as in poetry and in Wulfstan —influence of the poetic language (this contradicts Knispel's claim, cf. §68).
(c) Use in stereotyped expressions.
(d) Remnants of earlier patterns, not falling under the above headings.
(e) Statistical dispersion, which is a random manifestation of the combined interaction of these factors. This is the place to mention 'indirect' Latin influence, to demonstrate which is of course next to impossible.
(f) Use in dative absolute constructions.

From here he goes on to summarize the importance of these factors (a) to (f) in various OE texts (pp. 90-1). Space does not permit a full discussion of this important article. But three points deserve brief mention here.

§1228. The first is his observation that 'the more clear-cut a given pattern [in its formal distinctiveness], the higher the probability for

[290] The truth of this is strikingly illustrated in Dančev 1969, pp. 86-7, where Dančev points out how Ælfric's usage in Catholic Homilies sometimes fluctuates between a series of prepositional examples, a series of prepositionless examples, and then alternative use. He goes on: 'This reflects the typical instability of all doublet forms in any idiolect—the scribe [sic] does not seem able to make up his mind which form to use, occasionally getting fixed for a while in one groove. The same phenomenon attracted my attention several years ago when working on Ru1.'
[291] For what they are worth (see my review in RES 23 (1972), 461-3), the figures given by F. F. Gardner in her An Analysis of Syntactic Patterns of Old English (Mouton, 1971) also tend to confirm it.

the occurrence of prepositionless instances' (1969, p. 77). Thus, for instance, prepositions are less frequent with the dat. pl. *-um* than with the dat. sg. *-e*; with *sprecan* he found 242 examples of *wordum* with a preposition and sixty-six without against forty-three examples of *spræce* with a preposition and none without (1969, p. 79). The second point is the relation between the meaning of the noun and the presence or absence of a preposition. Words referring to parts of the body, such as *cneow, eage, toð*, and *tunge*, supply the bulk of prepositionless constructions, in contrast to nouns denoting instruments and weapons (only two examples without prepositions out of about 285) and nouns denoting material, clothes, money, vessels, and the like (only two examples without prepositions out of about 860); see 1969, pp. 79-81. Thirdly, there are 'recurrent collocations' (1969, pp. 85-7). Dančev found prepositions less common in three situations: first, in collocations of nouns like *HomU* 32. 189. 1 *uton god lufian inwerdre heortan eallum mode and eallum mægne* than when one of these nouns is used alone; second, in some collocations of verb + noun, e.g. *ÆLS* 27. 73 *þu scealt deaþe sweltan* (he found no prepositions with *sweltan*) than in others, e.g. *ÆLS* 6. 309 . . . *þæt ic mid mislicum deaðe þine munecas acwelle* and *ÆCHom* ii. 260. 17 *and Drihten on rode mid deaðe wæs geswefod*; and third, in certain collocations of adjective or pronoun + noun, e.g. when *ðis* + *word* occur together than when *word* occurs alone.

K. CONJUNCTIONS

1. INTRODUCTORY REMARKS

§1229. Conjunctions are traditionally divided into co-ordinating (subdivided according to the relationship between the elements joined; see §1685) and subordinating (subdivided according to the type of clause introduced; see §§2416-20).[292] The two cannot always be distinguished. MnE 'for' has caused grammarians difficulty and OE *forþon* can mean 'because' and 'for'. It can also mean 'therefore' and in this sense would be classified by some grammarians as a 'sentence adverb'. For my reasons for taking *forþon, swa*, and *þeah*, as co-ordinating conjunctions rather than 'sentence adverbs' when they do not introduce subordinate clauses, see §1101.

---

[292] As a possible alternative for the term 'conjunction', Collinson (*TPS* 1941, p. 88) suggests 'clause-introducer'—his English rendering of Sandfeld's *mot introducteur*, which included 'the so-called relatives'. We need not adopt it.

§1230. Subordinating conjunctions can be formally divided into seven types, five of which have MnE equivalents:

MnE	OE
1. 'that'	þæt
2. 'so that'	swa þæt
3. 'so . . . that'	swa . . . þæt
4.	þæs þe
5.	þæs . . . þæt
6. 'to the end that'	to þam þæt/þe
7. 'to this end . . . that'	to þi . . . þæt/þe

We can therefore speak of prepositional conjunctions (6 and 7) and non-prepositional conjunctions (1-5). We can speak of simple conjunctions (1), grouped conjunctions (2, 4, and 6), and divided conjunctions (3, 5, and 7). MnE has no exact equivalent for types 4 and 5, in which þæs is used adverbially; see §1141. For practical purposes, the best grouping is a twofold one—non-prepositional conjunctions, simple, grouped, and divided (i.e. items 1-5), and prepositional conjunctions or formulae, grouped and divided (items 6-7). The latter consist basically of a preposition + an oblique case of þæt (+ þæt or þe). The case used depends on the preposition. Some of the prepositional formulae can be used adverbially, e.g. forþon (see §1229) and ærþæm (§2723).

2. ALPHABETICAL LISTS

a. Notes

§1231. These lists contain co-ordinating conjunctions, including 'sentence adverbs' (see §1229), and subordinating conjunctions, including those which introduce noun clauses (see §§1956-61 and 2059-63). Relative pronouns (§§ 2103-4) are excluded. The aim is completeness but to save repetition the meanings and functions of conjunctions discussed elsewhere in this book are not given here. These can be found through the Index of Words and Phrases. Non-prepositional and prepositional conjunctions are listed separately. Not all spelling variants[293] nor all possible combinations of the co-ordinating conjunctions[294] are given.

---

[293] Haddock (Part II) gives a list of variants in the *Lindisfarne Gospels*.
[294] See Wülfing, ii. 685, and my §§1709-862. Bately notes that certain combinations appear in some 'Alfredian' texts, but not in others; see *Ang.* 88 (1970), 448-57. Further work along these lines may be justified when full collections are available.

b. Alphabetical list of non-prepositional conjunctions

§1232.

ac, ah
æghwæþer (ge) . . . ge . . . ge
ægþer . . . and
ægþer (ge) . . . ge . . . ge
ægþer . . . oþþe . . . oþþe
ær
alswa
and, ond, on (see Miller's Bede, pp.
    xxvi-xxviii)
butan, buton
eac
ealswa
elcor (see BTS, s.v. elcor IVa)
[elles][295]
eþþa 'or'
forutan 'without, besides, except'
furþum
ge (. . . ge) (eac)
gehwæþer ge . . . ge 'both . . . and'
gehwæþere
gif
hu
humeta
huru
hwæder
hwær
hwæþer (. . . þe)
hwæþere
hwanon
hwider
hwilum . . . hwilum
hwonne
hwy
loc, loca + an interrogative (§§ 2383
    and 3363-4)
na, ne, no
nahwæþer . . . ne (. . . ne)
nalles, nealles

naþor ne . . . ne (. . . ne)
næfre
næs
nefne, nemne, nymþe
no þy ær
nu
ono (see Miller's Bede, pp. xxix-
    xxxiii, and §§3107 and 3672)
oþþe (. . . oþþe), oþþon
sam (. . . sam)
siþþan (but see §2666)
soþhwæþere
soþlice
swa, alone and in combination; see the
    Index of Words and Phrases
swelce, swilce, swylce, alone and in
    combination; see the Index of Words
    and Phrases
þa
þadder, þæder, þædres
þa hwile þe
þanecan þe
þanne
þanon
þær
þæs, alone and in combination; see the
    Index of Words and Phrases
þæt
þe (. . . þe)
þeah, þeana, þeh
þeahhwæþere
þenden
þider
þon ma þe
þonne
þy læs (þe)
þy (. . . þy)
weald

---

[295] Steche (p. 17) tentatively lists *elles* as an adverbial conjunction. But, in view of its genitive origin, it seems perhaps safer to follow BT and *OEG*, §668, and to take it as an adverb. See also Nusser, pp. 24-7.

c. Alphabetical list of prepositional conjunctions

§1233.

æfter + *dat., instr.*
ær + *dat., instr.*
amang + *dat.*
betwix + *dat., instr.*
for + *dat., instr.*
[of + *dat.*] (*see* §2664)

(on)gemang + *dat.*
oþ + *acc.*
to + *gen., dat., instr.*
under + *dat.*
wiþ + *acc., gen., dat. instr.*

L. INTERJECTIONS

1. INTRODUCTORY REMARKS

§1234. It is no easier to define or classify interjections than any other part of speech; see §48. Inga Offerberg made a brave attempt to do so in her unpublished fil.lic. dissertation, 'A Study On Old English Interjections' (University of Stockholm, 1967) but was forced to use the term 'loosely and traditionally' (p. 17).[296] In this use, an 'interjection' is a word which habitually expresses an exclamation but which plays no part in the syntax of the sentence; indeed, as Mustanoja (p. 621) puts it, 'it is functionally equivalent to a whole sentence, i.e., it expresses an idea which is complete in itself'. Offerberg (p. 15) provides two useful illustrations of this—*Bede* 96. 18 *Wala wa: þæt is sarlic, þætte swa fæger feorh 7 swa leohtes ondwlitan men scyle agan 7 besittan þeostra aldor* and *Coll* 36 *sceaphyrde, hæfst þu ænig gedeorf? Gea, leof, ic hæbbe*, where, she remarks, '*wala wa* corresponds to *þæt is sarlic* and *gea* to *ic hæbbe gedeorf*'.

§1235. An interjection may be imitative of a natural sound (e.g. *haha* and *hehe*, which, according to *ÆGram* 279. 15, *getacniað hlehter on leden and on englisc*); may express an emotion (e.g. *eala* 'alas'); or may come close to giving a command (e.g. *efne* 'behold'). But—as the examples suggest—the distinctions cannot be pressed. 'Primary' interjections—ejaculations which never had any other function, e.g. *eala* and *haha*—are sometimes distinguished from

---

[296] This work offers a valuable collection of material with some useful comments. It is well in advance of some published Ph.D. theses. Offerberg's comments on 'what looked like patterns of OE colloquial speech . . . fragments of "Spoken Old English"' (p. 8) are of special interest; see, for example, pp. 64–5 and 120 of her work. My section on interjections was in draft before she sent me a copy of this dissertation. But I have made some alterations and additions as a result of reading it. I am grateful. On interjections in *Bede*, see Miller's edition, pp. xxix–xxxiii.

'secondary' interjections—those which originally or primarily belong to another grammatical category, e.g. the adverb *nu* and the interrogative *hwæt*.

§1236. To these 'secondary' interjections we can perhaps add *þær*; Nagashima (pp. 152 and 156) draws our attention to examples from the Old and New Testaments in which (he suggests) *þær* represents Latin *ecce*, e.g. *Matt(WSCp)* 28. 2 *7 þær wearð geworden micel eorþbifung*, Latin *et ecce terrae motus factus est magnus*. But the fact that at pp. 152-3 and 156-8 he quotes similar OE examples where there is no *ecce* in the Latin—such as *Matt(WSCp)* 8. 26 *7 þær wearð geworden mycel smyltness*, Latin *et facta est tranquillitas magna*—argues against the direct equivalence of *þær* and *ecce*. None the less, there may be something in his suggestion that an 'intrusive *þær*' not represented in the Latin Bible sometimes has 'evocative-interjectional' force, e.g. *John(WSCp)* 9. 13 and 11. 39 *Ða cwæð Martha to him þæs swustor þe þar dead wæs*, Latin *dicit ei Martha soror eius qui mortuus fuerat*.

§1237. Interjections are not all used in the same way. Many of them tend to occur initially to express strong feeling. They may be contextually as well as syntactically independent of what follows, e.g. *WHom* 5. 33 *Eala, eala, ac þa wæs mycel blis 7 bot seo betste . . .* , or contextually related to a following statement, e.g. *WHom* 17. 64 *Eala, eala, soð is þæt ic eow secge*; to a following exclamatory clause (with or without a vocative), e.g. *GD* 191. 23 *Eala, þu burh, þu Equine, þæt þe þus gelimpeð!*, *GD* 215. 25 *Eala, þæt min sawl efensargaþ þises wifes sare*, *BlHom* 161. 29 *Eala hu swiþe eadge wæron þa æþelan cennende Sancte Iohannes*, and *ÆGram* 227. 14 *o si haberem, eala gyf ic hæfde*; to a following imperative, e.g. *ÆLS* 7. 177 *Eala ge Romanisce arfæste symle gehelpað us hraðe*; to a following question, e.g. *Bo* 9. 20 *Hwæt la hwæt, sint þis nu þa god . . . þe þu ealne weg gehete þam monnum þe þe heorsumian woldan?*; or (as Offerberg puts it at p. 23) to 'a noun, which constitutes a complete clause, in poetic fragmentary language of great emotional intensity', as in *Wan* 94 *Eala beorht bune! Eala byrnwiga!* But the initial position is not obligatory. Offerberg (p. 55) notes that it is 'characteristic of *la* that it is often inserted in clauses, thus being literally an interjection or a *betwuxalegednys*, as Ælfric terms it [*ÆGram* 278. 1]. It is also placed in final position. In either case *la* often appears to be closely attached to the preceding word and to have no distinct meaning of its own.' She further observes (p. 78) that 'the lament *wa* generally occurs in combination with *la*: *wala*, *walawa.* Uncompounded it is rare except when followed by a noun or pronoun in the dative, as in *wa me.*'

2. LIST OF INTERJECTIONS

a. Notes

§1238. The list which follows is intended purely for initial reference and therefore gives only the most obvious meaning for each interjection. Offerberg's dissertation (§1234) offers the most complete coverage at present in existence. But see also Wülfing (ii. 686-95) and Mustanoja (pp. 620-40). The interjections are placed in alphabetical order in one list. There is no attempt to make any of the distinctions referred to in the preceding sections.

b. Alphabetical list

§1239.

æ alas!

æala, æla alas! O!

æfne behold!

afæstla O certainly! See *ÆGram* 280. 13.

ea O! alas!

eala alas!

efne, efne nu behold, indeed, truly!

egele, egla, eglaeg [= Latin *euge* in *Ps(K)* 69. 4 and elsewhere]

enu, eono, ono behold!

eow, eowlæ, eulæ, eule, euwa [of uncertain meaning]

gea yea!

georstu O!

gese, gyse yes!

haha and hehe getacniað hlehter on leden and on englisc (ÆGram 279. 15)

?hela [= Latin *heu* in *Ps(J)* 119. 5]

henu, heono, hona behold!

hig, hig hig, higla, higlahig, hilahi alas! See *ÆGram* 280. 13.

hui, huig alas! See *ÆGram* 278. 10.

hu (la) (nu) how (now)! come!

huru indeed, surely, at least. See Meyer, *Ang. B.* 53 (1942), 87-90.

hwæt ah! lo!

la lo! ah! yes!

na no! See *ÆHom* 13. 225.

nese no!

nic no!

nu [= Latin *ecce*]

nula [= Latin *heia*]. See *ÆGram* 228. 1.

ono behold! look here!

sehde, sehþ(e), seþþe behold!

tæg tæg [= Latin *puppup*][297]

?uton. See §916.

wa, wæ woe!

weg la (weg), weilawei, wilawei [= Latin *euge*]. See Björkman, *Archiv,* 114 (1905), 164.

wel (la) (ga) well! ah!

wellawell well, well. See *ÆGram* 280. 13.

---

[297] See H. D. Meritt, *Fact and Lore about Old English Words* (Stanford, 1954), 188.

III

THE SIMPLE SENTENCE:
ELEMENTS

A. CASE

1. INTRODUCTORY REMARKS

§1240. The extent to which the OE case-forms overlapped has already been discussed (§§8-15). In the light of *Or* 168. 16 . . . *þæt he heora swicdomes wið Alexander fremmende wære*, we can argue whether *tacna* in *ÆCHom* i. 344. 26 . . . *betwux ðam heofenlicum mihtum þe Godes tacna gefremmað* is a genitive after *gefremmað* or an early example of *a/u* confusion (*OEG*, §§49 and 377). In *ÆTemp* 24. 2, MS G has *þæt his trendel underscyt ðære sunnan* where MS *A* reads *þa sunnan*. The possibility that the latter is a genuine idiom and not a scribal error is confirmed by the fact that *undersceotan* appears with a personal passive in *CP* 27. 16 . . . *ðonne hi ne beoð mid nanre sylle underscotene ðæs godcundlican mægenes*; see §834. Such examples are perhaps not very important in themselves. But they remind us that there are many verbs in OE which can take more than one case; see §§1089-92. We may shrug off as another instance of this variation Ælfric's use of the accusative in *ÆCHom* i. 268. 11 *Deofol mot ælces mannes afandigan* and of the genitive three lines later in *ÆCHom* i. 268. 14 *Swa swa man afandað gold on fyre, swa afandað God þæs mannes mod*. But it is more difficult to dismiss the appearance of these two cases in the same sentence, as in *ÆCHom* ii. 482. 32 *Hwæt ða hæðengyldan, ða ðe þæt tempel and þæra goda gymdon, cwædon to þam ealdormen* . . . and *LS* 8. 453 *and þæt fyr heora ne æthran ne furþum an hær heora heafdes*. An example from the poetry is

Dream 78	Nu ðu miht gehyran, hæleð min se leofa,
	þæt ic bealuwara weorc gebiden hæbbe,
	sarra sorga,

where *weorc* and *sarra sorga* are parallel. Fluctuations like these seem to me strong signs that the concept of case was beginning to weaken. None the less, it remains a very real one in OE. A good example is *ÆCHom* ii. 84. 15 *He gearcað urne godan willan to fultumigenne, and he fylst ðam willan gegearcodne*, where the fact that *gegearcodne* is accusative agreeing with *urne godan willan* and not dative agreeing with *ðam willan* adds considerably to the emphasis already given it by its position in the sentence; see §851 fn. 219.

2. THE NOMINATIVE

a. The case of the subject

§1241. The nominative, answering the question 'Who?' or 'What?', is the case of the subject and its appositional elements, e.g. *ÆCHom* i. 450. 22 *Se biscop ða underfeng ða madmas, ÆCHom* i. 8. 7 *Paulus se apostol cwæð* . . . , and *ÆCHom* i. 302. 28 *and se ðe ne gelyfð, he bið geniðerod.* The syntax of the subject is discussed in §§1482–527.

b. The case of address

§1242. In the absence of a special vocative form, the nominative is the case of address, either with or without an interjection, e.g. *ÆCHom* i. 158. 19 *La leof, do þæt ic mæge geseon* but *ÆCHom* i. 258. 15 *Leof, tæce us hu we magon us gebiddan.* Interjections are frequently found before the personal pronouns, e.g. *ÆCHom* ii. 400. 4 *Eala ðu goda lareow* and *ÆLS* 5. 396 *Eala ge ungesæligan.*

§1243. The actual vocative expression may be one word such as a noun, e.g. *ÆCHom* i. 74. 35 *Drihten*, or an adjective, e.g. *ÆCHom* i. 316. 32 *Gea, leof.* It is, I suppose, arguable that in examples like *ÆCHom* i. 6. 31 *Clypa and ne geswic ðu, ðu* is a nominative of address, not the subject. I doubt it. But the point is terminological. See further §§887–91. But phrases such as I now quote (without spelling out the components) are to be found: *ÆCHom* ii. 114. 23 *leof Drihten, ÆCHom* ii. 114. 4 *Drihten leof, ÆCHom* i. 48. 5 *Min Drihten, ÆCHom* i. 336. 23 *Broðor min, ÆCHom* i. 34. 11 *þu Bethleem, Iudeisc land, ÆLS Pref* 38 *ðu leof, ÆCHom* ii. 310. 7 *ðu earma, ÆCHom* i. 528. 3 *Ðu mannes bearn, ÆCHom* ii. 400. 4 *Eala ðu goda lareow, ÆCHom* i. 28. 20 *men ða leofestan, ÆCHom* i. 32. 5 *Mine gebroðra þa leofostan,* and (with idiomatic separation of heavy groups) *ÆCHom* ii. 552. 19 *Eala ðu goda ðeowa and getrywe*; see §1247. Other combinations include *Bede* 348. 10 *Mine broðor mine þa leofan, Dream* 78 *hæleð min se leofa,* and *GuthB* 1076 *Min þæt leofe bearn.* As will be seen, the elements qualifying a noun may precede or follow it. Appositional elements may be added, e.g. *ÆCHom* i. 34. 11 above, *ÆCHom* i. 48. 3 *Drihten Hælend,* and

ÆCHom i. 546. 8 *Eala ðu eadige Godes cennestre, symle mæden Maria, tempel ðæs Halgan Gastes. . . .*

§1244. The person or thing addressed may, of course, appear elsewhere in the sentence in another case, e.g. *ÆCHom* ii. 86. 30 *Sy ðe, Drihten, lof, eces wuldres Cyning.* This merely reflects the fact that the vocative stands outside the structure of the sentence as far as agreement of case is concerned.

§1245. The basic rule for the use of strong and weak forms of the adjective set out in §102 generally holds here. The combination weak form of adjective + noun is hard to find in early prose. Wülfing (i, §122. 3) cites *Bede(B)* 486. 3 *goda hælend*, but *goda* may be a genitive plural since MS *C* has *duguþa* and MS *Ca dugoþa*. Krohn's only example (p. 14) is *GD(H)* 70. 6 *leofa drihten*, where the earlier version in MS *C* has *min drihten.* We also find *Bede(B)* 134. 24 *cyning leofusta.* But here again MS *B* is in solitary splendour, for MS *O* has *þu cyning* and MS *Ca cyning.* In Ælfric too the adjective is strong when used alone, e.g. *ÆCHom* ii. 252. 28 *sy þu hal, leof*, or with a noun, e.g. *ÆCHom* ii. 114. 23 *leof drihten* and *ÆCHom* ii. 114. 4 *drihten leof.* The examples *leofa man* and *leofa cild*, attributed by Schrader (p. 29) to Wulfstan, are not his; they belong to *HomU* 45. 289. 16 and 17. However, the phrase *leofan men*, as in *WHom* 10c. 3, is a favourite of Wulfstan, but not his monopoly; see Stuart, *EStudies*, 45 (1964), 39-42.

§1246. The use of weak forms in the poetry where we would expect strong ones is common; see §114. Examples in vocative expressions include *GenA* 1916 *leofa*, *Beo* 1854 *leofa Beowulf*, and *Beo* 1216 *Beowulf leofa.* But note *GenA* 2784 *min swæs frea.*

§1247. There is a general tendency to have a weak form of the adjective after *þu* or *ge* in vocative expressions in the early prose, e.g. *Solil* 13. 13 *Ðu, se aldsta feder, and þu wisesta, GD* 122. 18 *þu arwyrgda, nalæs þu gebletsoda*, and *CP* 207. 14 *Eala ge ungewitfullan Galatæ*; in the later prose, e.g. *ÆCHom* i. 372. 20 *Ðu leofa Drihten* and *ÆLS* 5. 396 *Eala ge ungesæligan and soðlice earmingas*; and in the poetry, e.g.

ChristA 275 Eala þu mæra middangeardes
        seo clæneste cwen ofer eorþan
        þara þe gewurde to widan feore

and

ChristA 348   Eala þu halga   heofona dryhten,
                  þu mid fæder þinne   gefyrn wære
                  efenwesende   in þam æþelan ham.

A comparison of *Bede(T)* 78. 19 *broþor þu leofesta* with *Bede(B)*
broðor se leofusta suggests that the personal pronoun was felt to be
the equivalent of a demonstrative or possessive. The contrast between forms with and without *þu* or *ge* is nicely pointed by examples
involving the splitting of heavy groups, such as *ÆCHom* ii. 552. 19
Eala þu goda ðeowa and getrywe and *ÆCHom* ii. 554. 7 *Ðu yfela*
ðeowa and sleac. But there are occasional exceptions in the later
prose—perhaps I should say very occasional; they include *ÆLS*
Pref 38 *þu leof* and *ÆCHom* ii. 108. 2 *Cumað ge bletsode mines*
Fæder, where it is tempting to read *gebletsode*. But this would
probably be wrong, for (as Malcolm Godden has told me), all other
manuscripts except Bodley 340 have *gebletsode* for *bletsode* and in
ÆHom 11. 409 *Cumað, ge gebletsodan mines heofonlican Fæder*,
MSS *M*, *R*, and *T*, all read *gebletsode* for *gebletsodan*.

c. The case of the complement

§1248. The nominative is the usual case of what is traditionally
called the complement, e.g. *soð witega* and *toweard* in *ÆCHom* i.
190. 15 . . . *þæt he wære soð witega, ðe toweard wæs* and *unge-*
leafful in *ÆCHom* i. 202. 5 *þa wearð he ungeleafful þæs engles*
bodungum. In such clauses or sentences the verb *beon/wesan* or
weorþan is merely a link; see §604.

§1249. Most of the elements and combinations which can serve as
subjects can also serve as nominative complements. But other elements can serve as complements; see §§1584-5.

§1250. The nominative is, of course, the case of the second participle when it forms a passive combination with *wesan* or *weorþan*;
see §§759-62.

§1251. The nominative is also found with verbs of rest or motion in
what may be either a complement or an appositional element, e.g.
ÆHom 5. 7 *Se Hælend þa sæt þær, of ðam siðfæte werig*, *ÆHom*
6. 2 . . . *be Lazare, þe seoc læg*, and *ÆHom* 4. 22 . . . *hu mæg þonne*
standan his rice staþolfæst? (For further examples see Visser, i,
§§221-2, 227, 233-4, and 237.) It also occurs with *þyncan* used

personally, e.g. *ÆCHom* ii. 570. 15 *Soðlice on ðam micclum dome ælcum ænlipium men ðincð to lytel his agen ingehyd him to gewitnysse* and *ÆCHom* ii. 82. 18 *and we earfoðlice him filiað tomerigen, seðe nu todæg is ure folgere geðuht*, or impersonally, e.g. *ÆHom* 6. 205 *and þincð him æþryt þæt he embe þæt þence.*

d. Other uses of the nominative

§1252. The nominative is sometimes found in the 'naming constructions' discussed in §§1473-81, e.g. *ÆCHom* i. 10. 21 *swa þæt he wæs gehaten Leohtberend* and *ÆCHom* ii. 82. 34 *He gecigde Drihten his Andfenga* (but cf. *ÆCHom* ii. 84. 4 *Ða nolde he gecigan God mildheortne*). In examples like *ÆCHom* i. 30. 6 *of ðære byrig Nazareð* and *ÆCHom* i. 200. 34 *to hire magan Elisabeth, Nazareð* and *Elisabeth* are probably to be regarded as uninflected datives rather than as nominatives; cf. *ÆCHom* i. 32. 32 *þeos towritennys asprang fram ðam ealdormen Cyrino: Cyrinus is gereht Yrfenuma.* On examples like *ÆCHom* ii. 358. 3 *He hæfde ænne broðor, Tuna gehaten*, where the participle seems nominative in form, see §1474.

§1253. The nominative is natural in such examples as *ÆCHom* ii. 226. 26 *ða Iudeiscan . . . geeuenlæcende heora fæder, þæt is, deofol . . . ;* cf. *ÆCHom* i. 228. 4 *gif he geuenlæcð deofle. . . .* Further on the *þæt is* construction, see §§323-7.

§1254. For the nominative after *butan* and *nemne*, see §§3630 and 3649. On the possibility that OE had a nominative absolute, see §§3832-45. On the nominative and infinitive, see §§3779-81.

3. THE ACCUSATIVE

a. The case of the 'direct object'

§1255. 'The great function of the Accusative is to form temporary compounds with the verb, as the great function of the Genitive is to form temporary compounds with the noun' (GL, p. 207). The accusative answers the question 'Whom?' or 'What?' and is traditionally said to be the case which follows a verb used 'transitively' (on the term, see §§602-6) or the case of the 'direct object' and its appositional elements, e.g. *ÆCHom* i. 32. 5 *Ure hælend, Godes Sunu . . . gemedemode hine sylfne . . . , ÆCHom* i. 322. 12 *He sende ðone Halgan Gast to eorðan . . .* , and *ÆCHom* i. 202. 3 *. . . þæt he sceolde . . . sunu habban, Iohannem ðone Fulluhtere.* Wülfing's promised treatment (i, §96) did not appear.

§1256. This statement must be modified for OE (and many other IE languages), inasmuch as some 'transitive' verbs govern a 'direct object' in the genitive or dative, while others of similar meaning take the accusative, e.g. *ÆCHom* ii. 266. 33 *Etað þisne hlaf* but *ÆCHom* ii. 168. 3 . . . *þæt hi nanes ætes on ðære fare ne onbirigdon* and *ÆCHom* i. 338. 20 . . . *and ða Iudeiscan boceras . . . þæt tældon* but *ÆCHom* i. 156. 10 *Seo menigu . . . ciddon ðam blindan*. Others can take the accusative and either one or both of the genitive and dative, e.g. *ÆCHom* i. 48. 4 . . . *onfoh minne gast*, *ÆCHom* i. 308. 5 . . . *hi . . . deaðes onfoð*, and *BlHom* 119. 11 *Ac ge onfoþ þæm mægene Halges Gastes*. . . . See further §§602-3. But the accusative remains the case most commonly found after 'transitive' verbs in OE. For this reason no verbs governing only the accusative are given in the List of verbal rections; see §1091 on this and other limitations in that list. On verbal rection see §§1081-92 and on the syntax of the 'direct object', §§1565-80.

§1257. The accusative is found after some impersonal verbs; see §1027.

§1258. A distinction is often made between 'the inner or internal object' and 'the outer or external object'. Thus, Moore writes (p. 12): 'The fundamental distinction is between the *External* and the *Internal* Object; in the External the action is directed to an object outside; in the Internal the action does not go outside itself. "Fight the foe" embodies an External Accusative, "Fight the good fight" an Internal Accusative.' These may sometimes be distinguished in OE. Thus we can detect the inner object—which 'serves to define more narrowly or to explain more fully the contents of the verb' (GL, §332)—in *ÆHom* 9. 32 . . . *þæt witan sceolon cyðan heora word openlice*, *ÆHom* 12. 156 *Ðær man Godes lof singð*, *ÆHom* 12. 157 *þær man Godes lare segð*, and *ÆHom* 22. 76 *and he him sylf wolde singan his gebedu*. The outer object is seen in *ÆCHom* i. 78. 10 *He ða gesamnode ealle þa ealdorbiscopas*, *ÆCHom* ii. 448. 29 *Ne ondræt Iob on idel God*, and *ÆCHom* i. 16. 30 *þa nam he micelne graman and andan to þam mannum*. But the distinction is not always obvious and need not be pressed; consider *ÆCHom* i. 20. 7 . . . *and he and his wif ða bearn gestryndon*, *ÆCHom* ii. 266. 33 *Etað þisne hlaf*, *ÆCHom* ii. 334. 23 *Ðu scealt eft ðinne lichaman underfon*, and *ÆHom* 19. 61 *Ne mot nan man his lima ne his gesceapu forceorfan*.

§1259. The so-called 'cognate accusative' (which occurs when the verb and its object are etymologically related) is a special case of the

'internal accusative', e.g. *BlHom* 63. 18 *7 hie demaþ heora domas,*
ÆCHom ii. 138. 33 *ðaða hi ða fare ferdon,* and *ÆCHom* ii. 476. 16
se cyning . . . leofode his lif on eawfæstre drohtnunge. The object in
such examples is of course pleonastic. But Nader's observation
(1879, pp. 7–8) that the cognate accusative hardly ever occurs without an adjective to avoid such pleonasm is clearly not true for OE.

b. Verbs with two accusatives

§1260. On verbs which take a double accusative, see §1083. Whether an example like *ÆCHom* i. 106. 33 . . . *ða tungelwitegan*
tocneowon Crist soðne mann . . . Hi oncneowon hine soðne Cyning
. . . is to be explained as a double accusative or an accusative and
unexpressed infinitive is a matter of terminology; see §§3766–76.

c. Other uses of the accusative

§1261. The accusative is used adverbially to express extent of space,
time, and other measurements, and to express degree; see §§1382–8.

§1262. When it is expressed, the subject of the accusative and infinitive construction is by definition accusative.

§1263. On the accusative with naming constructions, see §§1474–8
and with prepositions, §§1177–219. On the possible existence of
'accusative absolutes' see §§3832–45.

4. THE GENITIVE

a. Introductory remarks

(1) Problems of classification

§1264. Classifying and defining the various uses of the genitive
offers many problems. Too much can be made of them; as GL
observes (p. 207), 'the great function of the Accusative is to form
temporary compounds with the verb, as the great function of the
Genitive is to form temporary compounds with the noun. Beyond
this statement everything is more or less extra-grammatical, and
sharp sub-divisions are often unsatisfactory.'

§1265. Moore (pp. 35–45) offers a semi-semantic classification—
possessive ('belonging to a person'), partitive ('belonging to a class'),
descriptive ('belonging to a particular class'), and genitive of relation

('belonging to a special reference'). The last can be subsumed under the first, for—as Moore himself observes (p. 43)—'all usages within it are at root *possessive*'. As my own investigations progressed, it became clear that this threefold division is justified *as far as the genitive with nouns and pronouns* is concerned provided we remember that the compartments are not watertight. The possessive is usually descriptive, the partitive sometimes possessive and usually descriptive. So the descriptive may be possessive and/or partitive; consider *BlHom* 183. 22 *scepes heafod* and *Beo* 676 *Beowulf Geata*. But there are also descriptive genitives which involve no element of possession, e.g. *ÆCHom* i. 310. 28 *an lamb anes geares* and *ÆCHom* ii. 158. 17 *wines drenc*. However, Moore's attempt to embrace genitives with adjectives, verbs, and prepositions, caused him to erect his false fourth category—syntactic rather than semantic—and sowed the seeds of confusion. So my basic classification is formal— the genitive with nouns and pronouns, with adjectives, with prepositions, and with verbs, and its adverbial uses.[1] But some discussion of semantic and syntactical distinctions is inevitable.

§1266. The 'possessive' genitive—the most common use with nouns—is sometimes 'subjective', e.g. *ÆCHom* ii. 32. 20 *Godes mildheortnys* ('God showed mercy') and sometimes 'objective', e.g. *ÆCHom* i. 22. 17 *Godes ege* ('They feared God'). But the distinction cannot always be made; see §§1280-3.

§1267. The 'possessive' genitive may denote possession and something more, e.g. *ÆCHom* i. 200. 33 *æfter þæs engles bodunge*, where —as *ÆCHom* i. 200. 25 *on þam dæge bodode se heahengel Gabrihel ðam clænum mædene Godes tocyme* . . . makes clear—the archangel is the agent of the Annunciation. (So we sometimes hear of the 'genitive of agency'.) On the other hand, the 'possessive' genitive, as usually defined and exemplified, does not necessarily denote actual possession, e.g. *ÆCHom* i. 104. 3 . . . *þis godspel . . . þe belimpð to ðysses dæges ðenunge* '. . . the service for today' and *ÆCHom* i. 78. 1 . . . *on þære forman Cristes bec* 'in the first book about Christ'. An attempt is made in §§1284-6 to distinguish these and other shades of meaning.

§1268. The 'partitive' genitive, which 'stands for the Whole to which a Part belongs' (GL, p. 235), may be used with any word which denotes partition—including nouns (e.g. *ÆCHom* i. 92. 34

---

[1] Holtbuer, pp. 34-40, endeavours to use genitive combinations as proof or otherwise of Cynewulfian authorship. I am not convinced.

sumne dæl þæs felles), adjectives (e.g. *ÆCHom* i. 34. 11 *wacost burga*), pronouns (e.g. *ÆCHom* i. 580. 5 *eower sum*), numerals (e.g. *ÆCHom* ii. 18. 15 *an þæra wæs Sibylla*), and verbs (e.g. *ÆCHom* i. 72. 17 . . . *ic unforhtmod ðæs drences onfo*). For references to further discussions, see the General Index.

§1269. 'The Genitive Case . . . is akin to the Adjective, with which it is often parallel' (GL, p. 230). So we can speak of an adjectival or 'qualifying' genitive; cf. *ÆCHom* ii. 30. 7 *on mannes hiwe* with *ÆCHom* ii. 30. 10 *on þam menniscum hiwe*. This is not always a separate function, for it can be found in many genitives, including the simple 'possessive' (cf. *ÆCHom* i. 60. 4 *æt his witena handum* with *ÆCHom* i. 84. 8 *fram moderlicum breostum*), 'the genitive of agency' (cf. *ÆCHom* i. 200. 33 *æfter þæs engles bodunge* with *ÆCHom* i. 544. 31 *to engelicum spræcum*), and the partitive (cf. *ÆCHom* i. 450. 21 *goldes . . . hypan* with *ÆHom* 21. 256 *fif gyldene hringas*).

§1270. On the various types of genitives which have been detected with verbs and prepositions and in the adverbial uses, see the relevant discussions in the pages which follow.

§1271. To avoid undue bulk, the examples quoted are mostly from Ælfric. Except where otherwise stated, the remarks made hold for the earlier prose and for the poetry.

(2) *The parts of speech involved*

§1272. All parts of speech may govern a genitive except adverbs, conjunctions, and interjections. Not all governing words can be used in conjunction with all types of genitive. But it is not necessary to spell out the exceptions. The adverbial genitive is of course independent of any governing word.

§1273. The governing noun or pronoun may be in any case, including the genitive, e.g. *ÆCHom* i. 270. 20 (*seo halgung*) *þæs mæran naman Godes*. On non-repetition of the governing word, see §§95-6, and on the relative position of the governing word and its genitive(s), see §§1304-30.

§1274. The genitive of a noun denotes possession in the third person unless it is in apposition with a first or second person pronoun, as in *Or* 120. 14 *eower Romana brocu*. The 3rd pers. possessive *sin* was superseded by the genitive of the third person pronoun—*his, hire, hira*; see §§290–3. A demonstrative may occur in place of a possessive genitive, e.g. *ÆCHom* i. 86. 23 *Ac ðaða he wæs on ðissere beðunge geled, þa wearð se lichama eal toslopen*; see further §§303–10.

§1275. That forms like *min* and *ure, þin* and *eower*, and *his, hire*, and *hira*, retained a pronominal force which their modern equivalents lack is clear from the examples quoted in §296 and from others like *ÆCHom* i. 240. 33 *Ne mæg se standan . . . ac tylað his sylfes*. Shipley (p. 90) detects similar pronominal usages in *GenA* 984 *and his blod ageat*, ‖ *Cain Abeles* and *JDay ii* 168 *and heora heortan . . .* ‖ *synscyldigra*, and is supported for the former by Breitkreuz (p. 8): ‘Dass *his* [in *GenA* 984] nicht etwa als ein unflektiertes Adjektiv, sondern als reiner Genitiv aufzufassen ist, geht aus folgender Stelle hervor’ [‘That *his* . . . should be understood not as an uninflected adjective but as a pure genitive, is clear from the following passage’]: ‘*Gen* 272 *þurh his anes cræft. anes* ist hier die Apposition zum Genitiv *his*. Ebenfalls [Likewise] *Gen* 1587 *his selfes bearn* [*GenA* 1593].’ Examples like *Beo* 2147 *on* [*min*]*ne sylfes dom, ChristA* 9 *þin sylfes weorc*, and *And* 1417 *on þines sylfes hand*, suggest that Breitkreuz is not necessarily right. On the problems involved, see §§483–6.

§1276. This use of the genitive of the personal pronoun is most frequent when the pronoun is accompanied by *self*, e.g. *HomU* 21 *for his synnum and ure sylfra* (see further §484); *eal*, e.g. *WHom* 8c. 91 *He is ure ealra fæder; an*, e.g. *Beo* 2533 *ne gemet mannes, nefne min anes; begen*, e.g. *Solil* 25. 15 *incer beigra wealdend*; and *twegen*, e.g. *GenA* 1834 *freondlufu* ‖ *. . . uncer twega*. Here we can compare MnE ‘our fate’ but ‘the fate of us all/alone/two’ and so on.

§1277. But it does occur without such words. We find the subjective genitive in *ÆCHom* i. 242. 20 *to eower agenre ðearfe* and other examples in §296 and in *OEG,* §705. Most of the possible examples of the objective use of the genitive of the pronoun are ambiguous either in form, e.g. *Gen* 22. 16 *ac ðe wæs min ege mare þonne hys lif* (*ÆGram* 95. 2 *mei locutio, min spræc* notwithstanding), or in meaning; for examples of the latter, see §1281.

§1278. The inflected possessives of the first and second person are used for both subjective and objective possession, e.g. *BlHom* 23. 10 *þonne beo we urum Hælende fylgende* and *BlHom* 81. 22 *7 eac þa þe on helle synt biddaþ þinre onlesnesse 7 þinre hælo* (subjective) but *Solil* 55. 16 *uton gelyfan þæt god si on uncrum fultume* and

PPs 59. 4 . . . *þam þe ege ðinne elne healdað* (objective). There are many ambiguous examples. Thus *BlHom* 23. 23 *7 he onfeng þa ilcan gecynde for urum lufon þe he ær gesceop* might mean 'because of his love for us' or 'to win our love'.

§1279. In general, it can be said that we find examples of all the parts of speech which can have a genitive in most of the remaining genitival functions. Again there is no need to spell out exceptions.

b. With nouns and pronouns

(1) Genitives denoting possession

§1280. The function described as 'possessive' embraces a wide variety of genitives, most of which can be used with nouns referring to animates human and non-human, to materials, and to abstract qualities. The system of classification popular in the early dissertations—based on the type of nouns which were related—was too mechanical to be of any value even if it had worked. We must attempt one based on function. Basically the 'possessive' implies that the genitive *x* has or possesses *y*, e.g. *ÆCHom* i. 32. 5 *Godes sunu*, *ÆCHom* i. 422. 12 *ðære cyrcan madmas*, *ÆCHom* i. 14. 9 *anes treowes wæstm*, and *ÆCHom* i. 4. 29 *ord ælcere leasunge and yfelnysse*. The subjective genitive, e.g. *ÆCHom* i. 62. 33 *mines Drihtnes lare* ('The Master taught'; cf. *ÆHom* 2. 84 . . . *se Hælend . . . lærde þæt folc*), *ÆCHom* ii. 32. 20 *Godes mildheortnys*, and *ÆCHom* ii. 10. 8 *hire mægðhad*, is often distinguished from the objective genitive, e.g. *ÆCHom* ii. 8. 21 *ure sawla Alysend* ('He saves our souls'; cf. *ÆHom* 3. 129 *and Crist swa alysde þa ðe gelyfað on hyne*), *ÆCHom* i. 22. 17 *Ða wæs þa sume hwile Godes ege on mancynne*, *ÆCHom* ii. 602. 12 *and seo soðe lufu Godes and manna*. Both involve possession—in *ÆCHom* i. 62. 33 above, the Master has something to teach and in *ÆCHom* ii. 8. 21 above, our souls have a Saviour. The two can occur side by side, e.g. *ÆCHom* i. 300. 16 *Sy ðam arleasan ætbroden seo gesihð Godes wuldres*.

§1281. But the distinction cannot always be made. Sometimes this is because there is an ambiguity in the actual meaning or because both senses may be intended, e.g. *John(WSCp)* 5. 42 *Ac ic gecneow eow þ ge nabbaþ godes lufe on eow* ('You do not love God' or 'God does not love you') and *ÆCHom* i. 84. 4 *Hi wæron þæs Hælendes gewitan*: the Innocents were Christ's witnesses and witnesses for Christ. Sometimes it is because we can resolve the phrase in either way without affecting the meaning. Thus *ÆCHom* i. 8. 24 *An angin is ealra þinga, þæt is God Ælmihtig* can mean 'All things have a beginning—God' or 'God begins all things' and (transforming the latter) 'All things are begun by God'. The same difficulty can be observed with the genitive of pronouns, e.g. *Solil* 25. 15 *Se hlaford is incer beigra wealdend, ge ðin ge þæs hlafordes* ('He rules us' or 'We have Him as our ruler'?) and *WHom* 7. 76 *Witodlice witan we moton*[2] *hu we Criste geleanian eal þæt he for us 7 for ure lufan þafode* ('because He loved us' or 'so that we might love Him'?). See further §1277.

§1282. Already in OE such difficulties are sometimes avoided by the use of prepositions; cf. the variant readings at *Bede* 362. 28, where MS *T* and others have *swa mycel lufu godcundre lare* (where the love might come from the word of God) while MSS *O* and *Ca* have . . . *lufu to godcundre lare*, and note *CP* 409. 13 *for ðæm lufum ðe hi to him habbað* and *ÆCHom* ii. 318. 8 . . . *Cristes lufe on us*.

§1283. The folly of pressing the distinction too far can be seen when we consider phrases like *WHom* 6. 123 *Cyrus hatte Persa cyning, GenA* 2667 *folces weard*, and *Mald* 26 *wicinga ar.* QW (p. 62) describes phrases like the latter as objective. Daniels (p. 20) quarrels with Mohrbutter's description (p. 77) of the first as objective and prefers to see it as subjective. We can argue interminably without getting around the obvious truth that in all three both ideas are involved—'The Persians had a king called Cyrus' and 'A King called Cyrus ruled the Persians', and so on. There is therefore little point in following QW (p. 62) in viewing these as the 'two primary groups of usage'. Only confusion can result from the use of the alternative terms 'active' for the 'subjective', and 'passive' for the 'objective', genitive; see GL (p. 232) and QW (p. 62). *Godes lufu* may mean 'God loves us' and so can be called 'active', as opposed to 'We love God'— 'passive'. But both can be transformed into a passive—'We are loved by God' and 'God is loved by us'.

§1284. As already noted, both the subjective and objective genitives involve possession. So too does the genitive in *Or* 66. 2 *7 biddende þæt hie . . . þæs gewinnes sumne ende gedyden* and in the impersonal *Jud* 272 *þa wæs hyra tires æt ende*. The idea is also present in what Muxin calls respectively the 'characteristic' genitive (his §12), e.g. *BlHom* 7. 29 *Seo readnes þære rosan . . . seo hwitnes þære lilian*; the 'possessive locative' genitive (his §19), e.g. *ÆCHom* ii. 214. 1 *to eallum leodum þæs æðelan eardes*; the 'possessive temporal' genitive

---

[2] Should *moton* be between *geleanian* and *eal* rather than here?

(his §19), e.g. *Lit* 9 *on pentecostenes mæsse æfen*; and the 'qualifica-tive relative-qualitative' genitive (his §32), e.g. *Or* 18. 18 *of hwæles hyde . . . 7 of seoles* and *Or* 18. 20 *fiftyne mearðes fell.* (This is defined as the genitive which qualifies by revealing both the quality of the object qualified and its essence or real nature. Cf. *Or* 18. 21 *twegen sciprapas . . . oþer sy of hwæles hyde geworht, oþer of sioles* with *Or* 18. 21 *berenne kyrtel oððe yterenne.*)

§1285. GL (p. 231) calls 'the attention of the student . . . to the variety of forms which possession may take. *Statua Myronis*, "Myron's statue", may mean: 1. A statue which Myron owns; 2. Which Myron has made; 3. Which represents Myron.' There is no doubt that posses-sion is involved in type (1) examples such as *ÆCHom* i. 134. 21 *to Godes huse* and *ÆHom* 21. 216 *Drihtnes scrin.* I can see a sense in which it is present in type (2), e.g. *ÆCHom* i. 14. 33 *ealle his weorc ðe he geworhte* and *Luke(WSCp)* 3. 4 *on Isaias bec þæs witegan.* But it seems somewhat more remote from type (3) examples like *Or* 54. 23 *He . . . geworhte anes fearres anlicnesse of are*, *ÆCHom* i. 288. 15 *On hwilcum dæle hæfð se man Godes anlicnysse on him*, *ÆHom* 26. 19 *ealle þa anlicnyssa þæra ærenra goda*, and *ÆCHom* i. 78. 1 *Matheus awrat, on þære forman Cristes bec. . . .* However, the argument is terminological; the relationships are real.

✕ §1286. It is even more difficult to discern the idea of possession in examples like *ChronA* 91. 26 (901) *syx nihtum ær ealra haligra mæssan* (cf. *Ch* 1188 . . . *ðæt æghwilc messepriost gesinge fore Oswulfes sawle twa messan*); *Lch* ii. 26. 6 *wiþ eagna miste* (cf. *Lch* ii. 308. 3 *gif mist sie fore eagum . . .*); *LS* 10. 109. 53 *þurh sarlicne utgang þæs manfullan lifes* (cf. *Bede* 346. 7 *bi utgonge . . . of Ægypta londe*); *ChristB* 673 *wiges sped* (cf. *Ex* 153 *on ðam spildsiðe spede* and *El* 1181 *æt wigge sped*); *Bede* 46. 7 *to gebeorghe ðæs sæs* (cf. *HomU* 26 *wið þa biteran þing gebeorh*); and *ÆCHom* i. 176. 24 *gescead ægðer ge godes ge yfeles* (cf. *WHom* 9. 44 *gescead betweox soðe 7 unsoðe*). Further examples of genitives with little or no possessive elements will be found in the sections which follow.

§1287. The 'absolute' or 'elliptical' genitive—exemplified by MnE 'He worships at St. Martin's' and 'I met her at my mother's'—is unknown in OE. Its use in later periods is discussed by Logeman (*Archiv*, 117 (1906), 283); Swæn (*Jespersen Gram. Misc.*, pp. 275-86); and van der Gaaf (*EStudies*, 14 (1932), 49-65).

(2) *Genitives which describe or define*

§1288. As already noted in §1269, many genitives can be replaced by adjectives and so can be said to describe or define. Among them are the possessive genitive (see §1269 and cf. *ÆCHom* i. 12. 16 *ne næfre se yfela ræd ne com of Godes geþance, ac com of þæs deofles* with *ÆCHom* i. 84. 34 *seo godcundlice wracu* and *ÆCHom* i. 62. 31 *ðas deoflican facn*); the possessive 'locative' and 'temporal' genitives (see §1284 and cf. *CP* 415. 15 *ðæs londes wif* with *GD(H)* 50. 14 *æt utlendisceum mannum* and the two qualifying elements in *ÆCHom* i. 80. 15 *ealle ða hysecild . . . fram twywintrum cilde to anre nihte*); the 'characteristic' genitive (see §1284 and cf. *ÆCHom* ii. 58. 13 *on wynsumum wines swæcce* with *ÆCHom* ii. 58. 31 *to winlicum swæcce* and the two elements in *ByrM* 14. 15 *swete hunig and wynsumes swæcces*); the 'qualificative relative-qualitative' genitive (see §1284 and compare the two elements in *Or* 18. 21 quoted there); and the genitive which says that *x* is about *y* (see §1285 and cf. *BlHom* 111. 16 . . . *þonne we gehyron Godes bec us beforan reccean 7 rædan, 7 godspell secggean* with *BlHom* 15. 28 *Hwæt we nu gehyrdon þis halige godspel beforan us rædan*). Since not all nouns and noun groups have a corresponding adjective, this transformation is not always possible, e.g. *Luke(WSCp)* 3. 4 *on Isaias bec* and (with partitive genitives already qualified by adjectives) *ÆCHom* ii. 334. 15 *ealra goda God* and *ÆCHom* ii. 584. 29 *ungerim deorwurðra wyrta and deorwurðra gymstana*. But unqualified partitive genitives can be replaced by adjectives or by nouns not in the genitive; cf. *ÆCHom* i. 34. 11 *wacost burga* with *ÆCHom* i. 476. 30 *se mærosta mann*, *ÆCHom* i. 18. 6 *nan ðing yfeles* with *ÆHom* 1. 184 *nan unrihtwisnyss ne yfel*, *ÆCHom* ii. 584. 11 *ungerim goldes* with *ÆCHom* ii. 494. 16 *mid ungerimum folce*, and *GenA* 1866 *brego Egipto* with *GenA* 2229 *ides Egyptisc*.

§1289. The terms 'descriptive' and 'defining' are, however, traditionally used of the genitive in a narrower sense. Thus Moore (pp. 40-3) divides his 'descriptive genitive—belonging to a particular class' into the genitive which expresses 'definition proper' (this is also known as 'appositive'[3]), the genitive of quality, and the genitive of value (or price).[4] These can be detected in OE.

§1290. The 'appositive' or, as Muxin (§5) calls it, the 'identifying' genitive is seen in *ÆCHom* i. 262. 25 *Godes nama*, *VSal* 2 13 *to*

---

[3] This is not a happy term. A genitive can define without being appositive, e.g. *ÆCHom* i. 410. 25 *ða tid hire geneosunge*; see below.

[4] He also includes the 'genitive of purpose'; see §1293.

Romes byrig, and *VSal 2 39 on Ierusalemes lande,*[5] where the genitives do not denote possession, but can be replaced by a noun in
apposition, e.g. *ÆCHom* i. 12. 31 *and God him sette naman Adam,
ÆCHom* i. 568. 5 *to þære byrig Hierusalem*, and *ÆLS* 11. 11 *on
þam lande Armenia*; by an adjective, e.g. *ÆCHom* i. 30. 6 *fram Galileiscum earde* and *ÆCHom* i. 34. 11 *Iudeisc land*; or by the first
element of a compound, e.g. *Or* 2. 15 *Romeburg* and *ChronE* 23. 2
(604) *Lundenwic*. Such 'appositive' genitives are clearly distinct from
examples like *ÆHom* 5. 196 *þone Kyning . . . heofenan and eorðan*,
where the genitives denote possession and also describe—cf.
ÆCHom ii. 22. 22 *Maria . . . is seo heofenlice cwen*—but cannot be
replaced by an appositional element. *ÆHom* 23. 12 *on Romana
byrig* and *ÆCHom* i. 32. 19 *Romana rice* are not strictly appositive,
since *Romana* is a genitive plural introducing a different notion and
denoting possession—which the genitive singular *Romes* would not
do. This, as Muxin (§5) points out, is the basic distinction.

§1291. Wülfing (i, §43) did not take this point. Some of his examples are possessive. Some, remarks Einenkel (p. 70), are nearer
related to the qualitative or partitive genitive while others are of
biblical origin. Muxin (§5) augments the two appositive examples
cited by Einenkel (pp. 70-1). But the idiom is not common in OE
and I have no reason to quarrel with Einenkel's pronouncement
(p. 71) that 'looking at it broadly, we receive the impression that the
genitive of apposition does not belong to the true Germanic stock of
phrases'.

§1292. It is no difficult task to follow Moore (pp. 41-2) and to say
that the genitive of material or contents is exemplified by *ÆCHom*
ii. 196. 5 *ormæte stream wæteres*,[6] *ÆCHom* ii. 292. 12 *hunies
beobread*, and *ÆCHom* ii. 436. 4 *eal purpuran reaf*; the genitive of
quality by *ÆCHom* ii. 10. 12 *nan wifhades mann* and (as frequently,
with an adjective qualifying the genitive) *ÆCHom* ii. 120. 18 *hwites
lichaman and fægeres andwlitan menn* (physical characteristic),
ÆCHom i. 38. 9 *to anes geleafan sibbe* (mental), and *ÆCHom* ii.
298. 17 *haliges lifes mann* (moral); and the genitive of value or price
by *John(WSCp)* 6. 7 *on twegera hundred penega wurþe hlafes* and
Matt(WSCp) 27. 7 *þæs hælendes wurð*.

---

[5] GL (p. 231) distinguishes this 'appositional' genitive from the 'epexegetical' in Latin
examples which are like *Bo* 102. 32 *ðæt ilce yfel filgde ðære gifernesse*. But in both types
the genitive serves the same function as an appositional element.

[6] Examples like this are very close to partitive. Where do *ÆCHom* i. 580. 26 *wæteres
drence* and *ÆCHom* ii. 158. 17 *wines drenc* belong?

§1293. The trouble with such semantic sub-divisions is that they are never-ending. Thus March (p. 154) enriches our repertoire with a genitive of age, e.g. *ÆCHom* i. 310. 28 *an lamb anes geares* and *ÆCHom* ii. 40. 10 *anes geares lamb*; of size, e.g. *LS* 10. 113. 1 *fenn unmætre mycelnysse*; and of weight, e.g. *Deut* 22. 29 *fiftig yntsena seolfres*. To these could be added genitives of colour and smell, e.g. *BlHom* 73. 21 . . . *spica, seo is brunes heowes 7 godes stences*; of space, e.g. *ÆCHom* i. 562. 26 *geond hundteontig mila neawiste*; of distance, e.g. *Luke(WSCp)* 24. 13 *on fæce syxtig furlanga*; of duration of time, e.g. *ÆCHom* i. 244. 20 *ðreora daga fæsten*; of point of time from which, e.g. *ÆCHom* i. 80. 22 *on ðam twelftan dæge Cristes acennednysse*; of purpose, e.g. *ÆGram* 5. 14 *for intingan greciscra namena* and perhaps *Matt(WSCp)* 21. 13 *min hus . . . ge worhtun þ to þeofa cote* (but see §1295); of result, e.g. *Ch* 1188*H* 1. 7 *fore aedleane ðæs aecan 7 ðaes towardon lifes* (so Carlton 1970, p. 90); of cause, e.g. *ÆCHom* i. 36. 3 *to edleane his geswinces* and *ÆCHom* ii. 590. 15 *wite þæs weorces*;[7] and of origin, e.g. *Bede* 222. 10 *se nyhsta wæs scyttisces cynnes*; and so on. Balašova (*UZLIJ*, vyp. 3 (1956), 41–2) adds a genitive of attribution of one person to another, a genitive expressing that the person belongs or pertains to another, e.g. *Beo* 1961 *Hemminges mæg,* ‖ *nefa Garmundes*.

§1294. After contemplating these possibilities, one is almost ready to embrace Muxin's twofold classification: the 'qualificative qualitative' genitive (his §28) (the genitive which qualifies and denotes a quality)—cf. *CP* 93. 23 *ða word wisdomes* with *Max i* 165 *wislicu word, ÆCHom* i. 210. 28 *rihtwisnysse weorc* with *ÆHom* 2. 261 *þeowtlice weorc,* and *ÆCHom* ii. 10. 12 *nan wifhades mann* with *ÆCHom* i. 198. 5 *butan wiflicre bysnunge*—and the 'qualificative quantitative-qualitative' genitive (his §30) (the genitive which qualifies and denotes a quality which involves a quantity)—e.g. *Lch* i. 72. 26 *þreora trymessa wæge* and *ÆLS* 3. 36 *æfter geares fyrste*. The terms may be complicated. The idea is simple.

§1295. The question may be asked: 'How do these two differ from Muxin's "characteristic" genitive (his §12, my §1284) and his "qualificative relative-qualitative" genitive (his §32, my §1284)?' The answer seems to me that, whereas the idea of possession is very strongly present in, and indeed essential to, the last two—the rose has redness, the whale has a skin—it is absent from, or only remotely

---

[7] Imelmann may be right in so explaining *Jud* 156–8. But it is hard to see the relevance of this to *Jud* 329 *mærra madma*. See the ASPR note on *Jud* 158. On the possibility that *Jud* 329 may be partitive, see §1302.

present in, the first two. Thus (to refer to some of the examples quoted in the previous sections), there is no real sense in which a year possesses a lamb, a hundred miles a neighbourhood, Greek names a sake, a deed punishment, a year a period, or even wisdom words. Those examples into which the idea of possession enters more strongly are those which could be otherwise classified, e.g. *ÆCHom* ii. 196. 5 *ormæte stream wæteres* and *Lch* i. 72. 26 *þreora trymessa wæge* (partitive?) and *Matt(WSCp)* 21. 13 *min hus . . . ge worhtun þ to þeofa cote* (possessive rather than final?). I do not wish to press the point too far. But we can, I think, make a valid distinction between a possessive genitive which is usually (if not always) adjectival —and therefore descriptive—and a descriptive or defining—but basically non-possessive—genitive. The latter's similarity in function to the adjective will be apparent from a consideration of *ÆCHom* i. 436. 11 . . . *haliges lifes men, and swiðe gecneordlæcende on boclicum smeagungum, ÆCHom* ii. 332. 28 . . . *Furseus, æðelboren for worulde, arwurðes lifes, and gelyfed swiðe*, and *ÆCHom* ii. 74. 29 *Se merigenlica tilia and þære ðriddan tide. . . .*

(3) The partitive genitive

§1296. Strictly speaking, the partitive genitive represents the whole from which a part is taken. Muxin (§16) is right to point out the difference between what he calls the 'partitive' genitive, e.g. *BlHom* 73. 17 *an pund deorwyrþre smyrenesse* and *ÆCHom* i. 92. 34 *sumne dæl þæs felles* (in which a *part* is taken) from the 'elective' genitive —sometimes known as the 'cognate' or 'emphatic' genitive—e.g. *ÆCHom* i. 44. 5 *ealra worulda woruld, ÆCHom* ii. 14. 16 *ealra halgena Halga*, and *ÆCHom* ii. 334. 15 *ealra goda God* (in which *one of a kind* is chosen). But we can reasonably use the term 'partitive' for both.

§1297. Examples like *ÆCHom* ii. 606. 26 *heora nan, ÆCHom* ii. 158. 1 *naht ðyllices, ÆCHom* i. 18. 6 *nan ðing yfeles, ÆHom* 4.276 *þæra gedwolmanna . . . ealle*, and *ÆHom* 17. 5 *geond eall þære foresædan scire*, are often described as partitive, which in a strict terminological sense they are obviously not. But it seems pedantic to put them in a separate class from clearly partitive but otherwise parallel examples like *ÆCHom* ii. 18. 15 *An þæra, ÆCHom* ii. 518. 4 *aht witniendlices, ÆCHom* i. 138. 22 *sum ðing godes, ÆCHom* i. 540. 6 *Sume ðæra haligra gasta*, and *ÆCHom* i. 244. 18 *ðæs folces micelne dæl*. On the overlap between the partitive and other genitives, see §1265.

§1298. Without wishing to multiply examples, we can say that the partitive genitive occurs with nouns denoting partition, e.g. *ÆCHom* i. 32. 26 *swa micel getel mancynnes* and *ÆCHom* i. 536. 26 *þæt getel Godes gecorenra*; mass, measure, quantity, and extent, e.g. *ÆCHom* i. 72. 26 *ðreo tida dæges*, *ÆCHom* i. 564. 18 *þreora mila dries færeldes*, *Matt(WSCp)* 10. 42 *anne drinc cealdes wæteres*, *Bo* 67. 31 *se suðeastende þisses middaneardes*, *Lch* iii. 76. 4 *ane cuppan gemeredes huniges 7 healfe cuppan clænes gemyltes spices*, and *Luke(WSCp)* 12. 42 *hwætes gemet*; with nouns meaning 'multitude', 'crowd', 'people', and the like, e.g. *ÆHom* 20. 142 *of ðæs folces meniu, ÆCHom* ii. 352. 10 *ungerime meniu hwittra manna*, and *BlHom* 79. 30 *þæt geleaffulle folc Iudea*; and with adjectives of quantity used absolutely as nouns, e.g. *ÆCHom* ii. 584. 11 *ungerim goldes* (cf. *ÆCHom* ii. 494. 16 *mid ungerimum folce*) and *WHom* 6. 69 *folces unlytel* (cf. *WHom* 20. 24 *wæter unlitel*).

§1299. It is also found with numerals, both cardinal and ordinal, e.g. *ÆCHom* i. 422. 23 *nigontyne wera and wifa his hiwisces* and *ÆCHom* ii. 520. 30 *se ðreotteoða ðyses heapes* (but see §§548 and 567 for examples of agreement between numeral and noun); with demonstratives, e.g. *Or* 88. 4 *7 þær wurdon mid hungre acwealde, þær heora þa ne gehulpe þa þær æt ham wæron*; with *fela*, e.g. *ÆCHom* i. 24. 18 *fela wundra* (cf. *ÆCHom* i. 426. 18 *fela gewinn*); with indefinites like *sum*, e.g. *ÆCHom* i. 580. 5 *eower sum* and *ÆCHom* i. 540. 6 *sume ðæra haligra gasta* (cf. *ÆCHom* i. 608. 23 *sume ðas tacna* and see §§409-16), and *hwæt*, e.g. *ÆCHom* ii. 430. 7 *hwæt lytles*;[8] and with interrogative pronouns, e.g. *Matt(WSCp)* 19. 16 *hwæt godes do ic . . . ?*, *Met* 28. 1 *Hwa is on eorðan nu unlærdra . . . ?*, *CP* 165. 1 *Hwæt is ðienga ðe bieterre sie . . . ?*, and *Matt(WSCp)* 6. 27 *Hwylc eower . . . ?*

§1300. In examples like *Or* 17. 1 *. . . þæt he ealra Norðmonna norþmest bude*, *Or* 112. 3 *. . . for þon hie cuþon on horsum ealra folca feohtan betst 7 ærest*, and

Met 26. 54   Hio gedwolan fylgde
          manna swiðost   manegra þioda,
          cyninges dohtor,

the partitive genitive may depend on the pronoun rather than on the superlative adverb. But it seems to depend on the adverb in *CP* 367. 23 *. . . ðonne sculon we hie ealra ðinga ærest 7 geornost læran ðæt hie ne wilnigen leasgielpes*, *Bede* 358. 1 *7 him swiðe þæt his freond*

---

[8] Heltveit (1977, *passim*) offers more examples with the indefinites. See also my indexes.

beweredon 7 ealra swiðust þære eadigan gemynde Cuðberht, and

GenB 334   Fynd ongeaton
    þæt hie hæfdon gewrixled   wita unrim
    þurh heora miclan mod   and þurh miht godes
    and þurh ofermetto   ealra swiðost.

§ 1301. The partitive genitive may also be dependent on a relative pronoun, e.g. (with *þæt* 'what') *Or* 32. 19 *7 swa þeah þæt þær to lafe wearð þara Thelescisa;* (with *þætte* 'which') *CP* 60. 15 *ac ðæt þætte oðre men unaliefedes doð he sceal wepan;* (with *þe* 'who') *Or* 100. 7 *þa deadan . . . þe heora folces ofslagen wæron;* (with *se ðe* 'whoever') *Bede* 146. 21 *. . . se ðe lifigende wære þæs hades* (see Wülfing, i, § 255); (with *swa hwæt swa* 'whatever') *CP* 203. 10 *. . . swa hwæt sua hie ongietan mægen ðæs godcundan wisdomes;* and (with *swa hwylc swa* 'whichever') *Bede* 416. 5 *. . . swa hwylcne hiora swa him se tan æteawde.* On examples involving combinations of *eall,* the relative *þæt,* and a partitive genitive, see § § 457 and 2227–8.

§ 1302. In a few examples in the poetry we find what seems to be a partitive genitive with no governing word expressed:

Beo 1366   No þæs frod leofað
    gumena bearna,   þæt þone grund wite

—but *frod gumena bearna* could be taken together as the subject—

El 324   . . . þæt hio þære cwene   oncweðan meahton
    swa tiles swa trages,   swa hio him to sohte,

and possibly

Jud 325   . . .   wagon ond læddon
    to ðære beorhtan byrig,   Bethuliam,
    helmas ond hupseax,   hare byrnan,
    guðsceorp gumena   golde gefrætewod,
    mærra madma   þonne mon ænig
    asecgan mæge   searoþoncelra.

§ 1303. The genitive of a noun used partitively follows the noun, pronoun, or numeral, which governs it much more frequently than the genitive of a pronoun; cf. § § 1308–15. But this is a tendency which is often overcome by demands of style; see the examples quoted above, especially those from Ælfric in § 1297. The two can, of course, be separated, e.g. *CP* 165. 1 *Hwæt is ðienga ðe bieterre sie . . . , ChronA* 48. 8 (755) *7 hiera se æþeling gehwelcum feoh and feorh gebead,* and *ÆHom* 4. 276 *Eac þæra gedwolmanna þe dwelodon embe Crist . . . ealle heo oferswiðde mid soðum geleafan.*

(4) *The position and agreement of the attributive genitive*

§1304. The position of the partitive and other genitives used with nouns, adjectives, numerals, verbs, and prepositions, has been discussed in the relevant place in this chapter or others; see the General Index. Here we are concerned only with the attributive genitive used with nouns or noun-equivalents.

§1305. We can perhaps best begin with two obvious remarks: first, that in OE the attributive genitive can (with the qualifications made below) precede or follow the governing noun, and second, that in MnE the genitive precedes whereas the 'of' phrase follows the noun. The development of the latter—in so far as a study of it is relevant —has been considered in §1203, where I conclude that the decision whether the *of* construction is the equivalent of a possessive genitive in OE must be a personal one. But it will be obvious that if the genitive in post-position was ultimately to disappear, it must gradually have become less common. The figures given by investigators naturally vary from selected corpus to selected corpus. Yerkes (pp. 233-41) offers a detailed comparison between the practices of Wærferth and the reviser in the placing of attributive genitive nouns or noun phrases. The following table (which gives approximate percentages in brackets) emerges from figures given by Timmer (1939, pp. 51-2):

Attributive genitives in	Pre-position		Post-position	
	Proper Names	Others	Proper Names	Others
GD(C), books i and ii	82 (10.6)	293 (38)	38 (5)	360 (46.4)
GD(H), books i and ii	100 (14.5)	321 (46.5)	36 (5)	233 (34)

Thomas (pp. 65-6) makes an arbitrary and dubious distinction between the texts in (*b*) and (*c*) below:[9]

My ref.	His date	Texts	Adnominal genitives in		Periphrastic genitives
			post-position	pre-position	
(*a*)	end 9th–beginning 10th centuries	*CP, Bo, Or, Bede*	47.5	52.0	0.5
(*b*)	Latter part 10th–beginning 11th centuries	*Mart, BlHom, BenR*	30.5	68.5	1
(*c*)	11th century	*GD(H), ÆCHom, Gospels*, etc.	22.2	76.6	1.2

[9] Fries quotes Thomas's figures in *Lang*. 16 (1940), 206, but dates group (*c*) 'c. 1100'!

The figures denote percentages. These differing figures allow us to reach the unsurprising conclusion that the change to complete pre-position of inflected genitives was under way in OE. However, the fact that in *GD(H)* over twenty-five per cent of proper names in the genitive and over forty per cent of genitives other than those of proper names are in post-position suggests what a quick glance at a few pages of Ælfric or Wulfstan will show to have been the situation —that the transition was not complete in OE. Mustanoja (p. 77) observes rather vaguely that 'the inflectional postpositive genitive disappears from the living language at the beginning of the ME period'. Thomas, refuting Curme's statement (*MP* 11 (1913–14), 157) that 'in 1200 A.D. the triumph of the English analytic form is almost complete', is more definite: 'During the thirteenth century, the postpositive genitive practically disappears' (p. 102) and 'the triumph of the periphrastic genitive is not "almost complete" until the latter half of the fourteenth century' (p. 118). Compare Fries (*Lang.* 16 (1940), 205): 'before the end of the 13th century, the post-positive inflected genitive has completely disappeared'.[10] Timmer's statement (1939, p. 72) 'that it seems safe to assume as the time of transition [for the genitive of proper names] the 11th century (probably first half)' is of course based on supposition.

§1306. Full collections would no doubt enable someone to produce comparative figures for all the extant OE texts. But there is little chance that these would do more than confirm that the move to pre-position had begun and no guarantee that they would reflect the situation in spoken OE. I do not intend to concern myself with the relative percentages of genitives in pre- and post-position in the different texts.[11] Behaghel's observation (*DS* iv, §1566) that there were three stages in the development of the position of the non-partitive genitive in Germanic—first, all genitives are in front of the governing noun; second, genitives of things and abstracts can be behind it; third, genitives referring to persons, including finally even proper names, can be behind it—raises the fascinating possibility that by the time it reached ME the attributive genitive had gone round in a circle. This cannot be explored here. None the less, we can agree with Kirch (*PMLA* 74 (1959), 508–9) when he rejects Jespersen's suggestion (*GS*, 4th edn. (1923), §80) that 'the usage of the genitive noun before the modified noun was brought into Old English

---

[10] Judgement on this point lies outside my brief.

[11] Timmer (1939, *passim*) gives figures for *GD, Bede, Bo, ApT*, and Wulfstan. But in my opinion his arguments are often muddled. Thomas (*passim*) offers a variety of figures and examples from a wide selection of OE (and ME) texts.

from Scandinavian'. Kirch was in fact tilting at a windmill, for later (in *GS*, 9th edn. (1938), §80), Jespersen put this forward merely as a possibility, with the comment that 'in these delicate matters it is not safe to assert too much, as in fact many similarities may have been independently developed in both languages'.

§1307. Timmer (like Behaghel) was concerned with making what might be called semantic distinctions between proper names, names of persons, things, and abstracts, and pronouns. But—apart from occasional comments (e.g. 1939, p. 56)—he neglected what is probably the more important question of the syntactic structure of the phrase, although Sweet (*NEG* ii, §§1796-7) had emphasized the importance of this in 1898. Both aspects demand attention.

§1308. The regular position of the dependent possessives, whether declined or not, is before the noun and its qualifying element(s), e.g. *ÆCHom* i. 90. 25 *þinum ofspringe* and *ÆCHom* i. 34. 6 *to his halgan gelaðunge*; see further §§294-5, where the exceptions in prose and poetry are discussed. Curme (*MP* 11 (1913-14), 167) suggests that this regularity might have helped to establish pre-position as the norm for nouns; ' "his book" might have influenced "John's book" '.

§1309. There is no simple rule for the genitives of nouns, for they occur—both alone and in combination—in pre- and post-position. There can be no doubt that intonation and stress were factors here. But Curme's attempt (*MP* 11 (1913-14), 168) to use them as criteria failed, as it was bound to do and as he himself admitted. The particular rock on which it split was *John(WSCp)* 8. 39 *gif ge Abrahames bearn synt wyrceað Abrahames weorc*, which he mistranslated 'If you were *Ábraham's* children, ye would do the *wórks* of Abraham', but which could equally carry different stress, 'If you are Abraham's *chíldren*, do Abraham's *wórks*'. None the less, we can describe the situation in syntactic and semantic terms.

§1310. When the phrase consists of two nouns only or two nouns and a preposition, the genitive is regularly in pre-position whether it is that of a proper noun, e.g. *ÆCHom* i. 30. 15 *Godes engel*, *ÆCHom* i. 78. 16 *Israhela folc*, and *ÆLS* 32. 31 *on Norðhymbra lande*; of a word applicable to humans, e.g. *ÆCHom* ii. 30. 7 *on mannes hiwe* and *ÆCHom* i. 84. 13 *martyra blostman*; or of the name of a thing or quality, e.g. *ÆCHom* i. 32. 8 *for middangeardes alysednysse*, *ÆCHom* i. 34. 8 *on lifes bec*, *ÆCHom* i. 40. 9 *wisdomes geswutelung*, *ÆCHom* ii. 16. 8 *sibbe Ealdor*, and *ÆCHom* i. 52. 10 *synna micelnysse*.

§1311. In such phrases in the prose, pre-position is firmly established as the rule when the genitive is that of a proper name. I have noted no examples of the type ☆*engel Godes*—note the reversal of the Latin order in *Mart* 2 100. 4 *forþon he is cweden on gewritum frater domini, drihtnes broðor*—or of the type ☆*eðel Scotta*—Sweet (*NEG* ii, §1796) points out that the order 'is absolutely fixed in semi-compounds such as *Engla-lond*'. But there are some in the poetry, e.g. *Beo* 524 *sunu Beanstanes, Brun* 7 *afaran Eadweardes*, and *Beo* 2327 *gifstol Geata*. Even with the names of persons, things, and qualities, post-position is so markedly less frequent than pre-position in these phrases in the prose of all periods that it is difficult to find examples like *ÆCHom* i. 4. 1 *fram frymðe middangeardes, ÆCHom* i. 78. 4 *fram eastdæle middangeardes*, and *ÆCHom* i. 288. 34 *on ðrynnysse hada*.

§1312. An unqualified governing noun can be preceded or followed by a genitive qualified by an adjective or adjectives, e.g. *ÆCHom* i. 52. 22 *swa miccles lareowes geleafan* and *ÆCHom* ii. 10. 31 *ealra Cristenra manna moder* but *ÆCHom* i. 2. 18 *þurh gebylde mycelre lare* and *ÆCHom* ii. 14. 23 *heafod ealra haligra manna*; by a possessive, e.g. *ÆCHom* i. 34. 7 *ures geleafan gafol* but *ÆCHom* i. 28. 25 *to trymminge eowres geleafan*; by a numeral, e.g. *ÆCHom* i. 28. 6 *geond feowertigra daga fyrst* but *ÆCHom* i. 288. 34 *on annysse anre godcundnysse*; by a demonstrative (+ an adjective), e.g. *ÆCHom* ii. 6. 1 *þæs Fæder wisdom* and *ÆCHom* ii. 48. 15 *þære Halgan Ðrynnysse toclypung* but *ÆCHom* i. 198. 13 *Sunu þæs Hextan* and *ÆCHom* ii. 48. 13 *on naman ðære Halgan Ðrynnysse*; and by other combinations of which space does not permit exemplification.

§1313. When the governing noun is qualified, an unqualified genitive may precede both the governing noun and its qualifiers, follow them, or come between them. This last idiom is discussed below (§§1316-24). But we find pre-position of the genitive in *ÆCHom* i. 24. 7 *of Noes eltstan suna* and *ÆCHom* ii. 468. 17 *þurh Godes micclan cyste*, where the adjective is weak after the genitive (see §113), and in the unusual pattern seen in *BlHom* 45. 24 *on Godes þone soþan þeowdom* and *BlHom* 241. 8 *of Godes þam halgum*, which may be compared with examples like *BlHom* 13. 10 *ure se trumesta staþol* and *ÆCHom* i. 364. 5 *ðurh his ðæs mæran Forryneles and Fulluhteres ðingunge* (see §§103-12).[12] Post-position of the

---

[12] *BlHom* 45. 24 and *BlHom* 241. 8 seem to me sufficient to justify J. E. Cross's refusal (private communication, 1971) to follow Herzfeld in inserting *þegn* in *Mart* 2 44. 21 *þis is se weg mid þy þe drihtnes* [*þegn*] *se leofa Benedictus astah on heofon*. But whether they

unqualified genitive is seen in *Bo* 139. 17 *sio fiorðe boc Boeties, Or* 124. 20 *þær wæs ungemetlic wæl geslagen Persa, ÆCHom* i. 270. 20 *seo halgung þæs mæran naman Godes, ÆCHom* ii. 602. 12 *seo soðe lufu Godes*, and *ÆCHom* i. 84. 14 *on middeweardan cyle ungeleaf-fulnysse.*

§1314. When both nouns are individually qualified, we find the same three possibilities—the genitive group may occur before, after, or in the middle of, the governing group. The last is discussed below (§§1316-24). Pre-position seems to be restricted to situations in which the governing noun is qualified only by an adjective, e.g. *ÆCHom* i. 308. 34 *on his Fæder swiðran hand, ÆCHom* ii. 478. 12 *to ðines Suna Hælendes Cristes clænan geþeodnysse, ÆCHom* ii. 162. 34 *þæs arleasan preostes niðfullan ehtnysse*, and (with *Godes* intervening in the genitive group) *BlHom* 217. 12 *manigra Godes þeowa gastlic fæder*. In these we can substitute a possessive for the genitive combination (cf. *ÆCHom* i. 34. 6 *to his halgan gelaðunge*). Any possessive or demonstrative in such a group agrees with the genitive noun even when it is preceded by a preposition governing the adjective + noun, e.g. *ÆCHom* ii. 478. 12 above and *ÆCHom* ii. 156. 8 *on ðæs munuces soðan lufe*; see §1317. Post-position offers a wider variety of combinations, e.g. *ÆCHom* i. 28. 4 *on þam þriddan dæge his þrowunge, ÆCHom* i. 10. 25 *on þam norðdæle heofenan rices, ÆCHom* ii. 8. 11 *æt þæm twelf mægðum Israhela ðeoda, ÆCHom* i. 32. 34 *soð yrfenuma þæs ecan Fæder, ÆCHom* i. 166. 17 *uppan ðam scylfe þæs heagan temples, ÆCHom* i. 100. 5 *se forma dæg ðyssere worulde*, and *ÆCHom* i. 36. 36 *micel menigu heofenlices werodes God herigendra and singendra.* . . .

§1315. The genitive groups in post-position involve nouns of all kinds—proper, concrete referring to persons and things, and abstract. So the choice between pre- and post-position probably depended on stylistic and rhetorical considerations rather than on the meaning of the noun in the genitive: consider the variations in *ÆCHom* ii. 14. 22 *and he is ealra halgena Halga, forþan þe he is heafod ealra haligra manna, ÆCHom* ii. 16. 7 *Fæder þære toweardan worulde and sibbe Ealdor*, and *ÆCHom* i. 122. 29 *swa eac he alysde us fram ure sawla*

are sufficient to support Kaske's proposal (ΠΑΡΑΔΟΣΙΣ. *Studies in Memory of Edwin A. Quain* (Fordham U.P., 1976), 47-59) to take *Iohannis . . . mid þy fullwihte* in

Hell 135   swylce git Iohannis   in Iordane
                  mid þy fullwihte   fægre onbryrdon
                  ealne þisne middangeard

as 'by the baptism of John' is less certain. The combination *git Iohannis* certainly looks like 'you and John' (nominative); see §257.

synnum ðurh anfenge ures flæsces; compare *ÆCHom* i. 306. 34 *on ða swiðran hand his Fæder* with *ÆCHom* i. 308. 34 *on his Fæder swiðran hand*; and note examples like *ÆCHom* i. 234. 4 *and þam he sceal aheardian þe nane behreowsunge nabbað heora misdæda* and *ÆCHom* ii. 526. 14 *and ðurh his fultum wæstm brohton godra weorca*, in which verbs intervene between the governing nouns and the genitive groups. As a general rule, however, it may be said that the more qualifiers there are, the more frequent is post-position.

§1316. We turn now to those examples in which one or more qualifying elements (hereafter termed 1) precede a genitive noun (2) and a governing noun (3), e.g. *Or* 28. 13 *an lytel sæs earm* and *ÆCHom* i. 34. 30 *se Ælmihtiga Godes sunu*. The question is: with which element *can* (as opposed to *does*) 1—the qualifying elements—agree? The answer is fivefold: 1 can agree (*a*) with 2 only; (*b*) with 3 only; (*c*) partly with 2 and partly with 3; (*d*) with 2 or 3 without any change of sense; or (*e*) with 2 or 3 with a change of sense. In practice, of course, examples of (*d*) and (*e*) conform to either (*a*) or (*b*) because the qualifying elements agree with either 2 or 3. But we need to distinguish those examples in which the agreement of the qualifiers cannot be changed—(*a*) and (*b*)—from those in which it can —(*d*) and (*e*).[13]

§1317. Type (*a*)—(1 + 2) + 3—is exemplified in *ÆCHom* ii. 10. 31 *ealra cristenra manna moder*. Examples such as these involve preposition of the genitive group; see §§1305-14. In the remaining four groups, a genitive noun—either alone or with its own qualifying elements—intervenes between the qualifying elements of the governing noun and that noun itself.

§1318. Type (*b*)—1 + (2 +) 3—involves a noun used alone in the genitive. Unambiguous examples are most common with the proper noun *God*, e.g. *ÆCHom* i. 36. 1 *Se Godes Sunu*, *ÆCHom* i. 402. 16 *ðone forman Godes cyðere Stephanum*, *ÆCHom* i. 134. 29 *sum Godes mann*, *ÆCHom* ii. 414. 10 *nan oðer Godes Sunu*, and *Bede*

---

[13] Thomas divides his 871 examples (some of them ME) into twenty-two groups (pp. 139-52 and Appendix II). Groups 20 and 21 involve apposition, which I discuss in §1325. The remaining twenty are all variations of my patterns (*b*), (*c*), (*d*), and (*e*). Basically my (*b*) embraces his 3, 10 (some examples), 14, 15, 16 (one example), 19; my (*c*) embraces his 12, 13, 16 (one example), 18, 22; my (*d*) embraces his 1, 2, 9, 11; and my (*e*) embraces his 4, 5, 6, 7, 8, 10 (some examples), 17. (Here and there a few examples belong to other groups.) Thomas (pp. 112 and 152-3) says in effect that his 5 (e.g. *Or* 16. 28 *þone ilcan sæs earm*) and his 7 (e.g. *BlHom* 13. 2 *se lifigenda Godes Sunu*) belong to my group (*d*). But I think a change of agreement would give a different sense in these and similar examples.

56. 12 *þæt weorc þæs Godes wordes*, if *þæs* goes with *wordes*; compare *ÆCHom* i. 276. 23 *se God* (§333) and see §1320.[14] But examples occur with other nouns, e.g. *BlHom* 7. 31 *se Cristes brydbur*, *ÆCHom* ii. 100. 31 *þas twa ælmessena cynn*, *ÆCHom* i. 580. 25 *to anum wæteres drence*, and *ÆCHom* ii. 10. 12 *nan wifhades mann*. These examples of type (*b*)—in which the qualifying elements could not be inflected to agree with the noun in the genitive—can be distinguished from typical examples of type (*d*) such as *ÆCHom* ii. 58. 13 *on wynsumum wines swæcce*, where ☆*on wynsumes wines swæcce* would involve no change of sense, and of pattern (*e*) such as *ÆCHom* i. 40. 2 *þinne godes wurðscipe* 'thy dignity of [being] a god', where ☆*þines godes wurðscipe* would mean something different. Further on this, see §§1320-4.

§1319. Type (*c*)—in which a genitive group intervenes so that the qualifying elements agree partly with 2 and then partly with 3—is seen in *Bo* 8. 25 [*se wisdom*] *adrigde þa mines modes eagan* (or is *þa* an adverb?), *BenR* 20. 5 *seo foresæde þæs lareowes hæs and þa fulfremedan þæs lærincmannes weorc*, *GD(H)* 23. 21 *sum mæres lifes munuc* and 96. 31 *seo forecwedene ðæs halgan weres fostormodor*, *ÆCHom* i. 384. 4 *eal ðæs wælhreowan caseres folc*, and *ÆCHom* i. 48. 15 *eall ðæra Iudeiscra teona*.

§1320. Type (*d*)—defined as that in which 1 can agree with either 2 or 3 with no real change in meaning—is seen in MnE 'the King's son' and, by virtue of the fact that *þære* can be genitive singular or dative singular, in OE examples like *LawAf* 75. 1 *for þære sinwe wunde* and *ÆCHom* i. 464. 3 *to ðære sawle awyrdnysse*. There are also examples like *ÆCHom* i. 136. 6 *ðæs Hælendes tocymes* and *ÆCHom* i. 132. 35 *for ðæs hundredes ealdres geleafan*, in which *ðæs* can go with either or all of the nouns in the genitive; cf. *Bede* 56. 12 (§1318). But most OE examples of type (*d*) must conform to either type (*a*) or type (*b*), since the genitives *þæs, þisses, þara*, and *þissa*, are unambiguous. That these two possibilities did in fact exist is attested by pairs of examples involving demonstratives (on these, see below); adjectives, e.g. *HomU* 1. 102. 24 *alles middæneardes rice* but *BlHom* 27. 15 *eal eorþan rice*; and other words, e.g. *HomU* 2. 118. 1 *on anes eagæn beorhtnes* but *Bede* 136. 3 *an eagan bryhtm* and *Luke (WSCp)* 7. 2 *sumes hundred mannes þeowa* but *Luke(WSH)* 7. 2 *sum*

---

[14] Thomas (p. 52) says that he found 199 examples—at Appendix II, p. 5, the figure is 209—of the type *Ps(P)* 45. 4 *seo Godes burh* and six of the type *Ps(P)* 47. 7 *on þæs Godes byrig*. Unfortunately, he does not distinguish the remaining five at pp. 144-5 or in Appendix II. They are clearly exceptional. But *Bede* 56. 12 may be an example.

hundred mannes þeowa. Note also *ÆCHom* i. 498. 27 *nan synna for-gifenys* and compare *Exod(B)* 11. 5 *ealre ðære nytena frumcennedan*—type (*a*)—with *Exod(L)* 11. 5 *ealle þara nytena frumcennedan*—type (*c*).

§1321. When a type (*d*) phrase consists of a demonstrative and two nouns, the demonstrative usually agrees with the nearest noun, that in the genitive. Occasionally, perhaps on the analogy of examples like *ÆCHom* i. 30. 17 *se Godes engel* (see §1318), the demonstrative agrees with the governing noun. Thus, we find *GD(C)* 56. 28 *þisses ylcan Bonefacies cyrican* but *GD(H)* 56. 27 *on þissum* [Hecht emends to *þisses*] *ilcan Bonefacies cyrcean, ÆCHom* i. 32. 28 *þæs caseres gebann* but *ÆCHom* ii. 376. 25 *se hiredes ealdor, ÆLS* 29. 206 *þæs drihtnes þægen* but *ÆLS* 29. 249 *þone drihtnes ðægen,* and *ÆCHom* i. 426. 20 *ðæra deofla frofor* but *ÆLS* 31. 1206 *þurh þære deofla grimetunge.*[15] When we compare *Mart* 2 74. 12 *ymb þa drihtnes fotlastas* with *Mart* 2 76. 12 *þæs hælendes fotlastas* and *ÆCHom* ii. 286. 24 *to ðam hiredes hlaforde* with *ÆCHom* i. 462. 29 *þæs mædenes Sunu,* it is tempting to blame the preposition for the un-usual agreement. But we have examples like *ÆCHom* ii. 376. 25 *se hiredes ealdor* with no preposition and examples like *ÆCHom* i. 458. 21 *be ðæs apostoles hæse, ÆCHom* i. 458. 26 *into ðæs cyninges bure,* and *ÆCHom* i. 460. 9 *ðurh ðæs Hælendes tocyme,* where, despite the preposition, the demonstrative is in the genitive. Some idea of the comparative frequency of the two types can be gained from Thomas's figures, though they are not always complete and not always in agreement. In Appendix II he cites only seven examples like *se hundredes ealdor* in the whole of *ÆCHom* i—126. 8, 21; 128. 19; 132. 31; 248. 21, 31; 374. 15—and four in *ÆCHom* ii—258. 7; 286. 21, 25, 29. In all of them except *ÆCHom* i. 374. 15 *þone deofles ðen,* the intervening noun is either *hundredes* or *hir(e)des.* Opening *ÆCHom* i at random, I found six examples like *þæs mædenes Sunu* in just over two pages—458. 21, 26; 460. 9; 462. 24, 28, 29. In his whole corpus, he found only 107 examples like *se hiredes ealdor* (eighty-three of his type 1 and twenty-four of his type 2).

§1322. Ælfric uses the more common idiom at *ÆLS* 32. 190 *æt þæs halgan byrgene* 'at the saint's tomb' (cf. *ÆLS* 32. 233 *to þam halgan*). *ÆLS* 32. 165 *to þam halgan bodige* and *ÆLS* 32. 175 *þone halgan lichaman* are usually translated 'to the holy body' and 'the

---

[15] Sisam's suggestion (p. 185 fn. 2) that *þære* in this example may be genitive plural arises from the rarity of *þurh* + dative in Ælfric, not from problems of agreement.

holy body'. The odds are that this is right, but—in view of variations like those seen in *ÆCHom(Gg. 3. 28)* i. 88. 4 *fram ðam blodes gyte*, where MSS *D, E, T, Vit*, all have *þæs*—the possibility exists that they are examples of the less common pattern and should be translated 'to the body of the saint' and 'the body of the saint'. The difference is, of course, exquisite. But the tendency for the demonstrative to agree with the noun in the genitive is so strong that it sometimes prevails in contexts where it would seem that the demonstrative must go with the governing noun, e.g. *ÆGram* 2. 16 *seo cæg, ðe ðæra boca andgit unlicð*, where the sense is 'the meaning of books' rather than '[the] meaning of those books', *ÆCHom* ii. 602. 15 *þæs synfullan deað* 'the death of a sinner', and *ÆCHom* ii. 232. 27 *þæs manfullan mannes deað* 'the death of a wicked man'.

§1323. Group (*e*)—those in which 1 can agree with 2 or 3 but in which a change of agreement involves a change of sense—can be illustrated by MnE 'The bold general's son' which in rapid speech might actually mean 'The general's bold son'. In OE too examples of this type often involve a demonstrative + an adjective; cf. *ÆCHom* i. 386. 35 *ðæs Ælmihtigan Godes Sunu* (as it stands, type (*a*)) with *ÆCHom* i. 34. 30 *se Ælmihtiga Godes Sunu* (as it stands, type (*b*))[16] and consider the effect of a change of agreement in *CP* 245. 4 *se egeslica Godes dæg*, *CP* 431. 29 *on ðære ilcan Salomonnes bec*, *Or* 16. 28 *þone ilcan sæs earm*, *ÆCHom* i. 402. 16 *ðone forman Godes cyðere*, *ÆCHom* i. 380. 19 *ðisne deofles ðen*, and *ChronE* 225. 8 (1089) *se arwurða muneca feder 7 frouer*. But examples also occur without demonstratives but with strong forms of adjectives and other words declined strong, e.g. *Beo* 2774 *eald enta geweorc*, *Mart* 2 70. 15 *micel cnihta weorod*, *BlHom* 207. 32 *manigfealdlice ciricean þegnas*, *Bede* 122. 23 *oðerne cyninges þegn*, *Or* 28. 13 *an lytel sæs earm*, and *BlHom* 145. 27 *oþre Cristes þegnas* (cf. *Matt(WSCp)* 24. 24 *þonne cumað lease Cristas*).

×§1324. Of course, no ambiguity arises in any of these examples because the inflexions enable us to decide whether they belong to type (*a*) or to type (*b*). But there are examples in which this is not so. Thus *ÆCHom* i. 84. 12 *mid ðære reðan ehtnysse hatunge* could be type (*a*), 'with the hatred of fierce persecution', or type (*b*), 'with the fierce hatred of persecution', and in *ÆCHom* i. 10. 14 *nigon engla werod* the context decides in favour of 'nine troops of angels' and against 'a troop of nine angels'. The fact that such ambiguities have to be resolved by the use of the 'of' periphrasis points to the

---

[16] Despite Thomas (pp. 54, 140, and elsewhere), there is a difference—if only of emphasis.

main reasons for distinguishing types (*d*) and (*e*) in OE: first, as the loss of distinction in the inflexion of the demonstratives and the strong form of the adjective increased, the number of ambiguous examples became greater, and second (as Thomas (pp. 111 ff.) suggests), the possibility exists that examples of type (*d*)—in which change of inflexion could produce no change in meaning—may have contributed to this loss of inflexions. For, as Thomas observes (p. 177), 'a significant advance in the use of the adnominal periphrastic genitive did not take place until loss of inflection in the definite article and strong adjective had set in'. This topic cannot be pursued here. But see Thomas, *passim* (especially pp. 49 ff., 111 ff., 177, and 180-2). Further examples of attributive and other genitives will be found in Wülfing (i, §§47-9); Timmer 1939, *passim*; Sprockel, pp. 129-34; and (for the poetry) Shipley, *passim*; Nader (1882), *passim*; and Nadler (*passim*). See also the various theses on individual texts. There is a lot of valuable material in Thomas's thesis. Zatočil 'Zur Stellung des adnominalen Genitivs im Althochdeutschen und Altenglischen', *Sborník Prací Filosofické Fakulty Brněnské University*, 11 (1962), 119-31, is concerned only with translations of Scripture and is more interested in OHG than in OE.

§1325. Two nouns in apposition in the genitive can be placed together before the governing word, e.g. *ChronA* 82. 10 (890) *Ælfredes cyninges godsunu*; after it, e.g. *ChronA* 124. 3 (984) *seo halgung þæs æfterfilgendan bisceopes Ælfheages* and *LS* 10. 104. 1 *on þam dagum Æþelredes, þæs mæran kyninges Myrcna*; or split around it, e.g. *ÆCHom* i. 78. 3 *on Herodes dagum cyninges*, *ÆCHom* i. 194. 21 *of Dauides cynne, þæs maran cyninges*, *ÆCHom* ii. 146. 10 *ðæs cyninges sweoster Ecgfrides*, and *ÆCHom* i. 330. 25 *to ðæs heahfæderes wununge Abrahames*.

§1326. Ekwall (pp. 6-7) cites several examples like MS Bodleian 579, f. 1ᵛ *a Leofsuna gewittnisse a Wunforda* 'on Leofsunu's testimony in Wunford' and *ChK* 936 *on ealles ðæs hiredes gewitnesse on Baðon* 'on all the community's testimony at Bath'. These certainly invite comparison with *ChronE* 256. 29 (1127) *þes Caseres wif of Sexlande*, *ChronE* 267. 29 (1140) *þe kinges suster of France*, and the like. But they have *a* and *on*, not *of*, and so are not on all fours, since the prepositional phrase may depend on the governing noun and not on the genitive. The same is true of *ChronD* 154. 7 (1017) *Bryhtric Ælfeges sunu on Defenascire*, cited by Klaeber (*Kock Studies*, p. 109).

§1327. Three important factors in signalling the respective relationships of the various genitives or genitive groups when two or more
are used together are first, inflexion; second, the fact that a genitive
noun displaces the article in pairs like *seo cirice/Godes cirice* and 'the
book'/'John's book'; and third, the fact that proper nouns do not
normally serve as the governing noun of a genitive (group), since collocations such as *ÆCHom* ii. 16. 8 *sibbe Ealdor*, 'my sister's John',
and 'our people's God', are unusual. I can illustrate these points,
which are made by Abruzzo in *PL* 1 (1969), 399–406, by analysing
two examples which he quotes. In *Bede* 106. 20 *Onhyrede he on þon
þa bysene þæs ærestan heordes Godes cirican Sce Petres þæs apostoles*,
the third point is illustrated by the fact that *Godes*—alone of the
three genitives—is in pre-position to its governing noun, while the
presence of *þæs* between *Sce Petres* and *apostoles* signals that they
are in apposition; this illustrates the second point. But in *Bede* 206.
25 *7 þurh upstige on heofonas þæs midligendes Godes 7 monna,
monnes Hælendes Cristes*, the inflexions play a crucial part in signalling that *Godes* is in post-position to *þæs midligendes* and that
monnes is in apposition with—not in pre-position to—*Hælendes
Cristes*. The inflexional ending *-es* certifies that *midligendes*, which
on the negative evidence of BT(S) appears only here, is a noun and
therefore goes not with *Godes*—that would require ☆*þæs midligendan
Godes*—but with *7 monna*. The fact that the pl. *monna* is followed
immediately by the sg. *monnes* shows that *monnes* goes with *Hælendes
Cristes* and that the last phrase does not mean '[of] man's Saviour
Christ'; that would require the gen. pl. *monna* in this sentence.

§1328. Like other groups (§§1464–72), genitive groups involving
two nouns and/or adjectives joined by *and* or *ge* are found grouped
in pre-position, e.g. *ÆCHom* i. 356. 11 *and Godes and mædenes
Bearn* and *ÆCHom* i. 440. 6 *on Iohannes and on ealra þæra apostola
gymene*; grouped in post-position, e.g. *ÆCHom* i. 196. 19 *gymene
ægðer ge ðære meder ge þæs cildes* and *ÆCHom* i. 48. 31 *se soða
dema lybbendra and deadra*; or split, e.g. *ÆCHom* i. 496. 3 *Lazarus,
Marthan broðer and Marian, ÆCHom* i. 346. 14 *Godes lufe and
manna*, and *ÆCHom* ii. 592. 35 *ongean Cristes gesetnysse and ealra
his halgena*. A possessive and a noun genitive can also be split, e.g.
ÆCHom i. 38. 25 *ðin efenðeowa and ðinra gebroðra* and *ÆCHom*
ii. 396. 23 *heora sawla hælðe and heora freonda*.

§1329. This non-repetition of the governing noun with a second
genitive after *ond* or *ge* seen in *ÆCHom* i. 496. 3 (§1328)—'Lazarus,
Martha's brother and Mary's [brother]'—and the like is found not

only with *ond* and *ge*, but also with *ond na*, e.g. *ÆCHom* i. 172. 10 *Godes æhta and na deofles*; with *ac*, e.g. *ÆCHom* i. 12. 16 *ne næfre se yfela ræd ne com of Godes geþance, ac com of þæs deofles*; with *ne*, e.g. *ÆCHom* i. 474. 4 . . . *þæt he nære for his agenum synnum, ne for his maga, blind geboren*; with *oþþe*, e.g. *ÆCHom* i. 82. 21 *his eorðlice rice, oþþe æniges oðres cyninges*; in comparative clauses, e.g. *ÆCHom* i. 132. 34 and *ÆCHom* ii. 430. 9 (space forbids quotation); and in adjective clauses, e.g. *ÆCHom* i. 30. 7 *to Iudeiscre byrig, seo wæs Dauides*. Other interesting examples include *ÆCHom* i. 324. 25 *Se man ðe næfð Godes Gast on him nis he Godes* and *ÆCHom* i. 126. 34 *Manega oðre men bædon Drihten, sume for heora agenre hæle, sume for heora bearna, sume for leofra freonda*. But the noun is often repeated when the second genitive requires a plural form of it, e.g. *ÆCHom* ii. 478. 6 *ofer hire heafod and ofer ealra ðæra mædena heafdu* and *ÆCHom* i. 292. 18 *æt nanes Iudeisces mannes byrgene ne æt nanes oðres gedwolan, ac æt rihtgelyfedra manna byrgenum*. This is perhaps unexpected in view of the frequent appearance of the idiom *on hiera bedde* 'in their beds'; see §§87-91.

§1330. When two nouns govern the same genitive, the second is often accompanied by the third person possessive, e.g. *ÆCHom* ii. 14. 19 *Adames forgægednys and his synn*, *ÆCHom* i. 544. 15 *Cristes lichaman and his blodes*, and *ÆCHom* i. 166. 24 *ealles middangeardes welan and his wuldor*. But it need not be, e.g. *GD(C)* 30. 21 *Equities cytan 7 mynster*, *GD(H)* 21. 24 *Libertines mycelan eadmodnysse 7 geþwærnysse*, *ÆHom* 27. 7 *ure misdæda 7 synna*, and *ÆCHom* i. 2. 15 *his gebyrd and goodnys*.

c. With adjectives

(1) Genitives which describe or define

§1331. Adjectives which *prefer* the genitive include those meaning 'happy', 'grateful', 'generous', 'innocent', 'worthy', 'agreeable', 'mindful of', 'full', 'bold', 'ignorant', 'believing', 'desirous', 'ready', and their opposites. Adjectives of measure and extent like *brad* and *eald* are also found with the genitive. For lists and the necessary qualifications, see §§197-210 and 218-19.

(2) The partitive genitive

§1332. When used independently, *nan, eall*, and indefinites like *sum, ælc*, and *ænig*, are found with the partitive genitive (§§1296-7); see the indexes. So too are adjectives of quantity used independently in the positive degree, e.g. *Bede* 174. 14 *monige þara broðra* and *Bede(O)* 208. 25 *7 hiora heriges þær wæs micel ofslagen* (see further §432); in the comparative degree, e.g. *Bede* 236. 18 . . . *þæt þær micle ma moncynnes adronc on þæm wætre, þonne mid sweorde ofslegen wære, Bo* 101. 7 *swa mid læs worda swa mid ma*, and *Or* 82. 8 . . . *þæt he þæs gewinnes mehte mare gefremman*; and in the superlative, e.g. *Bo* 54. 8 *mæst bearna, Or* 128. 18 *ealra læst*, and *Or* 74. 22 *Seo ilce burg Babylonia, seo ðe mæst wæs 7 ærest ealra burga, seo is nu læst and westast.*

§1333. A superlative form of an 'adjective proper' may govern a partitive genitive when used alone, e.g. *Or* 114. 10 *on Olinthum þa burg, seo wæs fæstast 7 welegast Mæcedonia rices* and *Or* 242. 19 *for þon he wæs eallra monna mildheortast*; with a demonstrative, e.g. *Or(C)* 224. 24 *Scipia, se besta 7 se selesta Romana witena 7 þegena* and *Bo* 41. 16 *se ealra forcuþesta*; and in the combination demonstrative + adjective + noun, e.g. *CP* 199. 23 *on ðæm ealra læstan ðingum* and *Bo* 54. 9 *ðæt deorwyrðeste ðing ealra þissa weoruldgesælða.* Two or more superlatives may accompany the same partitive genitive, e.g. *Or* 72. 9 *for þon hit ealra Romana ænlicost wæs 7 cræftegast* and *Or* 74. 23 . . . *ealra weorca fæstast 7 wunderlecast 7 mærast.* But a partitive genitive is not essential with a superlative, e.g. *Or* 18. 6 *þa mæstan, Or* 18. 5 *se betsta hwælhuntað*, and *Or* 18. 13 *mid þæm fyrstum mannum on þæm lande.*

§1334. As the examples cited above show, the partitive genitive is found in the prose immediately before the adjective, immediately after it, and separated from it. The same variations occur in the poetry, e.g. *Beo* 3181 *manna mildust, GenB* 578 *idesa seo betste, Beo* 2382 *þone selestan sæcyninga*, and *El* 1201 *seleste* || *mid Iudeum gumena.*

§1335. The partitive genitive is, however, rarely if ever found with positive or comparative forms of 'adjectives proper'. Shipley's remark (p. 106) is equally applicable to the positive: 'The partitive genitive after comparatives is extremely rare in Anglo-Saxon, though its rarity is probably due more to the infrequency of the thought than to any grammatical obstacle to its expression.' Most apparent examples can be otherwise explained. Thus, in *Bede* 306. 10 *þara se ærra* . . . 'the former of these', *ærra* can be viewed as a numeral and in *Beo* 525 *Ðonne wene ic to þe wyrsan geþingea, wyrsan* is best explained as a genitive plural.

(3) *The genitive expressing comparison?*

§1336. Some earlier writers spoke of the possibility of an OE genitive of comparison. It rests on slender foundations. Wülfing (i, §245) disposed of the example proposed by Nader (1882, p. 5). Shipley (p. 106) rightly remarked that there are no examples in the poetry; those like *El* 1109 *Ða cwom semninga sunnan beorhtra* ‖ *lacende lig* which Rössger (pp. 357-8) proposed involve the regular dative of comparison.

§1337. Only the example cited by Wülfing himself (i, §10a) prevents us from dismissing the idea out of hand. This is *Bo* 71. 21 *Gif þu þe wilt don manegra beteran 7 weorðran, þonne scealt þu þe lætan anes wyrsan.* However, Small (1929, pp. 84 ff.) compares *manegra beteran 7 weorðran* and *anes wyrsan* and the similar phrases in *Sol* 268. 17 *Gif ðu ðe wyle don moniges betran, ðonne do ðu ðe anes wyrsan* with *CP* 4. 13 *Ure ieldran* ‘ “Our elders”, not “Older ones than we” ’, *Vain* 35 *He . . .* ‖ *. . . feoþ his betran* ‘ “He hates his superiors” ’, and *Mald* 276 *þa his betera leg* ‘ “Since his lord lay dead” ’. I share his view that the genitives before the comparatives denote possession, though some comparison is inevitably involved, and accept both his translation of *Bo* 71. 21—‘If you wish to make yourself the better and superior of many, then you must let yourself become the inferior (underling) of one person’—and his conclusion (p. 88) that ‘the *genitive* came into use with comparatives whenever the comparatives left the function of an adjective and assumed that of a noun. This in itself eliminates once and for all the possibility as well as the necessity of interpreting such a genitive as the case of comparison.’

d. With verbs

(1) *General remarks*

§1338. Verbs which take the genitive can be divided into those which take the genitive only, e.g. *friclan* ‘to desire’; those which take the genitive or another case, e.g. *onfon* ‘to receive’, which is found with accusative, genitive, or dative; and verbs of double rection like *lettan* ‘to hinder someone (accusative) from something (genitive)’ and *þancian* ‘to thank someone (dative) for something (genitive)’. An attempt has been made in §§1081-8 to group these verbs according to meaning. But the results are tendencies, not rules; see §1089 and the alphabetical List of verbal rections in §1092.

§1339. The genitives found with verbs have been variously classified. Little emerges except fuel for terminological or other arguments. Erickson (*Arch. L.* 6 (1975), 77) asserts that OE verbs 'may be said . . . to govern surface genitives only when the genitive remains after the deletion of the accusative or dative noun upon which it depends and when it itself has not been raised so as to receive normal object inflection'. The genitive in *ÆCHom* i. 618. 33 *Uton forði brucan þæs fyrstes ðe us God forgeaf* can be called 'objective' and 'partitive'. That in *ÆCHom* i. 88. 1 *heora siblingas . . . þa ðe wyllað mines forðsiðes fagnian* has been variously described as 'objective', 'causal', and 'descriptive' (QW, p. 63).[17] Ardern (p. xxviii) classifies genitives after verbs of ceasing, lacking, and depriving, as 'ablatival'. Genitives like *wuldras* in *And* 523 [*God*] *wuldras fylde* || *beorhtne boldwelan* are usually described as instrumental—cf. *Phoen* 626 *Heofonas sindon* || *fægre gefylled . . .* || *. . . þines wuldres, PPs* 64. 5 *Ealle we ðin hus ecum godum* || *fægere fyllað*, and *PPs* 64. 12 *þonne beoð þine feldas fylde mid wæstmum*—but there is an element of the subjective in it; cf.

Christ C 972   Swa se gifra gæst   grundas geondseceð;
hiþende leg   heahgetimbro
fylleð on foldwong   fyres egsan,
widmære blæst   woruld mid ealle,
hat, heorogifre

and MnE 'Lord, Thy glory fills the temple'. With the verbs *beon*, *wesan*, and *weorþan*, there are even more possibilities: 'possessive' or 'subjective', e.g. *CP* 211. 3 . . . *sume cuædon ðæt hie wæron Apollan, sume cuædon ðæt hie wæron Saules, sume Petres, sum cuæð ðæt he wære Cristes*; 'origin', e.g. *Bede* 224. 4 . . . *wæs Englisces cynnes* and *Or* 190. 16 . . . *buton he æþeles cynnes wære*; descriptive, e.g. *Bede* 100. 26 . . . *þæt ic eom milde 7 eaðmodre heortan*, Latin . . . *quia mitis sum et humilis corde*, and *ÆCHom* i. 230. 26 *His lichama wæs grapigendlic, and ðeah hwæðere unbrosnigendlic; he æteowde hine grapigendlicne and unbrosnigendlicne, forðan ðe his lichama wæs þæs ylcan gecyndes ðe he ær wæs, ac wæs hwæðere þeah oðres wuldres*; and partitive, e.g. *Or* 80. 6 *7 þara scipa wæron III M þe hiora mete bæran* and *Ps(P)* 17. 39 *Hy clypodon, and næs þara þe hig gehælde*. Only this last need be pursued.

(2) *The partitive genitive*

§1340. It is clear that some variations between the accusative and the genitive with the same verb are due to the fact that the accusative

---

[17] Without entering into the specific problem with which he is concerned, I note that Stanley omits the genitive from his list of constructions with verbs of rejoicing in *NM* 72 (1971), 405.

is expressing the whole, the genitive a part; as Grimm put it (*Deutsche Grammatik*, iv. 646), 'der Acc. drückt reine, sichere Wirkungen aus, der Gen. gehemmte, modificierte'. Muxin (pp. 159 ff.) remarks that the number of OE verbs capable of so distinguishing a partitive genitive object from a non-partitive accusative object is small, but that they are widely used. Some of his examples are convincing; cf. *Gen* 42. 36 *næbbe ic Iosep* with *Or* 80. 8 . . . *hwær hie landes hæfden þæt hie mehten an gewician, Bede* 28. 21 . . . *þæt hi ðonne ma of þam wifcynne him cyning curan þonne of þam wæpnedcynne* with *Or* 44. 21 . . . *oððe hie him woldon oðerra wera ceosan*, and *ÆCHom* i. 366. 15 *forðan ðe se soða God* . . . *hæfð geunnen ðone wurðmynt his gecorenum* with *Mald* 176 . . . *þæt þu minum gaste godes geunne.* . . . Others are less so. I can detect no difference between *Beo* 1490 *ic me mid Hruntinge* ‖ *dom gewyrce* and *Beo* 1387 *wyrce se þe mote* ‖ *domes ær deaþe*; it would be naive to argue that Beowulf is suggesting that lesser mortals must be content with partial *dom*. What is cited as *þis leoht* . . . *habbaþ* becomes less convincing as a reference to the whole when we read the full text *BlHom* 21. 13 *þis leoht we habbaþ wið nytenu gemæne* 'we share this light with the beasts of the field'. The apparent contrast between *wearp* . . . *ænne stan* and *wæteres weorpan* disappears when we have the sentences in front of us (they read *ÆCHom* ii. 156. 8 *se niðfulla deofol* . . . *wearp ða ænne stan to ðære bellan* and *Beo* 2790 *he hine eft ongon* ‖ *wæteres weorpan*), for *wæteres* is an 'instrumental' genitive and does not imply that Wiglaf resisted a temptation to drown Beowulf. However, these are differences of classification, not of principle. For, as Muxin goes on to point out (pp. 163 ff.), the distinction was not always made even with those verbs where it was possible; consider, for example,

Ch 1492   þis is Alfwoldes bisceopes cwyde þ is ðæt he geann þæs landes æt Sandforda in to þam mynstre . . . 7 he geann his hlaforde feower horsa . . . 7 feower scyldas 7 IIII spera 7 twegen helmas 7 twa byrnan . . . 7 Alfwolde munuce XX mancsa goldes 7 anes horses 7 anes geteldes . . . 7 Wulfgare his mæge twegra wahryfta 7 twegra setlhrægla 7 þreo byrnan 7 Godrice his aðume twegra byrnena . . . 7 Kenwolde helm 7 byrnan 7 Boian anes horses. . . .

§1341. That the distinction would have disappeared even if the inflexional system had not been reduced is more than likely. It is so obvious that the Picts were not going to be content with *part* of a king (*Bede* 28. 21 in §1340) and that even the wives of soldiers who have been on active service for fifteen years do not need *all* other men to achieve satisfaction (*Or* 44. 21 in §1340), that it was supererogatory to point it out by grammatical means. But its loss was of course assisted by such symptoms of the general decay of the case system as the use of the dative by the side of a non-partitive accusative seen in *BlHom* 29. 6 *ac he wolde urum hiwe onfon* against *BlHom* 29. 2 . . . *se Ælmihtiga* : . . *onfeng þæt hiw ure tyddran gecynde* (Muxin, p. 164) and by the frequent use with verbs of the genitive and the accusative without any syntactic or semantic differentiation (Muxin, pp. 171 ff.). This is seen both with pairs of verbs with similar meanings—thus *neos(i)an* 'to seek' prefers the genitive, e.g. *And* 483 *Wolde ic anes to ðe,* ǁ *cynerof hæleð, cræftes neosan . . .* , whereas *secan* 'to seek' has the accusative, e.g. *And* 225 *Gewat him þa se halga . . .* ǁ *. . . eðel secan,* but not (as far as I have observed) the genitive—and with the same verb, e.g. *biddan*—compare *ÆCHom* ii. 572. 8 *ac we sceolon nu cnucian, and infær biddan to heofenan rice* with the last clause in *BlHom* 227. 11 *þa bædon hine his discipulos þæt hie mostan huru sume uncyme streownesse him under gedon for his untrumnesse; þa cwæð he, Bearn, ne bidde ge þæs,* where no partition is involved—and (though Muxin (p. 171) does not acknowledge this) even *neos(i)an*—compare *GuthB* 1000 . . . *an ombehtþegn, se hine æghwylce* ǁ *daga neosade* with *Beo* 115 *Gewat ða neosian, sypðan niht becom,* ǁ *hean huses.*

§1342. So, as we might expect, the distinction ultimately disappeared. Whether it was always intended where it can be detected is doubtful; cf. *ÆHom* 1. 206 *7 God us þeah geuðe for his godnesse þære sunnan leoht* with *ÆHom* 1. 202 *7 eac he geuþe þære ylcan wununge Adames ofspringe*; *ÆCHom* i. 366. 15 *forðan ðe se soða God . . . hæfð geunnen ðone wurðmynt his gecorenum* with *ÆHom* 4. 295 *Uton herian urne Drihten, and þæt halige Godes word eac swilce lufian and mid geleafan gehealdan. Ðæs us geunne se ælmihtiga Wealdend . . .* ; and *ÆCHom* i. 72. 9 *. . . se yldesta hæðengylda . . . cwæð þæt he nolde gelyfan buton Iohannes attor drunce* with *ÆHomM* 14. 20 *Se cyning bebead . . . þæt ælc mann drunce þæs deorwurðan wines* and *Exod* 7. 25 *Ac hi ne mihton drincan seofon dagum of ðam wætere.* It is easy enough to put the last two in a different category from *ÆCHom* i. 72. 9. But how significant are the differences? The phrases *þæs deorwurðan wines* and *of ðam wætere* are clearly partitive—no one man could drink all the wine and the Egyptians had no desire to drink all the water. But equally clearly, there is no implication that John is to drink all the poison. He himself uses the genitive in his reply—*ÆCHom* i. 72. 17 *ic unforhtmod ðæs drences onfo*—and does not drink until two thieves have drunk—and died. The same point emerges if we compare examples like *Matt(AV)* 20. 23 'Ye shall drink indeed of my cup' and *1 Cor(AV)* 10. 21 'Ye cannot drink the cup of the Lord and the cup of devils'. So, while the genitive or its equivalent often denotes that the writer intends a reference to a part, it is dangerous to conclude that the use of the accusative always implies the whole in contrast to a part. It may have merely the negative significance that the writer does not want to stress that he is referring to a part. However, as we have already seen, the distinction is sometimes a real one; it seems reasonable to distinguish *ÆCHom* i. 160. 33 *Deor habbað hola, and fugelas habbað nest* (the whole) from *Conf 4* 356 *Se ðe þara mihta hæbbe, arære cirican Gode to lofe*, *WHom* 8c. 6 *gyf he þære ylde 7 ðæs andgytes hæfð þæt he hit understandan mæg*, and *ÆLS* 26. 260 *Ic hæbbe of þam stocce þe his heafod on stod* (part). The oft-quoted *ÆCHom* i. 414. 28 . . . *ðonne he ne moste þæs fyrstes habban ðe he gewilnode* probably belongs in this last group, but *þæs fyrstes* may show the influence of *wilnian*.

e. With prepositions

§1343. On the genitive with prepositions, see §§1177-219.

f. Functional equivalents

§1344. The following sometimes serve as equivalents of the genitive of nouns in its various functions: the declined possessive (§§289-310); the genitive of personal pronouns and of demonstratives (§§246 and 338-9); the dative of possession (§§304-10); other case forms of nouns and pronouns (§§1089 and 1380-1); adjectives (§§1269 and 1288); prepositional phrases, including those with *of* (§§1167 and 1203); adverbs (§§1389-407); compound nouns, e.g. *BlHom* 9. 32 *se wuldorcyning* (but *BlHom* 67. 13 *wuldres cyning*); and compound adjectives, e.g. *And* 1308 *domgeorn* (but *And* 959 *domes georn*). See further Muxin, *passim*.

5. THE DATIVE AND INSTRUMENTAL CASES

a. Introductory remarks

§1345. The OE instrumental—a syncretic case combining forms and functions of cases such as the locative and ablative—was itself subsumed under the dative; see §§6 and 8. The original function of the 'dative proper' seems to have been to indicate personal involvement or interest; cf. MnE constructions with 'to' and 'for'. But the term 'personal' hardly fits such examples as the second *him* in

ÆHom 21. 82 *Hi namon þa to wisdome þæt hi wurþodon him for godas þa sunnan and þone monan . . . and him lac offrodan, ÆCHom* i. 100. 9 . . . *se Ælmihtiga . . . het þæt hi wæron to tacne dagum and gearum,* and *ÆLS* 8. 52 . . . *þæt ge beoð þeowan synne and stanum.* So I shall speak of the 'dative of interest'. The instrumental was broadly concerned with 'the means or manner of an action' (QW, p. 67)—cf. MnE constructions with 'by' and 'with'—while the locative expressed 'position in space, time, or situation' (Ardern, p. xxx). But in OE the dative is used in lieu of the instrumental where the latter does not exist and often interchanges with it even where it does. As a natural corollary, the instrumental forms sometimes intrude into the realm of the 'dative proper'. The sentences which follow show that variation between the two cases in individual examples has no syntactical importance: *Mark(Ru2)* 16. 15 *bodigaþ godspel elce gescæfte,* where *Li* has *alle ł eghuelcum sceafte; Bede* 176. 23 *togeteledum þy geare* (dative and instrumental in the same phrase); *Bede(T)* 252. 4 *þy gemyndgadan gere,* where MS *B* has *þam gemyngodan geare;* and *ÆCHom* i. 306. 31 *and hi habbað swa miccle maran edlean æt Gode, swa micclum swa heora wuldor is læsse mid mannum.* Anderson draws our attention to some irregular uses of the instrumental in Northumbrian texts in *PMLA* 50 (1935), 946-56. So there is no point in following Kress in his attempt to distinguish the two cases on syntactical grounds; see §8 fn. 1. We must be content with describing the actual uses of the composite dative/instrumental in OE, bearing in mind these observations by Amos (p. 128):

> Lichtenheld, Groth, and others are right to point out the reduced use of the instrumental case in later Old English. But the case was always available to a writer who wished to use it. Neither a preference for nor the avoidance of the instrumental case provides sufficient grounds for dating a text, especially since scribal alterations will tend to disguise authorial practice.

§1346. The OE dative survives in a sense in MnE sentences like 'He gave me the book' and 'He gave the girl a kiss'. It is however a commonplace that prepositions gradually superseded simple case-forms in practically all the functions of the dative/instrumental discussed below. It is also a commonplace that the process was well under way in OE; see §1226. So if we look at it theoretically, without recourse to the manuscript, the insertion of *mid* above the line in *Bo* 14. 11 *Swa eac se suðerna wind hwilum mid miclum storme gedrefeð þa sæ* could have been made by the original scribe when he realized his error or by a later reader to whom the dative without a preposition was unacceptable.

§1347. My own impression is that the percentage of prepositions did not increase significantly during the OE period. It is supported by some evidence; see §§1227-8. According to Trnka (p. 163), the use of the case-form without a preposition was preserved to a greater extent in the poetry than in the prose. Dančev (1969, p. 90) suggests a 'consciously archaic use for stylistic reasons'. But Green (1913, §140) observes that for the expression of personal agency 'after Cædmon the tendency in poetry is entirely towards the analytical'; but see further §§1365-78, especially §1370. There is room for more work here on both prose and poetry when full concordances are available. But imponderables like the demands of metre, the personal preference of authors, and possible Latin influence, will complicate the argument. On prepositions which govern the dative/instrumental see §§1177-219.

§1348. Visser (i, §§316-51) uses the term 'indirect object' to cover not only the traditional 'indirect object' as in the type *He sealde his sweord ðam cyninge*, but also a wide variety of datives including the types *he Gode þancode, him tweonode, he him gewat, ic wæs him leof, he wæs me freond, he wæs mara eallum gesceaftum*, and *us is to donne hit*. We can, I think, be more precise.

b. With verbs

(1) The case of the 'direct object'

§1349. Certain OE verbs govern the dative of what would today be the 'direct object', e.g. *gecweman* in *ÆHom* 19. 79 *Se man þe butan wife wunað hogað hu he Gode gecweme*, and *ofhreowan* used impersonally in *ÆHom* 17. 140 . . . *7 him hearde ofhreow. . . .* Some, of course, can take more than one case; see the List of verbal rections. On the problems involved (terminological and otherwise), see §§602-6 and 1081-2.

(2) The case of the 'indirect object'

§1350. The dative of interest is common with verbs which take an accusative and a dative, e.g. *ÆCHom* i. 16. 7 *and sealde ðam fixum sund and ðam fugelum fliht*, *ÆCHom* i. 36. 8 *and se engel cydde Cristes acennednysse hyrdemannum*, and *ÆCHom* ii. 182. 8 *'Agif me minne sunu'*. Traditionally, the words in the dative in examples like these, where the verbs involve some sort of giving, are called 'indirect objects'; on the extent of the intrusion of *to* into this domain in OE, see §1210. But one can take something away as well as give it by means of the simple dative, e.g. *Bo* 7. 17 *þa ongan he smeagan 7 leornigan on him selfum hu he þ rice þam unrihtwisan cyninge aferran mihte* and *ÆCHom* ii. 182. 9 '*Hwæt la, ætbræd ic ðe þinne sunu?*'. It is pedantic and indeed (as Ball shows in *RES* 22 (1971), 468) danger-ous to distinguish the indirect object or dative of advantage from the dative of separation or of disadvantage; 'dative of interest' can cover both categories. On the position of these datives in their clause see §§3889 and 3907.

§1351. The 'dative of interest' remains in the dative in OE passive constructions, e.g. *ÆCHom* ii. 440. 23 *Maria geceas þone selestan dæl, se ðe ne bið hire næfre ætbroden*. The type 'The girl was given the book' is not found in OE; see §§834 and 839.

(3) The ethic dative

§1352. Another special case of the dative of personal interest is the ethic dative—'the dative when used to imply that a person, other than the subject or object, has an indirect interest in the fact stated' (*OED*, s.v. *ethical* a. 3). No OE examples of the ethic dative so defined have come to my notice or to that of Visser (i, §695). *Vain* 81 *gif me se witega ne leag*, cited by Mätzner (ii. 227), cannot stand in the light of the first two lines of the poem:

Vain 1   Hwæt, me frod wita   on fyrndagum
                  sægde, snottor ar,   sundorwundra fela!

§1353. Some writers on OE syntax, e.g. Sorg (pp. 10-19 and 34-7) and Ropers (pp. 24-6), have described as 'ethic' those datives which refer to the subject or object of the sentence. There is little point in extending the definition to include persons directly involved in the action. Such examples belong to one of the categories discussed above. L. Schmid, *Der ethische Dativ im Englischen* (Tübingen diss., 1922) is not concerned with OE or ME.

(4) Other uses with verbs

§1354. The dative/instrumental is used reflexively (see §§271-4), with inflected infinitives in the type *us is hit to donne* (see §§934-44), and with second participles in the dative absolute construction (see §§3804-31).

c. With nouns and adjectives

(1) General

§1355. Here we are frequently concerned with what can broadly be called the dative of interest, e.g. (with nouns) *ÆCHom* i. 4. 34

to ecum forwyrde þam ðe him onbugað and to ecere myrhðe ðam þe him þurh geleafan wiðcweðað, ÆCHom i. 42. 5 forðan þe hit næs nan neod þam Ælmihtigum Scyppende þæt he of wife acenned wære, and ÆCHom i. 100. 10 . . . and het þæt hi wæron to tacne dagum and gearum, and (with adjectives) ÆCHom i. 228. 4 And is nu hellegeat belocen rihtwisum mannum, and æfre open unrihtwisum, ÆCHom ii. 126. 3 . . . þeah ðe heo mannum unðancwurðe sy, and ÆCHom ii. 244. 17 . . . þæt him selre wære þæt he geboren nære. Here again there is no need to import semantic considerations by distinguishing the dative of advantage, e.g. the first clauses in ÆC Hom i. 4. 34 and ÆCHom i. 228. 4 (both quoted above) from the dative of disadvantage, e.g. the second clauses in the same sentences.

§1356. What might be called a dative of specification is found with some adjectives, e.g. ÆCHom i. 422. 7 Ic wæs blind bam eagum, Max i 82 bu sceolon ærest ‖ geofum god wesan, Dan 257 dydon swa hie cuðon ‖ ofne on innan, aldre generede, and Jud 230 scirmæled swyrd, ‖ ecgum gecoste. But this shades into the dative of interest and might indeed be said to occur with nouns, as in ÆCHom i. 100. 10 (§1355). For details of the dative with adjectives of various meanings see §§192-6 and 211-17.

(2) Denoting possession

§1357. The dative of possession, seen in the examples which follow, is another variety of the dative of interest: ÆCHom i. 136. 23 and wuldor þinum folce Israhele (cf. Luke(WSCp) 2. 32 . . . 7 to þines folces wuldre Israhel), ÆCHom i. 384. 22 Godes gelaðung wurðað þisne dæg ðam mæran apostole Paule to wurðmynte (cf. Lch ii. 138. 22 . . . on weorðmynde þara twelfa apostola), ÆLS 8. 52 . . . þæt ge beoð þeowan synne and stanum (cf. ÆCHom i. 172. 20 þonne bið he deofles ðeowa), and Beo 1961 hæleðum to helpe (cf. Beo 1830 hæleþa to helpe—or is hæleþa parallel to þegna?—and GenB 2176 freomanna to frofre—or is freomanna dependent on Hwæt or parallel to gasta?); the dative is certainly the regular idiom in the poetry with to helpe and to frofre. On this use of the dative, see further §§304-10.

(3) Expressing comparison

§1358. What can be called a dative of comparison occurs after adjectives meaning '(un)like' and '(in)comparable with', e.g. ÆCHom ii. 32. 32 and micclum fægnodon þæt heo wæs þam breðer gelic, ðam ðe heo hwene ær ðurh ða egeslican bifunge ungelic wæs, ÆCHom

i. 148. 24 *þonne bið he wiðmeten nytenum and na mannum*, and *ÆCHom* i. 442. 28 . . . *swa micclum swa þis halige mæden, Godes modor, is unwiðmetenlic eallum oðrum mædenum*. Those meaning 'like' can occur in the comparative, e.g. *ÆCHom* i. 154. 17 *nis heo hwæðere ðe geliccre ðære ecan worulde*, or in the superlative, e.g. *ÆCHom* ii. 30. 36 *þa wearð he færlice astreht, and slapendum gelicost læg*. Here we have the positive or negative comparison of equality.

§1359. A negative comparison of equality, e.g. *PPs* 95. 7 *Nis þe goda ænig on gumrice* || *ahwær efne gelic*, is the equivalent of a comparison of inequality. Small (1929, pp. 20-2) sees in this negative comparison of equality a true dative function and regards it as 'a semantic "bridge" ' which helped to bring about the use of the Germanic dative to express inequality in the combination 'comparative form of an adjective + dative', which, according to him, 'is not one that belongs to the genuine IE dative; . . . [it was] taken over by the Germanic dative along with other ablative, instrumental, and locative functions . . .' and so became a genuine native Germanic idiom. See further Small 1929, pp. 97-100.[18]

§1360. The combination of a comparative form of an adjective and a dative can be used to express a comparison of inequality only when the two things compared would be in the same case—either nominative or accusative—and are related to the same verb-form, as in the MnE examples 'He is taller than I' and 'She loves him more than me'. The conjunction *þonne* can of course also be used in these two situations. In other situations, the dative cannot be used whereas the conjunction can, e.g. MnE 'It is better to die than to be disgraced' and 'He said it more in sorrow than in anger'. See further Small 1929, pp. 18-19. Both occur in

Rid 40. 46   Ic eom fægerre   frætwum goldes,
            þeah hit mon awerge   wirum utan;
            ic eom wyrslicre   þonne þes wudu fula
            oððe þis waroð   þe her aworpen ligeð,

where *þonne* + nominative after *fægerre* and the dative after *wyrslicre* would have been syntactically acceptable.

---

[18] This book—*The Germanic Case of Comparison with a special study of English*—is a model investigation which deserves study as both an example in method and a masterly handling of the subject. Note particularly the observation that it 'was begun solely through a kind of intellectual curiosity aroused in the course of a previous study, and so there is no thesis to defend or hypothesis to justify' (p. 97).

§1361. Small makes two important points (1924, pp. 122-3, and 1929, p. 19 fn. 2, respectively):

From the available evidence, however, it is the writer's opinion that the clause-construction (i.e. the particle construction), being the more general in application and being capable of alone expressing all possible relations, is more elementary than the case-construction

and

It has not been sufficiently emphasized in the past, and often not recognized, that in no IE language has the case-construction stood as the *sole* means of expressing any phase of comparison. The particle has always 'overlapped' the case as far back as the records go, and the particle has *always* tended to supersede the case as the languages developed.

Visser (i, §349) notes that examples like ☆*him nan hlaford leofra nære* are ambiguous—'(1) "there was no lord dearer to them", (2) "there was no lord more beloved than he" '—and that this 'may have furthered the use of *þonne*, where the second interpretation was meant'.

§1362. The dative comparison of inequality is most common in the poetry, e.g.

Rid 40. 62　　Ic mesan mæg　　meahtelicor
　　　　　　　　　ond efnetan　　　ealdum þyrse

and

El 505　　　　　　　　　　　　ond him nænig wæs
　　　　　ælærendra　　oðer betera
　　　under swegles hleo　　syðþan æfre.

Small (1929, pp. 38-51) quotes all the examples from the poetry of comparisons of inequality made with the dative case (fifty examples) and with the particle *þonne* where the dative could have been used (sixty-two examples), gives a list of poems in which there are none of the former (1929, pp. 52-3) and in which there are no comparisons of inequality (1929, pp. 53-4), and concludes (1929, pp. 54-5) 'In other words, out of all the one hundred and twelve expressions of comparison where the case is syntactically possible it has been used by the poets fifty times, a remarkably high proportion of 45 per cent. This means that in the language of the poets the case method was still of equal importance with the particle in the expression of comparison.'

§1363. The dative comparison of inequality occurs spasmodically in the early prose; see Wülfing, i. 65, and Small 1929, pp. 56-67. Small (1929, pp. 56-8) found two examples in *Boethius*—*Bo* 79. 16

and *Bo* 63. 4 *þonne bið ælc dysig man þy unweorðra þe he mare rice hæfð ælcum wisum men*—giving a proportional strength of case-form against *þonne* of only four per cent compared with forty-five per cent in the *Metres*. The three examples in *Cura Pastoralis*—*CP* 106. 11, 114. 23, and 301. 12 *Ac se ure Aliesend, ðe mara is 7 mærra eallum gesceaftum . . .*—give a figure of five per cent (Small 1929, pp. 63–4) and the four in Gregory's *Dialogues*—*GD(C)* 91. 7, *GD(C)* 173. 11, *GD(C)* 217. 3, and *GD(C)* 266. 22 *hwæt hafað ma se snottra man þam dysigan*—a figure of seventeen per cent (Small 1929, pp. 65–7). Small (1929, p. 64) found none in the *Soliloquies* or *Orosius*. The highest percentage, according to his figures (1929, pp. 58–63), is fifty-five per cent in *Bede*, 'for in the whole five books there are only twelve instances of the overlapping particle-construction to offset these fifteen datives'. Small sees in these 'the general influence (not slavish translation) of the more compact (synthetic) Latin'.

§1364. The dative comparison of inequality is even less frequent in later prose. Small's one example from the *Blickling Homilies*—*BlHom* 163. 19 . . . *se mon Sancte Iohannes, se wæs mara 7 selra eallum oþrum mannum*—gives a figure of approximately six per cent (1929, pp. 67–8). Why it should occur when we find twenty lines later *BlHom* 165. 3 *Ic hine secge maran 7 selran þonne ænigne witgan* is a mystery. For the rest, the highest number occur in the Gospel translations (twenty-three examples) and in *Liber Scintillarum* (twenty-four examples), where Latin influence is strong (Small 1929, pp. 69–74). There are none in MS *H* of Gregory's *Dialogues* and none in Ælfric—apart from six in which the second element is a numeral; on these, see §§573 and 3239–42—or in Wulfstan (Small 1929, pp. 78–80). So, in Small's words (1929, p. 80)

Because of the lack of a continuous record of the language from generation to generation, we should not expect to find, and indeed we do not find, a steady and gradual decline in the use of the dative. But the evidence *does* enable us to assert that at the time of the earliest connected prose records the dative of comparison held about one-fifth of the field of expression that lay within its function, that the particle encroached more and more upon this fifth, and that by the beginning of the eleventh century the case had passed out of use.

On the possibility of an instrumental of comparison, see §3261.

d. The case of the instrument

§1365. One needs to distinguish verbs which take the dative/instrumental of 'direct object', e.g.

Rid 2. 6   streamas staþu beatað,   stundum weorpaþ
             on stealc hleoþa   stane ond sonde,
             ware ond wæge,

from those which take a 'direct object' and a dative/instrumental of means, e.g. *PPs* 64. 5 *ealle we ðin hus ecum godum* ‖ *fægere fyllað*, and those which take only a dative/instrumental of means, e.g. *Rid* 12. 1 *fotum ic fere*. Kress's classification would have been clearer and simpler if he had done this. Here we are not concerned with the first construction; see § 1082.

§ 1366. While on the one side the dative/instrumental of means shades into that of agency (see § 1372), on the other it shades into that of manner. Hence the use of the dative/instrumental to form adverbs; see §§ 1408–27. That the lines of demarcation are inevitably hazy has been shown in §§ 802–5 and 1410.

§ 1367. The means or instrument by which something is effected can be expressed by the dative/instrumental alone as well as by a preposition. The case-form alone is found in the early prose when the means or instrument is a part of the body, e.g.

Bede 224. 13   . . . þætte ne meahten godo beon, þa ðe monna hondum geworhte wæron of eorðlicum timbre, oððe of treom, oððe of stanum: þara trea æcyrfe 7 lafe oððe fyre forbærnde wæron, oððe in hwylchwugu fatu geheowad wæron mennisces broces, oððe cuðlice utworpen wæren 7 in forhogdnisse hæfde, 7 fotum treden 7 in eorðan gehwyrfde wæron

(but *Bede* 130. 13 *þa instæpe sette he mid þa swiðron hond him on ðæt heafod* and *CP* 357. 19 *Aworpen man bið a unnyt 7 gæð mid wo muðe, 7 bicneð mid ðæm eagum, 7 trit mid ðæm fet, 7 spricð mid ðæm fingre*) or something associated with it, e.g. *Bede* 40. 31 *7 eac oðre monige . . . ða wæron missenlicum cwealmnyssum ðreste 7 ungeheredre leoma toslitnysse wundade* and *Bede* 380. 23 . . . *ða hrægl ðam ðe* [*hie*] *Gode ðone gehalgodan lichoman . . . gyredon* (but *Bede* 376. 31 . . . *se leofa biscop Eadbyrht wæs mid grimre adle ðread 7 gestanden*, *Bede* 376. 15 . . . *ðara hrægla dæl þe se halga lichoma mid gegyrwed wæs*, and *Bede* 376. 28 . . . *ond þone lichoman gegyredon mid neowum hrægle*) (see further Dančev 1969, pp. 92–3); a natural phenomenon, e.g. *Bede* 430. 30 *Seo stow þær seo denu wæs ðe þu gesawe wallende lege 7 strongum celum egeslice beon . . .* (but *Bede* 52. 26 . . . *Chaldeas bærndon Hierusaleme weallas 7 ða cynelican getimbro mid fyre fornaman . . .*); or an abstract, e.g. *Bede* 34. 19 *7 swylce eac sticcemælum his þam halwendan trymnyssum wæs gelæred . . .* (but *Bede* 56. 22 *Ða wæs gestrangod Augustinus mid trymnysse þæs eadigan fæder*).

§1368. But Wülfing's list contains no examples of the case-form alone in what one might think would be its most common function —the expression of the material external instrument. I have found none. Such examples occur in the poetry, e.g. *Beo* 679 *forþan ic hine sweorde swebban nelle* (but *Beo* 574 . . . *þæt ic mid sweorde ofsloh* ‖ *niceras nigene*) and

Ex 197   Hæfdon hie gemynted   to þam mægenheapum
                to þam ærdæge   Israhela cynn
                billum abreotan

(but

GenA 2856   þær þu scealt ad gegærwan,
                bælfyr bearne þinum,   and blotan sylf
                sunu mid sweordes ecge . . .).

The categories already noted for the early prose can also be distinguished in the poetry, viz., a part of the body, e.g. *PPs* 138. 3 *þu me gehiwadest handa þinre* (but *PPs* 137. 7 *þu me geræhtest recene mid handa*) or something associated with it, e.g.

Rid 45. 3   on þæt banlease   bryd grapode,
                hygewlonc hondum,   hrægle þeahte
                þrindende þing   þeodnes dohtor

(but

GenA 1571   þæt he ne mihte   on gemynd drepen
                hine handum self   mid hrægle wryon);

a natural phenomenon, e.g. *GenA* 166 *Gesette yðum heora* ‖ *onrihtne ryne, rumum flode* (but *GenA* 156 *ac stod bewrigen fæste* ‖ *folde mid flode*) and *PPs* 88. 18 *and hine halige ele handum smyrede* (but *PPs* 132. 2 *unguentum* . . . ‖ *mid þy Aaron his beard oftast smyrede*); or an abstract, e.g. *CEdg* 4 *eac hi igbuend oðre worde* ‖ *beornas Baðan nemnaþ* (but *Met* 20. 55 . . . *nemdest eall swa ðeah* ‖ *mid ane noman ealle togædre*) and *Beo* 24 *lofdædum sceal* ‖ *in mægþa gehwære man geþeon* (but *GenB* 450 *wolde* . . . ‖ *mid mandædum men beswican*).

§1369. The dative/instrumental alone expressing the means can still be found in the later prose. As in the early prose, the material external instrument requires the preposition, e.g. *ÆCHom* ii. 334. 8 *gewæpnod mid hwitum scylde and scinendum swurde* and *ÆLS* 32. 109 . . . *and tigdon hine þærto mid heardum bendum and hine eft swuncgon langlice mid swipum*. But we find examples without prepositions with parts of the body or things associated with it, e.g. *ÆLS* 6. 164 *swa þæt he samcucu læg sweltendum gelic and fleow eall blode* and *ÆLS* 4. 210 *þær manna lic lagon . . . þa weollon eall maðon* (but *ÆCHom* ii. 312. 25 *and bat his tungan þæt heo on blode fleow* and *ÆCHom* ii. 312. 27 *mid hæran gescrydd*); with natural phenomena, e.g. *ÆCHom* ii. 310. 7 *elles ðu earma scealt yfelum deaðe sweltan* and *ÆCHom* ii. 232. 32 *se bið dead ecum deaðe* (but *ÆHom* 2. 107 *and se brosnigenda lichama . . . bið mid deaþe fornumen*); and with abstracts, e.g. *ÆCHom* i. 44. 15 *þa oðre six wæron gecigede ðisum namum* and *ÆCHom* ii. 64. 3 *þa spræc God to his witegan Samuhele ðisum wordum* (but *John(WSCp)* 10. 3 *7 he nemð his agene sceap be naman*, Latin *et proprias oues uocat nominatim*, and *ÆCHom* i. 482. 24 *þaða he spræc to anum Samaritaniscan wife mid ðisum worde*). We find a fluctuation in usage in *ÆCHom* ii. 334. 9 *Ða ðry englas gelicere beorhtnysse scinende wæron, and ðære sawle wunderlice wynsumnysse mid heora fiðera swege on belæddon, and mid heora sanges dreame micclum gegladodon.*

§1370. Did the preposition make perceptible gains against the simple case-form for the expression of instrumentality in the OE period? I have not noted any significant change in the prose, though at times I have had the impression that the simple case-form may be slightly less common in the later writings. Much the same can be said about the poetry. In view of the fact that he confuses agency and instrumentality and does not consider all examples of the latter (see §805), Green's observation (1913, §140) that 'after Cædmon the tendency in poetry is entirely towards the analytical' cannot be taken as conclusive. So my tentative answer to my question must be 'No'. This is in accordance with the general views expressed in §§1223-6. But there is room for more work here. Anyone doing it will have to pay particular attention to the points made by Dančev which I summarize in §§1227-8.

e. The case of agency?

§1371. As I pointed out in §805, it is a disputed question whether there are clear examples in which the personal agent is expressed by means of an OE case form alone. Indeed, in §833 I have given voice to doubts whether the idea of personal agency in the sense in which we understand it was recognized at all by Anglo-Saxon speakers or writers. But as with prepositions like *þurh, fram*, and *of* (see §833), so with the simple dative/instrumental we must ask the question: Are there examples in which (modern readers can reasonably feel that) the idea of personal agency was clearly expressed?

§1372. We can best approach what Visser (iii, §1988) calls 'this . . . ticklish problem' by remarking that the distinction between the ideas of means, personal agent, and person concerned or interested, cannot always be clearly drawn; consider

GenA 1762   Wriðende sceal
              mægðe þinre   monrim wesan
              swiðe under swegle   sunum and dohtrum,
              oðþæt fromcyme   folde weorðeð,
              þeodlond monig   þine gefylled,

Beo 991   Ða wæs haten hreþe   Heort innanweard
              folmum gefrætwod,

and

Beo 126   Ða wæs on uhtan   mid ærdæge
              Grendles guðcræft   gumum undyrne

(Green (1913, p. 96) observes that 'very near the actual agent is such a "potential" example as [Beo] 991-2', though he classifies it as expressing instrument or means), and four examples which are quoted by Mustanoja (p. 105) and repeated by Visser (iii, §1988), viz.

Dan 91   an wæs Annanias,   oðer Azarias,
              þridda Misael,   metode gecorene,

Dan 149   oðþæt witga cwom,
              Daniel to dome,   se wæs drihtne gecoren,
              snotor and soðfæst,

ÆCHom i. 58. 17 and [Iohannes] wearð ða him inweardlice gelufod (Sweet, R. 12, p. 209, has the note 'him, dative instead of the regular fram him'), and WHom 5. 109 Ac for þæra gebeorge þe him syn gecorene. . . . It is arguable whether those who are to people the earth in GenA 1762 are instruments or agents, and the note on ÆCHom i. 58. 17 above would never have been written if Ælfric had chosen the adjective leof instead of the participle gelufod. We cannot rely on the test of transforming such 'passive' constructions into their active form. We have no guarantee that the participles are verbal rather than adjectival (Green 1913, p. 118) and cannot be certain of the active form (Visser iii, §1988).

§1373. Green (1914, pp. 515-16) is confident that the simple dative/instrumental did express personal agency:

The Agent, i.e. the person functioning as the logical subject of passive expressions, seems to have been one of the first categories in Germanic to require the elucidative services of prepositions. Altogether there are but spare remnants in WULFILA, the BEOWULF and the EDDIC poems of that prepositionless form of agency which, judging by the testimony of related Indo-European languages, must have been characteristic of the older stages of the Germanic dialects. But even these remnants furnish a sufficient and conclusive evidence.

But in my opinion the 'conclusive evidence' melts away when exposed to the heat of investigation; Green's protestations (1913, p. 113, 1914, p. 516, and elsewhere) do not convince me that his examples are not datives of interest or instrumentality. All his OE examples are drawn from the poetry. Most of them fall readily into the two categories noted, e.g. (dative of instrumentality) *GenA* 1762, *Beo* 991, and *Beo* 126 (all in §1372) and

GenA 1967   þa wæs guðhergum   be Iordane
                     wera eðelland   wide geondsended,
                     folde feondum,

and (dative of interest) *Dan* 91, *Dan* 149 (both in §1372), and *Beo* 12 *Ðæm eafera wæs æfter cenned*. A few are disputed, e.g. *Beo* 1068 *Finnes eaferum* and *Beo* 646 *þæm ahlæcan*, but can be otherwise explained; see the standard editions. I postpone the discussion of the best of Green's examples to §1375.

§1374. Possible instances in the prose are even scarcer and no more convincing. Neither Wülfing (i, §91) nor Bacquet (pp. 556–74) notes any. I have already shown that it is possible to dismiss examples like *ÆCHom* i. 58. 17 *and wearð ða him inweardlice gelufod* and *ÆCHom* i. 58. 7 *He wæs on mægðhade Gode gecoren* (§1372). The more persuasive prose examples are discussed in §1375.

§1375. The best of Green's examples are

Beo 2842   Biowulfe wearð
                  dryhtmaðma dæl   deaðe forgolden,

GenA 1999   Gewiton feorh heora
                fram þam folcstyde   fleame nergan,
                secgum ofslegene,

and

Sat 557   þa wæs on eorðan   ece drihten
              feowertig daga   folgad folcum,
              gecyðed mancynne. . . .

The translation 'by' is convenient for these three and modern readers may well see in them the dative of personal agency. Similar examples can be found in the prose, e.g. *ÆCHom* i. 270. 18 *þa ðreo forman gebedu beoð us ongunnene on ðysre worulde, ac hi beoð a ungeendode*

on þære toweardan worulde and ÆCHom i. 502. 23 *Hi ða heora
biscop rædes befrunon, hwæt him be ðam to donne wære*. But all
can be seen as expressing instrumentality or interest and therefore
provide a flimsy foundation on which to erect a dative/instrumental
of personal agency in OE.

§1376. Whether we call them this is a question of labels—with
which Green seems unnecessarily concerned. He is too eager to
equate constructions without prepositions and constructions with
them—'it is safe to conceive of an unaltered and uniform mode of
thought thruout' (1913, p. 97)—and too eager to attribute to the
Anglo-Saxons a linguistic self-consciousness they may not have possessed—'it cannot be doubted, however, that tho one form served at
the same time for several functional types, these types were well
differentiated in the consciousness of the speaker' (1913, p. 118).
I am reluctant to assume that Anglo-Saxon speakers were conscious
of the distinction between 'A son was born to Mary' and 'A son was
borne by Mary' in sentences in which both 'to Mary' and 'by Mary'
represent a simple dative.

§1377. Green's discussion on OE (1913, pp. 95–105) shows clearly
that the dative/instrumental was used in various ways. But he seems
over-dominated by his anxiety to prove that there were in Germanic
two datives of agency—'the instrumental agent [which], in the last
analysis, was a comitative agent' and 'the dative [which], on the
other hand, developed the function of agency from its basic signification of personal interest' (1913, p. 114). It is, however, open to us
to say that, as far as the OE examples at any rate are concerned, the
dative/instrumental expressing instrumentality or means and the dative
of interest retained whatever individuality they may have had and
that the alleged transition of these two into dative/instrumentals of
agency did not take place. As I see it, the basic problem is again our
lack of native informants. We have no means of knowing that the idiom
in *ÆHom* 14. 228 *Crist geceas fisceras him sylfum to folgerum* is the
active form of that seen in *ÆCHom* i. 58. 7 *He wæs on mægðhade
Gode gecoren*, for *gecoren* may be an adjective; cf. *ÆHom* 18. 96
Oþre beoð gecorene and Gode gecweme, *ÆHom* 14. 167 *and seo
swiðre hand getacnode þa gecorenan halgan*, and *ÆHom* 14. 128 *mid
ðam gecorenum*. Even if *ÆHom* 14. 228 does correspond to *ÆCHom*
i. 58. 7, we have no grounds for assuming that *Gode* in *ÆCHom* i.
58. 7 must express the nominative agent *God* rather than the dative
of the person interested *him sylfum*.

§1378. It follows that in my opinion there is no question of an *increase* in the use of prepositions to express personal agency during the OE period. As far as the concept was present in OE (see §833), it was expressed by means of a preposition from the earliest period.

f. With prepositions

§1379. On the dative/instrumental with prepositions, see §§1177–219.

6. THE ADVERBIAL USE OF CASE-FORMS

a. Introductory remarks

§1380. Case forms (other than the nominative) of nouns, noun phrases, and pronouns, commonly serve as adverbs in OE. Here we are mainly concerned with uses without prepositions. A few prepositional phrases are quoted for comparison; but see further §§1167–9.

§1381. We find some overlap in the use of the various cases—as Andrew notes (*Postscript*, §94), 'we have, for instance, in prose the four forms *ungemet* (acc.), *ungemetes* (gen.), *ungemete* (instr.), *ungemetum* (dat. pl.)'—and the inevitable terminological problems. Thus, BT says of *ungemet* (s.v.) that 'where the word seems to be used with an adjective or with an adverbial force, it is given . . . as part of a compound'; *fif pund* in *HomU* 36. 228. 6 *and ælc an hagelstan wegeð fif pund* can be described as the direct object of *wegeð* or as an accusative of extent; and, since OE does not rigidly distinguish the accusative of motion to from the dative of rest at a place (see §1177(4)), *ham* in *ÆCHom* ii. 62. 13 *Abraham ða ham gecyrde* may be accusative 'used adverbially after verbs of motion' (BT, s.v. *ham*) or an endingless locative (*OEG*, §572). However, it seems best to treat the cases in their turn and to deal with these problems as they arise. Campbell (*OEG*, §668) gives a brief discussion and lists examples. See also Nicolai (pp. 19–22) and Einenkel (*Ang.* 22 (1899), 495, repeated in *Ang.* 26 (1903), 556-7; *Ang.* 26 (1903), 539; and *Ang.* 27 (1903-4), 173 and 183). The still-cited article by Gibbs— 'On the Adverbial Genitive Case in English', *American Journal of Science and Arts*, 45 (1843), 96-102—is concerned with MnE.

b. The accusative

(1) The accusative of extent

§1382. The accusative of extent is found referring to space, time, and degree. With reference to space, it is found with verbs, e.g. *ÆCHom* i. 108. 31 *Ne glad he ealne weig him ætforan* and *ÆCHom* ii. 506. 14 *He arærde him munuclif on micelre digelnysse, twa mila fram ðære ceastre Turoniscre ðeode*, and with adjectives, e.g. *ÆCHom* i. 20. 31 *Wyrc þe nu ænne arc, þreo hund fæðma lang, and fiftig fæðma wid, and þritig fæðma heah*. But a preposition—not necessarily one governing the accusative—can be used, e.g. *ÆCHom* i. 22. 25 *And hi . . . toferdon geond ealne middangeard, ÆCHom* ii. 190. 26 *þa becom se mæsta hunger ofer eallum middanearde seofon gear tosomne*, and *ÆCHom* i. 78. 29 *. . . þæt hi . . . þurh oðerne weg hine forcyrdon*.

§1383. The accusative of extent in time answers the question 'How long?'. It occurs alone, e.g. *ÆCHom* ii. 190. 26 (§1382), *ÆCHom* ii. 74. 35 *To hwi stande ge her ealne dæg ydele?, ÆCHom* i. 178. 10 *Moyses se heretoga fæste eac feowertig daga and feowertig nihta*, and (with the noun repeated or varied) *ÆCHom* i. 20. 8 *and he leofode nigon hund geara and þrittig geara* and *ÆCHom* ii. 330. 17 *. . . ren wæs forwyrned ðam wiðerweardum folce to ðreora geara fyrste, and syx monða fæce*, or with a preposition, e.g. *ÆCHom* ii. 298. 23 *He geheold Cristes setl geond ðrittig geara fæc*. But the dative is sometimes found, either alone—compare *ÆCHom* ii. 490. 8 *þas ðry dagas ge beoð gedrehte . . .* with *ÆCHom* ii. 490. 10 *. . . and hi ðrim dagum ne onbirigdon ætes ne wætes*—or with a preposition, e.g. *ÆCHom* i. 64. 13 *Bicgað eow pællene cyrtlas, þæt ge to lytelre hwile scinon swa swa rose.*

§1384. Yamakawa (1980, pp. 1-19) offers a fuller treatment— based on the W-S *Gospels, Beowulf, Blickling Homilies*, and part of Ælfric's *Lives of Saints*—of 'the adverbial accusative of duration and its prepositional equivalent' in OE. He distinguishes four basic patterns containing respectively a numeral ('(for) five years'), a definite article ('(for) the night'), an indefinite article ('(for) a long time'), and a possessive ('(in) all my life'); gives separate lists of the corresponding OE examples in each of his texts; cites similar examples in which the dative appears; and notes the existence of 'cognate accusatives' such as *BlHom* 33. 16 *7 eal his lif he lifde buton synnum* and of two similar examples with the dative in *BlHom* 167. 33 *. . . forþon þe he her on eorþan engelice life lifde* and *BlHom* 213. 10. The adverbial accusative is much more common than the dative or the prepositional phrase in the *Gospels* (32, 1, 2), *Beowulf* (35, 0, 8), and *Blickling Homilies* (35, 0 (he rightly excludes his examples 26 and 27, which I analyse as datives of degree or measure), and 2). But the figures in Ælfric's *Lives of Saints* are 23, 0, 17—a point of historical significance or personal preference? The prepositions used are *binnan* + dative (3 examples), *for* + dative (4), *geond* + accusative (5), *on* + dative (9), *þurh* + accusative (1), and *to* + dative (7). Yamakawa offers some important observations on the semantic differences between these various expressions and so paves the way for his treatment of ME (1980, pp. 20-39) and of MnE (*Hitotsubashi Journal of Arts and Sciences*, 23 (1982), 1-52).

§1385. The accusative singular neuter is used adverbially to express degree. It may refer to an action, e.g. *ÆCHom* ii. 536. 2 . . . *ne dera∂ him nan ∂ing on ∂am ecan e∂ele, þæt he on wege þyses lifes andlyfene underfeng* and *ÆCHom* ii. 122. 11 *þa ne mihte se papa þæt ge∂afian, þeah ∂e he eall wolde* (for this idiom see §3532); to a quality, e.g. *ÆHom* 20. 370 *seo geogu∂ . . . wæs þa geweaxen, and to wige ful strang*; or to a quantity, e.g. *ÆLS* 6. 359 *and he wunode . . . on his agenum mynstre em feowertig geara*. But there are other ways of expressing degree, e.g. the instrumental *micle* in *ChronA* 89. 31 (897) *Ac hi wæron micle swiþor gebrocede . . . mid ceapes cwilde 7 monna, ealles swiþost mid þæm þæt manige þara selestena cynges þena . . . for∂ferdon* and the prepositional phrase *mid ealle* in *ÆCHom* ii. 178. 26 . . . *and het o∂erne munuc awurpan ut þæt glæsene fæt mid ele mid ealle*. . . .

(2) *The accusative of motion to*

§1386. Sentences like *Or* 17. 3 *He sæde þeah þæt þæt land sie swiþe lang norþ þonan, Or* 17. 16 *7 siglde ∂a east be lande swa swa he meahte on feower dagum gesiglan*, and *ÆCHom* ii. 62. 13 *Abraham ∂a ham gecyrde*, are frequently quoted as examples of the simple accusative expressing motion to a place or the point reached. But *norþ* and *east* may be adverbs (see *OED*, s.vv.) and *ham* may be a locative (see §§14 and 1381). The combination preposition + accusative is, however, well attested, e.g. *ÆCHom* i. 10. 17 *Ðæt teo∂e werod . . . awende on yfel* and *ÆCHom* i. 318. 16 . . . *þæt his hrof astige o∂ heofon*. But both the genitive and the dative are found with prepositions, e.g. *ÆCHom* i. 28. 16 *ealle . . . arisa∂ of dea∂e him togeanes* and *ÆCHom* i. 74. 16 *Iohannes . . . eode wi∂ þæs Hælendes*.

(3) *The accusative of time when?*

§1387. Wülfing (i, §119b) cites examples in which the accusative allegedly answers the question 'when?'. It is hard to see how they differ from those in his §119a which answer the question 'how long?' and there seems no justification for the sub-division. They are quite different from the examples cited by Mustanoja (pp. 107–8), in which 'the ME common case ("accusative") used to indicate the time "when" obviously goes back to the OE and early ME instrumental dative of time'.

§1388. Similarly, Daniels fails to carry conviction when he writes (p. 145) that the accusative indicates, not only the time how long, but also the time when something happens. All the examples he cites belong to the former category. Those which could possibly refer to 'time when' can also be explained as duration of time, e.g. *WHom* 14. 37 *þas halgan tid* 'throughout the holy season', *WHom* 14. 57 *þæt lencten* 'during lent', and *HomU* 45. 289. 26 *þas halgan tid alce niht* 'throughout every night during the holy season'.

c. *The genitive*

(1) *Introductory remarks*

§1389. The genitive singular neuter of pronouns, adjectives, and the numeral *an*, and the genitive singular of nouns (either alone or in combination with qualifying elements), is used adverbially in OE. It may express degree, e.g. *ealles* 'entirely'; manner, e.g. *þonces* 'unwillingly'; place, e.g. *hamweardes* 'at home'; and time, e.g. *dæges* 'by day'. Shipley (p. 109) adds 'condition'—presumably on the strength of *weas* 'by chance'—and Carlton (1970, p. 90) describes *Ch* 1188 *fore aedleane ðæs aecan 7 ðaes towardon lifes* as a 'genitive of result'. I am content to describe these as genitives of manner and definition respectively.

§1390. The genitive singular occurs more often than the genitive plural. The strong masculine ending *-es* is most common, sometimes being analogically extended to feminine nouns, e.g. *ÆCHom* ii. 182. 33 *Ne mæg ic nateshwon buton mynstre nihtes wunian* and *Ps(P)* 13. 6 *unþearfes*, and to adverbs, e.g. *CP* 169. 13 *hidres ðædres* (cf. *CP* 59. 5 *hider 7 ðider*) and *ChronA* 86. 4 (894) *hamweardes* (cf. *Or* 44. 17 *hamweard*). But the genitive singular of weak nouns does occur, e.g. *ÆCHom* i. 170. 13 *agenes willan*. Whether *neadunge* in *ÆCHom* i. 112. 6 and *neadunga* in *ÆCHom* i. 216. 5 are genitives or datives cannot be determined. The gen. pl. -*a* occurs in *ealra* 'completely' and *geara* 'formerly' (Shipley, p. 111), and in combinations like *ÆCHom* i. 236. 11 *sumera ðinga eaðelicor* 'somewhat easier'. On other -*a* endings in adverbs, see *OEG*, §§665-6.

(2) *Manner and degree*

§ 1391. The adverbial genitive may answer the question 'How?', 'In what way?' (manner) or 'To what extent?' (degree). The distinction between the two is sometimes clear. Thus we can reasonably detect manner in *ÆCHom* i. 148. 26 *forðan ealle hyra unlustas hi sceolon gebetan sylfwylles on þyssum life, oððe unþances æfter ðyssum life* and degree in *ÆHom* 12. 45 . . . *þæt ge ealles ne beon þære lare bedælede*. But they shade into one another in words like *elles* 'else' and *endemes* 'equally', and elements of space or time can intrude, e.g. in *þwyres* 'crosswise' and *samtinges* 'together, immediately'.

§ 1392. Adverbial genitives of manner and degree include *æghwæs* 'in every respect', *ælces þinges* 'in every respect', *ealles, ealra* 'completely', *nealles* 'not at all', *ehsynes* 'with one's eye', *elles* 'else', *endebyrdes* 'in order, for order', *endemes* 'equally', *hwæthweganunges* 'somewhat', *lytesna* 'almost', *ungemetes* 'very, excessively', *micles* 'much, very', *ofermodes* 'in his pride', *nides* 'of necessity', *niðes, niða* 'hatefully, maliciously', *rimes* 'in number', *samtinges* 'together, immediately', *sumes* 'somewhat', *sumera ðinga* 'somewhat', *þæs* 'so, therefore', *(un)þances* '(un)willingly', *unþearfes* 'needlessly', *þwyres* 'crosswise', *(un)gewealdes* '(un)willingly', *weas* 'by chance', *welhwæs* 'altogether', *(un)willes* '(un)willingly', and *ungewisses* 'ignorantly'. The genitives *þances* and *willes* can be used alone or in combination with nouns and pronouns in the genitive, e.g. *WHom* 13. 49 *Godes þances, HomU* 47. 302. 21 *his agenes þances*, and *ÆCHom* ii. 334. 25 *his willes*. There are also compounds, e.g. *ÆCHom* i. 82. 27 *sylfwilles*.

(3) *Means or instrument*

§ 1393. The genitive of means or instrument is an alternative name for some genitives of manner rather than a special category. Thus the opening phrases in *ÆCHom* i. 212. 16 *Agenes willan and agenre gymeleaste he bið gebunden, ac þurh Godes mildheortnysse he bið unbunden* can be described as instrumental genitives—note the *þurh* phrase and cf. *ÆCHom* i. 228. 30 *be his agenum willan*—or as genitives of manner. The same is true of some defining genitives with adjectives, e.g. *Or* 21. 16 *twegen fætels full ealað oððe wæteres*, of genitives of place like *ÆCHom* i. 118. 22 *we ne magon gecyrran þæs weges ðe we comon*—cf. *ÆCHom* i. 78. 30 *þurh operne weg*—and of *WHom(BH)* 20. 61 *Ac mæst ælc swicode 7 oðrum derede wordes 7 dæde.*

§1394. Some scholars have been reluctant to admit the use of this genitive in the plural. Brodeur (p. 166), rejecting the translation '. . . excellently entertained' for *Beo* 2035 . . . *duguða biwenede*, remarks that 'although the dative plural *duguðum* is, very occasionally, used with adverbial force, the genitive plural *duguða* is not so used anywhere else'. For my objections to such arguments from silence, see *Neophil.* 52 (1968), 297. Green (1913, p. 100) hovers between emending *duguða* to *duguðe* or to *duguðum*, which he explains as a dative of agency, thereby replacing one difficulty with another; see §1371. Leslie (pp. 74-5) says of *Ruin* 33 *gleoma gefrætwed* that 'it is more likely . . . that *gleoma* is the instrumental of a *u* stem noun *gleomu*' than a genitive plural because 'genitive plurals used adverbially are few and mainly of relatively colourless nouns like *þing* and *gear*'. None of these writers refers to *niða* in *Beo* 845 *niða ofercumen*, *Beo* 1439 *niða genæged*, or *Beo* 2206 *niða genægdan*, which is usually explained as an instrumental genitive plural. We could, I suppose, read dat. sg. *-e* in all places. Of course, if we emend apparent examples or otherwise dismiss them because the idiom is rare, we finally make it non-existent and so justify ourselves. But the five examples reinforce one another and gain support from *ealra, geara,* and *sumera þinga.*

(4) *Place*
§1395. The adverbial genitive of place may be used to modify a verb, either alone, e.g. *ChronA* 86. 3 (894) *þa he þa wæs þiderweardes . . .* , or with another adverb, which may in turn modify it, e.g. *ChronA* 86. 1 (894) *7 wæs se cyng þa þiderweardes on fære*, or on which it may itself be dependent, e.g. *WHom* 12. 10 *þa syððan toferdon hy wide landes, GenA* 2706 *æghwær eorðan, ChristC* 1001 *londes ower*, and *Wife* 7 *hæfde ic uhtceare* ‖ *hwær min leodfruma londes wære.*

§1396. Smithers (*Schlauch Studies*, pp. 420-7) proposes to read 'an adverbial genitive *andeges* "in the high seat"' for *an dæges* in *Beo* 1935 *þæt hire an dæges eagum starede* and to translate ☆*hire andeges* as 'in the seat of honour in relation to (i.e. next) her'. But the notion that an adverbial genitive could govern a pronoun seems unlikely;

a preposition is called for. This is not my only reason for rejecting the emendation, but the matter cannot be pursued here.

§1397. Adverbial genitives of place include *hamweardes* 'homewards', *gehwæðeres* 'on every side', *innanbordes* 'at home, not abroad', *suðweardes* 'southwards', *togeanes* 'back, in return', *tomiddes* 'in the midst', *toweardes* 'hither', *þærtomiddes* 'in the midst', *þid(e)res*, *þiderweardes* 'thither', *þwyres* 'crosswise', *uppweardes* 'upwards', *utanbordes* 'abroad', and *utweardes* 'outwards'.

§1398. The genitive may refer to 'place where', e.g. *ChronA* 86. 3 (894) *þa he þa wæs þiderweardes, 7 sio operu fierd wæs hamweardes* . . . , or to 'place whither', e.g. *Or* 166. 18 *7 he se cyning his handa wæs uppweardes brædende wið þæs heofones* and *CP* 71. 6 *Sua bið sio costung æresð on ðæm mode 7 ðonne fereð utweardes to ðære hyde*. It may also give the direction or path of a movement, e.g. *Or* 21. 4 *7 þonne rideð ælc hys weges, ÆCHom* ii. 312. 1 *ðwyres* 'crosswise', *ÆCHom* i. 118. 21 *Ure eard soðlice is neorxnawang, to ðam we ne magon gecyrran þæs weges ðe we comon, WHom* 12. 10 (§1395), and *ÆLet* 2(D). 43 *7 þa siððan toferdon þa apostolas wide landes geond ealle þas world*.

§1399. It is possible to take *utanbordes* in *CP* 3. 11 *7 hu man utanbordes wisdom 7 lare hieder on lond sohte* as expressing 'place where'—'men [who were] abroad'—or 'place whence'—'men [from] abroad'. But since none of the other adverbial genitives listed above refers to 'place whence', the first explanation of *utanbordes* seems right. So I know of no reason for following Wentersdorf (*NM* 71 (1970), 610) when he translates *ful wide . . . feorres folclondes* in

Wife 45   . . .   sy æt him sylfum gelong
          eal his worulde wyn,   sy ful wide fah
          feorres folclondes,   þæt min freond siteð
          under stanhliþe . . .

as 'very far away . . . from his distant land-grant' or Greenfield (p. 144) when he sides with Gordon and Gollancz in translating *forð onetteð lænan lifes* in

Phoen 451   þær him nest wyrceð   wið niþa gehwam
          dædum domlicum   dryhtnes cempa,
          þonne he ælmessan   earmum dæleð,
          dugeþa leasum,   ond him dryhten gecygð,
          fæder on fultum,   forð onetteð,

> lænan lifes   leahtras dwæsceþ,
> mirce mandæde,   healdeð meotudes æ
> beald in breostum . . .

as 'hasteneth forth from this frail life'. In the first, Mackie's 'in a distant land' is supported by *Wife 7 hæfde ic uhtceare || hwær min leodfruma londes wære*, and in the second, we are in my opinion bound to follow the ASPR punctuation above and, taking *lænan lifes* with *leahtras*, to translate 'quenches the sins of the transitory life'.

(5) *Time*

§ 1400. The adverbial genitive defines the time within which something happens, e.g. *ÆCHom* i. 472. 28 *anes dæges* 'within one day', *ÆCHom* ii. 176. 3 *ydæges* 'on the same day', *ÆCHom* i. 80. 30 *þæs geares þe Crist acenned wæs, Beo* 2269 *dæges ond nihtes*,[19] and *Phoen* 37 *wintres ond sumeres*. The genitive here is akin to the partitive, whereas that in *ChronE* 57. 22 (796) *7 Eanbald arceb [forð-ferde] on ·iiii· idus Aug' þæs ilcan geares* and *ChronE* 57. 1 (793) *7 litel æfter þam þæs ilcan geares on ·vi· idus Iañr earmlice heðenra manna hergung adiligode Godes cyrican in Lindisfarena ee* may be possessive. However, the distinction between *þes ilcan geares* in *ChronE* 57. 23 (796) *7 þes ilcan geares forðferde Ceolwulf ꝧ*, which is clearly adverbial, and *þi ilcan geare* in *ChronE* 17. 1 (519) *7 þi ilcan geare hi gefuhton wið Bryttas* is a fine (if not undetectable) one. Perhaps the genitive stresses the implication '*sometime* in that year'.

§ 1401. Adverbial genitives of time include *dæges* 'by day', *ydæges* 'on the same day', *dæglanges* 'for a day', *geara* 'formerly', *ungeara* 'lately', *instæpes* 'at once', *nihtes* 'by night', *sæmtinges* 'immediately', *simles* 'always', *singales* 'continually, always', *sumeres* 'in the summer', *þærrihtes* 'immediately', *þæs* 'after', and *wintres* 'in the winter'.

§ 1402. Examples like *Or* 140. 12 *þy æfterran geare þæs, Or* 108. 15 *on ðæm æfterran geare þæs*, and *Or* 194. 6 *on þæm teoþan geare þæs þe Hannibal won on Italie*, suggest that *þæs* may originally have expressed point of time from which—literally 'from that'. But I suspect that even in the earliest literary texts it was almost fossilized in the sense 'after', whether used as an adverb *þæs* or as a conjunction

---

[19] We find *nihtes* alongside *in dæge* in *Rim* 44 and *neahtes* alongside *on dæg* in *MSol* 395; cf. my § 1390. But Shipley's comments on this (p. 111) seem more portentous than is justified by the examples in the poetry; see GK, s.v. *dæg*.

þæs (þe); on a possible exception—the refrain in *Deor*—see §§1404-5. Other examples in which the genitive of a noun or pronoun indicates the starting point of a period of time include *ÆCHom* i. 28. 4 . . . *on þam þriddan dæge his þrowunge*, *ÆCHom* i. 28. 9 . . . *on ðam feowerteogoðan dæge his æristes*, *ÆCHom* i. 312. 10 *þæs ymbe fiftig daga* (sometimes wrongly translated 'about fifty days after'; see §1219), and *ÆCHom* ii. 496. 29 *æfter ðrim monðum ðises*. Prepositions, of course, may also occur; compare *Or* 88. 1 *7 sona þæs, þy æfterran geare* with *Or* 86. 29 *sona æfter þæm* and *Or* 168. 26 *raðe þæs* with *Or* 164. 27 *raþe æfter þæm*.

§1403. For showing the end of a period of time, there are three constructions with *ende*. The first is seen in *Dan* 523 *swefn wæs æt ende*, where *swefn* is nominative; the second, with the nominative of *ende* + a genitive of what is at an end, in

And 1055   cempan coste   cyning weorðadon,
                wyrda waldend,   þæs wuldres ne bið
                æfre mid eldum   ende befangen

and *Phoen* 364 *þonne him weorþeð ‖ ende lifes*; and the third in *ChristC* 1028 . . . *weorþeð foldræste ‖ eardes æt ende* (literally '[it] shall be at the end of the earthly rest, the dwelling'), *JDay* i 2 *feores bið æt ende ‖ anra gehwylcum*, and *Jud* 272 *þa wæs hyra tires æt ende*. Sweet, in a note in his *Reader* withdrawn by Onions (Sweet, *R.* 8, p. 220), plausibly explained the third construction as a blend of the first and second. Timmer (*Judith* 272, note) rejected this theory on the odd ground that the third construction 'occurs more often in Old English' and went on to suggest that 'the genitives are perhaps semi-adverbial'. I prefer to regard them as possessive and am inclined to accept Sweet's explanation. A further complication is presented by *Ex* 267 *fyrst is æt ende ‖ lænes lifes*, where *fyrst* is the subject of *is*. If *lænes lifes* is not dependent on *fyrst*—'the period of the transitory life is at an end'—we have an apparent fusion of the first and third patterns above.

(6) *Reference or respect?*

§1404. The standard grammars do not, as far as I have observed, speak of an OE genitive of reference or respect and I have not found it necessary to erect this category myself. But it is called in by Kemp Malone and others to explain the genitives in *Deor* 7 *þæs ofereode*;

þisses swa mæg—the refrain which appears six times in all—and *þæs cynerices* in

Deor 24   Sæt secg monig   sorgum gebunden,
               wean on wenan,   wyscte geneahhe
               þæt þæs cynerices ofercumen wære.

Like Kemp Malone, Erickson (*Arch. L.* 6 (1975), 77–84) assumes that the same explanation fits both passages. But he questions the former's view on two grounds: 'there appears, however, to be no convincing evidence that Old English had genitives of respect or indeed that the OE verbs *ofergan* and *ofercuman* could be used impersonally'.[20] But the two passages can be construed in different ways without recourse to either of these explanations.

§1405. If we follow Kemp Malone in taking the genitives in *Deor* 7 *þæs ofereode; þisses swa mæg* as 'genitives of reference or respect', we will translate 'It passed over in respect of that; it can (pass over) in respect of this.' Erickson remarks that 'the Wardale translation of the refrain . . .—"The sorrow of that passed; so may the sorrow of this"—is *surely correct*' [my italics] (op. cit., p. 83 n. 7), and argues that 'these genitives are not predicate pseudo-subjects as they would be if the constructions were really impersonal, but in fact real subjects or at least what remains of the real subjects after Postal-type deletions have taken place' (op. cit., p. 81). This—like the proposed MnE parallels—fails to carry conviction; it (almost) forces us to believe that the Anglo-Saxons (who were *surely ignorant* of Postal-type deletions) were capable of using the nominative and the genitive interchangeably; the OE personal construction is typified by *Or* 218. 3 . . . *þæt ilce yfel ofereode* . . . and *CP* 395. 26 *Ðyses middangeardes ansien ofergæð*, where 'deletion' of *ansien* has not occurred. Wahlén (pp. 69–86) offers material the cumulative effect of which—though not decisive—is to suggest that the impersonal use of *ofergan* without a formal subject *hit* is more likely to be idiomatic OE. Accepting this and explaining *þæs* and *þisses* as genitives of point of time from which (see §1402), we can (I think) translate: 'It passed over from that; it can from this.' The exact reference of *þæs* and *þisses* is a literary, not a syntactical, problem.

[20] Schibsbye (*EStudies*, 50 (1969), 380–1) tried unsuccessfully to solve the second problem for *Deor* 7 by understanding *man* as subject of *ofereode* and taking *þæs* and *þisses* as 'objective complements'; he translates 'a man . . . managed to survive in that; so may a man . . . in this'. But see §376.

§ 1406. Let us now turn to *Deor* 24. The verb *ofercuman* governs the accusative[21] and the personal passive seen in *Or* 178. 5 *þa wæron Cartainiense swa ofercumene . . .* is idiomatic; see § 856. To produce a similar pattern, Erickson (op. cit., p. 81) postulates 'deletion' of a 'nominative, something with features similar to English *rule(r)*'. Again, this fails to carry conviction. We will do better to supply nom. *wea* from *wean* in the preceding line. This is no more violent than supplying nom. *burg* in *ÆCHom* i. 30. 7 *to Iudeiscre byrig, seo wæs Dauides*, acc. *hyge* in *Wan* 17 from nom. *hyge* in *Wan* 16, *he* in *Beo* 68 from *him* in *Beo* 67, or nom. *fugel* in *Phoen* 140 from *fugles* in *Phoen* 125, and can easily be paralleled from MnE.

§ 1407. We must, however, conclude that one of Erickson's points is well taken: 'there appears . . . to be no convincing evidence that Old English had genitives of respect' (op. cit., p. 77).

d. The dative and instrumental cases

(1) Introductory remarks

§ 1408. The dative/instrumental alone can denote the means or instrument and occasionally may perhaps denote the agent; see §§ 1365–70 and 1371–8. The main adverbial functions of these cases are to express manner, accompaniment, degree or measure, place, time, and cause.

§ 1409. The use of the dative *weorce* seen in *BlHom* 217. 22 *7 him wæs þæt swiþe myccle weorce þæt he swa ungefulwad forðferan sceolde*—for further examples see BT, s.v. *weorc* VII, and the ASPR note on *Jud* 93—can be compared with the use of prepositional phrases such as those seen in *Or* 194. 8 *eallum Romanum to ðæm mæstan ege*, *BlHom* 51. 9 *eal hit him wyrþ to teonan*, and *BlHom* 225. 27 *Wæs he toþæs arfæst þæt him wæs æghweþer on weorce ge þæt he leng from Cristes onsyne wære, [ge] ðæt he þone gesawe.*

(2) Manner

§ 1410. The dative/instrumental of means or instrumentality (§§ 1365–70) shades into that of manner in examples like *Bede* 322. 2 *þa semninga gehyrdon we þa abbudissan inne hludre stefne cleopian,*

---

[21] The example cited by BTS (s.v. *ofercuman* III)—*LS* 4. 75. 8—in which *ofercuman* is supposed to govern the genitive, is the result of a scribe misconstruing *þæs* as a demonstrative and not a relative; we should read *þæs wuldorge*[*wor*]*c*.

Bede 346. 20 *Ond he forðon fægre ænde his lif betynde 7 geendade,*
Bede 42. 10 *7 þa godcundan geryno clænan muðe 7 clænre heortan*
halgedon 7 fremedon,

GenA 1   Us is riht micel   ðæt we rodera weard,
                wereda wuldorcining,   wordum herigen,
                modum lufien!,

and

GenA 1917   and geþancmeta   þine mode
                on hwilce healfe   þu wille hwyrft don. . . .

Hofer (p. 386) detects a local as well as an instrumental element in
the last two examples and others like them.

§1411. Davis (Sweet, *Pr.* 9, p. 47) and Quirk and Wrenn (QW, p. 67)
see in this acceptance of the endings of the dat. sg. *-e* and the dat. pl.
-um to express means and manner the source of their use to form
adverbs. So we find *PPs* 54. 10 *fæcne* 'maliciously', *BlHom* 49. 6
nede 'of necessity', *ÆCHom* i. 126. 6 *yfele* 'grievously', *Beo* 741
unwearnum 'irresistibly', *Or* 17. 5 *styccemælum* 'here and there', and
ÆCHom i. 508. 12 *stæpmælum* 'step by step'. For further examples,
see Kress, pp. 30-1; Wülfing, i, §§91-2; Hofer, pp. 396-8; and *OEG*,
§668. On constructions like *ÆCHom* i. 74. 26 *astrehtum handum*,
see §§3810-11.

(3) *Accompaniment*

§1412. The dative/instrumental of accompaniment—which is akin
to that of manner—is found alone with verbs of motion, e.g. *Bede*
132. 6 *þa for he him togegnes ungelice weorode, ChronA* 74. 28
(878) *7 he lytle werede unieþelice æfter wudum for,* and

GenA 2453   Comon Sodomware,
                geonge and ealde,   gode unleofe
                corðrum miclum,

and with verbs of rest, e.g. *ChronA* 46. 28 (755) *7 þa geascode he*
þone cyning lytle werode on wifcyþþe on Merantune, Dream 69
Reste he ðær mæte weorode, and *Dream* 123 *þær ic ana wæs* ‖ *mæte*
werede. It also occurs, of course, governed by a preposition, e.g.
(with verbs of motion) *Bede* 270. 23 . . . *þæt he geseah Ceaddan*
sawle his broðor mid engla weorude of heofonum astigan and

GenA 2045   Him þa Abraham gewat   and þa eorlas þry
                þe him ær treowe sealdon   mid heora folcgetrume,

and (with verbs of rest) *Bede* 158. 8 . . . *mid his þegnum þe him mid*
wæron and *Beo* 1127 *Hengest ða gyt wælfægne winter wunode mid*

Finne. For further examples see Kress, pp. 19–21, and Green 1913, §138.

§1413. There is no doubt that some prepositional phrases expressing accompaniment must be construed with nouns or pronouns, and not with verbs, e.g. *Bede 152. 24 7 hine mid ealle his weorode adilgade* and *ChronA 76. 1 (878) 7 hiene mon þær ofslog, and dccc monna mid him*, and that others can be so taken, e.g. *ChronA 84. 20 (894) swa oft swa þa oþre hergas mid ealle herige utforon* and

ChristB 517   We mid þyslice   þreate willað
                   ofer heofona gehlidu   hlaford fergan.

The same possibility arises with similar phrases without prepositions, e.g. *ChronA 74. 28, ChronA 46. 28, Dream 69* (all in §1412), and *ChronA 76. 2 (878) 7 þæs on Eastron worhte Ælfred cyning lytle werede geweorc æt Æþelinga eigge.* In my opinion however, such examples provide support neither for Kershaw's proposition (p. 162) that in

Wan 6   Swa cwæð eardstapa,   earfeþa gemyndig,
                 wraþra wælsleahta,   winemæga hryre,

'as the text stands, *hryre* can hardly be taken otherwise than as a loose causal or comitative instrumental' nor for the Bliss–Dunning translation based on it—' "remembering the fierce battles accompanying the deaths of his kinsmen", i.e. "the fierce battles in which his kinsmen died" '. See further my comments in §65 and in *ASE* 4 (1975), 14–15. The adjectival and adverbial use of phrases (both with and without prepositions) is discussed at greater length elsewhere; see the General Index.

(4) *Degree or measure*

§1414. The dative/instrumental of manner shades into that of degree or measure. This may modify a verb, e.g. *ÆCHom* i. 130. 16 *and hi micclum ure mod gladiað* and *ÆCHom* i. 242. 33 . . . *he cyðde hu micclan he lufað his Fæder*; an adjective or participle, e.g. *ÆCHom* ii. 462. 31 . . . *we sind miccle rottran þonne ða fugelas* and *ÆCHom* ii. 462. 34 *Mannes gecynd is micclum gewurðod* . . . ; an adjective + a noun, e.g. *ÆCHom* i. 306. 31 *and hi habbað swa miccle maran edlean æt Gode* . . . ; another expression of degree, e.g. *ÆCHom* ii. 462. 28 . . . *hu miccle swiðor wile God foresceawian urne bigleofan*; an expression of time, e.g. *ÆCHom* i. 206. 13 *lytle ær*, *ÆCHom* i. 102. 29 *feower þricum lator*, and *ÆLS* 32. 3 *þrim gearum ær he forðferde*; and an expression of place, e.g. *BlHom* 193. 12 *þrim milum fram Rome byrig.* It will be observed that the modified element is frequently a comparative, as in *ÆCHom* ii. 462. 31, *ÆCHom* i. 306. 31, *ÆCHom* ii. 462. 28, and other examples quoted above, in *ChronA* 91. 28 (901) *7 he heold þæt rice oþrum healfum læs þe xxx wintra*, and in *CP* 5. 24 . . . *7 woldon ðæt her ðy mara wisdom on londe wære ðy we ma geðeoda cuðon.* On this last construction see §3339.

§1415. Callaway (*MLN* 37 (1922), 129–34) rightly concludes that in examples involving an expression of time such as those in §1414 and *Or* 208. 22 *Æfter þæm þe Romeburg getimbred wæs DC wintrum* . . . , the dative is used in a construction of native origin. The same is true of the other datives of degree or measure in the previous section. But Callaway's usual acumen seems to me to desert him when he claims (ibid.) that *Or* 208. 22 and the like embody, not the dative of measure or the 'dative denoting degree of difference' but 'the Quasi-Durative Dative of Time', in which 'the dative gives the time of one event by referring to another event either antecedent or subsequent thereto, and of necessity expresses at once both time when and time how long . . .'. His first argument—that in examples like *Or* 56. 13 *Ær þæm þe Romeburg getimbred wære xxgum wintrum, Læcede-moniæ 7 Mesiane, Creca leode, him betweonum winnende wæron xx wintra* . . . , Latin *Anno vicesimo ante Urbem conditam Lacedaemonii contra Messenios propter spretas virgines suas in solemni Messeniorum sacrificio, per annos viginti bellantes, ruinae suae totas Graeciae vires inplicuerunt*, 'the writer purposely uses the dative to designate time when and the accusative to designate time how long'—is inconclusive; it could just as easily be said that the writer purposely uses the dative to designate the 'degree of difference'. And his second argument—that 'in most of the examples of the Quasi-durative Dative in *Orosius*, the Old English dative translates a Latin ablative, singular, of time when'—in my opinion demonstrates that he is wrong. The dative plural *xxgum wintrum* in *Or* 56. 13 above cannot possibly denote time when; that would require a dative singular parallel to the Latin *anno vicesimo*. So it is a dative of degree or measure with the comparative *ær*, parallel to *ÆCHom* i. 206. 13 *lytle ær* and *ÆLS* 32. 3 *þrim gearum ær he forðferde.* The same is true of all the examples of the alleged 'Quasi-durative Dative', for all involve dative plurals like *xxgum wintrum*.

(5) *Place*

§1416. The dative can denote place where, e.g. *Bede* 26. 27 . . . *æfter rime fif Moyses boca, ðam seo godcunde æ awriten is* and

Sea 14   hu ic earmcearig   iscealdne sæ
                  winter wunade   wræccan lastum.

But this, as Hofer (pp. 399–401) and Quirk and Wrenn (QW, p. 66) agree, is rare; a preposition + the dative is usual even in the early texts. But *Bo* 68. 21 *forðæm hi hine ne magon tobrædan geond ealle eorðan, þeah hi on sumum lande mægen; forðæm þeah he sie anum gehered, þonne bið he oðrum unhered; þeah he on þam lande sie mære, þonne bið he on oðrum unmære* provides two examples of the dative alone apparently expressing place where alongside three with the preposition *on*.

§1417. The dative of place whither is found with the preposition *to*, e.g. *ÆCHom* i. 376. 28 *He ða leat to ðæs caseres eare. ÆCHom* ii. 462. 22 *we gelyfað þæt he gegæð Gode* and *ÆCHom* ii. 554. 23 *and ge sylfe him gegað þurh godum geearnungum* seem to offer examples with no preposition; see further BTS, s.v. *gegan* B. II. (1). But they can be described as datives of interest—'he goes into God's keeping' and 'you yourselves obey him'—and, in the absence of any incontestable examples, are better so taken.

§1418. The uninflected form *ham* after verbs of motion, as in *ÆHom* 17. 245 *Far þe ham to þinum hiwum*, can be taken as accusative; see §1386.

§1419. Hofer (p. 385) sees the dative denoting the space over or through which a movement takes place in three examples from the Junius MS, all with dat. sg. *foldwege* or *flodwege*. They are *GenA* 2873 *and onette* || *forð foldwege, GenA* 2511 *Gewit þu nergean þin* || *feorh foldwege*, and *Ex* 105 *sæmen æfter* || *foron flodwege*. These are akin to the dative of means; we need not erect a separate category.

§1420. An element of place can be detected in some datives of specification (see §1356), e.g. *ÆCHom* i. 422. 7 *Ic wæs blind bam eagum*, and in some datives which could be called manner, attendant circumstances, or even means, e.g. *ÆCHom* ii. 30. 19 . . . *and gemette ealle hire bearn mid ormætre cwylminge cwacigende eallum limum* and the examples in §1419. Whether *neah* in *Bede* 38. 6 *þa com he to swiðstremre ea, seo floweþ neah ðære ceastre wealle, GuthA* 172 *Him wæs engel neah*, and the like, is an adjective, an adverb, or a preposition, is a matter of terminology.

(6) *Time*

§1421. Schrader (p. 19) suggests that the dative answers the question 'How long?' and the instrumental the question 'When?'. All his datives are plural, e.g. *ÆCHom* ii. 490. 10 *and hi ðrim dagum ne onbirigdon ætes ne wætes*, and all his instrumentals are singular, e.g. *ÆGram* 148. 4 *ic tæce gyt to dæg oððe sume dæg* and *ÆCHom* ii. 134. 25 *þa gesæt he sume dæge*, where we have respectively the uninflected form *dæg* and the dat. sg. *dæge*. This distinction, of course, cannot stand. But the dative/instrumental can express both point of time when and duration of time how long.

§1422. The former needs little exemplification: *Or* 226. 17 *þære ilcan niht*, *ChronA* 88. 27 (894) *Đa þy ylcan gere* . . . (but *ChronA* 88. 14 (895) *Ond þa sona æfter þæm on ðys gere* and *ChronA* 84. 1 (893) *Her on þysum geare* . . .), the last clause in *ÆCHom* i. 180. 17 *We lybbað mislice on twelf monðum: nu sceole we ure gymeleaste on þysne timan geinnian, and lybban Gode, we ðe oðrum timan us sylfum leofodon* (but note alongside *oðrum timan* the two uses of the prep. *on*), and *ÆCHom* ii. 182. 26 *þa gecom he sume dæge to hyre cytan*. More examples will be found in Hofer, pp. 401-2, Kress, p. 31, and Wülfing, i, §93.

§1423. Schrader (p. 19) cites as examples of the dative expressing duration of time *ÆCHom* ii. 490. 10 (§1421), *ÆCHom* ii. 368. 35 *Efne ic beo mid eow eallum dagum*, and *ÆCHom* ii. 286. 25 *Oðrum dagum þu underfenge me on minum limum*. The last is certainly point of time; Thorpe translates 'on other days . . .'. And the other two could be so taken—*ðrim dagum* as 'on three days' and *eallum dagum* 'on all days'. So too in *ÆCHom* i. 154. 26 *Se mona deð ægðer ge wycxð ge wanað: healfum monðe he bið weaxende, healfum he bið wanigende*, we can follow Thorpe's 'for half a month . . . for a half' or can translate 'in one half . . . in the other'. This does not seem surprising, for the difference between the two is often notional. For example, it seems clear that the accusative *ane niht* denotes duration of time 'throughout a night' in *ÆCHom* i. 290. 14 *þa wacode se bisceop ane niht on Godes cyrcan*; Ælfric goes on: *ÆCHom* i. 290. 16 *Hi comon ða þæs on mergen to ðam gemote*. But few reading Thorpe's translation 'Then the bishop watched one night in God's church' would ponder whether 'one night' implied duration or point of time. And when one considers examples like *Or* 19. 13 *gyf man on niht wicode, 7 ælce dæge hæfde ambyrne wind* and *Bede* 390. 2 *7 ofer þæt ealle ðy dæge ne ablan 7 þære æfterfylgendan nihte, ða hwile ðe he wacian meahte—swa swa ða sægdon ða ðer onwearde wæron*—*þæt he a hwæthwugu spræce*, one can sympathize with Wülfing's failure (or refusal) to distinguish between time when and time how long (i, §§93 and 125). The same difficulty is apparent when we compare the translations which follow of three examples discussed by Yamakawa (1980, pp. 10–12): the two apparent accusative singulars in *BlHom* 127. 34 . . . *hongaþ leohtfæt, 7 þa beoð simle mid ele gefylde 7 æghwylce niht byrnaþ; 7 to þon leohte 7 beorhte scinaþ ælce niht* . . . (Morris and Yamakawa 'all the night . . . each night') and the dative singular in *BlHom* 91. 28 *7 syx dagum ær þissum dæge gelimpeþ syllice tacn æghwylce ane dæge* (Morris and Yamakawa 'each day'); and when we consider the fluctuations between accusative and dative singular forms in the examples cited in BTS, s.v. *niht* 'IV. (1) used to mark an occasion or a point of time'. Indeed, I have begun to wonder whether forms in *-e* such as *æghwylce* and *ælce* in *BlHom* 127. 34 may not be dative singular feminine by analogy with masc. *-e*, as in *BlHom* 91. 28 above; cf. *nihtes* (§1390) and note *Bede(T)* 90. 30 *æghwelce niht* but *Bede(O, Ca) æghwylcre niht*.

§1424. However, those who are reluctant to accept that *ÆCHom* ii. 490. 10 and *ÆCHom* ii. 368. 35 (both in §1423) express point of time can follow Callaway (*MLN* 37 (1922), 138) in regarding them as 'durative datives' imitating the Latin durative ablative; he compares *ÆCHom* ii. 368. 35 with *Matt* 28. 20 *et ecce ego uobis cum sum omnibus diebus usque ad consummationem saeculi* (where all the OE versions printed by Skeat have the accusative except for *Li allum dagum*). For, when we are confronted with the oft-quoted pair *Exod* 12. 15 *7 etað ðeorf seofon dagas*, Latin *septem diebus azyma comedetis*, but *Exod* 12. 19 *Ne beo nan gebyrmed mete seofon dagum on eowrum husum*, Latin *septem diebus fermentum non inuenietur in domibus uestris*, we cannot deny that the OE dative could be used to express what seems to be duration of time. But in my opinion the accusative in *Exod* 12. 15 is the native idiom and the dative in *Exod* 12. 19 is an imitation of the Vulgate use of the ablative 'to denote the time during which anything takes place, which is denoted in Cl.L. by the Acc. case' (Nunn, p. 25). Here I agree with Callaway (loc. cit., p. 136) that 'the presence of an adjective of measure [such as *eall, long, micel*] was only a slight factor in the development of the Durative Dative Proper in Old English'[22] and that 'the chief factor in the use of the dative to denote duration of time in Old English (both in West-Saxon and in Northumbrian) was the presence, in most instances, of a durative ablative in the Latin original'. The

---

[22] Indeed, I doubt its relevance. But see Callaway, ibid., pp. 135–6.

evidence he presents (ibid., pp. 136–41) is strong: *Jul* 508 *widan feore* is the only example he found in the poetry 'and that is in a poem known to be based on a Latin original';[23] 'the construction is practically unknown in the more original prose (the *Anglo-Saxon Chronicle* and Wulfstan)'; none of the forty-six ablatives of time how long noted by Callaway in *Orosius* is rendered by a durative dative, forty by an accusative; and the dative of time how long begins to appear under Latin influence in Ælfric's translation of the Old Testament and in the Rushworth, Lindisfarne, and West-Saxon, Gospels. But in all these except Lindisfarne, the accusative predominates, as the following table, based on Callaway's figures, shows:

Text	Duration of time expressed by			
	Latin ablative	OE accusative	OE dative	Other OE construction
Old Testament	140	80	8	52
West-Saxon Gospels	37	33	2	2
Rushworth Gospels				
(*incomplete figures*)	19	14	5	—
Lindisfarne Gospels	39	16	22	1

Further support comes from the history of the durative dative in the kindred Germanic languages. So, as Callaway sums up (ibid., pp. 140–1),

this conclusion seems irresistible . . . the True Durative Dative of Time . . . is a construction foreign to Old English and, probably, to the Germanic languages as a whole. . . . More than that: the durative dative proper never became naturalized in Old English (West Saxon and Northumbrian) or, probably, in the Germanic languages as a whole; in each, time how long was habitually expressed by an accusative, not by a dative, even in translations of late Latin texts abounding in ablatives of time how long.

§1425. The dative answers the questions 'How many times?', 'How often?', e.g. *Or* 244. 8 *feower siþan* and *Josh* 6. 15 *seofon siðon* (on the use of undeclined forms immediately before the qualified noun see *OEG*, §683), and, shading into point of time, *ÆCHom* i. 176. 2 *hwilon* 'sometimes' and *ÆCHom* i. 154. 17 *hwiltidum* 'at times'.

§1426. The dative also answers the question 'On which particular occasion?', e.g. *Or* 82. 7 *þriddan siþe*, *ÆCHom* i. 492. 12 *oðre siðe*,

---

[23] We find *widan feore* in *Prec* 23 and *to widan feore* in *Ex* 548, in *ChristA* 230 and 277, and in *ChristC* 1343 and 1543. Doubts about the metrical validity of *widan feore* have been raised; see R. Woolf, *Juliana* (London, 1955), note on line 191.

and *Prec* 27 *feorþan siðe*. For further examples of this and the previous idiom, see Wülfing, i, §§93 and 125, and my §591.

(7) *Cause*

§1427. The existence of a causal instrumental in OE seems to be established by examples like *ChronA* 62. 23 (836) *7 þy fultumode Beorhtric Offan þy he hæfde his dohtor him to cuene, BlHom* 23. 35 *Eal þis he þrowode for ure lufan 7 hælo, þy he wolde þæt we þæt heofenlice rice onfengon*, and *ÆCHom* i. 82. 28 *ac hit wære to hrædlic . . . ; þi forhradode Godes engel þæs arleasan geþeaht*, where *þy/þi* carries the sense 'for that [reason]' and is used either as an adverb 'therefore' or a conjunction 'because'. But many possible examples of a causal dative/instrumental can be otherwise explained. Thus *ðe* in *ÆCHom* ii. 538. 11 *gif ðu unwær bist, þu bist ðe swiðor geswenct* expresses neither cause nor degree (§3337) and *þysse andsware* in *ÆCHom* ii. 482. 26 *Me stent ege þysse andsware*, translated by Thorpe as 'through this answer', could be an objective genitive. Those of Hofer's examples (pp. 393-6) which do not involve *þy* (as does *Ex* 349) can be otherwise explained or described—as datives of means (*GenA* 2000 and *Dan* 277), of degree (*GenA* 422), of specification (*Dan* 258), and with a verb which takes the dative (*GenA* 1523).

B. APPOSITION

1. DEFINITION AND INTRODUCTORY REMARKS

§1428. The definition of apposition given by Pei and Gaynor (PG, p. 16) has been adopted with modifications: 'the use of paratactically joined linguistic forms occurring in the same clause or sentence which refer to the same referent and which have the same or similar grammatical form and function, but not the same meaning'. This definition allows us to exclude:

(1) asyndetically and syndetically co-ordinated groups, e.g. *ÆCHom* ii. 360. 32 *heofonwara, eorðwara, helwara, Beo* 1022 *hroden hildecumbor, helm, and byrnan*, and *ÆCHom* i. 4. 31 *tacna and wundra and ehtnysse*;

(2) idiomatically separated groups (§§1464-72);

(3) elements joined by *ac, oþþe, ne*, and the like;

(4) appositional and descriptive genitives[24] (§§1288-91);

---

[24] Peltola includes these (1960, pp. 166-7), thereby offending against his own principles (1960, p. 160).

(5) other case and prepositional phrases dependent on nouns;
(6) 'appositional *swa*-phrases': see §§3320-1;
(7) some *þæt is* constructions[24] (§§44(3) and 1443);
(8) sentences and adjective clauses.[24]

§1429. Ries proposed a twofold division of appositional constructions into 'appositions proper', e.g. 'Mr Bones the butcher', and
'appended groups', e.g. 'Mr Bones, much esteemed in this town'; see
TPS 1941, pp. 47-9. These can be distinguished in OE, e.g. *ÆCHom*
ii. 386. 4 *Crist is ana mannes Bearn, anes mannes and na twegra,
mædenes and na weres* but *ÆCHom* i. 358. 18 *his Fæder liflic on-
sægednys, on lambes wisan geoffrod* and *BlHom* 115. 18 *7 we him
fleondum fylgeaþ 7 hine feallendne lufiaþ.* Both can occur in the
same sentence, e.g. *ÆCHom* i. 32. 5 *ure Hælend, Godes Sunu,
euenece and gelic his Fæder.* But the distinction between 'appositional' and 'predicative' is not always clear. Thus Visser (i, §645)
sees an 'objective complement' in *fleondum* and *feallendne* in *BlHom*
115. 18 above. Peltola (1960, p. 162) observes that we 'may hesitate
between the appositional and the quasi-predicative character' of *reþe
cwellere* in *ÆLS* 19. 5 *and he rixode twentig geara reðe cwellere* and
finds a similar problem with *ÆLS* 10. 119 *He is hundredes ealdor
and hæfð godes ege swyðe rihtwys wer* (1960, pp. 170-1).[25] So there
is no point in following Ries. Peltola (1960, pp. 164-7), after discussing various methods of classification, comes down in favour of
a threefold division—extraposition, loose apposition, close apposition—based on 'the "closeness" of the construction'. As we shall
see, this system is open to certain criticisms which make its use
dangerous. Indeed, Peltola himself is forced to admit (1960, p. 172)
that 'the loose apposition cannot be strictly distinguished from an
expression in extraposition on the one hand, or from a close apposition on the other'. So, instead of adopting a ready-made classification, I have tried to answer the following questions:

What elements are found in apposition?

Do elements in apposition always agree in case?

What positions in the sentence do these elements occupy?

In what combinations and functions do they occur?

§1430. However, it must be stressed that certain distinctions cannot be made because they depend on a knowledge of the rhythms
and intonation patterns of OE. The same is true in MnE, for it is
impossible for us to decide whether five or six people were injured

---

[25] In classifying this and similar examples as 'extraposition', he departs unnecessarily from
the meaning which—he says (1960, p. 167)—was given the term by its coiner Jespersen.

when we read 'A London bus driver his wife the conductress and three passengers were injured today when a tree fell on the bus in which they were travelling.' Much of Peltola's classification (1960, *passim*) depends on the assumption that OE rhythmic and intonation patterns were identical with those of MnE and on the arbitrary identification of particular OE sentences with one possible MnE equivalent rather than with another. Thus he writes (1960, p. 186) of 'the development of the loose appositional construction *Ælmær, Ælfrices sunu* (with a pause between the IC's [Immediate Constituents]) to the close construction *Ælmær Ælfrices sunu* (name + byname, without a pause)'. I can see no basis for such remarks.

2. APPOSITIONAL ELEMENTS

§1431. Appositional groups usually consist of one or more of the following elements: nouns, adjectives, demonstratives, possessives, numerals, and personal pronouns, e.g. *ÆCHom* i. 80. 19 *Stemn is gehyred on heannysse, micel wop and ðoterung, ÆCHom* i. 4. 20 *Crist ure Drihten, ÆCHom* i. 146. 33 *He cwæð, se apostol Paulus, BlHom* 71. 4 . . . *heora cining cymeþ, milde 7 monþwære, ChronA* 70. 26 (871) *Sidroc eorl se gioncga, BlHom* 175. 22 *se heora lareow, Bede* 136. 7 *gif þeos lar owiht cuðlicre 7 gerisenlicre brenge* . . . , Latin *si haec noua doctrina certius aliquid attulit* . . . ,[26] *Matt(WSCp)* 20. 21 *þas mine twegen suna, ÆCHom* ii. 396. 32 *Sume hi comon feorran* (see §§402-16), and *ÆCHom* i. 402. 31 . . . *hi wæron gesamnode binnan ðære byrig Hierusalem, six hund ðusend manna.* . . . To these can be added infinitives and noun clauses, e.g. *Or* 52. 8 *Hit is unieðe to gesecgenne hu monege gewin siþþan wæron* . . . , *ÆCHom* i. 394. 15 *ac hit ne fremede him swa gedon,* and *ÆCHom* i. 42. 13 *þæt is ece lif, þæt hi ðe oncnawon soðne God,* and participles and participial phrases; see the General Index. As Bliss (1958, p. 10) notes, verbs may stand in apposition to one another, e.g. *Beo* 306 *Guman onetton, sigon ætsomne*; see further §§1529 and 1923. Adverbs and adverbial modifiers such as case and prepositional phrases may also be in apposition with one another, e.g. *ChronA* 88. 27 (894) *Ða þy ylcan gere onforan winter* . . . , *ChronA* 84. 1 (893) *Her on þysum geare,* and *ÆCHom* i. 170. 32 *upp on ane dune.*

§1432. A sentence may, of course, contain more than one appositional group, e.g. *ChronA* 70. 26 (871) and *ChronA* 88. 27 (894)— both in §1431—*ÆCHom* i. 202. 9 *his wif, hyre magan, Elisabeth,*

---

[26] Wülfing rightly argues that *owiht* here and *auht* in *Bo* 25. 19 are substantival rather than adverbial, as Einenkel suggested; see *Ang.* 27 (1904), 240.

ÆCHom i. 540. 17 *heahfæderas, eawfæste and wuldorfulle weras on heora life, witegena fæderas,* and *ÆCHom* ii. 362. 25 . . . *se Halga Gast, seðe is þæs Fæder Gast, and þæs Suna, heora begra Lufu and Willa, him bam efenedwistlic.*

§1433. Those seeking more examples than are quoted in these sections will find them in Wülfing, i (detailed references below), Bauch (Abschnitt I), Peltola 1960 (*passim*), and in most of 'the eighteen German dissertations' and of 'the prose text dissertations'.

3. APPOSITIVE PARTICIPLES

§1434. Participles such as those in *CP* 151. 24 *Ac monige scylda openlice witene beoð to forberanne* and *ÆCHom* ii. 132. 24 *Cuthberhtus se halga biscop, scinende on manegum geearnungum* . . . are often described as appositive. The term has its uses, though the difficulty of distinguishing appositional elements from attributive and predicative ones is especially apparent here; see §685 and Callaway 1901, pp. 153 and 181. As Callaway—to whom this discussion is much indebted—points out (1901, pp. 150-3), such appositive participles usually appear in post-position. They are often uninflected.[27] When inflected, they are almost invariably declined strong. But there are even in Ælfric examples in which a participle in pre-position comes close to being appositive, e.g. *ÆCHom* ii. 90. 15 *Se weg is seo fortredene heorte fram yflum geðohtum* . . . (where *fortredene* is a weak form) and *ÆLS* 27. 117 *Eala þu scinende rod swiþor þonne tungla* (where *scinende* may be strong or weak; see §1247). Appositive participles are most common in the nominative, but the dative is demanded in *ÆCHom* ii. 180. 20 *Se wælhreowa ehtere Thesalla* . . . *draf hine [Benedictus] ætforan him ridendum*, even though the reference is to the subject. They may govern nouns, e.g. *ÆCHom* ii. 578. 28 *and þæt folc . . . ham gewende, ðancigende þam Ælmihtigan ealra his goda* and *ÆCHom* ii. 598. 23 *and gescyld þine ðeowan þinum mægenðrymme underðeodde*, but need not, e.g. *ÆCHom* ii. 172. 26 *Hwæt la, ne æteowode ic inc bam slapendum* . . . ? and *ÆCHom* ii. 182. 2 *and he ða þearle ablicged aweg tengde*. . . . For full statistics and lists of examples, see Callaway 1901, pp. 154-267.

§1435. Callaway (1901, pp. 268-70) distinguishes three functions for the appositive participle. It may be equivalent to a dependent

---

[27] The frequency with which *-ende* appears for *-endne* in the accusative singular masculine may be due to the sequence of homorganic consonants and/or to confusion with *ja*- or *i*- nouns. Visser (ii, §§1011-15) gets himself into a tangle over this variation. See §§1438-9.

adjective clause and may be either limiting, e.g. *ÆCHom* ii. 186. 23
. . . *he cyðde his forðsið on ær sumum his leorningcnihtum mid him
drohtnigendum and sumum oðrum on fyrlenum stowum wunigendum*,
or non-limiting, e.g. *ÆCHom* ii. 128. 32 *Ongann ða Augustinus mid
his munecum to geefenlæcenne þæra apostola lif, mid singalum
gebedum and wæccan and fæstenum Gode ðeowigende*. . . . It may
be equivalent to a dependent adverb clause, e.g. *ÆCHom* ii. 250. 28
Se Hælend ða stod on ðam domerne gelædd (time) and

Beo 480   Ful oft gebeotedon   beore druncne
                   ofer ealowæge   oretmecgas

(time or cause). It may be 'substantially equivalent to an Independent Clause' and denote either an accompanying circumstance, e.g.
ÆLS 5. 457 [*þa cwelleras*] *on niht behyddon his halgan lichaman
. . . secgende him betwynan þæt huru ða cristenan ne becuman to his
lice*, or repeat the idea of the principal verb, e.g. *ÆLS* 3. 522 *and
Æffrem þa spræc mid greciscum gereorde, god herigende*. There is
a certain artificiality here. All appositive participles are to some
extent attributive; *Beo* 480-1 could just as easily be rendered 'The
warriors who were drunk . . .' as 'The warriors, when (because) they
were drunk . . .'. There is some idea of time in *ÆLS* 5. 457. So the
figures for the three divisions given by Callaway (1901, p. 270) with
such exactitude must be viewed with suspicion. But we need not
deny that the distinctions can often be made. However, it is only fair
to say that Callaway himself recognized the existence of these—and
other—difficulties of classification (1901, pp. 144-9, 268-70, 271-
2, 278, and so on). For further discussion and further examples—
including appositive participles denoting manner and means, time,
cause, purpose, concession, and condition—see Callaway 1901, pp.
270-96. On the distribution of appositive participles in 'Alfredian'
texts, see further Liggins, *Ang.* 88 (1970), 314-15.

§1436. Callaway discusses the origin of the appositive participle
(1901, pp. 297-320 and 349-51), concluding that in some uses it is
native and in others foreign: 'Anglo-Saxon was favorable to the
appositive participle with pronounced adjectival (descriptive) force,
but was unfavorable to the appositive participle with strong verbal
(assertive) force' (1901, p. 351). Indeed, 'all present participles with
a direct object are due to Latin influence' (ibid.). The 'flexibility and
grace' of Ælfric's style—in contrast to 'the unwieldiness and the
monotony of Ælfred's style'—results from the former's skilful handling and the latter's neglect of many functions of the appositive participle (1901, p. 352). These judgements cannot be pursued here. But
cf. §§3825-6.

4. CONCORD

§1437. Appositional elements can, of course, be in apposition with any appropriate part of the sentence—subject, object, complement, genitive and dative phrases, adverbs, adverbial modifiers, and so on. Where concord is possible, the usual principles apply. Agreement in number is the rule, except when collective nouns are involved, e.g. *ChronA* 74. 10 (876) *7 hie þa under þam hie nihtes bestælon þære fierde se gehorsoda here . . .* ; see also §1440. Agreement in gender, too, is normal, but there are occasional exceptions; see §§43-4. Agreement in case is by definition the rule. When such agreement is lacking, we must either suspect the form involved or say that the elements are not really in apposition. Aberrant forms are most common with participles (§§1438-40) and with foreign names, e.g. *ÆCHom* ii. 490. 21 *binnon ðære scire Babilonia, ÆCHom* i. 30. 10 *on þære byrig Bethleem, ÆCHom* i. 200. 34 *to hire magan Elisabeth,* and *ÆCHom* ii. 308. 4 *mid twam mæssepreostum Euentius and Theodolus.* These are to be explained as uninflected datives; cf. *ÆCHom* i. 66. 30 *þisum twam gebroðrum Attico and Eugenio, Or* 224. 3 *ongean Aristonocuse þæm cyninge,* and *El* 391 *in Bethleme.* But, despite Barela (p. 49) and Peltola (1960, pp. 197-8), *Solil* 4. 5 *Wilna ðe to gode hælend modes and lichaman* and *ÆLS* 14. 39 *ðam hælende Criste ealra woruldra alysend* may not be examples of lack of concord, for *hælend* and *alysend* may be dative singular; see *OEG,* §633.

§1438. Problems of agreement would seem likely to arise with appositive participles because they are often uninflected. In practice, uninflected or improperly inflected forms of such participles usually cause no more difficulty than the occasional uninflected adjective such as *toweard* in *BlHom* 117. 30 *. . . ealle þa tacno 7 þa fore-beacno þa þe her ure Drihten ær toweard sægde* and *biter ond beaduscearp* in

Beo 2702   þa gen sylf cyning
                        geweold his gewitte,   wællseaxe gebræd
                        biter ond beaduscearp,   þæt he on byrnan wæg;

consider *Or* 88. 12 *. . . 7 him sædon from burgum 7 from tunum on eorþan besuncen, Judg* 16. 7 *Gif ic beo gebunden mid seofon rapum of sinum geworhte . . . , LS* 23. 751 *geic eac gebiddan þeahhwæðere for me on þyssere worulde hleorende . . . , Beo* 372 *Ic hine cuðe cnihtwesende,* and

GuthB 1259   ...   nelle ic lætan þe
                 æfre unrotne   æfter ealdorlege
                 meðne modseocne   minre geweorðan,
                 soden sorgwælmum.

Since *biddan* can take the accusative of the person asked or the accusative of the thing asked for, *unabeden* in *ÆCHom* ii. 372. 15 *God bead mancynne þæt hi hine biddan sceoldan, and he wile syllan unabeden þæt þæt we us ne wendon þurh ure bene* may be nominative singular masculine—BT, s.v., has 'unasked'—or accusative singular neuter—Thorpe has 'unprayed for'. But the difference is of little or no significance.

§1439. One might expect the absence of acc. sg. masc. *-ne* to be an especially fertile source of ambiguity. In practice the context is almost always decisive, as with *standende* in *ÆCHom* i. 46. 30, 46. 32, 48. 7, and 48. 31 *and se eadiga cyðere Stephanus hine geseah standende, forðan ðe he wæs his gefylsta* and *acenned* in *ÆCHom* ii. 596. 25 *Ic gelyfe on ænne God . . . and on ænne Crist, Hælend Drihten, þone ancennedan Godes Sunu, of ðam Fæder acenned ær ealle worulda . . . acennedne na geworhtne. . . .* So too in *ÆCHom* ii. 446. 28 *Ne beheolde ðu la minne ðeowan Iob, þæt nan man nis his gelica on eorðan, bilewite man and rihtwis, ondrædende God and yfel forbugende*, where strictly speaking the nominative participles and adjectives in the last phrase should be accusative agreeing with *Iob* or genitive agreeing with *his*. Cases of real ambiguity are exceptional. We perhaps need the Latin *Vt clericum suum cadendo contritum aeque orando ac benedicendo a morte reuocauerit* to be sure of the sense of *Bede* 22. 16 *Ðæt he his preosta ænne of horse fallende 7 gebrysedne gelice gebiddende 7 bletsigende fram deaðe gecyrde.* It is not clear who is particularly singled out as rejoicing in *ÆCHom* i. 56. 34 *nu todæg hi underfengon Stephanum blissigende on heora geferrædene* or in *ÆHomM* 15. 328 *and god sylf ne geþafode þæt ic gescynd wurde, ac butan besmitennysse he asende me ongean, on his sige blissigende and on eowre alysednysse.* Since the subject of *weallan* can be what flows (e.g. *Beo* 2693) or its source (e.g. *Beo* 515), *hioroweallende* in

Beo 2777   Bill ær gescod
            —ecg wæs iren—   ealdhlafordes
            þam ðara maðma   mundbora wæs
            longe hwile,   ligegesan wæg
            hatne for horde,   hioroweallende
            middelnihtum,   oð þæt he morðre swealt

may be nominative—BT glosses it 'fiercely boiling'—or accusative—Klaeber gives 'welling fiercely'. But even these ambiguities—the most serious I have noticed—cannot be said to be really serious.

§1440. Fluctuation between singular and plural forms of participles used with collective nouns is to be expected, e.g. *ÆCHom* i. 30. 22 *þa færlice . . . wearð gesewen micel menigu heofenlices werodes God herigendra and singendra . . .* and *ÆCHom* i. 596. 29 *þa betwux ðisum eode eall þæt folc to Egeas botle, ealle samod clypigende and cweðende. . . .*

§1441. Examples in which lack of concord certifies that the elements are not strictly in apposition—even though they refer to the same referent—can be divided into five groups. First and second, there are the naming and the vocative constructions discussed in §§1474-7 and 1244. Third, there are the expressions which have 'the character of an exclamation or a parenthetic remark . . . placed in extraposition, characterized by the absence of concord' (Peltola 1960, p. 198), e.g. *Bede* 336. 21 *Ono seo foresprecene Cristes þeowe Hilde abbudisse—ealle þa þe hy cupon . . . gewunedan heo modor cegean 7 nemnan* ('initial extraposition'; see further Wülfing, i. 348-9), *ÆLS* 3. 255 *and siþþan to ðan sancte þe on ðæra cyrcean læg Mercurius se martyr mid mycclum wurðmynte* ('medial extraposition', according to Peltola—though *Mercurius se martyr* may belong to the adjective clause), and *ÆCHom* i. 200. 30 *[ure Hælend] seðe æfre wæs wunigende on godcundnysse mid his Fæder, and mid þam Halgan Gaste, hi ðry an God untodæledlic* ('final extraposition'). In *ÆCHom* ii. 238. 2 *Iohannes se Godspellere awrat þæt Drihten cwæde to Nichodeme, an ðæra Iudeiscra ealdra, ðaða he mid geleafan his lare sohte . . . , an* seems to agree with *he* rather than *Nichodeme*, but is probably better described, following Peltola, as in extraposition. Despite Klaeber (3, p. xciii fn. 9), I would also include here

Beo 1830   Ic on Higelace wat
                   Geata dryhten,   þeah ðe he geong sy,
                   folces hyrde,   þæt he mec fremman wile
                   wordum ond weorcum . . . ,

translating 'As for Higelac, I know the lord of the Geats, [I know] that he . . .'; for the general construction cf. *Beo* 1180-3; for *witan* with accusative of a person see *Beo* 181 (note *cupon* in *Beo* 180) and *ChristA* 384; for *witan* with an accusative object and a noun clause, see *Ex* 291-3 and *And* 603-4; for *on Higelace* 'as for Higelac' cf. *on mec* 'as for me' in *Beo* 2650 (in both passages, I agree with the Wrenn–CH translation).

§1442. Fourth, there are examples in which uninflected forms of foreign names stand at the beginning of a sentence and are taken up by personal pronouns in the genitive or dative case which is syntactically required, e.g. *Or* 12. 19 *Nilus seo ea hire æwielme is neh þæm clife þære Readan Sæs, Or* 8. 28 *Affrica 7 Asia hiera landgemircu onginnað of Alexandria*, and *Or* 12. 16 *Seo Ægyptus þe us near is, be norþan hire is þæt land Palastine*. On these, see §§298 and 3880–1.

§1443. Fifth, there are *þæt is* constructions like *ÆCHom* i. 154. 22 *Nu hæbbe we þæt leoht on urum mode, þæt is Cristes geleafa* and *ÆCHom* ii. 226. 26 . . . *swa eac ða Iudeiscan smeadon niðfullice ymbe Cristes cwale, geeuenlæcende heora fæder, þæt is deofol*, in which the elucidating noun is nominative after *is*. This seems to be the rule; cf. §44(3). Examples like *ÆCHom* ii. 94. 26 *Witodlice ðam oðrum þe æt Godes weofode þeniað, þæt is, mæssepreostum and diaconum is eallunge forboden ælc hæmed*, 'to the others—that is— to priests and deacons', where the elucidating element is in apposition with that which it elucidates, are the exception in my collections.

§1444. In examples like *ÆCHom* i. 484. 26 *Herodes hiwode hine sylfne unrotne* and *ÆCHom* ii. 24. 27 *þa gesawon hi hine adligne*, we can (I suppose) speak of apposition or of accusative and infinitive constructions with *beon* or *wesan* unexpressed. See §§3766–76.

5. TAUTOLOGIC ELEMENTS

a. Anticipatory pronouns

§1445. A pronoun in the appropriate case, gender, and number, may anticipate a noun without or with qualifiers, e.g. *LS* 34. 682 *And he Malchus andwyrde* and *ÆCHom* i. 146. 33 *He cwæð, se apostol Paulus* . . . ; composite groups, e.g. *ÆCHom* ii. 172. 17 *þa ða hi awocon, se ealdor and his profost* . . . ; and infinitives and noun clauses, e.g. *Or* 52. 8, *ÆCHom* i. 394. 15, and *ÆCHom* i. 42. 13 (all in §1431). In these examples, the second appositional element may have been explanatory or emphatic, according to the intonation.

§1446. The two elements may be side by side, e.g. *LS* 34. 682 (§1445), or separated by (for example) an adverb alone, e.g. *LS* 34. 688 *He þa Malchus nyste hwæt he cweðan sceolde*; a verb (and its modifiers), e.g. *Bede* 26. 2 *Hit is welig þis ealond on wæstmum* and *ÆCHom* ii. 172. 17 (§1445); or larger syntactical units, e.g. *Bede* 274. 10 . . . *þæt heo eac swylce for hine se ðe him þa stowe gesealde a þa stondendan munecas þær to Drihtne cleopodon.* . . . For further examples, see Wülfing, i. 343 ff.

b. Recapitulatory pronouns

§1447. A personal pronoun or a demonstrative is often used tautologically and/or anacoluthically as a grammatical substitute for a preceding word or group of words. I agree with Peltola (1960, p. 167) that the reason may be either to help the speaker control the sentence-structure or to give emphasis; see further §§1893-6. The element 'recapitulated' may be a noun without or with qualifiers, e.g. *ÆCHom* i. 102. 22 *Swa eac treowa, gif hi beoð on fullum monan geheawene, hi beoð heardran, ÆCHom* ii. 18. 19 *Swa gelice eac se hæðena cyning Nabuchodonosor, he geseah ehsynes þæs lifigendan Godes Sunu,* and *WPol* 75. 77 *Bisceopes dægweorc, ðæt bið mid rihte his gebedu ærest*; a composite group, e.g. *BlHom* 237. 23 *Se eadiga Matheus þa and se haliga Andreas hie wæron cyssende him betweonon*; a pronoun, e.g. *ÆCHom* i. 96. 17 *Ac we ðe sind to Godes anlicnysse gesceapene . . . we sceolon of deaðe arisan* and (perhaps) *ÆCHom* i. 260. 32 *Se ðe ðis hylt, he bið Godes bearn*; or a noun clause, e.g. *ÆCHom* i. 160. 27 *þæt is þæt we sceolon smeagan hwæt he tæce, and hwæt him licige, and þæt mid weorcum gefyllan.*

§1448. The recapitulated element occurs initially or very near the beginning of the sentence and may be followed immediately by the recapitulating pronoun, e.g. *ÆCHom* ii. 18. 19 (§1447), or separated from it by (for example) an adverb alone, e.g. *CP* 35. 14 *Sua sua Saul se cyning, æresð he fleah ðæt rice*; an adjective clause, e.g. *ÆCHom* i. 96. 17 (§1447); another subordinate clause, e.g. *ÆCHom* i. 102. 22 (§1447); or a clause and other elements, e.g. *ÆCHom* i. 268. 26 and *ÆCHom* i. 154. 16 *þeos woruld, þeah ðe heo myrige hwiltidum geðuht sy, nis heo hwæðere ðe geliccre ðære ecan worulde.* For further examples see Peltola's first seven types of extraposition, which belong here (Peltola 1960, pp. 168-70).

6. ELEMENTS WHICH AMPLIFY THE GOVERNING ELEMENT

a. Introductory remarks

§1449. Attempts to distinguish too rigidly between 'descriptive' and 'limiting' appositional elements founder on the same rocks as attempts

to distinguish 'descriptive' and 'limiting' adjective clauses (§§2271-
83): elements which limit also describe; the speaker or writer often
intends no such distinction; and the classification will often depend
on the hearer's or reader's knowledge. Consider the phrase 'Winston
Churchill, the war-time Prime Minister of Great Britain'. To those
who in the 1950s had never heard of Winston Churchill the American
author of *Richard Carvel*, the words added to the name were merely
descriptive; for them there was only one Winston Churchill. In the
1970s, when his grandson has become a public figure, they are limiting. In a thousand years they may again be merely descriptive. I have
no doubt that similar variations existed in OE. We may, with Peltola
(1960, pp. 164-5), see *ÆCHom* i. 58. 3 *Iohannes se godspellere* and
ÆCHom i. 202. 4 *Iohannem ðone Fulluhtere* as examples of limiting
(restrictive) apposition. If we quote the first example in full—*Iohannes se godspellere Cristes dyrling*—we can probably agree that
Cristes dyrling is descriptive as long as *se godspellere* is there. But
Peltola's claim (ibid.) that *Hilarius se gelæreda biscop*—I have not
been able to trace this—exemplifies descriptive apposition which
'does not determine the referent, but gives information about it' is
meaningless without the context and/or further knowledge; there
may have been a frivolous monk called Hilarius. Again, the notion
that in *Scs Stephanus, se forma cyþere*—also untraced—and *ÆCHom*
ii. 596. 13 *Hælend Crist* 'the referent is completely determined by
each of the IC's' (ibid.) is false; other St. Stephens had churches dedi-
cated to them in Anglo-Saxon England (see F. G. Holweck, *A Bio-
graphical Dictionary of the Saints* (St. Louis, 1924)) and *Hælend*
would not have meant Christ to uninstructed pagans.

§1450. So I have not tried in the sections which follow to distinguish 'restrictive' and 'non-restrictive' apposition (Carlton 1970,
p. 49). But since to a greater or lesser degree every apposition with
which we are concerned 'offers a solution to the "problem" contained
in the governing word' (Peltola 1960, p. 173), we can perhaps try to
analyse the semantic relationship of the two elements, bearing in
mind that the various categories inevitably shade into one another.

b. Elements augmenting proper names

§1451. Such elements may indicate rank or title, e.g. *ÆCHom* i.
78. 8 *Herodes cyning, ÆCHom* i. 30. 1 *se Romanisca casere Octauianus,* and *ÆCHom* ii. 284. 6 *Gregorius se halga papa*; occupation, sex,
or relationship, e.g. *ÆCHom* i. 2. 11 *ic Ælfric munuc and mæssepreost, ÆCHom* ii. 4. 21 *of ðam halgan mædene Marian* and *ÆCHom*

i. 16. 10 *ðone mann Adam*, and *ÆCHom* i. 30. 5 *Ioseph Cristes fosterfæder*; physical and mental characteristics, e.g. *ChronA* 70. 26 (871) *Sidroc eorl se gioncga* and *ÆCHom* i. 392. 1 *Saulus se arleasa*; some particular aspect which the writer wishes to stress, e.g. *ÆCHom* ii. 526. 6 *Crist, cristenra manna Heafod, Ordfruma ælcere gife* and *ÆCHom* i. 286. 8 *We sprecað ymbe God, deaðlice be Undeaðlicum, tyddre be Ælmihtigum, earmingas be Mildheortum*; or a geographical category, e.g. *ÆCHom* ii. 490. 21 *binnon ðære scire Babilonia.*

c. Clarifying elements

§1452. The second element may clarify by explaining the first, e.g. *ÆCHom* ii. 260. 24 *Eft soðlice se Scyppend . . . his handgeweorc alysde, Adames ofspring* and *ÆCHom* ii. 586. 35 *seo gastlice cwen, Godes gelaðung, oððe gehwilc halig sawul*; by translating it, e.g. *ÆGram* 119. 14 *tempus tid, modus gemet, species hiw, figura gefegednyss, coniugatio gepeodnyss, persona had, numerus getel*; or by making it more specific, e.g. *ÆCHom* i. 170. 32 *upp on ane dune*, *ÆCHom* i. 58. 24 *Eft on fyrste, æfter Cristes upstige to heofonum*, *ÆCHom* ii. 372. 19 *me is neod to farenne*, and (with pronouns which are not tautologic) *ÆCHom* i. 272. 27 *swa eac we sceolon manega cristene men Criste on annysse gehyrsumian* and *ÆCHom* ii. 472. 31 . . . *us his apostolum.*

d. Enumerating elements

§1453. The second element may list the components of the first, which may be a noun, e.g. *ÆCHom* i. 508. 27 *Godes ðeowas . . . sangeras and ræderas and sacerdas* and *ÆCHom* ii. 360. 32 *ealle gesceafta, heofonwara, eorðwara, helwara . . .* , or a numeral (+ a noun), e.g. *ÆCHom* ii. 430. 25 *þas feower nytenu getacnodon ða feower godspelleras, Mattheus, Marcus, Lucas, Iohannes*; or may amplify it by a pair of antonyms, e.g. *ÆCHom* i. 526. 17 . . . *ealle þa ðe hi gemetton, ægðer ge yfele ge gode.*

e. Repetitive elements

§1454. The second element may repeat the first, either without (significant) addition or variation, e.g. *ÆCHom* i. 20. 16 *and se ylca seðe ableow on Adames lichaman and him forgeaf sawle, se ylca forgyfð cildum sawle and lif* and *ÆCHom* i. 168. 23 *Eaðe mihte God, seðe awende wæter to wine . . . eaðelice he mihte awendan ða stanas to hlafum*, or with a qualifying attribute or adjunct, e.g. *ÆCHom* i.

92. 25 *and se heretoga Moyses and eal Israhela mægð, ealle hi ymb-*
snidon heora cild . . . , ÆCHom ii. 456. 17 . . . *and ic on minum*
flæsce God geseo, ic sylf and na oðer, and *ÆCHom* ii. 604. 35 *Hi*
wæron æfre þry and an, þry on hadum and an on Godcundnysse.

f. Partitive apposition

§ 1455. Partitive apposition occurs when one element (usually the
second) limits the other by specifying a particular part of it, e.g.
ChronA 76. 8 (878) *Hamtunscir se dæl se hiere behinon sæ was,*
ChronA 87. 1 (894) *swa hergode he his rice þone ilcan ende þe*
Æþered his cumpæder healdan sceolde (where a twelfth-century
hand has inserted *on* after *he* in an endeavour to 'regularize' the syntax), *ÆCHom* i. 178. 27, *ÆCHom* i. 28. 1 [*Crist*] *þone deofol ge-*
wylde and him of anam Adam and Euan, and heora ofspring, þone
dæl ðe him ær gecwemde . . . , and *ÆCHom* ii. 594. 15 . . . *ic ðas*
twa bec, him to lofe and to wurðmynte, Angelcynne onwreah, ðam
ungelæredum; ða gelæredan ne beðurfon þyssera boca. . . . In these
the second element seems an afterthought, but is essential to the
sense, as it is in MS Cotton Otho B. XI, f. 262ʳ *Nim henneægero*
þone geolocan and similar passages from the *Leechdoms*; see Torkar,
Ang. 94 (1976), 334. The same is true of examples involving *sum,*
such as *ÆCHom* ii. 592. 2 . . . *hi sume beoð fullice geclænsode*; see
§§ 409–16.

§ 1456. Another form of partitive apposition occurs when the first
element is amplified by a pair of near-synonyms, e.g. *ÆCHom* ii.
500. 16 *He . . . mannum geheolp, wædligum and wanscryddum.*

§ 1457. Flamme (p. 85) sees a form of partitive apposition in *BlHom*
11. 17 . . . *mid syxtigum werum, þæm strengestum þe on Israhelum*
wæron—'die Apposition vertritt einen partitiven Genetiv . . . mit 60
der stärksten Leute, welche . . .' ['the apposition stands for a partitive genitive . . . "with sixty of the strongest men who . . ."']. But it
is more likely to mean 'the sixty strongest' rather than 'sixty of the
strongest'. We may, however, note that in *Gen* 1. 27 *God gesceop ða*
man to his anlicnysse, to godes anlicnysse he gesceop hine; werhades
and wifhades he gesceop hi partitive (or descriptive?) genitives
replace the appositional accusatives *masculum* and *feminam* of the
Latin *Et creavit Deus hominem . . . masculum et feminam creavit eos.*

g. Sentence apposition

§ 1458. This name is given to an element which expresses the speaker's
opinion on the statement in the other element, e.g. *ÆCHom* ii. 166. 20

þa het Benedictus beran þa tocwysedan lima on anum hwitle into his gebedhuse, and beclysedre dura anrædlice on his gebedum læg, oð þæt tocwysede cild, þurh Godes mihte, geedcucode: wunderlic ðing and *ÆCHom* ii. 186. 5 *Wunderlic gesihð, þæt an deadlic man mihte ealne middaneard oferseon.* See further Peltola 1960, p. 171.

7. THE ORDER OF THE ELEMENTS

§1459. Anticipatory and recapitulatory pronouns are found next to the element with which they are in apposition or separated from it; see §§1445-8.

§1460. The same is true of elements which amplify the governing element. These are frequently found side by side, conforming to the normal OE rules of element order for subject, object, or whatever they happen to be, e.g. *ÆCHom* i. 392. 1 *Saulus se arleasa beswang ða cristenan, ÆCHom* i. 432. 30 *and ge habbað ænne Hlaford, God Ælmihtigne, ChronA* 82. 9 (890) *Æþelstan, se wæs Ælfredes cyninges godsunu,* and *ÆCHom* ii. 4. 20 *He wæs todæg acenned of ðam halgan mædene Marian.* But they may be separated by a noun, or nouns, e.g. *ChronE* 83. 9 (890) *Æðelstan, se wæs Ælfredes godsune cyninges* and *ÆCHom* ii. 86. 30 *Sy ðe, Drihten, lof, eces wuldres Cyning*; by an adverb, e.g. *ÆCHom* i. 506. 32 *se heahengel ða Michahel*; by a prepositional phrase, e.g. *ÆCHom* ii. 36. 24 *ða sende he his bydel toforan him, Iohannem þone fulluhtere*; by a verb alone or with its subject or modifiers, e.g. *ÆCHom* ii. 72. 30 *swa swa se witega cwæð Isaias, ÆCHom* i. 192. 20 *and he forði a on ecnysse wunað on forwyrde wælræw deofol,* and *ÆLS* 37. 143 *Drihten crist ic andette þæs ælmihtigan Fæder Sunu*; or by a clause, e.g. *ÆCHom* i. 134. 26 *[Maria] gebrohte þæt cild þe heo acende, Hælend Crist.*

§1461. When one of the elements is a proper name and the two elements are together, there are in theory four possible arrangements— ☆*cyning Ælfred* 'King Alfred', *Ælfred cyning* '☆Alfred King', *se cyning Ælfred* 'the King Alfred', and *Ælfred se cyning* 'Alfred the King'. Of these, the starred forms are not (often) found, although their counterparts are common. Traugott (p. 106) writes:

Rank titles which are primarily biblical, for example, *heahfædere* 'patriarch' or are late borrowings do not occur after the noun. This suggests that the *Alfred cyning* construction had become fixed or 'fossilized' in earlier OE. New terms that came into use in later OE occurred before the noun on the model of adjectives and also possibly on the model of biblical Latin phrases such as *Dominus Christ* 'Lord Christ' [*heahfædere* and *Alfred* both *sic*].

This might be taken to imply that there were examples like ☆*heah-fæder Abraham*. So far I have noted none, though I have found *BlHom* 161. 26 *from Arones dohtrum þæs heahfæder* and *ÆCHom* i. 46. 10 *be ðam heahfædere Abrahame*. Nor have I found ☆*hlaford Crist*. On the evidence of *BenR* 1. 9 *drihtnum Criste soðum cyninge*, *drihten* in *LPr iii* 18 *drihten god* may be adjectival. But my collections are incomplete. We do, however, find *Sat* 280 *hælend God*, *ChristA* 358 *hælend Crist*, and *PPs* 98. 10 *hælend drihten*, alongside *drihten/dryhten hælend* in *Sat* 218, 575, and 682, *And* 541 and 1407, and *El* 725. In all these the order reflects the demands of alliteration. But *BlHom* 67. 3 *On þyssum dæge ure Drihten Hælend wæs weorþod 7 hered from Iudea folce; forþon þe hie ongeaton þæt he wæs Hælend Crist* and *BlHom* 11. 21 *se gesibsuma cyning ure Drihten Hælend Crist* cannot be explained in this way. There is room for more work here.

§1462. Mutt (*NM* 69 (1968), 584) says that 'no considerations other than those of euphony and rhythm seem to have governed the place of the apposition'. This seems unlikely, and proves to be based on faulty reading of Peltola (1960, p. 197). Meaning and emphasis must at least sometimes have been relevant. Indeed, according to Brunner (ii. 33), 'Nur wenn auf dem Gattungsnamen besonderer Nachdruck lag, wurde er mit dem bestimmten Artikel nachgestellt, z.b. *Ælfred se cyning*' ['The common noun occurred in post-position with the "definite article" only when it carried special emphasis . . .']. However, this line of argument cannot be pursued without native informants. Only a knowledge of intonation and rhythm and of the audience could tell us whether in *se cyning Ælfred, se cyning* and *Ælfred* are equivalents or whether *Ælfred* is in restrictive apposition. Similarly it is impossible for us to tell whether *se cyning* in *Ælfred se cyning* is stressed or is a half-apologetically mentioned afterthought. Indeed, despite Peltola (1960, p. 197), we cannot even be sure that there was always a difference between them.

§1463. Brunner (ii. 33) and Christophersen (p. 173) agree that in the oldest times the pattern *Ælfred cyning* was the rule; the exceptions which have come to my notice involve geographical names, e.g. *Or* 186. 17 *ofer munt Iof*; see further Peltola 1960, pp. 183–5. In *ChronA* 64. 29 (853) *þa wæs domne Leo papa on Rome*, we can take *domne* as complement, *Leo papa* as subject; see Shannon, p. 21. This accords with the general assumption that IE lacked an article and is confirmed, according to Peltola (1960, pp. 178–9 and 181), by the fact that the tendency in OE is for writings not derived from

Latin originals to prefer the pattern *Ælfred cyning* and for those based on Latin to prefer one of the forms with the article. Christophersen (p. 173) says that 'the new construction (*se cyning Ælfred*) began to appear in the 9th century' and that in early ME this and the type *Ælfred se cyning* 'appear to have been about equally frequent'. But we have no means of knowing that both of these types were not in spoken use in the eighth century and no way of deciding whether they arose simultaneously; note that Shannon (p. 21) found only three examples like *ChronA* 60. 14 (823) *Baldred þone cyning* against six like *ChronA* 70. 22 (871) *se cyning Æþered* in the *Parker Chronicle* 734-871, where the type *ChronA* 72. 9 (871) *Ælfred cyning* is the most common. Similar fluctuations are apparent in combinations involving possessives or adjectives (Shannon, pp. 20-2). It is impossible for us to determine the factors which decided the order of these appositional elements and pointless to erect 'rules'; we must agree with Peltola (1960, p. 179) that here 'the use of the article is irregular'.

C. THE SPLITTING OF GROUPS

§1464. Here we are concerned with groups joined by conjunctions, such as MnE 'Tom and Jack and all the boys came', 'Tom came, and Jack and all the boys' and 'Then came Tom and Jack and all the boys'; on examples like *Lch* ii. 180. 28 *do on claŏ, ofersmit mid ele, lege on þone magan*, see §1576. These three patterns all appear in OE. But the 'split' construction seen in the second is more common than in MnE, partly no doubt because of the variety of element orders possible there, but even more (in my opinion) because of a dislike of 'heavy' groups; see below. The split element can be said to be essential for the meaning, but not for the grammar, of the sentence. As Biswas (*Journal of the University of Gauhati*, 26-7, no. 1 (1975-6), 75) says, it 'may be withdrawn without affecting the structure as a whole or dissolving it. In fact, the split elements are semantic components only.' On examples like *BlHom* 91. 32 *blodig wolcen mycel*, see §169.

§1465. Such splitting is most frequent with the conjunction *ond*, either alone, e.g. *ÆCHom* ii. 554. 7 *Þu yfela ŏeowa and sleac*, or with *samod* or *eac*, e.g. *ÆCHom* i. 490. 28 *Ure Drihten ferde to sumere byrig . . . and his gingran samod* and *ÆCHom* i. 376. 10 *and he het ŏone dry him to gefeccan, and eac ŏa apostolas*. But it is found with other conjunctions, e.g. *ÆCHom* i. 190. 9 . . . *ægŏer ge ŏære ealdan æ ge ŏære niwan*, *ÆCHom* i. 82. 21 . . . *his eorŏlice rice oþþe æniges oðres cyninges, ÆCHom* i. 162. 13 *He nolde his heafod befon mid gyldenum cynehelme, ac mid þyrnenum,* and *ÆCHom* i. 64. 8 . . . *þæt hi næfre ær swa clæne gold ne swa read ne gesawon.* Groups containing nouns, pronouns, and adjectives, in all cases, alone and in combination, prepositional phrases, and adverbs, can be so divided. On verb groups see §§1573-8. Klaeber (*Kock Studies,* pp. 107-8) offers more examples.

§1466. When the divided group serves as subject, complement, or direct object, of its clause, the separation can be by a verb (group) alone, e.g. *ÆCHom* i. 62. 31 . . . *eower mod is awend and eower andwlita;* by an infinitive, e.g. *ÆCHom* ii. 462. 2 . . . *þæt he ne mæg his gytsunge ðeowian, and Criste samod;* by a participle, e.g. *ÆCHom* ii. 202. 21 . . . *wearð micel ðunor gehyred and stemn;* or by a verb and other elements, e.g. *ÆCHom* i. 334. 6 . . . *þæt heora bliss ðe mare sy, and lufu to heora Drihtne.* With adjectives and genitives, the separation can be by a noun alone, e.g. *ÆCHom* ii. 554. 7 (§1465) and *ÆCHom* i. 346. 14 *Godes lufe and manna,* or by a noun and other elements, e.g. *ÆCHom* ii. 354. 21 *Maran cyle ic geseah and wyrsan* and *ÆCHom* ii. 446. 5 . . . *ure andgit and eac swiðor þæra ungelæredra.* In *Some of the Hardest Glosses in Old English* (Stanford, 1968), 52, Meritt rightly disposes of the ghost word *onriptid* (f.) 'harvest' (BTS, s.v.) by means of a split construction: *mycel wæstm bið and god on riptid.* Prepositional groups are frequently divided by participles, e.g. *ÆCHom* ii. 252. 33 . . . *on him wunigende and on heora bearnum* and *ÆCHom* ii. 402. 8 . . . *of rixum gebroden oðða of palmtwygum,* but there are other patterns, e.g. *ÆCHom* i. 320. 28 *swa sceal se lareow don* . . . *ærest on him sylfum ælcne leahter adwæscan, and siððan on his underðeoddum.* Further examples will be found in the sections which follow.

§1467. But, as I have already said, the split construction is only one of three possibilities. We find all the elements of a subject grouped together before a verb in *ÆCHom* i. 434. 24 . . . *þæt seo cwen Triphonia and Decius dohtor Cyrilla to Cristes geleafan* . . . *gebogene wæron* and *ÆCHom* i. 118. 23 *Se frumsceapena man and eall his ofspring wearð adræfed of neorxena wanges myrhðe* (for the singular verb see §30). All the elements are grouped together after the verb in *ÆCHom* i. 18. 25 *ac sceolde Adam and his ofspring tyman on asettum tyman* . . . and *ÆCHom* i. 598. 30 *þas ðrowunge awriton þære ðeode preostas and ða ylcan diaconas ðe hit eal gesawon.* They are separated in *ÆCHom* i. 434. 18 *Soðlice seo cwen Triphonia gesohte ðæs halgan sacerdes fet Iustines mid biterum tearum, and hire dohtor Cyrilla samod, ÆCHom* i. 358. 29 . . . *ða gastlican drohtnunga þe Crist siððan gesette, and his apostoli,* and (in the accusative and infinitive construction) in *ÆCHom* ii. 476. 22 *þa het se apostol ðone cyning cuman to cyrcan mid his folce, and ealle ða mædenu samod.* In examples like the second-last, the verb is of course singular in agreement with the first element of the subject, the second element being (as it were) an optional afterthought. What Reszkiewicz (1966*a*, p. 320) calls 'incomplete or pseudo-splits' occur in examples like *Gen* 8. 16 *Gang ut of ðam arce, ðu 7 þin wif 7 ðine suna 7 heora wif,* where the first portion of the subject [*ðu*] is idiomatically unexpressed after *gang.* We may compare examples like *ÆCHom* i. 174. 2 *þonne he bið belocen on hellewite on ecum fyre, he and ealle his geferan,* where the first subject is repeated with the second. Reszkiewicz quotes *Gen* 22. 3 [*Abraham ða aras on þære ylcan nihte*] *7 ferde mid twam cnapum to þam fyrlenum lande, 7 Isaac samod, on assum ridende* without the words in square brackets and sees a 'pseudo-split' there too. But we have a wide separation of *Abraham . . . 7 Isaac.* His other 'pseudo-split' (*ÆLS* 26. 4) can be similarly explained.

§1468. The same three arrangements are found with objects—all elements together after the verb, e.g. *ÆCHom* i. 46. 31 *Efne ic geseo heofenas opene, and mannes Sunu standende æt Godes swiðran;* all elements together before the verb, e.g. *ÆCHom* i. 218. 13 . . . *swa þæt we ure unðeawas and ealle leahtras and ðone deofol oferwinnan;* and the split construction, e.g. (with only verb or infinitive intervening) *ÆCHom* i. 236. 15 . . . *hu he of ðam lame flæsc worhte and blod, ban and fell, fex and næglas* and *ÆCHom* ii. 462. 2 . . . *þæt he ne mæg his gytsunge ðeowian and Criste samod,* and (with more intervening elements) *ÆCHom* ii. 240. 29 *Drihtnes ðrowunge we willað gedafenlice eow secgan on Engliscum gereorde, and ða gerynu samod.*

§1469. Space prevents such full exemplification of the various arrangements possible with complements—*ÆCHom* i. 10. 34 *þa wearð he and ealle his geferan forcuþran and wyrsan þonne ænig oðer gesceaft* but *ÆCHom* i. 86. 4 *and he eal innan samod forswæled wæs, and toborsten* and *ÆCHom* i. 116. 18 . . . *þæt he soð God wære and soð Cyning;* with genitives—see §1328; with datives— *ÆCHom* ii. 196. 5 *and of ðam stane arn ormæte stream wæteres eallum ðam folce and heora orfe to genihtsumnysse* but *ÆCHom* ii. 572. 30 *into ðam ecan fyre, þe ðam deofle is gegearcod and his awyrigedum englum;* with prepositional phrases—*ÆCHom* i. 190. 30

. . . *to alysenne ealne middangeard fram deofles anwealde and fram hellewite* but *ÆCHom* i. 320. 29 . . . *ærest on him sylfum ælcne leahter adwæscan, and siððan on his underðeoddum*; with adjectives —see §§166-71; and with adverbs—*ÆHom* 19. 180 *ealle mine synna þe ic sið and ær gefremode* but *ÆCHom* i. 164. 20 *Wel ðrowað se man, and Gode gecwemlice.*

× §1470. A fourth possibility is suggested by Plummer, who in his note on the passage claims that *ChronA* 32. 16 (661) *7 Eoppa mæssepreost be Wilferþes worde 7 Wulfhere cyning brohte Wihtwarum fulwiht ærest* 'is a good instance of an antique construction by which, when two names depend on the same noun, the second name is put in the direct case. This is preserved in A, B, C. In E it is altered to the more modern construction': *ChronE* 34. 30 (661) *7 Eoppa preost be Wilferðes worde 7 Wulfheres cininges brohte Wihtwarum fulwiht ærost manna*. Plummer goes on, 'Professor Earle remarks that the spread of Latin culture resuscitated, and perhaps somewhat extended the use of flexion. There is another instance, 1057 D, *ad init.*' I cannot accept this. The alleged parallel—*ChronD* 187. 34-7 (1057)—is clearly corrupt; cf. the reading of *ChronE*. Earle's notion suggests that inflexions were toys, whereas the fact that the two versions both give sense demonstrates that they were vital clues. The agreement of A, B, and C, against E—the passage is missing from D—suggests to me the possibility of error by the scribe of the lost exemplar of A, B, and C, rather than alteration by the scribe of E or its archetype. I suggest that the erring scribe in haste and carelessness mentally grouped the wrong elements in the split construction by linking Eoppa and Wulfhere rather than Wilferþ and Wulfhere and so wrote *Wulfhere cyning* nominative instead of the genitive which was in the original and was preserved by the scribe of the archetype of E. The fact that the erring scribe preserved *brohte* rather than writing *brohton/brohtun* may be further evidence of his carelessness or of the fact that *-e* may be a preterite plural indicative ending; see §§18-20.

§1471. Similar splitting of groups is of course a feature of the poetry, e.g. *Beo* 431 *þæt ic mote ana and minra eorla gedryht* ‖ . . . *Heorot fælsian* (but *Wid* 45 *Hroþwulf ond Hroðgar heoldon lengest* ‖ *sibbe ætsomne*); *Beo* 437 . . . *þæt ic sweord bere oþðe sidne scyld,* ‖ *geolorand to guþe* (but *Beo* 94 [*se Ælmihtiga*] *gesette sigehreþig sunnan ond monan*); *ChristA* 12 *þæt se cræftga cume ond se cyning sylfa*[28] (but *Jul* 339 *we þa heardestan* ‖ *and þa wyrrestan witu*

[28] Despite Reszkiewicz (1966a, pp. 320-1), this type—in which two elements referring to the same referent are separated—is not restricted to poetry; for examples from the prose see §§169-70.

geþoliað); and *Wid* 79 *Mid Scottum ic wæs ond mid Peohtum* (but
Wid 57 *Ic wæs mid Hunum and mid Hreðgotum*).

§1472. In my opinion this splitting of groups joined by conjunctions
was not, originally at any rate, due to considerations of emphasis and
style. It was rather one of the characteristic tendencies of the language. (Reszkiewicz (1966a, pp. 321 ff.) has some interesting remarks
on this point.) There seems to have been a dislike of 'heavy' groups,
and perhaps in the early stages even an inability to handle them, arising from the same sense of insecurity in the face of a complicated
sentence I have detected elsewhere; see §§1893-6. But in view of
the variations cited above—and there are many more such examples
—it is clear that it did become at times a matter of style or emphasis. This certainly seems to me the reason for the different constructions in *ÆCHom* i. 434. 18 *Soðlice seo cwen Triphonia gesohte ðæs
halgan sacerdes fet Iustines mid biterum tearum, and hire dohtor
Cyrilla samod, biddende þæs halgan fulluhtes*—where the fact that
two were converted is emphasized by the separation of the two
nominative groups—and *ÆCHom* i. 434. 23 *þaða þæs caseres
ðegnas gehyrdon þæt seo cwen Triphonia and Decius dohtor Cyrilla
to Cristes geleafan, and to ðam halwendum fulluhte gebogene wæron,
hi ða mid heora wifum gesohton ðone halgan sacerd, and bædon
miltsunge and fulluhtes*, where the *þaða* clause repeats the now-
known fact of the conversion. But there are of course times when
splitting would weaken the force, e.g. *ÆCHom* i. 64. 29-33, *ÆCHom*
i. 296. 13-17, and *ÆCHom* ii. 456. 3 *Ealle ðas costnunga deofol, and
ðæra æhta lyre, his bearna deað and his agen untrumnys, his wifes ge-
witleast, and his freonda edwit, ne mihton awecgan Iob of his modes
anrædnysse, ne fram his micclan geleafan, ðe he to þan Ælmihtigan
Gode symle hæfde.*

D. NAMING CONSTRUCTIONS

§1473. When the name is the complement of a passive periphrasis
of a verb of naming, it is naturally in the nominative, e.g. *ÆCHom*
i. 104. 29 . . . *is ðes freolsdæg Godes swutelung gecweden*, *ÆCHom*
i. 10. 22 . . . *he wæs gehaten Leohtberend*, and *Luke(WSCp)* 15. 19
nu ic neom wyrðe þ ic beo þin sunu nemned.[29] We must assume that
the same is true with *hatte*, e.g. *ÆCHom* i. 84. 27 *Rachel hatte
Iacobes wif* and *ÆHom* 22. 52 . . . *ænne heretogan se hatte Gallicanus*, though—because of the frequent lack of distinction between

---

[29] See Hahn, p. 164 fn. 593, for a list of OE verbs which translate Latin *voco*. Nagucka's
article (*SAP* 11 (1980), 27-39) came to my attention when this book was at press.

the nominative and accusative of nouns in OE (§9)—none of my examples demonstrates it.

§1474. The combination of a second participle of a verb of naming + a name is often used with a noun. When this noun is in the nominative, as in *ÆHom* 2. 11 *an wundorlic wæterscipe, Bethsaida gehaten*, the name must again be taken as nominative. In examples like *ÆCHom* ii. 358. 3 *He hæfde ænne broðor, Tuna gehaten, mæssepreost and abbud*, both *Tuna* and *gehaten* may be nominative or accusative in form—cf. *ÆLS* 11. 11 *on þam lande Armenia* and on uninflected participles see §42(2). But in the light of examples like *ÆLS* 5. 124 . . . *and gefette ænne mæssepreost Policarpus gehaten halig wær and snotor* and *ÆLS* 8. 9 . . . *and betæhte hi anum fulum wife Afrodosia geciged sceandlic on þeawum*, they are to be taken as nominative. The same holds in *ÆCHom* ii. 308. 5 *ætforan ðam casere, Aurelianus genamod*, where *Aurelianus* could be dative; cf. *ÆCHom* ii. 308. 4 *mid twam mæssepreostum, Euentius and Theodolus*. So the participle + name phrase is independent and in effect paratactic.

§1475. Similar paratactic constructions are found with the noun *nama*, e.g. *ÆCHom* i. 562. 33, *ÆCHom* i. 570. 32 *On þære tide wæs sum oðer witega on Iudea lande, his nama wæs Abacuc, se bær his ryfterum mete to æcere*, and *ÆCHom* ii. 96. 19 *he cuðe sumne mann on Romebyrig, his nama wæs Seruulus*; with *hatte*, e.g. *Or* 66. 30 . . . *he læg mid Latinus wife, Lucrettie hatte, Or* 70. 8 . . . *under þæm twæm consulum, Tita 7 Publia hatton, BlHom* 201. 21, and *BlHom* 175. 21 *An ceaster is on Iudea lande, hatte Nazareþ, of þære com se heora lareow;*[30] and with *is/wæs (ge)haten*, e.g. *Or* 140. 15 *þa bæd his fæder—wæs eac Fauius haten—þæt þa senatum forgeafen þæm suna þone gylt, ChronE* 207. 4 (1070), *ChronE* 205. 11 (1070) . . . *þet se cyng heafde gifen þ abbotrice an Frencisce abbot Turolde wæs gehaten*, and (with inflected participles) *Or* 112. 9 *he begeat Arues dohtor him to wife* . . . *Olimphiade wæs hatenu* and *Or* 44. 24 *On þære ilcan tide wurdon twegen æþelingas afliemde of Sciþþian, Plenius 7 Scolopetius wæron hatene*. As far as I have observed, Ælfric uses this last construction rarely (but see *ÆLet* 4. 302 in §2305) and avoids *hatte*; he prefers the ptcs. *gehaten* or *geciged*, the *his nama* idiom—all these are exemplified above—or the adjective clause, as in *ÆHom* 27. 17 *On þære halgan bec þe hatte Uita Patrum* . . . and *ÆHom* 1. 174 . . . *þurh þone soðan Wisdom, þe is Word gehaten on þisum godspelle*.

---

[30] *Hatte* does not occur in *Beowulf*. But it is found in other poems, especially the *Riddles*; see GK, s.v. *hatan, nominari*.

§1476. When the person or thing named is the object of a verb of naming, the name can be nominative or accusative; cf. MnE 'George always calls my baby girl "He"' and 'George always calls my baby girl "Him"'. OE examples with the nominative include *Or* 20. 12 *for ðy hit man hæt Wislemuða, Or* 12. 8 *þæt land þe mon hætt seo læsse Asia*, and *ÆCHom* ii. 82. 34 *He gecigde Drihten his Andfenga*, and with the accusative *Or* 14. 17 *þæt lond mon hætt þa ealdan Sciþþian 7 Ircaniam, Lch* iii. 190. 14 *þone dæg 7 ða niht þe we hata𐥋 bissextum* (cf. nom. *bissextus* in *Lch* iii. 206. 7 . . . *þ bissextus cume*), and *ChronD* 195. 32 (1066) *se steorra . . . þone sume men hata𐥋 þone fæxedon steorran*. Inevitably, there are ambiguous examples: *Or* 18. 10 *þa deor hi hatað hranas*—Sweet actually prints '*hranas*', though it is hard to see why he singles out this and a few more, e.g. *Or* 266. 13 and 14, from examples like *Or* 8. 2 *Oceanus . . . þone man garsecg hateð* and *Or* 8. 19 . . . *neah þære byrig þe mon hateð Theodosia* (where *Theodosia* might be accusative; cf. *Or* 14. 31 *oð Donua þa ea*)—*Bede* 52. 5 . . . *of ðam lande þe mon hateð Ealdsaxan*, and *ÆCHom* i. 92. 13 *ac God . . . gehet hine Abraham*. Examples of this sort predominate in my collections and are cited in support of their conflicting claims by Wülfing (i. 225)—*hatan* occurs mostly with a double accusative—and by Ardern (p. xxv)—as 'objective complement' after *hatan* the nominative 'appears to be the normal usage, though the more logical Accus. is sometimes found'. Ambiguous examples are, of course, valueless as evidence. Both usages are idiomatic. I must leave it at that.

§1477. In all the examples cited, the naming element is a noun. But it can be an adjective, which may also be nominative, e.g. *Or* 10. 7 *þone garsecg mon hæt Indisc* and *Or* 8. 16 *neh þæm garsecge þe mon hateð Sarmondisc*, or accusative, e.g. *ÆIntSig* 76 *Hwi namode Crist . . . Abel rihtwisne . . . ?* and *ÆCHom* ii. 84. 4 *Ða nolde hi gecigan God mildheortne*. Ambiguity, of course, exists when the nominative and accusative form of the adjective are the same, e.g. *Or* 8. 18 *þæt fen þe mon hateð Meotedisc*. My collections are not complete and it may be coincidental that my examples with the nominative are early and those with the accusative late. The reverse would have been less surprising in the light of the loss of inflexions. But we may note Brunner's suggestion (ii. 50) that the nominative is the earlier use— 'eigentlich ist es wohl ein Vokativ als Rufkasus' ['actually it is probably a vocative as a case for naming/calling (someone/something)'] —and that the accusative is the result of Latin influence.

§1478. The noun *nama* too is found in the nominative and accusative. The possessor of the name may be in the genitive, e.g. *BlHom*

197. 27 *sum rice man . . . þæs nama wæs Garganus* and *Matt(WSCp)* 1. 21 *⁊ þu nemst hys naman Hælend*, or in the dative, e.g. *ChronA* 120. 8 (975) *eorla ealdor þam wæs Eadweard nama* and *ÆCHom* i. 12. 31 *and God him sette naman Adam*.

§1479. The dative/instrumental of *nama* is occasionally found accompanied by a preposition, e.g. *Bede* 404. 31 *Swylc him eac in ða tid fulwihtes se gemyndega papa Petrus to naman scop* and (in translations of the Gospels) *Luke(WSCp)* 1. 5 . . . *wæs sum sacerd on naman Zacharias* and *Luke(Li)* 1. 5 *wæs . . . sacerd sum mið noma Zacharias*, Latin *fuit . . . sacerdos quidam nomine Zacharias*. It also occurs with *oþer*, e.g. *CP* 173. 16 *Gregorius . . . se wæs oðrum noman genemned Nanzanzenus* and *Or* 102. 2 *Laucius, þe oþre noman wæs haten Genutius*. But the dat. sg. *naman* does not seem to occur as a rendering of abl. *nomine* 'by name' in the construction *homo nomine X*, though it appears in *Luke(WSCp)* 1. 59 *⁊ nemdon hyne hys fæder naman Zachariam*, Latin *et uocant eum nomine patris eius Zachariam*. Hahn (pp. 163–82) analyses the way in which OE glossators handled the naming constructions in the Vulgate and comes to the conclusion (p. 173) that 'their invariable failure, in translating the expression "in name", to use for the Latin ablative of specification its closest parallel in Germanic, the dative, shows that this construction was wholly alien to OE'. The rest of her discussion on OE (both here and in *Lang.* 37 (1961), 476–83) is devoted to denying the view (which has been advanced) that *Beo* 78 and 1457 are examples of the construction seen in Latin *homo Iulius nomen*— a construction which (she concludes) was lacking in Gothic and OE.

§1480. Dančev (1969, p. 50), however, notes the use of the dative in examples like *ÆCHom* i. 96. 29 *þu bist geciged niwum naman* and *ÆCHom* i. 358. 10 *Crist is manegum naman genemned* alongside those with the preposition *mid*, e.g. *ÆCHom* i. 276. 13 *Nu ealle ðas ðing synd mid anum naman genemnode, gesceaft*, or *be*, e.g. *ÆCHom* ii. 164. 25 *Æt fruman he hine clypode be his naman, Benedicte, þæt is, Gebletsod*. *LS* 8. 436, which he quotes as an example with *þurh*, is entirely different in kind.

§1481. The names of places are occasionally found after *æt*, either uninflected or in the dative, and either without a verb of naming, e.g. *CP* 311. 6 *Koka ealdormon towearp ða burg æt Hierusalem*, or with one, e.g. *Or* 19. 22 *to þæm porte þe mon hæt æt Hæþum* and *ChronA* 16. 23 (552) *in þære stowe þe is genemned æt Searobyrg*, where *æt* was later erased.

E. THE SUBJECT

1. FORMS

a. Introductory remarks

§1482. The grammatical subject of a finite verb is in the nominative case. It is sometimes unexpressed; see §§1506-16. But normally we find one of the following elements or combinations in the nominative case: a noun (or participle) alone or in combination with a demonstrative and/or a possessive and/or an adjective or adjectives, e.g. *ÆCHom* i. 10. 18 *God hi gesceop ealle gode*, *ÆCHom* ii. 90. 14 *þæt sæd þe feoll be ðam wege mid twyfealdre dare losode, ðaða wegferende hit fortrædon and fugelas tobæron* (the participle is used alone in other cases also, e.g. *ÆCHom* i. 360. 31 *stemn clypigendes on westene*), *ÆCHom* i. 210. 29 *se nacoda assa bið mid reafum gesadelod*, and *ÆCHom* i. 192. 6 *Ure se Ælmihtiga Scyppend . . . gesceop mancynn*;[31] a demonstrative and/or possessive + a weak form of an adjective or participle, e.g. *ÆCHom* i. 106. 19 *þa Iudeiscan ðe on Crist gelyfdon wæron him gehendor stowlice*; a strong form of the adjective (see §1484); a demonstrative or personal pronoun, e.g. *ÆCHom* ii. 480. 5 *Hwæt ða Drihten arærde micelne wind, and se gelæhte ealne þone lig* and *ÆCHom* i. 8. 8 *We sind Godes gefylstan*; the neuters *hit, þæt*, and *þis* (see §§1485-90); a numeral alone or in combination with a noun (alone or qualified as above) or a pronoun, e.g. *ÆCHom* i. 10. 10 *Ðas þry hadas sindon an ælmihtig God*; an indefinite alone or in combination, e.g. *ÆCHom* i. 224. 26 *Nu cwyð sum man on his geðance*; an uninflected or inflected infinitive (see §§1537-9); and a noun or adjective clause (see §§1927, 1962-6, and 2103). More examples will be found in the appropriate sections of chapter II. Apposition may, of course, be involved; see §§1428-63.

§1483. The subject of an infinitive need not be expressed, but when it is, it is normally in the accusative case; see §3722.

b. The strong form of the adjective

§1484. According to Andrew (*Postscript*, §86), 'strong adjectives can function as nouns in all cases both singular and plural except the

---

[31] Hess's 'Old English Nominals', *PLL* 6 (1970), 302-13, is a discussion (based on Ælfric's 'Life of St. Oswald') of nouns, pronouns, and phrases which include one or the other, by 'one who has had orientation and experience in anthropological linguistics'. It adds little to our knowledge.

nominative singular'. In theory it is hard to see why what occurs in the plural—for example, *BlHom* 31. 9 *ac hine ealle halige þær herigaþ* and *Beo* 1594 *Blondenfeaxe, ‖ gomele ymb godne ongeador spræcon*—should be impossible in the singular. In fact it is possible; the neuter singular nominative strong form of an adjective occurs in, for example, *Lch* i. 74. 10 . . . *þ hit sona nænig lað ne bið* and *PPs* 92. 8 *Huse þinum halig gedafenað*. These represent an intermediate stage in the process of 'functional change' which is probably complete in examples like *ChristC* 1332 *hwæþer him yfel þe god under wunige*, where *yfel* and *god* are traditionally classified as nouns, no doubt because of examples like *Bo* 37. 20 . . . *hi ne magon weorðan togædere gemenged, þe ma ðe þ good ⁊ ðæt yfel magon ætgædere bion*, where the adjectives would be declined weak. Examples of such singulars are not common. But this is not because they are impossible, but because the need for them rarely arose. It rarely arises in MnE either, where we find the same tendency for the singular to refer to a thing or quality, e.g. 'Good is better than evil', and the plural to persons, e.g. 'The good die young'. None the less, we need not follow Andrew (*Postscript*, §§86 and 111) in arguing that emendation is essential in *Beo* 850 *deaðfæge deog*. If we do not want to take *deaðfæge* as the subject, we can explain it as appositional or attributive to an unexpressed *he*.

c. Hit, þæt, *and* þis

§1485. These neuter singular pronominal forms can be used in the nominative as subjects of finite verbs; for fuller exemplification of these uses—especially of *hit*—than is possible below, see Visser, i, §§44–64. *Hit* can be used with no specific referent as the subject of an impersonal verb, e.g. *Or* 234. 6 *hit hagolade seofon niht*, or of a verb used impersonally, e.g. *Or* 128. 24 *swa hit her beforan sægð*. But it is often absent, especially with expressions which do not refer to natural phenomena, e.g. *Or* 40. 26 *swylc her ær beforan sæde*; see further §§1031–5. As far as I have observed, *hit* is not used with the impersonal passive constructions like *ÆCHom* i. 514. 6 *forðam him bið geðenod mid his ðearfena þenunge* which are discussed in §§834–58. This is to be expected, since in the corresponding active form *him* would be the dative object of the verb and *his ðearfena þenung* the subject; cf. *ÆHom* 25a. 9 *he þenað Criste; and Crist þenað hym*.

§1486. All three pronouns can be used as subjects referring forward or back to a specific referent. They rarely anticipate a noun. We find tautologic *hit* doing so, e.g. *Bede* 26. 2 *Hit is welig þis ealond*; see §§1445-6. But I have not found examples corresponding to the modern use of 'it' to give emphasis, as in 'It's food that I want'. This is not surprising, since OE achieves the same emphasis by giving the noun initial position, e.g. *ÆCHom* ii. 234. 3 *Min Fæder is ðe me wuldrað*, or by starting with the verb, e.g. *BlHom* 29. 33 *Næs his gemet þæt he hine costode*. However, as Visser (i, §63) points out, there are sporadic examples with *þæt*, e.g. *WPol* 127. 183 *þæt is laðlic lif þæt hi swa maciað*.

§1487. But the pronouns under discussion often anticipate a clause, thereby avoiding a heavy subject at the beginning of a sentence and perhaps achieving emphasis, e.g. *Or* 108. 24 . . . *þa gewearð hit . . . þætte sume Romana wif on swelcum scinlace wurdon . . .* , *BlHom* 29. 30 *forþon þis næs gecweden be Criste þæt his fot æt stane opspurne, ah be halgum monnum, ÆCHom* i. 112. 4 *forðan ðe þæt is rihtwisnys þæt gehwylcum sy his agen cyre geðafod, ÆCHom* ii. 340. 10 *Hit is awriten, Lufa ðinne nextan swa swa ðe sylfne*, and *ApT* 32. 2 *Lareow, ne ofþingð hit ðe gif ic þus wer geceose*. However, constructions with no anticipatory pronoun are also common, e.g. *CP* 77. 1 *Forðæm wæs ðurh ðone witgan gecweden: Dooð eow clæne, ÆCHom* i. 148. 4 *Gif wife getimige þæt heo hire wer forleose . . .* , and *ÆCHom* i. 150. 26 *Wite gehwa eac þæt geset is on cyrclicum þeawum, þæt we sceolon on ðisum dæge beran ure leoht to cyrcan*. See further Pogatscher, pp. 294-6, and my §§1964 and 1967.

§1488. *Hit* occasionally anticipates an uninflected or inflected infinitive, e.g. *Or* 52. 8 *Hit is unieðe to gesecgenne hu monege gewin siþþan wæron . . .* and *Coll* 112 *Forþam plyhtlic þingc hit ys gefon hwæl*. But examples without *hit* predominate, e.g. *CP* 151. 8 . . . *hwilum bið god wærlice to miðanne his hieremonna scylda, ÆCHom* i. 236. 11 *Nu is geðuht þæt him sy sumera ðinga eaðelicor to ærærenne ðone deadan of ðam duste, þonne him wære to wyrcenne ealle gesceafta of nahte*, and *Coll* 8 *Leofre ys us beon beswungen for lare þænne hit ne cunnan*.

§1489. When referring back to a noun, the recapitulatory pronoun may agree with it in gender, e.g. *Or* 24. 12 *Brittannia þæt igland hit is norðeastlang; 7 hit is eahta hund mila lang 7 twa hund mila brad*, where the first *hit* is tautologic; see further §§1447-8. But recapitulatory *hit* is often used without regard to the gender and/or number of its antecedent, e.g. *BlHom* 175. 33 *Hwæt is se Crist? . . . Hit is seþe þes dry Simon sagað þæt he sy, ÆCHom* ii. 266. 33 *Etað þisne hlaf, hit is min lichama, ÆCHom* ii. 274. 8 . . . *se heofenlica mete . . . and þæt wæter . . . hæfde getacnunge Cristes lichaman and his blodes . . . Hit wæron ða ylcan ðe we nu offriað*, and *ÆCHom* i. 172. 8 *Eorðe and eall hire gefyllednys, and eal ymbhwyrft and þa ðe on ðam wuniað, ealle hit syndon Godes æhta.* On constructions involving *hit/þæt/þis* + *beon/wesan*, see further §§44(5), 323-7, and 342.

§1490. A recapitulatory pronoun may also refer back to an idea already expressed in a previous clause or sentence, e.g. *CP* 429. 16 *Ac forðæmðe hi her syngiað, 7 hit him no ne hreowð . . . , GenB* 816-26, where *hit* (nom.) is used twice in this way,[32] *John(WSCp)* 1. 19 *7 þ is Iohannes gewitnes*, and *BlHom* 71. 2 *þis wæs geworden, forþon þæt se witedom wære gefylled. . . .*

d. Introductory þær

§1491. The word 'there' in examples like MnE 'There is a green hill far away' carries little or no stress—cf. 'There at last is a green hill' —and has no local significance. It anticipates and takes the grammatical place of a subject which is yet to be expressed. It is variously called 'expletive', 'existential', and so on; see Nagashima, p. 135. I follow him in using the term 'introductory'.

§1492. When used initially *þær*, like MnE 'there', is often clearly local in reference rather than introductory, e.g. *ÆCHom* i. 52. 5 *þider ðe Stephanus forestop, mid Saules stanum oftorfod, ðider folgode Paulus, gefultumod þurh Stephanes gebedu. þær nis Paulus gescynd þurh Stephanes slege, ac Stephanus gladað on Paules gefærrædene.* (I disagree with Andrew, *SS,* §72, about this example.) That the weakening of *þær* in this function is the source of introductory *þær* is suggested by the numerous instances in which there is doubt about which we have. Among these doubtful examples, in my opinion, are the following, which the writers named in brackets give as examples of introductory *þær*: *ÆCHom* i. 22. 23 *þa wæron þær swa fela gereord swa ðær manna wæron* (Andrew, *Postscript,* §73), *BlHom* 213. 32 *þa sæt þær sum þearfa æt ðæm burggeate* (Visser, i, §66), and *Beo* 32 *þær æt hyðe stod hringedstefna* (Nagashima, p. 160).

---

[32] It seems best to take *hit* (acc.) in line 824 and *hit* (nom.) in lines 825 and 826 as all referring back to the *þæt* clauses which begin in lines 816 and 820. To take *hit* in line 825 as the subject of *mæg . . . hreowan* with no specific referent seems an unnecessary break in the sequence.

§1493. But something close to introductory *þær* certainly occurred in OE. According to Andrew (*Postscript,* §73), it 'appears to be a late prosaism in Old English; instances are exceedingly rare in *ASC* or *Bede*, but they are abundant in Ælfric'. Even the best examples in the *Chronicle* are somewhat dubious; consider *ChronA* 60. 11 (823) . . . *on Ellendune . . . 7 þær wæs micel wæl geslægen, ChronA* 90. 20 (897) *þa æt sumum cirre þæs ilcan geares comon þær sex scipu to Wiht,* and *ChronE* 142. 20 (1012) *forþam þær wæs gebroht win suðan.* Nagashima (pp. 140-5) agrees that examples in *Bede* are rare; he groups *Bede* and *Cura Pastoralis* as presenting a contrast to *Orosius*, a text which (he says) 'testifies to the establishment of the introductory *þær* in OE'; we may note, however, that his selected corpus did not include *CP* 127. 1-5, which contains six examples which both Bacquet (p. 266) and I take as introductory. But see §1497. Examples like *Or* 8. 4 *þeah þe sume men sægden þæt þær nære buton twegen dælas: Asia, 7 þæt oþer Europe* and *Or* 132. 12 *ac he hit for þæm ne angan þe þær wæs eorþbeofung on þære tide* are reasonably convincing, even in full context. Others quoted by Nagashima himself and by Visser (i, §66, and iii, §1829) are less so. But certainly we see the beginnings of introductory *þær* in eW-S.

§1494. In Ælfric there are more clear examples than in the earlier texts; they include *ÆCHom* i. 40. 24 *Nis þeahhwæðre seo godcundnys gemenged to ðære menniscnysse, ne ðær nan twæming nys* and *ÆCHom* ii. 400. 24 *Paruuli petierunt panem, nec erat qui frangeret eis: þæt is, on urum gereorde, Ða lytlan cild bædon him hlafes, ac þær næs nan mann ðe þone hlaf him betwynan tobræce.* But inevitably there are dubious ones, e.g. *ÆCHom* i. 22. 23 (§1492) and *ÆCHom* i. 174. 33 *gif þonne ure mod nimð gelustfullunge, þonne sceole we huru wiðstandan, þæt ðær ne beo nan geðafung to ðam yfelan weorce.* Nagashima (pp. 146-58) notes similar contrasts in other Ælfrician texts, in Wulfstan, and in the Gospels.

§1495. The view expressed by Andrew (*Postscript,* §74) that 'the evidence is against the use of expletive *ðær*' in *Beowulf* has been disputed with some success by Quirk (*London Mediaeval Studies,* 2 (1951), 32): 'as for the poetry, one cannot agree with Mr. Andrew's dismissal of the considerable evidence of existential *there* in *Beowulf*'. Quirk instances *Beo* 1063, 2231, 2555, 2762, and 2105 *þær wæs gidd ond gleo,* and suggests possible occurrences in the Cynewulfian poems, e.g. *El* 114 *þær wæs borda gebrec ond beorna geþrec.* Nagashima (pp. 159-64) gives many of Quirk's examples and adds more. Some of these do not convince, e.g. *Beo* 32 (§1492) and

Beo 1063   þær wæs sang ond sweg   samod ætgædere
                  fore Healfdenes   hildewisan . . . ,

where *þær* could anticipate line 1064.

§1496. We must, however, admit that some sort of introductory *þær* existed in OE. Quirk (loc. cit.) implies that its comparative scarcity in translated texts may be due to the fact that there is no corresponding idiom in Latin. But two points argue that we should not be too eager to follow Nagashima (p. 143) in speaking of 'the *establishment* [my italics] of the introductory *þær* in OE'. First, there are alternative constructions now lost or used differently, e.g. *CP* 467. 31 *Is hit lytel tweo ðæt ðæs wæterscipes welsprynge is on hefonrice, Bo* 55. 28 *Ac ðæt nis nan man þte sumes eacan ne ðyrfe, ÆHom* 8. 48 *and þe nis nan neod þæt þe hwa ahsige, Or* 50. 13 *Hwa is þætte ariman mæge . . . , Gen* 1. 3 *God cwæð ða: Gewurðe leoht, ÆCHom* i. 10. 14 *Her sindon nigon engla werod, ÆCHom* i. 290. 3 *Arrius hatte an gedwolman, ÆCHom* i. 330. 3 *Sum rice man wæs,* and *ÆCHom* i. 272. 8 *On ðam ecan life ne bið nan costnung ne nan yfel.* An interesting contrast presents itself in *ÆCHom* ii. 442. 17 *Witodlice on ðam toweardan life, ðe Maria getacnode, ne beoð ðas neoda, ne ðas ðenunga; þær we beoð gefedde, and we ðær nænne ne afedað; þær bið fulfremed þæt Maria her geceas,* where *þær* occurs three times with local reference after an initial clause in which MnE would have introductory 'there'. Nagashima's figures (based on a selected corpus in each case) show that in all the texts he studied, these alternatives were more common than introductory *þær* in contexts where the latter is a theoretical possibility.

§1497. Second, there are differences of usage between OE and MnE. We must not expect that introductory *þær* will always be at the beginning of the sentence or before its verb; OE idiom demands that we accept sentences like *CP* 127. 1 *Gif ðær ðonne sie gierd mid to ðreagenne, sie ðær eac stæf mid to wreðianne* as exemplifying introductory *þær*. But we may balk at *Or* 17. 20 *Ða læg þær an micel ea up in on þæt land* (Nagashima, p. 165) and *ÆCHom* ii. 504. 30 *Ða comon þær fleogende twegen fægre englas* (*Postscript,* §73), where *ða* and *þær* seem to be as much 'continuative' in function as temporal or local, but are scarcely introductory. (On the interchangeability of *þa* and *þær* in the 'continuative' function see Nagashima, pp. 150 and 158.) Indeed, Nagashima himself agrees that 'OE introductory *þær* has, even when it has lost much of its local meaning, a much stronger demonstrative-evocative force than PE *there*' (p. 150) and concludes that 'apart from local meaning, OE *þær* had developed an introductory function, including as its subdivisions a demonstrative-evocative and an interjectional function' (p. 164); on this see §1236. Though it is, of course, impossible to be sure about OE stress and intonation, this proposition seems to me very plausible. But it does mean that OE introductory *þær* and its MnE equivalent were not identical. There seems little point in further argument. We may, however, note that its absence in OE where we would have it in MnE may create an impression of awkwardness for a modern reader, e.g. *ÆCHom* ii. 348. 14 *On ðam timan wæs sum þegen Drihtelm gehaten, on Norðhymbra lande, bilewite on andgyte, gemetegod on ðeawum, arfæst on life, and his hiwrædene to ðam ylcan gewissode.*[33]

2. QUALIFYING ELEMENTS

§1498. Qualifiers of the subject such as demonstratives, possessives, indefinites, adjectives, and numerals, are of course in the nominative case. So too are elements in apposition with the subject or joined to it by *ond, ac,* and the like. The relative pronoun of an adjective clause which qualifies the subject agrees in gender and number with its antecedent, but not necessarily in case; see §2338. Other qualifying elements which do not agree in case include genitives and genitive groups (§§1269 and 1288), datives and dative groups (§§1355-6), and prepositional phrases. On participial phrases see §§1434-40, on *self* §§472-3, and on the 'ethic' dative §§1352-3.

§1499. Demonstratives, possessives, indefinites, adjectives, and numerals, are normally found before their headword, but occasionally after it; for further details of the possible arrangements see the relevant sections of chapter II. Separation can occur in the prose when the qualifying element is, for example, a participial phrase, e.g. *ÆLS* 26. 2 *wæs sum æðele cyning Oswold gehaten on Norðhymbra lande gelyfed swyþe on god*; a genitive phrase, e.g. *ÆLS* 26. 31 *and wurdon fela gehælde untrumra manna and eac swilce nytena*; a prepositional phrase, e.g. *ÆLS* 26. 40 *Seo stow is gehaten Heofonfeld on englisc wið þone langan weall þe þa Romaniscan worhtan*; or an adjective clause, e.g. *ÆLS* 26. 30 *Seo ylce rod siððan þe Oswold þær arærde* . . . . As has been shown in §§1459-63 and 1517-18, both appositional elements and the various parts of compound subjects may be

---

[33] These sections on introductory *þær* were ready for the press when Breivik's 'A Note on the Genesis of Existential *There*' (*EStudies*, 58 (1977), 334-48) came into my hands. After several readings of his article, which makes no mention of Nagashima, I was almost convinced that introductory or existential *þær* did not exist in OE. But I remained unconvinced by his claim to have demonstrated that 'if *there₂* [introductory] did indeed derive from *there₁* [locative], the separation must have occurred before the OE period' (p. 346).

placed side by side or separated by various elements ranging from a single word to a clause. Separation is much more common in the poetry; see (*inter alia*) §§150-7 and 3959.

§1500. Because of such variations in position, it is sometimes possible to take a case phrase or a prepositional phrase as adnominal or adverbial, e.g. *Or* 14. 18 *þæs landes is xliii þeoda, wide tosetene . . .* , *ÆCHom* i. 74. 25 *And he eode cucu and gesund into his byrgene, and astrehtum handum to Gode clypode . . .* (where *astrehtum handum* can be described as adnominal, adverbial, or absolute; see §§3810-11), *Luke(WSCp)* 9. 38 *þa clypode an wer of þære menego*, and *Matt(WSCp)* 27. 29 *and wundon cynehelm of þornum*. Further on this see Curme, *MP* 11 (1913-14), 149 ff.

§1501. When the element which qualifies a singular subject is a phrase introduced by the prep. *mid*, the verb is normally singular, e.g. *ChronA* 64. 7 (845) *Her Eanulf aldorman gefeaht mid Sumur sætum*, *ÆCHom* i. 62. 17 *þa se uðwita Graton samod mid þam cnihtum feoll to Iohannes fotum*, and *Mald* 51 *þæt her stynt unforcuð eorl mid his werode*. See further Hittle, pp. 16-18. Bauch's suggestion (pp. 62-3) that there is an example with *æfter* in *Phoen* 539-43 seems dubious to me; *stefn* may be accusative.

§1502. Examples of the type 'The captain with three of his men were taken prisoner'—described by Sweet (*NEG*, §2152) as 'ungrammatical' (but see Visser, i, §95)—occur sporadically in all periods of English. In OE, of course, the preposition is *mid*. We can explain the plural verb in *ChronA* 86. 1 (894) *7 wæs se cyng þa þiderweardes on fære, mid þære scire þe mid him fierdedon* as due to the collective noun *scir* (see §82) and that in *ChronA* 68. 3 (860) *7 wiþ þone here gefuhton Osric aldorman mid Hamtunscire 7 Æþelwulf aldormon mid Bearrucscire* as due to the fact that it is followed by two singular subjects joined by *ond*—despite Sprockel (ii. 214); see §29. Unambiguous examples occur in *ApT* 36. 9 *Mid þam þe Apollonius þæt geseah, he mid his aðume and mid his dohtor to hyre urnon and feollon ealle to hire fotum* and *Mald* 100 *þær ongean gramum gearowe stodon ‖ Byrhtnoð mid beornum*. But these are exceptional.

3. REPETITION, NON-REPETITION, AND NON-EXPRESSION, OF THE SUBJECT

§1503. A subject may be repeated in what is grammatically the same clause by anticipatory and/or recapitulatory pronouns, e.g.

LS 34. 429 *And he ða ure hælend se þe unborenum cildum lif sylð on heora modra innoðe . and se þe mid his anwealde ða forsearedon ban wecð of deaðe . and se þe eac lazarum to life gewende . and hine ymbe þreo dagas ðæs þe he bebyrged wæs of deaðe awehte . he sylf synderlice mid his agenre dæde þas seofon halgan þe on ðam scræfe slepon he hi awehte ða of ðam slæpe,* where both are exemplified (see further §§1445-8), or by part or all of itself (see §§1453-5). This phenomenon is very common when the first subject is qualified by an adjective clause, as in *LS* 34. 429 above and in the examples quoted in *Guide,* §148. But, despite Carkeet (p. 46), it is not restricted to such contexts; consider *Bede* 342. 20 (§2562). There is room for more work here.

§1504. When the same noun differently qualified serves as the subject of two or more clauses, it can be but need not be repeated, e.g. *ÆCHom* ii. 58. 1 *þa six wæterfatu getacnodon six ylda ðyssere worulde. Seo forme yld wæs . . . Seo oðer yld wæs . . . Seo þridde yld wæs . . . Seo feorðe fram Dauide . . . Seo fifte yld wæs . . . Seo sixte yld stent nu. . . .*

§1505. When the same subject serves for more than one simple sentence or co-ordinate clause, it can be repeated by a personal pronoun, but need not be. This is true whether the parataxis is syndetic or asyndetic. For examples see §§1690-702 and 1712-17 and 1752 respectively.

§1506. So far I have spoken of non-repetition rather than non-expression of the subject because in all the examples so far treated the 'missing' subject is the same as that of the verb of a preceding simple sentence or co-ordinate clause. I use the term 'non-expression' (and the adjective 'unexpressed') to imply that a subject which is not the same as that of a preceding simple sentence or co-ordinate clause has to be supplied from a noun, pronoun, or verb,[34] in the same clause, or in a neighbouring principal or subordinate clause, or (in extreme cases) in a distant clause. I prefer 'non-expression' to 'omission' because to speak of 'omission' of *ic* in *Beo* 2252 *Nah, hwa sweord wege* is to disregard the possibility that we have here 'a genuine archaism' (Ardern, p. xxv) and to speak of 'omission' of *hit* in *BlHom* 45. 3 *7 her sægþ on þyssum bocum þæt . . .* suggests that

---

[34] Ohlander (p. 107) remarks that 'the practice of omitting the subject . . . should no doubt partly be ascribed to the fact that in the parent language [Old English] the subject-pronoun was seldom necessary, since the subject was generally sufficiently indicated by the personal ending of the predicate verb'. In my opinion the verb endings were too ambiguous for this to have played much part, even in OE; see §§16-22.

this pattern developed from that in *Or* 128. 24 *swa hit her beforan sægð*, whereas they may be independent idioms or *hit* may be a later insertion. See further Pogatscher, pp. 294 ff.

§ 1507. Inevitably there is some no-man's land. We have seen in §§ 1487-8 that *hit, þæt*, or *þis*, may anticipate an infinitive or a noun clause, but need not. Visser objects to the notion that these infinitives or noun clauses can be the subject of the verb in a clause in which a pronoun subject does not appear. He speaks of *restan* in *Beo* 1792 *Geat unigmetes wel,* ‖ *rofne randwigan restan lyste* as being 'used by way of complement' to *lyste* (ii, § 899) and says of examples like *ÆCHom* i. 316. 23 . . . *þæt him wærlicor wære, þæt hi sumne dæl heora landes wurðes æthæfdon* . . . that 'the probability of this [second] clause not being a causative complement, but the subject, is slight, since it is never placed before the verb' (i, § 32). Similarly, he argues (i, § 27) that in examples like *Or* 46. 8 *Siþþan wæs hiera þeaw þæt hi ælce geare . . . tosomne ferdon*, the *þæt* clause is an adjunct of cause rather than the subject of *wæs*; the difficulty of this explanation 'may be accounted for by the assumption that modern linguistic feeling is entirely different from what it was at the time'. The problem is admittedly terminological. But one might almost as well argue that *sio ælmesse* could not be the subject of *gehreowe* in *CP* 324. 7 *7 him ðonne gehreowe sio ælmesse*, which Visser (i, § 31) cites as an example in which 'the complement of the verb is . . . a noun in the zero case'! The order in such clauses does not testify that the element which follows the verb cannot be the subject; it is explicable in terms of OE style and rhythm. We could get around the difficulty by saying that the infinitive in *Beo* 1792 and the *þæt* clauses in *ÆCHom* i. 316. 23 and *Or* 46. 8 (all quoted above) are in apposition with an unexpressed *hit* rather than subjects. But this creates another difficulty and there seems little point in arguing.

§ 1508. Non-expression of the subject can take different forms. Three types are discussed here. The first—which could almost be called non-repetition—occurs when the grammatical subject of the second of two paratactic clauses is an unexpressed plural pronoun which would refer back to a collective noun or two singular elements in the first. Examples after *ond, ac*, and the like, include *ChronA* 101. 15 (921) *þy ilcan siþe for se here of Huntandune 7 of East Englum 7 worhton þæt geweorc æt Tæmeseforda* (collective noun); *ÆCHom* i. 374. 18 *Se dry Simon and se wælhreowa Nero sind mid deofles gaste afyllede, and syrwiað ongean ðe* and *ChronA* 64. 20

(851) *7 him gefeaht wiþ Æþelwulf cyning 7 Æþelbald his sunu . . . and þær þæt mæste wæl geslogon . . .* (two singular nouns); *ÆCHom* i. 374. 27 *On ðone oðerne dæg com Paulus into ðære byrig, and heora ægðer oðerne mid micelre blisse underfeng and wæron togædere bodigende . . .* (reciprocal pronouns); and *Or* 80. 22 *Xerxis . . . þa þærto for mid eallum þæm mægene þe he ðærto gelædan mehte, 7 þær feohtende wæron III dagas . . .* (singular noun and prepositional phrase). When there is no preceding conjunction, as in *ChronA* 88. 7 (894) *þa ne mehte seo fird hie na hindan of faran, ær hie wæron inne on þæm geweorce; besæton þeah þæt geweorc utan sume twegen dagas . . .* and *Beo* 3030 *Weorod eall aras; ‖ eodon unbliðe under Earnanæs*, modern readers are more aware of the unexpressed subject. The pronoun can, of course, be expressed in the interests of clarity, style, or emphasis, e.g. *ChronE* 95. 6 (910) *7 mycel sciphere hider com suþan of Lidwicum 7 hergedon swiðe be Sefærn ac hi þær mæst ealle siððan forforon, ChronA* 86. 20 (894) *. . . 7 wæs se micla here æt ham. þa foron hie to . . . , ChronA* 78. 9-15 (885), and *ChronA* 85. 18-22 (894), where *hie* in line 20 indicates a change of subject.

§1509. Second, we have sentences in which an unexpressed subject has to be inferred from a word or group of words not in the nominative case in the same clause or in a neighbouring one. Examples in which the subject can be inferred from a word in another case in the same clause include *BlHom* 233. 2 *Broþor, hwyder wille feran mid þys medmyclum scipe?, BlHom* 99. 29 *. . . oþþe eal se wela þe him dæghwamlice gesamnodan, Phoen* 111 *Siþþan hine sylfne æfter sundplegan ‖ heahmod hefeð*, and *Mald* 20 *and bæd þæt hyra randas rihte heoldon.*

§1510. A nominative subject has to be inferred from an oblique case in a preceding clause in *BlHom* 13. 28 *ah hie a moton mid him gefeon, þær leofað 7 rixað a buton ende on ecnesse, ÆCHom* i. 196. 17 *þaða Ioseph þis smeade, þa com him to Godes engel and bebead him þæt sceolde habban gymene ægðer ge ðære meder ge þæs cildes*, and *Beo* 67 *Him on mod bearn, ‖ þæt healreced hatan wolde . . .* (in these the clause without a subject is subordinate to the preceding clause); in *Or* 114. 8, *Or* 110. 31 *His forme gefeoht wæs wið Atheniense 7 hie oferwonn, ÆCHom* i. 106. 24 *Ða easternan tungelwitegan gesawon niwne steorran beorhtne, na on heofenum betwux oðrum tunglum, ac wæs angenga betwux heofenum and eorðan*, and

Phoen 179 ne mæg him bitres wiht
scyldum sceððan, ac gescylded a
wunað ungewyrded . . .

(in these the two clauses are in syndetic parataxis); in *Or* 70. 6 *On
þæm dagum wæron þa mæstan ungetima on Romanum . . . under
þæm twæm consulum, Tita 7 Publia hatton, Bo* 54. 1 *On swilcum 7
on oðrum swelcum lænum 7 hreosendum weorðscipum ælces mennisces modes ingeþanc bið geswenced mid ðære geornfulnesse 7 mid
ðære tiluncga; wenð þonne þ hit hæbbe sum healic god gestryned . . .*
(where *hit* suggests that *mod* (n.) and not *ingeþanc* (m.) is the understood subject of *wenð*), *WHom* 17. 48 *Ðis mæg to heorthoge æghwylcum bisceope, beþence hine georne be þam þe he wille, Beo*
2877–82, and

Beo 665	Hæfde Kyningwuldor
Grendle togeanes,	swa guman gefrungon,
seleweard aseted;	sundornytte beheold
ymb aldor Dena,	eotonweard' abead

(in these the two clauses are in asyndetic parataxis);[35] and in *Law VAs.*
1. 1 *Gif se hlaford þonne wille ðone man mid woh fordon, berecce
hine þonne, gif he mæge, on folcgemote* (where the presence of the
reflexive *hine* may be noted; cf. § 889 and *WHom* 17. 48 above),
BenR 72. 4 *Gif his saule gyltas cþerum monnum digle beoð and him
sylfum cuðe, mid his andetnesse onwreo ða his abbode, WHom* 20c.
101,

Beo 143	. . . se þæm feonde ætwand.
	Swa rixode ond wið rihte wan,
	ana wið eallum . . .

(though Maisenhelder (p. 68) sees *ana* as the subject of *rixode*), and
Rid 12. 3 *Gif me feorh losað, fæste binde ‖ swearte Wealas* (in these
the clause without a subject is the principal clause). Examples in
which a nominative subject can be inferred from an oblique case in
a following clause include the two examples quoted in § 373 and *Beo*
1188 *Hwearf þa bi bence, þær hyre byre wæron. Beo* 1168 *Spræc ða
ides Scyldinga* is separated by nineteen lines of direct speech from
Beo 1188 *Hwearf þa.* . . . But [*Wealhþeow*] could be supplied from
the general context and from *ic* in *Beo* 1184 as well as from *hyre* in
Beo 1188. For a similar instance with no equivalent of *hyre*, see *Bo*
9. 18–30. On *Mald* 212 see Robinson, *JEGP* 75 (1976), 35–7. A complicated example involving different kinds of clauses, *BlHom* 95. 12–
19, is analysed by Pogatscher (p. 281).

---

[35] Andrew (*SS*, §§ 90–1, and *Postscript*, § 53) seeks to eliminate these and some dozen
other examples in *Beowulf* on the grounds that they 'may easily be due to scribal error'.
This is sometimes possible, e.g. in *Beo* 1903–4. But Andrew's emendations cannot be
accepted in all examples.

§1511. Third are those sentences in which an unexpressed subject in a principal clause has to be inferred from a nominative in a neighbouring subordinate clause or vice versa. Examples in which a preceding subordinate clause provides the subject for a following principal clause are not common, but include *CP* 25. 8 *ðeah ðe hi næfre leorningcnihtas næren, wilniað ðeah lareowas to beonne, Jud* 106 . . . *þæt he on swiman læg,* || *druncen and dolhwund. Næs ða dead ða gyt,* and perhaps *Beo* 469 [*Heregar*] *se wæs betera ðonne ic!* || *Siððan þa fæhðe feo þingode.* They occur most often in examples like *ÆLS* 12. 138 *Gif he hwæt tobrece ongean godes willan bete þæt georne*; see further Pogatscher, p. 279, and Visser, i, §13. I have found no certain examples in which a following subordinate clause provides the subject. The dual pronoun *wit* can be supplied for *Beo* 539 *Hæfdon swurd nacod* from the preceding or following subordinate clause, while it seems better to follow Carnicelli (69. 26) and to insert [*we*] in *Solil* 32. 3 *Forði me þincð swiðe dysig man þe wilnat þ* [*we*] *hine eallunga ongytan swilcne swilc he is þa hwile þe we on þysse worlde beoð* than to omit *þ* with Endter (for *þ* is supported by the form *wilnat*) or to assume non-expression of the subject. Endter and Carnicelli agree in inserting [*we*] in *Solil* 18. 16 and [*þu*] in *Solil* 24. 1; see Wülfing, i, §225.

§1512. I have not found any certain examples in which the unexpressed subject of a subordinate clause has to be supplied from a following principal clause.[36] It is, however, very easy to find subordinate clauses in which an unexpressed subject has to be inferred from an immediately or closely preceding governing clause. Space does not permit full exemplification here, but it will be seen from the examples given by Pogatscher (p. 278 and *passim*) that the phenomenon is more common in poetry than prose. The clause from which the subject has to be inferred is usually a principal clause, but may in its turn be subordinate to another clause. The following are typical:
(noun clauses)

Beo 2518
                    Nolde ic sweord beran,
    wæpen to wyrme,   gif ic wiste hu
    wið ðam aglæcean   elles meahte
    gylpe wiðgripan . . .

and *HomU* 35. 222. 24 *Hwæt, he drihten þa openlice cydde on þam worde, þa he cwæþ þæt an sunnandæg of deaþe arise, þæt* . . . ;

---

[36] Pogatscher's example 32 (p. 264) is actually not one. The *hig* missing after *þa* 'when' in Bright's *Reader* 139. 28 appears in both manuscripts; see *Nic(A)* 512. 12 (*hig*) and *Nic(B)* 513. 12 (*hyg*).

(adjective clause) *GenA* 97-102; (clause of place) *Beo* 286 *Weard maðelode, ðær on wicge sæt,* || *ombeht unforht*; (clauses of time) *Beo* 1486 *þæt ic gumcystum godne funde* || . . . *breac þonne moste* and *Wan* 19-29;[37] (clause of purpose) *BlHom* 247. 24 *Min Drihten Hælend Crist, send þinne þone Halgan Gast, þæt awecce ealle þa þe on þisse wætere syndon*;[38] (clauses of result) *BlHom* 65. 29 7 *se Alysend þysses menniscan cynnes hine sylfne geeaþmedde þæt of hehþe þæs fæderlican þrymmes to eorþan astag* . . . and *Beo* 565-9; (clause of reason) *BlHom* 191. 34 *Gefeoþ ge 7 wynsumiaþ, forþon þe micle mundboran gegearwod habbað*; (comparative clause) *Or* 86. 7 7 *nu sume men secgað þæt þa [tida] beteran wæren þonne nu sien*; (concessive clause) *Beo* 2343 . . . *ond se wyrm somod,* || *þeah ðe hordwelan heolde lange*; and (conditional clause) *MCharm* 4. 6 *Ut, litel spere, gif her inne sie* (cf. *MCharm* 4. 12 *Ut, lytel spere, gif hit her inne sy*).

§1513. This non-expression of a pronoun subject which can be supplied from a preceding clause must be accepted as idiomatic OE. Pogatscher (p. 278) argues that it goes back to WGmc. It could, of course, go back further. But the fact that it occurs (or survives) only spasmodically is hard to explain. Pogatscher's notion (p. 286) that the subject is unexpressed when it hovers ('vorschwebt') before the hearer's mind is impossible to apply in practice; here I agree with Andrew (*Postscript,* §§ 75-7). Alistair Campbell, in his lectures at Oxford, said what Pogatscher perhaps meant when he observed that 'always it is, if not the strictly grammatical, at least the psychological subject of what precedes that one omits'. But even this does not explain the principle on which the subject is sometimes expressed and sometimes not in what appear to us parallel situations. Pogatscher (pp. 275 ff.) rightly rejects the idea that all the examples are the result of scribal error. In attempting to revive this notion, Andrew finds himself committed to what seems to me the unlikely suggestion that 'a scribe unaccustomed to poetic usage' is responsible for

---

[37] The examples cited by Pogatscher (pp. 263-4) and Andrew (*Postscript,* § 76) of *siþþan* clauses with an unexpressed subject are sufficient in my opinion to certify that this is another. Dunning and Bliss's argument in their note to *Wan* 23a that 'the *ic* in 23b is superfluous, since if the subject of a co-ordinate clause is the same as that of the preceding clause it is not *normally* expressed' [my italics] is another instance of the fallacious argument that 'since X is uncommon, Y cannot be an example'. See Böhme, Part V, for more examples of temporal clauses with unexpressed subjects.

[38] In this example and in *BlHom* 147. 18 *Hwylc is of us Drihten þæt hæbbe swa hwite saule swa þeos halige Marie?* (where the *þæt* clause could be classified as consecutive with the subject unexpressed) *þæt* may be a relative pronoun with lack of concord. On this problem see §§ 2139-44 and 2806. On examples like *BlHom* 207. 11 . . . *þa swaðo* . . . *ðe ic ær sægde þæt þær ærest on ðæm marmanstane gemeted wæron,* see § 1980.

the 'signal violation of poetic idiom' which he detects in such examples as *Beo* 286 (§1512). I am afraid that the reason for the spasmodic appearance of the idiom lies buried with its users.

§1514. The same is true of those examples in which there is no referent in the immediate context for the unexpressed subject. These are naturally too long to quote here, but I give references to a few, with the nearest referent from which the subject can be inferred in brackets: *Bo* 9. 29 (9. 15 *se wisdom* and 9.20 *him*), *BlHom* 189. 17 (189. 4 *Neron . . . he* and 189. 6 *þe*), and *Phoen* 140 (125 *fugles* and 127 *wrixleþ*). We could add *Beo* 1020 (1010 *cyning* and 1017 *Hroðgar*). The difficulty of *Beo* 1590b—of which Andrew (*Postscript*, §49) says 'no sense . . . can be made'—can be reduced, if not removed, by placing 1588b-90a in parentheses; see §1717. But it is comparable with the other three examples. See further Pogatscher, pp. 289-90.

§1515. A special problem exists in

Cæd(M) 1   Nu scylun hergan   hefaenrices uard,
                    metudæs maecti   end his modgidanc,
                    uerc uuldurfadur . . . ,

where MSS *L* and *T* agree with *M* in having no *we*, whereas some other manuscripts have *Nu we*, which is of course supported by Bede's *debemus*. The notion that a first person nominative pronoun could be unexpressed when there was no possible grammatical referent derives no support from *GenA* 870, *GenA* 1098, *GenB* 828, or *GenB* 885 (Sarrazin, *EStudien*, 38 (1907), 183, and Dobbie's ASPR note), and virtually none from *And* 1487 (Pogatscher, p. 285), where there is a clear sequence *And* 1478 *ic . . .* (1481) *Mycel is to secganne . . .* (1487) *Hwæðre git sceolon* || *. . . reccan.* So, despite the difficulty of the order Adv.VOS, it may be—as Christopher Ball (private communication), comparing *Benedicite, omnia opera . . .* , has suggested— that the original subject of *scylun* was *uerc uuldurfadur* and that *we* was a later insertion. If this is true, we may have to attribute the initial misunderstanding to Bede himself or to his informants. See Mitchell, in progress (*b*).

§1516. For reasons of convenience, other types of non-expression of the subject have been considered elsewhere; see the General Index. However, it can be said here that Amos is on firm ground when she writes (p. 135): 'There is no reason to trust that the unexpressed subject—or its replacement by a personal pronoun or *hit*—can validly indicate the relative dating of Old English literature.'

· 4. THE POSITION OF THE SUBJECT AND ITS ASSOCIATED ELEMENTS

§1517. As already noted in the appropriate sections, elements which qualify or are in apposition with a headword which is the subject of its clause can be grouped with it—either before or after—or can be separated from it by various elements.

§1518. On the position of the subject in relation to the verb, object, and other clause or sentence elements, see chapter IX, *passim*.

5. SUBJECT–VERB AGREEMENT

§1519. Normally the subject and verb agree in number and in person (though there is no distinction of forms in the plural); see §26. Dual pronouns take plural verbs; see §28.

§1520. Some apparent exceptions to this general rule involve collective nouns, numerals, indefinites, and the like; see §32. Many of the examples cited by Stoelke (*passim*) belong here. Others involve verb forms in *-eþ*, e.g. *Bede(B, O, Ca)* 80. 11 *Of heortan utgangeð yfele geþohtas* (where *Bede(T)* has *utgongað*) and *PPs* 86. 1 *Healdeð his staðelas halige beorgas*, or *-e*, e.g. *Bede* 438. 9 *ðy læs him ætwite 7 on edwit sette his geðoftan* and *GenA* 954 *þeah þe hie him from swice*. These can be taken as indicative and subjunctive plurals respectively; see §§18-20. So many more of the examples cited by Stoelke (*passim*) disappear and with them his observation (p. 75) that in *Or* 122. 10 . . . *þær we for eowerre agenre gnornunge moste* and the like 'die dritte Person Singularis hat den Versuch gemacht, nicht nur die Numerusgrenze, sondern auch die Personengrenze zu überschreiten' ['the third person singular has tried to cross not only the boundary of number but also that of person']. In *WHom(BH)* 20. 52 *7 us stalu 7 cwalu, stric 7 steorfa, orfcwealm 7 uncoðu, hol 7 hete 7 rypera reaflac derede swiðe þearle, derede* (which appears in all the manuscripts) may be singular after a group of nouns viewed as one entity (§30) or a preterite indicative plural in *-e* (§19). Neither it nor any of the other examples cited by Mohrbutter (p. 54) provides any support for Bethurum's assertion (p. 360) that 'a singular verb with a plural subject is not unusual in Wulfstan's writings (see Dunkhase [she means Mohrbutter], p. 54)'.

§1521. Some examples in which an inconsistency in number may be due to the presence of an ambiguous form of a pronoun or adjective have been discussed in §77. Even in *BlHom* 53. 8 *forþon þe he heold ær his æhta him to wean 7 to wlencum 7 forwyrndon þam Drihtnes þearfum*, the ambiguous *him* might have triumphed over the unambiguous *he* and *his* to produce the pl. *forwyrndon*. Such an error is more likely on the part of a scribe than that of an author.

§1522. Other examples too in which lack of concord has been detected can be explained. Stoelke (p. 77) finds it in *Or* 178. 6 *ac hie gewearð þæt hie wolden to Romanum friþes wilnian*, where *gewearð* is impersonal, and (p. 16) in *Beo* 1131, a much discussed passage in which *deð* has been emended to *doð*, read as a plural, or taken with *oþer . . . gear*. But there remains a hard core of examples in which a plural subject is (or appears to be) preceded by a singular verb in real defiance of the rule of subject–verb concord. These occur in early prose, e.g. *Or* 116. 33 *On þæm gefeohte wæs ærest anfunden Sciþþia wanspeda*, *CP* 77. 15 *On ðæm selfan hrægle . . . wæs eac awriten ða naman ðara twelf heahfædera*, *CP* 157. 4 *Eac wæs gesewen on ðæm wage atifred ealle ða heargas Israhela folces*, and *CP* 411. 32 *Swa bið on ðisse menniscan gecynde manige on beteran hade 7 on beteran endebyrdnesse wyrsan, 7 on wyrsan hade 7 on wyrsan endebyrdnesse beteran*; in later prose, e.g. *ÆCHom* i. 316. 8 *ne heora nan næfde synderlice æhta, ac him eallum wæs gemæne heora ðing*, *ÆCHom* i. 330. 7 *forðan ðe him is cuð þæra eadmodra manna naman*, and *ÆHom* 15. 112 *Hym wæs behaten, gif hy heoldon Godes æ, eorðlice wæstmas, and Crist witodlice behet þæt ece lif þam þe his word healdað*; and in the poetry, e.g. *Men* 184 *Winterfylleð, swa hine wide cigð ‖ igbuende Engle and Seaxe*, *Rid* 8. 7 *stille on wicum ‖ siteð nigende*, *Max i* 122 . . . *snyttro in breostum, ‖ þær bið þæs monnes modgeþoncas*, *Prec* 4 *Do a þætte duge, deag þin gewyrhtu*,

Wan 92   Hwær cwom mearg? Hwær cwom mago?   Hwær cwom
                                                        maþþumgyfa?
             Hwær cwom symbla gesetu?   Hwær sindon seledreamas?,

Soul i 57   Ne mæg þe nu heonon adon,   hyrsta þa readan
             ne gold ne seolfor   ne þinra goda nan,
             ne þinre bryde beag   ne þin boldwela,
             ne nan þara goda   þe ðu iu ahtest,

where *Soul ii* 54 has *magon*, and *Men* 206 . . . *þæt us wunian ne mot wangas grene, ‖ foldan frætuwe*.

§1523. I would group *cigð* in *Men* 184 and *siteð* in *Rid* 8. 7 as scribal weakenings of plural forms through the stages *cigað* > *cigeð* and *sittað* > *sitteð* respectively; see §20. But we cannot dismiss the rest so easily. Schrader (p. 16) suggests that 'bei vorstehendem Prädicate ist dem Gedanken das Subject oft nicht so präsent, wie bei nachstehendem, und es steht daher zuweilen im Singular trotz pluralem Subjecte' ['with a preceding predicate the idea of the subject is often not as present in the mind as when the predicate follows, and it is thus sometimes in the singular despite the plural subject']. This would seem to imply that the author committed himself to a singular verb before formulating the actual grammatical subject. The idea has some merit. Thus in *ÆHom* 15. 112 Ælfric probably intended a singular subject corresponding to *þæt ece lif*, and in *Max i* 122 the sg. *snyttro* may have influenced *bið*. Schrader's explanation might also embrace those plural subjects in which we can detect a collective notion. Examples from the prose are *CP* 157. 4 'the whole pantheon', *CP* 411. 32 'a great number', *ÆCHom* i. 316. 8 'everything', and perhaps *CP* 77. 15 and *ÆCHom* i. 330. 7 in which *(ða) naman* might equal 'a list'. In the poetry there is a collective idea in *gewyrhtu* in *Prec* 4, but the word could be feminine singular; see BTS, s.v. In *Wan* 92 *gesetu* might imply 'a group of buildings', but the *cwom* which goes with it might be the result of repeating a formula, either automatically or for artistic effect. It is hard to see a collective idea in *ÆCHom* i. 314. 8 *and wæs æteowed bufon heora ælcum swylce fyrene tungan*, where Schrader (p. 16) detects lack of concord. I think he is wrong. Since *æteowed* is not declined, we can argue that *wæs æteowed* is impersonal and that *fyrene tungan* is not its subject: 'there was an appearance like tongues of fire'.

§1524. These examples so reinforce one another that it is tempting to suggest that the *lectio difficilior mæg* in *Soul i* 57 may be right— *(ge)hyrst* is not used in the singular as far as I have observed and may have a collective notion 'jewellery'—and that *magon* in *Soul ii* 54 may be a correction by a scribe who was a grammatical purist. I can, however, find no defence for *mot* in *Men* 206, where the emendation *moton* seems obligatory; I am unwilling to accept the notion that the combination singular verb + plural subject was as common as is suggested by Bethurum (see §1520) and Brook (p. 84): 'when a plural subject follows its verb, the verb is often, but not invariably, in the singular'.

§1525. When two singular subjects are joined by *ond*, the verb may be singular or plural; see §§29-30. When two singular subjects are joined by *oððe*, the verb is normally singular, e.g. *ÆCHom* i. 242. 4 *ac se hyra oððe se medgylda ne gedyrstlæcð . . . , Beo* 1762 *eft sona bið,* || *þæt þec adl oððe ecg eafoþes getwæfeð,* and *Rid* 40. 23 *Ic eom on stence strengre micle* || *þonne ricels oþþe rose sy.* An exception is *El* 508 . . . *þara þe wif oððe wer on woruld cendan.* Here *oððe* comes close to meaning 'and'; there may be a lack of grammatical concord, but the plural verb is not illogical, since it takes two to make a child.

§1526. When two or more singular subjects are joined by *ne* in a principal clause, the verb normally precedes the subject and is singular, e.g. *BlHom* 25. 31 *nis þær ege ne geflit ne yrre ne nænig wiþerweardnes, ÆCHom* i. 18. 23 *Ne þorfte Adam ne eal mancynn þe him siððan of acom deaðes onbyrian gif . . . , Beo* 1735 *no hine wiht dweleð* || *adl ne yldo,* and *Phoen* 14. In *Phoen* 60 *þær ne hægl ne hrim hreosað to foldan, ne windig wolcen,* we find what appears to be a plural verb following two singular subjects in what must be taken as a principal clause. However, in view of the sg. *gehreoseð* in *ChristC* 938 and of the not uncommon *-eð/-að* confusion in the *Exeter Book* (e.g. *Phoen* 488 and 511), the verb may be singular; see §19. In subordinate clauses, the verb normally follows the subject and is singular, e.g.

GuthA 655   . . .   to þam leofestan
              ecan earde,   þær is eþellond
              fæger ond gefealic   in fæder wuldre,
              ðær eow næfre   fore nergende
              leohtes leoma   ne lifes hyht
              in godes rice   agiefen weorþeð. . . .

A plural verb is found in *And* 1422 . . . *ne synu ne ban on swaðe lagon.* . . . But a singular verb may precede two subjects in subordinate clauses even in the late prose, e.g. *ÆCHom* i. 370. 18 . . . *þæt him ne bið getiðod naðor ne synna forgyfenys ne infær þæs heofenlican rices* and (with introductory *þær*) *ÆCHom* ii. 8. 7 . . . *swa þæt ðær nys naðor gemencgednys ne todal.* MnE too has the singular.

§1527. When all the subjects joined by *oððe* or *ne* are plural, the verb is naturally plural, e.g. *ÆCHom* i. 318. 28 . . . *wæron hi Ebreisce oððe Grecisce oððe Romanisce oððe Egyptisce* . . . and

Sea 82   næron nu cyningas   ne caseras
              ne goldgiefan   swylce iu wæron.

When they differ in number, the verb agrees with the nearest subject, e.g. *ÆLS* 31. 1270 . . . *þæt hi ealle ne mihton ne fisceras ne he sylf gefon ænne sprot, ÆGram* 259. 18 *ne lingua nec manus oculiue peccent, ne tunge ne handa oððe eagan syngion, Phoen* 134–9, and

Jul 590   Næs hyre wloh ne hrægl
                ne feax ne fel   fyre gemæled
                ne lic ne leoþu.

F. THE VERB

1. INTRODUCTORY REMARKS

§1528. I have already discussed in §§594-1099 the types of verbs which existed in OE, their paradigms, the uses of the moods and tenses (with references forward where appropriate), the development of periphrastic forms, verbal rection, and other topics which are at least partly morphological. Here I deal with verbal problems which seem more properly syntactical—though I do not stand too strongly on the distinction. The subjects, objects, and complements, of verbs are, of course, discussed elsewhere in this chapter.

2. APPOSITION

§1529. The two finite verbs in examples like *Beo* 306 *Guman onetton,* ‖ *sigon ætsomne* can be said to be in apposition. Writing of the poetry, Bliss (1958, p. 11) remarks: 'It seems probable that when two consecutive finite verbs stand in apposition to each other the second does not open a new clause.' Despite this and the fact that the example quoted above could be translated 'The warriors hastened, marching together', I have taken it and similar constructions as examples of parataxis; see §§1690-8. The difference is terminological.

3. REPETITION, NON-REPETITION, AND NON-EXPRESSION, OF VERBS

§1530. The patterns occurring in OE do not differ significantly from those in MnE if allowance is made for the obvious differences in element order and inflexions.[39] An independent verb may be repeated, either alone, e.g. *ÆCHom* ii. 104. 12 *swa swa Crist sylf cwæð be sumon rican menn on his godspelle: he cwæð '. . .'* and

---

[39] A. Ya. Antipova, in 'Glagol'noe zameščenie v drevneangliĭskom yazyke' (Verbal substitution in Old English), *Vestnik Leningradskogo gosudarstvennogo universiteta*, No. 8, vyp. 2, Series: Literature, History, Language (Leningrad, 1963), 125-36, uses the term 'verbal substitution' to mean the expression of the verbal element in the sentence by an incomplete verb, as in *Gewislice ic hæbbe . . . gif hi ðorftan*, and *Sua dide*. She concludes that elements of analysis appear in the structure of English before analytical verb forms. This accords with my findings.

ÆCHom i. 168. 26 *Ne lifað na se man be hlafe anum, ac lifað be ðam wordum ðe gað of Godes muðe*, or with its complement, e.g. *ÆCHom* i. 302. 19 *Him is gemæne mid stanum, þæt he beo wunigende; him is gemæne mid treowum, þæt he lybbe*, or be replaced by a synonym, e.g. *ÆCHom* ii. 448. 23 *Ne behydde ic mine synna, ne ic on minum bosme ne bediglode mine unrihtwisnysse.* One element of a periphrasis is often repeated, e.g. the verb in *ÆCHom* i. 274. 9 *Swa we sceolon eac, gif bið an ure geferena on sumre earfoðnysse, ealle we sceolon his yfel besargian* and the infinitive in *ÆCHom* i. 168. 1 *Se Hælend com to mancynne forði ðæt he wolde ealle ure costnunga oferswiðan mid his costnungum, and oferswiðan urne ðone ecan deað mid his hwilwendlicum deaðe*. Part of a periphrasis may have to be understood from another form of the same verb, e.g. *ÆCHom* i. 568. 2 . . . *Sennacherib, Syria cyning, manega leoda mid micclum cræfte to his anwealde gebigde, and swa wolde eac þone gelyfedan cyning Ezechiam*. Different participles may be combined with the same form of the verb 'to be', e.g. *ÆCHom* i. 542. 26 *Sume hi wæron mid wæpnum ofslagene, sume on lige forswælede, oðre mid swipum ofbeatene* . . . and *ÆCHom* i. 282. 12 *and ðæs Ælmihtigan Godes Sunu is æfre of ðam Fæder acenned, and æfre mid him wunigende.*

§1531. Repetition of a simple verb or of (part of) a periphrasis is stylistic and therefore the exception rather than the rule. The variations in *ÆCHom* i. 96. 17-26 and ii. 376. 27-31 will show how effective repetition can be when carefully employed by a master. On the use of *don* to avoid repetition of a preceding verb see §665.

§1532. A simple verb or a periphrasis is sometimes not expressed in a clause or sentence which requires the same form as that which precedes, e.g. *ÆCHom* i. 286. 1 *Oðer ðing deð seo hætu, and oðer seo beorhtnys, ÆCHom* i. 544. 32 *Blindum hi forgeafon gesihðe, healtum færeld* . . . , *ÆCHom* ii. 48. 4 *Hwilc fulluht sealde he? His agen fulluht*, and *ÆCHom* i. 286. 17 *Hwa mæg mid wordum ðære heofenan freatewunge asecgan? Oððe hwa ðære eorðan wæstmbærnysse?* Such non-expression is occasionally extended to situations in which a different form of the same verb is required, e.g. *ÆCHom* i. 284. 17 *Ælc ðæra þreora is God, þeahhwæðere hi ealle an God* and *ÆCHom* ii. 530. 16 *þæt gerip is micel, and ða rifteras feawa*. See also Brooks's note on *And* 1376.

§1533. The verb 'to be' is sometimes unexpressed when it cannot be understood from a preceding clause or sentence. Visser (i, §231) explains this as due to the 'semantic "emptiness"' of the copula. Examples include *ÆCHom* i. 56. 33 *Gyrstandæg sungon englas 'Gode wuldor on heannyssum'*, *ÆCHom* ii. 316. 20 *Micel mildheort- nys þæs Metodan Drihtnes, þæt we beon gecigede swa gesæliglice ures Scyppendes frynd*, *Beo* 3062 *Wundur hwar þonne* || *eorl ellenrof ende gefere . . .*, *Beo* 2297 *ne ðær ænig mon* || *on þære westenne*, and perhaps *Beo* 2035 *dryhtbearn Dena, duguða biwenede* (which I discuss in *Neophil.* 52 (1968), 297). See §3864 and also Roberts, *NQ* 224 (1979), 58.

§1534. It is sometimes doubtful whether we have an independent use of *magan, *sculan*, and the like, or ellipsis of an infinitive; see §§1000-8 and Visser, i, §234, s.v. *sceal.*

4. THE INFINITIVES

a. Introductory remarks

§1535. A full list of the functions of the simple (uninflected) and inflected infinitives, with references to relevant discussions, will be found in §971. The morphology and some of those functions have been discussed in §§920-71. Here we are concerned with those situ- ations in which the infinitives function more or less as nouns, i.e. as subject, object, or complement, of a simple sentence or clause, or in apposition with one of these elements. It will be pointed out below that some at least of the problems discussed are terminological; it is for this reason that the infinitive expressing purpose is discussed here. We may also note the varying uses of the words 'predicate' and 'predicative'; see initially Callaway (1913, p. 5 and *passim*), Bock 1931, pp. 132 ff., and my §§1540-3.

§1536. On the origin of the various constructions with the infini- tives, see Callaway 1913, chapter xiv; van der Gaaf, *EStudies*, 16 (1934), 81 ff.; and Bock 1931, *passim*.

b. As subject

§1537. Bock (1931, p. 247) tells us that 'einen reinen Infinitiv als Subjekt gibt es im Ae. Nicht'[40] and that 'in der Schriftsprache . . .

---

[40] The apparently striking contradiction between this remark and that of Visser (ii, §901) arises from careless expression on Visser's part. His statement that the simple infini- tive is of 'frequent occurrence . . . in this position' in OE simply does not square with his citation (ii, §898) of six examples, all of which show Latin influence, and indeed almost contradicts what he says in ii, §898.

nimmt der [to] Infinitiv nie die erste Stelle im Satz wie jedes nomi-
nale Subjekt ein' ['there is no use of a pure infinitive as the subject
of a sentence in OE . . . in the literary language . . . the [to] infinitive never stands at the beginning of the sentence as any noun subject
does']. This requires only slight qualification if we accept the idea
that an infinitive is not the subject unless it has first position in the
sentence (on this see below), for the infinitives rarely occur as S in
the pattern SVO. *Mark(WSCp)* 12. 33 *7 lufigean his nehstan swa
hine sylfne þæt is mare eallum onsægdnyssum* (cited by Visser, ii,
§898) is influenced by the Latin *et dilegere proximum* . . . and because of the tautologic *þæt* does not show the infinitive as the subject. Better examples are *Prog* 3 (*Cockayne*) 208. 3 *Stanes asendan
seocnysse ge[tacnað]. Cidan on swefnum ceapes eacan ge[tacnað]*
and *Matt(WSCp)* 20. 23 *to sittanne on mine swiþran healfe oððe on
wynstran nys me inc to syllanne*. But they are hard to parallel and
they too show Latin influence.

§1538. Some writers, however, describe infinitives as the subject
even when they do not have initial position. They include Callaway
(1913, chapter i), who criticizes his predecessors and classifies as
subjects infinitives which to others modify adjectives (§§1546-7),
serve as complements (§1541), or are in apposition (§1547). He in
turn is criticized by Bock (1931, pp. 124-54), whose rule seems to
be that unless an infinitive is at the head of its sentence, it is not the
subject. Visser (ii, §§898-915) perhaps straddles both camps; he
lists the infinitives in many of these patterns as subjects, but speaks
of some of them as complements. Space forbids further discussion.
What is in dispute is not OE idiom, but matters of classification and
terminology.

§1539. These writers were not unaware that certain constructions
were grammatically ambiguous—at least for modern scholars. Thus
Callaway (1913, p. 9) says that in sentences such as *CP 401*. 15 *Ic
eow secgge hwæt eow arwyrðlicost is to beganne* and *ÆCHom* ii.
386. 3 *Ðis fers is swiðe deoplic eow to understandenne* 'the infinitive seems to me, as a rule, to be subjective; but it is possible, of
course, that the pronoun or noun is subjective instead of objective,
and that the infinitive is adverbial and modifies the adjective'. This in
fact must be the situation in his third example—*Bo* 118. 6 *þæt is
[wundorlic þ ðu sægst 7 swiðe] earfoðlic dysegum monnum to
ongitanne*—(which he quotes in truncated form without the portion
I place in square brackets), for it is impossible to accept that the
initial *þæt* can be first the nominative subject of *is* and then the

accusative object of the infinitive. It must also be the situation in *ÆCHom* ii. 542. 27 *Ælc ehtnys bið earfoðe to þolienne*, where *ælc ehtnys* is nominative and cannot be the object of the infinitive. So there are examples in which the infinitive cannot be the subject of the verb 'to be'. But, as far as I can see, there are none in which it must be. Even in *Or* 74. 7 *swa ungeliefedlic is ænigum menn þæt to gesecgenne*, *Solil* 40. 4 *ac for þæs ðincges lufum þe ðe rihtre ys to lufianne þonne þæt*, and *GuthB* 1065 *Nis me earfeðe || to geþolianne þeodnes willan*—examples about which Callaway (1913, pp. 9-10) is 'less doubtful'—the infinitive need not be the subject of *(n)is*, which may be used impersonally with no expressed subject; compare my remarks in §1546 about the alternative but less common pattern with *hit* seen in *Or* 134. 15 *hit is ungeliefedlic to secganne*. The same is, I believe, true for examples like *ÆCHom* i. 216. 34 *be ðam is gelimplicor þonne mare to reccenne þonne nu sy*. See further §§934-44.

c. As complement

§1540. The term 'complement' (Visser, ii, §916) or 'predicate nominative' (Callaway 1913, p. 73) is sometimes used of the infinitives in examples like *ÆCHom* i. 490. 9 *Hwæt is lange lybban buton lange swincan?* and *ÆCHom* ii. 574. 2 *Hwæt is to cweðenne 'Ne cann ic eow' buton þæt ic ne worhte eow ðyllice?* On the analogy of *ÆCHom* i. 386. 10 *Hwæt eart ðu, leof hlaford?* we can describe these infinitives as 'nominative'. Whether they are the subject or complement of the copula is, I suppose, arguable. See further Callaway 1913, pp. 73-5, and Bock 1931, pp. 151-2.

§1541. The same two possibilities arise in *Mark(WSCp)* 9. 47 *betere þe is mid anum eagan gan on godes rice* . . . and *Matt(WSCp)* 19. 24 . . . *eaðelicre byð þam olfende to ganne þurh nædle eage* . . . , which Callaway (1913, pp. 14 and 11) classifies as 'subjective'. But some writers describe them as examples of the dative + infinitive construction; see §1547.

§1542. There is room too for difference of opinion about the classification of examples like *Or* 50. 16 *þeah swa hwelcne mon swa lyste þæt witan* . . . , *Beo* 1792 *Geat unigmetes wel, || rofne randwigan restan lyste*, *Coll* 112 *Gebeorhlicre ys me faran to ea* . . . , and *Coll* 8 *Leofre ys us beon beswungen*. Visser (i, §33, and ii, §899) hesitates between classifying these infinitives as causative objects, complements to impersonal colligations, or subjects. He is in the same dilemma (i, §33, and ii, §903) over similar examples with inflected infinitives, including *Or* 42. 12 *Eac me sceal aðreotan ymbe Philopes . . . to asecgenne, BlHom* 63. 5 *us is mycel þearf to witenne þæt Iudas nu is cwylmed . . . , ÆCHom* i. 360. 29 *Us gelustfullað gyt furður to sprecenne be ðan halgan were . . .* , and *Beo* 473 *Sorh is me to secganne . . .* , but seems to take the infinitive as subject in *GD(C)* 39. 21 *. . . þæt us nu nære alyfed to farene* and even in *ÆCHom* ii. 40. 15 *þis nis nu alyfed nanum men to donne*, where *þis* could (I suppose) be construed as object of *to donne* but where Visser's observation (iii, §2140) that 'the only word that can be apprehended as the subject is the infinitive' is not true. Whether the infinitive in such examples can be described as the subject seems to me to depend on whether the verb or phrase in question is found with the nominative of a thing (as opposed to the nominative of a person) as subject —a question which it is often impossible to answer; see §§1039-40. The distinction is important here. The nom. *setl* in *ÆCHom* i. 310. 3 *deman gedafnað setl* justifies us in explaining the infinitives in *ÆC Hom* ii. 318. 15 *Us gedafenað to donne dugeðe on sibbe . . . and eft on ehtnysse ure lif syllan for ðone soðan God . . .* as subjects of *gedafenað* (on the number of the verb see §30). But *ÆCHom* ii. 40. 6 *and we behofiað þæt we wisra lareowa trahtnunga . . . understandan* cannot in my opinion certify that in *Luke(WSCp)* 12. 12 *halig gast eow lærð on þære tide þa þing þe eow specan gebyrað* the infinitive *specan* is the subject of *gebyrað*. (I do not think that the need to make this particular distinction here vitiates my remarks in §1025.)

d. After verbs of motion and rest

§1543. To Callaway (1913, chapter v), the infinitive with verbs of rest or motion in examples like *LS* 14. 292 *And þa þær com fleogan drihtnes ængel* is predicative. He notes that other names have been proposed, including 'modal' and 'coordinate' (1913, p. 89). The interchangeability of the infinitive in this construction with a present participle—as in *ÆCHom* ii. 504. 30 *Ða comon þær fleogende twegen fægre englas*, where the participle has been variously described as appositive, verbal, or adverbial expressing manner—underlines the folly of taking names too seriously. See further Callaway 1913, pp. 221-4, and my §§967-9.

e. In apposition

§1544. Infinitives which explain or elaborate nouns are sometimes described as appositional, e.g. *ÆCHom* i. 360. 14 *Oðer forhæfednysse cynn is deorwurðre and healicre* . . . ; *styran his modes styrunge mid singalre gemetfæstnysse, and campian dæghwamlice wið leahtras, and hine sylfne ðreagian* . . . and *ÆCHom* ii. 244. 8 *Mihte ic hæbbe mine sawle to syllenne.* Here too belong examples with *þæt* such as *Mark (WSCp)* 12. 33 (§1537) and *Bede* 78. 22 *forðon hyngran, þyrstan, hatian, calan, wærigian—al þæt is of untrymnesse þæs gecyndes.*

§1545. Callaway, who gives more examples like the above (1913, pp. 75-7), also classifies as appositional certain infinitives with *ægðer, oðer,* and the like, e.g. *Or* 178. 9 *7 he him geswor on his goda noman þæt he ægþer wolde, ge þæt ærende abeodan* . . . *ge eac him þæt anwyrde eft gecyþan* and *CP* 355. 21 *forðæm he wisse ðæt hit bið swiðe unieðe ægðer to donne, ge wið ðone to cidanne ðe yfel deð, ge eac sibbe wið to habbenne.* Apposition seems the best ex-planation. But there are others. In *Or* 178. 9 we could say that *wolde* was used *apo koinou* governing *ægþer* and the two infinitives or that *ægþer* . . . *ge* . . . *ge eac* is a conjunctional combination. This last explanation, however, does not fit *CP* 355. 21 and is not supported by *Or* 44. 8 *7 him untweogendlice secgan het þæt hie oðer sceoldon, oþþe ðæt lond æt him alesan, oþþe he hie wolde mid gefeohte fordon 7 forherigan* and *Or* 120. 30 *þæt hie siþþan oþer sceoldon, oþþe for metelieste heora lif alætan, oþþe Somnitum an hand gan* (unless *oðer*—contrary to the dictionaries and grammars—can be taken as a conjunction) or by *Solil* 2. 10 . . . *forgife me þæt me to ægðrum onhagige: ge her nytwyrðe to beonne, ge huru þider to cumanne,* where *ægðrum* cannot be a conjunction.

§1546. Examples with *hit* like *Coll* 112 *Forþam plyhtlic þingc hit ys gefon hwæl* and *Bede* 2. 10 *Forþon hit is god godne to herianne 7 yfelne to leanne,* in which the infinitive can be said to be in appo-sition with *hit,* are rare. Examples known to me in addition to those quoted include *CP* 51. 5, *Or* 134. 15, 238. 2, and *HomU* 44. 283. 15. See further Visser, ii, §§907 and 908. The more usual pattern is seen in *Coll* 116 *Forþam leofre ys me gefon fisc* and *Matt(WSCp)* 17. 4 *god ys us her to beonne.* But in all four quoted examples the infini-tive may modify the adjective, with *hit* (where it occurs) as an empty subject; cf. *ÆGram* 135. 3 *tempus est arandi, hit ys tima to erigenne.* Both these possibilities exist in *Or* 52. 8 *Hit is unieþe to gesecgenne hu monege gewin siþþan wæron.* . . . But, despite Callaway (1913, p. 12), we cannot really take the infinitive as subject with *hit* as its object in *Or* 52. 8 any more than we can in *Coll* 112 and *Bede* 2. 10. So we had better conclude that in *ÆCHom* i. 94. 33 *Eaðe mihte þes cwyde beon læwedum mannum bediglod, nære seo gastlice getacning.*

Hit ðincð ungelæredum mannum dyselig to gehyrenne; ac gif hit him dyslic þince, þonne cide he wið God, þe hit gesette, na wið us, þe hit secgað the first two instances of *hit* are not objects of the infinitives but empty subjects of *ðincð*, while the second two refer to *þes cwyde* (or *seo gastlice getacning*), with lack of concord which can be paralleled (§47), but here may be due to the sequence *hit ðincð . . . hit ðincð*. In *ÆCHom* i. 394. 15 *ac hit ne fremede him swa gedon* too, where Callaway (1913, p. 15) classifies the infinitive as subject, *hit* is more likely to be an empty subject than a pronoun anticipating appositional *gedon* or a pronoun object of *gedon*. Thus we find that there are examples in which an infinitive not in first position cannot be the subject, but none in which it must be. We reached the same conclusion—*mutatis mutandis*—in §1539.

§1547. Fröhlich (pp. 68-70) lists *Or* 34. 31 *Ac þæt is to wundrianne þæt þa Egipti swa lytle þoncunge wiston Iosepe . . .* as an example of the type *hit is to* + infinitive. If this means that *þæt* in *Or* 34. 31 and *þis* in *ÆCHom* ii. 40. 15 *þis nis nu alyfed nanum men to donne* are to be taken as empty subjects, I cannot prove that he is wrong. But I doubt it. For reasons given above, I am not prepared to agree that the infinitive must be the subject in *Or* 34. 31 or even (despite Callaway 1913, p. 19) in *ÆCHom* ii. 40. 15, though here this solution is attractive. So again we are left with infinitives which can be appositional or which can be modifiers of an adjective or participle. To these alternatives can be added for *ÆCHom* ii. 40. 15 the possibility that we have the dative and infinitive construction; see §1541. But again, the form of the OE idioms is not in dispute—merely their parsing and classification by modern scholars.

f. As object

§1548. Many of Callaway's examples of what he calls the 'objective active infinitive' (1913, chapter ii) can be classified as accusative and infinitives, e.g. *ÆCHom* ii. 422. 28 *and se apostol abæd him wæter beran* (subject accusative unexpressed) and *ÆCHom* i. 604. 14 *Swa swa dæges leoht forwyrnð gehwilcne to gefremmenne þæt þæt seo niht geðafað*; on these see §§3745-51.

§1549. As noted in §955, some verbs have only the uninflected objective infinitive, e.g. *cunnian* (*ÆCHom* i. 450. 18 *and uton cunnian . . . ðone reðan wiðersacan . . . gegladian*); some have only the inflected infinitive, e.g. *smeagan* (*ÆCHom* ii. 146. 5 . . . *he sylf smeade þæt hus to aræraenne*); some have both, e.g. *beginnan* (*ÆCHom*

ii. 142. 13 *þa begann se wer dreorig wepan* but *ÆCHom* i. 22. 21 . . . *and begunnon þa to wyrcenne*). Callaway lists the verbs which belong to these three groups (1913, pp. 36, 43-4, and 58-9, respectively) and attempts to explain what differentiates their use (1913, pp. 60-71). He argues that (with the inevitable exceptions) verbs which take a direct accusative object have the uninflected infinitive, verbs which take other cases have the inflected infinitive, and verbs which take the accusative and at least one other case have both infinitives. But in §3723 I take issue with his classification of examples.

§1550. On the infinitives after *agan*, the 'modal' auxiliaries, and *(w)uton*, see §§932-3, 996-9, and 954. Callaway (1913, chapters iv and vi) speaks of these as 'predicative' rather than 'objective'. This too is a matter of terminology, as he himself recognizes.

§1551. Callaway (1913, p. 78) rightly dismisses a few examples in which other writers have construed infinitives as objects of prepositions.

g. Expressing purpose

§1552. Problems of terminology crop up also with the infinitive of purpose or the final infinitive. One is apparent when we consider *OrW* 29 *þonne him frea sylle* ‖ *to ongietanne godes agen bibod* and *Or* 42. 28 *7 ealle þa æðelestan bearn þara Atheniensa hi genoman 7 sealdon þæm Minotauro to etanne* . . . , in which Callaway (1913, pp. 47 and 142) classifies the infinitives as objective ('. . . grants to him to understand/the understanding of . . .') and final ('and gave [the children] to the Minotaur to eat/for eating') respectively, whereas Bock (1931, p. 158) sees the noun as direct object of the finite verb in both, with the infinitive expressing purpose. Bock (1931, pp. 157-60) notes several other pairs of examples in which Callaway makes a similar distinction.

§1553. These two possibilities—probably meaningful only to modern readers of OE—arise only when both the finite verb and the infinitive are transitive. Thus, we can take *Or* 54. 10 *Ac him Cirus his nefa gesealde Ircaniam þa þeode on anwald to habbanne* to mean either 'Cyrus gave him the people to have in his power' or 'Cyrus gave him to have the people in his power' and *ÆLS* 4. 226 *and heora fæder wæs cristen þam alyfde se casere heora cristendom to healdenne* to mean either '. . . whom the emperor allowed their Christianity to hold' or 'whom the emperor allowed to hold their Christianity'. (This difficulty has been discussed by Pope (*Ælfric*, i. 329, note to *ÆHom* 6. 22). But there are dangers in using the position of a pronoun object as evidence; see §2940. I cannot understand why Visser (i, §623) cites several examples of this sort as displaying 'absence of object'.) When either the infinitive or the verb is intransitive, the infinitive must go with the verb, e.g. *Matt(WSCp)* 8. 21 *alyfe me ærest to farenne* [*7 bebyrigean minne fæder*] and *ÆCHom* i. 542. 19 . . . *þæt hi on ðam micclum dome ofer twelf domsetl sittende beoð to demenne eallum mannum.* But even now we are not out of the terminological wood. Thus Callaway (1913, p. 136) classifies both *gretan* in *Beo* 2009 *Ic ðær furðum cwom* ‖ *to ðam hringselè Hroðgar gretan* and *secean* in *Beo* 267 *We þurh holdne hige hlaford þinne* ‖ . . . *secean cwomon* as examples of 'the uninflected final infinitive'. But both exemplify BT's statement (s.v. *cuman* II) that '*cuman* is used with the infinitive expressing manner or purpose'. (On the interchangeability of the infinitive and the present participle after verbs of motion, see §§967-9.) Whether we have manner or purpose seems to me to depend, in part at least, on the time-relationship of the two verbs. If the actions of the infinitive and the finite verb are contemporaneous—as in *Beo* 291 *Gewitaþ forð beran* ‖ *wæpen ond gewædu*—we can scarcely speak of purpose. If they are not—as in *Beo* 1274 *þa he hean gewat,* ‖ *dreame bedæled, deaþwic seon*—we can reasonably do so.

§1554. So we can agree that both infinitives often do express purpose, e.g. (uninflected) *ÆCHom* ii. 372. 24 *and ic wille faran fandian ðæra* and *ÆCHom* ii. 242. 35 *He eode eft sittan siððan mid his ðegnum,* and (inflected) *ÆCHom* ii. 372. 21 *Se færð to sceawienne his tun* . . . and *ÆCHom* i. 82. 27 . . . *he* . . . *seðe sylfwilles to ðrowienne middangearde genealæhte* (where *sylfwilles* seems decisive), though Mann, in 'Die Entstehung der finalen Infinitivs im Englischen' (*Archiv*, 187 (1950), 10-24), argues that the expression of purpose was originally restricted to the uninflected infinitive. For further examples—many dubious, as Callaway himself recognizes—and for the differences in the uses of the two infinitives when they express purpose, see §§2940-51 and Callaway 1913, chapter x.

5. THE PARTICIPLES

a. Morphology

§1555. The morphology of both present participles and second participles (§§23-4) has been discussed in §§101, 974, and 983.

b. Summary of uses

§1556. Both participles can be used alone or in participial phrases in the following functions: independently (as nouns) to form (part of) elements of a clause or sentence such as subject or object; attributively (as adjectives)—note the variation participle + noun, demonstrative + participle in *ÆCHom* i. 350. 12 *Behreowsigendum mannum he miltsað, ac he ne behet þam elcigendum gewiss lif oð merigen*; predicatively; appositively; and (in combination with *beon/wesan, weorþan*, and *habban*) to form verbal periphrases. The verbal force carried by the participles varies from example to example and the distinctions must not be pressed too rigidly. Occasionally we find a participle with a comparative or superlative form, e.g. *Bede* 394. 5 . . . *þær he hattra ⁊ beornendra wæs* and *Alex* 7. 13 *þa wæs ðær seo wæstmberendeste eorþe* (see also §101); with the prefix *un-*, e.g. *Met* 11. 13 *unawendende* (MS *J unawendendne*) and *LawIICn(G)* 81 *unawend* (MS *B unawended*); and with the suffix *-lic(e)*, e.g. *Bo(C)* 129. 8 *unandwendlic* (MS *B unawendendlic*) and *Bo(C)* 144. 15 *unanwendendlice* (MS *B unawendendlice*). We can detect an almost fossilized participial adjective in *ÆCHom* i. 136. 5 *þa wæs ðes man swiðe oflyst ðæs Hælendes tocymes*—the infinitive *oflystan* is not recorded; a more strongly verbal participle in *ÆCHom* ii. 292. 13 *ðone geðrowodan Crist* 'the Christ who had suffered, the crucified Christ'; and almost adverbial force in *ÆCHom* ii. 142. 23 *Cuðberhtus se halga siððan gefremode mihtiglice wundra, on ðam mynstre wunigende* (time), *ÆCHom* ii. 504. 30 *Ða comon þær fleogende twegen fægre englas* (manner), and *ÆCHom* ii. 130. 18 *and hi sylfe geðeoddon Cristes gelaðunge, on hine gelyfende* (cause). The difficulty of deciding whether a participle is predicative, appositive, or verbal—seen in some of the examples already cited and in *ÆCHom* i. 46. 16 . . . *and hu hi siððan feowertig geara on westene wæron mid heofenlicum bigleofan dæghwonlice gereordode* (where Thorpe has a comma after *wæron*)—has been discussed in §§975-9 and 984-5.

§1557. For references to the discussions on these uses, see the table of contents of chapter II and the General Index. Visser gives many examples (ii, §§1009-13, 1016, and 1144-7; iii, §§1790-5, 1890-1, 1894, and 2145-7). But his conclusions are not always acceptable.

§1558. The parallel use of present participles and finite verbs is seen in examples like *ÆCHom* i. 426. 29, *ÆCHom* i. 538. 14, *ÆCHom* ii. 340. 32, *ÆCHom* ii. 396. 20, and *ÆCHom* ii. 490. 21

and hi ða wunodon binnon ðære scire Babilonia, wyrcende miccle
wundra, onlihtende ða blindan, and deafum hlyst forgeafon, reoflige
geclænsodon, and deoflu fram wittseocum mannum afligdon.

§1559. On the interchangeability of infinitives and present participles in certain constructions see §§967-9 and 980 and note *BlHom*
237. 22 *and he ineode on þæt carcern mid his discipulum and he*
geseah þone eadigan Matheus ænne sitton singende.

§1560. Visser (ii, §1013) notes *BlHom* 245. 27 *Se haliga Andreas*
þa cwæð '. . .'. And þus cweþende, fyren wolc astah of heofonum . . .
as an example of a 'dangling or misrelated participle'. On absolute
participles see §§3804-46.

c. Position

§1561. In general, the position of participles and participial phrases
would seem to be based on rhetorical and stylistic rather than on
syntactical considerations; consider, for example, *ÆCHom* i. 52. 5
þider þe Stephanus forestop, mid Saules stanum oftorfod, ðider
folgode Paulus, gefultumod þurh Stephanes gebedu.

§1562. When used alone, the participle may precede or follow the
word it qualifies, either immediately or separated by other elements,
e.g. *ÆCHom* i. 390. 19 *Feallende he forleas lichamlice gesihðe,*
arisende he underfeng his modes onlihtinge, ÆCHom ii. 336. 7 *þa*
deoflu feohtende scuton heora fyrenan flan, and *ÆCHom* i. 340. 1
Ðaða he hit gemette, he hit bær on his exlum to ðære eowde blis-
sigende.

§1563. When combined with other elements to form a phrase, the
participle may precede or follow these elements, e.g. (with an object)
ÆCHom i. 370. 27 *. . . he gewende to Romebyrig, bodigende godspel*
but *ÆCHom* i. 560. 5 *Dionisius . . . ferde to Franclande, cristendom*
bodigende; (with a prepositional phrase) *ÆCHom* i. 46. 31 *Efne ic*
geseo . . . mannes Sunu standende æt Godes swiðran but *ÆCHom* i.
46. 32 *Iudei ða, mid micelre stemne hrymende, heoldon heora earan*;
and (with a noun phrase) *ÆCHom* ii. 30. 19 *. . . and gemette ealle*
hire bearn . . . cwacigende eallum limum but *ÆCHom* i. 596. 16 [*ðu*
gode rod] *nu æt nextan minum wilnigendum mode gegearcod.* The
participle may also be placed between two elements which it governs,
e.g. *ÆCHom* ii. 138. 21 *. . . oðþæt min sawul heonon siðige, of*
andwerdum life gelaðod to heofonan.

§1564. Like the participle alone, the participial phrase may precede the word it qualifies, e.g. *Luke(WSCp)* 23. 46 *and þus cweþende he forþferde*, or (more frequently, judging from my collections) follow it, either immediately, e.g. *ÆCHom* ii. 70. 22 *Se hehsta stæpe is on mægðhades mannum, þa ðe fram cildhade clænlice Gode þeowigende, ealle middaneardlice gælsan forhogiað*, or separated by other elements, e.g. *ÆCHom* i. 2. 25 *For þisum antimbre ic gedyrstlæhte, on Gode truwiende, þæt ic ðas gesetnysse undergann.*

G. THE OBJECTS

1. INTRODUCTORY REMARKS

§1565. Traditionally the accusative elements in a sentence like *ÆCHom* i. 180. 4 *and syle ðone oþerne dæl hungrium men* are called the direct object and the dative elements the indirect object. But complications arise because certain verbs which in MnE are regarded as transitive in that they take a direct object take the genitive or dative in OE, while others take the accusative and either the genitive or dative or both; see §§603 and 1089. The terminological and practical difficulties which can stem from this will be apparent to any reader of Visser's discussion of what he calls 'Verb with complement B. No distinct subordination (verb + object)' (Visser, i, §§315-709). Nothing but confusion can, however, result from following Visser in using the term 'indirect object' of *Gode* in *Bo* 13. 28 *Ðonca nu Gode* (i. 307), *him* in *Or* 32. 9 *him com . . . Godes wraco* (i. 288), *him* in *Or* 74. 32 *he him hamweard ferde* (i. 323), and *Gode* in *CP* 222. 21 *. . . ða lac beoð Gode ealra andfengeost* (i. 328). I use the terms 'indirect object' and 'direct object' only when it seems essential. The former is used in the traditional way, the latter embraces accusative, genitive, and dative, objects of verbs which in MnE are regarded as transitive or which take a direct object not found in MnE, e.g. *sittan* in *Bede* 478. 2 *Sæt he þæt bisceopsetl seofon 7 þritig wintra . . .* ; see Visser, i. 118. On these terms see further Collinson, *TPS* 1941, p. 127.

2. FORMS AND QUALIFYING ELEMENTS

§1566. With the addition of the reflexive pronoun (§§265-78), the elements and combinations which are found in the subject (§1482) can appear as objects in the case(s) appropriate to the governing verb. *Mutatis mutandis*, the remarks made about elements which qualify

the subject (§§1498-502) apply here. It would be superfluous to give examples; sufficient will be found in the appropriate parts of chapter II and in the sections which follow, as well as in 'the prose text dissertations' and 'the eighteen German dissertations'.

§1567. Visser (i, §§527-31) has made out a good case for the proposition 'that in the course of time *so* in the collocations of the type "I think so" gradually assumed the function of a quasi-object, almost passing into the sense "that" ' (i, §527). But he immediately adds the significant qualification that 'one of the respects in which it keeps differing from a "real" object is that it cannot be the subject of the corresponding passive construction ("*So was thought")'. So he was rightly doubtful whether '*swa* was apprehended as an object' in *Beo* 797 *ðær hie meahton swa* and the like (i, §§557 and 573). I am in full agreement with Ericson (*JEGP* 30 (1931), 19): 'Certain it is that translators of Old English as well as later grammarians have been too quick to label *swa* a pronoun, either relative or demonstrative.' For my reasons see §§2379-82; *Ang.* 81 (1963), 300; *RES* 15 (1964), 140; and *NM* 70 (1969), 75-8.

3. VERBS OF SINGLE RECTION

§1568. These are verbs like *ofslean* which can take only one object, e.g. *Or* 156. 12 *he ofslog micel þæs folces*, as opposed to those like *þancian* which can take two, e.g. *BlHom* 203. 30 *Hie . . . to ham foran 7 sona þæm Ælmihtigan Gode . . . þancudan þæs siges*. But this one object may vary in case even in the same sentence; see §1089. For details of the case(s) governed by these verbs, see §§1081-92. On verbs which may be compounded with an adverb or preposition, see §§1060-80.

4. VERBS OF DOUBLE RECTION

§1569. The combinations which can be governed by these verbs have been set out in §§1083-90. See also §1260 and Novikov, *IAF* 4 (1971), 114-21.

5. REPETITION AND NON-REPETITION OF THE OBJECTS

§1570. As in MnE, a noun object is repeated when clarity demands it, e.g. *ÆCHom* i. 54. 17 *Gif ðu offrast ðine lac to Godes weofode, and þu þær gemyndig bist þæt ðin broðor hæfð sum ðing ongean ðe, forlæt ðærrihte ða lac ætforan ðam weofode, and gang ærest to þinum breðer, and þe to him gesibsuma; and ðonne ðu eft cymst to ðam weofode, geoffra ðonne ðine lac.* Repetition by variation is of course characteristic of the poetry, e.g. *GenA* 1720 . . . *þæt him Abraham idese brohte,* ‖ *wif to hame.* But writers also use the term ‘repetition’ of sequences involving noun object . . . pronoun object, e.g. *ÆCHom* ii. 420. 34 *swa þæt an sunderhalga geband þone apostol, and hine gelædde to þæs cynges domerne,* or pronoun object . . . noun object, e.g. *Dan* 134 *þa him unbliðe andswarode* ‖ *wulfheort cyning, witgum sinum.* These need no further exemplification.

§1571. Tautologic repetition is not uncommon in the early prose, e.g. *Or* 30. 10 *And he Ninus Soroastrem Bactriana cyning . . . he hine oferwann, Bede* 456. 14 *7 forþon þe he hine Wilfrið . . . wisne onfunde,* and *CP* 309. 11 *Ond eft ðæm gifrum suiðe hrædlice him willað fylgan leohtlicu weorc . . . ;* see further §§1445-8. There is, however, no need to follow Visser (i, §603) in seeing tautology in examples like *Ps(P)* 33. 10 *ac þa þe God seceað, ne aspringeð him nan good,* where we have the *'sepe* relative; see §§2172-4.

§1572. Ohlander (p. 107 fn. 1) speaks of ‘the handy term “omission” ’. I would call it ‘misleading’, as it is by no means certain that the object in question was ever there to be omitted. So I use the term ‘non-repetition’. As far as I have observed, this occurs in OE only when the unexpressed object has to be understood from a specific word in another clause. Ohlander defines his group I examples (pp. 109-11) as exemplifying both ‘the object not understood from some specific word in a coordinate sentence’ (p. 109) and then ‘the omission of the object when understood from the situation or context generally’ (p. 111). I have not found—in his collections or elsewhere —any examples which conform to the second definition. In some of those he cites in his group I an object can be understood from a preceding clause which is not co-ordinate or the verb can be taken as intransitive, e.g. *Beo* 92 *cwæð þæt se Ælmihtiga eorðan worhte,* ‖ *wlitebeorhtne wang, swa wæter bebugeð* and

El 1120   Nu we seolfe geseoð   sigores tacen,
                 soðwundor godes,   þeah we wiðsocun ær
                 mid leasingum.

That the former is a possible explanation is shown by examples like *Bede* 28. 18 *Mid þy Peohtas wif næfdon, bædon him fram Scottum, Bede* 52. 21 *Cyðdon him . . . butan hi him maran andlyfne sealdon, þæt hi woldan him sylfe niman . . . ,* and perhaps *Or* 64. 29 *þa hie*

him þæs getygðedon, þa hæfdon hi him to wifum, where *hi* might be
the subject or the object of *hæfdon*. (Further examples will be found
in Wülfing, i, §234). The rest of Ohlander's group I examples can be
otherwise explained, e.g. *leode* in *Beo* 24 can be taken as dative
singular with *gelæsten*, or occur in disputed passages, e.g.

Beo 28   hi hyne þa ætbæron   to brimes faroðe,
                  swæse gesiþas,   swa he selfa bæd,
                  þenden wordum weold   wine Scyldinga—
                  leof landfruma   lange ahte,

where, if we do not wish to accept what the scribe wrote as evidence
for an intransitive use of *agan*, we can supply [*land*] as the object of
ahte from the compound *landfruma*. Here, I would say—in the
words of Ohlander (p. 105)—that 'the element to be understood or
supplied is so self-evident that the gap is mentally filled in by the
audience more or less unreflectingly' and would add that some other
apparent textual difficulties would disappear if we accepted the principle that an object is not always expressed when it can be supplied
in this way. For a possible example, see my discussion of *Beo* 14 in
§3120.

§1573. But once we have eliminated these and similar sentences, we
find that an overwhelming majority of unexpressed objects in OE—
and this is true of the examples cited by Ohlander (pp. 105-27), by
Klaeber (3, p. xcii fn. 9), and by Visser (i, §§613-14 and 624)—
exemplify non-repetition in one co-ordinate clause of an object
already expressed in another. This is scarcely surprising, for an object
governed by two verbs is rarely repeated in English of any date. We
can distinguish two main types in OE.

§1574. First, there is the pattern which prevails in MnE in which
the direct object is expressed with the second verb only, e.g. (both
verbs governing the same case) *ÆCHom* i. 2. 18 *ic geseah and gehyrde mycel gedwyld*, (the verbs governing different cases) *ÆCHom*
i. 270. 14 *and we sceolon lufian and filigan urum Drihtne*, and (prob-
lematic because of the varying rections involved) *ÆCHom* i. 78. 15
of ðe cymð se Heretoga seðe gewylt and gewissað Israhela folc and
ÆCHom i. 6. 21 . . . *þæt hi sceoldon læran and tæcan eallum
þeodum.*[41] Occasional examples of this type with no co-ordinating
conjunction occur in the poetry, e.g. *El* 207 . . . *swa se ealda feond* ||
forlærde ligesearwum, leode fortyhte.

---

[41] Since *brucan* can take the accusative as well as the genitive, the examples cited by
Visser (i, §624) do not necessarily exemplify 'absence of causative object (= in genitive)'.
He is perhaps following Ohlander, who fell into the same trap (pp. 125-6).

§1575. The second main pattern is that in which the direct object is expressed with the first verb only—rightly described by Ohlander (p. 113) as 'the normal way in OE . . . of letting two verbs govern one object'. Examples include those in which both verbs govern the same case, e.g. *ÆCHom* i. 460. 15 *Ac we ne underfoð gold ne seolfor, ac forseoð* and *ÆCHom* i. 376. 29 *and he bletsode ðone hlaf and tobræc and bewand on his twam slyfum*, or different cases, e.g. *ÆCHom* i. 268. 20 *gif he agylte, he hit georne gebete and syððan geswice*. The pattern here is SV nounO *and* V or S pronounO V *and* V; see §3907.

§1576. This pattern occurs in both prose and poetry with no conjunction, e.g. *Lch* i. 384. 20 *nim eorþan, oferweorp mid þinre swiþran handa under þinum swiþran fet, ÆCHom* i. 56. 17 *We secgað eow Godes riht; healdað gif ge willon*, and *Beo* 553 *Me to grunde teah ǁ fah feondscaða, fæste hæfde ǁ grim on grape.*

§1577. The separation of two verbs by a common object seen in some of the examples quoted above is, of course, one particular manifestation of the dislike of 'heavy' groups discussed in §1472. This phenomenon is still not understood by all writers. Visser (i, §§155 and 158) cites *ÆCHom* i. 516. 4 *Gif ðin hand oððe ðin fot þe æswicige, ceorf of þæt lim and awurp fram ðe* and *LS* 8. 335 *þa aras he and gelæhte hine be þam swuran and cyste and clypte* as examples of the 'absolute use of verbs' which normally require an object, while Sprockel (ii. 172-4) regards *ChronA* 100. 15 (920) *Her . . . for Eadweard cyning to Mældune 7 getimbrede þa burg 7 gestaðolode ær he þonon fore* as exemplifying 'omission' of the personal pronoun.

§1578. But the two verbs need not be separated, for the order may be varied for stylistic reasons, e.g. (with OSV *and* V) *ÆCHom* i. 14. 29 *ealle gesceafta God gesceop and geworhte on six dagum*; (with OVS *and* V twice) *ÆCHom* i. 332. 9 *Hine geswencte seo wædlung and afeormode; þone oðerne gewelgode his genihtsumnys and bepæhte*; and (with OV *and* VS) *ÆCHom* ii. 440. 12 *þa ealle gesceop and geworhte an God.*

§1579. There are, of course, other situations apart from these two in which an object need not be repeated. These cannot be fully exemplified; see further Ohlander, pp. 118 ff. But we find the indirect object expressed in the first clause only in *WHom* 20(*C*) 51 *Ne þrælas ne moton habban . . . þæt þæt heom on Godes est gode men geuðon 7 to ælmesgife for Godes lufan sealdon;*[42] a direct object understood from a dative in a preceding clause in *Bede* 44. 16 *þa compedon hi wið heora feondum 7 him mycel wæl on geslogan 7 of heora gemærum adrifon 7 aflymdon* (on the status of *on* see §§1067-73); a direct object understood from an object governed by a preposition in *Or* 132. 27 *Siþþan he for... 7 wið hie ealle gefeaht 7 oferwon;* and perhaps the reverse in *Lch* ii. 348. 8 *7 hæbbe him scenc fulne ealað 7 drype þriwa halig wæter on* (but see again §§1067-73).

6. THE POSITION OF THE OBJECTS

§1580. *Mutatis mutandis*, the remarks made about the position of the subject (§§1517-18) apply here. See further chapter IX.

H. THE COMPLEMENT

1. INTRODUCTORY REMARKS

§1581. As already noted in §606, I use the term 'complement' in the traditional way to describe elements which complete the sense of a sentence containing copula verbs such as *beon/wesan, weorþan, þyncan*, and others; for a chronologically arranged list of such verbs in English see Visser, i, §236. Verbs of rest or motion may also be added, though here nominative elements can be described as appositional; see §§976-9 and 1251. More examples than those given below will be found in Visser, i, §§240-314a. I am indebted to him for some of mine.

2. FORMS

a. Nominative elements

§1582. When the complement is a noun, adjective, or participle, it is in the nominative case, agreeing with the subject. For examples, see §§1248-51 and Visser, i, §§333-66, where Visser gives numerous instances of the idioms seen in *Pan* 15 *Se is æghwam freond* and *BlHom* 213. 11 *Wæs he . . . eallum his geferum leof.* Other combinations can of course occur, such as an adjective + a genitive, e.g. *CP* 429. 22 *he bið manigra wita wyrðe*, and an adjective + an infinitive, e.g. *CP* 173. 10 . . . *ðylæs sio earc si ungearo to beranne.*

---

[42] Visser (i, §625) wrongly includes this and two similar examples in his group in which 'the expressed direct object of the first verb functions as indirect object to the second verb'.

§1583. Other elements which occur in the nominative are pronouns, e.g. *John(WSCp)* 9. 9 *ic hit eom*, *ÆLS* 10. 191 *Hwæt eom ic manna þæt ic mihte god forbeodan?*, *Gen* 27. 32 *Hwæt eart þu?*, and *BlHom* 175. 34 *Hit is se þe þes dry Simon sagað þæt he sy*, and numerals, e.g. *Bo* 85. 6 *Hwæt, ic þonne ær sæde þ þ hehste good 7 sio hehste gesælð an wære*, *BlHom* 79. 23 *Ealles þæs folces wæs, þe se casere Titus innon Ierusalem beferde, þrittigun syþum hund teontig þusenda*, and *Jul* 678 *þær xxx wæs* ‖ *ond feowere eac*. . . .

b. *Other elements*

§1584. First, we have genitives of [adjectives +] nouns, which can denote possession, e.g. *GD* 252. 2 . . . *þæt hit oþres mannes wære* and *ÆCHom* i. 304. 34 . . . *forðan ðe ælc hæðen man bið deofles*, or origin, e.g. *Bede* 222. 10 *Se nyhsta wæs Scyttisces cynnes*, or can describe, e.g. *BlHom* 57. 18 *Manige men beoð heardre heortan* and *ÆCHom* i. 30. 27 *þam ðe beoð godes willan*. Next, there are pronouns in the genitive and possessives, e.g. *CP* 139. 1 *Se ðe ne gimð ðara ðe his beoð*, *John(WSCp)* 16. 15 *Ealle þa þing þe min fæder hæfð synt mine*, *Mark(WSCp)* 10. 40 *Soðlice nis hit na min inc to syllene* . . . , and *BlHom* 117. 23 *Nis þæt eower* . . . *þæt ge witan þa þrage*. . . .

§1585. Other elements which can serve as complements are the adverb *swa*, e.g. *Bede* 286. 16 *Ac hwæðre witað ge þæt hit swa nis* and *BlHom* 179. 2 *Eal hit is swa, ne leoge ic*; infinitives (see §§ 1540-2); adjective clauses, e.g. *Coll* 242 7 *beo þæt þy eart*; adverb clauses, e.g. *ÆCHom* i. 274. 6 *Se ðe þe mundað swa swa fæder, he bið swylce he ðin heafod sy*; noun clauses, e.g. *ÆCHom* i. 138. 30 *þæt is þæt we sceolon ure unclænnysse* . . . *adwæscan*; sentences, e.g. *ÆCHom* i. 138. 25 *þæt is, we sceolon ure yfelnysse behreowsian*; adverbs other than *swa*, e.g. *Bo* 81. 5 *ac hit is þeah þara* [= *þær*] and *Matt(WSCp)* 14. 23 *he wæs ana þær*; prepositional phrases, e.g. *Bo* 101. 2 *Ne mæg nan oðru gesceaft be him selfum bion* and *BlHom* 231. 14 *þry dagas nu to lafe syndon*; and combinations of the last two, e.g. *Bede* 30. 19 . . . *Orcadas þa ealond, þa wæron ut on garsecge butan Brotone* and *ÆTemp* 70. 12 *On winterlicere tide hi* [*Pliade*] *beoð on niht uppe 7 on dæg adune*.

c. *In the accusative and infinitive construction*

§1586. Here the complement is naturally in the accusative when it is declinable, e.g. *Bede(B)* 36. 17 *þonne wite þu me cristenne beon*,

BlHom 85. 33 *þonne þu wysctest þæt þu wistest Crist on rode ahan-genne* . . . , and *GenA* 1346 *Ic þe godne wat,* || *fæsthydigne.* Other elements can, of course, serve as complements here too, e.g. *Bede* 408. 21 *Ðara cynna monig he wiste in Germanie wesan* and *LS* 7. 62 *Mid þy þa Eufrosina þone munuc þær wiste.* . . . On the status of the examples without *beon/wesan*, see §§3766-76.

3. QUALIFYING ELEMENTS

§1587. *Mutatis mutandis*, the remarks made in §§1498-502 about the elements which qualify the subject are applicable here.

4. THE POSITION OF THE COMPLEMENT

§1588. This is discussed in chapter IX.

J. ADVERBIAL ELEMENTS

1. TYPES

§1589. In addition to adverbs (§§1100-50), the following occur in adverbial functions: combinations of two adverbs ('adverb phrases'), e.g. *Or* 34. 6 *swa wel* and *ÆHom* 17. 175 *ealles to swiþe*; adverb clauses (§§2416-3721); case forms, e.g. *ealles* in *ÆHom* 17. 175 above, and case phrases ('noun phrases'), e.g. *Or* 226. 17 *þære ilcan niht* and *BlHom* 193. 12 *prim milum* (§§1380-427); prepositional phrases (§§1158-67); and the infinitives which express purpose (§§1552-4 and 2940-51). Other suggested adverbial uses of the infinitives are dismissed in §959.

2. FUNCTIONS

§1590. The threefold classification proposed by QW (p. 91)— ' "adverbs" may be adjective-modifiers, verb-modifiers, or sentence-modifiers'—will serve with some qualification. First, 'adjective-modifiers' may modify an adverb, a numeral, a noun, a pronoun, a prepositional phrase, or a conjunction; for examples, see §1100. Second, the term 'verb-modifier' embraces not only adverb and adverb phrases, but also—despite Brown (1970, p. 63)—the other adverbial elements already distinguished. Third, the term 'sentence-modifier' —otherwise 'sentence adverb' (Onions, pp. 17-18) or 'clause modifier' (Brown 1970, p. 63)—has already been qualified in §§1101-3.

§1591. On the overlap in the functions of adjectives and adverbs, see §1108.

3. POSITION AND STRESS

§1592. 'Adjective modifiers' (as qualified above) immediately precede the word they modify.

§1593. For the rest, we can agree with QW (p. 91) that 'the free variation available to Ælfric in the position of adverbs is available today likewise'. So much depends on the writer's purpose. Thus we find repetition in *ÆCHom* i. 176. 27 *Mid þam ylcum ðrim ðingum þe se deofol ðone frumsceapenan mann oferswiðde, mid þam ylcan Crist oferswiðde hine*; parallelism in *ÆCHom* i. 144. 24 *Ðam ungeleaffullum mannum com Crist to hryre, and þam geleaffullum to æriste*; chiasmus in *ÆCHom* i. 8. 28 *He hylt mid his mihte heofonas and eorðan, and ealle gesceafta butan geswince*; a co-ordinate group not split in *ÆCHom* i. 372. 5 *He ða cwæð to ðam folce and to ðam dry*; and co-ordinate groups split in *ÆCHom* ii. 402. 8 *Spyrte bið . . . of rixum gebroden oððe of palmtwygum* (with a conjunction) and *ÆCHom* ii. 30. 26 *þa earman bearn ne mihton ða leng for sceame on þære byrig aðolian, for ðære atelican cwacunge . . .* (with no conjunction). Passages which are worthy of analysis but are too long to quote include *ÆCHom* ii. 376. 27–31 and *ÆCHom* ii. 602. 31–604. 2. Similar examples could be cited from earlier prose and from the poetry. But some attempt is made in chapter IX to define more accurately the position of adverbial elements within the clause.

§1594. The examples cited above will show how impossible it is for the modern scholar to write authoritatively about the stress of adverbial elements in the prose. The metrical 'rules' may make it perhaps a little less difficult for the poetry, but even here much remains controversial; see §3953.

K. NEGATION

1. INTRODUCTORY REMARKS

§1595. The OE adverbs of negation are listed and discussed in §§1126–33. Here we are primarily concerned with their use—either singly or in combination with one another or with negative adjectives and/or pronouns such as *nan* and *nænig*—in simple sentences or principal clauses expressing statements. But most of the 'rules' formulated hold for co-ordinate and subordinate clauses if allowance is made for the principles of element order formulated in the relevant chapters. Examples from such clauses have therefore been included where necessary. Special problems concerning negation—including the influence of a negative in a principal clause on the mood of the verb of a subordinate clause—are discussed elsewhere as they become relevant; see the General Index.[43]

§1596. Early writers on negation in OE started from the idea expressed by Mourek—see *Ang.* 35 (1911-12), 188 fn. 1—that Germanic originally distinguished qualitative (or sentence) negation—in which *ni* immediately before the verb negated the whole contents of the utterance—from quantitative (or word) negation—in which *ni* before a word or words other than a verb negated the individual concept expressed therein. Knörk and Rauert worked along these lines. Rauert, for example, saw qualitative negation in *Or* 152. 1 *ac Lisimachus ne mehte Demetriase wiðstondan* (p. 5); quantitative negation in *CP(H)* 345. 19 *To ðæm gebanne ðæs tohopan nan monn mæg cunnan* (p. 72)—MS *Ci* has *nan man ne mæg cuman*, which exemplifies the next category!; qualitative and quantitative negation in *CP* 129. 23 *Ne mæg nan mon twam hlafordum hieran* (p. 77); and qualitative and multiple quantitative negation in *Or* 194. 18. . . . *þæt heora nan ne mehte nanes wæpnes gewealdan* (p. 99).

§1597. Whether Mourek's distinction was a real one and, if so, whether it was valid for PrGmc. is a question outside the scope of this work.[44] But, as Schuchardt (pp. 8-9) saw from his study of

---

[43] V. M. Coombs gives a 'transformational-generative analysis of the negative operation' in Gothic, OHG, OS, OE, and ON, in 'A Semantic Syntax of Grammatical Negation in the older Germanic Dialects' (Ph.D. diss., Champaign, 1974); see *DAI* 35 (1975), 7889A. This thesis was reprinted (under the same title) as Göppinger Arbeiten zur Germanistik, 177 (1976).

[44] If we accept the conclusion that *Beowulf* and perhaps OE poetry in general preserved the alleged difference better than the prose—see Einenkel, *Ang.* 35 (1911-12), 189 ff.— we have a somewhat circular argument in its favour. But I cannot myself see why negating the verb is so different from negating any other word. The difference *in kind* between the alternatives 'Everybody/Nobody in the army knew about it' and 'The army knew/did not know about it' escapes me. Why *un-* in *unfeor* in *GenA* 2082 *oðþæt hie Domasco* ‖ *unfeor wæron* expresses qualitative negation (Knörk, pp. 39-40) also escapes me. Moreover, judging from the examples cited by Knörk (pp. 45-6), both *ne* conjunction and *ne* adverb immediately before a verb express qualitative negation. This may account for the failure of some subsequent writers to recognize the vital difference between these two words; see §§ 1602 and 1835 fn.

My sections on negation were completed some years before the appearance of Coombs's article 'Beowulf Negative Indefinites: The Klima Hypothesis Tested', *Orbis* (Louvain) 24 (1975), 417-25. She offers some useful remarks on previous writings on the topic (pp. 417-

Beowulf and as a comparison of the four examples just cited will show, the distinction does not hold for OE. Einenkel was led to ask (*Ang.* 35 (1911-12), 192) 'ob hier eine klare Scheidung der quantitativen von der qualitativen Negation noch vorliegt, oder ob man nicht eher von einer einheitlichen Verbalnegation reden könnte, zu welcher die alten quantitativ negierten Satzteile die Verstärkungen stellen und abgeben'.[45] We had better take the hint and scrap the terms; Einenkel's failure to do this sometimes results in confusion, e.g. at *Ang.* 35 (1911-12), 193. However, Knörk and Rauert—as well as Schuchardt—give numerous examples of the various negative elements. For 'a distinction between what may be called the serious and the ironical use of the negative sentence', see Williams, pp. 26 ff.

§1598. The use of negatives in certain subordinate clauses requires special consideration; for details see the General Index, s.v. negation.

2. THE ADVERB *NE* USED ALONE

§1599. The OE verb is most commonly negated by the adverb *ne* immediately preceding it, no matter what the order of the other elements. The negated verb is normally in initial position in principal clauses in the prose, e.g. *Bo* 38. 14 *Ne mæg se wela gedon þ se gitsere ne sie gitsere*, *Bo* 97. 6 *Ne mæg ic þæs oðsacan, ÆCHom* i. 6. 13 *Ne sende se deofol ða fyr, ÆCHom* i. 40. 18 *Næs þæt word to flæsce awend*, and *ÆCHom* i. 42. 9 *Ne oncneow heo weres gemanan*; on the same order in nexus questions see §§1644-5. Most of the exceptions involve personal pronoun subjects, e.g. *Or* 190. 29 *He næs buton seofontienewintre, CP* 33. 19 *He nolde beon cyning*, the first clause in *ÆCHom* ii. 110. 33 *He ne andwyrde ðam wife æt fruman, na for modignysse, ac he nolde his cwyde awendan*, and *ÆCHom* ii. 112. 4 *He nolde syllan intingan þam Iudeiscum. . . .*[46] Such sentences might give some support to *ÆCHom* ii. 40. 15 *þis nis nu alyfed nanum men to donne*, which, remarks Andrew (*SS*, §72), 'might easily be

19) and concludes—much to my satisfaction—that her 'generative-transformational analysis of the Old English indefinite quantifiers and indefinite adverbs found in the text of *Beowulf* demonstrates that in the deep structure distinct categories of qualitative and quantitative negation, previously based on a syntactical analysis of the surface structure alone, collapse' (p. 425).

[45] 'whether there is here still a clear division between qualitative and quantitative negation, or whether one should not rather speak of a uniform verbal negation, which is intensified by the old quantitatively negated phrases'.

[46] Many of the alleged examples cited by Bacquet (pp. 130-3) are inadmissible because they begin with *ond* or (like the second clause in *ÆCHom* ii. 110. 33 above) with *ac*. See further my review of Bacquet (*NM* 67 (1966), 86-97), where I give my reasons for rejecting his theory that S *ne* VO represents the *ordre de base*, while *ne* VSO is a type of *déclarative marquée*, and §3935.

a misreading of *Nis ðis'*. However, examples like *CP* 27. 25 *Ða hierdas næfdon 7git* and *ÆHom* 7. 207 (§1606), where the subject is a noun, are exceptional.

§1600. The usual principles of prose element order of course apply in co-ordinate clauses introduced by *ond, ac, ne*, and the like, and in subordinate clauses, where the verb does not normally have initial position after the conjunction; see the Indexes. Hence we find, for example, *ÆCHom* i. 168. 1 *ac he ne dorste Cristes fandian, gif him alyfed nære* and *ÆCHom* i. 168. 30 *gif se lichama næfð mete*. . . .

§1601. These patterns are often found in the poetry too, e.g. (principal clauses) *Beo* 38 *ne hyrde ic cymlicor ceol gegyrwan* and *Beo* 190 *ne mihte snotor hæleð* || *wean onwendan*; (co-ordinate clauses) *Beo* 182 *ne hie huru heofena Helm herian ne cupon* and *Beo* 599 *ac he lust wigeð,* || . . . *secce ne wenep*; and (subordinate clauses) *Beo* 1167 *peah pe he his magum nære* || *arfæst æt ecga gelacum* and *Beo* 2332 *swa him gepywe ne wæs*. But there are many more exceptions than in the prose. Common ones include examples with a noun or pronoun subject preceding a negated verb in a principal clause, e.g. *Beo* 50 *men ne cunnon* || *secgan to soðe* . . . and *Beo* 80 *He beot ne aleh*, examples with stressed *na/no* immediately before the verb (§1619), and examples without *ne* before the verb in a clause or sentence with another negative element (§§1620-6). But the demands of metre produce many more, such as *Beo* 180 *Metod hie ne cupon* (with initial object) and *Dream* 35 *pær ic pa ne dorste* . . . (with initial *pær* in a principal clause expressing place where).

§1602. In both prose and verse, *ne* not before a finite verb is a conjunction, e.g. *ÆGram* 259. 18 *ne lingua nec manus oculiue peccent, ne tunge ne handa oððe eagan syngion*; see further §§1832-41. This renders impossible the recent attempt to revive Conybeare's reading of *Wife* 18 *ða ic me ful gemæc ne monnan funde*; for details see my comments in *NM* 73 (1972), 224-6. Some apparent exceptions to this 'rule' in the prose which are due to Latin influence are discussed by Andrew (*SS*, §§75-6). There is one qualification: when one (or more) of two (or more) infinitives dependent on the same auxiliary is negated, adv. *ne* or *na* precedes the (first) negated infinitive, e.g.

Beo 183   Wa bið þæm ðe sceal
          þurh sliðne nið   sawle bescufan
          in fyres fæþm,   frofre ne wenan,
          wihte gewendan,

Bo 103. 9, and *ÆHom* 3. 104 (both in §1614). See further Einenkel, *Ang.* 35 (1912), 208-9. The position of adv. *ne* in examples like *Ex* 427 *Ne behwylfan mæg heofon and eorðe* ‖ *his wuldres word* is presumably to be attributed to the demands of metre. On *uton ne* + infinitive see §916.

3. THE ADVERB *NE* USED WITH OTHER NEGATIVES

a. In the prose

§1603. Negative adverbs and pronoun/adjectives—most of which exemplify contracted *ni* + an initial vowel, *h*, or *w*; see §§1129-31 —are frequently used in the prose in combination with *ne*. Two negatives do not cancel out to make one positive, as they do in Latin; on this see further Most, p. 92. For modern readers, at any rate, the effect of multiple negation is to emphasize. Joly (1972, p. 39) distinguishes 'négation simple immanente (*ic ne secge*)' from 'négation composée transcendante (*ic ne secge na/naht*)' and observes that 'la différence est d'ordre expressif et stylistique . . . La négation transcendante est catégorique et marque une dénégation forte en vieil anglais' ['the difference is of an expressive and stylistic order . . . The transcendent negative is categorical and indicates a strong denial in OE'].[47]

§1604. It would be pointless to exemplify all the possible arrangements. They include combinations of *na* (*ne* + *a*) or *no* (*ne* + *o*) and *ne* (see §1605); of *ne* and another negative adverb or adverb phrase, e.g. *GD(C)* 155. 30 *he swa þeah nanum gemete him to þon hyran nolde*, *Bo* 61. 11 *7 þonne hi gegadrad hæfð, þonne eowað he hi, nallas ne hilð* (see further §1621), *BlHom* 163. 8 *heo þonne þæs bearnes noht lata ne wæs*, *ÆCHom* i. 16. 16 *heo ne geendað næfre*, and *ÆHom* 6. 219 *næfð he his næfre forgyfenysse*; of *ne* and a negative adjective or pronoun, e.g. *CP* 47. 10 *Nis ðæs ðonne nan tweo*, *Bo* 79. 16 *forþam ðe nan mihtigra þe nis*, *BlHom* 87. 16 *Næs þa nænig ylding*, and *ÆHom* 7. 10 *and eower nan ne befrinð hwider ic fare nu*; and of *ne* and two (or, occasionally, more) other negatives, e.g. *Bo* 102. 6 *7 nan heort ne onscunode nanne leon, ne nan hara nænne hund, ne nan neat nyste nænne andan ne nænne ege to oðrum*, *BlHom* 51. 31 . . . *þæt wite . . . þe næfre nænig ende ne becymeþ*, and *ÆHom* 5. 124 *for ðam ðe þa Iudeiscan noldon næfre brucan nanes þinges mid þam hæþenum*.

[47] The 'stylistics' of the OE negative are discussed by Schuchardt in the unpublished part of his dissertation—he also deals with metre; by Marchand (*EStudies*, 20 (1938), 198-204); and by Joly (1972, *passim*).

§1605. When both *na* and *ne* negate the verb, we find either *na ne* V, e.g. *Bo* 16. 9 *gif þu hi na ne underfenge* and *ÆHom* 3. 112 *and hi na ne nydde on naðre healfe*, or *ne* V *na*, e.g. *GD* 226. 4 *7 seo þruh ne mæg na unc begen ymbfon*, *GD* 256. 3 *þaþa he ne forhtode na ymb his agenne deað*, *ÆHom* 4. 19 *and ne wunaþ na on sibbe*, and *ÆCHom* i. 210. 6 *ac we ne sind na genedde*. But when *na* negates some other element in the sentence it usually immediately precedes that element, both in combinations involving *na . . . ac*, e.g. *ÆCHom* i. 16. 21 *forðan ðe he nis na Scyppend, ac is atelic sceocca* (on this pattern see further §§1756-8), or without a following *ac* clause, e.g. *BlHom* 33. 36 *Weorþian we forþon Drihtnes godcundnesse, gif he nære soþ God . . . , na him englas ne þegnodon* and *ÆHom* 1. 169 *Nis he na gesceapen, ne he nis na gesceaft*. As the last example shows, the position of *na* in relation to the negated verb depends on the syntax of the particular clause.

§1606. Analysis of these examples shows that the position of *na* varies according to the type of sentence or clause and the elements which are negated and/or stressed. This is true of all negative elements, including a verb negated by the immediately preceding adverb *ne*. Thus, in *ÆCHom* i. 288. 1 *Hwæt wenst ðu hu miccle swiðor is Godes . . . miht . . . Him ne wiðstent nan ðing* and (as I read it, contrary to Andrew, *SS*, §72) *ÆCHom* i. 52. 7 *þær [on heofenan rice] nis Paulus gescynd þurh Stephanes slege* respectively, *him* and *þær* carry the stress and are therefore in initial position. The unusual phenomenon of a noun subject before a negated verb at the beginning of the second sentence (§1599) in *ÆHom* 7. 207 *Ne sprecð he [nan mann] na of him sylfum, ac sprecð swa hwæt swa he gehyrð. Se Halga Gast ne sprycð na, swa swa se Hælend cwæð . . .* is due partly to a desire for emphasis and partly to the demands of alliteration and stylistic parallelism. Parallelism too may explain the fact that introductory *þær* precedes a negated verb in the principal clause in *ÆCHom* i. 176. 7 *þær næs eac nan geðafung, forðon ðe ðær næs nan lustfullung*. The factors enunciated above should serve to explain the pattern of any individual sentence. The rigid 'rules' formulated by Einenkel on the basis of a limited corpus (*Ang.* 35 (1911-12), 203 ff.) do not hold—as he himself is forced to admit. There is room for further work here.

§1607. Davis (Sweet, *Pr.* 9, p. 58) says that 'in a negative sentence the particle is prefixed to every finite verb, and, in addition, to every word which may have a contracted negative form: *hit na ne feoll* "it did not fall"; *hie ne namon nanne ele* "they took no oil"'. This requires qualification. First, the verb in a negative sentence is not always preceded by adv. *ne*; see §§1627-30. Second, not all elements which can be negated by the addition of *ne* are so negated; consider *Bede* 52. 33 *7 ne wæs ænig seðe bebyrignysse sealde þam ðe . . . , Or* 254. 8 *. . . þæt he fleah 7 forbead þæt hiene mon god hete* (cf. *Or* 262. 21 *7 forbead þæt mon na ðær eft ne timbrede* and see §§2039-46), *BlHom* 223. 31, *BlHom* 223. 36 *Ne gehyrde nænig man on his muþe oht elles nefne Cristes lof . . . , ÆHom* 7. 156 *Ne mihte nan wana beon þam welwillendan Hælende ænig his limena,* and *ÆHom* 11. 551 *and ðar ne bið nan anda on heora ænigum.* But the strength of the tendency to negate adverbs and adjective/pronouns in prose sentences with adv. *ne* prefixed to the verb must not be underestimated; see §1628.

b. In the poetry

§1608. Here we find combinations of *na/no* and *ne*, with *na/no* usually following *ne*, e.g.

Dan 695   Sæton him æt wine   wealle belocene,
                 ne onegdon na   orlegra nið . . .

and *Mald* 268 *He ne wandode na æt þam wigplegan,* but sometimes preceding it, e.g. *Beo* 450 *no ðu ymb mines ne þearft* ‖ *lices feorme leng sorgian.* However, *na/no* also occurs alone; for details see §§1614-19. Alliteration does not seem to be a factor here.

§1609. But there is much less piling up of negatives in the poetry than in the prose. *Næfre* stands without *ne* before the verb in seven of the eight clauses in which it appears in *Beowulf* and in *Beo* 250 if we accept the manuscript reading; cf. *MCharm* 8. 10 (§909) and see Robinson, *Tennessee Studies in Literature,* 11 (1966), 155-8. The exception is *Beo* 1460 *næfre hit æt hilde ne swac* ‖ *manna ængum.* Even this example is to the point, for we have *ængum*—not *nængum,* which would be normal in the prose. The alliterations would be unaffected if all these elements were negated. But one of the two instances in *Beowulf* in which *æfre* appears in a negated clause tells a different story—*Beo* 1101, where *æfre* is essential for the alliteration. In the other (*Beo* 2600) *æfre* does not alliterate and *næfre* would be possible if we accepted *sibb* as accusative singular feminine. A comparison of the Klaeber and Wrenn–Bolton texts illuminates the point. Since *wynn* fluctuates between the *jo*-stem and the *i*-stem declension (see Klaeber, 3, p. lxxxv), I see no reason why *sibb* should not. But I am certainly not advocating emendation to *næfre.*

§1610. The reluctance to multiply negatives can be illustrated with negative and positive adjective/pronouns too. *Nan* appears twice in *Beowulf*. It is the only negative in *Beo* 988 *þæt him heardra nan hrinan wolde*, where (on the analogy of *Beo* 803 below) we could have had *nolde*. In

Beo 798   Hie þæt ne wiston   . . .
                 . . .   . . .   :   þone synscaðan
                 ænig ofer eorþan   irenna cyst,
                 guðbilla nan,   gretan nolde,

guðbilla nan (803a) is subsidiary to the alliterating *ænig*, which demands *nolde*; *guðbilla an* would not have given the required sense. *Nænig* occurs three times in subordinate clauses with a negated verb (*Beo* 242, 859, and 1514); *ænig* is possible in all three, but would involve double alliteration in a *b* line in *Beo* 859. But *nænig* appears five times with a verb which is not negated by *ne*—twice in co-ordinate clauses (*Beo* 157, 598) and three times in principal clauses with initial *nænig*[*ne*] (*Beo* 691, 1197, and 1933). *Nænig* is essential to the sense in all of these except in *Beo* 157, where the co-ordinate clause is introduced by conj. *ne*. On *Beo* 949 see §1611.

§1611. *Ænig* occurs in twenty-four negative clauses in *Beowulf*, including *Beo* 2006, where *ne* is an editorial insertion. In the three examples of *ænige þinga* (*Beo* 791, 2374, and 2905), *ænige* is essential for the alliteration, just as *nænige (ðinga)* is in *Met* 10. 16 and 19. 37. The positive form is essential for alliteration in three of the six principal clauses beginning with a negated verb (*Beo* 2493, 2548, and 2734), but not in the other three (*Beo* 2416, 2772—where it does however alliterate—and 3080). In the fifteen other negative sentences in *Beowulf* which contain *ænig*, it is essential for the alliteration in all but seven—*Beo* 793, 842, 1461, 1851, and 3054, where it does not alliterate, and *Beo* 802 and 2007, where it does. So there is no syntactical parallel in *Beowulf* to support the emendation of *ænigre* to *nænigre* (or some other form of *nænig*) in

Beo 948   heald forð tela
                 niwe sibbe.   Ne bið þe ænigre gad
                 worolde wilna,   þe ic geweald hæbbe,

though it would of course be quite acceptable in prose. The emendation, however, seems inevitable for reasons of alliteration, since (apart from the 'irregularities' discussed by Klaeber (3, pp. 280–1) and the 'inconsistencies' detected by Lehmann and Tabusa, *The Alliterations of the 'Beowulf'* (Austin, Texas, 1958), pp. 8–12) failure of alliteration in *Beowulf* can be rectified by an obvious addition to the text (e.g. *fela* in 586 and *dom* in 954) or by a reasonable emendation (e.g. *hildplegan* to *lindplegan* in 1073). We may say that the scribe's 'error' reflects his feeling that *ænigre* was to be expected in *Beowulf*[48] and that the poet's use of a variant acceptable in prose demonstrates that OE poets—like Chaucer, who used both *toos* and *toon* 'toes' in rhyme, and Byron, who wrote 'Whate'er she loveth, so she loves thee not'—were willing to choose—without regard to strict linguistic propriety—that alternative which suited them best if two different forms of a word were available. However, free variants involving alliteration are necessarily fewer than, and different in kind from, those involving rhyme.

§1612. So *ænig* is much more common in negative clauses in *Beowulf* than *nan* (two examples) and *nænig* (eight examples (excluding *Beo* 949 (§1611)), in four of which it is the only negative). In sixteen of its twenty-four appearances, *ænig* is essential for the alliteration. In the other eight, the poet could have written *nænig*. It would be easy to multiply examples in the poetry in which *ne* appears before the verb in clauses containing other words which could be but are not negated. Sometimes the positive form is demanded by the alliteration, e.g. *And* 360 *æðele be æðelum. Æfre ic ne hyrde*, *El* 572 *ne ær ne sið æfre hyrdon*, and *Dream* 110 *Ne mæg þær ænig unforht wesan*. But this is not always so, e.g. *And* 493 *swa ic æfre ne geseah ænigne mann* and

Men 101   Ne hyrde ic guman a fyrn
           ænigne ær   æfre bringan
           ofer sealtne mere   selran lare,

in both of which *nænigne* and *næfre* would have supplied the alliteration. See Knörk (pp. 44 ff.) for more examples. Jespersen (*Neg.*, p. 58) notes that examples like *And* 360 and 493 run contrary to 'a universal tendency' to join the negative element to the first of two words whenever there is logically a possibility of attracting it to either. They are not alone in this in OE.

§1613. There is room for more work here. But on the evidence so far provided we can conclude first, that the fact that multiple negation

---

[48] If, following most editors, we emend *nænigum* to *ænigum* in *Dream* 47 *opene inwidhlemmas. Ne dorste ic hira nænigum sceððan*, we are postulating the opposite error on the part of the scribe. This emendation is supported, not only by the examples from *Beowulf*, but also by *Dream* 110 *Ne mæg þær ænig unforht wesan*. Here we would have to justify the scribe's alteration in the same way as Swanton (in his note to the line, where he accepts the lack of alliteration) attempts to justify its retention—by saying that 'double negation is common OE usage'. The scribe's *nænig* for *ne ænig* in *Sea* 25 *urigfeþra; ne ænig hleomæga* is an easily explicable error of a different sort.

was less common in the poetry than in the prose is due partly, but not entirely, to the demands of alliteration, and second, that when two forms of a word were available, Anglo-Saxon poets (like their successors) were prepared to choose the alternative more suited to their purpose.

4. NEGATIVES OTHER THAN THE ADVERB *NE* USED ALONE

a. Na/no *negating words other than finite verbs*

§1614. In the prose, words (other than finite verbs) and phrases are regularly negated by *na/no*, e.g. *ChronE* 3. 6 (—) *mid langum scipum na manegum*, *GD* 321. 1 *he gerihte na fullfremedlice his lif*, *GD* 263. 11 *an þara is þe na mid flæsce bewrigen is* (but *GD* 263. 15 *se gast se þe na mid þy flæsce nis bewrigen*), *Bo* 103. 9 *Ac ða lufe mon mæg swiðe uneaðe oððe na forbeodan*, and *ÆHom* 3. 104 *þas þing gedafenode soðlice to donne, and eac þa oðre na to forlætene.*

§1615. In the poetry, too, words (other than finite verbs) and phrases can be negated by *na/no*, e.g. *Beo* 244 *No her cuðlicor cuman ongunnon* || *lindhæbbende*, *Beo* 567 *syðþan na*, *Beo* 754 *no þy ær* (on this see §§1800–2),

Beo 1534   Swa sceal man don,
            þonne he æt guðe   gegan þenceð
            longsumne lof;   na ymb his lif ceearað

(where he must be concerned about *lof*), *Beo* 1355 *no hie fæder cunnon*, and

Beo 541   No he wiht fram me
            flodyþum feor   fleotan meahte,
            hraþor on holme,   no ic fram him wolde.

The use of *no* before a stressed pronoun seen in the last two examples is a common one in the poetry; see Andrew, *SS*, §81.

§1616. *Na* is regularly used in the prose—especially by Ælfric— to negate one of two alternative words or phrases, either the first, e.g. *ÆCHom* i. 54. 15 . . . *þonne hlyste he godes rædes, na of minum muðe, ac of Cristes sylfes*, *ÆCHom* i. 126. 23 *þes hundredes ealdor genealæhte ðam Hælende na healfunga ac fulfremedlice*, and *ÆCHom* i. 58. 5 *and he hine lufode synderlice, na swa micclum for ðære mæglican sibbe swa for ðære clænnysse his ansundan mægðhades,* or the second, e.g. *ÆCHom* i. 352. 18 *forðan ðe he wæs Godes bydel and na God, ÆCHom* i. 400. 12 *Godes miht þe gehælde, na ic,* and *ÆCHom* i. 368. 21 *and seo is mid gecorenum mannum getimbrod, na mid deadum stanum.* In this function, *na* may accompany a negated verb, e.g. *ÆCHom* i. 146. 9 *Næs seo eadige Maria na ofslegen ne gemartyrod lichomlice ac gastlice* (see §§1605-6). But it is of course not obligatory, e.g. *ÆCHom* i. 92. 3 *Ne beo ðu geciged heononforð Abram ac Abraham*; see further §1757.

§1617. As far as I have observed, *nalles*—not *na*—is the word used in the poetry to negate one of two alternative words or phrases; see §1760. But with alternative clauses or sentences, *ne* (adv.) . . . *ac, na . . . ac,* and *nalles . . . ac,* all occur in both prose and poetry; see §§1756-61.

b. Na/no *negating finite verbs*

§1618. *Na/no* is occasionally found negating finite verbs in the prose. In examples like *GD(C)* 213. 28 . . . *þæt hit na gehran þæs scræfes hrofe . . . ac feoll swiðe feorr* (where O has *no ne*), *na* negates the first of two alternative verbs. The influence of a following *ac* may also be responsible for *na* in *ÆCHom* i. 550. 28 *Na beoð þa eadige þe for hynðum . . . heofiað; ac ða beoð eadige ðe heora synna bewepað.* But there are instances where this is not so, e.g. *GD* 218. 7 *7 swa þeah he na forhogode, ÆCHom* i. 128. 33 *Soð ic eow secge, na gemette ic swa micelne geleafan on Israhela ðeode,* and *ChronA* 132. 25 (1001) *7 eac fela godra hama þe we genemnan na cunnan*; see Wülfing, ii, §594, and Einenkel, *Ang.* 35 (1911-12), 191, for more. Even if we do not agree with Andrew (*SS,* §79) that these 'must be scribal errors' to the extent of emending, we must admit that their rarity in the prose makes their status dubious. Emphasis will not do as an explanation for such a spasmodic phenomenon.

§1619. The usage is better attested—though still not common—in the poetry. There *na/no* carries stress when it negates a verb. It usually precedes the verb, as in *Beo* 136 . . . *morðbeala mare ond no mearn fore* and *Wan* 96 . . . *genap under nihthelm swa heo no wære,* but occasionally follows it, e.g. *Sea* 66 . . . *læne on londe. Ic gelyfe no . . .* and *El* 1081 *A min hige sorgað,* ‖ . . . *ond geresteð no.* In *Phoen* 72 . . . *wlitigum wæstmum, þær no waniað o, no* is unstressed and should probably be emended to *ne* as a scribal anticipation of *o*.

c. Nalles

§1620. The forms *nealles, nalles, nallæs, nallas, nales, nalæs, nalas,* and *næs,*[49] can be taken together for syntactical purposes, although Wülfing (ii, §593) suggests that originally there may have been two words—*nalles* = *ne ealles* and *nalæs* = *na læs*. GK (s.v. *næs*) sees *næs* not as a contraction of *nalles*, but as a combination of *ne + gese, gise*. As far as I have observed, none of these forms appears in the works of Ælfric or Wulfstan.

§1621. Examples in which *nalles* negates a finite verb are rare. All those I have noted in the prose have a negative adverb between *nalles* and a verb which is one of a contrasted pair, e.g. (with *ne*) *Bo* 61. 11 *7 þonne hi gegadrad hæfð, þonne eowað he hi, nallas ne hilð* and *Lev* 1. 17 *Ætbrede of þa feþeru, næs ne ceorfe,* and (with *na ne*) *Gen* 27. 12 . . . *7 þæt he wyrge me næs na ne bletsige.* But initial *nalles* immediately precedes a verb without *ne* in

> *Met* 9. 34   Nalles sorgode   hwæðer siððan a
> mihtig drihten   ametan wolde
> wrece be gewyrhtum   wohfremmendum. . . .

§1622. In sentences in which one of two alternative words (other than finite verbs) or phrases is negated, *na/no* is usual in the prose (§1616), but *nalles* sometimes serves, e.g. *Bede* 4. 25 *nalæs mid anes mannes geþeahte ac mid gesægene unrim geleaffulra witena, CP* 31. 6 *on hira unðeawum, nals on hira lare, BlHom* 5. 5 *Heo wæs ful cweden, næs æmetugu,* and (with *na*) *BlHom* 95. 19 *Næs na mid golde ne mid godwebbenum hræglum, ac mid godum dædum 7 halgum we sceolan beon gefrætwode.* In the poetry, where *na/no* does not occur in these patterns, *nalles* is (as far as I know) the rule; see §1617. Two examples must suffice: *Beo* 338 . . . *for wlenco, nalles for wræcsiðum, ‖ ac for higeþrymmum* and *Beo* 3019 *oft nalles æne.*

§1623. *Nalles* may also negate a single word or phrase in both prose, e.g. *CP* 27. 14 *Hie ricsedon, næs ðeah mines ðonces, CP* 263. 15 *ðonne beo him suiðe egefull ðæt ece wite, nalles ðeah sua egeful ðæt hie ealneg ðurhwunigen on ðæm ege,* and (with *na*) *ApT* 18. 5 *gemildsa me nacodum, forlidenum, næs na of earmlicum birdum*

---

[49] This form is still sometimes confused with *næs < ne wæs*; for an example see Brown 1970, pp. 80–1.

geborenum, and poetry, e.g. *Beo* 3089 *nealles swæslice* and *El* 817 *nalles feam siðum*. But *na/no* is certainly more common in this function in the prose and (I would say, pending full collections) in the poetry.

§1624. According to Andrew (*SS*, §82), the use of *nalles* 'as a head-word to negate a sentence' is restricted to the poetry. Typical examples are *Met* 9. 34 (§1621), *Beo* 1441 *Gyrede hine Beowulf* || *eorlge-wædum, nalles for ealdre mearn*, and *Beo* 2873 *Nealles folccyning fyrdgesteallum* || *gylpan þorfte*. For an example in the prose involving *Nalæs . . . ac*, see §1759.

d. Other negative adverbs

§1625. Other negative adverbs may be used in prose and poetry in clauses without *ne* before the verb. They include *næfre*, e.g. *GD* 257. 5 *forþon þe næfre synfulle men gecyrdon to cwiðnesse þære soðan dædbote gif nænige bysene ne wæron godra manna* and *Beo* 247 *Næfre ic maran geseah* || *eorla ofer eorþan* (see further §1609), and *nænige þinga*, e.g. *Bede* 82. 6 *forðon se seolfa willa nænge þinga buton synne beon mæg* and

Met 19. 37	Ic nat hu ic mæge	nænige ðinga
	ealles swa swiðe	on sefan minum
	hiora dysig tælan	swa hit me don lysteð.

In these, the negative element negates the adverb and the combination in effect negates the clause more emphatically than adv. *ne* would have done.

e. Negative adjective/pronouns

§1626. Negative adjective/pronouns occur in clauses whose verb is not negated by adv. *ne* in prose, e.g. the second clause in *GD* 325. 34 *ne geworhte ic næfre nænine wom ðe, ne ic noht yfeles gedyde in ðinum geleafan, GD* 332. 1 *ac wolde þæt men wiston þæt him nænig syn ungebeted butan wrace aleoðod wære, ÆCHom* i. 288. 5 *Him is nan ðing digle ne uncuð*, and *ÆCHom* ii. 310. 24 *and eac hine sylfne for nahte tealde*, and (more commonly; see §§1609-10) in the poetry, e.g. *Beo* 598 *nymeð nydbade, nænegum arað* || *leode Deniga* and *Beo* 691 *Nænig heora þohte þæt he þanon scolde*. On the examples from the poetry, see further §§1611-13.

f. Conclusions

§1627. Davis (Sweet, *Pr.* 9, p. 58) lays it down that 'in a negative sentence the particle [*ne*] is prefixed to every finite verb'. This rule requires qulification in two ways—apart from the obvious one implied in the words 'negative sentence', which excludes sentences in which the influence of *na* (§§1614-17) or *nalles* (§§1622-3) is restricted to specific words (other than finite verbs) or phrases. First, *na/no* sometimes appears instead of *ne* in both prose and poetry (§§1618-19). Second, there are those sentences just discussed which contain negatives such as *næfre* and *nænig* but in which the verb does not have prefixed *ne*. To these can be added co-ordinate clauses introduced by conj. *ne*, e.g. *Num* 23. 25 *Ne ðu hine wyrige, ne ðu hine bletsa* and the examples in §1832. More examples are given by Knörk (pp. 40-4), Rauert (pp. 71-6), and Schuchardt (*passim*).

§1628. As already noted in §1607, this failure to use *ne* immediately before the verb of a negated sentence is one form of exception to the general rule that OE prose prefers the multiple negative. However, the tendency to use adv. *ne* is very strong in the prose. Complete figures are not available. But Einenkel (*Ang.* 35 (1911-12), 191-2) found that *ne* was missing in less than ten per cent of negative sentences in Books iii and iv of Gregory's *Dialogues* and in less than four per cent in Books iv and v of *Boethius*. Rauert's examples of multiple negation in 'Alfredian' texts (pp. 76-100) occupy almost five times as much space as those in which adv. *ne* does not appear in negated sentences (pp. 71-6). My own impression is that the higher of the two figures given by Einenkel would certainly not be exceeded —and probably not approached—in the works of Ælfric and Wulfstan, while Jespersen (*Neg.*, pp. 64-5) reports that there is only one such exception in *Apollonius*—*ApT* 34. 22 *ne ondræt þu ðe æniges þinges.*

§1629. Complete figures are lacking for the poetry too. But the already-noted reluctance of poets to pile up negatives (§1609) is apparent from certain statistics about the use of adv. *ne*, which are based partly on Klaeber's Glossary to *Beowulf* and partly on Knörk's collections. (The figures are necessarily approximate because of problems of interpretation and emendation.) First, in the majority of 138 sentences in *Beowulf* in which *ne* immediately precedes the verb, it is the only negative. Second, *ne* is not found before the verb in 86.5 per cent of the 111 negative sentences in *Beowulf* contained in the table which follows—a striking contrast indeed to the percentages for the prose given in the preceding section.

Sentences containing	without adv. *ne*	with adv. *ne*
næfre	7	1
nænig	5	3
nan	1	1 (?) (*Beo* 803; see §1610)
na/no not immediately before verb	35	5
ne conj. (excluding disjunctive phrases)	27	5
nalles not negating a specific word only	21	0
Total	96	15

Third, in the great majority of sentences in Knörk's selected corpus of the poetry, adv. *ne* immediately before the verb is the only negative. Fourth, Knörk's corpus contains some 241 negative sentences without adv. *ne* prefixed to the verb (pp. 40-4), e.g. *Sea* 25 *ne ænig hleomæga ‖ feasceaftig ferð frefran meahte* and *Wid* 40 *Nænig efeneald him eorlscipe maran ‖ on orette*, against 103 with multiple negation (pp. 59-63), e.g. *Wan* 9 *Nis nu cwicra nan. . . .* In other words, adv. *ne* is not prefixed to the verb in seventy per cent of the sentences which contain another negative. This figure, though not as high as that for the 111 examples in *Beowulf*, is still in striking contrast to the figures for the prose cited above. There is room for more work on this aspect—and indeed others—of negation in OE. But the contrast between prose and poetry in respect of multiple negation is clearly marked and cannot be explained solely by the demands of alliteration.

§1630. BT(S), s.v. *nawiht* II, notes the use of *naht/noht* as an adverb 'not' negating words other than verbs. (In *Ps(A)* 88. 20 (23) *nowiht fromað se fiond in him* represents Latin *nihil proficiet inimicus in eo*.) Here it differs from its MnE descendant 'not', which can negate verbs as well as other words. *Naht/noht* occurs in sentences with *ne* before the verb, e.g. *Bo* 12. 27 *gesege me, nu þu cwist þ ðu noht ne tweoge þte God þisse worulde rihtwisige* (where *noht* reinforces *ne*), *Bo* 26. 30 *Ne mæg hus naht lange standan . . .* , *BlHom* 163. 8 (§1604), and *JDay i* 22, and in sentences without *ne* before the verb, e.g. *Bede* 138. 12, *Bede* 178. 18 *Gelomp noht micelre tide æfter his slege . . .* , *BlHom* 43. 25 *þonne sægde Sanctus Pauwlus þæt he gesawe naht feor from þæs mæssepreostes sidan . . .* , and *GuthB* 1168. See also §446.

5. OTHER METHODS OF NEGATION

§1631. As in MnE, a negative is implied in contexts not negative in form in rejected conditions (§§3608-10) and in rhetorical questions (§1641).

§1632. Negation can also be expressed by negative prefixes and suffixes (§1133), by the use of *to* (§§1142-3), and by understatement, e.g. *Beo* 2897 *lyt swigode* ‖ *niwra spella se ðe næs gerad* and *Dream* 69 *Reste he ðære mæte weorode*. On the last see further Mitchell 1976*a*, pp. 29-31.

IV

THE SIMPLE SENTENCE: TYPES

A. INTRODUCTORY REMARKS

§ 1633. Here we are concerned with the structure of simple sentences and principal clauses, i.e. with the expression of non-dependent statements, questions, explanations, and commands or wishes. *A défaut de mieux*, I retain the traditional concepts of simple and complex sentences (§ 1876), while avoiding the term 'multiple sentence' for reasons given in § 1685. I am aware that there are problems of terminology (see Collinson, *TPS* 1941, pp. 120-1) and of definition (are 'No!' and 'Mad?' sentences?) and that the 'sentence' is not always the unit of spoken English (as a study of most tape-recorded conversations will show). Indeed, I am not convinced that the sentence as traditionally defined and understood was always the unit of written OE prose and poetry; see §§ 1879-82 and 3956-7. I have a great deal of sympathy with H. Pilch when he says 'Wir werden, wie ich glaube, in der Syntax nicht wesentlich weiter kommen, wenn wir nicht auf den Satz als undefinierte und universale Obereinheit in der Syntax verzichten und ihn ersetzen durch ein Netzwerk von Relationen zwischen syntaktischen Gruppen bestimmter Sprachen' ['We will not, I think, make any significant progress in the study of syntax unless we abandon the sentence as a vague, universal, supreme syntactic unit, and replace it with a network of relationships between syntactic groups in particular languages'] ('Matrix der altenglischen Satztypen', *Linguistique contemporaine. Hommage à Eric Buyssens*, edd. Jean Dierickx and Yvan Lebrun (Brussels, 1970), 167). But no practical alternative has yet emerged. Systems such as those adopted by Jespersen, Sandfeld, and West (see my Introduction), are not entirely satisfactory and have not achieved wide recognition. Pilch's own 'matrix' is not yet fully developed; see Pilch's *Altenglische Grammatik* (Munich, 1970) and Lars-G. Hallander's review of it in *SN* 50 (1978), 135-41.

§ 1634. Problems of classification are presented by the ambiguous demonstrative/relative, e.g.

Beo 194   þæt fram ham gefrægn   Higelaces þegn
               god mid Geatum,   Grendles dæda;

      se wæs moncynnes   mægenes strengest
      on þæm dæge   þysses lifes,
      æþele ond eacen,

where *se* may mean 'he, that one' or 'who', and by ambiguous adverb/
conjunctions, e.g.

Beo 126   Ða wæs on uhtan   mid ærdæge
      Grendles guðcræft   gumum undyrne;
      þa wæs æfter wiste   wop up ahafen,
      micel morgensweg,

where *ða* in line 126 is usually taken as 'then', as in Klaeber's punctuation above, but where Andrew (*Postscript,* §16) argues that it
means 'when'. These problems are discussed in §§2109-21 and 2418
respectively. Cross-references are provided for other problems which
have been discussed elsewhere.

§1635. Direct speech—in which the words of a speaker are quoted
verbatim—is a special form of non-dependent speech. The difference
consists solely in the presence in direct speech of an introductory or
parenthetic verb of speaking by which the reporter certifies or claims
that he is actually using the speaker's own words. It is discussed in
§§1935, 1939, and 1949. P. W. Pillsbury (*Descriptive Analysis of
Discourse in Late West Saxon Texts* (Mouton, 1967), 17-19) restricts
his study to examples of direct speech in the belief that this is the
nearest we can get to a live informant. The suggestion is attractive
and at first glance seems worth pursuing. But the qualifications Pillsbury himself has to make reinforce my feeling that this line of investigation will not produce anything very solid. In any event Pillsbury
himself was not really concerned with establishing the norms of OE
colloquial speech. The title is misleading: 'the purpose of this investigation was to formulate a description of the inflectional characteristics and syntactic behavior of eleventh century English nouns' (p. 15)
in 'all [*sic*] the dialogue passages in eleventh century prose texts'
(inside of cover). Its interest is not in OE for its own sake: 'the purpose here is to test an analytical procedure against a specific language
corpus' (p. 24). Nothing that is not known about the OE noun
emerges. Much that is known does not emerge because the corpus is
limited.

§1636. The absence from OE manuscripts of inverted commas or
any specific device for marking direct speech causes little real difficulty, but some inconsistency; consider *ÆCHom* i. 2. 29-4. 7, *ÆCHom*
i. 48. 9-25, and *ÆCHom* i. 98. 10 *þæt stænene sex þe þæt cild*

*ymbsnað getacnode ðone stan ðe se apostol cwæð, 'Se stan soðlice
wæs Crist'. He cwæð wæs for ðære getacnunge, na for edwiste*, where
the second *wæs* should be in inverted commas. But occasionally the
actual punctuation will depend on knowledge of something outside
the text, e.g. *ÆCHom* i. 8. 7 *Paulus se apostol cwæð, 'We sind Godes
gefylstan', and swa ðeah ne do we nan þing to Gode, buton Godes
fultume.*

§1637. On 'represented' speech see §§1945 and 1984.

B. NON-DEPENDENT STATEMENTS

§1638. In affirmative statements the most common element orders
are SV, e.g. *ÆCHom* i. 4. 2 *Manega lease Cristas cumað on minum
naman, cweðende 'Ic eom Crist'* and *ÆCHom* i. 10. 12 *He gesceop
tyn engla werod,* and adv. VS, e.g. *ÆCHom* i. 4. 14 *þonne cymð se
Antecrist* and *ÆCHom* i. 10. 26 *þa gefæstnode he þisne ræd.* In
negative statements, *ne* usually occupies initial position immediately
followed by the verb, e.g. *ÆCHom* i. 82. 33 *Ne forseah Crist his
geongan cempan* and the similar sentences in §3935. But these
orders are not obligatory and departures from them—sometimes,
but not always, for reasons of style, emphasis, and the like—are
common, even in simple statements. See further chapter IX.

§1639. The verb is in the indicative mood. On repetition, non-
repetition, and non-expression, of the subject in statements, see
§§1503-16.

C. NON-DEPENDENT QUESTIONS

1. INTRODUCTORY REMARKS

§1640. Here I propose to follow Jespersen's terminology (*Ess.*,
pp. 304-5):

There are two kinds of questions: 'Did he say that?' is an example of the one
kind, and 'What did he say?' and 'Who said that?' are examples of the other.
　In the former kind—nexus-questions—we call in question the combination
(nexus) of a subject and a predicate. We may therefore continue with the negative counterpart: 'Did he say that, or did he not (say that)?' and thus make it
into a disjunctive or alternative question. The answer to a simple nexus-question
is *yes* or *no*; the answer to a disjunctive question like 'Is it black or white?' or

'Did he drink sherry or port?' is one of the two alternatives (or else 'neither').
. . .

In questions of the second kind we have an unknown quantity x, exactly as in an algebraic equation; we may therefore use the term x-questions. The linguistic expression for this x is an interrogative pronoun or pronominal adverb.

Jespersen's examples of x-questions include 'Who said that?' and 'When did he say it?'. In OE, we see nexus questions in *ÆCHom* i. 46. 7 *Is hit swa hi secgað?*, *ÆCHom* i. 136. 30 *Hwæðer ic mote lybban oðþæt ic hine geseo?*, and (with the negative alternative expressed) *Matt(WSCp)* 22. 17 *ys hyt alyfed þ man casere gaful sylle þe na?*, and x-questions in *ÆCHom* ii. 184. 8 *hwæt hæfst þu gedon?* and *ÆCHom* i. 136. 28 *Ela, hwænne cymð se Hælend?* These are considered in more detail below. Further examples will be found in Bacquet, pp. 183-231. To save undue repetition, I remind the reader that *don* is not used as an auxiliary in OE; see §§665-9. So questions of the type 'Did he say it?' do not occur.

§1641. Rhetorical questions do not constitute a third class. Both types may be so used. So we find rhetorical nexus questions in *Bo* 73. 24 *Hwæðer ge nu secan gold on treowum?*, *ÆCHom* i. 430. 34 *Hwæt la, eart ðu to dry awend . . . ?*, and *ÆLS* 9. 72 *Eart þu la god?*, and rhetorical x-questions in *Or* 50. 13 *Hwa is þætte ariman mæge hwæt þær moncynnes forwearð . . . ?* and *ÆCHom* ii. 188. 19 *Hwa mæg on worulde ealle ða wundra gereccan . . . ?* The obvious answer is sometimes given, e.g. *Bo* 39. 28 *Wenst ðu þ se godcunda anweald ne mihte afyrran þone anweald þam unrihtwisan kasere . . . ? Gise, la gese; ic wat þæt he mihte, gif he wolde.* A genuine question may be made rhetorical by the inclusion of the answer, e.g. (in a *butan* phrase) *ÆCHom* i. 94. 32 *Hwæt getacnað þæs fylmenes ofcyrf on ðam gesceape, buton galnysse wanunge?* and (in a *butan* clause) *ÆCHom* i. 348. 24 *ac hwa mæg beon eadig, buton he his Scyppendes wununge on him sylfum hæbbe?*

§1642. *Mutatis mutandis*, the rules for negatives laid down in §§ 1595-632 apply to negative questions too. On element order in questions which are in asyndetic parataxis or are introduced by *ond, ac*, or *oððe*, see §§1868-71. The subject is expressed except with those impersonal verbs which are used without one; see §§1031-5.

2. NEXUS QUESTIONS

§1643. As the examples in §§1870-5 show, nexus questions can be asked in two ways in OE—with the element order VS or with introductory *hwæðer* 'whether' and the order SV.

§1644. In both positive and negative questions with the order VS, the mood of the verb is indicative, e.g. *CP* 43. 3 *Petrus lufastu me?*, *Bo* 12. 16 *Gelefst ðu þ sio wyrd wealde þisse worulde, Solil* 36. 16 *ne lyste þe fægeres wifes . . . ?*, and *ÆCHom* ii. 256. 12 *ne ondrætst ðu ðe god?* With those 'auxiliary' verbs which do occur in OE we find vSV and the indicative, as in MnE, e.g. *Bo* 17. 17 *Habbe ic þe awer benumen þinra gifena . . . ?*, *Bo* 12. 12 *Mot ic nu cunnian hwon þinre fæstrædnesse . . . ?*, *ÆHom* 12. 12 *Mæg he, la, inn faran to his modor innoðe eft, and swa beon geedcenned?*, and *ÆHom* 8. 234 *and ne mæg se Eallwealdend, gif ðu hine lufast, his leoman þe asendan, and eac þe lufian?*

§1645. The order VS is not peculiar to questions. It is sometimes found in positive statements, e.g. *ÆCHom* i. 102. 20 *Is hwæðere æfter gecynde on gesceapennysse ælc lichamlice gesceaft . . . mægen-fæstre on fullum monan . . .* (cf. *ÆCHom* i. 46. 7 *Is hit swa hi secgað?*), and is the regular order in negative statements, e.g. *ÆCHom* i. 376. 21 *Ne ondræde ic ðine awyrgedan gastas . . .* (cf. *ÆCHom* i. 376. 23 *Ne ondrætst ðu ðe, Petrus, Simones mihta . . . ?*). The context almost always resolves the potential ambiguity for the modern scholar, e.g. *Matt(WSCp)* 20. 13 *Đa cwæð he andswarigende hyra anum: Eala þu freond, ne do ic þe nænne teonan. Hu, ne come þu to me to wyrceanne wið anum peninge?*; both the context and the Latin should have shown Einenkel that he was wrong when he took *GD* 258. 22 *. . . ne bodað nu na þes middangeard his ende . . .* as a question (*Ang.* 35 (1912), 204–5). The same is true in imperative sentences like *CP* 109. 5 *Weahsað ge 7 monigfaldiað 7 gefyllað eorðan* and *BlHom* 191. 21 *ne beoð ge nu unrote ac gefeoþ mid me*, where the order VS occurs and the verb is in form either indicative or imperative. For the Anglo-Saxon speaker, however, intonation must have been the guide. The same can be said of sentences with other orders, e.g. (imperatives with V . . . vSV) *Matt(WSCp)* 19. 14 *Lætað þa lytlingas and nelle ge hig forbeodan cuman to me* and (questions with OSV . . . OSV . . . SV) *Bo* 71. 25 *Anwaldes ðu wilnast? . . . Gilpes þu girnst? . . . þu woldest nu brucan ungemetlicre wrænnesse?*

§1646. As I am reluctant to accept the notion that OE *ac* can serve as an interrogative particle except in literal glosses, I would add to these examples three more nexus questions with initial *ac* and element order SV, viz. *Bede* 68. 27, *LS* 10. 162. 21, and *Beo* 1987. For full citation of these and a general discussion of the problem, see Mitchell 1977, pp. 98-100.

§1647. Exclamatory *hwæt (la)* sometimes introduces nexus questions as well as statements and exclamations, e.g. (positive questions) *ÆHom* 14. 136 *Hwæt, bið æfre wyrse ænig þing on worlde þonne swylc dæd . . . ?* and *ÆCHom* i. 430. 34 *Hwæt la, eart ðu to dry awend . . . ?*, and (negative questions) *ÆCHom* ii. 452. 13 *. . . and Drihten him cwæð to, Hwæt la, ne beheolde ðu minne ðeowan Iob . . . ?* (where the ambiguous *beheolde* should be taken as indicative rather than as subjunctive under the influence of *cwæð*; cf. *Gen* 27. 36 (§1650) and *ÆCHom* i. 64. 16 *Hwæt la, ne mæg se Ælmihtiga Wealdend þurhteon þæt he do his ðeowan rice . . . ?* Again intonation must have removed the ambiguity I detect in examples like *Bo* 113. 30 *Hwæt wenað þa yfelan þ hi bion bedælde ðara wita . . . ?* (where, despite Bacquet (p. 185 fn. 2), *hwæt* could mean 'why?') and *ÆCHom* ii. 572. 34 *Hwæt ne cann se ðe ealle ðing cann?* I hesitate to follow Visser (iii, §1454) when he suggests that *hwæt* is an interrogative particle with the order SV in *LS* 34. 516 and 532 (here he has the support of Skeat's punctuation and of Andrew, *SS*, §60) and in *WaldB* 14—these can all be taken as non-dependent exclamations —or in *PPs* 107. 10, where the poet has made a Latin question into a statement. For the reverse see *Or* 50. 13.

§1648. *Hu*, which is common in *x*-questions and in exclamations, occurs either alone or in combination with *la* as the equivalent of Latin *nonne* in negative nexus questions which demand an affirmative answer, e.g. *Matt(WSCp)* 13. 27 *Hlaford hu ne seow[e] þu god sæd on þinum æcere?*, Latin *nonne bonum semen seminasti in agro tuo?*[1] Bacquet (pp. 220-8) offers numerous examples from the 'Alfredian' texts. They include *Solil* 16. 9 *hu ne hæfð he sawle?* and *Bo* 87. 21 *Hu ne meaht þu geðencan?* To these may be added *ÆCHom* ii. 432. 31 *Hu ne is þis seo miccle Babilon ðe ic sylf getimbrode . . . ?*, *ÆCHom* ii. 20. 12 *Hula ne wurpe we þry cnihtas into ðam fyre?*, and *ÆCHom* i. 388. 1 *La hu, ne is ðes se wælhreowa ehtere cristenra manna?* Here again the order is VS and the mood indicative.

§1649. The same is true in positive nexus questions demanding the answer 'No'. These are most commonly introduced by *cwyst ðu/ cweðe ge* representing Latin *numquid*, e.g. *Gen* 37. 8 *Cwyst ðu la, byst ðu ure cyning . . . ?*, Latin *Numquid rex noster eris?*, *John*

---

[1] *Matt(Li)* 13. 27 reads *drihten ahne god sed ðu geseawu in lond ðinum? Ahne* also represents *numquid* in the glosses, e.g. *John(Li)* 4. 29 *hueðer ł ahne he is Christus?*, Latin *numquid ipse est Christus?* (So too does *ah*, e.g. *Ps(A)* 29. 9 *ah ondetteð ðe dust?*, Latin *numquid confitebitur tibi pulvis?*) We can accept Visser's conclusion (iii, §1461) that such examples of *ahne* 'were probably only literal translations and did not reflect the language as it was spoken at the time'.

(WSCp) 18. 17 *Cwyst ðu, eart ðu of ðyses leorningcnihtum . . . ?
Nicc ne eom ic*, Latin *numquid . . . ?*, and *John(WSCp)* 4. 29 *Cweðe
ge, is he Crist?*, Latin *numquid ipse est Christus?*

§1650. In *Gen* 27. 36 *Cwyst þu, ne heolde þu me nane bletsunge?*
(cf. *ÆCHom* ii. 452. 13 (§1647)), Latin *Numquid non reseruasti . . .
et mihi benedictionem?*, Esau's negated question desperately demands
the answer 'Yes'. But in *Gen* 27. 38 *La fæder, hæfdest ðu gyt ane
bletsunga?*, Latin *Num unam . . . tantum benedictionem habes, pater?*,
he seems to have given up hope. Ogura (1979, pp. 21-2) gives more
such examples and adds three with *secgan*, viz. *Luke(WSCp)* 6. 39,
11. 12, and (with an interesting contrast) 11. 11 *Hwylc eower bitt
his fæder hlafes . segst þu sylð he him stan . oððe gif he byt fisces
sylð he him næddran for fisce*. In all of these, the verb of the actual
question is indicative.

§1651. Positive nexus questions demanding the answer 'No' can also
be introduced by *wen(e)st þu/wen(e)stu*, e.g. *Bo* 29. 28 *Wenst þu
mæge seo wyrd þe gedon þ þa þing þin agnu sen þa ðe heora agene
gecynd þe gedon fremde?*, where the Latin has a statement beginning
Numquam 'Never', and *CP* 405. 11 *Gif hwelc wif forlæt hiere ceorl,
7 nimð hire oðerne, wenestu recce he hire æfre ma, oððe mæg hio
æfre eft cuman to him swa clænu swa hio ær wæs?*, Latin . . . *numquid revertetur ad eam ultra? Numquid non polluta et contaminata
erit mulier illa?* See further §1983. The use of *cwyst þu, segst þu,
wenst þu*, and their variants, as interrogative equivalents is discussed
by Ogura in a forthcoming article in *NM*.

§1652. Non-dependent nexus questions introduced by *hwæþer* are
with few exceptions characterized by two things—the element order
S(. . .)V and the subjunctive mood, e.g. *Ps(P)* 29. 9 *Hwæðer þe þæt
dust herige on þære burgene oþþe hwæðer hit cyðe þine rihtwisnesse?*,
Latin *Numquid confitebitur tibi pulvis aut annuntiabit veritatem
tuam?* As Nusser (pp. 183-4) and Andrew (*SS*, §60) point out, these
characteristics suggest that such questions were originally dependent;
on this see §§1658-9.

§1653. The only examples which do not have S(. . .)V are those in
which the verb is impersonal, e.g. *Bo* 29. 9 *Hwæþer þe nu licien
fægru lond?* and similar instances given by Bacquet, pp. 203-4—in
these 'the indirect object . . . occupies the place of the subject, which
it semantically is' (Campbell, *RES* 15 (1964), 191); a few which are
clearly due to Latin influence, e.g. *Bede* 68. 22 *Hwæðer moton*

twegen æwe gebroðor twa geswustor in gesinscipe onfon . . . ?,
Latin *Si debeant duo germani fratres singulas sorores accipere . . .?*;
and perhaps some in which two alternatives are expressed; on these
see §§1873-4.

§1654. The great majority of non-dependent nexus questions introduced by *hwæþer* have the present subjunctive. Examples with
the present indicative like *Matt(WSCp)* 20. 15 *hwæþer þe þin eage
manful ys . . . ?*, Latin *an oculus tuus nequam est . . . ?* are exceptional but are easily explicable as the result of Latin influence. The
preterite is rare, but does occur, e.g. *Bo* 62. 14 *Gif þu nu gesawe
sumne swiðe wisne man þe hæfde swiðe gooda oferhyda 7 wære
þeah swiðe earm 7 swiðe ungesælig, hwæðer ðu wolde cweðan þ he
wære unwyrðe anwealdes 7 weorðscipes?*, where *wolde* (ambiguous
in form) is preterite subjunctive in a rejected or imaginary condition.
I have noted no unambiguous preterite indicatives.

§1655. Many of the questions with the present subjunctive are
rhetorical. Some demand—a few even give—the answer 'No', e.g.
Bo 56. 9 *Hwæðer nu good hlisa 7 foremærnes seo for nauht to
tellenne? Nese, nese . . . , Bo* 73. 24 *Hwæðer ge nu secan gold on
treowum? ic wat þeah þ ge hit þær ne secað, ne finde ge hit no*, and
Met 19. 15 *Hwæþer ge nu willen wæpan mid hundum ‖ on sealtne
sæ . . . ?* Sometimes a positive answer is expected, e.g. *Bo* 60. 10
Hwæðer þa welegan nu næfre ne hingrige ne ne þyrste ne ne cale?,
and even given, e.g. *Bo* 28. 27 *Hwæþer nu gimma wlite eowre eagan
to him getio hiora to wundriganne? Swa ic wat þ hi doð.*

§1656. But such questions can be genuine, e.g. *Bo* 35. 28 *Eala,
hwæðer ge netenlican men ongiten hwilc se wela sie 7 se anwald
. . . ? þa sint eowere hlafordas 7 eowere waldendas, næs ge heora,
ÆCHom* i. 136. 30 *Hwæðer ic mote lybban oðþæt ic hine geseo?*,
and *ÆHom* 26. 53 *oððe hwæðer þin miht þe mæge forwyrnan
. . . ?*, Latin *sed forte recognitionem peccati prohibet potestas
imperii.* For further examples and syntactical comment see Bacquet,
pp. 191-4; Behre, pp. 244-7, 256-7, and 260-1; and Visser, ii, §854.

§1657. In the questions which have a negative answer, 'we are', says
Hotz (p. 42), 'in presence of subject matters merely imaginary, merely
supposed a moment to exist for argument's sake, and the subj. is the
subj. of unreality'. In the others, he goes on, 'the subj. appears to
express astonishment, wonder, about the subject matter'. We can perhaps add doubt. See further Traugott, pp. 73 and 101-2.

§1658. The combination of the order SV and the subjunctive mood means that it is possible to take some examples as non-dependent or dependent questions; consider *ÆHom* 5. 73 *Hys discipuli þa sædon digellice him betwynan, Hwæðer ænig man him brohte mete hider?* (so Pope) and compare Thorpe's punctuation of *ÆCHom* i. 236. 32 with that adopted by Pope in *ÆHom* 21. 419. The same ambiguity seems to exist in nexus questions introduced by *cwyst ðu*, e.g. *GD(H)* 146. 1 *la, leof, sege, ic þe bidde, cwyst þu, hwæþer hit sy to gelyfenne . . . ?*, Latin *dic, quæso te, numquidnam credendum est . . . ?*, and *Matt(WSCp)* 26. 25 *Cwyst þu lareow hwæðer ic hyt si?*, Latin *numquid ego sum rabbi?*

§1659. The editors of *OED* long ago summed it up thus (s.v. *whether* II. 2): 'Introducing a simple direct question, thus becoming a mere sign of interrogation (but often with verb in subjunctive, and almost always without inversion of subject and verb, as if depending on a principal clause understood . . .).' There is little more to be said except that, pending full collections, I would tentatively omit 'often' and 'almost' when speaking of the OE usage, and that sentences like *John(WSCp)* 7. 52 *Cwyst þu þ þu si galileisc?*, Latin *numquid et tu galilaeus es?*, and *John(WSCp)* 4. 29 *Cweðe ge is he Crist?*, Latin *numquid ipse est christus?*, suggest that the examples from the Gospels at any rate are likely to be non-dependent; see §1658 and Gorrell, pp. 356-7. But, despite Schrader (§75), *cwyst þu* governs a noun clause of dependent statement introduced by *þæt* in *ÆLS* 5. 169 *Cwyst þu la þæt nære nan lyfigende god . . .* 'Thou sayest that . . .'.

§1660. *Hwæðer (ðe)* occasionally glosses Latin *an*, e.g. *Mark(WSCp)* 3. 4 and *Mark(WSH)* 3. 4 *Đa cwæð he alyfð restedagen wel to donne hwæðer ðe yfele sawle gehælen hwaðer to forspillen*, Latin *et dicit eis licet sabbatis bene facere an male animam saluam facere an perdere.*

3. *X*-QUESTIONS

§1661. As in MnE, positive *x*-questions in OE are introduced by interrogative pronoun/adjectives (see §§346-60) or by interrogative adverbs (see §§1147-50). The verb is usually indicative. The element order is normally Interrog. VS . . . ?, e.g. *Bo* 137. 25 *Hwæt wenst þu bi þære goodan wyrde . . . ?* and *ÆCHom* i. 78. 6 *Hwær is Iudeiscra leoda cyning . . . ?*, unless one of the OE 'auxiliaries' is used. Then the order is vSV, e.g. *CP* 133. 10 *Eala, hwy is ðis gold adeorcad?*, *Bo* 143. 17 *Hwæt hæbbe ic forgiten þæs þe wit ær spræcon?*, *ÆHom*

8. 239 *Hwæt mage we eow secgan swutellicor be þysum . . . ?*, and *ÆHom* 12. 11 *Hu mæg se ealda mann eft beon acenned?* Further examples will be found in the sections listed above.

§1662. Since non-dependent nexus questions introduced by *hwæþer* usually have the order S(. . .)V and the subjunctive (see §1652), they cannot often be confused with non-dependent *x*-questions introduced by the pronoun *hwæþer* 'which (of two)?', e.g. *Solil* 51. 18 *Hweðer ðincð þe þonne betre, þe ðæt soð þe seo soðfestnes?* and *ÆCHom* i. 222. 20 *Hwæðer cweðe we, ðe ure ðe ðæra engla?* A few difficult examples involving alternatives are discussed in §§1873-4.

§1663. There are some variations from these norms. The subject of course comes first when it is the interrogative itself, e.g. *Bo* 15. 20 *Eala Mod, hwæt bewearp þe on ðas care . . . ?* and *ÆHom* 11. 143 *Hwa dorste æfre gewilnian þæs wynsuman eardes . . . ?* The indirect object but logical subject of an impersonal verb follows it immediately, e.g. *Or* 182. 22 *Hu þyncð eow nu Romanum hu seo sibb gefæstnad wære . . . ?* and *Matt(WSCp)* 21. 28 *Hu þincð eow . . . ?*; see Bacquet, pp. 203-4. A pronoun subject immediately follows its verb. But when the subject is a noun group it may be preceded by another element or elements, e.g. *CP* 105. 5 *Hwæt getacniað ðonne ða twelf oxan . . . ?*, *CP* 171. 2 *Hwæt mæg ðonne elles seo earc tacnian buton ða halgan ciricean . . . ?*, *Bo* 67. 12 *Hu licað þe nu se anwald 7 se wela . . . ?*, *CP* 197. 22 *Hwæt tacnað us ðonne Saul buton yfle hlafurdas?*, and *ÆHom* 13. 20 *Hu mæg la se blinda lædan þone blindan . . . ?* (cf. *ÆHom* 13. 24 *Hu miht þu la geseon þæt mot . . . ?*). But other arrangements occur because of the demands of emphasis or style, e.g. *Bo* 38. 28 *Hwæt godes is se wela ðonne, ðonne he ne mæg þa grundleasan gitsunga afyllan þæs gitseres . . . ?* and *ÆHom* 4. 21 *Gif se sceocca soðlice is on him sylfum todæled, hu mæg þonne standan his rice staþolfæst?* Bacquet (chapter V, *passim*) has a valuable collection of examples illustrating the variations in 'Alfredian' texts.

§1664. *X*-questions are negated according to the patterns set out in §§1595-632 but otherwise match their positive counterparts. A few examples must suffice: *Bo* 126. 5 *Oððe hwa ne wafað þæs . . . ?*, *Bo* 126. 18 *Oððe hwy ne wundriað hi þæs . . . ?*, *Bo* 56. 6 *Hwi nis nu anweald to tellanne . . . ?*, *Bo* 124. 5 *Oððe hwy ne magon ge gebidan gecyndelices deaðes . . . ?*, *ÆCHom* i. 378. 8 *Hwi ne cwest ðu nan word?*, and *ÆCHom* i. 114. 4 *Hwi ne sceal he ðonne rihtlice wrecan þæt yfel . . . ?* Other elements may intervene between the interrogative and the negated verb, e.g. *Solil* 16. 8 *Hwi gyf ic sawle lufige, hu ne lufige ic minne freond?*

§1665. The type of apposition seen in MnFr. *Le professeur où est-il?* occurs in OE, e.g. *GD(C)* 136. 10 *Se halga wer for hwan ne cuþe he þa deogolnysse þære godcundan sceawunge* . . . ?, *CP* 133. 11 7 *ðæt æðeleste hiew hwy wearð hit onhworfen?*, and *ÆCHom* i. 410. 21 *þæt ðwyre mod* . . . *hwæt deð hit buton swilce hit lecge stan ofer stane?* In these examples the two elements agree in case. But this is not always so, e.g. *ÆCHom* i. 346. 3 *þas Godes ðegnas* . . . *hwider gescyt ðonne heora endebyrdnesse* . . . ? and *ÆHom* 9. 44 *Se be-hydda wisdom and se bedigloda goldhord, hwilc fremu is ænigum on aðrum þæra?* Such constructions are not restricted to questions; see §§44(3) and 1441.

§1666. As in MnE, contracted questions occur in which the subject, verb, and sometimes other elements, must be understood from a pre-ceding clause, e.g. *Solil* 17. 12 *For hwi?*, *Solil* 26. 5 *Hwilce bebodu?*, *ÆCHom* i. 144. 27 *Hu ðonne?*, *ÆCHom* i. 278. 24 *Hwi swa?*, and *ÆCHom* i. 320. 2 *Hwi ofer Criste on culfran hiwe? Hwi ofer Cristes hirede on fyres gelicnysse?* See §3874.

§1667. There are occasional *x*-questions, both positive and negative, in which the subject precedes a verb which is either subjunctive or ambiguous in form. They fall into three groups. The first includes *ÆCHom* i. 314. 20 *La hwæt þis beon sceole?* and *LS* 34. 532 *La hwæt þis æfre beon scyle þæt ic her wundres gehyre?*, where the order may be due to the presence of an interjection (see §1671 and Andrew, *SS*, §60) and the subjunctive perhaps expresses surprise.

§1668. In the second group the interrogative word is itself the sub-ject, the order is that normal in non-dependent *x*-questions, and we should expect the indicative. Goodwin (p. 74, line 3) is not followed by Gonser in emending *þince* to *þincð* in *LS* 10. 157. 50 *þa geseah he þone foresprecenan broðor Wigfrið, cwæð þa þus to him: And nu broþor Wigfrið, ac hwylc þince þe nu, þæt se preost sig, be þam þu gyrstandæge cwæde* . . . ?, Latin . . . *sanctus Guthlacus* . . . *inquit: O Frater Wilfride, quomodo tibi nunc videtur ille Clericus, de quo hesterno die judicare promisisti?* Here we may have to do with some-thing approaching 'represented speech' (see §§1945 and 1984), with the subj. *þince* due to the influence of *cwæð* (see §2033). In

Met 28. 44   Hwa þegna ne mæge
         eac wafian   ælces stiorran,

> hwy hi ne scinen   scirum wederum
> beforan ðære sunnan . . . ?,

we may have a contracted form of the pattern seen in

Met 28. 32   Hwa is weoruldmonna   þæt ne wafige,
                  hu sume steorran   oð ða sæ farað
                  under merestreamas,   þæs ðe monnum ðincð?

Both questions demand the answer 'None'; we may compare

Met 10. 68   Hwæt þonne hæbbe   hæleþa ænig,
                  guma æt þæm gilpe,   gif hine gegripan mot
                  se eca deað   æfter þissum worulde?,

where *hwæt* is the object, the order the normal interrogative one, and the answer demanded is 'Nothing'. The subjunctive—which is common in *x*-questions in the *Boethius* and the *Metres*; see §§1669-70—perhaps emphasizes the speaker's attitude and the nature of the question. Here we may compare *Mark(WSCp)* 10. 26 *7 hwa mæg beon hal?*, Latin *et quis potest saluus fieri?* with *Mark(Li)* 10. 26 *7 hua mæge hal wuosa?*

§1669. The third group consists of examples in which the interrogative is not the subject. They include *Bo* 10. 17 *Hwy þu la Drihten æfre woldest þ seo wyrd swa hwyrfan sceolde?*, *Bo* 71. 15 *Hwæt þu þonne mæne mid þære gidsunge þæs feos . . . ?*, *Met* 19. 10 *Hwy ge nu ne settan on sume dune* || *fiscnet eowru . . . ?*, and *PPs* 79. 12 *Forhwan þu towurpe weallfæsten his?* Further examples will be found in *Bo* 46. 7, *Bo* 139. 7, and (from the *Metres*) in Henk (p. 12). *Bo* 68. 9 *Eala, wuldur þisse weorulde, ea, forhwy þe haten dysige men mid leasre stemne wuldor, nu þu nane neart?* is best explained as belonging here, with the order OVS (see §3918) to emphasize the connection between *þe* and the preceding vocative; but see Bacquet, p. 194. Behre offers comment and examples (pp. 244-7, 256-7, and 260-1). Analogous to these are examples such as

Met 10. 18   Eala, ofermodan,   hwi eow a lyste
                  mid eowrum swiran   selfra willum
                  þæt swære gioc   symle underlutan?

and

Met 10. 63   þeah ge nu wenen   and wilnigen
                  þæt ge lange tid   libban moten,
                  hwæt iow æfre þy bet   bio oððe þince?,

in which the indirect object of an impersonal verb occupies the place of the subject, which logically it is.

§1670. No one explanation will account for all the subjunctives. Henk (p. 13) rightly detects the subjunctive of unreality ('der conj. der Irrealität') in *Met* 19. 10 and similar examples which demand the answer 'No'. Wülfing (ii. 72) detects uncertainty in examples like *Bo* 71. 15; this explanation would also do for *Bo* 10. 17. (See further Hotz, pp. 41 ff.) But here too—as with nexus questions introduced by *hwæþer* (§§1658-9)—the order S(. . .)V and the subjunctive suggest that these questions may originally have been dependent; see further Horn, *AngB.* 27 (1916), 82-4.

D. NON-DEPENDENT EXCLAMATIONS

§1671. Without intonation patterns and native informants we are sometimes hard put to decide whether we have a non-dependent exclamation or statement, e.g. *ÆCHom* i. 438. 12 *Eft he cwæð to Iohanne, 'Loca nu, her stent þin modor'*, or a non-dependent exclamation or question, e.g. *ÆCHom* i. 252. 21 *Gif ge cunnon, þa ðe yfele sind, syllan ða godnysse eowrum bearnum, hu micele swiðor wile eower Heofonlica Fæder forgyfan godne gast him biddendum*. The presence or absence of an interjection or of a vocative is no criterion. Neither is essential to an exclamation and both may be linked to non-dependent statements, questions, and commands, as well as to exclamations; see §§1234-9 and consider *ÆCHom* i. 78. 13 *Eala þu Bethleem, Iudeisc land, ne eart ðu nateshwon wacost burga on Iudeiscum ealdrum*, where the order *ne* ind.VS could signal a negative statement, question, or exclamation. The order VS can be decisive in positive sentences; thus *ÆHom* 14. 136 *Hwæt, bið æfre wyrse ænig þing . . . ?* is a question. But it is not infallible. Thus Thorpe, faced with the pattern *Gif . . . , hu miccle swiðor* vSV in *ÆCHom* ii. 462. 25, *ÆCHom* i. 68. 23 (where the *hu micele* clause depends on *ðu tæhtest*), and *ÆCHom* i. 252. 21, ended the sentences with a question mark, an exclamation mark, and a full stop, respectively. Neither the order SV nor S . . . V can decide between positive statements and positive exclamations, e.g. *ÆCHom* i. 46. 26 *Hwæt ða Iudeiscan þa wurdon þearle on heora heortan astyrode, ÆCHom* ii. 518. 27 *Hwæt ða Turonisce þone halgan gelæhton*, and *Beo* 1 *Hwæt, we Gardena . . . || . . . þrym gefrunon*. The interjections and/ or the context may seem to decide for exclamations in examples like *Solil* 43. 10 *Wa la wa! hwæt þu me for hæardne lætst!, ÆCHom* ii. 322. 15 *Wa ðan ðe strang bið to swiðlicum drencum . . . !, ÆCHom* ii. 488. 12 *Eala þu cyning, þas fulan wuhta þu sceoldest awurpan of ðinum rice . . . !* (where we have the 'predicative' preceding the subject; cf. Jespersen, *Ess.*, p. 127), *ÆCHom* ii. 518. 14 *Eala, hwilc heofung holdra and geleaffulra hlude ða swegde . . . !*, *ÆCHom* ii. 78. 32, where two exclamations joined by *and* both have the order S . . . V, *Beo* 11 *þæt wæs god cyning!*, *Hell* 76 *Eala Gabrihel, hu þu eart gleaw and scearp* || *. . . !*, and *Hell* 99 *Eala Hierusalem . . . ,* || *hu þu in þære stowe stille gewunadest!* Yet there is room for difference of opinion in some of these examples.

§1672. The mood in non-dependent exclamations is indicative. So *Bo* 34. 10 *Æala, hwæt se forma gitsere wære, þe ærest þa eorþan ongan delfan æfter golde . . . ?* and the corresponding passage in the *Metres* (*Met* 8. 55) are questions; see §1670, where the possibility is mooted that we may have to understand a principal clause on which the *x*-question is dependent. The same possibility arises with certain clauses introduced by *hu* or *þæt*. *ÆCHom* i. 288. 1 *Hwæt wenst ðu hu miccle swiðor is Godes andweardnys . . .* and *ÆCHom* i. 442. 8 *. . . hu miccle swiðor wenst þu þæt he nu todæg þæt heofonlice werod . . . sendan wolde* in their different ways come close to being dependent exclamations. Are we to understand some sort of principal clause to govern that introduced by *hu* in *ÆCHom* i. 130. 10 *Hu miccle swiðor miht ðu, þe ælmihtig God eart, þurh ðine hæse gefremman swa hwæt swa ðu wilt* or those introduced by *þæt* in *Bo* 34. 6 *Eala þ ure tida nu ne mihtan weorþan swilce* (where the negative certifies that we have an exclamation, not a wish, even though the Latin reads *Vtinam modo nostra redirent* || *In mores tempora priscos!*; see §1974 and cf. *Bo* 50. 3 *Eala þte þis moncyn wære gesælig . . .* , which represents *O felix hominum genus . . .*) and *GD* 191. 23 *Eala, þu burh, þu Equine, þæt þe þus gelimpeð!?* Further on this problem in both prose and poetry, see §§1972–5.

§1673. In all the examples already quoted, the exclamation has been a clause and the subject has been expressed. More patterns could be added, e.g. *ChristC* 1488 *Hwæt, me þeos heardra þynceð!* (with 'predicative' before the verb; cf. §1671),

GenB 418   . . .   þær geworht stondað
    Adam and Eue   on eorðrice
    mid welan bewunden,   and we synd aworpene hider
    on þas deopan dalo,

and

ChristB 403   Halig eart þu, halig,   heahengla brego,
    soð sigores frea,   simle þu bist halig,
    dryhtna dryhten!

But, as in MnE, neither a subject nor a verb is essential in the exclamatory clause, e.g. *ÆCHom* ii. 166. 23 *wunderlic ðing!*, *ÆCHom* i. 596. 24 *Unriht wisdom, þæt se halga wer swa ðrowode!*, *ÆCHom* ii. 480. 15 *Rihtlice swa, þæt he . . . !*, *ÆCHom* ii. 92. 15 *þwyrlice ðing, ðe heora hlafordas doð geswencte fram carum*, *ÆCHom* i. 66. 25 *Eala ðu cniht, ðe þurh ðines flæsces lust hrædlice ðine sawle forlure!*, *Wan* 94 *Eala beorht bune! Eala byrnwiga! || Eala þeodnes þrym!*, and

Sat 163   Eala drihtenes þrym!   Eala duguða helm!
                Eala meotodes miht!   Eala middaneard!
                Eala dæg leohta!   Eala dream godes!
                Eala engla þreat!   Eala upheofen!

See further §§1533 and 3864.

§1674. On what may be parenthetic exclamations in OE poetry, e.g. *Beo* 1422 *Flod blode weol—folc to sægon— || hatan heolfre*, see §3854.

E. NON-DEPENDENT COMMANDS AND WISHES

§1675. Positive and negative commands, wishes, exhortations, or suggestions, which are capable of (non-)fulfilment are usually expressed by the first person plural present subjunctive, the second person singular and plural imperative, the second person singular and plural present subjunctive, and the third person singular and plural present subjunctive. These constructions and associated problems—including ambiguous verb-forms, the presence or absence of the pronoun subject, and the relative order of subject and verb—have been discussed in §§879–919. Behre (p. 18 fn. 1) rightly points out that 'in OE, as in other Germanic languages, the adhortative subjunctive . . . does not occur in the 1st pers. sing.'.

§1676. Ælfric has the pedagogic glosses *ÆGram* 142. 1 *Tempore fvtvro utinam amer, eala gif ic beo gelufod gyt* (and so on through the Latin present subjunctive passive) and *ÆGram* 200. 3 *Fvtvro utinam uelim, eala gyf ic wylle gyt*. I have not met this idiom—*gif* + present subjunctive expressing a possible wish for the future—in my reading. *ChristC* 1312, with *Eala þær we nu magon . . . geseon*, is so taken in ASPR. But it seems better to follow Schaar (pp. 76–8) in taking it as a conditional clause; cf. *Gen* 13. 16 (§3603) for an impossibility expressed as an open condition. But *gif* does occur with the preterite subjunctive expressing an unrealized or impossible wish; see §§1680–1.

§1677. The principles established for negatives in §§1595–632 apply here. Thus we find *ne* VS in *BlHom* 191. 21 *Ne beoð ge nu unrote*; *ne* and another negative in *GD* 255. 28 *Ne wundra þu naht, Petrus, Luke(WSCp)* 9. 3 *Ne nyme ge nan þing . . .* , and *ÆCHom* i. 258. 23 *And ne læd ðu na us on costnunge*; and a verb not negated by adv. *ne* in *MCharm* 8. 10 *Næfre ge wilde to wuda fleogan, Num* 23. 25 *Ne ðu hine wyrige, ne ðu hine bletsa*, Latin *Nec maledicas ei, nec benedicas* (where *ne . . . ne* are correlative conjunctions), and

PPs 118. 10   Ic þe mid ealre   innancundre
                 heortan sece;   ne þu huru me
                 fram þinum bebodum   feor adrife,

Latin *In toto corde meo exquisiui te . Ne repellas me a mandatis tuis*, where the carelessness of the poet-translator of the *Paris Psalter* is perhaps again in evidence. If *ne* is the adverb, it should precede the verb, as it does in the prose versions, e.g. *Ps(A)* 118. 10 *ne adrif ðu mec from bibodum ðinum*. As it stands, it is a conjunction; see §1832.

§1678. Neither *Num* 23. 25 nor *PPs* 118. 10 justifies the suggestion, made in ASPR iii. 293, that in

Prec 21   Ðriddan syþe   þoncsnottor guma
             breostgehygdum   his bearn lærde:
             Ne gewuna wyrsa,   widan feore,
             ængum eahta,   ac þu þe anne genim
             to gesprecan symle   spella ond lara
             rædhycgende

eahta can be taken as an imperative negated by *ne*. That is just not OE. Initial *ne* in such a sequence must be the adverb and must be immediately followed by the verb, as in *Beo* 1384 *Ne sorga, snotor guma*. So—as GK (pp. 140 and 837) rightly have it—*gewuna* is imperative. For *eahta* to be imperative, we should require either initial *no/na*, as in *Beo* 366 *no ðu him wearne geteoh* ‖ *ðinra gegncwida*, or *ne* immediately before the imperative, as in *Beo* 1760 *oferhyda ne gym, mære cempa*.

§1679. Wishes which are unrealized or impossible are expressed by the preterite subjunctive of a finite verb or 'modal' auxiliary in what can be described as the protasis of a conditional sentence with aposiopesis or non-expression of the principal clause; see *OED*, s.v. *if* I. 7. That Ælfric at least was conscious of this possibility is shown by *ÆGram* 125. 16 *utinam legissem in iuuentute, eala gif ic rædde on iugoðe, þonne cuðe ic nu sum god*. But whether the original function of such clauses was the expression of a wish or of a condition remains a matter for debate; see §3620.

§1680. The idiom takes three forms in OE. Firstly, we have *gif* + preterite subjunctive, e.g. *Luke(WSCp)* 19. 42, *ÆLS* 3. 520 *þa sæde se biscop, Eala gif ic hæfde þine synna ana, ÆCHom* ii. 308. 15 *Eala gif ðu wære hund,* and

Met 9. 53   Eala, gif he wolde,   ðæt he wel meahte,
                 þæt unriht him   eaðe forbiodan!

Secondly, we have *þær* + preterite subjunctive, e.g. *Bo* 110. 15 *Eala, ðær hi ne meahton* (Wülfing (ii, §1117) reads *þæt*. But see §1974), *Deut (Lambeth* 427) 32. 29 *Eala þær hig hogodon 7 understodon,* Latin *utinam saperent et intelligerent, Met* 24. 4,

Soul i 138   Eala, min dryhten,
                 þær ic þe moste   mid me lædan,
                 þæt wyt englas   ealle gesawon,
                 heofona wuldor,   swylc swa ðu me ær her scrife!,

and

Met 8. 39   Eala, þær hit wurde   oððe wolde god
                 þæt on eorðan nu   ussa tida
                 geond þas widan weoruld   wæren æghwæs
                 swelce under sunnan,

where Fox, Grein, and Assmann, unnecessarily emend *þær* to *þæt*. Other possible examples with *þær* are *Sat* 107 (see Meroney, *JEGP* 41 (1942), 205–7); *El* 978; and *Jul* 570 (see Strunk's note on this line, Small 1924, p. 141, but Klaeber, *Ang.* 29 (1906), 271). Thirdly —but rarely—there is the inverted pattern VS, e.g. *CP* 445. 36 *Eala wære he auðer, oððe hat, oððe ceald—Rev* 3. 15 *utinam frigidus esses, aut calidus!*—and perhaps *Bo* 23. 10 *Eala, wæran þa ancras swa trume 7 swa ðurhwuniende, ge for Gode ge for worulde, swa swa þu segst; þonne mihte we micle þy eð geþolian swa hwæt earfoþnessa swa us on become* (Sedgefield's semi-colon could be replaced by a comma to give a conditional sentence) and

GenB 368   Wa la, ahte ic minra handa geweald
                 and moste ane tid   ute weorðan,
                 wesan ane winterstunde,   þonne ic mid þys werode—

(where a semi-colon before *þonne* is a possible alternative to the comma).

§1681. A comparison of *ÆGram* 141. 6 *utinam amarer, eala gif ic wære gelufod* and *ÆGram* 125. 14 *utinam legerem nunc, eala gif ic rædde nu* with *ÆGram* 141. 12 *utinam amatus essem vel amatus fuissem, eala gif ic wære fulfremedlice gelufod oððe gefyrn* and *ÆGram* 125. 15 *utinam legerem heri, eala gif ic rædde gyrstan dæg* illustrates that the preterite subjunctive could express impossible wishes in the present or in the past and that the distinction had to be made by adverbs. That it could also express a possible wish for the future is clear from examples like *CP* 9. 5 *forðy ic wolde ðætte hie ealneg æt ðære stowe wæren*; see further §2007. But the fact that the preterite subjunctive (which often refers to the future-in-the-past in dependent desires and elsewhere) is the only way in OE of expressing what is unrealized or impossible means that it can express an impossible wish in the future. So with some of the quoted examples, such as *ÆLS* 3. 520, *Met* 9. 53, and *Soul i* 138, there are two possibilities: the speaker may conceive that his wish is impossible in the future as well as unrealized in the present or he may still have the hope that it may be realized in the future—'for with God all things are possible'. Further on the timelessness of the preterite subjunctive expressing the unrealized or the unreal in OE, see *Guide*, §§179. 4 and 198, and §§3606–7.

§1682. Other methods of expressing non-dependent commands and the like are discussed in §§916–19.

V

PARATAXIS AND THE 'MULTIPLE SENTENCE'

A. INTRODUCTORY REMARKS

§1683. The term 'parataxis' is used here in a purely formal sense to mean a construction in which sentences or clauses are not formally subordinated one to the other. When no conjunctions are involved, as in *Beo* 702 *Com on wanre niht* || *scriðan sceadugenga. Sceotend swæfon* . . . and

Beo 516   Git on wæteres æht
           seofon niht swuncon;   he þe æt sunde oferflat,
           hæfde mare mægen,

we have 'asyndetic parataxis'. When conjunctions such as *ond* or *ac* are present, as in *Beo* 748 *he onfeng hraþe* || *inwitþancum ond wið earm gesæt*, we have 'syndetic parataxis'. Opposed to 'parataxis' is 'hypotaxis', which implies the use in a sentence of one or more of the relative pronouns or subordinating conjunctions discussed in chapter VII, e.g.

Beo 2633   Ic ðæt mæl geman,   þær we medu þegun,
                 þonne we geheton   ussum hlaforde
                 in biorsele,   ðe us ðas beagas geaf,
                 þæt we him ða guðgetawa   gyldan woldon,
                 gif him þyslicu   þearf gelumpe,
                 helmas ond heard sweord,

or of the order VS, e.g. *ÆCHom* i. 94. 33 *Eaðe mihte þes cwyde beon læwedum mannum bediglod, nære seo gastlice getacning.* On the problems involved in making these distinctions, see initially Quirk, pp. 72–4.

§1684. Asyndetic and syndetic parataxis may occur in the same sentences with words, e.g. *WHom* 7. 131 *gitseras, ryperas 7 reaferas 7 woruldstruderas*, *Beo* 133 *wæs þæt gewin to strang*, ||*lað ond longsum!*, and

El 726   ond þu geworhtest   þurh þines wuldres miht
              heofon ond eorðan   ond holmþræce,
              sæs sidne fæðm,   samod ealle gesceaft

(but cf. *And* 887 *þær wæs wuldres wynn, wigendra þrym,* ‖ *æðelic onginn*); with accusative and infinitive constructions, e.g.

Beo 1114   Het ða Hildeburh   æt Hnæfes ade
                     hire selfre sunu   sweoloðe befæstan,
                     banfatu bærnan,   ond on bæl don
                     eame on eaxle;

and with clauses, e.g. *ChronA* 70. 11 (871), *ÆCHom* ii. 148. 8 . . . *and hi ðone halgan swiðe halsodon, heora cneow bigdon, and mid tearum bædon* . . . , *ÆCHom* i. 480. 16 *Efne nu blinde geseoð, and ða healtan gað, and hreoflige men synd geclænsode, deafe gehyrað, and ða deadan arisað,* and

Beo 1151   Ða wæs heal roden
           feonda feorum,   swilce Fin slægen,
           cyning on corþre,   ond seo cwen numen,

where *wæs* is expressed only once. On the joining of prepositional phrases, see §§1170-6. There is room for more work here.

§1685. A multiple (or compound) sentence is traditionally defined for MnE as a sentence consisting of two or more co-ordinate clauses, i.e. clauses joined together by co-ordinating conjunctions such as 'and' ('cumulative'), 'but' ('adversative'), '(either . . .) or' ('alternative'), and 'for' ('illative'). Several difficulties arise here for the student of OE syntax. First, the term 'co-ordinating' is misleading because such OE conjunctions as *ond* and *ac* are frequently followed by the element order S . . . V, which is basically subordinate. Failure to recognize this has led many scholars astray; see §1731. Second, the distinction between 'cumulative', 'adversative', 'alternative', and 'illative', cannot always be drawn with certainty because the 'co-ordinating' conjunctions of OE frequently overlap these boundaries. So I avoid these terms as far as possible, contenting myself with the semantic division used below. (On 'sentence adverbs' see §1101.) Third, there is the question whether or not the presence of a conjunction such as *ond* or *ac* is essential to a multiple sentence or (to put it another way) whether a sequence like *Beo* 7 *he þæs frofre gebad,* ‖ *weox under wolcnum, weorðmyndum þah* (in which the subject is expressed only with the first verb) constitutes a multiple sentence. Andrew (*SS,* §85) seems to think so, for he quotes this as an example of an idiom 'which is wrongly called parataxis but is really asyndetic co-ordination'; see §1693. All these questions involve matters of definition about which decisions are hardly necessary. It is better to do without the term 'multiple sentence' for OE.

§1686. There are problems of more moment where personal preference is the only criterion available today and may have been the
determining factor even in OE. These include the ambiguous adverb/
conjunctions such as *þa*, *þonne*, and *þær*, and the ambiguous demon-
strative/relative *se*; see §1634. Campbell (1970, p. 95), after asking
whether *Ða* in

Beo 917   Ða wæs morgenleoht
              scofen ond scynded.   Eode scealc monig
              swiðhicgende   to sele þam hean . . .

was to be translated 'Then' or 'When', observed: 'I think that such
passages were open to personal interpretation, and that reciters
would indicate their view of the passage by intonation.' I agree,
though, as I point out in *NQ* 223 (1978), 390-4, and in §§2422-3
and 2536, it is in my opinion an over-simplification to think of the
terms 'ambiguous adverb/conjunction' and 'ambiguous demonstra-
tive/relative' as necessarily implying that the choice was simply between a subordinate clause and an independent sentence in the
modern sense of the terms. So does Andrew (*SS*, pp. 17-18), though
he remarks that they 'are better taken as subordinate'. This accords
with his view that such 'immature and almost childish' sequences as
'Then . . . Then' involve 'simply a lack of grammatical subordination'
and are to be distinguished from examples in which parataxis is 'a
rhetorical device by which a subordinate relation is idiomatically
expressed by a coordinately juxtaposed sentence' as in MnE 'Knock
and it shall be opened' (*SS*, p. 87). Despite these remarks and his further observations (*SS*, p. 95), it is arguable that parataxis is no less
dramatic than hypotaxis in examples like *Bo* 102. 25 *Ða ongon he
biddan heora blisse; ða ongunnon hi wepan mid him* (see *Guide*,
§182), *ÆCHom* i. 66. 9-14, *ÆCHom* i. 228. 28-34, *ÆCHom* ii.
108. 19 *Me hingrode, and ge me ætes forwyrndon; me ðyrste, and ge
me drincan ne sealdon; ic wæs cuma, and ge me underfon noldon; ic
wæs nacod, nolde ge me wæda tiðian; ic wæs untrum and on cwearterne, nolde ge me geneosian*, *Dream* 42b-69, *Beo* 739-49, and
(despite Andrew, *SS*, §110)

Beo 126   Ða wæs on uhtan   mid ærdæge
               Grendles guðcræft   gumum undyrne;
               þa wæs æfter wiste   wop up ahafen,
               micel morgensweg.

Indeed, Rynell (pp. 31-6 and *passim*) argues for the paratactic nature of much OE poetry. Whether we accept Rynell's views or not,[1]

---

[1] Some of Rynell's arguments seem to suggest that the poet was rather more conscious
of the distinction between the periodic and the paratactic than is likely to have been the
case, e.g. the sentence on p. 31 beginning 'Similarly, it is held. . . .'

it is undeniable that Andrew's determination to find hypotaxis whenever he possibly could led to the creation of a series of elaborate and often untenable rules; see in particular §§2109-21, 2444-8, 2522-4, and 2536-8.

§1687. Parataxis does not necessarily involve monotony, for it can offer a variety of sentence structure. The point is well made by A. H. Smith for the Parker Chronicle (*The Parker Chronicle 832-900* (Methuen OE Library, 3rd edn., 1951), 15). However, the amount of work which has appeared on parataxis in this text alone—it includes that by Rübens, pp. 10-28; Shannon, pp. 8-18; Zuck, pp. 82-3; Sprockel, pp. 71-7; and J. Turville-Petre, 'The Narrative Style in Old English', *Maxwell Studies*, pp. 116-25—reveals the impossibility of pursuing the subject here, either with reference to the Parker Chronicle itself or to OE prose and poetry in general.

§1688. It is a widely held opinion that parataxis preceded hypotaxis in the development of language; as Mann (*Archiv*, 180 (1942), 88) puts it: 'Wenn wir nach der Entstehung der Konjunktionen forschen, also nach den Hilfsmitteln, die einen Nebensatz dem Hauptsatz unterordnen, müssen wir von der Erkenntnis ausgehen, daß sich die moderne Sprachform der Unterordnung aus der der Beiordnung (Asyndese-verbundene Parataxe-Hypotaxe) entwickelt hat.'[2] Similarly, Small (1924, p. 125) observes that 'it may be laid down as a general principle that in the progress of language parataxis precedes hypotaxis'. I do not propose to pursue this problem here. But see §2431 and, for fuller discussions on parataxis and hypotaxis in works which deal with OE (and for reference to others), Schücking, pp. ix-xxiv; Rübens, pp. 1-7; Small 1924, pp. 125-32 and 154; Möllmer, pp. 2-8 and 113-14; Klaeber, 'Eine Randbemerkung zur Nebenordnung und Unterordnung im Altenglischen', *AngB.* 52 (1941), 216-19; Mann, 'Die Entstehung von nebensatzeinleitenden Konjunktionen im Englischen', *Archiv*, 80 (1942), 86-93; Rynell; and the works cited in §§1879-82. For examples of both types of parataxis, see the works by Schücking and Rübens; 'the prose text dissertations'; 'the eighteen German dissertations'; Steche; and W. Kopas, *Die Grundzüge der Satzverknüpfung in Cynewulfs Schriften* (Breslau, 1910).

§1689. Problems involving non-dependent questions, including co-ordination and the use of *ac* as an interrogative particle, are discussed elsewhere; see the Indexes.

---

    [2] 'In our search for the origin of conjunctions, that is, for the means by which one clause is subordinated to another, we must begin by recognizing that the modern linguistic form of subordination has developed out of juxtaposition (asyndesis-bound parataxis-hypotaxis).'

B. ASYNDETIC PARATAXIS

1. THE SUBJECT OF THE VERBS IS THE SAME, BUT IS NOT REPEATED

§1690. We start with those examples which involve what may be called 'semi-subordination'; see §§1923-4. In these the second clause is logically subordinate to the first and its finite verb can often conveniently be rendered by a MnE participle. This occurs in both prose and poetry and is particularly common with *willan* (expressing purpose), e.g. *ÆCHom* ii. 144. 7 *Se halga ða het him bringan sæd; wolde on ðam westene wæstmes tilian* and *Beo* 1292 *Heo wæs on ofste, wolde ut þanon,* ‖ *feore beorgan*; with *wenan* and *þencan* (expressing cause), e.g. *ÆCHom* ii. 388. 23 *Ðaða Drihten ðam scipe genealæhte, ða wurdon hi afyrhte, wendon þæt hit sum gedwimor wære, ÆCHom* i. 82. 10 *þa het he forðy acwellan ealle ða hysecild . . . : ðohte gif he hi ealle ofsloge, þæt se an ne ætburste þe he sohte,* and

Beo 2183   Hean wæs lange,
     swa hyne Geata bearn   godne ne tealdon,
     . . .   . . . ;
     swyðe wendon,   þæt he sleac wære . . . ;

with verbs of saying (sometimes shading into the expression of cause), e.g. *ÆCHom* i. 86. 15 *Fela ðæra læca he acwealde; cwæð þæt hi hine gehælan mihton and noldon, ÆCHom* ii. 502. 34 *Æfter ðisum gemette Martinus þone deofol, se axode ardlice hwider he siðode, sæde þæt he wolde his wiðerwinna beon on eallum his færelde,* and

Beo 198   Het him yðlidan
     godne gegyrwan;   cwæð, he guðcyning
     ofer swanrade   secean wolde . . . ;

and with verbs of requesting and commanding, e.g. *ÆCHom* ii. 152. 10 *Hereberhtus ða swiðe hohful wearð, and feol to his fotum mid flowendum tearum, bæd þæt he moste him mid siðian . . . , ÆCHom* ii. 190. 32 *þa æt nextan aras Pharao . . . and þæt Israhela folc eall on ðeowte gebrohte, het hi wyrcan his burhweallas,* and (with *heht* repeated)

Beo 1807   Heht þa se hearda   Hrunting beran
     sunu Ecglafes,   heht his sweord niman,
     leoflic iren;   sægde him þæs leanes þanc. . . .

§1691. 'Semi-subordination' occurs occasionally with other verbs, e.g. *BlHom* 223. 6 *Ða wæs heora sum reðra 7 hatheortra ðonne þa opre; gebrægd ða his sweorde, mynte hine slean* (on this example see §1693); *ÆCHom* i. 414. 17 *He wand þa swa swa wurm; ne mihte geðolian þa egeslican gesihðe ðæra awyrgedra gasta* (expressing cause); *Beo* 1441 *Gyrede hine Beowulf* ‖ *eorlgewædum, nalles for ealdre mearn* (expressing concession); and

Beo 2369   þær him Hygd gebead   hord ond rice,
                beagas ond bregostol;   bearne ne truwode,
                þæt he wið ælfylcum   eþelstolas
                healdan cuðe,   ða wæs Hygelac dead

(expressing cause). The variations in the editorial punctuation of the examples quoted in this and the preceding section should be noted.

§1692. The evidence presented by Callaway (1901, *passim*) confirms my impression that the present participle is more common in this function in the prose, e.g. *ÆCHom* i. 78. 31 *Efne ða Godes engel æteowode Iosepe . . . on swefnum, cweðende, 'Aris . . .'* and *ÆCHom* i. 74. 6 *Hi ða begen þone apostol gesohton, his miltsunge biddende.* However, finite verbs in 'semi-subordination' and present participles sometimes occur in the same sentence with no obvious distinction, e.g. *ÆCHom* ii. 546. 14 *Gregorius awrat be sumum geðyldigan were, Stephanus gehaten, se forlet ealle woruldðing, and forfleah manna gehlyd, beeode his gebedu, on sumum mynstre drohtniende* and *ÆCHom* ii. 144. 24 *ac an ðæra fugela eft fleogende com ymbe ðry dagas þearle dreorig, fleah to his foton, swiðe biddende þæt he on ðam lande lybban moste. . . .*

§1693. Two verbs can (appear to) be involved in a 'semi-subordinate' pattern, either without *ond*, e.g. *BlHom* 223. 6 (§1691) and *Beo* 1807 (§1690), or with it, e.g. the well-known *Bo* 102. 2 *Ða sceolde se hearpere weorðan swa sarig . . . 7 sæt on ðæm muntum ægðer ge dæges ge nihtes, weop 7 hearpode . . .* and *ÆCHom* ii. 406. 34 *Sum hiredes hlaford . . . com æfter fyrste to ðam treowe, sohte wæstm ðæron and nænne ne gemette.* Both patterns can occur in the same sentence, e.g. *ÆCHom* ii. 518. 18 *Seo burhwaru wolde . . . þone halgan geniman, and Pictauienscisce þearle wiðcwædon; woldon habban ðone ylcan þe hi ær alændon to ðam biscopdome of heora burhscire, cwædon þæt he wære heora munuc æt fruman, and woldon hine habban huru swa deadne.* Sometimes the verbs are clearly of the same 'rank', e.g. *weop 7 hearpode* 'weeping and harping' in *Bo* 102. 2. Sometimes they are clearly not, e.g. in *BlHom* 223. 6 (§1691), where *gebrægd* is in effect the main clause of the whole sentence, *mynte* expresses purpose—'he drew his sword, intending to kill him'

—and the initial '*Đa wæs . . .*' clause comes close to being causal. Sometimes there is room for difference of opinion, e.g. in *ÆCHom* ii. 518. 18, in *ÆCHom* ii. 406. 34, which can be rendered as 'he came seeking fruit and finding none' or 'he came seeking fruit, but found none', and in *Beo* 306 *Guman onetton, ‖ sigon ætsomne . . .*, where the verbs can be said to be in apposition (§1529) and where we can translate 'The warriors hastened, advancing together' or 'the warriors hastened and advanced together' or 'the warriors hastened; they advanced together . . .'. Andrew (*SS*, §85) detects what 'is wrongly called parataxis but is really asyndetic co-ordination' in examples like *Beo* 7 *he þæs frofre gebad, ‖ weox under wolcnum weorðmyndum þah*. The difference is terminological; *weox* and *þah* could just as easily be described (in Andrew's words) as 'performing the function of a defining clause' (*Postscript*, §60); see §1696.

§1694. The reverse pattern—in which the first clause is logically subordinate to the second—often occurs when the relationship is one of time, sometimes shading into cause, e.g. *ÆCHom* i. 46. 35 *þa leasgewitan ða ledon heora hacelan ætforan fotum sumes geonges cnihtes, se wæs geciged Saulus. Ongunnon ða oftorfian mid heardum stanum ðone eadigan Stephanum, ÆCHom* i. 402. 24 *God ða oncneow þæt ða Iudeiscan nanre dædbote ne gymdon . . . : sende him ða to Romanisc folc and hi ealle fordyde*, and *ÆCHom* ii. 312. 22 *And heo sona swa dyde . . . and mid arwurðnysse hi ealle bebyrigde; efste ham siððan to ðam earman casere*. Despite the inconsistencies in Thorpe's punctuation, these three do not differ syntactically: the second clauses have initial verb accompanied by either *ða* or *siððan*, have a subject which is the same as that of the preceding clause but is not repeated, and describe an action which follows that of the preceding clause. Here too belong *CP* 121. 13, *CP* 227. 10, and *Bo* 135. 32— sentences with initial V in the present tense and *þonne* which are cited by Bacquet (p. 587) as appearing in lively and picturesque description. We can add *CP* 121. 14 *Đonne cymð his hlaford on ðæm dæge ðe he ne wenð, ond on ða tiid ðæt he hine ær nat; hæfð hine ðonne siððan for ænne licettere*. For further examples see *ÆCHom* i. 28. 5 and 244. 29, *ÆCHom* ii. 306. 12 and 502. 29, and (with the relevant clauses in subordination) *ÆCHom* ii. 356. 4 *and man afunde ða þæt his gewuna wæs, þæt he worhte his weorc to seofon nihtum, and sealde on ðone Sæternes dæg; nam ða of his cræfte him bigleofan, and dælde ðone ofereacan þearfum mid estfullum mode*. Two such subjectless clauses appear in succession in *ÆCHom* ii. 346. 32 and *ÆCHom* ii. 348. 24 *He aras þa þærrihte, and eode to circan, and þurhwunode on gebedum ealne þone merien. Dælde syððan his æhta on ðreo, ænne dæl his wife, oðerne dæl his cildum, þriddan þearfum. Forlet syððan ealle woruldþing. . . .* The subjectless verb is preceded by an adverbial group in *ÆCHom* ii. 334. 35 *He ða up gesæt . . . and swa untrum leofode twegen dagas. Eft ða on ðære þriddan nihte middan, astrehte his handa on gebedum. . . .*

§1695. The first of two clauses or sentences in asyndetic parataxis may express a condition required for the fulfilment of the second, e.g. *ÆCHom* ii. 564. 12 *Ageot ele uppon wæter oððe on oðrum wætan, se ele flyt bufon, ÆHom* 27. 6 *Uton nu . . . andettan ure misdæda 7 synna . . . 7 uton geswican æfre ælces yfeles 7 don to gode þone dæl þe we magon; þonne gebeorge we us sylfum wið ece wite 7 geearniað us heofena rice . . . ,* and

GenB 256　　　　　　　　　　　Lof sceolde he drihtnes wyrcean,
　　　dyran sceolde he his dreamas on heofonum,　　and sceolde his
　　　　　　　　　　　　　　　　drihtne þancian
　　þæs leanes þe he him on þam leohte gescerede　　þonne læte he
　　　　　　　　　　　　　　　his hine lange wealdan.

On the relationship between unfulfilled wishes and conditional clauses, see §3620.

§1696. The relationship between the two clauses in the examples discussed so far has been adverbial. But, as Andrew points out, the second clause may occasionally be described as 'performing the function of a defining clause' (*Postscript*, §60) or as 'equivalent to an Adjectival clause or phrase' (*SS*, §106). Examples of the former include *ChronC* 142. 22 (1012) *. . . 7 hine þær ða bysmorlice acwylmdon . ofterfodon mid banum 7 mid hryðera heafdum* 'pelting him . . .',

Beo 1994　　　　　　　　　　ic ðe lange bæd,
　　þæt ðu þone wælgæst　　wihte ne grette,
　　lete Suð-Dene　　sylfe geweorðan
　　guðe wið Grendel,

and—after '*swa don* or the like', where they are 'particularly common' (*SS*, §104)—*ÆCHom* ii. 138. 7 *Ða dyde Cuðberhtus swa his gewuna wæs, sang his gebedu on sælicere yðe* and

Beo 1534　　　　　　　　　　Swa sceal man don,
　　þonne he æt guðe　　gegan þenceð
　　longsumne lof;　　na ymb his lif cearað.

§1697. Examples in which the second clause is the equivalent of an adjective clause or phrase are frequent in naming constructions (see

§1475) and are occasionally found with *beon/wesan*, e.g. *ChronA* 94. 20 (906) *Her on þys geare gefor Ælfred, wæs æt Baðum gerefa* and

Sat 75   Eft reordade   oðre siðe
                feonda aldor.   Wæs þa forht agen,
                seoððan he ðes wites   worn gefelde.

To Andrew (*Postscript,* §62), *wæs* clauses such as that in

Beo 2208   he geheold tela
                fiftig wintra—   wæs ða frod cyning,
                eald eþelweard—   oð ðæt an ongan
                deorcum nihtum   draca ricsian

'are all adverbial'. They could be adjectival. But the point is one of terminology.

§1698. A study of the foregoing examples will show that the types of asyndetic parataxis discussed here can occur in both principal and subordinate clauses. Inconsistency in punctuating them seems to be the rule in modern editions of both prose (see §1694) and poetry (see *SS,* §§85-9, and *Postscript,* §§60-3, where Andrew makes some valuable points, though I do not agree with all the details).

2. THE SUBJECT OF THE VERBS IS THE SAME AND IS REPEATED

§1699. The same subject can however be repeated by a personal pronoun in the second of two clauses in asyndetic parataxis in both prose and poetry. Examples from the prose include *Or* 228. 11 *Ac siþþan se þridda dæl on his gewealde wæs, he beswac begen þa suna: oþerne he ofslog, (oþerne adræfde,) Or* 262. 22 *7 he fordyde þara Iudena xi hund m: sume he ofslog, (sume on oþer land gesealde,) sume he mid hungre acwealde, ÆCHom* i. 64. 35 *Se gytsere hæfð ænne lichaman and menigfealde scrud; he hæfð ane wambe and þusend manna bigleofan, ÆCHom* i. 74. 30 *þu heolde minne lichaman wið ælce besmittennysse . . . þu settest on minum muðe þinre soðfæstnysse word,* and *ÆCHom* i. 64. 21 *Ge gehældon untruman on þæs Hælendes naman, ge afligdon deoflu, ge forgeafon blindum gesihðe. . . .* In such examples the parallel clauses carry equal 'rank' and emphasis—despite the inconsistencies in punctuation. So too, of course, do the bracketed clauses, in which the pronoun is not repeated.

§1700. Sometimes the pattern of the sentence suggests scribal omission of a subordinating conjunction, e.g. *ÆCHom* i. 186. 1 *Oft*

gehwa gesihð fægre stafas awritene, þonne heraðð he ðone writere and
þa stafas, and nat hwæt hi mænað (where *þonne* could be inserted
after *Oft*) and *ÆCHom* i. 38. 22 *ac Iohannes se Godspellere . . .*
wolde hine gebiddan to þam engle þe him to spræc, þa forwyrnde se
engel him ðæs (where *þa* after *ac* would make a neat complex sentence). In these two, the element order would suit either a principal
or a subordinate clause. But in *ÆCHom* i. 60. 21 *On ðam oðrum*
dæge eode se apostol be ðære stræte, þa ofseah he hwær sum uðwita
lædde twegen gebroðru, the first clause is less likely to be subordinate.
Thorpe's punctuation and translations suggest an unwillingness to
accept the two sentences in these examples as equal and independent. But they could be. See §2544.

§1701. Examples from the poetry include

Beo 2788	He ða mid þam maðmum mærne þioden,
	dryhten sinne driorigne fand
	ealdres æt ende; he hine eft ongon
	wæteres weorpan,
Beo 925	Hroðgar maþelode— he to healle geong,
	stod on stapole, geseah steapne hrof
	golde fahne ond Grendles hond—,
Beo 459	Gesloh þin fæder fæhðe mæste;
	wearþ he Heaþolafe to handbonan
	mid Wilfingum,
Beo 963	Ic hine hrædlice heardan clammum
	on wælbedde wriþan þohte
	. . . . . . ;
	ic hine ne mihte, þa Metod nolde,
	ganges getwæman . . . ,

and

JDay ii 21	Ic gemunde eac mærðe drihtnes
	. . . . . .
	Ic gemunde þis mid me.

Many more could be cited.

§1702. Andrew (*Postscript*, §51) formulates the rule that in such
clauses in the poetry 'the subject, if unchanged, is not expressed'.[3]
So he speaks of 'the forbidden otiose "he" in the paratactic clause'
in examples like

---

[3] He refers to them twice in §51 as examples of 'the co-ordinate *ond*-clause', but his
general heading to the section ('*The Asyndetic Co-ordinate clause*'), his examples, and his
discussion, make it clear that he means clauses without *ond*; cf. the opening sentence of
Postscript, §56.

Beo 2337   Heht him þa gewyrcean   wigendra hleo
              eallirenne,   eorla dryhten,
              wigbord wrætlic;   wisse he gearwe,
              þæt him holtwudu   helpan ne meahte

(*Postscript*, §61) and of 'the otiose pronoun' in *Beo* 925 (§1701)
(*Postscript*, §57). His rule compels him to suggest the elimination of
both instances of *he* in

Beo 2724   Biowulf maþelode—   he ofer benne spræc,
              wunde wælbleate;   wisse he gearwe,
              þæt he dæghwila   gedrogen hæfde,
              eorðan wynne

(*Postscript*, §§57 and 61). To eliminate the 'offending' pronouns
in these examples, in the others cited by Andrew (*SS*, §100, and
Postscript, chapter v), and in all similar ones in the poetry, demands
impossible violence to the manuscript texts and the acceptance of
the proposition—untenable in this particular instance—that what is
common and often important (if not essential) to the sense in the
prose cannot possibly occur in the poetry.

3. THE SUBJECT OF THE FIRST VERB APPEARS IN A DIFFERENT CASE IN THE SECOND CLAUSE

§1703. Examples such as *ÆCHom* i. 380. 18 *Broðer, þu wære Gode
gecoren ær ic, ðe gedafnað þæt þu ðisne deofles ðen mid ðinum
benum afylle* (where the first clause is in a causal relationship to the
second) and *ÆCHom* ii. 510. 31 *Martinus eac com to anes mannes
huse, his cnapa wæs awed wunderlice ðurh deofol and arn him togeanes mid gyniendum muðe* (where *his* can conveniently be translated 'whose')—similar examples will be found at *ÆCHom* i. 336. 6
and 352. 1—raise again the problem of punctuation. Thorpe's
comma perhaps comes closer to expressing the proper relationship
than would a full stop; see further Andrew, *SS*, §107. No such problem arises in examples like *ÆCHom* i. 134. 1 *Geleafa is ealra mægena
fyrmest; buton þam ne mæg nan man Gode lician*, though some may
prefer a full stop to a semi-colon; *þam* can scarcely be taken as a
relative pronoun.

4. THE SUBJECTS OF THE VERBS ARE DIFFERENT AND BOTH ARE EXPRESSED

§1704. This form of asyndetic parataxis may vary from simple
enumeration or cataloguing to highly moving and effective rhetoric;

see further §§1896, 2115, and 2121. As examples of narrative sequence we may quote *ChronA* 60. 26 (827) *Ærest Ælle SuþSeaxna cyning se þus micel rice hæfde, se æfter wæs Ceawlin . . . se þridda wæs Æþelbryht . . . se feorþa wæs Rædwald . . . fifta wæs Eadwine . . . eahtoþa wæs Ecgbryht Wesseaxna cyning, ÆCHom* i. 130. 4 *Maria and Martha wæron twa geswystru . . . ; hi cwædon to Criste . . . þes ðegen cwæð to Criste . . . Drihten cwæð . . . þas word sind lustbære to gehyrenne . . . ,*

Beo 758   Gemunde þa se goda,   mæg Higelaces,
             æfenspræce,   uplang astod
             ond him fæste wiðfeng;   fingras burston;
             eoten wæs utweard,   eorl furþur stop,

and

Dream 50   Feala ic on þam beorge   gebiden hæbbe
              wraðra wyrda.   Geseah ic weruda god
              þearle þenian.   þystro hæfdon
              bewrigen mid wolcnum   wealdendes hræw,
              scirne sciman,   sceadu forðeode,
              wann under wolcnum.   Weop eal gesceaft,
              cwiðdon cyninges fyll.   Crist wæs on rode.

§1705. Many other examples could be quoted, including *ÆCHom* i. 132. 9 *þæt godspel cwyð, 'On þa yttran þeostru'. Ða yttran þeostru sind þæs lichaman blindnyssa wiðutan. Ða inran þeostru sind þæs modes blindnyssa wiðinnan* (where the first sentence is explained by those which follow); *BlHom* 13. 6 *Lufian we hine nu . . . þonne ne læteþ he us no costian ofer gemet, ÆCHom* i. 256. 13, and *ÆCHom* i. 86. 34 *Swa ricene swa ic gewite, ofsleað ealle ðas Iudeiscan ealdras, ðe ic on cwearterne beclysde, þonne beoð heora siblingas to heofunge geneadode . . .* (in all of which the clause which contains a command or exhortation also contains a condition for the following clause); *Beo* 702 *Com on wanre niht ‖ scriðan sceadugenga. Sceotend swæfon . . .* and

Beo 1114   Het ða Hildeburh   æt Hnæfes ade
              hire selfre sunu   sweoloðe befæstan,
              banfatu bærnan,   ond on bæl don
              eame on eaxle.   Ides gnornode,
              geomrode giddum

(in which the relationship is temporal, shading into causal);

Beo 1907   no þær wegflotan   wind ofer yðum
              siðes getwæfde;   sægenga for,

> fleat famigheals   forð ofer yðe,
> bundenstefna   ofer brimstream⌐ꞔ

(where it is causal or adversative); and

Beo 1600   Næs ofgeafon
>   hwate Scyldingas;   gewat him ham þonon
>   goldwine gumena.   Gistas setan
>   modes seoce   ond on mere staredon

(where it is concessive or adversative). Other relationships are, of course, possible; see Schücking, pp. 139-48, and Kopas, pp. 80-4.

§1706. In conformity with his rule 'that, in poetry as in prose, the type with conjunctive order could only stand after *ond* and was never asyndetic' (*SS*, §99), Andrew (*SS*, §§97-9) suggests the insertion of *ond* between the last two clauses in examples like

Beo 470   Siððan þa fæhðe   feo þingode;
>   sende ic Wylfingum   ofer wæteres hrycg
>   ealde madmas;   he me aþas swor.

This is unnecessary, for the order S . . . V can occur in principal clauses in both prose and poetry; see §§3914-15 and 3944.

5. THE SUBJECTS OF THE VERBS ARE DIFFERENT, BUT THE SECOND IS UNEXPRESSED

§1707. On non-expression of the subject in all types of clause, see §§1503-16.

6. THE SAME VERB SERVES FOR DIFFERENT SUBJECTS

§1708. As in MnE, the same verb may serve for more than one subject, e.g. *ÆCHom* i. 310. 13 *Petrus bodade on Iudea lande, Paulus on hæðenum folce, Andreas on Scithia, Iohannes on Asia, Bartholomeus on India, Matheus on Ethiopia, and swa heora gehwilc on his dæle.* . . .

C. SYNDETIC PARATAXIS

1. INTRODUCTORY REMARKS

§1709. Many of the conjunctions discussed in the sections which follow can, of course, join elements other than clauses or sentences, including nouns and pronouns, e.g. *ÆCHom* i. 4. 3 *tacna and wundra* (see §§95-6) and *Beo* 431 *ic . . . ana ond minra eorla gedryht* (but the dual serves in place of combinations like MnE 'you and I'); numerals, e.g. *GenA* 1169 *fif and sixtig* (see §144); adjectives, e.g. *ÆCHom* ii. 290. 21 *micele and manega fixas* (see §§555-60); participles, e.g. *ÆCHom* i. 60. 9 *fægnigende and cweðende . . .* ; infinitives, e.g. *ÆCHom* i. 6. 21 *. . . hi sceoldon læran and tæcan eallum þeodum*; adverbs, e.g. *GenA* 225 *nean and feorran* and *El* 198 *dæges ond nihtes*; combinations of these, e.g. *ÆCHom* i. 4. 14 *mennisc mann and soð deofol*; and phrases of various kinds, e.g. *ÆCHom* i. 2. 23 *buton þam mannum anum ðe þæt Leden cuðon, and buton þam bocum ðe Ælfred cyning snoterlice awende of Ledene on Englisc* and *ÆCHom* i. 596. 3 *mid bliðum mode fægnigende and þæt folc lærende*. The linked elements need not be grammatically identical, e.g. *Beo* 431 above, *ÆCHom* i. 208. 23 *hæðen and ungetemed*, *ÆCHom* ii. 246. 9 *ealle gewæpnode and mid leohtfatum*, and *ÆCHom* i. 2. 26 *For þisum antimbre ic gedyrstlæhte . . . and eac forðam þe menn behofiað godre lare*; Shannon (p. 20) gives more examples. The joining of verbs, clauses, and sentences, by *ond* and other 'co-ordinating' conjunctions, is discussed in the sections which follow.[4] If we analyse these according to whether the subject is repeated or expressed or unexpressed, we find the same five patterns here as we found in asyndetic parataxis. For reasons of space and convenience, I cite mostly examples involving *ond* and discuss them in §§1712-39.[5] The order of elements is treated separately for each conjunction or group of conjunctions.

§1710. Emphasis or intensification can be achieved by coupling two adjectives or adverbs of (quasi-)synonymous or of opposite meaning, e.g. *GenB* 265 *leoht and scene*, ‖ *hwit and hiowbeorht*, *GenA* 118 *side and wide*, *GenA* 1206 *swa men doþ*, ‖ *geonge and ealde*, and *GenA* 225 *nean and feorran*; see further Peltola, *NM* 70 (1969), 36-7, and Maisenhelder, p. 65. The coupling of two verbs can also give emphasis, e.g. *ÆCHom* i. 2. 19 *ac forþan þe ic geseah and gehyrde mycel gedwyld on manegum Engliscum bocum*.

§1711. On the splitting of groups joined by *ond*, see §§1464-72.

---

[4] I have not attempted a full treatment of *ond, ac, ge, ne*, and other such conjunctions, when they join clauses, sentences, or elements other than verbs. On these uses, see initially Kohonen, 'Observations on Syntactic Characteristics of Binomials in Late Old English and Early Middle English Prose', *NM* 80 (1979), 133-63, and the works by I. Koskenniemi and others to which he refers.

[5] R. D. Smith, 'Co-ordination of Linguistic Units in Selected Old English Prose of the Early Eleventh Century' (M.Phil. thesis, University College, London, 1971) deals with MnE 'and' and OE *ond* from a transformational viewpoint.

2. CONJUNCTIONS MEANING '(BOTH . . .) AND'

a. Ond

(1) The subject

§1712. If we ask whether the second clause contains a subject,[6] we can distinguish the same five patterns as in asyndetic parataxis. First, there are the examples in which the subject of the verbs is the same, but is not repeated, e.g. *ChronA* 70. 12 (871) *þa gemette hie Æþelwulf aldormon on Englafelda 7 him þær wiþ gefeaht 7 sige nam, ÆCHom* ii. 328. 29 *ac he hæfde geðyld . . . And forbær þus eaðelice, BlHom* 27. 26 . . . *þæt ure Drihten æfter þæm fulwihte fæstte, 7 eac wæs costad,* and

Beo 3016   ne mægð scyne
          habban on healse   hringweorðunge,
          ac sceal geomormod,   golde bereafod
          oft nalles æne   elland tredan. . . .

In examples like *ÆCHom* i. 48. 3 *and he clypode, and cwæð . . . And gebigde his cneowu, mid micelre stemne clypigende . . . And he mid þam worde ða gewat to ðan Ælmihtigum Hælende* (the problems of punctuation are, of course, modern; see §§1879-82) and *WHom* 6. 169 *He æt 7 dranc, 7 ægðer he þolode ge cyle ge hætan,* it can be argued that the variations reflect the demands of rhythm and emphasis. But the non-repetition of *he* in the last clause in *ÆCHom* i. 182. 16 *Ða genam se Hælend þa fif hlafas and bletsode and tobræc and todælde betwux ðam sittendum: swa gelice eac þa fixas todælde* is difficult for modern readers to explain.

§1713. A distinction can be made in the examples in which the same subject is not repeated after *ond*. When the first of the two finite verbs expresses the idea of rest or motion, the second verb often denotes what the agent was doing when resting or moving, e.g. *ÆCHom* i. 246. 2 *and se witega læg and slep, BlHom* 123. 21 *hwæt stondaþ ge her 7 þyses wundriað . . . ?,* and *ÆCHom* ii. 166. 6 *Hi urnon to ablicgede and woldon þæt fyr mid wætere ofgeotan,* and so performs the function of a participle or infinitive; see §§967-9. Here we have something similar to the 'semi-subordination' seen in such examples of asyndetic parataxis as *ÆCHom* ii. 152. 10 *Hereberhtus . . . feol to his fotum mid flowendum tearum, bæd þæt he moste him mid siðian . . .* which are discussed in §§1923-4. But

---

[6] Bacquet sometimes failed to ask this question—with serious consequences; see my review in *NM* 67 (1966), 88.

usually the verbs joined by *ond* express actions which occur in (close) sequence rather than simultaneously. This occurs with verbs of rest, e.g. *BlHom* 101. 2 *ah heora lichoman licggað on eorðan 7 beoþ to duste gewordne*, and of motion, e.g. *ÆCHom* i. 30. 30 *Hi comon ða hrædlice, and gemetton Marian and Ioseph and þæt cild geled on anre binne*, as well as with other verbs, e.g. *ÆCHom* i. 6. 31 *Clypa and ne geswic ðu, ahefe þine stemne swa swa byme and cyð minum folce heora leahtras . . .* , *ÆCHom* i. 10. 23 *. . . [he] cwæð on his heortan þæt he wolde and eaðe mihte beon his Scyppende gelic*, and *ÆCHom* i. 34. 20 *Maria acende ða hire frumcennedan sunu . . . and hine mid cildclaðum bewand and . . . on anre binne gelede*. States as opposed to actions can also be denoted, e.g. *ÆCHom* i. 30. 7 *. . . to Iudeiscre byrig, seo wæs Dauides and wæs geciged Bethleem*.

§1714. The second group embraces those examples in which both clauses have the same subject, which is repeated by a personal pronoun in the second clause, e.g. *ChronA* 72. 5 (871) *7 þæs ofer Eastron gefor Æþered cyning 7 he ricsode v gear*, *ÆCHom* i. 98. 35 *þes monað is monða anginn, and he bið fyrmest on geares monðum*, *ÆCHom* i. 194. 24 *Ure alysednysse anginn we gehyrdon on ðisre dægþerlican rædinge . . . and we sind getealde betwux Godes bearnum*, *JDay i* 22 *Ufan hit is enge ond hit is innan hat*, and *JDay ii* 24 *Ic gemunde þis mid me, and ic mearn swiðe, || and ic murcnigende cwæð. . . .*

§1715. Andrew (*Postscript,* §48) rightly remarks that 'in Old English as in other periods of English, the subject of a co-ordinate clause, if the same as that of the principal sentence, is *normally* [my italics] not expressed'. We may compare *Beo* 3087 *Ic wæs þær inne and þæt eall geondseh* and *Beo* 1766 *oððe eagena bearhtm || forsiteð ond forsworceð*—where there is no change of subject and no pronoun with the second verb—with *Beo* 2138 *holm heolfre weoll ond ic heafde becearf . . .* and *Beo* 109 *ne gefeah he þære fæhðe, ac he hine feor forwræc*—where there is a change of subject and a pronoun is expressed. But he goes on—with a not unfamiliar lapse in logic—to construe 'normally' as 'always' and to argue that *he* after *ac* in *Beo* 599, *Beo* 2834, and

Beo 2897   Lyt swigode
        niwra spella   se ðe næs gerad,
        ac he soðlice   sægde ofer ealle

'is otiose, since there is no change of subject'. This cannot stand even for examples after *ac* in *Beowulf* in the light of *Beo* 438, 773, 2084, 2522, 2598, 2850, 2976, and

Beo 739   Ne þæt se aglæca   yldan þohte,
                     ac he gefeng hraðe   forman siðe
                     slæpendne rinc

—all of which support the so-called 'otiose' pronoun in Andrew's three examples. That it does not apply after *ond* in the poetry seems clear to me from examples like *JDay i* 22 and *JDay ii* 24 (both in §1714) and from one example in *Beowulf* itself—

Beo 1748   þinceð him to lytel,   þæt he lange heold,
                     gytsað gromhydig,   nallas on gylp seleð
                     fætte beagas,   ond he þa forðgesceaft
                     forgyteð ond forgymeð,   þæs þe him ær God sealde,
                     wuldres Waldend,   weorðmynda dæl.

§1716. The next two patterns need only be exemplified. The third is that in which the subject of the first verb appears in a different case in the second clause, e.g. *ChronA* 72. 6 (871) *7 he ricsode v gear 7 his lic liþ æt Winburnan* and

Beo 920   swylce self cyning
                     of brydbure,   beahhorda weard,
                     tryddode tirfæst   getrume micle,
                     cystum gecyþed,   ond his cwen mid him
                     medostigge mæt   mægþa hose.

In the fourth, the subjects of the verbs are different and both are expressed, e.g. *ChronA* 70. 17 (871) *7 Æþelwulf aldormon wearþ ofslægen 7 þa Deniscan ahton wælstowe gewald* and *Beo* 2138 and *Beo* 109 (both in §1715).

§1717. The fifth group comprises examples in which the subjects of the two verbs are different, but the subject of the second is unexpressed, e.g. *ChronA* 70. 27 (871) . . . *7 þa hergas begen gefliemde, 7 fela þusenda ofslægenra, 7 onfeohtende wæron oþ niht.* These have been discussed in §§1514–15. One apparent example (see *Postscript,* §49) can perhaps be avoided by repunctuation:

Beo 1584   He him þæs lean forgeald,
                     reþe cempa,   to ðæs þe he on ræste geseah
                     guðwerigne   Grendel licgan,
                     aldorleasne,   swa him ær gescod
                     hild æt Heorote—   hra wide sprong,
                     syþðan he æfter deaðe   drepe þrowade,
                     heorosweng heardne—   ond hine þa heafde becearf.

§1718. The punctuation of a series of clauses beginning with *ond* presents problems for the modern editor which were unwittingly solved—perhaps in different ways—by the Anglo-Saxon reader or hearer familiar with the intonation patterns and syntax of the language. In this connection, a comparison of Earle and Plummer's punctuation of the Parker manuscript's annal for 871—*ChronA* 70. 11-72. 17—with that adopted by Whitelock—Sweet, *R. 15*, 6. 1-40—will prove instructive. Both editors agree that a comma is appropriate before *ond* when the subject of the verb after *ond* is not expressed, whether it is the same as the subject of the preceding verb (e.g. *ChronA* 70. 12-14) or different (e.g. *ChronA* 70. 27-8). But when the subject of the verb after *ond* is expressed, there is marked inconsistency not only between but also within the editions, especially when the subjects are different; consider the variations before the clauses beginning *7 þær wearþ* in *ChronA* 70. 23, 72. 2, and 72. 3 and before those in which *ond* is immediately followed by the subject in *ChronA* 70. 17 (first *ond* clause), 70. 17 (second *ond* clause), and 70. 24. The two editions differ in *ChronA* 72. 5-6—the only example in the annal in which the same subject is expressed with both verbs. Both editions have a comma before *7 þæs* in *ChronA* 70. 11. Earle and Plummer have a comma before *7 þæs geares* in *ChronA* 72. 15, where the *Reader* has a semi-colon. Apart from this, they agree that a heavier stop than a comma is necessary before clauses or sentences of the pattern *ond* adverb VS. But they fluctuate between a semi-colon, a full stop beginning a new sentence, or a full stop beginning a new paragraph; see the examples beginning in *ChronA* 70. 18 (*7 þæs*), 70. 22 (*7 þa*), 70. 28 (*7 þæs*), 70. 31 (*7 þæs*), 72. 4 (*7 æfter þissum gefeohte*), 72. 5 and 9 (*7 þæs*), 72. 11 (*7 þæs geares*), and 72. 16 (*7 þy geare*). So the question 'What is a multiple sentence?' again arises. But again we should not spend too much time on it. The Anglo-Saxons did not compose according to modern rules of punctuation; see §§ 1879-82.

(2) *Element order*

§ 1719. All the basic orders are found after *ond* in both early and late prose. For reasons of space I usually give here only examples from Ælfric's *Catholic Homilies*—Shannon (pp. 9-14) gives them from the *Parker Chronicle* 734-891—and do not exemplify all possible variations.

§ 1720. The order SV is seen in *ÆCHom* i. 24. 2 *and we besettað urne geleafan and urne hiht on eow,* i. 4. 16 *And se gesewenlica deofol þonne wyrcð ungerima wundra,* i. 4. 11 *and þa synd ða bydelas þæs ecan forwyrdes,* i. 4. 19 *and þeos weoruld bið siððan geendod,* i. 24. 35 *and hit weox swa swa oðre cild doð,* and (with the indirect object in emphatic position) i. 24. 16 *And þyssere mægðe God sealde and gesette æ.*

§ 1721. The order S . . . V is seen in *ÆCHom* i. 20. 7 *and he and his wif ða bearn gestryndon,* i. 14. 15 *and Adam him eallum naman gesceop,* i. 46. 24 *and ge ðone rihtwisan Crist niðfullice acwealdon,* i. 26. 35 *and Crist on ðære hwile to helle gewende,* and i. 44. 19 *and hi ða mid gebedum and bletsungum to diaconum gehadode wurdon.*

§ 1722. The direct object (§ 1565) has initial position in the patterns OSV, e.g. *ÆCHom* i. 56. 20 *and ða yfelan we mynegiað* and i. 18. 25 *and his nan man ne onbyrigde,* and OVS, e.g. *ÆCHom* i. 404. 11 *and þa lafe ðæs hungres ofsloh se Romanisca here* and i. 120. 10 *and him filigde micel menigu.*

§ 1723. When one of the adverbs *þa* and *þonne* immediately follows *ond,* the order is VS, e.g. *ÆCHom* i. 14. 13 *And þa wæs Adam swa wis . . . ,* i. 176. 15 *and þa wearð he oferswiðed,* ii. 542. 24 *and ðonne genihtsumað seo unrihtwisnys,* and ii. 14. 12 *and þonne bið seo ealde forgægednys geendod.* Here, as in examples like *ÆCHom* i. 24. 29 *and eft þaða he man gewearð, þa wæs he acenned of þam clænan mædene Marian,* where the correlative pattern discussed in § 2576 is preserved, the influence of the adverb prevails by drawing the verb into pre-subject position. The same is true of *þær,* e.g. *ÆHom* 11. 568 *and ðær soðlice bið on ece dæg ðe næfre ne geendað,* and probably of *þider* and *þanon,* though there are no examples in my collections.

§ 1724. The existence of these examples establishes the syntactical possibility of the numerous clauses with *ond þa* VS, *ond þær* VS, and *ond* adverb group VS, which occur in the *Anglo-Saxon Chronicle,* e.g. *ChronA* 70. 22 (871) *7 þa gefeaht se cyning Æþered . . . , ChronA* 72. 22 (873) *7 þa namon Mierce friþ . . . , ChronA* 70. 16 (871) *7 þær wæs micel wæl geslægen . . . , ChronA* 70. 23 (871) *7 þær wearþ se cyning Bagsecg ofslægen, ChronA* 70. 11 (871) *7 þæs ymb iii niht ridon ii eorlas up,* and *ChronA* 72. 5 (871) *7 þæs ofer Eastron gefor Æþered cyning.* But Malcolm Parkes has raised with me the possibility that in some of these examples and in similar ones elsewhere, there may have been scribal confusion between the *positura*—which according to Isidore was a *nota sententiarum* used to mark the end of something, to separate it from what followed—and the Tironian sign for the Latin word *et,* and therefore that sometimes at any rate *7* in OE manuscripts does not stand for *and* but marks the beginning of a new sentence with *þa/þær/þonne* (adverb group) VS. There is of course no way of proving this for any particular instance. But *ond* may be less frequent in the *Chronicle* than the standard editions suggest. See further Mitchell 1980*a*, p. 391.

§1725. But after other adverbs and after prepositional phrases, the element order fluctuates, as it does in clauses not introduced by *ond*, e.g. *ÆCHom* ii. 72. 11 *And swa getrymde his leorningcnihta geleafan Hælend Crist* . . . but *ÆCHom* i. 50. 4 *and swa se ðe wæs neoðor on endebyrdnesse wearð fyrmest on ðrowunge*; *ÆCHom* ii. 578. 6 *and of eallum leodum comon menn to gehyrenne Salomones wisdom* but *ÆCHom* i. 14. 10 *and mid þære eaðelican gehyrsumnysse þu ge-earnast heofenan rices myrhðu* and *ÆCHom* i. 10. 6 *and þurh his willan he hi ealle geliffæste*; and (in successive sentences) *ÆCHom* ii. 18. 5 *Be mancynnes æriste witegode Isaias, 'þa deadan sceolon arisan* . . .' but ii. 18. 7 *Be ðam dome Dauid cwæð to Gode, 'þu, Drihten . . .'.*

§1726. A negated verb can occur immediately after *ond*, e.g. *ÆCHom* i. 10. 1 *and ne mæg nan þing his willan wiðstandan*; cf. §§3924 and 3934–5. But the influence of *ond* often postpones the verb, e.g. *ÆCHom* i. 154. 14 *and we ne magon on ðissum life þæs ecan leohtes brucan* and *ÆCHom* i. 18. 25 *and his nan man ne onbyrigde*; cf. §1721.

§1727. The order VS is even found with no intervening element between *ond* and the verb, e.g. *ÆCHom* i. 492. 4 *and bið his yfelnys mannum cuð*, i. 2. 29 *and beoð fela frecednyssa on mancynne*, i. 316. 2 *and bugon to fulluhte on ðam dæge ðreo ðusend manna*, and i. 44. 21 *and wæs gemenigfylld þæt getel cristenra manna þearle on Hierusalem*. (I have deliberately excluded examples such as *ÆCHom* i. 230. 21 *þa on niht com him to Godes engel and lædde hi ut of ðam cwearterne and stod on merigen þæt cweartern fæste belocen*, where the influence of initial *þa* may be responsible for the position of the verb in the last clause.)

§1728. In *ond* clauses in which the subject is not repeated or expressed, we find *ond* VO, e.g. *ÆCHom* i. 14. 18 *and næbbe nænne fultum*; *ond* OV, e.g. *ÆCHom* i. 26. 14 *and þa deoflu todræfde*; *ond* adv. V, e.g. *ÆCHom* i. 182. 2 *and þær sæt mid his leorningcnihtum*; and *ond* adv. OV, e.g. *ÆCHom* ii. 28. 32 *and ðær hire hæle gefette*.

§1729. That the dictum 'even co-ordinating conjunctions are syntactically subordinating' (Campbell 1970, p. 93 fn. 4) still has some validity in late OE is clear from examples like *ÆCHom* i. 402. 15 . . . *swa þæt hi oftorfodon mid stanum ðone forman Godes cyðere Stephanum, and Iacobum, Iohannes broðer, beheafdodon* and *ÆCHom* i. 430. 31 *þa færlice, mid ðam ðe he gesæt, comon ðæs caseres cempan and hine gelæhton and to ðam cwellere gelæddon.* That its validity was not universal is clear from many of the examples already quoted and from others such as *ÆCHom* ii. 64. 32 and *ÆCHom* i. 14. 19 *And God þa geswefode þone Adam and þapa he slep ða genam he an rib of his sidan and geworhte of ðam ribbe ænne wifman and axode Adam hu heo hatan sceolde.*

§1730. In view of the subsequent disappearance of the order S . . . V it would be surprising if the dictum were universally valid in OE. Several factors are relevant here. First we must remember the tendency of pronoun objects to precede the verb; see §3907. Second, there are the demands of rhythm and emphasis. Here the reader will have to consider each example for himself without feeling bound to accept Bacquet's conclusion that the order *ond* . . . V is the norm and the order *ond* V is 'marqué'; see Mitchell, *NM* 65 (1964), 133 fn. 5, and ibid. 67 (1966), 92.

§1731. A third factor is that the order SV became increasingly common during the OE period, both after *ond* and elsewhere. As I have already pointed out—see especially *NM* 65 (1964), 132-3 and 138 ff.—I have no doubt of the truth of this. I give my reasons for rejecting Bacquet's claim (p. 753) that

la syntaxe de position est donc encore, dans la seconde moitié du XIe siècle, celle que nous avons observée dans les écrits alfrédiens, celle aussi des documenst [*sic*] kentiques ou merciens qui datent de la première moitié du IXe siècle. Une période de deux siècles et plus s'est écoulée sans que la langue évolue en ce domaine, alors que d'autres systèmes tel que le système modal, sont en cours de modification au début du Xe siècle[7]

in *NM* 67 (1966), 92, 94, and 95-7. The establishment of full statistics must be left to others. They are not yet available, mainly because (as I have noted in the places cited in the next sentence) previous writers have failed to recognize the influence of *ond* (and *ac*) in postponing the verb. Among them are Fourquet (see *NM* 67 (1966), 87-8); Rothstein, Barrett, and Bacquet (see *NM* 65 (1964), 117-19);

---

[7] 'The syntax of position is thus still, in the second half of the eleventh century, that which we have observed in Alfredian writings, and that also of the Kentish or Mercian documents dating from the first half of the ninth century. A period of two centuries and more has elapsed without the language evolving in this domain, whereas other systems, such as the modal system, are in the process of modification at the beginning of the tenth century.'

Shores (see *NM* 71 (1970), 611-14); Carlton (see *MÆ* 40 (1971), 183); Gardner (see *RES* 23 (1972), 462); Millward (see *EStudies*, 55 (1974), 387); and Sprockel (see *RES* 25 (1974), 453). To these can be added Shannon (see her pp. 9-14, where *ond* is suppressed in at least one example and where vital distinctions are not made) and Zuck (see his pp. 73-6, where he suppresses *ond* in ten examples). No doubt the catalogue is incomplete. But it is complete enough to suggest that it is more than time for those who intend to write on the order of elements in OE to take to head Alistair Campbell's last formulation of what should long ago have been a truism (Campbell 1970, p. 93 fn. 4):

Failure to recognise that even co-ordinating conjunctions are syntactically subordinating has often led scholars to quote clauses which are opened by such conjunctions without the conjunctions, which alone make their word-order possible. Such mal-quotation is frequent in Bosworth–Toller's *Anglo-Saxon Dictionary*, and renders much of the material in Paul Bacquet, *La Structure de la phrase verbale à l'époque Alfrédienne*, Paris, 1962, irrelevant. See also my review of the latter work, *Review of English Studies*, New Series, XV (1964), 190-193.

§1732. On element order in non-dependent commands introduced by *ond* see §905.

(3) *The relationships expressed*

§1733. The conjunction *ond* is often purely cumulative, e.g. *ÆCHom* i. 4. 3 *tacna and wundra*, *ÆCHom* i. 2. 23 *buton þam mannum . . . and buton þæm bocum . . .* , and *ÆCHom* i. 42. 25 *Se oxa oncneow his hlaford and se assa his hlafordes binne*. Closely akin to this is its use in narrative sequences, e.g. *ÆCHom* i. 228. 28 and *ÆCHom* i. 58. 12 *Se Hælend ða het þa ðenigmen afyllan six stænene fatu mid hluttrum wætere and he mid his bletsunge þæt wæter to æðelum wine awende*. In these functions *ond* is unemphatic. But it can sometimes give emphasis to a group of words, e.g. *Ch* 1381 *ðæt is ðæt Leofenað and his twegen yrfewardas after him gesyllan ælce geare xv leaxas, and ða gode, ðam biscope* and *ÆCHom* i. 50. 25 *Swiðor he besorgade . . . and rihtlice swiðor*; to a statement, e.g. *Matt(WSCp)* 26. 69 *þa com to hym an þeowyn 7 cwæð: 7 þu wære mid þam galileiscean hælynde*; to a transition in narrative or thought, e.g. *ÆCHom* i. 42. 30 *Ðyllice word Maria heold aræfnigende on hire heortan. And þa hyrdas gecyrdon ongean wuldrigende and herigende God . . .* and *ÆCHom* i. 10. 31 *And swiðe rihtlice him swa getimode . . .* ; or to a question, e.g. *ÆLet* 1. 16 *And hu mihtan þa halgan weras þa wunigan butan wife?* The varying degrees of emphasis which *ond* may give cannot always be accurately distinguished; consider *ÆCHom* i. 12. 28 and the difficulties of punctuation discussed in §1718.

§1734. But the relationship between two clauses introduced by *ond* may be other than cumulative or sequential. *ÆLS* 8. 220 *Se munt byrnð æfre swa swa ma oðre doð. þa getimode hit ymb twelf monað æfter Agathes þrowunge and Ethna up ableow* is often cited as an example 'where *and* = *þæt*' (BTS, s.v. III. 3). A clause introduced by *ond* can often be replaced by an adjective clause, e.g. *ÆCHom* i. 510. 1 *þær is ahangen sum glæsen fæt mid sylfrenne racenteage, and þæs wynsuman wætan onfehð* (same subject not repeated); *ÆCHom* ii. 40. 4 *þes is min leofa Sunu, and he me wel licað* (same subject repeated); *ÆCHom* ii. 158. 3 *þa wæs þær gehende sum munuclif and heora abbud wæs þa niwan forðfaren* (subject of first clause appears in a different case—with a change of number—in the second clause); and *ÆCHom* i. 336. 10 and i. 336. 8 *ða gemette he be wege sumne licðrowere licgende eal tocinen and nahte his feðes geweald* (in both of which the subject of the second clause has to be understood from an oblique case in the first clause). On this, see further Klaeber, *Ang.* 27 (1904), 264–5.

§1735. The relationship between the two clauses is often adverbial. Thus the clause introduced by *ond* may express purpose, e.g.*ÆCHom* i. 18. 12 *þa com God and axode hwi he his bebod tobræce*; result, e.g. *ÆCHom* i. 10. 29 . . . *þa becom Godes grama ofer hi ealle, and hi ealle wurdon awende of þam fægeran hiwe* . . . (see Glogauer, §5); or comparison, e.g. *CP* 307. 8 . . . *Crist, ðe simle anes willan wæs 7 God Fæder, us salde bisne.* . . . The first clause could be replaced by a clause of time, e.g. *ÆCHom* i. 16. 12 *and he worhte ða þone man mid his handum and him on ableow sawle* and many other narrative sequences; by a causal clause, e.g. *ÆLet* 1. 42 *He sceal þæt folc læran to geleafan mid bodunge and mid clænum þeawum þam cristenum gebysnian. And his lif ne sceal beon swylce læwedra manna*; or by a conditional clause, e.g.*ÆCHom* ii. 564. 13 *Ageot wæter uppon ðone ele and se ele abrecð up and swimð bufon, ÆCHom* ii. 294. 31 *Wurde ure miht geedniwod, þonne towurpe we ðis deofolgild, ÆHom* 3. 21 *uton hine ofslean and his yrfweardnyss ure byð syððan*, and *HomU* 36. 229. 22 (see §3691). In *ÆCHom* ii. 500. 21 *Ða næfde Martinus nan ðing to syllenne þam nacodan ðearfan, þe ðær swa ðearle hrymde, buton his gewædum þe he wel behofode, and hæfde ær his ðing þearfum gedælede, and* introduces an explanatory clause. On 'causal' *and* clauses, see further §§3169–71.

§1736. The first clause in sentences like *ÆCHom* i. 424. 8 *Se Æl-mihtiga Fæder ures Hælendes is Scyppend ealra gesceafta, and ðu cwyst þæt ic me gebiddan sceole to dumbum stanum, ða ðe sind agrafene ðurh manna handa* could be replaced by a concessive clause. But we could equally well translate *ond* as 'but' and describe the relationship as adversative; compare *ÆCHom* i. 100. 34 *God gesceop ealle gesceafta and deofol nane gesceafta scyppan ne mæg* and *Beo* 1604 *wiston ond ne wendon, þæt hie heora winedrihten || selfne gesawon* (see Glogauer, §4). See further §§3516-18, 3525, and 3668-70.

§1737. The relationships described here are real; for more examples, see Maisenhelder, pp. 62-79. But it would, I think, be misleading to say that *ond* can mean 'who' or 'so that' or 'but' or the like. Maisen-helder (p. 62) says: 'In allen Fällen also, wo *and* den Sinn von "daß, aber, als, bis, denn" erhält, liegt dies nicht etwa an der Bedeutung von *and*, sondern an dem Inhalt und gegenseitigen Verhältnis der durch *and* verbundenen Sätze.'[8] The truth of this will be apparent from a consideration of *ÆCHom* i. 160. 23 *Se man gesihð and fylið Gode, seðe cann understandan God, and god weorc wyrcð. Se man gesihð and nele Gode fylian, seðe understent God, and nele god wyrcan.*

§1738. Certain relationships can of course be indicated or stressed by the presence of a suitable adverb or conjunction after *ond*, e.g. (cumulative or sequential) *ÆCHom* i. 2. 27 . . . *and eac*, i. 4. 4 *and eac swylce*, and i. 52. 20 *and þær to eacen*; (temporal) *ÆCHom* i. 42. 29 . . . *and heo geseah ða* . . . and *ÆCHom* i. 14. 30 *and on ðam seofoðan dæge he geendode his weorc*; (consecutive) *ÆCHom* i. 50. 4 . . . *and swa se ðe wæs neoðor on endebyrdnysse wearð fyrmest on ðrowunge* and *ÆCHom* ii. 372. 33 *and swa gehwæt* 'and so on'; and (adversative) *ÆCHom* i. 8. 8 . . . *and swa ðeah ne do we nan ðing to gode.*

(4) Ond *as a preposition?*

§1739. BT recognized *and* as 'prep. dat. acc.'. But in BTS (s.v. *and*, prep.) we are told that 'in the examples given under II [i.e. those with the accusative] *and = an, on*'. An analysis of some of the BT(S) examples and of others like them by Maisenhelder (pp. 47-50) sup-ports Holthausen's refusal (s.v. *and*) to acknowledge *and* as a preposi-tion. In my opinion none of the examples demands acceptance; I

---

[8] 'Thus, in all instances where *and* has the sense of "that", "but", "when", "until", "for", this is not the result of the meaning of "and" but of the meaning and interrelation-ship of the sentences linked by "and".'

agree with Campbell (BTC, s.v. *and*, prep.): 'the word probably does not exist; in all citations we have *and*, conj., or an error for *an, on*'.

b. Other conjunctions

§1740. *Eac* is occasionally used initially without *ond* in a cumulative or resumptive sense 'and, also, too', e.g. *ÆCHom* i. 402. 17 . . . *and Iacobum, Iohannes broðer, beheafdodon. Eac ðone rihtwisan Iacobum hi ascufon of ðam temple and acwealdon* . . . and *ChristA* 301 *Eac we þæt gefrugnon.* . . . But it is more often used in combinations such as *swa eac*, e.g. *ÆCHom* i. 138. 27 *Eac swa þa unclænan nytenu getacniað ure unclænan geþohtas and weorc, ða we sceolon symle acwellan* . . . (Thorpe's translation is wrong here), *ÆCHom* i. 2. 27 *ond eac*, i. 4. 4 *and eac swylce*, and i. 6. 16 *ne eac*. See further BT(S), s.v. *eac*.

§1741. *Ge* is found alone in the sense 'and', e.g. *BlHom* 127. 8 *is þonne on westan medmycel duru þæt mannes heafod ge þa sculdro magan in* and *Phoen* 523 *soðfæst ge synnig*. The combination *ge eac* also occurs, e.g. *BlHom* 15. 4 *be þisse ondweardan tide, ge eac be þære toweardan.*

§1742. Combinations of *æghwæþer/ægþer* and *ge* mean 'both . . . and'. They join words, e.g. *ÆCHom* i. 18. 4 *ægðer ge god ge yfel* (but see §1744) and (with *and eac* introducing a third element) i. 246. 20 *and ægðer ge men ge ða sucendan cild and eac ða nytenu*; phrases, e.g. *ÆCHom* i. 184. 18 *ægðer ge þurh his godnysse ge ðurh his mihte*; infinitive groups with a common auxiliary verb, e.g. *Bede* 192. 8 . . . *þonne mæg seo godcunde arfæstnisse þurh geearnunge swa micles monnes æghwæðer ge lengre fæc þisses lifes þe forgifan, ge þec eac þæs ecan lifes ingonges wyrðne gedon*; and clauses, e.g. *ÆCHom* i. 298. 22 *and ða bec þurhwuniað on cristenre ðeode, ægðer ge ðær þær ða apostoli lichamlice bodedon, ge þær ðær hi na ne becomon*. More than two elements can be combined, e.g. *Or* 50. 19 *ægðer ge on monslihtum ge on hungre ge on scipgebroce ge on mislicre forscapunge*, *ÆCHom* i. 246. 20 above, and *ÆCHom* i. 392. 10 *ægþer ge mid lare ge mid gebedum ge mid gewritum.*

§1743. We also find *ægðer ge . . . and*, e.g. *ÆCHom* ii. 46. 20 *Uton habban ægðer ge ðære culfran unscæððignysse and ðæs fyres bryne* (cf. *ÆCHom* i. 246. 20 (§1742)), and some examples of *ægðer* without an immediately following *ge*, e.g. *CP* 195. 21 . . . *ðæt hi ægðer hæbben eagan innan ge utan* and *ÆCHom* ii. 20. 35 *We sceolon ægðer*

*gelyfan Godes wundra and eac mid micelre lufe geðancian þam
Heofonlican Fæder.*

§1744. In some of the quoted examples, *ægþer* may be parsed as a
pronoun, e.g. *ÆCHom* i. 18. 4 (§1742). But in others, e.g. *ÆCHom*
i. 298. 22 (§1742), it cannot be. Hence we must follow BTS (s.v.
ægþer III) in distinguishing a conjunctional use. See further §§461
and 1813–17.

§1745. The meaning 'both . . . and' may also be conveyed by *ge . . .
ge*, e.g. *Bede* 318. 12 . . . *ge mid bysenum heofonlices lifes ge eac mid
monungum* and *BlHom* 51. 7 . . . *ge on lande ge on oþrum þingum ge
on oþrum gestreonum*; *ge . . . and*, e.g. *ÆLS* 1. 171 *Seo sawul . . .
mæg underfon ge godne wyllan and yfelne*; and *ge . . . and eac*, e.g.
ÆCHom ii. 200. 26 . . . *ge ærðan ðe hi þa Readan Sæ ofereodon,
and eac siððan on ðam westene.*

§1746. Further on the combinations so far discussed, see BT(S),
s.vv., and Nusser, pp. 48–55. On combinations meaning 'not only . . .
but also', see §§1777–99.

§1747. Neither the word 'both' nor the combination 'both . . . and'
occurs in OE; see *OED*, s.v. *both*. In examples like *Or* 148. 12 *7 hie
butu ofslog, ge þone cyning ge þa cwene, butu* is one object of *oflsog*.

§1748. Ericson (1932, p. 19) says that initial *swa* 'may serve as a
mere transitional link between clauses or at the head of a sentence.
In such examples, the modal signification is so low that the *swa*
approximates "and".' It is, however, not clear to me which particular
sentences among those he quotes were meant to exemplify this.

§1749. *Swylce* 'likewise, also' often links clauses, e.g. *BlHom* 33. 33
*he wæs soþ man, þy hine dorste deofol costian, swylce he wæs soþ
God, þe him englas þegnedon* and

Beo 828   Hæfde East-Denum
                 Geatmecga leod   gilp gelæsted,
                 swylce oncyþðe   ealle gebette,
                 inwidsorge. . . .

§1750. Schücking (§46) notes that *hyrde ic* serves as a kind of co-
ordinator, marking a transition to something different, in examples
like

Beo 59

Ðæm feower bearn   forðgerimed
in worold wocun,   weoroda ræswa[n],
Heorogar ond Hroðgar   ond Halga til,
hyrde ic þæt [. . .   wæs On]elan cwen,
Heaðo-Scilfingas   healsgebedda.

§1751. The use of *oððe* in the sense 'and' is not recognized by BT(S) or GK. But the suggestion has been made for certain examples in the poetry. I would dismiss *Gifts* 12 and 13, *Dan* 140, and *Dan* 321 and *And* 334 (which can be compared with one another); in all of these 'or' gives satisfactory sense. In *PPs* 135. 23, MS *oþ* seems to be an error; ASPR v emends to *And*. In *Beo* 649 the sense is 'until', as in *ChronA* 86. 14 (894), *PPs* 139. 11, and elsewhere; whether *oþþe* stands for *oþþæt* is discussed in §2755. The same may be true in

Beo 3002

syððan hie gefricgeað   frean userne
ealdorleasne,   þone ðe ær geheold
wið hettendum   hord ond rice,
æfter hæleða hryre,   hwate scildwigan,
folcred fremede,   oððe furður gen
eorlscipe efnde;

Beowulf's final deed of valour ended his life and his reign. The fact that we find (for example) *Ex* 1 *feor and neah*, *Wan* 26 *feor oþþe neah*, and *Wife* 25 *feor ge neah* (Glogauer, §1) does not prove that the three *conjunctions* mean the same. Nor can I see that *oþþe* means *ond* in

Wan 26

hwær ic feor oþþe neah   findan meahte
þone þe in meoduhealle   min mine wisse,
oþþe mec freondleasne   frefran wolde,
weman mid wynnum

and similar examples cited by Glogauer (§3). But in

Beo 2474

. . .   syððan Hreðel swealt,
oððe him Ongenðeowes   eaferan wæran
frome fyrdhwate

and

And 744

Ge synd unlæde,   earmra geþohta
searowum beswicene,   oððe sel nyton,
mode gemyrde,

neither 'or' nor 'until' suits. So at the moment we are forced to concede the seemingly unlikely possibility that *oþþe* can mean both 'or' —excluding what precedes—and 'and (furthermore)'—with no

exclusion of what precedes.[9] Sequences like *ÆLS* 17. 24 and *ÆCHom*
ii. 330. 24 *Se ðeoda lareow sæde mancynne, þæt dyrne forligeras
oððe deofolgyldan, sceaðan and reaferas, oððe reðe manslagan,
gytseras and drinceras, þe dollice lybbað, nabbað Godes rice on
roderlicere heofonan*, and the plural verb in *El* 508 . . . *þara þe wif
oððe wer on woruld cendan* seem to reinforce this possibility. Nusser
(p. 23) also has these examples and offers more from later periods.
Liebermann (*Archiv*, 151 (1926), 79–80) adds two from the *Laws*.
There is room for more work here by the lexicographers.

3. CONJUNCTIONS MEANING 'BUT', 'HOWEVER', AND THE LIKE

a. Ac

(1) *The subject*

§1752. The five patterns discussed in detail for *ond* in §§1712–17
occur with *ac* and can be exemplified here without further comment.[10] When the subject of both verbs is the same, it is normally
not repeated in the *ac* clause, e.g. *ÆCHom* i. 16. 21 *forðan ðe he nis
na Scyppend ac is atelic sceocca*, but can be, e.g. *ÆCHom* i. 12. 10
*ne hi ne magon nu, ne hi nellað nane synne gewyrcan, ac hi æfre
beoð ymbe þæt an. . . .* On Andrew's unnecessary attempt to eliminate the latter pattern from the poetry, see §1715. The subject of
the first verb may appear in the *ac* clause in a different case, e.g.
ÆCHom i. 4. 16 *And se gesewenlica deofol þonne wyrcð ungerima
wundra . . . ac his tima ne bið na langsum*. When the two verbs have
different subjects, both are usually expressed, e.g. *ÆCHom* i. 8. 2
*For wel fela ic wat on þisum earde gelæredran þonne ic sy ac God
geswutelað his wundra þurh ðone þe he wile*, but the second is sometimes not expressed, e.g. *ÆCHom* i. 106. 24 *Ða easternan tungelwitegan gesawon niwne steorran beorhtne, na on heofenum
betwux oðrum tunglum, ac wæs angenga betwux heofenum and
eorðan*; on this see further §§1503–16.

(2) *Element order*

§1753. *Mutatis mutandis*, the remarks made about element order
after *ond* in §§1719–32 apply after *ac*. Its influence in postponing

---

[9] Andrew (*Postscript*, §§99 and 102) discusses the three *Beowulf* examples. He is hope-
lessly wrong about *Beo* 649, probably right about *Beo* 3006, and unconvincing about
Beo 2475.

[10] The following item, which appears in some bibliographies under *ac*, refers to *ac* (fem.)
'oak': (F. A.) Wood, *JEGP* 13 (1914), 499.

the verb has too often been overlooked and all the basic element orders occur after it, both when a subject is not expressed in the *ac* clause, e.g. *ÆCHom* i. 16. 21 (§1752) (*ac* V) and *ÆCHom* ii. 62. 20 *God fæder ne sparode his agenum Bearne ac for us eallum hine to deaðe sealde* (*ac* . . . V), and when one is, e.g. *ÆCHom* i. 8. 3 *ac God geswutelað his wundra* . . . , i. 12. 20 *ac God ne gesceop hine na to deofle*, and i. 12. 11 *ac hi æfre beoð ymbe þæt an* (SV); *ÆLS* 31. 1358 *ac he æfre openum eagum and upahefenum handum his gebeda ne geswac*, *ÆCHom* ii. 122. 21 *ac eal folc ðone eadigan Gregorium to ðære geðincðe anmodlice geceas*, and *ÆCHom* ii. 62. 24 *ac se ramm hine spelode* (S . . . V); *ÆCHom* i. 210. 15 *ac þone wacan assan he geceas him to byrðre* (OSV); *ÆCHom* i. 180. 9 *ac þæt fæsten tælð God* and ii. 362. 6 *ac hit nyston eorðlice men ær Cristes ðrowunge* (OVS); *ÆCHom* ii. 6. 16 *ac sende se Fæder his ancennedan Sunu to þrowunge* and *ÆCHom* i. 610. 3 *ac ne mænde Drihten ðas tacna on ðære godspellican witegunge* (VS); and *ÆCHom* i. 6. 22 *ac þæra is nu to lyt ðe wile wel tæcan* (where MnE would use expletive 'there'). As with *ond*, fluctuation is apparent when *ac* is immediately followed by an adverb or an adverbial element, e.g. *ÆCHom* i. 4. 6 *ac for his gecorenum he gescyrte þa dagas* (SV), *ÆCHom* ii. 220. 13 *ac buton ælcere foresceawunge his yrsunge gefremað* (OV), *ÆCHom* i. 84. 34 *ac buton yldinge him becom seo godcundlice wracu* (OVS), and *ÆHom* 21. 580 *ac þar wæs gehende an hæþen tempel* (VS). Again, there is no syntactical rule; considerations of style and emphasis are decisive.

§1754. Like *ond* (§1723), *ac* does not normally affect the element order in correlative sentences involving *þa*, *þonne*, and the like, e.g. *ÆCHom* i. 208. 18 *Ac ðaða Crist com to mancynne, þa awende he ure stuntnysse to gerade* and *ÆCHom* i. 38. 16 *ac siððan se heofenlica cyning urne eorðlican lichaman underfeng, siððan gecyrdon his englas to ure sibbe*.

§1755. *Ac* may be reinforced by another conjunction or by an adverb. We find, for example, *ÆCHom* i. 554. 5 *ac swiðor*, *ÆCHom* i. 86. 6 *ac ðeah*, *ÆCHom* i. 84. 5 *ac* . . . *þeah*, and *ÆCHom* i. 32. 25 *ac eac swylce*.

§1756. When one of two alternatives is to be negated, it can be either the first or the second. When it is the first, we find in OE the patterns *na/no* (hereafter abbreviated to *na*; see §1128) or adv. *ne* or *nalles* . . . *ac*. Logically, the negative word should appear immediately before the first of the contrasted words, phrases, or clauses.

In the prose, such negation is usually effected by *na* with words, phrases, and clauses, as in *ÆCHom* i. 198. 16 *na lichamlice ac gast-lice, ÆCHom* i. 210. 1 *Ne cwædon hi na Ure Hlaford, ne Ðin Hlaford, ac forðrihte Hlaford, ÆCHom* i. 158. 25–30, *ÆCHom* i. 402. 10 *na to ðam weorcstanum, oððe to ðære getimbrunge, ac . . . to ðam ceastergewarum, ÆCHom* i. 80. 30 *na swa þeah þæs geares . . . ac æfter twegra geara ymbryne, ÆCHom* i. 106. 4 *na ðurh stemne ac ðurh tacn, ÆCHom* i. 2. 18 *na þurh gebylde mycelre lare ac forþan þe ic geseah and gehyrde mycel gedwyld*, and (with idiomatic nega-tion of the verb) *ÆCHom* i. 136. 26 *ac hit næs na him getiðod, ac wæs getiðod þisum ealdan men, ÆCHom* i. 100. 26 *ac se monandæg nis na fyrmest daga on þære wucan, ac is se oðer*, and *ÆCHom* i. 16. 11 *. . . he ne cwæð na 'Geweorðe man geworht', ac he cwæð 'Uton gewyrcan mannan to ure anlicnysse'.* These last three examples should be contrasted with *ÆCHom* i. 142. 16 *Ðas twa fugelcyn ne singað na, swa swa oðre fugelas, ac hi geomeriað . . .* , where the verbs themselves are contrasted.

§1757. But what is logical is not always what is said. Sometimes the negative *na* is placed before the wrong word, as in *CP* 181. 16 *Be ðæm we magon suiðe swutule oncnawan ðæt se eaðmodnesse lareow . . . na ne cuæð: Biddað ac: Secgað ⁊ bebeodað* and *ÆCHom* i. 204. 21 *Ne synd we na Abrahames cynnes flæsclice, ac gastlice*; cf. *ÆC Hom* i. 198. 16 *na lichamlice ac gastlice.* But more frequently we find that the negative—in the form of the adv. *ne*—is attracted to the verb and that the first of the contrasted elements is not negated, e.g. *ÆCHom* i. 94. 17 *He cwæð þæt he ne come to ðy þæt he wolde þa ealdan æ towurpan ac gefyllan* and *ÆCHom* i. 610. 3 *ac ne mænde Drihten ðas tacna on ðære godspellican witegunge, ac ða egefullan tacna þe ðam micclan dæge forestæppað*; these differ from *CP* 181. 16 above in that they do not have *na*. In examples like *ÆC Hom* i. 92. 3 *Ne beo ðu geciged heononforð Abram, ac Abraham . . . ne ðin wif ne beo gehaten Sarai, ac beo gehaten Sarra* and *ÆCHom* i. 234. 19 *Ne getimode þam apostole Thome unforsceawodlice, þæt he ungeleafful wæs Cristes æristes, ac hit getimode þurh Godes forsceawunge*, the repetition of the verb produces a logical construc-tion. For the same phenomena in MnE and other languages, see Jespersen, *Neg.*, pp. 45–8.

§1758. Both patterns discussed in §§1756–7 are found contrasting a false or rejected cause with a true or accepted one, e.g. (with *na*) *ÆCHom* i. 2. 18 (§1756) and (with a negated verb) *ÆCHom* i. 34. 23 *Næs þæt cild forði gecweden hire frumcennede cild swilce heo*

oðer siððan acende, ac forði þe Crist is frumcenned of manegum
gastlicum gebroðrum; see further §§3180-94.

§1759. The combination *nalles* (or one of its variants; see §1620)
. . . *ac* occasionally occurs in the prose outside Ælfric and Wulfstan,
e.g. *Bede* 4. 25 *nalæs mid anes mannes geþeahte ac mid gesægene*
unrim geleaffulra witena, BlHom 197. 8 *Heo þonne nalles on goldes*
wlite 7 on seolfres ne scineþ, ac on sundorweorþunge . . . heo ge-
wuldrad stondeþ, and *BlHom* 121. 11 *Nalas þæt wolcn þær þy forþ*
com þe ure Drihten þæs wolcnes fultomes þearfe hæfde æt þære
upastignesse, oþþe þæt wolcn hiene up ahofe, ah he þæt wolcn him
beforan nam, where (despite Andrew, *SS,* §82) *nalas* stands 'as a
head-word to negate a sentence'.

§1760. My observations so far confirm Andrew's statement (*SS,*
§§81-2) that *nalles,* not *na,* (. . . *ac*) is used in the poetry to negate
one of two alternative words or phrases, e.g. *Beo* 3021, *Beo* 3019 *oft*
nalles æne, ChristC 1170 *monge nales fea,* and

Beo 338   Wen'ic þæt ge for wlenco,   nalles for wræcsiðum,
                   ac for higeþrymmum   Hroðgar sohton.

§1761. With alternative clauses, *nalles . . . ac* is much more common
in the poetry than in the prose, e.g. *Beo* 562, 2503, 2596, and

Beo 2832   Nalles æfter lyfte   lacende hwearf
                   middelnihtum,   maðmæhta wlonc
                   ansyn ywde,   ac he eorðan gefeoll
                   for ðæs hildfruman   hondgeweorce.

But the other patterns already noted in the prose—viz., *na . . . ac*
and *ne* verb . . . *ac*—also occur in the poetry when clauses are involved. When *na . . . ac* is used, *na* is frequently followed by a stressed
pronoun, as in

Beo 445   Na þu minne þearft
                   hafalan hydan,   ac he me habban wile
                   dreore fahne,   gif mec deað nimeð;

see further Andrew, *SS,* §81. But it can occur in other contexts, e.g.

Beo 2306   þa wæs dæg sceacen
                   wyrme on willan;   no on wealle læ[n]g
                   bidan wolde,   ac mid bæle for,
                   fyre gefysed.

Many of the examples of *ne . . . ac* involve *ne wæs* or its contraction *næs*, e.g.

Beo 2506

ne wæs ecg bona,
ac him hildegrap   heortan wylmas,
banhus gebræc

and *Beo* 2975 *næs he fæge þa git,* || *ac he hyne gewyrpte.* But there are examples with other verbs, e.g. *Beo* 109 *ne gefeah he þære fæhðe, ac he hine feor forwræc.* Here again (as in §§1596-7), we see the impossibility of always distinguishing word and sentence negation.

§1762. The first clause may contain a virtual negative, e.g.

Beo 2897

Lyt swigode
niwra spella   se ðe næs gerad,
ac he soðlice   sægde ofer ealle. . . .

§1763. When the second element is to be negated, there are several possibilities. When an element other than a clause is involved, we find *(ond) na* immediately before it, e.g. *ÆCHom* ii. 572. 7 *Drihten cwæð on oðrum godspelle 'Cnuciað and eow bið geopenod'; ac we sceolon nu cnucian . . . na ðonne, ÆCHom* i. 400. 12 *Godes miht þe gehælde, na ic, ÆCHom* i. 40. 13 *forðan ðe he is God and na gesceaft, ÆCHom* i. 352. 18 *forðan ðe he wæs Godes bydel ond na God,* and *ÆCHom* i. 36. 2 *on dæge and na on nihte.*

§1764. The conjunction *ond* occasionally has an almost adversative sense when it introduces a negative clause; see §§1736-7. But *ac* is more common. The negated clause may contain only the adv. *ne,* e.g. *ÆCHom* i. 244. 27 *þa wearð se witega afyrht, and wolde forfleon Godes gesihðe, ac he ne mihte,* or the adv. *ne* reinforced by *na,* e.g. *ÆCHom* i. 12. 19 *þonne wite he þæt God gesceop to mæran engle þone þe nu is deofol; ac God ne gesceop hine na to deofle,* or by other negatives, e.g. *ÆCHom* i. 302. 13 *Stanas sind gesceafta, ac hi nabbað nan lif ne hi ne gefredað.* We find a virtual negative in an *ac* clause in *ÆCHom* i. 6. 22 *ac þæra is nu to lyt ðe wile wel tæcan and wel bysnian.*

§1765. On element order in non-dependent commands introduced by *ac,* see §906.

§1766. Two positive clauses can be contrasted by *ac,* e.g. *ÆCHom* ii. 572. 7 (§1763), *ÆCHom* i. 8. 2 *For wel fela ic wat on þisum earde gelæredran þonne ic sy, ac God geswutelað his wundra þurh ðone þe he wile*, and *ÆCHom* i. 302. 11 *He cwæð, 'Bodiað eallum gesceafte'; ac mid þam naman is se mann ana getacnod.* Schücking (§50, Anm. 1) errs in citing *Beo* 696 as an example of this sort. *Nænig* in *Beo* 691 provides a negative for *Ac* in *Beo* 696 as well as for *ac* in *Beo* 694.

(3) *The relationships expressed*

§1767. What meaning or meanings does *ac* have in OE? This question has been discussed by many writers, including Schücking (pp. 91-3), Schuchardt (pp. 71-6), Williams (pp. 148-65), and Glogauer (*passim*). Williams (p. 163) finds himself in complete agreement with Schuchardt (p. 74) when he said that for the period of *Beowulf* we must reject any specialized conjunctional meaning for *ac*. According to Williams (pp. 148-50), '*ac* in *Beowulf* is always an external sign of the phenomenon I have called "antithetic expansion" ', which 'is represented concretely by examples like "He isn't crying, he's laughing" '. He distinguishes this from 'concessive expansion', exemplified by 'He is weak/not strong but he fights well' but takes no cognizance of the fact that 'but' also has a 'contrastive' use, e.g. 'He has a house of his own, but (= whereas) his brother lives in a flat'; see Collinson, *Lingua*, 1 (1947-8), 329. Williams is able to maintain his proposition for *Beowulf* (it seems to me) only by much ingenuity and it will become apparent that I do not accept it either for *Beowulf* or for OE in general.

§1768. Glogauer (p. 22) follows Schücking (§50) in distinguishing three functions of *ac*—adversative ('die adversative'), annulling ('die aufhebende'), and causal ('die begründende'). But he adds a fourth —continuative ('die die Erzählung fortführende'). I shall discuss these in reverse order.

§1769. Glogauer adds his fourth category—continuative *ac*— under the heading '*Ac = ond*' (pp. 21-2). His sole OE prose example is *CP* 30. 12 *forðon hi nan mon ne dear ðreagean ðeah hi agylten, ac mid þæm bioð synna swiðe gebrædda, þe hi bioð swa geweorðode.* But, even though the Latin has *et in exemplum culpa vehementer extenditur* . . . , there is sufficient opposition between the two clauses to justify the translator's *ac* in Williams's sense—either they are reprimanded for their sins or the sins increase. However, it can be said that, if we had *ond*, we would perhaps see a consecutive relationship 'and so . . .'; see Williams, p. 152. From the poetry Glogauer cites *Beo* 804, *Beo* 1576, and

Beo 2141   næs ic fæge þa gyt;
            ac me eorla hleo   eft gesealde
            maðma menigeo,   maga Healfdenes,

as sentences in which *ac* comes close to being a connecting or linking
conjunction ('eine Konj. der Zusammengehörigkeit'). I do not see
how these and his other examples differ from many others involving
ac. According to Schaar (p. 173), *ac* in *Phoen* 5 and *Phoen* 26 'is =
copulative *ond*'. There is no justification for this; in both, *ac* follows
a clause containing a negative and means 'but'. Andrew's emendation
(*Postscript*, §99) of *ac* to *eac* or *ec* in *Beo* 1448 is unnecessary; there
is enough contrast between the coat of mail which guards the body
and the helmet which guards the head to justify *ac*. As Klaeber (3,
Glossary, s.v. *ac*) remarks: 'the adversative (mostly contradictory-
adversative, cf. Ger. "sondern") function appears with varying degrees
of logical strictness; occasionally it shades off into the connective-
adversative type (almost = *and*, 1448)'. Whether the formula '*ac* =
ond' ever holds is a question of semantics which cannot be pursued
here.

§1770. I turn now to the causal or explanatory function ('die begründende Funktion'). As Schücking (p. 91) and Glogauer (pp. 22–4)
point out, the reason why something is not so often seems to be expressed in a following *ac* clause. Typical examples from the poetry
include *Beo* 705, *Beo* 2832, and

Beo 445   Na þu minne þearft
            hafalan hydan,   ac he me habban wile
            dreore fahne,   gif mec deað nimeð.

(This, says Glogauer, can often be explained by assuming a mental
leap which misses out the adversative clause to which *ac* really belongs and attaches *ac* to the explanatory clause.) They are not alone.
Sedgefield translates *ac* in *Bo* 15. 25 *þonne eart ðu on gedwolan, ac
swylce hiora þeawas sint* as 'for'. Thorpe does the same for *ÆCHom*
i. 100. 34 *God gesceop ealle gesceafta, and deofol nane gesceafta
scyppan ne mæg, ac he is yfel tihtend and leas wyrcend*. . . . BT (s.v.
ac II) propose *ac* in *Beo* 740 and *GenA* 2159 (on these, see Liggins
1955, pp. 210–11), and Schaar (p. 173) adds *ac* in *GuthA* 259 and
310. However, the causal relationship—if indeed present—is not
uppermost in these examples; see Williams, pp. 151–3, and Liggins,
loc. cit. But there are some in which it does seem to be. Liggins
(1955, pp. 211–12) observes that there are seven passages in the
'Alfredian' translations and two in Ælfric in which 'the function of
ac is purely explanatory'. They include *CP* 147. 12 *Ac hit is ðeah*

suiðe earfeðdæde ðæt mon lustlice ðone lareow gehieran wille ðe mon ne lufað, ÆCHom i. 104. 29, and *ÆCHom* i. 478. 5. Van Dam (p. 40) gives references to five sentences in which '*ac* was used as a coordinating conjunction to express causality'. Other possible examples include the second *ac* in *ÆCHom* i. 36. 16, which Thorpe translates as 'for'. But this could be compared with *ÆCHom* i. 94. 17 and the like; see §1757.

§1771. Next there is the function described as 'aufhebende' or 'annulling'. Schücking's examples (p. 92) include

Beo 2475   oððe him Ongenðeowes   eaferan wæran
                   frome fyrdhwate,   freode ne woldon
                   ofer heafo healdan,   ac ymb Hreosnabeorh
                   eatolne inwitscear   oft gefremedon—

'will er den Krieg, so Wünscht er nicht den Frieden'—and *Beo* 2897 (§1762)—'redet er, so schweigt er nicht'. Other names given to it are 'explanatory' or 'enhancing' or 'substitutive'; see Quirk, pp. 51–4. The essential feature is that the first expression—a negative one—is annulled or enhanced or replaced by the second: 'if he wants war, he does not wish for peace' and 'if he speaks, he is not silent'.

§1772. Full consideration of the meanings of *ac* must be left to the lexicographers. However, I have reservations about Williams's claim (pp. 162–3) that his 'antithetic expansion' covers all the adversative examples cited by Schücking, and assert that his rule cannot be extended to OE in general, for we can detect not only the function in which two mutually exclusive propositions are contrasted, e.g. *ÆHom* 1. 48 *Godes bearn . . . þa þe na of blodum ne of flæsces willan ne of þæs weres willan ac ða þæ of Gode synd acennede*— this comes close to the annulling—but also the explanatory (§1770). We can perhaps add the contrastive (§1767), e.g. *ÆCHom* i. 8. 2 (§1752), and the adversative or concessive, e.g. *ÆCHom* i. 302. 11 *He cwæð, 'Bodiað eallum gesceafte'; ac mid þam naman is se manna ana getacnod*; see further Glogauer, §35, and my §§3519–20. But Quirk's claim (pp. 50–1) that *ac* sometimes has 'a non-concessive "subject-changing"' function is dubious; see Campbell, *RES* 7 (1956), 66–7.

b. Other conjunctions

§1773. *OED* (s.v. *but* C. III. 23) recognizes *bute* as an 'adversative conjunction' in *ChronA* 90. 18 (897) *næron nawðer ne on Fresisc gescæpene ne on Denisc, bute swa him selfum ðuhte þæt hie nyt-wyrðoste beon meahten*; see further BTS, s.v. *butan* C. II. (2). Varnhagen (pp. 33-4) quotes this and similar examples as 'instances . . . which serve to show the state of transition from the original exceptive to the adversative meaning'; they include *ChronE* 123. 1 (978) *Her on þissum geare ealle þa yldestan Angelcynnes witan gefeollan æt Calne of anre upfloran butan se halga Dunstan ærcebiscop ana ætstod uppon anum beame* and

GenB 681	Hit nis wuhte gelic
elles on eorðan,	buton swa þes ar sægeð,
þæt hit gegnunga	from gode come.

Varnhagen's position is sound; all his examples are transitional in that *butan* can always mean 'except' and can always be taken as governing the clause which follows. This is true of *Or* 17. 4 (Wülfing, ii. 649); of *Gen* 15. 10 (Schrader, p. 75); of *Beo* 1559 (Mather, p. 15); of all the relevant examples quoted by Gehse (pp. 38-52); and of all the examples of 'concessive-equivalent' *butan* clauses cited by Quirk (pp. 62-3; see my §3500).

§1774. On the use of *þonne* in an adversative sense 'then, yet, but', see BT, s.v. *þanne* A. IV, and Glogauer, §12. This is particularly common in *gif* clauses, e.g. *ÆCHom* i. 134. 18 *þæt is feowertig daga, gif hit hysecild wære; gif hit þonne mædencild wære . . . hundehtatig daga.*

§1775. The adversative relationship can be expressed by other words or combinations, including *ÆCHom* i. 84. 33 *Eornostlice, BlHom* 17. 7 *hwæþre,*[11] *ÆHom* 23. 195 *þeah, BlHom* 215. 2 *þeah hweðre,* and *ÆCHom* ii. 352. 22 *swa ðeah.* We find *ac swa ðeah hwæðere* in *ÆCHom* ii. 364. 25.

§1776. On the uses of *furþum, huru, soðlice,* and *witodlice,* see BT(S), s.vv. On *forþon* '?however', see §§3081-4.

c. 'Not only . . . but (also)'

§1777. The combination *þæt an*—see *ÆGram* 241. 7 *dumtaxat, þæt an, tantummodo, þæt an*—appears occasionally in positive sentences in the sense 'only', e.g. *GD* 180. 20 *gedo me þæt an to are, agif me minne agenne sunu,* Latin *solummodo pietatem in me exhibe,*

---

[11] Glogauer's suggestion (§10) that *hwæðre/hwæðere* in *Dream* 24, *Dream* 57, and elsewhere, equals *forðam* does not compel acceptance—or indeed understanding.

mihique unicum filium redde, and (accompanied by *þæt*) *GD* 176. 17
. . . *sum wif . . . þa weallode wide dæges 7 nihtes geond þa muntas
7 þa dena, geond þa wudas 7 þa feldas, 7 þæt an þæt heo þær
gereste þær hi seo werignes genydde þæt heo restan sceolde*, Latin
. . . *ibique tantummodo quiescebat*. . . . It is, however, more common in negative clauses in the sense 'not only'.

§1778. According to Rissanen (1967*b*, p. 410), 'no really independent adverb "only" seems to have existed in OE'. *An* was not so
used, except as the result of mechanical glossing; see Rissanen 1967*b*,
pp. 424-5. The exact status of *ana* is uncertain; see §§536-44. The
phrase *for an* appears four times as a translation of *tantum(modo)*
and five times in senses varying from 'only' to 'indeed'; see Rissanen
1967*a*, pp. 183-4, and 1967*b*, p. 420.

§1779. Rissanen (1967*a*, p. 177) speaks of 'the stereotyped use of
þæt an in the sense "that alone", "only", in translations from Latin'
and believes (1967*a*, p. 182) that 'the OE constructions *(ne) þæt an
þæt* and *(ne) þæt an* were literary in character'—for *(ne)* read *(na/
nalles)*; see §1784—and 'were probably never accepted in the
spoken language'. In support of this view, he notes (1967*a*, p. 182)
that 'both expressions are recorded mainly in texts which are influenced by Latin'; for details of its distribution, see the table given by
Rissanen 1967*b*, p. 423. There are no examples in the *Chronicle* or
the Charters and only one in the poetry, viz.

Met 11. 48   Nis hit no þæt an   þæt swa eaðe mæg
                 wiðerweard gesceaft   wesan ætgædere
                 symbel geferan,   ac hit is sellicre
                 þæt hiora ænig ne mæg   butan oþrum bion.

This goes back to *Bo* 49. 14 *no þ an þæt . . . ac*, a construction which
is not represented in the Latin original (metre 8 of book ii) but
which occurs elsewhere in *Boethius* in imitation of Latin *non solum
. . . sed (etiam)*.

§1780. This—and Rissanen's subsequent discussion—would seem
to suggest that the constructions were in origin calques. But elsewhere (1967*b*, p. 422), Rissanen gives some support to the theory
that 'OE *þæt an* "only" goes back to a primitive Germanic usage' and
'was no longer current in the spoken language in the OE period'. I
shall return to this point later.

§1781. The combination *þæt an* seems to vary in meaning and function. Sometimes it can be explained as a purely mechanical gloss for

solum—*an* representing as it were the sense of *solus* and *þæt* certifying that it was neuter. (For strong forms of *an* in the sense 'alone',
see §§541-2.) Thus, in *Coll* 116 *Forþam leofre ys me gefon fisc
þæne ic mæg ofslean, þonne fisc þe na þæt an me ac eac swylce mine
geferan mid anum slege he mæg besencean oþþe gecwylman*, Latin
*Quia carius est mihi capere piscem quem possum occidere, quam
illum qui non solum me sed etiam meos socios uno ictu potest mer-
gere aut mortificare*, it is possible that *þæt an* for *solum* is just as
mechanical a gloss as *he mæg* for *potest*, where the position of *he*
certifies that it is tautologic and not part of the relative pronoun;
see §§2185-7. But there are situations in which *þæt an* can be otherwise explained. In *GD* 253. 24 *7 þæt an hi magon in me gewyrcan,
þæt heom God selfa on me alyfeð*, Latin *tantum in me possunt
facere, quantum ipse permiserit*, and *Bede* 440. 4 . . . *7 nales ðæt an
þæt ic on weorce 7 on worde 7 eac hwylce þæt ic on þæm med-
mestan geðohte gesyngode* . . . , Latin . . . *non solum quae opere uel
uerbo, sed etiam quae tenuissima cogitatione peccaui* . . . , the sequence *þæt an* . . . *þæt* can be translated either 'only what' or 'that
only which'. The translation 'that only, that alone'—as opposed to
'only'—is almost obligatory in examples like *GD* 180. 20 *gedo me
þæt an to are, agif me minne agenne sunu*, Latin *Solummodo pietatem in me exhibe, mihique unicum filium redde*, and *ÆCHom* i.
12. 11 *ac hi æfre beoð ymbe þæt an, hu hi magon Gode gehyrsumian
and him gecweman*; see further Rissanen 1967a, pp. 171-3. It is a
possible alternative to 'only' in examples like *Bo* 26. 17, *GD(C)*
161. 28 *nis hit na ræded, þæt he gebæde in heora cwale, ac þæt an,
þæt he þreade þa scylde þe hi þurhtugon, CP* 94. 16, and *CP* 162. 1
*7 ne sceal he no ðæt an bodigean his hieremonnum hu ða synna him
wiðwinnað ac he him sceal eac cyðan mid hwelcum cræftum he him
wiðstondan mæg*, Latin *Sed quia non solum debent innotescere,
qualiter vitia impugnent, verum etiam quomodo custoditae nos virtutes roborent* . . . ; here *þæt an*—like *þis an* in *GD* 216. 24 . . .
þonne cweðað ge þis an þæt drihten selfa . . . *his sylfes weorc geworhte*—may anticipate the noun clause. In *BenR* 31. 2 . . . *gif
munuc inne on his heortan eaðmod bið and na þæt an, ac eac swylce
utene mid his lichoman eaðmodnesse* . . . *gebycnige*, Latin . . . *si non
solum corpore sed et corde, LS* 1 *(CCCC* 198, f. 386ᵛ) . . . *for þon ne
forlæte ic þe æfre. Ac ic þe gefreolsige of ealra frecennesse 7 nalæs
þæt an ac simle ealle þine breþere*, and similar examples quoted by
Rissanen (1967a, pp. 181-2), *þæt an* follows the clause to which
'only' refers. Here we can translate *þæt an* as 'that only, that alone'
referring back to a preceding word or phrase or can take it as a use of
þæt an 'only' in contexts where in MnE we should have to repeat

that word or phrase—'not only in his heart' and 'not only you'. Is
the latter explanation possible? Rissanen (1967*a*, p. 180, and 1967*b*,
p. 417) thinks that *þæt* in *þæt an* is sometimes at any rate pleonastic. Erickson (1973, pp. 77 and 85) speaks of 'an apparently func-
tionless demonstrative "that" ' and of 'an otiose pronoun *þæt*'. I
would suggest that this is an anachronistic view and that *þæt an* became an accepted gloss for 'only'; one can almost hear the excited
discussion (or the drowsy exposition) in the monastic schools. That
this artificial usage could exist alongside the idiomatic *þæt an* 'that
only, that alone' is no harder to believe than the well-known fact
that *for þam þe* can mean 'because' and 'for those who' or that
for þæm/ðæm can have the vastly different functions it has in *Or*
17. 35 *Swiþost he for ðider, toeacan þæs landes sceawunge, for
þæm horschwælum, for ðæm hie habbað swiþe æþele ban on hiora
toþum.* . . .

§1782. I turn now to OE methods of rendering 'not only . . . but
(also)'. We see OE coping with this pattern from its own resources in
those situations in which exclusive *an* can be used in apposition with
a noun or pronoun, e.g. *GD* 190. 20 *7 he sona aweg adraf nalæs na
þa nunnan ane ac ealle þa wif*, Latin *non solum eandem Dei famulam,
sed omnem quoque feminam . . . expulit*, *BlHom* 13. 5 *Ne herede
heo hine no mid wordum anum, ac mid ealre heortan*, *BlHom* 13. 6
*Lufian we hine nu 7 his noman mycclian næs no on gesundum
þingum anum, ac eac swylce on wiðerweardum þingum . . .* , and
ÆCHom ii. 368. 6 *Ne bidde ic na for ðisum anum, ac eac swilce for
ða ðe on me gelyfað þurh heora word*. For further examples see
Rissanen 1967*b*, pp. 411–12. The order of the juxtaposed elements
may be reversed, e.g. *CP* 41. 21 . . . *oft him gebyreð ðæt hie weorðað
bereafod ðara giefa ðe him God for monigra monna ðingum geaf,
næs for hiera anra*, Latin . . . *ipsa sibi plerumque dona adimunt, quae
non pro se tantum modo, sed etiam pro aliis acceperunt*, and the first
may be repeated to give emphasis, e.g. *BenR* 130. 11 *Hyrsumnesse
god and duguð þæt is a ðam abbode to gegearwienne . . . na him
anum, ac eac swylce ælc broðor oþrum estelice hyrsumige*.

§1783. But, as Rissanen (1967*a*, p. 178) points out, the translators
were in a quandary when they came to dealing with sentences in
which there was 'no noun or pronoun to which *an* could be attached
without altering the sense of the Latin original'. Here, I believe, they
used *þæt an* 'only' as what—despite Erickson (1973, p. 77)—I still
regard as 'a conventional correlative'. I would suggest that originally
this took two basic forms. When the juxtaposed elements in OE were

words or phrases, the original pattern—which I shall call (*a*)—was *na/nalles þæt an . . . ac (. . .) (eac) (swylce* or the like). When they were clauses, the conj. *þæt* was added to the first element and sometimes to the second to form what I shall call pattern (*b*). These two patterns were later confused; see §§1790-1.

§1784. Ælfric uses *na* for the initial negative (*ÆCHom* ii. 468. 18). In *Orosius*, we find *nales* (*Or* 30. 27), while the OE *Boethius* fluctuates between *no* (*Bo* 49. 14), *nalles* (*Bo* 33. 28), and *nalles no* (*Bo* 113. 31). An accompanying verb may be negated, e.g. *Bo* 121. 6 *. . . þonne nis hit no ðæt an þ hi nyllað þisse þinre race gelefan*, or not, e.g. *ÆCHom* ii. 468. 18 *He hine geseah na þæt an mid licham- licere gesihðe. . . .* The negative *na/nalles* is not obligatory if the verb is negated, e.g. *BlHom* 137. 10 *Nis hit þæt an þæt him anum þæm apostolum wære geofu seald.* The second element can be *ac* alone (*Or* 128. 33), *ac eac* (*Or* 40. 4), *ac eac swelce* (*Or* 30. 28), *ac swylce eac* (*Bede* 290. 10), *ac þeah* (*Bo* 50. 18), *7 eac* (*Bede* 440. 5), *ac . . . eac* (*BlHom* 85. 15), and so on.

§1785. We find the pattern without the conj. *þæt*—pattern (*a*)— in sentences in which exclusive *an* could not be used in apposition. The juxtaposed elements can be adjectives or participles, e.g. *GD* 213. 6 *nalles þæt an cwic, ac eac swylce æghwæs he wæs ansund*, Latin *non solum vivus sed etiam incolomis*, and *GD* 304. 13 *nales þæt an geseonde ac eac swylce fandiende 7 prowiende*, Latin . . . *non solum videndo, sed etiam experiendo patiatur* (v.l. *patitur*); finite verbs, e.g. *Bede* 228. 23 *Ac to gelyfanne is, þæt swylc deað þæs æfestan monnes nales þæt an swylce synne adilgode ac swylce eac his geearnunge toycte*, Latin *Sed credendum est, quia talis mors uiri religiosi non solum talem culpam diluerit, sed etiam meritum eius auxerit*, and *CP* 101. 21, where *no ðæt an . . . ac* translates Latin *non solum . . . sed* but the juxtaposition of the repeated *wiln(i)að* misrepresents the juxtaposition in the Latin; infinitives, e.g. *CP* 163. 1 *7 ne sceal he no ðæt an bodigan his hieremonnum hu ða synna him wiðwinnað, ac he him sceal eac cyðan mid hwelcum cræftum he him wiðstondan mæg*, Latin *sed quia non solum debent innotescere quali- ter vitia impugnent, verum etiam quomodo custoditae nos virtutes roborent*, where the translator repeats the subject and finite verb;[12] adverbs, e.g. *ChrodR* 1. 61. 14 *na þæt an æne oððe tuwa oððe þriwa ac gelome*, Latin *primo . . . non solum et secundo ac tertio, quinimmo crebrius*; noun phrases, e.g. *Bede* 212. 12 *þa geseah he nales þæt an*

---

[12] When the juxtaposed elements are infinitives, the tendency is to repeat the subject and the finite verb.

þa maran gefean þara eadigra gasta, ac swylce eac þa mæstan gefleoto 7 gewinn þara wærgra gasta, Latin . . . *uidit non solum maiora beatorum gaudia sed et maxima malignorum spirituum certamina;* and case and prepositional phrases, e.g. *Bede* 484. 20 . . . *nales þæt an hwilce dæge ac eac swilce hwilce cyne compes oþþe under hwilcum deman hie middangeard oferswiðden* . . . , Latin . . . *non solum qua die uerum etiam quo genere certaminis uel sub quo iudice mundum uicerint.* . . . It seems perverse to deny that in these examples the translators used *na/nalles þæt an* as the direct equivalent of *non solum.*

§1786. They frequently did the same when they could have used exclusive *an* in apposition with the first of two juxtaposed nouns or pronouns, e.g. *Bede* 290. 10 *nales þæt an oðerra leoma ac swylce eac þære tungan onstyrenesse biswicade,* Latin *non solum membrorum ceterorum sed et linguae motu caruit, Coll* 117 *na þæt an me ac eac swylce mine geferan,* Latin *non solum me sed etiam meos socios, ApT* 10. 19 *na þæt an his find ac eac swilce his frind,* Latin *non tantum inimici sed etiam amici,* and *ArPrGl* 1 *JJC* 92. 9 *na for þissum þæt an ic bidde fæder ac for þam þe to gelyfenne syndon,* Latin *non pro his tantum rogo pater sed pro eis qui credituri sunt.* Similar examples occur in texts perhaps not so closely influenced by the Latin, e.g. *ÆCHom* ii. 468. 18 and *ÆCHom* ii. 468. 21 *Folga me na þæt an on fotlicum gange ac eac swilce on godra ðeawa geefenlæcunge.*[13] These and other examples cited by Rissanen (1967a, pp. 180-1, and 1967b, pp. 417-18) confirm that pattern (a)—*na/nalles þæt an . . . ac (. . .) (eac) (swylce)*—became an accepted expression in OE prose for 'not only . . . but also' when words (including finite verbs) and phrases were juxtaposed. Indeed, it sometimes appears in sentences containing exclusive *an*, e.g. *BenR* 111. 5 *Na þæt an be munecum anum is þis to healdenne, ac eac swylce be arwyrðum canonicum,* Latin *non solum autem monachum sed etiam* . . . , and *HomS* 36. 155 *7 þa godcundan hadas syndon gewanode for hyra sylfra gewyrhtum 7 geearnungum 7 nalas þæt an Godes þeowas ane syndon ac eac swylce cyningas 7 bisceopas 7 ealdormen* . . . , and (as in MnE) is sometimes misplaced, e.g. *GD* 332. 5 . . . *ic eom . . . genyded þæt ic nalæs þæt an forhtige þa synne þe ic on me sylfum ongyte, ac eac swylce þa ic on me na ne ongyte,* or misused, e.g. *LS* 34. 86.

§1787. We turn now to pattern (b). Here I shall distinguish (b1) *na/ nalles þæt an þæt . . . ac (. . .) (eac) (swylce),* in which *þæt* is not

---

[13] Erickson (1973, pp. 82-3) mistakenly (I believe) uses the existence of examples like these as an argument in favour of his 'complementation' theory.

added to the second element, from pattern (*b*2), in which it is. As I
see it, these were the original patterns when two clauses or some elements in two fully expressed clauses were contrasted. OE examples
of pattern (*b*2) include *CP* 95. 15 *Se lareow sceal . . . foreðencean na
ðæt an ðætte he ðurh hine nan woh ne bodige, ac eac ðæt he nane
ðinga ðæt ryht to suiðe . . . ne bodige* (where the verb is repeated and
the objects are juxtaposed); *Bo* 49. 13 *7 þeah hi beoð swa geþwæra
þætte no þ an þæt hi magon geferan beon, ac þy furðor þ heora
furðum nan buton oðrum beon ne mæg* (where the verb is repeated
in a different number and the complements are juxtaposed); and *Bo*
13. 25 *Eac þ wæs swiðe micel pleoh þ ðu swa wenan sceoldes; næs
hit no þ an þ þu on ungemetlicum ungesælðum wære, ac eac þ þu
fulneah mid ealle forwurde* and *BenR* 14. 5 . . . *þæt is, þæt he sceal
rædan and racian oþra manna saulum, sumum mid olæcungum,
sumum mid þreaungum, sumum mid lare, no þæt an, þæt he sceole
symle gyrnan, þæt he him þæs befæsten eowdes nanne æfwirdlan
næbbe, ac eac þæt he mæge gefeon be þæm wæstme heora godra
weorca* (in both of which the only element common to both clauses
is the subject). In these sentences, the two noun clauses introduced
by *þæt* can be explained as being in apposition with *þæt an* 'that
alone/only (. . .) that (conj.)'. *CP* 193. 20 . . . *ne sceal he no ðæt an
don ðæt he ana wacie, ac he sceal eac his friend wreccan*, though not
an example of pattern (*b*), neatly illustrates the construction I have
in mind.

§1788. Pattern (*b*1), without the second conjunction, is not a MnE
pattern. But such non-repetition of *þæt* is idiomatic in OE, not only
in contrasts between true and false causes (§3182), in the second of
two clauses compared by means of *þonne* (§§3228-9 and 3232-5),
and elsewhere, but also in the idiom under discussion here, e.g. *ApT*
14. 14 *Hlaford Apolloni, gif ðu þissere hungrigan ceasterwaru gehelp-
est, na þæt an þæt we willað þinne fleam bediglian, ac eac swilce,
gif þe neod gebirað, we willað campian for ðinre hælo*, Latin *Domine
Apolloni, Si esurienti civitati subveneris, non solum fugam tuam cela-
bimus sed, si necesse fuerit, pro salute tua dimicabimus*. We can say
that, in sentences like this, two noun clauses—one introduced by
þæt, one with idiomatic non-expression of *þæt*—are in apposition
with *þæt an* 'that alone'. Rissanen (1967*b*, pp. 413-14) cites many
similar examples. They include (with the same subject repeated)
BlHom 85. 15 *7 nis no þæt an þæt he him ure witu ondræde, ac he
wile eac oþre of urum bendum alesan*; (with the same subject and
verb repeated, as in *ApT* 14. 14 above) *Bo* 121. 6 *Ac gif ic me wende
to þises folces dome, þonne nis hit no ðæt an þ hi nyllað þisse þinre*

race gelefan, ac hi hit nyllað furðum geheran and *ÆCHom* i. 140. 9
*na þæt an þæt he wolde mann beon for us . . . ac eac swylce he
wolde beon þearfa for us*; (with the same subject not repeated) *Bede*
132. 1 *Dyde se cyning swa hit ær cweden wæs; nales þæt an þæt he
ðone wreccan to cwale ne gesealde, ac eac swylce him gefultumade
þæt he to rice becwom*; and (with different subjects) *Or* 48. 32 *Ac
siþþan Crist geboren wæs, þe ealles middangeardes is sibb 7 frið,
nales þæt an þæt men hie mehten aliesan mid feo of þeowdome, ac
eac þeoda him betweonum buton þeowdome gesibbsume wæron.*
The same subject appears twice in the first clause in *Or* 30. 26 and in
GD(H) 109. 22, where it also appears in the second clause. Pattern
(*b*) is seen in part in *VercHom* 3. 87 *7 næs na þæt an þæt he ðam
apostolum sylfum þas lare bebead*, where there is no second clause.

§1789. We have already seen in §1786 that exclusive *an* appears
tautologically in examples of pattern (*a*). It is also found in sentences
containing pattern (*b*), e.g. *BlHom* 129. 1 and *BlHom* 137. 10 *Nis
hit þæt an þæt him anum þæm apostolum wære geofu seald ac eac
ðonne eallum manna cynne forgifnes wæs seald ealra synna.*

§1790. This is not the only evidence that the translators were not
completely at ease when dealing with *non solum . . . sed etiam*. As
Rissanen (1967*b*, p. 413) points out, the use of type (*b*) patterns like
Bede 110. 24 *Forðon nales þæt aan þæt he Cristes geleafan onfon ne
wolde, ac swylce eac unalyfedre forlegenesse 7 egeslicre wæs be-
smiten, swa þæt he eode to his fæder wife* to render Latin *Siquidem
non solum fidem Christi recipere noluerat, sed et fornicatione pol-
lutus est . . . ita ut uxorem patris haberet*, while satisfactorily retaining the sense of the original, 'made the translation syntactically
heavy' and 'the expression most emphatic'. A further pointer is that
patterns (*a*) and (*b*) themselves became confused. This is easy to
understand; they were not completely natural idioms (see §§1796–9)
and the fact that *þæt* was optional after *ac (. . .) (eac) (swylce)* in
pattern (*b*) could have led to the feeling that it was optional after
þæt an and so to its intrusion into places in which pattern (*a*) was
appropriate. Thus pattern (*b*1)—with *þæt an þæt*—is out of place
in *Bede* 48. 29 *7 nalæs þæt an þæt ðas ðing dyden weoruldmen, ac
eac swylce þæt Drihtnes eowde 7 his hyrdas* (where the juxtaposition is between subjects); in *Bede* 302. 23 *Ond þa Wilferð biscop in
þære þeode godcunde lare lærde, nales þæt an þætte from yrmðum
ecre niðrunge, ac swylce eac from þæm manfullan wæle hwilwendlicre
forwyrde generede* (where two prepositional phrases are juxtaposed);
and in *Bede* 474. 10 *Wæs þæt wunderlico stihtung þære godcundan*

*foreseonesse, þætte se arwyrða wer nales þæt an þæt he in Eastran
forðferde of þissum middangearde to Gode Fæder, ac eac swylce
mid þy þætte þy dæge Eastran mærsode wæron, þe hie næfre ær
gewunedon in þæm stowum weorþade beon* (where the juxtaposition
is between a temporal phrase and a temporal clause). But if the verb
had been repeated, as in *Bo* 26. 17 *Hwæt we gewislice witon unrim
ðara monna þe þa ecan gesælða sohton nalles þurh þ an þ hi wilnodon ðæs lichomlican deaðes, ac eac manegra sarlicre wita hi ge-
wilnodon wið þæm ecan life*, or varied, as in *GD(H)* 125. 18 . . .
*forþam þe þa toglidenan stanas þæs wages na þæt an þæt hi his limu
tocwysdon, ac hi eac swylce mid ealle his ban tobrysdon*, pattern
(*b*1) or (*b*2) would have been in order. Rissanen (1967*a*, pp. 178-80,
and 1967*b*, pp. 415-16) discusses these and similar examples in more
detail, comparing them where possible with their Latin originals.

§1791. It is interesting to note that in this last example, *GD(H)* 125.
18, the omission of *þæt hi* after *na þæt an* and of *hi* after *ac* would
give pattern (*a*), with two verbs juxtaposed—this can be compared
with the combinations of a noun clause and an adjective clause discussed in §1980—but that, if we wished to repeat the subject in
Bede 228. 23 *Ac to gelyfanne is þæt swylc deað þæs æfestan monnes
nales þæt an swylce synne adilgode, ac swylce eac his geearnunge
toycte*, where pattern (*a*) appears and is rightly reproduced in Miller's
translation 'But we must believe that such a death of a pious man not
only did away with such sin, but also increased his merits', we should
have to use pattern (*b*), which would appear in MnE as 'But we must
believe not only that such a death . . . , but also that it . . .'. Further
examples of confusion arising from the repetition or non-repetition
of subject and/or verb will be found in Rissanen 1967*a* and *b, passim.*

§1792. Erickson (1973, *passim*) argues that the pattern seen in *Bo*
13. 25 and *Bo* 121. 6 (§§1787 and 1788 respectively) is 'embedded'
in examples such as *ApT* 14. 14 and those like it quoted or referred
to in §1788—though (according to him) it needs *hit wæs* after *ac*
in *Bo* 13. 25 and *hit is þæt* after *ac* in *Bo* 121. 6 for completeness—
and that the patterns we actually find are the result of 'deletion' of
'embedded material' such as *nis/næs hit* and *hit is/wæs* from 'under-
lying structures' of this sort.[14]

---

[14] Erickson's article makes no mention of either Rissanen 1967*a* or 1967*b*, in which (as
far as I can see) Rissanen anticipated him in everything of value he had to offer. It reveals an
imperfect knowledge of OE syntax, e.g. the statements that *na* and *næfre* 'can be found
only when a negative verb also occurs' (1973, p. 78) and that 'the appearance of *na* pre-
supposes a negative verb' (1973, p. 83)—this erroneous idea is fundamental to his theory—

§1793. In *Bo* 13. 25 (§1787) and *Bo* 121. 6 (§1788), we can agree that the 'surface structure' does conform to the patterns which Erickson would see embedded. But there are examples in which this is not true. Thus Erickson (1973, p. 81) expands his version of *VercHom*, f. 119ᵛ, *forþan we witon þæt be urum geþohtum we sceolan beon demede fram gode and nales þæt an þæt he ure lichoman sceawað ac eac swylce ure geþohtas* by inserting *nis hit* before *nales* and *hit is* after *ac*. [15] In my opinion this is impossible; *nales þæt an* logically belongs with *ure lichoman* 'not only our bodies' (cf. *GD* 332. 5 (§1786)— 'not only those sins'), the second *þæt* clause with its juxtaposed objects is parallel to the first, and both are the objects of *we witon*— which is the right thing to insert, if we must insert. Erickson (1973, p. 79) similarly inserts *nis hit* before *na* and *hit is* after *ac* in his version of *VercHom*, f. 113ᵛ, *ðonne ys þæt twelfte mægen þære sawle þæt man hæbbe Godes soðan lufe 7 ure nehstena 7 na þæt an þæt we lufien þa þe ure frynd synt for Gode ac eac þæt we for Godes lufe 7 for his ege lufion þa þe ure fynd syndon*. At first glance, this seems possible. But a moment's reflection shows that it is possible only because *þæt twelfte mægen* is neuter. If the homilist had written *seo twelfte cyst*, we would have to read *seo* for *hit*; here too the *þæt* clauses are parallel. It is not difficult to find examples outside Erickson's which do not allow the insertion of *hit is*, e.g. *GD(C)* 161. 28 (§1781) and *ÆCHom* i. 140. 7 *Se Ælmihtiga Godes Sunu wæs swiðe gemyndig ure neoda on eallum ðingum; na þæt an þæt he wolde mann beon for us, ðaða he God wæs, ac eac swylce he wolde beon þearfa for us, ðaða he rice wæs*, where—if anything is to be supplied —it would be respectively *hit is ræded* and *he wæs gemyndig*.

§1794. But in these examples and in similar ones involving juxtaposed clauses, it is unnecessary to insert anything. As the Latin shows, we do not need to insert *hit is* or to take the *þæt* clauses as the objects of *selle* in *CP* 81. 24 *Eac him mon scolde sellan ða breosð ðæs neates toeacan ðæm boge, ðæt is ðæt he geleornige ðæt he selle Gode his agne breosð, ðæt is his inngeðonc; nalles na ðæt an ðæt he on his breostum ðence ðætte ryht sie, ac eac ða spone ðe his ðeawa giemað to ðæm illcan mid his godum biesenum*, Latin *Et non solum pectore quae recta sunt cogitet, sed spectatores suos ad sublimia*

and the apparent belief (1973, p. 84 and p. 88 fn. 23) that the rules for verb position in OE are the same as those in MnE. And, as Erickson himself has to admit (1973, p. 81), it presents a theory which cannot explain all the examples.

[15] I do not quarrel with his insertion of *þæt he sceawað* after *eac swylce*. But positive *hit is* would in fact do just as well before *nales* here and in other examples in which Erickson inserts *nis hit*, if either were possible. As I point out (§1792 fn. 14), he mistakenly believes that any sentence containing a negative element must contain *ne* + verb.

armo operis invitet . . . , and OE *na þæt an þæt* . . . *ac eac swilce*, which (as we have already seen) is one OE equivalent of MnE 'not only . . . but also' and Latin *non solum . . . sed etiam*, provides all the information needed in *ApT* 14. 14 (§1788). Erickson's 'embedded structures' are in my opinion irrelevant here. They are irrelevant too in examples like *ÆCHom* i. 32. 21 *Se nama gedafenað þam heofon-lican Cyninge Criste, þe on his timan acenned wæs, seðe his heofon-lice rice geyhte, and ðone hryre, þe se feallenda deofol on engla werode gewanode, mid menniscum gecynde eft gefylde. Na þæt an þæt he ðone lyre anfealdlice gefylde, ac eac swylce micclum geihte* and in *ÆCHom* i. 56. 5 *Witodlice þurh ðines feondes lufe þu bist Godes freond; and na þæt an þæt ðu his freond sy, ac eac swilce þu bist Godes bearn, þurh ða rædene þæt þu þinne feond lufige*, in which Ælfric himself repeats material for emphasis. In the latter, for example, he could have written ☆*Witodlice þu bist na þæt an Godes freond þurh ðines feondes lufe ac eac swilce Godes bearn þurh ða rædene þæt þu þinne feond lufige*, using pattern (*a*).

§1795. Further arguments against Erickson's theory are the fact that the examples which it cannot explain (1973, p. 81) present no difficulty to the simple-minded, and the fact that some of his expla-nations are so complicated as to be comical; consider what he does to *ÆCHom* ii. 468. 18 (1973, pp. 82-3) and to the examples from the OE gloss to Ælfric's *Colloquy*, where the glossator was merely put-ting OE words above the Latin ones (1973, pp. 83-4).

§1796. The origin of *þæt an* 'only' has been discussed by Rissanen (1967*b*, pp. 421-7). In his view 'the occurrence of the adverb *þat-ain(ei)* "only" in Gothic and *þat eina* in ON seems to support the theory that OE *þæt an* "only" goes back to a primitive Germanic usage' (1967*b*, p. 422). I am inclined to see this as one possible strand in a complicated pattern. The direct ON equivalent of *þæt an* is *þat eitt*; see CV, s.v. *einn*, adj., A. III. β. The direct OE equivalent of *þat eina* is *þæt ana*, which occurs in the Lindisfarne Gospels; see Rissanen 1967*a*, p. 177 fn. 2. In both OE and ON, it is not clear whether the forms in -*a* are weak neuter or adverbial; see §540 and CV, loc. cit. Here then we can see what Rissanen (1967*b*, p. 424) describes as 'the construction inherited from primitive Germanic . . . the adverbial *þæt an* which corresponds syntactically with the Gothic and OIcel. types'. But he also says that 'it seems that the phrase *þæt an* was no longer current in the spoken language in the OE period' (1967*b*, p. 422) and that 'this type had perhaps become obsolete and the OE translators were uncertain about its syntactic "correctness" ' (1967*b*, p. 424).

✕ §1797. Two other strands—both already discussed—can be detected. First, there is the fact that *þæt an (. . .) þæt* can often be literally translated 'that alone/only (. . .) that (conj.)' (§1787). Here there is no question of any element being tautologic or otiose or of the expression being an obsolete and not understood heritage of PrGmc. It is good natural OE.

§1798. Second, there is the possibility that—at least in Gothic and OE—the usage could in places be a calque, a mechanical glossing device: *ni þatainei* for *οὐ μόνον* and *na þæt an* for *non solum* (§1785).

§1799. The OE evidence, I think, allows us to say *either* that these three strands were all present in OE *þæt an, or* that the PrGmc. usage —if it ever existed (and here further work on ON usage is called for) —had died out in OE and that *þæt an* 'only' combined the other two strands only. This is not the place to adjudicate. It is, however, clear that the construction was not always understood by translators and/or scribes; consider the variant readings and different versions at *BenR* 2. 1, *GD* 138. 1, and *VercHom* 3. 90, and see Rissanen 1967*b*, pp. 424–7.

d. Adversative phrases involving a negative + þy/þon + a comparative

§1800. Perhaps the best-known of these combinations is *no ðy ær*, which occurs six times in *Beowulf* and (as far as I am aware) nowhere else in the prose or the poetry. In all six examples it can be translated literally—'no sooner for that/because of that'—or 'yet (. . .) not'. In four of them—*Beo* 753 *he on mode wearð ‖ forht on ferhðe; no þy ær fram meahte, Beo* 1502, 2081, and 2373—the reference of *þy* is to a preceding principal clause—'He was afraid; he could not get away faster because/though he was afraid'—and *no þy ær* can be described as a co-ordinating adversative conjunction.[16] In the remaining two—*Beo* 2160 and

Beo 2462   Swa Wedra helm
           æfter Herebealde   heortan sorge
           weallinde wæg;   wihte ne meahte
           on ðam feorhbonan   fæghðe gebetan;
           no ðy ær he þone heaðorinc   hatian ne meahte
           laðum dædum,   þeah him leof ne wæs—

the reference is to a following concessive clause introduced by *þeah*; here *no þy ær* is correlative with *þeah*.

[16] Nader (*Ang.* 11 (1888–9), 451) suggests that in *Beo* 2373 *no ðy ær* is a subordinating conjunction. But see Schücking, §53.

§1801. But are these the true explanations? It is interesting that Small, in his treatment of examples like

Beo 2275   He gesecean sceall
                hord on hrusan,   þær he hæðen gold
                wara wintrum frod;   ne byð him wihte ðy sel,

(Small 1926 and 1930, *passim*), did not mention *no þy ær*. For, as it is explained above, it presents an exception to his dictum that 'the form *the* immediately before the comparative . . . always . . . refers to a condition or object previously named or understood, and is functionally a true case of comparison, meaning not "by that", but "than that" or "than before" '. The reader is referred to my discussion on this point in §§3243-50, but must carry out his own tests. It is my opinion, however, that if Small had considered these six examples, he would have had no difficulty in making the first four conform: *Beo* 754 '. . . no sooner than before [he became afraid]'; *Beo* 1502 '. . . no sooner than before [she seized him]'; *Beo* 2081 '. . . no sooner than before [he ate Hondscio]'; and *Beo* 2373 '. . . no sooner than before [Hygelac was dead]'. But I find it hard to detect any 'condition or object previously named or understood' in the remaining two (*Beo* 2160 and 2462) and cannot fit in either 'no sooner than before' or 'no sooner than that'. These last two passages have in common the fact that *no þy ær* . . . could be correlative with the following *þeah*. But while 'no sooner for that' or 'yet (. . .) not' reads quite naturally in *Beo* 2160, the presence of lines 2464b-65 makes it awkward in line 2466, for lines 2464b-65 and 2466-7 are parallel, not contrasted. We achieve some sort of consistency if we accept that *no þy ær*, recorded only in *Beowulf*, means 'no sooner for that' or 'yet (. . .) not'. But, since it may be a personal idiosyncrasy of one poet, we can say either that it presents an exception to Small's rule or that the *Beowulf* poet used it appropriately in the first four, inappropriately in the last two, examples discussed above.

§1802. The closest parallel in the poetry to the phrase *no þy ær* is found in

Dan 753   No þæt þin aldor   æfre wolde
                godes goldfatu   in gylp beran,
                ne ðy hraðor hremde,   ðeah ðe here brohte
                Israela gestreon   in his æhte geweald,

where the negative element is supplied by the co-ordinating conj. *ne* and the phrase is correlative with *þeah*. The ASPR *Concordance* reveals that only twelve more examples of the combination negative + *þy/þon* + comparative occur in the poetic corpus.

§1803. *No ðy hraðor*, with its variants, seems to be the most common of these patterns in the prose, where it occurs correlatively with *þeah*, e.g. *Bo* 5. 30 *7 þeah hwa gegaderie ealle þas andweardan god, þonne ne mæg he no þe raðor beon swa welig swa he wolde*, *Solil* 17. 18 *nese, ne do ic hi na ðe raðor gelice, þeah ic hy togædere nemne*, and *ÆCHom* i. 224. 5 *þeah man deadne mannan mid reafe bewinde, ne arist þæt reaf na ðe hraðor eft mid þam men*. In these and similar examples cited by Burnham (p. 32), the literal translation 'no sooner for that' is at best strained.

§1804. Phrases involving *ær* without a correlative conj. *þeah* occur occasionally in the prose, e.g. *Bede* 400. 19 *7 ic ða word geherde 7 nohte ðon ær þære ærninge blon*, Latin *Et ego audiens nihilominus coeptis institi uetitis* (where Miller has both worlds by translating 'And I heard the words and yet did not any the sooner stop racing') and *GD* 152. 16 *witudlice þa nunnan nahte þy ær næron onwænde fram heora þam ærran unþeawum*.

§1805. The phrase *nohte þon læs* is sometimes used correlatively with *þeah* as a translation of Latin *nihilominus*, e.g. *Bede* 412. 5 *7 þeh ðe he gewiss geworden wære þurh ða ætewnesse þære gesihðe, nohte þon læs he his fore gegearwede mid ðæm gemyndgadum broðrum*, Latin *Ipso uero, tametsi certus est factus de uisione, nihilominus temtauit iter dispositum cum fratribus memoratis incipere*. Other combinations include *na þy læs*, e.g. *Or* 228. 31 *7 he þeh siþþan na þy læs ne hergeade on Romane*, and *nohte ðon ma*, e.g. *CP* 163. 18 *Ond suaðeah nu, ðeah se lareow ðis eall smealice 7 openlice gecyðe, ne forstent hit him noht, ne him nohte ðon ma ne beoð forlætna his agna synna*. . . . See further Burnham, pp. 31–2, and Quirk, pp. 79–80.

4. CONJUNCTIONS MEANING '(EITHER ...) OR'

a. Oþþe 'or'

§1806. The etymology and variant forms of *oþþe* are discussed, with bibliographical references, by Nusser (pp. 1 ff.).

§1807. In the pattern A *oþþe* B, *oþþe* means 'or'. The choice offered may be between two subjects, e.g. *ÆCHom* i. 242. 4 *ac se hyra oððe se medgylda ne gedyrstlæcð* . . . (where, following the usual practice in English, the verb is singular); two objects, e.g. *ÆCHom* i. 138. 24 *Ure yfelan geðohtas oððe weorc we sceolon alysan mid fif scyllingum*;

two complements, e.g. *ÆCHom* i. 344. 5 *Seraphim sind gecwedene byrnende oððe onælende*; two phrases, e.g. *ÆCHom* i. 354. 1 . . . *ðurh martyrdom oððe þurh oðre halige geearnunga*; or two principal or subordinate clauses with the same or different subjects, e.g. *ÆC Hom* i. 186. 10 *ne bið na genoh þæt we þæs tacnes wundrian oþþe þurh þæt God herian, ÆCHom* i. 112. 5, *ÆCHom* i. 246. 5 *Hi axodon hine hwæt he wære oððe hu he faran wolde, ÆCHom* i. 60. 26, and *ÆLS* 14. 63 *oferswyð his drycræft oððe he þe oferswyðe.*

§1808. In the pattern A *oððe* B *oððe* C . . . , *oððe* also means 'or', e.g. *ÆCHom* i. 318. 28 . . . *wæron hi Ebreisce oððe Grecisce oððe Romanisce oððe Egyptisce oððe swa hwilcere ðeode swa hi wæron, ÆCHom* i. 250. 7, *ÆCHom* ii. 590. 9 . . . *treowa oþþe streaw oððe ceaf,* and *ÆCHom* ii. 590. 23 . . . *and þæt man cyde buton steore intingan, oþþe oðrum olæce mid leasre lyffetunge, oþþe man biddendne ðearfan misræce, oððe ær mæle hine gereordige, oððe ungemetlice gæmnige.* Like MnE 'or', *oþþe* need not be expressed between every alternative, e.g. *ÆLS* 36. 378 . . . *se þe lufað on eorþan his eorðlican fæder modor oððe bearn oþþe wif ofer god* . . . and *ÆCHom* ii. 588. 23 *Swa hwa swa getimbrað, ofer ðisum grundwealle, gold, oððe seolfor, oððe deorwurðe stanas, oþþe treowa, streaw oþþe ceaf, anes gehwilces mannes weorc bið swutel.*

§1809. The relationship between the alternatives varies. Sometimes they are mutually exclusive, e.g. in *ÆCHom* i. 318. 28 (§1808) (if they are Hebrews, they cannot be Greeks or Romans or Egyptians or anything else), *ÆLS* 14. 63 (§1807) (only one can win), and *Beo* 1490 *ic me mid Hruntinge* || *dom gewyrce, oþðe mec dead nimeð!* Sometimes we are merely offered two synonyms, near synonyms, or variants, e.g. *Solil* 66. 31 . . . *þonne wat ic swiðe lytel oððe nanwiht,* three sentences in §1807—*ÆCHom* i. 242. 4, i. 138. 24, and i. 344. 5—and *Beo* 2252 *Nah, hwa sweord wege* || *oððe feormie fæted wæge.* Two opposites may be linked by *oþþe* to make a whole, e.g. *LS* 34. 277 *eall þæt he ær agylte læsse oþþe mare, GenA* 1047 *feorran oððe nean* 'anywhere', and *ChristC* 1052 *ær oþþe sið* 'ever'. In some of these at any rate *ond* would have done as well. It is hard, for example, to follow BTS (s.v. *oþþe* I(1)) in believing that alternatives are really presented in the last two examples. See further §1710. We can follow Nusser (pp. 16 ff.) in distinguishing the former as 'strong' ('starke') alternatives and the latter as 'weak' ('schwache'). The latter concept embraces what Schücking (§48) called the 'varying' ('variierende') *oððe*. I do not agree with Nusser (p. 18) that this function is restricted to subordinate clauses in *Beowulf;ÆLS* 21. 145

and geond fif monþas feawa daga wæron þæt ðær næron gehælede huru ðry untrume, hwilon fif oððe syx, seofon oððe eahta, tyn oððe twelf, syxtyne oððe eahtatyne seems to exemplify it, as well as examples like *ÆCHom* i. 242. 4 (§1807). But he rightly points out that the line cannot always be drawn with certainty.

b. Oþþe ... oþþe 'either ... or'

§1810. The pattern *oþþe* A *oþþe* B (*oþþe* C) means 'either A or B (or C)'. Clause elements are contrasted in *ÆCHom* i. 6. 35 ... *gif ic nolde oðrum mannum cyðan, oððe þurh tungan oððe þurh gewritu, þa godspellican soþfæstnysse, ÆHom* 18. 27 *Gif hwa bið on þære tide ymbe hys tilunge, oððe on his huse, oððe on hys æcere* ..., and (with the contrasted elements in apposition with a preceding element) *ÆCHom* i. 532. 8 ... *ond onfon edlean ealra ure dæda, oððe wununge mid Gode for godum geearnungum, oþþe hellewite mid deofle for mandædum* and *ÆCHom* ii. 328. 12 ... *þæt ælc ðær underfo swa hwæt swa he on lichaman adreah, oððe god oþþe yfel.* Three alternatives are presented in *ÆCHom* ii. 146. 31 *on nanum heolstrum heofenan, oþþe eorðan, oþþe sæ ðriddan,* three in *ÆHom* 30. 99, and four in *ÆLS* 37. 133 ... *þa ðe wæron forscyldegode oþþe þurh manslihte oððe þurh morþdæda oððe þurh drycræft oððe dyrne forliger.*

§1811. Various patterns occur when clause elements are contrasted. The subject can occur before the first *oþþe* and be repeated after the second *oþþe,* e.g. *Bede(B)* 246. 32 *7 ealle Scottas ... oðþe heora treowe sealdon þ hi riht mid him healdan woldon oððe hi ham to heora eþle comon,* Latin *ut ... Scotti omnes ... aut his manus darent aut suam redirent ad patriam.* It can occur after both the first and second *oþþe,* e.g. *ÆLS* 17. 200 *þæt getimað þonne swa for twam intingum oþþe god swa þreað ure ðwyrlican dæda oððe he ure afandað on ðære frecednysse. ÆCHom* i. 592. 12 *þa sarnyssa on ðyssere worulde oððe hi sind leohte and acumenlice, oððe hi sind swære* ..., with the subject expressed three times, is strictly speaking anacoluthic. But the same subject need not be repeated, e.g. *ÆLS* 13. 58 *oððe he mid geameleaste huru us gebysgað oþþe mid smeagungum smealice us hremð* (where *he* follows the first *oððe*), *ÆLS* 28. 109 ... *buton us drihten Crist oþþe his leoht forgife oþþe us læde onweg* (where *Crist* precedes the first *oððe*), and *Bede* 482. 2 *me symble swete 7 wynsum wæs, ðæt ic oþþe leornode oþþe lærde oððe write* (where we have three alternatives). Nusser, to whom I owe some of the foregoing, offers more examples (pp. 32–4).

§1812. In most of the sentences quoted above, the alternatives are 'strong' rather than 'weak' (§1809). But some of those involving clause elements may show the 'weak' or 'varying' alternative, e.g. *ÆCHom* i. 6. 35 (? 'in any way') and *ÆHom* 18. 27 (? 'anywhere').

c. Ahwæþer/auþer/aþor (. . .) oþþe . . . oþþe *'either . . . or'*

§1813. The first element, which also appears as *awþer, aþer*, and *owþer*, gives eMnE *outher*. The disjunctive sense originally belonged to it and was taken over by *æghwæþer/ægþer*, MnE 'either'; see further *OED*, s.vv., and Nusser, pp. 35–9 and 44. The confusion must have begun early; in *Bo* 108. 13, for example, MS *C* has *awðer . . . oþþe . . . oþþe*, MS *B ægþer . . . oþþe . . . oþþe.*

§1814. The main point to be established about this combination in OE is the status of this first element. The problem arises even in the early prose. Frequently *auþer* or its variant is clearly pronominal. Thus in *CP* 23. 7 . . . *ðylæs hine auðer oððe his lif oððe his lar to upahebbe*, it is the subject of *upahebbe*. In *CP* 445. 36 *Eala, wære he auðer, oððe hat oððe ceald*, it is the complement. In *Or* 290. 21 *þa oferhogode he þæt he him aðer dyde, oþþe wiernde oþþe tigþade*, *Bo* 137. 21 *Ælc wyrd is nyt þara þe auðer deð, oððe lærð, oððe wyrcð*, and *BenR* 71. 15 . . . *gif he aðor dyde, oðþe ofergimde, oðþe forgeat, oðþe tobræc ænig þing on þære hyrsumnesse þe he onhyrsumode* . . . (where there are three variants), it is the neuter object of *dyde/deð*. In such examples *oþþe . . . oþþe* means 'either . . . or' and presents variants which are in apposition with the pron. *auþer*. In all these examples, *oþþe* intervenes—usually (but not always) immediately—between the pronoun and the first variant.

§1815. But there are examples in which *auþer* cannot be parsed as a pronoun. They include *Or* 18. 25 *Eal þæt his man aþer oððe ettan oððe erian mæg þæt lið wið ða sæ, Bo* 108. 12 *7 ða dysegan nanwuht nellað onginnan ðæs ðe hi him awðer mægen to wenan oððe lofes oððe leana, Bo* 146. 25 . . . *oððe þæs gewittes ænig dæl þe him forgifen is auþer oððe hrorum neatum oððe unhrorum*, and (continuing *BenR* 71. 15 in §1814) *BenR* 71. 17 . . . *aþer oðþe on kycenan oþþe on hederne oðþe on mynstres bæcerne oþþe on wyrtune oðþe on ænigum oðerum cræfte* . . . (where there are five variants).[17]

---

[17] Nusser (p. 42) rightly sees that, in this and similar examples, *aþer* cannot be a pronoun. His reason for describing it as 'ganz konjunktional' ['entirely conjunctional'] is that there are more than two variants. That this is a false line of argument is demonstrated by *BenR* 71. 15 (§1814), for there—as Nusser, rightly but inconsistently, says (p. 43)—'*aðor* ist offenbar als Pronomen anzusehen' ['*aðor* is clearly to be regarded as a pronoun'].

A later example involving two clauses is *LawCn* 1020. 18 . . . *7 nan man swa dyrstig ne sy, þæt he aðor oððe cypinge wyrce oððe ænig mot gesæce þam halgan dæge.* In these examples too *oþþe* intervenes —usually (but not always) immediately—between *aþor* and the first variant. The exact status of *aþor* in these examples is a problem of terminology. It is not a pronoun. It is not on all fours with MnE 'either' in 'either . . . or', where we call 'either' an adverb or a conjunction; see *OED*, s.v. It clearly represents a transitional stage.

§ 1816. These examples cited above involve both clause elements and clauses. Most of them and of the examples quoted by Nusser (pp. 39–44) seem to me to present 'strong' alternatives (§ 1809). Here I disagree with Nusser (p. 45). But, as we have already seen, the dividing line is not always clear and there are examples of the 'weak' and the 'varying' functions, e.g. *BenR* 71. 17 (§ 1815) and *Solil* 38. 3 *Hwæt wille ic ma cwæðan aðer oððe be mete oððe be drince oððe be baðe oððe be welan oððe be wyrðscype oððe be ænigum worldlusta?*

d. Ahwæþer/auþer/aþor . . . oþþe ?'*either* . . . *or*'

§ 1817. The transition referred to in § 1815 is carried a stage further in OE. *OED* (s.v. other, *conj.* and *adv.*[2]) states that 'there is no trace in OE of *awðer* (*aðer*) or *oðer* taking the place of the first member of the alternative *oððe* . . . *oððe* . . .'. This requires qualification; there is, as Nusser (pp. 43–4) points out, a *trace*, for the combination *aþor* . . . *oþþe* does occur with no *oþþe* to support the *aþor*. In most of the examples *aþor* is to be parsed as a pronoun. These include *Solil* 58. 25 . . . *oððe, gyf heo æallu æce wæren, hweðer heora enig æfter ðisse weorlde on ðam æcan lyfe awðer dide, wexse*[18] *oððe wanede, HomU* 34. 200. 2 *he forbyt ælcum men aðor to bycganne oððe to syllanne,*

Creed 41   Ic haligne gast   hihte beluce,
                     emne swa ecne   swa is aðor gecweden,
                     fæder oððe freobearn,   folca gereordum,

and (with *auðer* following the alternatives)

Met 20. 41   Næs æror ðe   ænegu gesceaft
                        þe auht oððe nauht   auðer worhte. . . .

---

[18] MS *werse.* Carnicelli's *wexse* (85. 14) seems preferable to Endter's *weoxe.* Carnicelli rejects Jost's insertion of *oððe* before *wexse* for reasons which suggest that he was unaware of the fact that it would be normal. But, on the evidence of the other examples presented here, it need not be inserted.

But one can see the beginnings of 'either . . . or' in *HomU* 34. 200. 2 above. In examples like *HomU* 47. 303. 12 *hit is forboden on halgum bocum swyþe deope, þæt nan cristen man ne mote his ælmessan ahwæþer behatan oððe to bringan, ne his wæccan ne his broces bote secean ahwider, buton to Criste sylfum and to his halgum and to cyrcean*, where *ahwæþer* cannot be a pronoun, we are almost compelled to parse it as a conjunction.

e.   Oþer (. . .) oþþe . . . oþþe *'either . . . or'*

§1818. In this combination, as in that discussed in §§1813-16, *oþþe* intervenes—usually (but not always) immediately—between the pronoun and the first variant. In many examples, *oþer* is a pronoun, e.g. *Or* 68. 27 . . . *7 eac gesworen hæfdon ðæt hie oþer forleosan woldon, oþþe hira agen lif oþþe Porsennes þæs cyninges* and *Or* 44. 20 . . . *oð heora wif him sendon ærendracan æfter, 7 him sædon þæt hie oðer dyden, oðþe ham comen oððe hie him woldon oðerra wera ceosan*. In both of these, we have acc. neut. sg. *oþer* as object of a verb with two variants in apposition with it. In the first example, *lif* is unexpressed in the second alternative. In the second, there is strictly a lack of logic, because the *hie* who are the subject of *dyden* and *comen* are not the subject of *woldon*.

§1819. I have found no examples of this combination in which *oþer* cannot possibly be parsed as a pronoun. But there are some in which it seems to me unlikely to be one, e.g. *Or* 44. 8 *7 him untweogendlice secgan het þæt hie oðer sceolden, oððe ðæt lond æt him alesan, oþþe he hie wolde mid gefeohte fordon 7 forherigan* and *Or* 120. 30 . . . *þæt hie siþþan oþer sceoldon, oþþe for metelieste heora lif alætan, oþþe Somnitum an hand gan*, in both of which we would need [*don*] to govern *oðer* if it were a pronoun object. These examples probably represent a transitional stage similar to that noted with *aþor (. . .) oððe . . . oððe* in §1815. This stage is clearly seen in *Or* 138. 31 . . . *to tacne þæt hie oþer woldon oððe ealle libban oþþe ealle licgean*, where *oþer* can be taken as object of *woldon* or with the first *oððe* as a conjunction *oþer . . . oððe* 'either'. This is, of course, not on all fours with MnE 'either . . . or'; see again §1815.

§1820. The combination *oþer þara (. . .) oþþe . . . oþþe* sometimes occurs in *Orosius*. Here *oþer* is a pronoun, either the subject, e.g. *Or* 136. 19 *oðer þara is, oððe hie hit nyton, oððe hi hit witan nyllað*; the complement, e.g. *Or* 294. 25 *ac ælc com oþer þara, oþþe on hie selfe, oþþe on þa eorþan*; or the object, e.g. *Or* 114. 23 *7 þæt he oðer ðara dyde, oþþe hie gesemde, oþþe him gefultumade þæt hi hie oferwinnan mehten.* I have noted no examples in which *oþer* is not a pronoun.

§1821. The same cannot be said of the combination *oþer twega (. . .) oþþe . . . oþþe,* which appears most often in *Boethius,* but is not restricted to it; see further Wülfing, i, §359b, Nusser, pp. 44-6, and Bately, *Ang.* 88 (1970), 450. In examples like *Bo* 53. 19 *þa wilniað oðer twega, oððe him selfe ricsian, oððe hi to ðæra ricena freondscipe gepiodan* and *Bo* 137. 8 . . . *þ hio oðer twega do, oððe hine þreatige . . . oððe him leanige, oðer* is clearly a pronoun object. In *Bo* 63. 29 *þonne þa rican beoð oðer twega, oððe on ælðeode oððe on hiora agenre gecyððe,* we can parse *oðer* as a pronoun complement or take *oðer twega oððe* as a conjunction 'either'. In *Bo* 26. 1 *Hwæt, ælc þara þe þas woruldgesælþa hæfð oþer twega oððe he wat þ hi him fromwearde beoð oððe he hit þonne nat* and *Bo* 30. 14 *Gif ðu heore mare selest, oþer twega oððe hit þe derað, oððe hit ðe þeah unwynsum bið, oððe ungetæse, oððe frecenlic, eall þ þu nu ofer gemet dest,* only the latter possibility seems to present itself, unless we supply [*hit is*] before *oþer.* Such instances are at least transitional.

§1822. The examples quoted above involve both clause elements and clauses. Most of them involve 'strong' alternatives (§1809). But, as we see from *Bo* 29. 3 *þeah hi Godes gesceaftes sien, ne sint hi no wið eow to metanne, forðæm þe oþer twega oððe hit nan god nis for eow selfe, oððe þeah forlytel god wið eow to metane,* this is not always true.

§1823. Nusser (p. 46) cites two examples from the poetry in which *oðer twega* unsupported by *oððe* introduces two variants separated by *oððe,* viz.

WaldA 8   Nu is se dæg cumen
                    þæt ðu scealt aninga   oðer twega
                    lif forleosan   oððe langne dom
                    agan mid eldum

and

Mald 207   hi woldon þa ealle   oðer twega,
                    lif forlætan   oððe leofne gewrecan.

In these, *oðer* can clearly be taken as a pronoun.

§1824. All the evidence then suggests that *oþer* was not used alone as a conjunction in OE; see BTC, s.v.

f. Swa . . . swa *'either . . . or'*

§1825. The elements contrasted by *swa . . . swa* can play an independent part in the sentence, e.g. *BlHom* 101. 29 below and *ÆCHom* ii. 406. 12 . . . *þa gesceadwisan men ðe andgit habbað and be agenum willan wyrcað swa god swa yfel*, where *god* and *yfel* are objects, or be in apposition with another element, e.g. *BlHom* 23. 6 below, *ÆLS* 11. 32 *þa cwæð se dema þæt hi oþer þæra dydon, swa hi þam godum geoffrodon and arwurðnysse hæfdon swa hi ða offrunge forsawon and gescynde wurdon*, *ÆCHom* i. 602. 27 *and se gemænelica dom dæghwomlice genealæhð, on ðam underfehð anra gehwilc be ðam ðe he geearnode on lichaman, swa god swa yfel*, and *ÆGram* 260. 12 *siue uir siue mulier swa hwæþer swa hit sy, swa wer swa wif*. The combination is frequently followed by a *swa* clause, e.g. *BlHom* 101. 29 *7 anra manna gehwylc sceal forþberan swa god swa yfel swa he ær dyde*,[19] *BlHom* 23. 6 *7 nu eft sceolon oþerne eþel secan, swa wite swa wuldor, swe we nu geearnian willaþ*, and (after six *swa . . . swa* patterns)

ChristB 589 . . .   þæt nu monna gehwylc
      cwic þendan her wunað, geceosan mot
      swa helle hienþu swa heofones mærþu,
      swa þæt leohte leoht swa ða laþan niht,
      swa þrymmes þræce swa þystra wræce,
      swa mid dryhten dream swa mid deoflum hream,
      swa wite mid wraþum swa wuldor mid arum,
      swa lif swa dead, swa him leofre bið
      to gefremmanne, þenden flæsc ond gæst
      wuniað in worulde.

We have a single *swa* 'or' in

Jul 87   Dem þu hi to deaþe, gif þe gedafen þince,
      swa to life læt, swa þe leofre sy

and four alternatives—'either . . . or . . . or . . . or' in *Or* 106. 12 . . . *on swelce healfe swelce hie þonne winnende beon woldan, swa suþ, swa norþ, swa east, swa west. . . .* On this construction, see further Nusser, pp. 34-5, Glogauer, §25, and Ericson 1932, pp. 58-9.

§1826. When used with *swa* (. . . *swa*), *swa hwæþer swa/swæþer* sometimes shades from a pronominal use 'either . . . or . . . , whichever . . .' into the conjunctional use 'whether . . . or'; see BT(S), s.v. *swæðer* II and *HomU* 34. 201. 10 (§2363 fn. 76). Wülfing (i, §351) says that in *Bo* 101. 6 *Forðæm ðu ne þearft nauht swiþe wundrian*

---

[19] Morris translates *swa . . . swa* here as 'both . . . and'. But see Ericson 1932, pp. 59-60.

ðeah we spyrien æfter ðæm ðe we ongunnon, swa mid læs worda swa mid ma, swæðer we hit gereccan magon, swæðer is completely set or fixed ('erstarrt') as a conjunction. Sedgefield glosses it as a pronoun 'whichever (of two)', but translates it '. . . with less or more words, as we can show it forth'. Burnham (p. 38) claims that 'swæðer may become adverbial, the construction otherwise remaining the same, as in' *LawIIIEg* 7. 1 *Gyf he þonne ne mæge, gewylde man hine swaðor man mæge, swa cwicne swa deadne.* There is room for more work here when the full collections are available.

g. Other words and combinations

§1827. Glogauer (§6) notes that the conj. *ær* sometimes introduces what is in effect the second of two alternatives. He sees a 'potential' function—'it is more likely that . . .'—in

And 1435   Soð þæt gecyðeð
    mænig æt meðle   on þam myclan dæge,
    þæt ðæt geweorðeð,   þæt ðeos wlitige gesceaft,
    heofon ond eorðe,   hreosaþ togadore,
    ær awæged sie   worda ænig
    þe ic þurh minne muð   meðlan onginne

and an 'alternative' function—'rather than . . .'—in

Beo 1368   Ðeah þe hæðstapa   hundum geswenced,
    heorot hornum trum   holtwudu sece,
    feorran geflymed,   ær he feorh seleð,
    aldor on ofre,   ær he in wille,
    hafelan beorgan.

§1828. *Elles* 'else' is used alone to introduce the second of two alternatives, e.g. *ÆCHom* ii. 310. 6 *Beorh ðe, ic bidde, and forlæt ðone biscop, elles ðu earma scealt yfelum deaðe sweltan.* It also occurs with *oþþe*, e.g. *LawVIIIAtr* 26 *Gif mæssepreost manslaga wurðe oððe elles manweorc to swiðe gewurce . . .*, and with *þe*, e.g. *LS* 34. 742 *. . . þæt ic þurh nan þincg ne mæg gecnawan hwæðer þys sy Ephesa byrig þe elles ænig oþer.* See further Nusser, pp. 24 and 27-8.

§1829. The appearance of *or* in Thorpe's version of *ÆCHom* ii. 318. 17 *. . . for ðone soðan God or for sumne broðer* is the result of error; the manuscript has *oððe*.

§1830. Two alternatives may be presented by the use of correlative pronouns, e.g. *ÆCHom* i. 256. 20 *Oðer is þæt hwa rice beo gif his*

*yldran him æhta becwædon; oðer is, gif hwa þurh gytsunge rice ge-
wurðe,* or correlative adverbs, e.g. *ÆCHom* i. 184. 2 *Hwilon we beoð
hale, hwilon untrume.* See further §§1863-7. A negative alternative
can be implied by the use of *oðer* 'one of two' without a correlative,
e.g. *ÆCHom* i. 576. 2 *For mandædum wæron þa twegen sceaðan ge-
witnode ðe mid Criste hangodon, ac heora oðer mid micclum geleafan
gebæd hine to Criste*; cf. MnE 'One prayed [but the other did not]'.

§1831. On disjunctive clauses involving *sam . . . sam* or the element
order VS, see §§3435 and 3443-8 respectively.[20] On disjunctive
questions, see §§1662 and 1868-75.

5. NEGATIVE CONNECTIVES

a. Introductory remarks[21]

§1832. I must first remind the reader that it is essential—in Campbell's words (*RES* 15 (1964), 193 fn. 1)—'to distinguish *ne*, conjunction, from *ne*, negative adverb; except directly before a verb, *ne*
is always the former'. It is also important to note that the verb in a
clause introduced by conj. *ne* need not be itself negated by adv. *ne*,
e.g. *Bede* 160. 16 *Ferde he geond eall ge þurh mynsterstowe ge þurh
folcstowe, ne he on horses hricge cuman wolde, BlHom* 223. 31 *Ðis
wæs soðlice eadig wer, ne wæs æfre facen ne inwid on his heortan ne
he nænigne man unrihtlice fordemde ne nænigum yfel wið yfele
geald,* and

Beo 168 no he þone gifstol gretan moste,
       maþðum for Metode, ne his myne wisse.

This is also true of sentences containing negative pronouns and adverbs; see §§1607 and 1627-9.

§1833. Combinations of one positive and one negative clause or of
two (or more) negative clauses can occur in asyndetic parataxis, e.g.
ÆCHom i. 10. 14 *Her sindon nigon engla werod: hi nabbað nænne
lichaman* and *Exod* 20. 13-15 *Ne sleh ðu. Ne synga ðu. Ne stel ðu,*
or with *ond*, e.g. *ÆCHom* i. 22. 23 *þa wæron þær swa fela gereord*

---

[20] Morris's notion that *oþþe . . . sam* in *BlHom* 53. 17 means 'or . . . or' is wrong. See
BT, s.v. *sam-hwilc.*
[21] In these remarks I am especially indebted to Jespersen (*Neg.*, pp. 103 ff.). All quotations from him which appear here are taken from these pages. Andrew has a good chapter
on 'Negative words and sentences' in *SS* (pp. 62-71). For his comments on *Beowulf*, see the
subject index to *Postscript* (p. 157). Miyabe (*Poetica* (Tokyo), 2 (1974), 25-35) discusses
negative sentences in *Beowulf*. See also Mitchell, in progress (*a*).

swa ðær manna wæron; and heora nan nyste hwæt oðer cwæð and
ÆCHom i. 14. 17 *Nis na gedafenlic þæt þes man ana beo and næbbe
nænne fultum.* [22]

§1834. A positive clause can be followed by a negative one introduced by the conjunction *ne*, e.g. *ÆCHom* i. 580. 16 *Ac God sceawað
þæs mannes heortan, and na his æhta, ne he ne telð hu miccle speda
we on his lacum aspendon* and *ÆCHom* ii. 124. 8 *Efne nu ðis folc is
mid swurde þæs heofonlican graman ofslegen, and gehwilce ænlipige
sind mid færlicum slihte aweste, ne seo adl ðam deaðe ne forestæpð,
ac ge geseoð þæt se sylfa deað þære adle yldinge forhradað.* These
two and some similar examples are quoted by Andrew (*SS*, §77). He
says: 'Normally, however, a *ne*-clause after an affirmative sentence
has a particular shade of meaning which may be rendered by an
adverbial phrase introduced by "without".' So he translates the
second example above '. . . each one individually is destroyed by sudden stroke without any preceding illness . . .'. His 'however' applies
to the first example. I cannot see why; it could be translated 'God
looks on the heart of man . . . without reckoning the greatness of the
riches we spend in gifts to Him . . .'. But 'and . . . not' will often do
as well. (The examples from *Beowulf* offered by Andrew in *SS*, §78,
do not all conform to this pattern.) A positive clause follows a negative clause in many of the examples involving *ne . . . ac* which are discussed in §§1752–72.

§1835. As Jespersen remarks, when the ideas in two negative clauses
'have at least one element in common, it is usual to join them more
closely by means of some negative connective'. He lists seven possible
arrangements and notes various simplifications which may occur
when three or more ideas are involved; some of these occur in OE
and are treated below. These seven types involve negative conjunctions (*nc*[1] and *nc*[2]), and/or conjunctions (*c*), or negative adverbs or
pronouns (*n*): (1) *nc*[1] *A nc*[1] *B* 'Nor seeks nor finds he mortal blisses';
(2) *nc*[1] *A nc*[2] *B* 'He neither loves nor hates her'; (3) *nc A c B* 'I neither
saw or desired to see any people'; (4) *A nc B* 'He moved nor spoke';
(5) *n A nc B* 'The royal Dane does not haunt his own murderer,
neither does Arthur' and 'Never attaching herself much to us, neither
us to her'; (6) *n A nc*[1] *B nc*[2] 'I can know nothing nor themselves
neither'; and (7) *n A n B nc* 'I'll not spend beyond it. I'll ne're run in
debt neither'. (The examples are Jespersen's.) The tautologic negatives

[22] *CP* 371. 24 is on all fours with this example. Bacquet's remarks about it (p. 178) are
completely misconceived.

of OE add more possibilities, but they are treated as the equivalent of *n*.[23]

§1836. The elements represented by *A* and *B* in these formulae may be words, e.g. *ÆCHom* i. 352. 6 *ne dranc he wines drenc ne nanes gemencgedes wætan ne gebrowenes* and *ÆCHom* i. 2. 22 *and me ofhreow þæt hi ne cupon ne næfdon þa godspellican lare*; phrases of various kinds, e.g. *ÆCHom* i. 44. 26 *ac hi ne mihton his wisdome wiðstandan ne ðam Halgum Gaste* and *ÆCHom* i. 212. 29 . . . *seðe nele for nanre ehtnysse bugan fram Criste, ne for swurde, ne for fyre, ne for wætere, ne for hungre, ne for bendum*; or clauses, e.g. *ÆCHom* i. 56. 21 *Ne beo se rihtwisa gymeleas on his anginne ne se yfela ortruwige ðurh his unrihtwisnysse*. Whether we have two clauses or one in examples like *ÆCHom* i. 10. 2 *Ne mæg nan gesceaft fulfremedlice smeagan ne understandan ymbe God* is a terminological question which could also be asked of examples like *ÆCHom* i. 352. 6 and i. 44. 26 (both quoted above); such non-repetition of a verb is idiomatic in all periods of English and needs no further discussion. In the sections which follow we are most concerned with examples involving two or more clauses, but examples of other patterns are cited when necessary.

§1837. Jespersen makes a vital point when he remarks: 'The connectives are often termed disjunctive, like (*either* . . .) *or*, but are really different and juxtapose rather than indicate an alternative; this is shown in the formation of Lat. *neque* . . . *neque*, which are negative forms of *que* . . . *que* "both . . . and" '; see further BT(S), s.v. *ne*, and *OED*, s.vv. 'ne', 'neither', and 'nor'. This is neatly illustrated by examples like *ÆCHom* i. 80. 33 *Næs he æðelboren, ne him naht to þam cynecynne ne gebyrode* and *ÆCHom* i. 272. 8 *On ðam ecan life ne bið nan costnung ne nan yfel; forði ðær ne cymð nan deofol ne nan yfel mann*. The variation in Thorpe's translation of the latter may seem without point: 'In the life eternal there will be no temptation and no evil; for there will come no devil nor evil man who may trouble or hurt us.' But both arrangements are idiomatic not only in MnE, but also in OE, as *ÆCHom* i. 154. 13 *Nu sind we ute belocene fram ðam heofenlican leohte, and we ne magon on ðissum life þæs ecan leohtes brucan; ne we his na mare ne cunnon buton swa micel swa we ðurh Cristes lare on bocum rædað* shows.

---

[23] Nusser (pp. 86–8, 108–9, and elsewhere) fails to make the fundamental distinction between *n* and *nc*. All his OE examples conform to one of the patterns listed above. His 'negative Rückbeziehung' ['retrospective negative'] (p. 86) seems to equal Jespersen's (4), while his 'negative Wechselbeziehung' ['interrelating negative'] (p. 108) seems to embrace Jespersen's (1) and (2). His classification can be safely disregarded.

§1838. The conj. *ne* may be reinforced by *eac*, e.g. *ÆCHom* i. 98. 26 *nis ðeah þæs forðy ðæs geares ord, ne eac on ðisum dæge nis mid nanum gesceade; furðon*, e.g. *ÆCHom* ii. 144. 9 *He seow ða hwæte on beswuncenum lande, ac hit to wæstme aspringan ne moste, ne furðon mid gærse growende næs*; and the like; see Nusser, pp. 102-3.

§1839. According to Andrew (*SS*, §74), 'we can lay down the general rule that *ne* never introduces a principal sentence unless it is followed immediately by the verb'. Andrew's point is that only adv. *ne* can introduce a principal sentence and that it would be wrong to print *ÆCHom* i. 56. 21 *Ne beo se rihtwisa gymeleas on his anginne ne se yfela ortruwige ðurh his unrihtwisnysse* as two independent sentences introduced by *ne*. We can restate his position thus: when the conj. *ne* 'nor' introduces the *second* of two alternative or juxtaposed clauses, it cannot begin a new sentence. Andrew did not ask whether the conj. *ne* 'neither' in the combination *ne . . . ne* 'neither . . . nor' could introduce a new sentence; on this see §1843.

§1840. There are certainly clauses with initial *ne* in both prose and poetry whose co-ordination with a previous clause is obscured by the fact that the editor has punctuated. *Ne, : ne*, or *; ne*. Repunctuation is not always necessary; consider *ÆHom* 1. 251 (§1843). But it is often attractive and sometimes indeed inescapable; consider *Solil* 67. 10 . . . *þu hy ne myht ful sweotole geseon swilce swilc heo is, forðam þu ne eart ðer þær heo is. Ne þin lichaman þær beon ne mæg . . .* , *ÆCHom* ii. 94. 29-96. 1, *ÆCHom* i. 12. 15 *and hi næfre ne gebigde ne ne nydde mid nanum þingum to þam yfelan ræde; ne næfre se yfela ræd ne com of Godes geþance, ac com of þæs deofles, swa swa we ær cwædon*, and

Beo 506   Eart þu se Beowulf,   se þe wið Brecan wunne,
                 on sidne sæ   ymb sund flite,
                 ðær git for wlence   wada cunnedon
                 ond for dolgilpe   on deop wæter
                 aldrum neþdon?   Ne inc ænig mon,
                 ne leof ne lað,   belean mihte
                 sorhfullne sið,   þa git on sund reon;[24]

for further examples see *SS*, §74, and Suter, §40.

§1841. Exceptions such as *Matt(WSCp)* 21. 27 *ne ic eow ne secge . . .* , Latin *nec ergo dico uobis*, and others quoted by Andrew (*SS*,

---

[24] Andrew's indecision about how to explain the following three and a half lines *Beo* 513-16a—see *SS*, §26, and *Postscript*, §21—does not reduce the attractiveness of his notion that the clause beginning *ne inc* should be part of Unferth's question; see *SS*, §78. It must, however, be said that not all the examples cited by Andrew in that section are of the same kind.

§§ 75-6) can be explained as slavish renderings of the Latin, though this will not do for examples like *PPs* 118. 10 *ne þu huru me* || *fram þinum bebodum feor adrife*, Latin *ne repellas me a mandatis tuis*. But there are more principal clauses with conj. *ne* at their head which do not contain the second of two alternative or juxtaposed propositions and cannot be made co-ordinate with a previous clause, e.g. *Bo* 25. 2 *Ne nanwuht ne bið yfel ær mon wene þ hit yfel sie . . . , Bo* 106. 18 *Gif ðu ðonne hwone gesihst ðe mæg don þ þ he don wile, ne ðe ðonne nauht ne tweoð þ se hæbbe anwald* (cf. *Bo* 106. 20 *Ne tweoð me ðæs nauht), ÆCHom* ii. 230. 29 *We menn beoð mid synnum acennede: ne we ne beoð be agenum dihte acennede, ne we ne lybbað swa lange swa us lyst, ne we swa ne sweltað swa we sylfe geceosað* 'neither . . . nor . . . nor', and

ChristC 1316   Ne þæt ænig mæg   oþrum gesecgan
                  mid hu micle elne   æghwylc wille
                  þurh ealle list   lifes tiligan. . . .

I suspect that full collections will reveal more examples. But even these suggest that we are not bound to accept Andrew's view that *ne* does not begin a new sentence in examples like *Bo* 76. 33, *ÆCHom* i. 6. 16, *Beo* 862, *Beo* 1071, and *Beo* 2922; see *SS*, § 78. There is room for further work here.

b. The patterns

§1842. We turn now to a consideration of the seven patterns (already described in § 1835) by which, according to Jespersen, two negative ideas can be connected. I have not found examples of all of them in OE. But an eighth—*n A c B*—is exemplified in § 1852. The most common seem to be pattern (5) and the ancestor of pattern (2) described below.

§1843. On pattern (1)—*nc*[1] *A nc*[1] *B*—Jespersen writes:

In the old Germanic languages we had correspondingly Got. *nih . . . nih*, and (with a different word) OHG (Tatian) *noh . . . noh*; but in *ne . . . ne* as found in ON, OS and OE the written form at any rate does not show us whether we have this type (*ne* corresponding to Got. *nih*) or the unconnected use of two simple negatives, corresponding to Got. *ni . . . ni.*

This is too sweeping for OE. I have no doubt that we have this pattern (1) in examples in which two words other than finite verbs, two phrases, or two clauses, are joined by *ne . . . ne* in mid-sentence, e.g. *GD(C)* 257. 23 *ða ymb middeniht utan, þæs þe he sylfa sæde me, ne he eallunga ne slep ne he fullmedomlice wacian mihte* (MS *O* omits the second *ne*, which is of course the adverb), *BlHom* 25. 31 *nis þær ege ne geflit ne yrre ne nænig wiþerweardnes, ÆCHom* i. 248. 34 *forðan ðe nan man nære wyrðe ne þæs geleafan ne ðæs ecan lifes . . .* , and *ÆHom* 6. 219 *. . . næfð he his næfre forgyfenysse, ne on ðissere worulde, ne on ðære toweardan.* All these examples contain the usual tautologic negation, but it will be noted that the finite verbs are not always negated by adv. *ne*; see § 1832. I also have no doubt that we have in OE examples in which a principal clause introduced by conj. *ne* is followed by another clause similarly introduced. Some of these are clearly due to direct imitation of a Latin original, e.g. *BenR* 74. 22 *Ne nan broðor wið operne ne þeode, ne mid his geþeodrædenne ne lette on unþæslicum timan,* Latin *Neque frater ad fratrem jungatur horis incompetentibus, ÆGram* 259. 18 *ne lingua nec manus oculiue peccent, ne tunge ne handa oðða eagan syngion, ÆGram* 260. 5 *nec laudo nec uitupero, ne ic ne herige ne ic ne tæle,* and *Num* 23. 25 *Ne ðu hine wyrige, ne ðu hine bletsa,* Latin *Nec maledicas ei, nec benedicas.* Again it will be noted that, while some finite verbs are negated by adv. *ne*, others are not. But my collections contain a few clear examples in which this pattern occurs without direct Latin influence, e.g. *Exod* 12. 9 *Ne ne eton ge of ðam nan ðing hreawes ne mid wætere gesoden* (where the Latin *Non comedetis ex eo crudum quid, nec coctum aqua* calls for *Ne eton*; cf. *ÆCHom* ii. 264. 4 *Ne ete ge of ðam lambe nan ðing hreaw, ne on wætere gesoden*), *Bo* 36. 14 *Ne nan mon ne mæg ðæm gesceadwisan mode gederian, ne him gedon þ hit sie ðæt ðæt hit ne bið* (the Latin has nothing corresponding to this), *ÆCHom* ii. 230. 29 (§ 1841), and

ChristA 78   Ne we soðlice   swylc ne gefrugnan
in ærdagum   æfre gelimpan,
þæt ðu in sundurgiefe   swylce befenge,
ne we þære wyrde   wenan þurfon
toweard in tide.

Again I suspect that there may be more examples. But *ÆHom* i. 251 *Ne furðon ænne sticcan ne ænne stæf we næfdon ne ane oflætan to urum mæssan gode gyf he us ne foresceawode him sylf þæt on ær* is not one. Nor is it an exception to the rule that *ne* not immediately before a verb is a conjunction. Though imperfect, the immediately preceding passage—*ÆHom* 1. 248 *gold 7 seol(for : : : : ne mi)hte nan mann macian to wecgum gyf God ne geworhte þa oran to þam* —is sufficient to show that the initial *ne* is a conjunction introducing a clause co-ordinate with the preceding principal clause. Both are apodoses of rejected or imaginary conditions. So it conforms to Andrew's rule (§ 1839). Nevertheless, I would be inclined to follow

Pope in printing *Ne furðon*. . . . For a comparable situation in MnE, cf. my sentence above beginning 'Nor is it an exception . . .'.

§1844. We can now see that Jespersen's assertion that the written form alone does not reveal unambiguous OE examples of the pattern nc^1 *A* nc^1 *B* is not true when the juxtaposed elements are words *other than finite verbs*, phrases, or clauses. We can also see that in these situations we can distinguish conj. *ne* from adv. *ne* at the beginning of sentences, despite the first clause of Nusser's footnote (p. 109): 'Besonders wenn das erste *ne* an der Spitze eines Satzes steht, aber auch sonst, läßt sich in ae., me. und ne. Beispielen nicht immer ganz sicher entscheiden, ob das erste *ne* nicht neg.-rückbez. Konj. ist.'[25] But the problem noted by Jespersen and Nusser does arise when we consider sentences in which finite verbs are juxtaposed.

✕ §1845. The first *ne* seems to be an adverb in *ÆCHom* i. 320. 14 *He ne hrymde ne he biterwyrde næs ne he sace ne astyrede* (would the conj. *ne* have preceded the first *he*?) and *ÆCHom* i. 572. 2 *La leof, ne geseah ic næfre ða burh, ne ic ðone seað nat* (would the conj. *ne* have produced the order VS?). The contrast between conj. *ne* and adv. *ne* is perfectly illustrated in the last two clauses in *BlHom* 89. 10 *Ac þu Drihten scyld minre iugoþe, 7 min onunwisdomes ne wes þu gemyndig, ne ne ahwyrf þu þine onsyne ne þine mild-heortnesse from me, ne þu ne gecyr on erre from þinre þeowene*; in the sequence *ne ne ahwyrf þu*, we have conj. *ne* followed by adv. *ne*. This sequence is quite common and quite unambiguous, e.g. *CP* 193. 24 *Ne slapige no ðin eage, ne ne hnappigen ðine bræwas* (Millward, p. 32, prints what I regard as an impossible *ne* for *no*[26]), *Lev* 25. 4 *ne saw ðu þonne ne ne rip ne ðinne wingeard ne wyrc*, Latin *agrum non seres et uineam non putabis, Exod* 20. 4–5 *Ne wyrc ðu ðe agrafene godas, Ne ne wurða*, Latin *Non facies tibi sculptile. Non adorabis ea, neque coles, ÆCHom* ii. 40. 16 *He ne wiðerode ongean, ne ne feaht þe swiðor þe lamb deð*, and (with coalescence of adv. *ne*) *ÆCHom* i. 2. 22 *and me ofhreow þæt hi ne cuþon ne næfdon þa godspellican lare*. But what is the function of the first *ne* in *ÆCHom* i. 320. 14 and the last two examples or of the second *ne* in *ÆCHom* ii. 46. 18 *ne deð seo culfre na swa ne leofað heo be nanum deaðe*? Millward (p. 31 fn. 3) assumes 'that a construction is not co-ordinated by *ne* unless *ne* appears twice'. This is not justified, for (as

---

[25] 'Especially when the first *ne* stands at the beginning of a sentence, but also in other situations, it is not always possible to tell for sure in OE, ME, and MnE, examples whether the first *ne* is not a retrospective negative conjunction.'

[26] I would emend *ne* to *na* before *ecan* in *BlHom* 81. 3 *Cuþlice þæt tacnaþ þæt þas lareowas ne sceolan Godes domas nawþer ne na wanian ne ne ecan* and in similar examples.

we have already seen) verbs in negative clauses need not be preceded
by adv. *ne*. We may think (or feel) that the first *ne* in the first three
sentences is the adverb and that—since Millward's assumption is
wrong—Andrew (*SS, §73*) is right when he says that in *ÆCHom* ii.
46. 18 'the second *ne* is of course the conjunction'. But we cannot
prove these propositions. In the first three examples the first *ne* may
be a conjunction 'neither'[27] and in the fourth, Millward's view that
we have the adverb may be right: 'The dove does not do so; it does
not live by any death.' Millward is certainly right when she says (p. 31
fn. 3) that 'it cannot be demonstrated that *ne + ne* does not become
simply *ne* when two occurrences of the form appear together'. But it
would require the wisdom of Solomon to decide which remained.
Thus, in *Exod* 22. 28 *Ne tæl ðu, ne wirig ðu þines folces ealdor*,
Latin *Non detrahes et principi populi tui non maledices*, the second
ne would be an adverb if *tæl* is absolute and intransitive (this would
be at least unusual), but would be a conjunction if the object goes
with both verbs; since the construction is imperative, the order VS
is perhaps not as decisive for adv. *ne* as it would be in a statement.
On element order in non-dependent commands introduced by *ne*, see
§§904-10 and 1677-8.

§1846. In the poetry, the problem arises more frequently because
element order is a less reliable test there and/or because of the
phenomena subsumed under Kuhn's Law of Sentence Particles. Typical examples include

Beo 887　　　　　　　　　he under harne stan,
　　　　　æþelinges bearn　　ana geneðde
　　　　　frecne dæde,　　ne wæs him Fitela mid

and

Beo 179　　　　　　　　　helle gemundon
　　　　　in modsefan,　　Metod hie ne cuþon,
　　　　　dæda Demend,　　ne wiston hie Drihten God . . . ;

for more, see Schuchardt, pp. 28 ff.

§1847. The nearest we get in OE to Jespersen's pattern (2)—
nc[1] *A nc*[2] *B*—occurs most commonly in the form *nahwæþer/naðor
ne . . . ne*, e.g. (with two words juxtaposed) *ÆCHom* i. 278. 7 *Se is
Fæder seðe nis naðer ne geboren ne gesceapen fram nanum oðrum*

---

[27] Even if we had *næfre noldon ne ne mihton* in *ÆCHom* i. 12. 8 . . . *swa þæt hi næfre
ne mihton ne noldon syððan fram his willan gebugan*, it would not, I think, disprove this
contention. I can see no reason for denying the *possibility* that conj. *ne* could coalesce with
a verb.

and *ÆCHom* i. 564. 29 . . . *swa þæt nateshwon næs gemet on ðam earde naðor ne hæðen ne Iudeisc* . . . ; (with two phrases) *ÆCHom* i. 404. 22 *ac hi næron his gemyndige, naðor ne ðurh lufe ne þurh ege*; (with a noun and a clause) *ÆCHom* ii. 238. 8 *ac eow eallum nis cuð naðor ne seo getacnung ne hu hit gedon wæs*; and (with two clauses) *Solil* 45. 3 *naðer ne hi þeder gelice eaðe cumað, ne hi þer gelice eaðe ne beoð.* For further examples and variant spellings of *nahwæþer*, see Nusser, pp. 113-16.

§1848. This formula is, of course, the ancestor of the modern pattern (2) 'neither . . . nor'. But it does not exactly conform to it, because the conj. *ne* always immediately follows *nahwæþer/naðor* (cf. *a(w)ðer/oþer* . . . *oþþe* in §§1813-17) and because the exact function of *nahwæþer/naðor* is sometimes in doubt. In examples like *ÆCHom* i. 278. 7 and i. 564. 29 in §1847, *naðor* may be the nominative of a pronoun 'neither (of two)', serving respectively as complement and subject; in that event, we have pattern (1) nc^1 A nc^1 B. We might have a neuter accusative form in examples like *ÆCHom* ii. 38. 6 *ne dranc he naðor ne win ne beor ne ealu ne nan ðæra wætan ðe menn of druncniað*, for *naðor* can mean 'neither of more than two', e.g. *Ch* 427 *and ic bebeodæ on Godæs ælmihtiges naman ðæt nauðær næ sie to ðon geðurstig, ne cyning næ bisceop, ne nanes hades man, þæt þas minæ gife on wændæ oððæ gewanie*, Latin *Necnon et hoc praecipio in nomine omnipotentis dei, quod nullus rex aut episcopus, uel aliquis alius potens, sit tam audax ut huius meae donationis condictum commouere seu confringere praesumat.*

§1849. But there are examples in which *nahwæþer/naðor* cannot be a pronoun. They include *BlHom* 45. 14 . . . *þæt hi þonne ne mihtan nawþer ne him sylfum ne þære heorde þe hi ær Gode healdan sceoldan, nænige gode beon* (*nawþer* cannot be either the object of *mihtan* or the complement of *beon*); *ÆHom* 9. 204 *and [ða Iudeiscan] nabbað nu naðor ne þone Fæder ne hine* (the pronominal form would be *naðorne*); and *ÆCHom* i. 18. 6 . . . *ac God hi gesceop swa bilewite þæt hi ne cuðon nan ðing yfeles, naðor ne on gesihðe ne on spræce ne on weorce* (*naðor* would give no sense read as a pronoun).

§1850. Whether *naþor* in these examples is described as an adverb qualifying *ne* to give a compound conjunction *naþor ne*—in which case we have pattern (2) nc^1 A nc^2 B—or as a conjunction—in which case we have nc^2 nc^1 A nc^1 B^{28}—is a terminological problem.

---

[28] Andrew's attempt (*SS*, §84, and *Postscript*, §99) to prove that *noðer* is not a conjunction can be dismissed. His discussion of *Beo* 2124 overlooks the point made by Jespersen and discussed in §1837.

But it must be noted that OE *naþor* is not a conjunction in the same sense as MnE 'neither', for it is always accompanied by *ne* (or *na*) when it can be translated 'neither'; compare the comments on *a(w)ðer oþþe . . . oþþe* in §1817.

§1851. The combination *naþer na . . . na* occurs in *ChronF* 130. 24 (995) . . . *hi ne brahtan nan gewrit naþer na of þam cinge na of þan folce*; here *na* seems to be a conjunction. But see §1855.

§1852. Pattern (3)—*nc A c B*—appears in OE, e.g. *Beo* 2922 *Ne ic te Sweoðeode sibbe oððe treowe* ‖ *wihte ne wene* and in

JDay ii 256   ne cymð þær sorh ne sar   ne geswenced yld,
             ne þær ænig geswinc   æfre gelimpeð,
             oððe hunger oþþe þurst   oððe heanlic slæp,
             ne bið þær fefur ne adl   ne færlic cwyld,
             nanes liges gebrasl   ne se laðlica cyle.

As Glogauer (§2) points out, the homily based on this poem substitutes *ne* for *oððe*: *HomU* 26. 139. 26 *ne cymð þær sorh ne sar ne ænig geswinc ne hungor ne ðurst ne hefelic slæp ne byð þær fefor ne adl ne færlic cwyld ne nanes liges gebrasll ne se laðlica cyle*. But there is another pattern which Jespersen failed to note and which I call pattern (8)—*n A c B*. This occurs in OE, e.g. *Bede* 196. 30 *Næfre ofer þis ic owiht ma spreco oððe demo hwæt . . . ðu Godes bearnum selle*, *ÆCHom* i. 284. 8 *Nis na se Fæder ana Ðrynnys, oððe se Sunu Ðrynnys, oððe se Halga Gast Ðrynnys . . .* , and *Beo* 2252 *Nah, hwa sweord wege* ‖ *oððe feormie fæted wæge*, and in MnE, e.g. 'It's not George or Harry, but Tom'.

§1853. Pattern (4)—*A nc B*—contains (in Jespersen's words) 'a negative conjunction "looking before and after" and rendering both A and B negative'. As far as I have observed, it is restricted to examples in which A and B are substantives or pronouns, e.g. *ÆCHom* ii. 252. 6 *forðan ðe Herodes ne he eac ne mihte nænne gylt on him to deaðe afindan* and

Beo 1099   . . .   þæt ðær ænig mon
           wordum ne worcum   wære ne bræce,
           ne þurh inwitsearo   æfre gemænden . . . ,

or adverbs, e.g. *GuthB* 1118 *ær ne sið*. These examples predate those noted by *OED*, s.v. (*ne adv.* and *conj.*[1] B. 1. c.). But the *OED* definition fits them: '*conj.* . . . = Nor. . . . with omission of preceding negative (sometimes expressed in what follows)'. Examples of this sort must be distinguished from those like *ÆCHom* i. 316. 7 *and wearð eall seo geleaffulle menigu swa anmod swilce hi ealle hæfdon ane*

heortan and ane sawle, ne heora nan næfde synderlice æhta ac him
eallum wæs gemæne heora ðing ne ðær næs nan wædla betwux him,
where both clauses introduced by conj. *ne* are preceded by a positive
clause to which the negative does not look back.

§1854. Jespersen's pattern (5)—*n A nc B*—is common in OE, e.g.
(with words other than finite verbs juxtaposed) *ÆCHom* i. 286. 4
Swa eac Crist ana underfeng ða menniscnysse and na se Fæder ne se
Halga Gast, ÆCHom i. 44. 26 *ac hi ne mihton his wisdome wið-*
standan ne ðam Halgum Gaste . . . , and *ÆCHom* i. 10. 2 *Ne mæg*
nan gesceaft fulfremedlice smeagan ne understandan ymbe god; (with
two phrases juxtaposed) *BlHom* 95. 19 *Næs na mid golde ne mid*
godwebbenum hræglum ac mid godum dædum 7 halgum we sceolan
beon gefrætwode and *ÆCHom* i. 134. 16 . . . *swa þæt heo ne come*
into Godes temple ne on anum bedde mid hire were ær ðam fyrste þe
we ær cwædon; and (with two clauses) *ÆCHom* i. 18. 28 *Næs him*
gesceapen fram Gode ne he næs genedd þæt he sceolde Godes bebod
tobrecan and *ÆCHom* i. 302. 13 *Stanas sind gesceafta ac hi nabbað*
nan lif ne hi ne gefredað. Here too tautologic negatives are common;
they occur in some of the examples above and in *ÆCHom* i. 96. 15
Witodlice se fyrenfulla bið earmra ðonne ænig nyten, forðan þe þæt
nyten næfð nane sawle, ne næfre ne geedcucað, ne þa toweardan
wita ne ðrowað. But again we find verbs not negated by adv. *ne*, e.g.
BlHom 223. 31 *Ðis wæs soðlice eadig wer, ne wæs æfre facen ne*
inwid on his heortan, ne he nænigne man unrihtlice fordemde, ne
nænigum yfel wiþ yfele geald; ne hine nænig man yrne ne grammodne
ne funde, ac he wæs a on anum mode. So we cannot be sure that
sentences with two juxtaposed finite verbs, such as *ÆCHom* i. 2. 22
and me ofhreow þæt hi ne cuþon ne næfdon þa godspellican lare
exemplify pattern (5)—*n A nc B*—or pattern (1)—*nc[1] A nc[1] B*
—since the first *ne* may be an adverb or a conjunction; see §1845.
Sometimes a tautologic negative produces a pattern which is strictly
neither pattern (1) nor pattern (5), e.g. *Bede* 206. 22 *On þara East-*
rana mærsunge swa þeah he nowiht oðres ne ne gelyfde ne ne weor-
ðode ne ne bodode buton þæt ylce þæt we . . . , Latin *In quo tamen*
hoc adprobo, quia in celebratione sui paschae non aliud corde tene-
bat, uenerabatur et praedicabat quam quod nos. Here the absence of
a verb for the OE adjective clause is noteworthy. But it is another
example of imitation of the Latin. If we take the first *ne* as a conjunction in *ÆCHom* i. 12. 8 . . . *swa þæt hi næfre ne mihton ne*
noldon syððan fram his willan gebugan, it too begins *n nc[1] A* and so
exemplifies the same pattern. If (as seems to me more likely) it is an
adverb, we have pattern (5).

§1855. Some examples with *na/no* quoted by Nusser (pp. 92–3) involve similar problems. The probability that *na* can serve as a conjunction has been established in §1851. Whether the second *na* in *BenR* 54. 7 *Se mynstres hordere si gecoren of þære gesamnunge, wis, on geripedum þeawum, syfre and na oferettol, na drefend, ne teonful, ne lofgeorn, ac God ondrædende* is an adverb or conjunction is, I suppose, arguable. But in either event we have pattern (5). *Bede (T)* 402. 27 reads *þonne ne eart ðu fullfremedlice no on riht gefullwad*. MS *O* also has *no*. But MSS *B, C,* and *Ca*, have *ne*, which must be a conjunction, thus giving pattern (5). Whether *no* is an adverb, giving asyndetic parataxis, or a conjunction, giving pattern (5), is again arguable. There is no doubt that we have pattern (5) in

Beo 1392   Ic hit þe gehate: no he on helm losaþ,
                  ne on foldan fæþm,   ne on fyrgenholt,
                  ne on gyfenes grund,   ga þær he wille!

But in

Beo 541   No he wiht fram me
                  flodyþum feor   fleotan meahte,
                  hraþor on holme,   no ic fram him wolde,

we may have two adverbs, giving asyndetic parataxis, or pattern (1) nc^1 *A* nc^1 *B*, or pattern (5) *n A nc B*. All these problems are in the event terminological.

§1856. I have so far noted one example of pattern (6)—*n A* nc^1 *B* nc^2—viz. *ÆHom* 5. 105 *ne swanc se Fæder ne se Sunu naðor on þam micclan weorce*, but none of pattern (7)—*n A n B nc*.

§1857. When the subject of two or more juxtaposed clauses is the same it may be repeated in both or all of them, e.g. *ÆCHom* i. 320. 14 *He ne hrymde ne he biterwyrde næs ne he sace ne astyrede* and *ÆCHom* ii. 44. 21 *He ne cidde ne he ne hrymde betwux mannum ne he sace ne astyrede ne he biterwyrde næs*, but need not be, e.g. *ÆCHom* i. 96. 15 and *ÆCHom* i. 2. 22 (for both these see §1854), and *ÆCHom* ii. 40. 16 *He ne wiðerode ongean ne ne feaht.* . . . On this point Andrew (*SS,* §73) says 'that, even when the subject does not change, the pronoun, contrary to ModE idiom, is usually repeated in the co-ordinate clause'. But both usages occur in MnE—we could translate the last sentence either 'He did not resist and did not fight' or 'He did not resist nor did he fight'—and we cannot really say that one is more 'usual' than the other. The same is true in OE; whether the subject is repeated or not depends on such factors as the closeness of the connection—consider *ÆCHom* i. 12. 8–11—and the needs of clarity, emphasis, and style.

6. CONJUNCTIONS MEANING 'FOR'

§1858. These conjunctions—typified by MnE 'for'—are traditionally known as 'illative'. They present serious problems of classification. As Haber points out (*American Speech*, 30 (1955), 151),
'the only practical conclusion is that the conjunction ['for'] has two
uses, subordinating and coordinating, and that punctuation is of no
significance in determining either'. In other words, MnE 'for' can
sometimes be replaced by 'because'. The situation in OE is even more
complicated, for *forþon* and its variants can mean 'therefore' (§3010)
and 'because' (§§3033-6) as well as 'for'. The use of OE *for* as a
conj. 'for, because' is late; see §3037. Liggins (1955, pp. 213-14)
points out that *forþon* sometimes approaches MnE colourless 'now',
with not even a weak explanatory function, e.g. *Or* 100. 10. In such
examples, she remarks, it comes close to being an interjection rather
than an adverb or a conjunction. See §§3081-4.

§1859. Neither element order, the absence of *þe* (despite Rübens,
p. 32), nor any other criterion I am aware of, can tell us whether
forþon introduces a co-ordinate or a subordinate clause in *Or* 17. 35
*Swiþost he for ðider, toeacan þæs landes sceawunge, for þæm
horschwælum, for ðæm hie habbað swiþe æþele ban on hiora toþum,
ÆHom* 6. 137 *Is swaþeah oðer ærist on urum sawlum þe ure Hælend
deð dæghwamlice on mannum, þonne seo sawul arist of ðære synna
deaðe, for ðam se ðe syngað, hys sawul ne leofað, buton heo þurh
andetnysse eft acucige,* and

Beo 415   þa me þæt gelærdon   leode mine,
              þa selestan,   snotere ceorlas,
              þeoden Hroðgar,   þæt ic þe sohte,
              forþan hie mægenes cræft   minne cuþon.

Indeed, it is not even certain that the presence of *þe* certifies that we
have a subordinate clause. Inverted uses are possible even if we
accept that *forþon þe* was originally a conjunction and there is nothing inherently improbable about Thorpe's punctuation and translation of *ÆCHom* i. 410. 23 *Ac ðonne seo sawul bið to hire witnunge
gelæd, ðonne bið eal seo getimbrung hire smeagunge toworpen;
forðan ðe heo ne oncneow ða tid hire geneosunge* '. . . ; for it knew
not the time of its visitation'—especially when we compare *Matt
(WSCp)* 5. 3 *Eadige synt þa gastlican þearfan, forþam hyra ys heofena
rice,* Latin *Beati pauperes spiritu quoniam ipsorum est regnum
caelorum,* with *Matt(WSCp)* 5. 4 *Eadige synt þa liðan forþam þe hi
eorðan agun,* Latin *Beati mites quoniam ipsi posidebunt terram,* and

BlHom 25. 22 *Wa eow þe nu hlihaþ, forþon ge eft wepað on ecnesse* with *BlHom* 25. 20 *Eadige beoþ þa þe nu wepað, forþon þe hi beoþ eft afrefrede.* On this see further §§3014-18.

§1860. We may similarly argue whether *þy* in *BlHom* 23. 35 *Eal þis he þrowode for ure lufan 7 hælo; þy he wolde þæt we þæt heofenlice rice onfengon* (so Morris) and *nu* in *ÆCHom* i. 102. 17 *Ic wene þæt ic swunce on ydel, ðaða ic eow to Gode gebigde: nu ge cepað dagas and monðas mid ydelum wiglungum* (so Thorpe) introduce co-ordinate or subordinate clauses. See §3925.

§1861. Other words which sometimes serve an illative function include *ono* (§§1862 and 3107) and *soðlice* and *witodlice* (§§3166-8). On *ond* and *ac* introducing explanatory clauses, see §§3169-71 and 1770. On the expression of cause in asyndetic parataxis see §3165.

7. OTHER WORDS

§1862. Pope (*Ælfric*, i. 102) remarks of Ælfric that

he tends also, in paratactic sequences, to ease transitions by an assortment of introductory adverbs, ranging from the local *þær* and temporal *þa* to the more or less logical *eornostlice* 'therefore, accordingly', the adversative *þeah-hwæðere*, and the vaguely asseverative *soþlice* and *witodlice*. These last, corresponding more or less to Latin *vero*, are used more sparingly in the early prose than in the later, rhythmical variety, where they are sometimes almost meaningless fillers.

This use of introductory adverbs or co-ordinating conjunctions—see §1101—is, of course, not restricted to Ælfric. Among those found in other authors (and in some cases in Ælfric) are: *forþon* 'therefore'; *huru* 'indeed'; *ono*, which serves as a weak connective in OE (see Miller, i, pp. xxix ff., and Liggins 1955, p. 213); *swa* 'thus, so'; *þæs* 'therefore, after'; *weald* 'perhaps'; and other local and temporal adverbs. Space does not permit citation of examples; they can be conveniently found in BT(S), s.vv.

D. CORRELATION NOT INVOLVING SUBORDINATION

1. NOUNS, ADJECTIVES, PRONOUNS, AND NUMERALS

§1863. Two or more alternatives may be contrasted by the correlative use of nouns, adjectives, pronouns, and/or numerals, in asyndetic or syndetic parataxis, e.g. *ÆCHom* i. 224. 14 *Twa lif sind soðlice:*

þæt an we cunnon, þæt oðer us wæs uncuð ær Cristes tocyme. þæt an lif is deadlic, þæt oðer undeadlic. Ac se hælend com and under-feng þæt an lif and geswutelode þæt oðer. þæt an lif he æteowde mid his deaðe, and þæt oðer mid his æriste. Similarly, we find *ÆC Hom* i. 234. 2 *þam mannum . . . and þam . . .* , *ÆCHom* ii. 440. 4 *an . . . oðer, ÆCHom* i. 248. 16 *se . . . se oðer, ÆCHom* i. 254. 30 *se rica . . . se oðer, ÆCHom* i. 332. 9 *Hine . . . þone oðerne, ÆCHom* i. 256. 20 *oðer . . . oðer, ÆCHom* ii. 546. 4 *oðre ðing . . . oþre . . . oðre,* and *ÆCHom* i. 360. 8 *oðer . . . and se ylca.* On correlative *sum . . . sum* and *sum . . . oþer,* see §394.

§1864. Parataxis shades into comparison in examples like *ÆCHom* ii. 574. 1 *Drihten ne oncnæwð hi, forðan ðe hi sind oðre, oþre hi wæron;* see Andrew, *SS,* §105, and Brown 1970, p. 79. For further examples involving *oþer,* see §§508-10.

§1865. On the ambiguous demonstrative/relative, see §§2109-21, and on the correlation of demonstratives and relatives, §§2261-2.

2. ADVERBS

§1866. Alternatives may also be contrasted by the use of correlative adverbs, e.g. *ÆCHom* i. 470. 27 *For mislicum intingum . . . hwilon . . . hwilon . . . hwilon . . . hwilon, ÆCHom* i. 410. 26 *On manegum gemetum . . . hwiltidum . . . hwilon . . . hwilon,* and *ÆCHom* i. 184. 2 *Hwilon . . . hwilon . . . nu . . . and eft.* Other combinations may express successive action, e.g. *ÆCHom* ii. 82. 25 *ærest . . . syððan,* or repeated action, e.g. *ÆCHom* ii. 302. 9 *æne and oðre siðe* and *ÆC Hom* i. 232. 10 *Tuwa . . . nu æne and eft oðre siðe.*

§1867. On the problem of the ambiguous adverb/conjunction, see §2418, and on correlation involving subordination, see the appropriate sections of chapter VII.

E. ELEMENT ORDER IN PARATACTIC NON-DEPENDENT QUESTIONS

1. X-QUESTIONS

§1868. If an interrogative is expressed or repeated in an *x*-question which is in asyndetic parataxis with a preceding question or which is introduced by *ond, ac,* or *oððe,* the normal order is VS, e.g. *ÆCHom*

i. 136. 28 *Ela, hwænne cymð se Hælend? Hwænne bið he acenned? Hwænne mot ic hine geseon?*, *ÆCHom* i. 254. 7 *And hwilc is se Fæder?*, *ÆCHom* i. 156. 18 *Ac hwæt dyde se blinda?*, and *ÆHom* 25c. 6 *ac hwi ehtst þu min?*, unless the interrogative itself is the subject, e.g. *ÆCHom* i. 286. 9 *ac hwa mæg weorðfullice sprecan be ðam . . . ?*, *ÆCHom* i. 286. 19 *Oððe hwa heraðꞵ genihtsumlice ealra tida ymbhwyrft?*, and (perhaps) *ÆCHom* i. 254. 5 *Ac hwa is ure Fæder?* So Andrew (*SS*, §60) is right when he says that in *BlHom* 155. 35 *Hwæt wille ge nu? hwæt ic hire doo?* 'the second *hwæt* can only be a scribal error for *þæt*'; cf. *BlHom* 15. 24 *Hwæt wilt þu þæt ic þe do?* On examples like *Bo* 139. 7, where two questions joined by *ond* both have SV with the subjunctive, see §1669. In *PPs* 113. 5 *Oððe þu, Iordanen, for hwi gengdest on bæcling?*, *þu, Iordanen* is vocative and we might have expected *þu* after *gengdest*.

§1869. When neither the interrogative nor the subject is repeated, we naturally enough find patterns like that in *ÆCHom* i. 184. 30 *Hwa sylð nu wæstm urum æcerum and gemenigfylt þæt gerip of feawum cornum . . . ?* But when the subject is repeated and the interrogative is not, the influence of the conjunction can draw the subject before the verb, e.g. *ÆCHom* ii. 108. 9 *Drihten hwænne gesawe we ðe hungrine, and we ðe gereordodon? oððe þurstigne, and we ðe scencton? oððe hwænne wære ðu cuma, and we ðe underfengon? oððe hwænne gesawe we ðe untrumne oþþe on cwearterne, and we ðe geneosodon?* and *ÆCHom* ii. 108. 24 *La leof, hwænne gesawe we ðe hungrine . . . and we ðe noldon ðenian?* In the anacoluthic *ÆCHom* i. 338. 24 *Hwilc eower hæfð hundteontig sceapa, and gif he forlysð an ðæra sceapa, ðonne forlæt he ða nigon and hundnigontig on westene and gæð secende þæt an ðe him losode?, ðonne [ne] forlæt he . . .* is either a nexus question or an *x*-question with tautologic *he*.

2. NEXUS QUESTIONS WITHOUT AN INTERROGATIVE WORD

§1870. When two or more nexus questions with no interrogative are in syndetic parataxis, the first has the order VS; see §1644. When the second question is both nexus and negative, the adv. *ne* produces or preserves the order VS, e.g. (after *ond*) *ÆHom* 13. 124 *Hu mæg la se blinda lædan þone blindan and hu ne feallað hy begen on sumne blindne seað?*—cf. *Luke(WSCp)* 6. 39 *Segst þu, mæg se blinda þæne blindan lædan? Hu ne feallaþ hig begen on þæne pytt?*, where the questions are in asyndetic parataxis—and (after *oþþe*) *CP* 377. 7 *Hu nytt bið se forholena cræft oððe ðæt forhyd[d]e gold? Oððe gif*

*hwelc folc bið mid hungre geswenced, 7 hwa his hwæte gehyt 7
oðhielt, hu ne wilt he ðonne hiera deaðes?*, where the first is an *x*-
question.

§1871. But when the second question is a positive nexus introduced
by *ond* or *oððe*, the subject may precede the verb, e.g. *ÆCHom* i.
306. 22 *Drihten, Drihten, la hu ne witegode we on ðinum naman,
and we adræfdon deoflo of wodum mannum, and we micele mihta
on þinum naman gefremedon?, ÆCHom* i. 480. 6 *Eart ðu se ðe toweard is, oþþe we oðres andbidian sceolon,* and *ÆCHom* ii. 80. 25
*La hu, ne mot ic don þæt ic wille? . . . Oððe ðin eage is yfel, forðan
þe ic eom god?*; cf. *Matt(WSCp)* 20. 15 *oþþe ne mot ic don þ ic wylle
hwæþer þe þine eage manful ys forþam þe ic god eom,* where *hwæþer*
produces the order S . . . V.

3. QUESTIONS INTRODUCED BY *HWÆþER*

§1872. *Hwæþer* may introduce both *x*-questions ('which of two
. . . ?') and nexus questions (☆'Whether . . . ?'). With both single
(§§1652–60 and 1662) and double questions, the two can usually
be distinguished by element order and mood—VS and the indicative for *x*-questions, e.g. *Bo* 122. 28 *Gif þu ne deman moste, hwæ-
ðerne woldes þu deman wites wyrðran, þe ðone þe ðone unscyldgan
witnode, ðe ðone þe þ wite þolade?* 'Which would you judge worthier
of punishment, [either] him who . . . or him who . . . ?', but S(. . .)V
and the subjunctive for nexus questions, e.g. *Bo* 20. 30 *Hwæðer ðe
ðu hi forseo . . . þe þu gebide hwonne hi ðe sorgiendne forlæten?*
'Are you to despise them . . . or to wait till they leave you sorrow-
ing?'. Analogous patterns occur when a dative pronoun is the semantic subject; cf. *Solil* 51. 18 *Hweðer ðincð þe þonne betre, þe ðæt soð
þe seo soðfestnes?* (*x*-question), Latin *Quod horum duorum putas
esse præstantius?*, with *Bo* 29. 9 *Hwæþer þe nu licien fægru lond?*
(nexus). For further examples, see Nusser, pp. 160–6.

§1873. But there are some problems. In *CP* 117. 9 *Hwæðer ic cume
ðe mid ege ðe mid lufe?* we have SV and a nexus question. If we believe the order VS in *CP* 117. 7 *Hwæðer wille ge ðæt ic cume to eow,
ðe mid gierde ðe mid monnðwære gæste?*, we will see an *x*-question
—'Which do you wish: that I come to you with a rod or with gentleness of spirit?'. But this possibility does not arise in *Solil* 22. 3
Hweðer geleornodest þu, þe myd þam eagum, þe mid þam ingeþance?
or in *Solil* 19. 1 *hwæðer woldest þu ðonne þinne cniht . . . cunnan,
þe mid ðam utram gewitum, þe mið þam inran?*—I cannot accept

Bacquet's 'how' (p. 215 fn. 1). So, despite the order VS, the EETS translation of *CP* 117. 7 as a nexus question seems justified: 'Do ye wish me to come to you with a rod, or with gentleness of spirit?'. None the less, the difference in order between *CP* 117. 7 and *CP* 117. 9—which is present in both *H* and *C* manuscripts—is odd. *LS* 8. 131 *Hwæðer is ðe leofre þe ðu nu onfo þa costnunga þe near þinum ende?* seemed to me clearly an *x*-question—'Which is your choice—that you receive the temptations now or nearer your end?'. But in view of the preceding examples, the EETS translation is at least a possibility: 'Whether is dearer to thee to receive temptations now or nearer thy end?'. *Matt(WSCp)* 21. 25 *Hwæðer wæs Iohannes fulluht þe of heofonum þe of mannum*, Latin *baptismum Iohannis unde erat e caelo an ex hominibus*, perhaps confuses the two kinds of question. Do we translate the question in *ÆCHom* i. 222. 18 *Se bydel wæs ymbscryd mid scinendum reafe, forðan ðe he bodade þa blisse þisre freolstide, and ure mærða. Hwæðer cweðe we, ðe ure ðe ðæra engla? We cweðað soðlice, ægðer ge ure ge heora* as an *x*-question —'Which do we say—ours or the angels'?'—or, following BT, as a nexus—'Shall we say ours or the angels'?'.

§1874. None of these examples has the unambiguous subjunctive which usually accompanies non-dependent nexus questions introduced by *hwæþer* with the order SV. So the possibility exists that we have what is strictly a tautologic *hwæþer* introducing disjunctive nexus questions with the order VS and verb-forms which are in effect indicative.

§1875. The combinations involved in double questions with *hwæþer* can be characterized as *hwæþer (. . .) (þe) . . . þe* and *hwæþer (. . .) (oþþe) . . . oþþe*; typical examples include *ÆLS* 14. 38 *Hwæðer is to lufigenne oððe hwam lac to offrigenne, ðam hælende Criste ealra worulda alysend oþþe Apolline ealra deofla ealdre?* (*x*-question) and *Bo* 20. 30 *Hwæðer ðe ðu hi forseo . . . þe þu gebide hwonne hi ðe sorgiendne forlæten?* (nexus question).

VI

THE COMPLEX SENTENCE

A. INTRODUCTORY REMARKS

§1876. A complex sentence consists of a principal clause and one or more subordinate clauses. The latter are clauses introduced by a relative pronoun or by a subordinating conjunction as defined in §§1229-30. On the problems of terminology involved, see §1633.

§1877. Sentences such as *ÆCHom* i. 290. 9 *God wæs æfre, and æfre wæs his Wisdom of him acenned, and se Wisdom is his Sunu, ealswa mihtig swa se Fæder,* which contain a principal clause, a clause or clauses introduced by the 'co-ordinating' conjunction *and,* and a subordinate clause or clauses, are sometimes called 'multiple- (or compound-)complex'. For the reasons given in §1685, I avoid this term. As far as I am aware, traditional grammar has no special term for sentences like *ÆCHom* i. 288. 19 *þurh þæt gemynd se man geðencð þa ðing ðe he gehyrde, oþþe geseah, oþþe geleornode,* which consist of one principal clause and two or more subordinate clauses joined by a 'co-ordinating' conjunction. But they exist. Most of the problems which concern sentences like these have already been discussed in chapter V. Those which remain are dealt with as they arise.

✕ §1878. A full treatment of the types of sentence discussed in the two preceding paragraphs would demand a study of the development of OE sentence-structure and style in both prose and poetry. Such a task cannot be attempted here. But I plan to outline some of the major syntactical considerations involved. Anyone contemplating further work on OE sentence structure should take cognizance of three articles in Russian by G. G. Alekseeva: ['The Structure of Complex Sentences with Consecutive Subordination in Old English'], *IAF* 3 (1965), 214-27; ['The Particularities of the Inner Predicative Structure of Complex Sentences and Subsequent Subordination in Old English'], *IAF* 3 (1965), 228-37; and ['The Correlation of Nominal Parts in Complex Sentences with Consecutive Subordination in Old English'], *Vestnik Leningradskogo Universiteta,* series 8 (1976), vyp. 2, 111-20. These offer suggested structural models and some statistics on the relative frequency of the various patterns the author detects in a limited corpus. Kivimaa (pp. 147-8) offers comments and references to discussions on 'common Germanic features' in subordinate clauses.

B. PUNCTUATION

§1879. The first consideration is punctuation. It is clear that modern *readers* cannot always grasp the exact nuance an Anglo-Saxon reader, or reciter, conveyed to his *hearers*, and that even when they can, they cannot convey it to others by modern punctuation, which is concerned with MnE as a written rather than a spoken medium, whereas in OE (one ventures to think) we generally have to do with the rhythms and clause terminals of something closer to speech than to formal writing. Thus, when a modern editor looks at *ÆCHom* ii. 66. 22 *Babilonia seo Chaldeisca burh is gereht gescyndnys seo getacnað helle* . . . , he sees what seems to be a clear-cut example of the ambiguous demonstrative-relative in which he has to decide whether to follow Thorpe's *gescyndnys. Seo* or Andrew's *gescyndnys, seo* (*SS*, §49). But examples like *ÆCHom* ii. 96. 19 *He cwæð þæt he cuðe sumne man on Romebyrig, his nama wæs Seruulus, ðearfa on æhtum, and welig on geearnungum* (where all manuscripts have either a *punctus* before *his, ðearfa,* and *and,* and a *punctus versus* after *geearnungum* or a *punctus* after *geearnungum* only) and *ÆCHom* ii. 510. 31 *Martinus eac com to anes mannes huse his cnapa wæs awed wundorlice ðurh deofol* (where none of the manuscripts has any original punctuation before *his*) suggest that the problem is not quite so simple. The fact that in both of them *his* cannot be a relative pronoun and seems unlikely to introduce what we think of as a new sentence suggests to me—as I have pointed out in *NQ* 223 (1978), 390-4, and in §1686—that it is an over-simplification to think of the terms 'ambiguous demonstrative/relative' and 'ambiguous adverb/conjunction' as necessarily implying that the choice was simply between a subordinate clause and an independent sentence in the modern sense of the words. That the sentence as traditionally defined and understood was always the unit of OE prose and poetry should not be taken for granted; consider for example annal 1001 in the *Parker Chronicle* which, says Zuck (p. 91), 'has a cluster of thirty-four clauses, the longest in the corpus',[1] *ÆCHom* i. 614. 3

---

[1] I make it thirty-three + two in the later addition. The clauses beginning 7 *ðær* (*ChronA* 132. 5, 9, 20, and 23) may exemplify the scribal confusion between the *positura* and the 'Tironian sign' used for Latin *et* and OE *and* which is discussed in §1724. If so, we could distinguish five sentences or 'clause clusters' rather than one. If not, the same might well be true!

Behealdað þas fictreowa and ealle oðre treowa, þonne hi spryttað, ðonne wite ge þæt hit sumor læhð, and *And* 474-80, where we have the problem of the *apo koinou* clause which I have discussed in *NM* 70 (1969), 78-81; see further §§3789-803.

✕ §1880. How then should we punctuate OE texts in modern editions? 'In medieval punctuation', says Harlow (*RES* 10 (1959), 18-19), 'grammatical principles will be found to be secondary to rhetorical'. Hence punctuation in OE manuscripts cannot be a reliable guide to the grammatical nature or function of individual clauses. Modern punctuation is syntactical, produces modern sentences, and so forces unnecessary and irrelevant decisions on editors. It may be true that, as Shippey (p. 199 fn. 29) says, 'there is now little doubt that Old English poetic sentences were longer and better organised than early editors thought, and that repeated words such as *forþon . . . forþon* or *þa . . . þa* were used to signal clause boundaries rather than sentence ones'. But I believe that sometimes at any rate there should be doubt—in prose as well as in poetry—and that failure to recognize this is leading to the acceptance of over-sophisticated syntactical patternings which can in turn lead to the imposition of over-sophisticated literary interpretations. Hence my belief that the time has come to introduce a new system of punctuation of OE texts. I have made some suggestions in *RES* 31 (1980), 385-413.

§1881. In the hope that they will be pursued, I venture some further considerations. I accept Bately's claim (*The Literary Prose of King Alfred's Reign: Translation or Transformation?* (An Inaugural Lecture, 4 March 1980, privately circulated), 19-20) that there are passages in both *Or* and *Bo* in which 'the unit is not the phrase or the sentence but the paragraph *or even larger section*' (my italics). I agree with Clemoes that 'Ælfric wrote in intonation paragraphs'[2] and am confident that the unit of OE poetry is the verse paragraph (Mitchell 1980a, p. 411). (Here I note that Alistair Campbell believed that 'no attentive reader of OE poetry can fail to observe that the poets are highly skilled in the composition of long continuous paragraphs' and saw it as a virtue in Andrew that he recognized this (Lecture Notes). In his lectures, Campbell construed *Phoen* 424-42 as one continuous paragraph, with *Is þon gelicast* (424) picked up by *swa* (437) and 426b-37a under the government of *þonne* (426b).) However, I

---

[2] P. Clemoes, *Liturgical Influence on Punctuation in Late Old English and Early Middle English Manuscripts* (Occasional Papers, Number 1, printed for the Department of Anglo-Saxon) (Cambridge, 1952), 17. I denote this by 'Clemoes, *Punctuation*' in this and the next section.

think it extremely unlikely that we shall ever recover the timing and intonation patterns of OE with sufficient accuracy to decide the exact relationship between OE paragraphs (as we shall do better to call them) and MnE sentences or to solve such problems as the ambiguous demonstrative/relative or the ambiguous adverb/conjunction. A study of these and other problems in the poetry with particular reference to Kuhn's Law will be necessary; thus Campbell (Lecture Notes) argued that in *GuthA* 84, *hafað* (87b) 'is a sentence-particle and could not be delayed in its clause in the way the [ASPR] punctuation suggests; we need a dash or colon at *bona*'. See further § 3947. For the prose, someone might risk a comparative study of the punctuation of different manuscripts of selected prose texts in an attempt to see whether Dunning and Bliss's observation concerning the Exeter Book (*The Wanderer*, p. 11) is true of any OE prose texts: '. . . it cannot be claimed that the punctuation is fully·systematic; on the other hand, it is far from being random.'[3] The other manuscripts of poetic texts are likely to be less fruitful here; see Mitchell 1980*a*, pp. 396–7. But the suggestion by R. D. Stevick that variations in spacing between groups of letters in the manuscripts of *Beowulf* and of Ælfric's *Grammar* provide clues to timing, intonation, and '"prominence" (or sentence accent)', in OE seems ill-founded.[4] It is unlikely to throw any light on the problems just mentioned. The same is true of Maling's 'Sentence Stress in Old English' (*Linguistic Inquiry*, 2 (1971), 379–99), which promises in the title more than it provides in the text; it is concerned solely with *Beowulf* and does not make me any more certain of how to punctuate it or how to stress it.

§ 1882. There are thus daunting difficulties in the creation of a new system of punctuation for OE texts. Such a system will involve at least a partial retention of the OE system whose loss was lamented

---

[3] One could make a similar point about *Paradise Lost*, where (I believe) the inconsistencies in the punctuation and spelling of the manuscript of Book I and of the first edition may be at least partly due to the fact that, when the text was read aloud to Milton, he made alterations according to a system when the reader stumbled but did not necessarily do so when he read correctly; cf. Clemoes, *Punctuation*, p. 20.

It is with great interest that I now note the suggestion made by M. B. Parkes, 'Punctuation, or Pause and Effect', *Medieval Eloquence Studies in the Theory and Practice of Medieval Rhetoric*, ed. James J. Murphy (University of California Press, 1978), 138–9, that 'one might adduce a general principle about medieval punctuation. Medieval scribes and correctors punctuate where confusion is likely to arise (if their Latin is sufficient to recognize the fact) and do not always punctuate where confusion is not likely to arise, even when they are concerned with the *sententia literae*.'

[4] *Suprasegmentals, Meter, and the Manuscript of* Beowulf (The Hague, 1968)—reviewed by Wrenn, *MÆ* 38 (1969), 309–10, and by Ball, *RES* 21 (1970), 476–8—and *English and Its History: The Evolution of a Language* (Boston, 1968), 291–7.

by Clemoes (*Punctuation*, p. 20). It will have to present an agreed consensus on the syntax of individual constructions and will at times certainly have to disregard manuscript punctuation because of the possibility of scribal error; see Clemoes, *Punctuation*, p. 17 fn. 1.[5] However, it need scarcely be said that the time is not yet ripe for its introduction. So, in general, I have in this book reproduced the punctuation of my chosen edition, despite my ever-growing dissatisfaction with both editorial and manuscript punctuation. But I have departed from it, usually silently, in those places where I believe that it distorts the syntax too much. I am aware of and regret the resulting inconsistencies.[6] When I began my work, I knew that there was a problem. I was not aware of its magnitude. I hope that a consistent and accepted system of punctuation for OE texts will arise as a result of discussion. My experience has convinced me that one is needed. My inconsistencies will probably bring the reader to the same conviction.

C. SUBORDINATION AND HYPOTAXIS

§1883. As pointed out in §1683, hypotaxis is the opposite of parataxis and implies the use in a sentence of one or more of the relative pronouns or subordinating conjunctions discussed in chapter VII. It is commonly held that parataxis preceded hypotaxis in the development of language; see §1688. The main types of subordinate clause are noun clauses (dependent statements, questions, exclamations, commands, and wishes); adjective (or relative) clauses; and adverb clauses (place, time, purpose, result, cause, comparison, concession, and condition). For further details, see initially the Table of Contents to chapter VII.

§1884. This is the classification proposed in the Joint Committee Report. Every grammatical system is a Procrustean bed. I have chosen to lie in that which is most familiar, for the proposed alternatives— such as those of Jespersen (*A System of Clauses* (Society for Pure English, Tract 54, 1940) and *Ess.*, pp. 349-73) and Sandfeld (*TPS* 1941, pp. 87-9)—have not achieved sufficient recognition to warrant their use in a descriptive grammar. Clauses are therefore

---

[5] To the works cited in this discussion and the bibliographical items mentioned in them should be added the following, all of which concern the poetry: Emerson, *MP* 23 (1925-6), 393-405; Wyatt and Chambers, *Beowulf*, pp. xxix-xxx; Klaeber, 3, p. clxiv; and Slay, *TPS* 1952, pp. 13-14.

[6] Nor have I been able to solve the problem of punctuation in Latin texts, e.g. the Vulgate, where R. Weber, B. Fischer, *et al.* (edd.) *Biblia Sacra iuxta Vulgatam Versionem* (Stuttgart, 1969), does not use punctuation at all.

classified first according to their function (expression of purpose, result, and so on) and are then subdivided according to the introductory conjunction (*þæt, swa,* and so on) or to the syntactical method of expressing the function (e.g. inversion expressing condition).

§1885. Even those who are unwilling to accept what I say in §§1879-82 will have to admit that there are no infallible criteria for distinguishing principal from subordinate clauses. The context, clause order, and element order, sometimes serve as guides. Mood can be decisive, e.g. *ÆCHom* ii. 252. 34 *ær hi sind gebundene ær hi beon geborene* 'they are bound before they are born'. The vital clue of intonation is denied to us. This means that we cannot use the criterion of metre with any certainty. Punctuation has already been discussed and discarded. A Latin original can be a dangerous guide, for there is no guarantee that the translator was trying to give an accurate representation of the Latin construction and no certainty that he could do so if he wanted to, since the two languages were not necessarily at the same stage of development or equipped with the same devices. The introductory word is not conclusive when an ambiguous demonstrative/relative or adverb/conjunction is involved (see Klaeber, *AngB*. 52 (1941), 216-19, and my §§2109 and 1686). Doubts can even arise with conjunctions which might be thought unambiguously subordinating; see, for example, my comments on *forþon þe* in §§2424 and 3011 and on *oð þæt* in *NQ* 223 (1978), 390-4. However, the ambiguity is frequently of importance only to a classifier. Thus, while the repetition of *nu* suggests correlation and therefore the use of a comma rather than of a stop after *earde* in

Sat 228   Nu is gesene   þæt we syngodon
                 uppe on earde.   Sceolon nu æfre þæs
                 dreogan domlease gewinn   drihtnes mihtum,

the relationship is causal whether the first clause is regarded as principal or subordinate, and it does not seem of great moment whether we have a stop or comma after *nytenum* in *Exod* 9. 10 . . . *7 swellendae blædran 7 wunda wurdon on ðam mannum 7 on þam nytenum,* [11] *Swa þæt ða dryas ne mihton standan.* . . . (Despite Klaeber (ibid.), both Grein and Crawford have the comma.)

§1886. Problems of classification and terminology involving subordinate clauses are discussed in the course of chapter VII; see §§1926-30.

D. CORRELATION AND ANTICIPATION

§1887. One of the most marked characteristics of the OE complex sentence is the frequency with which the constituent clauses are firmly linked by the use of correlative adverbs and conjunctions, correlative demonstrative and relative pronouns, or pronouns which make a principal clause complete and anticipate a following noun clause.

§1888. Words which are used correlatively and can be either adverbs or conjunctions include *ær, nu, siþþan, þær, þa, þanon, þider, þonne*, and (much less frequently) the prepositional formulae. Van Dam found that *forþæm/þam/þan* adverb was correlative with the conjunction in only eighteen of 303 examples in which it occurred without *þe* (p. 42) and in only seventeen of 166 examples in which it occurred with *þe* (pp. 45 and 48); for a fuller discussion of this problem, see §§3072-80. Adams listed only two such examples involving formulae with *mid* (pp. 189-93) and none with formulae involving *ær* (pp. 215-20); in the latter the simple adverb *ær* does, however, occur.[7] When two successive clauses are introduced by one of these words or phrases, we cannot always be sure whether we have a complex sentence, two principal clauses in asyndetic parataxis, or (as I have suggested in §1879) something between the two.

§1889. The difficulty of distinguishing subordinate adverb clauses from principal clauses when the introductory words are the same in form can be resolved either by doubling the word when it is used as a conjunction, e.g. *swa swa, þa þa*, or *þær þær*, or by adding *þe* to the word which introduces the subordinate clause, e.g. *þanon þe, þeah þe*, and *forþon þe*, though (as pointed out in §1885) this is not always conclusive. The former is a favourite device of Ælfric, but is not restricted to him; see Pope *Ælfric*, i. 102-3. As far as I have observed, most conjunctions seem to prefer one of these devices rather than the other; thus, I have found *þa þe* rare in the prose (Adams, pp. 23-4 and 186) and unknown in the poetry, and have no examples of ✩*swa þe*, ✩*þanon þanon*, or ✩*forþon forþon*. Full collections may, however, reveal some examples, for *þær þe* occurs twice in the poetry—in *Dan* 627 and *Sat* 639—and occasionally in the prose, e.g. *VercHom* 6. 88 *þærðe þis god ne wære, nænige þinga ure goda on hyra onsyne gefeollon*, where it means 'if'. But *þonne* is usually found alone. We find *þonne þe* very occasionally in the prose,

---

[7] Carkeet (*passim*) either was unaware of or took no cognizance of the infrequency of the correlative use of prepositional formulae.

e.g. *GD* 206. 26 . . . *þonne þe he sceawaþ þa godan fremian 7 weaxan to Godes wuldre* and *ÆCHom* i. 48. 9, and once in the poetry—*Sat* 150, where it is better taken as 'when' than 'than when'; see §2588. The doubled form is not found in the poetry; appears occasionally in *Bo* and *CP* (Adams, p. 185), e.g. *CP* 127. 20 *7 ðonne, ðonne hie hie habbað, dæges 7 niehtes hie fundiað to bigietenne* . . . ; but is avoided by Ælfric. See further Adams, p. 25, and Möllmer, p. 26.

§1890. There is, of course, no difficulty in distinguishing the two types of clause when the adverb and conjunction are different, e.g. *þeah* . . . *hwæþre* 'though . . . yet', *gif* . . . *þonne* 'if . . . then', and *ÆCHom* i. 60. 11 *Mid þam ðe se apostol Iohannes stop into ðære byrig Ephesum, þa bær man him togeanes anre wydewan lic to byrigenne* 'when . . . then' or 'as . . . then'. These examples remind us that words like *þær, þa, þonne,* and *þeah,* can occur correlatively not only with one another but also with other words or formulae. The details must be sought in the appropriate sections of chapter VII and in the monographs.

§1891. The problem of the ambiguous demonstrative/relative can be resolved by using *þe* with the latter in sequences like *se . . . se þe* 'he . . . who'; see §2221 (and §2208). In examples like *ÆCHom* i. 68. 26 *þæt þæt we mid gitsigendum eagum agylton, þæt we nu mid wependum eagum bereowsiað* and *ÆCHom* i. 578. 23 . . . *and hi ðeah, æfter stemne anre hæse, þæt þæt hi hæfdon forgeaton, þæt þæt* means 'that which' or 'what'. But the same meaning can be conveyed by *þæt,* e.g. *ÆCHom* i. 14. 7 . . . *buton þu do þæt ic þe hate and forgang þæt ic þe forbeode,* or by *þe,* e.g. *ÆCHom* i. 462. 31 *and forði ic sprece ðe he me het*; see further §§2126-33 and 2322-4.

§1892. Noun clauses may be introduced by *þæt, þæt þe,* or *þætte,* and can usually be identified without difficulty; see §§1929-30. The neut. dem. *þæt* or *þis* or the neut. pron. *hit* is frequently used in the nominative to anticipate a principal clause, e.g. *ÆCHom* i. 42. 13 *þæt is ece lif, þæt hi ðe oncnawon soðne God, ÆCHom* ii. 412. 4 *Ðis is þæt fyrmeste weorc and se fyrmesta willa, þæt we gelyfon on ðone ancennedan Godes Sunu,* and the first *þæt* in

GenB 595   þæt is micel wundor
    þæt hit ece god   æfre wolde
    þeoden þolian,   þæt wurde þegn swa monig
    forlædd be þam lygenum   þe for þam larum com.

This pattern is still possible in MnE, e.g. 'It is not true that he is ill', though when writing formally we can say 'That he is ill is not true'

—a construction not possible in OE. These anticipatory pronouns also occur in other cases, e.g. (accusative object of a verb) *Or* 172. 2 *þæt gefremede Diulius hiora consul, þæt þæt angin wearð tidlice þurhtogen, CP* 181. 18 *7 eac we magon oncnawan ðæt, ðæt ða earman 7 ða untruman sient to retanne*, the third *þæt* in *ÆCHom* i. 224. 30 *Se godspellere Matheus awrat on Cristes bec, þæt manega halige menn, ðe wæron on ðære ealdan æ forðfarene, þæt hi arison mid Criste; and þæt sædon gehwilce wise lareowas, þæt hi habbað gefremod heora ærist to ðam ecan life, swa swa we ealle don sceolon on ende þisre worulde*—Ælfric here uses for emphasis a construction which he usually seems to avoid—*WHom* 6. 193 *Ðonne is us mycel þearf þæt we eac þæt understandan þæt hit to ðam dome nu georne nealæcð, hit* in *GenB* 596 above, and

Mald 5   þa þæt Offan mæg   ærest onfunde
                  þæt se eorl nolde   yrhðo geþolian . . . ;

(accusative after a preposition) *ÆCHom* ii. 318. 7 *Iohannes se apostol awrat . . . þæt we oncneowon Cristes lufe on us þurh þæt, þæt he sealde hine sylfne for us*; (genitive) *ÆLS* 32. 211 *Men þa þæs wundrodon hu þa weargas hangodon, ÆCHom* i. 146. 28 *Rihtlice swa halig wif wæs þæs wyrþe þæt heo moste witigian embe Crist*, and *GenB* 432 *Hycgað his ealle* ‖ *hu ge hi beswicen*; and (dative) *ÆCHom* i. 94. 1 *And þæt tacn wæs ða swa micel on geleaffullum mannum, swa micel swa nu is þæt halige fulluht, buton ðam anum þæt nan man ne mihte Godes rice gefaran.* . . . But noun clauses with anticipatory pronouns in cases other than the nominative are less common than noun clauses without such pronouns in prose and poetry of all periods and become increasingly rare as time goes by. Further on this topic see §§1963–5, 1967, and 1929.

§1893. To a speaker or writer of MnE, many of these correlative adverbs and demonstratives and many of the anticipatory pronouns are tautologic. But they allowed the Anglo-Saxon to control his sentence by completing one syntactical unit before beginning another. In my opinion, they are similar in nature and origin to recapitulatory elements such as *hie* in *CP* 5. 13 *Ure ieldran, ða ðe ðas stowa ær hioldon, hie lufodon wisdom* . . . and *ðæt* in *Bo* 102. 29 *7 þ unstille hweol ðe Ixion wæs to gebunden Leuita cyning for his scylde, ðæt oðstod for his hearpunga*, where the pronouns repeat the antecedent of the intervening adjective clauses, and similar elements in *Bede* 342. 20–6 and in *ÆCHom* i. 28. 1 *and [Crist] him of anam Adam and Euan and heora ofspring, þone dæl ðe him ær gecwemde*. See further *Guide*, §148.

§1894. I believe that this fondness for correlation, anticipation, and recapitulation, may have its origin in a 'feeling of insecurity in the face of the complicated sentence' (*Guide*, §150) which is sometimes apparent in the early prose (see *Guide*, §§139, 148, and 172) and which is a natural corollary of the move from parataxis to hypotaxis discussed in §§2421–32. That these devices go back to an earlier paratactic stage of the spoken language is suggested by a study of the early annals in the *Chronicle* and of the poetry, where oral delivery —which was in my opinion slower than in most modern recordings; see §3971—would favour devices which made for easier comprehension; consider *ChronA* 46. 28 (755) *7 þa geascode he þone cyning lytle werode on wifcyþþe on Meran tune, 7 hine þær berad, 7 þone bur utan be eode ær hine þa men onfunden þe mid þam kyninge wærun; 7 þa ongeat se cyning þæt . . .* ; *ChronA* 42. 5 (716) *Her Osred Norþanhymbra cyning wearþ ofslægen, 7 se hæfde vii winter rice æfter Aldferþe; þa feng Coenred to rice, 7 heold ii gear; þa Osric 7 heold xi gear*;

Beo 277		Ic þæs Hroðgar mæg
	þurh rumne sefan	ræd gelæran,
	hu he frod ond god	feond oferswyðeþ . . . ;

and

Beo 126	Ða wæs on uhtan	mid ærdæge
	Grendles guðcræft	gumum undyrne;
	þa wæs æfter wiste	wop up ahafen,
	micel morgensweg.	

§1895. Carkeet (1976, p. 49) objects to my exposition of this 'traditional view' concerning the origin of the correlative system on the grounds that 'it is loosely stated'—the fact that he quotes only ten of my words from some seven lines (*Guide*, §150) robs this criticism of some of its sting—that 'it fails to explain why the pairs very often consist of identical words', and that it 'also fails to deal with the frequency of *þe* in the conjunctions'. I discuss Carkeet's theory about the origin of conjunctions in §§2421–32; my remarks here should be read in conjunction with those sections. But let me restate my basic thesis, this time (I hope) less 'loosely'. I believe that these phenomena reflect the paratactic origin of OE sentence-structure and a resulting inability in the early stages to handle a complex sentence without, as it were, expressing one idea completely before beginning another. This would account for both the separation of antecedent and relative and the recapitulation of the antecedent by a demonstrative or personal pronoun. It would account for the anticipation of a coming noun clause by a neuter demonstrative or personal pronoun. It would explain why correlative adverbs and conjunctions are often identical in form and, as I point out in Mitchell, at press (c), §11, would account for the way in which the relative order of a principal and a subordinate clause varies (among other factors) according to the nature of the latter. In short, all the phenomena discussed by Carkeet are quite naturally explained by the assumption that parataxis preceded hypotaxis, that early writers were insecure in the face of the complicated sentence, and that—as their confidence grew— they used these devices for stylistic and rhetorical ends. This last stage would naturally result in the evolution of devices to distinguish the principal from the subordinate clause by marking formally distinctions already made by intonation. Hence the use of *þe* with conjunctions, the doubling of a word when it served as a conjunction, and the variations between the orders VS in a principal clause and S(. . .)V in a subordinate clause, the last of which are most consistently observed with those conjunctions which correspond in form to an adverb; see chapter IX.

§1896. Before I conclude this discussion, I must repeat that I am not suggesting and—*pace* one reviewer of my *Guide*[8]—did not suggest there that 'a feeling of insecurity in the face of the complicated sentence' is symptomatic of all the prose of the earlier period or of the prose of all periods; the notion is absurd.[9] Nor am I suggesting that the poets knew only parataxis; see §§1686-7. But the power and elegance of OE prose and the beauty and mystery of OE poetry are topics outside the scope of this book.

---

[8] Seiffert in *EPS* 10 (1967), 63-4. My views are very close to those expressed by Sweet in the Introduction to his edition of *Cura Pastoralis*, pp. xl-xli.

[9] A critical history of the development of OE prose is not part of my brief. But, while it is an acknowledged commonplace that it did develop, more detailed study of the syntax of individual authors is still required to illuminate the process. Liggins (1955, *passim*) gives some valuable pointers. Thus, she notes (1955, pp. 533-4) that Ælfric's skill in handling participial constructions is in marked contrast to the clumsiness displayed by the translators; analyses his individual preferences in the expression of cause (1955, pp. 537-41); and concludes (1955, p. 537): 'If the analysis of one aspect of OE prose style has not led to a revised opinion of it as a whole, it has served to reveal some of the details of the technique of its most attractive author, and of Ælfric's superiority to the other writers of the ninth, tenth and eleventh centuries.' Other contributions include those on Ælfric by Waterhouse (*ASE* 5 (1976), 83-103, and *ASE* 7 (1978), 131-48) and Godden (*The Old English Homily and Its Backgrounds*, edd. P. E. Szarmach and B. F. Huppé (New York, 1978), 99-117); that on Wulfstan by Hollowell (*Neophil.* 61 (1977), 287-96); and those on sentence-structure cited in §1922. The methods adopted, and the results achieved, by K. Manabe in *Syntax and Style in Early English Finite and Non-finite Clauses c.900-1600* (Tokyo, 1979) will also repay study.

E. THE ORDER AND ARRANGEMENT OF CLAUSES

§ 1897. Following Nesfield (pp. 143-4), we may usefully contrast loose sentences—which continue running on after grammatical completeness has been reached—with periodic sentences—which are not grammatically complete until the close. The distinction applies both to simple and to complex sentences, e.g. *Mald* 54 *Feallan sceolon* || *hæþene (æt hilde)* but *Mald* 40 *we willaþ mid þam sceattum us to scype gangan*, and *ÆCHom* i. 34. 33 *Maria wæs ða cuma ðær (swa swa þæt godspel us segð)* but *ÆCHom* i. 174. 20 *Buton se deofol gesawe þæt Crist man wære, ne gecostnode he hine*. But it must not be pressed too far; consider *ÆCHom* i. 166. 18 *Gif ðu Godes Sunu sy, feall (nu adun)* and (in its context) *ÆCHom* i. 168. 15 *Cwæð þa on his geðance, þæt he fandian wolde (hwæt he wære)*.

§ 1898. West (p. 103) observes that his study 'shows that the cumulative, or loose, sentence has always been the predominant sentence type in written English, back through *Beowulf*'. His limited study cannot be taken as authoritative,[10] but he probably states a general truth, though we can perhaps omit the word 'written'. The time is

[10] It is based on a very limited corpus indeed; fails to make some essential distinctions —simple and complex sentences are not distinguished, 'there are no compound sentences as such' (p. 13), and all types of subordinate clauses are lumped together; and introduces what seems to me the peculiar concept of the 'intermediate sentence' (pp. 13-15). The last is not, as one might suspect, another name for a clause used *apo koinou*, but is used of sentences like *ChronA* 84. 17-20 (894), which—if the verb governing *foregisla vi* had been expressed—would (according to West) have comprised a periodic sentence followed by a simple sentence. The problem is complicated by our inability to decide whether some clauses are principal or subordinate—which, according to Andrew (*Postscript*, pp. vii-viii), produces the 'curious superstition' that in *Beowulf* the pattern 'principal + temporal clause' is permissible while the pattern 'temporal + principal clause' is not; see §§ 2536-8—and by the *apo koinou* clauses discussed in §§ 3789-803. In view of all these uncertainties, blanket percentages such as those produced by West are of little value.

The sections which follow owe a great deal to Miss Ruth Waterhouse of Macquarie University, N.S.W., who has helped me, not only by sending me a copy of her article (Waterhouse 1976), but also in correspondence and personal discussion. I acknowledge the debt gratefully. My reading of her thesis (Waterhouse 1978) confirms me in my opinion that our knowledge of OE syntax and style will benefit from detailed study of the structure of sentences containing one subordinate clause or more and of the factors affecting the position and length of the clauses. But all types of sentences will have to be considered; see my comments in § 1901, fn. 13.

Significant differences in the use of clauses in Wærferth's translation of Gregory's *Dialogues* and in the revision in MS *H* (made at Worcester during or just before the first half of the eleventh century) are discussed by Yerkes (pp. 314-38). He concludes (p. 339) that 'virtually every linguistic change introduced into Wærferth's translation by the reviser and discussed or cited above either brings the translation more into accord with normal PresE or does not have any effect on its modernity'. An important restatement of Yerkes's findings will be found in the Introduction and Conclusion to his *Syntax and Style in Old English* (Binghamton, N.Y., 1982).

not yet ripe for a full consideration of the problem; see §1922. But some points must be made.

§1899. In English of all periods, adverb and adverb phrases in clauses with the order SV(O) tend to follow the verb (and object), and most types of subordinate clauses tend to follow their principal clause, the likeliest exceptions being perhaps conditional and temporal clauses,[11] and indefinite adjective clauses used as subjects. (The presence or absence of correlation is an important factor; see §1925.) In general such sentences will be loose rather than periodic, though there are exceptions, e.g. 'He completed what he could'. The pattern of repetition with variation and advance so common in OE poetry also favours the loose rather than the periodic structure. Exemplification of these points would be superfluous.

§1900. On the whole, sentences in which a subordinate clause precedes the principal clause tend to be periodic, but an addition to the principal clause may make the sentence loose, e.g. *ÆCHom* i. 296. 3 *Ðaða hi up to heofonum starigende stodon, ða gesawon hi ðær twegen englas on hwitum gerelan, þus cweðende, Ge Galileisce weras, hwi stande ge ðus starigende wið heofenas weard?* The same is true of sentences in which the subordinate clause falls within the principal clause, e.g. *ÆCHom* i. 184. 3 *forðy is þis lif, swa swa we ær cwædon, þære sæ wiðmeten* (periodic) but *ÆCHom* i. 186. 13 *þa fif hlafas ðe se cnapa bær getacniað þa fif bec ðe Moyses se heretoga sette on ðære ealdan æ* (loose).

§1901. As we have seen, complex sentences consisting of two clauses can be arranged so that the subordinate clause comes before, after, or within, the principal clause.[12] If we take P = the principal clause and Sp = a subordinate clause qualifying or modifying (elements in) the principal clause, we can represent these symbolically as Sp | P; P | Sp; and P | (Sp) (round brackets denoting an interpolated or intercalary

---

[11] Möllmer (pp. 9-10 and 20-1) observes that subordinate *þa* and *þonne* clauses regularly follow the principal clause. But this conclusion leans too heavily on figures from the poetry and so reflects the 'curious superstition' referred to in the previous footnote. He is not justified in using it to support a theory about the origin of subordinate clauses. However, Robinson (1973, p. 472) makes a point about the value of syntactical glosses for the study of clause order which should be taken up by future investigators. See further David Yerkes, *Syntax and Style in Old English* (Binghamton, N. Y., 1982), 98-9.

[12] The fourth possible arrangement—principal clause within the subordinate clause—occurs in Latin (GL, §686), but not in English. In examples like *Or* 17. 33 *þa Finnas, him þuhte, 7 þa Beormas spræcon neah an geþeode*, we have to do with a parenthesis; see §3849.

clause),[13] respectively. These two-clause patterns have not been allotted an alphabetical symbol. The subordinate clause itself or elements in it can in turn be qualified or modified by another subordinate clause which immediately follows it or is interpolated in it. I shall call such a clause Ss. This pattern—which I shall call type A— can occur in two basic arrangements. Type A1, with P first, is seen in ÆCHom i. 34. 28 *He wæs mid wacum cildclaðum bewæfed þæt he us forgeafe ða undeadlican tunecan þe we forluron on ðæs frumsceapenan mannes forgægednysse* and (with an extra Ss) ÆCHom i. 18. 21 *Ða deadan fell getacnodon þæt hi wæron ða deadlice. þe mihton beon undeadlice gif hi heoldon þæt eaðelice Godes bebod*, where we have P | Sp | Ss and P | Sp | Ss | Ss respectively. An example of P | Sp like ÆCHom ii. 530. 13 *Se lareow gearcað Godes weg þonne he mannum bodað lifes word* will become P | Sp | Ss in dependent speech, e.g. ÆCHom ii. 512. 29 *Ne sæde ure Hælend þæt he swa wolde beon mid purpuran gehiwod oþþe mid helme scinende þonne he eft come mid engla ðrymme*. Type A1 with intercalary Ss —P | Sp | (Ss)—is seen in ÆCHom i. 120. 20 *Se lareow Hægmon cweð on ðissere trahtnunge þæt seo dun þe se Hælend of astah getacnode heofenan rice.* . . .

§1902. We have type A2, with Sp first—Sp | Ss | P—in ÆCHom i. 52. 27 *Gif ge forgyfað þam mannum þe wið eow agyltað, þonne forgyfð eow eower Fæder eowere synna* and (with intercalary Ss)— Sp | (Ss) | P—in ÆCHom i. 54. 24 *Gif ðonne se cristena mann, þe ðin broðor is, ðe ahwar geyfelode, þæt ðu scealt miltsigende forgifan.* See further §1905.

§1903. We have already seen in ÆCHom i. 18. 21 (§1901) that type A1, which Waterhouse (1976, p. 174) calls the 'gradient' construction because each clause is subordinate to its predecessor, can have more than one Ss. There is, of course, a practical limit to the number of subordinate clauses which can follow a principal clause. But we find six subordinate clauses and a parenthetic *cwæð Orosius* in *Or* 40. 23-7, all of them qualifying or modifying (elements in) the

---

[13] Finer distinctions can be made to take account of the position of the intercalary clause relative to the subject, verb, and/or object, of the principal clause. Waterhouse (1976, p. 185, and 1978, pp. 92-6) has some valuable suggestions; see §1907. Future workers undertaking more detailed analyses than space permits here will need to make use of the distinctions she has so rightly drawn. They will also need to follow her where I have not in distinguishing the various types of subordinate clauses instead of using the blanket symbol S, since the arrangement of sentences largely depends on the types of subordinate clauses involved. It is impossible for me to treat this topic fully here. But the table at the end of this chapter (§1925) attempts to describe some important tendencies.

preceding clause and so giving the sequence P | *cwæð Orosius* | Sp | Ss | Ss | Ss | Ss | Ss. In *WHom* 5. 88–96 we have nine subordinate clauses, all of them except the last—which is co-ordinate with the clause it follows—qualifying or modifying (elements in) the preceding clause. So we have the sequence P | Sp | Ss | . . . | Ss | Ss + Ss, where the symbol + indicates that two clauses are co-ordinate; see further §1910. (Here the co-ordinate clauses are adjective clauses sharing the same introductory word *þe*. I do not here differentiate this pattern from that in which two clauses of the same kind occur in co-ordination with the introductory word repeated or (as I point out in the preceding footnote) from that in which the subordinate clauses in co-ordination are of different types.)

§1904. The + Ss clause in *WHom* 5. 88–96 can be said to level out the gradient. The same is true of a clause co-ordinate with the principal clause—+ P—or with a subordinate clause attached to the principal clause—+ Sp. Thus we find the sequence P + P | Sp + Sp | Ss | Ss in *ÆCHom* i. 328. 3 *Biscopas sind þæs ylcan hades on Godes gelaðunge, and healdað þa gesetnysse on heora biscepunge, swa þæt hi settað heora handa ofer gefullude menn, and biddað þæt se Ælmihtiga Wealdend him sende ða seofonfealdan gife his Gastes, seðe leofað and rixað a butan ende*, where the gradient continues after levelling out. See further §1910.

§1905. In general, long sequences of subordinate clauses such as these follow the principal clause. When a principal clause does not begin a sentence, it is usually preceded by only one clause (the pattern Sp | P in §1901), e.g. *ÆCHom* ii. 144. 15 *Gif se Ælmihtiga eow ðises geuðe, brucað þæra wæstma and me ne biddað*—Sp | P + P; cf. the examples of pattern Ba2 in §1906. But two subordinate clauses (or more) precede in the type A2 pattern Sp | Ss | P, e.g. *ÆCHom* i. 174. 20 *Buton se deofol gesawe þæt Crist man wære, ne gecostnode he hine* and Sp + Sp | Ss + Ss | P + P, e.g. *ÆCHom* i. 6. 24 *Gif þu ne gestentst þone unrihtwisan, and hine ne manast, þæt he fram his arleasnysse gecyrre and lybbe, þonne swelt se arleasa on his unrihtwisnysse, and ic wille ofgan æt ðe his blod.*[14] On the possibility of pattern Ba3 (Sp | Sp | P), see §1907. There are occasional examples of three subordinate clauses preceding the principal clause, e.g. *CP* 261. 16 *Se ðe for us gebæd to his Fæder, ðeah he him emnmiehtig sie on his godhade, ða ða him mon on bismer to gebæd,*

---

[14] Similar patterns may occur in MnE. Thus, the sentence which appears in different forms as sentences 59, 60, and 61, in Quirk, §11. 82, could be rephrased as Sp | Ss | P— 'That you would help me if you could is of small comfort'.

ða swugode he (where it could be argued that *se* is an antecedent) and *ÆCHom* i. 178. 27 *Swa swa Godes æ us bebyt þæt we sceolon ealle þa ðing þe us gesceotað of ures geares teolunge Gode þa teoðunge syllan, swa we sceolon eac on ðisum teoðingdagum urne lichaman mid forhæfednysse Gode to lofe teoðian.* We find four in *ÆLS(Jul)* 17. 257 *Gif hwa nu wundrige hwi god wolde forgifan þam yfelum mannum agenne freodom þone* [other MSS *þonne*] *he wat on ær þæt hi yfel don willað. Nu cweðe we þæt hit ne gerist nanum ricum cynincge þæt hi ealle beon þeowe menn ðe him þenian sceolon.* . . .

§1906. The essence of the type A pattern is that it has only one Sp clause or one sequence of co-ordinate Sp clauses. But a principal clause or elements in it can be qualified or modified by two subordinate clauses which are not co-ordinate with or dependent on one another. Following Waterhouse (1976, p. 175), we can describe this as the 'two-to-one' construction. There are three basic patterns which I shall call Ba1, Ba2, and Ba3. Type Ba1—P | Sp | Sp—is seen in *ÆCHom* i. 50. 9 *He is gecweden protomartyr, þæt is se forma cyðere, forðan ðe he æfter Cristes ðrowunge ærest martyrdom geðrowode,* in *ÆCHom* i. 90. 28 *Ðis is min wed þæt ge healdan sceolon betwux me and eow, þæt ælc hysecild on eowrum cynrene beo ymbsniden,* and (with the addition of Ss) in *ÆCHom* i. 82. 17 *Ac he cydde syððan his facenfullan syrewunge, hu he ymbe wolde, gif he hine gemette, ðaða he ealle his efenealdan adylegode for his anes ehtnysse.* But the principal clause need not come first. We find type Ba2— Sp | P | Sp—in *ÆCHom* i. 26. 25 *þeah ðe eal mennisc wære gegaderod, ne mihton hi ealle hine acwellan, gif he sylf nolde, ÆCHom* i. 146. 21 *þaða se Symeon hæfde gewitegod þas witegunge be Criste, þa com þær sum wuduwe, seo wæs Anna gehaten,* and (with the addition of Ss) in *ÆCHom* i. 122. 33 *Mid þam ðe he forbead þam gehæledum hreoflian þæt he hit nanum men ne cydde, mid þam he sealde us bysne þæt we ne sceolon na widmærsian ure weldæda.* . . .

§1907. Type Ba3—Sp | Sp | P—is mathematically possible, but seems unnatural in MnE; consider 'Before he entered the house, in order that he should not leave fingerprints he put on rubber gloves'. It must not be confused with type A2 as seen in examples like 'Before he entered the house which he intended to burgle, he put on rubber gloves' and *ÆCHom* i. 174. 20 (§1905)—Sp | Ss | P. Waterhouse (1976, pp. 185-6) refers to four examples of what she describes as 'two-to-one' constructions with a 'both preceding arrangement' and has kindly given me the references. On my criteria, none of the four is Sp | Sp | P. I would call *ÆLS* 31. 175-6 Sp + Sp | P. Waterhouse

(1976, p. 178) does not distinguish these two patterns, but later included *ÆLS* 31. 175-6 among her co-ordination examples (1978, pp. 96-7).[15] Two—*ÆLS* 29. 273-4 and *ÆLS* 16. 180-3—can be Sp | Sp | P only if we accept Waterhouse's dictum (1976, p. 185) that 'where the interpolated clause precedes both subject and verb of the head clause, it is classed as preceding, even though it may follow some part of the head clause'. This seems to me an unnecessary over-simplification.[16] *ÆLS* 29. 273-4 begins with a nominative element which is repeated by a personal pronoun in the second subordinate clause and in the principal clause which ends the sentence. I would classify *ÆLS* 16. 180-3 as Sp | Ss | P | (Sp) + (Sp). I discuss the fourth example (*ÆLS* 11. 123-5) in §1915.

§1908. In the 'two-to-one' constructions so far discussed, the head clause P has been the principal clause of the sentence. But it may be a subordinate clause in dependent speech, e.g. *ÆCHom* i. 48. 34 *ac ðeahhwæðere is geþuht, gif ænig todal beon mæg betwux martyrum, þæt se is healicost seðe ðone martyrdom æfter Gode astealde*;[17] cf. §§1901 and 1917.

§1909. In examples of type Ba, as in those of type A, an Sp can be intercalary, e.g. *ÆCHom* i. 152. 17 *Ða men þe beforan þam Hælende ferdon, ciddon ongean ðone blindan þæt he suwian sceolde*, *ÆCHom* i. 182. 25 *Seo sæ, þe se Hælend oferferde, getacnað þas andweardan woruld, to ðære com Crist and oferferde*, and *ÆCHom* i. 96. 1 *ac gif hit him dyslic þince, þonne cide he wið God, þe hit gesette, na wið us, þe hit secgað*. An Sp can in turn be qualified or modified by an Ss, e.g. *ÆCHom* i. 132. 11-15 and *ÆCHom* i. 44. 9 *We rædað on ðære bec þe is gehaten Actus Apostolorum, þæt ða apostolas gehadodon seofon diaconas on ðære gelaðunge þe of Iudeiscum folce to Cristes geleafan beah, æfter his ðrowunge, and æriste of deaðe, and upstige to heofenum.*

§1910. Both types A and Ba can be augmented by a clause or clauses introduced by conjunctions such as *ond*, *ac*, *oþþe*, and *ne*. So we

---

[15] A finer classification can of course be obtained if desired by distinguishing the various types of subordinate clauses and by indicating whether two co-ordinate clauses of the same type share the same introductory word or formula or not. See §§1901 fn. 13 and 1903.

[16] Waterhouse (1978, pp. 98-100 and *passim*) persists in this over-simplification. But she has shown that a finer classification can—and indeed must—be obtained here too, this time by distinguishing the nature of the element of the principal clause which precedes the subordinate clause. See initially Waterhouse 1978, pp. 92-6.

[17] Mathematically speaking, there are other ways of arranging one principal clause P and two subordinate clauses Sp and/or Ss. But we can, I think, safely eliminate those involving two Ss clauses (P | Ss | Ss, Ss | P | Ss, and Ss | Ss | P); those in which Ss immediately follows P (P | Ss | Sp and Sp | P | Ss); and those with initial Ss (Ss | P | Sp and Ss | Sp | P).

find variations of type A in *ÆCHom* i. 32. 17 *He wæs acenned on þæs caseres dagum þe wæs Octauianus gehaten, se gerymde Romana rice to ðan swiðe þæt him eal middangeard to beah, and he wæs forði Augustus geciged, þæt is geycende his rice, ÆCHom* i. 54. 22 *Gif ðu ðonne þinum cristenum breðer deredest, þonne hæfð he sum ðing ongean ðe, and þu scealt be Godes tæcunge hine gegladian, ær ðu ðine lac geoffrige,* and *ÆCHom* i. 34. 23 *Næs þæt cild forði gecweden hire frumcennede cild swilce heo oðer siððan acende, ac forði þe Crist is frumcenned of manegum gastlicum gebroðrum,* and of type Ba in *ÆCHom* i. 58. 19 *Witodlice ðisum leofan leorningcnihte befæste se Hælend his modor, þaþa he on rode hengene mancynn alysde, þæt his clæne lif ðæs clænan mædenes Marian gymde, and heo ða on hyre swyster suna ðenungum wunode* and *ÆCHom* i. 22. 31 *Eft ðonne hi deade wæron, þonne cwædon þa cucan þæt hi wæron godas and wurðodon hi and him lac offrodon.* Combinations of types A and Ba also occur, e.g. *ÆCHom* i. 82. 17, *ÆCHom* i. 122. 33 (both in §1906), *ÆCHom* i. 50. 14 *þa leasan gewitan, ðe hine forsædon, hine ongunnon ærest to torfienne; forðan þe Moyses æ tæhte, þæt swa hwa swa oðerne to deaðe forsæde, sceolde wurpan ðone forman stan to ðam ðe he ær mid his tungan acwealde* and

ÆLS 15. 159   Se feorða godspellere is Iohannes Cristes moddrian sunu, se wæs Criste swa leof þæt he hlynode uppan his breoste, on ðam þe wæs behyd eall se heofonlica wisdom, swylce he of ðam drunce þa deopan lare þe he siððan awrat on wundorlicor gesetnyssa, swa þæt he oferstah ealle gesceafta and þa word geopenade þe englas ne dorston.

§1911.   A third arrangement is, however, possible in a complex sentence consisting of one principal and two subordinate clauses—one subordinate clause—Sc—may modify or qualify the complex sentence made up by the other clauses. MnE examples include 'Blessed are those who are sorrowful, because they shall be comforted' and 'If he is found guilty, it is certain that he will get a long sentence'. Here the patterns can be described as P | Sp | Sc and Sc | P | Sp respectively. I shall call examples like these type Bb or 'one-to-two' constructions.[18]

---

[18] Waterhouse (1976, p. 179 and *passim*) regards the 'two-to-one' construction (type Ba) as 'standard' and the 'one-to-two' construction (type Bb) as 'deviant' from it. As she says (1976, p. 193), quoting *ÆLS* 28. 157-9 (where the last clause may be Sp or Sc), the two shade into one another. But we do not refuse to distinguish the indicative from the subjunctive because there are ambiguous forms. The distinction between Sp and Sc is easily made when one subordinate clause (Sp) is an essential part of the principal clause, e.g. the dependent question in *ÆCHom* i. 14. 4 (§1912)—this could be replaced by a noun or pronoun object—and the limiting adjective clause in *Gen* 2. 11 *An ea of ðam hatte Fison, seo* [dem. or rel. pron.?] *gæð onbutan ðæt land ðe is gehaten Euilað, ðær ðær gold wyxð*—this could be replaced by a participial construction *Euilað gehaten.* But in an example like *ChronE* 3.12

§1912. We find type Bb1—P | Sp | Sc—in examples like *ÆCHom*
i. 14. 4 *Gyse hu mihte Adam tocnawan hwæt he wære, buton he
wære gehyrsum on sumum þince his Hlaforde, ÆCHom* i. 82. 28 *ac
hit wære to hrædlic gif he ða on cildcradole acweald wurde, swilce
ðonne his tocyme mancynne bediglod wære*, and (with intercalary
(Sp)) *ÆCHom* i. 122. 23 *ac se inra mann, þæt is seo sawul, bið
micele atelicor, gif heo mid mislicum leahtrum begripen bið* and
ÆCHom i. 124. 2 *Witodlice ne bið us mid nanum oðrum edleane
forgolden, gif we good for gylpe doð, buton mid helle susle; forðan
ðe gilp is an heofodleahter.* If the *þe* clause is restrictive in *ÆCHom*
i. 12. 12 *Swa mihton eac þa oðre þe ðær feollon don, gif hi woldon*
we have type Bb1—P | (Sp) | Sc. But it may not be, in which case
we have type Ba1—P | (Sp) | Sp.

§1913. Type Bb2—Sc | P | Sp—appears in *ÆCHom* i. 26. 25 *þeah
ðe eal mennisc wære gegaderod, ne mihton hi ealle hine acwellan gif
he sylf nolde, ÆLS* 5. 195-8, *ÆLS* 13. 33 *gif he ðonne nele his
fultum us don ne ure bene gehyran, þonne bið hit swutol þæt we mid
yfelum dædum hine ær gegremedon*, and (with intercalary (Sp))
ÆCHom i. 124. 17 *ac gif heora wena soð wære, ðonne nolde Drihten
asendan þone ðe he sylf gehælde to þam sacerde mid ænigre lace.* We
also have Sc | P | Sp in *ÆCHom* i. 12. 20 *ac God ne gesceop hine na
to deofle; ac þaða he wæs mid ealle fordon and forscyldgod þurh þa
miclan upahefednysse and wiðerweardnysse, þa wearð he to deofle
awend, seðe ær wæs mære engel geworht* if the adjective clause is
restrictive. But in the whole context it may not be, in which case we
have type Ba2—Sp | P | Sp.

§1914. I have found occasional examples of type Bb3—Sc | Sp | P
—e.g. *ÆCHom* i. 52. 34 *witodlice gif hwa furðon ænne man hata ð
on ðisum middangearde, swa hwæt swa he to gode gedeð, eal he hit
forlyst* and (with co-ordination and an Ss clause) *ÆCHom* i. 54. 2
*þeah ðe ic aspende ealle mine æhta on ðearfena bigleofan, and ðeah
ðe ic minne agenne lichaman to cwale gesylle, swa ðæt ic forbyrne
on martyrdome; gif ic næbbe ða soðan lufe, ne fremað hit me nan*

(—) 7 *gif hwa eow wiðstent we eow fultumiað þ ge hit magon gegangan*, classification must
be a matter of opinion. My feeling is that the *þ* clause is more closely linked to the principal
clause than the *gif* clause and so I would read it Sc | P | Sp. Yet I can see a case for Sp | P | Sp
or even for Sp | P | Sc. But we are now down to feelings.

However, as Waterhouse has pointed out, the 'two-to-one' and the 'one-to-two' constructions are different in kind from the gradient constructions of type A. Hence I call them Ba
and Bb rather than B and C. I regret that, despite my advice to the contrary, Waterhouse in
her thesis (Waterhouse 1978) failed to distinguish these two types from one another and
from subordinate clauses which are co-ordinate with one another when compiling her final
figures.

ðing, and of type Bb4—P | Sc | Sp—e.g. *ÆCHom* i. 16. 14 *forði is se man betera—gif he gode geðihð—þonne ealle ða nytenu sindon*, where the emphatic parenthesis introduces a minatory note. This complex is in turn modified by Sc + Sc | Ss and an independent exclamatory clause (not quoted). The same three clause types—principal, conditional, and comparative—are arranged in *ÆCHom* i. 96. 5-7 as type Bb1 (P | Sp | Sc).

§1915. By definition, no pattern involving two Scs and one P is possible. But two other patterns are theoretically possible. The first is Sp | Sc | P, which I shall call Bb5. On the analogy of *ÆCHom* i. 52. 34, quoted in §1914 as an example of type Bb3, an OE equivalent of 'Whatever good he does—if he hates even one man on this earth—he will lose it all' could occur. One of Waterhouse's 'both preceding' examples (1976, pp. 185-6) comes close to being one— *ÆLS* 11. 123 *Se þe soðlice gelyfð on þone lyfigendan fæder and on his ancennedan sunu and on þone halgan gast þeah þe he dead beo he bið swa þeah cucu*. But the fact that the initial adjective clause may be used *apo koinou* with both of the following *hes* complicates the situation. So too does the fact that *se* may be an antecedent relative repeated by *he* in the principal clause; this would give us P | (Sp) | (Sc)—a variant of type Bb1. However, I cannot see *ÆLS* 11. 123 as Sp | Sp | P or as Sc | Sp | P.

§1916. The last possible pattern is type Bb6—Sp | P | Sc. Examples include *ÆLS* 4. 207 *Gif þu nelle me ofslean asend me to þam casere þæt ic þær deað þrowige for minum drihtne criste*,[19] *ÆLS* 9. 48 *and þæt þu on deaðe sylst for drihtnes naman þu hit sylst for þan þe þu hit ne miht mid þe aweg lædan*, and (with more than three clauses) *ÆCHom* i. 446. 30 *þa ðe on mæigðhade wuniað blission hi, forðan ðe hi geearnodon þæt beon þæt hi heriað* and *ÆCHom* i. 446. 33 *þa þe on clænan wudewanhade sind, herion hi and arwurðion, forðan ðe swutol is þæt hi ne magon beon clæne buton ðurh Cristes gife, seoðe wæs fulfremedlice on Marian ðe hi herigað*, where the pattern is Sp | P + P | Sc | Ss | Ss | Ss. It will be noted that some of the examples of patterns Bb5 and Bb6 quoted above involve an

---

[19] It is possible, as Waterhouse points out (private communication, July 1977) that a *gif* clause can be separated from its principal clause. If we do this, *ÆLS* 4. 207 is type Ba2 (Sp | P | Sp). The same difficulty arises in *ÆLS* 1. 143-5, *ÆLS* 3. 186-8, and in *ÆLS* 5. 70-4, which I would classify as Sp | P + P | Sc because P + P is in effect an inseparable unit. This kind of difficulty could be advanced as an argument for not distinguishing the 'two-to-one' pattern (type Ba) from the 'one-to-two' pattern (type Bb), since (as Waterhouse reminds me) the degree of tightness of the relationship may vary with the types of clauses involved. But, as I have already said (§1911 fn.), I believe that the distinction can sometimes be made and therefore is worth making.

indefinite adjective clause which serves as the subject of the principal clause but is recapitulated by a personal pronoun which in MnE would be tautologic.

§1917. So far all the clauses designated P in these 'one-to-two' constructions have been the principal clauses of the sentence. That they can be subordinate is clear from examples of dependent speech like *ÆCHom* i. 82. 12 [*Herodes*] *ðohte gif he hi ealle ofsloge, þæt se an ne ætburste þe he sohte* and *ÆCHom* ii. 336. 12–18, with the sequence P | Sp | Ss | (Ss) | Sc | Ss | Ss | Sc, where the first Sc clause modifies the preceding complex of four clauses and the second modifies the complex of two Ss's which precedes it. Other examples in which an Sc modifies a complex of more than two clauses include *ÆCHom* i. 48. 9–13. An Sc clause may itself contain one or more coordinate clauses. Both these phenomena are illustrated in *ÆCHom* i. 12. 12 *Swa mihton eac þa oðre þe ðær feollon don, gif hi woldon; forþi ðe God hi geworhte to wlitegum engla gecynde, and let hi habban agenne cyre, and hi næfre ne gebigde ne ne nydde mid nanum þingum to þam yfelan ræde.*

§1918. Waterhouse (1976, pp. 177 and 192–3, and private communication) notes occasional examples of what may be 'three-to-one' or 'four-to-one' constructions. In some of these it is not clear whether the last clause is Sp, referring to the principal clause only, or Sc, referring to the complex. Thus, in *ÆLS* 21. 223 *Aþelwold þa se arwurða and se eadiga bisceop þe on ðam dagum wæs on Winceastre bisceop bead his munecum eallum þe on ðam mynstre wunodon þæt hi ealle eodon endemes to cyrcan*, we have P | (Sp) | Sp | Sp if the second *þe* clause is non-restrictive. But we have P | (Sp) | Sp | Sc— a 'two-to-one' construction followed by a 'one-to-three' (in other words, a combination of types Ba and Bb)—if the *þe* clause is restrictive, as it is in *ÆLS* 32. 133 *þa æfter fyrste syððan hi afarene wæron com þæt landfolc to þe þær to lafe wæs þa þær heora hlafordes lic læg butan heafde*. Again, in *ÆLS* 28. 157 *þa halgan þe we heriað and heora gelican forsawon þisne middaneard þeah þe he myrge wære þa ða hi on life wæron forþan þe hi gewilnodon þæs ecan*, we have, according to Waterhouse (1976, p. 193), either a 'four-to-one' construction or a 'three-to-one' modified by Sc. I prefer the latter classification, because saints can wish for eternal life only in this world; they have it in the next. A clear example of a 'four-to-one' construction occurs in dependent speech in *ÆLS* 24. 125 *and se hælend foresceawode syððan he to heofonum astah þæt he sende þam cyninge swa swa he ær gecwæð ænne of ðam hundseofontigum*

*þe he geceas to bodigenne se wæs Tatheus gehaten þæt he gehælde
ðone cynincg*, where (disregarding the two introductory clauses) we
have P | (Sp) | Sp | Sp | Sp.

§1919. Other variations in sentence-structure demand mention.
Rhetorical repetitions are common, e.g. *ÆCHom* i. 168. 23 *Eaðe
mihte God, seðe awende wæter to wine, and seðe ealle gesceafta of
nahte geworhte, eaðelice he mihte awendan ða stanas to hlafum*; see
further §§1893-4.

§1920. Another variation is the arrangement in which material
which properly belongs to a subordinate clause appears before the
subordinating conjunction. This occurs in the prose and (more frequently) in the poetry. The subordinate clause precedes the principal
clause in examples like *Bede* 444. 24 *7 he monige forð acigde buton
yldincge þæt hi heora mandæda hreowe dydon*, Latin *ac longe
lateque diffamatum multos ad agendam et non differendam scelerum
suorum paenitudinem prouocauit*, *Solil* 26. 21 *Uncuð þeh ic wære,
ðonun cume* [*ic*] . . . , *LawAfEl* 21 *Sunu oððe dohtor gif he of-
stinge, ðæs ilcan domes sie he wyrðe, ÆCHom* i. 138. 17 *Eac on
heora orfe, swa hwæt swa frumcenned wære, bringan þæt to Godes
huse and hit ðær Gode offrian*, and perhaps *Wid* 142 *lof se gewyrceð,
‖ hafað under heofonum heahfæstne dom.*[20] But, in what seems the
more common manifestation of this peculiarity, the principal clause
comes first and material from the subordinate clause appears in it.
Here, as in the preceding group, the OE arrangement would be unacceptable today. Examples include *Solil* 34. 8 *Ðara fif þinga þu
ondrest þæt þu scyle sum forleosan, Solil* 57. 13 *and ða ðreo ðing ic
gehure þæt þu nu gewislice wast, CP* 83. 22, *CP* 171. 14 *Ða saglas is
beboden ðæt scoldon beon mid golde befongne, Or* 18. 31 *7 norðe-
weard he cwæð, þær hit smalost wære, þæt hit mihte beon þreora
mila brad to þæm more*, and

Wan 58   Forþon ic geþencan ne mæg   geond þas woruld
              for hwan modsefa   min ne gesweorce.

I discuss this and similar examples in *NM* 69 (1968), 58-9. Klaeber
(*Kock Studies*, pp. 112-15) gives more from the poetry. Other possible

[20] Kock (*Ang.* 45 (1921), 130) writes: '*Se*, of course, is a demonstrative. Holthausen
transforms it into a relative. That is bad for three reasons and good for none. It involves
extraordinary word-order, want of parallelism, and meagre sense.' Holthausen's interpretation is, however, possible. The syntax is supported by the examples cited above. Parallelism
is not essential in every sentence in OE poetry. The assumption that *lof* and *dom* are necessarily identical is a dangerous one; 'he who performs *lof* will win *dom*' seems a possible
translation until the lexicographers prove otherwise.

examples are *ÆLS* 1. 83 *Nu wylle we eow sum þing be eowre sawle sæccgan, sceortlice gif we magon* (where, however, *sceortlice* may be *apo koinou*), *Beo* 14 (§3120),

Beo 1355   no hie fæder cunnon,
           hwæþer him ænig wæs   ær acenned
           dyrnra gasta

(but *cunnon* may be taken *apo koinou* with two objects; see §§1969 and 3119-20), and

Wife 45   sy æt him sylfum gelong
           eal his worulde wyn,   sy ful wide fah
           feorres folclondes,   þæt min freond siteð . . . ,

where *fah* may belong in the *þæt* clause '. . . that my friend sits outcast'.

§1921. In his lectures Alistair Campbell was wont to draw attention to 'a somewhat similar artifice' in the poetry by which 'an adverbial element is deliberately placed in contiguity to a verb to which it does not belong'. The phrase precedes the verb, e.g. *on ræste* in

Beo 120   Wiht unhælo,
           grim ond grædig,   gearo sona wæs,
           reoc ond reþe,   ond on ræste genam
           þritig þegna

and *ealle* in

GuthA 119   Oþer him þas eorþan   ealle sægde
             læne under lyfte,   ond þa longan god
             herede on heofonum,   þær haligra
             sawla gesittað   in sigorwuldre
             dryhtnes dreamas.

See further Klaeber, ibid.

§1921a. Occasionally we find material which belongs to the principal clause placed in a subordinate clause, e.g.

GenB 618   Gif giet þurh cuscne siodo
             læst mina lara,   þonne gife ic him þæs leohtes genog
             þæs ic þe swa godes   gegired hæbbe,

PPs 57. 5   God heora toðas   grame gescæneð
             þa hi on muðe   mycle habbað,

and

Jul 465   Ic sceal þinga gehwylc
             þolian ond þafian   on þinne dom,

        womdæda onwreon,   þe ic wideferg
        sweartra gesyrede,

where *swa godes, mycle,* and *sweartra,* respectively belong to the preceding principal clause. Further examples, including some from the prose, are discussed in §§2226-30. Wagner (pp. 69-70) cites

Beo 205   Hæfde se goda   Geata leoda
                cempan gecorone   þara þe he cenoste
                findan mihte

and

Beo 2867   ... þonne he on ealubence   oft gesealde
                healsittendum   helm ond byrnan,
                þeoden his þegnum,   swylce he þrydlicost
                ower feor oððe neah   findan meahte ...

among examples in which a superlative belonging to the principal clause appears in a subordinate clause. Such an interpretation is not essential; see §2266.

§1922. These examples are far from exhausting the variety of OE sentence-structure. There is more work to be done here. This will involve consideration of the nature of the principal clause—are the patterns different with statements, questions, exclamations, and commands or wishes?—and of the order of the different types of subordinate clauses in relation to the principal clause and to one another; here Waterhouse's work is already beginning to show important results. Even more exciting is the possibility that such studies will throw further light on the stylistic preferences of prose writers and poets; the work of Liggins on *Orosius* (*Ang.* 88 (1970), 319-20) and of Schaar on the *Cynewulf* group has already pointed the way and here too that of Waterhouse seems likely to produce further advances.[21]

[21] However, Schaar's methods and conclusions are far from acceptable as they stand. On the (in)validity of his test for distinguishing principal and subordinate clauses, see §2445. He seems to me to belong to the 'hypotaxis good, parataxis bad' school; see, for example, his pages 153 and 325. His observation (p. 184) that *Dream* has 'a marked tendency towards syndetic combinations' is completely untrue of lines 44-77 and of dubious validity for lines 1-43. The difference he draws between 'loose variation' and 'close variation' (pp. 184-234) does not seem as clear-cut to me as it does to him—consider *Ex* 447-515 and his own conclusions (especially p. 325, top)—and I doubt the truth of the simple equations 'close variation = vernacular tradition', 'loose variation = Latin influence' (his pp. 324-5); cf. Sisam's observations in *PBA* 18 (1932), 315. Because he wrote in 1949, Schaar's work on 'the testimony of the parallels' (pp. 235-309) is outdated. He points out on p. 235 that 'Kail . . . held that the Anglo-Saxon poetical parallels are rather parts of a large stock of formulas, from which the poets may have drawn independently.' He is not to be seriously condemned in 1978 for failing in 1949 to realize the full implications of this remark. The application of the oral-formulaic theory to OE poetry was begun by Lord with an analysis of *Beowulf* in 1949; see Robinson, *Speculum*, 45 (1970), 285 fn. 4. Magoun's influential

But the value of clause order as a criterion for punctuation must not be exaggerated; see my comments in *NM* 70 (1969), 78-81.

F. SEMI-SUBORDINATION

§1923. This is a blanket term for those constructions in which an OE finite verb can conveniently be rendered by a MnE participle. It is most frequently used of constructions with *wolde* like *ÆCHom* ii. 306. 4 *þa ferde heo to Hierusalem, mid fullum geleafan, wolde ða rode findan ðe Crist on ðrowade* '. . . wishing to find the cross' and *ÆCHom* ii. 474. 23 *Ða com þæs landes menigu mid leohtfatum and mid taperum, mid store and mid mislicum offrungum; woldon ðam godspellere swa swa gode offrian* '. . . wishing to make offering to the evangelist'; the variation in Thorpe's punctuation is noteworthy. These and similar examples with verbs of thinking, saying, and other meanings, are discussed in §§1690-1.

§1924. The term can also be applied to *swa* clauses such as those in *GD(C)* 116. 3 *. . . 7 sæde þæt he sylfa nære nænig gewita þæs mægnes 7 þæt dyde þæt he dyde swa he hit nyste* (the reviser's version is discussed below) and

And 260   Him ða ondswarode   ælmihti god,
                 swa þæt ne wiste,   se ðe þæs wordes bad,
                 hwæt se manna wæs   meðelhegendra,
                 þe he þær on waroðe   wið þingode.

(Here I follow Burnham, Kock, and Brooks, rather than ASPR ii. 107.) Such clauses, says Burnham (p. 15), may 'be regarded as weakened result or modal clauses. They are usually accompanied by a negative. *Swa* must be interpreted in these cases as a rather characterless connective, shading into concession, result, or manner, as the case may be, and, with the negative, corresponding to Modern English "without", "not being".' In view of this comment, it is interesting to note that the reviser of Gregory's *Dialogues* replaced *swa he hit nyste* by *nytende* when he wrote *GD(H)* 116. 3 *7 cwæð þæt he nære na gewita þæs mægenes, þe he nytende worhte*. Further on this use of *swa*, see §§3476-80.

article—a revision of a lecture given in London in January 1952—appeared in *Speculum*, 28 (1953), 446-63. The basic insecurity of the foundations on which Schaar's last two paragraphs (p. 326) rest had long before been exposed by Sisam in *PBA* 18 (1932), 328-9 fn. 16. These and other criticisms could be developed at greater length.

G. THE POSITION OF SUBORDINATE CLAUSES:
A TABLE

§1925.

Kind of Clause	References (in addition to the General Index)	Tendencies
Noun	Gorrell, pp. 466–9	Never at the beginning of a sentence in OE; the pattern 'That he is here is true' does not appear in my collections.
Adjective	Grossmann, pp. 79–87; Anklam, pp. 113–24	Definite adjective clauses usually follow the antecedent (though not necessarily immediately) and are therefore usually found within, or at the end of, the clause to which they refer. Indefinite adjective clauses are commonly found at the beginning of a sentence.
Place	Andrew, *Postscript*, §23	Definite local clauses frequently precede the principal clause in the prose when it contains a correlative. This is rarely allowed by modern editors in the poetry. But they can follow or occur within the principal clause. Indefinite local clauses are often found at the beginning of a sentence.
Time: *þa* and *þonne* clauses	Andrew, *Postscript*, §2	Clauses introduced by *þa* and *þonne* frequently precede the principal clause in prose when it contains a correlative. This is rarely allowed by modern editors in the poetry. But they can follow or occur within the principal clause.
oð (þæt) clauses	Adams, p. 127	Almost invariably in final position.
Other temporal clauses	Adams, p. 158	These can precede, follow, or occur within, the principal clause.
Purpose	Shearin 1903, pp. 55–8	Clauses of purpose follow the clause on which they depend, either immediately or after (part of) another clause. There are rare examples in which the clause of purpose has initial position in its sentence.

Table (*cont.*)

Kind of Clause	References (in addition to the General Index)	Tendencies
Result	Benham, p. 239	As far as I have observed, clauses of result invariably follow the clause on which they depend, either immediately or after (part of) another clause.
Cause	Liggins 1955, *passim*. It is part of her system of classification	Explanatory clauses follow the principal clause. Clauses of 'true Reason' (see §3015) usually follow the principal clause, even when it contains a correlative causal adverb, but may precede it or be interpolated in it.
Comparison	Small 1924, pp. 70-7 and 120-1; Ericson 1932, pp. 9-19 and 42-58	Clauses expressing inequality, clauses with *swa* + adj. (+ noun)/adv. + *swa* or *þy* + a comparative + *þy*, and clauses involving a hypothesis, follow the principal clause. Clauses with *swa* + a comparative + *swa* may precede or follow the principal clause. When two clauses are compared, the comparative clause may precede or follow the principal clause.
Concession	Burnham, pp. 95–108	*þeah (þe)* clauses regularly precede a principal clause which contains a correlative. Otherwise they precede or follow the principal clause or can be interpolated in it.
Condition	Mather, pp. 71-2; Gorrell, p. 466	*Gif* clauses regularly precede a principal clause which contains correlative *þonne*. Otherwise they precede or follow the principal clause or can be interpolated in it. Clauses introduced by *butan* and *nymþe* tend to follow the principal clause.

INDEXES

THERE are three Indexes—the General Index, the Index of Words and Phrases, and the Index of Passages Particularly Discussed. References are to section numbers except when p(p). precedes the number. Volume I contains the General Index to §§1-1925, Volume II the complete General Index and the other two Indexes. Footnote numbers are given only when there is more than one footnote to the section cited. For the reason given in §4000, there is no Index of Persons containing the names of nineteenth- and twentieth-century scholars whose work is referred to in the course of this book. For Ælfric, Cynewulf, Wulfstan, and other OE writers, see the General Index. The word-by-word system of alphabetization has been used.

In the General Index, the head word is the (primary) noun, e.g. 'pronouns, personal', 'vowels, unstressed', and 'phrases, prepositional', except when that arrangement seemed perverse, pedantic, or misleading, e.g. 'element order', 'linguistic facts', and 'literary considerations'. For reasons of space, the number of cross-references is limited. Thus, the various functions of the periphrastic forms with present participles discussed in §§685-94 are not given separate entries and entries such as 'conjunctions, co-ordinating' must be used in conjunction with those under *and, ac, oþþe*, and the like, in the Index of Words and Phrases. For the same reasons, there is no entry 'syntax, differences between Old English and Modern English'. The reader seeking such information should find it by referring to the phenomenon in which he is interested; thus, the entry 'pronouns, anaphoric' will lead him to §71. Cross-references such as that in §174 are not included. Entries under such items as 'sentences', both 'simple' and 'complex'; 'speech', both 'dependent' and 'non-dependent'; and 'clauses', 'principal', 'co-ordinate', and 'subordinate'; are necessarily highly selective, for many syntactical phenomena can occur in all these units. Entries involving square brackets, such as (s.v. 'case') '*see also* [case], concord' indicate that the reader is to search within the entry 'case'; contrast (also s.v. 'case') 'accusative *see* case, accusative', which refers to the separate entry 'case, accusative'.

The General Index must be treated as a supplement to the Contents. Thus, under 'concord' the reader is referred to '1-47 *see* Contents' and under 'agreement' to 'concord'. This explains why the General Index does not contain such entries as 'concords, the basic OE 25-47' or 'agreement between subject and predicate 26-39', but does contain the entries 'predicate, agreement with subject 26-39' and 'subject(s), agreement with predicate 26-39'. So it is imperative that invitations to '*see* Contents' be accepted, even though the penalty for non-acceptance is less severe than that described in Luke 14. 24. The Contents can also be used to advantage in entries which consist merely of figures, especially those in which there are no section numbers distinguished by italic type or accompanied by the words '*see* Contents' and/or '*especially*' to denote that the sections so distinguished serve as a useful introduction to the topic in question. Thus, under 'poetry, OE, usages', no discussions on nouns (§§54-96 in the Contents) are listed, whereas concord (§§1-47) and adjectives (§§97-219) attract entries. Again, the entry under 'adjectives, inflexions, strong and weak forms' directs the reader first to the main discussion ('97-141 *see* Contents') and then to the use of one or both of these forms in the nominative of address (§§1245-7), as subject (§1484), and in poetry (§3964). Further references to their use in poetry will be found in the entries 'poetry, OE, syntax influenced by metre and/or alliteration' (§139) and 'poetry, OE, usages' (§§105, 114, 122, 127, and 134).

Similar use can, of course, be made of the Index of Words and Phrases, which also embraces prefixes such as *ge-* and endings such as *-an, -en, -on,* and *-un,* but is not exhaustive and does not include references to items mentioned merely by way of illustration, such as *se wisdom,* Ælfric, and the like, in §54. The criterion is that the mention must be of syntactical significance, for example the fact that the endings cited above are not distinctive for mood (§22) and that *syn* and *syndon* can be both indicative and subjunctive (§2). References to such items as *freos* in *Dan* 66 (§62) and *hryre* in *Wan* 7 (§65), in which the use of a particular form in a particular context is in question, will be found through the Index of Passages Particularly Discussed.

The Index of Passages Particularly Discussed is intended to contain references both to *OES* and to all my articles and reviews up to December 1983, including those at press and in progress. But it is occasionally difficult to decide when a passage has been 'particularly' discussed. My criterion has been this: 'particular' discussion means that I have thrown, or have attempted to throw, some light (however dim) on the interpretation of the passage cited. Sometimes the case is clear—for inclusion *CP* 304. 6, for exclusion *CP* 304. 19 (on these two, see Mitchell 1979*a*, pp. 39-40) and the seven examples from Visser i, §323, discussed at Mitchell 1979*b*, pp. 541-2. Where there is doubt, e.g. *Alex* 14. 1 and *Bede* 480. 21 (on these two, see §486 and Mitchell 1972, p. 230, and 1979*a*, pp. 43-4), I have generally included the reference.

Having been sternly advised that 'anyone can write the book but only the author can write the indexes', I have forced myself to do so. I am entirely responsible for the Index of Words and Phrases and for the Index of Passages Particularly Discussed. The General Index has been edited from my draft by Jennifer Speake, whose patient and skilful assistance I gratefully acknowledge. I also thank Vera Keep for characteristic concern above the call of duty in offering, at the setting stage, suggestions about the layout of the General Index which have made it much easier to use, and Martin Garrett for careful help with the checking of the other two Indexes. I have tried to make the Indexes helpful rather than burdensome, selective rather than overwhelming, by attempting to ensure that the headings are the meaningful ones and that the sections included are those which contain significant discussion or reference. Some of the omissions are therefore deliberate. Others are the unintended result of 'a wobbling of the mental knees' which afflicted me as I approached the finishing line of what proved to be a longer race than I expected at the start. Those failings which remain are my responsibility. I can only crave indulgence both from the reader who finds that too much has been included and from the reader who finds that too much has been omitted, at the same time expressing the hope that somehow or other both will find what they seek.

GENERAL INDEX

Boethius (*cont.*)
    1185, 1363, 1628, 1784, 1821, 1881,
    1889

caesura, metrical, separation of elements by
    122, 150-7, 175-7, 295
case 1-47 *see* Contents, 94, 1240-427 *see*
    Contents
    changes in use with prepositions 1222-8
    classification or terminology 195-6, 1243,
       1260, 1264-71, 1280-303 *passim*,
       1339-40, 1345, 1350, 1355-6, 1371-
       8, 1381
    concord 33-47 *see* Contents; ~, different
       cases governed by same preposition-
       in same sentence 1173, 1177, 1183,
       1186, 1207, 1218, 1222, 1441; ~,
       different cases in similar construc-
       tions 1240, 1341-2, 1380-427 *pas-
       sim*
    instrumental, subsumed under and some-
       times confused with dative 6, 8 and
       fn., 1345
    locative 8, 14, 1345, 1381
    prepositions replace endings 2, 8, 13,
       1346-7, 1367-70, 1376-8, 1380-427
       passim
    with prepositions 1177-219
    syncretism 8-15, 603, 851, 1223
    system, collapse 2, 8-15, 49-50, 62-5,
       858, 1081, 1099, 1220-2, 1240,
       1341, 1470
    vocative 106, 114, 137, 163, 295, 1242-
       7, 1477, 1671
case, accusative 1255-63 *see* Contents
    adverbial 1382-8 *see* Contents
    cognate 1259, 1384
    as complement 1586
    of degree 1382-5
    double 835-7, 1083, 1476; ~, alter-
       native constructions 1083
    of extent 1381, 1382-5
    with impersonal verbs 1027, 1257
    with infinitives 937, 1539
    passive of verbs with double accusative
       835-7, 1083
    passive of verbs with single accusative
       744-858 *see* Contents, 835-7, 841-2
    with prepositions 1177-219
    with present participles 980-1
    reflexive 266-9, 277, 1052-3, 1055
    of time 1382-5, 1387-8
    with verbs 1027, 1082, 1083-7, 1090,
       1091-2, 1257
case, dative 1345-79 *see* Contents
    of accompaniment 1412-13
    with adjectives 192-6, 197-8, 200, 201,

    204 fn., 205-7, 209, 211-17, 218-
    19, 1355-64, 1582
    adverbial 76, 1408-27 *see* Contents
    of agency 762, 805, 1371-8
    of cause 1427
    cognate 1384
    comitative 1412-13
    of comparison 1358-64
    of degree or measure 1414-15
    distributive 415 n. 3
    ethic 1352-3
    functions (descriptive terms otherwise
       unlisted) 1345, 1350, 1355-6, 1377,
       1419-20, 1424, 1427
    with impersonal verbs 1027, 1082
    of indirect object 1350-1
    of indirect object with *to* 1210
    as object of infinitive 937
    of instrument or means 762, 803, 1365-
       70, 1372, 1410-11, 1420
    instrumental case subsumed under and
       sometimes confused with 6, 8 and
       fn., 1345
    of interest 1345, 1350-1, 1352, 1355-6,
       1357, 1372, 1417
    of manner 1410-11, 1412, 1414, 1420
    of person on whom obligation or neces-
       sity falls 936, 938, 941-2
    personal pronoun + *self* 487-91
    of possession 304-10, 338, 1357
    overlap or conflict with prepositional
       phrases 2, 8, 13, 1346-7, 1367-70,
       1376-8, 1380-427 *passim*
    with prepositions 1177-219
    reflexive 271-4, 277, 487-91 (with *self*),
       1052-3, 1055, 1058
    of time 1415, 1421-6
    with *to*, source of usage 1212
    after *þurh* in Ælfric, Introduction
    uninflected 1252, 1381, 1421
    with verbs 1027, 1082, 1084-7, 1090,
       1091-2, 1349-54
case, genitive 1264-344 *see* Contents
    in absolute constructions, *see* 432 fn.
       113
    'absolute' use with *micel* 432 fn. 113
    'primarily an Adjectival Case' 100, 1269,
       1288, 1290, 1295
    with adjectives 192-6, 197-210, 218-19,
       1300, 1331-7, 1582
    adverbial 1272, 1389-407 *see* Contents
    of agency 1267
    with *an* 534-5, 1276
    appositive 1289-91
    attributive, concord 1304-30
    of cause 1293, 1339
    characteristic 1284, 1288, 1295

of comparison 1336-7

as complement 1584

of condition 1389

of degree 1389, 1391-2

descriptive or defining 1265, 1288-95, 1331, 1339, 1389, 1393, 1584

'elliptical' unknown in OE 1287

functions (descriptive terms otherwise unlisted) 1265, 1267, 1289-93, 1296, 1339, 1584

governed by demonstrative 314

governed by superlative 187, 1300, 1332-3

with impersonal verbs 1027-8

as object of infinitive 937

of instrument or means 1340, 1393-4

of manner 1389, 1391-2, 1393

non-expression of governing element 1287, 1302

of noun + weak form of adjective + noun 113

numeral with *sum* 389-92, 395, 397-400

objective 1266, 1277-8, 1280-4, 1339, 1427

of phrases, rivalry with 1202-3, 1305-6, 1324

order and position of elements 113, 143-4, 147, 149, 348, 1303, 1304-30, 1334

of origin 1293, 1339, 1584

partitive 299, 348, 379, 381-2, 395-401, 402-16, 417, 419-20, 424, 426-32, 435-9, 442-3, 445, 450, 455-7, 459, 461-2, 465-8, 503, 506 fn. 124, 517, 522, 534-5, 548-50, 561-2, 567, 1265, 1268, 1288, 1291, 1292 fn., 1295, 1296-303, 1332-5, 1339, 1340-2, 1400

of personal pronouns 300, 301, 483-6, 1275-6

of place 1284, 1288, 1293

possessive 1265-7, 1274, 1280-7, 1288, 1290-1, 1295, 1337, 1339, 1403, 1584

with prepositions 1177-219

of purpose 1293

qualificative qualitative 1294-5

qualificative   quantitative-qualitative 1294-5

qualificative relative-qualitative 1284, 1288. 1295

of reference or respect 1404-7

reflexive 270, 277, 1052-3

of result 1293, 1389

subjective 1266, 1277-8, 1280-4, 1339

of time 1284, 1288, 1293, 1389, 1400-3

with verbs 1027-8, 1082, 1085-6, 1090, 1091-2, 1338-42

case, nominative 1177, 1241-54 *see* Contents, 1482-527 *see* Contents

in complement 1248-51, 1582-3

with infinitive 957-8, 1539, 1540-2

cause:

accepted, actual, suggested, and rejected or denied 1758

expressed by *for* 1187

expressed by infinitives 959

expressed in parataxis 1690-1, 1693-4, 1703, 1705, 1735, 1768, 1770, 1772

expressed by participles 1435

expressed by prepositional phrases 802-33a *passim*

or agent or instrument expressed by prepositional phrases 812, 813, 817, 818, 833a

'Cædmonian' poems, usages 829 fn.

Cædmon's Hymn, usages 1223

change, functional 50, 1484

Charters, usages 112, 1779

chiasmus 161, 1593

Christ and Satan, usages 476, 628

Chronicle, usages 33 fn., 112, 313 fn., 441, 690 fn., 710, 799, 878, 1185, 1424, 1493, 1718, 1779, 1894

classification or terminology:

prepositions, adverbs, prepositional adverbs, postpositions, separable prefixes, or inseparable prefixes 280, 924, 926, 1060-80 *see* Contents

'clause modifiers' 1103

clause order 1895, *1897-922*, 1925

adjective clauses 1925

causal clauses 1925

with collective noun subjects 80-6

clauses of comparison 1925

clauses of concession 1925

clauses of condition 1925

in dependent speech 1908, 1917-18, 1925

noun clauses, not found in initial position in sentence 1892, 1925

clauses of place 1925

in poetry, Andrew describes a 'curious superstition' 1898 fn., 1899 fn.

clauses of purpose and result 1925

semi-subordination 1690-7

syntactical criterion 1885, 1922

clauses of time 1925

clause(s):

negative(-equivalent), expressing command, wish, or the like 879-919 *passim*, 1675-81; ~, originally had

numerals as 325, 565, 1583
participles as 1582
prepositional phrases as 671, 1158, 1585
sentences as 1585
split 1466, 1469
term discussed 39 fn., 604-6, 608, 1581
determines number of verb 'to be' after
    þæt 47(3), 323-7, 342, 565
repeated with verb 1530
compounds:
    expressing extent or degree 1146
    expressing instrument 803
    expressing time 593
    nominal, in poetry 158
    numerical 587, 593
computers, use of, Introduction
'concatenative constructions' 410, 414
concession:
    expressed by parataxis 1691, 1705, 1736,
        1767, 1772
    expressed by participles and participial
        phrases 1435
    reinforcement by sentence elements 1755
concord 1-47 *see* Contents
    begen 551
    lack of in parallel expressions 42(8),
        44(3), 751 fn. 186, 986 (*ÆLS* 21.
        351), 1172, 1240, 1244, 1252, 1437-
        43, 1470, 1474-7, 1489, 1665
'concrete', term applied to sentences 653-
    64, 783, 784 fn. 200
condition(s):
    'conditional' infinitive 959
    expressed in adjective clauses 649
    expressed by imperative or jussive sub-
        junctive 617, 882, 1695, 1705, 1735
    expressed by parataxis 617, 882, 1695,
        1705, 1735
    expressed by participles 1435
    genitive of 1389
    rejected or imaginary 1631, 1843
conjunction(s) 1229-33 *see* Contents
    adversative 1685, 1752-805 *see* Contents,
        1736, 1738
    alternative 1685, 1806-31 *see* Contents
    classification or terminology 571, 924,
        1229, 1662, 1685, 1739, 1744,
        1806-31 *passim*, 1832-57 *passim*,
        1858-60, 1872-5
    co-ordinating 741, 1709-862 *see* Con-
        tents; ~, influence on element order
        (often overlooked) 1078, 1685,
        1729-31, 1753; ~, repetition of ele-
        ments after 166; ~, to be distinguished
        from sentence adverbs 1101; ~, *see
        also* co-ordination; parataxis; cumula-
        tive 1685, 1709-51 *see* Contents

divided, term explained 1230
doubling 1889, 1895
grouped, term explained 1230
illative 1685, 1858-61, 1862
(references to) lists of 1231 fn., 1232-
    3, 1775-6, 1861, 1862
negative co-ordinating 1832-57 *see* Con-
    tents
non-prepositional, term explained 1230
    ~, *see also those listed in* 1232
non-repetition 1788, 1790, 1808
origin 1157, 1230, 1233
prepositional, correlation 1888 and fn.;
    ~, formation 1157, 1230, 1233;
    ~, term explained 1230; ~, *see also
    those listed in* 1233
simple, term explained 1230
subordinating, preceded by material be-
    longing to subordinate clause 1920-1;
    ~, *þe* not always a sign 1859, 1885,
    1889
þæt, oblique cases 318
þe 'than' 573-4
contrast, expressed by parataxis 1766-7,
    1772
co-ordination 29-31, 46, 495-7, 1040,
    1051, 1170-6, 1525-7, 1709-862
    passim, 1877, 1897-922 *passim*
correlation:
    clauses of condition 1116-17
    complex sentences 1885, 1887-96
    expressing alternatives 1863-7
    indefinites 379, 393, 394, 403, 407,
        435, 443-4, 459, 505, 508-10,
        512
    prepositional formulae 1888 and fn.
Cura Pastoralis, usages 691, 710, 738 and
    fn., 771-6, 878, 1110 fn., 1185,
    1363, 1493, 1889
Cynewulf, usages 251, 878, 1265 fn., 1495,
    1922 and fn.

Daniel (poem), usages 792
dative and infinitive 1541, 1547
degree:
    adverbs 1135-45
    expressed by accusative 1382-5
    expressed by dative 1414-15
    expressed by genitive 1389, 1391-2
    expressed by other means 1146
demonstrative/relatives, the ambiguous 47,
    52, 69, 322, 324, 327, 404, 1634,
    1686, 1879, 1885, 1891
demonstratives 311-45 *see* Contents
    alternating with personal pronouns or
        possessives 303-10, 320-1, 338, 344,
        1274

verbs, auxiliary and 'verbal' 599; ∼, continuous tenses 682-701; ∼, perfect tenses 702-43 *passim*; ∼, periphrastic forms 665, 703-21, 724 fn. 72, 727, 757-8; ∼, possibly compound 1060-80; vocative expressions 295, 1243

elements:
adverbial 1589-94 *see* Contents
in alternative constructions 1806-31, 1863-7
anticipatory 666
appositional 1428-63 *see* Contents
augmenting proper names 1451
clarifying 1452
enumerating 1453
governed by a comparative or superlative 182, 187
independent, participles function as 1435; ∼, vocative expressions 1244
in 'not only . . . but (also)' patterns 1777-99
in parataxis 1683-875 *passim, especially* 1684
recapitulatory 666, 1454
repetitive 1454
involved in splitting of groups 1464-72
elision of -*e*, in *ne* 1129-31, 1761, 1845 fn. 27
'ellipsis' 1287
emendation:
attitudes to 1572
dangers of 15, 20, 68
on metrical grounds, Introduction
examples, choice of, Introduction
excess, *to* does not always express 1142-3
exclamations:
classification or terminology 348, 357, 1647-8, 1671-2
element order 1078, 1671
expressing extent or degree 1146
non-dependent 705, 1647-8, 1671-4
non-expression of elements 1533, 1673
parenthetic 323-7, 1674
(plu)perfect periphrases in 705
Exodus (poem), usages 476
explanatory use of finite verbs after *don* 666
extent:
accusative of 1381, 1382-5
adverbs of 1135-45
other means of expressing 1146
extraposition 44(3), 1429 and fn., 1441, 1448

fact:
expressed by *beon/wesan* 658-9, 662
expressed by indicative mood 877
expressed by subjunctive mood 877

formulae, poetic, oral-formulaic theory 1922 fn.; ∼, unthinking or mechanical use 376, 1182, 1523
prepositional, infrequently correlative 1888 and fn.; ∼, formation 1157, 1230, 1233; ∼, not always fossilized 1781; ∼, must be distinguished from relative combinations containing preposition + demonstrative (antecedent) + (. . .) *þe/þæt* 1781; ∼, term explained 1230
fractions 578-80
French, influence on English 189 fn., 801, 811, 1193, 1202 and fn.
futurity:
expressed by *beon/wesan* + inflected infinitive 945-8
expressed by infinitives 945-8
expressed by present tenses of *beon/ wesan* 652, 657-64
expressed by present tenses of subjunctive 1676
expressed by present tenses of *weorþan* 672
expressed by **sculan* or *willan* + infinitive 947, 1023-4

gender 55-71, *see* Contents
agreement of antecedent and pronoun 45-7
agreement of noun/pronoun and appositive element 43
agreement of noun/pronoun and attributive element 40
agreement of subject and adjective/participle 33-8
agreement of subject and complement 39, 323
changes in nouns 62-5, 68
concord, lack of 38, 63-5, 66-8, 69-71, 551
distinctions in OE 3, 55-61
distinctions survive in adjectives, participles, and pronouns 66-8
feminine or neuter forms used referring to male and female 38, 551
loss in OE 62-8
non-repetition of *se* with nouns of different gender 337
nouns with more than one 62-5
syntactical criterion 65, 67, 256
Genesis A and/or *B*, usages, Introduction fn., 476, 878
Germanic languages, influence on English 188 fn., 259, 1796-9
glosses, syntactical 1158a, 1899 fn.
Glosses, usages 63, 64 fn., 66, 68, 109-12,

numerals (*cont.*)
    with dative of possession 307
    formation 570-87 *see* Contents
    genitive case with *sum* 389-92, 395,
        397-400
    with genitive case 1292-3, 1299
    'indefinite' 589
    indefinite use 588-90
    number of verb after *þæt* with numeral
        complement 325
    position when used as qualifiers 143,
        145-6, 149
    in post-position 164
    predicative use 415(3)
    with prepositional phrases 1159, 1162,
        1201
    qualifying adjectives as nouns 133
    qualifying nouns 123, 125, 133
    as subject 1482
    with *sum* 389-92, 395, 397-400
numerals, cardinal:
    an 523-47 *see* Contents
    an with 545
    an, is there a weak declension? 529, 537-
        44
    other than *an* 548-54 *see* Contents
    se with 331
    sum with 389-92, 395, 397-400 (*cf.*
        479), 415
    swelc with 505
    used in forming numerals 570-87 *see*
        Contents
numerals, compound:
    cardinal 555-60
    forms affected by metre 558, 1218
    ordinal 569
numerals, ordinal:
    declension, formation, and functions
        566-9
    with personal pronoun and *self* 479
    used in forming numerals 570-87 *see*
        Contents
numerals, Roman 554, 569

object(s) 1565-80 *see* Contents
    only accusative object accompanied by
        inflected participle in (plu)perfect
        periphrasis 709
    accusative becomes subject of passive
        periphrasis 834-58
    cases 602-7, 1565
    causative 1028, 1040, 1082 fn. 248,
        1090, 1574 fn.
    classification or terminology 937-44,
        1539-42, 1565, 1572
    cognate 754, 1259, 1384
    dative, not made subject of a passive

periphrasis whether direct or indirect
    834, 838-40, 843-7, 848-54, 856-8
different forms with verbs 1081-92
different types in (plu)perfect periphrasis
    712-19
direct, case 1255-63 *see* Contents, 1338,
    1349, 1365, ~, term discussed 1565
genitive, not made subject of passive
    periphrasis 834, 838-40, 843-7,
    848-54, 856-8
indirect, case 1350-1; ~, with imper-
    sonal verbs in non-dependent ques-
    tions 1653, 1663, 1669; ~, term dis-
    cussed 1348, 1565; ~, *to* + dative
    1210
infinitive as 931, 954-5, 971, 999, 1090,
    1548-51, (1566)
infinitive as direct object of 'modal' verbs
    999
inner or internal 1258
non-expression 1570-9 *passim*
(non-)repetition 1570-9
noun clauses as 1090, 1566, 1892
outer or external 1258
possessive as 299
of reflexive verbs 1052
second participles alone do not take one
    984
split 1466, 1468
term discussed 39 fn., 602-6, 608, 1565
obligation:
    expressed by *agan* 932-3
    expressed by *beon/wesan* + inflected
        infinitive 932-3, 934-44, 945
    expressed by *habban* + inflected infini-
        tive 950-3
    expressed by **sculan* 933
Old English:
    archaic or primitive 109-12, 117-20,
        122, 139-40, 225, 232, 290-3, 336,
        372-5, 527, 540, 697, 1226-7, 1347,
        1780, 1796, 1799
    colloquial, Introduction, 275 fn., 302,
        312, 668, 1211, 1234 fn.
    limited corpus, Introduction
    how long did it last? 15
    an oligometochic language? 973
omission, term avoided 1506, 1572
Orosius, usages 109, 141, 419, 423, 428-9,
    463, 690 fn., 691, 764, 786, 799,
    1110 fn., 1185-6, 1424, 1493, 1784,
    1819-20, 1881, 1922

paragraph:
    unit of OE prose 1881
    verse, unit of OE poetry 1881
parataxis 1683-875 *see* Contents

expressed by infinitive 959
expressed by parataxis 617, 1735, 1738, 1769
rhythm 889, 891, 914, 1032, 1201, 1430, 1462, 1507, 1712, 1730

St. Chad, usages 110-12
Scandinavian languages, influence on English 801, 1225 fn. 288, 1306
scribal imprecision, may produce unexpected mood 601
semi-subordination 626, 1690-7, 1713, 1923-4
sentence apposition 1458
'sentence modifiers' 1101-3, 1137, 1590
sentence structure 1146, 1876-925 *see* Contents
    as test of authorship 1922
    variations express extent or degree 1146
sentences:
    as antecedents or 'postcedents' 342, 1490
    as complements 1585
    complex 1876-925 *see* Contents; ~, term explained 1876
    compound, term avoided 1685
    'concrete' 653-64, 783, 784 fn. 200
    loose or cumulative 1897-922 *passim*
    loose structure normal in prose and poetry 1898-900
    multiple, term avoided 1633, 1685, 1718, 1877
    in parataxis 1683-875 *passim*
    periodic 1897-922 *passim*
    simple 1240-682 *see* Contents; ~, classification or terminology 1633-4; ~, elements 1240-632 *see* Contents; ~, types 1633-82 *see* Contents
    not always unit of OE prose and poetry 1633, 1879, 1881
sequence of moods 876
sex v. gender, conflicts in agreement 25, 47, 55, 68, 69-71, 292, 484, 486
S F(F), Nickel's abbreviation 681
short titles of OE texts, pp. xxx-xxxv
Soliloquies, usages 691, 1363
speech, dependent:
    sequence of tenses 859-64
    tense 637
    verbal periphrases in 703 fn., 771 and fn.
speech, direct 703 fn., 1635-6
speech material(s), qualifying elements separated from noun by 149-57, 175-7, 234, 295
speech, non-dependent 859-64, 1635
    classification or terminology 875, 877,

880a, 881, 885 fn., 887, 1645, 1647-8, 1671; ~, dependent or non-dependent 354, 1652, 1658-9, 1670, 1672
    verbal periphrases in 771 and fn.
speech, represented 1668
statement(s), non-dependent 1638-9, 1645, 1647, 1671; ~, element order 1638
statistics, use, Introduction, 750
stress and/or emphasis 220, 233, 315, 320, 328-9, 341, 409 fn. 102, 475-6, 478, 481, 483, 491, 518, 523-4, 558, 604, 793, 1146, 1309, 1472, 1486-7, 1497, 1508, 1594, 1606, 1710, 1712, 1730, 1733, 1857, 1881
style 172, 317, 686, 793, 962-4, 1146, 1303, 1315, 1347, 1436, 1462, 1472, 1507, 1508, 1531, 1561, 1578, 1593, 1603 fn., 1606, 1638, 1663, 1687, 1704, 1857, 1878, 1881, 1893-6, 1919, 1922 and fn.
subject/object 937-44, 1539-42
subject(s) 1482-527 *see* Contents
    agreement with predicate 26-39 *see* Contents
    change 256, 320-1
    classification or terminology 348, 937-44, 1500, 1507, 1539-42
    infinitives as 841-2, 931, 971, 1482, 1507, 1537-9
    nominative the case of 1241
    non-expression 256, 370-6, 496-7, 879-80, 883-910 *passim*, 913-14, 916-17, 1032, 1404 fn., 1503-16, 1673; ~, of formal *hit* 749, 834-58 *passim*, 1025-51 *passim*, 1485
    (non-)repetition (of part) 1503-6, 1508, 1690-702, 1712-17, 1728, 1734, 1752-3, 1785 and fn., 1788, 1791, 1857, 1869
    noun clauses as 835-7, 841-2, 1482, 1892
    number when two subjects joined by *and* 29-31
    in asyndetic parataxis 1690-708 *see* Contents
    in syndetic parataxis 1712-18, 1752
    possessive as 299
    of reflexive verbs 1052
    repetition of subject and finite verb 1785 and fn., 1788
    se as subject-changer 320-1
    split 1466-7
subtraction, formation of numerals by 573-7
suffixes:
    adjectival 51 fn.
    negative 1133, 1632

minimal distinctions 2, 4, 16-22, 600-2

verbs 594-1099 *see* Contents, 1528-64 *see* Contents

absolute, expressing reciprocity 288; ~, intransitive and/or reflexive uses 266-8, 270-2, 602, 605-7, 1054-8

with accusative 1027, 1082, 1083-7, 1090, 1091-2, 1257

with double accusative, passive 835-7, 1083

with accusative and noun clause or infinitive (phrase), passive 835-7, 841-2, 845

alone, expressing reciprocity 288

basic paradigms 1093-9 *see* Contents

classification or terminology 594, 600-10, 611-50 *passim*, 651-80 *passim*, 685-94, 711 fn., 722-33, 734-42, 749, 755, 762-81, 786-801, 806, 851, 865-73, 875, 877, 881, 885 fn., 908-10, 1052-8, 1060-80 *passim*, 1089-90, 1529, 1534, 1535-54

(possibly) compound 1060-80 *see* Contents

concord 26-32, 79-86, 323-7, 395, 433, 452, 561-5, 1467, 1501-2, 1508, 1519-27

constructed with prepositions 1060-80 *passim*, 1081-92 *passim*, 1167-9

with dative 1027, 1082, 1084-7, 1090, 1091-2, 1349-54

denominative, used reflexively 1054

distinguished according to rection 1090

durative or imperfective 691, 722 and fn. 168, 740, 783

finite, anticipatory use of *don* before 666; ~, explanatory use after *don* 666; ~, repetition by synonyms 1530; ~, and subject, repetition 1785 and fn., 1788; ~, vary with infinitives 967-9, 1713; ~, vary with present participles 1558, 1692, 1713

full or with full meaning, *don* 665-9; ~, 'modal' verbs 1000-1, 1006-8; ~, term discussed 594

with genitive 1027-8, 1082, 1085-6, 1090, 1091-2, 1338-42

governing only prepositions, passive 855

governing reflexive pronouns 266-8, 270-2, 607, 747, 1052-9 *passim*

groups split by object 1575-7

imperfective or durative 691, 722 and fn. 168, 740, 783

with infinitives 932-58 *see* Contents, 971

inflexions, ambiguity, loss, or variation 2, 16-24 *see* Contents, 49, 243, 601-

1a, 613-50 *passim*, 874-919 *see* Contents, 921, 1099, 1506 fn., 1520, 1647; ~, 'could in most cases [*sic*] functionally be dispensed with' 16 *cf.* 1506 fn.

inseparable 1060-80 *passim*

(references to) lists of 722 fn. 169, 1082-92 *passim*

mutative or perfective 722 and fn. 168, 740, 783

non-denominative, used reflexively 1054

non-expression 1532-4, 1673; ~, of *beon/wesan* 988

(non-)repetition 665, 711, 1530-1, 1708, 1785 and fn., 1787, 1788, 1790-1, 1836

with prepositional phrases 1028, 1083, 1087-92, 1158, 1167-9

with prepositions 1060-80 *passim*, 1081-92 *passim*, 1167-9

preterite-present, term explained 991 fn.

reflexive constructions 265-78, 607, 747, 1052-9

with reflexive pronouns rendering Latin passives 747

repetition, avoided by use of *don* 665; ~, *habban* in (plu)perfect periphrases 711

separable 1060-80 *passim*

verbs, auxiliary:

beon/wesan, with full verb *(ge)weorþan* 674; ~, with passive 673, 734, 786-801; ~, with (plu)perfect 702, 734-42

don not one in OE 665-9, 1099

habban, with full verb *(ge)weorþan* 674; ~, with (plu)perfect 702-4, 705-33, 734-42 *passim*

hatan 679-80

with inflected and/or uninflected infinitives 955

lætan 680

onginnan/aginnan/beginnan 675-8

term discussed or explained 594, 599, 610, 991

weorþan, with full verb *habban* 670; ~, with passive 673, 734, 786-801; ~, with (plu)perfect 702, 734-42

verbs, impersonal (use) 1025-51 *see* Contents. [*Note: I regret that I have not consistently observed the strict definition of 'impersonal' proposed in §1025; see, for example, §§1251 and 1349. In these and similar contexts, the word should be in inverted commas.*]

with accusative 1027, 1257

verbs, impersonal (use) (*cont.*)
  beon/wesan 945
  classification or terminology 602, 607, 1025–30
  with dative 1027, 1082
  expressing commands 898
  expressing wishes 898
  with genitive 1027–8
  with infinitive 971, 1029
  magan 374, 1037
  in non-dependent questions 1642, 1653, 1663, 1669
verbs, intransitive (use):
  beon/wesan and *weorþan* as (plu)perfect auxiliaries 702, 734–42
  constructions with second participle not to be confused with passives 834 fn.
  habban as (plu)perfect auxiliary 702–4, 705–33, 734–42 *passim*
  with infinitives 936, 945, 967–9
  'intransitive verb' sometimes shorthand for 'verb used intransitively' 606
  in periphrastic (plu)perfect 691, 702, 706 (Table 3), 720–2, 727–33, 734–42, 868
  with prepositional adverbs 1065–6, 1074–5
  used reflexively 1053–4, 1058
  rendering Latin passive 747
  term explained 602–6, 1065 fn.
verbs, 'modal' auxiliary 990–1024 *see* Contents
  except *agan* prefer uninflected infinitive 955, 971, 996–9
  basic paradigm 1095
  classification or terminology 991, 1009
  with infinitives as periphrases for simple subjunctive 1009, 1014
  with infinitives expressing commands, wishes, or the like 917–18
  a special use of *magan* 370, 374
  in nexus questions 1644
  non-expression of infinitive with 1002–8
  sculan or *willan* with infinitive expressing future 1009, 1023–4
  term discussed 610, 751 fn. 185, 991
verbs, periphrastic (forms) 681–858 *see* Contents
  none with *don* in OE 665–9, 1099
  element order, possible lines of research 599
  (plu)perfect 638, 641, 644, 702–43 *see* Contents; ~, expressing state or action 724–33, 734–42; ~, non-repetition of *habban* 711; ~, patterns listed 702–21

with present participle 682–701 *see* Contents; ~, expressing aspect 694, 868, 871; ~, expressing command or wish 881; ~, not identical in function with MnE equivalents 683–94; ~, patterns listed 683–4
repetition of one element 1530
term explained 608–10, 681
verbs, rection 602–6, 834–58, 1081–92 *see* Contents, 1240, 1255–7
  adjective and verb combinations 1082
  compound verbs 1091–2
  double 835–42, 848–54, 856–8, 1083–8, 1260, 1569
  impersonal verbs 1027–30
  infinitive inflected or uninflected 932–3, 954, 996–9, 1549–50
  list 1091–2
  list (possibly) incomplete 852, 1091
  noun and verb combinations 1082, 1088
  single 1568
  triple 1088
verbs, semantic classification:
  of accusing 1085
  of admonishing and exhorting 1037; ~, used in impersonal constructions 1037
  of addressing and answering 1082
  of asking, enquiring, and requesting 1085
  of benefit and profit or loss 1082
  of beginning, continuing, and ending 955, 979, 985
  of believing or disbelieving 1082
  of caring or neglecting 1082
  of causing 665–8, 680. 726 fn., 731, 955, 981
  of changing 691
  of commanding and requesting 955, 1690
  of delaying 955
  of depriving or taking away 1085, 1086
  of desiring or needing 1082
  of emotion 1053, 1082
  of enjoying and using 1082
  of explaining 1037
  of giving or refusing 1082, 1086. 1210
  of happening and becoming 1037
  of helping or harming 1082
  of inclination, intention, and will 955
  of liking or disliking 1082
  of making or constructing 1053
  of mental activity or perception 955, 981, 1053, 1082; ~, used in impersonal constructions 1032, 1037
  of motion and/or rest 274, 691, 699, 955, 967–9, 979, 981, 985. 1053–4,

1122, 1251, 1412, 1543, 1581, 1713

of naming 1473–81

of natural phenomena, used in impersonal constructions 1032, 1037

of permitting 955, 1037

of physical action or sense perception 691, 955, 981, 1053–4, 1082

of physical action or 'affections', used in impersonal constructions 1032, 1037

of pleasing or displeasing 1082

of possessing and ruling 1053, 1082

of refusing 1086

of remembering or forgetting 1082

of rest, idea of motion sometimes inherent 1122

of seeming 985

of serving or resisting 1082

of speaking 1690, 1901 fn.; ~, in impersonal constructions 1037; ~, in periphrases with present participle 691; ~, with prepositions 1210, 1228; ~, in semi-subordination 1690

of thanking 1086

see also list of verbal rections (§§1091–2)

verbs, transitive (use):

auxiliaries *beon/wesan* and *weorþan* in passive, *habban* in (plu)perfect 734

rection 1255–6

in periphrastic (plu)perfect 702–4, 705–21, 723–33, 734–5, 743, 868

with prepositional adverbs 1065–71

used reflexively 1053–7

term discussed 602–6, 843, 1065 fn.

'transitive verb' sometimes shorthand for 'verb used transitively' 606

'verbal', Bliss's term 599

'verbal substitution', Antipova's term 1527 fn., *see also* 665

voice:

active infinitive with verb in passive 957

distinctions in OE 7, 600(1)

'medial' 1053

voice, active 594–1099, *see* Contents
impersonal constructions 1036–43

voice, passive 600(1), 744–858 *see* Contents

auxiliary *beon/wesan* 600(1), 673, 734–5, 748–801, 1099

auxiliary *weorþan* 600(1), 673, 734–5, 748–801, 1099

cognate object becomes subject of periphrasis 754

with dative of interest 1351, 1372

'double passive group' 754

formed from double accusative 835–7, 1083

impersonal 834–58, 1030, 1044, 1045–51, 1485; ~, formal subject *hit* not used 1485; ~, or indirect, term explained 749; ~, used in OE when verb does not take accusative object in active voice 834, 840, 843–7, 848–58 *see* Contents (for possible exceptions see 851 and fnn.; for apparent exceptions see 856–8)

infinitive in accusative and infinitive 751–4, 761, 988

man + active form a substitute 369

periphrases with present participles not used with a passive sense 694

periphrastic 744–858 *see* Contents; ~, expressing action or state 724–42, 749, 766–7, 768 fn., 786–801, 806; ~, expressing command or wish 881; ~, with *lætan* 680; ~, non-repetition of participle 757; ~, patterns with verbs which govern only one accusative object listed 750–6; ~, time-reference 782–5; ~, with verbs other than *beon/wesan* and *weorþan* 680, 748, 800 fn.

with verbs of double rection 835–42, 848–54, 856–8

personal, or direct, term explained 749; ~, used in OE when subject would have been accusative object in active voice 834–58; ~, used rather than impersonal when choice existed 843–7

regular (or true), and 'adjectival': are they to be distinguished? 763–5; ~, and constructions with second participles of intransitive verbs to be distinguished 834 fn.

synthetic 746

verb with active infinitive 957

ways of expressing 746–8

vowels, unstressed, obscuration 14–15, 18–20, 22

wishes:

or clauses of condition 1679–80

expressed by passive voice 881

not expressed by *magan* + infinitive 1013

non-dependent 879–919 *see* Contents, 1645, 1671, 1675–82; ~, expressed by impersonal verb 898

polite, expressed by *wolde* 1022

unrealized or impossible 1676, 1679–81